The Book of Saints

The Book of Saints

A Comprehensive Biographical Dictionary

Dom Basil Watkins, OSB
on behalf of the Benedictine monks of
St Augustine's Abbey, Ramsgate

Eighth Edition
Entirely revised and reset

t&t clark

LONDON · NEW YORK · OXFORD · NEW DELHI · SYDNEY

T&T CLARK
Bloomsbury Publishing Plc
50 Bedford Square, London, WC1B 3DP, UK
1385 Broadway, New York, NY 10018, USA

BLOOMSBURY, T&T CLARK and the T&T Clark logo are trademarks of Bloomsbury
Publishing Plc

First edition published 1921

This edition first published in 2015 by Bloomsbury Academic
Reprinted 2017, 2018, 2019 (twice), 2020

A catalogue record for this book is available from the British Library.

ISBN: HB: 978-0-56766-414-3
PB: 978-0-56766-456-3
ePDF: 978-0-56766-413-6
ePub: 978-0-56766-415-0

The book of saints: a comprehensive biographical dictionary/edited by Dom Basil
Watkins, OSB on behalf of the Benedictine monks of St Augustine's Abbey,
Ramsgate. – Eighth Edition, Entirely revised and reset.
pages cm
Includes bibliographical references and index.
ISBN 978-0-567-66414-3 (hardback : alk. paper) – ISBN 978-0-567-66456-3
(pbk.: alk. paper) 1. Christian saints–Biography–Dictionaries. I. Watkins,
Basil, editor. II. St. Augustine's Abbey (Ramsgate, England)
BX4655.3.B66 2015
282.092'2–dc23
[B]
2015017473

Typeset by Deanta Global Publishing Services, Chennai, India
Printed and bound in Great Britain

To find out more about our authors and books visit www.bloomsbury.com and
sign up for our newsletters.

Contents

List of Illustrations   viii

Introduction   x

Abbreviations   xii

Saints: Entries A to Z   1

Bibliography   783

Glossary to *The Book of Saints*   784

Appendix to *The Book of Saints*: Lists of National Martyrs   793

List of Illustrations

Frontispiece   Holy Family © Mondadori Portfolio/Getty Images   v

A   St Anthony Abbot and St Agatha © De Agostini/Getty Images   1

B   Pope Benedict XVI celebrates a special mass for the sick in Lourdes, South of France on September 15, 2008. Bernadette Soubirous's portrait. © Eric VANDEVILLE/Gamma-Rapho via Getty Images   84

C   Chapel of Our Lady of the Miraculous Medal, Catherine Labouré and Virgin Mary © Godong/UIG via Getty Images   117

D   Saint Dorothy and the Infant Christ, ca 1460. Artist: Francesco di Giorgio Martini (1439-1501) © Fine Art Images/Heritage Images/Getty Images   167

E   Edward The Confessor, Anglo-Saxon king of England, 1070s. © Ann Ronan Pictures/Print Collector/Getty Images   193

F   Saint Francis Xavier © DeAgostini/Getty Images   232

G   Saint Gregory the Great between his parents by Giuseppe Franchi, copy after the lost paintings at Sant Andrea in Clivio Scauri, today San Gregorio Magno in Rome, oil on canvas, 1611 © DEA/VENERANDA BIBLIOTECA AMBROSIANA/De Agostini/Getty Images   268

H   Hildegard of Bingen receiving the Light from Heaven, c.1151 (vellum) © German School/Getty Images   300

I   Portrait of Saint Ignatius of Loyola, founder of the Society of Jesus or Jesuits by Giuseppe Franchi, oil on canvas © Photo By DEA/VENERANDA BIBLIOTECA AMBROSIANA/De Agostini/Getty Images   324

J   Mother Teresa and John Paul II at Vatican in Rome, Italy on February 05, 1992. © Photo by Livio ANTICOLI/Gamma-Rapho via Getty Images   336

K   SKOREA-VATICAN-POPE-RELIGION-HISTORY © JUNG YEON-JE/ AFP/Getty Images   412

L   Wooden plaque of St Lucy of Syracuse, Spanish, 17th century. © Science and Society Picture Library/Getty Images   415

M   Maximilian Kolbe © Universal History Archive/UIG via Getty images   451

N   St Nicholas of Myra © Photo by DeAgostini/Getty Images   534

O   Stone figure of St Oswald by anonymous mediaeval © Hans Wild/The LIFE
     Picture Collection/Getty Images   551

P   St Perpetua comforting her father © DeAgostini/Getty Images   561

Q   Carthaginian Bishop Quotvultdeus © DeAgostini/Getty Images   626

R   Tobias and the angel © Leemage/UIG via Getty Images   630

S   Scholastica © Hulton Archive/Getty Images   659

T   'St Teresa of Avila before the Cross', c1621–1663. Artist: Guido Cagnacci
     © Ann Ronan Pictures/Print Collector/Getty Images   700

U   Legend of St Ursula. Martyrdom of the Pilgrims and the Funeral of Ursula,
     by Vittore Carpaccio, 1493, 15th Century, oil on canvas, cm 271 x 560.
     © Mondadori Portfolio/Getty Images   735

V   St Veronica with the Holy Kerchief. © Universal Images Group/Getty Images   741

W   Saint Wenceslas © DeAgostini/Getty Images   761

X–Z   St Zacharius © Hulton Archive/Getty Images   775

Introduction

This book contains biographical entries for all those who have been formally canonized or beatified by the Roman Catholic Church to date (2015), as well as for those who have had their local veneration approved by the church as a whole. Together with these, entries are provided for those listed in both the old (last edition 1924) and the revised (2004) Roman Martyrologies. The result is claimed to be the only complete dictionary of all the saints listed in both Martyrologies – in any language.

The major hagiographical event since the last edition of this work in 2002 has been the publication of the revised Roman Martyrology. This actually occurred just as the last edition went to press, and no use could be made of it then. This new martyrology was the result of a directive of the Second Vatican Council of the Roman Catholic Church forty years before, that the church's veneration of saints should conform to historical reality and not to obviously false legends. Since the previous martyrology dated from the sixteenth century, and had been only lightly revised subsequently, the work required in revisions and additions was enormous. The result is a massive tome of 844 pages, which unfortunately has not yet been translated into English from the original Latin. It had a second edition in 2004, and counts as an official document of the Magisterium of the Roman Catholic Church.

When the first edition of the 'Book of Saints' was published in 1921, it was intended as an alphabetical listing of all the saints then listed in the Roman Martyrology, as well as for others selected according to the personal interests of the editors. The apparatus provided the date of each saint, his or her liturgical status and, for religious, the congregation or Order to which he or she belonged. The liturgical apparatus became obsolete in 1970 when the Roman Catholic Church revised its liturgy, and the attribution to the various Orders was unfortunately over-indulgent towards various false and tendentious historical claims made on behalf of these Orders.

So, the apparatus in this edition has been completely replaced. The emphasis is now on each saint's listing in the Roman Martyrology, and on his or her liturgical veneration in the Roman Catholic Church as a whole (if any). The revision of the Martyrology has meant the deletion of a large number of saints now considered spurious. It is made clear in the apparatus whether saints are still venerated liturgically, whether they used to be venerated but are so no longer, whether they are in both the old or new Martyrologies, in the new Martyrology only or whether they have been deleted in the revision of the Martyrology. The mention of any affiliation to a religious order is now to be found in the text.

Entries are listed in strict alphabetical order, as follows: First by the first word of the Christian name, then by surname (if any) or cognomen. Compound Christian names are hyphenated. There are no entries with surname first. Those entries for consecrated religious are by their names in religion, as given by the official documents published in Rome, even if they are better known by their baptismal names or nicknames. Different religious congregations have differing traditions regarding surnames: the Franciscans tend to replace these by a cognomen derived from the person's place of birth and the Carmelites drop surnames altogether. For the purpose of listing, the surnames (where known) of all of these have been restored (e.g. 'Teresa-of-the-Child-Jesus Martin'). Names in bold type refer to saints or blesseds listed in the revised Roman Martyrology, those in bold italics to those who are not so listed, bold italics in brackets to those have been actually deleted from the Roman Martyrology, and those in normal italics to variant names of individuals listed elsewhere.

A name is given in the familiar English form or in the form most familiar in England (e.g. 'James' not 'Jacques'), without any offence intended to national sensibilities. This policy of only using English names is intended to avoid any tendentious selection of languages in which to list names – it is no longer the case that European national languages can expect a privileged status worldwide, and some saints are claimed by competing national groups. An exception is made for certain obsolescent English forms that are widely divergent from the original (e.g. 'Dionysius' is listed as such and not as 'Dennis', and 'Louis' not as 'Lewis'). Anglo-Saxon names have been generally left in the familiar Latinized forms rather than being rendered as they were actually pronounced, but dog-Latin versions of vernacular names have mostly been avoided (these usually add 'us' or 'is' to the end, e.g. 'Guerricus' for 'Guerric').

As regards geographical names, the policy in this book is that any existing familiar English form, as employed in the national media of the United Kingdom, is used in preference. Also, contemporary names are used in preference to historical ones (even at the risk of apparent anachronism).

The entries for New Testament saints presume that the reader has access to a copy of the Bible, so narrative descriptions for these saints are minimal. Only those Old Testament characters listed in the Roman Martyrology have been included.

In order to save space, most individual listings of early martyrs included in group descriptions in the Martyrologies have been deleted. Also deleted have been most of those entries referring to so-called saints not in the Martyrologies. There are an unmanageably enormous number of these, existing in unofficial local venerations or in historical documentation.

This book is intended primarily to be a work of reference, which entails that a critical attitude is taken towards historical evidence (especially early legends). This is an expression of conformity to the hagiographical norms expressed by the Second Vatican Council. No attack on anybody's devotional attachments or practices is intended as a result.

Readers are welcome to draw attention to any mistakes or omissions.

Book of Saints, Eighth Edition

Apparatus and abbreviations

Names in **bold upright font** are of saints and beati listed in the present edition of the Roman Martyrology (2004).

Names in ***bold italic font*** are of those whose cultic venerations have either not been approved, or have been approved by local hierarchies only. These are not listed in the Roman Martyrology.

Names bracketed in ***(bold italic font)*** are those who have been deleted from the Roman Martyrology, with the implication that veneration is not approved. This is either because there is substantial doubt about the existence of those concerned, or that they were unworthy of being listed.

{1}	In the present General Calendar of the Roman Catholic Church, revised 1969.
{1 –group}	In the General Calendar, only as one of a group (usually of national martyrs).
{2}	In the revised Roman Martyrology (2004), but not in the General Calendar.
{2?}	Possibly should have been included in the revised Roman Martyrology.
{2 –add}	Recent beatifications and canonizations.
{3}	In the former General Calendar before 1969, as revised 1942.
{4}	In the old Roman Martyrology (English translation 1937).
{4 –deleted}	Deleted in the revision of the Roman Martyrology.

?	date or status uncertain
A.	Apostle
a.	'ante' (before, in time)
Bl, BB	Blessed (single & plural)
C	century
Comp(s)	Companion(s)
c.	'circa' (about, in time)
cf.	see under
d.	died
p	'post' (after, in time)
q.v.	which see
St, SS	Saint (single & plural)

A

Aaron the Priest (St) {2}

1 July
He features as the brother of Moses in the Pentateuch of the Old Testament, the first priest of Israel after the Exodus.

Abb cf. **Ebba.**

Abbo (Goeric) of Metz (St) {2}

19 September
d. 647. He succeeded St Arnulf as bishop of Metz (France) in 627. Other details are untrustworthy.

Abda, Ebedjesu and Comps (SS) {2, 4}

16 May
C4th. They numbered forty, and were martyred at Kashkar in the persecution ordered by Shah Shapur II (who tried to eliminate Christianity from the Persian Empire between 341 and 380). The two named were bishops, the latter of the city (the ruins of which are on the other side of the river Tigris from the present Wasit in Iraq).

Abdon and Sennen (SS) {2, 3}

30 July
C3rd? They were martyred at Rome and buried on the Via Portuense. According to their unreliable acta, they were Persian noblemen brought to Rome as prisoners of war who helped imprisoned Christians there and buried the bodies of martyrs. Their cultus was confined to particular calendars in 1969.

Abercius (St) {2, 4}

22 October
C3rd. Asserted to have succeeded St Papias as bishop of Hierapolis in Phrygia (Asia Minor), he was imprisoned for campaigning against paganism but was released and died in peace. He composed his own epitaph, which was discovered in 1882 and is an important early witness of the church's dogmatic teaching.

(Abibas) (St) {4, deleted}

3 August
His fictional legend is that he was the second son of the rabbi Gamaliel who taught St Paul (Acts 5:34; 22:3), became a Christian like his father and died aged seventy-nine. His alleged relics were found at Capergamala near Jerusalem in 415, together with those of SS Stephen, Gamaliel and Nicodemus.

(Abibus of Edessa) (St) {4, deleted}

15 November
He was listed as a C4th deacon of Edessa (Syria, now Urfa in Turkey), who was martyred by burning during the reign of Licinius and buried with his friends, SS Gurias and Samonas.

(Abilius of Alexandria) (St) {4, deleted}

22 February
According to Eusebius (the only source), the first three bishops of Alexandria in Egypt were SS Mark, Anianus and Abilius, the last from the year 84.

Ablebert cf. **Emebert.**

Abraham (St) {2}

9 October
He is the spiritual father of Jews, Christians and Muslims and features in the Book of Genesis in the Old Testament.

Abraham (Abraamios) of Arbela (St) {2}

31 January
d. 345. A bishop of Arbela (now Arbil in northern Iraq), he was martyred at Telman in the reign of Shah Shapur II of Persia.

Abraham of Clermont (St) {2, 4}

15 June
d. c.480. Born along the Euphrates river, during a persecution in Persia he went to Egypt but was abducted as a slave by brigands for five years. When he escaped, he sailed to Gaul, where he became a hermit near Clermont-Ferrand, France. Eventually he became abbot-founder at the monastery of St Cyriac there. He is a patron against fever.

Abraham Kidunaia (St) {2, 4}

29 October
d. ?366. He fled from wealth and a prestigious marriage to become a hermit near Edessa (Syria) but was ordained for a town called Beth-Kiduna, which he completely converted to Christianity. St Ephrem was his friend and wrote his biography.

Abran cf. **Gibrian**.

Abrunculus of Clermont-Ferrand (St) {2}

4 January
d. 490. From Autun, he became bishop of Langres (France) but was expelled by the Arian king of Burgundy. Then he took over from St Sidonius Apolloninaris as bishop of Clermont-Ferrand. He has been mistakenly duplicated as 'Aprunculus' in the revised Roman Martyrology on 14 May.

Abudemius (St) {2, 4}

15 July
C4th. From the Aegean island of Tenedos (Greece, now Bozcada in Turkey), he was martyred in the reign of Diocletian.

Abundius and Comps (SS) {2, 4}

16 September
d. 304. They were martyred at Mount Soracte on the Flaminian Way near Rome. Their untrustworthy acta assert the following: Abundius was a priest who raised John, the son of a senator Marcian, from the dead. These three were then killed together with Abundantius, a deacon, on the orders of Emperor Diocletian and their relics were taken to Rome.

Abundius and Irenaeus (SS) {2, 4}

23 August
d. ?258. According to their legend, they were martyrs of Rome who were drowned in a public sewer during the persecution of Valerian.

Abundius of Como (St) {2, 4}

2 April
d. 468. A Greek, he became bishop of Como (Italy) in 449. As a capable theologian, he was sent by Pope St Leo to Emperor Theodosius II on a mission which helped prepare for the Council of Chalcedon in 451. He is depicted with a deer, or in the act of resurrecting a dead child.

Abundius of Cordoba (St) {2, 4}

11 July
d. 854. A parish priest of Ananelos near Cordoba when the Umayyad caliphs ruled Spain, he was involved with the 'martyr movement' and became embroiled in inter-religious polemic. He defended Christianity before the caliph's Islamic tribunal, was beheaded as a result and then fed to the dogs.

Abundius of Rome (St) {2, 4}

15 April
d. ?564. The 'Dialogues' of St Gregory the Great mention the humble and grace-filled life of this sacristan of St Peter's in Rome, and he is still venerated there.

Acacius has many variants: 'Achatius', 'Achacius', 'Acathius', 'Achathius', 'Achates', 'Agatius' or 'Agathius'.

Acacius of Amida (St) {2, 4}

9 April

C5th. Bishop of Amida in Persia (now Diyar-bakir in Turkish Kurdistan), he ransomed Persian prisoners of war from the proceeds of the sale of the sacred vessels of his cathedral. The Shah, Bahram V, was so impressed that he ceased to persecute his Christian subjects.

(Acacius of Ararat and Comps) (SS) *{4, deleted}*

22 June

The story of the Roman army officer Acacius and his ten thousand soldiers, allegedly martyred on Mount Ararat in Armenia, was popular in the Middle Ages. It is fiction.

Acacius of Byzantium (St) {2, 4}

8 May

d. ?303. A Cappadocian centurion in the Roman army in Thrace, he was tortured and beheaded at Byzantium (later Constantinople) in the reign of Diocletian. Emperor Constantine later built a basilica there in his honour.

Acacius of Melitene (St) {2}

17 April

d. ?435. He was bishop of Melitene in Roman Armenia (now Malatya in Turkey), and was unjustly deposed by his flock after opposing Nesorius at the Council of Ephesus.

Acacius of Miletus (St) {2, 4}

28 July

d. c.310. He was martyred at Miletus (Asia Minor), the reign of Licinius.

Achard cf. **Aichard**.

Achard of Avranches (St) {2}

29 April

d. 1172. He was a canon regular of St Victor at Paris before becoming bishop of Avranches

(France) in 1161. He wrote much on spiritual and controversial subjects before his death at the Premonstratensian abbey of La Lucerne d'Outremer in Normandy.

Acharius (St) {2}

27 November

d. ?640. A monk at Luxeuil under St Eustace and bishop of Noyon-Tournai from 621, he helped St Amandus of Elnone, oversaw the establishment of the diocese of Thérouanne near Calais (France) and arranged that his friend St Omer was made the first bishop.

Achilles of Alexandria (St) {2, 4}

13 June

d. 312. Successor of St Peter the martyr as patriarch of Alexandria (Egypt), he ordained the heresiarch Arius. Nevertheless, he was praised by St Athanasius and despised by the schismatic Meletians for the orthodoxy of his doctrine.

Achilles Kiwanuka (St) {1 –group}

3 June

d. 1886. He was a clerk in Buganda (Uganda) before becoming a courtier of King Mwanga, on whose orders he was martyred. Cf. **Charles Lwanga and Comps**.

Achilles Thaumaturgus (St) {2}

15 May

d. c.330. Bishop of Larissa in Thessaly (Greece), he was at the first ecumenical council of Nicaea. In 986, his city was sacked by Tsar Samuel of Bulgaria and his relics taken to Prespa.

Achilles Puchala (Bl) {2}

19 July

1911–43. A Franciscan Conventual friar, he was shot with Bl Herman Stepień at

Borowikowszczyzna during the Nazi occupation of Poland. Cf. **Poland, Martyrs of the Nazi Occupation of**.

Acindynus and Comps (SS) {2, 4}

2 November
C4th. Along with many Persian priests and clerics, they were martyred in the reign of Shah Shapur II. Also named are Pegasius, Aphthonius, Elpidiphorus and Anempodistus.

Acisclus (St) {2, 4}

17 November
d. ?304. He was martyred in Cordoba (Spain), probably in the reign of Emperor Diocletian. The old Roman Martyrology mentions his sister Victoria as a fellow martyr, but she has been deleted.

Acontus and Comps (SS) {2, 4}

5 September
? They were martyred at Porto near Rome (Italy). The companions were Nonnus, Herculanus and Taurinus.

Ada (Adrehild) (St) {2}

4 December
d. p692. She was an abbess of the nunnery of St Julien-des-Prés at Le Mans (France).

Adalbero of Würzburg (St) {2}

6 October
?1010–90. A nobleman from Lambach near Linz (Austria), he was a student at Paris with St Altman of Passau. When he became bishop of Würzburg in 1045 he supported Pope St Gregory VII against Emperor Henry IV, which led to his exile to an abbey (which he had helped to found) in his native town. He died there and his cultus was approved in 1883.

Adalbert of Egmond (St) {2}

25 June
d. 705. A Northumbrian monk, he trained under St Egbert of Iona in Ireland and accompanied St Willibrord to Friesland in 690 as a deacon, the headquarters of his own mission developing into the abbey of Egmond (Netherlands) with himself as first abbot. This was the oldest monastery in the present Netherlands.

Adalbert Nierychlewski (Bl) {2}

7 February
1903–42. He was a priest in Poland of the Congregation of St Michael the Archangel, and was arrested by the occupying Germans at Cracow in 1941. He died after torture at Auschwitz. Cf. **Poland, Martyrs of the Nazi Occupation of**.

Adalbert (Vojtech) of Prague (St) {1, 4}

23 April
956–97. Born in Bohemia (Czech Republic) and educated by his namesake of Magdeburg, he became bishop of Prague in 983 but gave up and went to Rome to be a Benedictine monk. He tried and failed twice again, in the process preaching in Poland, Hungary and Kievan Rus, before being martyred by the Old Prussians near Danzig (now Gdansk in Poland). He is called the apostle of the Catholic Slavs.

Adalgott II of Disentis (St) {2}

3 October
d. 1160. A monk under St Bernard at Clairvaux, he became abbot at the Benedictine monastery of Disentis and bishop of Chur (Switzerland) in 1150. An excellent pastor, he founded a hospital for poor people. Another abbot of the same monastery, Adalgott I who died in 1031, was also venerated as a saint in the Middle Ages, but his cultus was never confirmed.

Adalhard (Adalard, Alard) of Corbie (St) {2}

2 January

d. 826. A grandson of Charles Martel, he grew up at the court of Charlemagne and became the mayor of the palace before entering the abbey of Corbie in Picardy (France) before moving to Montecassino. However, he served as a courtier again until exiled by Emperor Louis the Pious from 814 to 821. Then he was allowed to return to Corbie, whereupon he founded the great abbey of New Corbie (Corvey near Paderborn) in Germany and also the nunnery of Herford. He was a strict monastic reformer as well as an active participant in affairs of state, but opposed the universal imposition of the Benedictine rule for monasteries in the Empire being implemented by St Benedict of Aniane. He died at Corbie, and was enshrined there. Some of his writings survive.

Adam Arakawa (Bl) {2 –add}

5 June

d. 1614. He was a married Japanese lay catechist of the diocese of Fukuoka, who was martyred at Shiki near Amakusa in Nagasaki. He was beatified in 2008. Cf. **Japan, Martyrs of**.

Adam Bargielski (Bl) {2}

8 September

1903–42. He was a Polish parish priest martyred at the Dachau concentration camp near Munich (Germany). Cf. **Poland, Martyrs of the Nazi Occupation of**.

Adam of Fermo (St) {2}

16 May

d. c.1210. A hermit, he became the Benedictine abbot of San Sabino on Monte Vissiano near Fermo (Italy), and his shrine is in that city's cathedral.

Adamnan of Coldingham (St) {2?}

31 January

d. ?680. An Irish pilgrim, he became a monk at Coldingham in Scotland (near Berwick) under the abbess St Ebba, and his cultus was confirmed in 1898 for St Andrew's and Edinburgh. However, he is not listed in the Roman Martyrology.

Adamnan (Adam, Aunan, Eunan) of Iona (St) {2}

23 September

?625–704. From Co. Donegal (Ireland), he became abbot of Iona (Scotland) in 679 and supported the Roman observance of Easter against the Celtic one (without converting his monastery). He wrote a biography of St Columba, and was an influential lawgiver in Ireland.

(Adauctus) *(St) {4 –deleted}*

7 February

d. 304. An Italian minister of finance to Emperor Diocletian at the latter's capital at Nicomedia (Asia Minor), he was listed as executed after his religion was discovered. His fate was shared by the entire Phrygian town of Antandro which was burnt, and the two incidents are connected by Rufinus.

Adel~ (names beginning with), also cf. **Alde~**.

Adelaide, Empress (St) {2}

16 December

c.930–99. A daughter of the king of Burgundy and widow of Lothair II of Italy, she was rescued from persecution and married by Emperor Otto I. Again widowed (in 973), she was harassed by her son but became regent of the Holy Roman Empire when old before retiring to a nunnery. She was friendly with the abbots of Cluny, who supported her.

Adelaide of Vilich (St) {2}

5 February
d. 1015. Her father, the count of Gelder, founded the Benedictine nunneries of Vilich near Bonn and Our Lady of the Capitol at Cologne (Germany), and she was abbess of each in turn. Her cultus was confirmed for Cologne in 1966.

Adelelm (Alleaume, Lesmes, Elesmes) of Burgos (St) {2}

30 January
d. 1097. Born near Poitiers (France), he became a soldier but met St Robert of Chaise-Dieu on returning from a pilgrimage to Rome and joined his Benedictine monastery. In 1079, he was sent to Burgos (Spain) and founded the monastery of St John outside the city walls with the help of the king and queen of Castile. A church dedicated to him stands on the site.

Adelin of Celle (St) {2}

3 February
d. c.690. From Gascony (France), he accompanied St Remaclus first to Solignac near Limoges (France) and then to Stavelot (Belgium) and Maastricht (Netherlands). He became a hermit near Dinant (Belgium) and helped to found the abbey of Celle near Liege, where he died.

Adelina (St) {2}

20 October
d. 1125. A granddaughter of King William I of England and sister of Bl Vitalis of Savigny, she became abbess of a Benedictine nunnery in Normandy (France) that her brother had founded, later called Les Dames Blanches de Mortain.

Adelphius (St) {2}

11 September
d. c.670. A grandson of St Romaricus and his successor in 653 as abbot of Remiremont in the Vosges (France), he died at the abbey of Luxeuil.

Adelphus (St) {2, 4}

29 August
C5th. He has an ancient cultus at Metz (France) as a bishop there, but nothing is known of his life.

Adelpret (Bl) {2}

20 September
d. 1172. The second bishop of Trent (now in Italy), he was strenuous in the defence of the rights of poor people and of his church, and as a result was ambushed and murdered at a place called Povereto near Trent.

Adelric (Alaric) (St) {2}

29 September
C10th. Son of a duke of Swabia, he was sent to be educated at the Benedictine abbey of Einsiedeln (Switzerland). He became a monk and priest there, and later a hermit on an island in the Zurich See.

Adeodatus cf. **Deusdedit**.

Aderald (St) {2}

20 October
d. 1002. As archdeacon of Troyes (France), he led a pilgrimage to the Holy Land and then founded the abbey of the Holy Sepulchre at Samblières to house the relics that he had collected.

(Adheritus) (St) {4 –deleted}

27 September
C2nd? He was allegedly a Greek who succeeded St Apollinaris as bishop of Ravenna (Italy). His shrine has been in the basilica

of St Apollinaris in Classe since the early Middle Ages.

Adilia cf. **Adela**.

Adjutor (Ayutre) (St) {2, 4}

30 April
d. 1131. The Norman lord of Vernon-sur-Seine (France), he went on the First Crusade, returned and became a monk at Tiron. Later, he became a hermit near the monastery.

Adjutus cf. **Avitus**.

Ado of Vienne (St) {2 ,4}

16 December
d. 875. A Burgundian monk of Ferrières, he became headmaster of the abbey school of Prüm near Trier (Germany), but the jealousy of some monks drove him away to Rome. He eventually became bishop of Vienne in 859, and did well. He compiled a martyrology which was a remote ancestor of the old Roman Martyrology, but seems unfortunately to have resorted to deliberate and unscrupulous forgery and invention to do so. The errors thus perpetrated have had a long history.

Adolf and John (SS) {2, 4}

27 September
d. 825. They were two brothers from Seville (Spain) who had a Muslim father and a Christian mother. They were martyred in Cordoba for refusing to accept Islam.

Adolf Kolping (Bl) {2}

4 December
1813–65. Born near Cologne (Germany), he was initially a shoemaker working twelve hours a day but managed to study for the priesthood, being ordained in 1845. He was parish priest at the industrial town of Elberfeld, then became a cathedral canon in 1849 and founded a Catholic association of apprentices, the 'Kolping Family'. This was a 'people's academy in the people's style', offering opportunities for study in a family environment and aiming at the intellectual and spiritual improvement of the working class. There were 26,000 members in Europe and America at his death. He was beatified in 1991.

Adolf Ludigo Mkasa (St) {1 –group}

3 June
1886. He was originally a herdsman, then a martyr of Buganda (Uganda). Cf. **Charles Lwanga and Comps**.

Adolf of Osnabrück (St) {2}

30 June
?1185–1224. A nobleman of Westphalia (Germany), he resigned a canonry at Cologne to become a Cistercian at Camp. He became bishop of Osnabrück in 1216, and was known as 'the almoner of the poor' by his charity. Adolf Hitler (baptized a Catholic) was named after him.

Adrian III, Pope (St) {2, 4}

8 July
d. 885. He became pope in 884 and immediately set out for the diet of Worms, intending to seek aid from the Germans against the Muslims. He died on the way near Modena (Italy) and was buried at the abbey of Non-antola outside that city. His cultus was confirmed in 1892 for Nonantola.

Adrian and Eubulus (SS) {2}

5 and 7 March
d. 308. They went to visit the Christians in Caesarea in the Holy Land, were seized and then martyred two days apart (Adrian first).

Adrian of Canterbury (St) {2}

9 January

d. 710. An African abbot of Nerida near Naples (Italy), he was asked by Pope Vitalian to become archbishop of Canterbury but declined and nominated St Theodore of Tarsus instead. The pope sent him to England anyway, to help St Theodore and (according to St Bede) to keep an eye on him. He became abbot of SS Peter and Paul (later renamed after St Augustine) at Canterbury, established a famous school there and became known for his scholarship. His body was discovered in 1091 and his cultus was established afterwards.

Adrian Fortescue (Bl) {2}

9 July

1476–1539. Born at Ponsbourne in Herts (England), he was a cousin of Anne Boleyn and was married to Anne Stonor. A Knight of St John, he refused the oath of supremacy to King Henry VIII and was beheaded on Tower Hill, London. He was beatified in 1895. Cf. **England (Martyrs of)**.

Adrian van Hilvarenbeek (St) {2}

9 July

d. 1572. He was a Premonstratensian canon, one of the **Gorinchem martyrs** (q.v.).

(Adrian of Argyropolis) *(St)* {4, deleted}

26 August

Early C4th? He is listed as a martyr of Nicomedia (Asia Minor) who was enshrined at Argyropolis, but is probably a duplicate of the following.

Adrian of Nicomedia (St) {2, 3}

8 September

? He was martyred at Nicomedia (Asia Minor), and that is all that is known. According to his unreliable legend, he was a pagan army officer at the court of Emperor Diocletian who helped Christian prisoners and was himself imprisoned. His work was taken up by his wife, St Natalia. All the prisoners being martyred, she took his relics to Byzantium from where others took them to Rome. The former Senate House in the Forum was his church, but his cultus was confined to local calendars in 1969.

Adrian Takahashi Mondo and Comps (BB) {2 –add}

7 October

d. 1613. He was a married Japanese layperson of Arima in Hyōgo, and was martyred there with his wife Jane Takahashi. With them were martyred Leo Hayashida Sukeemon, his wife Martha Hayashida, his son Diego Hayashida and his daughter Mary-Magdalen Hayashida; also Leo Takedomi Kan'emon and his son Paul Takedomi Dan'emon. They were beatified in 2008. Cf. **Japan, Martyrs of**.

Adrio (St) {2, 4}

17 May

C4th? He was martyred at Alexandria (Egypt), either by pagans or by Arians. The old Roman Martyrology listed two companions, Victor and Basilla, who have been deleted.

Ae~; this prefix is often rendered 'A~' or 'E~'.

Aedesius (St) {2, 4}

9 April

d. 306. A Lycian and brother of St Apphian, he was at Alexandria (Egypt) studying philosophy in the reign of Galerius and rebuked a judge who was forcing consecrated virgins into prostitution. As a result, he was tortured and drowned in the sea.

Aedilburga cf. **Ethelburga**.
Aegidius cf. **Giles**.
Aelgifu cf. **Elgiva**.

Aelred (St) {2}

12 January
1109–66. A priest's son from Hexham in Northumberland (England), he became master of the palace of King David of Scotland before joining the Cistercians at Rievaulx (Yorks) in 1133. He became abbot of Revesby and then of Rievaulx in 1147, and combined personal austerity with gentleness in office. He has left several ascetical and exegetical writings.

Affrosa cf. **Daffrosa**.

Afra of Augsburg (St) {2, 4}

7 August
d. 304. She is described as an unbaptized prostitute at Augsburg (Germany) who converted and was martyred. A great abbey in the city was dedicated to her.

(Afra of Brescia) (St) {4 –deleted}

24 May
? Listed as a martyr of Brescia (Italy), she is connected by an unreliable legend with SS Faustina and Jovita.

Africa (Martyrs of)
Under the Roman Empire, 'Africa' meant what is now the Maghrib. There were many martyrs there as it was a stronghold of Latin Christianity, and the following are listed in the revised Roman Martyrology:

{2, 4}

17 October
C3rd? A group of 270 were mentioned as martyred at Volitanum.

{2, 4}

22 July
C3–4th. 'Martyrs of Massyla' were praised by St Augustine and by Prudentius.

{2, 4}

11 February
Early C4th. The 'Guardians of the Holy Scriptures' in Numidia died rather than hand the sacred texts over to the authorities when this was required in the reign of Diocletian. (The willingness of others to obey led to the Donatist schism.)

{2, 4}

5 April
C5th. A large group was killed at Regia in Mauretania in the reign of King Genseric, an Arian Vandal. They were celebrating the Easter Mass, and the lector had his throat pierced by an arrow while intoning the 'Alleluia'.

{2, 4}

16 December
d. c.480. A large group of women was killed in the reign of King Hunneric, an Arian Vandal.

The following have been deleted from the Roman Martyrology:

30 October
? A group of between 100 and 200 were listed as martyred in an early persecution.

6 January
Early C3rd? A group of both sexes was listed as burnt in the reign of Septimus Severus.

(Agabius) (St) {4 –deleted}

4 August
d. c.250. He was listed as an early bishop of Verona (Italy), but his existence is uncertain.

Agabus (St) {2, 4}

13 February
C1st. The church prophet mentioned in the Acts of the Apostles (9:28; 21:10-12), he is often depicted as a Carmelite because of a worthless medieval legend.

Agape, Chionia and Irene (SS) {2, 4}

1 April
d. 304. Their acta state that they were three unmarried sisters who were in a group of martyrs burnt at Thessalonica (Greece) in the reign of Diocletian, except for Irene who was taken from the group and abused in a brothel for two days before being martyred on 5 April.

(Agape of Terni) (St) {4 –deleted}

15 February
Mid C3rd? The discredited legend of St Valentine of Terni alleges that he founded a community of virgins and that this martyr was one of them.

Agapitus I, Pope (St) {2, 4}

22 April
d. 536. Born in Rome and archdeacon there, he was elected pope in May 535 and had to go on an embassy to Emperor Justinian in order to persuade him not to reconquer Italy from the Ostrogoths. While in Constantinople, he deposed Patriarch Anthimus for Monophysitism and then died. His body was returned to Rome. Some of his letters survive.

Agapitus of Palestrina (St) {2, 3}

18 August
? He was allegedly a teenager aged fifteen who was martyred at Palestrina near Rome. He has an ancient cultus and is the city's patron, but his acta are unreliable. His cultus was confined to particular calendars in 1969.

(Agapitus of Ravenna) (St) {4 –deleted}

16 March
C4th? He was listed as an early bishop of Ravenna (Italy).

(Agapitus of Synnada) (St) {4 –deleted}

24 March
C3rd? He was listed as a bishop in Phrygia (Asia Minor).

Agapius of Cirta and Comps (SS) {2, 4}

4 May
d. ?259. The Spanish bishops, Agapius and Secundinus, were exiled to Cirta in Numidia (now Algeria) in the reign of Valerian and were martyred there together with the virgins Tertulla and Antonia, a soldier Emilian and a woman with her twins.

Agapius of Caesarea (St) {2, 4}

21 November
d. 306. From Caesarea in the Holy Land, he had been imprisoned three times as a Christian and the fourth time was chained to a murderer to be thrown to the wild animals in the amphitheatre. His companion was pardoned, but he refused to renounce his faith and was mauled by a bear. The next day he was weighted with stones and thrown into the sea.

Agabius of Novara (St) {2, 4}

10 September
C5th. He was listed as succeeding St Gaudentius as bishop of Novara in Piedmont (Italy) in 417.

Agatha (St) {1, 3}

5 February
d. ?251. One of the most famous Latin virgin martyrs (also venerated in the East), she was

killed at Catania (Sicily). Her unreliable legend states that her breasts were amputated as part of her martyrdom, and she is thus depicted with a knife or shears and with a plate holding her breasts. Her name is in the Roman Canon of the Mass, and she is the patroness of bell-founders, wet-nurses (of both because of her breasts) and of jewellers.

Agatha Chŏn Kyŏng-hyŏb (St) {1 –group}

26 September
Cf. **Sebastian Nam I-gwan and Comps**.

Agatha Kim A-gi (St) {1 –group}

24 May
Cf. **Augustine Yi Kwang-hŏn and Comps**.

Agatha Kwŏn Chin-i (St) {1 –group}

31 January
Cf. **Augustine Pak Chŏng-wŏn and Comps**.

Agatha Kim A-gi (St) {1 –group}

24 May
Cf. **Augustine Yi Kwang-hŏn and Comps**.

Agatha Kwŏn Chin-i (St) {1 –group}

31 January
Cf. **Augustine Pak Chŏng-wŏn and Comps**.

Agatha Lin Zhao and Comps (St) {1 –group}

28 January
1817–58. From Qinglong in Guizhou (China), when young she took a private vow of virginity and became a headmistress. She was beheaded with SS Jerome Lu Ting-mei (a schoolteacher) and Laurence Wang Bing (a prosperous farmer), catechists, at Maokou in the same province after they had been denounced as Christians. Cf. **China, Martyrs of**.

Agatha Yi and Teresa Kim (SS) {1 –group}

9 January
d. 1840. They were strangled in prison at Seoul in Korea after being flogged. The former was a virgin whose parents had already been martyred, and the latter was a widow. Cf. **Korea, Martyrs of**.

Agatha Yi Kan-nan (St) {1 –group}

20 September
Cf. **Laurence Han I-hyŏng and Comps**.

Agatha Yi Kyŏng-i (St) {1 –group}

31 January
Cf. **Augustine Pak Chŏng-wŏn and Comps**.

Agatha Yi So-sa (St) {1 –group}

24 May
Cf. **Augustine Yi Kwang-hŏn and Comps**.

Agathangelus and Cassian (BB) {2}

7 August
d. 1638. Two French Capuchins (the former from Vendôme, the latter from Nantes), they went to Egypt in the 1630s to help in ecumenical work with the Coptic Church. Failing in this because of the public immorality of some local Catholics, they went to Ethiopia disguised as Coptic monks. Their arrival was reported to the Negus (Emperor) Fasilidas by a German Protestant, and they were stoned to death at Gondar after a three-day public ordeal during which they were offered their freedom if they accepted the doctrines of the native Ethiopian church. They were beatified in 1906.

(Agatho) (St) {4 –deleted}

7 December
d. 250. He is apparently identical to St Besas, one of the companions of **SS Julian and Eunus**.

Agatho, Pope (St) {2, 4}

10 January
c.577–681. Born in Palermo in Sicily, he may have been a Latin or Byzantine rite monk before becoming pope in 678. His legates presided over the sixth ecumenical council at Constantinople against Monothelitism in 680. He also restored St Wilfrid to the bishopric of York after the latter's diocese had been divided.

(Agatho and Triphina) (SS) {4 –deleted}

5 July
? Nothing is known about these Sicilian martyrs, not even the sex of the latter-named.

(Agathoclia) (St) {4 –deleted}

17 September.
? Her legend in the old Roman Martyrology describes her as the servant of a pagan woman who ill-treated her in order to force her to apostatize. She was eventually condemned and burnt. She is the patron of Mequinenza in Aragon, and has thus been described as a Spaniard.

Agathonicus, Zoticus and Comps (SS) {2, 4}

21 August
C3rd The former was a patrician who was martyred near Byzantium (later Constantinople), while the latter were a philosopher and some of his disciples martyred at about the same time. A basilica was built in their honour at Constantinople.

Agathopodes and Theodolus (SS) {2, 4}

4 April
d. 303. The former was a deacon and the latter a young lector of the church at Thessalonica (Greece). They were martyred in the reign of Emperor Maximian Herculius for refusing to hand over the sacred texts.

Ageric (Aguy, Airy) of Verdun (St) {2, 4}

1 December
d. 588. Successor of St Desiderius as bishop of Verdun in 554, he was highly regarded by SS Gregory of Tours and Venantius Fortunatus, his contemporaries. He was buried in his own home, which became a church and then the Benedictine abbey of St Airy.

Aggaeus cf. **Haggai**.

Agil (Aile, Ail, Aisle, Ayeul, Ely) (St) {2}

30 August
c.580–650. A Burgundian nobleman, he became a monk at Luxeuil under St Columban and his successor St Eustace and accompanied the latter on a missionary journey to Bavaria in ?617. He then became the first abbot of Rebais near Paris (France).

Agileus (St) {2, 4}

25 January
C3–4th. A martyr at Carthage in Roman Africa, he was highly venerated by the African and Roman churches. His relics were taken to Rome, and St Augustine preached an extant sermon in his honour.

Agilulf (St) {2, 4}

31 March
d. 751. He became archbishop of Cologne in ?746. In the C11th, he was confused with a monk martyred by barbarians and was hence listed as a martyr, and was also supposed to have been abbot of Stavelot-Malmédy in Belgium. Both of these assertions are false.

Agnellus of Naples (St) {2, 4}

14 December
End C6th. A hermit and then abbot of San Gaudioso near Naples (Italy), he is one of the patron saints of that city. The tradition is that

he used to raise sieges by displaying a banner of the cross.

Agnellus of Pisa (Bl) {2}

13 March
d. 1235 or 1275. From Pisa (Italy), he was received as a Franciscan by St Francis and sent by him first to found a house in Paris and then to be the first provincial superior in England. Arriving at Dover in 1224, he founded a friary at Canterbury and also at Oxford, where he established a famous school and where he died. His cultus was confirmed in 1892 for Pisa.

Agnes (St) {1, 3}

21 January
C3–4th. A Roman girl aged about twelve, she was martyred and buried on the Via Nomentana in Rome where a basilica was built for her in the reign of Constantine. She is mentioned in the Roman Canon of the Mass, was praised by Prudentius and SS Ambrose and Damasus and, as a virgin martyr, is a special guardian of chastity. This was despite her age, as she had reached the age of consent for girls in the Roman Empire. Her acta are untrustworthy. Her attribute is a lamb (a pun on her name).

Agnes of Assisi (St) {2}

16 November
1197–1253. She was the younger sister of St Clare, whom she followed to the Benedictine convent of Panso near Assisi (Italy) when aged sixteen and thence to San Damiano. She was the first Poor Clare abbess of Monticelli at Florence, opened convents at Padua, Venice and Mantua and died at San Damiano three months after St Clare.

Agnes of Bagno (Bl) {2?}

4 September
Early C12th. She was a Camaldolese nun at Santa Lucia near Bagno di Roma in Tuscany (Italy) and has her shrine at Pereto. Her cultus was confirmed in 1823, but she is not listed in the Roman Martyrology.

Agnes de Beniganim cf. **Josephine-Mary-of-St-Agnes Albiñana**.

Agnes of Bohemia (St) {2}

2 March
1200–82. Born at Prague (Czech Republic), she was the daughter of the king of Bohemia and was educated by the Cistercian nuns of Trzebnica (Poland). She refused to marry and, with the help of the pope, she founded and entered a Poor Clare convent at Prague which was staffed by five nuns sent by St Clare from Assisi. She remained there for the rest of her life, forty-six years, and was canonized in 1989.

Agnes Cao Kuiying (St) {1 –group}

1 March
1821–56. From a Catholic family of Guizhou (China), she was orphaned when young, settled at Xingyi and was briefly married to a violent and cruel man. In her widowhood, she was a disciple of St Augustus Chapdelaine and helped the missionaries in Guangxi (China) as a catechist. She was martyred at Xilinxian by being stuffed into a cage in prison which only permitted her to stand, and being left to die. Cf. **China, Martyrs of**.

Agnes-of-Jesus Galand (Bl) {2}

19 October
1602–34. Born in Puy-en-Velay (France), when aged seven she set out to be a 'slave of the Holy Virgin' and joined the Dominicanesses at Langeac in 1623. She was made prioress, but was deposed through calumny. She was mystically involved in prayer for Fr Olier, Abbot of Pébrac (who opened the first seminaries in France) and was beatified in 1994.

Agnes Kim Hyo-ju (St) {1 –group}

3 September
Cf. **John Pak Hu-jae and Comps**.

Agnes Lê Thị Thành (St) {1 –group}

12 July
d. 1841. Born of Christian parents at Bai Den, Vietnam, she became a wife and mother. For sheltering priests in her house during the persecution ordered by Emperor Thiệu Trị, she was arrested and viciously tortured, and as a result, she died in prison at Ninh Bình. Cf. **Vietnam, Martyrs of**.

Agnes of Poitiers (St) {2}

13 May
d. 588. She was the adopted daughter of Queen St Radegund, and was made abbess of Holy Cross at Poitiers (France). St Caesarius of Arles provided her with a rule for her monastery, but she had to be deposed in 589 after a revolt among the nuns. She was a friend of St Venantius Fortunatus.

Agnes Segni of Montepulciano (St) {2}

20 April
d. 1317. From Tuscany (Italy), when aged nine she entered a nunnery at Montepulciano and went on to be founding superior of a Dominican nunnery in the city in 1306. She was a famous mystic, and is the patron of the city.

Agnes Takea (Bl) {2}

10 September
d. 1626. She was a Japanese, the wife of Bl Cosmas Takea, and was beheaded at Nagasaki in the 'Great Martyrdom' with BB Charles Spinola and Comps. Cf. **Japan, Martyrs of** and **Great Martyrdom at Nagasaki**.

Agoard, Aglibert and Comps (SS) {2, 4}

24 June
? This large group was martyred at Creteil near Paris (France).

Agricius (St) {2, 4}

13 January
d. 330. Predecessor of St Maximinus as bishop of Trier (Germany), he was at the Council of Arles in 314. A biography of the C11th claimed that he obtained the Holy Coat (a garment venerated at Trier as having been worn by Christ) from St Helen in Jerusalem.

(Agricola) (St) {4 –deleted}

3 December
? He was listed as a martyr in Pannonia (modern Hungary), but with no biographical details.

Agricola of Avignon (St) {2}

2 September
d. 700. Patron of Avignon (France) since 1647, he was allegedly a monk at Lérins for sixteen years before becoming the coadjutor and successor of his father, St Magnus, as bishop of Avignon in 660. He founded a daughter house of Lérins in the city as well as a nunnery, and allegedly drove away a flock of storks by his blessing. His story is only documented from the C15th.

Agricola (Arègle, Agrèle) of Châlon sur Saône (St) {2, 4}

17 March
d. 580. A bishop of Châlon sur Saône (France), he was praised by St Gregory of Tours for the austerity of his life.

Agricola of Nevers (St) {2}

26 February
End C6th. He was bishop of Nevers (France) from c.570.

(Agrippina) *(St)* *{4 –deleted}*

23 June
C3rd? She was listed as a Roman virgin martyr. There are competing shrines to her in Mineo (Sicily) and in Constantinople.

Agrippinus (Arpinus) of Naples (St) {2, 4}

9 November
C3rd. A bishop of Naples with an ancient cultus, his relics are under the cathedral's high altar together with those of SS Eutychius and Acutius (alleged companions of St Januarius).

Aguy cf. **Agericus** or **Agrecius**.

Aibert (Aybert) (St) {2}

7 April
d. 1140. Born near Tournai (Belgium), he became a Benedictine monk at St Crispin's Abbey there, was cellarer and provost for twenty-three years and then became a hermit. He celebrated two masses daily by choice, one for the living and one for the dead.

Aichard (Achard) of Jumièges (St) {2, 4}

15 September
C7th. Born at Poitiers (France), the son of a Merovingian courtier, when young he became a monk at Ansion near Poitiers. After thirty-nine years there, he became abbot at Quinçay and then at Jumièges, where he succeeded St Philibert. His community there allegedly numbered almost a thousand.

Aidan (Maedoc) of Fearns (St) {2}

31 January
d. 626. From Connaught (Ireland), he became a monk in his youth under St David in Wales before founding a monastery at Fearns in Co. Wexford and becoming its first superior and bishop. His biography is semi-legendary. He is the principal patron of the diocese of Fearns.

Aidan of Lindisfarne (St) {2}

31 August
d. 651. An Irish monk of Iona (Scotland), he was sent to evangelize Northumbria (England) in 635 at the request of its king, St Oswald. He founded a monastery at Lindisfarne and became bishop there, and his fruitful apostolate is described in St Bede's 'Ecclesiastical History'. He also founded monasteries at Melrose, Hartlepool and Gateshead, thus introducing the Irish monastic tradition into England. He died at Bamburgh, and is sometimes represented with a stag (owing to a legend that he saved a hunted deer by praying to make it invisible).

Aignan cf. **Anianus**.

Aigulf (Ayou, Ayoul) of Lérins (St) {2, 4}

3 September
d. 675. From Blois (France), the unreliable legend is that he became a monk of Fleury and was sent to Montecassino in order to find the relics of St Benedict. This was because Fleury had just converted to the Benedictine observance. In c.670, he was sent to be abbot of Lérins and to effect a similar conversion, but some of the brethren there, resenting this, took him and four other monks to an island off Corsica and murdered them. The Roman Martyrology merely lists them as martyred by Saracen pirates.

Ailbe (Ailbhe) of Emly (St) {2}

12 September
d. ?528. He was allegedly the first bishop of Emly in Co. Tipperary (Ireland).

Aimé cf. **Amatus**.

Aimo Taparelli (Bl) {2}

1 August
1395–1495. Born in Savigliano in Piedmont (Italy) of the family of the counts of Lagnasco,

he became a Dominican and was appointed chaplain to Bl Duke Amadeus of Savoy. He was also inquisitor-general for Lombardy and Liguria. His cultus was confirmed in 1856 for Turin and the Dominicans.

Airald (Ayruld) (Bl) {2}

2 January
d. 1146. A Carthusian prior of Portes near Belley (France), he was made bishop of St John of Maurienne in Savoy in 1132. His cultus was confirmed for Maurienne in 1863.

Airy cf. **Agericus**.
Aisle cf. **Agil**.
Ajou cf. **Aigulf**.
Ajutre cf. **Adjutor**.
Aladius cf. **Albaud**.

Alan de Solminihac (Bl) {2}

31 December
1593–1659. A nobleman born in Périgord (France), when aged twenty he became the abbot of the decayed Augustinian abbey of Chancelade and seriously set out to reform it. In 1637 he became bishop of Cahors, and similarly worked to reform a degraded diocese and to fight the errors of Jansenism. He was beatified in 1981.

Alban (St) {2}

22 June
d. ?287. A pagan soldier at Verulamium in Roman Britain, he was converted to Christianity by a persecuted priest sheltering in his house and was martyred instead of him on a hill outside the town. The record of this, in St Bede's 'Ecclesiastical History', is the only narrative witness to the Romano-British church. St Bede placed the martyrdom in the context of the persecution of Diocletian, but this has been doubted and that of Decius

proposed. King Offa of Mercia later built an abbey on the site of the martyrdom, around which grew the city of St Albans. His attribute is a cross on a pole.

(Alban of Mainz) *(St) {4 –deleted}*

21 June
d. c.400. He was allegedly a Greek priest of Naxos in the Cyclades, who was sent into exile by the Arians to Mainz (Germany), where he became a missionary. The local Arians killed him, and an abbey at Mainz was dedicated in his honour.

Alban-Bartholomew Roe (St) {2}

21 January
d. 1642. Born in Suffolk (England) of Protestant parents, he went to Cambridge University, was converted at Douai and became a Benedictine monk at Dieuleward (now Ampleforth) in 1612. He worked in London and the Home Counties from 1615 until he was martyred at Tyburn with Bl Thomas Green after a long imprisonment. He was canonized in 1970. Cf. **England (Martyrs of)**.

Alberic of Cîteaux (St) {2}

26 January
d. 1109. One of the three founders of the Cistercians, he was at first a hermit at Collan near Châlons-sur Marne (France), then he followed St Robert to Molesmes in 1075 and became his prior there. They both went to Cîteaux in 1098. St Alberic was prior there as well, and succeeded St Robert as abbot in 1099.

Alberic Crescitelli (St) {1 –group}

21 July
1863–1900. From near Benevento (Italy), he attended the Pontifical Seminary for Foreign Missions at Rome and, after being ordained

in 1887, went as a missionary to Shanxi (China). He was captured in the Boxer Rebellion at a village called Yanzibian near Yangpingguan and beaten almost to death. The following day he was dragged to a river by his ankles over a stony road, tortured and dismembered and finally beheaded. His body parts were thrown into the river. Cf. **China, Martyrs of.**

Albert cf. **Alpert.**

Albert and Vitus (SS) {2}

2 September
d. 1096. A soldier of Bergamo (Italy), he was badly wounded and vowed that he would become a consecrated religious if cured. After a pilgrimage to St James at Compostella, he founded the Benedictine abbey of St James at Pontida outside Bergamo and put it under the Cluniac obedience. His relics, formerly enshrined at Bergamo, were returned to Pontida (which survives as a working monastery) in 1928, and he is venerated with a monk-disciple named Vitus.

Albert of Bergamo (St) {2}

11 May
d. 1279. An Italian peasant farmer and a Dominican tertiary, he was persecuted by his wife and relatives for helping poor and destitute people. He died at Cremona (Italy), and his cultus was confirmed for there in 1728.

Albert of Cashel (St) {2}

8 January
C8th. He is the patron of Cashel in Ireland, and has an unreliable extant biography. According to this, he was an Anglo-Saxon missionary in Ireland and Bavaria who visited Jerusalem and who died and was buried in Regensburg in Bavaria (Germany).

Albert Chmielowski (St) {2}

25 December
1845–1916. Born at Igołomia in Russian Poland near Cracow, he studied in Warsaw and St Petersburg but was involved in the Polish insurrection of 1863 against Russia and was exiled to Western Europe, where he studied painting. He found Christian faith in painting religious pictures and moved to Cracow (then under the Hapsburgs) where he shared his life and earnings from his painting with the poor. In 1880 he became a Franciscan tertiary, being called 'another Francis', and his followers became the 'Albertine Fathers and Sisters'. He was canonized in 1989.

Albert of Colle (Bl) {2}

17 August
d. 1202. He was a priest and hermit on Monte Torrecelli near Colle di Val d'Else in Tuscany (Italy).

Albert the Great (St) {1, 3}

15 November
c.1200–80. A nobleman from Swabia (Germany), he joined the Dominicans while at the University of Padua, became a lecturer in theology at Cologne and Paris and recognized the genius of his pupil, St Thomas Aquinas. Then he became provincial superior of the Dominicans in Germany and bishop of Regensburg for two years from 1260. The rest of his life was spent teaching and writing in Cologne, where he was the pioneer in applying Aristotelianism to theology and where his immense output dealt with all contemporary branches of scholarship (hence his nickname, 'Doctor Universalis'). He was declared a doctor of the Church in 1931, being thus equivalently canonized, and is the patron of scientists.

Albert Hurtado Cruchaga (St) {2}

18 August
1901–52. Born in Viña del Mar (Chile) of a poor family, he became a Jesuit in Santiago and chaplain of the youth movement of 'Catholic Action' there. In 1944 he started 'El Hogar del Christo', a series of homes for homeless people, and in 1947 he founded the 'Chilean Trade Union Association' in order to promote the church's social teaching. He died of pancreatic cancer, and was canonized in 2005.

Albert of Jerusalem (St) {2}

14 September
d. 1214. An Italian canon regular, he was in turn prior-general of the Augustinians, bishop of Bobbio and of Vercelli and, in 1205, Latin Patriarch of Jerusalem under Pope Innocent III. He established his residence at Acre, and helped St Brocard organize the hermits of Carmel, writing a rule for them. Thus he is the co-founder of the Carmelites. He was killed by a corrupt master of a hospital at Acre in the Holy Land whom he had deposed.

Albert of Louvain (St) {2, 4}

24 November
d. 1192. Born at Keizersberg near Louvain (Belgium), he was elected bishop of Liege in opposition to Emperor Henry VI, who had his own candidate. The pope supported him, and he was ordained at Rheims in 1192, but he was murdered by three German knights two months later and was regarded as a martyr.

Albert-Mary Marco Alemán and Comps (BB) {2 –add}

d. 1936. They are the Carmelite Martyrs of Madrid, Spain. Bl Albert-Mary was the superior of the Carmelite friary at Ayala in Madrid, and when the Spanish Civil War began, he and his community went into hiding. However he was betrayed, and imprisoned after refusing to deny his faith. He was then shot and buried in a common grave. His eight companions were young friars of the Onda friary at Castellón, who were arrested, taken to Madrid and shot. They were beatified in 2013. Cf. **Spanish Civil War, Martyrs of** and list in appendix.

Albert Marvelli (Bl) {2 –add}

5 October
1918–46. From Ferrara in Italy but brought up in Rimini, as a teenager he was much involved in Catholic Action. He was noted for going about on his bicycle performing works of charity, and this continued after he became a schoolteacher. During the war he saved several Jews from deportation, and after it he joined the city council. As a member of the Christian Democratic Party everybody, including his ideological opponents, respected him. He was killed on his bicycle in a road accident and was beatified in 2004.

Albert of Montecorvino (St) {2}

5 April
d. 1127. A son of Norman immigrants, he became bishop of Montecorvino near Salerno (Italy) but went blind when old and was provided with a coadjutor. The latter treated him with cruelty, which he bore with patience.

Albert of Sassoferrato (Bl) {2}

7 August
d. 1350. He was a monk of Santa Croce di Tripozzo in the Marches (Italy), later a Camaldolese monastery, and his cultus was confirmed for the Camaldolese in 1837.

Albert of Trapani (St) {2}

7 August
c.1240–1307. From Trapani (Sicily), he joined the Carmelites there and went to

Messina as a priest. He became provincial superior in 1296. His special work was the conversion of Jews to Christianity, at which he was very successful. His cultus was confirmed in 1454.

Albertina Berkenbrock (Bl) {2 –add}

1919–31. She was from a farming family at São Luis in Santa Catarina state, Brazil, and as a child was placid and happy, having a special devotion to St Aloysius Gonzaga. However, when aged twelve, an employee of her father's whom she had befriended tricked her into going into a wood, whereupon he followed with the intention of raping her. She fought hard and successfully to prevent this, so he cut her throat and accused another man of the crime. However, he eventually confessed to this and to two other rape-murders, and while in prison testified that she had preferred to die rather than submit to rape. This was instrumental in her beatification in 2007.

Albertinus (St) {2}

13 April
d. 1294. He became a monk of Fonteavellana near Urbino in Italy, the chief monastery of a Benedictine congregation (united to the Camaldolese in 1570) in 1250 and served as prior-general of said congregation from 1275. His cultus was confirmed in 1782.

(Albina) (St) {4 –deleted}

16 December
Mid C3rd? The old Roman Martyrology stated that she was a virgin martyr of Gaeta in the Campagna (Italy), where her ancient shrine is located. The Eastern tradition is that her body was miraculously transported there from Caesarea in the Holy Land, where she was martyred.

Albinus (Aubin) of Angers (St) {2}

1 March
d. 550. From Vannes (France), he became a monk and abbot of Tincillac near Angers, then bishop of Angers in c.530. He played an important part at the third council of Orleans in 538. The abbey of St Aubin at Angers was dedicated to him, and he has a shrine and pilgrimage centre at St Aubin de Moeslain.

(Albinus of Lyons) (St) {4 –deleted}

15 September
End C4th? Listed as the successor of St Justus as bishop of Lyons after 381, he was supposed to have built the church of St Stephen there as his cathedral.

Albuin of Buraburg (St) {2}

26 October
d. ?786. He was an English monk called Witta ('Blond'), who Latinized his name when he went on the German mission with St Boniface. He became bishop of Buraburg in Hesse in 741.

Albuin of Brixen (St) {2}

5 February
d. ?1006. A nobleman of Carinthia (Austria), he became bishop of Säben in 977 and transferred the see to Brixen in the South Tyrol (now in Italy).

Aldebrand (Bl) {2}

1 May
d. 1170. Born near Cesena (Italy), he became provost of Rimini where he preached vigorously against licentiousness and once had to flee for his life as a result. In 1170 he became bishop of Fossombrone, where he is the principal patron.

Aldegund (Orgonne) (St) {2, 4}

30 January

630–84. Sister of St Waldetrude, she was the abbess-founder of Maubeuge in Flanders (France).

Alderic (Audry) of Le Mans (Bl) {2}

7 January

d. 856. Chaplain of Emperor Louis the Pious and bishop of Le Mans (France) from 832, he was a saintly bishop and a capable public official. Some of his writings are extant.

Aldetrude (Adeltrude) (St) {2}

25 February

d. 526. Her extant biography is unreliable. According to it, she was a daughter of SS Vincent Madelgar and Waldetrude, was sent as a girl to her aunt St Aldegund at Maubeuge in Flanders (France), later became that nunnery's second abbess, died in 696 and was succeeded by her sister, St Madalberta. The revised Roman Martyrology has her 170 years earlier.

Aldhelm (St) {2}

25 May

639–709. Born in Wessex (England), he became a monk at Malmesbury, studied under St Adrian at Canterbury, became headmaster of the Malmesbury abbey school and then was made abbot in 675. He was made first bishop of Sherborne in 705 while remaining abbot of Malmesbury, where his shrine was established. The first English scholar of note, he wrote poetry in English and Latin (although none of his English work is extant). He loved books, and has been called the first English librarian.

Alexander (St) {2, 4}

21 September

? He was martyred at Baccana (Italy), twenty miles from Rome on the Via Cassia, and was formerly listed as a bishop.

(Alexander) (St) *{4 –deleted}*

30 January

C3rd? The old Roman Martyrology listed him as an elderly martyr of the reign of Decius, but he may be the same as St Alexander of Jerusalem.

(Alexander) (St) *{4 –deleted}*

27 March

C3rd. The old Roman Martyrology listed him as a soldier who was martyred in Pannonia (now in Hungary) in the reign of Maximian Herculius, and he may be the anonymous martyr of Thrace celebrated on 13 May.

(Alexander I, Pope) (St) *{4 –deleted}*

3 May

C2nd? He was listed by St Irenaeus as having been pope for about six years (other sources differ), but not a martyr. (The Roman church was probably still an informal federation of Christian synagogues at the time.) His acta as a martyr are fictitious. Unusually, he was deleted from the revised Roman Martyrology despite being in the General Calendar before 1969.

(Alexander, Abundius, Antigonus and Fortunatus) (SS) *{4 –deleted}*

27 February

? They are listed as martyrs either in Rome (according to the old Roman Martyrology), or in Thessaly (according to St Bede).

Alexander, Eventius and Theodolus (SS) {2, 3}

3 May

C3rd–4th. Roman martyrs, they were buried on the Via Normativa. The first was later confused with Pope St Alexander I, but is now considered to be the St Alexander mentioned in the Roman Canon of the Mass. Their cultus was confined to local calendars in 1969.

(Alexander, Heraclius and Comps) *(SS)*
{4 –deleted}

22 October
? Their legend is that St Alexander was a bishop who was successful in converting Jews and pagans, who was tortured and martyred together with St Heraclius, a soldier guard converted by his example, and others.

(Alexander and Theodore) *(SS) {4 –deleted}*

17 March
? Nothing is known about these alleged martyrs.

Alexander of Alexandria (St) {2}

26 February
c.250–326. Patriarch of Alexandria (Egypt) from 312, he condemned Arius (one of his clergy) for heresy and favoured the young St Athanasius, whom he ordained deacon. He was also faced with the schism of the rigorist Meletians. He died just after he and St Athanasius had attended the first ecumenical council at Nicaea (325), which definitively condemned Arianism. A few of his writings have survived.

Alexander of Bergamo (St) {2}

26 August
C3rd–4th. He was martyred at Bergamo (Italy). His unreliable legend connected him with the Theban Legion (q.v.).

Alexander Blake (Bl) {2}

4 May
d. 1590. He was a London ostler who was executed with Bl Nicholas Horner on the charge of having aided Bl Christopher Bales, a priest. He was beatified in 1987. Cf. **England (Martyrs of)**.

Alexander Briant (St) {2}

1 December
?1561–81. From Somerset, he converted while studying at Oxford and was ordained at Douai in 1578. He worked in Somerset until seized in London in 1581 and severely tortured in order to make him disclose the whereabouts of Fr Robert Parsons SJ. He joined the Society of Jesus in prison before being tried and condemned for alleged complicity in a fictitious plot. He was executed at Tyburn with SS Ralph Sherwin and Edmund Campion and was canonized in 1970. Cf. **England (Martyrs of)**.

Alexander Carbonarius (St) {2}

11 August
C3rd. A philosopher who became a charcoal burner as an exercise in humility, he was made bishop of Comana in Pontus (Asia Minor) on the recommendation of St Gregory Thaumaturgus and was martyred by being burnt. These events were described by St Gregory of Nyssa.

Alexander of Constantinople (St) {2, 4}

28 August
d. 336. Bishop of Constantinople from 313 to 336 during the Arian controversy, he was at the First Council of Nicaea in 325 and spoke out against Arius. The tradition is that his prayers led to Arius dying in a public toilet when his bowels prolapsed.

(Alexander of Corinth) *(St) {4 –deleted}*

24 November
d. 361. He was listed as a martyr of Corinth (Greece) in the reign of Julian.

Alexander Crow (Bl) {2}

30 November
d. 1586. A shoemaker from York, he was ordained at Rheims and was a priest in Yorkshire for two years before being seized while baptizing a child at South Duffield. He was executed at York and was beatified in 1987. Cf. **England (Martyrs of)**.

(Alexander of Fermo) *(St)* *{4 –deleted}*

11 January
Mid C3rd? He was allegedly a bishop of Fermo near Ancona (Italy), martyred in the reign of Decius. His presumed relics are enshrined in the cathedral there.

Alexander of Fiesole (St) {2, 4}

6 June
d. 823. A bishop of Fiesole near Florence (Italy), he appealed to the emperor to restore certain properties of his diocese which had been alienated, and was consequently ambushed and drowned near Bologna by his opponents. He is no longer listed as a martyr.

Alexander of Jerusalem (St) {2, 4}

18 March
d. c.250. A fellow student with Origen in Alexandria, he became bishop of his native city in Cappadocia (Asia Minor) and was imprisoned for his faith in the reign of Severus. He afterwards became coadjutor to Narcissus in Jerusalem, and this is the first recorded example of the transfer of a bishop and of coadjutorship. He founded a library and a school for the exiled Origen, and died in prison at Caesarea in the reign of Decius.

Alexander of Pidna (St) {2}

14 March
d. c.390. He was martyred at Pidna in Macedonia, and enshrined at Thessalonica (Greece).

Alexander of Philomelium and Comps (St) {2}

13 July
Early C4th. He was martyred at Philomelium in Phrygia (Asia Minor) with thirty soldiers.

Alexander Rawlins (Bl) {2}

7 April
d. 1595. Possibly from Gloucestershire, he was educated at Rheims and ordained in 1590. He was captured and executed while on the York mission and was beatified in 1929. Cf. **England (Martyrs of)**.

(Alexander of Rome) *(St)* *{4 –deleted}*

9 February
? He was listed as martyred at Rome with thirty-eight companions.

Alexander (Sándor) István (Bl) {2 –add}

8 June
1914–53. From a working-class family of Szolnok in Hungary, he migrated to Budapest in 1936 in order to join the Salesians as a lay brother and to train as a printer for that order. After the Communist takeover his printing works were forcibly shut down, but he continued catechetical work with young people in secret. As a result he was arrested, tortured and hanged. He was beatified as a martyr in 2013.

Alexander Sauli (St) {2, 4}

11 October
1534–92. From Milan (Italy), he became a Barnabite priest and a zealous preacher and confessor, being for a time the spiritual director of St Charles Borromeo. He became superior of his congregation and was made bishop of Aleria in Corsica for twenty years in 1569, completely reforming the diocese. He was transferred to Pavia just before his death, and was canonized in 1904.

(Alexander of Thessalonica) *(St)* *{4 –deleted}*

9 November
Early C4th?. He was listed as martyred at Thessalonica (Greece).

(Alexander of Verona) *(St)* *{4 –deleted}*

4 June
C8th? Nothing is known about this alleged bishop of Verona (Italy).

(Alexandra of Amisus and Comps) *(SS)*
{4 –deleted}

20 March
d. c.300? They were listed as a group of women of Amisus in Paphlagonia (Asia Minor) burnt in the reign of Diocletian. The others named are Claudia, Euphrasia, Matrona, Juliana, Euphemia, Theodosia and Derphuta with her sister.

Alexandria (Martyrs of)

The contests between paganism, heresy and Christianity were especially vicious at Alexandria (Egypt) during the Roman Empire, and many died in both official persecutions and in the rioting for which the city was notorious. The following anonymous groups are listed in the Roman Martyrology:

{2, 4}

10 August
d. 257. St Dionysius left a description of a violent persecution in the reign of Valerian, when inhuman tortures were used.

{2, 4}

7 February
d. 356. While St Athanasius was celebrating Mass, an Arian army officer ordered his congregation to be massacred (he himself escaping).

{2, 4}

21 March
d. 357 or 358. The Catholic Churches were sacked on a Good Friday by the pagans and Arians during the reign of the Arian Emperor Constantius II, and many worshippers died. St Athanasius wrote about this event, which he blamed on George, the Arian bishop imposed on his see.

{2, 4}

28 February
d. 262. Many Christians were considered to be martyrs who had died after nursing the sick during an epidemic in the reign of Valerian, in contrast with the pagans who abandoned them in fear.

{2, 4}

21 May
d. 372. When St Athanasius was exiled and replaced by the Arian George during the reign of Constantius II, many of his followers were killed or themselves exiled during the season of Easter. The old Roman Martyrology named a priest Secundus, who has been deleted.

{2, 4}

17 March
d. 392. During the reign of Theodosius there was a riot between the Christians and the worshippers of Serapis, who had the main temple in the city. Many died, and the temple of Serapis was destroyed by Patriarch Theophilus in the following year.

Alexandrina-Mary da Costa (Bl) {2 –add}

13 October
1904–55. From a peasant family of Balasar in Portugal, she was an ordinary girl until aged fourteen. Then, she jumped twelve metres from a window in order to avoid rape by a gang of violent intruders and was left partially paralysed. This paralysis became total and irreversible five years later. She received the mystical grace of suffering as Christ suffered in his Passion every Friday, and of being a reminder to others of the effects of sin. She suffered diabolic temptations, and evidently

ate nothing except the Holy Eucharist in the last thirteen years of her life. She was beatified in 2004.

Alexis Choemon and Comps (BB) {2 –add}

12 January
d. 1629. Three related laymen were martyred at Hanazawa (Yonezawa, Yamagata). Alexis died with Candidus 'Bōzu' (nickname; real surname unknown) his brother-in-law, and Ignatius of Hanazawa who was a nephew of Candidus. They were beatified in 2008. Cf. **Japan, Martyrs of**.

Alexis Falconieri (St) {1 –group, 3}

17 February
1200–1310. He is patron of studies in the Servite order. Cf. **Servites, Founders of**.

Alexis of Nagasaki (Bl) {2}

10 September
d. 1622. A Japanese catechist and a Dominican novice, he was burnt in the 'Great Martyrdom' at Nagasaki with BB Charles Spinola and Comps. Cf. **Japan, Martyrs of** and **Great Martyrdom at Nagasaki**.

Alexis Nakamura (Bl) {2}

27 November
d. 1619. A Japanese layman of the family of the daimyos of Hirado, he was beheaded with Anthony Kimura and Comps at Nagasaki. Cf. **Japan, Martyrs of**.

Alexis of Rome (St) {2, 3}

17 July
C4th. The cultus of this saint was suppressed for the Latin rite in 1969, although it remains popular in the East. The remote source of the story seems to be a certain Mar Riscia, a holy man of Edessa (Syria, now Urfa in Turkey). The developed legend, which spread to the West on the opening of the Greek monastery of SS Boniface and Alexis on the Aventine in Rome in the C10th, concerns a Roman senator's son who fled his wedding to become a beggar and eventually returned home to live unrecognized as a menial beneath a staircase (which is his attribute).

Alexis Sobaszek (Bl) {2}

1 August
1895–1942. He was a Polish priest killed at Dachau concentration camp in Germany. Cf. **Poland, Martyrs of the Nazi Occupation of**.

Alexis U Se-yŏng (St) {1 –group}

11 March
Cf. **Mark Chŏng Ui-bae and Alexis U Se-yŏng**.

Alexis Zaryckyj (Bl) {2}

30 October
1912–63. A priest of Lvov in the Soviet Union (now Lviv in Ukraine), he died in the gulag at Dolinka in Karaganda in the Caucasus. Cf. **Nicholas Čarneckyj and Comps**.

Aleydis of Skarenbeke (St) {2}

11 June
d. 1250. A young Cistercian nun of La Cambre at Brussels (Belgium), she became blind, leprous and paralysed and had to go into isolation from her community. She offered up her sufferings for souls in Purgatory and had visions of their being set free as a result. Her biography was written by a contemporary, and her cultus was confirmed in 1907.

Alferius (St) {2}

12 April
930–1050. A Norman nobleman of Salerno (Italy), he went on an embassy to France, fell ill at the abbey of Chiusa, recovered and

became a monk at Cluny under St Odilo. The duke of Salerno obtained his return, and he founded the abbey of La Cava outside the city. This spawned hundreds of affiliated houses of the Cluniac observance in southern Italy. His cultus was confirmed in 1893 for La Cava.

Alfonso cf. **Alphonsus**.

Alfred (St) {2}

15 August
d. 874. A monk of Corvey in Lower Saxony (Germany), he became bishop of Hildesheim in 851 and was known in the Holy Roman Empire for his peace and goodwill. He supported monasticism, upheld canon law and was devoted to Our Lady.

Alfreda cf. **Etheldritha**.
Algeric cf. **Agericus**.
Alice cf. **Adelaide**.

Alice-Mary-Jadwiga Kotowska (Bl) {2}

11 November
1899–1939. A sister of the Congregation of the Sisters of the Resurrection, she was shot at Laski Piasnica near Wejherowo in Poland. Cf. **Poland, Martyrs of the Nazi Occupation of**.

Alix le Clerc cf. **Mary-Teresa-of-Jesus Le Clerc**.
Allan cf. **Elian**.
Alleaume cf. **Adelemus**.
Alloyne cf. **Bavo**.

Allucio (St) {2}

23 October
d. 1134. Born near Pescia in Tuscany (Italy), he was a herdsman before the town made him superior of the almshouse at Val di Nievole. His followers were called 'Brethren of St Allucio'. His cultus was confirmed in the C19th.

Allyre cf. **Illidius**.

Almachius (St) {2}

1 January
d. 391. An Eastern hermit, while in Rome he publicly protested against the gladiatorial contests in the amphitheatre. The prefect ordered him killed, and the Emperor Honorius allegedly abolished such games as a consequence (if so, without full effect).

Alonzo cf. **Alphonsus**.

Aloysius Andritzki (Bl) {2 –add}

3 February
1914–43. He was an ethnic Sorb from Radibor (Germany), and as a young man helped to propagate both the faith and Sorbian culture. He became a diocesan priest of Meissen in 1939, but quickly became the target of Nazi hostility because of his public criticism of their policies. He was arrested and sent to Dachau, where he was murdered by lethal injection while suffering from typhoid. He was beatified as a martyr in 2011.

Aloysius-Gonzaga Gonza (St) {1 –group}

27 May
d. 1886. A page at the court of King Mwanga of Buganda (Uganda), he was imprisoned after being baptized and killed with a spear after a few weeks. Cf. **Charles Lwanga and Comps**.

Aloysius Gonzaga (St) {1, 3}

21 June
1568–91. A nobleman born at Castiglione delle Stiviere in Tuscany (Italy), as a boy he was a page at the courts of Tuscany, Mantua and Spain but joined the Jesuits when aged seventeen despite his family's opposition. Professed in 1587, he was a disciple of St Robert Bellamine. He died at Rome of the after-effects of plague after nursing sufferers of that disease.

Canonized in 1726, he is the protector of young students and patron of Christian youth. A contemporary likeness is extant.

Aloysius Guanella (Bl) {2}

24 October
1842–1915. A shepherd-boy on the Swiss border before he became a priest of Como (Italy), he was much influenced by St John Bosco and founded the 'Servants of Charity' and the 'Daughters of Our Lady of Providence' in order to relieve distress of any kind. He established his congregations in the United States to help Italian immigrants and wrote much on popular piety. He died at Como and was beatified in 1964.

Aloysius Liguda (Bl) {2}

8 December
1898–1942. A Polish priest of the Society of the Divine Word, he was deported to Dachau and martyred there. Cf. **Poland, Martyrs of the Nazi Occupation of**.

Aloysius Orione (St) {2}

12 March
1872–1940. Born in Tortona (Italy), he became a priest there after being influenced as a teenager by St John Bosco. He started his 'Little Work of Divine Providence' in order to help needy people, modelled on the charism of St Joseph Cottolengo, and founded five religious congregations to help, namely the 'Sons', 'Hermits', and 'Brothers of Divine Providence'; the 'Little Sisters of Charity' and the 'Blind Sacramentine Sisters'. He also had worldwide missionary interests and worked for reunion with the Orthodox. He was canonized in 2004.

Aloysius-Mary Palazzolo (Bl) {2}

15 June
1827–86. From Bergamo (Italy), he was ordained in 1880 and proved to have a similar charism to that of St John Bosco. He was involved in the Christian education of children and adults, and also in caring for sick and poor people and for the children of manual workers. He founded the 'Poor Little Sisters' and the 'Brothers of the Holy Family' to further these ends. He was beatified in 1963.

Aloysius Rabatá (Bl) {2}

8 May
c.1430–90. He became a Carmelite at Trapani (Sicily) and became superior of the friary at Randazzo. He was attacked, hit on the head and died later as a result, meanwhile refusing to identify his unknown assailant. His cultus was confirmed for the Carmelites in 1841.

Aloysius Scrosoppi (St) {2}

3 April
1804–84. From Udine (Italy), he became a priest there and, with his brother Charles who was superior of the city's Oratory, started helping destitute girls. This led to the foundation of the 'Sisters of Providence', which spread through Europe. He followed his brother into the Oratory and succeeded him as its superior, where he remained until it was suppressed by the Italian government. He was beatified in 1981 and canonized in 2001.

Aloysius Stepinac (Bl) {2}

10 February
1898–1960. Born in Krašic, Croatia (then part of Hungary), he became a diocesan priest of Zagreb in 1930 and was energetically involved in charitable activities. He was made archbishop in 1937, and did not support the racist policies of the fascist government of Croatia established after the German invasion of Yugoslavia but tried to help its victims. After the Communist takeover in Yugoslavia he was tried in 1946 and sentenced to hard labour for sixteen years, commuted to house

arrest in his home town in 1951. He was made a cardinal in 1953, and there is evidence that he was killed by poisoning. He was beatified as a martyr in 1998.

Aloysius Variara (Bl) {2 –add}

15 January
1875–1923. From Asti in Italy, he became a Salesian at Turin in 1891 and went to Agua de Dios in Colombia in 1894. He was ordained in 1898, and opened a leprosarium for young people in 1905. To help run this he founded the 'Daughters of the Sacred Hearts of Jesus and Mary', and kept in touch with the sisters after being transferred to various other places in Colombia and Venezuela. He died at Cucuta in Colombia, and was beatified in 2002. His congregation has become international in scope.

Aloysius Versiglia and Callistus Caravario (SS) {1 –group}

25 February
d. 1930. The former was born near Tortona (Italy) in 1885, joined the Salesians in 1885 and went to China in 1906. He became vicar-apostolic of Suzhou in 1921. The latter was from Lombardy, born in 1903, who joined the Salesians in 1918, went to China and became pastor of Linjou in 1928. While accompanying Bl Aloysius on a pastoral visit to that place with three young Christian women, his group was ambushed at Litaoqui in Guandong by robbers intent on rape. The two men intervened, were beaten to death and their bodies were burnt on the bank of the river Beijiang. Cf. **China, Martyrs of.**

Alpais of Cudot (Bl) {2}

3 November
d. 1211. Born in Cudot near Sens (France), she helped her peasant family on the farm until bedridden with leprosy while still a child. It was alleged that for a long time her only food was the Eucharist. Her patience and gentleness made such an impression that her cultus was informally maintained until confirmed for Sens in 1874.

Alpert (Albert) (St) {2}

5 September
d. ?1073. He was the founder and first abbot of the monastery of Butrio near Tortona (Italy).

Alphaeus and Zacchaeus (SS) {2, 4}

17 November
d. 303. Cousins, they were beheaded in Caesarea in the Holy Land in the reign of Diocletian. The former was a local reader and exorcist, the latter was a deacon from Gadara (now in Jordan).

Alphege the Martyr (St) {2}

19 April
d. 1012. A Benedictine monk of Deerhurst near Gloucester (England), he became bishop of Winchester in 984 and archbishop of Canterbury in 1005. When the Danes invaded in 1011 he refused to leave his people, and when held to ransom he refused to let the money of the poor be used. His captors soon lost patience, pelted him with bones during a drunken feast at Greenwich and then killed him with an axe. This is an early example of a martyr witnessing to justice rather than strictly to faith.

Alpherius cf. **Alferius.**

Alphius, Alexander and Zosimus (SS) {2, 4}

28 September
Early C4th. They were martyred at Caledon in Pisidia (Asia Minor). According to legend in the old Roman Martyrology, one Mark was a shepherd of Antioch in Pisidia who converted Alphius, Alexander and Zosimus his

brothers, also Nicon, Neon, Heliodorus and thirty soldiers 'in various places', implying that several groups of martyrs were conflated. Apart from the three brothers, all these have been deleted.

Alphius, Philadelphus and Cyrinus (SS) {2, 4}

10 May
C3rd. They are patrons of Lentini in Sicily and have a popular cultus in Australia based on the shrine at Silkwood in Queensland. They were possibly brothers who were martyred in the reign of Decius.

Alphonsa-of-the-Immaculate-Conception Muttathupadathu (St) {2}

28 July
1910–46. Born in Kudamaloor in Kerala (India) in the Malabarese rite, she avoided an arranged marriage as a teenager by burning her feet and was allowed to join the Poor Clares at Bharananganame in 1927. Initially healthy, her health quickly broke down for a period of five years until she was healed after asking the intercession of St Cyriac. She was then professed in 1935, but her health gave way again, and the rest of her life was a physical torment. She was canonized in 2008.

Alphonsus-Mary Fusco (Bl) {2}

6 February
1839–1910. From Angri near Nocera, Italy, the only child of peasant farmers, he was ordained as a diocesan priest in 1863 and ministered in his home town. In 1878 he helped to found the congregation of the Baptistine Sisters of the Nazarene in order to teach and care for poor orphan children at their 'Little House of Providence'. Other houses were opened throughout Italy before his death. He was beatified in 2001.

Alphonsus-Mary Liguori (St) {1, 3}

1 August
1696–1787. A nobleman born near Naples (Italy), he started his career as a lawyer but became a priest instead in 1726. The need to catechize the rural peasantry led him to found the 'Congregation of the Holy Redeemer' (Redemptorists) in 1749. He was forced to become bishop of Sant' Agata de' Goti for thirteen years in 1762, until his health failed and he returned to his congregation. He wrote much on theology, spirituality, ethics and history, was canonized in 1839 and declared a doctor of the Church in 1871.

Alphonsus López López and Comps (BB) {2}

d. 1936. They were six Franciscan Conventuals from the friary at Granollers in Spain. During the civil war they were expelled from their friary by Republicans, and initially allowed to live with family and friends. But in the summer they were seized and killed, some by shooting and others by beating on various dates. They were beatified in 2001. Cf. **Spanish Civil War, Martyrs of**.

Alphonsus-Mary Mazurek (Bl) {2}

28 August
1891–1944. From Baranowka in Poland, he became a Discalced Carmelite friar, becoming a teacher at his order's minor seminary and prior of the friary at Czerna. He was beaten and shot at Nawojowa Gora. Cf. **Poland, Martyrs of the Nazi Occupation of**.

Alphonsus de Mena (Bl) {2}

10 September
d. 1622. Born at Logroño (Spain), he became a Dominican at Salamanca, went to Japan and was burnt at Nagasaki in the 'Great Martyrdom' with BB Charles Spinola and Comps. Cf. **Japan, Martyrs of** and **Great Martyrdom at Nagasaki**.

Alphonsus Navarete (Bl) {2}

1 June
d. 1617. From Valladolid (Spain), he became a Dominican missionary in the Philippines and then the provincial vicar in Japan in 1611. After converting thousands to Christianity he was beheaded on the island of Takashima with BB Leo Tanaka and Ferdinand-of-St-Joseph Ayala. He was beatified in 1867. Cf. **Japan, Martyrs of**.

Alphonsus de Orozco (St) {2}

19 September
1500–91. Born at Oropesa in Castile (Spain), as an undergraduate at Salamanca University he was inspired to become an Augustinian friar by the sermons of St Thomas of Villanueva. He was a preacher at the court of King Philip II and a prolific and important spiritual author in Spanish. He was canonized in 2002.

Alphonsus Pacheco (Bl) {2}

7 July
1550–83. From Minayá in Catalonia (Spain), he joined the Jesuits in 1566 and became a missionary priest in Goa (Portuguese India). After a difficult career he was killed in the district of Salsette (near Bombay) with **Rudolf Acquaviva and Comps**.

Alphonsus Rodríguez (St) {2}

30 October
1531–1617. From Segovia (Spain), he became a married wool merchant but lost his family and joined the Jesuits as a lay brother when aged forty-four. He was doorkeeper of the college of Montesión at Palma on Mallorca from 1580 to 1604, and managed to edify the whole island by the way he performed this duty. He was canonized in 1888.

Alpinus of Lyons (St) {2}

15 September
C4th. He succeeded St Justus as bishop of Lyons (France).

Altfrid cf. **Alfred**.
Altheus cf. **Tathai**.
Althryda cf. **Etheldritha**.

Altmann (Bl) {2}

8 August
c.1020–91. From Westphalia (Germany), he became a canon at Paderborn and then at Aachen, chaplain to Emperor Henry III and bishop of Passau in 1065. He supported Pope St Gregory VII against Emperor Henry IV and was exiled, but he maintained his influence. He was a zealous supporter of the Augustinian Canons Regular and founded and reformed several of their abbeys, including that of Göttweig where he was buried.

Alto (St) {2}

9 February
C8th. A wandering Irish hermit, he settled in a wood near Augsburg (Germany) which the Frankish king Pepin gave to him and built a church which St Boniface consecrated in 750. This later became the abbey of Altomünster. His alleged relics are preserved there.

Aluinus cf. **Alvitus**.

Alvarez of Cordoba (Bl) {2}

19 February
d. c.1430. A Dominican at Cordoba (Spain) from 1368, he was a successful preacher in Andalusia, France and Italy, and his reform friary that he founded in 1423 became a noted centre of piety and scholarship. He opposed Peter de Luna, the last antipope of Avignon. His cultus was confirmed for Cordoba in 1741.

Álvaro del Portillo (Bl) {2 –add}

23 March
1914–94. From Madrid, Spain, he was a civil engineer when he joined Opus Dei in 1935. He was one of the first three priests of Opus Dei to be ordained, in 1944, and went on to be their secretary general. In 1975 he succeeded St Joseph Mary Escrivá as superior, and was made the first prelate when Opus Dei became a prelature in 1985. For this he was consecrated as a titular bishop in 1991. He wrote extensively on pastoral and ecclesiological themes, especially on the role of the laity in the modern church. He died at Rome, and was beatified in 2014.

Alypius the Stylite (St) {2}

26 November
d. p610. From Adrianople in Paphlagonia (Asia Minor), he became a hermit nearby and allegedly spent fifty-three years as a stylite on a pillar. Cf. **Stylianos**.

Alypius of Tagaste (St) {2}

15 August
d. c.430. A friend and disciple of St Augustine, he was baptized with him in Milan (Italy) in 387. Afterwards they spent some time together as monks at his home town of Tagaste in Roman Africa before Alipius visited the Holy Land and then became bishop of Tagaste in 393. As such he was St Augustine's chief supporter.

Amabilis of Riom (St) {2}

18 October
C5th. Apparently he was cathedral precentor at Clermont (France) and then parish priest at Riom in the Auvergne. He is invoked against fire and snakes.

Amadeus degli Amedei (St) {1 –group, 3}

17 February
d. 1265. He became superior of the foundation on Monte Senario at Florence in 1233. Cf. **Servites, Founders of**.

Amadeus of Lausanne (Bl) {2}

27 August
c.1110–59. Son of Bl Amadeus of Clermont, he was educated at Cluny and was at the court of Emperor Henry V before joining the abbey of Clairvaux under St Bernard. In 1139 he became abbot of Hautecombe in Savoy; he was made bishop of Lausanne in 1144 and became co-regent of Savoy and chancellor of Burgundy before he died. His eight sermons on Our Lady are dogmatically important.

Amadeus IX of Savoy, Duke (Bl) {2}

30 March
1435–72. Born at Thonon, he became reigning duke of Savoy (now in France) in 1455 and endeared himself to most of his subjects. A sufferer of epilepsy, he had to abdicate in favour of his wife but was the remote ancestor of the Italian royal family. He died at Vercelli (Italy). His cultus was confirmed for Savoy in 1677.

Amador cf. **Amator**.

Amalberga This has variants: Amelberga, Amalburga, Amalia, Amelia.

Amalberga of Maubeuge (St) {2, 4}

10 July
d. 690. Born in Brabant in the Low Countries, she was a niece or sister of Bl Pepin of Landen, wife of Count Witger and mother of SS Gudula, Emebert and Reineldis. Witger became a monk at Lobbes and a nun at Maubeuge in Flanders (France).

Amalberga of Munsterbilzen (St) {2}

10 July
Late C8th. She was veiled as a nun at Munsterbilzen in Belgium (near Maastricht) by St Willibrord. Her relics were transferred to the abbey of St Peter at Ghent (Belgium) in 1073.

Amandus and Junian (SS) {2}

16 October
C6th. The former was a hermit in a forest in Limousin (France), and the latter was his disciple and had the village of St Junien named after him.

Amandus of Bordeaux (St) {2, 4}

18 June
C5th. He succeeded St Delphinus as bishop of Bordeaux (c.404) and converted and catechized St Paulinus of Nola, who wrote about him.

Amandus of Elnone (St) {2}

6 February
d. 677. Born near Nantes (France), after fifteen years as a hermit at Bourges he visited Rome and was ordained as a missionary bishop. He worked in what is now French Flanders and in Belgium, founding many monasteries, and apparently became bishop of Tongeren-Maastricht. That he preached to the Slovenes in Carinthia and to the Basques in Navarre is uncertain. He died as a nonagenarian in retirement at Elnone near Tournai (Belgium), his best-known foundation. The place is now named Saint-Amand-les-Eaux after him.

Amandus of Strasbourg (St) {2}

26 October
C4th. He was the first bishop of Strasbourg (now in France). There are many obscure saints of this name in the Frankish territories in the period C4th–C8th, but he is the only one listed in the Roman Martyrology.

(Amantius, Alexander and Comps) (SS) {4 –delete}

6 June
? According to their legend, Amantius was a bishop of Noyon (France) who evangelized around Carcassonne and who had three brothers who were priests. The four were martyred near Carcassonne.

(Amantius of Città del Castello) (St) {4 –delete}

26 September
d. c.600? He is described as a priest of Città del Castello near Perugia (Italy), and a valued acquaintance of Pope St Gregory the Great at Rome.

Amantius of Como (St) {2, 4}

8 April
d. 449. He succeeded St Provinus as bishop of Como (Italy).

Amantius of Rodez (St) {2, 4}

4 November
C5th. He was listed as the first bishop of Rodez in France.

Amaranthus (St) {2, 4}

7 November
C3rd. He was mentioned by St Gregory of Tours as having been martyred at Albi (France), but details are lacking.

Amasius (St) {2}

23 January
d. 356. A Greek refugee from the Arians, he became second bishop of Teano (Italy) in 346.

Amator, Peter and Louis (SS) {2, 4}

30 April
d. 855. They were martyred at Cordoba (Spain) under the Umayyad Emir for preaching in public. Amator was a priest from Martos near Cordoba, Peter was a monk and Louis was a layman.

Amator of Autun (St) {4 –delete}

26 November
C3rd? He was listed as a bishop of Autun (France).

Amator of Auxerre (St) {2, 4}

1 May
d. 418. He was bishop of Auxerre (France). His extant biography is unreliable.

Amatus of Nusco (St) {2, 4}

30 September
d. 1093. He was a bishop of Nusco near Naples (Italy). It has been alleged that he was a Benedictine monk beforehand.

Amatus (Amé, Aimé, Amado) of Remiremont (St) {2, 4}

13 September
d. 629. From Grenoble (France), he was a monk and hermit for over thirty years at the abbey of St Maurice of Agaune (Switzerland) before joining St Eustace at Luxeuil. There he inspired St Romaric to found the Columbanian double monastery of Remiremont in 620, and became its first abbot.

Amatus Ronconi (St) {2}

8 May
d. ?1292. From Saludecio near Rimini (Italy), he became a Franciscan tertiary and made four pilgrimages to Compostella after spending an extended period living as a hermit. Meanwhile he devoted his life to the assistance of pilgrims, and built several chapels and resting places for them. He died in his home town. His cultus was confirmed for Rimini in 1776, and he was canonized in 2014.

Amatus of Sion (St) {2, 4}

13 September
d. 690. Abbot of Agaune, he became bishop of Sion in the Vallais (Switzerland) (not of Sens, as claimed). A false accusation led to his banishment first to the abbey of Péronne and then to that of Breuil, where he died as a monk.

(Ambicus, Victor and Julius) (SS) {4 –delete}

3 December
Early C4th? They were listed as martyred at the imperial capital of Nicomedia (Asia Minor) in the reign of Diocletian.

Ambrose of Agaune (St) {2, 4}

2 November
d. c.520. He was abbot of Agaune near St Moritz (Switzerland), not to be confused with another of the same name who died in 582.

Ambrose Barlow (St) {2}

10 September
d. 1641. From near Manchester, Edward Barlow was baptized as a Catholic, raised as a Protestant but re-converted and studied for the priesthood at Douai and Valladolid. He became a monk of St Gregory's at Douai in 1615 but transferred his stability to the Spanish abbey of Cellanova. He worked in southern Lancashire for twenty-four years and was imprisoned and released four times before being captured at Leigh and executed at Lancaster. He was canonized in 1970. Cf. **England (Martyrs of)**.

(Ambrose of Cahors) (St) {4 –delete}

16 October
Mid 8th? He was described as a bishop of Cahors (France) who resigned to be a hermit and died at a place in Berry now called St-Ambrose-sur-Arnon.

Ambrose Fernández (Bl) {2}

7 January
1551–1620. From Sisto in Portugal, he went as a fortune hunter to Japan but joined the Jesuits as a lay brother in 1577. He died of a stroke in the notorious prison of Suzuta at Omura and was beatified in 1867. Cf. **Japan, Martyrs of**.

(Ambrose of Ferentino) (St) {4 –delete}

16 August
Early C4th? He was allegedly a centurion martyred at Ferentino in central Italy in the reign of Diocletian, but his acta have their earliest documentary witness from the C14th.

Ambrose Kibuka (St) {1 –group}

3 June
d. 1886. A page at the court of King Mwanga of Buganda (Uganda), he was burnt alive in the year after his baptism. Cf. **Charles Lwanga and Comps**.

Ambrose of Milan (St) {1, 3}

7 December
?339–97. Born in Gaul, where his father was praetorian prefect, he became a lawyer at Rome and then the governor of Liguria and Emilia while in his early 30s. He was based in Milan (Italy), the imperial capital in the West, at a time when the church was disturbed by Arianism. While he was keeping order at the election of a new bishop he found himself elected by acclamation after a child shouted 'Ambrose for bishop!' Despite being unwilling and only a catechumen, he was ordained on 7 December 374, became a great pastor and was the most influential churchman of the time in Italy (the popes included). Well known for his charitable activities, his writings, his ability in administration and his fervent opposition to Arianism, he also opposed the misuse of secular power, as in his famous rebuke of Emperor Theodosius I over a massacre at Thessalonica. He is one of the four great Latin Fathers and a doctor of the Church, and his attributes are a whip or a beehive (as a reference to the sweetness of his preaching). He died on 4 April.

Ambrose Sansedoni (Bl) {2, 4}

20 March
1220–87. From Siena, he joined the Dominicans in 1237 and studied with St Thomas Aquinas under St Albert the Great at Cologne. A superb preacher (his vehemence was supposed to have hastened his death), he preached in Germany, France and Italy and was also master of the pope's palace. His attribute is a model of his native city, and his cultus was confirmed in 1622.

Amé cf. **Amatus**.

(Amiterno, Martyrs of) (SS) {4 –delete}

24 July
? The old Roman Martyrology listed eighty-three soldiers allegedly martyred at Amiterno in the Abruzzi, Italy. This spurious entry was apparently taken from a very garbled reference to the 83rd milestone on the road from Rome to L'Aquila.

(Ammon, Theophilus, Neoterius and Comps) (SS) {4 –delete}

8 September
? They were a group of twenty-five listed as martyred at Alexandria in Egypt.

Ammon, Zeno, Ptolemy, Ingen and Theophilus (SS) {2, 4}

1 June
d. 249. The first four were soldiers and the last a civilian, and they were at the trial of a Christian in Alexandria (Egypt) who was wavering. They gave vocal support and were themselves beheaded.

(Ammon of Heraclea and Comps) (SS) *{4 –delete}*

1 September
Early C4th? They were listed as a deacon and forty young women whom he had converted, martyred at Heraclea in Thrace (European Turkey) in the reign of Licinius.

(Ammonius and Alexander) (SS) *{4 –delete}*

9 February
? They were listed as martyred at Soli on Cyprus.

Amorion, Martyrs of (SS) {2, 4}

6 March
d. 848. An Arab incursion into the Byzantine Empire resulted in the capture of forty-two army officers who were imprisoned first in the fortress of Amorion in Phrygia. Later they were taken to Syria, and after a long imprisonment were beheaded on the banks of the Euphrates river.

Amos the Prophet (St) {2, 4}

15 June
He is the third of the minor prophets in the Old Testament.

(Ampelus and Gaius) (SS) *{4 –delete}*

20 November
d. ?302. Nothing is known of them, although they have been presumed to have been martyred at Messina (Sicily) in the reign of Diocletian.

Apphian (St) {2, 4}

2 April
Early C3rd. A young man of Caesarea in the Holy Land, he went into the governor's house and interrupted his sacrifice to his domestic idols with a rebuke. For this he was tortured to death. His brother was St Aedesius.

Amphilochius of Iconium (St) {2, 4}

23 November
d. a.403. A cousin of St Gregory Nazianzen, he studied with him and St Basil at Constantinople and was a lawyer in Constantinople before being made bishop of Iconium (Asia Minor, now Konya in Turkey) by St Basil in 373. He was one of the Cappodocian Fathers, opposing Arianism, and writing an important work on the divinity of the Holy Spirit against Macedonianism. He also presided at the synod of Side, which condemned the Messalian assertion that prayer is the only means of salvation. Most of his writings have been lost.

(Amphion of Nicomedia) (St) *{4 –delete}*

12 June
d. p325. He was bishop of Epiphania in Cilicia during the persecution of Galerius, was later made bishop of Nicomedia (Asia Minor) and attended the First Council of Nicaea. He wrote against the Arians.

(Ampliatus, Urban and Narcissus) (SS) *{4 –delete}*

31 October
C1st. They are mentioned in St Paul's letter to the Romans (16:8-12), and feature in the legends associated with St Andrew in Greece.

Anacletus, Pope (St) {3 –delete}

13 July

This is an alternative name for Pope St Cletus in ancient sources. The original composers of the old Roman Martyrology mistakenly thought that they were two separate people, hence there was a spurious celebration in the General Calendar before 1969.

Anacletus González Flores (Bl) {2 –add}

1 April

1888–1927. From a poor family of Guadalajara in Mexico, he studied for the priesthood but discerned that he did not have a vocation and became a lawyer instead in 1922. He was a leader of the Catholic Association of Mexican Youth, and publicly opposed the anti-Catholic policies of the Mexican government. After the beginning of the Cristero rebellion he organized support for the rebels, and as a result was arrested and framed for an assassination that he had not perpetrated. He was viciously tortured in prison before being executed, and was beatified in 2005. Cf. **Mexico, Martyrs of**.

(Ananias, Azarias and Misael) (SS) {4 –deleted}

17 July

They are the three young men who feature in the Book of Daniel in the Old Testament as having been thrown into a furnace and surviving. They have been deleted from the Roman Martyrology, because the book was written in the C2nd BC, and they are fictional characters.

Ananias of Arbela (St) {2, 4}

22 November

d. 345. He was martyred at Arbela in Persia on the orders of the archmagus of the Zoroastrian state cult during the persecution ordered by Shah Shapur II. He was whipped three times with such severity that bits of flesh were ripped off his body, and died as a result the following night.

Ananias of Damascus (St) {2, 4}

25 January

C1st. He was the disciple who baptized St Paul (cf. Acts 9), and his dubious legend states that he evangelized Damascus, Eleutheropolis (near Gaza) and other places before being martyred.

Anastasia (St) {1, 3}

25 December

d. ?304. Traditionally she was martyred at Sirmium (now Srem Mitrovica in Serbia), but her acta are worthless and little is known of her. Her relics were taken to Constantinople, and her cultus in Rome developed around her basilica by the Forum, where many Byzantine officials used to live. She was the only saint commemorated at Christmas, and her name is in the Roman Canon of the Mass.

(Anastasia and Cyril) (SS) {4 –delete}

28 October

Mid C3rd. Their dubious and distasteful story, recounted in the old Roman Martyrology, involves a Roman woman being publicly mutilated in the reign of Valerian and a bystander who had done her a kindness being martyred with her. There is doubt concerning their historical existence.

(Anastasius) (St) {4 –delete}

5 December

? No information is given about this martyr.

Anastasius I, Pope (St) {2, 4}

19 December

d. 401. He became pope in 399. The Roman Martyrology, St Jerome, St Augustine and St Paulinus of Nola all praised his poverty and pastoral concern. He held a synod against Origenism in 400 and was succeeded by his son, Innocent I.

Anastasius, Felix and Digna (SS) {2, 4}

14 June

d. 853. They were two monks and a nun of the double monastery of Tábanos, near Cordoba (Spain) in the time of the Muslim Umayyad emirs. Anastasius had been a deacon at a church in the city, and Felix was a Berber monk from Asturias. They were executed for preaching at Cordoba.

(Anastasius, Placid, Genesius and Comps) (SS) {4 –delete}

11 October

? They were listed as martyrs in the old Roman Martyrology, but with no details.

(Anastasius I of Antioch) (St) {4 –delete}

21 April

d. 599. Patriarch of Antioch (Syria), he opposed the imperial innovations in Christology by Justinian and was exiled for twenty-three years by Justin II. He was restored by Maurice with the aid of St Gregory the Great. He is not to be confused with his namesake of Sinai.

Anastasius II of Antioch, the Younger (St) {2, 4}

20 April

d. 609. He succeeded St Anastasius I as patriarch of Antioch (Syria), and was horribly murdered during a rebellion of the Syrian Jews against the tyrannical Emperor Phocas (who had ordered a persecution against them).

Anastasius of Brescia (St) {2, 4}

20 May

d. ?610. Bishop of Brescia in Lombardy (Italy), he helped to convert the Lombards from Arianism.

(Anastasius of Camerino and Comps) (SS) {4 –delete}

11 May

Mid C3rd? According to his legend, he was an army tribune involved in the persecution by the Emperor Decius who was converted by the courage of those being tortured under his authority. A few days after this, he and his entire household were arrested and beheaded. Their shrine is at Camerino in the Marches (Italy).

Anastasius of Cluny (St) {2}

16 October

c.1020–85. A rich and well-educated Venetian, he became a monk at Mont-Saint-Michel in Normandy but left because of a simoniac abbot and joined Cluny under St Hugh in 1066. He went to preach to the Muslims in Spain for seven years by order of the pope in 1073, then returned to Cluny. Afterwards he was a hermit near Toulouse and died on his way back to Cluny again.

(Anastasius Cornicularius) (St) {4 –delete}

21 August

Mid C3rd? According to his legend (a duplication of that of St Anastasius of Camerino), he was an army officer ('Cornicularius' was a rank) who was converted by the example of St Agapitus at Salone near Palestrina (Italy), and was then martyred. The old Roman Martyrology, however, confused him with St Anastasius the Fuller in placing his martyrdom at Salona in Dalmatia (Croatia).

Anastasius the Fuller (St) {2, 4}

25 August

? A cloth fuller from Aquileia near Venice (Italy), he moved to Salona (near Split in Croatia) and openly professed his faith, even painting a cross on his front door. He was executed by drowning.

Anastasius of Lérida *(St)*

11 May
? The patron of Lérida (Spain), he is claimed to have been a native of that city but may be a duplication of one of the martyrs called Anastasius.

Anastasius the Monk (St)

22 July
Cf. **Maximus the Confessor and Comps**.

Anastasius-James Pankiewicz (Bl) {2}

20 April
1882–1942. A Polish Franciscan friar, he was deported to Dachau by the Nazis but died of ill-treatment on the way at Hartheim near Linz in Austria. Cf. **Poland, Martyrs of the Nazi Occupation of**.

Anastasius of Pavia (St) {2, 4}

30 May
d. c.680. A convert from Arianism, he became bishop of Pavia near Milan (Italy) in 680.

Anastasius the Persian (St) {2, 3}

22 January
d. 628. Magundat had been a soldier of the Persian Shah Chosroes II, but he converted, was baptized as Anastasius and became a monk at Jerusalem. In the Persian invasion he was taken to the Shah at Caesarea and executed. His head was eventually enshrined in the Roman church of SS Vincent and Anastasius, but his cultus was confined to local calendars in 1969.

Anastasius the Sinaite (St) {2}

21 April
d. c.700. A monk from the Holy Land, he became abbot of St Catherine's at Sinai and was prominent in the Christological controversies of the period, leaving many ascetical and theological works (all of which were later edited). The most famous of these is the *Hodegos* or *Guide*.

(Anastasius of Suppentonia) *(St) {4 –delete}*

11 January
d. c.570? He is described in the 'Dialogues' of St Gregory the Great as a notary of the Roman church who became abbot of Suppentonia (Castel Sant'Elia) near Nepi (Italy). He and his monks then died in quick succession 'at the summons of an angel'. The work is not now regarded as a reliable historical source.

(Anastasius of Terni) *(St) {4 –delete}*

17 August
Mid C6th? He was listed as a bishop of Terni (near Rome) at the time when the Empire was re-conquering Italy from the Ostrogoths. The tradition was that he had been a Syrian hermit near Perugia, but this is thought to be the result of confusion between a hermit-martyr and a bishop of Terni.

Anatolia and Victoria (SS) {2, 4}

10 July
? They were martyred outside Rieti near Rome. St Jerome wrote that they were sisters denounced as Christians by rejected suitors. The old Roman Martyrology replaced Victoria with Audax, a soldier.

Anatolius of Constantinople (St) {2}

3 July
d. 458. He was patriarch of Constantinople from 449.

Anatolius Kiriggwajjo (St) {1 –group}

3 June
d. 1886. From a family of herdsmen, he became one of the pages of King Mwanga

of Buganda (Uganda) and was martyred. Cf. **Charles Lwanga and Comps**.

Anatolius of Laodecia (St) {2, 4}

3 July
C3rd. From Alexandria (Egypt) and head of the Aristotelian school there, he became bishop of Laodecia (Latakia, Syria) in 269. He was a great philosopher and mathematician, and his writings were commended by St Jerome.

Anatolius of Milan (St) {2, 4}

24 September
C2nd. He is venerated as the first bishop of Milan (Italy). The worthless tradition is that St Barnabas appointed him, and that he died at Brescia. The old Roman Martyrology listed him as 'Anathalo'.

Ancestors of Christ (St) {2}

24 December
On this date the revised Roman Martyrology commemorates all the ancestors of Christ mentioned in the two genealogies given for him in the New Testament.

Andéol cf. **Antiochus**.

Andeolus (St) {2, 4}

1 May
? He was martyred near Viviers on the Rhône in France. His worthless legend is that he was a subdeacon of Smyrna, sent as a missionary by St Polycarp.

Andochius, Thyrsus and Felix (SS) {2, 4}

24 September
? They were martyred near Autun in France. Their worthless legend makes the first a priest of Smyrna and the second a deacon, who were sent by St Polycarp to Autun where they lodged with Felix, a rich merchant whom they converted and who died with them.

Andrew (St) {1, 3}

30 November
C1st. The elder brother of St Peter was the first-called of the Apostles (hence his Greek title of 'Protoclete') and features in the Gospels, but he did not become one of the 'Inner Council' of SS Peter, James and John. There is no scriptural evidence for his career after the resurrection. Patristic authors preserved the traditions that he evangelized Scythia (now the coast-lands of Romania) and the heartland of modern Greece, being martyred at Patras. The tradition that he was executed on a diagonal cross is late. Later authors, under the influence of disputes over ecclesiastical precedence, claimed him as the founder of the churches at Byzantium (i.e. Constantinople) and at Kiev. Hence he is the patron of the Patriarchate of Constantinople and of the Ukraine, as well as of Scotland. His alleged body has been at Amalfi (Italy) since it was stolen from Constantinople in 1210, but his head (formerly at Rome) has been returned.

Andrew, John, Peter and Anthony (SS) {2, 4}

23 September
d. p881. After the Muslim Aghlabids of Tunisia conquered Syracuse in Sicily they deported these four, then tortured and executed them.

Andrew Abellon (Bl) {2}

15 May
1375–1450. He was the prior of the royal Dominican friary of St Mary Magdalen at Saint-Maximin (France), and also Aix (where he died) and at Marseilles. He was a talented painter. His cultus was confirmed in 1902 for Aix and the Dominicans.

Andrew Avellano (St) {2, 3}

10 November
1521–1608. From Castronuovo near Naples (Italy), he became an ecclesiastical lawyer before joining the Theatines and had a very successful apostolate, especially in Lombardy where he became a friend and counsellor of St Charles Borromeo. He died at Naples when he was about to say Mass. Though he was canonized in 1712, his cultus was confined to local or particular calendars in 1969.

Andrew Bauer (St) {1 –group}

9 July
Cf. **Gregory Grassi and Comps**.

Andrew Bessette (St) {2}

6 January
1845–1937. Born at Saint-Grégoire-d'Iberville in Quebec (Canada), he was a manual worker in the United States before joining the Congregation of the Holy Cross in 1870. For thirty-four years he did domestic work at the college at Côtes des Neiges and developed a great devotion to St Joseph, which bore fruit when he founded the sanctuary of St Joseph at Montreal in 1904. He was canonized in 2010.

Andrew Bobola (St) {2}

16 May
1592–1657. A Polish nobleman, he joined the Jesuits at Vilnius (Lithuania) in 1611 and spent his life reconciling Orthodox believers with the Catholic Church. He was captured by a gang of Cossacks at Ivanava (Bielarus) and was tortured and partially flayed before being killed. He was canonized in 1938.

Andrew Caccioli (Bl) {2}

3 June
d. 1254 or 1264. From Spello near Assisi (Italy), he was a wealthy priest before becoming one of the first disciples of St Francis. He supported a strict interpretation of the Franciscan rule against the innovations of Br Elias and was persecuted and imprisoned as a result. He died at the friary he had founded at Spello, and his cultus was confirmed for there in 1738.

Andrew the Calabite (St) {2, 4}

20 October
d. 767. A monk of Crete, he went to Constantinople and publicly denounced as heresy the iconoclastic policy of Emperor Constantine V. The latter had him tortured, then abandoned him to a mob of iconoclasts who paraded him through the city and lynched him.

Andrew Chŏng Hwa-gyŏng (St) {1 –group}

23 January
d. 1840. He was a catechist and helper of St Laurence Imbert at Seoul in Korea, and ran his house as a refuge for persecuted Christians. As a result, he was viciously beaten in prison, and he succumbed to his injuries. Cf. **Korea, Martyrs of**.

Andrew-of-Anagni Conti (Bl) {2}

17 February
d. 1302. A nobleman from Anagni (Italy), he was a nephew of Pope Alexander IV but became a Franciscan lay brother and then a hermit in the Apennines, staying that way despite an offer to make him a cardinal. He was much troubled by demons, and is invoked against them. He died at Rome, and his cultus was confirmed for Anagni in 1724.

Andrew Corsini (St) {2, 3}

6 January
1302–73. A nobleman of Florence (Italy), he spent his early teens in hedonism but joined the Carmelites when aged sixteen and became austerely penitential all his life. He studied at

Paris and Avignon, was made prior at Florence and became bishop of Fiesole nearby in 1360. He was charitable to the poor and an effective mediator between the warring factions of the time. He was canonized in 1724, and his cultus was confined to particular calendars in 1969.

Andrew of Crete (St) {2}

4 July
c.660–740. From Damascus (Syria), he was a monk at Mar Saba and then at the Holy Sepulchre in Jerusalem. Then he became a deacon at Hagia Sophia at Constantinople and finally archbishop of Gortyna in Crete in 692. He wrote many homilies and panegyrics of saints, and invented the Byzantine liturgical hymn form called the 'canon'.

Andrew Dotti (Bl) {2}

31 August
1256–1315. A nobleman and military officer from Borgo San Sepolcro (Italy), he joined the Servites with St Philip Benizi at Florence in 1278 and went on preaching expeditions with him. He died as a hermit at Vallucola near Montevecchio, and his cultus was confirmed for Borgo San Sepulcro and the Servites in 1806.

Andrew Dũng Lạc (St) {1 –group}

21 December
1785–1839. A Vietnamese priest, he was arrested at Hanoi and ordered to trample on a crucifix. On his refusal, he was beheaded with St Peter Trường Văn Thi. Cf. **Vietnam, Martyrs of.**

Andrew-Charles Ferrari (Bl) {2}

2 February
1850–1921. From near Parma (Italy), he became a priest and the rector of the seminary there before becoming bishop of Como

in 1891. He was made archbishop of Milan in 1894, taking the name Charles in honour of St Charles Borromeo, and proved a model bishop. He was loyal to the teachings of the church at the time of the Modernist crisis, and sought to put them into practice at a time of great social change. He died of throat cancer and was beatified in 1987.

Andrew of Florence (St) {2, 4}

26 February
C9th. The bishop of Florence (Italy) formerly listed in the Roman Martyrology as being of the C5th is now listed as being four hundred years later.

Andrew-Hubert Fournet (St) {2}

13 May
1752–1834. Born at Saint-Pierre-de-Maillé near Poitiers (France), he became parish priest of his native town and served as such, at the risk of his life, through the French Revolution. He, with St Jane-Elizabeth Bichier des Ages, founded the 'Daughters of the Cross' for nursing and teaching in 1807. He died at La Puye and was canonized in 1933.

Andrew dei Franchi Boccagni (Bl) {2}

26 May
1335–1401. Born in Pistoia near Florence (Italy), he became a Dominican there and was made bishop in 1378. He resigned and went back to his old friary one year before he died. His cultus was confirmed for Pistoia in 1921.

Andrew Gallerani (Bl) {2}

19 March
d. 1251. A military officer of Siena (Italy), he accidentally killed a man whom he had heard blaspheming and was exiled. He lived a life of unusual penance and charity and was allowed to return, whereupon he founded the

'Brothers of Mercy' (which lasted until 1308). His cultus was confirmed for Siena in 1798.

Andrew-of-Palazuelo González-Díez González Núñez and Comps (BB) {2 –add}

d. 1936–37. They were thirty-one Franciscan Capuchin friars, plus one oblate, of the convents of El Pardo and Jesus de Mediaceli in the diocese of Madrid. They were martyred in separate incidents during the Spanish Civil War, and were beatified in 2013. Cf. **Spanish Civil War, Martyrs of** and list in appendix.

Andrew-of-Peschiera Grego (Bl) {2}

19 January
1400–85. From Peschiera on Lake Garda near Verona (Italy), he became a Dominican at Brescia when aged fifteen, studied at Florence and then did missionary work in the Valtellina on the Swiss border. The 'Apostle of the Valtellina', his cultus was confirmed for Verona and Como in 1820.

Andrew Hibernon (Bl) {2}

18 April
1534–1602. Born near Murcia (Spain) of impoverished nobility, he worked to support his sister but was robbed of his savings and joined the Conventual Franciscans in reaction as a lay brother. However, he transferred to the Alcantarines (reformed Franciscans) at Elche, and converted many Muslims by his frank simplicity. He died while setting up a friary at Gandia, and was beatified in 1791.

Andrew Iščak (Bl) {2}

26 June
1888–1941. A priest of Lwow in Poland (now Lviv in Ukraine), he was killed by soldiers of the Red Army at Sykhiv near Lwow after that area of Poland had been annexed by the Soviet Union. Cf. **Nicholas Čarneckyj and 24 Comps**.

Andrew Kaggwa (St) {1 –group}.

26 May
d. 1886. The royal band-master at the court of King Mwanga of Buganda (Uganda), he was baptized in 1881 and later beheaded. Cf. **Charles Lwanga and Comps**.

Andrew Kim Tae-gŏn (St) {1 –group}

16 September
d. 1846. A Korean nobleman, he was ordained at Macao (the first Korean to become a priest). On his return, he worked as a missionary for two years before being arrested and beheaded at Sainamhte. Cf. **Korea, Martyrs of**.

Andrew Longhin (Bl) {1 –add}

26 June
1863–1936. From Fiumicello near Padua in Italy, he became a Franciscan Capuchin friar at Venice and became local superior before being made bishop of Treviso in 1902. He was outstanding in taking care of the spiritual welfare of the diocesan clergy and in promoting catechesis and Catholic social action. He was beatified in 2002.

Andrew of Montereale (Bl) {2}

18 April
1397–1480. From Mascioni near Rieti (Italy), when aged fourteen he became an Augustinian friar at Montereale. He was an itinerant preacher in Italy and France and served as provincial superior of Umbria. He was noted for his fasting. His cultus was confirmed for Rieti in 1764.

Andrew Nguyễn Kim Thông Nam (St) {1 –group}

15 July
c.1790–1855. A Vietnamese catechist and village leader of Mỹ Tho in the Mekong Delta, he was arrested during the persecution ordered by Emperor Minh Mạng and

sentenced to exile. He died of hardship on the road, loaded with chains and a yoke designed to prevent him lying down. Cf. **Vietnam, Martyrs of.**

Andrew of Phú Yên (Bl) {2}

26 July
?1625–44. From Phú Yên in central Vietnam, he was converted by Fr De Rhodes, a famous Jesuit missionary in Vietnam, and became a catechist. In 1644 the emperor ordered foreign missionaries to be expelled and Christianity suppressed; Bl Andrew was ordered to be executed as an example by the city governor. He was beatified in 2000. Cf. **Vietnam, Martyrs of.**

Andrew Sola y Molist (Bl) {2 –add}

25 April
1895–1927. From Taradell near Barcelona in Spain, he became a Claretian and went to Mexico as a missionary in 1923. He immediately had to go into hiding and practised his ministry in secret, initially at León in Jalisco. After ignoring a warning that he was on a government death list, he was arrested and shot because of his priesthood at Rancho de San Joaquín during the Cristero War, together with BB Joseph-Trinity Rangel Montaño and Leonard Pérez Larios. He was beatified in 2005. Cf. **Mexico, Martyrs of.**

Andrew de Soveral and Comps (BB) {2}

16 July
d. 1645. Jesuit missionaries from Portugal had started to evangelize the native peoples of Rio Grande do Norte, at the easternmost tip of Brazil, when the Dutch West India Company invaded in 1630 and established a government at Recife. The people of the two parishes at Natal and Cunhaú were brutally persecuted by the Calvinist Dutch. Those attending Mass at the chapel at Cunhaú were massacred along with their priest, Bl Andrew, on 16 July 1645. Those of Natal were rounded up, taken to a site 20 km from the city and later massacred with their priest, Bl Ambrose-Francis Ferro, after vicious tortures. The two priests and twenty-eight companions were beatified in 2000. Cf. list of martyrs in appendix under **Brazil**.

Andrew Tokuan (Bl) {2}

18 November
d. 1619. A Japanese layman born in Nagasaki, he was a member of the Confraternity of the Holy Rosary and was burnt alive with Bl Leonard Kimura for sheltering missionaries. He was beatified in 1867. Cf. **Japan, Martyrs of.**

Andrew Trần Văn Trong (St) {1 –group}

28 November
1817–35. A Vietnamese soldier, he became a priest and a member of the Paris Mission Society. During the persecution ordered by Emperor Minh Mạng he was ordered to trample on a crucifix. On his refusal he was imprisoned, tortured and beheaded at Khám Đường near Hué in central Vietnam. It is recorded that his mother caught his severed head. Cf. **Vietnam, Martyrs of.**

Andrew the Tribune & Comps (SS) {2, 4}

19 August
d. ?303. Their story is that they were an officer and some men of the army of the Emperor Galerius on an expedition against the Persians. They were denounced as Christians, took refuge in the Taurus Mountains (in southern Asia Minor) but were followed and killed.

Andrew Tường (St) {1 –group}

16 June
Cf. **Dominic Nguyên and Comps.**

Andrew Wang Tiangqing (St) {1 –group}

22 July
Cf. **Joseph Wang Yumei and Comps**.

Andrew Wouters van Heynoert (St) {2}

9 July
d. 1572. One of the martyrs of **Gorinchem** (q.v.), he was a secular priest at Heynoert near Dordrecht (Netherlands) who had been living a scandalous life. When the Calvinist 'Sea-Beggars' captured him and tried to make him apostatize, however, he refused and was hanged with the other martyrs.

Andrew Yakichi (St) {2}

2 October
d. 1622. An eight-year-old, he was one of a family of four Japanese martyred at Nagasaki. His father Louis was burnt, while he, his mother Lucy and brother Francis were beheaded. Cf. **Japan, Martyrs of**.

Andrew Yamamoto Shichiemon (Bl) {2 –add}

12 January
Cf. **Louis Amagasu Iemon and Comps**.

Andrew Yoshida (Bl) {2}

1 October
d. 1617. A Japanese layman, he was a member of the Confraternity of the Holy Rosary and was martyred at Nagasaki with Bl Caspar Hikojiro for sheltering missionaries. They were beatified in 1867. Cf. **Japan, Martyrs of**.

Andrew Zoerard (St) {2}

17 July
d. 1031–34. A Polish hermit, he was associated with a Benedictine monastery on the mountain of Zobar near Nitra (Slovakia) and was the spiritual father of St Benedict of Skalka. He was canonized in 1083.

(Andronicus and Athanasia) (SS) {4 –deleted}

9 October
C5th? According to their legend, they were a married couple of Antioch in Syria, the husband being a banker or silversmith. When their children died they separated to become hermits in Egypt and, after many years, occupied adjoining cells without recognizing each other until Athanasia died. Their veneration is popular in Egypt and Ethiopia.

(Anectus) (St) {4 –deleted}

27 June
Early C4th? Cardinal Baronius, the reviser of the old Roman Martyrology, probably made a guess at placing this alleged martyr at Caesarea in the Holy Land in the reign of Diocletian.

Angadresima (St) {2}

14 October
d. ?695. Abbess of Oröer-des-Vierges near Beauvais (France), she was a cousin of St Lambert of Lyons and had been professed as a nun by St Ouen.

Angela of Foligno (St) {2}

4 January
?1248–1309. She was a rich, self-indulgent married woman of Foligno near Rome (Italy), but converted and became a Franciscan tertiary before her husband and children all died. Then she lived a penitential life as the leader of a large group of tertiaries of both sexes, and had many supernatural and mystical experiences which she recounted to her confessor and which he published. Her cultus was

confirmed in 1693, and she was equivalently canonized in 2013.

Angela-of-the-Cross Guerrero González (St) {2}

2 March

1846–1932. Born in Seville (Spain), she tried in turn to join the Carmelites and Sisters of Charity, but her health failed her. Then she became a seamstress and eventually founded her own institute in 1875, the 'Society of the Cross', in order to help the poor in their own homes and to have a charism based on bearing one's cross in following Christ. She was canonized in 2003.

Angela-of-St-Joseph Lloret Martí and Comps (BB) {2}

20 November

1875–1936. Born near Alicante (Spain), she became superior-general of the 'Sisters of Christian Doctrine' who were a congregation devoted to catechesis. Their mother house at Valencia was suppressed in 1936 at the start of the Spanish Civil War, the seventeen sisters there were imprisoned for three months and were then executed in the autumn at Paterna. They were beatified in 1995. Two sisters had died in prison before the execution. Cf. **Spanish Civil War, Martyrs of** and list in appendix.

Angela de'Merici (St) {1, 3}

27 January

1474–1540. She was born on the shores of Lake Garda near Verona (Italy), was orphaned when young and then devoted herself to educating girls and nursing sick women. She was joined by others, and thus was founded the congregation of the Ursulines in 1535. They were the first teaching order of women religious ever founded. She died at Brescia and was canonized in 1807.

Angela Salawa (Bl) {2}

12 March

1881–1922. Born near Cracow (then in Austria, now in Poland), she became a domestic servant there when aged sixteen. She took a private vow of chastity and did works of charity in her spare time, especially for the sick and wounded during the First World War. In 1917 her health started to fail, and she retired to a shed where she spent five years in solitude before dying, offering her poverty and continual prayer for God's glory in the new nation of Poland and in the world. She was beatified in 1991.

Angela-Mary Truszkowska (Bl) {2}

10 October

1825–99. A Polish noblewoman born at Kalisz, then in Russian Poland, when young she devoted herself to caring for the poor and needy. A conversion experience in 1848 led her to try her vocation with the Visitation nuns. Failing, she founded the 'Felician Sisters' in 1855 (with a contemplative branch in 1860), and re-founded them in Austrian Galicia in 1865 after their suppression in Russia. The congregation has become international. She was beatified in 1993.

Angelico (Fra) Cf. **John of Fiesole**.

Angelina of Marsciano (Bl) {2}

14 July

1377–1435. A noblewoman born at Montegiove in Umbria (Italy), she was married when fourteen and widowed when seventeen. She then founded a convent of Franciscan tertiaries at Foligno in 1397, became the superior and founded fifteen other houses of the new congregation by the time it received papal approval in 1428. Her cultus was confirmed for Foligno in 1825.

Angelus

This is the original Latin form of a name common in Latin countries: 'Angelo' in Italy, 'Ange' in France, 'Angel' in Spain and 'Anjo' in Portugal. It derives from St Michael the Archangel.

Angelus-Darius Acosta Zurita (Bl) {2 –add}

25 July
1908–31. From Naolinco in Veracruz state, Mexico, he became a diocesan priest and was appointed to the parish of the Annunciation in Veracruz city. The state authorities enacted a statute called the 'Tejeda Law' in 1931, specifying a small maximum number of priests allowed to minister in the state. Bl Angel-Darius ignored this, having been ordained the same year. On the day that the law took force a squad of soldiers entered his church during a baptism and shot him. He was beatified in 2005. Cf. **Mexico, Martyrs of**.

Angelus of Acquapagana (Bl) {2}

19 August
1271–1313. After being a Camaldolese monk at Val de Castro he became a Silvestrine hermit at Acquapagana near Camerino (Italy). His cultus was confirmed for Camerino in 1845.

Angelus-of-Chivasso Carletti (Bl) {2}

12 April
d. 1495. From Chivasso near Turin (Italy), he was a lawyer and senator of Monferrato but then became a Franciscan at Genoa instead. He filled important offices in his order, wrote a standard text on casuistry (the 'Summa Angelica'), preached among the Muslims and Waldenses and was known for effecting conversions. His cultus was confirmed for Monreale and Cuneo in 1753.

Angelus-of-Foligno Conti (Bl) {2}

27 August
1226–1312. From Foligno (Italy), he became an Augustinian friar when aged twenty and was a friend of St Nicholas of Tolentino. He founded three houses of his order in Umbria, and his cultus was confirmed for Foligno in 1891.

Angelus-of-Acri Falcone (Bl) {2}

30 October
1669–1739. From Acri near Bisignano in Calabria (Italy), he became a Capuchin with difficulty in 1690 after failing twice in trying to become a consecrated religious. His career as a preacher was initially a failure, but then it succeeded spectacularly. He died at Acri and was beatified in 1825.

Angelus of Furcio (Bl) {2}

6 February
1246–1327. From near Chieti in the Abruzzi (Italy), he became an Augustinian friar, studied theology at Paris and then had a life-long career as professor of theology at Naples University. He also served a term as his order's provincial, but refused to become a bishop. His cultus was confirmed for Naples and Vasto in 1888.

Angelus of Gualdo (Bl) {2}

15 January
?1265–1325. From Nocera in Umbria (Italy), when young he completed a barefoot penitential pilgrimage to Compostella in Spain before becoming a Camaldolese lay brother. He spent forty years immured in his cell and was known for his simplicity, innocence and gentleness. His cultus was confirmed for Nocera in 1825.

Angelus of Jerusalem (St) {2, 4}

5 May
1145–1225. Born in Crusader Jerusalem of convert Jewish parents, he was one of the first

hermits on Mount Carmel and was chosen to obtain papal approval for the common rule written for them by St Albert. After visiting Rome he stopped to preach in Sicily and was killed by a man whose crimes he had denounced. He is listed as a martyr.

Angelus of Massaccio (Bl) {2}

8 May
d. 1458. A Camaldolese monk of Santa Maria di Serra in the Marches (Italy), he was martyred by heretics called Fraticelli because of his preaching on church dogma against them. His cultus was confirmed for Iesi in 1842.

Angelus-Augustine Mazzinghi (Bl) {2}

16 August
1377–1438. He became a Carmelite in his native city of Florence (Italy) and went on to be professor of theology, prior at Frascati and at Florence and provincial superior. He was extremely edifying as a consecrated religious, and his cultus was confirmed in 1761 for Florence.

Angelus Orsucci (Bl) {2}

10 September
1573–1622. From Lucca (Italy), he became a Dominican there, studied at Valencia and went to be a missionary in the Philippines and then in Japan. He was captured, imprisoned for four years in atrocious conditions at Omura and then burnt at Nagasaki in the 'Great Martyrdom' with BB Charles Spinola and Comps. Cf. **Japan, Martyrs of** and **Great Martyrdom at Nagasaki.**

Angelus Paoli (Bl) {2 –add}

17 January
1642–1720. From Agrigento in Tuscany (Italy), he was a pious teenager who spent his time teaching catechism to poor children.

In 1660 he joined the Calced Carmelites at Siena, and after ordination was sent to Pisa. He was subsequently at Cupoli, Monte Catino and Fivizzano. He had a special devotion to the Passion, and to practical charity towards poor people. In 1687 he transferred to Rome, where he nursed in the city's hospitals as well as serving as novice-master for his community. He was beatified in 2010.

Angelus Scarpetti (Bl) {2}

15 February
d. c.1306. From Borgo San Sepulcro in Umbria (Italy), he joined the Augustinian friars and was a fellow student of St Nicholas of Tolentino. He was known for his miracles, and one story was that he resurrected a man who had been executed despite his intercession for a pardon. The claim that he founded several friaries in England is not confirmed. His cultus was confirmed for Borgo San Sepulcro in 1921.

Angilbert (St) {2}

18 February
d. 814. An important figure at the court of Charlemagne, he filled several major offices and was noted for his poetry as well as having two illegitimate sons by the emperor's daughter. The emperor gave him the abbey of St Riquier as a reward, and he converted from a rather dissipated life to being a reforming abbot, having about 300 monks in his community. He introduced the continual celebration of the Divine Office in relays, thus influencing later Cluniac custom.

Angus the Culdee (St) {2}

11 March
d. ?824. The composer of a well-known metrical hymn to the saints called the Felire ('Festilogium'), he was alleged to have been a monk at Clonenagh in Co. Laois (Ireland) and

became abbot-bishop there. Although famous in his day, there is no early biography of him nor any evidence of contemporary liturgical veneration.

Anianus of Alexandria (St) {2, 4}

25 April
d. ?67. Eusebius and the apocryphal Acts of St Mark describe him as a shoemaker who was second bishop of Alexandria (Egypt) after St Mark. He formerly had a church dedicated to him in the Velabro at Rome.

Anianus of Orleans (St) {2, 4}

17 November
d. 453. The fifth bishop of Orleans (France), it was left to him to organize the defences of the city at the approach of the Huns under Attila. He allegedly had a meeting with the latter and averted a siege.

Anicetus, Pope (St) {2, 3}

17 April
d. 166. A Syrian, by tradition he became pope in 155. He was visited by St Polycarp to discuss the date of Easter, and this is historically the first evidence for an individual bishop of Rome acting on his own authority. He also fought against the Gnostics. His cultus was suppressed in 1969 after he had been falsely celebrated as a martyr for centuries.

Anicetus, Photius and Comps (SS) {2, 4}

12 August
Early C4th. They were martyrs of Nicomedia (Asia Minor) in the reign of Diocletian. Their unreliable acta mention companion martyrs, now deleted from the Roman Martyrology.

Anicetus Kopliński (Bl) {2}

16 October
1875–1941. He was a Polish Franciscan Capuchin friar who was gassed at Auschwitz on the same day as Bl Joseph Jankowski was beaten to death there. He was a friend of Bl Fidelis Chijnacki. Cf. **Poland, Martyrs of the Nazi Occupation of**.

Anicetus-Adolf Seco Gutiérrez (St) {2}

9 October
Cf. **Innocent-of-Mary-Immaculate Canoura Arnau and Comps**.

Anne (St) {1, 3}

26 July
C1st. The name of the mother of Our Lady is not mentioned in the New Testament, and the earliest reference to SS Joachim and Anne as being her parents is in the 'Protoevangelium of James', an apocryphal work written in c.170. St Anne's cultus emerged in the East in the C6th and in the West in the C8th, but it did not become general in the latter until the C14th. It then became very popular. The two are now celebrated together.

Anne-Mary Adorni (Bl) {2 –add}

7 February
1805–93. From Fivizzano (Italy), she moved to Parma as a teenager and was married into the ducal family there. Widowed in 1844, she began to visit women in prison and also to help and educate poor young girls in danger of making a living out of prostitution. She attracted disciples, and hence founded two congregations: The Handmaidens of Blessed Mary Immaculate and the Institute of the Good Shepherd of Parma. She died at Parma and was beatified in 2010.

Anne An Xinzhi and Comps (St) {1 –group}

11 July
1900. She was with SS Mary An Guozhi her daughter-in-law, Anne An Jiaozhi her granddaughter-in law and Mary An Linhua her

granddaughter when they were seized by a gang of Boxers at their village of Liugongyin in Anping county, southeastern Hebei (China). After being invited to abandon their faith they were beheaded. Cf. **China, Martyrs of**.

Anne-of-St-Bartholomew García (Bl) {2}

7 June
1549–1626. From Almendral near Avila (Spain), she initially took part in her family's work of shepherding but then joined St Teresa's reformed convent at Avila as its first lay sister, becoming the founder's secretary and companion in her journeys to make foundations throughout Spain. In 1606 she was sent to introduce the reform into France as a choir nun, and was prioress at Pontoise and Tours. She founded the English convent at Antwerp in 1612 and died there. She has left some religious verse. She was beatified in 1917.

Anne-Rose Gattorno (Bl) {2}

6 May
1831–1900. From a rich family of Genoa in Italy, she married and had a family but lost her husband and her wealth. This led to a spiritual conversion, and she became a Franciscan tertiary, receiving the stigmata in 1862. In 1866 she founded the 'Daughters of St Anne, Mother of Mary Immaculate' at Piacenza for active works of mercy. Her institution had become international by the time she died at Rome. She was beatified in 2000.

Anne-Mary Janer Anglarill (Bl) {2 –add}

11 January
1800–85. From Cervera near Lerida (Spain), she joined the Sisters of Charity in 1819 and was in charge of a hospital in her home town by 1832, but anti-clerical influences and the Carlist war led to her exile to France. She returned in 1844, and in 1857 took over the hospital at Urgell. There she founded the Sisters of the Holy Family of Urgell, dedicated to the education of girls and ignorant young women. She died at Talarn near Lerida, and was beatified in 2011.

Anne-Mary Javouhey (Bl) {2}

15 July
1779–1851. From Jallanges in the Côte d'Or (France), when she was young during the French Revolution she used to shelter and care for persecuted 'non-juring' priests (those refusing the oath of loyalty to the government). After the persecution had passed she founded the 'Sisters of St Joseph of Cluny' at Cabillon in 1805. This mother house was moved to Cluny seven years later, and the sisters started missionary work worldwide. She herself worked on the missions in West Africa and French Guiana for several years. She died in Paris and was beatified in 1950.

Anne Jin'emon (Bl) {2 –add}

12 January
Cf. **Louis Amagasu Iemon and Comps**.

Anne Kajiya (Bl) {2 –add}

6 October
Cf. **John Hashimoto Tahyōe and Comps**.

Anne Kim Chang-gŭm (St) {1 –group}

20 July
Cf. **Mary-Magdalen Yi Yŏn-hŭi and Comps**.

Anne Line (St) {2}

27 February
1565–1601. From a Calvinist family of Great Dunmow in Essex, she converted when aged twenty and was driven from home as a result. She married a fellow convert in 1585, but he was exiled, and she was left destitute in 1594. Then she kept a safe house for priests in London and took private vows. After a raid during a Mass at her house she was arrested

and hanged at Tyburn for sheltering priests. She was canonized in 1970. Cf. **England (Martyrs of)**.

Anne-of-the-Angels Monteagudo (Bl) {2}

10 January
1601–86. Born in Arequipa in Peru, she joined the Dominicanesses there in 1618. Believing that the monastery should be like a seminary of holiness for the laity, she got permission from the bishop to help those coming to her with prayers, advice and help. Her last decade was one of severe physical suffering, and she was beatified in 1985.

Anne Pak A-gi (St) {1 –group}

24 May
Cf. **Augustine Yi Kwang-hŏn and Comps**.

Anne (Anna) the Prophetess (St) {2, 4}

3 February
C1st. Cf. the Gospel of St Luke, 2:36-38 (other traditions are apocryphal).

Anne Schäffer (St) {2}

5 October
1882–1925. From Mindelstetten near Regensburg (Germany), she wished to become a missionary sister but scalded both legs with boiling lye while working in a laundry when aged nineteen. The injuries did not heal, leaving her bedridden. She recognized a call to share mystically in the sufferings of Christ crucified, and received the stigmata in 1910. Despite her infirmity she maintained an active apostolate through a voluminous correspondence. She died of a brain injury caused by falling out of bed, and was canonized in 2012.

Anne-Mary Taigi (Bl) {2}

9 June
1769–1837. She was the daughter of a chemist in Siena (Italy), and when her father's business failed she went to Rome to work as a domestic servant. She married a butler of the Chigi family, had seven children and lived the normal life of a married working-class woman. She reached a high degree of holiness, however, and had the charisms of prophecy and the reading of thoughts. Many high churchmen and noble seculars sought her advice. She was beatified in 1920.

Anne Wang (St) {1 –group}

22 July
Cf. **Joseph Wang Yumei and Comps**.

Annemund (St) {2}

28 September
d. ?658. He was a Frankish courtier who became archbishop of Lyons (France) in c.650, and welcomed SS Benedict Biscop and Wilfrid on their journeys to Rome. He was the victim of a political assassination ordered by Ebroin, mayor of the palace.

Anno of Cologne (St) {2, 4}

4 December
d. 1075. He was the son of a poor knight of Swabia, and when he became the prince-archbishop of Cologne (Germany) in 1056 many of that city despised him for it. However, he had a crowded, important and not always edifying career in the church and in politics, and founded the abbey of Siegburg (which survived until closure in 2011). He retired there to do strict penance for the last year of his life.

Annunciata Cocchetti (Bl) {2}

23 March
1800–82. From near Brescia (Italy), her family was rich, but she was orphaned, moved to Milan and, on the advice of Fr Luke Passi, settled at Cemmo in the Camunico valley and opened a girls' school in 1831. In 1842 she

joined the 'Teaching Sisters of St Dorothy', founded at Venice by Fr Luke and, when he died, the bishop of Brescia encouraged her to found an independent congregation, the 'Sisters of St Dorothy at Cemmo', in 1866. She was beatified in 1991.

(Ansanus the Baptizer) (St) {4 –deleted}

1 December
Early C4th? His legend is that he was of the Anician family of Rome, became a Christian when aged twelve and was handed over to the authorities by his father. He escaped, and gained his nickname by converting many at Bagnorea and Siena before being recaptured and beheaded.

Anselm of Canterbury (St) {1, 3}

21 April
d. 1109. From Aosta in Piedmont (Italy), he became a Benedictine monk at Bec under Bl Herluin, then was abbot there and succeeded Lanfranc as archbishop of Canterbury (England) in 1093. He was soon exiled by King William II, however, and was at the council of Bari in 1098 where he helped to reconcile the Byzantine-rite bishops of the area of south Italy just conquered by the Normans. The next king, Henry I, invited him back but exiled him again after he disputed the king's right to invest bishops. He only returned permanently in 1106. His philosophical and theological work was a bridge between the patristic authors (especially St Augustine) and the scholastics, and is still of importance (especially his presentation of the 'ontological argument'). His biography was written by his secretary, a monk of Canterbury Cathedral called Eadmer. He was declared a doctor of the Church in 1720.

Anselm II of Lucca (St) {2, 4}

18 March
1036–86. Born at Mantua (Italy), he was chosen to be bishop of Lucca by his uncle, Pope Alexander II, but initially refused to be invested by Emperor Henry IV. Pope St Gregory VII later persuaded him to accept for a while, but then he fled his diocese and became a Cluniac monk at Polizone. The pope made him return, but his attempt to reform the cathedral canons at Lucca caused them to rebel, and he fled again. He then became the papal legate in Lombardy, and was a strong supporter of Pope St Gregory as well as being a noted scholar and canonist (a collection by him of canon laws is extant). He died at Mantua.

Anselm of Nonantola (St) {2}

3 March
d. 803. Duke of Friuli and brother-in-law of the Lombard King Aistulf, he became a monk and founded the abbeys of Fanano and Normantola (Italy) together with attached hospitals and hostels. Banished to Montecassino by the next king, Desiderius, after seven years he was restored by Charlemagne when the Lombard kingdom had been conquered by the Franks.

Anselm Polanco Fontecha and Philip Ripoll Morata (BB) {2}

7 February
d. 1939. Bl Anselm was born near Palencia (Spain), joined the Augustinian friars and became bishop of Teruel in 1935. Bl Philip, his vicar-general, was born in Teruel. When the city was captured by the Republicans in 1938 during the Spanish Civil War, the two were imprisoned for thirteen months. At war's end, they were taken hostage by disbanded soldiers and shot in a gorge near Gerona. They were beatified in 1995. Cf. **Spanish Civil War, Martyrs of**.

Ansfrid (Bl) {2}

3 May
d. 1008. Duke of Brabant in the Low Countries and an imperial knight, he founded the

convent of Thorn in 992 for his wife and daughter, and became a Benedictine monk at his other foundation of Heiligen. But he was made archbishop of Utrecht (Netherlands) in 994, which he remained until he went blind in 1006. Then he retired to Heiligen to die.

Ansgar (Oscar) (St) {1}

3 February
801–65. A nobleman from near Amiens (France), he was educated at the abbey of Corbie in Picardy when St Adelard was abbot and St Paschasius Radbert was schoolmaster. After becoming a monk there he was transferred to New Corbie in Lower Saxony (Corvey near Paderborn), whence he was taken by King Harold of Denmark to evangelize his subjects. After a missionary expedition to Sweden he was made first archbishop of Hamburg in 832 after the Franks conquered the Saxons, and his mission territory covered Denmark, Scandinavia and northern Germany as well. After Hamburg was destroyed by the Vikings in 845 his see was united to that of Bremen. His personal missionary efforts in Sweden met with initial success but with eventual failure, and Christianity was only firmly established there in the C11th. He died at Bremen and is the patron of Denmark.

Ansovinus (St) {2}

13 March
d. 868. A hermit near Torcello, he accepted appointment as bishop of Camerino (Italy) on condition that he was exempt from having to support and provide soldiers (this was standard practice for bishops as feudal lords at the time).

Ansuerus and Comps (SS) {2}

15 July
d. 1066. A noble of Schleswig, he became a Benedictine monk and then abbot of St Georgenburg near Ratzeburg south of Lübeck (Germany), which abbey became a centre of evangelization among the indigenous Slavs east of the river Elbe. He and twenty-eight of his community were stoned to death in an anti-Christian rebellion by them. They are listed as martyrs.

Antherus, Pope (St) {2, 4}

3 January
d. 236. A Greek, he was pope for only a few weeks after Pope St Pontian. There is no record of his having been a martyr. He was the first pope to be buried in the catacomb of St Callistus, and part of his epitaph survives.

Anthelm (St) {2, 4}

26 June
1105–78. A noble from Chignin in Savoy (now in France), he was ordained when young and became a Carthusian at Portes after a chance visit there. In 1139 he became prior of the Grande Chartreuse, and was instrumental in setting the Carthusians up as a separate religious order. In 1152 he became prior of Portes, and he reluctantly became bishop of Belley in 1163. He was such a model bishop that he was universally loved in his diocese, but he showed his personal preference by visiting his original monastery whenever possible.

Anthimus, Leontius and Euprepius (SS) {4 –deleted}

27 September
They were listed (with reserve) in the old Roman Martyrology as brothers of SS Cosmas and Damian who were martyred with them. They never existed.

Anthimus of Nicomedia (St) {2, 4}

24 April
d. 303. Bishop of Nicomedia (Asia Minor), he was martyred in the reign of Diocletian

(whose capital the place was). There followed a pogrom of local Christians.

Anthimus of Rome (St) {2, 4}

11 May
Late C3rd. His story is that he was a priest of Rome who converted a prefect in the reign of Diocletian and was thrown into the Tiber. He escaped, but was beheaded and was buried on the Via Salaria, twenty-two miles from Rome.

(Antholian and Comps) (SS) *{4 –deleted}*

6 February
Mid C3rd? St Gregory of Tours lists them as martyrs of Auvergne (France) in the reigns of Valerian and Gallienus. The companions were Cassius, Maximus, Liminius and Victorinus.

Anthonius cf. **Anthimus**.

Anthony and Hierax (SS) {2}

23 August
C10th. They were Byzantine-rite hermits at the monastery of St Philip near Lócri in Calabria (Italy).

(Anthony, Merulus and John) (SS) *{4 –deleted}*

17 January
C6th? The 'Dialogues' attributed to St Gregory the Great mention these three monks of the monastery of St Andrew on the Coelian Hill in Rome, describing their virtues and miracles. The work is not now regarded as a reliable historical source.

Anthony Bajewski (Bl) {2}

8 May
1915–41. A Polish Franciscan Conventual friar, he died of ill-treatment at Auschwitz. Together with Bl Pius Bartosik, he had been a colleague of St Maximilian Kolbe before the Nazi invasion, and they supported each other in the camp. Cf. **Poland, Martyrs of the Nazi Occupation of**.

Anthony Baldinucci (Bl) {2}

7 November
1665–1717. From Florence (Italy), he became a Jesuit in 1681 and was a home missionary in the Abruzzi and Romagna. He had some very unusual methods of preaching and of calling people to penance, such as whipping himself until bloody. He died at Pofi and was beatified in 1893.

Anthony Beszta-Borowski (Bl) {2}

15 July
1880–1943. He was a Polish priest shot by the Nazis at Bielsk Podlaski. Cf. **Poland, Martyrs of the Nazi Occupation of**.

Anthony Bonfadini (Bl) {2}

1 December
?1402–82. From Ferrara (Italy), he became a Franciscan there and was sent to the Holy Land. Having returned, he died at Contignola near Faenza, and his cultus was confirmed for Faenza in 1901.

Anthony Chevrier (Bl) {2}

2 October
1826–79. From Lyons (France), he became parish priest at St Andrew's Church there in 1860. Following the advice of St John Vianney to arrange for the catechizing of poor children for first communion, he founded the catechesis centre of 'La Providence du Prado', and tertiary Franciscan congregations of priests and sisters to run it. He also took charge of a new parish in the suburbs across the river Rhône, then in a separate diocese. He was beatified in 1986.

Anthony della Chiesa (Bl) {2}

22 January
1394–1459. A nobleman from near Vercelli in Piedmont (Italy), after he became a Dominican he was prior of the friaries of Como, Savona, Florence and Bologna, and was a helper of St Bernardine of Siena in his apostolate. His cultus was confirmed for Vercelli in 1819.

Anthony-Mary Claret (St) {1}

24 October
1807–70. From Salent in Catalonia (Spain), he was a weaver before being ordained in 1835. He devoted himself to home missions, and he formed the 'Missionary Sons of the Immaculate Heart of Mary', nicknamed the 'Claretians', with the group of priests who helped him. He became bishop of Santiago de Cuba in 1850 and was appointed royal confessor to Queen Isabella II in 1856, in both offices having great difficulty from anti-clericalism. He and the queen went into exile together in 1868, and he died at Fontfroide in France after having attended the First Vatican Council and spoken in favour of papal infallibility. He was known for his charisms of prophecy and miracles, and was canonized in 1950.

Anthony Daniel (St) {2}

4 July
1601–48. From Dieppe in Normandy (France), he became a Jesuit in 1621 and went as a missionary to the Huron nation in what is now Ontario (Canada), east of Lake Huron in 1634. He was at a fortified Huron settlement called Teanaostaye when it was attacked by an Iroquois raiding party during the war between the Hurons and the Iroquois. St Anthony tried to give the villagers time to escape by staging a diversion, which he did by advancing to meet the raiders while holding a crucifix. They shot him and threw his body into the burning chapel. He was canonized in 1930. Cf. **John Brébeuf and Comps**.

Anthony Daveluy and Comps (SS) {1 –group}

30 March
d. 1866. From Amiens (France), he was sent to Korea as a missionary priest, where he became coadjutor to St Simeon Berneaux for twenty years and wrote many works in Korean. He was seized in Keutori, interrogated before the royal tribunal, imprisoned, tortured and killed with a sword at Suryong. He had five companions in martyrdom: Peter Amaître, a priest aged twenty-nine from Amgoulême; Martin-Luke Huin, a priest aged thirty from Langres; Luke Hwang Sŏk-tu, a Korean layman convert who had given much help to SS Simeon and Anthony, especially in translating into Korean; Joseph Chang Chu-gi, who was a Korean catechist aged sixty-four and Thomas Son Cha-sŏn, another catechist. They were canonized in 1984. Cf. **Korea, Martyrs of**.

Anthony Deynan (St) {1 –group}

6 February
d. 1597. A Japanese native of Nagasaki, he was an acolyte and a Franciscan tertiary who was crucified when aged thirteen. Cf. **Paul Miki and Comps** and **Japan, Martyrs of**.

Anthony Durcovici (Bl) {2 –add}

20 December
1888–1950. A Romanian, he was born at Bad Deutsch-Altenburg in Austria, studied in Rome after his ordination and migrated to Romania where he was prefect of the Latin-rite seminary at Bucharest and then professor and rector of the Theological Academy. He was made bishop of Iaşi in 1947, but was deposed by the Communists in 1949. He died in prison at Sighetu Marmaţiei, and was beatified as a martyr in 2014.

Anthony-of-Ancona Fatati (Bl) {2}

9 January

c.1410–84. Born at Ancona (Italy), he was in turn archpriest at Ancona, vicar-general of Siena, canon at St Peter's at Rome, bishop of Teramo and finally bishop of Ancona. He has a cultus in all these places.

Anthony Faúndez López and Comps (BB) {2 –add}

d. 1936. These four are the Martyrs of the Franciscan Friars Minor of Murcia in Spain, killed by Republican militia during the civil war. Bl Anthony Fáundez López was a friar, killed at Bullas. Bl Bonaventure Muñoz Martínez was another friar, killed at Cuello de Tinaja with Bl Peter Sánchez Barba, a diocesan priest of Cartagena who was also a Franciscan tertiary. Bl Fulgentius Martínez García was another diocesan priest and tertiary, martyred at Espinardo. They were beatified as a group in 2013. Cf. **Spanish Civil War, Martyrs of** and list in appendix.

Anthony Fernandes (Bl) {2}

15 July

Cf. **Ignatius de Azevedo and Comps**.

Anthony Francisco (Bl) {2}

25 July

d. 1583. Born at Coïmbra (Portugal), he became a Jesuit in 1570. After being sent to India he took charge of the mission of Arlin on the island of Salsette, near Bombay, and was martyred with Bl **Rudolph Acquaviva** (q.v.).

Anthony Franco (Bl) {2 –add}

2 September

1585–1626. A Neapolitan nobleman, he studied as a lawyer but was ordained in 1610. At that time, southern Italy and Sicily were ruled by Spain, and after a period at the Spanish royal court he was appointed Major Chaplain of Sicily and Territorial Prelate of Santa Lucia del Mela near Messina. Despite being one of the most important ecclesiastical dignitaries on the island he lived a life of remarkable penance, including fasting on bread and water and sleeping on the floor. This shortened his life, and he died in his city aged only forty. The instruments of penance that he used have been the focus of miraculous cures. He was beatified in 2013.

Anthony-of-St-Anne Galvão di França (St) {2}

23 December

1739–1822. From near São Paolo in Brazil, his family was wealthy and he became an Alcantarene Franciscan at Rio de Janeiro in 1760. In 1768 he was made preacher and public confessor at São Paolo, and founded the famous nunnery of Our Lady of Light in the city. He died and was buried there, and was canonized in 2007.

Anthony-Mary Gianelli (St) {2}

7 June

1789–1846. Born at Cereta near Genoa (Italy) of a poor family, he was ordained in 1812 after a benefactress paid for his education and served as a parish priest before becoming bishop of Bobbio in 1838. He founded the 'Sisters of Our Lady of the Garden' and was a very successful bishop both pastorally and in administration. He died at Piacenza and was canonized in 1951.

Anthony González (St) {1 –group}

24 September

1593–1637. From León (Spain), he was one of the group of Dominican missionaries with St Laurence Ruiz. After they had been seized and imprisoned in chains, he was subjected to the water torture twice in order to induce apostasy. He died of a fever in prison before the others were martyred, but was canonized as a martyr himself with them. Cf. **Laurence Ruiz and Comps** and **Japan, Martyrs of**.

Anthony Grassi (Bl) {2}

13 December
d. 1671. He was a priest of the Oratory at Fermo in the Marches (Italy) and was its superior from 1635 until his death. He had the charism of the reading of consciences and was a great spiritual director. One story is that his serenity of manner became more marked after he was struck by lightning. He was beatified in 1900.

Anthony the Great (St) {1, 3}

17 January
?251–356. He is regarded as being the father of all monks. Born at Coma in Upper Egypt, he was orphaned in his youth and gave away the property he inherited in order to become a hermit on the outskirts of his village. This was not unusual at the time, but he was the first in then going into the real desert, and he spent a long time in seclusion fighting diabolic temptations. Afterwards he became famous throughout Egypt and beyond, and became a strong supporter of St Athanasius against the Arians. He gathered many disciples, having a more public base at Pispir on the Nile and also a completely isolated oasis retreat (the 'Inner Mountain') in the Eastern Desert, where he died and where the Coptic monastery bearing his name still flourishes. St Athanasius wrote his biography, which was translated into Latin and which introduced the monastic ideal to Rome. His attribute is the tau-cross, and he is often represented with a pig (which symbolizes his temptations).

Anthony van Hoornaert (St) {2}

9 July
d. 1572. He was a Franciscan friar, one of the **Gorinchem** martyrs (q.v.).

Anthony Ishida and Comps (BB) {2}

3 September
d. 1632. A Japanese Jesuit, he was burnt at Nagasaki with five companions: BB Bartholomew Guttierez, Vincent Carvalho and Francis-of-Jesus Ortega, Augustinians; Jerome-of-the-Cross de Torres, a secular priest, and Gabriel-of-St-Mary-Magdalen of Fonseca, a Franciscan lay brother. They had been tortured for over a month beforehand in order to induce apostasy. Cf. **Japan, Martyrs of**.

Anthony Kimura and Comps (Bl) {2}

27 November
1595–1619. Of the family of the daimyos of Hirado-jima and a relative of Bl Leonard Kimura, he was beheaded at Nagasaki (Japan) with ten companions: BB Thomas Koteda, Leo Nakanishi, Alexis Nakamura, Michael Sakaguchi, John Iwanaga, Bartholomew Seki, Matthias Nakano, Matthias Kozaka, Romanus Motayama and John Motayama. Cf. **Japan, Martyrs of**.

Anthony Kauleas (St) {2, 4}

12 February
829–901. From near Constantinople, he became a monk and abbot of the Theotokos monastery there before being appointed patriarch in 893, the second after Photius. He tried to reconcile the factions which had arisen in the time of the latter.

Anthony of Kiev (St) {2}

7 May
983–1073. From Lubich near Chernigov (Ukraine), he became a monk on Mount Athos (Greece), then part of the Byzantine Empire. On his return in 1013, he founded a monastic settlement in some riverside caves at Kiev, and this was the start of the famous

Pechera (Caves) monastery there. He chose St Theodosius of Kiev to succeed him and retired to be a hermit just before his death.

Anthony Kim Sŏng-u (St) {1 –group}

29 April
d. 1841. He was the father of a family at Seoul in Korea, and ran a house church at his home. As a result he was arrested and strangled in prison. Cf. **Korea, Martyrs of**.

Anthony Kiuni (Bl){2}

10 September
1572–1622. A Japanese, he became a Jesuit at Omura and was burnt at Nagasaki during the 'Great Martyrdom' with Charles Spinola and Comps. Cf. **Japan, Martyrs of** and **Great Martyrdom at Nagasaki**.

Anthony of Korea (Bl) {2}

10 September
d. 1622. A Korean catechist helping the Jesuits in Japan, he was beheaded at Nagasaki during the 'Great Martyrdom' with Charles Spinola and Comps. Cf. **Japan, Martyrs of** and **Great Martyrdom at Nagasaki**.

Anthony of Lérins (St) {2, 4}

28 December
d. c.520. Born in Lower Pannonia (now Hungary), he was a hermit at several places in the Alps before he became a monk at Lérins (France).

Anthony Leszczwicz (Bl) {2}

17 February
1890–1943. He was a priest of the Congregation of the Clerics of Mary who was burnt to death at Rosica by the Nazis. Cf. **Poland, Martyrs of the Nazi Occupation of**.

Anthony Lucci (Bl) {2}

25 July
1681–1752. Born in the Abruzzi (Italy), he joined the Franciscans in 1698, studied at Naples and Rome and became a consultant for various dicasteries of the Curia at Rome. The pope chose him to be bishop of Bovino, where he became known for his charity to the poor. He was bishop for twenty-three years, and was beatified in 1989.

Anthony Middleton (Bl) {2}

6 May
d. 1590. From Middleton Tyas in Yorkshire (England), he was ordained at Rheims in 1586 and martyred for his priesthood at Clerkenwell in London. Cf. **England (Martyrs of)**.

Anthony-of-Amandola Miglorati (Bl) {2}

25 January
?1355–1450. Born at Amandola in the Marches (Italy), he became an Augustinian friar and a friend and disciple of St Nicholas Tolentino. His cultus was confirmed for Fermo in 1759.

Anthony-of-St-Dominic of Nagasaki (Bl)

8 September
Cf. **Dominic Castellet and Comps**.

Anthony-of-St-Francis of Nagasaki (Bl) {2}

27 August
d. 1627. A Japanese catechist and a fellow worker with Bl Francis-of-St-Mary of Mancha (q.v.), he was burnt at Nagasaki with him and thirteen others. Cf. **Japan, Martyrs of**.

Anthony Neyrot (Bl) {2}

10 April
d. 1460. From Rivoli near Turin (Italy), he became a Dominican but was captured by

Muslim pirates on the way to Naples and taken to Tunis. There he apostatized to Islam and married but repented after a few months, put on his Dominican habit and publicly proclaimed Christ. He was stoned to death, and his cultus as a martyr was confirmed for Turin in 1767.

Anthony Nguyễn Đích (St) {1 –group}

12 August
Cf. **James Đỗ May Năm and Comps**.

Anthony Nguyễn Hữu Quỳnh (St) {1 –group}

10 July
1768–1840. A Vietnamese physician, he became a catechist attached to the Paris Foreign Mission Society and was killed by strangling after two years' imprisonment at Đồng Hời in central Vietnam. With him was martyred St Peter Nguyễn Khắc Tự. Cf. **Vietnam, Martyrs of**.

Anthony-Julian Nowowiejski (Bl) {2}

28 May
1858–1941. He was the archbishop of Plock in Poland, and died of starvation and ill-treatment in a prison at Działdowo. Cf. **Poland, Martyrs of the Nazi Occupation of**.

Anthony of Padua (St) {1, 3}

13 June
1195–1231. From Lisbon (Portugal), when young he joined the Canons Regular but transferred to the Franciscans at Coïmbra in 1212. He set off for the Maghreb in order to preach to the Muslims but illness and stormy weather brought him to Italy instead. He met St Francis, who helped him establish himself as a preacher against heresy and as a thaumaturge. He died at Padua and was canonized the following year, being especially popular in intercession as a finder of lost objects. In

1946 he was declared a doctor of the Church, being responsible for introducing Augustinian theology to the nascent Franciscans. He is represented with the Christ-Child and a lily.

Anthony Page (Bl) {2}

20 April
d. 1593. Born in Harrow in Middlesex, he studied at Oxford and Douai and was ordained at Soissons in 1591. On Candlemas in 1593 a great search for priests ordered for the North found him at Haworth Hall near York. He was executed at York and was beatified in 1987. Cf. **England (Martyrs of)**.

Anthony Patrizi (Bl) {2}

28 March
d. 1311. From Siena (Italy), he became an Augustinian friar at Monticiano and became the superior of the friary. His cultus was confirmed for the Augustinian friars in 1804.

Anthony Pavoni (Bl) {2}

9 April
?1326–74. From Savigliano south of Turin (Italy), he became a Dominican and superior of the friary in his native town before becoming inquisitor-general for Liguria and Piedmont. He was killed by Waldensian heretics at Bricherasio on leaving a church after preaching a sermon against them, and his cultus was confirmed for Turin and the Dominicans in 1856.

Anthony Primaldo and Comps (SS) {2}

14 August
d. 1480. The city of Otranto, on the heel of Italy, was briefly captured by the Ottoman Turks in 1480, and they gave the inhabitants the choice between conversion to Islam or death. Led by St Anthony, an elderly and pious artisan, eight hundred and twelve citizens chose death and were beheaded with their bishop in

the cathedral. The city never recovered. Their cultus was approved for Otranto in 1771, and they were finally canonized in 2013.

Anthony-Mary Pucci (St) {2}

12 January

1819–92. From Poggiole in Tuscany (Italy), he became a Servite in 1843 and was appointed parish priest of Viarregio. He was a model pastor, especially in his care for the poor and the sick, and was canonized in 1962.

Anthony Rewera (Bl) {2}

1 October

1868–1942. A Polish priest, he died of ill-treatment at the concentration camp at Dachau. Cf. **Poland, Martyrs of the Nazi Occupation of**.

Anthony Rosmini (Bl) {2 –add}

1797–1855. From a noble family of Rovereto near Trent (then part of the Hapsburg Empire), he became a doctor of the University of Padua before being ordained at Chioggia in 1823. At an audience Pope Pius VII encouraged him to undertake original work on philosophy, and as a result he wrote on many subjects. However, his writings drew opposition, especially concerning moral conscience, and were placed on the Index for a time. They were vindicated just before his death at Stresa. His other major work was the foundation of the 'Institute of Charity', nicknamed the Rosminians. They became very popular in England after 1835, and were the first to wear the religious habit in public there since the Reformation. They also introduced many other popular Catholic devotions.

Anthony Sanga (Bl) {2}

10 September

d. 1622. A Japanese catechist, he suffered in the 'Great Martyrdom' at Nagasaki with Charles Spinola and Comps. Cf. **Japan, Martyrs of** and **Great Martyrdom at Nagasaki**.

Anthony Schwartz (Bl) {2}

15 September

1852–1929. From a large family near Vienna (Austria), his father was a theatrical musician, and he started a career as a singer but entered the Vienna seminary instead, being ordained in 1875. His work as a hospital chaplain brought him in contact with the sufferings of young workers and apprentices, and he founded a religious community to help them: the 'Christian Workers of St Joseph Calasanz'. He aimed at their Christian and moral formation, publicly fought the way they were exploited and was one of the pioneers of the church's social teaching as expressed in the encyclical *Rerum Novarum*. This caused controversy, which he avoided answering. He died at Vienna and was beatified in 1998.

Anthony-Martin Slomšek (Bl) {2}

24 September

1800–62. From a peasant family of Slom in Stryia, Austria (now in Slovenia), he was ordained in 1824 and served as a parish priest and seminary spiritual director before being made bishop of Lavant in 1846. He transferred the see to Maribor in 1859 and was zealous for the evangelization of the Slovene people, as well as being visitor-apostolic for the declining Benedictine monasteries of central Europe. He died at Maribor and was beatified in 1999.

Anthony Soares (Bl) {2}

15 July

Cf. **Ignatius de Azevedo and Comps**.

Anthony Świadek (Bl) {2}

25 January

1909–45. A Polish priest, he died of ill-treatment at the concentration camp at Dachau near Munich (Germany). Cf. **'Poland, Martyrs of the Nazi Occupation of.'**

Anthony and John of Tlaxcala (BB) {2}
{1 –group}

23 September
?1516–29. Native Mexicans born near Tlaxcala (Mexico), they were converted and set
off to evangelize Oaxaca with a Dominican
tertiary. They wished to destroy any idol
they came across and, when they came to
a village called Cuauhtinchán, Bl Anthony
went into a temple to do so while Bl John
waited outside. The residents beat the latter to death, and did the same to the former
when he came out to remonstrate. They were
beatified in 1990.

Anthony Torriani (Bl) {2}

24 July
d. 1694. Born at Milan (Italy), he became a
physician there after studying at Padua. He
joined the Augustinian friars and, after several apostolic journeys including one where
he spent three years at Compostella (Spain),
he died at Aquila in the Abruzzi (Italy). His
cultus was confirmed for Aquila in 1759.

Anthony Turner (Bl) {2}

20 June
d. 1679. From Dalby Parva (Leics), he was a
graduate of Cambridge who became a Jesuit
in 1653 and was executed at Tyburn with BB
Thomas Whitbread and Comps. Cf. **England,
Martyrs of**.

Anthony-of-St-Bonaventure of Tuy (Bl) {2}

8 September
1588–1628. From Tuy in Galicia (Spain), he
studied at Salamanca, became a Franciscan
and went to Manila (Philippines). There he
was ordained and went to Japan, where he
reconciled over 2700 apostates before being
burnt alive at Nagasaki with BB Dominic
Castellet and Comps. Cf. **Japan, Martyrs of**.

Anthony-of-Stroncone dei Vici (Bl) {2}

8 February
1391–1461. From Stroncone (Italy), he
became a Franciscan lay brother when aged
eleven. Despite his lowly status he was chosen to help Bl Thomas Bellacci in his work in
Tuscany against the dualist heretics called the
'Fraticelli'. After more than a decade at this
he was recalled to the friary of the Carceri at
Assisi and lived a life of penance. His cultus
was confirmed for Assisi and the Franciscans in 1687. In 1809 his relics were forcibly
seized by the citizens of Stroncone.

Anthony Vom (Bl) {2}

10 September
d. 1622. A three-year-old, he was martyred
during the 'Great Martyrdom' at Nagasaki
with his father, Bl Clement Vom, and Charles
Spinola and Comps. Cf. **Japan, Martyrs of**
and **Great Martyrdom at Nagasaki**.

Anthony Weerden (St) {2}

9 July
d. 1572. He was a Franciscan friar, one of the
Gorinchem martyrs (q.v.).

Anthony Yamada (Bl) {2}

19 August
d. 1622. He was a Japanese sailor on the ship
taking BB Louis Flores and Comps to Japan,
and was beheaded at Nagasaki with them. Cf.
Japan, Martyrs of.

Anthony-Mary Zaccaria (St) {1, 3}

5 July
1502–39. From Cremona (Italy), he was medical student before becoming a secular priest.
As such he was known for his enormous apostolic zeal, and the work that he undertook as
a result probably shortened his life. In 1530
he founded the 'Clerks Regular of St Paul',

usually known as the Barnabites as their headquarters in Milan were at the church of St Barnabas. He died at Cremona and was canonized in 1897.

Anthony Zawistowski (Bl) {2}

4 June
1882–1942. A Polish priest, he was beaten to death at the concentration camp at Dachau with Bl Stanislaus Starowieyski. Cf. **Poland, Martyrs of the Nazi Occupation of.**

Anthusa of Eumenia (St) {2}

18 April
C8th. She was a daughter of Emperor Constantine V at Constantinople, and did not share her father's fanatical adherence to iconoclasm. As a princess she practised the corporal works of mercy, and after he died she became a nun and died as abbess of the nunnery of Eumenia in the city.

Anthusa of Mantineion (St) {1, 3}

27 July
C8th. A hermit, she became superior of a nunnery near Constantinople and openly defied the iconoclast edicts of Emperor Constantine V. She was interrogated by him and tortured, but the empress protected her from further harm, and she lived to a ripe old age.

(Anthusa the Younger) (St) {4 –deleted}

27 August
? She was allegedly a virgin martyred in Persia by being sewn up in a sack and dropped into a well.

Antidius (Antel, Antible, Tude) (St) {2, 4}

17 June
d. ?411. Bishop of Besançon (France), he was killed by invading Vandals at Ruffey, although he was erroneously listed as a C3rd disciple of St Froninus and his successor as bishop.

Antioch (Martyrs of) {4 –deleted}

The following anonymous groups were listed in the old Roman Martyrology as having been martyred at Antioch (Syria). They have all been deleted from the new edition:

24 December
d. 250. Forty unmarried women were killed in the reign of Decius.

11 March
d. c.300. Many in the reign of Maximian were viciously tortured to death.

6 November
d. 637. Ten (or more) were killed when the Muslims captured the city.

Antiochus (St) {2, 4}

13 December
Early C4th. He was martyred on the island off southwest Sardinia which now bears his name, San'Antiocho.

Antiochus of Anastasiopolis (SS) {2, 4}

15 July
C3–4th. St Antiochus, a brother of St Plato of Ancyra, was martyred at Anastasiopolis in Galatia (Asia Minor). His fanciful legend alleged that, after his beheading when milk spurted from the neck instead of blood, Cyriac the executioner was converted and was himself martyred. The latter has been deleted from the Roman Martyrology.

Antiochus (Andeol) of Lyons (St) {2, 4}

13 August
d. c.500. A priest of Lyons (France), he was sent to Egypt to persuade St Justus, the city's bishop, to return after the latter had fled to become a monk. Failing in this, he became bishop himself.

Antipas (St) {2, 4}

11 April
d. c.90. Cf. Rev. 2:13. He was the 'faithful witness' put to death at Pergamum (Asia Minor), but the allegation that he was killed by being roasted inside a bronze statue of a bull has been deleted from the Roman Martyrology.

Antolianus (St) {2}

6 February
C3rd. He was martyred at Clermont-Ferrand (France).

Antonia of Florence (Bl) {2}

29 February
1400–72. From Florence (Italy), she was widowed when young and became a Franciscan Conventual tertiary. As superior of the convent at Aquila she introduced the original rule of the Poor Clares, and had St John Capestrano as a guide. She suffered much from a painful illness before she died. Her cultus was confirmed for Aquila in 1847.

Antonia Messina (Bl) {2}

17 May
1919–35. Born near Nuoro in Sardinia, she was a pious child in the context of a traditional peasant society. She was out collecting firewood for the family's bread oven after Mass one Sunday when she was a victim of attempted rape and suffered fatal head injuries in defending her virginity. She was beatified as a virgin martyr in 1987.

Antonia-Mary Verna (Bl) {2 –add}

25 December
1773–1838. From a small village near Turin (Italy), as a teenager she began catechizing village children and realized the need in rural areas where there were no schools. In 1806 she

and several companions founded the Sisters of Charity of the Immaculate Conception of Ivrea for this work. She died at Turin, worn out in the efforts needed to respond to the needs that she perceived. She was beatified in 2011.

(Antonina of Cea) *(St) {4 –deleted}*

1 March
Early C4th? The old Roman Martyrology listed her as a martyr in the persecution of Diocletian who suffered at 'Cea'. A deliberate medieval forgery identified the place as being in Spain, and another opinion placed her at Nicaea. This would make her identical with the following.

Antonina of Nicaea (St) {2, 4}

4 May
C3–4th. She was severely tortured at Nicaea (now Iznik in Turkey), being hung up for three days and imprisoned for two years before being burnt. Her developed legend states that she was a virgin of Byzantium who was condemned to be sexually abused in a brothel but was allowed to escape temporarily by St Alexander, a soldier, who changed clothes with her. He has been deleted from the revised Roman Martyrology. The old Roman Martyrology placed her at Nicomedia on this date, and duplicated her at Nicaea on 12 June.

Antoninus of Apamea (St) {2, 4}

2 September
C4th. Aged twenty, he was martyred by pagans at Apamea in Syria after he had destroyed some idols.

Antoninus of Caesarea and Comps (SS) {2, 4}

13 November
d. 308. They were martyred in the reign of Galerius at Caesarea in the Holy Land. Manatha

was a virgin and was burnt, while Antoninus, Nicephorus, Zebinas and Germanus were beheaded.

Antoninus Fantosati and Joseph-Mary Gamboro (SS) {1 –group}

7 July
d. 1900. St Antoninus was born in 1842 at Santa Maria in Valle (Italy), became a Franciscan at Spineta and went to China in 1867. After serving as a missionary in Hubei for eighteen years he was made vicar-general of Upper Hubei and vicar-apostolic of South Hunan in 1892. During the Boxer uprising he was travelling by boat to Henyang with St Joseph-Mary Gambaro, who was a Franciscan priest born near Novara (Italy) in 1869. They were ambushed on the river by Boxers, stoned and beaten to death. Cf. **China, Martyrs of**.

Antoninus Fontana (St) {2, 4}

31 October
d. 661. He was bishop of Milan (Italy) for one year. St Charles Borromeo enshrined his relics.

Antoninus of Piacenza (St) {2, 4}

30 September
? He was martyred at Piacenza (Italy). His alleged blood, kept in a phial, is claimed to have the same properties as that of St Januarius at Naples.

Antoninus Pierozzi (St) {2, 3}

2 May
1389–1459. From Florence (Italy), he became a Dominican at Fiesole and was made prior of the Minerva convent at Rome while still young. In 1436 he founded San Marco at Florence, and reluctantly became archbishop of the city in 1446. He was known to care for his people, especially the poor ones, and was a writer on moral theology and international

law. Canonized in 1523, his cultus was confined to local calendars in 1969.

(Antoninus of Rome) (St) {4 –deleted}

22 August
C2nd? He was listed as beheaded on the Via Aurelia outside Rome.

Antoninus of Sorrento (St) {2, 4}

14 February
d. 830. A Benedictine monk of one of the daughter houses of Montecassino, he became a refugee hermit because of war until he settled at Sorrento (Italy) as abbot of the monastery of St Agrippinus. He is the patron of Sorrento.

(Anysia) (St) {4 –deleted}

30 December
Early C4th? According to her legend she was a young woman of Thessalonica (Greece) who was killed by a soldier after she refused to let him take her to a pagan sacrifice.

Anysius (St) {2, 4}

30 December
d. ?406. The successor of St Ascholius as bishop of Thessalonica (Greece), he was the representative of Pope St Damasus in Illyria and a friend of SS Ambrose and John Chrysostom.

Août cf. **Augustus**.

(Apelles and Lucius) (SS) {4 –deleted}

22 April
C1st? The old Roman Martyrology described them as 'from among the first disciples of Christ', usually equated with those mentioned in Rom. 16:10, 21. Traditionally St Apelles was bishop of Smyrna (now Izmir, Turkey) and St Lucius bishop of Laodicea.

(Apellius, Luke and Clement) *(SS)*
{4 –deleted}

10 September
They are a duplication in the old Roman Martyrology of SS Apelles and Lucius, with an unknown Clement added.

Aper (Apre, Epvre, Evre) of Toul (St) {2, 4}

15 September
C6th. He became bishop of Toul (France) in 500. According to tradition he had been a lawyer from Trier before being ordained.

Aper of Vienne (St) {2}

4 December
C7th. He was a priest of Vienne (France) who renounced his patrimony and became a penitential hermit in a cell that he built himself.

Aphrahat (Aphraates) (St) {2}

29 January
d. ?378. A Persian, he was a hermit first at Edessa and then at Antioch (Syria), and opposed Arianism in the reign of Valens. His identification with the famous Syriac patristic writer is uncertain.

(Aphrodisus of Alexandria and Comps) *(SS)*
{4 –deleted}

30 April
? He was listed as a priest, martyred at Alexandria (Egypt) with about thirty of his people.

Aphrodisius of Béziers (SS) {2, 4}

28 April
? He is venerated as the first bishop of Béziers (France). His legend, recounted by St Gregory of Tours, makes him an Egyptian who sheltered the Holy Family during their flight into Egypt and who was martyred with three others named Caralippus, Agapius and Eusebius. These have been deleted from the Roman Martyrology.

Apian cf. **Appian**.

(Apollinaris and Timothy) *(SS)* *{4 –deleted}*

23 August
These two were venerated at Rheims (France). Apparently the former was St Apollinaris of Ravenna and the latter was St Timothy at Rome, and a local legend was invented to explain why they were celebrated on the same day at Rheims when their real identities had been forgotten.

Apollinaris the Apologist (St) {2, 4}

8 January
d. c.180. Claudius Apollinaris was a bishop of Hierapolis in Phrygia (Asia Minor) who wrote an *Apology for Christianity* dedicated to the Emperor Marcus Aurelius as well as other works. None is extant. He was an effective opponent of Montanism.

Apollinaris of Ravenna (St) {1, 3}

20 July
C2nd. Traditionally the first bishop of Ravenna (Italy), he is venerated as a martyr at Classe outside the city (where his basilica now stands). His acta, describing him as a disciple of St Peter, are fictions of the C7th. His cultus was confined to local calendars in 1969, but has been re-established in the General Calendar.

(Apollinaris Syncletica) *(St)* *{4 –deleted}*

5 January
C4th? She is the heroine of a religious romance which alleges that she disguised herself as a boy in order to live undiscovered in the hermitage of one of the Egyptian saints called Macarius.

Apollinaris (Aiplonay) of Valence (St) {2, 4}

5 October
d. c.520. Elder brother of St Avitus of Vienne, he was a very successful bishop of Valence (France) and is the patron of that diocese.

Apolline cf. **Apollonia**.

(Apollo, Isacius and Codratus) (SS) {4 –deleted}

21 April
They form part of the legend of St George, and are described as domestic servants of the Empress Alexandra, wife of Diocletian, who were martyred at Nicomedia. The problem with this is that Alexandra never existed.

Apollonia of Alexandria (St) {2, 3}

9 February
d. 249. An elderly deaconess of Alexandria (Egypt), she was martyred in the reign of Decius. According to her legend she had her teeth torn out with pincers before being threatened with burning unless she apostatized. She replied by jumping into the fire. Her attribute is a tooth in pincers, and she is invoked against toothache. Her cultus was confined to local calendars in 1970.

Apollonia of Nagasaki (Bl) {2}

10 September
1622. A Japanese widow, she was beheaded at Nagasaki in the 'Great Martyrdom' with BB Charles Spinola and Comps. Cf. **Japan, Martyrs of** and **Great Martyrdom at Nagasaki**.

(Apollonius and Eugene) (SS) {4 –deleted}

23 July
? They were listed as Roman martyrs, the former being tied up and used as an archery target and the latter beheaded.

(Apollonius and Leontius) (SS) {4 –deleted}

19 March
? These two were listed as martyred bishops in the Hieronomian Martyrology, but nothing is known about them. They have been claimed for Braga in Portugal.

Apollonius and Philemon (SS) {2, 4}

8 March
d. ?305. Philemon was an actor and musician at Antinoë (Egypt) and was converted by the deacon Apollonius of the same city. They were arrested, brought to Alexandria, tied up and thrown into the sea in the reign of Diocletian.

Apollonius of Alexandria (St) {2, 4}

10 April
? He was a priest martyred at Alexandria (Egypt). The old Roman Martyrology mentioned five companions.

Apollonius the Apologist (St) {2, 4}

21 April
d. 185. A Roman senator, he was betrayed as a Christian by one of his slaves and beheaded. His 'apologia', or the defence of Christianity that he made at his trial, has survived in an Armenian text.

(Apollonius of Brescia) (St) {4 –deleted}

7 July
? The shrine of this alleged bishop of Brescia in Lombardy (Italy) is in the cathedral there. He is mentioned in the unreliable acta of SS Faustinus and Jovita.

Apollonius of Sardis (St) {2, 4}

10 July
? From Sardis (Asia Minor), he was flogged and crucified at Iconium (now Konya, Turkey).

Appian of Caesarea (St) {2}

2 April
d. 306. He was martyred at Caesarea in the Holy Land during the persecution of Galerius.

Appian of Commacchio (St) {2}

4 March
C8th. From Liguria (Italy), he became a monk at the abbey of Ciel d'Oro at Pavia before going on to be a hermit at Commacchio on the Adriatic and evangelizing the surrounding area.

(Apronian) (St) *{4 –deleted}*

2 February
d. ?304. According to his legend he was a Roman jailer who was converted when taking St Sisinnius before the tribunal, forthwith declared his new faith and was himself martyred. Cf. **Saturninus and Sisinnius**.

Aprunculus of Clermont-Ferrand (St) {2}

14 May
He is the same person as Abrunculus on 4 January. The duplication in the revised Roman Martyrology is a mistake.

Aptonius (St) {2}

26 October
d. ?567. He was a bishop of Angoulême (France).

Aquila and Priscilla (SS) {2, 4}

8 July
C1st. What is known of them is found in the Acts of the Apostles. They were among the Jews banished from Rome by Emperor Claudius, and they set up as tent makers at Corinth. St Paul lodged with them there (Acts 18:3).

(Aquila of Alexandria) (St) *{4 –deleted}*

20 May
d. 311. His legend states that he was martyred at Alexandria (Egypt) ripped apart with iron wool-carding combs in the reign of Maximinus Daia.

(Aquilina of Byblos) (St) *{4 –deleted}*

13 June
d. 293. According to her unreliable acta, she was a twelve-year-old girl who was tortured and martyred at Byblos in the Lebanon.

(Aquilinus, Geminus, Eugene and Comps) (SS) *{4 –deleted}*

4 January
End C5th? Numbering seven, they were listed as killed in Roman Africa by the Arian Vandal King Hunneric. Their acta are lost, but were known to St Bede in the C8th. The companions were Marcian, Quintus, Theodotus and Tryphon.

(Aquilinus, Geminus, Gelasius and Comps) (SS) *{4 –deleted}*

4 February
C3rd? They are listed as martyrs at 'Forum Sempronii' (a poor guess is that this is Fossombrone in central Italy), but nothing is known about them. The companions were Magnus and Donatus.

(Aquilinus and Victorian) (SS) *{4 –deleted}*

16 May
? They are listed by St Bede in his martyrology as having been martyred in Isauria (central Asia Minor), but nothing is known about them.

Aquilinus of Evreux (St) {2, 4}

19 October
d. c.690. From Bayeux (France), he was a soldier in the Frankish army for forty years.

On his return from fighting the Visigoths, he and his wife agreed to spend their lives in works of charity, and they moved to Evreux. St Aquilinus was soon made bishop there, but he avoided public life.

(Aquilinus of Milan) (St) {4 –deleted}

29 January
C7th?. His history has been very badly confused. According to the tradition, he was a Bavarian priest at Cologne (Germany) who fled the likelihood of being made a bishop, went to Paris and then to Milan (Italy). He preached against the Manichaean heretics there and was killed as a result. However, the evidence suggests that he was of the C7th and was martyred by the Arian Lombards. His shrine is at Milan.

(Arabia, Martyrs of) {4 –deleted}

22 February
d. ?306. There was a noteworthy pogrom of Christians in the Roman province of Arabia during the reign of Galerius. This province was in southwest Syria, with Bostra as its capital.

Ararat (Martyrs of) cf. **Acacius and Comps**.

(Arator of Alexandria and Comps) (SS) {4 –deleted}

21 April
? He was listed by the old Roman Martyrology as a martyred priest of Alexandria (Egypt), but nothing further is known about him. His companions were Felix, Fortunatus, Silvius and Vitalis. The new Roman Martyrology has replaced him with Aristus.

Arbogast (St) {2, 4}

21 July
C6th. Born in Aquitaine (not in the British Isles), he became a hermit in Alsace (France) and was forced to become the bishop of Strasbourg by the Frankish king. He was a wise and humble bishop, who directed that he should be buried in the criminals' graveyard but who later had a church built over his grave. He is depicted as walking on a river.

Arcadius (St) {2, 4}

12 January
d. ?304. A prominent Roman African citizen of Caesarea in Mauretania (near Algiers), he died after being slowly mutilated in the reign of Maximian Herculius.

Arcadius, Probus and Comps (SS) {2, 4}

13 November
d. 473. They were from Andalucia (Spain) and were taken to Africa by the Arian Vandal King Genseric, where they were the first to be martyred in the Vandal persecution. The companions were the brothers Paschasius, Eutychian and Paulillus. Paulillus was a small child, and when he would not apostatize he was severely beaten and enslaved.

Archangela Girlani (Bl) {2}

25 January
1460–95. From Trino (Italy), she became a Carmelite at Parma in 1477 and was the founding superior of the Carmel at Mantua. She was a model religious, and her cultus was confirmed for the Carmelites in 1864.

Archangelus Piacentini (Bl) {2}

10 August
d. 1460. From Calafatimi (Sicily), he was a hermit at Alcamo when Pope Martin V suppressed the hermitages of the island. He then joined the Franciscan Observants at Palermo, became provincial superior and helped them spread throughout Sicily. His cultus was confirmed for Mazzara in 1836.

Archangelus Tadini (St) {2}

20 May
1846–1912. From Verolanuova near Brescia (Italy), he was ordained for the diocese of Brescia in 1870 and became parish priest of Botticino Sera in 1887, where he remained for the rest of his life. He had a great interest in the welfare of factory workers, especially women, and founded the 'Worker Sisters of the Holy House of Nazareth' to help educate the latter. He was canonized in 2009.

Archelaus, Cyril and Photius (SS) {2, 4}

4 March
C3–4th. They were martyred at Nicomedia (Asia Minor) with seventeen companions.

(Archelaus of Kashkar) (St) {4 –deleted}

26 December
C3rd? He is listed as a bishop of Kashkar on the Tigris (Iraq), a great opponent of Manichaeism, but the writings on the subject bearing his name are not by him.

Archippus (St) {2, 4}

20 March
C1st. St Paul referred to him twice (Phil. 2; Col. 4:17). Derivative tradition considered him to be the first bishop of Colossae in Asia Minor.

Arcontius of Viviers (St) {2, 4}

10 January
d. c.740. A bishop of Viviers (France), he is recorded as having been killed by a mob for having defended the interests of his diocese but is no longer listed as a martyr.

(Ardalion) (St) {4 –deleted}

14 April
d. c.300? He is described as having been an actor somewhere in the East, who suddenly proclaimed himself a Christian while engaged in ridiculing Christianity on stage. His audience then arranged that he was roasted alive in the marketplace. The same story is told about others, such as SS Genesius and Gelasius.

Ardan (Ardaing, Ardagne, Ardagnus) (St) {2}

11 February
d. 1066. He was a Benedictine abbot of Tournus near Autun (France) and was remembered for his charity to the sufferers of a famine from 1030 to 1033.

Ardo Smaragdus (St) {2}

7 March
d. 843. From Languedoc, he was a Benedictine monk of Aniane near Montpellier (France) when St Benedict of Aniane was abbot there. He became the school headmaster and St Benedict's secretary, travelling companion, biographer and successor as abbot when St Benedict went to Aachen. His cultus was peculiar to Aniane.

Aredius (Yrieux) (St) {2}

25 August
d. 591. From Limoges (France), after service at the Frankish court he became the abbot-founder of the monastery of Atane in the Limousin, afterwards named St Yrieux after him. He was a noted evangelist throughout France. Other variants of his name are Yriez, Yriel, Ysary, Ysère and Yséry.

Aregle cf. **Agricola**.

Ares, Promus and Elias (St) {2}

14 December
d. 308–9. These three set out on a journey from Egypt to Cilicia to support local Christians in the persecution of the Emperor Maximinus. At Caesarea in the Holy Land they were seized, deprived of their eyes and feet and taken to

Ascalon. There Ares was burnt alive, and the other two were beheaded.

(Aresius, Rogatus and Comps) *(SS)*
{4 –deleted}

10 June
? They were listed as seventeen Roman African martyrs. Some martyrologies identify them with **Theodolus, Saturninus and Comps** (q.v.).

(Aretas of Rome and Comps) *(SS)*
{4 –deleted}

1 October
? They are listed in the old Roman Martyrology as numbering five hundred and four and as having been martyred at Rome. One opinion is that they are a duplication of the martyrs of **Najran** (q.v.).

(Aretius and Dacian) *(SS)* *{4 –deleted}*

4 June
? They were listed as martyred at Rome and buried in the catacombs on the Appian Way.

Argariarga cf. **Osmanna**.

Argeus, Narcissus and Marcellinus (SS)
{2, 4}

2 January
Early C4th. Their legend alleges that they were three brothers who joined the army of the Emperor Licinius. St Marcellinus was only a boy and, when he refused to perform military duties, he was flogged, imprisoned and then thrown into the Black Sea at Tomi (on the coast of Romania). His brothers were beheaded.

Argimirus (St) {2, 4}

28 June
d. 856. Born near Cordoba (Spain), he became a high-ranking Muslim of that city but was dismissed from office on suspicion of being a secret Christian. Shortly afterwards he became a monk, openly renounced Islam, proclaimed Christ and was beheaded.

Ariadne (St) {2, 4}

18 September
? She was martyred at Prymnessus in Phrygia (Asia Minor). Her legend states that she was the Christian slave of a local nobleman who had her flogged for refusing to join the pagan celebration of his birthday. She ran away and took refuge in a cleft in a rock which miraculously opened and then closed, thus entombing her.

Arialdus (St) {2}

27 June
d. 1066. A deacon of Milan (Italy), with the support of the emperor he made a stand against the simony prevalent at the time, especially that of the reigning archbishop. He was excommunicated, imprisoned on an island in Lake Maggiore and then killed there by two priests supporting the archbishop. His cultus as a martyr was confirmed for Milan in 1904.

(Arian, Theoticus and Comps) *(SS)*
{4 –deleted}

8 March
Early C4th? According to the legend, Arian was the governor of Thebes (Egypt), and he and his four companions were converted at Alexandria after witnessing the martyrdom of SS Apollonius and Philemon. The presiding judge ordered them to be drowned in the sea, but dolphins brought their bodies ashore.

Arigius (St) {2}

1 May
535–604. Bishop of Gap (France) for twenty years, he was a great pastor.

(Aristaeus and Antoninus) *(SS) {4 –deleted}*

3 September
? They have been associated with Capua (Italy), but there is no local record of them there. The former is probably an Egyptian martyr and the latter a duplication of St Antoninus of Apamea.

Aristarchus of Thessalonica (St) {2, 4}

4 August
C1st. He is the travelling companion and fellow worker of St Paul, mentioned in Acts 20:4, 27:2 and Phil. 24. Unhistorical legend makes him first bishop of Thessalonica (Greece) and a sharer in St Paul's martyrdom at Rome.

Aristides the Apologist (St) {2, 4}

31 August
d. c.150. An Athenian philosopher, he wrote an *Apology for Christianity* to the Emperor Hadrian in 125. This was preserved by being incorporated into the text of the story of Barlaam and Josaphat.

(Aristion) *(St) {4 –deleted}*

22 February
C1st? Traditionally one of the seventy-two disciples, he was alleged to have been martyred either at Salamis in Cyprus or at Alexandria in Egypt.

(Aristobolus) *(St) {4 –deleted}*

15 March
C1st. He is mentioned in St Paul's letter to the Romans (16:11), and is traditionally one of the seventy-two disciples. The legends identifying him with Zebedee the father of SS James and John, and placing him in Britain, are fictions.

(Ariston and Comps) *(SS) {4 –deleted}*

2 July
Late C3rd? A group of ten (the others being Crescentian, Eutychian, Felicissimus, Felix, Justus, Marcia, Symphorosa, Urban and Vitalis), they were listed as martyred in the Campagna (Italy) in the reign of Diocletian. Details are lacking.

Aristus (St) {2}

21 April
? He was a priest, martyred at Alexandria (Egypt), and seems to be the source of the 'Arator' in the old Roman Martyrology.

(Arius ('Macarius') of Petra) *(St) {4 –deleted}*

20 June
d. c.350. Arius was a bishop of Petra (Jordan) who was present at the council of Sardica in 347. The Arians managed to get him exiled to Africa, where he died. He has never had a cultus, but Cardinal Baronius inserted him into the old Roman Martyrology and arbitrarily changed his name to Macarius to distinguish him from Arius, the heresiarch.

Armagilus (Armel, Ermel, Ermyn) (St) {2}

16 August
C6th. Allegedly a cousin of St Sampson and born in south Wales, he was a missionary in Cornwall (England) where St Erme is named after him and in Brittany (France) where he founded monasteries at Saint-Armel-des-Boscheaux and Ploermel. He is represented holding the Devil on a chain or tied up with his priestly stole, and sometimes with armour under his vestments.

Armand cf. **Ormond.**

Armentarius of Pavia (St) {2, 4}

30 January
d. p731. As bishop of Pavia (Italy) he obtained the independence of his diocese from the archbishop of Milan.

Armogast, Archinimus and Saturninus
(SS) {2, 4}

29 March
d. ?462. Palace courtiers at Carthage in Roman Africa, they were singled out in the Arian persecution arranged by the Vandal King Genseric. They were tortured, put to work in the mines and then enslaved as cowherds but were not killed as their persecutors did not want them venerated as martyrs. However they are listed as such.

Armon cf. **Germanus of Auxerre**.

Arnold Janssen (St) {2}

15 January
1837–1909. Born at Goch (Germany), after he was ordained he founded the 'Missionary Society of the Divine Word' in 1875 at Steyl in the Netherlands in order to help in foreign missions. He also founded two congregations for women: the 'Missionary Servants of the Holy Spirit' and the 'Servants of the Holy Spirit for Perpetual Adoration'. He was canonized in 2003.

Arnold Rèche (Bl) {2}

23 October
1838–90. From near Metz (France), he became a coachman and muleteer in Charleville before joining the 'Brothers of the Christian Schools' in 1862. He taught at Rheims from 1863 to 1877, but found it hard to keep discipline. Then he was made novice-master at Thillois in 1877 and gave great edification. He became rector of the institute's retirement home in Rheims just before he died of a stroke, and was beatified in 1987.

Arnulf of Gap (St) {2}

19 September
d. ?1075. Born at Vendôme (France), he joined the Benedictine abbey of the Holy Trinity there and became the bishop of Gap in 1063. He is the principal patron of the city.

Arnulf of Metz (St) {2, 4}

18 July
?582–640. A nobleman from near Nancy (France), he was a high official at the Frankish Austrasian court before he and his wife agreed to become consecrated religious. She became a nun, but he was made bishop of Metz (France) in 616 before he could become a monk. When he retired as bishop he became a hermit near Remiremont. He was the progenitor of the Carolingian dynasty.

Arnulf of Soissons (St) {2, 4}

15 August
c.1040–87. From Flanders, for some years he was a soldier in the royal army of France and then became a hermit at the Benedictine abbey of St Médard at Soissons (France). He was forced to become the city's bishop in 1081, but was expelled by a rival and retired to the abbey of Oudenbourg (Belgium) which he had founded.

Arpinus cf. **Agrippinus**.

Arsacius (Ursacius) (St) {2, 4}

16 August
d. 358. His story is that he was a Persian soldier in the Roman army who converted and became a hermit in a tower overlooking Nicomedia (Asia Minor). He foretold the earthquake of 358 which destroyed the city, and was found dead in his tower by refugee citizens.

Arsenius of Armi (St) {2}

15 January
d. 904. He was a Byzantine-rite hermit at Armi near Reggio di Calabria (Italy).

Arsenius of Corfu (St) {2}

19 January
C10th. Born in Constantinople of Jewish descent, he became the first bishop of Corfu (Greece) and is a patron of the island.

Arsenius the Great (St) {2, 4}

8 May
d. ?449. A Roman of senatorial rank, he was chosen by Emperor Theodosius I to be the tutor of his mentally subnormal sons, Arcadius and Honorius, in 383. In 393 he fled to Egypt in disgust and became a monk and disciple of St John the Short at Scetis, where his erudition, austerity and silence enhanced his reputation among the native Copts. After Scetis was devastated by barbarians in 434 he moved to Troë near Memphis, where he died. He features in the *Apophegmata Patrum*.

Artald (Arthaud, Artaud) of Belley (Bl) {2}

6 October
1101–1206. A courtier of Savoy (now in France), he became a Carthusian at Portes in 1120 and founded a monastery at Arvières-en-Valromey in 1140. He was appointed bishop of Belley in 1188, but resigned two years later and returned to Arvières where he died a centenarian. His cultus was approved for Belley in 1834.

Artemas of Puteoli (St) {2, 4}

25 January
C3–4th. He was martyred at Puteoli (Pozzuoli near Naples, Italy). His fictional legend describes him as a schoolboy of who was stabbed to death by his pagan confreres with their pens. A similar story is told of others.

Artemius and Paulina (SS) {2, 4}

6 June
? They were martyred on the Via Aurelia, just to the west of Rome. According to their unreliable legend, Artemius was the governor of a Roman prison. Candida was his wife, and Paulina his daughter. They were converted by St Peter the Exorcist and baptized by St Marcellinus, then Artemius was beheaded, and the two women were buried alive under a cairn. Candida has been deleted from the Roman Martyrology.

(Artemius the Great Martyr) *(St) {4 –deleted}*

20 October
d. 363. A high courtier under Emperor Constantine, he was made prefect of Egypt by Emperor Constantius. He was a zealous Arian and persecuted St Athanasius and the Orthodox in Egypt. There is no indication that he repented of this, but he was beheaded as a Christian in the reign of Julian and was venerated as a martyr.

Artemis Zatti (Bl) {2 –add}

15 March
1880–1951. He was from Reggio Emilia in Italy, but his family emigrated and settled at Bahia Blanca in Argentina when he was in his teens. In 1900 he joined the Salesians as a lay brother, but contracted tuberculosis and was sent to Viedma in the Andes. There he was cured, and became responsible for the pharmacy and the hospital, depending only on donations for funds. He died of cancer of the liver and was beatified in 2002.

(Artemon) *(St) {4 –deleted}*

8 October
Early C4th? He was listed as a priest of Laodicea in Phrygia (Asia Minor), burnt in the reign of Diocletian.

Arthellais (St) {2}

3 March
d. c.570. One of the patrons of Benevento (Italy), she was alleged to have fled there

from Constantinople in order to escape the unwelcome attentions of Emperor Justinian.

Arthur Bell cf. **Francis Bell**.

Artiston (St) {2}

13 December
C4th. He was martyred at Porto Romano (now the town of Fiumicino) at the mouth of the Tiber (Italy).

Asaph (St) {2}

1 May
d. c.600. A monk, he was allegedly a disciple of St Kentigern and his successor as abbot and bishop at the place now named after him in north Wales. Many of his relatives also became saints and gave their names to localities, for example Deiniol and Tysilo.

Ascension-of-the-Heart-of-Jesus Nicol Goñi (Bl) {2 –add}

24 February
1868–1940. From Tafalla in Navarra, Spain, she became a Dominicaness at Huesca in 1885. In 1913 she headed a group of sisters to a mission at Porto Maldonado in the Amazonian forests of Peru. In 1918, together with the local bishop, she founded the 'Dominican Missionary Sisters of the Rosary' as an indigenous Peruvian congregation. She was beatified in 2005.

Asclas (St) {2, 4}

20 January
Early C4th. He was martyred at Antinoë (Egypt) in the reign of Diocletian by being thrown into the Nile.

Asclepiades (St) {2, 4}

18 October
d. 218. He succeeded St Serapion as bishop of Antioch (Syria) in 211, and was listed as

a martyr in the old Roman Martyrology. This seems to be because of his sufferings during the persecution in the reign of Septimus Severus.

Asella (St) {2, 4}

6 December
d. p385. St Jerome wrote in praise of this Roman abbess, relating that she became a nun when aged ten and then a recluse in a small cell two years later. Disciples gathered around her and these became a sizeable community.

Asicus (Ascicus, Tassach) (St) {2}

14 April
C5th. An early disciple of St Patrick in Ireland, he became first abbot and bishop of Elphin in Co. Roscommon, of which diocese he is the patron. He was a coppersmith, and some examples of his handiwork survive.

Aspren (Aspronas) (St) {2, 4}

3 August
C2nd–3rd. By tradition he was the first bishop of Naples (Italy) and was healed, baptized and ordained by St Peter. He dates from the end of the second century in reality.

Assumpta (Assunta) Marchetti (Bl) {2 –add}

1 July
1871–1948. From Lombrici di Camaiore near Lucca, Italy, as a teenager she wished to become a nun, but family responsibilities prevented this until 1895. In that year she emigrated to Brazil at the invitation of her brother, a missionary priest among the expatriate Italians there, and joined the new congregation of Missionary Sisters of St Charles Borromeo or Scalabrinian Sisters. She was based at São Paolo, where she founded an orphanage and where she died. She was beatified in 2014.

(Asteria) (St) {4 –deleted}

10 August
Early C4th? According to her dubious acta, she was a sister of St Grata who helped with the burial of St Alexander and was martyred at Bergamo (Italy).

Asterius (St) {2, 4}

19 October
C3rd. A Roman priest, he buried the body of Pope St Callistus after the latter's martyrdom and was himself thrown into the Tiber at Ostia as a result by order of Emperor Alexander Severus. His body was recovered and enshrined in the cathedral at Ostia.

(Asterius of Petra) (St) {4 –deleted}

10 June
d. p362. Formerly an Arian, he converted to orthodoxy, became bishop of Petra (now in Jordan) and published an account of the Arian machinations at the council of Sardica (347). He was banished to Libya by Constantius, recalled by Julian and is last heard of in 362.

Athan cf. **Tathai**.

Athanasia (St) {2, 4}

18 April
C9th. Born on the island of Aegina off Piraeus (Greece) of an ancient Greek family, she lost her first husband in warfare against the Muslims. She remarried, but the couple separated by mutual consent to become consecrated religious, and she turned their former house at Timia into a convent which she ruled as abbess. She died there after spending several years at Constantinople as an imperial adviser.

(Athanasius, Anthusa and Comps) (SS) {4 –deleted}

22 August
Mid C3rd? According to the acta of St Anthusa (which resemble those of St Pelagia of Tarsus), Athanasius was a bishop of Tarsus in Cilicia who baptized Anthusa, a lady of Seleucia, and two of her slaves, Charisius and Neophytus. The three men were martyred in the reign of Valerian, while she lived for twenty-three years afterwards.

Athanasius of Alexandria (St) {1, 3}

2 May
?296–373. Born in Alexandria (Egypt), he became a deacon under St Alexander there and denounced Arius as a heretic. After having accompanied St Alexander to the Council of Nicaea in 325 he became patriarch himself in 328 and was the outstanding champion of Christ's divinity against Arianism. For this he was exiled five times between 336 and 366, initially to Trier, then to Rome (where he helped introduce an awareness of monasticism with his translation of the life of St Anthony and by taking two monks with him), and then to the Egyptian desert among the monks. He was an outstanding theologian, pastor and churchman and is a doctor of the Church.

Athanasius the Athonite (St) {2}

5 July
c.920–1004. From Trebizond (now Trabzon in Turkey), he became a monk on the Bithynian Olympus and then migrated to the colony of hermits on Mount Athos. There he founded the 'Great Laura', the first cenobitic monastery, with the help of his friend, the Emperor Nicephorus Phocas. This was the start of the great monastic republic of Athos, which survives, and he became superior of sixty communities on the mountain by the time of his death. He was killed when the dome of his monastery's church fell in.

Athanasius Bazzekuketta (St) {1 –group}

27 May
d. 1886. He was a page at the court of King Mwanga of Buganda (Uganda), and the royal

treasurer. Baptized in 1885, he was martyred by order of the king a year later. Cf. **Charles Lwanga and Comps**.

Athanasius of Jerusalem (St) {2, 4}

5 July
d. 452. When the Council of Chalcedon condemned Monophysitism in 451, the Monophysites in Jerusalem deposed the bishop St Juvenal in favour of their candidate, Theodosius. St Athanasius, a deacon, protested at this and was beheaded by members of the garrison.

Athanasius of Naples (St) {2, 4}

15 July
832–72. Son of the duke of Naples (Italy), he was made bishop there when aged eighteen. After twenty years he was a target of extortion by his ruling relatives, who imprisoned and exiled him. He died at Veroli, but his body was eventually transferred back to Naples.

Athenodorus (St) {2, 4}

7 November
C3rd {4 –deleted}. Born in Neocaesarea in Cappodocia (Asia Minor), he was a brother of St Gregory Thaumaturgus, was converted with him and studied with him under Origen at Caesarea in the Holy Land. He became a bishop of an unknown town in Pontus and was martyred in the reign of Aurelian.

Athenodorus (St) {2, 4}

7 December
d. ?304. According to the Roman Martyrology he was martyred in Syria in the reign of Diocletian. He died after being tortured and before he could be executed; his would-be executioner dropped dead, and no one else dared to be the replacement.

(Athenogenes) (St) {4 –deleted}

18 January
? The old Roman Martyrology listed him as an old theologian burnt in Pontus who left in writing a hymn that he sang at his martyrdom. St Basil identified this with the Byzantine vespers hymn, *Phos Hilaron*. He is identical with St Athenogenes of Sebaste.

Athenogenes of Sebaste (St) {2, 4}

16 July
d. c.305. He was a martyred bishop of Sebaste (now Sivas) in Asia Minor, who wrote a hymn declaring the divinity of the Holy Spirit. The ten disciples mentioned in the old Roman Martyrology have been deleted.

Atheus cf. **Tathai**.
Athilda cf. **Alkeld**.

Atilanus Cruz Alvarado (St) {1 –group}

1 July
Cf. **Justin Orona Madrigal and Atilanus Cruz Alvarado**.

Attalas (St) {2, 4}

10 March
d. 626. A Burgundian monk of Lérins (France), he transferred to Luxeuil under St Columban and accompanied him to Bobbio in Lombardy (Italy) where he helped him found the abbey and succeeded him as abbot in 615. In his abbacy the monks of Bobbio rebelled against the severity of the Columbanian rule.

(Atticus) (St) {4 –deleted}

6 November
? He was listed by the old Roman Martyrology as having been martyred in Phrygia (Asia Minor), but no details survive.

Attilanus (St) {2, 4}

5 October
d. 1009. From near Zaragoza (Spain), he became a monk and then prior at Moreruela under St Froilan as abbot. They were ordained together as bishops, Froilan of León and Attlianus of Zamora.

Atto (Attho) of Pistoia (St) {2}

22 May
d. 1153. From either Badajoz (Spain) or Florence (Italy), he became a monk at Vallombrosa near the latter city and then abbot-general of the congregation of that name. He was made bishop of Pistoia, and wrote biographies of SS John Gualbert and Bernard degli Uberti.

Attracta (Athracht) (St) {2}

11 August
C5th. Possibly a contemporary of St Patrick in Ireland, she was a hermit at Killaraght on Lough Gara in Co. Sligo and then at Drum near Boyle in Co. Roscommon. Both places became nunneries under her direction.

Aubert cf. **Autbert**.
Aubierge cf. **Ethelburga**.
Aubin cf. **Albinus**.

(Auctus, Taurion and Thessalonica) *(SS)* *{4 –deleted}*

7 November
? These were listed as martyrs of Amphipolis near Thessalonica (Greece).

(Audas and Comps) *(SS) {4 –deleted}*

16 May
d. ?420. They were listed as a Persian bishop with seven priests, nine deacons and seven virgins, martyred at the start of a general persecution in the Sassanid Persian Empire.

Audöenus (Aldwin, Ouen, Owen, Dado) (St) {2}

24 August
c.600–84. A Frankish courtier from near Soissons (France), he founded the abbey of Rebais in Brie and became bishop of Rouen in 641. He died at a place now named after him near Paris.

Audomarus cf. **Omer**.
Audrey cf. **Etheldreda**.

Augulus (Aule) (St) {2, 4}

30 April
C7th. He was a bishop of Viviers (France) who founded the first hospital in the city and redeemed many captives. Fictitious legend made him a C4th martyr at London.

(Augustalis) *(St) {4 –deleted}*

7 September
Mid C5th? He was listed as a bishop in Roman Gaul, possibly at Arles (France).

Augustina Pietrantoni (St) {2}

13 November
1864–94. Born at Tivoli near Rome to a large peasant family, she became a Sister of Charity and a nurse at the Santo Spiritu Hospital at Rome. The atmosphere in the hospital was anti-religious, and there she was fatally stabbed by a patient. She asked for mercy for him before she died, and was canonized in 1999.

Augustine and Felicity (SS) {2}

16 November
d. c.250. They were martyred at Capua (Italy).

Augustine Caloca Cortés (St) {1 –group}

25 May
Cf. **Christopher Magallanes Jara and Augustine Caloca Cortés**.

Augustine of Canterbury (St) {2, 4}

27 May
d. 604. He was prior of St Andrew's monastery on the Coelian Hill in Rome when he was sent by Pope St Gregory the Great with forty companions to evangelize the pagan Anglo-Saxons in Britain. He was ordained bishop for the mission at Arles on the way. The missionaries landed at Ebbsfleet on Thanet in the Kingdom of Kent in 597, converted the king, St Ethelbert, with many of his subjects and established the primatial English diocese at Canterbury. St Augustine succeeded in establishing the Latin Church in England, but failed to establish relationships with the Celtic Christians. He died shortly after St Gregory, and the two are venerated as the 'apostles of the English'. There is no historical evidence that he was a Benedictine.

Augustine (Eystein) Erlandssön (St) {2}

26 January
d. 1188. He was the bishop of Nidaros in Norway, and defended the interests of his diocese against secular rulers as well as promoting the faith.

Augustine Fangi (Bl) {2}

22 July
d. 1493. From Biella in Piedmont (Italy) he joined the Dominicans there and had a busy apostolic career united with physical sufferings until he died at Venice. His cultus was confirmed for Biella in 1872.

Augustine-Mary García Tribaldos and Comps (BB) {2 –add}

30 July
d. 1936. They are the Martyrs of the Brothers of the Christian Schools at Madrid, Spain. Bl Augustine-Mary was the superior of the school at Bujedo, and at the start of the Spanish Civil War he and fifteen of his confreres were arrested by Communist militia, taken to the Casa de Campo and shot. They were beatified in 2013. Cf. **Spanish Civil War, Martyrs of** and list in appendix.

Augustine of Hippo (St) {1, 3}

28 August
354–430. He was born in Tagaste in Roman Africa, his mother (St Monica) was a fervent Christian, but his father was a pagan. He trained as a rhetorician and practised that profession at Tagaste, Carthage, Rome and Milan. As a young man he was attracted to Manichaeism and fathered a child (St Adeodatus) out of wedlock. He was converted by the influence of St Ambrose of Milan and his mother's prayers, helped by St Paul's theology and the use of neoplatonic philosophy. Being baptized in Milan by St Ambrose in 387, he went back to Africa and lived in quasi-monastic seclusion with a few friends for three years until his ordination for the city of Hippo as priest and then as bishop. As a pastor his literary output was enormous (especially famous are his 'Confessions', 'The City of God' and 'The Trinity'), and his influence on Latin patristic and early medieval theology was absolute. His need to combat especially the heresies concerning grace of Donatism and Pelagianism led him to develop the doctrine of grace and free will in an authoritative manner. Two letters of his advising religious communities were much later incorporated into a formal rule bearing his name, which became very popular in the Middle Ages. He is a doctor of the Church. His alleged relics are at Pavia (Italy).

Augustine Kažotić (Bl) {2}

8 August
1260–1323. From near Split in Dalmatia (Croatia), he became a Dominican, preached

in Croatia and Hungary and was made bishop of Zagreb. He had the charisms of gentleness and healing. Later he was transferred to Lucera (Italy), for which place his cultus was confirmed in 1702.

Augustine Nguyễn Văn Mới (St) {1 –group}

19 December
Cf. **Francis-Xavier Hà Trọng) Mậu and Comps**.

Augustine Novellus (Bl) {2}

19 May
d. 1310. From Taormina (Sicily), he obtained a degree in law at Bologna and became chancellor of the Kingdom of Sicily under King Manfred. Being left for dead after the battle of Benevento against Charles of Anjou led him to join the Augustinian friars as a lay brother, but he was soon persuaded to accept ordination, and he eventually became his order's prior-general and the pope's confessor and legate. His cultus was confirmed for Siena, where he died, in 1759.

Augustine Ota (Bl) {2}

25 September
d. 1622. From the island of Hirado-jima off Japan, he was a catechist before being imprisoned and beheaded at Iki. He became a Jesuit in prison. He was beatified in 1867. Cf. **Japan, Martyrs of**.

Augustine Pak Chŏng-wŏn and Comps (SS) {1 –group}

31 January
d. 1840. They were a group of six who were martyred in Korea after being tortured in prison. St Augustine was a catechist, and the others were Agatha Yi Kyŏng-i, Agatha Kwŏn Chin-i, Mary Yi In-dŏg a virgin, Mary-Magdalen Son So-byŏg and Peter Hong Pyŏng-ju, also a catechist. Cf. **Korea, Martyrs of**.

Augustine Phan Viết Huy (St) {1 –group}

13 June
d. 1839. A Vietnamese soldier, he was ordered to trample on a crucifix during the persecution ordered by Emperor Minh Mạng. He did so, but repented, publicly proclaimed his faith and was sawn in half with St Nicholas Bùi Viết Thể at Hué. Cf. **Vietnam, Martyrs of**.

Augustine Roscelli (St) {2}

7 May
1818–1902. Born in Casarza Ligure (Italy), he was initially a shepherd but became a parish priest in Genoa in 1846 and spent innumerable hours in the confessional. He also set up a vocational training centre for young women with no other means of support apart from prostitution, and worked as chaplain in the city's orphanage and prison. He founded the 'Sisters of the Immaculata' to help run the training centre in 1876. He was beatified in 1995 and canonized in 2001.

Augustine Schoeffler (St) {1 –group}

1 May
1822–51. From Mittelbronn in Lorraine (France), he joined the 'Paris Society for Foreign Missions' and was sent to Vietnam. He worked as a priest there for three years before being arrested during the persecution ordered by Emperor Tự Đức. After a period of imprisonment he was beheaded at Sơn Tây. Cf. **Vietnam, Martyrs of**.

Augustine Thevarparampil (Bl) {2 –add}

1891–1973. He was from a 'dalit' (Untouchable) family of Ramapuram in Kerala, India, and was ordained as a diocesan priest in 1921. As parish priest of his home town, he developed his apostolate to his fellow dalits, who were in a state of extreme poverty and social deprivation owing to their low status. As a result thousands converted, and he obtained the nickname of 'Kunjachan' or 'little father' by which he was generally known. He was beatified in 2006.

Augustine Webster (St) {2}

4 May
d. 1535. A Carthusian at Sheen in Surrey, he was made prior of Axholme (Lincs). He visited the London Charterhouse together with St Robert Lawrence of Beauvale to consult its prior, St John Houghton, about the religious policy of King Henry VIII. They were arrested at the London Charterhouse, executed at Tyburn for denying the king's supremacy in spiritual matters and were canonized in 1970. Cf. **England (Martyrs of)**.

Augustine Yi Kwang-hŏn and Comps (SS) {1 –group}

24 May
d. 1839. They were a group of nine who were beheaded together at Seoul in Korea after being imprisoned for some time. St Augustine was the father of a family who held bible-reading sessions in his home. The others were Agatha Kim A-gi, a wife and mother who was baptized in prison, Agatha Yi So-sa, Anne Pak A-gi, Barbara Han A-gi, Damian Nam Myŏng-hyŏg, a catechist, Lucy Pak Hŭi-sun, Mary-Magdalen Kim Ŏ-bi and Peter Kwon Tŭ-gin. Cf. **Korea, Martyrs of**.

Augustine Yu Chin-gil (St) {1 –group}

22 September
d. 1839. Cf. **Paul Chŏng Ha-sang and Augustine Yu Chin-gil**.

Augustine Zhao Rong (St) {1 –group}

21 March
1746–1815. From Wuchuan in Guizhou (China), he was a warden in a prison in which Christians were being held and was converted by their example. In 1781 he was ordained and went to do missionary work in western Sichuan. He was arrested in 1815 and, being already ill, died in prison after torture sometime in the season of spring. Cf. **China, Martyrs of**.

Augustus of Bourges (St) {2, 4}

7 October
d. c.560. An abbot at Bourges (France), he was a friend of St Germanus of Paris and discovered the body of St Ursinus (the evangelizer of the district).

Augustus Chapdelaine (St) {1 –group}

29 February
1814–56. The ninth child of a peasant of Normandy (France), he joined the 'Paris Society of Foreign Missions' and went to China to be a missionary priest in Guangxi in 1852. He was arrested at Xilinxian while giving instruction in the faith, and was given three hundred strokes of a bamboo cane in order to induce apostasy. Then he was kept in a very small cell in prison before being beheaded. Cf. **China, Martyrs of**.

Augustus Czartoryski (Bl) {2}

8 April
1858–93. A prince, he was born in Paris of a noble Polish family living in exile, and was initially set to be involved in contemporary Polish nationalistic aspirations. However, he was already aware of a call to the religious life when St John Bosco said Mass in the chapel of the family palace, and eventually became a Salesian in 1887. He was ordained a year before he died of tuberculosis, a disease from which he had suffered most of his life. He was beatified in 2004.

Augustus-Andrew Martín Fernández (St) {2}

9 October
Cf. **Innocent-of-Mary-Immaculate Canoura Arnau and Comps**.

Aulaire cf. **Eulalia of Barcelona**.

Aunacharius of Auxerre (St) {2, 4}

25 September
d. 604. From near Orleans (France), he was educated at the Burgundian court and became bishop of Auxerre in 561. He ordered the Divine Office to be recited in all his diocesan churches.

Aurea Banzai (Bl) {2 –add}

12 January
Cf. **Louis Amagasu Iemon and Comps**.

Aurea (Aura) of Cuteclara (St) {2, 4}

19 July
d. 856. She was a Muslim from Cordoba (Spain) who converted to Christianity and became a nun at Cuteclara for over twenty years. Her family denounced her as an apostate from Islam, and she was beheaded.

Aurea of Ostia (St) {2, 4}

20 May
? She has an ancient cultus at Ostia Antica near Rome, but her acta are fictional. She is the patron of the former cathedral there.

Aurea of Paris (St) {2, 4}

4 October
d. ?666. A Syrian, she was appointed by St Eligius as superior of the nunnery of St Martial at Paris (France) in 633. She died in an epidemic with 160 of her community.

(Aurelia and Neomisia) (SS) {4 –deleted}

25 September
? Their story is that they were from Asia Minor and went on pilgrimage to the Holy Land and to Rome. At Capua (Italy) they were waylaid by pirates, but escaped under the cover of a thunderstorm, took refuge at Macerata near Anagni and died there.

Aurelia Arambarri Fuente and Comps (BB) {2 –add}
d. 1936. They were four members of the congregation of Servants of Mary, Ministers to the Sick who were martyred in the diocese of Madrid during the Spanish Civil War. Three of them were killed by anarchists at Aravaca on 6 December, and one at Las Rozas the day beforehand. They were beatified in 2013. Cf. **Spanish Civil War, Martyrs of** and list in appendix.

(Aurelia of Strasbourg) (St) {4 –deleted}

15 October
Early C11th? According to her unreliable legend, she was a French princess and was attached to a Benedictine abbey at Strasbourg in Alsace (France) for fifty-five years as a hermit.

Aurelian of Arles (St) {2, 4}

16 June
d. 551. Bishop of Arles (France) from 546, he was Pope Vigilius's legate for Gaul and founded two monasteries (one for each sex) at Arles. The customaries that he gave them were based on the rules of SS Caesarius and Benedict.

(Aurelius and Publius) (SS) {4 –deleted}

12 November
C2nd? They were listed as two bishops who wrote against the Montanists and who were martyred.

Aurelius Ample Alcaide and Comps (BB) {2}

d. 1936. They were twelve Franciscan Capuchins, five Capuchiness nuns and an Augustinian Discalced nun (Bl Josepha-of-the-Purification Masiá Ferragut, related to three of the Capuchinesses) who were killed during the Spanish Civil War in various places during August and September 1936. Cf. **Spanish Civil War, Martyrs** of and lists in appendix.

Aurelius of Carthage (St) {2}

20 July
d. c.430. Bishop of Carthage and metropolitan of Roman Africa, he was a friend of St Augustine of Hippo and an early opponent of Pelagianism. He asked the help of the civil authorities against the activities of the Donatists.

Aurelius-Mary Villalón Acebrón and Comps (BB) {2}

d. 1936. Seven members of the 'Brothers of Christian Schools' who were teaching in the college of Almería (Spain), they were killed after the local 'Revolutionary Committee' ordered the liquidation of priests and religious. They were beatified in 1993. Cf. **Spanish Civil War, Martyrs of** and list in appendix.

Aureus, Justina and Comps (SS) {2}

16 June
C5th. Aureus was bishop of Mainz (Germany), and went into exile with his sister Justina when the Huns invaded. They then returned and were massacred with the congregation while he was saying Mass.

Ausonius of Angoulême (St) {2}

22 May
C4–5th. He is venerated as the first bishop of Angoulême (France).

Auspicius of Toul (St) {2}

8 July
C5th. Mentioned as bishop of Toul (France) by Sidonius Apollinaris, he had a shrine at Saint-Mansuy.

(Auspicius of Trier) (St) {4 –deleted}

8 July
? Claimed to be the fourth bishop of Trier (Germany) in succession to St Maternus, he is probably a duplication of St Auspicius of Toul.

Austin cf. **Augustine**.

Austindus (St) {2}

26 July
d. 1068. From Bordeaux, he joined the Benedictine abbey of Saint-Orens at Auch (France), became its abbot and entered it into the Cluniac congregation. In 1041 he became the city's archbishop and fought against simony.

Austreberta (St) {2, 4}

10 February
?635–704. From near Thérouanne in Artois (France), she was the daughter of St Framechild and the Count Palatine Badefrid and was clothed as a nun at Ponthieu by St Omer. She became abbess of St Philibert's foundation at Pavilly in Normandy.

Austregisil (Aoustrille, Outrille) of Bourges (St) {2, 4}

20 May
551–624. From Bourges (France), he was educated as a courtier but became a monk at Saint-Nizier in Lyons instead, going on to become abbot there and bishop of Bourges in 612.

Austremonius (Stremoine) of Clermont-Ferrand (St) {2, 4}

1 November
C3rd. Traditionally one of seven missionaries sent from Rome to evangelize Gaul, he preached in the Auvergne and became the first bishop of Clermont-Ferrand (France).

Audomar (Omer) (St) {2}

1 November
?595–670. From near Constance (Germany), he became a monk at Luxeuil and bishop of Thérouanne (which missionary diocese then embraced what is now French Flanders and the Pas-de-Calais) in ?637. In order to evangelize the area, he enlisted the help of many missionary monks who founded numerous monasteries. He himself founded the monastery of Sithiu with St Bertin, and this was the nucleus of the future town of St Omer.

Autbert of Avranches (St) {2}

10 September
d. ?725. Bishop of Avranches (France), he founded the famous abbey of Mont-St-Michel off the coast of Normandy.

Autbert of Cambrai-Arras (St) {2, 4}

13 December
d. c.670. Bishop of Cambrai-Arras, he was a great patron of monastic life and founded many monasteries in northern France, including the great abbey of St Vedast at Arras. His attribute is a baker's peel.

Autbert of Landevennec (St)

1 February
d. 1129. A Benedictine monk of Landevennec in Brittany (France), he became chaplain to the nunnery of St Sulpice near Rheims and has a cultus in that city.

Autel cf. **Augustalis**.

Autonomous (St) {2, 4}

12 September
C3rd. According to the Byzantine tradition he was an Italian bishop who fled to Bithynia (Asia Minor) during the persecution by Diocletian. There he was martyred after success as a missionary.

Auxanus (Ansano) (St) {2, 4}

3 September
d. ?589. He was a bishop of Milan (Italy), where he has a popular cultus.

Auxentius (St) {2, 4}

14 February
C5th. A Persian born in Syria, he was a guard in the service of Emperor Theodosius II before becoming a hermit on the mountain of Scopa in Bithynia near Constantinople. He successfully defended his orthodoxy against false accusations at the Council of Chalcedon in 451.

(Auxentius of Mopsuestia) (St) {4 –deleted}

18 December
Early C4th? He is described as a soldier in the army of Emperor Licinius who was persecuted for refusing to join in pagan rites, but survived and went on to become bishop of Mopsuestia near Antioch (Syria).

(Auxibius) (St) {4 –deleted}

19 February
C1st? He was traditionally baptized by St Mark and made first bishop of Soli in Cyprus by St Paul.

Aventinus of Chartres (St) {2}

4 February
d. ?511. He was the successor of his brother, St Solemnis, as bishop of Chartres (France).

Aventinus of Larbouch (St) {2}

7 June
C8th. Born at Bagnères in the Pyrenees (France), he became a hermit in the valley of Larbouche and was killed there by the Arabs.

Aventinus of Troyes (St) {2, 4}

4 February
d. ?537. From central France, he was the almoner of St Lupus of Troyes but left that

city to become a hermit at the place later named St Aventin after him.

Avertanus (St) {2}

25 February
d. ?1386. Born in Limoges (France), he became a Carmelite lay brother there but died outside Lucca (Italy) while on a pilgrimage to the Holy Land with Bl Romeo.

Avertinus (St) {2}

5 May
d. 1189. He was a deacon under St Thomas Becket at Canterbury (England), and went with him into exile. When St Thomas was martyred, he returned to Tours and eventually became a hermit at Laventie near Lille.

(Avitus) (St) {4 –deleted}

27 January
? The old Roman Martyrology lists an African martyr of this name, who may be linked with the St Avitus who is anachronistically celebrated as the apostle and first bishop of the Canaries.

Avitus (Avy) of Micy (St) {2, 4}

17 June
d. ?530. A monk of Menat in Auvergne (France), he became abbot of Micy near Orleans and then was allegedly a hermit in the hills of Perche (west of Chartres) where he formed a new monastery which he ruled, gathering the disciples who joined him. He is

probably the 'Adjutus' listed in the old Roman Martyrology on 19 December.

Avitus of Vienne (St) {2, 4}

5 February
c.450–518. From the Auvergne (France), he was the brother of St Apollinaris, bishop of Valence, and son of St Hesychius, bishop of Vienne. He succeeded the latter and was a popular bishop and writer, having also the respect of the ruling Arian Burgundians. He converted their king, St Sigismund, to orthodoxy from Arianism. Many of his letters survive.

Aybert cf. **Aibert**.

(Azadas and Comps) (SS) {4 –deleted}

22 April
d. 341–2. The old Roman Martyrology had a long list of martyrs under the Persian Shah Shapur II. Those named were Azadas, a eunuch at court; the bishops Milles, Acepsimas, Mareas and Bicor; the priests James, Aithalas and Joseph; the deacons Azadas and Abdjesus and the virgin Tarbula with her servant as well as twenty other bishops, over 250 clerics and many monastics. The revised Roman Martyrology lists only Milles under his correct name of **Maryáhb**.

(Azas and Comps) (SS) {4 –deleted}

19 November
Early C5th. They were listed as a group of about 150 soldiers martyred in Isauria (central Asia Minor) in the reign of Diocletian.

B

Babylas and Comps (SS) {2, 4}

24 January
d. c.250. He was bishop of Antioch (Syria) and St John Chrysostom gave two homilies in his honour, asserting that he refused an emperor (possibly Philip the Arabian) admission to his cathedral. He died in chains while awaiting execution in the reign of Decius, and his relics were enshrined near the famous shrine to Apollo at Daphne near the city. His companions were three youths, Epolonus, Prilidan and Urban, who were pupils of his and who were also martyred.

Babilla cf. **Basilla**.

Balbina (St) {2, 4}

31 March
d. a.595. The old Roman Martyrology describes her as the daughter of the Roman martyr Quirinus, who was baptized by Pope St Alexander I, became a consecrated virgin and was buried after her martyrdom on the Appian Way near her father. All this is unreliable. Her shrine was later established on the Aventine, and the new Roman Martyrology only refers to this.

Baldomer (St) {2, 4}

27 February
d. c.660. A locksmith at Lyons (France), he became a monk and subdeacon at the monastery of St Justus there. He is a patron of locksmiths.

Baldus of Tours (St) {2}

7 November
d. ?552. He was a bishop of Tours, and was remembered for what he did when he found that his predecessor had left a large sum of money in the cathedral treasury. He distributed it all in alms.

Baldwin of Rieti (St) {2}

24 July
d. 1140. An Italian Cistercian monk of Clairvaux under St Bernard and one of the latter's favourite disciples, he was sent to Rieti (Italy) to be abbot of San Pastore there. He is the town's principal patron.

Balsamus (St) {2}

24 November
d. 1232. The tenth Benedictine abbot of Cava near Salerno (Italy), his cultus was approved in 1928.

Balthasar Kagayama Hanzaemon and Comp (BB) {2 –add}

15 October
d. 1619. A married layman, he was martyred with his son James at Hiji near Ōita in the diocese of Fukuoka. They were beatified in 2008. Cf. **Japan, Martyrs of**.

Balthasar-of-Chiavari Ravascieri (Bl) {2}

17 October
d. 1492. A Franciscan companion of Bl Bernardine-of-Feltre, his cultus was confirmed for Pavia (Italy) in 1930.

Balthasar de Torres (Bl) {2}

20 June
1563–1626. Born in Granada (Spain), he became a Jesuit in 1579, taught theology at Goa (India) and Macao (China) and went to Japan in 1606. He was burnt at Nagasaki with Francis Pacheco and Comps. Cf. **Japan, Martyrs of**.

Balthasar Uchibori and Comps (BB) {2 –add}

21 February
d. 1627. From Fukae, he was martyred with his two sons, Anthony and Ignatius, at Shimabara

near Nagasaki. They were beatified in 2008. Cf. **Japan, Martyrs of**.

Balthild cf. **Bathild**.
Baptist or Baptista cf. **John-Baptist**.

Baptist Spagnoli (Bl) {2}

20 March
1447–1516. His family was from Spain, but he was born at Mantua (Italy) and studied at Padua. In 1463 he joined the Carmelites at Ferrara and became the superior-general of the order in 1513. He was famous as a Latin poet, having written over 50,000 lines of Latin verse, and is a good example of contemporary Christian humanism in Italy. His cultus was confirmed for Mantua and the Carmelites in 1885.

Baptista Varrano (Bl) {2}

31 May
1458–1527. Born at Camerino (Italy), daughter of the Duke of Varrano, she became a Poor Clare at Urbino in 1481 and was made abbess of the nunnery of St Clare, founded by her father, in 1499. Her cultus was confirmed for Camerino in 1843.

Barbara (St) {2, 3}

4 December
? The new Roman Martyrology lists her as a virgin martyr of Nicomedia (Asia Minor). According to her fictional acta, first written in the C7th, she was a young woman who was imprisoned in a tower by her paranoid father who then had her condemned for becoming a Christian and was himself killed by lightning. Her cultus was suppressed in 1969. Her attribute is a tower.

Barbara Cho Chŭng-i (St) {1 –group}

29 December
Cf. **Benedicta Hyŏn Kyŏng-nyŏn and Comps**.

Barbara Ch'oe Yŏng-i (St) {1 –group}

1 February
Cf. **Paul Hong Yŏng-ju and Comps**.

Barbara Cui Lianzhi (St) {1 –group}

15 June
1849–1900. A Catholic of Xiaotan in Hebei (China), she was the mother of two priests and was killed in the Boxer uprising. After another son, her daughter-in-law and seven other Christians were massacred at Liushuitao, she tried to escape by night but was caught on the road at Qianshengzhuang. She was tortured before being killed. Cf. **China, Martyrs of**.

Barbara Han A-gi (St) {1 –group}

24 May
Cf. **Augustine Yi Kwang-hŏn and Comps**.

Barbara Kim and Barbara Yi (St) {1 –group}

27 May
d. 1839. The former was a widow and the latter, a fifteen-year-old virgin. They died together of disease in prison at Seoul in Korea. Cf. **Korea, Martyrs of**.

Barbara Ko Sun-i (St) {1 –group}

29 December
Cf. **Benedicta Hyŏn Kyŏng-nyŏn and Comps**.

Barbara Kwŏn-hŭi (St) {1 –group}

3 September
Cf. **John Pak Hu-jae and Comps**.

Barbara Yi (St) {1 –group}

27 May
Cf. **Barbara Kim and Barbara Yi**.

Barbara Yi Chŏng-hŭi (St) {1 –group}

3 September
Cf. **John Pak Hu-jae and Comps**.

Barbatian (St) {2, 4}

31 December
C5th. A priest of Antioch (Syria), he went to Rome and became known by Empress Galla Placidia, who built a monastery for him at the seat of the imperial government at Ravenna and who employed him as an adviser.

Barbatus (Barbas) (St) {2, 4}

19 February
?612–82. Born in Benevento (Italy), he became his city's bishop in 663. An opponent of Monothelitism, he organized resistance in the siege by Emperor Constans II and later took part in the condemnation of that heresy by the Sixth Ecumenical Council at Constantinople. He had to help suppress a local snake cult adopted by Lombard immigrants, an interesting example of pagan survival in Italy.

Barbe cf. **Barbara**.

Bardo (Bl) {2}

11 June
982–1053. A Benedictine monk of Fulda in Hesse (Germany), he served as abbot of Werden and then of Hersfeld before becoming archbishop of Mainz in 1031. He served as the imperial chancellor and was known for his love of the poor, of animals and also of rigorous penances which Pope St Leo IX advised him to mitigate. The new Roman Martyrology lists him as a beatus.

(Bardomian, Eucarpus and Comps) *(SS)* *{4 –deleted}*

25 September
? They were listed as twenty-eight, martyred in Asia Minor.

Barlaam (St) {2, 4}

19 November
d. ?303. Martyred at Antioch of Pisidia (Asia Minor) in the reign of Diocletian, he was praised in an extant homily by St Basil.

(Barlaam and Josaphat) *(SS)* *{4 –deleted}*

27 November
They are the main characters of a Christian adaptation of a Buddhist legend which is among the works attributed to St John Damascene and is possibly by him. They were inserted into the old Roman Martyrology only in the C16th.

Barnabas (St) {1, 3}

11 June
C1st. A Cypriot and the patron of Cyprus, he was a very early Christian disciple and shared St Paul's early career as an apostle (cf. **Acts of the Apostles**). Traditionally he died a martyr on Cyprus, although Milan implausibly claims him as its first bishop. He is liturgically celebrated as an apostle, and his attribute is a pile of stones.

Barnard (St) {2}

22 January
777–842. From near Lyons (France), he was educated at the court of Charlemagne and became a soldier but resigned, founded the abbey of Ambronay and became a monk and then abbot there in 803. He was made bishop of Vienne (France) in 810, and took part in attempts at church reform. His cultus was confirmed in 1903.

Barnoch cf. **Barrog**.

Barontius and Desiderius (SS) {2, 4}

26 March
C7th. The former was a noble of Berry (France) who became a monk at Lonrey near

Bourges but then travelled to Pistoia (Italy) to be a hermit as a result of a vision. The latter was his companion in his austere life there.

Barr cf. **Finbarr**.

(Barsabas and Comps) *(SS)* *{4 –deleted}*

11 December
Mid C4th? They were listed as a Persian abbot and his monks, martyred in the reign of Shah Shapur II. Possibly they are the same as those below or SS Simeon Barsabae and Comps.

Barsanuphius *and John* (SS) {2, 4}

11 April
d. c.540. They were famous recluses at a monastery near Gaza in the Holy Land, the latter being the disciple and secretary of the former. Many letters of direction of theirs survive, as their help was sought by all sorts of people, and their joint cultus in the East is popular. However, only St Barsanuphius has been listed in the Roman Martyrology.

Barsen (Barso, Barsas) (St) {2}

15 October
d. 379. A bishop of Edessa in Syria (now Urfa in Turkey), he was exiled to the desert between Egypt and Libya by the Arian Emperor Valens and died there.

Barsimaeus (Barsamja) (St) {2, 4}

30 January
C3rd. According to the old Roman Martyrology, he was a bishop of Edessa (Syria) martyred in the reign of Trajan. The new edition corrects this, making him a confessor (not a martyr) in the persecution of Decius.

Bartholomea Bagnesi cf. **Mary-Bartholomea Bagnesi**.

Bartholomea Capitanio (St) {2}

26 July
1807–33. Born at Lovere near Bergamo (Italy), she tried her vocation with the Poor Clares but discerned a more active vocation and so opened a school at home in 1824 and a hospital in 1826. She was also a correspondent on spiritual matters with the local young people and clergy. In 1832 she founded the 'Sisters of Charity of Lovere' together with St Vincenza Gerosa, and was the inspiration of her institute during the year before she died. She was canonized in 1950.

Bartholomew (St) {1, 3}

24 August
C1st. He is listed among the twelve Apostles in the synoptic gospels and is identified with Nathaniel in the first chapter of the gospel of St John. Nothing is known about his career, and the traditions are late and conflicting. Eusebius states that he was in 'India' before St Pantaenus, and the Roman tradition has him being martyred in Armenia. His alleged relics are enshrined on the eponymous island in the Tiber in Rome, and his attribute is a flaying knife.

Bartholomew 'Aiutami-Cristo' (Bl) {2}

28 January
d. 1224. From Pisa, he became a Camaldolese lay brother at the monastery of St Frediano there. His nickname means 'Christ help me', which he continually repeated. His cultus was confirmed for Pisa and the Camaldolese in 1857.

Bartholomew Amidei (St) {1, 3 –group}

17 February
Cf. **Servites, Founders of**.

Bartholomew de Bregantia (Bl) {2}

27 October
c.1200–70. From Vicenza (Italy), he made his vows as a Dominican to St Dominic at Padua.

He became Latin bishop of Limassol (Cyprus) in 1252 and bishop of Vicenza in 1256. His cultus was approved for Vicenza in 1793.

Bartholomew of Cervere (Bl) {2}

21 April

1420–66. From Savigliano in Piedmont (Italy), he became a Dominican, taught theology at Turin and became the inquisitor for Piedmont. He was killed by heretics at Cervere near Fossano and his cultus was confirmed for the Dominicans in 1853.

Bartholomew Chŏng Mun-ho (St) {1 –group}

13 December
Cf. **Peter Cho Hua-sŏ and Comps**.

Bartholomew Fanti (Bl) {2}

5 December

1443–95. From Mantua (Italy), he became a Carmelite there and became famous as a preacher and spiritual director of St John-Baptist Spagnuolo, among others. He also had the charism of healing. His cultus was confirmed for Mantua in 1909.

Bartholomew-of-the-Martyrs Fernández (Bl) {2}

16 July

1514–90. From Lisbon in Portugal, he became a Dominican in 1528, going on to teach philosophy and theology and being appointed the royal preacher. In 1559 he was ordained bishop of Braga, and set about reforming his large diocese. His theological writings have been of enduring influence. He died in retirement at the Dominican convent at Viana do Castelo and was beatified in 2001.

Bartholomew Gutiérez (Bl) {2}

3 September
1538–1632. A Mexican, he became an Augustinian friar at Puebla in 1596, was ordained

and was then sent to Manila in 1606. He became prior at Ukusi in Japan in 1612, and was an effective missionary until his betrayal and imprisonment in 1629. He was burnt at Nagasaki with Bl Anthony Ishida and Comps. Cf. **Japan, Martyrs of**.

Bartholomew Kawano Shichiyemon (Bl) {2}

10 September

d. 1622. A Japanese layman, he was beheaded at Nagasaki with BB Charles Spinola and Comps in the 'Great Martyrdom'. His son Peter was beheaded the next day with BB Caspar Koteda and Comps. Cf. **Japan, Martyrs of** and **Great Martyrdom at Nagasaki**.

Bartholomew Laurel (Bl) {2}

27 August

d. 1627. From Mexico City, he became a Franciscan lay brother, studied medicine in Manila from 1609 and went to Japan in 1622. He was burnt at Nagasaki with Francis-of-St-Mary of Mancha and Comps. Cf. **Japan, Martyrs of**.

Bartholomew Longo (Bl) {2}

5 October

1841–1926. From Campagna (Italy), he became a lawyer in Naples and married a widowed client who had property in the valley of Pompei near the city. There he founded a sanctuary to Our Lady 'of Pompei' in 1876 and worked hard to promote Marian devotions and to further charity, especially towards the children of prisoners. He founded the 'Daughters of the Rosary', a congregation of Dominican tertiaries. He was beatified in 1980.

Bartholomew Mohioye (Bl) {2}

19 August

d.1622. A Japanese sailor on the ship carrying BB Louis Flores and Comps to Japan, he was beheaded at Nagasaki with them{2} Cf. **Japan, Martyrs of**.

Bartholomew-Mary dal Monte (Bl) {2}

24 Dec
1726–78. From Bologna (Italy), he was educated by the Jesuits there and became a priest after being inspired by St Leonard of Port Maurice. He became a famous and effective home missionary, preaching in about sixty Italian dioceses apart from his own, and was zealous against Jansenism and Enlightenment scepticism. He was merciful towards sinners, however. He died at Bologna and was beatified in 1997.

Bartholomew Pucci-Franceschi (Bl) {2}

6 May
d. 1330. From Montepulciano (Italy), he was a wealthy married layman who obtained his wife's permission to become a Franciscan. He was an example of a 'fool for Christ's sake', and his cultus was confirmed for Montepulciano in 1880.

Bartholomew of Rossano (St) {2}

11 November
d. 1065. A Calabrian Greek from Rossano (Italy), he followed St Nilus to Grottaferrata near Frascati and is regarded as the second founder of this surviving Basilian monastery of the Italo-Greek rite. He was also a noted writer of Greek hymns.

Bartholomew Sheki (Bl) {2}

27 November
d. 1619. A Japanese layman of the family of the daimyos of Hirado-jima, he was beheaded at Nagasaki with BB Thomas Koteda and Comps. Cf. **Japan, Martyrs of**.

Bartholomew of Simero (St) {2}

19 August
d. 1130. After leading the life of a hermit he founded the Byzantine-rite monastery of Simero in Calabria (Italy).

Bartholus Buonpedoni (Bl) {2}

14 December
d. 1300. Initially a secular servant at a Benedictine abbey at Pisa (Italy), he became a Franciscan tertiary before being ordained a priest of the diocese of Volterra when aged thirty. He was at the parish of Peccioli before contracting leprosy, and he spent the last twenty years of his life helping his fellow lepers. His cultus was confirmed for Colle di Val d'Elsa in 1910.

Basil, Ephrem and Comps (SS) {2, 4}

7 March
C4th. A group of missionary bishops, Basil, Ephrem, Eugene, Agathodorus, Elpidius, Etherius and Capito were martyred in the Crimea. SS Nestor and Arcadius were perhaps martyred in Cyprus, and have been deleted from the Roman Martyrology.

Basil of Ancyra (St) {2, 4}

22 March
d. 362. A priest of Ancyra (Asia Minor, now Ankara in Turkey), he was a fervent opponent of Arianism and was tortured before being martyred in the reign of Julian.

Basil of Antioch (St) {2}

20 November
C3rd. He was a martyr of Antioch in Syria.

Basil the Elder and Emmelia (SS) {2, 4}

30 May
d. 349, 372 resp. The parents of SS Basil the Great, Gregory of Nyssa, Peter of Sebaste and Macrina the Younger as well as six other children, they were distinguished laypeople of Caesarea in Cappadocia (Asia Minor, now Kayseri in Turkey) who were exiled for a time in the reign of Galerius. St Basil was a lawyer

whose mother was St Macrina the Elder. She was herself a disciple of St Gregory Thaumaturgus, a disciple of Origen.

Basil of Constantinople and Procopius Decapolita (SS) {2, 4}

27 February
d. 741. They were friends and monks of Constantinople and were imprisoned for witnessing against the iconoclast policy of the Emperor Leo III. After his death they were released.

Basil the Great (St) {1, 3}

2 January
c.330–79. Born of a distinguished family at Caesarea in Cappodocia (Asia Minor, now Kayseri in Turkey), his parents, three siblings and paternal grandparents are also saints (cf. **Basil and Emmelia**). After studying at Constantinople and Athens, he visited the famous monks of Egypt, Syria and the Holy Land before founding a monastery on the Iris river in Pontus. This led to the writing of his 'Rules', still standard for Eastern monasticism. In 370 he became metropolitan of Caesarea and spent the rest of his short life fighting against Arianism which was being favoured by the imperial court at Constantinople. His influence was absolutely dominant in Cappadocia, and his writings helped establish the Catholic doctrine of the Trinity, especially as regards the divinity of the Holy Spirit. He also left a collection of letters which became standards in Greek rhetoric and edited the Byzantine eucharistic liturgy named after him. He is one of the four 'Great Doctors' in the West and one of the three 'Holy Hierarchs' of the East, being portrayed with a characteristic long dark beard.

Basil Hopko (Bl) {2 –add}

28 July
1904–76. From Hrabské in eastern Slovakia (then part of the Hapsburg Empire), he was ordained in the Greek-Catholic rite in 1929 and became parish priest of Prague. In 1941 he was attached to the seminary at Prešov, and was ordained as auxiliary bishop in 1947. The new Communist regime suppressed the Catholic Church of the Greek-Catholic rite in 1950, declaring that it was now part of the 'Czechoslovak Orthodox Church', and Bl Basil was arrested and imprisoned. He was released in 1964, but was only able to act as bishop of his rite openly from 1968. He was beatified as a martyr in 2003, owing to the torture and mistreatment that he suffered while in prison.

Basil-Anthony-Mary Moreau (Bl) {2 –add}

1799–1873. A child of the French Revolution born at Laigné-en-Belin, he was ordained as a diocesan priest of Le Mans in 1821. He became the vice-rector and spiritual director of the seminary, and in 1837 founded a congregation of auxiliary priests, the 'Congregation of the Holy Cross', to assist the parish clergy to repair the ravages of the Revolution. In 1841 he founded the 'Marianite Sisters of the Holy Cross', initially as housekeepers for priests but later as a more generally apostolic sisterhood. These twin congregations later spread to the United States. He died at Le Mans and was beatified in 2007.

Basil of Parion (St) {2}

12 April
d. 735. He was a bishop of Parion on the Sea of Marmara, and supported the veneration of images. For this he was imprisoned and exiled by Emperor Leo the Isaurian, but died in peace.

Basil Velyčkovskij (Bl) {2}

30 June
1903–73. He was the bishop of the Catholic Church of the Ukrainian rite, based in what

is now Lviv (Ukraine). Before the Second World War the city was Lwow in Poland, and he was a Byzantine-rite Redemptorist, but it was then annexed by the Soviet Union, and the Byzantine-rite Catholics were violently suppressed. Bl Basil was imprisoned for ten years from 1945, and was secretly consecrated bishop of the underground church in 1963. He was arrested again in 1969, and exiled in a dying condition in 1972. He died at Winnipeg in Canada, but was beatified as a martyr because his death is thought to have been the result of poison. Cf. **Nicholas Čarneckyi and Comps**.

(Basileus, Auxilius and Saturninus) (SS) {4 –deleted}

27 November
? They were martyred at Antioch in Syria. Basileus was a bishop, but of where is unknown.

Basileus of Amasea (St) {2, 4}

26 April
d. ?312. Bishop of Amasea in Pontus (Asia Minor), he was drowned in the Black Sea in the reign of Licinius for giving shelter to St Glaphyra. His acta are unreliable.

Basilides (SS) {2, 4}

12 June
? He was martyred on the Aurelian Way, twelve miles west of Rome. The old Roman Martyrology listed Tripos, Mandal and twenty companions and put the event in the reign of Aurelian, but these details have been deleted.

(Basilides, Cyrinus, Nabor and Nazarius) (SS) {3 –deleted}

12 June
Formerly listed in the old Roman Martyrology as having been martyred in the reign of Diocletian, they had their cultus suppressed in 1969. Basilides seems to be a duplicate of the one in the previous entry, Cyrinus to be St Quirinus of Sisak and the last two to be unknown Milanese martyrs.

Basilides of Alexandria (St) {2, 4}

30 June
d. 202. A soldier of the guard of the prefect of Egypt, he defended St Potamioena the Elder from the hostility of the spectators when detailed to be her executioner and was converted. He was shortly afterwards martyred in the reign of Septimus Severus. His story is in the history by Eusebius.

Basiliscus of Comana (St) {2, 4}

22 May
C4th. Bishop of Comana in Pontus (Asia Minor), he was beheaded near Nicomedia in the reign of Maximin, and his body was dumped into a river. It was recovered and taken back to Comana.

(Basilissa and Anastasia) (SS) {4 –deleted}

15 April
C1st? Their legend has it that they were disciples in Rome of SS Peter and Paul, whose bodies they buried and who were themselves martyred in the reign of Nero. Their existence is doubtful.

Basilissa of Nicomedia (St) {2, 4}

3 September
Early C4th. The Roman Martyrology lists her as a virgin martyr in Nicomedia (Asia Minor). Other details have been deleted.

Basilla of Rome (St) {2, 4}

22 September
d. 304. She was a Roman martyr buried on the old Salarian Way outside the city. Her legend, which is a commonplace in hagiographical literature, states that she was a young

woman who was martyred after refusing to marry a pagan patrician to whom she had been betrothed.

Basilla of Sirmium (St) {2, 4}

29 August
C3rd–4th. The old Roman Martyrology listed her as having been martyred at Smyrna (Izmir in Turkey), but this has been corrected to Sirmium (now Srem Mitrovica in Serbia).

Basinus (St) {2}

4 March
d. 705. The abbot of St Maximin's Abbey at Trier (Germany), he succeeded St Numerian as bishop of the city and was of great assistance to St Willibrord and his companion Saxon missionaries. He retired to his abbey in old age to die.

(Basolus) (St) {4 –deleted}

26 November
C6th? His legend is that he was from Limoges and was a monk at Verzy near Rheims (France) before becoming a wonder-working hermit for forty years on a hill overlooking the city.

(Bassa, Paula and Agathonica) (SS) {4 –deleted}

10 August
? They are listed as having been martyred at Carthage in Roman Africa.

Bassa and Sons (SS) {2, 4}

21 August
d. 304. She was martyred on the Greek island of Halona, and her three sons, Theognius, Agapius and Pistius, at Edessa in Greece (not the Syrian city). Their cultus is ancient, but their acta are unreliable.

Bassian of Alexandria and Comps (SS) {2, 4}

14 February
? They were martyrs of Alexandria (Egypt). Bassian, Tonion, Protus and Lucius were thrown into the sea; Cyrion a priest, Agatho an exorcist and Moses were burnt and Dionysius and Ammonius were killed with the sword. The old Roman Martyrology garbled the first four as 'Bassian, Anthony and Protolicus'.

Bassian of Lodi (St) {2, 4}

19 January
d. 413. A Sicilian bishop of Lodi in Lombardy (Italy), he was highly regarded by his friend St Ambrose whom he attended to on his deathbed.

(Bassus, Dionysius, Agapitus and Comps) (SS) {4 –deleted}

20 November
? A group of forty-three, they were listed as martyred at Heraclea in Thrace (European Turkey).

(Bassus of Nice) (St) {4 –deleted}

5 December
C3rd? He was listed as a bishop of Nice (France), martyred by being pierced with two large nails.

Bathild (Balthild) (St) {2}

30 January
d. 680. A Saxon girl sold as a slave to the mayor (comptroller) of the palace of the Frankish king of Neustria (France), she ended up as queen by marrying King Clovis II in 649. She was regent from 656 (when her husband died) until 664 when her eldest son Clotaire III took power, and two other sons later became kings. She founded the abbey of Corbie and the double monastery (for nuns and monks) at Chelles and became a nun at

the latter, the rule of which was derived from those of SS Columban and Benedict. Her contemporary biography is reliable.

Baudelius (St) {2, 4}

20 May
? A married man from Orleans (France), he was a zealous Christian and was martyred at Nîmes. His cultus has left 400 churches in France and north Spain dedicated to him.

Baudolinus (St) {2}

10 November
C8th. He was a hermit, allegedly from a noble family, who lived in a hut on the bank of the river Tanaro in southern Piedmont (Italy). His shrine was initially at Forum Fulvii, and when that place was abandoned in favour of Alessandria in 1168 his relics were taken there. He is the patron of the city.

Baudry cf. **Balderic**.

Bavo (St) {2}

1 October
d. a.659. From Hesbaye near Liege (Belgium), he led an immoral life when young but was widowed and then converted to a life of penance by a sermon by St Amandus of Elnone. He founded an abbey (later named after him) on his property at Ghent and ended up as a hermit in a cell nearby. He is patron of the city.

Bean of Ireland (St) {2}

16 December
? The revised Roman Martyrology merely lists him as a hermit of Ireland.

Bean of Mortlach (St) {2}

26 October
d. ?1032. He was the first bishop of Mortlach (Scotland), the see of which was transferred to Aberdeen early in the C12th. There is confusion between him and other saints of the same name.

Beatrice I of Este (Bl) {2}

10 May
?1191–1226. Daughter of the Marquis d'Este of Ferrara (Italy), she was orphaned as a child and ran away from home to become a Benedictine nun at Solarola near Padua when aged fourteen. She died aged twenty at the nunnery at Gemola which she had founded, and had her cultus confirmed for Ferrara in 1763.

Beatrice II of Este (Bl) {2}

18 January
d. 1262. A niece of the above, she lost her fiancé when young and then had founded for her the Benedictine nunnery of St Anthony at Ferrara (Italy), becoming a nun there in 1254. Her cultus was confirmed for Ferrara in 1774.

Beatrice d'Ornacieaux (Bl) {2}

25 November
d. 1309. She joined the Carthusian nuns at Parmenie when aged thirteen and had a mystical devotion to the Passion. She also suffered from diabolic manifestations. She died at the nunnery of Eymieux near Valence (France), which she had helped to found.

Beatrice da Silva Meneses (St) {2}

17 August
1424–90. A Portuguese noblewoman born at Ceuta in Morocco, when aged twenty she accompanied a Portuguese princess to the Spanish court at Toledo and quickly became a nun at the Cistercian nunnery of St Dominic of Silos there. Later she founded the Congregation of the Immaculate Conception ('Conceptionists'), which had the Benedictine

rule under her but which was given the rule of St Clare after her death. She died at Toledo and was canonized in 1976.

Beatus (St) {2, 4}

9 May

C7th? He is venerated as the apostle of Switzerland, and his hermitage is pointed out at Beatenberg near Interlaken (Bern). Nothing certain is known of his life.

Beatus and Bantus (SS) {2}

25 July

Early C7th. They were hermits near Trier (Germany) when St Magneric was bishop there.

Bede the Venerable (St) {1, 3}

25 May

673–735. Born near Wearmouth in Sunderland (England), he was a child-oblate in the abbey there under St Benedict Biscop and was transferred to the foundation at Jarrow. There he remained all his life as a scholar and teacher of his brethren, becoming a polymath and one of the most learned men then in western Europe. In contrast he took part in no important events, apart from his ordination by St John of Beverley. His major work, the *Ecclesiastical History of the English People*, makes him the progenitor of English historiography and is the only coherent source for the early Anglo-Saxon church. His works on biblical exegesis (his main interest) were very popular in the Middle Ages, and he also helped to establish the counting of years from the birth of Christ. His cultus was not fully established in England before the Reformation (hence some Protestants refer to him as 'Venerable Bede' instead of 'St Bede'), but he was declared a doctor of the Church in 1899. His attribute is a water-jug.

Bede the Younger (St) {2}

10 April

d. ?883. An important official at the court of Emperor Charles the Bald, he became a Benedictine at the abbey of Gavello south of Padua (Italy). He refused to become a bishop. His relics have been at the abbey of Subiaco since the C19th.

Bega (Bee, Begh) of St Bees (St) {2}

6 September

d. c.660. She was allegedly an Irish girl who fled a threatened marriage, and founded a nunnery on St Bees Head in Cumbria (England). She has been confused with a nun at Hackness near Whitby (England) under St Hilda, who had her shrine at the abbey of Whitby before the Reformation.

Begga of Andenne (St) {2, 4}

17 December

d. 693. Daughter of BB Pepin of Landen and Ida and sister of St Gertrude of Nivelles, she married Ansegis (son of St Arnulf of Metz) and was the mother of Pepin the Short, the founder of the Carolingian dynasty. As a widow she founded and governed a nunnery at Andenne on the Meuse (France).

Bellinus (St) {2, 4}

26 November

d. 1147. Allegedly a German, as bishop of Padua (Italy) he energetically opposed simony and was hence assassinated. He is venerated as a martyr.

Benedict

This name is in Latin, Benedictus; in Italian, Benedetto; in French, Benoît; in Spanish, Benito; in Portuguese, Bento; in Catalan, Benet; in German, Benedikt; in medieval English, Benet. The Greek equivalent is Makarios.

Benedict II, Pope (St) {2, 4}

8 May
d. 685. A Roman, he was elected pope in 683, but his consecration was delayed a year while awaiting confirmation from the emperor in Constantinople. He then reigned for eleven months and was noted for his practical charity to poor people.

Benedict XI, Pope (Bl) {2, 4}

7 July
1240–1304. From Treviso (Italy), Nicholas Boccasini joined the Dominicans and became their ninth master-general before being made cardinal of Ostia and papal legate. He was elected pope in 1303. His cultus was confirmed for Perugia in 1736.

Benedict of Aniane (St) {2}

12 February
c.750–821. A Visigoth named Witiza, he served at the Frankish courts of Pepin and Charlemagne before becoming a monk near Dijon in 773. In 779 he founded his own abbey on his patrimony in the Aniane gorge in Languedoc, and this became the centre of reform of the monasteries in France and Germany under imperial encouragement. In 813 Emperor Louis the Pious built for him a model abbey called Kornelimünster near the imperial capital of Aachen. In 817 he presided at a synod of abbots at Aachen which imposed the Benedictine rule and a common customary on all the monasteries of the Empire, thus definitively establishing the Benedictines as a religious order.

Benedict of Benevento and Comps (SS) {2, 4}

12 November
d. 1003. From Benevento (Italy), he became a Camaldolese monk and went as a missionary to Poland with companions named John, Matthew and Isaac. They settled at Miedzyrzec near Gniezno, but the little community was massacred by robbers together with a local servant of theirs called Christian. Their cultus was confirmed in 1508.

Benedict Biscop (St) {2}

12 January
?628–?690. A Northumbrian noble, when a young man he made two pilgrimages to Rome and became a monk at Lérins during the second of them. Returning with St Theodore, he became abbot of St Peter's in Canterbury (England) and then founded the twin monasteries of Wearmouth and Jarrow (675–82) in Northumbria. In these he introduced Roman liturgical customs and chant and used the rule of St Benedict in compiling the customary. The abbeys became famous for scholarship of high quality (the library was probably the best in Anglo-Saxon England) and craftwork which (especially in stone and glass) was novel in Saxon England. He was the spiritual father of St Bede.

Benedict (Bénézet) of the Bridge (St) {2}

14 April
d. 1184. A Savoyard shepherd, he apparently received a vision of an angel telling him to build a stone bridge over the Rhône at Avignon (France). This he did, with the help of the bishop and certain miracles.

(Benedict of Campania) *(St)* {4 –deleted}

23 March
d c.550. The story in the 'Dialogues' attributed to St Gregory the Great is that this hermit was thrown into a furnace somewhere in the Campania (Italy) by some Goths commanded by Totila and kept unharmed by a miracle. The 'Dialogues' are not now regarded as a reliable historical source.

Benedict Crispus (St) {2, 4}

11 March
d. 725. He was archbishop of Milan (Italy) from 680.

Benedict of Kawachi (Bl) {2 –add}

6 October
Cf. **John Hashimoto Tahyōe and Comps**.

Benedict-Joseph Labre (St) {2}

16 April
1748–83. From near Boulogne-sur-Mer (France), his family ran a shop, but he tried his vocation with the Carthusians and Cistercians before becoming a pilgrim-beggar. He wandered from shrine to shrine in western Europe, living off alms but never accepting money. Being absolutely destitute and subject to serious privations, he is the best example in the West of the 'fool for Christ's sake' more familiar in the Russian tradition. He died in Rome and was canonized in 1883.

Benedict-of-St-Philadelphus Massarari (St) {2, 4}

4 April
1526–89. Nicknamed 'The Negro' because of his colour, he was born near Messina in Sicily of African serf parents. He became a hermit and then a Franciscan lay brother at Palermo. Starting as the cook, he went on to become an excellent superior and novice-master of the friary before becoming the cook again when old (which he preferred). He was canonized in 1807.

Benedict of Mazerac (St) {2}

22 October
C9th. From Patras (Greece), he fled as a refugee with ten companions to Nantes (France) and founded a small monastery at Mazerac nearby.

Benedict Menni (St) {2}

24 April
1841–1914. From Milan (Italy), he helped to transfer wounded soldiers from the railway station to the hospital run by the Hospitallers of St John of God in 1859, and this led him to join them in 1860. In 1866 he went to Barcelona to restore a children's' hospital and to found a badly needed mental hospital. He founded the 'Hospitaller Sisters' in 1880 and their new Spanish province in 1884. He became superior-general in 1909 but had to resign owing to calumny which exiled him from Italy and Spain. He died in Paris and was canonized in 2000.

Benedict of Nursia (St) {1, 3}

11 July
d. 550. He is primarily celebrated as the compiler of the monastic rule named after him, in itself anonymous and based on an earlier document called the Rule of the Master (possibly also by him). An ancient tradition equates him with the hero of the second 'Dialogue' attributed to St Gregory the Great, which is the only biographical source and which is now regarded as of dubious authenticity. The rule and dialogue lack cross references. According to the latter he was a young man from Nursia (now Norcia in Umbria, Italy) who went to study at Rome but fled in disgust and became a hermit near the ruins of Nero's villa at Subiaco. There he established a monastic colony before moving to Montecassino in about 530 and founding the abbey there, where he died. There are competing claims for his relics at Montecassino and Fleury (France), but both involve a loss of continuity of veneration. His rule gradually took precedence in the monasteries of Merovingian France and apparently became familiar in Saxon English monasticism through the agency of SS Wilfrid and Benedict Biscop. It was prescribed for the

Carolingian Empire from 817 and was absolutely dominant in Western monasticism for over two centuries after, at a time when monasteries were the centres of the surviving civilization. For this reason St Benedict was declared patron of Europe in 1964. There is no evidence for his cultus at Rome before the C10th.

Benedict de'Passionei (Bl) {2}

30 April
1560–1625. From Urbino (Italy), he was a lawyer there before joining the Capuchins at Fano in 1584. He was the companion of St Laurence of Brindisi in the latter's travels in Austria and Bohemia, but returned to Italy to die at Fossombrone. He was beatified in 1867.

Benedict Ricasoli (Bl) {2}

20 January
d. 1107. From Coltiboni near Florence (Italy), he became a Vallumbrosan monk in a monastery founded by his parents and then a hermit. His cultus was confirmed for Fiesole in 1907.

Benedict of Quinçay (St) {2, 4}

23 October
Before C9th. His dubious story alleges that he was a bishop of Sebaste (formerly Samaria) in the Holy Land who fled persecution by Emperor Julian and settled as a hermit at Quinçay near Poitiers (France). The site subsequently became an abbey. The revised Roman Martyrology merely lists him as a priest.

Benedict of Skalka (St) {2}

17 July
d. ?1034. Trained by St Andrew Zorard, he became a hermit on Mount Zobor near Nitra (Slovakia) and was famous for his austerity and prayerfulness. He was killed by marauders in 1012 and was canonized in 1083.

Benedict-of-Jesus Valdivieso Sáez (St) {2}

9 October
Cf. **Innocent-of-Mary-Immaculate Canoura Arnau and Comps**.

Benedicta Cambiagio Frassinello (St) {2}

21 May
1791–1858. From near Genoa (Italy), she married John-Baptist, a young farmer, and they mutually agreed to live in celibacy two years later. In 1825 she entered the Ursulines at Bressino and he the Somaschi as a lay brother, but she had to leave because of her health and settled at Pavia. There the bishop encouraged her to open an institute in 1828 to care for derelict girls and to turn them into respectable wives and mothers. Her husband left the Somaschi to help, which lost them the bishop's approval and they moved back to their old farm at Ronco and founded the 'Benedictine Sisters of Providence' for this work. She was canonized in 2002.

Benedicta Hyŏn Kyŏng-nyŏn and Comps (SS) {1 –group}

29 December
d. 1839. She was a widow and catechist who was beheaded at Seoul in Korea with six others after various tortures. The others were Barbara Cho Chŭng-i the widow of St Sebastian Nam I-gwan, Barbara Ko Sun-i the wife of St Augustine Pak Chŏng-wŏn, Elizabeth Chŏng Chŏng-hye the daughter of St Cecilia Yu So-sa and sister of St Paul Chŏng Ha-sang, Mary-Magdalen Han Yŏng-i a widow, Mary-Magdalen Yi Yŏng-dŏg the sister of St Catherine Yi and Peter Ch'oe Ch'ang-hŭb a catechist. Cf. **Korea, Martyrs of**.

(Benedicta of Laon) *(St)* *{4 –deleted}*

8 October
? She was listed as martyred near Laon (France), but further details are conflicting.

Benedicta of Rome (St) {2, 4}

6 May
C6th. St Gregory the Great, in his fourth dialogue, wrote that this nun of St Galla's nunnery in Rome had her death foretold to her by St Peter in a vision. She has been kept in the revised Roman Martyrology.

(Benedicta of Sens) (St) *{4 –deleted}*

29 June
? The old Roman Martyrology listed her as a consecrated virgin near Sens (France). Later legends describe her as sister of SS Augustine and Sanctian from Spain, the three of them being martyred in Gaul in the reign of Aurelian.

Benedictine Martyrs of the Reformation (BB) {2}

1 December
d. 1539. Three Benedictine abbots, with two (possibly four) other monks, were executed during the dissolution of the monasteries in England and were beatified as martyrs in 1895. However, the abbots and their communities had signed the Oath of Supremacy demanded by King Henry VIII, and there is no record of their having publicly recanted. The wish to save their abbeys seems to have been their primary motivation in their vacillating attitude towards the government, and this was a factor in their favour at their beatification.

Bl Thomas Beche (or Marshall) became abbot of Colchester St John's in 1535 and refused to surrender his abbey. His private remarks showing his disgust at the government's religious policy were enough for him to be arrested and executed at Colchester, although the records of his trial (which survive) describe him as trying to explain these remarks away. It is clear, however, that he remained orthodox. He was martyred on 1 December.

Bl Hugh Cook (or Faringdon) became abbot of Reading in 1520. What happened to him in 1539 is not very clear, and an anonymous pamphlet in his defence has been a major source. He was possibly implicated in the conspiracy of the Marquess of Exeter. He was executed with Bl John Eynon, parish priest of St Giles' in Reading, and Bl John Rugg, a retired prebendary of Chichester living at the abbey. These two are often claimed as monks, but there is no record of their having taken vows. The date of their execution is unknown; the Roman Martyrology notionally lists them on 15 November, together with the following.

Bl Richard Whiting became abbot of Glastonbury in 1525. He refused to surrender his abbey, and was executed on Tor Hill on 15 November with two of his brethren, Bl John Thorne, the treasurer, and Bl Roger James, the sacrist. The records are poor, but it seems that they were condemned at Wells for robbery, having concealed precious items in various places in the abbey in order to save them from seizure.

All these have a common liturgical cultus in the Order of St Benedict.

Bénézet cf. **Benedict of the Bridge**.

Benignus of Dijon (St) {2, 4}

1 November
? He is venerated as a martyred priest, and had an abbey erected over his shrine at Dijon (France). The legend connecting him with St Polycarp of Smyrna is worthless.

Benignus of Milan (St) {2, 4}

20 November
d. c.470. He was archbishop of Milan (Italy) when the Heruli, led by Odoacer, took the city.

Benignus of Todi (St) {2, 4}

13 February
Early C4th. A priest of Todi in Umbria (Italy), he was martyred in the reign of Diocletian.

(Benignus of Utrecht) (St) {4 –deleted}

28 June
C6th? He was a bishop mentioned in a decretal of Pope Pelagius II as wanting to resign, but it is not clear from which see. Chartres (France) is a possibility. He seems to have retired to Utrecht (Netherlands), where his shrine was established.

Benild (St) {2, 4}

15 June
d. 853. A woman of Cordoba (Spain) when it was a Muslim city, she was inspired to speak out against Islam by the example of a priest being killed and was herself burnt the following day. Her ashes were thrown into the Guadalquivir River in order to prevent her veneration.

Benildus Romançon (St) {2}

13 August
1805–62. From Thuret near Clermont-Ferrand (France), he became a Brother of the Christian Schools and proved the feasibility of combining a career as a teacher with a life of prayer and of fidelity as a religious. He had an externally uneventful career as headmaster at Saugues, where he died. He was canonized in 1967.

Benincasa of La Cava (Bl) {2}

10 January
d. 1194. He became the eighth abbot of his Benedictine monastery of La Cava near Salerno (Italy) in 1171 and sent a hundred monks to occupy the new Sicilian royal monastery at Monreale. His cultus was confirmed in 1928.

Benincasa of Monticchiello (Bl) {2}

9 May
1376–1426. From Florence (Italy), he became a Servite at Montepulciano and went on to be a life-long hermit, first near Siena and then in an inaccessible cave at Monticchiello. His cultus was confirmed for the Franciscans in 1829.

Benjamin (St) {2, 4}

31 March
d. 420. A Persian deacon, he was imprisoned and released on condition that he ceased preaching. On his not obeying, he was tortured and killed in the reign of Shah Varanes by being impaled on a knotty stick inserted into his anus.

Benjamin-Julian Alfonsus Andrés (St) {2}

9 October
Cf. **Innocent-of-Mary-Immaculate Canoura Arnau and Comps**.

Benno of Meissen (St) {2, 4}

16 June
d. 1106. Possibly from Hildesheim (Germany) and educated at the abbey there, he became a canon at Gozlar. Being made bishop of Meissen in 1066, he was almost alone among the German bishops in supporting Pope St Gregory VII against Emperor Henry VI. After the latter's submission he concentrated on evangelizing the Sorbs. He was canonized in 1523 and is patron of Munich.

Bentivolius da Bonis (Bl) {2}

25 December
d. 1232. From San Severino in the Marches (Italy), he was one of the earliest disciples of St Francis. His cultus was confirmed for San Severino in 1852.

Benvenuta Bojani (Bl) {2}

30 October
d. 1292. The seventh of seven daughters of a noble couple of Cividale in Friuli (Italy), when young she became a Dominican tertiary

and lived a severely penitential life in her parents' household, doing housework, praying and working miracles. Her cultus was approved for Udine in 1763.

Benvenutus of Gubbio (Bl) {2}

27 June

d. ?1232. He was a nobleman of Gubbio (Italy) who became a disciple of St Francis and was devoted to nursing lepers. He died at Corneto in Apulia.

Benvenutus Mareni (Bl) {2}

5 May

d. 1289. From Recanati near Loreto (Italy), he became a Franciscan lay brother and mostly worked in the kitchen. He was subject to supernatural phenomena. His cultus confirmed for Recanati in 1796.

Benvenutus Scotivoli (St) {2, 4}

22 March

d. 1282. From Ancona (Italy), he studied law at Bologna with St Sylvester Gozzolini before becoming archdeacon of Ancona. He was made bishop of Osimo in 1264, and restored the loyalty of the citizens to the Papacy. The assertion that he was a Franciscan is based merely on a grey hood found in his tomb and is hardly adequate. The revised Roman Martyrology describes him as dying on the bare earth 'in the Franciscan spirit'.

Berard of Carbio and Comps (SS) {2, 4}

16 January

d. 1220. They were sent by St Francis to convert the Muslims in Iberia and the Maghrib, and went from Italy to Coïmbra (Portugal). They started preaching in Seville, were driven out and tried again in Morocco, where they were beheaded. Berard, Otto and Peter were priests, and Adjutus and Accursius were lay

brothers. The protomartyrs of the Franciscans, they were canonized in 1481.

Berard of Maris (St) {2}

3 November

d. 1130. He became cardinal-archbishop of Marsi, a rural district to the east of Rome in 1109 (the cathedral of this diocese is at Pescina), and his cultus there was confirmed in 1802.

Bercham cf. **Berthanc**.

Bercharius (St) {2, 4}

26 March

d. 685. A monk originally of Luxeuil (France), he was made the first abbot of Hautvilliers at its foundation by St Nivard of Rheims. After going on pilgrimage to Rome and the Holy Land he founded an abbey at Moutier-en-Der but was stabbed one night by a monk whom he had rebuked, and died after expressing his forgiveness. He is not listed as a martyr now.

Berctuald cf. **Brithwald**.

Beregisus (St) {2}

2 October

d. p725. As a priest he was the confessor of Pepin of Heristal, with whose help he founded the abbey of Saint-Hubert in the Ardennes (Belgium) and was first abbot. This monastery was for canons, not monks.

Berengarius (Berenger) (St) {2}

26 May

d. 1093. From near Toulouse (France), he became a Benedictine at Saint-Papoul near Carcasonne (France) and served as novice-master, almoner and master of works. He was known for his charity and patience.

Berenice, Domnina and Prosdoca (SS) {2, 4}

14 April
C4th. A mother with her two daughters from Antioch (Syria), they allegedly fled to Edessa (now Urfa in Turkey) to escape persecution but were seized and drowned themselves on the way back in order to escape abuse by their escorting soldiers. Such action is now condemned as suicide by the church, and the Roman Martyrology now describes them as having drowned while trying to escape.

Berlindis (St) {2}

3 February
d. c.700. A niece of St Amandus, she became a nun at Moorsel near Alost (Belgium) and then a hermit at Meerbeke when her nunnery was destroyed.

Bernard, Mary and Grace (SS) {2}

21 August
d. c.1180. Ahmed, Zaida and Zoraida were children of Mansur, the Muslim emir of Lérida in Catalonia (Spain). Ahmed converted, became a Cistercian monk named Bernard at Poblet near Tarragona and, when old, he tried to convert his siblings. He was successful with the two sisters, but a brother had the three of them executed as apostates from Islam.

(Bernard of Arce) *(St) {4 –deleted}*

14 October
C9th. He was listed as a pilgrim, either a Saxon or a Frank, who died as a hermit at Arpino in Campania (Italy) after having been to Rome and the Holy Land.

Bernard II of Baden (Bl) {2}

15 July
1428–58. Margrave of Baden (Germany), he left his brother as regent and, as an ambassador of Emperor Frederick III, tried in several

European courts to arrange a crusade against the Turks. He failed, died at Moncalieri in Piedmont (Italy) and his cultus was confirmed for there and for Turin in 1769.

Bernard Calbó (St) {2}

25 October
d. 1243. A Cistercian monk in Catalonia (Spain), he was the first abbot of Santas Creus near Tarragona before becoming bishop of Vich in 1233.

(Bernard of Carinola) *(St) {4 –deleted}*

12 March
d. 1109. From Capua (Italy), he was the first bishop of Carinola in Campania, having transferred the diocese thereto from Forum Claudii in 1100 after thirteen years as a bishop. He was very old when he died. It is unusual for a known historical figure to be deleted from the Roman Martyrology.

Bernard of Clairvaux (St) (1, 3)

20 August
1090–1153. A nobleman born near Dijon (France), in 1112 he joined the new abbey of Cîteaux with (it is asserted) thirty friends and relatives whom he had persuaded to enter. He was sent to be first abbot of the new foundation at Clairvaux in 1115 and transformed the struggling Cistercian congregation into a spectacular success, founding sixty-eight abbeys. He became one of the most famous and influential men in western Europe and was popular as an adviser of those in power, secular as well as ecclesiastical. His theological writings, of which the most famous are the 'Treatise on the Love of God' and the 'Commentary on the Song of Songs', were highly influential and led him to be declared a doctor of the Church in 1830. He proclaimed the Second Crusade at Vézelay in 1146 and the disaster that this proved to be cast a shadow over his later life

and vitiated his political judgement. He died at Clairvaux and was canonized in 1174. His attribute is a white dog.

Bernard of Hildesheim (Bl) {2}

20 July
d. 1153. Bishop of Hildesheim (Germany), he served for twenty-three years despite being blind.

Bernard-Francis de Hoyos (Bl) {2 –add}

29 November
1711–35. From Torrelobatón near Valladolid (Spain), where his father was secretary to the city council, he entered the Society of Jesus at a young age and was ordained in 1735. He died a few weeks later of typhoid, aged twenty-four. During his studies for the priesthood he helped to propagate devotion to the Sacred Heart in Spain with great success. He was beatified in 2010.

Bernard-of-Corleone Latini (St) {2}

19 January
1605–67. A shoemaker from Corleone in Sicily, he was reputed the best swordsman in the island before fatally wounding an opponent and taking sanctuary in the Capuchin church at Palermo. There he became a lay brother in 1632, and was famous for his austerity. He was beatified in 1768 and canonized in 2001.

Bernard Lichtenberg (Bl) {2}

5 November
1875–1943. From Breslau, Germany (now Wroclaw, Poland), he became a parish priest in Berlin and provost of its cathedral in 1938. Active politically, he protested at the treatment of the Jews by the Nazis and they sent him to the concentration camp at Dachau. He died on the way and was beatified in 1996.

Bernard of Menthon (St) {2, 4}

15 June
d. 1081. He was the vicar-general of the diocese of Aosta in the Alps (Italy) for forty years and was especially solicitous for the welfare of the many travellers crossing the mountain passes. He founded hospices, run by Canons Regular, in the two passes now bearing his name. He died at Novara. A breed of dog is named after him, and he is the patron of mountaineers.

Bernard of Parma (St) {2, 4}

4 December
1055–1133. From Florence (Italy), he gave up brilliant prospects to become a monk at Vallumbrosa and went on to become abbot-general of that congregation before being made a cardinal in 1097 and bishop of Parma in 1106. He was active against simony and schism, was exiled twice but was a great success as a bishop. He died at the abbey of Cavana, which he had founded.

Bernard the Penitent (Bl) {2}

19 April
d. 1182. A Provençal criminal, he was sentenced by his bishop to seven years' penance, which he spent on pilgrimage in Europe and to the Holy Land. He did this while wearing seven heavy iron rings around his body. Afterwards he became a hermit at Sithiu at Saint-Omer (France) and then a monk at the Benedictine abbey there.

Bernard-of-Offida Peroni (Bl) {2}

23 August
1604–94. From near Ancona (Italy), he became a Capuchin lay brother at Offida, was some time at Fermo and then became the collector of alms at Offida. He was famous for his wisdom and working of miracles, and also

for his concern for poor and sick people. He was beatified in 1795.

Bernard of Rodez (St) {2}

9 October
d. 1110. From Rodez near Albi in France, he became an Augustinian canon and helped with the foundation of the abbey of Montsalvy nearby, which he governed as abbot.

Bernard Scammacca (Bl) {2}

11 January
d. 1487. From Catania (Sicily), his family was wealthy, and he was a delinquent youth, until he was seriously wounded in a duel. Then he repented for his conduct, joined the Dominicans and did continuous penance for his past excesses. His cultus was approved for Catania in 1825.

Bernard-Mary-of-Jesus Silvestrelli (Bl) {2}

9 December
1831–1911. A Roman, he tried to join the Passionists in 1853, but his health failed him. He entered successfully at Morrovalle near Macerta in 1856 in company with St Gabriel of Our Lady of Sorrows, having been ordained meanwhile. He was superior-general of his congregation from 1878 to 1907, was highly regarded by the popes and refused to become a cardinal out of humility. He spent his retired life at Moricone in the Sabine Hills, where he died of a fall. He was beatified in 1988.

Bernard of Tiron (St) {2}

14 April
1046–1117. From near Abbeville (France), he became a monk at St Cyprian's at Poitiers and was appointed prior of St Sabinus for twenty years. Then he became a hermit, was appointed abbot of St Cyprian's but went off to be a hermit again in a forest near Chartres.

His disciples there formed the nucleus of the abbey of Tiron and a new congregation, the Tironensians, which was an attempt to restore the full observance of the Benedictine rule. They spread in France and were important in Scotland, but mitigated their observance and were eventually merged with the Maurists. His cultus was confirmed in 1861.

Bernard Tolomei (St) {2 –add}

21 August
1272–1348. From Siena (Italy) and educated by an uncle who was a Dominican, he studied law and served the city in several offices, including that of mayor. In 1313 he became a hermit at Monteoliveto, ten miles from Siena, and there founded a new abbey. This was the start of the new congregation of the Olivetans. He and many of his monks died of the plague while nursing sufferers during an epidemic, and his body was lost, which is why he was canonized so late. His cultus was approved for Siena and the Olivetans in 1644, and he was canonized in 2009.

Bernard Vũ Văn Duệ (St) {1 –group}

1 August
1755–1838. A retired secular priest of Vietnam, he voluntarily gave himself up during the persecution of the Vietnamese church ordered by Emperor Minh Mạng. As a result he was beheaded at Nam Định with St Dominic Nguyễn Văn Hạnh. Cf. **Vietnam, Martyrs of**.

Bernardette cf. **Mary-Bernarda Soubirous**.

Bernardine-of-Siena degl'Albizzeschi (St) {1, 3}

20 May
1380–1444. From Massa Maritima (Italy), he became a Franciscan Observant in 1402. He preached his first sermon in 1417, and subsequently became the foremost Italian missionary preacher of the C15th. His special

subject was the Holy Name of Jesus, devotion to which he was instrumental in spreading. From 1438 to 1442 he was vicar-general of his order, and helped to improve its discipline. He died at Aquila and was canonized in 1450. His attribute is a plaque with the initials IHS, also three mitres at his feet (representing bishoprics that he had refused).

Bernardine-of-Fossa Amici (Bl) {2}

27 November
d. 1503. From near Aquila (Italy), he became a Franciscan Observant in 1445 and, after serving in various administrative posts, became an itinerant preacher in Italy, Croatia and Bosnia. He died at Aquila, where his cultus was confirmed in 1828.

Bernardine Realino (St) {2}

2 July
1530–1616. From near Modena (Italy), he became a lawyer but joined the Jesuits in 1564. He was at Naples for ten years, and then was the rector of the college at Lecce until his death. He was canonized in 1947.

Bernardine-of-Feltre Tomitano (Bl) {2}

28 September
1439–94. From Feltre in the Dolomites (Italy), he became a Franciscan Observant and was a teacher before finding his vocation as a vehement preacher, especially against usury. As a practical aid against this he helped in the setting up of 'monti di pieta' (charitable lending houses) in several Italian cities. His cultus was confirmed for Feltre and Pavia in 1728.

Bernold (Bernulf) of Utrecht (St) {2}

19 July
d. 1054. He was a bishop of Utrecht (Netherlands) and was zealous for the reform of his diocese.

Bernward (St) {2, 4}

20 November
c.960–1022. The grandson of the Count Palatine of Saxony (Germany), he was imperial court chaplain and tutor to Emperor Otto III before being made bishop of Hildesheim in 993. He was an accomplished artist, being skilled in architecture, painting, sculpture and metal working, and some of his work survives at Hildesheim. He apparently became a Benedictine monk before his death.

(Beronicus, Pelagia and Comps) (SS) {4 –deleted}

19 October
? They were listed as fifty-nine martyrs of Antioch (Syria) in an early persecution, but nothing else is known.

Bertha of Blangy (St) {2}

4 July
d. ?725. The daughter of a Frankish court official from Arras (France), when widowed she became a nun at her foundation at Blangy with her two daughters in ?686, and was subsequently abbess.

Berthold of Carmel (St) {2}

29 March
d. ?1188. From Limoges (France), he studied at Paris and then went to the Holy Land as a crusader. There he joined the Latin-rite hermits who had settled on Carmel and was appointed their superior by his brother Aymeric, Latin patriarch of Jerusalem. This was the start of the Carmelite order.

Berthold of Garsten (Bl) {2}

27 July
1090–1142. A nobleman born near Constance (Germany), he was widowed when aged thirty and became a monk at Sankt-Blasien in the

Black Forest. Eventually he became first abbot of the new foundation of Garsten in Styria (Austria), which abbey he made rich and famous. Much of his time was spent in hearing confessions. His cultus was confirmed for Linz in 1970.

Bertichram (St) {2}

30 June
d. ?623. From Autun (France), he was educated by St Germanus at Paris, became archdeacon there and was then made bishop of Le Mans. He was interested in agriculture, viniculture and in being charitable to the poor and to monks.

Bertilla of Chelles (St) {2}

5 November
d. ?705. A nun at Jouarre near Meaux (France), she served in various capacities there before becoming the first abbess of the great double monastery of Chelles which had been founded by Queen St Bathildis with nuns from Jouarre. (The foundation was not initially Benedictine.) She was abbess for fifty years, during which the foundation was a great success and attracted many Anglo-Saxon vocations.

Bertin the Great (St) {2, 4}

5 September
d. ?698. From near Constance (Germany), he became a monk at Luxeuil (France) under St Waldebert and went as a missionary to the Pas-de-Calais. Then he was made first abbot by St Omer of the new foundation of Sithiu, later named after him and now in the town of St Omer, and this was such a success that he made several further foundations. His attribute is a boat (since his monastery was then on an island in a fen).

Bertrand of Aquileia (Bl) {2}

6 June
1260–1350. From near Cahors (France), he was the papal auditor at Avignon before being made patriarch of Aquileia near Venice (Italy) in 1334. He was killed for opposing simony and the alienation of church property in his diocese and is listed as a martyr.

Bertrand of Comminges (St) {2}

16 October
d. 1123. A knight from Gascony (France), he became archdeacon of Toulouse and then bishop of Comminges in 1083. He restored the diocese (which is now united to Toulouse) during his fifty years as bishop.

Bertrand of Garrigues (Bl) {2}

6 September
d. 1230. From Garrigue near Nîmes (France), he was a secular priest but became a Dominican under St Dominic and helped to found the friary at Paris. He was a constant companion of St Dominic before becoming the provincial for Provence. He died at Toulouse, and his cultus was confirmed for Valence and the Dominicans in 1881.

Bertrand of Grandselve (Bl) {2}

11 July
d. 1149. Abbot of the Cistercian abbey of Grandselve near Toulouse (France) for twelve years, he was a noted visionary.

Bertulf of Bobbio (St) {2}

19 August
d. 639. A Frank, he became a monk at Luxeuil under St Eustace and then went to Bobbio in Lombardy (Italy) where he succeeded St Attalas as abbot in 627. He managed to obtain papal dispensation for his abbey from episcopal jurisdiction, the first such case recorded.

Bertwin (St) {2}

11 November
C7th. An Anglo-Saxon monk, he was ordained as a missionary bishop and evangelized the territory around Namur (Belgium), where he founded the abbey of Malonne.

Bessarion the Great (St) {2, 4}

6 June
C4th. There are several early Egyptian monks of this name who have been confused with him, but the one with this feast day was a disciple of St Anthony and of St Macarius at Scetis and features in the Apophtegmata Patrum.

Betharius (St) {2}

2 August
d. ?623. He was bishop of Chartres (France) from 595, but the extant biography is unreliable.

Bianor and Silvanus (SS) {2, 4}

10 July
C4th. They were beheaded in Pisidia (Asia Minor). Their acta are unreliable.

Bibiana (Vivian) (St) {2, 3}

2 December
? She was martyred at Rome, where she has a basilica to which her cultus was confined in 1969. Her acta are completely worthless, being medieval romantic fiction, hence the corresponding entries in the old Roman Martyrology are spurious and have been deleted.

Bilhild (St) {2}

27 November
C8th. From near Würzburg (Germany), she was married to the duke of Thuringia and founded the nunnery of Altmünster at Mainz when widowed, becoming its abbess.

Bili (St) {2}

23 June
d. ?914. He was a bishop of Vannes in Brittany (France), killed by the Vikings during a raid and venerated as a martyr.

Birgitta cf. **Brigid of Sweden**.

(Birillus) *(St)* *{4 –deleted}*

21 March
His legend states that he accompanied St Peter to Italy from Antioch (Syria) and was ordained by him as first bishop of Catania (Sicily). There is no historical evidence for this.

Birinus (St) {2, 4}

3 December
d. c.650. A priest of Rome who was possibly a monk, he volunteered to go to England as a missionary and was ordained bishop at Milan on the way. On arriving he converted King Cynegils of Wessex in 634. In 636 he established his cathedral at Dorchester on Thames (which was the remote ancestor of the diocese of Lincoln) and evangelized the surrounding area, which was then the power base of the kingdom. He is known as the apostle of Wessex.

Bladulf of Bobbio (St) {2}

1 January
d. c.630. He was a monk and disciple of St Columbanus at the latter's monastic foundation Bobbio in Lombardy (Italy).

(Blaise and Demetrius) *(SS)* *{4 –deleted}*

29 November
? They were listed as martyrs of Veroli (Italy), but nothing else is known.

Blaise of Sebaste (St) {1, 3}

3 February
d. c.320. According to his legendary acta, he was a bishop of Sebaste in Armenia who

saved the life of a boy who was choking on a fishbone and who was martyred in the reign of Licinius after being tortured with a wool-comb, which is his attribute. Thus a special 'Blessing of St Blaise' for diseases of the throat is available in the Latin rite on his feast day. The crusaders popularized his cultus in the West.

Blanca cf. **Alda**.
Blanche cf. **Gwen**.

Blandina Merten (Bl) {2}

18 May
1883–1918. Born to a pious peasant family near Koblenz (Germany), she was a clever girl and obtained her teacher's certificate in 1902. Her character was such that she was nicknamed 'the angel' in all seriousness. She joined the Ursulines at Ahrweiler in 1908 and taught at Saarbrücken and Trier before dying of tuberculosis. She was beatified in 1987.

Blane (St) {2}

10 August
C6th. A disciple of SS Comgall and Canice in Ireland, he became a bishop in Scotland and was buried at a monastery he had founded at Dunblane.

Blastus and Dionysius (SS) {2}

17 June
? They were martyred at a locality called Septem Palumbae on the old Salarian Way to the north of Rome.

Bodo (St) {2}

11 September
d. a.680. From Toul (France), he and his wife were influenced by his sister St Salaberga to separate and become consecrated religious.

He became a monk at Laon and founded three monasteries before being made bishop of Toul in 670.

Boethius (St) {2}

23 October
c.480–524. Anicius Manlius Torquatus Severinus Boethius was a Roman whose father was consul under King Theodoric the Ostrogoth, and who became consul himself in 510 after being educated at Athens and Alexandria. He was a notable philosopher, and his influence on medieval thought was profound. As well as attempting to translate all the works of Plato and Aristotle into Latin, he wrote several extant original works, the most famous being 'The Consolation of Philosophy' which he wrote in prison after being accused of treason by the king in 534. He was later executed at Pavia, for which city his cultus as a saint was confirmed in 1883, and is also venerated at the church of Santa Maria in Portico at Rome. His status as a martyr is dubious.

Bogumil (Theophilus) of Gniezno (St) {2}

10 June
d. 1182. From Dobrow on the Wartha river (Poland), he studied in Paris and became parish priest of his home town before becoming archbishop of Gniezno. He failed to win over his clergy despite his wisdom and zeal, but he founded the Cistercian abbey of Coronowa. In 1172 he resigned and became a Camaldolese monk at Uniejow. His cultus was approved for Wloclawek in 1925.

Boleslav Strzlecki (Bl) {2}

2 May
1896–1941. A Polish priest, he died of ill-treatment at the concentration camp at Auschwitz. Cf. **Poland, Martyrs of the Nazi Occupation of**.

Boleslava-Mary Lament (Bl) {2}

29 January
1862–1946. From Łowicz in Poland, in 1876 she went to Warsaw to work as a fine dressmaker but in 1892 started to care for derelict people. In 1903 her spiritual director, Bl Honoratus Koźmiński, advised her to go to Mohilev in Bielarus and found the 'Missionary Sisters of the Holy Family' to foster church unity with the Orthodox. They moved to St Petersburg in 1907, working with children and the poor until the Russian Revolution exiled them. Some stayed behind clandestinely, but Bl Boleslava re-established the mother house at Białystok in Poland, where she had a stroke two years before she died. She was beatified in 1991.

Bona cf. **Bova**.

Bona of Pisa (St) {2}

29 May
d. 1207. She was a hermit attached to the Canons Regular of St Martin at Pisa (Italy), and went on pilgrimage to the Holy Land, Compostella and Rome several times.

Bonajuncta Monetti (St) {1, 3 –group}

17 February
d. 1257. When the seven founders of the Servite order started their foundation community on Mt Senario, he had the task of collecting alms for them to live on. He was the second superior-general of the new order. Cf. **Servites, Founders of**.

Bonaventure (St) {1, 3}

15 July
1221–74. From near Viterbo (Italy), he was baptized as John but was nicknamed 'Good Fortune' by St Francis, who cured him miraculously when he was a toddler. He became a Franciscan when aged twenty, studied at the University of Paris under Alexander of Hales and taught there until elected minister-general of his order in 1257. His work in establishing it earned him the title of 'Second Founder', and he wrote an authoritative life of St Francis in order to foster its unity. He was made cardinal-bishop of Albano in 1273 and died during the Council of Lyons, for which he had helped to prepare. He was canonized in 1482. As one of the foremost medieval scholastics and a great mystical writer, he was declared a doctor of the Church in 1588.

Bonaventure Buonacorsi (Bl) {2}

14 December
d. 1315. From Pistoia in Tuscany (Italy), he was the leader there of the anti-papal Ghibelline party until he was converted in 1276 by St Philip Benizi, who was acting as a peacemaker between them and the pro-papal Guelfs. He joined the Servites and became a preacher of peace himself, being nicknamed 'the blessed'. His cultus was approved for the Servites in 1822.

Bonaventure Gran (Bl) {2}

11 September
1620–84. From near Barcelona (Spain), when his wife died he became a Franciscan at Escornalbu. His mystical charismata attracted attention, however, so he went to Rome and became the doorkeeper at St Isidore's friary. He founded several Franciscan retreat-houses in and around Rome, and his advice was valued by popes and cardinals. He died at Rome and was beatified in 1906.

Bonaventure of Miyako (St) {1 –group}

6 February
d. 1597. A Japanese Franciscan tertiary and a catechist helping the Franciscan missionaries

in Japan, he was crucified at Nagasaki with SS Paul Miki and Comps. Cf. **Japan, Martyrs of**.

Bonaventure of Potenza (Bl) {2}

26 October
1651–1711. From Potenza in Lucania (Italy), he became a Franciscan at Nocera and was a home missioner based initially at Amalfi, then at Ischia and at Naples. He died at Ravello and was beatified in 1775.

Bonaventure Tornielli (Bl) {2}

31 March
1412–91. From Forli (Italy), he became a Servite in 1448 and was a preacher in the Papal States and the Kingdom of Naples. He also served for a period as vicar-general of his congregation. He died at Udine, and his cultus was confirmed for Romagna and the Servites in 1911.

Bonet cf. **Bonitus**.

Bonfilius of Foligno (St) {2}

27 September
1040–?1115. From Osimo near Ancona (Italy), he entered the abbey at Storace and became its abbot. He was made bishop of Foligno in 1078, but resigned in 1096 after a pilgrimage to the Holy Land and retired to die at the abbey of St Mary of La Fara near Cingoli.

Bonfilius Monaldi (St) {1, 3 –group}

17 February
d. 1262. He had a vision of Our Lady in the cathedral in Florence (Italy) which led him to inspire his six companions to join him in founding the new order, and he was the first superior-general. Cf. **Servites, Founders of**.

Boniface I, Pope (St) {2, 4}

4 September
d. 422. A Roman, he was elected pope in 418, but the electoral college had split and he was troubled by an anti-pope, Eulalius. He resisted Pelagianism, and letters to him on the subject by St Augustine survive.

Boniface IV, Pope (St) {2, 4}

8 May
d. 615. From Valeria in the Abruzzi (Italy), he became pope in 608 and is remembered for dedicating the Roman Pantheon temple as a church (thus ensuring the building's survival). An unconfirmed tradition states that he had been a disciple of St Gregory and a monk at St Sebastian's.

(Boniface and Thecla) (SS) {4 –deleted}

30 August
d. c.250. They were apparently martyred in the reign of Maximian at Hadrametum in Roman Africa (now Sousse in Tunisia). According to their dubious acta they were the parents of the **Twelve Brothers** (q.v.).

Boniface of Crediton (St) {1, 3}

5 June
c.680–754. A Saxon called Winfrith from Crediton in Devon (England), he became a child-oblate at a monastery in Exeter when aged five and, when professed, went to Nursling near Southampton to be school headmaster. There he became a priest in 710 and went on a missionary expedition to Friesland in 716 which was a failure. He went to Rome in 718 to get the pope's approval for his subsequent outstandingly successful missionary effort in Germany, which earned him the title of apostle of that country. He became missionary bishop in 723 with full jurisdiction, and set up new dioceses as well as founding

many monasteries for both sexes based on the Benedictine ideal. Many Anglo-Saxon consecrated religious from England helped to fill these. He also helped to organize the church in France. In 747 he was made archbishop of Mainz but resigned in 752 to go on mission again to Friesland. He was killed with fifty-two companions at Dokkum by a gang of pagan robbers and was buried at his monastic foundation at Fulda in Bavaria, Germany.

(Boniface of Ferentino) (St) {4 –deleted}

14 May
C6th. He is mentioned in the 'Dialogues' of St Gregory the Great as a miracle-working bishop of Ferentino in Tuscany (Italy). This work is no longer regarded as a reliable historical source.

Boniface of Lausanne (St) {2}

19 February
d. 1260. From Brussels (Belgium), he was educated by the nuns at La Cambre near there, then studied and taught dogma first at the University of Paris and then at that of Cologne. In 1230 he became bishop of Lausanne but retired in 1239, whereupon he went back to La Cambre (by then Cistercian) as chaplain.

Boniface (Bruno) of Querfurt (St) {2, 4}

9 March
d. 1009. From near Paderborn (Germany), he accompanied his relative Emperor Otto III to Rome and there was clothed as a Camaldolese monk by St Romuald. In 1004 he became archbishop of Magdeburg in Germany with special responsibility for the Slavs and Balts of the German marches, and was killed with eighteen companions by pagan Prussians at Braunsberg (now Braniewo in Poland). Oddly, in the Roman Martyrology he is commemorated under his baptismal name of Bruno.

Boniface of Savoy (Bl) {2}

4 July
d 1270. Of the ducal family of Savoy, he was a Carthusian at the Grand Chartreuse before becoming bishop of Belley in 1232, episcopal administrator of Valence as well in 1239 and then archbishop of Canterbury (England) in 1241. He was very unpopular and experienced serious trouble trying to enforce his alleged rights of visitation, so he has never been venerated at Canterbury. He died while back in Savoy, was buried in Hautcombe abbey and his cultus was confirmed for Turin in 1830.

(Boniface of Tarsus) (St) {4 –deleted}

14 May
He was allegedly martyred at Tarsus at the start of the C4th, but his acta are fictitious and his cultus is unknown before the C9th. It was suppressed in 1969, and he has also been deleted from the Roman Martyrology. The church of St Alexis at Rome has his alleged relics.

Boniface of Valperga (Bl) {2}

25 April
d. 1243. Initially a Benedictine at Fruttuaria, he transferred to the Augustinian Canons Regular to become prior at St Ursus at Aosta in the Italian Alps in 1212. He became bishop of Aosta in 1219, and his cultus was confirmed for that place in 1890.

Boniface Żukowski (Bl) {2}

10 April
1913–42. A Polish Franciscan Conventual friar, he died of ill-treatment at the concentration camp at Dachau. Cf. **Poland, Martyrs of the Nazi Occupation of**.

Bonifacia Rodríguez Castro (Bl) {2 –add}

8 August
1837–1905. From Salamanca in Spain, she became a cord maker after the early death of her father, and her shop became a focus of charitable activity by a group of pious friends. Some of these joined her in 1874 to found the 'Servants of St Joseph' in order to help and protect female manual workers in the city. After the exile of her helper in this, Fr Francis Butiña SJ, she became sole superior but was removed after false accusations were made. She founded another convent at Zamorra, but her first foundation was not reconciled to her before her death. She was beatified in 2003.

Bonita of Alvier (St) {2}

16 October
C9–11th. She was a consecrated virgin, whose shrine is at Brioude in the Auvergne (France).

Bonitus (Bont) of Clermont (St) {2, 4}

15 January
d. c.710. From Auvergne (France), he was the Austrasian king's chancellor and prefect of Marseilles before becoming bishop of Clermont-Ferrand in 690 for ten years. Then he became a monk at Manglieu near Clermont, and died at Lyons after a pilgrimage to Rome.

Bononius of Lucedio (St) {2, 4}

30 August
d. 1026. From Bologna (Italy), he travelled to Egypt to become a hermit. After a period at Sinai he returned and became the abbot of Lucedio in Piedmont. A Camaldolese tradition makes him a disciple of St Romuald.

(Bonosus and Maximian) (SS) {4 –deleted}

21 August
d. 362. They were listed as two army officers of the Herculean cohort based at Antioch (Syria) who were tortured and beheaded on the orders of Emperor Julian after they refused to give up their cohort's banner bearing the Chi-Rho symbol in exchange for a pagan one.

Bonosus of Trier (St) {2}

17 February
d. 373. Bishop of Trier in Germany at a time when that city was a capital of the western Roman Empire, he was a disciple of St Hilary of Poitiers and worked zealously for the integrity of the church in his region.

(Bonus and Comps) (SS) {4 –deleted}

1 August
d. 257. He was listed as a priest, martyred at Rome with eleven companions (Faustus, Maurus, Primitivus, Calumniosus, Joannes, Exuperius, Cyril, Theodore, Basil, Castilus and Honoratus) in the reign of Valerian.

Boris and Gleb (SS) {2}

24 July
d. 1010. They were sons of St Vladimir the Grand Prince of Kiev, and when their father died they were killed by their brother Svyatopolk who wanted to succeed to the throne. Out of piety they refused either to fight for their rights or to allow themselves to be defended by their allies, and were thus venerated as 'passion bearers'. In the Russian church, this category of martyr does not need to die as a result of specific hatred of the faith, a traditional requirement for martyrs in the West (but cf. **St Alphege the Martyr**). In the West they used to be known as Romanus and David.

Botolph and Adulf (SS)

17 June
C7th. Their story is very confused and untrustworthy. According to it they were

Saxon noble brothers who became monks in the Low Countries. Adulf allegedly became bishop of Maastricht (a confusion with another of the same name), while St Botolph returned to England and founded a monastery at 'Ikanhoe'. This was thought to have been near Boston ('Botolph's town'), but is now thought to be Iken in Suffolk. Many English churches were dedicated to him, especially at town gates (there are good examples in the City of London), but his cultus was confined to England.

Botvid (St) {2}

28 July
d. 1100. A Swede from Södermanland west of Stockholm (Sweden), he became a convert in England and was a missionary back home until he was killed by a Finnish slave whom he had bought and was instructing.

(Bova and Doda) (SS) {4 –deleted}

14 April
C7th. They were sister and niece, respectively, of St Balderic, who founded a nunnery at Rheims (France) and made St Bova its first abbess. St Doda was apparently its second. He was never listed in the Roman Martyrology, but they were (as 'Bona and Doda') before their deletion.

Braulio of Zaragoza (St) {2}

18 March
?585–651. He was allegedly a monk at Zaragoza and a pupil and disciple of St Isidore of Seville. Becoming bishop of his native city in 631, he was one of the celebrated Iberian fathers and helped St Isidore in renewing the Visigothic church in Spain. He wrote several hagiographical works and has left a collection of letters.

Brendan the Voyager (St) {2}

16 May
d. ?578. From Fenit in Co. Kerry (Ireland), he was educated under St Ita and was later a disciple of St Finian of Clonard and of St Jarlath of Tuam. He founded many monasteries in Ireland, chief of which became Clonfert in Co. Galway, on which he imposed a very austere rule of life. He is chiefly famous for his legendary voyage to the 'Isles of the Blessed', written down in the C11th, which has been claimed as a possible discovery of America. This is extremely unlikely, although its feasibility has been shown by a journey in a replica craft. He is a patron of sailors.

Bretannio (St) {2, 4}

25 January
C4th. Bishop of Tomi (on the coast of Romania), he was exiled by Emperor Valens for being anti-Arian but popular protest forced his recall.

Brian Lacey (Bl) {2}

10 December
d. 1591. A Norfolk layman, he was hanged at Tyburn for sheltering priests together with St Eustace White and Comps. Cf. **England, Martyrs of**.

Brice (Brictius) (St) {2, 4}

13 November
d. 444. A disciple of St Martin of Tours at Marmoutier, as a priest he was ambitious and licentious but managed to be chosen as St Martin's successor as bishop of Tours (France) in 397. He was a bad bishop for twenty years until he was expelled and fled to Rome. There he repented, was allowed to return and was then such a success that he was honoured with popular and extensive veneration after his death.

(Brictius) *(St)* {4 –deleted}

9 July
d. ?312. Bishop of Martola near Spoleto in Umbria (Italy), he was imprisoned in the persecution of Diocletian but survived and was venerated as a confessor, dying in the reign of Constantine.

Brieuc (St) {2}

1 May
d. c.500. From north Dyfed (Wales), he was educated in Gaul by St Germanus of Auxerre and became a missionary in his native territory until driven out by invasion. Then he went to Brittany (France) with many followers and founded two abbeys, at Tréguier and St Brieuc.

Brigid (Bride) of Kildare (St) {2}

1 February
d. ?525. 'Mary of the Gael' was allegedly born near Dundalk, became a nun when young and is credited with founding the first nunnery in Ireland at Kildare. She is one of the most popular Irish saints and the junior patron of Ireland and very many legends have her as their subject. Her mercy and charity to the poor often feature in these. She is the special patron of those in the dairy industry, and a cow is her attribute. Unfortunately the historical evidence for her is poor, and one scholarly opinion nowadays is that she never existed but was the Christianization of a pagan deity.

Brigid-of-Jesus Morello (Bl) {2}

3 September
1610–79. A noblewoman of Rapallo near Genoa (Italy), she married and settled at Salsomaggiore near Parma, but her husband died of illness after the hardships of the Spanish invasion of 1636, and she took a private vow of chastity in 1640. Then she was recommended as the right person to run a new boarding school for girls at Piacenza, and this led to the foundation of the 'Ursuline Sisters of Mary Immaculate' in 1649 for this sort of work. She died after being seriously ill for twenty-four years and was beatified in 1998.

Brigid (Birgitta) of Sweden (St) {1, 3}

23 July
1303–73. A noblewoman born near Uppsala (Sweden), she married when aged fifteen and had a happy family life for twenty-eight years, having eight children. But her husband died when the couple were on a pilgrimage to Compostela, and she started to live a visionary life of penance. Her account of her visions of Christ survive in Latin translation, having been edited by others. She founded the mother house of her new religious Order of the Holy Saviour (the Brigettines) at Vadstena on the great lake of Vättern in 1344 and moved to Rome in 1350, where she died. She is depicted in the distinctive habit of her order (itself a result of a vision), with a chain or a heart marked with a cross or with a pilgrim's staff and flask. She was declared a patron of Europe in 2000.

Brinolf Algotsson (St) {2}

6 February
d. 1317. He was bishop of Skara in Sweden, and was famous for knowledge and pastoral zeal.

Brioc cf. **Brieuc**.

Britto (St) {2}

5 May
d. 386. Bishop of Trier (Germany) and metropolitan of Gaul, he fought Priscillianism but opposed the intervention of the secular power against that heresy.

Brixius cf. **Brice**.

Brocard (St) {2}

2 September
d. ?1231. He succeeded St Berthold as superior of the Frankish hermits on Carmel in the Holy Land and asked St Albert, Latin Patriarch of Jerusalem, to draw up a rule of life for them. This was the genesis of the Carmelites as a religious order. He was highly respected by the Muslims.

Bronislav Komorowski (Bl) {2}

22 March
1889–1940. A Polish priest, he was shot by the Nazis at the concentration camp of Stutthof near Gdynia in Poland together with Bl Marianus Górecki. Cf. **Poland, Martyrs of the Nazi Occupation of**.

Bronislav Kostkowski (Bl) {2}

27 November
1915–42. A Polish seminarian, he died of ill-treatment at the concentration camp at Dachau. Cf. **Poland, Martyrs of the Nazi Occupation of**.

Bronislav Markiewicz (Bl) {2 –add}

29 January
1842–1912. From Pruchnik in Poland (then part of the Hapsburg Empire), he became a parish priest of Przemyśl in 1867 but went to Italy to join the Salesians under St John Bosco in 1885. He returned in 1892, and left the Salesians to found indigenous Polish religious congregations, now known as the Michaelites, for both sexes in 1897. These are now international in scope. He was beatified in 2005.

Bronislava (Bl) {2}

29 August
1203–59. She was a noblewoman from Kamien in Silesia (Poland) and her cousin was St Hyacinth of Cracow. In 1219 she became a Premonstratensian nun at Zwierzyniec near Cracow, and died as a hermit. Her cultus was confirmed for Cracow in 1839.

Bruno the Carthusian (St) {1, 3}

6 October
a.1030–1101. From Cologne (Germany), he studied at Rheims and Paris, became a canon at Cologne and was then diocesan chancellor at Rheims. However, he left to become a hermit under St Robert of Molesmes and then withdrew with six companions to La Grande Chartreuse in the Alps near Grenoble in 1084, thus founding the Carthusian order of cenobitic hermits with the help of St Hugh of Grenoble. In 1090 Pope Bl Urban II, his disciple, called him to Rome to be his adviser, but he was allowed to found another monastery at La Torre near Squillace in Calabria. He died in retirement there.

Bruno the Great (St) {2}

11 October
?925–65. The youngest son of Emperor Henry I, he was devoted to his studies when young and became the arch-chancellor of the Empire under his brother Emperor Otto I in 951. In 953 he became duke of Lorraine and simultaneously archbishop of Cologne (Germany), thus uniting the ecclesiastical and secular power in one person as the prince-bishop. This sort of arrangement survived in the Holy Roman Empire until Napoleon, and with Bruno it worked well, although in later centuries it was the source of serious scandal. He raised educational standards, introduced the reform of Gorze to the monasteries in the diocese (he was commendatory abbot of Lorsch and Corvey) and was a central figure in the Ottonian imperial polity.

Bruno of Querfurt cf. **Boniface of Querfurt**.
Bruno of Saxony and Comps cf. **Ebstorf, Martyrs of**.

Bruno of Segni (St) {2, 4}

18 July

?1050–1123. From near Asti in Piedmont (Italy), he studied at Bologna and disputed with Berengarius concerning the latter's denial of the Real Presence in the Eucharist. His work on this subject was definitive for centuries. In 1079 he became bishop of Segni and was then papal librarian and cardinal legate. He retired temporarily to Montecassino and became its abbot in 1107, but was recalled in 1111 and died at Segni. He was canonized in 1183.

Bruno Seronum (St) {1 –group}

3 June

d. 1885. A soldier in the army of Mwanga, king of Buganda (Uganda), he was burnt alive a few weeks after his baptism. Cf. **Charles Lwanga and Comps**.

Bruno of Würzburg (St) {2}

27 May

?1005–45. Son of the Duke of Carinthia, he was an imperial counsellor before becoming bishop of Würzburg (Germany) in 1033. He founded many churches in his diocese and wrote several extant catechetical works. He was killed by a collapsing balcony at a banquet with Emperor Henry III at Peusenbeug (Austria) while they were on an expedition to Hungary.

Bruno Zembol (Bl) {2}

21 August

1905–42. He died of ill-treatment at the concentration camp at Dachau. Cf. **Poland, Martyrs of the Nazi Occupation of**.

Brychan *(St)*

6 April

? In legend he was a Welsh king associated with the region of Brecknock who had eleven sons and twenty-four daughters forming a clan of saints and who had other saints among his descendants. Nothing historical is known about him.

Budoc (Budeaux) *(St)*

9 December

C7th? From Brittany (France), he was allegedly educated in Ireland and became abbot of Youghal near Cork before returning to Brittany and succeeding SS Samson and Maglorius as bishop of Dol. There are several places in Devon and Cornwall (England) named after him.

(Bulgaria, Martyrs of) *(SS) {4 –deleted}*

23 July

C9th. The Bulgars migrated across the Danube to their present homeland in 679, but their first great ruler was Khan Krum who came to power in 804. He attacked the Byzantine Empire and managed to defeat and kill Emperor Nicephorus I in battle in 811. During his campaigns many Byzantine civilians were apparently killed because they were Christians, and these were reckoned as martyrs at Constantinople. The old Roman Martyrology had a horribly confused entry which blamed the emperor for the persecution. The Bulgars became Christian themselves in 865.

Burchard of Beinwil (Bl) {2}

18 May

C12th. He was a parish priest of Beinwil in the canton Aargau, Switzerland and has his shrine there.

Burchard of Würzburg (St) {2, 4}

2 February

d. 754. An Anglo-Saxon monk from Wessex, he joined St Boniface on mission in 732 and became the first bishop of Würzburg (Germany) in 741. He evangelized Franconia, founding many monasteries, and allegedly resigned in 753 to become a monk at Homburg near Frankfurt before he died.

C

Cadoc (Docus, Cathmael, Cadvael) (St) {2}

21 September

C6th. Of the royal family of Morgannwg (Wales), he became a monk and founded the great monastery of Llancarfan near Cardiff in 518. After extensive travelling he went to Brittany (France) with St Gildas in 547 and was a hermit on an island in the Morbihan until returning in 551. He allegedly became a bishop and was killed by the invading Saxons at 'Beneventum'. There is a church dedicated to another saint of the same name at Cambusland (Scotland).

Caecilia, Caecilianus cf. **Cecilia, Cecilianus**.

Caecilius of Carthage (St) {2, 4}

3 June

C3rd. According to the Roman Martyrology, he was a priest of Carthage who converted St Cyprian. The latter revered his memory, appropriating his name and taking care of his family after his death.

(Caerealis, Pupulus, Gaius and Serapion) *(SS) {4 –deleted}*

28 February

? They were martyred at Alexandria (Egypt). Gaius was added to the group by Baronius when he revised the old Roman Martyrology.

(Caerealis and Sallustia) *(SS) {4 –deleted}*

14 September

d. 251. Husband and wife, they were allegedly catechized by Pope St Cornelius and martyred at Rome in the reign of Decius.

Caesar de Bus (Bl) {2}

15 April

1544–1607. Born near Avignon (France), he converted from a sinful life in 1574 and became devoted to preaching and catechesis in response to the Council of Trent. When aged fifty-two he was ordained and founded the Congregation of the Fathers of Christian Doctrine ('Doctrinarians') to this end. He was beatified in 1975.

Caesaria of Arles (St) {2}

12 January

d ?529. Sister of St Caesarius of Arles, she was abbess of a nunnery founded in the city for her by her brother. Her talents were praised by SS Gregory of Tours and Venantius Fortunatus.

(Caesarius, Dacius and Comps) *(SS) {4 –deleted}*

1 November

? A group of seven, they were listed as martyred at Damascus (Syria).

Caesarius of Terracina (St) {2, 4}

1 November

? He was martyred at Terracina in Lazio (Italy) According to the old Roman Martyrology, he was an African deacon who suffered with a priest named Julian. However, these details have been deleted. There is a church dedicated to him near the Baths of Caracalla in Rome.

(Caesarius of Arabissus) (St) *{4 –deleted}*

28 December

d. 309. He was considered to have atoned for a rather immoral life by being nailed to the stake and burnt at Arabissus in Armenia in the reign of Galerius. He was the father of Eudoxius the Arian.

Caesarius of Arles (St) {2, 4}

27 August

470–542. From Châlon-sur-Saône (France), he became a monk at Lérins in 490 and bishop of Arles in 500. A great bishop, he chaired several local councils of the church, notably that of Orange in 529 which condemned semi-Pelagianism. He founded his namesake nunnery at Arles, made his sister St Caesaria its abbess and drew up an influential rule for it. He is one of the best examples of how the leaders of the church in western Europe had to take on much of the social and political responsibility for their people as the social structures of the Western Roman Empire fell into decay. He has left a collection of homilies.

Caesarius Nazianzen (St) {2}

25 February
d. 369. He is known from the extant funeral oration given by his brother, St Gregory Nazianzen. A doctor of medicine at the court of Constantinople, he resisted attempts by Emperor Julian to convert him back to paganism. He remained a catechumen nearly all his life, however, until almost killed in an earthquake at Nicaea.

(Caesidius and Comps) (SS) {4 –deleted}

31 August
C3rd. The unreliable acta of St Rufinus describe him as that saint's son, one of a group martyred at Lake Fucino east of Rome.

Caesidius Giacomantonio (St) {1 –group}

4 July
1873–1900. From Fossa Aquilana (Italy), he became a Franciscan and was sent to China in 1899. There he was posted to Hengyang in southern Hunan, but after only a month there was attacked by a mob of Boxers who spotted him saving the Blessed Sacrament from profanation. He was stoned and burnt alive with petrol. Cf. **China, Martyrs of**.

Cagnoald (St) {2}

6 September
d. ?632. Brother of SS Faro and Fara, he was a monk at Luxeuil under St Columban before becoming bishop of Laon (France).

Cairnech cf. **Carantoc**.
Caius cf. **Gaius**.

Cajetan (St) {1, 3}

7 August
1480–1547. A nobleman from Vicenza in Lombardy (Italy), he was in the curia at Rome from 1506 to 1517. On returning to Vicenza, he organized charitable work for sick and poor people there and at Rome and Venice. In 1523, together with Peter Caraffa (bishop of Chieti and later Pope Paul IV) and others, he founded the Congregation of Clerks Regular or 'Theatines' for that work. This became one of the great congregations of the Counter-Reformation, rejecting support from benefices and becoming involved in missionary work and in the Tridentine liturgical reform. He died at Naples and was canonized in 1671.

Cajetan Catanoso (St) {2}

4 April
1879–1953. From near Reggio Calabria (Italy), his family were pious landowners. He was ordained in 1902 and became a parish priest in his city. He encouraged the devotion to the Holy Face, fostered priestly vocations and was keen on arranging parish missions. In 1935 he founded the 'Daughters of St Veronica, Missionaries of the Holy Face' for prayer, catechesis and charitable works. He was canonized in 2005.

Cajetan Errico (St) {2 –add}

29 October
1791–1860. From a family which ran a pasta factory at Secondigliano near Naples in Italy, he became a diocesan priest in 1815 and was a schoolteacher for twenty years. Then he experienced a vision of St Alphonsus Liguori, who instructed him to build a church dedicated to Our Lady of Sorrows in his native village

and to found a new religious congregation dedicated to mission work. He did both, and the 'Missionaries of the Sacred Hearts of Jesus and Mary' was founded in 1836. It is now international in scope. Bl Cajetan died at Secondigliano and was canonized in 2008.

Cajetana (Gaetana) Sterni (Bl) {2}

26 November
1827–89. She was born at Cassola near Vicenza in Italy, but the family was at Bassano when her father died. She married when aged fifteen, but was a pregnant widow after eight months and then lost the baby. She then tried for a religious vocation, but her mother died and she had to take care of her younger siblings before finally being able to take charge of the town's poor-house in 1853. In 1860 she made religious profession and so founded the 'Daughters of the Divine Will', which has spread worldwide. She died at Bassano and was beatified in 2001.

Calais cf. **Carileff**.

(Calepodius and Comps) (SS) {4 –deleted}

10 May
d. ?222–232. Romans, they were massacred by a pagan mob in the reign of Alexander Severus. Calepodius, the first to be killed, gave his name to a catacomb. Palmatius, of consular rank, was killed with his family and forty-two of his household, while the senator Simplicius was killed with sixty-five of his family and household. Also killed were a married couple, Felix and Blanda.

Caletrix (St) {2}

4 September
d. a.573. He succeeded St Lubinus as bishop of Chartres (France), his native city, in perhaps 557.

Calimeius (St) {2, 4}

31 July
End C2nd. A Greek, he was educated at Rome by Pope St Telesphorus and became bishop of Milan (Italy). He evangelized the Po valley before being martyred in the reign of Commodus by being dropped down a well. His relics are in his church at Milan.

Callinicus and Basilissa (SS) {2, 4}

22 March
d. c.250. The Roman Martyrology lists them as martyrs in Galatia (Asia Minor), and has changed the gender of Callinicus from Callinica.

Callinicus, Himerius and Comps (SS) {2}

6 November
d. 638. They were soldiers taken captive during the first Muslim Arab invasion of the Holy Land when Gaza was conquered, and brought to Jerusalem. There St Sophronius encouraged them to remain loyal to their faith, and they were beheaded. The companions were: Stephen, two called Theodore, Peter, Paul, two called John and one of unknown name.

Callinicus of Gangra (St) {2, 4}

29 July
d. c.300. He was burnt at Gangra in Paphlagonia (Asia Minor), his native town. His acta are unreliable, but his veneration is popular in the East.

(Calliope) (St) {4 –deleted}

8 June
d. 250? She was perhaps beheaded somewhere in Greece, but details are lacking, and her acta are fictitious.

Calliopus (St) {2, 4}

7 April
Early C4th. He was crucified head-downwards at Pompeiopolis in Cilicia (Asia Minor) in the reign of Diocletian.

(Callistratus and Comps) (SS) {4 –deleted}

26 September
d. c.300. They were allegedly fifty soldiers killed in prison at Byzantium, possibly in the reign of Diocletian. Their acta are fictitious.

Callistus I, Pope (St) {1, 3}

14 October
d. ?222. A slave at Rome before his emancipation, he was made deacon by Pope St Zephyrinus and had responsibility for the catacomb now named after him. He became pope in 217, and showed leniency in the controversy as to whether the church could re-admit serious sinners to communion after penance. In this he was opposed by the rigorists, notably Tertullian and St Hippolytus. The latter, his bitter enemy, violently attacked him in writing in the 'Philosophumena' and was made anti-pope against him. He died a martyr, but his acta are fictitious.

(Callistus, Charisius and Comps) (SS) *{4 –deleted}*

16 April
C3rd. A group of nine, they were listed as thrown into the sea at Corinth (Greece).

(Callistus, Felix and Boniface) (SS) *{4 –deleted}*

29 December
? They are in all the old Western Martyrologies, but nothing is known about them.

Callistus Caravario (St) {1 –group}

25 February
Cf. **Aloysius Versiglia and Callistus Caravario**.

(Calocerus) (St) *{4 –deleted}*

18 April
? According to his late and unreliable acta, he was an official of Emperor Hadrian at Brescia (Italy) and was connected with SS Faustinus and Jovita.

(Calocerus of Ravenna) (St) *{4 –deleted}*

11 February
d. c.130. He was allegedly a disciple of St Apollinaris who succeeded him as bishop of Ravenna (Italy).

Calogerus (St) {2, 4}

18 June
C5th. A Greek, he became a monk at Rome and was a missionary on the Lipari Islands before becoming a hermit for thirty-five years near Girgenti (Sicily).

Cambrai, Martyrs of (BB) {2}

26 June
d. 1794. The convent of the Daughters of Charity at Arras was founded in 1656, and was running a girls' school and nursing in the town at the onset of the French Revolution in 1789. The sisters were allowed to carry on nursing in lay attire but were required to take the revolutionary oath in 1794. They refused, so were imprisoned and then guillotined at Cambrai. The superior was Mary-Magdalen Fontaine, and the other three were Jane Gérard, Frances Lanel and Teresa Fantou. They were beatified in 1920. Cf. **French Revolution, Martyrs of**.

Camelian of Troyes (St) {2}

28 July
C6th. He succeeded St Lupus as bishop of Troyes (France) in 478.

(Camerino, Martyrs of) *(SS)* {4 –deleted}

29 May
? The old Roman Martyrology listed an alleged 1525, martyred at Camerino near Ancona (Italy).

Camilla Gentili (Bl) {2}

18 May
C14th or C15th. Her cultus as a martyr was confirmed for Sanseverino in Italy in 1841 and her relics are in the Dominican church there. She was killed by an impious relative.

Camilla-Baptist da Varano (St) {2 –add}

31 May
1458–1524. From Camerino in Macerata (Italy), she was an illegitimate daughter of the city's prince but was included in his family. When she was twenty-one she received a conviction of a religious vocation, and despite much family opposition she became a Poor Clare at Urbino. Her father re-founded a nunnery next to his castle just for her in 1483, and she became abbess in 1500. In 1505 she was sent by the pope to make a new foundation at Fermo, and she died there of the plague. She wrote extensively, and is an important exponent of the Poor Clare spiritual tradition. She was canonized in 2010.

Camillus Constanzi (Bl) {2}

12 October
1572–1622. From Calabria (Italy), he became a Jesuit and went to Japan in 1605. In 1614 he was expelled to Macao but returned in disguise in 1621 and was caught and slowly burnt at Hirado. Cf. **Japan, Martyrs of**.

Camillus de Lellis (St) {1, 3}

14 July
1550–1614. From the Abruzzi (Italy), he became a soldier and proved to be a quarrelsome gambler. He set out to change his ways in 1575 and tried to become a Capuchin but a chronic, incurable infection in one leg prevented this, and he went on to be the director of a Roman hospital instead. He founded a confraternity to help with the nursing, and was ordained in 1584. His confraternity became a religious order, the 'Clerks Regular of a Good Death, Ministers of the Sick' usually known as Camillans, and this was approved in 1591. He died at Rome, was canonized in 1746 and was declared to be the patron of sick people and their helpers in 1886.

Camin cf. **Caimin**.

(Campania, Martyrs of) *(SS)* {4 –deleted}

2 March
C6th. St Gregory the Great wrote about eighty peasants killed during the Lombard invasion of southern Italy after refusing to worship the head of a goat.

Candelaria-of-St-Joseph Paz Castillo Ramírez (Bl) {2 –add}
1863–1940. From Altagracia de Orituco in Guarico state, Venezuela, she lost her father when aged seven, and her family descended into poverty. When aged twenty-four her mother died also, and she had responsibility for a large extended family. However, she also nursed victims of civil war and began to assist in the town's hospital in 1903. Helpers joined her, and this was the beginning of the 'Venezuelan Carmelite Sisters'. After the founding of two more hospitals, her congregation was affiliated to the Order of Carmel as tertiaries in 1925. She died at Cumana and was beatified in 2008.

(Candida of Carthage) *(St)* {4 –deleted}

20 September
d. ?300. She was listed as martyred at Carthage in Roman Africa, perhaps in the reign of Maximian Herculius (although her dates are disputed).

Candida-Mary-of-Jesus Cipitria y Barriola (St) {2}

9 August
1845–1912. Born in Guipúzcoa (Spain) of a working-class family, she founded the 'Daughters of Jesus' in Salamanca with an Ignatian charism in order to educate children of all backgrounds. A deep contemplative and lover of poverty, she had a universal interest in social justice and was canonized in 2010.

(Candida the Elder) (St) {4 –deleted}

4 September
C1st? Her legend is that she welcomed St Peter when he was passing through Naples on his way to Rome and was miraculously cured of an illness by him. Then she converted St Aspren, the city's alleged first bishop. She probably never existed.

Candida of Rome (St) {2, 4}

3 October
? She was one of a group of martyrs who were killed on the Ostian Way outside Rome. Her relics were enshrined in the church of St Praxedes in the C9th.

Candida of Whitchurch (St)

1 June
? The shrine of St Candida at Whitchurch Canonicorum in Dorset is the only one to survive the Reformation with its relics intact. These were examined in 1900, and it was found that she was about forty. Nothing else is known about her.

(Candida the Younger) (St) {4 –deleted}

10 September
C6th. She was described as a married woman with a family at Naples (Italy) who achieved sanctity as a wife and mother. Her relics were noted for exuding a liquid with miraculous properties.

(Candidus) (St) {4 –deleted}

3 October
? He was listed as martyred at a place called the 'Shaggy Bear' (ad Ursum Pileatum) on the Esquiline in Rome.

(Candidus, Piperion and Comps) (SS) {4 –deleted}

11 March
d. 254–9. A group of twenty-two, they were listed as martyred either at Carthage (Roman Africa) or at Alexandria (Egypt), probably in the reign of Valerian. Nothing further is known.

Canice (Cainnech, Kenneth) (St) {2, 4}

11 October
d. 599. The patron saint of Kilkenny (Ireland) was born in Ulster and learnt to be a monk under St Finian at Clonard, Co. Meath and St Cadoc in Wales. He travelled extensively as a missionary in Scotland and Ireland, perhaps founding the monastic settlement at St Andrew's (Scotland) and that at Kilkenny as well as several others.

(Cantidus, Cantidian and Sobel) (SS) {4 –deleted}

5 August
? They were martyred in Egypt, but nothing else is known.

Cantius and Comps (SS) {2, 4}

31 May
Early C4th. Cantius, Cantian and Cantianilla were three siblings of the Anicii family at Rome. They fled from Emperor Diocletian to Aquileia, but were executed there on

123

his orders. A panegyric in their honour by St Maximus of Turin survives. Protus, a fellow martyr described as their tutor, has been deleted from the Roman Martyrology.

Canute (Knut) IV, King of Denmark (St) {2, 3}

10 July

1043–86. An illegitimate son of King Sweyn III of Denmark and a great-nephew of King Canute the Great who ruled Denmark and England, he was a zealous Christian. When he became king himself he set out to establish the church in Denmark according to canon law and also instigated missionary activity among the Balts. He tried twice to invade England. One of his innovations was the introduction and enforcement of church tithes, and this helped to foster a revolt led by his brother which ended in his being killed at Odense. Thus he was regarded as a martyr, and his shrine was established at the Benedictine abbey that he had founded there. He was canonized in 1101, but his cultus has been confined to local calendars since 1969.

Canute (Knut) Lavard (St) {2}

7 January

d. 1137. He was duke of Schleswig (then part of Denmark) and a nephew of St Canute the King. He had to do much fighting against Scandinavian pirates and was also involved in missionary activity among the Slavs of eastern Holstein. He was a candidate for the Danish throne, and was assassinated as a result near Ringsted in a conspiracy headed by a relative who wished to supplant him. He was then venerated as a martyr and was canonized in 1169.

(Capitolina and Erotheis) *(SS) {4 –deleted}*

27 October

d. 304. They were listed as a lady and her maid who were martyred at Caesarea in Cappodocia (Asia Minor) in the reign of Diocletian.

Cappadocia (Martyrs of) (SS) {2, 4}

23 May

d. 303. Many Christians were tortured and killed in a pogrom in Cappadocia (Asia Minor) in the reign of Galerius.

Caprasius of Agen (St) {2, 4}

20 October

d. ?303. He was martyred at Agen on the Garonne (France) in the reign of Diocletian. His acta, including his connection with St Faith, are spurious.

Caprasius of Lérins (St) {2, 4}

1 June

d. c.430. He was a hermit on the Riviera island of Lérins (France) and was joined by SS Honoratus and Venantius. The three of them did a monastic tour of the East, and Venantius died in Greece. The other two returned to Lérins, where Honoratus founded the famous monastery and Caprasius succeeded him as abbot when he became bishop of Arles.

Caradoc (St) {2}

13 April

d. 1124. He was court harpist to King Rhys of Morgannwg (South Wales) before becoming a monk at Llandaff. He was ordained at Mynyw (St David's) and was a hermit on Barry Island but was harassed by pirates and moved to St Ismael's cell near Haroldston in Pembrokeshire, where he died. His shrine is at St David's.

Carantoc (St) {2}

16 May

C6th. The Roman Martyrology lists him as a bishop of Cardigan (Wales). He founded the church at Llangranog near there, and was also associated with Crantock in Cornwall and

Carhampton in Somerset (England). He has a cultus in Brittany, and may be identical to St Carantoc in Ireland who is described as accompanying St Patrick.

Caraunus (Chéron) (St) {2, 4}

28 May
C5th. A deacon from Rome, he evangelized the region around Chartres (France) and was martyred by robbers. An Augustinian monastery arose around his shrine.

Carileff (Calais) (St) {2}

1 July
C6th. From Aquitaine, he was a companion of St Avitus of Micy before becoming a hermit on his own and founding a monastery at Anille in Maine (France). This abbey was later named St Calais after him.

Carissima of Albi (St) {2}

7 September
d. c.600. From Albi (France), she was a hermit in a forest nearby and then a nun at Vioux. Her relics are in the cathedral of Albi.

Carmel-of-the-Child-Jesus González Ramos García Prieto (Bl) {2 –add}

1834–99. From Antequera near Malaga in Spain, she married a dissolute man when aged twenty-two and put up with his immorality for twenty years until her prayers and example converted him four years before he died. As a childless widow, she opened a small school for poor children at her home and was joined in this work by some young friends of hers. Thus was founded the Third Order congregation of the 'Franciscan Sisters of the Sacred Hearts of Jesus and Mary', which opened eleven houses in Spain during her lifetime. As well as educating poor children, they also held evening classes for workers and ran nursing homes for old people. She died in the town of her birth, and was beatified in 2007.

Carmel-Mary Moyano Linares and Comps (BB) {2 –add}

d. 1936. They are the ten Carmelite Martyrs of Córdoba, Spain who were killed during the civil war. Four were members of the community at Montoro, massacred on 22 July. The others belonged to the friary and minor seminary at Hinojosa del Duque. They were beatified in 2013. Cf. **Spanish Civil War, Martyrs of** and list in appendix.

Caroline Kóska (Bl) {2}

18 November
1898–1914. From near Tarnow in Austrian Galicia (now in Poland), she was one of a peasant family who were a focus of devotional activity in her parish. She was a prayerful, hard-working and charitable child. When the Russian army invaded at the start of the First World War, an enemy soldier seized her at her home and forced her into the forest in order to rape her. Her body was later found bearing the wounds of heroic resistance and with the throat cut, but with its virginity intact. She was beatified in 1987.

(Carponius, Evaristus, Priscian and Fortunata) (SS) {4 –deleted}

14 October
d. ?303. Their legend describes them as siblings who were martyred at Caesarea in the Holy Land in the reign of Diocletian. Their relics are at Naples (Italy).

(Carpophorus and Abundius) (SS) {4 –deleted}

10 December
Early C4th. They were listed as a priest and deacon, martyred in the reign of Diocletian.

The legend that this happened at Seville in Spain is false.

(Carpophorus of Como and Comps) *(SS)* *{4 –deleted}*

7 August
End C3rd? A group of soldiers, they were listed as martyred at Como (Italy) in the reign of Maximian Herculius. The companions were Exanthus, Cassius, Severinus, Secundus and Licinius.

Carpus of Thyatira and Comps (SS) {2, 4}

13 April
C2nd. A bishop of Thyatira (Asia Minor), he was seized with his deacon Papylus and the latter's sister Agathonica. They were taken to Pergamum to be martyred. Agathodorus, a servant of Papylus, has been deleted from the Roman Martyrology.

(Carpus of Troy) *(St)* *{4 –deleted}*

13 October
C1st. He is mentioned by St Paul in II Tim 4:13, but nothing else is known. The Byzantine Martyrology lists him as a bishop.

Carterius and Comps (SS) {2, 4}

2 November
d. c.320. They were soldiers burnt at the stake at Sebaste in Armenia in the reign of Licinius. The named companions were Styriacus, Tobias, Eudoxius and Agapius. Eastern menologies add Marinus, Oceanus, Eustratius, Nicopolitanus and Atticus.

Carthage (Carthach Mochuda) the Younger (St) {2}

14 May
d. 638. From Co. Kerry (Ireland), in 590 he founded a monastery at Rathin in Co. Westmeath and was abbot and bishop there (a common arrangement in the early Irish church). He wrote the monastery's rule in verse. The community was expelled in 635 and re-settled at Lismore, where it became famous as a place of studies. His cultus was confirmed in 1903 as the principal patron of Lismore. He is distinguished from Carthage the Elder, who succeeded St Kieran as bishop of Ossory in Co. Offaly and died around 540.

Carthusian Martyrs

Cf. **Augustine Webster, Humphrey Middlemore, James Walworth, John Davy, *John Houghton, John Rochester, Richard Bere, Robert Lawrence, *Robert Salt, Sebastian Newdigate, *Thomas Green, Thomas Johnson, *Thomas Redyng, *Thomas Scriven, *Walter Pierson, William Exmew, *William Greenwood,** and **William Horne** (all with separate entries). Those of the London Charterhouse who were starved to death at Newgate Prison are marked*.

Casilda of Briviesca (St) {2}

9 April
d. 1075. From Toledo (Spain) and a Muslim who converted to Christianity, she became a hermit near Briviesca in Burgos province. Her veneration is popular in Spain, especially at Burgos and Toledo.

Casimir Gostyński (Bl) {2}

6 May
1884–1942. A Polish priest, he was gassed at the concentration camp at Dachau with Bl Henry Kaczorowski. Cf. **Poland, Martyrs of the Nazi Occupation of.**

Casimir Grelewski (Bl) {2}

9 January
1907–42. A Polish priest, he was hanged at the concentration camp at Dachau with Bl Joseph

Pawlowski. Cf. **Poland, Martyrs of the Nazi Occupation of**.

Casimir of Poland (St) {1, 3}

4 March

1458–84. Born at Cracow, the third son of King Casimir IV of Poland, he was offered the crown of Hungary by a rebellious faction there in 1471 but refused to countenance the use of force and was briefly imprisoned by his disappointed father. As the heir to the Polish crown, he was Grand-Duke of Lithuania and served as regent in the absence of his father for two years from 1481, but refused to marry as he wished to stay celibate. He died of tuberculosis at Hrodno (Bielarus) on a visit to Lithuania and was buried at Vilnius. He is one of the patrons of Poland, and his attributes are a crown and a lily.

Casimir Sykulski (Bl) {2}

1 December

1882–1941. A Polish priest, he was shot at the concentration camp at Auschwitz. Cf. **Poland, Martyrs of the Nazi Occupation of**.

Caspar Bertoni (St) {2}

12 June

1777–1843. From Verona (Italy), he became a priest there in 1789 and founded a Marian oratory with some young people which became a focus of renewal for the diocese. He formed his priest-disciples into a congregation called the 'Stigmatine Fathers' in 1816. He was canonized in 1989.

Caspar de Bono (Bl) {2}

14 July

1530–1604. From Valencia (Spain), he became a silk merchant, then a soldier and finally a Minim friar. He served twice as corrector-provincial for the Spanish Minims and was beatified in 1786.

Caspar del Bufalo (St) {2}

28 December

1786–1837. From Rome, he was ordained there in 1808 and was exiled to Corsica for rejecting the Napoleonic polity. Returning in 1814, he went to Giano near Spoleto and founded there the first house of the 'Missioners of the Precious Blood' for home mission work in Italy. It was opposed, especially as regards its name, and was only approved after his death. He was canonized in 1955.

Caspar Cratz cf. **John Caspar Cratz**.

Caspar Hikojiro (Bl) {2}

1 October

d. 1617. The housekeeper of Bl Alphonsus Navarrete, he was beheaded with Bl Andrew Yoshida at Nagasaki. Cf. **Japan, Martyrs of**.

Caspar Koteda and Comps (Bl) {2}

11 September

d. 1622. Of the family of the daimyos of Hirado, he worked as catechist for Bl Camillus Costanzo and was martyred at Nagasaki with two companions, BB Francis Takeya and Peter Shichiyemon (both children) on the day after the 'Great Martyrdom'. They were beatified in 1867. Cf. **Japan, Martyrs of**.

Caspar Nishi Genka and Comps (BB) {2 –add}

14 November

d. 1609. He was a married lay catechist of the diocese of Nagasaki, and was martyred at Ikitsuki in Nagasaki together with his wife and son, Ursula Nishi and John Nishi Mataishi. They were beatified in 2008. Cf. **Japan, Martyrs of**.

Caspar Sadamatsu (Bl) {2}

20 June

d. 1626. From Omura (Japan), he became a Jesuit lay brother in 1582 and worked as secretary for several Jesuit provincials in Japan. The last of these was Bl Francis Pacheco, with whom he was burnt at Nagasaki. He was beatified in 1867. Cf. **Japan, Martyrs of**.

Caspar Stranggassinger (Bl) {2}

26 September
1871–99. From Berchtesgaden in Bavaria (Germany) of a peasant family, he joined the Redemptorists at Gars in 1893 and was ordained two years later. He became the vice-rector of the trainee missionaries and a teacher of Latin, but he regarded his personal sanctification as his chief work. He died after a short illness and was beatified in 1988.

Caspar and Mary Vas (BB) {2}

27 August
d. 1627. A Japanese married couple, they were Franciscan tertiaries who were martyred at Nagasaki with Francis-of-St-Mary of Mancha and Comps. Cf. **Japan, Martyrs of**.

Cassian cf. **John Cassian**.

Cassian of Autun (St) {2, 4}

5 August
C4th. An Egyptian (according to a C9th biography) and a noted thaumaturge, he became bishop of Autun (France) in 314.

Cassian of Benevento (St) {2}

11 August
C4th. He was bishop of Benevento (Italy) and his relics are at St Mary's Church there.

Cassian of Imola (St) {2, 3}

13 August
d. c.300. His story is that he was the headmaster of a school at Imola near Ravenna (Italy) and that he was martyred in the reign of Diocletian by being handed over to his pagan pupils, who slowly stabbed him to death with their pens. This is according to Prudentius and the Roman Martyrology. The cultus was confined to local calendars in 1969.

Cassian of Tangier (St) {2, 4}

3 December
d. c.300. During the trial of St Marcellus at Tangier in Roman Africa (now in Morocco) in the reign of Diocletian, Cassian as the recorder of the proceedings became indignant at the injustice being perpetrated, threw down his pen and declared himself to be a Christian. He was arrested and martyred a few weeks later. His acta are genuine, and he is mentioned in one of the hymns of Prudentius.

(Cassian of Todi) (St) {4 –deleted}

13 August
C4th? He is alleged to have been the successor of St Pontian as bishop of Todi (Italy) and to have been martyred in the reign of Maximian Herculius, but his acta are unreliable, and he may be a duplicate of St Cassian of Imola.

Cassius and Florentius (SS) {2, 4}

10 October
Early C4th. They were martyred at Bonn (Germany). The reference in the Roman Martyrology to 'many others' has been deleted.

Cassius and Victorinus (SS) {2, 4}

15 May
d. ?264. They were martyred by invading barbarians at Clermont-Ferrand (France). The Roman Martyrology added 'Maximus and companions', but these have been deleted.

Cassius of Narni (St) {2, 4}

29 June
d. 558. He was bishop of Narni near Rome from 537. St Gregory the Great wrote of him with approbation.

(Castor and Stephen) *(SS) {4 –deleted}*

27 April
? They were listed as martyrs of Tarsus in Cilicia (Asia Minor) in an early persecution, and may be a duplicate of Castor of Tarsus.

(Castor, Victor and Rogatian) *(SS) {4 –deleted}*

28 December
? All that is recorded is that they were martyred in Roman Africa.

Castor of Apt (St) {2}

21 September
d. 426. From Nîmes (France), he got married and settled at Marseilles, but he and his wife separated to become consecrated religious, and he founded a monastery at Manauque. Then he was forced to become the bishop of Apt. St John Cassian wrote the 'Institutes' at his request.

Castor of Koblenz (St) {2}

13 February
C4th. According to his legend, he was a Gascon who was ordained by St Maximinus of Trier and who evangelized the Moselle valley between there and Koblenz (Germany), settling at Karden. He is the patron of Koblenz.

Castor of Tarsus (SS) {2, 4}

28 March
? They were martyred at Tarsus in Cilicia (Asia Minor) in an early persecution. The Roman Martyrology used to list a companion, Dorotheus, but he has been deleted.

Castrensis (St) {2}

11 February
? He was a martyr of Castel Volturno near Capua (Italy). A legend, not accepted by the revised Roman Martyrology, asserted that he was one of the African bishops exiled by the Vandals.

Castritian of Milan (St) {2, 4}

1 December
C3rd. He was listed as bishop of Milan (Italy) from the year 95, the predecessor of St Calimerius, but lived in reality over a century later.

Castulus (St) {2, 4}

26 March
? He was a martyr buried on the Via Labicana in Rome. According to his legend (deleted from the Roman Martyrology), he was an official at the Roman palace of Emperor Diocletian, but he was tortured, imprisoned and buried alive in a sandpit because he used to give refuge to persecuted Christians.

(Castulus and Euprepis) *(SS) {4 –deleted}*

30 November
? Nothing is recorded about these Roman martyrs.

Castus and Emilius (SS) {2, 4}

22 May
d. 203. They were burnt at Carthage (Roman Africa), having repented after apostatizing under torture. Both St Cyprian and St Augustine praised them.

(Castus and Secundinus) *(SS) {4 –deleted}*

1 July
Early C4th? Their relics are at Gaeta near Naples (Italy). They are alleged to have been bishops, but their acta are unreliable.

Catald (St) {2, 4}

10 May
C7th. From Munster (Ireland), he was a pupil and then the headmaster of the monastery school at Lismore. He became bishop of Rachau, but went on a pilgrimage to the Holy Land. Then he was made bishop of Taranto at

the heel of Italy on his way back, and is the principal patron of that diocese. Two different persons may have been conflated in this tradition.

Catellus (St)

19 January
C9th. He was bishop of Castellamare in the south of Naples (Italy), and is the principal patron of that diocese despite his unconfirmed cultus.

Catherine of Alexandria (St) {1, 3}

25 November
Her fictitious and fanciful acta describe her as having been martyred at Alexandria (Egypt) in the reign of Maxentius. Her alleged relics are at the monastery named after her at Sinai, but the first evidence of her cultus (which became very popular in the Middle Ages) dates from the C9th. Her attribute is a cartwheel with a spiked rim (the 'Catherine wheel'). Her cultus was suppressed in 1969, only to be re-established later.

Catherine of Bologna (St) {2, 4}

9 March
1413–63. From Bologna (Italy), she was a maid of honour at the ducal court of Ferrara and joined a group of Franciscan tertiaries there. In 1432 this became a Poor Clare house, and she became prioress of a foundation at Bologna in 1457. Her charism was expressed in prayer for the conversion of sinners, and the visions she had led her to write the 'Revelations of the Seven Spiritual Weapons'. She was canonized in 1712. She is depicted holding the Christ-Child.

Catherine Chŏng Ch'ŏr-yŏm (St) {1 –group}

20 September
Cf. **Laurence Han I-hyŏng and Comps**.

Catherine Cittadini (Bl) {2}

5 May
1801–57. From Bergamo, Italy, she was orphaned when young and settled at Somasca with her sister. There they started a boarding school for girls, which act eventually led to the foundation of the congregation of the Ursuline Sisters of Somasca. This is now established worldwide. She was beatified in 2001.

Catherine-Mary Drexel (St) {2}

3 March
1858–1955. Born in Philadelphia, USA, she was the heiress to a banking fortune and a city socialite but was inspired to donate her wealth to missionary work among Native and African Americans. Pope Leo XIII asked her to found her own congregation, and she set up the 'Blessed Sacrament Sisters for Indians and Coloured People' at her family's summer mansion at Torresdale. She made forty-nine foundations, as well as setting up the Xavier University at New Orleans in 1915. Her canonization was in 2000.

Catherine Emmerich (Bl) {2}

(9 February)
1774–1824. From a peasant family near Coesfeld in Germany, she was physically frail but joined the Augustinian nuns at Agnetenberg in 1802. The nunnery was suppressed in 1811 and she became the domestic servant of an exiled French priest at Dülmen, but became bedridden two years later. She received the stigmata and experienced visions of the Passion, which were published in book form as the 'Dolorous Passion' by the poet Brentano in 1833. She died at Dülmen and was beatified in 2004.

Catherine-of-Genoa Fieschi (St) {2, 4}

15 September
1477–1510. She was a noblewoman of Genoa (Italy). The man she married when aged

sixteen lived a profligate life, and her own life was empty before she had a sudden conversion and became absorbed in piety and charitable works. Her husband started sharing her interests after he went bankrupt, and they worked in a local hospital until he died, and she became its director. She was a famous mystic (the 'Apostle of Purgatory'), and her experiences are described in the 'Vita e dottrina' (of which she was not the final editor, as it was published forty years after her death). She was canonized in 1737.

Catherine Jarrige (Bl) {2}

4 July

1754–1836. Born near St Flour in the Massif Central (France), she grew up as a lacemaker and entered the Dominican Third Order at Mauriac where she begged for poor people. After the Revolution she helped the non-juring clergy in many ways, and also worked in rebuilding the church after the Terror. She was beatified in 1996.

Catherine Labouré (St) {2}

31 December

1806–75. A farmer's daughter from the Côte d'Or (France), she became a Sister of Charity of St Vincent de Paul in 1830 and lived a very ordinary life until she died at the Enghien-Reuilly convent at Paris. She had a series of private visions of Our Lady, however, who instructed her in the design of, and devotion to, the 'Miraculous Medal'. This became popular throughout the church. She was canonized in 1947.

Catherine Mattei (Bl) {2}

4 September

1486–1547. From Racconigi near Cuneo in Piedmont (Italy), she was a daughter of a blacksmith and became a Dominican tertiary while working as a weaver at home. She set out to imitate the life of her namesake of Siena and received the stigmata, but was persecuted and fled to Carmagnola, where she died. Her cultus was confirmed for the Dominicans in 1808.

Catherine of Nagasaki (Bl) {2}

10 September

d. 1622. She was a Japanese widow who was beheaded in the 'Great Martyrdom' at Nagasaki, together with BB Charles Spinola and Comps. Cf. **Japan, Martyrs of** and **Great Martyrdom at Nagasaki**.

Catherine of Pallanza (Bl) {2}

6 April

?1437–78. From Pallanza near Novara (Italy), she became a hermit in the mountains above Varese near Milan when she was fourteen. She attracted disciples and founded the Augustinian nunnery of S. Maria del Monte. Her cultus was confirmed for Milan in 1769.

Catherine dei Ricci (St) {2}

2 February

1522–90. A noblewoman of Florence (Italy), she became a Dominican regular tertiary at Prato and served as novice-mistress and prioress, being influenced by Savanarola. She was a great mystic, having visions of the Passion and receiving the stigmata as well as being a thaumaturge. Thousands of people of all kinds visited her at her convent to seek her help. She died at Prato and was canonized in 1712.

Catherine of Siena (St) {1, 3}

29 April

1347–80. From Siena (Italy), she was the twenty-fifth child of a wool-dyer. Having made a vow of chastity when aged seven, she became a Dominican tertiary when aged fifteen, remaining at her parents' home and gathering all sorts of people as disciples by the example of her sanctity. She helped the poor of the city, nursed plague victims, lived a heroically penitential life and was very effective in converting obdurate sinners. The unity and welfare of the church was her special concern, and she persuaded Pope Gregory XI to return to Rome from Avignon in 1376 and also tried to heal the subsequent Great Schism. Apart from over four hundred letters, she wrote a 'Dialogue' which is of first importance in mystical theology. She died at Rome, whither she had been summoned by the pope, and was canonized in 1461. In 1939 she was declared patron of Italy and was declared a doctor of the Church in 1970 and a patron of Europe in 2000.

Catherine (Karin) of Sweden (St) {2}

24 March
?1331–81. A Swede, the fourth child of St Brigid, she married a German nobleman who was a life-long invalid. They lived in continence until he let her go to her mother in Rome in 1349. She accompanied her mother's body back to the Bridgettine nunnery at Vadstena in 1373 and became its abbess (her husband having died in 1351). In 1379 she obtained papal recognition of the Bridgettines and also promoted her mother's canonization. Her cultus was confirmed in 1484.

Catherine Tanaka (Bl) {2}

12 July
d. 1626. The wife of Bl John Tanaka, she was beheaded at Nagasaki (Japan) with Mancius Araki and Comps. Cf. **Japan, Martyrs of**.

Catherine (Kateri) Tekákwitha (St) {2}

17 April
1656–80. A Native American, her father was an Iroquois, and her mother was a Christian Algonquin. Born in what is now New York State (USA), she was orphaned when aged four and baptized by missionaries when aged twenty. Her family disapproved, and she fled to French Canada (now Quebec), where she took a vow of virginity and became known for her prayer, work and asceticism. She died at Sault aged twenty-four, and was canonized in 2012.

Catherine Thomás (St) {2}

5 April
1533–74. An orphan girl of Valdemuzza on Majorca (Spain), she kept the sheep of an uncle who abused her before she joined the Canonesses of St Augustine at Palma when aged sixteen. She became a 'fool for Christ's sake' and was subject to mystical and diabolic phenomena, allegedly being continually in ecstasy at the end of her life. She was canonized in 1930.

Catherine Volpicelli (St) {2}

(28 December)
1839–94. From a rich family of Naples, Italy, she was initially a socialite but turned to a life of prayer and was inspired by a French pious association, the 'Apostleship of Prayer'. In 1874 she founded the 'Servants of the Sacred Heart' at Naples. She died there and was canonized in 2009.

Catherine Yi (St) {1 –group}

26 September
Cf. **Sebastian Nam I-gwan and Comps**.

Catulinus and Comps (SS) {2, 4}

15 July
? They were martyred at Carthage (Roman Africa) and buried in the basilica of Faustus, and St Augustine preached a surviving panegyric on St Catulinus, a deacon. His companions

were named as Januarius, Florentius, Julia and Justa in the old Roman Martyrology, but these names have been deleted. Other martyrologies mention Pollutana.

Ceallach McAedh (St) {2, 4}

1 April
d. 1129. Possibly an Irish monk of Glastonbury (England), he studied at Oxford. When he became archbishop of Armagh (Ireland) in 1106 he was the last appointed by hereditary succession, as he initiated a reform of the Irish church which was continued by St Malachy, his successor whom he had chosen.

Ceccard of Luna (St) {2}

16 June
d. c.860. Bishop of Luna in Tuscany (Italy), he rebuked the inhabitants of Massa-Carrara for immoral behaviour, and they killed him. His cultus was confirmed for Massa in 1832.

Cecilia (St) {1, 3}

22 November
? One of the most celebrated of the Roman virgin martyrs, she is commemorated in the Roman canon of the Mass. Her acta are legendary, however, and all that is known for certain is that she was buried in the cemetery of St Callistus. She is traditionally associated with SS Valerian and Tiburtius, and the alleged relics of the three of them are at St Cecilia's in Trastevere. She is the patron of musicians and is usually depicted with a musical instrument.

Cecilia Eusepi (Bl) {2 –add}

10 January
1910–28. Born at Monte Romano near Viterbo (Italy), the youngest of eleven children, as a child she was inspired by the life of St Teresa of Lisieux and so joined the Order of the Servants of Mary as a tertiary when aged twelve. A year later she applied to become a religious of the order, and studied in order to become a missionary. However, she was afflicted with virulent tuberculosis and returned back to her family at Nepi where she died. While dying she wrote her spiritual autobiography, *The Story of a Clown*. She was beatified in 2012.

Cecilia Yu So-sa (St) {1 –group}

23 November
d. 1839. She was a widow aged seventy-nine at Seoul in Korea, who was imprisoned and had her property confiscated. She was interrogated twelve times and flogged before dying in prison. Cf. **Korea, Martyrs of**.

Cedd (St) {2}

26 October
d. 664. A Northumbrian and monk of Lindisfarne whose brother was St Chad, he was sent by St Finan to help in evangelizing Mercia (England) before being consecrated bishop of the East Saxons at London in 654. He founded monasteries at Tilbury and Bradwell (Essex), attended the Synod of Whitby (at which he renounced the Celtic rite) and founded a monastery (initially Celtic) at Lastingham near Malton (Yorks) to which he retired to die. (None of his monasteries survived the Viking incursions.)

Ceferino cf. **Zephyrinus**.

Celerinus and Comps (SS) {2, 4}

3 February
C3rd. He was imprisoned, tortured and martyred at Carthage. His grandmother Celerina and two soldier uncles, Laurence and Ignatius, had already suffered martyrdom.

Celestina-of-the-Mother-of-God Donati (Bl) {2 –add}

1848–1925. From Marradi near Florence in Italy, she wished to become a religious but was prevented by her father who wanted her to look after him. Eventually, when aged forty-one she opened a house with some young followers, together with her father, aunt and sister. This was the start of the 'Daughters of the Poor of St Joseph Calasanz', dedicated to educating and caring for poor children, especially those of prisoners. This spread throughout Italy. She died at Florence and was beatified in 2008.

Celestina Faron (Bl) {2}

9 April
1913–44. A Polish sister of the Congregation of the Servants of the Immaculate Conception, she died of ill-treatment on Easter Sunday at the concentration camp at Auschwitz. She had previously made a spiritual donation of her life for the conversion of a renegade priest, who subsequently repented. Cf. **Poland, Martyrs of the Nazi Occupation of**.

Celestine I, Pope (St) {2, 4}

6 April
d. 432. A Roman priest from the Campagna, he succeeded St Boniface I as pope in 422. He supported the campaign of St Germanus of Auxerre against Pelagianism, sent St Palladius to evangelize Ireland and confirmed the condemnation of Nestorius through his legates at the Council of Ephesus in 431. His cultus was suppressed in 1969.

Celestine V, Pope cf. **Peter Celestine**.

Celine Chludzińska Borzecka (Bl) {2 –add}

1833–1913. From a wealthy Polish landowning background at Orsza (now in Bielarus), she married when aged twenty and had four children, two of whom survived. Theirs was a very happy family, until her husband was paralysed by a stroke. They moved to Vienna where he lingered for five years until he died in 1874. The widow and her younger daughter then moved to Rome, where they were inspired by Fr Peter Sememko to found a female branch of the Ressurectionists. This they did at Rome in 1887 when they opened their first school, and in 1891 they established their first canonical community at Kety near Wadowice in Poland. Bl Celine governed the congregation until her death, and oversaw its spread to Bulgaria and the United States. She was beatified in 2007.

Celsus cf. **Ceallach**.

(Celsus and Clement) (SS) {4 –deleted}

21 November
? Only the names are listed of these Roman martyrs.

Ceneric (St) {2}

7 May
C7th. He was a deacon of Le Mans (France) who became a monk. After venerating SS Martin of Tours and Julian of Le Mans at their shrines, he became a hermit and lived an austere life.

Censurius of Auxerre (St) {2, 4}

10 June
C5th. He succeeded St Germanus as bishop of Auxerre (France) in 448, built a church in his honour there and was himself buried in it.

Centolla (St) {2, 4}

13 August
? She was martyred near Burgos (Spain). A companion, Helen, has been deleted from the Roman Martyrology.

Ceolfrid (Geoffrey) (St)

25 September

?642–716. A Northumbrian monk at the Yorkshire (England) monastery of Gilling, he transferred to the monastery of Ripon where he became novice-master. In 672 he transferred again to Wearmouth-Jarrow at the invitation of St Benedict Biscop, the founder, and eventually became abbot of the twin monasteries. St Bede was one of his monks. He arranged the production of the 'Codex Amiatinus' as a gift to the pope, and this survives at Florence as the oldest single-volume copy of the Vulgate and a witness of the high artistic standards of Saxon monasticism. He resigned in 716 and died at Langres (France) while on a pilgrimage to Rome. The popularity of his medieval cultus is evident by the surviving boy's name 'Geoffrey'.

Ceratius (Cérase) (St) {2}

6 June

d. ?452. The cultus of this bishop of Grenoble (France) was confirmed in 1903.

Cerbonius of Populonia (St) {2, 4}

10 October

d. ?575. A Roman African bishop, he was a refugee from the Vandals and settled at Populonia in Tuscany (Italy), allegedly becoming bishop there. The Lombards exiled him to Elba, where he died. He is the patron of Massa Maritima, into which diocese his own has been incorporated.

(Cerbonius of Verona) (St) {4 –deleted}

10 October

C5th. He is venerated as a former bishop of Verona in Italy, but is probably a duplicate of the above.

Cerneuf cf. **Serenus**.

Ceslaus (Bl) {2}

17 July

?1184–1242. From Kamien (Poland), he was a canon at Cracow before becoming a Dominican at Rome under St Dominic with St Hyacinth, his brother. He was made the provincial of Poland at Breslau in Silesia (now Wroclaw in Poland), preached in Silesia and Bohemia and was the spiritual director of St Hedwig of Silesia. He was a leader in the city's successful resistance to the Mongols in their incursion of 1240. His cultus was confirmed for Wroclaw in 1712.

Cetheus cf. **Peregrine of Aquila**.
Ch- cf. 'C-', 'K-', if names spelt thus initially are not found.

Chad (Ceadda) (St) {2}

2 March

d. 672. From Northumbria (England) and brother of St Cedd, he was educated at Lindisfarne under St Aidan and in Ireland before becoming abbot of the Columbanian monastery of Lastingham founded by his brother. During one of St Wilfrid's exiles he was made archbishop of York but was removed by St Theodore of Canterbury when St Wilfrid returned and went to Lichfield in 669 to evangelize the Mercians. He died there, and part of his relics is now at his namesake cathedral at Birmingham. His attributes are a church and a vine.

Chaeremon of Nilopolis and Comps (SS) {2, 4}

22 December

d. 250. A very old bishop of Nilopolis (Egypt), when the Decian persecution was instigated he took to the hills with some companions. They were never seen again and were probably eaten by animals or enslaved by nomads (the Sahara desert was greener in those days.)

Chaffre cf. **Theofrid**.

(Chalcedon, Martyrs of) *(SS)* *{4 –deleted}*

24 September
d. 304. They numbered forty-nine and were listed as martyred at Chalcedon, across the Bosporus from Byzantium (Constantinople). Possibly they were the city's church choir.

Charalampus and Comps (SS) {2}

10 February
C3rd. A priest, he was martyred at Magnesia (Asia Minor) in the reign of Septimus Severus with two soldiers named Porphyrius and Dauctus and three women.

Charitina (St) {2, 4}

5 October
Early C4th. She died under torture at Corycos in Cilicia (Asia Minor) in the reign of Diocletian.

Chariton (St) {2}

28 September
d. c.350. He was a hermit in a wadi in the Judaean Desert near Jerusalem, and founded a monastery in a series of caves along the sides of the gorge. Each cave contained a monk, with a larger cave used as the church. This became known as the Old Laura or the Laura of St Chariton, and was an extremely influential arrangement taken up by other monastic founders in the Holy Land. He himself founded several other monastic settlements. His traditional date is about a century earlier than that accepted by the revised Roman Martyrology.

Chariton and Comps (SS) {2}

1 June
Cf. **Justin Martyr**.

Charles of Austria, Emperor (Bl) {2 –add}

1 April
1887–1922. He was born as an archduke of the Hapsburg Empire and great-nephew of the reigning emperor, Franz-Joseph. He had a strong Eucharistic piety and was personally devoted to prayer and to the church's teaching on peace and social justice. In 1911 he married Princess Zita of Bourbon-Parma; the marriage was a love match, and they had eight children. In 1914 he became heir to the imperial throne when Archduke Franz Ferdinand was assassinated at Sarajevo, and became emperor on the death of Franz-Joseph in 1917. The First World War had overtaxed the resources of the empire, which was already in a state of disintegration into its component nationalities, and there was little he could do to prevent this. He rejected his wife's pleas that he assert his authority by force of arms, and was exiled to Madeira in 1917. There the family had to live in poverty, and he died of pneumonia exacerbated by the damp condition of their residence. He was beatified in 2004.

Charles of Blois (Bl) {2}

29 September
?1319–64. A nephew of King Philip VI of France, he married Joan of Brittany in 1341 and thus became Duke of Brittany. He spent the rest of his life fighting in defence of his title against his uncle, John de Montfort, apart from nine years spent in the Tower of London. He was killed in battle. His cultus was forbidden in 1368, but confirmed for Blois and St Brieuc in 1904.

Charles Borromeo (St) {1, 3}

4 November
1538–84. From Rocca d'Arona near Lake Maggiore (Italy), his uncle was Pope Pius IV and he was made a curial cardinal and

archbishop of Milan in 1560 when aged only twenty-two and not yet a priest. He was secretly ordained bishop in 1563 to avoid pressures to marry, became papal Secretary of State and was instrumental in the Counter-Reformation (especially in the Tridentine reform of the curia). In 1565 he became bishop of Milan which was in a state of serious decay as a diocese. The rest of his life was spent in renewing it thoroughly, and he became the greatest bishop of his day in Italy, with enormous influence. He was canonized in 1610.

Charles Cho Shin-ch'ŏl (St) {1 –group}

26 September
Cf. **Sebastian Nam I-gwan and Comps**.

Charles Eraña Guruceta and Comps (BB) {2}

18 September
1884–1936. From Guipúzcoa (Spain), he became a lay Marianist and ran a prestigious school in Madrid. After the start of the civil war he tried to find help from other Marianist communities in Ciudad Real, but these had been dispersed, and he was arrested with two confreres: Bl Fidelis Fuidio Rodriguez and Bl Jesus Hita Miranda. He was the first to be shot in the city on 18 September. Bl Jesus was martyred with a group of Passionists at Carrión de Calatrava on 25 September, and Bl Fidelis was martyred in the city on 17 October. They were beatified in 1995. Cf. **Spanish Civil War, Martyrs of**.

Charles de Foucauld (Bl) {2 –add}

1 December
1858–1916. From a distinguished family of Strasbourg in France, he became an army officer but lost his faith in the process. He served in the Sahara, and the experience led him to resign his commission and explore Morocco in 1883–4. He regained his faith and, being aware of a vocation to a life of prayer and asceticism, joined the Trappists, initially at Nazareth, in 1890. However, he was not suited to community life and left to live as a hermit at Nazareth. He was ordained in 1901, and then lived as a hermit in the Sahara, initially at Beni-Abbes and latterly at Tamanrasset, hoping to inspire the desert dwellers by his example. He was killed by Muslim fundamentalists. He had no disciples in his lifetime, but the writings he left led to the foundation of the 'Little Brothers of Jesus' in 1933 and the 'Little Sisters of Jesus' in 1936. He was beatified in 2005.

Charles Garnier (Bl) {2}

7 December
1606–49. From Paris (France), he became a Jesuit in 1634 and went as a missionary to the Huron nation in what was now Ontario (Canada), east of Lake Huron in 1636. He was a fellow missioner with St John Brébeuf, and died in a raid by the Iroquois almost six months after St John's martyrdom. He was canonized in 1930. Cf. **John Brébeuf and Comps**.

Charles Gnocchi (Bl) {2 –add}

28 February
1902–56. From San Colombano al Lambro near Lodi (Italy), he became a diocesan parish priest of Milan in 1925 but was transferred by Bl Albert-Ildephonsus Schuster, the archbishop, to the army to be a chaplain. During the Second World War he served on the Eastern Front, and on his return after Italy's surrender was imprisoned by the Germans for helping fugitive Allied prisoners of war. As a result of his experiences he founded the Pro Juventate Foundation to help war orphans and those maimed, especially the young. He died of cancer at Milan, and was beatified in 2009. His foundation is famous in Italy for aiding suffering children.

Charles the Good (Bl) {2}

2 March
d. 1127. A son of St Canute, king of Denmark, he went with his uncle Robert II on crusade to the Holy Land and succeeded him as count of Flanders in 1119. He was a wise and careful ruler, with a special concern for the poor, and was killed at Bruges (Belgium) in a conspiracy by some magnates. His cultus was confirmed for Bruges in 1883.

Charles the Great ('Charlemagne') (Bl)

28 January
742–814. The son of Pepin the Short, he became king of the Franks in 768 and was crowned as the first Holy Roman emperor in 800 by Pope St Leo III. He was successful in founding a great empire in the West around his capital at Aachen, and tried hard to raise the standards of church and state therein. But the political foundations were inadequate, and his empire did not long survive his death. His cultus was approved for Aachen in 1165 and was popular in the north of Germany and of France in the Middle Ages, partly owing to anti-papal nationalist sentiment. Pope Benedict XIV confirmed it in the C18th, despite the emperor's immoral private life and his unsoundness concerning the dogmatic validity of icons. He is the principal patron of Metten Abbey, but is not in the Roman Martyrology.

Charles-of-St-Andrew Houbin (St) {2}

5 January
1821–93. From near Maastricht (Netherlands), he joined the Passionists at Tournai in 1846, was ordained in 1852 and was then sent to London. He went to Dublin in 1857, where he spent the rest of his life (apart from 1866–74 at Sutton, Surrey). He sometimes had to spend all day in the confessional; such were the numbers coming to him, and converted many sinners and lapsed Catholics both in Britain and in Ireland. He had a great zeal for the sanctification of Ireland as a means to the conversion of Britain and prayed always for the unity of the church. He was canonized in 2007.

Charles Hyon Sŏng-mun (St) {1 –group}

19 September
d. 1846. He was a catechist at Seoul in Korea, and was involved in secretly bringing in foreign missionary priests. After many dangerous labours for the faith he was imprisoned with other Christians, and encouraged them in prison before being beheaded. Cf. **Korea, Martyrs of**.

Charles Leisner (Bl) {2}

12 August
1915–45. From Rees on the Rhine (Germany), he was involved in underground Catholic youth work under the Nazis at Münster. After being ordained deacon he was sent to the concentration camp at Dachau for criticizing Hitler in 1941 and was secretly ordained priest there in 1944. He died of tuberculosis just after his liberation and was beatified as a martyr in 1996.

Charles Liviero (Bl) {2 –add}

1866–1932. From a working-class family at Vicenza in Italy, he was ordained a diocesan priest of Padua in 1888. He became known for his witness against atheistic socialism and his work to put the church's social teachings into practice. In 1910 he was consecrated bishop of Città di Castello near Perugia, a diocese in which the church had lost the respect of secular society. He worked hard and successfully to remedy this, and to help him in his charitable works he founded the 'Sisters, Little Servants of the Sacred Heart'. He was famous for his care for poor people. He died in hospital at Fano as a result of a road accident, and was beatified in 2007.

Charles Lwanga and Comps (SS) {1 –group}

3 June
1885–87. The evangelization of the Kingdom of Buganda (the core of modern Uganda) started with the exploration of the area by the British in the latter part of the C19th, and saw competition between Catholic and Protestant missionaries in setting up local churches. In October 1885 the new Kabaka (King) Mwanga, who was an extremely corrupt and vicious young man, ordered the assassination of James Hannington, the newly arrived Anglican missionary bishop. Then he ordered a general persecution of his Christian subjects in May 1886, mainly because the Christians among his page-boys (Charles Lwanga was their leader) objected to being the casual targets of his licentiousness. Twenty-two Catholics, mostly courtiers aged between thirteen and thirty, were killed by being dismembered and burnt alive before the Kabaka's overthrow in September 1888. They were canonized in 1964, and are the protomartyrs of sub-Saharan Africa. A number of Protestants were killed as well. Cf. **Uganda** in lists of national martyrs in appendix.

Charles-Joseph-Eugene de Mazenod (St) {2}

21 May
1782–1861. From Aix-en-Provence (France) of a family in the high civil service, he was exiled by the French Revolution and was ordained on his return in 1811. He founded the 'Missionary Oblates of Mary Immaculate' in order to promote popular missions and to preach to the poor, and was made bishop of Marseilles in 1837. He thoroughly reformed his diocese. His canonization was in 1995.

Charles Meehan (Bl) {2}

12 August
1640–79. An Irish Franciscan, he was on his way home from Bavaria (where he had taken refuge from persecution), but his ship was wrecked on the north Welsh coast, and he was executed at Ruthin despite never having been a priest in Wales or England (he may have worked in Scotland). He was beatified in 1987. Cf. **Wales, Martyrs of**.

Charles-of-Sezze Melchiori (St) {2}

6 January
1613–70. From Sezze in the Campagna (Italy), he became a Franciscan in 1635 and famous for mystical experiences. It was alleged that he bore a visible wound caused by a ray of light from a consecrated host piercing his heart in 1648. He wrote several treatises on the spiritual life and also an autobiography. He died at Rome and was canonized in 1959.

Charles-Emmanuel Rodrígues Santiago (Bl) {2}

(13 July)
1918–63. The 'Lay Apostle of the Liturgy' was born at Caguas, Puerto Rico and had a hard childhood marked by the destitution of his family after a fire and by the onset of ulcerative colitis. The latter interfered with his formal education, but he was a voracious seeker after knowledge and became deeply committed to propagating the understanding of the church's liturgy. While working as an office clerk he edited a magazine on the subject and organized many initiatives to further his life's aim. He died of rectal cancer and was beatified in 2001.

Charles Spinola and Comps (SS) {2}

10 September
d. 1622. An Italian nobleman born at Prague, he became a Jesuit in 1584 and was on the Japanese mission from 1594 to 1618. Then he was seized, imprisoned for four years and finally burnt alive in the 'Great Martyrdom' at Nagasaki with twenty-two companions (seven Jesuits, six Dominicans, three Franciscans and

six laypeople), after having to watch twenty-nine others being beheaded. Cf. **Japan, Martyrs of** and **Great Martyrdom at Nagasaki**.

Charles Steeb cf. **John-Henry-Charles Steeb**.
Chef cf. **Theodore**.

Chelidona (St) {2}

13 October
d. 1152. From the Abruzzi (Italy), when young she became a hermit in a cave called the 'Morra Ferogna' near Tivoli and was clothed as a Benedictine nun at St Scholastica's nunnery at Subiaco nearby. She continued as a hermit, however. Her relics are in her abbey church, and she is one of the patrons of Subiaco.

Chely cf. **Hilary of Mende**.
Chéron cf. **Caraunus**.

Cherubin Testa (Bl) {2}

17 September
1451–79. He was an Augustinian friar at Avigliana in Piedmont (Italy), and his cultus was confirmed for the Augustinian friars in 1865.

Cheslav Jóźwiak and Comps (Bl) {2}

24 August
1919–42. A group of five Polish laymen, they were guillotined at a prison at Dresden in Germany. The others were BB Edward Kaźmierski, Edward Klinik, Francis Kęsy and Yarogniev Wojciechowski. Cf. **Poland, Martyrs of the Nazi Occupation of**.

Childomarca (St) {2}

19 June
d. ?682. She was a nun who took the veil at Bordeaux (France), but was moved to Rouen and was appointed abbess of Fécamp by St Wandrille. She showed hospitality to St Leodegar after his mutilation arranged by Ebroin, mayor of the palace of the king.

Chilian cf. **Kilian**.

China (Martyrs of) {1 –group}

9 July
Christianity has been in China for over a thousand years, but the Catholic Church only began to be established there with the arrival of the Portuguese in the region in the early sixteenth century. The Jesuits gained influence at the court of the Ming emperors, but Christianity was not easily compatible with the Confucianism of the State. When the Manchus overthrew the Ming dynasty in 1643, there was a wave of persecution. The protomartyr of the Chinese church was Bl Francis de Capillas who was martyred in Fujian in 1648. The Jesuits regained some influence at court, but persecution was renewed in 1717 and continued intermittently until the Western powers enforced toleration in the Treaty of Nanking in 1842. In 1900, as the empire was decaying, there was a two-month long xenophobic outburst, mostly in north-central areas, called the Boxer Rebellion. About 30,000 Catholics were massacred during this, mostly in the provinces of Hebei and Hunan. A total of 120 martyrs, natives and missionaries were canonized in 2000 (St John-Gabriel Perboyre was canonized in 1996.) They now have a common liturgical celebration in the General Calendar on 9 July. Cf. lists of national martyrs in appendix.

Chl- also cf. 'Cl-', 'Kl-'.
Chr- also cf. 'Cr-'.

Chrestus and Pappus (SS) {2}

3 April
Early C4th? They were martyred at Tomi, which is now Constanţa in Romania.

Christiana-of-the-Cross Menabuoi (Bl) {2}

4 January

d. 1310. According to her story, she fled from her home at Castello di Santa Croce in Tuscany (Italy) in order to avoid marriage and became a serving maid at Lucca. Then she returned to found an Augustinian nunnery. Her cultus was confirmed for San Miniato in 1776.

Christicola cf. **Cele-Christ**.

Christina the Astonishing (Bl) {2}

24 July

1150–1224. From near Liege (Belgium), she was orphaned in 1165 and had a cataleptic fit in 1182 which initiated a series of unbelievable mystical phenomena which lasted for the rest of her life (hence her nickname). These were recorded by a Dominican before she died at a convent at St Truiden.

Christina of Bolseno (St) {2, 3}

24 July

? She was possibly a Roman who was martyred at Bolseno in Tuscany (Italy). Her acta are legendary and have been confused with the fantastic stories concerning a probably fictional 'Christina of Tyre'. Her attributes are an arrow and a millstone. Her cultus was confined to local calendars in 1969.

Christina Bruzo (Bl) {2}

6 November

1242–1312. From Stommeln near Cologne (Germany), she was a Beguine at Cologne before becoming the housekeeper of the parish priest at Stommeln. From age eleven she was subject to an extraordinary series of mystical and paranormal phenomena which were recorded by a Dominican. Her cultus was confirmed for Cologne in 1908.

Christina Camozzi (Bl) {2}

13 February

1435–58. From Porlezza on Lake Lugano (Italy), she was the daughter of a doctor and led a worthless life until a sudden conversion caused her to become an Augustinian nun in 1454. She nursed in a hospital at Spoleto and practised extreme mortifications. Her cultus was confirmed for the Augustinians in 1834. (She is sometimes surnamed 'Visconti' in error).

Christina Ciccarelli (Bl) {2}

18 January

1481–1543. From Luco de Marsi in the Abruzzi (Italy), she became an Augustinian nun and prioress at Aquileia. Her cultus was confirmed for that place in 1841.

Christina the Persian (St) {2, 4}

13 March

d. 559. A young Persian woman, she was whipped to death in the reign of Shah Chosroes I.

Christinus Gondek (Bl) {2}

23 July

1909–42. A Polish Franciscan friar, he died of ill-treatment at the concentration camp at Dachau. Cf. **Poland, Martyrs of the Nazi Occupation of**.

Christopher (St) {2, 3}

25 July

? The Roman Martyrology lists him as a martyr in Lycia (Asia Minor) in the reign of Decius. Nothing is known about him, but many fanciful legends have been attached to his name. The most familiar has him as a giant carrying the Christ-Child across a river, and this is how he is usually represented. His cultus was confined to local calendars in 1969, but he remains a popular patron of travellers.

Christopher Bales (Bl) {2}

4 March
d. 1590. From Coniscliffe west of Darlington in Co. Durham, he was educated at Rome and Rheims and ordained priest at Douai in 1587. The next year he went to England and after two years was seized and hanged, drawn and quartered at Fleet Street in London with BB Alexander Blake and Nicholas Horner. He was beatified in 1929. Cf. **England, Martyrs of**.

Christopher Buxton (Bl) {2}

1 October
d. 1588. From Tideswell in Derbyshire (England), he was educated at Rheims and Rome and ordained priest in 1586. He was hanged, drawn and quartered at Canterbury and was beatified in 1929. Cf. **England, Martyrs of**.

Christopher of Collesano (St) {2}

17 December
C10th. He was from Collesano near Cefalù in Sicily and had two sons, SS Macarius of Collesano and Sabas the Younger, and a wife Kale. He got the permission of the latter to become a Byzantine-rite monk at Agira (Sicily), and later was a hermit at a place called Ktisma. His sons joined him there, and Kale founded a nunnery nearby. In 940 a famine forced the family to move to Calabria, where they founded a monastery dedicated to St Michael on Monte Mercurion. The threat of Muslim incursions forced them to move to Monte Latinion in the Basilicata, where he died.

Christopher-of-St-Catherine López de Valladolid Orea (Bl) {2 –add}

21 July
1638–90. He was born into a peasant family of Mérida in Spain, and after a historically obscure youth was ordained in 1663. He was an army chaplain, and then spent time as a hermit before joining a convent of Franciscan tertiaries at Córdoba. There he founded the Franciscan Hospitallers of Jesus the Nazarene, for men and women to nurse sick people. He was beatified in 2013.

Christopher Maccassoli (Bl) {2}

5 March
d. 1485. A nobleman from Milan (Italy), he became a Franciscan and eventually re-founded a friary at Vigevano near Milan. He was sought out by thousands for help and advice. His cultus was confirmed for Vigevano in 1890.

Christopher Magallanes Jara and Augustine Caloca Cortés (St) {1 –group}

25 May
d. 1927. They were two priests, shot at the orders of an army officer at Catatlán near Guadalajara in Mexico. Bl Augustine was born at San Juan Bautista del Teúl in 1898, and helped Bl Christopher catechize children while studying for the priesthood informally (the government had shut the established seminary at Guadalajara). He was ordained in 1923, and was appointed parish priest of Totalice and prefect of the re-founded seminary. During the Cristero War, government forces arrested him after he urged the seminarians to go into hiding, and he was imprisoned in the same cell as Bl Christopher. The two were executed together. Cf. **Mexico, Martyrs of**.

Christopher of Milan (Bl) {2}

1 March
d. 1484. From Milan (Italy), he became a Dominican and was a preacher famous in the Republic of Genoa and the Duchy of Milan. He had a friary founded for him at Taggia near Ventimiglia, where he died. His cultus was confirmed for Ventimiglia and the Dominicans in 1875.

Christopher Robinson (Bl) {2}

31 March
d. 1597. From near Carlisle, he was ordained at Rheims in 1592 and was a priest in Cumbria for five years before being captured at Penrith. He was executed at Carlisle on an uncertain date in late March and was beatified in 1987. Cf. **England, Martyrs of**.

Christopher of Romandiola (Bl) {2}

31 October
?1172–1272. A parish priest of the diocese of Cesena (Italy) at Romandiola, he became one of the early Franciscans after St Francis visited his village and was one of the first of the order in Gascony (France). He died at Cahors, and his cultus was confirmed for there in 1905.

Christopher of Tlaxcala (Bl) {2}

23 September
c.1514–27. A native Mexican born near Tlaxcala and converted by the Franciscans, he had a father who objected to his evangelizing. On a family feast day, the latter was encouraged by one of his wives to beat Bl Christopher badly and to throw him on a bonfire. He died that night, after having thanked his father for the gift of martyrdom. He was beatified in 1900 with BB Anthony and John.

Christopher Wharton (Bl) {2}

28 March
d. 1600. From Middleton near Ilkley in Yorkshire, he was a nephew of the first Lord Wharton and a fellow of Trinity College, Oxford before his conversion. He was ordained at Rheims in 1584 and was a priest in Yorkshire until he was captured at Carlton Hall near Leeds and executed at York. He was beatified in 1987. Cf. **England, Martyrs of**.

Chrodegang (St) {2}

6 March
d. 766. From near Liege (Belgium), he was the chief minister for Charles Martel from 737 and was made bishop of Metz (France) while retaining his secular office in 742 after Pepin had become ruler. He introduced the Roman liturgy to his diocese (displacing the Gallican rite), founded and restored several monasteries (notably Gorze) and organized his cathedral chapter into a canonry living a common life under a rule. This last innovation was extremely influential. He died at Metz, and his shrine was at Gorze until destroyed in the French Revolution.

Chrodogang (St) {2}

3 September
d. 775. The brother of St Opportuna, he became bishop of Sées in Normandy (France) but was assassinated by a relative to whom he had entrusted the administration of the diocese while on pilgrimage to Rome. The spelling of his name differs from that of the previous.

Chromatius of Aquileia (St) {2, 4}

2 December
d. ?407. Bishop of Aquileia (Italy) from 387, he was associated with the ascetic community there headed by St Jerome and Rufinus. He was consecrated bishop by St Ambrose in ?387, and loyally defended St John Chrysostom when the latter was exiled. He was a great theologian, but little of his writings survives.

Chromatius of Rome (St)

11 August
C3rd. He was allegedly prefect of Rome and father of St Tiburtius of Rome, but was not listed in the Roman Martyrology.

Chrysanthus and Daria (SS) {1, 3} {2, 3}

25 October
d. ?253. They were martyrs buried on the Salarian Way at Rome, but nothing else is known about them. Their legend describes them as a married couple, an Egyptian husband and a Greek wife, who were buried alive in a sand-pit at Rome. Their cultus was confined to particular calendars in 1969.

Chrysanthus González García and Comps (BB) {2 –add}

d. 1936. Sixty-four Marist Brothers, with two lay helpers, were martyred by Communist Republican authorities in the diocese of Lerida during the Spanish Civil War. This was as a result of a policy of completely eliminating the church from society, advised by representatives sent by Stalin from the Soviet Union. The martyrs were beatified in 2013. Cf. **Spanish Civil War, Martyrs of** and list in appendix.

Chrysogonus (St) {2, 3}

24 November
d. ?304. He was martyred at Aquileia near Venice (Italy) and has a basilica at Rome, but nothing else is known about him. His association with St Anastasia is legendary. Since 1969 his cultus is confined to his basilica in Trastevere, although he is mentioned in the Roman canon of the Mass.

Chuniald and Gislar (SS) {2}

24 September
C8th. They were missionary priests, possibly from Scotland or Ireland, who were based at Salzburg (Austria) and helped St Rupert of Salzburg to evangelize the surrounding areas.

Ciaran (Kieran, Kyran) the Younger (St) {2}

9 September
C6th. From the region of Connaught in Ireland, he was trained in the monastic life by St Finian of Clonard and became the abbot-founder of Clonmacnoise in County Offaly, on the Shannon. For this influential monastery he drew up an extremely austere monastic rule, known as 'the Law of Kieran'.

Cicco of Pesaro (Bl)

4 August
d. 1350. From Pesaro (Italy), he became a Franciscan tertiary and a hermit nearby. His cultus was confirmed for Pesaro in 1859, but he is not listed in the Roman Martyrology.

Cilinia (St) {2, 4}

21 October
d. p458. The mother of St Principius of Soissons and of St Remigius of Rheims, she died at Laon (France).

(Cindeus) (St) {4 –deleted}

11 July
d. c.300. He was listed as a priest of Pamphylia (Asia Minor), burnt alive in the reign of Diocletian.

Cinnia (St)

1 February
C5th. A princess of Ulster (Ireland), she became a nun near Clogher after having been baptized by St Patrick, who also received her vows.

Ciwa cf. **Kigwe**.
Clair cf. **Clarus**.

Clare-of-Rimini Agolanti (Bl) {2}

10 February
d. ?1326. A noblewoman of Rimini (Italy), she married twice and lived a sinful and worthless life as a wife. But her second husband died and her father and brother were killed in civil disturbances, after which she converted, became

a Franciscan tertiary, founded the nunnery of Our Lady of the Angels at Rimini and henceforth lived a life of rigorous penance. Her cultus was confirmed for Rimini in 1784.

Clare of Assisi (St) {1, 3}

11 August
?1194–1253. A beautiful young noblewoman from Assisi (Italy), she ran away from home to join St Francis and to follow his ideals. He heard her vows as a nun in 1212, found a refuge for her at the Benedictine nunnery of St Paul's in Assisi and then obtained a house by the church of St Damian for her and her sister St Agnes in 1215. She governed this first nunnery of the Poor Clares in absolute poverty for forty years, and was as much instrumental in spreading the Franciscan ideal as St Francis herself. She is often represented holding a monstrance, in reference to a story that she saved her nunnery from a raid by mercenary soldiers by exposing the Blessed Sacrament to them.

Clare Badano (Bl) {2 –add}

7 October
1971–90. Born at Sassello near Savona (Italy), she had a solid Christian upbringing as an only child and became a member of Focolare when aged nine. Her later life was that of a normal teenager, especially when the family moved to Savona. She had many friends, was good at sport and music and dreamed of being an air hostess. She died slowly of an osteosarcoma (bone cancer) and her loving resignation and prayer during this led her to be beatified in 2010.

Clare Bosatta de Pianello (Bl) {2}

20 April
1858–87. From Pianello Lario near Como (Italy), in 1877 she joined the 'Daughters of Our Lady of Providence' which had just been founded by Bl Aloysius Guanella at the Sacred Heart Hospital there. In 1886 she moved to Como and became the superior-general, but did not live long as such. She was devoted both to the interior life and to caring for the elderly and orphans. Her beatification was in 1991.

Clare Gambacorta (Bl) {2}

17 April
1362–1419. Daughter of the ruler of Pisa (Italy) and sister of Bl Peter Gambacorta, she was a widow at fifteen and tried to join the Poor Clares. Her father prevented this, but allowed her to become a Dominican nun in 1378. She became the prioress of her own foundation in the city and set out to reform her order. Her cultus was confirmed for Pisa and the Dominicans in 1830.

Clare-of-the-Cross of Montefalco (St) {2, 3}

17 August
?1275–1308. From Montefalco near Spoleto (Italy), she became a Franciscan tertiary hermit with her sister at Montefalco, but her sister founded the Augustinian nunnery of the Holy Cross in 1290 and she became the second abbess. (The circumstances of their change in rule are obscure). She was a great mystic with a special devotion to the Passion, and the Instruments of the Passion were allegedly visible on her heart (probably scar tissue caused by heart attacks) when this was examined after her death. She was canonized in 1881.

Clare Yamada (Bl) {2}

10 September
d. 1622. She was beheaded in the 'Great Martyrdom' at Nagasaki (Japan) with her husband, Bl Dominic Yamada, and Charles Spinola and Comps. Cf. **Japan, Martyrs of** and **Great Martyrdom at Nagasaki**.

Clarentius of Vienne (St) {2, 4}

26 April
d. c.620. He succeeded St Etherius as bishop of Vienne (France).

(Clarus of Vexin) (St) {4 –deleted}

4 November
C9th? His story is that he was from Rochester in Kent (England), went to France and became a hermit near Cherbourg. Then he wandered about and ended up at a locality called Vexin near Beauvais, where he was killed by a noblewoman after he had rejected her advances. His shrine was at his namesake village of Saint-Clair-sur-Epte, and he is invoked against sore eyes (probably because of his name: 'Clear').

Clarus of Marmoutier (St) {2, 4}

8 November
d. ?396. From Tours (France), he was a monk at Marmoutier under St Martin and became a hermit nearby.

Clarus of Nantes (St) {2}

10 October
C4th. He was a bishop of Nantes, by false Gallican tradition a disciple of St Peter and apostle of Armorica (Brittany, France).

Clarus of Vienne (St) R.

1 January
d. c.660. From near Vienne (France), he became a monk at the monastery of St Ferreol and then abbot of St Marcellus at Vienne. His cultus was confirmed in 1903.

(Clateus of Brescia) (St) {4 –deleted}

4 June
? He was allegedly a bishop of Brescia (Italy) who was martyred in the reign of Nero. This is unhistorical; if he existed, he may have been of the early C4th.

Claudia Thévenet Cf. **Mary-of-the-Incarnation Thévenet.**

Claudius, Asterius, Neon and Comps (SS) {2, 4}

23 August
d. 303. Three brothers of Aegea in Cilicia (Asia Minor), they were betrayed as Christians by their stepmother (who coveted their property) and were either crucified or beheaded. Traditionally associated with them are Donvina (a mistake for 'Domina') and Theonilla, but these have been deleted from the Roman Martyrology.

(Claudius, Crispin and Comps) (SS) {4 –deleted}

3 December
? Nothing is known about these African martyrs. The companions were listed as Magina, John and Stephen.

(Claudius, Hilaria and Comps) (SS) {4 –deleted}

3 December
d. ?283. Allegedly a military tribune at Rome, his wife, two sons (Jason and Maurus) and seventy soldiers, they feature in the legendary acta of SS Chrysanthus and Daria.

(Claudius, Justus, Jucundinus and Comps) (SS) {4 –deleted}

21 July
C3rd? They were listed as eight companions of St Julia, martyred with her at Troyes (France) in the reign of Aurelian. Their shrine was at the abbey of Jouarre near Meaux.

Claudius, Lupercus and Victorius (SS) {2, 4}

30 October
d. ?303. Sons of the centurion St Marcellus, they were beheaded at León (Spain) in the reign of Diocletian.

(Claudius, Nicostratus and Comps 1) (SS)
{4 –deleted}

7 July
Late C3rd? They are in the unreliable acta of St Sebastian as having been martyred at Rome on the same day as that saint, but are probably identical with the Four Crowned Martyrs of Pannonia. The companions are Castorius, Victorinus and Symphorian.

(Claudius, Nicostratus and Comps 2) (SS)
{4 –deleted}

8 November
Early C4th? They were listed as martyred on the Via Labicana outside Rome in the reign of Diocletian, but have identical names to the above (except that Victorinus becomes Simplicius), and are almost certainly a duplicate of them.

Claudius of Besançon (St) {2, 4}

6 June
d. ?696. From Franche-Comté (France), he was initially a soldier but became a priest and a canon of Besançon. The he became a monk at Condat in the Jura, was made abbot and introduced the rule of St Benedict there. In 685 he became bishop of Besançon but remained abbot of his monastery, to which he retired to die and which was later named St Claud after him.

Claudius de la Colombière (St) {2}

15 February
1641–82. From near Grenoble (France), he became a Jesuit at Avignon in 1659 and went on to be the superior of the house at Paray-le-Monial. There he was the spiritual director of St Margaret-Mary Alacoque, and helped her in fostering the devotion to the Sacred Heart. He went to England in 1676 as the Duchess of York's chaplain, but was banished as a result of the Oates plot. He died at Avignon and was canonized in 1992.

Claudius Granzotto (Bl) {2}

15 August
1900–47. Born in S. Lucia del Piave (Italy), he left school when young, served in the army and then obtained a diploma in sculpture from Venice's Academy of Fine Arts. After working in his own studio for four years he joined the Franciscans in order to unite his art to holiness. He became a model friar as well as a sculptor with great spiritual and human sensitivity. He died of a brain tumour and was beatified in 1994.

Clear cf. **Clarus**.

Cleer (Clether) *(St)*

23 October
d. c.520. A Welsh nobleman, he emigrated to Cornwall (England) and settled at the place near Liskeard where St Cleer's chapel and well are now seen. He is possibly identical with the patron of St Clether, a village near Camerton in the same county.

Clement I, Pope (St) {1, 3}

23 November
d. ?101. By tradition he was the third successor of St Peter and pope for about a decade. The Roman church was most probably an informal federation of Christian synagogues at the time with no one overall leader, however. His letter to the church at Corinth, in which he attempted to settle some disputes there in the name of the Roman church, survives as one of the most important sub-apostolic writings. The so-called 'second letter' is not by him. He is mentioned in the Roman canon of the Mass and is venerated as a martyr, but nothing is known for certain about his life, and his acta are unreliable. His alleged relics were brought to Rome from the Crimea by SS Cyril and Methodius. His attribute is an anchor.

Clement and Agathangelus (SS) {2}

23 January
Early C4th. They were martyred at Ancyra (Asia Minor, now Ankara in Turkey) in the reign of Diocletian. Their acta are unreliable.

Clement-Ignatius Delgado y Cebrián (St) {1 –group}

12 July
1761–1838. A Spanish Dominican on the Vietnamese missions, he worked there for nearly fifty years, being made titular bishop of Mellipotamo and appointed vicar-apostolic of 'East Tonkin' (northeast Vietnam). He was seized during the persecution ordered by Emperor Minh Mạng, put into a small cage exposed to the elements and left to die. Cf. **Vietnam, Martyrs of**.

Clement of Elpidio (Bl) {2}

8 April
d. 1291. From Osimo (Italy), he became an Augustinian friar and was made superior-general in 1270. He drew up written constitutions which were approved in 1287, and is thus regarded as the order's second founder. His cultus was approved for Orvieto and the Augustinian friars in 1572.

Clement-Augustus von Galen (Bl) {2 –add}

22 March
1887. A nobleman from Dinklage near Oldenburg (Germany), he became a diocesan priest of Münster in 1904. In 1933 he became the bishop, and as such was outspoken on social issues and against the anti-Christian aspects of National Socialism. As a result he was involved in the drafting of the papal encyclical 'Mit Brennender Sorge' which was circulated in the German Catholic Church in 1937. His status was such that the Nazis did not dare to molest him personally, and he was able to travel to Rome to be made a cardinal in 1946. He died at Münster a month later and was beatified in 2005.

Clement-Mary Hofbauer (Dvorak) (St) {2}

15 March
1751–1820. The son of a Czech grazier of Tasswitz in Moravia (Czech Republic), he was a baker before becoming a hermit in 1775. Going to Rome, he was clothed as a consecrated religious at Tivoli near Rome. He joined the Redemptorists at Rome in 1783 and was sent to found a house at Vienna. This proving impossible, he established himself in Warsaw in 1787 with immediate success, and became vicar-general for Middle Europe in 1793. The house at Warsaw was closed by Napoleon in 1807, and he went back to Vienna for the rest of his life, where he was very popular as a preacher and missioner, being nicknamed the 'Apostle of Vienna'. He was canonized in 1909.

Clement Kyuyemon (Bl) {2}

1 November
d. 1622. From Arima in Japan, he was the housekeeper of Bl Paul Navarro, wrote his biography and was martyred with him and his two companions at Shimabara. Cf. **Japan, Martyrs of**.

Clement Marchisio (Bl) {2}

16 December
1833–1903. A Piedmontese, he was ordained in 1856 and became the parish priest of Rivalba near Turin in 1860, where he stayed for forty-three years. He was concerned for young people, especially for teenage girls moving to the towns from the villages in order to find a living. He built a hospital for them, trained such girls in weaving as an alternative to prostitution and founded the 'Daughters of St Joseph' to help him in 1877. He was beatified in 1984.

Clement of Metz (St) {2}

23 November
C4th? He is claimed as the first bishop of Metz (France), having been sent there as a missionary from Rome.

Clement of Ohrid and Comps (SS) {2}

27 July
Early C10th. Clement, Nahum, Gorazd, Angelarius and Sabas were priests assisting SS Cyril and Methodius on the mission to the Slavs of Great Moravia (roughly the present-day Czech Republic), but were expelled when the Latin clergy of the neighbouring German dioceses procured the suppression of the mission in 885. They migrated to Bulgaria, which had accepted Christianity in the Byzantine rite through their khan Boris, and founded a monastery at Ohrid (now in the republic of Macedonia). This became the main centre for the development of the infant Bulgarian church, and Clement became its first archbishop. He was the first author (as distinct from translator) to write in Church Slavonic, helped by Nahum, and the five are considered the apostles of Bulgaria and of Macedonia.

Clement Šeptyckyj (Bl) {2}

1 May
1870–1951. Archimandrite of the monastery at Univ, he died in the prison at Vladimir in the Soviet Union (now Bielarus). Cf. **Nicholas Čarneckyj and 24 Comps**.

Clement Vismara (Bl) {2 –add}

15 June
1897–1988. From a working-class family of Agrate Brianza (Italy), he saw active service in the First World War before being ordained as a missionary priest of the Pontifical Institute for Foreign Missions in 1923. He went to Burma, and established a new mission at Mong Lin in 1928. Despite primitive and dangerous conditions he founded other missions, until he was interned during the Second World War. The invading Japanese released him and let him alone, so he went to back to Mong Lin. In 1955 he transferred to Mong Ping, where he eventually died. Towards the end, the military dictatorship expelled all younger missionaries but again left him alone. He continued to work to help poor and disadvantaged people until his end. He was beatified in 2011.

Clement Vom (Bl) {2}

10 September
d. 1622. A Japanese, he was martyred in the 'Great Martyrdom' at Nagasaki with his three-year-old son, Bl Anthony Vom and Charles Spinola and Comps. Cf. **Japan, Martyrs of** and **Great Martyrdom at Nagasaki**.

Clementina Nengapeta Anuarite (Bl) {2}

1 December
1941–64. She was born near Isiro in northeastern Belgian Congo (now Congo-Kinshasa) to an animist family but was baptized in 1943, went in 1953 to the school run by the Sisters of the Holy Family at the Bafwabaka mission and joined them as a sacristan and cook. After the independence of the Congo, there was civil war, and the Simba faction seized the mission at the end of 1964. Thirty-four of the native sisters were rounded up and taken to Isiro to provide sexual relief for the soldiers, and Clementina was chosen by the commandant. She resisted on the grounds of her consecration, and he beat her to death. She was beatified as a virgin martyr in 1985.

Cleonicus and Eutropius (SS) {2, 4}

3 March
Early C4th. They were martyred at Amasea in Pontus (Asia Minor, the south coast of the Black Sea) in the reign of Maximian.

References to their having been soldiers and to a companion Basiliscus have been deleted from the Roman Martyrology.

Cleophas (St) {2, 4}

25 September
C1st. He was one of the two disciples who met Christ on the road to Emmaus (Luke 24). That is all that is known about him, but the old Roman Martyrology stated that he was martyred by the Jews in his house at Emmaus. He has been identified with Alphaeus, the father of St James the Less, and Hegesippus stated that he was a brother of St Joseph. Both of these suppositions lack foundation.

Cletus, Pope (St) {2, 3}

26 April
C1st. Allegedly the second successor of St Peter as pope (according to St Irenaeus), he is identical to St Anacletus. (The latter originated from the two versions of the name in the papal lists being taken to be different people.) His cultus was suppressed in 1969, but he is mentioned in the Roman canon of the Mass.

(Clicerius of Milan) *(St)* *{4 –deleted}*

20 September
d. ?438. Nothing is known about this alleged bishop of Milan (Italy).

Clinius (St) {2, 4}

30 March
d. p1030 Allegedly a Greek and a monk of Montecassino (Italy), he became the superior of the daughter house of St Peter in a forest near Pontecorvo.

Clodoald (Cloud) (St) {2, 4}

7 September
d. 560. A grandson of King Clovis, he was educated by St Clotilde, but he fled to Provence when his two brothers were murdered and became a hermit. He eventually became the abbot-founder of the abbey named after him near Paris (France).

Clodulf (Clou) of Metz (St) {2, 4}

8 June
d. c.660. He succeeded his father St Arnulf as bishop of Metz (France) in ?656. He was allegedly bishop for forty years, but the evidence is against this.

Cloelia Barbieri (St) {2}

13 July
1847–70. From near Bologna (Italy), she lost her father early in life and had a pious but poverty-stricken childhood. Despite having little education she taught the basics to the local poor children and also nursed, attracting several poor young women as helpers. When she was twenty-one, she started the 'Minim Sisters of Our Lady of Sorrows' with four of them under the patronage of St Francis of Paola. She died two years later of tuberculosis as a result of her being malnourished as a child, and was canonized in 1989.

Clotilde (St) {2, 4}

3 June
?474–545. Born at Lyons (France), she was a daughter of the king of Burgundy and married Clovis, the king of the Franks. She was instrumental in his conversion to Catholicism in 496, which event was of the first importance for the future of the church in the West. She was widowed in 511, and died by St Martin's tomb at Tours.

Clou cf. **Clodulf**.
Cloud cf. **Clodoald**.
Codratus cf. **Quadratus**.

(Codratus of Corinth and Comps) *(SS)*
{4 –deleted}

10 March
d. ?258. He was listed as martyred at Corinth (Greece) in the reign of Valerian with Dionysius, Cyprian, Anectus, Paul and Crescens. The Byzantine Martyrology lists another sixteen names.

Coemgen cf. **Kevin**.

Cointha (Quinta) (St) {2, 4}

8 February
d. 249. She was a native Egyptian martyred at Alexandria in the reign of Decius, allegedly by being dragged through the city by her feet.

Colan cf. **Gollen**.

Colette Boilet (St) {2}

6 March
1381–1447. From Corbie in Picardy (France), she was a carpenter's daughter who tried her vocation as a Benedictine and then as a Beguine before becoming a hermit at Corbie. Finally she recognized her true vocation as being that of restoring the Poor Clares to their original charism, especially as regards absolute poverty. She was made their superior by the anti-pope at Avignon in 1406 and established her Colettine reform in France, Germany and the Low Countries, founding seventeen new convents. She also helped St Vincent Ferrer in his work against the Great Schism. She died at Ghent and was canonized in 1807. Her attribute is a lamb, and she is depicted as a Poor Clare with bare feet (one of the distinguishing features of her reform).

Colman

This name was extremely popular in the early Irish church. There are ninety-six saints with it in the Donegal Martyrology, two hundred and nine in the Book of Leinster and others

recorded elsewhere. Many of these are apparently duplicates.

Colman of Cloyne (St) {2}

24 November
d. ?606. From Cork (Ireland), when a young man he was the royal bard at the court of Cashel but was baptized in middle age by St Brendan and became a monk and a priest. He preached in Munster, founded the abbey at Cloyne in Co. Cork and became its first bishop. His cultus was approved in 1903 as the principal patron of the diocese of Cloyne.

Colman of Dromore (St) {2}

7 June
C6th. Either from Argyll or Ulster (there are two traditions), he became the abbot-founder and bishop of Dromore in Co. Down (Ireland) and was allegedly the teacher of St Finian of Clonard. His cultus was approved in 1903 as principal patron of the diocese of Dromore.

Colman Macduagh (St) {2}

29 October
d. ?632. A nobleman of Ireland ('Macduagh' means 'Son of Duac'), he was a hermit on Arranmore Island in Co. Donegal and at Burren in Co. Clare before founding the monastery of Kilmacduagh in Co. Galway and becoming its abbot-bishop. He is the principal patron of the diocese.

Colman of Orkney (St) {2}

6 June
d. c.1010. He was a bishop of the Orkney Islands (Scotland) at a period when they belonged to Norway.

Colman (Coloman) of Stockerau (St) {2, 4}

17 July
d. 1012. He was a pilgrim from Ireland or Scotland passing through Austria on his way

to the Holy Land, and because he could not speak German he was seized as a spy, tortured and hanged at Stockerau near Vienna. Then he was honoured as a saint because his body (now at the abbey of Melk) worked miracles. He is a minor patron of Austria, but is no longer listed as a martyr.

Colmoc cf. **Colman of Dromore**.

(Cologne, Martyrs of) *(SS)* *{4 –deleted}*

15 October
Early C4th? They were listed as four hundred martyred at Cologne (Germany) in the reign of Maximian.

Colonia Sufetana, Martyrs of (SS) {2}

30 August
d. 399. The place was a town in Roman Africa, located in what is now central Tunisia. When an order by Emperor Honorius resulted in the destruction of a much venerated statue of Herculius, the pagan inhabitants revolted and indulged in a pogrom of their Christian neighbours. Sixty of them were martyred.

Columba (Columb) *(St)*

17 September
? There are two places in Cornwall (England) named after this saint, who is alleged to have been a young woman martyred by a pagan ruler.

Columba of Cordoba (St) {2, 4}

17 September
d. 853. From Cordoba (Spain), she became a nun at Tábanos, but her monastery was destroyed by the Muslims, and she went back to Cordoba. There she was urged to convert to Islam but reviled Muhammad instead and was beheaded.

Columba Gabriel (Bl) {2}

24 September
1858–1926. A Pole, born in what is now Ivanovo-Frankivsk in the Ukraine, she became a Benedictine nun at Lviv in 1882. Distinguished by her prayer, purity and love of neighbour, she was made abbess in 1897 but had to move to Rome in 1900 in order to escape unwelcome attention. In 1908 she founded the 'Benedictine Sisters of Charity', an active sisterhood which spread through Italy and to Romania and Madagascar. She was beatified in 1993.

Columba Guardagnoli (Bl) {2}

20 May
1467–1501. From Rieti in Umbria (Italy), she became a Dominican tertiary at Perugia, founded the convent of St Catherine there and won the respect of all in the city, including its rulers. She was alleged to have incurred the enmity of Lucrezia Borgia, however. Her cultus was confirmed for Perugia and Rieti in 1627.

Columba (Columcille) of Iona (St) {2}

9 June
d. ?597. The 'Apostle of Scotland' was of the Clan O'Neill and was born at Gartan in Co. Donegal (Ireland). He studied under St Finian at Clonard, became a monk at Glasnevin and founded monasteries at Derry and Durrow. He emigrated with twelve companions to Iona in Scotland in 563, not as a penance (as the story goes) but as part of the Irish settlement of Dalriada (Argyll) which started around 525. Iona became the greatest monastery in north Britain, and for thirty-four years he evangelized the Picts, Strathclyde Britons and Lothian Saxons as well as his fellow Irish settlers ('Scots'), the four races which made up the future kingdom of Scotland. The monastery's

influence extended to Northumbria. His biography was written by St Adamnan, and part of the Book of Psalms which he copied (the 'Cathach') survives.

Columba Kim Hyo-im (St) {1 –group}

26 September
Cf. **Sebastian Nam I-gwan and Comps**.

Columba Marmion (Bl) {2}

3 October
1858–1923. He was born at Dublin (Ireland) of an Irish father and French mother, and initially became a diocesan priest. However, in 1886 he became a monk at the Benedictine abbey of Maredsous in Belgium and helped found the abbey of Keizersberg in Louvain. In 1909 he was elected as abbot of Maredsous and became well known as a spiritual director and retreat giver; his conferences were published and are regarded as spiritual classics. He had to oversee the forced formation of the Maredsous congregation of Benedictines as a result of the disruptions of the First World War. He died in an influenza epidemic and was beatified in 2000.

Columba of Sens (St) {2, 4}

31 December
Early C4th. A Spanish refugee from persecution, with other Spaniards she was martyred at Meaux (France). Her shrine was at Sens before the Huguenots destroyed it. Her acta are not reliable.

Columban (St) {2, 4}

23 November
?543–615. From Leinster (Ireland), he was a monk at Bangor in Co. Down under St Comgall before becoming a wandering missionary with several companions in 580. Passing through England and Brittany, he founded the

great monastery of Luxeuil in Burgundy in 591 and was abbot for twenty years. His extremely austere rule there became very influential among the rural Frankish nobility, but started to be mitigated soon after his death by insertions from the Benedictine rule. He offended the Frankish court by outspoken criticism of its morals and the local church hierarchy by his insistence on the Celtic observance in his houses, and he was forced into exile in 610. In ?612 he founded the monastery of Bobbio in Lombardy (Italy), where he died. He has left several writings.

Comgall (St) {2}

10 May
d. ?622. An Ulsterman, he became a monk at Clonenagh under St Fintan and founded the great monastery of Bangor in Co. Down (Ireland) in ?555. He imposed a severe rule, but the house became a source of many missionary monks such as St Columban. He seems to have travelled to Scotland, Wales and Cornwall, but he died at Bangor. His cultus was confirmed in 1903.

Comgan of Loch Alsh (St) {2}

13 October
C8th. An Irish prince who was a brother of St Kentigern, he emigrated to Scotland with his nephew St Fillan and they became monks on Loch Alsh in Ross. He was buried on Iona.

Compiègne, Carmelite Martyrs of (BB) {2}

17 July
d. 1794. The Carmel at Compiègne was established in 1641, but it was suppressed in 1790 after the French Revolution and the sisters were forced to disperse and live in the town. They tried to maintain their common life as far as possible, however, and this was charged against them by the local Jacobins. Sixteen of them were taken to Paris, tried and

guillotined. They were the superior, Teresa-of-St-Augustine Lidoine, twelve choir sisters, a novice and two externs (the Soiron sisters, Teresa and Catherine). They were beatified in 1906. Cf. **French Revolution, Martyrs of**.

Conald cf. **Chuniald**.

(Concessa) *(St) {4 –deleted}*

8 April
? She was a martyr venerated at Carthage (Roman Africa).

Congar cf. **Cungar**.

Conleth (St) {2}

3 May
d. c.520. A hermit at Oldconnell in Co. Kildare (Ireland), he allegedly knew St Brigid and became spiritual director of her nunnery at Kildare. He was eventually made its first bishop and was known as a skilled metalworker, copyist and illuminator. He is the principal patron of the diocese of Kildare.

(Conon, Father and Son) *(SS) {4 –deleted}*

29 May
d. 275. They were allegedly tortured to death at Iconium (Asia Minor, now Konya in Turkey) in the reign of Aurelian. Their relics are at Naples. They are unknown in the East.

Conon the Gardener (St) {2, 4}

5 March
d. c.250. His story is that he was from Nazareth in the Holy Land and was a gardener at Mandona in Pamphylia (Asia Minor) before being martyred in the reign of Decius. He was forced to run before a chariot after having nails hammered into the soles of his feet. The old Roman Martyrology ascribed him to Cyprus in error.

Conon of Nesi (St) {2}

28 March
d. 1236. From Nesi near Messina in Sicily, as a young man he went on pilgrimage. On his return he found his parents had died, and so he gave away his property and became a Byzantine-rite hermit.

Conor O'Devany and Comp (BB) {2}

1 February
d. 1611. He was the Franciscan bishop of Down and Conor (Ireland) and was hanged at Dublin with Bl Patrick O'Loughlan, a fellow Franciscan priest. They were beatified as martyrs in 1992. Cf. **Ireland, Martyrs of**.

Conrad of Bavaria (Bl) {2}

14 February
?1105–54. The son of a duke of Bavaria (Germany), he studied at Cologne but became a Cistercian monk at Morimond before transferring to Clairvaux under St Bernard. He went to the Holy Land to be a hermit, but died at Modugno in Apulia (Italy) on his way back to visit St Bernard on his deathbed. His cultus was confirmed for Molfetta in 1832.

Conrad-of-Parzheim Birndorfer (St) {2}

21 April
1818–91. From a peasant family at Parzheim in Bavaria (Germany), he became a Capuchin lay brother in 1849 and spent over forty years as doorkeeper at his friary at Altötting. He had the charism of prophecy and discernment of consciences, and was famous for the charitable care he took of callers. He was canonized in 1934.

Conrad-of-Piacenza Confalonieri (St) {2}

19 February
1290–1354. A nobleman of Piacenza (Italy), while out hunting he started a forest fire for which a poor man was blamed and executed. In

reparation he gave away his possessions, let his wife join the Poor Clares and became a hermit and a Franciscan tertiary. Initially living near Piacenza, he ended up at a place called Neto in Sicily where he lived for thirty years.

Conrad of Constance (St) {2, 4}

26 November
d. 975. A nobleman, he became bishop of Constance (Germany) in 934. He managed to go on pilgrimage to the Holy Land three times and to avoid involvement in secular politics, an unusual feat for a bishop in the Ottonian Empire. He was canonized in 1123.

Conrad of Offida (Bl) {2}

14 December
?1237–1306. From Offida near Ascoli Piceno (Italy), he joined the Franciscans in 1251, became a hermit near Ancona and served as priest in that town. He was sympathetic to the eremitic and spiritual aspects of the Franciscan charism. He died at Bastia in Umbria while preaching and his cultus was confirmed for the Franciscans in 1817.

Conrad O'Rourke (Bl) {2}

13 August
Cf. **Patrick O'Healy and Comp**.

(Consortia) *(St)* *{4 –deleted}*

22 June
d. 570? Her story is that she founded a nunnery which had been endowed by the Frankish king Clotaire in return for her having miraculously healed his daughter. She was venerated at Cluny (France) but nothing is known for certain about her.

Constabilis (St) {2}

17 February
?1060–1124. From Lucania, he became a child-oblate and monk at the Benedictine abbey of Cava near Salerno (Italy) with St Leo as his abbot. In 1122 he became abbot himself and allegedly founded the town of Castelabbate (of which he is the patron). His cultus was confirmed in 1893.

(Constantine of Carthage) (St) *{4 –deleted}*

11 March
? The old Roman Martyrology lists him as a 'confessor at Carthage (Roman Africa)', which implies that he witnessed to the faith in a persecution and survived.

Constantine of Cornwall *(St)*

9 March
C6th? A village near Falmouth in Cornwall (England) and an island near Padstow are named after this alleged Cornish king who became a hermit. His story is unhistorical.

Constantine of Gap (St) {2, 4}

12 April
d. 529. He was the first bishop of Gap (France).

Constantine II of Scotland, King (St) {2}

11 March
d. 874. He died fighting pagan Danish invaders, was buried at Iona and is listed as a martyr.

Constantinople (Martyrs of) {2, 4}

The Roman Martyrology lists four anonymous groups of martyrs at Constantinople:

30 March
Mid C4th. The Orthodox who were tortured and killed in the reign of the Arian Emperor Constantius on the orders of the patriarch Macedonius.

8 February
d. 485. The community of the Dion monastery, which was massacred during the Acacian schism for delivering the notice of excommunication to Patriarch Acacius.

9 August

d. ?729. When Emperor Leo III instituted his iconoclast policy at Constantinople, one of its first public manifestations was the removal and destruction of the great icon of Christ over the Bronze Gate of the imperial palace. The soldier sent to accomplish this was lynched by a group of about ten citizens who were seized and executed either at once or eight months later. The Roman Martyrology does not give their names, which were: Julian, Marcian, Alexis, Demetrius, James, John, Leontius, Marcella, Peter and Photius.

8 July

Mid C9th. The Abrahamite monks who were killed in the reign of the iconoclast emperor Theophilus for defending the validity of icons.

Constantius of Ancona (St) {2, 4}

23 September

C5th. He was the sacristan at St Stephen's Church in Ancona (Italy), where his veneration is still popular.

Constantius of Aquino (St) {2, 4}

1 September

d. c.570. Bishop of Aquino (Italy), he is mentioned with approbation by St Gregory the Great.

Constantius Bernocchi (Bl) {2}

25 February

1410–81. From Fabriano in the Marches (Italy), he became a Dominican at Ascoli when aged fifteen and went on to teach theology at Bologna and Florence. He served as prior of various friaries, including that of Ascoli where he died. His cultus was confirmed for Ascoli in 1811.

Constantius of Perugia and Comps (SS) {2, 4}

29 January

C3rd. He was a bishop of Perugia (Italy). The Roman Martyrology no longer refers to

him as having been martyred with several companions.

(Constantius of Rome) (St) {4 –deleted}

30 November

C5th. He is listed in the old Roman Martyrology as a priest of Rome who opposed the Pelagians and was persecuted by them.

Contardus d'Este (St) {2}

16 April

d. 1249. A nobleman of Ferrara (Italy), he set out on a pilgrimage to Compostella but only got as far as Broni near Tortona where he died destitute.

Contardus Ferrini (Bl) {2}

17 October

1859–1902. From Milan (Italy), he took degrees in civil and canon law at Pavia University before teaching at Messina, Mutina and finally again at Pavia. He was a Franciscan tertiary, a member of the Society of St Vincent de Paul, a friend of the future Pope Pius XI and a model of a Catholic university professor. He died at Suna on Lake Maggiore and was beatified in 1947.

Conus of Cardossa (St) {2}

3 June

C13th. From Diano in Lucania (Italy), he became a Benedictine monk at Cardossa nearby. His relics were enshrined at Diano, and his cultus was confirmed for there in 1871.

Convoyo (St) {2}

5 January

d. 868. From Brittany (France), he was archdeacon of Vannes but then became a hermit, a monk at Glanfeuil and finally the abbot-founder of St Saviour's at Redon. He was driven from his monastery by the Norse and died in exile. His cultus was confirmed for Redon in 1866.

Corbinian (St) {2, 4}

8 September
d. 725. A Frank from near Fontainebleu (France), he became a hermit and then went to Rome in 709. There he was made a missionary bishop for Bavaria (Germany) by the pope in 717, and established himself at Freising. He founded the abbey of Obermais, where he died.

(Cordula) (St) {4 –deleted}

22 October
Her story is part of the fictional cycle of legends associated with St Ursula, and her cultus was suppressed in 1969.

(Corebus) (St) {4 –deleted}

18 April
C2nd? His story is that he was a prefect at Messina (Sicily) who was converted by St Eleutherius and martyred in the reign of Hadrian. The acta of St Eleutherius are fiction, however, and St Corebus probably never existed.

Corentin (St) {2}

12 December
C7–8th. A Cornish hermit, he became a bishop in Brittany (France), perhaps at Quimper where he is venerated. The village of Cury in the Lizard in Cornwall (England) is named after him.

(Corfu, Martyrs of) (SS) {4 –deleted}

29 April
C1st? The 'Seven Robbers' were allegedly converted by St Jason (cf. Acts 17:5) and martyred on the island of Corfu. The Byzantine Martyrology lists them as Euphrasius, Faustian, Inischolus, Januarius, Mannonius, Massalius and Saturninus.

Cormac McCullinan (St)

14 September
d. 908. He was apparently first bishop of Cashel in Co. Tipperary (Ireland) and was chosen as king of Munster in 902. He was killed in battle. The 'Psalter of Cashel', compiled by him, still exists, and his name is still used for boys.

Cornelius, Pope (St) {1, 3}

16 September
d. 253. He became pope in 251 after a fourteen-month vacancy caused by the Decian persecution. One of his most serious problems concerned the re-admission to communion of those who had apostatized during that persecution, and he advocated a lenient policy towards these. A rigorist faction denied that such people could be forgiven, however, and it elected Novatian as anti-pope. Cornelius's policy prevailed, helped by the support of such as St Cyprian of Carthage, and Novatian was excommunicated (his sect, however, survived for a long time). The persecution was revived and St Cornelius was exiled to Civita Vecchia where he died. St Cyprian described him as a martyr. His tomb in Rome is extant, and he is mentioned in the Roman canon of the Mass. His attribute is a cow or a cow's horn (a pun on his name).

Cornelius of Caesarea (St) {2, 4}

20 October
C1st. He was the centurion baptized by St Peter at Caesarea in the Holy Land (Acts 10), and was traditionally regarded as the first bishop of that city.

Cornelius van Wijk (St) {2}

9 July
d. 1572. From Wijk bij Duurstede near Utrecht (Netherlands), he became a Franciscan at

Gorinchem and was hanged at Briel as one of the **Gorinchem** martyrs (q.v.).

Cosconius, Zeno and Melanippus (SS) {2}

18 January
C3rd–4th. They were martyred at Nicaea (now Iznik) in northwestern Asia Minor.

Cosmas and Damian (SS) {1, 3}

26 September
Early C4th. Their story is that they were Arab brothers who practised medicine and who did not charge for their services (hence their nickname of 'Anargyrioi', or 'Money-less', in the East). According to tradition they were martyred at Cyrrhus near Antioch (Syria) in the reign of Diocletian, and their relics were taken to Rome. Their cultus was extremely popular in the West in the Middle Ages, and they are mentioned in the Roman canon of the Mass. Their attribute is an item of medical equipment (e.g. a mortar and pestle). Their acta are legendary, and assert that they were martyred with their mother Theodora and their brothers Anthimus, Euprepius and Leontius. These have been deleted from the Roman Martyrology.

Cosmas the Charcoal-burner cf. **Gomidas**.

Cosmas Shizaburo (Bl) {2 –add}

6 October
Cf. **John Hashimoto Tahyōe and Comps**.

Cosmas Takeya (St) {1 –group}

6 February
d. 1597. A Japanese Franciscan tertiary, he was an interpreter for the Franciscan missionaries and was crucified at Nagasaki with St Paul Miki and Comps. Cf. **Japan, Martyrs of**.

Cosmas Takeya Sozaburo (Bl) {2}

18 November
d. 1619. A Korean, he was taken to Japan as a prisoner of war. While there he joined the Confraternity of the Holy Rosary and sheltered Bl John of St Dominic, for which he was burnt at Nagasaki with BB Leonard Kimura and Comps. Cf. **Japan, Martyrs of**.

(Cottidus, Eugene and Comps) (SS) {4 –deleted}

6 September
? They are listed as having been martyred in Cappadocia (Asia Minor), Cottidus being a deacon, but nothing is known of them.

(Craton and Comps) (SS) {4 –deleted}

25 February
C3rd? Allegedly a philosopher and rhetorician from Athens, he was teaching in Rome when he was converted by St Valentine of Terni and martyred with his family in the reign of Aurelian.

(Crescens) (St) {4 –deleted}

27 June
C1st. He was a disciple of St Paul, who referred to him as having gone to Galatia in Asia Minor (2 Tim. 4:10). Thus he is traditionally the first bishop of the Galatians and was martyred there in the reign of Trajan. There are other traditions, seriously confused and unreliable, associating him with Vienne in France and Mainz in Germany (apparently as a result of confusing Galatia with Gaul).

Crescens of Myra (St) {2, 4}

15 April
? He was burnt at the stake at Myra in Lycia (Asia Minor).

(Crescens of Rome and Comps) *(SS)* *{4 –deleted}*

28 May

C3rd? He was listed as tortured and burnt at Rome with Dioscorides and Paul. The old Roman Martyrology added Helladius, who was not of the group.

Crescentia Hoss cf. **Mary-Crescentia Hoss.**

(Crescentian, Victor, Rosula and Generalis) *(SS)* *{4 –deleted}*

14 September

d. ?258. They are alleged to have been martyred in Carthage (Roman Africa) with St Cyprian.

(Crescentian of Rome) *(St)* *{4 –deleted}*

24 November

d. 309. He was allegedly racked in the presence of SS Cyriac, Largus and Smagagdus at Rome, dying as a result in the reign of Maxentius.

(Crescentian of Saldo) *(St)* *{4 –deleted}*

1 June

d. ?287. He was allegedly a soldier beheaded at Saldo in Umbria (Italy), but he may not have existed.

(Crescentian of Sassari) *(St)* *{4 –deleted}*

31 May

C2nd? He was allegedly martyred at Sassari (Sardinia) in the reign of Hadrian, being associated with SS Gabinus and Crispulus. His veneration is still popular there.

(Crescentiana) *(St)* *{4 –deleted}*

5 May

C5th? A church in Rome was dedicated to her as a martyr by the end of the C5th, but nothing else is known.

(Crescentius) *(St)* *{4 –deleted}*

14 September

d. c.300. An eleven-year-old son of St Euthymius, he fled with his father to Perugia (Italy) during the persecution ordered by Diocletian but was brought back to Rome when orphaned to be tortured and beheaded.

(Crescentius of Florence) *(St)* *{4 –deleted}*

19 April

End C4th. He was a subdeacon to St Zenobius at Florence (Italy) and a disciple of St Ambrose.

Crispin and Crispinian (SS) {2, 4}

25 October

d. ?285. Brothers who were shoemakers, they were allegedly beheaded at Soissons (France) in the reign of Diocletian but were probably Roman martyrs whose relics were transferred. Their veneration was popular during the Middle Ages (one legend had them living at Faversham in Kent, England) but has faded away. They were patrons of shoemakers, and their attributes are shoes or cobbling tools.

Crispin of Ecija (St) {2, 4}

20 November

C3rd. A bishop of Ecija in Andalusia (Spain), he was martyred by beheading.

Crispin-of-Viterbo Fioretti (St) {2}

19 May

1668–1750. From Viterbo (Italy), he became a Capuchin lay brother there and worked as a cook. Later he was at Tolfa, then at Rome and Albano and finally he died at Rome where his cultus is extremely popular. He had great spiritual wisdom, was heroic in nursing sick people and called himself the 'Capuchin's donkey'. He was canonized in 1982.

Crispin of Pavia (St) {2, 4}

7 January
d. 467. He was bishop during the pontificate of St Leo the Great, and signed the acts of the Council of Milan in 451.

Crispina (St) {2, 4}

5 December
d. 304. A married woman with several children from Thagura in Numidia (Roman Africa), she refused to offer pagan sacrifice and was tortured and beheaded in the reign of Diocletian. Her acta are genuine, and St Augustine preached two sermons about her.

(Crispulus and Restitutus) *(SS)* *{4 –deleted}*

10 June
C1st? They were possibly martyred at Rome in the reign of Nero. The old Roman Martyrology depends on Rabanus Maurus in assigning them to Spain, however.

(Crispus and Gaius) *(SS)* *{4 –deleted}*

4 October
C1st. They were the only ones that St Paul baptized at Corinth (1 Cor. 1:14), Crispus being ruler of the synagogue (Acts 18:8) and Gaius being probably referred to by St Paul as 'my host' (Rom. 16:23) and by St John as 'dearly beloved' in his third letter. Traditionally they became bishops of Aegina and Thessalonica (Greece), respectively, and were martyred.

St Cross
Churches with this dedication in England are commemorating not a saint but the cross of Christ.

Cronidas, Leontius and Serapion (SS) {2}

12 September
Early C3rd. During the reign of the Emperor Maximinus, they were martyred at Alexandria (Egypt) by being thrown into the sea.

Cuby cf. **Cybi**.

Cucuphas (Cugat, Guinefort) (St) {2, 4}

25 July
Early C4th?. A Punic nobleman from Scillis in Roman Africa, he went to Spain and was martyred near Barcelona. On the site arose the abbey of St Cugat del Valles, and he became one of the most popular of the Spanish martyrs. Prudentius wrote some poetry in his honour.

Cunegund the Empress (St) {2}

3 March
d. 1039. She was married to Emperor St Henry II in 999, and helped to found the new diocese of Bamburg and the nunnery of Kaufungen. A year after she was widowed she entered the latter as a nun, in 1025. It has been claimed that the marriage was not consummated (there were no children), and she has been liturgically celebrated as a virgin as a result.

Cunegund (Kinga) of Poland (St) {2}

24 July
d. 1293. A niece of St Elizabeth of Hungary and great-niece of St Hedwig, she was married to Boleslav V, prince of Cracow (Poland) and allegedly lived with him in celibacy. The couple tried hard to alleviate the sufferings caused by the Mongol incursions, and she died as a Franciscan tertiary in the nunnery she had founded at Sandecz. Her cultus was confirmed in 1690, and she is one of the patrons of Poland.

Cungar (Cumgar, Cyngar, Congar, Docuinus, Doguinus) (St) {2}

7 November
C6th. A Celtic monk, he founded a monastery at Congresbury in Somerset (England) and was buried there (the name means 'Cumgar's tomb'). His C12th biography is unreliable and

confuses him with other Welsh saints having similar names.

Cunibert of Cologne (St) {2, 4}

12 November
d. ?663. A Frankish courtier from Moselle (France), he became archdeacon of Trier (Germany) and then archbishop of Cologne in 623. He was regent of Frankish Austrasia while King St Sigebert III was a minor and founded many churches and monasteries. His shrine is at Cologne. His extant medieval biographies are unreliable.

(Curcodomus) *(St)* *{4 –deleted}*

4 May
C3rd? He was allegedly a Roman deacon who became a helper of St Peregrinus, first bishop of Auxerre (France).

Curé d'Ars cf. **John-Mary Vianney**.
Curitan cf. **Boniface**.

(Curonotus of Iconium) *(St)* *{4 –deleted}*

12 September
Mid C3rd? He was listed as a bishop of Iconium (Asia Minor, now Konya in Turkey), martyred in the reign of Valerian.

Cury cf. **Corentin**.

Cuthbert of Lindisfarne (St) {2}

20 March
d. 687. Possibly of Saxon parents (this is uncertain), he was a shepherd until he became a monk at Melrose (Scotland) in 651, which abbey followed Celtic traditions. He was guest-master at Ripon (England) until that monastery converted to Roman practices, upon which he returned to Melrose and became prior there and then at Lindisfarne. He accepted the verdict of the Synod of Whitby in 664 and helped convert his monastery to Roman customs; however, he went to Farne as a hermit in 676. In 684 he was made bishop of Lindisfarne, but resigned and returned to Farne just before he died. His relics were eventually enshrined at Durham in 995 and became the most popular focus of pilgrimage in the North of England in the Middle Ages. They were left in situ at the Reformation. He is depicted holding the severed head of St Oswald and accompanied by the swans and otters that he befriended as a hermit.

Cuthbert Mayne (St) {2}

30 November
1544–77. From near Barnstaple in Devon (England), his family was Protestant, and he became an Anglican minister, but he converted while studying at Oxford and was eventually ordained at Douai. In 1575 he went to Cornwall but was captured within a year and executed at Launceston. The protomartyr of the English seminaries, he was canonized in 1970. Cf. **England, Martyrs of**.

Cuthman (St)

8 February
C9th. He was a hermit at Steyning in Sussex (England), and when the church there was granted to the French abbey of Fécamp they appropriated his relics. He remained the patron of the town until the Dissolution, and is still liturgically celebrated in the local diocese. He is not in the Roman Martyrology.

Cybar cf. **Eparchius**.

Cybi (Cuby) (St)

8 November
C6th. He was abbot-founder of a monastery at Caer-gybi (Holyhead) on Anglesey (Wales). The popularity of his ancient veneration is evidenced by churches dedicated to him at

Llangibby (Gwent), Llangybi (Gwynedd) and at Tregony, Landulph and Cuby in Cornwall. The legends about him are unreliable.

Cynderyn cf. **Kentigern**.
Cynfarch cf. **Kingsmark**.

(Cyprian and Justina) *(SS)* *{4 –deleted}*

26 September
d. ?303. The legend is that Cyprian was a pagan astrologer who tried to seduce Justina, a Christian maiden, and was converted by her instead, both of them being beheaded at Nicomedia (Asia Minor) in the reign of Diocletian. The story is fictional, and the cultus was suppressed in 1969.

Cyprian of Calamitense (St) {2}

20 November
d. ?1190. He was abbot of the Byzantine-rite monastery of Calamitense in Calabria (Italy). He kept the rules and customs of Eastern monasticism with fidelity, was strict with himself but was generous to poor people and was a ready counsellor.

Cyprian of Carthage (St) {1, 3}

16 September
c.200–58. Thascius Cecilianus Cyprianus was a Roman African lawyer who became a Christian in ?245 and bishop of Carthage in 248. He was one of the earliest Latin church fathers, writing numerous theological treatises and letters. His support for the lenient policy of Pope St Cornelius in dealing with the lapsed was decisive against the rigorist party led by Novatian, but he erred in teaching that the baptism of heretics is invalid. He went into hiding during the persecution of Decius but was seized and martyred in the reign of Valerian. His acta are genuine, and he is mentioned in the Roman canon of the Mass.

Cyprian Iwene Tansi (Bl) {2}

20 January
1903–64. He was an Igbo from a farming family of the Aguleri region near Onitsha in Nigeria. He was brought up as an animist but was baptized when aged nine and went on to be ordained as the second indigenous priest of the Onitsha diocese in 1937. He was appointed the parish priest of Dunukofia, where his zeal and example led to a major increase in vocations. In response to his bishop's wish that a contemplative monastery be founded in his diocese, he became a Trappist Cistercian at Mount St Bernard near Leicester (England) in 1950. He was shocked when the decision was taken to make the foundation in Cameroon instead in 1963, but accepted this and was about to become novice-master there when he died at Leicester of an aneurysm. He was beatified in 1998.

Cyprian Subran (St) {2, 4}

9 December
C6th. Originally a monk at Périgueux in the Dordogne (France), he became a hermit nearby at the place where the village of Saint-Cyprien is now situated.

Cyprian of Toulon (St) {2}

3 October
d. p543. A monk at St Victor's Abbey at Marseilles (France), he was a disciple of St Caesarius of Arles and wrote his biography. He became bishop of Toulon in 516 and vigorously opposed the local semi-Pelagians.

Cyprilla (St) {2}

5 July
Early C4th. Her story is that, during the persecution of Diocletian, she was arrested and had burning charcoal and incense put in her hand that was being held over a pagan altar. She let

it burn out in her hand rather than let it drop onto the altar. Then she was dismembered and beheaded.

Cyr cf. **Quiricus and Julitta**.

(Cyrenia and Juliana) *(SS)* *{4 –deleted}*

1 November
d. 306. They were listed as burnt at Tarsus in Cilicia (Asia Minor) in the reign of Maximian.

Cyriac, Cyriaca
These names are also spelt Quiriacus, Quiriaca; or Kyriacus, Kyriaca; or Kiriacus, Kiriaca; or Dominicus, Dominica. The last pair are the Latin equivalents.

(Cyriac and Apollinaris) *(SS)* *{4 –deleted}*

21 June
? They are listed as Roman African martyrs, but nothing else is known.

Cyriac and Archelaus (SS) {2, 4}

23 August
? They were martyred at Ostia at the mouth of the Tiber (Rome). The old Roman Martyrology alleged that they were a bishop and deacon, and added a priest Maximus. These details have been deleted.

Cyriac and Claudian (SS) {2}

24 October
? They were martyred at Hierapolis in Phrygia (Asia Minor).

Cyriac, Largus and Comps (SS) {2, 3}

8 August
Early C4th. They were martyred and buried on the Ostian Way outside Rome, the companions being Crescentian, Memmia, Juliana and Smaragdus. The acta are unreliable, and nothing else is known. There was a church in Rome dedicated to St Cyriac, but his relics were transferred to S. Maria in Via Lata when it was demolished. The cultus was confined to particular calendars in 1969.

Cyriac and Paula (SS) {2, 4}

18 June
Early C4th. They were stoned to death at Malaga (Spain) in the reign of Diocletian.

(Cyriac, Paulillus and Comps) *(SS)* *{4 –deleted}*

19 December
Early C4th? They were allegedly martyred at Nicomedia (Asia Minor) in the reign of Diocletian. Listed also are Secundus, Anastasius and Sindimius. Nothing else is known.

(Cyriac of Ancona) *(St)* *{4 –deleted}*

4 May
? The unreliable acta of this patron of Ancona (Italy) describe him as a bishop of Jerusalem martyred in the reign of Julian. Jerusalem had no bishop of this name, so (if he existed) he was perhaps a bishop of Ancona martyred while on a pilgrimage in the Holy Land.

Cyriac of Bonvicini (St) {2}

19 September
d. 1030. He was abbot of a monastery at Bonvicini near Cosenza in Calabria (Italy), and is enshrined at the village now there.

Cyriac-Elias-of-the-Holy-Family Chavarra (St) {2}

3 January
1805–71. Born near Changanachary in Kerala (India), he was ordained in the Malabar rite in 1829 and started a religious foundation at Mannanam in 1831. This prospered, its work being preaching, spiritual missions and teaching in seminaries, and six other houses for men and one for women were also opened. There

was a schism in the Malabar rite when an Assyrian bishop arrived in the year 186, and Cyriac was made vicar-apostolic to counter this. He purified the Malabar liturgy as well as writing much. He was canonized in 2014.

Cyriac the Great (St) {2, 4}

29 September
d. 557. One of the famous monks of the Judaean Desert, as a teenager he went from Corinth to the Holy Land and became a monk under SS Euthymius and Gerasimus. During his long life (he died a centenarian) he opposed the Origenist errors popular among monks in the Holy Land at the time. His stone-built cell survives in the desert at Sousakim where he spent the latter years of his life as the only hermit able to survive in such a barren place, the driest in the Holy Land (just west of the southern part of the Dead Sea). His biography was written by Cyril of Scythopolis.

(Cyriac of Nicomedia and Comps) (SS) {4 –deleted}

7 April
? These eleven are listed as having been martyred at Nicomedia (Asia Minor).

Cyriac-Mary Sancha y Hervás (Bl) {2 –add}

26 February
1833–1909. From Quintana del Vidio, Spain, he was educated at Salamanca before becoming a diocesan priest of Osma in 1858. From 1862 to 1876 he was rector of the seminary at Santiago de Cuba (in Cuba), and founded the Institute of the Religious of Charity of Cardinal Sancha in 1869 while on the island. In 1876 he was consecrated auxiliary bishop of Toledo, and was bishop in turn of Ávila, Madrid, Valencia and finally Toledo which is the primatial see of Spain. He was made a cardinal in 1894. He died at Toledo and was beatified in 2009.

Cyriaca of Nicomedia (SS) {2, 4}

6 July
d. c.300. She was martyred at Nicomedia (Asia Minor) in the reign of Diocletian, and has her shrine at Tropea in Calabria (Italy). Her five virgin companions have been deleted from the Roman Martyrology.

Cyriaca (Dominica) of Rome (St) {2, 4}

21 August
d. c.300. She is described in the legend of St Laurence as a wealthy Roman widow who used to shelter persecuted Christians and whose house he used when distributing alms. It is now thought that she was of later date. She donated her family cemetery around the site of the basilica of St Laurence outside the Walls at Rome to the church, and her residence is traditionally marked by the church of S. Maria in Domnica on the Esquiline. There is an underground chapel and a catacomb at St Laurence named after her.

(Cyril, Aquila and Comps) (SS) {4 –deleted}

1 August
? The companions were Peter, Domitian, Rufus and Menander. Cyril seems to have been a bishop of Tomi (on the Black Sea coast of Romania), Peter was a duplicate of the apostle and Rufus was a martyr of Rome. The group was erroneously associated with Philadelphia in Roman Arabia.

Cyril and Methodius (SS) {1, 3}

14 February
d. 869 and ?885, respectively. The 'Apostles of the Slavs' were brothers from Thessalonica, sons of a government official. Constantine was a brilliant student at Constantinople and became a priest and a professor at the university there. Methodius became a provincial governor and ended up in a monastery

on the Bithynian Olympus. In 863 they went to evangelize Moravia, a Slav kingdom (now part of the Czech Republic), for which they translated the Scriptures and liturgical texts into Slavonic. This caused opposition from the local Latin clergy so they went to Rome for approval. There Constantine became a monk with the name Cyril and quickly died. Methodius got the necessary approval and returned to Moravia as bishop and legate, but continued to be opposed by the German clergy for his remaining sixteen years. His work was initially successful but not lasting in Moravia. It bore greater fruit in the other Slavic lands, and the brothers were declared co-patrons of Europe with St Benedict in 1980. They are liturgically celebrated on the anniversary of St Cyril; St Methodius died on 6 April.

(Cyril, Rogatus and Comps) (SS) *{4 –deleted}*.

8 March
? They are listed as Roman African martyrs with Cyril as a bishop, but nothing is known. Also listed are Felix, another Rogatus, Beata, Herenia, Felicity, Urban, Silvanus and Mamillus.

Cyril of Alexandria (St) {1, 3}

27 June
?376–444. From Alexandria (Egypt), he was a nephew of Patriarch Theophilus and became patriarch himself in 412. He fought the surviving paganism in Egypt (with violent results) and strongly opposed the Christological teachings of Nestorius, Patriarch of Constantinople. These were condemned at the Council of Ephesus in 431, at which he presided and which marked the height of the Egyptian church's influence. He was a great theologian and one of the greatest Eastern fathers, being venerated as the chief teacher of the Coptic and Ethiopian churches. He was declared a doctor of the Church in 1882.

Cyril of Antioch (St) {2, 4}

22 July
d. ?306. He became patriarch of Antioch (Syria) in 280 and endured the persecution of Diocletian, but seems not to have been a martyr.

Cyril of Axiopolis (SS) {2}

12 May
C3rd? He was martyred with six companions at Axiopolis on the Danube river near Ruse (Bulgaria).

(Cyril of Gortyna) (St) *{4 –deleted}*

9 July
d. 250. He was listed as an elderly bishop of Gortyna in Crete martyred in the reign of Decius.

Cyril of Heliopolis (St) {2, 4}

28 March
d. ?362. A deacon of Heliopolis (Baalbek) in Lebanon, he destroyed some idols there and was disembowelled by the townsfolk as a result in the reign of Julian. The city remained a pagan stronghold for another century.

Cyril of Jerusalem (St) {1, 3}

18 March
?315–86. From near Jerusalem, he became bishop of that city in c.350. He firmly opposed the Arians and spent a total of seventeen years in exile as a result. His fame derives from his set of catechetical lectures given in Lent to those being baptized at Easter, which led to his being declared a doctor of the Church in 1882.

Cyril-Bertrand Sanz Tejedor (St) {2}

9 October
Cf. **Innocent-of-Mary-Immaculate Canoura Arnau and Comps**.

(Cyrilla of Cyrene) *(St)* *{4 –deleted}*

5 July
d. c.300. She was listed as an old widow of Cyrene (Libya) who died under torture in the reign of Diocletian.

(Cyrilla of Rome) *(St)* *{4 –deleted}*

28 October
d. ?269. She was allegedly the daughter of St Tryphonia and features in the legendary acta of St Laurence. Nothing is known about her.

Cyrus and John (SS) {2, 4}

31 January
Early C4th. A physician and a soldier who had met in the desert after fleeing persecution in Alexandria (Egypt), they returned to the city to assist an imprisoned woman and her three daughters and were themselves martyred. Their shrine near Canopus became famous, and they are among the most popular martyrs of the Coptic Church.

(Cyrus of Carthage) *(St)* *{4 –deleted}*

14 July
? When Cardinal Baronius revised the old Roman Martyrology he inserted this otherwise unknown bishop on the basis of a reference in Possidus's biography of St Augustine where the latter is described as giving a sermon on his feast day. 'Cyrus' may simply be a copyist's error for 'Cyprian'.

Cyrus of Constantinople (St) {2}

7 January
d. 714. He was a monk in a monastery near Amastris on the Black Sea coast of Asia Minor when he was consecrated as patriarch of Constantinople in 705. In 712 he was deposed by the usurping Emperor Philippicus, and sent back to his monastery.

D

(Dadas, Casdoe and Gabdelas) *(SS)*
{4 –deleted}

29 September
d. ?368. They were listed as a married noble Persian couple and (probably) their son, who were at the court of Shah Shapur II and were martyred after vicious tortures.

(Dafrosa) *(St) {4 –deleted}*

4 January
? According to the worthless acta of St Bibiana, she was her mother and was martyred at Rome in the reign of Julian. She probably never existed.

Dagan cf. **Decuman**.

Dalmatius Moner (Bl) {2}

2 September
1291–1341. From near Gerona (Spain), he became a Dominican there and led an extremely austere life in the friary, refusing all positions of responsibility. His cultus was confirmed for Gerona in 1721.

(Dalmatius of Pavia) *(St) {4 –deleted}*

5 December
d. 304. He was listed as a bishop of Pavia (Italy) martyred in the reign of Maximian Herculius.

Dalmatius of Rodez (St) {2}

13 November
d. c.580. He became bishop of Rodez (France) in 524 and had to defend his people against persecution by the Arian Visigoths.

Damascus, Martyrs of cf. **Emmanuel Ruiz and Comps**.

Damasus, Pope (St) {1, 3}

11 December
?304–84. Born at Rome of Spanish parents, he became a deacon at the Spanish church of St Laurence there and went on to be elected pope in 366. (The election was violently contested, and there was an anti-pope, Ursicinus.) He effectively opposed heresies such as Arianism and Apollinarianism, revised the Roman liturgy and restored many churches and catacombs, composing famous inscriptions for martyrs' tombs therein. Also he commissioned his friend St Jerome to revise the Latin New Testament, which eventually resulted in the latter producing the Vulgate edition of the Bible.

(Damian) *(SS) {4 –deleted}*

12 February
? There were apparently two obscure martyrs confused in the old Roman Martyrology on this date. The first was a soldier martyred in Roman Africa or at Alexandria, and the second was a Roman whose relics were taken from St Callistus's catacombs to Salamanca (Spain).

Damian Fulcheri (Bl) {2}

26 October
c.1400–84. From Finario near Savona in Liguria (Italy), he became a Dominican there and went on to preach throughout northern Italy. He died at Reggio d'Emilia and his cultus was confirmed for Savona and the Dominicans in 1848.

Damian Ichiyata (Bl) {2 –add}

28 February
Cf. **Paul Uchibori Sakuemon and Comps**.

Damian Nam Myŏng-hyŏg (St) {1 –group}

24 May
Cf. **Augustine Yi Kwang-hŏn and Comps**.

Damian of Pavia (St) {2, 4}

12 April
d. 697. As a priest of Pavia (Italy), he opposed the Monothelites at the synod of Milan in

680, which influenced the third ecumenical council of Constantinople in condemning that heresy. In ?685 he was made bishop, and was a peacemaker between the Lombards and the emperor.

Damian of Sakai (Bl) {2 –add}

19 August
d. 1605. He was a Japanese lay catechist from Sakai, who was martyred at Yamaguchi. He was beatified in 2008. Cf. **Japan, Martyrs of**.

Damian-Joseph de Veuster (St) {2}

15 April
1840–89. Born at Tremelo (Belgium), he followed his brother in becoming a 'Picpus Father' in 1859 and went to Hawaii in 1864 (when it was still an independent country). He was on a mission on the 'Big Island' when the government announced a policy of deporting all lepers to a concentration camp at Kalaupapa on Molokai. He volunteered to join them in 1873, caught leprosy himself and died there sixteen years later. He was canonized in 2009.

Damian Yamichi Tanda (Bl) {2}

10 September
d. 1622. He was a Japanese layman beheaded in the 'Great Martyrdom' at Nagasaki with his five-year-old son, Michael Yamichi, and Charles Spinola and Comps. Cf. **Japan, Martyrs of** and **Great Martyrdom at Nagasaki**.

Danax (St) {2}

16 January
? He was a martyr at Valona, now Vlorë in Albania, and was allegedly a deacon killed while trying to conceal the sacred vessels of his church during a riot or invasion.

Daniel (Deiniol) of Bangor (St) {2}

11 September
d. 584. He founded the monasteries at Bangor in Gwynedd and at Bangor Isycoed in Clwyd (Wales) and allegedly became first bishop of the former place in 516. The cathedral and many Welsh churches are dedicated to him.

Daniel of Belvedere and Comps (SS) {2}

10 October
d. 1227. This group of early Franciscan missionaries was sent to Morocco by Brother Elias in order to convert the Muslims there. Daniel was the leader, having been the provincial superior of Calabria, and the others were Samuel, Angelus, Domnus, Leo, Nicholas and Hugolin. They arrived at Ceuta, preached in public and were initially arrested and imprisoned as insane. Later it was demanded that that they convert to Islam and on their refusal, they were beheaded. They were canonized in 1516.

Daniel Brottier (Bl) {2}

28 February
1876–1936. From La Ferté-Saint-Cyr near Blois (France), he was ordained and joined the 'Congregation of the Holy Spirit and the Immaculate Heart of Mary' at Orly in 1903 in order to become a missionary. His first posting to Senegal ruined his health very quickly, however, and he had to return in 1906. Then he organized home support for the missions, founding the 'Souvenir Africain' periodical and collecting money for the building of Dakar Cathedral. He also started the 'National Union of Combatants' for war veterans and restored a famous orphanage in Paris. He died of typhoid and was beatified in 1984.

Daniel Comboni (St) {2}

10 October
1831–81. Born in Limone sul Garda (Italy) of very poor parents, he became a priest in

Verona and dedicated his life to evangelizing Africa. He went to Khartoum (Sudan) in 1854 as a missionary but returned to Europe in 1864 in order to plead for the missions, in the process founding the 'Verona Fathers' in 1867 and the 'Missionary Sisters of Verona' in 1872. In 1877 he was made vicar-apostolic of Central Africa. He died at Khartoum and was canonized in 2003.

Daniel of Padua (St) {2, 4}

3 January
d. ?304. His story is that he was a convert Jewish deacon who helped St Prosdocimus, the first bishop of Padua (Italy), before being martyred. His alleged relics were found and enshrined in the C11th, and he is now considered to have been a martyr of the early C4th.

(Daniel the Prophet) *(St)* *{4 –deleted}*

21 July
The fourth of the Major Prophets of the Old Testament has been deleted from the Roman Martyrology, because his book was actually written in the C2nd BC, and he is a fictional character.

Daniel the Stylite (St) {2, 4}

11 December
d. 493. From near Samosata on the upper Euphrates (Syria), he started as a monk there but visited St Simeon the Elder on his pillar near Antioch in 452 and resolved to imitate him. This he did near Constantinople, where Emperor Leo I built him a series of pillars on which he lived for thirty-three years until his death. He was forcibly ordained in situ and descended to the ground only once in that time in order to rebuke the Monophysite Emperor Basiliscus. He was the oracle of the whole city.

(Darius, Zosimus, Paul and Secundus) *(SS)* *{4 –deleted}*

19 December
? They were listed as martyred at Nicaea (Asia Minor), but nothing else is known.

Dasius, Zoticus, Gaius and Comps (SS) {2, 4}

21 October
d. 303. Fifteen soldiers, they were martyred at Nicomedia (Asia Minor) in the reign of Diocletian.

Dasius of Dorostorum (St) {2, 4}

20 November
Early C4th? A Roman soldier, he refused to take part in the pagan celebration of Saturnalia and was martyred at Dorostorum in Moesia (Bulgaria). His relics are at Ancona (Italy), and his acta might have been derived from genuine sources.

(Dathus) *(St)* *{4 –deleted}*

3 July
d. 190. According to his legend he became bishop of Ravenna (Italy) in the reign of Commudus after the miraculous appearance of a dove over his head. His existence is doubtful.

(Datius, Reatrus and Comps) *(SS)* *{4 –deleted}*

27 January
Late C5th? They were listed as martyred in Roman Africa by the Arian Vandals.

Datius of Milan (St) {2, 4}

14 January
d. 552. A friend of Cassiodorus, he became bishop of Milan (Italy) after 530 but fled to Constantinople after his diocese was overrun by the Arian Ostrogoths. There he died after defending Pope Vigilius in the 'Three Chapters' controversy.

(Datvius, Julian, Vincent and Comps) (SS)
{4 –deleted}

27 January
? They were listed as martyred in Roman Africa.

David Galvan Bermúdez (St) {1 –group}

30 January
d. 1915. He was a priest of Guadalajara in Mexico, and after the revolution of 1911 caused offence by insisting on the sanctity of marriage. As a result he was abducted on the orders of army officers and shot without trial. Cf. **Mexico, Martyrs of**.

David Gunston (Bl) {2}

12 July
d. 1541. A son of Vice-Admiral Gunston (or Gonson), he was a knight of St John of Jerusalem at Clerkenwell (London) and was hanged, drawn and quartered at Southwark for refusing to accept King Henry VIII's spiritual supremacy. He was beatified in 1929. Cf. **England, Martyrs of**.

David of Himmerod (Bl) {2}

11 December
d. 1179. From Florence (Italy), he became a Cistercian monk at Clairvaux under St Bernard in 1131 and was sent to Germany in 1134 to found the abbey of Himmerod near Trier.

David of Menevia (St) {2}

1 March
d. c.600. The fame of the patron saint of Wales rests entirely on the polemical biography of Rhygyfarch, bishop of St David's, which was written in c.1090. It sets out to defend the independence of his diocese against the claims of Canterbury and is unreliable, being full of obvious anachronisms. It seems evident, however, that the saint was a great monastic founder, establishing a monastery at Mynyw (Menevia) where the city named after him now is and becoming its first bishop (being mentioned as present at the synod of Brefi in 545). The monks there followed an extremely austere rule. His cultus was approved in 1120, and his shrine became a great pilgrimage centre. The relics preserved there have recently been shown not to be his. His attribute is a leek, or a daffodil (perhaps a pun on his name).

David the King (St) {2}

29 December
He was the second king of the United Kingdom of Israel in the Old Testament, and the traditional author of the Psalms.

David Lewis (St) {2}

27 August
1616–79. From Gwent (Wales), he was educated at Abergavenny, became a convert, studied for the priesthood at Rome and became a Jesuit in 1644. He worked in South Wales for thirty-one years from 1648, based at Cwm in Gwent and using the alias 'Charles Baker'. As a result of the Oates plot he was executed at Usk and was canonized in 1970. Cf. **Wales, Martyrs of**.

David Okelo and Jildo Irwa (BB) {2 –add}

20 October
d. 1918. They belonged to the Acholi tribe in northern Uganda, and were young catechists (David was sixteen and Jildo, twelve). Christianity had just started to penetrate the area of the upper Nile, north of Lake Albert, and they volunteered to go to Paimol. This village was in an area where Christianity was being blamed by pagans for various misfortunes, and they were quickly kidnapped from the village and killed. They were beatified in 2002.

David Roldán Lara (St) {1 –group}

15 August
Cf. **Aloysius Batis Sainz and Comps**.

David of Thessalonica (St) {2, 4}

26 June
d. ?540. From Mesopotamia, he was a hermit outside Thessalonica (Greece) for seventy years. His alleged relics have been at Pavia (Italy) since 1054.

David Uribe Velasco (St) {1 –group}

12 April
1888–1927. From Buenavista de Cuellar in Mexico, he became a diocesan priest of Tabasco in 1913. During the government persecution of the church, he was arrested and given a death sentence, but the faithful of his parish at Chilapa obtained his pardon. However, when he was arrested a second time, there was no trial, but he was shot at the prison at San José in Chilpancingo, Mexico. Cf. **Mexico, Martyrs of**.

David of Västermanland (St) {2}

15 July
d. ?1082. According to the unreliable details concerning him, he was an English Cluniac Benedictine who joined the mission in Sweden headed by St Sigfrid and eventually founded a Benedictine abbey at Monkentorp (the last allegation is anachronistic). He is regarded as the first bishop of Västerås.

Davinus the Pilgrim (St) {2, 4}

3 June
d. 1051. An Armenian, he was on a pilgrimage to Rome and Compostella when he stopped off for a while as a hermit at Lucca (Italy). There he fell ill and died.

Dé cf. **Aidan of Fearns**.

Declan McErc (St) {2}

24 July
C5th? He is venerated as the first bishop of Ardmore in Co. Waterford (Ireland). His legendary biography alleges that he was a missionary in Ireland before St Patrick, but this is unhistorical.

Decorosus (St) {2, 4}

15 February
d. p680. From Capua (Italy), he became bishop there in 660. His shrine is at the cathedral.

Deel or Deille cf. **Deicola**.
Degadh cf. **Dagaeus**.

Deicola (St) {2, 4}

18 January
C7th. An Irish monk of Bangor, he accompanied St Columban to Burgundy and helped him to found the abbey of Luxeuil. When Columban was exiled, Deicola was too old to travel and founded the abbey of Lure in the Vosges instead. His name has many variants: Deicolus, Desle, Dichul, Deel, Delle, Deille.

Deiniol cf. **Daniel of Bangor**.

Delphina of Signe (Bl) {2}

26 November
d. ?1358. A noblewoman of Provence (France), she married St Elzear of Sabran in 1299 but they agreed not to consummate the marriage and became Franciscan tertiaries. In 1317 they went to the court of Naples (Italy), where she made friends with the queen. When she was widowed in 1323, she returned to Provence and lived in absolute poverty. She was buried at Apt, and her cultus was confirmed in 1694.

Delphinus of Bordeaux (St) {2, 4}

24 December

d. a.404. Bishop of Bordeaux (France) from 380, he fought the Priscillianists and was instrumental in converting St Paulinus of Nola.

(Demetria) *(St)* *{4 –deleted}*

21 June

d. ?363. The worthless acta of St Bibiana allege that she was her sister. She probably never existed.

Demetrianus of Antioch (St) {2}

10 November

d. c.260. He was a patriarch of Antioch in Syria, and when Shapur I, Shah of Persia, briefly conquered the city he was taken into exile. He died in captivity somewhere in Persia.

(Demetrius) *(St)* *{4 –deleted}*

14 August

? He was listed in the old Roman Martyrology as a Roman African martyr, but there is no other record of him.

(Demetrius, Anianus, Eustosius and Comps) *(SS)* *{4 –deleted}*

10 November

? They are listed as a group of twenty-three martyred at Antioch (Syria), Demetrius being a bishop and Anianus his deacon.

(Demetrius, Concessus, Hilary and Comps) *(SS)* *{4 –deleted}*

9 April

? A very unlikely group of martyrs, they were listed together as Roman although apparently from different places.

(Demetrius, Honoratus and Florus) *(SS)* *{4 –deleted}*

22 December

? They are listed as having been martyred at Ostia near Rome, and may be the same as SS Demetrius and Honorius.

(Demetrius and Honorius) *(SS)* *{4 –deleted}*

21 November

? They are listed as Romans who were martyred at Ostia.

Demetrius of Thessalonica (St) {2, 4}

9 April

d. c.300. He was probably a deacon who was martyred at Sirmium (Srem Mitrovica in Serbia) in the reign of Diocletian. His cultus flourished in Thessalonica, of which city he is the patron and where the legend grew up of his having been a military hero. As such he is one of the most popular saints in the Orthodox Church, being nicknamed the 'Great Martyr'. He is represented on horseback fighting a dragon, distinguishable from St George in having a red horse instead of a white one.

Democritus, Secundus and Dionysius (SS) {2, 4}

31 July

C3rd. They were martyred at Synnada in Phrygia (Asia Minor).

Denis, Dennis

These are the traditional French and English versions of **Dionysius**. They are only used nowadays in reference to certain Western saints, however, and the original name has been preferred in this book.

Denise cf. **Dionysia**.

Deodatus of Blois (St) {2}

24 April
C6th. From Blois (France), he became a hermit at the place where the abbey and village of Saint-Dyé-sur-Loire later developed. His biographies are legendary.

Deodatus (Dié, Didier, Dieu-Donné, Adéodat) of Nevers (St) {2}

19 June
d. 679. He was allegedly bishop of Nevers (France) for three years from 655 before becoming a hermit at Jointures in the Vosges, where he founded a monastery later named after him. It was alleged that he was also the hermit-founder of the monastery of Ebersheimmünster near Strasbourg (Alsace).

Deodatus of Nola (St) {2}

26 June
C5th. He was the successor of St Paulinus as bishop of Nola (Italy).

Deogratias (St) {2, 4}

5 January
d. 457. After the Arian Vandals had driven St Quodvultdeus into exile, there was no Catholic bishop in Carthage (Roman Africa) until St Deogratius was elected in 456. He died after a year. As bishop he helped the prisoners brought back by the Vandals after they had sacked Rome, selling all that the local church possessed in order to do so.

Dermot O'Hurley (Bl) {2}

20 June
d. 1584. He was archbishop of Cashel (Ireland) and was imprisoned, interrogated and tortured in the reign of Queen Elizabeth I. He was finally hanged in public at a locality called Hoggen Green, and was beatified in 1992. Cf. **Ireland (Martyrs of)**.

Deruvianus or Derwa cf. **Dyfan**.

Desideratus of Besançon (St) {2}

27 July
C5th. He is venerated at Lons-le-Saulnier in the Jura Mountains (France) as a bishop of Besançon who had been born there.

Desideratus of Bourges (St) {2}

8 May
d. 550. He was a Frankish courtier and succeeded St Arcadius as bishop of Bourges (France) in 543.

Desiderius of Cahors (St) {2}

15 November
d. 655. A Gallo-Roman nobleman, he was at the Frankish court before succeeding St Rusticus, his murdered brother, as bishop of Cahors (France) in 630. Some of his letters survive.

Desiderius of Langres and Comps (SS) {2}

23 May
d. ?411. Perhaps from Genoa, he became bishop of Langres (France) and was killed with many of his people in a barbarian incursion. It is thought that the barbarians were Vandals. He is alleged to have been killed in their camp after going there to beg mercy for his city.

Desiderius of Vienne (St) {2}

26 May
d. ?606. From Autun, he became bishop of Vienne (France) in 596 and was a correspondent of Pope St Gregory the Great, but was persecuted and exiled by Queen Brunhilde. He was eventually stoned to death at her instigation and that of an enemy bishop of Lyons at the place now called Saint-Didier-sur-Chalaronne.

Deusdedit (Adeodatus), Pope (St) {2, 4}

8 November
d. 618. A Roman, he became pope in 615 during the Lombard invasions and was remembered for his concern for the sick during an epidemic. He favoured the secular clergy, and there is no evidence that he had been a monk as has been claimed. The error probably arises from confusion with Deusdedit of Montecassino.

(Deusdedit of Brescia) (St) {4 –deleted}

10 December
d. c.700. Bishop of Brescia (Italy), he played a leading part in the Monothelite controversy in Italy.

Deusdedit of Montecassino (St) {2, 4}

9 October
d. ?834. A Benedictine monk of Montecassino (Italy), he became abbot in 828 and became known for his almsgiving. The Duke of Benevento tried to extort the abbey's property by ill-treating and imprisoning him, and he apparently starved to death in prison. He is no longer listed as a martyr.

(Deusdedit of Rome) (St) {4 –deleted}

10 August
C6th. According to the 'Dialogues' attributed to St Gregory the Great, he was a Roman shoemaker who gave to the poor every Sunday whatever was left over from his week's earnings after paying for the bare necessities of life.

Devasahayam Pillai (Bl) {2 –add}

14 January
1712–52. Born at Nattalam in Tamil Nadu (India), he came from a high-caste Hindu family from Kerala and became an important courtier in the Kingdom of Travancore there. However, he was converted by a Catholic Dutch soldier in the maharajah's army in 1745. As a result, he was arrested and condemned to death on false charges in 1748; he was only executed by shooting four years later. During the intervening period, he was continually tortured. His execution was in a forest at Aralvaimozhi, and he was beatified as a martyr in 2012. He is the first Indian layperson to be beatified.

Devereaux cf. **Dubricius**.

Devota (St) {2}

27 January
d. c.300. From Corsica, she died on the rack in the reign of Diocletian and is the patron of Corsica and Monaco. Her relics are at Monaco.

Dewi cf. **David**.
Deyniolen cf. **Daniel the Younger**.

(Diaconus –'Deacon') (St) {4 –deleted}

14 March
C6th. He was mentioned by St Gregory the Great as an anonymous deacon who was killed with two monks in the province of Marsi in Italy by the invading Lombards. Thus he was listed as 'Deacon' in the old Roman Martyrology.

Diana, Cecilia and Amata (BB) {2}

9 June
C13th. They were the founders of the first Dominican nunnery at Bologna. Diana de Andelo was a native noble girl who entered a local convent, was abducted by her parents but returned and helped transfer the community to Valle di San Pietro. Cecilia and Amata Romana came from the St Sixtus nunnery in Rome to introduce the Dominican rule there. Cecilia had been personally acquainted with

St Dominic. Their cultus was confirmed for Bologna and the Dominicans in 1891. The Roman Martyrology does not list Amata, and lists Cecilia on 4 August.

Dichu (St)

29 April

C5th. His story is that he was an Ulster (Ireland) pig farmer, the son of a chieftain, who opposed St Patrick at his landing but changed his mind, became his first convert and gave him the land at Saul (Co. Down) for his first church. His later life is obscure.

Dichul cf. **Deicola**.
Didier cf. **Desiderius**.
Dié cf. **Deodatus**.

Diego

This is a corrupt form of the Spanish name for St James the Great (Jacob); the original Sant Iago became San Diego. In modern times it has been Latinized to Didacus. The Portuguese version is 'Diogo'.

Diego Carvalho (Bl) {2}

22 February

1578–1624. From Coïmbra (Portugal), he became a Jesuit in 1594, went to Goa in 1600 and to Japan as a priest in 1609. In 1623 he was arrested with a number of his people, who together were taken to Sendai and immersed in the icy waters of a river until they died of hypothermia. He alone was beatified in 1867. Cf. **Japan, Martyrs of**.

Diego Kagayama Haito (Bl) {2 –add}

14 October

1565–1619. He was a married lay member of the Confraternity of the Rosary of the diocese of Fukuoka, and was martyred at Kokura near that city. He was beatified in 2008. Cf. **Japan, Martyrs of**.

Diego López Caamaño (Bl) {2}

24 March

1743–1801. From Cádiz (Spain), he became a Capuchin at Seville in 1759 and preached throughout Spain, especially in Andalucia, giving more than 20,000 sermons. He also had a fruitful ministry in the confessional. He died at Ronda and was beatified in 1894.

Diego Oddi (Bl) {2}

3 June

1839–1919. From a poor peasant family of Vallinfreda in Latium (Italy), he was influenced by Bl Marianus of Roccacasale in becoming a Franciscan at Bellegra in 1871. He begged for alms for his friary in the Subiaco region for forty years, and became known for continuous prayer, penance and cheerfulness. He was beatified in 1999.

Diego of San Nicolás (St) {2, 3}

12 November

c.1400–63. From a poor family at San Nicolás del Puerto near Seville (Spain), he became a Franciscan lay brother at Arrizafa and was appointed guardian of the friary on Fuerteventura in the Canaries in 1445. He was sent to Rome in 1450 and nursed the sick in an epidemic there. He died at Alcalá, back in Spain, and was canonized in 1588. His cultus was confined to local calendars in 1969.

Diego-Aloysius de San Vitores (Bl) {2}

2 April

1627–72. A nobleman born at Burgos (Spain), he became a Jesuit in 1640 and went to be a missionary in the Philippines in 1662. In 1668 he went to Guam and baptized 3,000 in three years. There he was joined by St Peter Calungsod, a young Filipino catechist who accompanied him. There were disturbances between the native Chamorros and immigrant Filipinos, however, causing anti-Christian agitation owing to which many lapsed. Bl Diego and St Peter visited one such lapsed Christian native, baptized his baby daughter with the consent of the mother and were killed as a result. Bl Diego was beatified in 1985, and St Peter (only) was canonized in 2012.

Diego Ventaja Milán and Emmanuel Medina Olmos (BB) {2}

30 August
d. 1936. They were the bishops of Almería and Guadix (Spain) and were killed after the 'Revolutionary Committee' of Almería ordered the liquidation of priests and religious in that city. They were beatified together in 1993. Cf. **Spanish Civil War, Martyrs of**.

Diego Yūki Ryōsetsu (Bl) {2 –add}

25 February
d. 1636. He was a Jesuit priest from Awa near Tokushima who was martyred at Ōsaka and beatified in 2008. Cf. **Japan, Martyrs of**.

Dieudonné cf. **Deusdedit** or **Adeodatus**.
Digna cf. **Emerita**.

(Digna of Todi) (St) {4 –deleted}

11 August
Early C4th? She was listed as a maiden of Todi in Umbria (Italy) who took to the mountains to escape the persecution of Diocletian and died a hermit.

Dimitri cf. **Demetrius of Thessalonica**.

Diodore, Diomedes and Didymus (SS) {2, 4}

9 October
? They were martyrs of Laodicea (Latakia) in Syria.

(Diodore, Marianus and Comps) (SS) {4 –deleted}

1 December
d. 283. They were listed as Roman martyrs of the reign of Numerian, and described as a priest, deacon and congregation who were discovered by the authorities while assembled for prayer in the catacomb of SS Chrysanthus and Daria and who were then walled up and left to die.

Diodore and Rhodopianus (SS) {2, 4}

30 April
Early C4th. Two deacons, they were martyred at Aphrodisiopolis in Caria (Asia Minor) in the reign of Diocletian.

(Diomedes, Julian and Comps (SS) {4 –deleted}

2 September
? They are merely listed as having been burnt, drowned, beheaded or crucified without any other details. The others are Philip, Eutychian, Hesychius, Leonides, Philadelphus, Menalippus and Pantagapes.

Diomedes Anargyrus (St) {2, 4}

9 June
? From Tarsus in Cilicia, according to his story he was a physician and practised among the poor free of charge (hence his surname meaning 'Moneyless'). He was seized at Nicaea (Asia Minor) but died while being taken to Nicomedia, where his body was beheaded.

Dionysia
This name is familiarly rendered as 'Denise'.

Dionysia, Dativa and Comps (SS) {2, 4}

6 December
C5th. According to Victor of Utica, who wrote an account of the persecution in Africa under

the Arian Vandal King Hunneric, this group included the widow Dionysia, her sister Dativa and her small son Majoricus who were all burnt at the stake. Emilius, a physician, and Tertius, a monk, were flayed alive and Boniface, Leontia, Sibidensis, Servius, Victrix and others were killed in ingenious ways.

Dionysius

In the Middle Ages, this name was usually rendered in English as Dennis (from the French Denis). 'Sydney' is a corrupt form of 'Saint Denis'.

Dionysius, Pope (St) {2, 4}

30 December
d. 268. A Roman, he became pope in perhaps 259 and successfully restored the church's life after the persecution of Valerian. He opposed the heresies of Sabellius and of Paul of Samosata.

(Dionysius, Emilian and Sebastian) (SS) {4 –deleted}

8 February
? The old Roman Martyrology lists them as Armenian monks, but nothing is known about them.

(Dionysius, Faustus, Gaius, Peter, Paul and Comps) (SS) {4 –deleted}

3 October
Mid C3rd? From Alexandria (Egypt), they were listed as persecuted in 250 in the Decian persecution, and then martyred in the reign of Valerian. There is confusion over the identities of each, despite their insertion into the old Roman Martyrology by Cardinal Baronius. 'Dionysius' seems to be the patriarch of Alexandria, and 'Faustus and Gaius' the same as the Gaius and Faustus listed in the old Roman Martyrology on 4 October and now transferred to the 3rd.

(Dionysius and Privatus) (SS) {4 –deleted}

20 September
? They were listed as martyrs of Phrygia (Asia Minor).

Dionysius and Redemptus (SS) {2}

29 November
d. 1638. Dionysius-of-the-Nativity Berthelot was a French navigator and cartographer who became a Carmelite at Goa (India) in 1635, was ordained in 1638 and sent on a Portuguese embassy to Aceh. This was a fervently Muslim kingdom on the north tip of Sumatra. Redemptus-of-the-Cross Rodriguez da Cunha, a Portuguese lay brother, went with him. The delegation was not well received, and they were killed. They were beatified in 1900.

Dionysius of Alexandria (St) {2, 4}

8 April
d. 265. From Alexandria (Egypt), he was a pupil of Origen and was his successor as head of the catechetical school of Alexandria before becoming patriarch in 248. He was exiled in the reign of Decius and again in that of Valerian but succeeded in remaining in control of his diocese. He was a great theologian and controversialist, but only the fragments preserved by Eusebius survive of his writings.

Dionysius the Areopagite (St) {2, 4}

3 October
C1st. Converted by St Paul at Athens (Acts 17:34), he traditionally became the first bishop of Athens. In the Dark Ages he was deliberately confused with St Dionysius of Paris, and also the works by the C5th mystical writer now called 'Pseudo-Dionysius' were ascribed to him. The identity of the latter is wholly unknown.

(Dionysius the Carthusian) (Bl)

12 March

1402–71. From Flanders, he obtained his doctorate at Cologne University when aged twenty-one and became a Carthusian at Roermond (Netherlands) in 1423. There he remained until his death, except for a period at a new foundation at 's-Hertogenbosch. He was a great and prolific mystical writer, being nicknamed the 'Ecstatic Doctor'. His cultus has not been confirmed, as the Carthusians never promote the causes of their members.

Dionysius of Corinth (St) {2, 4}

8 April

d. 180. Succeeding St Primus as bishop of Corinth (Greece), he had great authority in the church of his day and wrote many letters to other local churches, including that of Rome. Only fragments of these survive. The Byzantine martyrology lists him as a martyr, but the Roman Martyrology does not.

Dionysius Fujishima (Bl) {2}

1 November

d. 1622. Of a noble Japanese family near Arima, he became a Jesuit novice and was martyred with Bl Paul Navarro (q.v.). Cf. **Japan, Martyrs of**.

Dionysius of Milan (St) {2, 4}

25 May

d. ?361. The successor of St Protasius as bishop of Milan (Italy) in 351, he defended St Athanasius against the Arian Emperor Constantius and was thus exiled to Cappodocia with St Eusebius of Vercelli. He died there, but St Ambrose had his relics brought back to Milan by St Aurelius of Armenia.

Dionysius (Denis) of Paris and Comps (SS) {1, 3}

9 October

d. c.250. According to St Gregory of Tours (the sole source), he was sent from Rome with five other missionary bishops to evangelize Gaul and became the first bishop of Paris (France). In the reign of Decius he was beheaded with his two companions, Rusticus and Eleutherius, at a place near the city where the abbey named Saint-Denis after him was later founded. In the C9th Hilduin, a Gallican abbot of Saint-Denis, maliciously forged a set of acta linking the saint to St Dionysius the Areopagite and to the author of an anonymous C5th spiritual author now called the 'Pseudo-Dionysius'. This conflation of three separate persons led to a popular cultus in the Middle Ages, and a fraudulent entry in the old Roman Martyrology.

Dionysius Pamplona Polo and Comps (BB) {2}

d. 1936. From Teruel province (Spain), he joined the Piarists and became parish priest at Peralta de la Sal in Huesca (the birthplace of their founder, St Joseph Calasanz). He, five of his brethren there and seven other Piarists were shot in Monzón prison during the civil war and were beatified in 1995. Cf. **Spanish Civil War, Martyrs of** and list in appendix.

(Dionysius of Rome) *(St) {4 –deleted}*

12 May

d. 304. He was allegedly the uncle and guardian of St Pancras and went with him to Rome. They were seized, and St Dionysius died in prison in the reign of Diocletian, being listed as a martyr.

Dionysius Ssebuggwawo (St) {1 –group}

25 May
d. 1885. A servant of King Mwanga of Buganda (Uganda), he was caught teaching the catechism by the latter and was killed with a spear. He was the first victim of the Ugandan persecution. Cf. **Charles Lwanga and Comps**.

Dionysius of Vienne (St) {2, 4}

8 May
C4th. Allegedly one of the ten missionaries sent from Rome to Gaul with St Peregrine, he succeeded St Justus as bishop of Vienne (France).

Dioscorides of Myra (St) {2, 4}

10 May
? He was martyred at Myra (Asia Minor). The old Roman Martyrology had 'Smyrna' in error.

Dioscorus of Kynopolis (St) {2, 4}

18 May
d. ?303. The son of a lector at Kynopolis (Egypt), he was tortured in various ways before being beheaded.

Diruvianus cf. **Dyfan**.

Disibod (Disen) (St) {2}

8 July
C7th. Allegedly an Irish bishop, he went to Germany with some companions and evangelized the area around Mainz. Near there he founded a monastery later called Disenberg which, as a nunnery, became famous as the home of St Hildegard. Her biography of him is historically worthless.

Dismas cf. **Good Thief**.

Dius Thaumaturgus (St) {2}

19 July
C5th? From Antioch in Syria, he became a priest and an Acoemetite monk at Constantinople, founding the monastery of Diitikon.

Dizier cf. **Desiderius**.
Docco cf. **Cumgar**.
Docus cf **Cadoc**.

Dodo of Lobbes (St) {2}

29 October
C8th. From near Laon (France), he was a child-oblate at the abbey of Lobbes (Belgium) under St Ursmar, became a monk there and was later abbot of Wallers-en-Faigne.

Dogmael (St)

14 June
C5th–C6th. The patron of St Dogmael's, across the river from Cardigan (Wales), seems to have founded a monastery at St Dogmael's as well as in Anglesey and in Brittany.

Dolores cf. **Mary-of-Sorrows**.
Dometius cf. **Domitius**.

(Dominator of Brescia) (St) {4 –deleted}

5 November
d. ?495. He was listed as a bishop of Brescia in Lombardy (Italy).

Dominic
This is from the Latin Dominicus, which is the equivalent of the Greek name Cyriac.

Dominic and Gregory (BB) {2}

26 April
C13th. Two Spanish Dominicans, they were preaching in the Somontano district of Aragón (Spain), northeast of Zaragoza. During a thunderstorm they sheltered under a rock on

a mountainside near Perarú, but this rock was struck by lightning, and under its impact it fell on them and buried them. Their shrine is at Besians near Barbastro, and their cultus was confirmed for Barbastro in 1854.

(Dominic, Victor and Comps) (SS) {4 –deleted}

29 December
? Nothing is known about these Roman African martyrs. The companions are Primian, Lybosus, Saturninus, Crescentius, Secundus and Honoratus.

Dominic-of-the-Mother-of-God Barberi (Bl) {2}

27 August
1792–1849. From a peasant family near Viterbo (Italy), he became a Passionist in 1815 and served as superior at Lucca from 1831 and as provincial of south Italy from 1833. In 1841 he was sent to England as superior of his order's first house in England, at Aston (Staffs). He was hoping for the imminent conversion of the country as a whole and this, together with his unprepossessing appearance and poor English, led him to be treated with hostility by native Catholics and Protestants alike. His personal holiness inspired many individual conversions to the Roman Catholic Church, however, including that of John Henry Newman. He was taken ill on a train, died at Reading and was beatified in 1963.

(Dominic of Brescia) (St) {4 –deleted}

20 December
d. ?612. He succeeded St Anastasius as bishop of Brescia (Italy). His relics were enshrined by St Charles Borromeo.

Dominic Bùy Văn Uy (St) {1 –group}

19 December
Cf. **Francis-Xavier Hà Trọng Mậu and Comps**.

Dominic de la Calzada (St) {2, 4}

12 May
d. 1060. From Vitoria in the Basque Country (Spain), he became a hermit in Rioja after failing to become a monk at Valvanera. The work he took up was building a bridge, causeway and hospice as part of a pilgrim route to Compostella passing near his hermitage on the Oja River, and the site, now called La Calzada ('The Causeway'), itself became a pilgrimage centre.

Dominic Cám (St) {1 –group}

11 March
1859. He was a Vietnamese priest and Dominican tertiary who ministered in secret to imprisoned Christians. At length he was arrested during the persecution ordered by Emperor Tự Đức and ordered to trample on a crucifix. On his refusal he was beheaded, clutching the crucifix he had refused to profane. Cf. **Vietnam, Martyrs of**.

Dominic Castellet and Comps (BB) {2}

8 September
d. 1628. They were a group of twenty-two martyred at Nagasaki (Japan). Eleven were burnt alive: Bl Dominic was from near Barcelona (Spain) and, on becoming a Dominican, was sent to Japan where he became vicar-provincial. Martyred with him were two Dominican lay brothers, Thomas-of-St-Hyacinth of Nagasaki and Anthony-of-St-Dominic of Nagasaki; two Franciscans, Anthony-of St-Bonaventure of Tuy and Dominic of Nagasaki, and six laypeople: Lucy-Louise of Omura, Michael Yamada, John Tomachi, John Imamura, Paul Sadaya Aybara and Matthew Alvarez. Eleven were beheaded: Dominic, Michael, Paul and Thomas Tomachi (sons of John Tomachi); Laurence Yamada (son of Michael Yamada); Romanus and Leo Aybara (sons of Paul Sadaya Aybara); Louis,

Francis and Dominic Higashi (father and two sons), and James Hayashida. Cf. **Japan, Martyrs of**.

Dominic Collins (Bl) {2}

31 October
d. 1602. A Jesuit lay brother, he was imprisoned, interrogated and tortured before being hanged at Youghal near Cork. Cf. **Ireland, Martyrs of**.

Dominic-Nicholas Đinh Đạt (St) {1 –group}

18 July
d. 1839. A Vietnamese soldier, he was ordered to trample on a crucifix during the persecution ordered by Emperor Minh Mạng and complied. He immediately repented, wrote a letter to the emperor proclaiming his faith and so was strangled at Nam Định. Cf. **Vietnam, Martyrs of**.

Dominic de Guzman (St) {1, 3}

8 August
1170–1221. From Caleruega near Burgos (Spain), he became a canon regular at Osma Cathedral and went with his bishop, Bl Diego de Azevedo, to the south of France in 1202 in order to help the evangelical campaign against the Albigenses (which later turned into a crusade). The experience convinced him of the necessity of preaching the faith to ordinary people. The two of them opened a nunnery at Prouille for women converts from the Albigenses in 1206, which was the start of the Dominican order. This, the 'Friars Preachers', was approved in 1216 and was sent all over Europe by St Dominic in order to preach and teach. Together with the Franciscans, it represented a radical departure from the previously accepted norms of consecrated life which presumed stability in a monastery. The friars proved ideally suited to the urban civilization developing in the high Middle Ages, especially in the new universities. St Dominic died at Bologna after much journeying in western Europe and was canonized in 1234. He is represented as an elderly Dominican holding a lily, or with a dog or a rosary.

Dominic Henares (St) {1 –group}

25 June
d. 1838. A Spanish Dominican, he became the coadjutor bishop of the apostolic vicar for Vietnam, St Ignatius Delgado, in 1803. He was seized and beheaded with his catechist, St Francis Đỗ Minh Chiểu, at Nam Định during the persecution ordered by Emperor Minh Mạng. Cf. **Vietnam, Martyrs of**.

Dominic Higashi (Bl) {2}

8 September
d. 1628. He was a toddler aged two when he was beheaded with his father and brother at Nagasaki (Japan). Cf. **Dominic Castellet and Comps** and **Japan, Martyrs of**.

Dominic Huyên and Dominic Toại (St) {1 –group}

5 June
d. 1862. They were Vietnamese fishermen and family men, who were arrested during the persecution ordered by Emperor Tự Đức. They spent some time in prison being tortured in various ways, and were noted for encouraging fellow imprisoned Christians to keep the faith. They were finally beheaded at Tang Gia in north Vietnam. Cf. **Vietnam, Martyrs of**.

Dominic Ibáñez de Eriquicia (St) {1 –group}

14 August
1589–1633. Born in San Sebastian (Spain), he became a Dominican missionary in the Philippines and spent a decade as vicar-provincial in Japan before being martyred in Nagasaki

with St Francis Shoyemon. He was canonized in 1987 with St Laurence Ruiz and Comps. Cf. **Japan, Martyrs of**.

Dominic-of-the-Blessed-Sacrament Iturrate Zubero (Bl) {2}

7 April
1901–27. Born in Dima in the Basque Country (Spain), he joined the Trinitarians in 1914, was sent to Rome in 1919 and was ordained in 1925. A model religious, he had strong devotions to the Blessed Sacrament and to Our Lady and wished to go on foreign missions. However, he was appointed master of students at Cordoba instead and, while still in Rome, contracted tuberculosis and returned to Spain to die. He was beatified in 1983.

Dominic Jędrzejewski (Bl) {2}

29 August
1886–1942. A Polish priest, he died of ill-treatment at the concentration camp at Dachau. Cf. **Poland, Martyrs of the Nazi Occupation of**.

Dominic Jorjes (Bl) {2}

14 March
d. 1619. A soldier from Portugal, he settled in Japan and became the housekeeper of Bl Charles Spinola. He was burnt alive at Nagasaki with Bl Leonard Kimura and Comps (q.v.). Cf. **Japan, Martyrs of**.

Dominic Lentini (Bl) {2}

25 February
1770–1828. From a poor family of Lauria in Basilicata (Italy), he was ordained priest in 1794 and served as parish priest of his native town all his life. His life was manifestly centred on the Eucharist, on evangelical poverty and on prayer, and he was totally dedicated to evangelization in his district. He was effective in converting sinners because he obviously practised what he preached, and was devoted to Our Lady of Sorrows. He also set out to teach an authentic Christian culture to the young people who gathered at his house. He was beatified in 1997.

Dominic Loricatus (St) {2, 4}

14 October
995–1060. From Umbria (Italy), he spent his life doing penance for his parents who had given a deerskin to the local bishop to obtain his ordination. He never exercised his priestly functions, wore a coat of mail next to his skin (hence his surname), recited the Psalter once a day and fasted on bread and water. At first he was a hermit in Umbria, then a disciple of St Peter Damian at Fonteavellano and finally prior of a monastery at Frontale.

Dominic Magoshichi de Hyuga (Bl) {2}

12 September
d. 1622. A Japanese catechist and Dominican tertiary, he was burnt alive at Omura with Bl Thomas Zumarraga and Comps (q.v.). Cf. **Japan, Martyrs of**.

Dominic Mậu (St) {1 –group}

5 November
d. 1858. He was a Vietnamese Dominican priest, and during the persecution ordered by Emperor Tự Đức he publicly carried the rosary and exhorted Christians to keep the faith. As a result he was arrested and beheaded besides the river Hưng Yên in north Vietnam. Cf. **Vietnam, Martyrs of**.

Dominic Mạo (St) {1 –group}

16 June
Cf. **Dominic Nguyễn and Comps**.

Dominic of Nagasaki (Bl) {2}

8 September
d. 1628. A Japanese catechist, he took vows as a Franciscan while in prison at Omura with Bl Anthony-of-St-Bonaventure and was burnt with him at Nagasaki. Cf. **Dominic Castellet and Comps** and **Japan, Martyrs of**.

Dominic-of-the-Holy-Rosary of Nagasaki (Bl) {2}

10 September
d. 1622. A Japanese catechist and a Dominican novice, he was beheaded during the 'Great Martyrdom' at Nagasaki. Cf. **Charles Spinola and Comps** and **Japan, Martyrs of** and **Great Martyrdom at Nagasaki**.

Dominic Nakano (Bl) {2}

10 September
d. 1622. The nineteen-year-old son of Bl Matthias Nakano, he was beheaded at Nagasaki (Japan) in the 'Great Persecution'. Cf. **Charles Spinola and Comps**, **Great Martyrdom at Nagasaki** and **Japan, Martyrs of**.

Dominic Nhi (St) {1 –group}

16 June
Cf. **Dominic Nguyễn and Comps**.

Dominic Ninh (SS) {1 –group}

16 July
d. 1862. He was a young farmer of Âu Thi in north Vietnam, and refused to trample on a crucifix during the persecution ordered by Emperor Tự Đức. As a result he was beheaded. Cf. **Vietnam, Martyrs of**.

Dominic Ngôn (St) {1 –group}

22 May
d. 1862. He was a Vietnamese farmer and family man, and when a group of soldiers ordered him to trample on a crucifix he adored it instead. He was arrested, condemned by the local mandarin and beheaded at An Xá in central Vietnam. Cf. **Vietnam, Martyrs of**.

Dominic Nguyễn and Comps (SS) {1 –group}

16 June
d. 1862. He was a doctor of medicine, and was imprisoned with four farmers at Lăng Cốc in north Vietnam during the persecution ordered by Emperor Tự Đức. They suffered many tortures before being beheaded. The companions were Andrew Tường, Dominic Mạo, Dominic Nhi and Vincent Tường. Cf. **Vietnam, Martyrs of**.

Dominic Nguyễn Văn Hạnh (St) {1 –group}

1 August
1772–1838. He was a Vietnamese Dominican priest, and during the persecution ordered by Emperor Minh Mạng he was beheaded at Nam Định with St Bernard Vũ Văn Duệ. Cf. **Vietnam, Martyrs of**.

Dominic Nguyễn Văn Xuyên (St) {1 –group}

26 November
1788–1839. He was a Vietnamese Dominican priest, beheaded with St Thomas Đinh Viết Dụ at Nam Định during the persecution ordered by Emperor Minh Mạng. Cf. **Vietnam, Martyrs of**.

Dominic Phạm Trọng Khảm and Comps (SS) {1 –group}

13 January
d. 1859. He was a Vietnamese family man who was martyred with his son, St Luke Thìn, and a neighbour, St Joseph Phạm Trọng Tả, at Nam Định in north Vietnam during the persecution ordered by Emperor Tự Đức. Cf. **Vietnam, Martyrs of**.

Dominic Savio (St) {2}

9 March
1842–57. The son of a blacksmith at Riva de Chieri in the Piedmont (Italy), he became a pupil of St John Bosco (who wrote his biography). He died at Mondonio aged fourteen, having shown evidence of high sanctity, and is the youngest non-martyr so far canonized (in 1954).

Dominic Shobioye and Comps (BB) {2}

16 September
d. 1628. A Japanese layman, he was beheaded at Nagasaki with Michael and Paul Timonoya. Cf. **Japan, Martyrs of**.

Dominic of Silos (St) {2, 4}

20 December
c.1000–73. From Rioja (Spain), he became a monk and prior of San Millán de Cogolla in the Kingdom of Navarre but was exiled after quarrelling with the king. The king of Castile welcomed him and sent him to restore the Benedictine abbey of Silos (now named after him) which he achieved with great success. Under him the abbey became famous for the production of manuscripts, and was also involved in the ransoming of prisoners taken by the Muslims. At his shrine Bl Jane de Aza de Guzman prayed for a child, and on giving birth she named the boy Dominic in gratitude. He later founded the Dominicans.

Dominic of Sora (St) {2, 4}

22 January
951–1031. From Foligno (Italy), he became a priest at his home town and the abbot-founder of several Benedictine monasteries in middle Italy, including Sora in Lazio where he died.

Dominic Spadafora (Bl) {2}

21 December
d. 1521. From Palermo (Sicily), he joined the Dominicans after being a student at Padua and became a famous preacher in Italy. He died in the friary he had founded at Montecerignone near San Marino and his cultus was confirmed for Montefeltro in 1921.

Dominic Toại (St) {1 –group}

5 June
Cf. **Dominic Huyên and Dominic Toại**.

Dominic Tomachi (Bl) {2}

8 September
d. 1628. He was sixteen when he was beheaded with his three brothers at Nagasaki. Their father, Bl John Tomachi, was burnt. Cf. **Dominic Castellet and Comps** and **Japan, Martyrs of**.

Dominic Trạch (St) {1 –group}

18 September
1792–1842. He was a Vietnamese priest and Dominican tertiary beheaded at Nam Định in north Vietnam after refusing to trample on a crucifix during the persecution ordered by Emperor Minh Mạng. Cf. **Vietnam, Martyrs of**.

Dominic Tước (St) {1 –group}

2 April
d. 1839. A Vietnamese priest and a tertiary of the Dominicans, he died in prison from wounds inflicted on him at Xương Điền in north Vietnam during the persecution ordered by Emperor Minh Mạng. Cf. **Vietnam, Martyrs of**.

Dominic Vernagalli (Bl) {2}

20 April
d. 1218. From Pisa (Italy), he became a Camaldolese monk at the abbey of St Michael there and founded a hospital attached to the monastery. His cultus was confirmed for the Camaldolese in 1854.

Dominic Yamada (Bl) {2}

10 September
d. 1622. He was beheaded with his wife, Bl Clare, in the 'Great Martyrdom' at Nagasaki (Japan). Cf. **Charles Spinola and Comps**, **Japan, Martyrs of** and **Great Martyrdom at Nagasaki**.

Dominica cf. **Cyriaca**.

Dominica Ogata (Bl) {2}

10 September
d 1622. She was a Japanese laywoman beheaded at Nagasaki (Japan) in the 'Great Martyrdom'. Cf. **Charles Spinola and Comps**, **Japan, Martyrs of** and **Great Martyrdom at Nagasaki**.

(Dominica of Tropea) (St) {4 –deleted}

6 July
? Cardinal Baronius inserted this saint into his revision of the old Roman Martyrology. She was alleged either to have been martyred on the banks of the Euphrates and to have had her body carried by angels to Tropea in Calabria (Italy), or to have been a native of the latter place and martyred there. She was unknown in Tropea before the C16th, and seems to be a version of an apocryphal martyr of Nicomedia called Cyriaca.

(Domitian of Châlons) (St) {4 –deleted}

9 August
C4th? He was listed as succeeding his teacher St Donatian as third bishop of Châlons-sur-Marne (France).

Domitian of Lérins (St) {2, 4}

1 July
C5th. An orphan from Rome, he became a monk at Lérins (off the Riviera, France) and later founded the abbey of St Rambert-de-Joux near Belley. The sources referring to him are very unreliable.

Domitian of Melitene (St) {2}

10 January
d. ?602. He had been married, but was a widower and monk when he was elected to be bishop of Melitene in Roman Armenia (now Malatya). The rich gifts he received from the Emperor Maurice, a relative, he gave to the poor. He strove to convert local Zoroastrians.

Domitilla (St) {2, 3}

7 May
d. c.100. According to the revised Roman Martyrology, she was a niece of St Flavius Clemens the consul. The Emperor Domitian accused her of being an atheist on account of her Christianity, and exiled her with some others to the island of Ponza of Terracina. Afterwards she was martyred. According to the unreliable acta of SS Nereus and Achilleus, two foster-sisters Euphrosyna and Theodora suffered with her.

In the old Roman Martyrology, she was conflated with Flavia Domitilla, a great-niece of the Emperors Titus and Domitian, who married St Flavius Clemens and was exiled to Pantelleria for her faith. The confusion encouraged the suppression of the cultus in 1969.

(Domitius of Amiens) (St) {4 –deleted}

23 October
C8th. A canon of the cathedral of Amiens (France), he became a hermit at Saint-Acheul.

(Domitius of Caesarea and Comps) (SS) {4 –deleted}

23 March
d. 361. His story is that he was a Phrygian who heckled the pagan ceremonies held in a theatre in the presence of Emperor Julian at Caesarea in the Holy Land. He was beheaded, allegedly

together with Pelagia, Aquila, Eparchius and Theodosia although these probably do not belong with him.

(Domitius of Nisibis and Comps) (St) {4 –deleted}

7 August
C4th. He was allegedly a Persian monk martyred at Nisibis in Mesopotamia with two disciples in the reign of Julian, but is probably a duplicate of Domitius of Caesarea.

Domitius the Physician (St) {2, 4}

5 July
C5th. He was a hermit on the mountain of Quros in Roman Armenia, and was not a martyr. The myth attached to him was that he was a Persian hermit walled up in his cave near Cyrrhus (Syria) by order of Emperor Julian, and this story gave rise to his namesakes of Caesarea and Nisibis.

Domneva cf. **Ermenburga**.

Domnina of Anazarbus (St) {2, 4}

12 October
d. ?304. She was alleged to have died in prison from the effects of beating and torture at Anazarbus in Cilicia (Asia Minor).

(Domnina of Teramo and Comps) (SS) {4 –deleted}

14 April
d. ?269. They are listed in the old Roman Martyrology as having been martyred at Teramo in Umbria (Italy), but may belong to Terni instead if they ever existed.

Domninus of Caesarea (St) {2, 4}

5 November
d. 307. He was a young physician who was condemned to slavery in the mines, where he was treated with great cruelty. After surviving this for five years (which was unusual), he was ordered to be burnt. The Roman Martyrology has deleted the reference to companions, including Silvanus, Philotheus and Theotimus.

Domninus of Città di Castello (St) {2}

9 October
d. 610. He was a hermit at Città di Castello in Umbria (Italy).

Dorus (St) {2}

20 November
C5th. He was a bishop of Benevento in Campania (Italy).

Domninus of Thessalonica (St) {2, 4}

30 March
Early C4th. He was martyred at Thessalonica (Greece). The Roman Martyrology has deleted the reference to Victor and other companions.

(Domninus of Thessalonica-2) (St) {4 –deleted}

1 October
He is a straightforwardly mistaken duplication of the above in the old Roman Martyrology.

Domninus of Parma (St) {2, 4}

9 October
Early C4th. From Parma (Italy), he fled the persecution of Diocletian but was pursued and beheaded nearby at Borgo San Donnino, where his shrine now is.

Domninus of Vienne (St) {2, 4}

3 November
d. 657. He succeeded St Desiderius as bishop of Vienne (France), and was noted for ransoming captives.

(Domnio of Bergamo) *(St)* *{4 –deleted}*

16 July

End C3rd? He was listed as martyred at Bergamo in Lombardy (Italy) in the reign of Diocletian.

(Domnio of Rome) *(St)* *{4 –deleted}*

28 December

C4th. A Roman priest, he was remembered because SS Jerome and Augustine wrote in his praise.

Domnio of Salona (St) {2, 4}

11 April

d. 299. He was a bishop of Salona (now a suburb of Split in Croatia) who was martyred in the reign of Diocletian. The Roman Martyrology has deleted the reference to eight soldier companions.

Domnoc cf. **Modomnock**.

Domnolus of Le Mans (St) {2, 4}

1 December

d. 581. Abbot of a monastery near Paris (France), he became bishop of Le Mans in 559 and was a founder of many monasteries, churches and charitable institutions.

Donald *(St)*

15 July

C8th. He is alleged to have lived as a religious with his nine daughters in Glen Ogilvie near Coupar Angus (Scotland). The 'Nine Maidens' went to Abernethy after he died. His name is still popular for boys, despite his obscurity.

Donas cf. **Donatian**.

Donata and Comps (SS) {2, 4}

31 December

? The relics of these early Roman woman martyrs were in the catacombs of the Via Salaria.

Listed also are Paulina, Rogata, Dominanda, Serotina, Saturnina and Hilaria.

Donatian, Praesidius and Comps (SS) {2, 4}

6 September

C5th. An account survives by Victor of Utica of the persecution of the Catholics in ex-Roman Africa by Hunneric, Arian King of the Vandals. Almost five thousand were exiled in one year. These bishops, of what is now Tunisia, were driven into the desert to die, the others being Mansuetus, Germanus and Fusculus, while Laetus was burnt after imprisonment.

Donatian and Rogatian (SS) {2, 4}

24 May

d.304. They were martyred at Nantes (France) in the reign of Diocletian.

Donatian of Châlons-sur-Marne (St) {2, 4}

7 August

C4th. He was the second bishop of Châlons-sur-Marne (France).

Donatian (Donas) of Rheims (St) {2, 4}

14 October

d. 389. From Rome, he became bishop of Rheims (France) in 360. In the C9th his relics were taken to Bruges (Belgium), of which place he became the patron.

Donatus of Arezzo (St) {2, 3}

7 August

C4th. He was the second bishop of Arezzo in Tuscany (Italy), but through confusion with another of the same name was falsely celebrated as a martyr. He had no connection with Hilarinus with whom he was listed, who was a martyr of Ostia if he ever existed. His cultus was confined to local calendars in 1969.

(Donatus, Justus, Herena and Comps) *(SS)*
{4 –deleted}

25 February
d. c.250. A group of fifty, they were listed as martyred in Roman Africa in the reign of Decius.

(Donatus, Sabinus and Agape) *(SS)*
{4 –deleted}

25 January
? They were listed in the old Roman Martyrology, but nothing is known about them.

(Donatus, Secundian, Romulus and Comps) *(SS) {4 –deleted}*

17 February
d. 304. A group of eighty-nine, they were listed as martyred at Porto Gruaro (the old Concordia) near Venice (Italy) in the reign of Diocletian.

Donatus of Besançon (St) {2}

7 August
d. p558. Educated at the monastery of Luxeuil, he became bishop of Besançon (France) in 624 and founded a pair of monasteries for monks and nuns there. His 'Rule for Virgins' relies on the rules of SS Benedict and Columban.

(Donatus of Corfu) *(St) {4 –deleted}*

29 October
? All that is known about this extremely dubious saint is that his alleged relics were brought to Corfu (Greece) by a refugee priest from Asia Minor in c.600 and were enshrined at Kassiopi at the instigation of St Gregory the Great.

Donatus of Euraea (St) {2, 4}

30 April
d. late C4th. Bishop of Euraea in Epirus (now Albania), he was mentioned by the church historian Sozomen.

Donatus of Orleans (St) {2, 4}

19 August
C6th. From Orleans (France), he became a hermit near Sisteron in Provence (France) and has his shrine there.

Donatus Scotus (St) {2, 4}

22 October
d. ?875. From Scotland or Ireland, he was returning from a pilgrimage to Rome when he was made bishop of Fiesole near Florence (Italy) in ?829. He was a literary scholar, and cared for other pilgrims.

Donnan of Eigg and Comps (SS) {2}

17 April
d. 617. Allegedly a monk of Iona (Scotland) under St Columba, he became abbot-founder of a daughter monastery on the island of Eigg nearby. The entire community of fifty-three was allegedly massacred on Easter Sunday by Danish raiders. His existence has been questioned, but is accepted by the Roman Martyrology.

Dorcas cf. **Tabitha**.
Doris cf. **Dorothy**.

Dorotheus and Gorgonius (SS) {2, 3}

12 March
d. 303. They were among the first victims of the persecution ordered by Diocletian, being the palace-master and chamberlain at the emperor's capital at Nicomedia (Asia Minor). Their martyrdom by strangling is recorded by Eusebius. Their cultus was confined to particular calendars in 1969, and the Roman Martyrology now lists them with St Peter of Nicomedia.

Dorotheus of Tyre (St) {2, 4}

5 June
C4th. His life is obscure, but it is alleged that he was a priest of Tyre (Lebanon) who was

exiled in the reign of Diocletian, made bishop upon his return from exile and finally beaten to death at Varna (Bulgaria) in the reign of Julian.

Dorothy and Theophilus (St) {2, 3}

6 February
Early C4th. Dorothy was a virgin martyr of Caesarea in Cappodocia (Asia Minor), and was beheaded with Theophilus, a scholastic in the reign of Diocletian. Her acta are a romantic fiction. Her cultus, formerly very popular in the West, was suppressed in 1969. She is represented with roses or apples. The Roman Martyrology now lists the two together.

Dorothy of Montau (St) {2}

25 June
1336–94. A peasant girl from Montau in Teutonic (later East) Prussia, she married a wealthy swordsmith of Danzig called Albert. They had nine children, and she changed his harsh character by means of patience and prayer. After his death she became a hermit at Marienwerder (now Kwidzyn in Poland). Her cultus survived the Second World War in Poland, and was confirmed in 1976.

Dorymedon (St) {2, 4}

20 September
? He was martyred at Synnada in Phrygia (Asia Minor) the day after Trophimus.

Douceline cf. **Dulcelina**.
Dreux cf. **Drogo**.
Drillo cf. **Trillo**.

Droctoveus (Droctonius, Drotté) (St) {2, 4}

10 March
d. c.580. He was a disciple of St Germanus of Paris before becoming abbot of St Symphorian's Abbey at Autun (France). His former master then appointed him first abbot of his new monastery at Paris, later called Saint-Germain-des-Prés.

Drogo (Dreux, Druon) of Sebourg (St) {2, 4}

16 April
d. 1186. A Fleming from Artois (France), he lost his parents when aged twenty and, after disposing of his property, became a wandering shepherd and apparently went on pilgrimage to Rome nine times. Eventually he settled as a hermit near Sebourg in Hainault and lived on bread and water for forty-five years.

Drostan (St) {2}

11 July
C6th? From Ireland, he was a monk at Iona under St Columba and first abbot of Deer near Aberdeen. He is venerated as one of the apostles of Scotland and has a holy well near Aberdour.

Drosis (SS) {2, 4}

14 December
End C3rd. He was martyred by burning at Antioch (Syria), and St John Chrysostom preached an extant homily on his feast day there. Two companions, Zosimus and Theodore, have been deleted from the Roman Martyrology.

Dubricius (Dubric, Dyfrig) (St) {2}

14 November
d. ?545. One of the founders of monasticism in Wales, he established monasteries in the Wye Valley area from bases at Henllan and Moccas. He had jurisdiction over Caldey, appointed St Samson abbot there and later ordained him bishop. By tradition he was first bishop of Llandaff and then of Caerleon. He died in Bardsey.

Dubtach (Duthac) of Ross (St) {2}

8 March

d. 1065. A missionary bishop in Ross (Scotland), he had his shrine at Tain, which was a famous pilgrimage centre before the Reformation.

Dula (St) {2, 4}

25 March

? Her story is that she was a slave girl sold to a pagan soldier at Nicomedia (Asia Minor). She refused to be his concubine, as was his right under Roman law, and he killed her in anger.

(Dulas of Zepherinum) *(St)* *{4 –deleted}*

15 June

d. 300. His real name was Tatianus (the nickname 'Dulas' means 'servant'). He was imprisoned at Zepherinum in Cilicia (Asia Minor) and was savagely tortured over two days because he mocked the pagan gods. He died of the effects while being taken away for execution.

Dulce-of-the-Poor López Pontes de Souza Brito (Bl) {2 –add}

13 March

1914–92. She was born and died at Salvador (Brazil). The daughter of a university don, she started to help poor and homeless people in her early teens but could only join the Missionary Sisters of the Immaculate Conception in 1932. She started her apostolate by opening a doss-house for homeless men, and went on to found several large charitable institutions in her native city, including a hospital and orphanage. When she was dying she was visited by Bl John Paul II. She was beatified in 2011.

Dulcidius (Dulcet, Doucis) of Agen (St) {2}

17 October

d. c.450. He succeeded St Phoebadius as bishop of Agen (France).

Dunstan of Canterbury (St) {2}

19 May

909–88. From a noble family of Somerset (England), he was educated by the monks at Glastonbury, which was possibly the only monastery in England where any sort of monastic life had survived the Danish incursions. He became a royal courtier but vowed privately to become a monk and returned to Glastonbury as a hermit, where he practised the crafts of metalwork, manuscript illumination and embroidery for which he became famous. He was appointed abbot of Glastonbury by the king in 943 and made the abbey a centre of monastic renewal, introducing the Benedictine rule. His monastic zeal was increased by a period of exile at Ghent, where he saw the effects of continental monastic reform. After his recall in 957, this zeal bore fruit in collaboration with SS Ethelwold and Oswald, the three founding and reforming many monasteries and promulgating the 'Regularis Concordia' for their common observance. He became bishop of Worcester in 957 and archbishop of Canterbury in 960 and had great influence in affairs of state. Also the English custom of having cathedral priories was instigated by him, and he may have introduced monks at Canterbury Cathedral, where he died. He is often depicted holding the Devil by the nose with a pair of pincers.

Dwynwen *(St)*

25 January

d. c.460. Of the family of St Brychan, she settled as a hermit at Llanddwyn on Anglesey. The place became a great pilgrimage centre before the Reformation. The saying 'Nothing wins hearts like cheerfulness' is attributed to her, and she is the Welsh patron of true lovers.

Dwynwen cf. **Theneva**.
Dyfrig cf. **Dubricius**.

Dympna (Dymphna) (St) {2}

30 May

C7–9th. She was a virgin martyr of Gheel near Antwerp (Belgium). Her fanciful legend describes her as an Irish princess who fled with a priest from her incestuous father to that place, where they were killed by their pursuers. The story was invented for some relics found there in the C13th, and insane people were alleged to be cured at her shrine. She became their patron, and a great mental hospital was built that same century at Gheel.

E

Ead- cf. **Ed-**
Eadgith cf. **Edith**.

Eanswith (Eanswida) *(St)*

12 September
d. c.640. A granddaughter of King St Ethelbert of Kent (England), she was first abbess of a nunnery (the first in Saxon England) founded for her in 630 by her father the king at Folkestone. It was destroyed by the Danes in 867 but re-founded as a cell of Canterbury Cathedral Priory and transferred to the site of the present Anglican town church of St Mary and Eanswith in 1137 after incursions by the sea. Her alleged relics were rediscovered in that church in 1885, and are still there. She is not in the Roman Martyrology.

Eata (St) {2}

26 October
d. ?686. A disciple of St Aidan, he became abbot of Melrose in Scotland (a Celtic monastery) and received St Cuthbert as a monk there. After the council of Whitby, he accepted the Roman observances and became the first English bishop of Lindisfarne. He was made bishop of Hexham on a division of his diocese in 678, was at Lindisfarne 681–5 and then left that see to St Cuthbert when he went back to Hexham.

Eberhard cf. **Everard**.
Ebregisil cf. **Evergisil**.

Ebrulf (Évroul) of Ouche (St) {2, 4}

29 December
?617–706. From Bayeux in Normandy (France), he was at the Merovingian court before becoming a monk at Deux Jumeaux near his native city. Later he became abbot-founder of Ouche (later named after him) and also founded some smaller monasteries. The historian Oderic Vitalis was a monk under him.

Ecclesius (St) {2}

27 July
d. ?532. Bishop of Ravenna (Italy) from 521, he started the construction of the basilica of St Vitalis there and is commemorated by a mosaic therein.

Edan cf. **Aidan**.
Edilburga cf. **Ethelburga**.
Ediltrudis cf. **Etheldreda**.
Edith Stein cf. **Teresa -Benedicta- of- the-Cross Stein**.

Edith of Wilton (St) {2}

16 September
961–84. Daughter of King Edgar of England and of the nun St Wulftrude, she was taken to Wilton Abbey in Wiltshire as a baby and never left it. She was professed as a nun when aged fifteen, and refused either to become an abbess or to become queen when her father died. St Dunstan was at her deathbed. She is patron of Kent, because she was born at Kemsing near Sevenoaks.

Edmund, King (St) {2, 4}

20 November
d. 869. King of East Anglia (England) from ?855, he was killed after being taken prisoner in a Danish incursion, allegedly because of his faith. He is often depicted pierced with arrows, as according to tradition his captors used him for target practice before beheading him. The place where this happened is described as 'Hellesdon', which seems to be a field near Bradfield St Clare in Suffolk rather than the town in Norfolk. The place nearby where he was buried became a great abbey around which the town of Bury St Edmunds grew.

Edmund Arrowsmith (St) {2}

28 August
d. 1628. From a recusant farming family at Haydock near St Helens (Lancs), he studied at

Douai, was ordained priest in 1612 and went on the Lancashire mission the following year. In 1623, he became a Jesuit. He was hanged, drawn and quartered at Lancaster and was canonized in 1970. Cf. **England, Martyrs of**.

Edmund Bojanowski (Bl) {2}

7 August
1814–71. A Polish nobleman from Grabónog in the German Empire, after his university studies he devoted his life to works of charity in the rural areas of his ancestral locality. After founding a home for orphans he attracted some young women as disciples from the local peasantry, and thus founded the 'Sisters, Servants of Mary Immaculate' in 1858. This had twenty-two houses in Poland at the time of his death. He was beatified in 1999.

Edmund Campion (St) {2}

1 December
?1540–81. From London, he was a pupil at Christ's Hospital there, then a brilliant student at St John's College at Oxford. He became an Anglican deacon before he converted, whereupon he studied at Douai and at Rome where he became a Jesuit. He was ordained at Prague and was one year on the English mission where he was a great success. Then he was betrayed, tortured and hanged, drawn and quartered at Tyburn. He was canonized in 1970. Cf. **England, Martyrs of**.

Edmund Duke and Comps (Bl) {2}

27 May
d. 1590. From Kent, he was educated at Rheims and ordained at Rome in 1589. He went to the North with BB Richard Hill (a Yorkshireman ordained at Laon), John Hogg and Richard Holliday (also known as John). The four young priests were immediately seized and executed at Durham. They were beatified in 1987. Cf. **England, Martyrs of**.

Edmund Gennings (St) {2}

10 December
d. 1591. From Lichfield (Staffs), he was a convert who studied at Rheims and was ordained priest there in 1590. He was quickly captured on his return to England together with St Polydore Plasden during Mass at the house of St Swithin Wells in Gray's Inn Road (London). He was hanged, drawn and quartered at Gray's Inn Fields with St Swithin and was canonized in 1970. Cf. **England, Martyrs of**.

Edmund Rich (St) {2}

16 November
1180–1240. From a family of shopkeepers at Abingdon on the Thames (England), he was a student at Oxford and Paris before becoming professor of philosophy at Oxford in 1219. He became a canon of Salisbury Cathedral in 1222 and was made archbishop of Canterbury in 1233. His reforming zeal for justice and good ecclesiastical discipline made him unpopular with the king, his own cathedral priory and the papal legate among others so he secretly went into exile in 1235 to the Cistercian abbey of Pontigny. He died at Soissy, an Augustinian monastery, but his shrine was at Pontigny. The Cistercian claim that he became a monk of theirs seems to be false. There is a college at Oxford named after him.

Edmund Sykes (Bl) {2}

23 March
d. 1587. The son of a Leeds merchant, he was ordained at Rheims in 1581 and was a priest in York for four years before being deported. On his return there he was betrayed by his brother and was executed. He was beatified in 1987. Cf. **England, Martyrs of**.

Edward II, King of England

1307–27. After his revolting murder at Berkeley Castle, this body of this worthless king was acquired by the abbot of Gloucester with the intention of establishing it as a focus of pilgrimage to his abbey. His intention was so successful that the abbey was able to rebuild its church (now the cathedral) with the profits. This is a good example of the abuses that caused the act of canonization to be removed from the power of local churches and to be reserved to the Papacy.

Edward Bamber (Bl) {2}

7 August

d. 1646. From a recusant family near Poulton (Lancs), he studied at St Omer and Seville and was ordained at Cadiz in 1626. He was a priest in Lancashire for sixteen years before his capture during the Interregnum, and he was executed at Lancaster with BB Martin Woodcock and Thomas Whitaker. They were beatified in 1987. Cf. **England, Martyrs of**.

Edward Barlow cf. **Ambrose Edward Barlow**.

Edward Burden (Bl) {2}

29 November

d. 1588. A convert graduate of Oxford from Co. Durham, he was ordained at Rheims and was a priest at York, becoming known for his kindness and gentleness. He was executed there and was beatified in 1987. Cf. **England, Martyrs of**.

Edward Campion cf. **Gerald Edwards**.

Edward Catherick (Bl) {2}

13 April

d. 1642. From Carlton near Richmond (Yorks), he was educated at Douai and was on the English mission from 1635. He was executed at York and was beatified in 1929. Cf. **England, Martyrs of**.

Edward Cheevers (Bl) {2}

5 July

Cf. **Matthew Lambert and Comps**.

Edward Coleman (Bl) {2}

3 December

d. 1678. A Suffolk landowner, he was educated at Peterhouse in Cambridge but became a convert and the secretary of the Duchess of York (the sister-in-law of King Charles II). He was the first victim of the Oates plot, being executed at Tyburn on the charge of conspiring with foreign powers to re-establish the Catholic Church in England. Cf. **England, Martyrs of**.

Edward the Confessor, King of England (St) {2, 3}

13 October

1003–66. Born at Islip near Oxford, a son of King Ethelred the Unready, he spent much of his youth in exile at Normandy before becoming king in 1042. He was pious, generous and unambitious and was respected for his unworldliness and chastity (the rumour had it that his marriage was not consummated), but he lacked the ruthlessness, ambition and consistency needed for a successful contemporary ruler. He was more interested in prayer and hunting than in government but his reign was afterwards remembered for its prosperity, peace and justice. He founded Westminster Abbey, where he was buried and where his relics were enshrined on 13 October 1162, the year after his canonization. They remain in situ. The depiction on the Bayeaux Tapestry of a fair-haired man with a long beard is probably based on his actual appearance. His cultus was confined to particular calendars in 1969.

Edward Detkens (Bl) {2}

10 October

1885–1942. The auxiliary bishop of Plock in Poland, he died of ill-treatment by the Nazis in a prison at Działdowo. Cf. **Poland, Martyrs of the Nazi Occupation of**.

Edward Focherini (Bl) {2 –add}

27 December
1907–44. Born in Modena, Italy, he became a journalist in that city and the father of a large family. After the downfall of Mussolini when the occupying Germans were rounding up Jews in Italy for extermination, he worked hard to arrange the escape of many. The forging of documents giving them false non-Jewish identities was his speciality. As a result, he was arrested and deported to the concentration camp at Hersbruck in Germany, where he died. He was beatified as a martyr in 2013.

Edward Fulthorp (Bl) {2}

4 July
d. 1597. A Yorkshire landowner, he converted and was executed at York as a result together with BB Henry Abbot, Thomas Bosgrave and William Andleby. He was beatified in 1929. Cf. **England, Martyrs of**.

Edward Grzymala (Bl) {2}

10 August
1906–42. A Polish priest of the Congregation of Little Workers of Divine Providence, he was gassed at the concentration camp at Dachau with Bl Francis Drzewiecki. Cf. **Poland, Martyrs of the Nazi Occupation of**.

Edward James (Bl) {2}

1 October
d. 1588. From the village of Breaston near Derby, he was a student at St John's College in Oxford but converted and studied at Rheims and Rome. He was ordained priest in 1583, was executed at Chichester (Sx) and was beatified in 1929. Cf. **England, Martyrs of**.

Edward Jones (Bl) {2}

6 May
d. 1590. A convert from somewhere in the diocese of St Asaph (Wales), he studied at Rheims and was ordained in 1588, being captured two years later and executed in Fleet Street (London) with Bl Anthony Middleton. He was beatified in 1929. Cf. **England, Martyrs of**.

Edward 'the Martyr', King of England (St) {2}

18 March
d. 978. The son of Edgar the Peaceful, he succeeded him as king in 975 when aged thirteen. He was murdered at Corfe by a faction favouring his younger brother (a later allegation blamed his stepmother) and buried at Wareham (Dorset). He did not die for the faith, but the injustice of his death and his remembered goodness led to popular veneration and his relics were transferred to Shaftesbury Abbey. They are now at the Orthodox monastery at Brookwood (Surrey). The Roman Martyrology does not list him as a martyr.

Edward Oldcorne (Bl) {2}

7 April
d. 1606. From York, he was ordained priest at Rome and became a Jesuit in 1587. He was on mission in the Midlands from 1588 to 1606 and was executed at Worcester for alleged involvement in the Gunpowder Plot together with Bl Ralph Ashley. He was beatified in 1929. Cf. **England, Martyrs of**.

Edward Osbaldeston (Bl) {2}

16 November
1560–94. Of the Lancashire gentry, he was born at Osbaldeston Hall near Blackburn and was ordained at Rheims in 1585. He was a priest in Yorkshire but was betrayed by

a renegade priest who saw him in an inn at Tollerton. He was executed at York and beatified in 1987. Cf. **England, Martyrs of**.

Edward Poppe (Bl) {2}

10 June
1890–1924. From Moerzeke in Flanders (Belgium), he became a parish priest at Ghent before serving as rector of a religious community in his home region and then as director of clerics fulfilling their military service. His life-long interest was the re-evangelization of Flanders in the face of the growing secularization of society, and he wrote much to this end. He was beatified in 1999.

Edward Powell (Bl) {2}

30 July
d. 1540. A Welshman, he became a fellow of Oriel College in Oxford and a canon of Salisbury Cathedral, being known for his writings against Luther. As one of advisers of Queen Catherine of Aragon, he opposed the spiritual claims of King Henry VIII and was imprisoned for six years before being hanged, drawn and quartered at Smithfield (London) with BB Richard Featherstone and Thomas Abel. He was beatified in 1886. Cf. **England, Martyrs of**.

Edward-Joseph Rosaz (Bl) {2}

3 March
1830–1903. Born at Susa in Piedmont (Italy), he was ordained in 1854 and became a cathedral canon, the seminary rector and chaplain to nuns and prisoners. To help the poor and children of the diocese, he founded the 'Franciscan Missionary Sisters of Susa' in 1870. He became bishop in 1878 and proved to be a truly great pastor, being devoted to the Eucharist, Our Lady and the pope. His personal spirituality was based on 'lectio divina'. He was beatified in 1991.

Edward Shelley (Bl) {2}

30 August
d. 1588. A landowner of Warminghurst in Sussex, he was hanged at Tyburn for sheltering priests along with St Margaret Ward and BB John Roche, Richard Lloyd, Richard Leigh and Richard Martin. He was beatified in 1929. Cf. **England, Martyrs of**.

Edward Stransham (Bl) {2}

21 January
d. 1586. From Oxford, he was a student at St John's College there but converted, studied at Douai and Rheims and was ordained in 1580. From the following year he was on mission in London and Oxford until he was captured and executed at Tyburn. He was beatified in 1929. Cf. **England, Martyrs of**.

Edward Thwing (Bl) {2}

27 July
1560–1600. Related to St John of Bridlington and to Bl Thomas Thwing, he was born at Heworth Hall in Yorks and became professor of Hebrew and Greek at the college at Rheims before being ordained at Laon in 1597. He was a priest in Lancashire before being captured and executed at Lancaster with Bl Robert Nutter. He was beatified in 1987. Cf. **England, Martyrs of**.

Edward Waterson (Bl) {2}

8 January
d. 1593. A convert from London, he studied at Rheims and was ordained in 1592. He was immediately captured on his return to England and executed at Newcastle. He was beatified in 1929. Cf. **England, Martyrs of**.

Egbert of Iona (St) {2, 4}

24 April
d. 729. An Anglo-Saxon monk from Lindisfarne, he went to Ireland to study at an

unidentified monastery called 'Rathmelsigi' and remained there, helping to inspire missionary monks to go to the Germanic countries. Then he went to Iona (Scotland) and tried to introduce the Roman observance. He eventually succeeded, it being alleged that he died on the first Easter Sunday celebrated there on the date given by the Roman calculation.

(Egdunus and Comps) (SS) {4 –deleted}

12 March
d. 303. They were martyred at Nicomedia (Asia Minor) in the reign of Diocletian by being hanged head downwards over a fire.

Egidius cf. **Giles**.

Egwin (St) {2}

30 December
d. 717. An Anglo-Saxon nobleman and possibly a monk, he became bishop of Worcester (England) in 692 but was driven away by a hostile faction. He was reinstated after going to Rome for vindication, and probably founded Evesham Abbey where his shrine was established.

Eldrad (St) {2}

13 March
d. c.840. From Provence (France), he spent his large fortune in charity and then went on pilgrimage to Rome. After many wanderings he joined the abbey of Novalese in the Italian Alps below Mont Cenis pass, and became abbot for thirty years. He built much, including a hospice at the summit of the pass, and augmented the library. His cultus was approved in 1904.

Eleazar de Sabran (St) {2, 4}

27 September
1286–1323. A nobleman from Provence (France) married to Bl Delphina of Signe, he held the barony of Ansouis at home as well as the county of Ariano in the Kingdom of Naples. He went to the latter as tutor to the king's son, served as regent of the kingdom and died in Paris as its ambassador. He was noted for his honesty, penance and prayer at a time when these qualities were not common among his class. He was canonized in 1369.

Elesbaan (Caleb), Negus (St) {2, 4}

15 May
d. ?535. He was the Negus (king) of Axum in Ethiopia after that country became Christian and campaigned against the Jewish king of the Himyarites in the Yemen after the latter persecuted his Christian subjects. He abdicated to become a monk, allegedly at Jerusalem but actually near Axum. He is listed in the Roman Martyrology although he was almost certainly a Monophysite.

Eleuchadius of Ravenna (St) {2, 4}

14 February
C3nd. A Greek, he was converted by St Apollinaris of Ravenna (Italy) and was bishop-administrator for him in his absence. Then he succeeded St Adheritus as bishop and is alleged to have introduced the practice of the Divine Office to the West.

Eleutherius, Pope (St) {2, 3}

26 May
d. 189. A Greek deacon of Rome, he succeeded St Soter as pope in perhaps 174. Very little is known about him, and the story that he sent missionaries to Britain is a myth. His cultus was suppressed in 1969.

(Eleutherius, Anthia and Comps) (SS) {4- deleted}

18 April
d. 117–38. They were alleged to have been an Illyrian bishop, his mother and eleven others

who were martyred in the reign of Hadrian. Their acta are completely worthless, however, being medieval Byzantine fiction.

(Eleutherius and Leonides) (SS) {4- deleted}

8 August
? They were burnt, possibly at Byzantium (later Constantinople) but nothing is known for certain.

Eleutherius of Auxerre (St) {2, 4}

26 August
C6th. He was bishop of Auxerre (France) from 532.

(Eleutherius of Byzantium) (St) {4 –deleted}

20 February
d. c.310. Allegedly a bishop and martyr of Byzantium (later Constantinople), he is usually identified with St Eleutherius of Tarsia.

Eleutherius of Nicomedia (St) {2, 4}

2 October
End C3rd. He was martyred at Nicomedia (Asia Minor), but his acta are unreliable. The assertions that he was a solider and had companion martyrs have been deleted from the Roman Martyrology.

(Eleutherius of Rocca d'Arce) (St) {4 –deleted}

29 May
? The principal patron of Rocca d'Arce near Aquino (Italy) was alleged to have been a hermit, an English pilgrim and a brother of SS Grimwald of Pontecorvo and Fulk Scotti.

Eleutherius of Spoleto (St) {2, 4}

6 September
C6th. Abbot of a monastery at Spoleto (Italy), he was a thaumaturge and had some of his miracles described by St Gregory the Great (who himself experienced a cure). He

migrated to Rome and became a monk at St Gregory's monastery of St Andrew's.

Eleutherius of Tarsia (St) {2, 4}

4 August
Early C4th. He was a martyr of Tarsia in Bithynia (Asia Minor) and had a pilgrimage shrine there as well as a church in Constantinople. His acta are unreliable.

Eleutherius of Tournai (St) {2, 4}

20 February
d. c.530. From Tournai (Belgium), he became bishop there (possibly the first) in 486 and evangelized the Franks settling in the area. He allegedly died as a result of being attacked by some local Arians, but the extant biographies are unreliable and the Roman Martyrology does not list him as a martyr.

Eleutheropolis, Martyrs of (SS) {2}

17 December
d. 638. They were fifty soldiers massacred by the invading Muslim Arabs at Eleutheopolis in the Holy Land after the fall of the city of Gaza. Their names have survived: six named John, two named Paul, Photinus, two named Zitas, Eugenius, Muselius, Stephen, three named Theodore, five named George, Theopemptus, Sergius, Cyriac and Philoxenus from the Scythian cohort; Theodosius, Epiphanius, four called John, two called Theodore, Sergius, two called George, Thomas, Stephen, Conon, Paul, Paulinus, Caiumas, Abramius, Marmises and Marinus from the cohort of volunteers.

Elias, Jeremias, Isaias, Samuel and Daniel (SS) {2, 4}

16 February
d. 309. Five Egyptians, they went to visit some fellow Christian countrymen who had been condemned to the mines in Cilicia (Asia Minor). On the way back they were seized and

beheaded at Caesarea in the Holy Land. Eusebius was there at the time and wrote a graphic
account of the martyrdom.

Elias, Paul and Isidore (SS) {2, 4}

17 April
d. 856. Elias was a priest of Cordoba (Spain)
under Muslim rule and was killed with two
young monks, whom he was directing. St
Eulogius left an eye-witness account of the
martyrdom.

Elias Facchini (St) {1 –group}

9 July
Cf. **Gregory Grassi and Comps**.

Elias-del-Socorro Nieves (Bl) {2}

11 October
1882–1928. From a peasant family of Guanajuato State, Mexico, despite tuberculosis he
became an Augustinian friar at Yurira in 1904
and was ordained in 1916. In 1921, he was put
in charge of an extremely poor rural parish until
1927, when the 'Christero' guerrilla movement
against the persecution of the church by the
government broke out. He was ordered by the
latter to move to a city so as to be under obser-
vation but took to the hills instead and continued his rural ministry in secret. After fourteen
months he was captured with two ranchers by a
military patrol, recognized as a priest and shot
with them. He was beatified as a martyr in 1997.

Elias (Elijah) the Prophet (St) {2, 4}

20 July
He features as the first great prophet of Israel
in the books of Kings in the Old Testament.

Elias Spelaiotes (St) {2}

11 September
d. 960. From Reggio di Calabria (Italy), he
became a monk when aged nineteen and died
as a hermit in a cave at Meliculla (his surname

means 'Troglodyte'). He has been confused
with Elias of Thessalonica.

Elias the Younger (St) {2}

17 August
823–903. From Sicily, he was enslaved after
the Muslim conquest of the island in 831 but
was released and visited the holy places of the
East before founding a monastery at Salianae
in Calabria (Italy). He died at Thessalonica on
his way to Constantinople.

Elisha-of-St-Clement Fracasso (Bl) {2 –add}

1901–27. From Bari (Italy), she had a vision
of St Theresa of the Child Jesus on the
evening before her first Holy Communion
when aged ten, which eventually led her to
become a Carmelite nun in her home city in
1920. She died of meningitis seven years later,
on Christmas Day, and was beatified in 2006.

Eligius (Eloi, Eloy) of Noyon (St) {2, 4}

1 December
588–660. From a lowly background at Limoges (France), owing to his talent he became
the royal goldsmith and minter at the Frankish court at Paris and endowed many churches
and monasteries such as Solignac. In 640, he
left his post to become a priest, was made
bishop of Noyon and evangelized French and
Belgian Flanders. He had an extremely popular cultus in the Middle Ages. Some pieces
of precious metalwork allegedly by him survived to the French Revolution, but all but one
fragment were then destroyed.

Elijah cf. **Elias**.

Eliphius (Eloff) (St) {2}

16 October
C4th. Allegedly from Ireland or Scotland,
he was martyred at Soulosse near Saint-Dié

(France) and had his relics taken to Cologne (Germany) in the C10th.

Elisha the Prophet (St) {2, 4}

14 June

He was the disciple of Elijah, and has a cycle of stories about him in the Books of Kings in the Old Testament.

Elizabeth (St) {2, 4}

23 September

C1st. What is known about the mother of St John the Baptist is limited to the Gospel of St Luke.

Elizabeth Achler 'the Good' (Bl) {2}

25 November

1386–1480. From Waldsee in Württemberg (Germany), she became a Franciscan tertiary in 1400 and was a prodigious faster as well as a mystic and stigmatic. In 1403, she joined a community at Reute nearby and died there. Her cultus was confirmed for Constance in 1766.

Elizabeth-Anne Bayley Seton (St) {2}

4 January

1774–1821. From New York, she was a devout member of the Episcopalian Church until she was widowed with five children in 1804. Then she converted, was confirmed at Baltimore in 1806 and went on to found the first indigenous American sisterhood, the 'Sisters of Charity of St Joseph'. They worked to build up a parochial school system in the USA. She died near Baltimore and was canonized in 1975.

Elizabeth Canori Mora (Bl) {2}

4 February

1779–1825. A Roman, she married a young lawyer but he soon abandoned her with two daughters. This meant she had to earn her own living, but still managed to care for other needy families. She became a Trinitarian tertiary in 1807. Her husband repented shortly after her death and became a priest of the Franciscan Conventuals, as she had predicted. She was beatified in 1994.

Elizabeth-of-the-Trinity Catez (Bl) {2}

9 November

1880–1906. From near Bourges (France), she early recognized a Carmelite vocation and made a private vow of chastity when aged fourteen. She joined the Carmel at Dijon in 1901 and died of tuberculosis five years later, but her experience of contemplative prayer in the meantime led her to develop her doctrine of the indwelling of the Holy Trinity in the praying subject. She was beatified in 1984.

Elizabeth Chŏng Chŏng-hye (St) {1 –group}

29 December

Cf. **Benedicta Hyŏn Kyŏng-nyŏn and Comps**.

Elizabeth of Hungary (St) {1, 3}

17 November

1207–31. Born at Presburg in Hungary (now Bratislava in Slovakia), she was a daughter of King Andrew II and a niece of St Hedwig. When aged fourteen she married Ludwig IV, landgrave of Thuringia (Germany), and was happily married with three children until he died on crusade at Otranto. Then she was dispossessed (but was granted the city of Marburg) and became a Franciscan tertiary, living in poverty while helping the destitute. She was canonized in 1235. She is often depicted with her cloak full of roses.

Elizabeth-Bartholomea Picenardi (Bl) {2}

20 February

1428–68. From Mantua (Italy), when she lost her mother she became a Servite tertiary and collected a group of disciples from the Mantuan nobility, thus founding a new nunnery. Her cultus was confirmed in 1804 for Cremona, Mantua and the Servites.

Elizabeth of Portugal (St) {1, 3}

4 July
1271–1336. Daughter of the king of Aragon, when aged twelve she married King Denis of Portugal who was a capable ruler but an immoral and selfish person. At his dissolute {2} court she gave an example of Christian rectitude and charity and tried to make peace between the Iberian kingdoms. As a widow, she became a Franciscan tertiary at a Poor Clare convent at Coïmbra. She was canonized in 1625.

Elizabeth Qin Bianzhi and Simon Qin Qunfu (SS) {1 –group}

19 July
1846 & 1886–1900. She was a widow of Nanpeiluo in Hebei (China) with six children. After the Boxer rebellion they moved to Liucun near Renqin for safety but were betrayed. As they fled St Simon, a son, was caught and killed. St Elizabeth was shot dead with two daughters two days later (another son had already been killed). Cf. **China, Martyrs of**.

Elizabeth Renzi (Bl) {2}

14 August
1786–1859. From near Rimini (Italy), she joined the Augustinians at Pietrarubbia in 1807 but the community was suppressed in 1810 and she returned home. In 1824, she started to teach at the secondary school at Corriano, which lacked qualified teachers. To run it properly she eventually founded the 'Pious Teachers of Our Lady of Sorrows', which was approved as a diocesan institute with a charism based on the Seven Sorrows of Our Lady. She died at Corriano and was beatified in 1989.

Elizabeth of Schönau (St) {2, 4}

18 June
1126–64. When aged twelve she entered the Benedictine (not Cistercian) nunnery at Schönau near Bonn (Germany). After being professed in 1147, she became subject to visions which were described in the biography written by her brother Egbert, who was abbot of a neighbouring monastery. Some of these, such as those concerning St Ursula, seem to have been delusions but she was humble and bore her ill health with patience. She became abbess in 1157.

Elizabeth Vendramini (Bl) {2}

2 April
1790–1860. Born at Bassani near Vicenza (Italy), she refused to marry and, when aged twenty-seven, devoted herself to being 'poor with the poor' in order to help them and to find God in them. She went to Padua in 1828 and founded the 'Elizabethines', which were Franciscan tertiaries with St Elizabeth of Hungary as their patron. She was beatified in 1990.

Elmo cf. **Erasmus** or **Peter Gonzalez**.
Eloff cf. **Eliphius**.
Eloi cf. **Eligius**.

Elphege the Elder (or the Bald) (St) {2}

12 March
d. 951. He became a monk in unknown circumstances and was made bishop of Winchester (England) in 934. He was possibly related to St Dunstan whom he introduced to the monastic life and then ordained, together with St Ethelwold. ('Bald' refers to his tonsure, which was unusual in England at a time when monastic life had collapsed.)

(Elpidius, Marcellus, Eustochius and Comps) (SS) {4 –deleted}

16 November
d. 362. According to their story, Elpidius was an official at the court of the Arian emperor Constantius. After the accession of the pagan emperor Julian, he was martyred with several companions in an unknown place, by being tied to the tails of two wild horses and thus dragged about before being burnt alive. The problem with this story is that any high official at court at that time was most likely to have been an Arian himself, and hence would not have been regarded as a Catholic martyr. Also, Julian's policy was to avoid martyring Christians.

(Elpidius of Cappadocia) (St) {4 –deleted}

2 September
C4th. There are two villages called Sant' Elpidio near Fermo in the Marches (Italy), and these are alleged to have been the sites of monasteries founded by a hermit from Cappodocia (Asia Minor).

(Elpidius of Lyons) (St) {4 –deleted}

2 September
d. 422. He succeeded St Antiochus as bishop of Lyons (France). His shrine there (with many others in France) was destroyed by Calvinists in 1562.

Elpidius of San Elpidio (St) {2}

2 September
Before C11th. He is enshrined at the small town of San Elpidio a Mare near Fermo (Italy), but nothing is known about him.

Elvis (St)

22 February
C6th? He was allegedly one of the companions of St Breaca, and has an ancient church dedicated to him near Solvay in Cornwall (England). He may also be the patron of St Allen near Truro, but the traditions are seriously confused. His only contemporary importance lies in his name.

Elzear cf. **Eleazar**.

Emebert (Ablebert) (St) {2}

15 January
d. ?645. He was a bishop of Cambrai (Belgium).

Emerentiana (St) {2, 3}

23 January
C4th? She is a Roman martyr with an ancient cultus. Her unreliable legend describes her as being stoned to death after being discovered praying at the tomb of St Agatha, her recently martyred foster-sister. Her cultus was confined to local calendars in 1969, and details of the legend deleted from the Roman Martyrology.

Emeric of Hungary (St) {2, 4}

4 November
1007–31. Son of King St Stephen and crown prince of Hungary, he was tutored by St Gerard Sagredo and gave promise of being a model ruler but died before his father in a hunting accident. A pagan reaction followed. He was canonized with his father in 1083.

Emeric de Quart (Bl) {2}

1 August
d. 1313. He became bishop of Aosta in the Alps (Italy) in 1301, and his cultus was confirmed for there in 1881.

Emerita (SS) {2, 4}

22 September
? She was martyred at Rome and buried in the Commodilla cemetery on the Via Ostiense.

The subsequent legend duplicates her as a pair of virgins, Digna and Emerita, who were martyred in the reign of Valerian by being hanged by their hair and burnt with torches until they died. These details have been deleted from the Roman Martyrology.

Emetherius and Cheledonius (SS) {2, 4}

3 March
C4th? Allegedly two soldiers, they were martyred at Calahorra in Old Castile (Spain). Their acta have been lost, but both Prudentius and St Gregory of Tours mention them.

Emidius cf. **Emygdius**.

Emigdius (St) {2, 4}

5 August
C4th. He is alleged to have been a bishop and martyr at Ascoli Piceno (Italy) but his acta are unreliable. He has a cultus in California as a protector against earthquakes.

Emila and Jeremias (SS) {2, 4}

15 September
d. 852. Brothers from Cordoba (Spain), they preached against Islam in Arabic and were killed as a result in the reign of the Umayyad emir Abderrahman II. Emilas was a deacon.

Emilian de Cogolla (St) {2, 4}

12 November
d. 574. Initially a poverty-stricken shepherd in La Rioja (Spain), he became a hermit and then a priest of the church at Berceo near Tarazona. He went back to being a hermit, however, gathered a large number of disciples and thus founded the monastery of La Cogolla ('The Cowl'). He is a minor patron of Spain, having been invoked in the wars against the Moors.

Emilian of Cyzicus (St) {2, 4}

8 August
d. c.820. A bishop of Cyzicus on the south shore of the Sea of Marmara (Asia Minor), he died in exile for opposing iconoclasm.

Emilian Kovč (Bl) {2}

25 March
1884–1944. From an Eastern-rite Catholic family of Kosmach in western Ukraine, he studied in Lviv and Rome and became a diocesan priest of Ivano-Frankivisk in 1911. He worked in Galicia and in Bosnia (both then parts of the Hapsburg Empire) before becoming parish priest at Peremyshljany. This became part of Poland, but during the Second World War was first occupied by the Soviets and then by the Germans, both of which persecuted him and his Ukrainian parishioners. Finally he was taken to the concentration camp at Majdanek, where he celebrated the sacraments in secret for his fellow prisoners. He died in the camp hospital and was beatified as a martyr in 2001.

(Emilian of Rennes) (St) *{4 –deleted}*

11 October
? He is listed in the old Roman Martyrology as a hermit at Rennes in Brittany (France) but there is no record of him locally and he is possibly a duplication of St Melanius of Rennes.

Emilian of Silistria (St) {2, 4}

18 July
d. 362. He was martyred at Silistria (Bulgaria) in the reign of Julian.

Emilian Szramek (Bl) {2}

13 January
1887–1942. A Polish priest, he died of ill-treatment at the concentration camp at Dachau. Cf. **Poland, Martyrs of the Nazi Occupation of**.

Emilian of Valence (St) {2}

13 September
d. p374. He is venerated as the first bishop of Valence (France)

Emilian of Vercelli (St) {2}

17 May
C6th. He had been a hermit for forty years when he became bishop of Vercelli in Piedmont (Italy) and went on to die a centenarian.

Emiliana (St) {2, 4}

5 January
C6th. She was a paternal aunt of St Gregory the Great, who described her as living in community with two other maiden aunts (Amita and Tarsilla) in their own house at Rome.

(Emiliana) *(St) {4 –deleted}*

30 June
? There used to be a church dedicated to her in Rome, but nothing is known of her and there is a suspicion that the dedication originally came from a street name.

Emily cf. **Mary-Emily**.

Emily Bicchieri (Bl) {2}

3 May
1238–1314. From Vercelli (Italy), she induced her father to found a Dominican nunnery there and she became the first superior. She had the charism of prophecy. Her cultus was confirmed for Vercelli in 1769.

Emily de Vialar (St) {2}

24 August
1797–1856. From Gaillac near Albi (France), she lost her mother when still a child and kept house for her father until she was thirty-five while devoting herself to prayer and works of charity. Then she received a large inheritance and set about founding the 'Sisters of St Joseph of the Apparition' locally in 1832. She lost her money and also her prestige in Albi after a disastrous missionary expedition to Algiers but managed to establish a house at Marseilles in 1852. By the time she died her institute had spread through Europe and to Africa and Asia. She was canonized in 1951.

Emma cf. **Gemma**.

Emmanuel, Sabinus and Comps (SS) {2, 4}

26 March
? These four were martyred somewhere in Asia Minor, the other two being Codratus and Theodosius. The Roman Martyrology has deleted a reference to forty companions.

Emmanuel Basulto Jiménez and Comps (BB) {2 –add}

d. 1936. Bl Emmanuel Basulto Jiménez was the bishop of Jaén in Spain at the outbreak of the Spanish Civil War. He was shot with one of his priests, Bl Felix Pérez Portela, at Vallecas near Madrid on 12 Augustafter being maliciously accused of embezzling public funds in the context of vicious public hostility. They were beatified in 2013, together with two other diocesan priests, a seminarian and a layman killed in separate incidents. Cf. **Spanish Civil War, Martyrs of** and list in appendix.

Emmanuel Borrás Ferré and Comps (BB) {2 –add}

d. 1936–7. They are the martyrs of the Diocese of Tarragona. This diocese suffered the worst persecution of any of those in Spain during the Spanish Civil War, as the Communist Republican authorities in control there decreed the complete suppression of the church. This policy was implemented by killing every priest and male religious who could be found, a total which included the bishop and one hundred and forty-five others. Sixty-six diocesan priests were killed (including two seminarians), thirty-nine Salesians, twenty Benedictine monks from the abbey of Montserrat, seven Discalced Carmelites, seven Claretians, four Carmelite Tertiaries of Teaching (a congregation now extinct) and one Capuchin. They were beatified as a group, as a witness to what this diocese suffered, in 2013. Cf. **Spanish Civil War, Martyrs of** and list in appendix.

Emmanuel Domingo y Sol (Bl) {2}

25 January

1836–1909. Born at Tortosa (Spain) where he spent his life, he was ordained in 1860. Then he started the first Spanish Catholic newspaper directed at young men and founded the 'Institute of Diocesan Worker Priests' in order to give reparative adoration to the Blessed Sacrament as the centre of the priest's life and to encourage priestly vocations. This spread to Portugal, Italy and the USA. He also founded three congregations of sisters and the Pontifical Spanish College in Rome. Extremely charitable to everyone, especially to the poor and despised, he was beatified in 1987.

Emmanuel Gómez Gónzalez and Adilius Daronch (BB) {2 –add}

d. 1924. Bl Emmanuel was born in 1877, and was a diocesan priest of Braga in Portugal before transferring to Brazil in 1813. He joined the diocese of Santa Maria in the state of Rio Grande do Sul, and was responsible for the vast parish of Nonoai. The bishop asked him to visit the German colonists in a forested region near the border with Uruguay, and he took one of his altar-servers, Bl Adilius, who was fifteen years old. However, the area was infested with revolutionary guerrillas, who objected to his giving Christian burial to those

whom they had killed. Despite warnings they continued their tour, and were ambushed in a remote forest at Três Passos, tied to trees and shot. They were beatified as martyrs in 2007. Their shrine is at Nonoai.

Emmanuel González García (Bl) {2}

4 January

1877–1940. From Seville, Spain, he was ordained in 1901 and became a parish priest at Huelva where he developed a strong devotion to reparation to Jesus in the Blessed Sacrament. To this end he founded the 'Eucharistic Missionaries of Nazareth' and several lay societies. In 1920 he was made bishop of Malaga, but had to go into exile in 1931 as a result of the Spanish Civil War. He died at Palencia and was beatified in 2001.

Emmanuel Lê Văn Phụng (St) {1 –group}

13 July

?1796–1859. From Dan Nuoc in the Mekong Delta of Vietnam, he became a catechist but was imprisoned during the persecution ordered by Emperor Tự Đức. He exhorted his family and friends to forgive their persecutors before he was executed by beheading at Châu Đốc. Cf. **Vietnam, Martyrs of**.

Emmanuel Lozano Garrido (Bl) {2 –add}

3 November

1920–71. He was born at Linares (Spain), and joined the army in 1934. However, in the following year he contracted spondylitis and for the rest of his life was in a wheelchair and in constant pain. He helped to distribute Holy Communion during the Spanish Civil War in the face of anti-clerical violence, and afterwards became a journalist with a fierce devotion to the Eucharist. He was a prolific writer of articles for several magazines, under the byline of Lolo, even after he went blind in 1962. He also wrote several books on spiritual subjects. He died at Linares, and was the first professional journalist to be beatified, in 2010.

Emmanuel Medina Olmos (Bl) {2}

30 August
Cf. **Diego Ventaja Milán and Emmanuel Medina Olmos**.

Emmanuel Morales (St) {1 –group}

15 August
Cf. **Aloysius Batis Sainz and Comps**.

Emmanuel Nguyễn Văn Triệu (St) {1 –group}

17 September
?1756–98. A Vietnamese with Christian parents, he became a soldier but left the army, was ordained priest and worked with the missionaries of the Paris Mission Society. While visiting his mother at the imperial capital of Hué, he was arrested and beheaded on the orders of Emperor Cảnh Thịnh. Cf. **Vietnam, Martyrs of**.

Emmanuel Phụng (St) {1 –group}

31 July
d. 1859. He was a layman of Cây Mét near Saigon in Vietnam, and shared the imprisonment and beheading of St Peter Đoàn Công Quý during the persecution ordered by Emperor Tự Đức. Cf. **Vietnam, Martyrs of**.

Emmanuel Ruiz and Comps (BB) {2}

10 July
d. 1860. After the Crimean War there was great hostility shown to the Middle Eastern Christians in the Ottoman Empire. The Druzes in the Lebanon indulged in a pogrom of their Christian neighbours, and when news of this reached Damascus a Muslim mob sacked the Christian quarter and massacred about four thousand with the connivance of the authorities. A community of eight Franciscans and three Maronite brothers who had taken refuge with them were offered the choice of conversion to Islam or death, and were killed after their refusal. They were Emmanuel Ruiz (superior of the friary), Carmelus Volta, Engelbert Kolland, Francis Pinazo d'Arpuentes, Ascanius Nicanor, Nicholas Alberca, John-James Fernandez and Peter Soler (Franciscans); Francis, Mooti and Raphael Massabki (Maronite brothers). They were beatified in 1926.

Emmanuel (Manuel)-of-the-Holy-Family Sanz Dominguez (Bl) {2 –add}

8 November
1887–1936. From Sotodosos near Guadalajara in Spain, he was a railwayman and then a banker before he was inspired to restore the ancient monastic Order of St Jerome, which was on the verge of being suppressed owing to lack of vocations. He set up a new community in the derelict monastery of Santa María del Parral near Segovia in 1925, which proved to be the salvation of the order. On the outbreak of the Spanish Civil War he was arrested and later killed at Paracuellos del Jarama near Madrid. He was beatified in 2013. Cf. **Spanish Civil War, Martyrs of** and list in appendix.

Emmeram (Haimhramm) (St) {2, 4}

22 September
d. c.690. According to his unreliable biography, he was from Poitiers (France) and was on his way through Bavaria (Germany) on a missionary journey to the Avars when he was persuaded by the duke to stay at Regensburg and become its bishop. Then at the start of a journey to Rome he was waylaid by the duke's son who accused him of seducing a sister of his and ordered him to be blinded and deprived of his extremities. He died later as a result, was buried at Regensburg and was venerated

as a martyr at the abbey that was founded at his shrine.

Enda (Eanna) (St) {2}

21 March
d. ?542. Brother of St Fanchea, he is regarded as Ireland's earliest founder of monasteries, the principal one being Killeaney on Inishmore in the Aran Islands. He had many disciples who went on to become great monastic founders, such as SS Brendan and Finian.

Eneco (Enneco, Iñigo) (St) {2, 4}

1 June
d. c.1060. From Calatayud near Zaragoza (Spain), he became a Cluniac Benedictine monk at the Aragonese abbey of San Juan de la Peña and went on to become a hermit. The king appointed him abbot of Oña near Burgos, which abbey he elevated to great splendour. He won the respect of Jews and Muslims and was canonized in 1259.

Engelbert of Cologne (St) {2, 4}

7 November
?1186–1225. A son of the Count of Berg, as a child he became cathedral provost of Cologne (Germany) in 1203 but was excommunicated in 1206 for rebellion against the emperor and went on the Albigensian Crusade as an atonement. He became archbishop of Cologne in 1216 and (despite being a typical prince-prelate) he supported the secular clergy, restored monasteries and encouraged the new orders of friars. In 1221, he served as administrator of the Empire. He was killed on the orders of a nephew whom he had rebuked for plundering the nunnery of Essen and was venerated as a martyr.

England, Martyrs of

4 May
d. 1535–1681. From the Reformation to the C19th the Catholic Church was proscribed in England. The first 160 years of this period saw systematic persecution as government policy, initially under King Henry VIII who ruthlessly dealt with those who refused to accept his claim to spiritual supremacy. Martyrdoms were especially common under Queen Elizabeth I and King James I, but continued until the end of the C17th. All sorts of people suffered in various different places but the majority of them were regular and secular priests. This is because to work as a priest in England while having been ordained abroad was declared treason by statute, and the punishment specified for traitors was usually applied to condemned priests. This was to be half-asphyxiated by hanging, then to be disembowelled and dismembered while still alive. The Catholic laity were usually persecuted by the levy of fines because the government appreciated the extra revenue. Of the martyrs (including those of Wales), fifty-four were beatified in 1886, nine in 1895, one hundred and thirty-six in 1929 and eighty-five in 1987. So far forty-two have been canonized, including four Welsh martyrs (forty in 1970 and SS John Fisher and Thomas More in 1935), leaving a total of 242 beatified (including two Welsh martyrs). Before 2001 the forty saints of 1970 were celebrated together on 25 October, but then one feast day was established for all the English martyrs and the Welsh ones celebrated separately. Cf. lists of national martyrs in appendix.

Engratia (St) {2, 4}

16 April
d. ?304. She was a maiden who was tortured at Zaragoza (Spain), allegedly by being disembowelled and having one breast cut off. Although regarded as a martyr she apparently survived this treatment.

Ennodius (St) {2, 4}

17 July
473–521. Magnus Felix Ennodius was a Gallo-Roman nobleman from Arles in France

who became a professor of rhetoric at Milan (Italy) and lived a carefree married life until a serious illness caused a conversion. His wife became a nun and he was ordained, being made bishop of Pavia near Milan in 510. He was a poet and hymnographer and also a papal legate at Constantinople during the reign of the Monophysite emperor Anastasius I.

Enoch cf. **Kennocha**.

Eoban and Comps (SS) {2, 4}

5 June
d. 754. They are the companions of St Boniface who were killed with him at Dokkum. St Eoban was allegedly an Irishman, who became a monk in England and helped St Willibrord and then St Boniface on their missions. He was made bishop of Martelaar in the Netherlands by the latter. His shrine was at Erfurt in Thuringia (Germany). There were nine companions: Vintrugus (or Walter), a priest; Amandus, Sevibaldus and Bosa, deacons and Vaccarus, Gundecarus and Ellurus (or Atevulfus), monks. Despite sharing St Boniface's martyrdom they have never been liturgically commemorated with him.

Eogan cf. **Eugene**.

Eonius of Arles (St) {2}

18 August
d. 502. He was archbishop of Arles (France), and defended his church against the Pelagian heresy. He ordained St Caesarius, and nominated him to be his successor.

Epaphras (St) {2, 4}

19 July
C1st. He is mentioned by St Paul in his Letter to the Colossians (Col. 1:7, 4:12, also Phil. 23), and was hence traditionally regarded as bishop of Colossae and a martyr there.

The Roman Martyrology has deleted both assertions.

Epaphroditus (St) {2, 4}

22 March
C1st. He is referred to by St Paul (Phil. 2:25) as having been sent to the Philippians and hence has been traditionally regarded as the first bishop of Philippi in Greek Macedonia. The assertion in the old Roman Martyrology that he was made bishop of Terracina in Italy by St Peter is mythical and has been deleted.

Eparchius (Cybar) (St) {2, 4}

1 July
?504–81. A nobleman from Périgord (France), he became a monk at Sessac and then a hermit at Angoulême in 542.

Ephebus of Naples (St) {2}

23 May
C4th. He was a bishop of Naples (Italy).

(Ephesus, Martyrs of) (SS) *{4 –deleted}*

12 January
C8th? In his revision of the old Roman Martyrology Cardinal Baronius listed forty-two monks of a monastery at Ephesus (Asia Minor) who were killed on the orders of Emperor Constantine V for opposing his iconoclast policy. Baronius's literary source for this entry is now unknown, but it might have been referring to **Stephen, Basil and Comps**.

Ephrem the Syrian (St) {1, 3}

9 June
d. 378. A convert from Nisibis in Mesopotamia, it is probable that he was headmaster of the catechetical school there before the city was annexed by the Persian Empire in 363. Then he and most of the Christian population became refugees, and he settled at Edessa

(now Urfa in Turkey) where he became a deacon. He was the most prolific and famous of the Syrian Fathers, being especially known for his biblical commentaries and the Syriac hymns which he wrote to encourage the Catholic faith and to oppose Arianism (Arius had apparently invented the genre of popular hymns in the contemporary vernacular). The Mariological hymns are especially important dogmatically. He also led relief efforts in a famine which ravaged the district just before his death. He was declared a doctor of the Church in 1920. He is no longer regarded as having been a monk.

(Ephysius) (St) {4 –deleted}

15 January
d. ?303. He is alleged to have been martyred at Cagliari (Sardinia) in the reign of Diocletian but his acta are a worthless forgery. Nevertheless his veneration is popular on the island.

(Epicharis) (St) {4 –deleted}

27 September
Early C4th? She was listed as a Roman senator's wife who was martyred at Byzantium (later Constantinople) or at Rome.

(Epictetus and Comps) (SS) {4 –deleted}

9 January
d. ?250. They are listed as twelve Roman African martyrs, just possibly of the Decian persecution as St Cyprian wrote of a bishop called Epictetus. Named companions are Jucundus, Secundus, Vitalis and Felix.

(Epigmenius) (St) {4 –deleted}

24 March
d. c.300. Listed as a Roman priest martyred in the reign of Diocletian, he is probably the same as St Pigmenius.

Epimachus, Alexander and Comps (SS) {2, 3}

12 December
d. 250. They were tortured and burnt at Alexandria (Egypt) in the reign of Decius. With them were beheaded Ammonarion, a consecrated virgin, Mercuria, Dionysia and other women. The old Roman Martyrology listed another 'Ammonaria'. Epimachus is also listed in error in the old Roman Martyrology on 10 May together with St Gordian, and as such the two had a cultus in the former general calendar. This was suppressed in 1969.

Epimachus of Pelusium (St) {2}

30 October
d. c.250. He was from Pelusium (Egypt), and by tradition was a hermit there. During the persecution ordered by the emperor Decius he went to Alexandria and overturned the pagan altar on which the authorities were forcing Christians to offer sacrifice. For this he was tortured and beheaded.

(Epiphana) (St) {4 –deleted}

12 July
? An alleged martyr of Sicily, she is mentioned only in the unreliable acta of St Alphius.

(Epiphanius, Donatus and Comps) (SS) {4 –deleted}

7 April
? Nothing is written about these martyrs, except that Epiphanius was a Roman African bishop and that there were seventeen in the group. Rufinus and Modestus were also named.

Epiphanius of Pavia (St) {2, 4}

21 January
d. 496. From Pavia (then called Ticinum) near Milan (Italy), he became bishop there in 467. The city was destroyed by Odoacer in 476,

and Epiphanius was largely responsible for rebuilding it and renaming it Pavia. He travelled to Lyons to secure the release of thousands of Italians from captivity. He died at Pavia and his relics were taken to Hildesheim (Germany) in 962.

Epiphanius of Salamis (St) {2}

12 May
?315–403. A native of the Holy Land, he became a monk when young and founded a monastery near Eleutheropolis east of Gaza. He was a zealous opponent of heresy, especially of Arianism and Origenism, and his 'Panarion' or handbook of heresies became famous. He became bishop of Salamis in Cyprus in 367. When old he was deceived by Patriarch Theophilus of Alexandria and joined in the deposition of St John Chrysostom at Constantinople, but became aware of the deception and died on the voyage back to Cyprus.

Epipodius, Alexander and Comps (SS) {2, 4}

22 April
d. 178. Two young men and thirty-four others, they were martyred at Lyons (France) in the reign of Marcus Aurelius. The latter was martyred two days after the former.

(Epitacius and Basileus) (SS) {4 –deleted}

23 May
? They were allegedly early martyrs. The first-named is identified with the first bishop of Tuy in Galicia (Spain) and the second with a bishop of Braga in Portugal. The traditions are confused.

Equitius (St) {2, 4}

11 August
d. ?571. He is the subject of the first book of the Dialogues of St Gregory the Great, the only evidence of his existence, and is described as a monk who founded a large number of monasteries for men and women in the ancient province of Valeria east of Rome. His headquarters was at what is now Pescara. The Roman Martyrology has kept his listing.

(Erasmus of Antioch) (St) {4 –deleted}

25 November
? He is listed as having been martyred at Antioch (Syria) but may be a duplicate of St Erasmus of Formia.

Erasmus (Elmo, Erarmo, Ermo) of Formia (St) {2, 3}

2 June
d. ?303. A bishop of Formia near Gaeta (Italy), he was martyred in the reign of Diocletian and had his relics taken to Gaeta when his town was destroyed in a Muslim raid in 842. This is all that is known. A large amount of legendary material has been added to his story, however, and this led to his veneration being very popular in the Middle Ages. He is the patron of sailors, and is depicted being martyred by having his intestines wound out with a windlass. His cultus was confined to local calendars in 1969.

Erastus (St) {2, 4}

26 July
C1st. The city treasurer of Corinth (Greece) when St Paul was there, he is mentioned in Acts 19:22, Rom. 16:23 and 2 Tim. 4:20. Later traditions conflict; the Eastern tradition is that he became bishop of Caesarea Phillipi in the Holy Land, while the Roman tradition is that he became bishop of Philippi in Greek Macedonia and was martyred.

Erconwald (St) {2}

30 April
d. 693. Allegedly of the royal family of East Anglia (England), he became the abbot-founder of Chertsey in Surrey and founded a nunnery at Barking in Essex where his sister,

St Ethelburga, became abbess. He was made bishop of London by St Theodore of Canterbury in 675 and died at Barking. His shrine at St Paul's cathedral in London was destroyed in the Reformation.

Erembert (St) {2}

14 May

d. 674. From near Paris (France), he became a monk at Fontenelle in Normandy in c.640 and bishop of Toulouse in 656. In 668 he retired back to his abbey.

Erentrude (Ermentrude) (St) {2}

30 June

d. ?718. A sister or niece of St Rupert of Salzburg (Austria), she became abbess of the nunnery of Nonnberg at Salzburg which he had founded for her.

Ergoule cf. **Gudula**.

Erhard (St) {2}

8 January

d. 707. He was a missionary bishop working around Regensburg in Bavaria (Germany). His origin is uncertain, and he possibly became a Columbanian monk. He founded seven monasteries. His extant biography is unreliable.

Eric IX of Sweden, King (St) {2}

18 May

d. 1161. He became king of Sweden in 1150 but his reign is not well documented. He was alleged to have been a protector of the church and a just ruler and was nicknamed the 'Lawgiver'. In 1157 he started the Swedish conquest and colonization of Finland, which was later (and with little justification) called a missionary crusade. He was apparently killed in a brawl after attending church at Uppsala by rebels led by a Danish invader and was regarded as a martyr. He is the patron of Sweden.

Erizzo (Bl)

9 February

d. 1094. From Florence (Italy), he was the first disciple of St John Gualbert who founded the Vallumbrosan order. He himself became its fourth abbot-general, and his cultus was confirmed for the Vallumbrosans in 1600. However, he has not been listed in the Roman Martyrology.

Erkembodo (St) {2}

12 April

d. 742. Allegedly an Irishman, he succeeded St Bertin the Great as abbot of Sithiu at Saint-Omer (France), at which abbey the Benedictine rule had replaced that of St Columban. He established the abbey's greatness, and became bishop of Thérouanne nearby in 722 while retaining the abbacy.

Ermenburga ('Domneva') (St)

19 November

d. c.700. A princess of Kent (England), she married a prince of Mercia and was the mother of three royal Saxon abbesses: Mildred, Milburga and Mildgytha. When an old widow she founded a nunnery at Minster in Thanet (Kent), but resigned as abbess in favour of her daughter Mildred. Her nickname is a corruption of Domna (i.e. Lady) Ebba and is preserved in the name of the locality of Ebbsfleet where St Augustine landed. Her cultus remains alive at her nunnery and in the locality, but is unconfirmed.

Ermenfrid (St) {2}

25 September

d. c.670. A Frankish courtier, he became a monk at Luxeuil under St Waldebert and later founded the abbey of Cusance in Burgundy (France).

Ermengaud (St) {2, 4}

3 November
d. 1035. Bishop of Urgell in the Pyrenees (Spain) from 1010 till 1035, he had to restore Christian life there after the occupation by the Arabs. He built the cathedral, and gave its canons a rule of life based on that of St Augustine. He died of head injuries caused by a fall.

Ermengol cf. **Hermengaudius**.

Ermin (St) {2, 4}

25 April
d. 737. From near Laon (France), as a priest he became a monk at Lobbes near Charleroi (Belgium) and succeeded St Ursmar as abbot and bishop there in 711.

Ernest (St)

7 November
d. 1148. A Benedictine abbot of Zwiefalten in Swabia (Germany), he resigned in 1146 and went on the disastrous Second Crusade. He then allegedly preached in Persia and Arabia, was tortured to death at Mecca and had his body rescued by an Armenian priest. The story is unlikely. Although he would have met that fate if he were caught in Mecca, there would not have been any Christians there to notice. His name is still used for boys.

(Erotis) (St) {4 –deleted}

6 October
C4th. She is listed as having been burnt alive, possibly in Greece although she may be none other than the St Erotheis listed with St Capitolina.

Eskil (St) {2}

12 June
d. ?1038. He allegedly accompanied St Sigfrid on a missionary expedition to Sweden from England and became bishop of Strängnäss near Stockholm. He protested at a pagan festival being held by some apostate converts of his and they stoned him.

Ethbin (St) {2, 4}

19 October
d. c.600. Allegedly from Britain, he was educated in Brittany (France) by St Sampson and became a monk at Taurac in 554. The Franks raided the abbey and dispersed the community in 556, whereupon he went to Ireland and became a hermit (allegedly near Kildare).

Ethelbert and Ethelred (SS)

17 October
d. 670. Great-grandsons of St Ethelbert of Kent (England) and brothers of St Ermenburga, they had a claim to the Kentish throne and so were murdered by the chief counsellor of King Egbert at Eastry near Sandwich. The king founded Minster Abbey for their sister in expiation and their shrine was eventually established at Ramsey Abbey near Peterborough. Their status as martyrs is highly dubious, and their cultus became extinct in the Reformation.

Ethelbert of East Anglia, King (St)

20 May
d. 794. As king of East Anglia (England) he was about to marry a daughter of King Offa of Mercia but was ordered killed near Hereford by his future mother-in-law. His body was transferred to that city and he became one of several Saxon royals venerated as martyrs despite the secular nature of their deaths. His shrine was at Hereford Cathedral until the Reformation.

Ethelbert of Kent, King (St) {2}

25 February
560–616. He married Bertha, a Christian Frankish princess, and so knew about

Christianity when he received St Augustine and his missionary companions at Ebbsfleet in Thanet (England) in 597. His baptism followed, although not immediately, and was the first of a Saxon king. He went on to found the cathedral at Canterbury (fairly certainly not as a monastery) on the site of his palace as well as monasteries outside the city at Canterbury (St Augustine's) and at Rochester. He was notable in not forcing conversion on his subjects, but his personal example bore fruit.

Ethelburga of Barking *(St)*

11 October
d. ?675. She fled home, allegedly at the East Anglian royal court, to avoid marriage and St Erconwald, her brother, founded a nunnery for her at Barking in Essex (England). She was too young to become abbess, so St Hildelid was fetched from France to stand in until she was fit to govern. When she took over she proved a great success. Her cults was never confirmed.

Ethelburga (Aedilburga, Aubierge) of Faremoutiers (St) {2}

7 July
d. 695. An illegitimate daughter of King Anna of East Anglia, she became a nun at Faremoutiers-en-Brie (France) and was the third abbess after Burgundofara and Sethrida.

Ethelburga of Lyminge *(St)*

5 April
d. ?647. Daughter of King St Ethelbert of Kent (England), she married King St Edwin of Northumbria and took with her St Paulinus, who became bishop of York. There was a pagan reaction after her husband's death in battle and they both fled back to Kent, where she became abbess-founder of a nunnery at Lyminge near Folkestone in 660. This was destroyed by the Vikings but a new church

(which survives) was built in 965 adjacent to the old, apparently incorporating the niche of her original shrine in its south wall. This can still be examined.

Etheldreda (Ethelreda, Ediltrudis, Audrey) (St) {2}

23 June
d. 679. Daughter of Anna, king of East Anglia, and sister of SS Ethelburga, Sexburga and Withburga, she married twice but allegedly refused to consummate either marriage. The second time she was supported by St Wilfrid, who encouraged her to become a nun at Coldingham in 672. She then founded a great double monastery at Ely, and her pilgrimage shrine at the cathedral there was popular in the Middle Ages. Her hand survives in the Catholic Church at Ely, and her attribute is a budding rod or lily. The word 'tawdry' is a corruption of 'St Audrey' and refers to the quality of the merchandise once sold in her honour at Ely.

Ethelred cf. **Aelred**.

Ethelwold of Winchester (St) {2}

1 August
912–84. From Winchester (England), he was a royal courtier with St Dunstan, was ordained with him and became a monk of Glastonbury under him. In 955 he became abbot-restorer of Abingdon near Oxford and bishop of Winchester in 963. He ejected the secular canons from his cathedral and replaced them with Benedictine monks, and he also helped to re-found or restore many other monasteries: Chertsey, Peterborough, Thorney, Croyland, Winchester-Newminster and Ely. In this he worked with SS Dunstan and Oswald to re-establish monastic life in England after the Danish devastations and was the traditional author of the 'Regularis Concordia', the agreed standard of

observance for the country's monasteries. He was also known as a craftsman.

(Etherius of Auxerre) (St) {4 –deleted}

27 July
d. 573. He was bishop of Auxerre (France) from 563.

(Etherius of Nicomedia) (St) {4 –deleted}

18 June
Early C4th? He was listed as martyred at Nicomedia (Asia Minor) in the reign of Diocletian.

Etherius of Vienne (St) {2, 4}

14 June
C7th. He was a bishop of Vienne (France).

Eucharius of Trier (St) {2, 4}

8 December
C3rd. Traditionally the first bishop of Trier (Germany), he was anachronistically alleged to have been sent there by St Peter.

Eucherius of Lyons (St) {2, 4}

16 November
d. c.450. From a patrician family of Lyons (France), he was married but his wife died, whereupon he became a monk at Lérins and wrote some extant ascetical works. He became archbishop of Lyons in ?432 and was friendly with many of the great Gallo-Roman churchmen of the time. He retired to be a hermit in 441.

Eucherius of Orleans (St) {2, 4}

20 February
d. ?738. From Orleans (France), he was well educated, especially in theology, and became a monk at Jumièges near Rouen in 714. He became bishop of Orleans in 721 and opposed Charles Martel's policy of sequestering church property to help support his fight against the Arab invaders and to reward his followers. Thus he was exiled in 737, first to Cologne and then to the vicinity of Liege (Belgium) where he died at the abbey of St Truiden.

Eudo (Eudon, Eudes, Odo) (St) {2}

19 November
d. c.720. He was trained as a monk at Lérins before becoming the abbot-founder of Corméry-en-Velay in the Massif Central (France).

(Eudocia) (St) {4 –deleted}

1 March
d. ?98–117. Her story was that she was a Samaritan prostitute at Heliopolis (Baalbek) in the Lebanon who converted, became a penitent and was beheaded in the reign of Trajan.

(Eudoxius, Zeno, Macarius and Comps) (SS) {4 –deleted}

5 September
Early C4th? They were listed as a group of 1024 soldiers who refused to join in a pagan sacrifice at Melitene in Armenia and were martyred in the space of about a fortnight.

Eugendus (Oyend) (St) {2}

1 January
d. 516. He was a child-oblate aged seven at Condat Abbey in the Jura (France) near Geneva and later became abbot. The site is now the town of Saint-Claude.

(Eugene and Macarius) (SS) {4 –deleted}

20 December
Mid C4th? They were listed as two priests of Antioch (Syria) who were whipped, exiled to Roman Arabia (southern Syria) and beheaded on their return in the reign of Julian.

Eugene I, Pope (St) {2, 4}

2 June

d. 657. A Roman priest, he was elected to replace Pope St Martin in 654 while the latter was in exile in the Crimea for opposing the Monothelite teaching of Emperor Constans II. Becoming pope in reality the following year with the death of the exile, he continued the policy of opposition and was only saved from the fate of his predecessor by the preoccupation of the emperor with the Muslims.

Eugene III, Pope (Bl) {2, 4}

8 July

d. 1153. Born near Pisa (Italy) as Peter Paganelli, he was in the diocesan curia of Pisa before becoming a monk at Clairvaux under St Bernard in 1135. He was appointed as first abbot of the new Cistercian abbey of Tre Fontane near Rome and was elected pope in 1145. But the Romans wanted to establish a republic without having the pope as secular ruler, so he had to flee the city and stay away for most of his pontificate. St Bernard wrote an ascetical treatise for him, 'De Consideratione'. He allowed St Bernard to preach the Second Crusade, and his political judgement after the disaster that that proved to be was sounder than that of his old master. He died at Tivoli and his cultus was confirmed for the Cistercians and locally for Rome in 1872.

Eugene (Eoghan, Euny, Owen) of Ardstraw (St) {2}

23 August

C6th. Allegedly the first bishop of Ardstraw in Co. Tyrone (Ireland), he is apparently commemorated by Uny Lelant on St Ives Bay in Cornwall (England) and is also known in Brittany. He is the principal patron of the diocese of Derry (Ireland).

Eugene-of-the-Sacred-Heart Bossilkov (Bl) {2}

11 November

1900–52. From a Latin-rite peasant family of Belene near Pleven (Bulgaria), he joined the Passionists at Ere in Belgium in 1919 and, after his ordination at Nikopol in 1926 and his theological education at Rome, became a parish priest of the Nikopol diocese in Bulgaria. He became bishop in 1946, just after the Communist takeover of the country. The government policy was to destroy the Latin-rite church, which involved the expulsion of all foreign missionaries, confiscation of property and the suppression of religious institutions. In 1952, he was arrested, interrogated with torture and executed at Sofia after a show trial. He was beatified as a martyr in 1998.

Eugene of Carthage (St) {2, 4}

13 July

d. 505. Becoming bishop of Carthage (Roman Africa) in 481, he was almost immediately driven into exile in the desert by the conquering Arian Vandals. After being allowed to return twice he was at last exiled to Albi (France) in 496. The Roman Martyrology has deleted the reference to many companions, including his archdeacon and deputy, Salutaris and Muritta.

(Eugene of Milan) *(St)* *{4 –deleted}*

30 December

? He is listed as a bishop of Milan (Italy), but with no indication of date.

(Eugene of Paris) *(St)* *{4 –deleted}*

15 November

Late C3rd? He apparently accompanied St Dionysius from Rome to Paris (France) and was martyred at Deuil nearby. The assertion that he became archbishop of Toledo in Spain is fictitious, and his alleged relics there are spurious.

Eugene of Toledo (St) {2, 4}

13 November
d. 657. A Visigothic nobleman from Toledo (Spain), he became a monk and abbot at the Encratia monastery at Zaragoza and succeeded another of the same name as archbishop of Toledo in 646. He revised the local Gothic rite (now long extinct as such) and wrote some extant poetry.

Eugenia Joubert (Bl) {2}

2 July
1876–1904. Born in Yssingeaux near Le Puy (France), she entered the 'Holy Family of the Sacred Heart', newly founded by Mary Ignatius Melin at Le Puy. Their charism was devotion to the Sacred Heart as the bond of community life and to catechetical instruction of poor people. She ended up in Liege in Belgium, following the way of spiritual childhood (especially in obedience and humility), and was beatified in 1994.

Eugenia Picco (Bl) {2}

7 September
1867–1921. From Crescenzago near Milan, Italy, she was the daughter of a musician who abandoned his family. Despite being raised in a corrupt and irreligious environment, she early received an urge to prayer. As a result, she ran away from home when aged twenty and joined the new Congregation of the Little Daughters of Sacred Hearts of Jesus and Mary in Parma. In 1911, she became the superior-general, and was always faithful to her life's intention to 'suffer, be silent and love'. She was beatified in 2001.

Eugenia Ravasco (Bl) {2}

24 October
1845–1900. From Milan in Italy, she was taken to Genoa in 1852 and started to teach catechism to some neglected young girls in the city after 1863. The lack of educational opportunities for them led her to found the 'Sisters of the Sacred Hearts of Jesus and Mary', which was approved by the bishop in 1882, despite much opposition arising from the anti-clericalism fashionable at the time. She died at Genoa and was beatified in 2003. Her congregation has since become international in scope.

Eugenia of Rome (St) {2, 4}

25 December
End C3rd. She was martyred in the reign of Valerian and was buried on the Via Latina in Rome. Her fictitious acta describe how she disguised herself as a monk, became an abbot and was only exposed when she was accused of the impossible act of fornicating as a man with a woman. Such a story is a stock tale in early hagiography.

(Eulalia of Barcelona) (St) {4 –deleted}

12 February
d. ?304. Allegedly a native of Barcelona (Spain) who was martyred in the reign of Diocletian, she has acta which are derived from those of St Eulalia of Mérida. This leads to the conclusion that she is a duplicate of the latter. Her veneration is still popular (especially in her city).

Eulalia of Mérida (St) {2, 4}

10 December
d. 304. The most famous virgin martyr of Spain, she is mentioned by St Augustine and has a hymn in her honour written by Prudentius. She was allegedly burnt at the stake at Mérida when aged thirteen in the reign of Diocletian, but her acta are unreliable.

Eulampius and Eulampia (SS) {2, 4}

10 October
Early C4th. They were martyred at Nicomedia (Asia Minor) in the reign of Diocletian.

Their unreliable acta describe them as young children, brother and sister, whose example converted a couple of hundred others who were also martyred. These details have been deleted from the Roman Martyrology.

Eulogius of Alexandria (St) {2, 4}

13 June

d. ?607. A Syrian monk and abbot at Antioch, he became Melkite patriarch of Alexandria (Egypt) in 580. St Gregory the Great was his friend and correspondent and informed him of the sending of St Augustine and companions to England in a surviving letter.

(Eulogius of Constantinople and Comps) *(SS) {4 –deleted}*

3 July

d. 363–70. They were listed as twenty-two who were martyred at Constantinople in the reign of Valens for opposing Arianism.

Eulogius of Cordoba (St) {2, 4}

11 March

d. 859. Priest and seminary director of Cordoba (Spain) when that city was the capital of the Umayyad emirate, he was involved in the contemporary 'martyr movement' from 850 to 856 when several Christians courted martyrdom by publicly denouncing Islam. He wrote an account of them ('Memorial of the Saints') in which he tried to defend their status as martyrs (the church does not approve martyrdom resulting from gratuitously offensive behaviour towards non-Christians). He was about to become bishop of Toledo when he was executed for protecting St Leocritia, a young woman who had converted from Islam.

Eulogius of Edessa (St) {2, 4}

23 April

d. 387. A priest of Edessa in upper Mesopotamia (now Urfa in Turkey), he was banished to the Egyptian Thebaid by Emperor Valens for opposing Arianism but recalled and made bishop after the latter's death in 375.

Eumenes (St) {2, 4}

18 September

C7th. Bishop of Gortyna in Crete, he was exiled to the Egyptian Thebaid for opposing Monothelitism and died there. His relics were returned, and the miracles associated with them gave him the nickname 'Wonderworker'.

Euny cf. **Eugenius**.

(Euphemia, Dorothy, Thecla and Erasma) *(SS) {4 –deleted}*

3 September

? They were allegedly very early martyrs at Aquileia (Italy) and are venerated at Venice and in its former Adriatic possessions as well as at Ravenna.

Euphemia of Chalcedon (St) {2, 3}

16 September

d. ?303. Her acta are fictitious but she was certainly martyred at Chalcedon (across the Bosphorus from Constantinople) as a church was built on the site of her martyrdom in the reign of Constantine, and it was in this church that the ecumenical council of Chalcedon was held in 451. She is one of the most popular virgin-martyrs in the East but her cultus was confined to local calendars in the West in 1969.

Euphrasia (St) {2}

24 July

C5th. From Constantinople and related to the imperial family, when she lost her father at seven years of age she went to Egypt with her mother to join the Pachomian nuns at Tabennesis in the Thebaid. They took her but not her patrimony, which she left with her mother until the latter died. Then the emperor offered to marry her off, but she refused, asked him to give her fortune to charity and stayed in the nunnery until she died, aged about thirty. She has an early biography.

Euphrasia-of-the-Sacred-Heart-of-Jesus Eluvathingal (St) {2 –add}

29 August
1877–1952. From Kattoor near Trichur in Kerala, India, she was of the Syro-Malabar rite and joined the Congregation of the Mother of Carmel at Koonammavu in 1897. She became novice-mistress in 1904, and became superior of the new convent at Ollur in 1913. She resigned in 1916, but remained at that convent until her death. She became famous for her complete dedication to charity and prayer, and her letters to the local bishop concerning her spiritual life have survived. She was canonized in 2014.

Euphrasia Pelletier cf. **Mary-of-St-Euphrasia Pelletier**.

(Euphrasius of Africa) (St) {4 –deleted}

14 January
? He is listed as a bishop of Roman Africa and may be identical with Eucrathius, a correspondent of St Cyprian, or may have been a bishop martyred by the Arian Vandals.

Euphrasius of Clermont-Ferrand (St) {2}

14 January
d. 515–16. He succeeded St Abrunculus as bishop of Clermont-Ferrand (France), and was praised for his hospitality by St Gregory of Tours.

Euphronius of Autun (St) {2, 4}

3 August
d. p475. He became bishop of Autun (France) in 460 and was one of the greatest bishops of Gaul in the C5th. He was a friend of St Lupus of Troyes, and a letter of his to him survives.

Euphronius of Tours (St) {2, 4}

4 August
530–73. A nephew of St Gregory of Langres, he became bishop of Tours (France) in 556 and was remembered for helping to rebuild the city when it was burnt down.

(Euphrosyne) (St) {4 –deleted}

1 January
? Her legend describes her as a young woman of Alexandria (Egypt) who joined a monastery as a monk to escape marriage and lived as such for many years, her sex only being discovered when she was dying. Her historical existence is doubtful as the story is a common one in hagiography, and other examples of it feature St Pelagia the Penitent and St Eugenia of Rome.

Euplus (St) {2, 4}

12 August
d. 304. A native of Catania (Sicily), he was found in possession of a copy of the Gospels in contravention of an edict of persecution issued by Emperor Diocletian. He was tortured in order to induce apostasy before being martyred. His acta are genuine.

Euprepius of Verona (St) {2}

21 August
C3rd? He is venerated as the first bishop of Verona (Italy). A worthless tradition describes him as appointed by St Peter.

(Eupsychius of Caesarea -1) (St) {4 –deleted}

7 September
d. c.130. He is alleged to have been martyred at Caesarea in Cappadocia (Asia Minor) in the reign of Hadrian.

Eupsychius of Caesarea (2) (St) {2, 4}

9 April
d. 362. A young nobleman of Caesarea in Cappodocia (Asia Minor), when the emperor Julian visited the city he was arrested on a charge of having helped to destroy the temple of Fortune there and was then tortured and beheaded.

Eurosia (Orosia) (St) {2}

25 July
d. ?714. According to her legend she was from Bayonne in France (or from Bohemia) and was martyred at Jaca in the Aragonese Pyrenees (Spain) by Arab invaders. Despite doubts about her existence her cultus is popular and was confirmed for Jaca in 1902.

Eurosia Fabris Barban (Bl) {2 –add}

9 January
1866–1932. From a peasant family of Marola near Vicenza in Italy, typically for the time she only had two years at school because she was needed to help with the family farm. She was virtuous and had a pleasant personality, but married late after taking on the responsibility for two little orphan girls. She had nine children of her own, and welcomed many others into her home, being universally known as 'Mama Rosa'. Her home was regarded as an ideal Christian community, and three sons became priests. She died two years after being widowed and was beatified in 2005.

(Eusebia of Bergamo) (St) {4 –deleted}

29 October
Late C3rd? She was listed as martyred at Bergamo in Lombardy (Italy) in the reign of Maximian Herculius.

Eusebia of Hamay (St) {2}

16 March
d. c.680. Eldest daughter of SS Adalbald and Rictrude, as a child she was placed by her mother in the nunnery founded and run by St Gertrude, her grandmother, at Hamay near Douai (France). She became abbess when aged twelve (a typical example of hereditary succession in Frankish monasticism) but her mother thought that she was too young for the responsibility and she and her community moved to the nunnery at Marchiennes. Later, when she was more grown-up, they returned home to Hamay.

Eusebia Palomino Yenes (Bl) {2}

10 February
1899–1935. From the family of a poor farmworker at Camtalpino in Spain, she helped out with domestic duties at the local school run by the Daughters of Mary, Help of Christians on Sunday afternoons and so was inspired to join them in 1922. She was sent to the house at Valverde del Camino where, despite her unprepossessing appearance and lack of formal education, she became known for her kindness and spiritual wisdom. In 1932 she fell victim to a neuropathic disorder causing permanent and violent muscle spasms, and died after two and a half years of tranquil agony. She was beatified in 2004.

Eusebia of Saint-Cyr (St) {2}

30 September
d. 497. She was a nun of Saint-Cyr in Marseilles (France), who lived a holy life and died at an advanced age. In her later worthless legend, she became the abbess of a community of thirty-nine other nuns of the nunnery who were massacred by Muslim pirates in the C9th.

Eusebius, Pope (St) {2, 4}

17 August
d. 310. A Greek, he was pope for only a few months during a violent controversy at Rome over the reconciliation of those who had apostatized in the recent persecution. He died in exile in Sicily.

Eusebius, Charalampus and Comps (St) {2}

28 April
? They were martyred at Nicomedia (Asia Minor).

(Eusebius, Marcellus and Comps) (SS)
{4 –deleted}

2 December
Mid C3rd? They were listed as martyred at Rome in the reign of Valerian. Eusebius, a priest, was beheaded with Marcellus (his deacon), Neon and Mary; Adria and Hippolytus were whipped to death; Paulina died under torture and Maximus was thrown into the Tiber.

(Eusebius, Neon, Leontius, Longinus and Comps) (SS) {4 –deleted}

24 April
? They are listed as numbering forty in the Western tradition, nine in the Eastern, and have been incorporated into the legend of St George as witnesses of his martyrdom who were themselves martyred.

Eusebius, Nestabus, Zeno and Nestor (SS) {2, 4}

8 September
d. 362. They helped to destroy the main pagan temple at Gaza in the Holy Land during the reign of the emperor Julian and were lynched as a result by the townsfolk. Nestor was spared by the mob after the initial beating because of his good looks, but he died as a result of his wounds. Gaza remained a stronghold of paganism until its suppression in the Roman Empire later in the century.

(Eusebius, Pontian, Vincent and Peregrine) (SS) {4 –deleted}

25 August
d. ?192. Their relics were given to Vienne (France) by Pope St Nicholas in 863, and that is all that is known about them. Their acta are untrustworthy.

(Eusebius of Africa and Comps) (SS)
{4 –deleted}

5 March
? They are listed as martyrs of Roman Africa.

Eusebius of Bologna (St) {2, 4}

26 September
End C4th. A friend of St Ambrose of Milan, he became bishop of Bologna (Italy) about 370. He opposed Arianism, and discovered the alleged relics of SS Vitalis and Agricola.

Eusebius of Fano (St) {2}

18 April
d. ?526. He became bishop of Fano (Italy) in 502, and accompanied Pope St John I to Constantinople on the embassy ordered by the Arian King Theodoric the Ostrogoth. Like the pope, he was imprisoned on his return and died in custody. He is not listed as a martyr.

Eusebius of Milan (St) {2, 4}

8 August
d. 462. Probably a Greek, he succeeded St Lazarus as bishop of Milan (Italy) in 450 and was a zealous opponent of Monophysitism.

(Eusebius of Phoenecia) (St) {4 –deleted}

21 September
? He is listed as such as a martyr, but with no other details.

Eusebius of Rome (St) {2, 3}

14 August
C4–5th? He was allegedly a Roman parish priest who was under house arrest in the reign of Constantius for opposing Arianism. His house became the present Roman church named after him. His acta are a forgery.

Eusebius of St Gall (St) {2}

31 January
d. 884. An Irish pilgrim, he became a monk at the abbey of St Gall (Switzerland) and went on to become a hermit on the Victorsberg in Graubünden. There he was killed by a peasant with a scythe, allegedly because he had criticized the local lack of religion. He is not listed as a martyr in the Roman Martyrology.

Eusebius of Samosata (St) {2, 4}

22 June
d. c.380. Bishop of Samosata (Syria) from 361, he was a friend and colleague of SS Basil and Gregory Nazianzen in their fight against Arianism. He was exiled to what is now Bulgaria by the emperor Valens in 373, but recalled on his death. He was martyred at a place called Dolichium when an Arian woman dropped a brick on his head from the town wall.

Eusebius of Vercelli (St) {1, 3}

2 August
?283–371. From Sardinia, he became a cleric in Rome and was made bishop of Vercelli in Piedmont (Italy) in 340. He was the first bishop in the West to organize his cathedral clergy under a monastic rule. In 355 he refused to consent to the exile of St Athanasius for opposing Arianism and was himself exiled to the East, spending some time in Egypt, but he was allowed to return by Emperor Julian in 363 and then worked to get rid of Arianism in the Western church. He died in peace.

Eusicius (St) {2}

27 November
d. 542. He was a hermit on the banks of the river Cher (France), and was the founder and first abbot of the monastery of Celles.

(Eusignius) (St) {4 –deleted}

5 August
d. 362. Allegedly aged one hundred and ten and with sixty years of army service behind him, he was beheaded at Antioch (Syria) in the reign of Julian for refusing to offer pagan sacrifice.

(Eustace) (St) {4 –deleted}

12 October
? He is listed in the old Roman Martyrology as a priest and confessor of Syria, but the Bollandists considered that he was more likely to have been an Egyptian martyr if he existed at all.

(Eustace, Thespesius and Anatolius) (SS) {4 –deleted}

20 November
d. 235. They were listed as martyred at Nicaea (Asia Minor) in the reign of Maximinus Thrax.

Eustace Kugler (Bl) {2 –add}

10 June
1867–1946. From Neuhaus bei Nittenau in Bavaria (Germany), the son of the village blacksmith, he was not well educated and worked as a building labourer before joining the Brothers Hospitaller of St John of God at Regensburg. He became the Provincial of Bavaria in 1925, and set about providing the modern hospital that the city lacked. He managed both the funding, and the completion of the enormous project which led to one of the best hospitals in Germany. In his period of office the membership of the province doubled. He was noted for his humility, spirit of service and his quiet opposition to the Nazi ideology (he was unusual among opponents of the regime for being left unmolested). He died of stomach cancer, and was beatified in 2009.

Eustace of Luxeuil (St) {2, 4}

2 April
d. 629. A disciple of St Columban at Luxeuil (Burgundy), he became abbot in 613 when his master was forced into exile. He was allegedly in charge of six hundred monks, and under him the monastery became a great source of bishops and saints.

Eustace of Naples (St) {2}

29 March
C3rd. He was the seventh bishop of Naples (Italy) and his cultus was confirmed for there in 1884.

Eustace of Rome (St) {2, 3}

20 September
? His unreliable legend states that he was a Roman army officer with a wife Theopistes and two sons, Agapitus and Theopistus. He was converted by seeing a stag with a crucifix between its antlers while out hunting, and was martyred with his family in the reign of Hadrian. The Roman Martyrology now merely lists him as a martyr without companions, and his cultus was suppressed in the Roman rite in 1969.

Eustace White and Comps (SS) {2}

10 December
d. 1591. From Louth (Lincs), he was a convert who trained for the priesthood at Rheims and at Rome. Ordained in 1588, he went to work in the West Country but was quickly seized at Blandford Forum and was hanged, drawn and quartered at Tyburn (London) together with St Polydore Plasden. With them were hanged BB Brian Lacey, John Mason and Sidney Hodgson. He was canonized in 1970. Cf. England, Martyrs of.

(Eustathius of Ancyra) (St) {4 –deleted}

28 July
? According to his legend he was tortured and thrown into the local river at Ancyra (Asia Minor, now Ankara in Turkey), but was saved by an angel and died in peace.

Eustathius of Antioch (St) {2, 4}

21 February
d. ?338. From Side in Pamphylia (Asia Minor), he became bishop of Beroea (Syria) in 270 and patriarch of Antioch in 323. He was present at the Council of Nicaea and opposed the Arians in his preaching and writing. In 331 he was deposed by an Arian synod at Antioch and died in exile at Trajanopolis in Thrace. This led to a long-term schism at Antioch.

(Eusterius) (St) {4 –deleted}

19 October
C5th. He is listed as the fourth bishop of Salerno (Italy).

Eustochium Bellini (Bl) {2}

13 February
1444–69. Born to a nun in the degenerate Benedictine nunnery of St Prosdocimus at Padua (Italy), she was brought up there until a more observant community of nuns took over and she asked to become a nun with them. Although normally gentle and pious, she was subject to violent outbursts of hysteria and was thus suspected of witchcraft and of being possessed by a demon. Hence she was starved, ill-treated, imprisoned and almost burnt as a witch, which treatment she bore with patience and humility during her periods of lucidity. She was professed after the chaplain intervened in her favour, and then gained the respect of her community before she died. It was then discovered that she had burnt the

name of Jesus into the top of her breasts. She is locally venerated at Padua.

Eustochium of Bethlehem (St) {2}

28 September
c.370–419. The third and favourite daughter of St Paula, when her father died she and her mother toured the monastic sites in Egypt and then settled at Bethlehem with St Jerome. She helped him with his literary work, for example in his Vulgate translation of the Bible, and succeeded her mother as abbess at the nunnery that the latter had founded. She died there, in Bethlehem, and the Latin nunnery did not long survive her.

Eustochium Calafató (St) {2}

20 January
1437–68. A noblewoman of Messina (Sicily), she became a Poor Clare there in 1446 when only a child, and obtained permission from the pope in 1457 to found a nunnery of the Franciscan Observants at Montevergine in the city. She was canonized in 1988.

Eustochium van Lieshout (Bl) {2 –add}

30 August
1890–1943. From a farming family of Aarle-Rixtel in the Netherlands, he joined the 'Congregation of the Sacred Hearts of Jesus and Mary' in 1913 and was ordained in 1918. After serving as a parish priest around Rotterdam, he was sent to Brazil in 1925 where he spent ten years at Agua Suja in Romaria, six years at Poá and two in Belo Horizonte. He became famous for his concern for sick and poor people, and had the gift of healing through the intercession of St Joseph. He died of typhus at Belo Horizonte and was beatified in 2006.

(Eustochium of Tarsus) (St) {4 –deleted}

2 November
Mid C4th? From Tarsus in Cilicia (Asia Minor), she allegedly refused to sacrifice to Aphrodite in the reign of Julian and died under torture.

Eustochius of Tours (St) {2, 4}

19 September
d. 461. He succeeded St Brice as bishop of Tours (France) in 444.

Eustolia and Sosipatra (SS) {2, 4}

9 November
C6th. They may both have been daughters of Emperor Maurice at Constantinople (582–602), although Eustolia is alleged to have been born at Rome. They founded and entered a nunnery at Constantinople.

Eustorgius I of Milan (St) {2, 4}

18 September
d. a.355. A Greek, he became archbishop of Milan (Italy) in 315 and was zealous against Arianism. A remark in a letter of St Athanasius indicates that he may have been martyred as a result, but the Roman Martyrology does not accept this.

Eustorgius II of Milan (St) {2, 4}

6 June
d. 518. A Roman priest, he became archbishop of Milan (Italy) in 512. He was especially charitable to the poor, and ransomed many of his people captured by barbarian invaders.

(Eustorgius of Nicomedia) (St) {4 –deleted}

11 April
Early C4th? The old Roman Martyrology listed him as a priest of Nicomedia (Asia Minor). The Byzantine Martyrology alleged that he was martyred with Nestor, Filonus and Ceremonius.

Eustratius and Comps (SS) {2, 4}

13 December
Early C4th? According to their legend, Eustratius was an Armenian noble who was

arrested in the reign of Diocletian. Auxentius, a priest, and Mardarius, a friend, interceded for him and were beheaded. His servant, Eugene, was tortured to death and converted a soldier, Orestes, by his example. The latter was taken to Sebaste with Eustratius and both were burnt, on a gridiron and in a furnace, respectively.

(Euthalia and Sermilian) (SS) {4 –deleted}

27 August
? They are listed as brother and sister, martyred at Lentini near Catania (Sicily).

Eustratius Thaumaturgus (St) {2}

9 January
C9th. From Tarsus in Cilicia (Asia Minor), when young he ran away from home and became a monk at the Abgar monastery on the Bithynian Olympus (the present Ulu Dagh mountain) near Brusa (now Bursa). He was exiled for opposing iconoclasm, but died as abbot of the monastery of Agaru.

Euthymius of Alexandria (St) {2, 4}

5 May
d. 305? He is listed as a deacon and martyr of Alexandria (Egypt).

Euthymius the Great (St) {2}

20 January
378–473. From Melitene in Armenia, he became a priest and monk and had supervision of the monasteries of his native district. He went to Jerusalem in 406 and became one of the greatest of the fathers of the Judaean desert, founding several lauras. He opposed Nestorianism and Monophysitism and was a bulwark of orthodoxy in the Holy Land after the Council of Chalcedon, when the Monophysites seized the bishopric of Jerusalem. He induced the empress Eudoxia not to support them and helped to restore the bishop Juvenal to his position. His biography was written by St Cyril of Scythopolis, and he is highly venerated in Eastern monasticism.

(Euthymius of Nicomedia) (St) {4 –deleted}

24 December
d. 303. He was listed as martyred at Nicomedia (Asia Minor), the capital of the emperor Diocletian, after giving moral support to others facing martyrdom.

(Euthymius of Perugia) (St) {4 –deleted}

29 August
Early C4th? He was allegedly a Roman who fled with his wife and his son, St Crescentius, during the persecution of Diocletian and died at Perugia. He is venerated there, but his acta are untrustworthy.

Euthymius of Sardis (St) {2, 4}

34 December
d. 824. A monk before he became bishop of Sardis (Asia Minor), he was present at the second ecumenical council of Nicaea in 787 which upheld the adoration of icons. The emperor Theophilus tried to restore iconoclasm and exiled Euthymius for twenty-nine years, after which he was whipped to death.

Eutropia (St) {2, 4}

30 October
C3rd? She is listed as a martyr of Alexandria (Egypt) who died under torture.

(Eutropia of Auvergne) (St) {4 –deleted}

15 September
C5th. Mentioned by Sidonius Apollinaris, she is listed as a charitable widow of the Auvergne (France).

Eutropius, Zosima and Bonosa (SS) {2, 4}

15 July
? They were martyred at Ostia at the mouth of the Tiber (Italy).

Eutropius of Orange (St) {2, 4}

27 May
d. ?475. From Marseilles (France), he became bishop of Orange when that place had been devastated by the Visigoths and is described as supporting himself by farming. He is the source of a fictitious story concerning the first bishop of Orange (allegedly with the same name).

Eutropius of Saintes (St) {2, 4}

30 April
C3rd He is venerated as the first bishop of Saintes (France), and is alleged to have been a companion martyr of St Dionysius of Paris.

Eutychian, Pope (St) {2, 4}

8 December
d. 283. He was apparently from Tuscany (Italy), but other biographical details are lacking. He is no longer listed as a martyr.

(Eutychius and Domitian) (SS) {4 –deleted}

28 December
? They are listed as a priest and his deacon who were martyred at Ancyra (Asia Minor, now Ankara in Turkey).

Eutychius and Florentius (SS) {2}

23 May
d. 487? They were two monks who settled at Valcastoria near Norcia (Italy) and who were praised by St Gregory the Great.

Eutychius of Alexandria (St) {2, 4}

26 March
d. 356. He was a subdeacon of Alexandria (Egypt). When St Athanasius, patriarch of the city, was exiled in 356 for his anti-Arian views, one George (an Arian cleric) was set up as an anti-patriarch and instigated serious violence against the orthodox. Many were killed or seized and sent into exile, including Eutychius who was on the way to the mines as a prisoner when he died of exhaustion.

(Eutychius of Cádiz) (St) {4 –deleted}

11 December
C4th. He is venerated as a martyr at Cádiz (Spain) but nothing is certainly known about him.

Eutychius of Como (St) {2}

5 June
d. 539. He was a bishop of Como (Italy), who would regularly retire to a cave near his city to fast and pray.

Eutychius of Constantinople (St) {2}

6 April
d. 582. A monk from Amasea on the Black Sea coast of Asia Minor, he became patriarch of Constantinople in 553, dedicated the new church of Hagia Sophia there and was chairman at the fifth ecumenical council which was called in response to the continuing problem of the Monophysites. He opposed the emperor Justinian's plans to reconcile them and was exiled for twelve years.

(Eutychius of Ferentino) (St) {4 –deleted}

15 April
? This unknown martyr at Ferentino in the Roman Campagna was mentioned in the 'Dialogues' attributed to St Gregory the Great as having appeared to St Redemptus, bishop of the place, in a vision.

(Eutychius the Patrician and Comps) (SS) {4 –deleted}

14 March
d. 741. They were the numerous victims of a massacre of Christians by Muslim Arabs at

Carrhae in upper Mesopotamia (near Urfa in Turkey), which is the same place as the Haran associated with the patriarch Abraham.

Eutychius of Perinthus (SS) {2, 4}

29 September
C3rd? He is listed as a martyr of Thrace (in the south-eastern Balkans), either of Perinthus or of Heraclea. His two companions, Plautus and Heracleas, have been deleted from the Roman Martyrology.

(Eutychius the Phrygian) (St) {4 –deleted}

24 August
C1st. According to the apocryphal acta of St John, he was a disciple of St Paul who attached himself to St John, was with him at Patmos and who died in peace after being tortured for the faith. His identification with the young man who fell from a window at Ephesus (Acts 20) is based merely on the names being the same.

Eutychius of Rome (St) {2, 4}

4 February
? His acta are lost, but the inscription composed for his tomb by Pope St Damasus has survived and it asserts that he was imprisoned for twelve days without food and then thrown into a well.

Euvert cf. **Evortius**.

(Evagrius and Benignus) (SS) {4 –deleted}

3 April
? They were listed as martyred at Tomi in Scythia (on the coast of Romania).

(Evagrius, Priscian and Comps) (SS) {4 –deleted}

14 October
? They were listed as martyrs of Rome.

Evagrius of Constantinople (St) {2, 4}

6 March
d. ?378. He became archbishop of Constantinople in 370 for the few remaining Catholics in the city, after two decades during which the incumbent was an Arian. He was soon exiled by the emperor Valens and the place and time of his death are unknown.

Evangelist and Peregrine (BB) {2}

30 March
C12–13th. Noblemen of Verona (Italy), they were school friends who entered the local Augustinian friary together, were granted similar charisms in working miracles and who died within a few hours of each other. Their cultus was approved for the Augustinian friars in 1837.

Evaristus, Pope (St) {2, 3}

26 October
d. 107. He traditionally had Hellenic-Jewish ancestry but nothing is known for certain about him. Like all the early popes he used to have a cultus as a martyr, but this was suppressed in 1969.

(Evasius of Asti) (St) {4 –deleted}

1 December
Mid C4th? Allegedly the first bishop of Asti in Piedmont (Italy), the untrustworthy and late accounts given of him describe him as being driven from his diocese by Arians and being killed at Casale Monferrato in the reign of Julian.

(Evasius of Brescia) (St) {4 –deleted}

2 December
? He is listed as the first bishop of Brescia (Italy).

Eve of Liege (Bl) {2}

14 March
d. ?1266. A hermit on Mount Cornelius at Liege (Belgium) and associated with the

nunnery of St Martin, she took over the work of campaigning (with success) for the institution of the feast of Corpus Christi when Bl Juliana of Cornillon died. Her cultus was confirmed for Liege in 1902.

(Evellius) (St) {4 –deleted}

11 May
C1st? Allegedly a counsellor of Nero who was converted by the example of the first martyrs of Rome, he is connected in legend with St Torpes. They were supposedly martyred at Pisa, but their existence is very questionable.

Everard

This name is also rendered variously as Eberhard, Everhard, Evard, Erhard, Erard, etc.

Everard of Fréjus (St) {2}

16 December
d. 867. The count of Fréjus and an influential nobleman at the Frankish court, he founded a monastery of canons regular at Cysoing near Cambrai (France) and was enshrined there some years after his death.

Everard Hanse (Bl) {2}

31 July
d. 1581. From Northamptonshire, he was educated at Cambridge and became an Anglican minister before his conversion. Then he was ordained priest at Rheims in 1581 and was captured and executed at Tyburn (London) immediately on his return to England. On the scaffold he was heard to say 'Oh, happy day!' He was beatified in 1886. Cf. **England, Martyrs of**.

Everard von Nellenburg (Bl) {2}

25 March
1018–78. Count of Nellenburg, he was related to Pope St Leo IX and to Emperor St Henry II.

In 1050 he founded the Benedictine abbey of Schaffhausen on the Rhine (now in Switzerland) and became a monk there. His wife founded a nunnery nearby. The abbey was the nucleus of what is now the capital of a Swiss canton.

Evergisil of Cologne (St) {2, 4}

24 October
d. c.590. He became archbishop of Cologne in 580, was highly respected at the Merovingian court and went as an ambassador to Visigothic Spain. The Roman Martyrology accepts the legend that he was martyred by robbers.

Everild (Averil) (St)

9 July
Late C7th. From the Wessex (England) nobility, she ran away from home and was clothed as a nun with two companions by St Wilfrid, possibly at a place now called Everingham near Market Weighton in Yorkshire. An alternative site is at Nether Poppleton near York, which has the only other old church dedicated to her.

Evermod (St) {2}

17 February
d. 1178. A disciple of St Norbert, he became a Premonstratensian canon at Antwerp in Belgium before becoming superior of Gottesgnaden in 1134 and of Magdeburg in Germany in 1138. He evangelized the Slavs on the Elbe and became bishop of Ratzeburg near Lübeck (Germany) in 1154. As such he encouraged the dispossession of the native Slavs by inviting Saxons to colonize the area.

Evetius of Nicomedia (St) {2, 4}

24 February
d. 303. A 'Christian of secular dignity', he tore down and ripped up Diocletian's edict of

persecution against the Christians when this was publicly exhibited at Nicomedia (Asia Minor). For this he was tortured and burnt alive. His true name was unknown; 'John' was the arbitrary Latin appellation used in the old Roman Martyrology, 'Eleutherius' the Byzantine. The revised Roman Martyrology uses the name given.

(Evodius, Hermogenes and Callista) (SS) {4 –deleted}

25 April
? The old Roman Martyrology lists them thrice. On 2 August they we listed as the three sons of St Theodota, a martyr of Nicaea, and this is accepted in the revised edition. On 25 April and 2 September they were listed as having been martyred at Syracuse, and Callistus is feminized to Callista. No acta exist mentioning their martyrdom at Syracuse.

(Evodius of Antioch) (St) {4 –deleted}

6 May
C1st? He was allegedly the first bishop of Antioch (Syria) after St Peter and was the predecessor of St Ignatius. The historical evidence for his existence is poor.

Evodius of Rouen (St) {2, 4}

8 October
C5th. A Frankish archbishop of Rouen (France), he had his relics transferred to Braine near Soissons four hundred years after he died.

Evurtius (Euvert) (St) {2, 4}

7 September
C4th. A Roman subdeacon, he became bishop of Orleans (France). The Augustinian abbey of Saint-Euvert was built to house his shrine.

Evroul cf. **Ebrulf**.

Ewald the Dark and Ewald the Fair (SS) {2}

3 October
d. 695. Brothers from Northumbria (England), they were educated in Ireland, became monks and went on a missionary journey to Lower Saxony in Germany. Shortly after they started their apostolate they were martyred together at Aplerbeke near Dortmund (Germany). Their nicknames refer to the colour of their hair.

(Exsuperantia) (St) {4 –deleted}

26 April
? She has a cultus at Troyes (France) and had allegedly been a hermit, but nothing is known about her.

Exsuperantius of Cingoli (St) {2, 4}

24 January
C5th? Allegedly from Roman Africa, he was a bishop of Cingoli near Ancona (Italy).

Exsuperantius of Ravenna (St) {2, 4}

29 May
d. betw. 430 & 476. He was bishop of Ravenna (Italy) from 398.

Exsuperius (Soupire, Spire) of Bayeux (St) {2}

1 August
Late C4th? He became bishop of Bayeux (France) c.390. His shrine was established at Corbeil.

Exsuperius (Soupire) of Toulouse (St) {2, 4}

28 September
d. p411. Bishop of Toulouse (France) from ?405, he was a friend of St Jerome and was remembered for his charity to the poor in the Holy Land and in Egypt as well as back home to those dispossessed by the barbarian invasions.

Eystein cf. **Augustine Erlandssön**.

Ezechiel the Prophet (St) {2, 4}

23 July
He is the third of the Major Prophets of the Old Testament.

Ezechiel Moreno Diaz (St) {2}

19 August
1848–1906. From Alfaro in the Ebro valley (Spain), he joined the Augustinian Recollects when aged sixteen and was a missionary in the Philippines from 1869 to 1885. Then, after some time in Spain, he went to Colombia in 1888. He became bishop of Pasto, where he was much revered. He was canonized in 1992.

Ezra the Scribe (St) {2, 4}

13 July
He features in the books of Ezra and Nehemiah in the Old Testament.

F

Fabian, Pope (St) {1, 3}

20 January
d. 250. He succeeded St Antheros as pope in 236 and had a peaceful pontificate until his arrest at the start of the persecution of Decius and his subsequent death in prison. He was praised by St Cyprian, his contemporary. Some of his relics were taken to the basilica of St Sebastian which led to the two being celebrated together liturgically until 1969, when their celebrations were separated.

Fabiola (St) {2}

27 December
d. 400. A Roman noblewoman, she was married to a worthless husband and so divorced him and remarried. This caused scandal to the church, so she did public penance after being widowed and became a disciple of St Jerome, founding a hospital in the city with St Pammachius. In 395 she went to the Holy Land and tried to become a nun with St Jerome at Bethlehem, but he was not willing and she returned home and founded a hospice for pilgrims arriving at Rome. She was extremely popular among the common people of the city.

Fabius of Caesarea (St) {2}

31 July
d. 303 or 304. A soldier, he was beheaded at Caesarea in Mauretania (Roman Africa) in the reign of Diocletian for refusing to carry the vexillum (standard) which had pagan symbols on it.

(Fabician and Philibert) (SS) {4 –deleted}

22 August
? These alleged martyrs are venerated at Toledo (Spain).

Fachanan of Ross (St) {2}

14 August
Late C6th. He was allegedly the first bishop of Ross (Rosscarbery) in Co. Cork (Ireland) and founded a monastic school there at which St Brendan taught. He is the principal patron of the diocese of Ross, and the principal patron of the diocese of Kilfenora in Co. Clare (Ireland) might have been the same person.

Facius of Cremona (St) {2}

18 January
d. 1190–1272. He was born at Verona and was a goldsmith there, but moved to Cremona after he made enemies. There he founded a lay confraternity for the practice of charitable works, and became famous for his penitential life. He was made inspector of all the monasteries in the diocese of Verona despite being only a layman.

Facundus and Primitivus (SS) {2, 4}

27 November
Early C4th. From León (Spain), they were beheaded at a place in the region where the abbey and then the town of Sahagún grew up, the name being a corruption of St Facundus.

Fagan cf. **Fugiatus.**

(Faith, Hope and Charity) (SS) {4 –deleted}

1 August
C2nd? In Greek they are Pistis, Elpis and Agape; in Latin, Fides, Spes and Caritas. Their unreliable legend describes them as children, daughters of St Wisdom (Sophia or Sapientia), who were martyred with their mother at Rome in the reign of Hadrian.

Faith (Foy) of Conques (St) {2, 4}

6 October
C3rd. From Agen on the Garonne (France), she was martyred there in the reign of Maximian Herculius. Her shrine was established at the abbey of Conques where her golden reliquary made in 949 is a rare survival. Part of her relics was taken to Glastonbury, giving

rise to a cultus in England and to several church dedications. Her legends are fictitious. Her attribute is a gridiron.

Fal cf. **Fidolus**.

Falco of Cava (Bl) {2}

6 June
d. 1146. He became a Benedictine monk at Cava near Salerno (Italy) under St Peter and was prior of the daughter house of Cirzosimo before succeeding St Simeon as abbot in 1141. His cultus was confirmed for Cava in 1928.

Falcus of Palena (St) {2}

9 August
C9–10th. A Calabrian, he became a hermit in the Abruzzi (Italy), and his shrine is at Palena. His cultus was confirmed for Valva and Solmona in 1893.

Famian (Gebhard) (St) {2}

8 August
d. ?1150. From Cologne, he became a pilgrim and went to Rome, the Holy Land and finally to Compostella (Spain), near where he became a hermit for twenty-five years. When the Cistercian abbey of Osera was founded he joined it, but went on another pilgrimage to the Holy Land and died at Gallese in Umbria (Italy) on his way back. His name was only given to him after death, and refers to the fame deriving from miracles at his shrine.

Fandilas (St) {2, 4}

13 June
d. 853. An Andalusian, he was abbot of Peñamelaria near Cordoba (Spain), the capital of the Umayyad emirs. He was beheaded for preaching the futility of Islam.

Fantinus the Elder (St) {2}

24 July
C4th. From Syracuse (Sicily), he was converted by a hermit and converted his parents in turn, but they were martyred in the reign of Diocletian and he fled to Calabria. He died at Gioja.

Fantinus the Younger (St) {2, 4}

30 August
C10th. He was a Byzantine-rite abbot in Calabria (Italy), but his monastery was destroyed in a Muslim raid and he went to Corinth (Greece) and then to Larissa. He died at Thessalonica.

Fara (Burgundofara) (St) {2, 4}

7 December
d. 657. The daughter of a Frankish courtier, she was cured of a chronic illness as a child by the prayers of St Columban and developed a monastic vocation. Her father wanted her to marry but could not break her resolve, and ended up founding the nunnery of Faremoutiers near Meaux (France) for her. She was abbess there for thirty-seven years, and many Anglo-Saxon girls received their monastic training there. The old Roman Martyrology also listed her by error on 3 April. SS Faro and Cagnoald were her brother and sister.

Faro (St) {2, 4}

28 October
d. c 670. Brother of SS Fara and Cagnoald, he was a Frankish courtier who rose to the position of royal chancellor before he and his wife separated to become religious. It is uncertain which monastery he was in before he became bishop of Meaux (France) in 626. As such he was a great supporter of monasticism.

(Fausta) *(St)* *{4 –deleted}*

19 December
C3rd? She was allegedly the widowed mother of St Anastasia.

(Fausta, Evilasius and Maximus) *(SS)*
{4 –deleted}

20 September
d. 303. According to their story, Fausta was a teenager who was ordered to be tortured by Evilasius, a pagan magistrate. She converted him by her fortitude, and they then converted a praetor, Maximus, in the same way. The three were martyred at Cyzicus on the Sea of Marmara (Asia Minor) in the reign of Diocletian.

Faustina Kowalska cf. **Mary-Faustina Kowalska**.

Faustinian (St) {2, 4}

26 February
C4th. A bishop of Bologna (Italy), allegedly the second, he restored the life of his diocese after the persecution of Diocletian and then fought against Arianism.

Faustinus and Jovita (SS) {2, 3}

15 February
? They were martyred at Brescia (Italy). According to their unreliable acta, they were two brothers, noblemen, who were beheaded there in the reign of Hadrian. Their cultus, although ancient, was suppressed in 1969.

(Faustinus, Lucius and Comps) *(SS)*
{4 –deleted}

15 December
? Nothing is known about these Roman African martyrs. The companions were listed as Candidus, Caelian, Mark, Januarius and Fortunatus.

(Faustinus, Timothy and Venustus) *(SS)*
{4 –deleted}

22 May
d. ?362. They were martyred at Rome in the reign of Julian.

(Faustinus of Brescia) *(St)* *{4 –deleted}*

16 February
d. 381. He succeeded St Ursicinus as bishop of Brescia in Lombardy (Italy) c.360 As an alleged descendant of Faustinus and Jovita (q.v.) he compiled (or invented) their acta.

Faustinus Míguez (Bl) {2}

8 March
1831–1925. From the province of Orense in Spain, he joined the Piarists at Madrid and taught in various schools for almost fifty years, being inspired by the example of St Joseph Calasanz. He was also skilled in herbal medicine, founding a laboratory for research therein. Noting the illiteracy and marginalization of many poor young women in contemporary Spanish society, he founded the 'Calasanctian Institute of the Daughters of the Divine Shepherdess' in 1885 to help with their education. Dying at Getafe, he was beatified in 1998.

(Faustinus of Rome and Comps) *(SS)*
{4 –deleted}

17 February
? They were listed as martyrs of Rome, numbering fifty-five.

(Faustinus of Todi) *(St)* *{4 –deleted}*

29 July
C4th. This alleged disciple of St Felix of Martano has a church dedicated to him at Spoleto (Italy) and is venerated at Todi. He apparently died in peace after standing up for his faith during persecution.

(Faustus) (St) {4 –deleted}

16 July
d. c.250. A Greek, he was martyred in an unknown place by being crucified and being used for archery practice. Allegedly he took five days to die.

Faustus, Dius and Ammonius (SS) {2, 4}

8 September
d. ?311. They were priests who were martyred in Egypt in the reign of Diocletian, in the same persecution that saw the martyrdom of St Peter of Alexandria.

Faustus, Gaius and Comps (SS) {2, 4}

3 October
Mid C3rd. They are listed as disciples of St Dionysius of Alexandria (Egypt) who were persecuted in the reigns of Decius and Valerian. The companions were Peter, Paul, Eusebius, Chaeremon, Lucius and another two. Faustus lived long enough to be martyred under Diocletian, c.300.

The revised Roman Martyrology has conflated the entries in the previous edition for 'Dionysius, Faustus and Companions' on this day, 'Gaius, Faustus and Companions' on the day following and 'Faustus of Alexandria' on 19 November. These arose from mistaken duplications.

Faustus, Januarius and Martial (SS) {2, 4}

13 October
C3rd–4th. They were martyred at Cordoba (Spain).

(Faustus, Macarius and Comps) (SS) {4 –deleted}

6 September
d. 250. They numbered twelve and were beheaded at Alexandria (Egypt) in the reign of Decius.

Faustus of Milan (St) {4 –deleted}

7 August
C2nd? He was allegedly a soldier martyred at Milan (Italy) in the reign of Commodus.

Faustus of Riez (St) {2}

28 September
d. p485. From Brittany (France), he became a monk at Lérins and its abbot in 433. He was made bishop of Riez in 459, became very influential and fought against Pelagianism and Arianism. For this, he was exiled. He was the most distinguished defender of semi-Pelagianism against the teachings on grace of St Augustine.

(Faustus of Rome and Comps) (SS) {4 –deleted}

24 June
? A group of twenty-four unknown Roman martyrs, they may be identical with SS Lucilla, Flora and Comps (who numbered the same).

(Febronia) (St) {4 –deleted}

25 July
Early C4th? According to her story, she was a young nun of a nunnery at Nisibis in upper Mesopotamia (now on the border between Syria and Turkey) who was left behind with two others when the community fled the persecution of Diocletian. She was singled out to be tortured by the removal of the usual appendages before being beheaded. Her acta were allegedly written by one of the companions. There is doubt as to her having existed.

Felicia Meda (Bl) {2}

30 September
1378–1444. From Milan (Italy), she became a Poor Clare there in 1400 and was made abbess in 1425. Proving a success, she was sent to Pesaro to found a new nunnery in 1439. Her cultus was approved in 1812.

(Felician, Philippian and Comps) (SS)
{4 –deleted}

30 January
? They are listed as a group of one hundred and twenty-six Roman African martyrs.

Felician of Carthage (St) {2, 4}

29 October
C3rd? He was martyred at Carthage in Roman Africa. The old Roman Martyrology gave him companions, Hyacinth, Quintus and Lucius, and placed them somewhere in Lucania (Italy).

Felician of Foligno (St) {2, 4}

24 January
C3rd. From Foligno (Italy), he became a rhetorician at Rome but was sent back as bishop by Pope St Victor I. He evangelized Umbria but was arrested when very old in the reign of Decius and died on the road to Rome where he was to have been martyred. He is listed twice in error in the old Roman Martyrology, also on 20 October.

Felicissima (St) {2, 4}

26 May
End 3rd. She was martyred at Todi (Italy) in the reign of Diocletian. The old Roman Martyrology listed her as three males: Felicissimus, Heraclius and Paulinus.

(Felicissimus of Perugia) *(St) {4 –deleted}*

24 November
Early C4th? He was listed as martyred at Perugia (Italy).

Felicity of Rome (St) {2, 3}

23 November
? She was an early martyr of Rome who was buried on the Via Salaria, and may be the Felicity mentioned in the Roman canon of the Mass (usually taken to be the companion of St Perpetua). Her unreliable acta describe her as a widow martyred with her seven sons, and the old Roman Martyrology mistakenly equates these with the **Seven Brothers**. Her cultus was confined to local calendars in 1969.

Felicula of Rome (St) {2, 4}

13 June
Early C4th? She was martyred on the Via Arderatina outside Rome. According to her unreliable legend, she was the foster-sister of St Petronilla and, after the latter's martyrdom in the reign of Diocletian, was left in prison without food or drink for a fortnight and then thrown into a ditch to die.

Felim (Fidlemin) (St) {2}

9 August
C6th. Allegedly a disciple of St Columba, he founded a monastery at Kilmore in Co. Cavan (Ireland) and is the principal patron of the diocese of Kilmore.

(Felinus and Gratian) *(SS) {4 –deleted}*

1 June
C3rd? They were allegedly soldiers martyred at Perugia (Italy) in the reign of Decius. Their shrine is at Arona on Lake Maggiore.

Felix I, Pope (St) {2, 3}

30 May
d. 274. Allegedly a Roman, he became pope in 269. A letter forged by the Apollinarians in condemnation of the heresy of Paul of Samosata was accepted by the council of Ephesus as being by him. He had been venerated as a martyr, but apparently in mistake for another Felix and his cultus as such was suppressed in 1969.

(Felix II, Antipope) *(St) {3 –deleted}*

29 July
d. 365. He was archdeacon to Pope Liberius when the latter was exiled in 355 by Emperor

Constantius for opposing Arianism. He was then elected as antipope by the Arian faction at Rome and was confirmed in office by the council of Sirmium. When Pope Liberius returned he was driven into exile. The old Roman Martyrology listed him as a valid pope and also as a martyr, owing to the unreliable tradition that he opposed the emperor and was killed as a result. His cultus was confined to local calendars in 1969, and he has since been deleted from the Roman Martyrology.

Felix III, Pope (St) {2, 4}

1 March
d. 492. An alleged ancestor of St Gregory the Great, he became pope in 483 and firmly opposed Monophysitism. In 484, he condemned the 'Henoticon', an Imperial decree issued by Emperor Zeno and Patriarch Acacius of Constantinople in order to try to reconcile the Monophysites. This initiated the 'Acacian schism' between the two churches, which lasted until 518. The Roman Martyrology has chosen to keep his erroneous numeration, even though 'Felix II' was not a legitimate pope.

Felix IV, Pope (St) {2, 4}

22 September
d. 530. From near Benevento (Italy), he became pope in 526 and was remembered for his generosity to the poor of Rome. He approved the council of Orange in 529, which promulgated important doctrine on grace and original sin.

Felix and Adauctus (SS) {2, 3}

30 August
d. ?304. Their legend, which seems to be an embellishment of the inscription composed for their tomb on the Ostian Way at Rome by Pope St Damasus, is that the former was a Roman priest who had been condemned and was being taken to his place of execution. An unknown bystander was led by his example to proclaim his faith and was martyred with him (the name meaning 'the one added'). Their cultus was confined to local calendars in 1969.

(Felix and Constantia) (SS) {4 –deleted}

19 September
C1st? They are listed as martyrs of Nocera (Italy) in the reign of Nero, but there are two towns called Nocera in Italy with rival sets of relics. One is in Campania, the other in Umbria.

Felix, Cyprian and Comps (SS) {2, 4}

12 October
d. 483. Two bishops and allegedly 4964 Roman African Catholics, they were driven into the desert in modern Algeria by the Arian Vandal King Hunneric. There they died of privation, were eaten by wild animals or were killed or enslaved by the local Berbers. Their fate is recorded by Victor of Utica, their contemporary.

(Felix and Eusebius) (SS) {4 –deleted}

5 November
C1st? They were allegedly martyred at Terracina between Rome and Naples.

Felix and Fortunatus (SS) {2, 4}

14 May
Early C4th. They were martyred at Aquileia near Venice (Italy) in the reign of Diocletian, and were allegedly two brothers from Vicenza.

(Felix, Fortunatus and Achilles) (SS) {4 –deleted}

23 April
C3rd? A priest and two deacons, they were allegedly sent by St Irenaeus of Lyons to evangelize the district of Vienne (France) and were martyred in the reign of Caracalla. Their acta are unreliable.

Felix and Gennadius (SS) {2, 4}

16 May
? The shrine of these martyrs is at Uzalis in Roman Africa, but nothing is known about them.

(Felix and Januarius) *(SS)* *{4 –deleted}*

7 January
? They were allegedly martyred at one of the cities called Heraclea in the East, not the one near Cadiz (Spain) where they are venerated.

(Felix, Julia and Jucunda) *(SS)* *{4 –deleted}*

27 July
? Erroneously listed in the old Roman Martyrology as martyrs at Nola near Naples (Italy), the first is the famous Felix of Nola while the other two seem to be martyrs of Nicomedia (Asia Minor).

(Felix, Luciolus, Fortunatus, Marcia and Comps) *(SS)* *{4 –deleted}*

3 March
? A group of forty martyrs, claimed for Roman Africa on slender grounds.

Felix and Regula (SS) {2}

11 September
? They have a popular local cultus at Zürich (Switzerland). According to their untrustworthy legend they were a brother and sister who took refuge there in the reign of Maximian but who were discovered and beheaded.

(Felix, Symphronius, Hippolytus and Comps) *(SS)* *{4 –deleted}*

3 February
? They were possibly martyred in Roman Africa, if they existed at all. It is suspected that they are a duplication of other martyrs.

(Felix of Africa and Comps) *(SS)* *{4 –deleted}*

23 March
C5th. They are listed as twenty-four Roman African martyrs.

Felix-of-Nicosia Amoroso (St) {2}

31 May
1715–87. From Nicosia (Sicily), he was an apprentice shoemaker and tried and failed several times to become a consecrated religious. Finally he became a lay brother in the Capuchin friary at his home town and went begging for funds for its maintenance. He helped poor and sick people, reconciled habitual sinners and was canonized in 2005.

Felix of Bologna (St) {2, 4}

4 December
d. 431. A deacon at Milan (Italy) under St Ambrose, he later became bishop of Bologna.

(Felix of Brescia) *(St)* *{4 –deleted}*

23 February
? He is merely listed as a bishop of Brescia (Italy).

Felix of Cantalice (St) {2, 4}

18 May
1515–87. From a peasant family near Cantalice in Apulia (Italy), he started out as a farm labourer but became a Capuchin lay brother at Anticoli in 1543. In 1547, he went to the friary at Rome and begged daily for funds for its support for forty years. He became friendly with SS Charles Borromeo and Philip Neri, was especially attached to children and was an example of spiritual joy (being nicknamed 'Deogratias' from his constantly saying 'Thanks be to God'). He was the first Capuchin to be canonized, in 1712.

Felix of Como (St) {2, 4}

8 October
End C4th. He was consecrated bishop of Como (Italy), allegedly the first one there, by his friend St Ambrose.

Felix of Dunwich (St) {2}

8 March
d. ?646. From Burgundy, he became a missionary bishop. In 630 he went to East Anglia with its king St Sigebert (who had been baptized in exile) and became the 'Apostle of the East Angles' with the support of St Honoratus of Canterbury. He was a great success as a preacher, and established his base at Dunwich on the coast of Suffolk. This walled city has now been washed away by the sea and the church of St John, thought to have been his cathedral, was lost in 1540. His copy of the Gospels, written in c.630, survived as the 'Red Book of Dunwich' at Eye Priory and then at the magistrates' court at Eye before allegedly being cut up for tags at a local mansion in the mid-C19th. His is depicted with three rings on his right hand.

(Felix of Fondi) *(St)* *{4 –deleted}*

6 November
C6th. He featured in the 'Dialogues' attributed to St Gregory the Great as a monk at Fondi near Terracina (Italy) who had a tame poisonous snake guarding his garden. Some alleged saints in this probably unhistorical work are more obviously ridiculous than others, and the Roman Martyrology has deleted almost all of them.

Felix of Gerona (St) {2, 4}

1 August
Early C4th. He was martyred at Gerona in the persecution by the emperor Diocletian. According to his legend, he was a native of Roman Africa.

(Felix of Metz) *(St)* *{4 –deleted}*

21 February
C2nd? He is the alleged third bishop of Metz (France). The existence of that diocese is only certain from the C4th, however, and the earlier traditions may be fictitious.

Felix of Nantes (St) {2}

6 January
d. 582. He was bishop of Nantes (France) for about thirty-three years.

Felix of Nicosia cf. **Felix-of-Nicosia Amoroso**.

Felix of Nola (1) (St) {2, 3}

14 January
End C3rd. Born at Nola near Naples (Italy), his father was a soldier from Syria. He became a priest of Nola and was especially helpful to St Maximus the bishop when the persecution by Decius broke out. He had to suffer much himself, and was thus sometimes celebrated as a martyr. St Paulinus of Nola had a great devotion to him and wrote in his honour, which led to his cultus being one of the most popular in south Italy. However it was confined to local calendars in 1969.

Felix of Nola (2) (St) {2, 4}

15 November
C4–5th. A second St Felix of Nola is venerated as the principal patron of Nola near Naples, and is described as the town's first bishop who was venerated with fifty companions. The Roman Martyrology now accepts that he is not to be identified with the earlier St Felix of Nola who is described in the previous entry.

(Felix of Pavia) *(St)* *{4 –deleted}*

15 July
? This alleged bishop and martyr has a cultus at Pavia (Italy) but is otherwise unknown and may be the same as St Felix of Spoleto.

(Felix of Pistoia) *(St)* *{4 –deleted}*

26 August
C9th? Allegedly an early hermit of Pistoia in Tuscany (Italy), his alleged relics were found there in 1414. His existence is doubtful.

Felix of Rome (St) {2}

14 January
C3rd–4th. He was martyred on the Via Portuense outside Rome.

Felix of Seville (St) {2, 4}

2 May
? He is a martyred deacon venerated at Seville (Spain).

Felix of Salona (St) {2, 4}

18 May
d. 299. He was martyred at Salona in Dalmatia (Croatia) in the reign of Diocletian. Later it was alleged that he was a bishop either of Spoleto (Italy) or of Spello nearby.

(Felix of Sutri) *(St)* *{4 –deleted}*

23 June
Mid C3rd? He was allegedly a priest from Sutri near Viterbo (Italy) who had his face smashed in with a heavy stone at Civita Castellana nearby in the reign of Valerian.

Felix of Thibiuca (St) {2, 4}

15 July
d. 303. Bishop of Thibiuca in Roman Africa, he refused to hand over his church's copies of the Scriptures for destruction as required by an edict of Diocletian. Thus he was taken to Carthage, exiled to Italy and beheaded at Venosa. The old Roman Martyrology listed four spurious companions: Adauctus (cf. **Felix and Adauctus**), Januarius, Fortunatus and Septimus (cf. **Twelve Brothers**).

Felix of Thynissa (St) {2, 4}

6 November
C3rd. A Roman African, he died in prison awaiting martyrdom at Thynissa near Annaba (Algeria). St Augustine preached a sermon in his honour.

(Felix of Trier) *(St)* *{4 –deleted}*

26 March
d. c.400. He was consecrated bishop of Trier (Germany) by his friend St Martin of Tours in 386. However, those clerics who had elected him had also asked Maximus, the usurping emperor, for the death of the heretic Priscillian. So St Felix was refused communion by the pope and St Ambrose of Milan and resigned as a result, although his personal integrity was not in question. He is one of the few genuinely historical personages to have been deleted from the Roman Martyrology.

Felix of Valois (St) {2, 3}

20 November
?1127–?1212. According to his legend, he was a hermit near Meaux (France) who founded the Trinitarian order with St John of Matha in order to redeem Christians taken prisoners by Muslim raiders. The early Trinitarians kept no records, a defect which their successors made up for by forgery, and so his existence is dubious. His cultus was confirmed for the Trinitarians and for Spain in 1666, extended to the entire Latin church in 1694 but confined again to local calendars in 1969.

(Felix of Verona) *(St)* *{4 –deleted}*

19 July
? He was allegedly an early bishop of Verona (Italy).

Ferdinand-of-St-Joseph Ayalà (Bl) {2}

1 June
1575–1617. From near Ciudad Real (Spain), he became an Augustinian friar and went to Japan via Mexico in 1605 as vicar-provincial of the Augustinian mission there. He worked at Osaka and was beheaded at Omura, being beatified in 1867. Cf. **Japan, Martyrs of**.

Ferdinand-Mary Baccilieri (Bl) {2}

13 July
1821–93. From Campodoso near Modena (Italy), he tried his vocation with the Jesuits before being ordained as a diocesan priest of Bologna in 1844. In 1851, he was made parish priest of Galeazza, where he remained for forty-one years, the rest of his life. In order to educate poor girls of the parish, he founded the 'Mantellate Servite Sisters of Rome' in 1866, and this has since become an international congregation. He was beatified in 1999.

Ferdinand III of Spain, King (St) {2, 4}

30 May
1198–1252. King of Castile from 1217, he united his kingdom with that of León in 1230 and was able to follow up the crushing defeat of the Muslims by the Spanish Christians at Los Navos de Tolosa in 1212 by conquering Cordoba (1236), Murcia, Jaen, Cadiz and finally Seville in 1249. He consolidated his conquests by founding many church institutions (including the university of Salamanca), by practising tolerance towards his new Muslim and Jewish subjects (although not towards heretics) and by aiming at doing no injustice to anyone. He lived extremely frugally and penitentially, died at Seville and his cultus was confirmed for Spain in 1655.

Fergus (Fergustian) of Glamis (St) {2}

27 November
d. p721. An Irish missionary bishop, he worked in the regions of Strathearn, Caithness and Buchan in Scotland and died at Glamis near Forfar. He signed the acta of a Roman council in 721, describing himself as a Pict.

Fernando cf. **Ferdinand**.
Ferran cf. **Ferdinand**.

Ferreolus and Ferrutius (SS) {2, 4}

16 June
C4th? According to their legend, they were Gallo-Romans who studied at Athens and at Smyrna (now Izmir in Turkey) and were converted by St Polycarp. Returning as priest and deacon, they were sent by St Irenaeus of Lyons to evangelize the region around Besançon (France), where they were martyred after thirty years. In reality, they were probably martyred in the following century.

Ferreolus (Fergéol) of Grenoble (St) {2}

12 January
d. ?659. Bishop of Grenoble (France), he was allegedly killed by order of Ebroin, the mayor of the palace of the Neustrian kingdom. His cultus was confirmed in 1907.

Ferreolus of Limoges (St) {2}

18 September
End 6th. Bishop of Limoges (France), he was admired by St Gregory of Tours but his extant biography is fictitious.

Ferreolus of Uzès (St) {2}

4 January
d. 581. From Narbonne (France), he became bishop of Uzès near Avignon but was exiled by the king for three years, allegedly because he tried to convert the Jews of his diocese. He wrote a rule for a monastery that he founded (this relies in part on the rule of St Benedict).

Ferreolus of Vienne (St) {2, 4}

18 September
Late C3rd. A Roman army officer, traditionally the commanding officer of St Julian of Brioude (q.v.), during a persecution (probably of Diocletian) he was imprisoned for his faith in a latrine pit at Vienne (France) but escaped through the sewer. He was recaptured and beheaded.

Ferrutius of Mainz (St) {2, 4}

28 October
d. c.300. A Roman soldier stationed at Mainz (Germany), he tried to resign rather than take part in the prescribed pagan rituals but was imprisoned instead at Kastel nearby and died of ill-treatment.

Festus cf. **Faustus**.

Festus and Desiderius (SS) {2, 3 –group}

7 September
C4th. Festus was a deacon and Desiderius was a lector martyred at Benevento (Italy). Formerly they were included in the worthless legend of St Januarius of Benevento, and liturgically celebrated with him.

Fiacre (Fiacrius, Fiaker, Fèvre) (St) {2, 4}

30 August
d. c.670. From Ireland, he became a hermit at Kilferagh (named after him) in Co. Kilkenny before emigrating to France and becoming a hermit at Breuil near Meaux on a site given to him by the local bishop, St Faro. His cell grew into an abbey. His veneration is still popular and he is a patron of gardeners (his attribute is a spade) and of men suffering from venereal disease (he had no time for women).

Fibitius (St) {2, 4}

5 November
d. c.450. He was abbot of a monastery at Trier (Germany) before becoming bishop there.

(Fidelis) (St) {4 –deleted}

23 March
? An alleged Roman African martyr, he may be one of the companions of the St Felix listed on the same date.

Fidelis of Como (St) {2, 4}

28 October
Early C4th? A soldier, he was martyred at Samolito near Como in Lombardy (Italy). Most of his relics were taken to Milan by St Charles Borromeo, but some remain at Como.

Fidelis Chijnacki (Bl) {2}

9 July
1906–42. From Łodz in Poland, he worked at the Post Office of Warsaw and there joined 'Catholic Action', making those suffering from alcoholism his special care. In 1933, he joined the Capuchins, continuing his work with alcoholics. He was arrested by the Nazis in 1940 and held initially at Sachsenhausen and then at Dachau, where he died of starvation, abuse and overwork. Cf. **Poland, Martyrs of the Nazi Occupation of**.

Fidelis-of-Sigmaringen Roy (St) {1, 3}

24 April
1577–1622. From Sigmaringen in southern Germany, he travelled widely as tutor to a young nobleman before qualifying as a lawyer and doing much work for the poor at Ensisheim in Alsace. Then he became a Capuchin at Freiburg-in-Breisgau in 1612 and was appointed head of the mission to Graubünden canton in Switzerland by the newly founded Roman congregation of Propaganda Fide in 1622. The area was fanatically Protestant but his success was startling, so the Zwinglian preachers asserted that he was an agent of the Hapsburgs. As a result, he was martyred in the church at Seewis near Chur. He was canonized in 1746.

Fidentian, Valerian, Victoria and Comps (SS) {2, 4}

15 November
? They numbered twenty, and were martyred at Hippo Regius (Roman Africa). Fidentian was the bishop, and St Augustine preached in their honour. The old Roman Martyrology garbled their names to 'Secundus, Fidentian and Varicus'.

(Fidentius and Terence) (SS) {4 –deleted}

27 September
? The alleged relics of these martyrs were discovered at Todi (Italy) in the C12th and are venerated there. Nothing is known about them and their acta are fictitious.

(Fidentius of Padua) (St) {4 –deleted}

16 November
C2nd? He has a cultus at Padua but nothing is known about him. Traditionally he was a martyr, and Cardinal Baronius listed him as a bishop in his revision of the old Roman Martyrology (it is unclear as to why).

Fides cf. **Faith**.

Fidolus (Phal) (St) {2, 4}

16 May
d. c.540. The son of a Roman official in Auvergne (France), he was captured and sold as a slave by the invading Franks but redeemed by Aventinus, an abbot of a monastery near Troyes. Fidolus later became abbot himself at the place, later named Saint-Phal after him.

Fillan cf. **Foillan**.

Fina of San Gimignano (St) {2}

12 March
d. 1253. Born into a poor family at San Gimignano in Tuscany (Italy), she was never a nun but lived at home (possibly as a Benedictine oblate). She suffered a repulsive and paralysing breakdown in health when young and took six years to die in a state of serious neglect, being remembered for her patience.

Finan cf. **Finian**.

Finan of Lindisfarne (St) {2}

17 February
d. ?656. An Irish monk of Iona, he was chosen by his brethren to succeed St Aidan as bishop of Lindisfarne. He continued the evangelization of Northumbria (England) in partnership with its king St Oswin and founded monasteries at Gilling, Tynemouth and Whitby. He also sent missionaries to Mercia and East Anglia, consecrating St Chad for the Mercian mission. He was a staunch upholder of Celtic church traditions.

Finbar (Findbar, Barr) (St) {2}

25 September
C6th. A native of the region of Connaught in Ireland, he became a hermit at Gougane Barra and founded a monastery on the site of Cork (of which city he is considered the first bishop). The island of Barra in the Western Isles (Scotland) is named after him. His name means 'Blond'. He is the principal patron of the diocese of Cork.

Findbarr cf. **Finian**.

Fingar (Gwinear) (St) {2}

14 December
d. c.460. He was martyred at Gwinear near Hayle in Cornwall (England), and seems to have been a hermit in Brittany previously, as Plouvinger there is named after him and he is venerated there. The Roman Martyrology has not listed his alleged companions, including his sister Phiala.

Finian (Finnian) of Clonard (St) {2}

12 December
d. 549. From Myshall near Carlow (Ireland), he was a monk in Wales for some time before returning to Ireland and founding many monasteries and churches. The greatest of these was Clonard in Meath which became the foremost school in Ireland, famous for its biblical exegesis. Among its pupils were the so-called 'Twelve Apostles of Ireland', who helped to establish Christianity thoroughly in Ireland after the death of St Patrick's generation. He is the principal patron of the diocese of Meath.

Fintan of Clonenagh (St) {2}

17 February
d. 603. From Leinster (Ireland) and a disciple of St Columba at Terryglass, he became a hermit at Clonenagh in Co. Laois and founded a monastery for the disciples who came to him. Allegedly the austerity of this was such that neighbouring monasteries objected.

Fintan of Rheinau (St) {2}

15 November
d. ?878. From Leinster (Ireland), he was captured by Norse raiders and taken to the Orkneys to be a slave but escaped and went on pilgrimage to Rome. Then he became a monk at Farfa nearby before ending up as a hermit at the abbey of Rheinau on the Rhine in Zürich canton (Switzerland) for twenty-two years.

(Firmatus and Flaviana) (SS) *{4 –deleted}*

5 October
? They are venerated as martyrs at Auxerre (France), but nothing is known about them.

Firmin of Amiens (St) {2, 4}

25 September
? The reputed first bishop of Amiens (France) and a martyr, he is described as being from Pamplona in Spanish Navarre and a convert of St Saturninus of Toulouse.

(Firmin of Amiens, Abbot) (St) *{4 –deleted}*

11 March
? In his revision of the old Roman Martyrology Cardinal Baronius inserted an abbot of Amiens called Firmin. No such saint has ever been venerated there, and he seems to have conflated Firmian of Piceno and Firmin, third bishop of Amiens.

Firmin of Gevaudan (St) {2}

14 January
C5th. He succeeded St Privatus of Gevaudan as bishop of this area of the southern Massif Central (France), and is venerated at Mende.

Firmin of Metz (St) {2, 4}

18 August
C4th. He succeeded St Adelphus as bishop of Metz (France), but the statements about him are confused.

Firmin of Uzès (St) {2, 4}

11 October
d. p552. From Narbonne (France), he was educated by an uncle who was bishop of Uzès near Avignon and succeeded him as bishop in 538.

Firmina of Amelia (St) {2, 4}

24 November
C4th? From Rome, she died under torture at Amelia in Umbria (Italy) in the reign of Diocletian.

(Firmus) (St) *{4 –deleted}*

1 June
d. c.290. He was listed as an Eastern martyr, possibly of Egypt.

(Firmus and Rusticus) *(SS) {4 –deleted}*

9 August
d. c.290. They were allegedly two related citizens of Bergamo in Lombardy (Italy) who were martyred at Verona in the reign of Maximian, but their acta are not authentic and they may have been African martyrs whose relics were taken to Verona.

(Firmus of Tagaste) *(St) {4 –deleted}*

31 July
Early C4th. St Augustine wrote of him that he was 'firm by name but firmer by faith' because he endured torture rather than give up a fugitive sought by the authorities. On the basis of this, Cardinal Baronius inserted his name into the old Roman Martyrology.

First Martyrs of Rome cf. **Protomartyrs of Rome**.

Flannan (St) {2}

18 December
C7th. An Irish monk, he was ordained in Rome and was the first bishop of Killaloe in Co. Clare (Ireland), founded by St Lua. He was also a hermit for a while on the Flannan Islands, west of Lewis in the Western Isles (Scotland). He is the principal patron of the diocese of Killaloe.

Flavia Domitilla cf. **Domitilla**.

(Flavian and Elias) *(SS) {4 –deleted}*

20 July
d. 512 & 518 resp. They were the patriarchs of Antioch and of Jerusalem and were exiled to Petra (Jordan) by the Monophysite emperor Anastasius I. Flavian had refused to commit himself to opposing the council of Chalcedon and was deposed, and Elias had supported him by refusing communion to the intruded

patriarch Severus. Elias did not accept the council himself, however, and he is not venerated by the Orthodox. They died in exile and were inserted into the old Roman Martyrology despite being under contemporary Roman excommunication for having accepted the *Henoticon*.

(Flavian of Acquapendente) *(St) {4 –deleted}*

22 December
d. 362. Alleged to have been a prefect of Rome, in the reign of Julian he was branded on the forehead as a slave and exiled to Acquapendente in Tuscany (Italy), where he died. His acta are untrustworthy.

Flavian of Autun (SS) {2, 4}

20 July
d. 544 & 614. The fifteenth and the twenty-first bishops of Autun (France), both called Flavian, are listed as saints. The former only is in the Roman Martyrology.

(Flavian of Civitavecchia) *(St) {4 –deleted}*

28 January
Early C4th? He was listed as a deputy prefect of Rome, beheaded at Civitavecchia in the reign of Diocletian.

Flavian of Constantinople (St) {2, 4}

18 February
d. 449. A priest of Constantinople, he became patriarch there in 446 and made an enemy of Chrysaphius, a palace eunuch and adviser of Emperor Theodosius II, by refusing to make a donation to him on his election. Then Flavian denounced the Monophysitism of the monk Eutyches, who claimed to be interpreting the teaching of St Cyril of Alexandria, in 448 and informed Pope St Leo. The latter replied with his famous 'Tome' (an encyclical letter). Then his enemies at home and Dioscorus, the

patriarch of Alexandria, arranged for a council at Ephesus in 449, the so-called 'Robber Synod', at which Flavian was deposed and so badly beaten that he died three days later. He was vindicated at the Council of Chalcedon in 451, which accepted the Tome of Leo and definitively rejected Monophysitism.

Flavius and Companions (SS) {2, 4}

7 May
d. c.300. Totalling five, they were martyred at Nicomedia (Asia Minor) in the reign of Diocletian (whose capital the place was). The former Latin tradition was that he was the bishop who died with his two brothers, Augustus and Augustine. Eastern sources list the companions as Marcellinus, Macrobius and Eutyches.

Flavius Clemens (St) {2, 4}

22 June
d. 96. Brother of the emperor Vespasian and uncle of Titus and Domitian, he married St Domitilla (q.v.). He was consul with Domitian in 95, who had him executed in the following year for 'atheism' and 'Jewish customs'. This has been taken to refer to his conversion to Christianity.

(Flocellus) (St) {4 –deleted}

17 September
C2nd? From near Coutances (France), he was listed as a teenager who was tortured and thrown to the wild animals in the amphitheatre (allegedly at Autun) in the reign of Marcus Aurelius.

Flora and Mary (SS) {2, 4}

24 November
d. 851. They were two young women of Cordoba (Spain) when that city was the capital of the Umayyad emirate, and had Muslim fathers and Christian mothers. After choosing Christianity they were condemned as apostates under Islamic law and beheaded after a long imprisonment.

Flora of Beaulieu (Bl) {2}

5 October
d. 1347. From the Auvergne (France), when aged fourteen she joined the Hospitaller nuns of St John at Beaulieu near Rocamadour. She suffered some very interesting mystical and psychological phenomena associated with her spiritual sufferings.

Florence cf. **Florentina**, **Florentia** or **Florentius**.

Florentia (St) {2}

1 December
C4th. When St Hilary of Poitiers (France) was exiled to Phrygia (Asia Minor), he made a disciple of this virgin who followed him back home and became a hermit outside the city.

Florentina (Florence) (St) {2, 4}

28 August
C7th. From Cartagena (Spain), she was the sister of SS Leander, Fulgentius and Isidore. The family was orphaned when she was little and she was educated by St Leander, who wrote a rule for a monastic foundation that she made. She died at Ecija.

Florentinus, Hilary and Aphrodisius (SS) {2, 4}

27 September
C5th. They are listed as hermits martyred in Roman Gaul by invading barbarians, at a place which has been claimed as Sion in Valais (Switzerland), Sémont near Autun, Suint in the Charolais or Simond near Dijon (all in France). A companion Aphrodisius has been deleted from the Roman Martyrology.

Florentinus Asensio Barroso (Bl) {2}

9 August

1877–1936. Born near Valladolid (Spain), he was ordained in 1901 and became a lecturer in theology at the university there before being made the parish priest of the cathedral. He was a prolific and effective preacher and also confessor to consecrated religious, and was appointed the bishop of Barbastro at the start of 1936. The city was ruled by anticlerical republicans and, despite his goodwill and collaboration, he was imprisoned in July and tortured and mutilated before being shot. He was beatified in 1997. Cf. **Spanish Civil War, Martyrs of.**

Florentius of Città del Castello (St) {2}

13 November

C6th. He was a bishop of Città del Castello in Umbria (Italy), and was praised by Pope St Gregory the Great for his sanctity and the soundness of his doctrine.

(Florentinus of Trier) (St) {4 –deleted}

16 October

C4th. He is alleged to have been the successor of St Severianus as bishop of Trier (Germany), but there is serious doubt concerning the existence of both.

Florentius (St) {2, 4}

22 September

C5th. From Bavaria (Germany), he became a disciple of St Martin of Tours, who ordained him and sent him to evangelize Poitou (France). He eventually settled as a hermit on the Loire River near Angers, and along with the disciples who gathered around him, he formed the monastery which was later known as Saint-Florent-le-Vieil.

Florentius and Diocletian (SS) {2, 4}

11 May

d. 303. They were martyred at Osimo near Ancona (Italy) in the reign of Diocletian. The Roman Martyrology has deleted a companion Sisinnius, and corrected the name of Diocletian from Diocletius. The latter form seems to have been the result of a wish to avoid using the name of the persecuting emperor.

(Florentius and Felix) (SS) {4 –deleted}

25 July

C3rd? They were listed as two Roman soldiers martyred at Furcona near Aquila (Italy) in the reign of Maximinius Thrax.

(Florentius, Julian, Cyriac, Marcellinus and Faustinus) (SS) {4 –deleted}

5 June

d. 250? They were listed as beheaded at Perugia (Italy) in the reign of Decius.

Florentius of Cahors (St) {2}

4 July

C5th. He was bishop of Cahors (France), and was praised by St Paulinus of Nola.

Florentius of Orange (St) {2, 4}

17 October

d. ?524. He was a bishop of Orange near Avignon (France).

(Florentius of Seville) (St) {4 –deleted}

23 February

C5th? He was listed as a priest of Seville (Spain).

Florentius of Strasbourg (St) {2, 4}

7 November

d. a.614. From Ireland, he went to Alsace (France) in 664 and founded a monastery at Haslach in the Black Forest (Germany). In 678, he became bishop of Strasbourg and established an Irish monastery there. He is called the 'Apostle of Alsace'.

Florentius of Thessalonica (St) {2, 4}

13 October

C2nd? He was burnt at the stake at Thessalonica (Greece).

(Florentius of Trechâteaux) *(St) {4 –deleted}*

27 October

C3rd? He was allegedly martyred by the invading Allemani at Arc sur Tille near Dijon in Burgundy (France) and his shrine was established in a monastery named Trechâteaux nearby.

Florentius of Vienne (St) {2, 4}

3 January

d. p377. The old Roman Martyrology listed him as a bishop of Vienne (France) who was martyred in the reign of Gallienus in about 275, and he is locally venerated as a martyr-bishop. But the extant list of bishops of the city puts him in the C4th, and mentions him attending a council in 374.

Florian (St) {2, 4}

4 May

d. 304. He was thrown off the bridge at Lorch in Austria and drowned in the reign of Diocletian. His shrine is at Linz, part of his alleged relics are at Cracow (Poland) and he is the patron of Upper Austria.

Florian, Calanicus and Comps cf.
Eleutheropolis, Martyrs of.

Florian Stępniak (Bl) {2}

12 August

1912–42. A Polish Franciscan Capuchin friar, he was gassed at the concentration camp at Dachau with Bl Joseph Straszewski. Cf. **Poland, Martyrs of the Nazi Occupation of**.

Florida Cevoli (Bl) {2}

12 June

1685–1767. Born of a noble family in Pisa, at the age of eighteen she entered the Capuchin

Poor Clares of Citta di Castello. Her novice-mistress was St Veronica Giuliani, who became abbess in 1716. Bl Florida was made the prioress, and became abbess in turn in 1727. She encouraged a stricter observance and was well known in the neighbourhood for her charity. She was beatified in 1993.

Florinus (St) {2}

17 November

d. ?856. He was a parish priest in the Graubünden (Switzerland), and some of his relics are at his namesake church at Koblenz (Germany). His extant biographies are unreliable.

(Florus, Laurus, Proculus and Maximus)
(SS) {4 –deleted}.

18 August

C2nd? Their Byzantine legend, probably fictional, describes the first two as Illyrian brothers who were stonemasons and who were employed by the last two to build a temple. When it was finished they were all converted, so they then dedicated the building as a church and were thrown down a dry well as a result.

Florus (Flour) of Lodève (St) {2}

1 June

? He was the first bishop of Lodève near Montpellier (France) and his shrine is at Saint-Flour in the Massif Central.

Flosculus (Flou) of Orleans (St) {2, 4}

2 February

d. c.500. He was bishop of Orleans (France) and a contemporary of Sidonius Apollinaris.

Foellan (Foilan, Fillan) (St) {2}

9 January

d. c.710. From Ireland, he went to Scotland with St Kentigerna, his mother, and St Comgan, a relative, and became a missionary monk there. He died at Strathfillan in Perthshire.

Foillan (St) {2}

31 October

d. ?655. Brother of SS Fursey and Ultan, whom he accompanied to England from Ireland, he became abbot of a Celtic-rite monastery at Burgh Castle near Great Yarmouth (Norfolk) and helped to evangelize East Anglia. When his monastery was destroyed in a raid by King Penda of Mercia he went to the Low Countries, founded a monastery at Fosse in Brabant (Belgium) and was the spiritual director of the nunnery at Nivelles. He was murdered by robbers in the forest of Soignies and formerly venerated as a martyr.

Folcwin (St) {2}

14 December

d. 855. He became bishop of Thérouanne near Calais (France) in ?816. His shrine was established at the abbey of St Bertin at St Omer.

Fortis Gabrielli *(Bl)*

9 May

d. 1040. From Gubbio in Umbria (Italy), he became a hermit in the mountains near Scheggia but later joined the new monastic foundation at Fontavellana. His cultus was approved for Gubbio in 1756, but he is not in the Roman Martyrology.

Fortunata Viti cf. **Mary-Fortunata Viti**.

(Fortunatus, Felician, Firmus and Candidus) (SS) {4 –deleted}

2 February

? They are originally listed in the Martyrology of Usuard but nothing is known about them.

(Fortunatus, Felix and Comps) (SS) *{4 –deleted}*

26 February

? Nothing is known about this group of twenty-nine martyrs.

(Fortunatus, Gaius and Anthes) (SS) *{4 –deleted}*

28 August

Early C4th? They were martyred at Salerno (Italy) in the reign of Diocletian and have a popular local veneration there. Their acta are unreliable. Fortunatus may be the one of the same name associated with the 'Twelve Holy Brothers'.

Fortunatus and Hermagoras (SS) {2, 4}

12 July

C3rd. They were martyred at Aquileia (Italy). According to their spurious legend, St Hermagoras was a disciple of St Mark, by whom he was appointed first bishop of the city. Then he was beheaded in the reign of Nero with his deacon, Fortunatus. When the see of Aquileia was in schism from Rome in C6th, this legend was probably maliciously fabricated to give the church there a spurious apostolic foundation

(Fortunatus and Lucian) (SS) {4 –deleted}

13 June

? They were listed as Roman African martyrs.

(Fortunatus and Marcian) (SS) {4 –deleted}

17 April

? They were possibly martyrs of Roman Africa, not (as asserted) of Antioch.

Fourtunatus of Fano (St) {2}

8 June

End C6th. He was a bishop of Fano (Italy), and was remembered for ransoming captives.

Fortunatus of Naples (Bl) {2}

14 June
C4th. A bishop of Naples (Italy), he fought against Arianism and his cultus was confirmed in 1841.

(Fortunatus of Rome) (St) {4 –deleted}

15 October
? He was listed as martyred at Rome and buried on the Aurelian Way.

Fortunatus of Todi (St) {2}

14 October
C6th. From Poitiers, he became bishop of Todi in Umbria (Italy) and is remembered for saving his city from being sacked by the army of Totilla the Goth.

Fortunatus of Torrito (St) {2, 4}

1 June
d. c.400. A parish priest of Torrito near Spoleto (Italy), he was remembered for earning his living by manual labour and for being extremely charitable to the poor.

Fortunatus Velasco Tobar and Comps (BB) {2 –add}

d. 1936. Fourteen Salesians were martyred during the Spanish Civil War in several incidents, the most serious being when four of them were killed together at Guadalajara on 6 December. They were beatified in 2013. Cf. **Spanish Civil War, Martyrs of** and list in appendix.

Forty Martyrs of Sebaste (SS) {2, 3}

10 March
d. 320. They were forty soldiers killed by order of the emperor Licinius at Sebaste in Armenia (now Sivas in Turkey). According to their story, they were left naked for a night in winter on a frozen lake with a heated bathhouse on its shore for any who apostatized. One did apostatize, but his place was taken by one of the guards who was converted by the heroism of the rest. At daybreak all were dead except the youngest, St Melito, who was carried by his mother following the cart full of corpses until he also died and she added his body to the rest. This martyrdom is mentioned by Sozomen and preached upon by SS Basil, Gregory of Nyssa, Gaudentius of Brescia and other patristic writers. The cultus is very popular in the East but was suppressed in the Roman rite in 1969.

Foster cf. **Vedast**.

Four Crowned Martyrs (SS) {2, 3}

There are two groups of martyrs with this title, and they have been separated in the revised Roman Martyrology:

8 August
d. 306. A group of soldiers was martyred at Albano (Italy), namely Secundus, Severian, Carpophorus and Victorinus.

8 November
d. 306. Claudius, Nicostratus, Symphorian, Castorius and Simplicius were martyred somewhere in Lower Pannonia (around Belgrade in Serbia). They were stonemasons who refused a commission to carve a statue of the god Aesculapius, and were martyred at the request of the retired emperor Diocletian.

The relics of only four of them were taken to Rome, and they were later confused with the Albano group. Their acta are of great value, but because of the confusion the cultus was confined to local or particular calendars in 1969.

Fourteen Holy Helpers

8 August
There was a popular medieval devotion to these saints as especially helpful in time of

need. They were St Giles and the martyrs SS Acacius of Ararat, Barbara, Blaise of Sebaste, Catherine of Alexandria, Christopher, Cyriac of Rome, Dionysius of Paris, Erasmus of Formiae, Eustace of Rome, George, Margaret, Pantaleon and Vitus. Their collective cultus was suppressed in 1969.

Foy cf. **Faith**.
Fra Angelico cf. **John of Fielsole**.

Frambald (St) {2}

16 August
d. c.650. He was a courtier before becoming a hermit at Ivry near Paris (France), later migrating to the forest of Passais in Maine. He died at a place called Saint-Fraimault after him.

Franca Visalta (St) {2}

25 April
1170–1218. From Piacenza (Italy), when aged only seven she entered the Benedictine nunnery of St Sixtus there, was professed when aged fourteen and became the abbess in ?1198. Apparently she was too severe and was deposed, so she became a Cistercian nun in 1215. Then she was made abbess of the nunnery at Pittoli.

Frances-of-the-Sacred-Heart Aldea Araujo (Bl) {2}

20 July
Cf. **Rita-of-the-Sorrows Pujalte Sánchez and Frances-of-the-Sacred-Heart Aldea Araujo**.

Frances d'Amboise (Bl) {2}

4 November
1427–85. A noblewoman of Brittany (France), she married its duke who was a depressive, jealous and dissolute character, and eventually reformed him by prayer and patience. She

introduced the Carmelite nuns to Brittany, founded a nunnery at Nantes, became a nun there herself in 1460 when widowed and was made prioress in 1476.

Frances-of-Sales Aviat (St) {2}

10 January
1844–1914. Born near Châlons-sur-Marne (France), she left home in 1866, went to Troyes and teamed up with Bl Louis Brisson who had a mission to children and young people working in factories. On the advice of the superior of the local Visitation convent they founded the 'Oblate Sisters of St Francis de Sales' in 1868, which spread through France despite opposition. But they were suppressed by an anticlerical government in 1903 and she moved the mother house to Padua (Italy), where she died. She was canonized in 2001.

Frances Bisoka (Bl) {2}

27 August
d. 1627. A Japanese Dominican tertiary, she used to shelter missionaries in her house and was hence burnt alive at Nagasaki with BB Francis-of-St-Mary of Mancha and Comps. Cf. **Japan, Martyrs of**.

Frances Bussa de'Leoni of Rome (St) {2, 3}

9 March
1384–1440. A noblewoman of Rome, she was married for forty years from 1396 and reputedly never had an argument with her husband. She was a model wife and mother of six children, and obtained her husband's consent to live in continence and to practise contemplative prayer in 1414. She had many mystical experiences as well as many trials, such as the death of five of her children, her husband's banishment and the confiscation of their property. When she was widowed in 1436 she joined the house of regular Olivetan Benedictine oblates that she had founded at

Tor de' Specci ('Tower of Mirrors') in 1433. Her biography was written by her spiritual director and refers to her special devotion to, and awareness of, her guardian angel. She is a patron of motorists and of Benedictine oblates.

Frances-Xavier Cabrini (St) {2}

22 December

1850–1917. From near Lodi in Lombardy (Italy), the thirteenth child of her family, she became a teacher at a parish orphanage at Codogno in 1874 and founded the mother house there of the 'Missionary Sisters of the Sacred Heart' three years later. This became a diocesan institute of Lodi in 1880 and she hoped to send her sisters to China, but the pope advised her to concentrate on the United States where the Italian immigrants were in danger of losing their faith. She went with the first group of sisters to New York in 1889 and continued taking new groups across regularly, year by year. She ended up founding sixty-seven religious institutes to be run by her congregation as schools, hospitals and orphanages in Europe and in both of the Americas. Eventually she became a citizen of the USA and died of malaria at one of her hospitals in Chicago. She was canonized in 1946.

Frances-Anne-of-the-Sorrowing-Virgin Cirrer Carbonell (Bl) {2}

27 February

1781–1855. Born at Sencelles on Majorca (Spain) of a peasant family, she had lost all her near relatives by the time she was forty. While running her farm she catechized children and practised penance and humility. Joining the Sisters of Charity in 1851, she carried on catechizing and nursing in the parish and became the superior of her community. She died of a stroke immediately after Mass and was beatified in 1989.

Frances-of-the-Incarnation Espejo Martos (Bl) {2 –add}

6 November

1873–1937. From Martos (Spain), she entered the local convent of Trinitarian nuns in 1893 after being educated there as an orphan. In 1936 the convent was forcibly shut by Communists, so she went to live with her brother. On 12 January in the following year, however, she was arrested and shot because of her religious status at Las Casillas near Jaén together with Bl Victoria Valverde González and Isabel of St Raphael (a Clarissan nun not yet beatified). She was beatified as a martyr in 2006, the first Trinitarian nun to receive this honour.

Frances (Francisca) de Paula de Jesus Isabel (Bl) {2 –add}

14 June

1810–95. She is usually known by her nickname of Nhá Chica. Born into a poor family of São João del Rey in Minas Gerais, Brazil, she was orphaned when aged ten and spent the rest of her life as a single woman devoted to prayer and service to her neighbours. With time, she became famous for the quality of her spiritual advice. She died at Baependi and was beatified in 2013.

Frances of Rome cf. **Frances Bussa de'Leoni**.

Frances Schervier (Bl) {2}

14 December

1819–76. From Aachen (Germany), she was of a wealthy middle-class background. Practical concern for poor people led her to found the 'Franciscan Sisters of the Poor' in 1845. These were proved in service in the wars at the founding of the German Empire and comprised 41 houses in Europe and North America when she died at Aachen. She was beatified in 1974.

Francis-of-Nagasaki Adauctus (St) {1 –group}

6 February
d. 1597. A Japanese doctor of medicine from Miyako, he was a Franciscan tertiary and helped the missionaries as a catechist. Crucified at Nagasaki with SS Paul Miki and Comps, he was canonized with them in 1862. Cf. **Japan, Martyrs of**.

Francis of Assisi (St) {1, 3}

4 October
1181–1226. The son of a rich merchant of Assisi in Umbria (Italy), he was baptized as John but was nicknamed 'Frenchy', possibly because he could speak French. He joined his father's business and lived a carefree life until a spiritual conversion led him to a life of prayer and penance. His father disinherited him and he professed a state of absolute poverty for two years, restoring the chapels of St Damian and the 'Portiuncula' in his home town, before founding the Friars Minor in 1209. These were characterized by spiritual joy and complete poverty, individual and collective. He gathered five thousand disciples in ten years but the institutionalization of such a charism proved very difficult, and these difficulties persisted long after his death. His rule received papal approval in 1215, however, and his friars established themselves throughout western Europe, especially in university towns. They were ideally suited to the new urban environment. In 1219, after the first solemn chapter of his order at Assisi, he went to Egypt to try and convert the Muslims but was rebuffed with courtesy. He received the stigmata on Mount Alvernia (the first recorded case) in 1224, and died as a deacon. 'Il Povarello' (the 'Poor Little Man') is the most popular saint of the second Christian millennium, although sentiment has rather obscured the starker aspects of his prophetic and apocalyptic witness.

Francis Bell (Bl) {2}

11 December
1591–1643. A Worcestershire landowner, he was baptized as Arthur. Studying at Valladolid, he became a Franciscan, was ordained at Salamanca and was in turn chaplain to nuns in the Spanish Netherlands, superior of Douai friary, professor of Hebrew and first Provincial of the new Scottish province. Returning to England in 1634, he was seized by Parliamentary troops at Stevenage during the civil war and was executed at Tyburn. He was beatified in 1987. Cf. **England, Martyrs of**.

Francis-Xavier-Mary Bianchi (St) {2}

31 January
1743–1815. From Arpino in eastern Lazio (Italy), he became a Barnabite and was ordained priest Naples in 1767 in the face of his family's opposition. He was professor of theology at Naples University from 1778 and was also a noted spiritual director, but his main interest was in helping poor and derelict people, especially girls being forced into prostitution by poverty, and did so with such zeal and austerity that he ruined his health and lost the use of his legs from 1804. Nicknamed the 'Apostle of Naples', he died there and was canonized in 1951.

Francis Blanco (St) {1 –group}

6 February
d. 1597. From Monterey in Galicia (Spain), he studied at Salamanca and became a Franciscan at Villapando. Initially he worked as a missionary in Mexico, then at Manila and finally in Japan from 1594. He was crucified at Nagasaki and was canonized in 1862 with SS Paul Miki and Comps. Cf. **Japan, Martyrs of**.

Francis de Borja (St) {2, 3}

30 September
1510–72. A nobleman from Gandía near Valencia (Spain), he was related to the notorious

Italian Borgia family. Educated at the court of the emperor Charles V, he married in 1529 and was occupied as a courtier and in administering his estate at Gandía until he was widowed in 1546. The sight of his wife's body caused a spiritual conversion and he then became a Jesuit. He was elected superior-general of the Society in 1665 and made his chief work its development and strengthening, at which he was so successful that he became one of the most important figures of the Counter-Reformation. He founded new missions in the Americas, established the Jesuits in Poland and helped in the foundation of the German College in Rome. He died at Rome and was canonized in 1671, but his cultus was confined to particular calendars in 1969.

Francis-Xavier Cần (St) {1 –group}

20 November
803–1837. From Sou Mieng in northwest Vietnam, he was a catechist helping the missionary priests of the Paris Society and was strangled in prison at Hanoi in north Vietnam during the persecution ordered by Emperor Minh Mạng. His head was then cut off for public display. Cf. **Vietnam, Martyrs of**.

Francis-Ferdinand de Capillas (St) {1 –group}

15 January
1607–48. From Palencia (Spain), he became a Dominican at Valladolid and was sent to Manila, Taiwan and finally Fujian province in China. He was successful as a missionary, but when the Manchus invaded and overthrew the Ming Dynasty he was tortured and beheaded as a spy at Fuan. He was canonized in 2000 as one of the martyrs of China, and is the protomartyr. Cf. **China, Martyrs of**.

Francis Caracciolo (St) {1, 3}

4 June
1563–1608. From a noble Neapolitan family, he was born in the Abruzzi (Italy) and seems

to have suffered from a severe skin disease when young. This healed after he decided to become a priest and, after his ordination in 1588, he founded the congregation of the 'Minor Clerks Regular' at Naples with John Adorno. Perpetual adoration of the Blessed Sacrament was one of its main duties. He was the first superior-general of the new order, founded many houses and died at Agnone while establishing a house there. He was canonized in 1807, but his cultus was confined to local or particular calendars in 1969.

Francis-of-Paola Castelló y Aleu (Bl) {2}

22 September
1914–36. From Lugo in Spain, as a young man studying in Barcelona and Lerida he joined several sodalities and Catholic youth movements and was arrested as a result by the anticlerical Republican authorities. After a trial which found him guilty of sedition as a result of his missionary work, he was shot. He was canonized in 2001. Cf. **Spanish Civil War, Martyrs of**.

Francis Ch'oe Kyŏng-hwan (St) {1 –group}

12 September
d. 1839. A catechist of Seoul in Korea, after being arrested he refused to deny his faith as demanded and was imprisoned. In prison he persisted in prayer and catechesis and as a result was tortured to death. Cf. **Korea, Martyrs of**.

Francis Coll y Guitart (St) {2}

2 April
1812–75. From Vich in Catalonia (Spain), he joined the Dominicans just in time for their thirty-eight-year suppression in Spain. After ten years as an exclaustrated priest-religious, he obtained Petrine faculties as a roving missionary and spent twenty-three years preaching in Catalonia, mostly on the mysteries

of the Rosary. He founded the 'Dominican Sisters of the Annunciation' in 1856 to teach in rural areas. He died after some years of senile decay and was canonized in 2009.

Francis-Mary Croese of Camporosso (St) {2}

17 September

1804–66. From a peasant family near Ventimiglia (Italy), he became a Capuchin lay brother at the friary at Genoa in 1821 and was there for forty years as the alms-gatherer. He died of cholera while nursing victims of an epidemic and was canonized in 1962.

Francis Dachtera (Bl) {2}

23 August

1910–44. A Polish priest, he was used in medical experiments at the concentration camp at Dachau and died as a result. Cf. **Poland, Martyrs of the Nazi Occupation of**.

Francis Díaz del Rincón (St) {1 –group}

28 October

1713–48. From Seville (Spain), he became a Dominican at Ecija and was sent to China in 1736. He worked in the Fujian mission until he was captured and executed in prison. Cf. **Francis Serrano Frias and Comps**.

Francis Dickenson (Bl) {2}

13 April

d. 1590. A Yorkshireman and a convert, he studied for the priesthood at Rheims and was ordained in 1589. He was quickly captured on his return to England and hanged, drawn and quartered at Rochester (Kent) with Bl Miles Gerrard. Other sources have their execution on the 30th. He was beatified in 1929. Cf. **England, Martyrs of**.

Francis Đỗ Minh Chiểu (St) {1 –group}

25 June

d. 1838. He was a catechist helping St Dominic Henares, and was seized and beheaded with him at Nam Định during the persecution ordered by Emperor Minh Mạng. Cf. **Vietnam, Martyrs of**.

Francis Drzewiecki (Bl) {2}

10 August

1908–42. He was a Polish priest, a 'Son of Divine Providence' and was deported to the concentration camp at Dachau where he was put to digging on the farm. He was able to keep the Blessed Sacrament with him. He was gassed with Bl Edward Grzymala. Cf. **Poland, Martyrs of the Nazi Occupation of**.

Francis Faà di Bruno (Bl) {2}

27 March

1825–88. Born at Alessandria in Piedmont (Italy), he was in the officer corps of the army of the Kingdom of Sardinia for seven years before obtaining a doctorate in mathematics at Paris and becoming a lecturer at Turin University in 1856. He was a man of many talents, being an inventor, sacred musician and writer as well as a mathematician. Being inspired by St John Bosco, he was ordained in Rome in 1876 and founded the 'Little Sisters of Our Lady of Suffrage' in 1881 together with a church of the same name at Turin, so that the Office of the Dead could be said continually for the souls in Purgatory. He was beatified in 1988.

Francis-Anthony Fasani (St) {2}

29 November

1681–1742. From Lucera in Apulia (Italy), he became a Franciscan Conventual, went on to be provincial superior and introduced necessary reforms. Based mainly at Lucera, he became known there for the grace of levitation in prayer. He died in that city and was canonized in 1986.

Francis Fogolla (St) {1 –group}

9 July
Cf. **Gregory Grassi and Comps**.

Francis Galvez and Comps (Bl) {2}

4 December

1567–1623. From Utiel near Valencia (Spain), he became a Franciscan at Valencia in 1591, went to Manila in 1609 and was in Japan for two years from 1612 until persecution broke out. He returned secretly in 1618 and was eventually burnt alive at what is now Tokyo with BB Jerome de Angelis and Simon Yempo. He was beatified in 1867. About fifty were executed with them, but documentation is lacking in their cases. Cf. **Japan, Martyrs of**.

Francis Gárate Aranguren (Bl) {2}

9 September

1857–1929. Born in Guipozcoa (Spain), he joined the Jesuits as a lay brother in 1874 and ended up as the gatekeeper of the University College of Deusto at Bilbao. His life and the way he performed his duties there for forty-one years led him to be beatified in 1985.

Francis de Geronimo (St) {2}

11 May

1642–1716. From near Taranto in Apulia (Italy), he was educated by the Jesuits, ordained priest in 1666 and became a Jesuit in 1670. The rest of his life was spent as a preacher in south Italy, especially in Naples where he gathered huge congregations and converted many obdurate sinners. He also had great care for poor people (which the city did not lack). He was canonized in 1839.

Francis Gil de Frederich (St) {1 –group}

22 January

1702–45. From Tortosa (Spain), he became a Dominican at Barcelona and was sent first to the Philippines and then to north Vietnam in 1732. There he was captured, imprisoned for several years and beheaded at Checo in north Vietnam with St Matthew Alonso de Leziniana on the orders of Emperor Trịnh Doanh. Cf. **Vietnam, Martyrs of**.

Francis-Xavier Hà Trọng Mậu and Comps (SS) {1 –group}

19 December

d. 1839. A Vietnamese catechist and a Dominican tertiary, he was executed at Bắc Ninh in north Vietnam with four fellow Dominican tertiaries. St Augustine Nguyễn Văn Mới was a poor labourer, St Dominic Bùy Văn Uy was a nineteen-year-old catechist, Stephen Nguyễn Văn Vinh was a peasant and Thomas Nguyễn Văn Đệ was a tailor. They refused to trample on a crucifix during the persecution ordered by Emperor Minh Mạng, and were tortured in prison before being strangled. Cf. **Vietnam, Martyrs of**.

Francis Higashi (Bl) {2}

8 September

d. 1628. A Japanese five-year-old, he was beheaded at Nagasaki with his father, Louis, and his brother, Dominic. Cf. **Dominic Castellet and Comps** and **Japan, Martyrs of**.

Francis Ingleby (Bl) {2}

3 June

d. 1586. Born at Ripley (Yorks), he studied at Oxford, the Inner Temple and Douai and was ordained at Laon. After two years as a priest at York the deference he was being shown in social intercourse with Catholics gave him away and he was executed at York. He was beatified in 1987. Cf. **England, Martyrs of**.

Francis Jaccard (St) {1 –group}

21 September

1799–1838. From Savoy, he became a priest of the Society of Foreign Missions at Paris and was sent to south Vietnam in 1826. He was imprisoned during the persecution ordered by Emperor Minh Mạng, and viciously whipped before being garrotted. With him was martyred St Thomas Trần Văn Thiện. Cf. **Vietnam, Martyrs of**.

Francis Jägerstätter (Bl) {2 –add}

1907–43. He was from St Radegund in Upper Austria, and took the name of his stepfather when his mother married (he was illegitimate). He married and became a farmworker and sexton in his home village, having three daughters and an ordinary life but thinking deeply about his faith. He voted against the unification of Austria with Nazi Germany, the only one in his village to do so. He concluded that any participation in the war being fought by the Nazis after 1939 would be a serious sin. As a result, when he was called up he refused to cooperate, so was tried for sedition at Berlin and executed. He was beatified as a martyr in 2007.

Francis-of-St-Mary of Mancha and Comps (BB) {2}

27 August

d. 1627. He was burnt alive at Nagasaki with Bartholomew Laurel (a Mexican Franciscan), Caspar Vas (a Japanese doctor who was a Franciscan tertiary, in whose house Bl Francis was captured), and Anthony-of-St-Francis of Nagasaki, a Japanese catechist. Beheaded with them were Mary Vas (Caspar's wife) and six Franciscan tertiaries: Louis Matsuo Soyemon, a neighbour of the Vas couple; Francis Kuhioye, baptized in prison; Thomas Wo Jinyemon, formerly a domestic worker for the Jesuits; Luke Kiyemon, a builder of hiding places; Michael Kizayemon, another carpenter; and Martin Gómez, who had concealed fugitive Franciscans. On the same day or on the previous one four Dominican tertiaries were burnt: Francis Kurobioye, a catechist; Gaius Jinyemon, formerly a Buddhist monk from Korea;

Mary-Magdalen Kiyota, from a daimyo's family, and Frances Bisoka. They were beatified in 1867. Cf. **Japan, Martyrs of**.

Francis and Jacinta Marto (BB) {2}

4 April

1908–19 & 1910–20 resp. They were children of a peasant family of Aljustrel near Fátima (Portugal), and were keeping a flock of sheep with their cousin, Lucia de Jesus, on 13 May 1917 when they saw an apparition of the Blessed Virgin Mary. This apparition was repeated once a month for five months, and led to the founding of the famous Marian shrine of Fátima. Bl Francis died at home eighteen months later, and Bl Jacinta died at Lisbon two years and four months later. They were beatified in 2000.

Francis-the-Carpenter of Miyako (St) {1 –group}

6 February

1597. A Japanese baptized by the Franciscans in Nagasaki, he came to watch the martyrdom of SS Paul Miki and Comps. He was seized and killed with them. Cf. **Japan, Martyrs of**.

Francis-Xavier de Montmorency-Laval (St) {2}

6 May

1623–1708. A nobleman born near Evreux (France), he was ordained when aged twenty-four, renounced his patrimony and became vicar-apostolic of New France (Canada and Louisiana) in 1658. He founded the diocese and seminary of Quebec in 1674 and was the first bishop until his retirement in 1684. He was canonized in 2014.

Francis Morales (Bl) {2}

10 September

d. 1622. From Madrid, he became a Dominican and worked on the Satsuma mission in

Japan for twenty years. In 1608 he went to Fushimi and thence to Nagasaki in 1614, where he was burnt with BB Charles Spinola and Comps in the 'Great Martyrdom'. Cf. **Japan, Martyrs of**.

Francis-of-St-Bonaventure of Musashino (Bl) {2}

12 September

d. 1622. A Japanese catechist from Musashino near Tokyo, he worked with Bl Apollinaris Franco, became a Franciscan in prison and was burnt with him at Omura. Cf. **Thomas-of-the-Holy-Sprit Zumarraga and Comps** and **Japan, Martyrs of**.

Francis Néron cf. **Peter-Francis Néron**

Francis Pacheco and Comps (SS) {2}

20 June

1566–1626. A Portuguese, he became a Jesuit at Lisbon and was sent to Macao in 1592. He worked in Japan and served as rector of the college at Macao until he finally returned to Japan in 1617 to work in secret as provincial and as administrator of the diocese of Arima. He was burnt alive at Nagasaki with Balthasar de Torres (Spanish Jesuit); John-Baptist Zola (Italian Jesuit); Caspar Sadamatsu (Japanese Jesuit lay brother); Vincent Caum (Korean); Peter Rinsei, Michael Tozo, Paul Shinsuke and John Kisaku (Japanese). The last five became Jesuits in prison before their martyrdom. They were beatified in 1867. Cf. **Japan, Martyrs of**.

Francis Page (Bl) {2}

20 April

d. 1602. Born at Antwerp, his family was from Harrow in Middlesex. After his conversion he studied at Douai, was ordained in 1600, quickly captured on his return to England and became a Jesuit in prison before his execution at Tyburn (London). He was beatified in 1929. Cf. **England, Martyrs of**.

Francis-of-Jesus-Mary-and-Joseph Palau y Quer (Bl) {2}

20 March

1811–72. Born at Aytona near Lérida (Spain), he overcame family opposition to enter the Barcelona Carmel in 1832. But this was burnt down in an anticlerical riot before he was ordained in 1836, so he spent the next four years as an itinerant preacher in Spain. When this became too dangerous he went into exile in France, but he returned to Barcelona in 1851 to open a school of adult catechesis. This in turn was suppressed in 1854 and he returned to preaching throughout Catalonia and the Balearics. At Ciudadela in Majorca he founded the 'Tertiary Sisters of Carmel', which later split to become the 'Carmelite Missionaries' and the 'Teresan Carmelite Missionaries', also the 'Carmelite Tertiary Brothers of Charity' (which became extinct in the civil war). He died at Tarragona and was beatified in 1988.

Francis of Paola (St) {1, 3}

2 April

1416–1507. From a poor family of Paola in Calabria (Italy), when aged thirteen he started living as a hermit on the coast nearby. He established a monastery for the disciples who had gathered around him in 1454, and thus founded the new order of Minim Friars. The name means 'the least', and they obliged themselves to a perpetual Lent by a fourth religious vow. The pope ordered him to go to Plessis-les-Tours in France to assist King Louis XI on his deathbed in 1482 and he was prevented from returning by the king's successors, who valued his holiness. He died at Plessis, was canonized in 1519 and was declared patron of seafarers in 1943.

Francis-of-St-Michael de la Parilla (St)
{1 –group}

6 February
d. 1597. From near Valladolid (Spain), he became a Franciscan lay brother and went with St Peter-Baptist of San Esteban from Manila to Japan in 1593. They were captured at Osaka three years later, crucified at Nagasaki and canonized in 1862. Cf. **Paul Miki and Comps** and **Japan, Martyrs of**.

Francis Patrizi (Bl) {2}

26 May
d. 1328. From Siena (Italy), he was inspired by a sermon of a Servite friar, Bl Ambrose Sansedoni, and was received into that order by St Philip Benizi after his mother died. He had the charism of reconciling enemies. He died in Siena and his cultus was approved for there in 1743.

Francis-of-Calderola Piani (Bl) {2}

13 September
d. 1407. From Calderola near Camerino (Italy), as a Franciscan he was a successful preacher and had the charism of reconciling enemies. He died at Colfano and his cultus was confirmed for Camerino in 1843.

Francis de Posadas (Bl) {2}

20 September
1644–1713. From Aracoeli near Cordoba (Spain), he became a Dominican in his native town and spent his life giving missions throughout southern Spain before dying at Aracoeli. He was beatified in 1818.

Francis Regis Clet (St) {1 –group}

18 February
1748–1820. From Grenoble (France), he joined the 'Congregation of the Mission' (the Lazarists) and went on to be the director of the seminary at the mother house in Paris. After the French Revolution broke out, he was sent to China in 1791 and worked there under great difficulty for thirty years in Hubei before being betrayed by an apostate. He was seized, tortured and garrotted at Hangzhou. Cf. **China, Martyrs of**.

Francis Rogaczewski (Bl) {2}

11 August
1892–1940. He became priest of a Polish-speaking parish in what was about to become the Free City of Danzig in 1918, and as such was an immediate target of Nazi invaders when war broke out between Germany and Poland. He was arrested on the same day, 1 September 1939, and was imprisoned and tortured for eleven months before being shot. Cf. **Poland, Martyrs of the Nazi Occupation of**.

Francis Rosłaniec (Bl) {2}

14 October
1889–1942. A Polish priest, he was gassed at the concentration camp at Dachau with Bl Stanislaus Mysakowski. Cf. **Poland, Martyrs of the Nazi Occupation of**.

Francis van Rouga (St) {2}

9 July
d. 1572. He was a Franciscan friar, one of the **Gorinchem** martyrs (q.v.).

Francis de Sales (St) {1, 3}

24 January
1567–1622. A nobleman from near Annecy in Savoy (now in France), he was a law student at Paris and Padua before becoming a priest in 1593. Over the next four years he set about reconciling the Calvinist inhabitants of the Chablis to the church, with enormous success (he allegedly made over eight thousand converts), and was made coadjutor bishop of

Geneva in 1599. He was never able to visit the Calvinist stronghold of Geneva city. In 1602, he became bishop, and excelled as a pastor and a spiritual writer. He took care over the standard of his clergy and their preaching, founded a seminary at Annecy and became beloved by his people. His most famous writing is the 'Introduction to the Devout Life'. He became acquainted with St Jane de Chantal in 1604 and helped her to found the Visitation order of nuns. He died at Lyons, was canonized in 1665, declared a doctor of the Church in 1877 and patron of journalists in 1923.

Francis-Xavier Seelos (Bl) {2}

4 October
1819–67. From Füssen in Bavaria, Germany, he early received a vocation to provide spiritual care for German-speaking migrants to the USA and joined the Redemptorists at New York in 1843. After being ordained in Baltimore in 1844 he was based at Pittsburgh and the cities in Maryland before serving as an itinerant preacher in the eastern USA. He died of yellow fever at New Orleans and was beatified in 2000.

Francis Serrano Frias (St) {1 –group}

28 October
1691–1748. From Granada (Spain), he became a Dominican there and was sent to Fujian in China in 1725. In 1746, he was imprisoned, and strangled in prison two years later at Fuzhou. St Francis was made titular bishop of Tipasa while in custody. With him were martyred SS Joachim Royo Pérez, John Alcober Figura and Francis Díaz del Rincón. Cf. **China, Martyrs of**.

Francis Shoyemon (St) {1 –group}

14 August
d. 1633. A Japanese catechist and Dominican novice, he was martyred at Nagasaki with St Dominic Ibáñez de Erquicia and was canonized in 1987 with SS Laurence Ruiz and Comps. Cf. **Japan, Martyrs of**.

Francis Solano (St) {2}

14 July
1549–1610. From Montilla in Andalucia (Spain), he became a Franciscan Observant there in 1569 and went to South America after twenty years of apostolic activity in Spain. He worked among the native Americans on the Plata estuary as well as with the colonists in Peru, at Trujillo and at Lima. He died at Lima and was canonized in 1726.

Francis Spinelli (Bl) {2}

6 February
1853–1913. From Milan (Italy), he became a diocesan priest at Bergamo in 1875 and founded the 'Sisters, Adorers of the Blessed Sacrament' with Catherine Comensoli in 1882. They suffered serious difficulties and accusations, so moved to Rivolta in the diocese of Cremona in 1889. The bishop there learnt that the charges against them were false and approved the foundation. Bl Francis' motto was 'Love the Eucharist, take care of the poor, and forgive everything.' He was beatified in 1992.

Francis Spoto (Bl) {2 –add}
1924–64. From Raffadali near Agrigento in Italy, he was ordained as a priest of the 'Missionary Servants of the Poor' in 1951 and was elected superior-general in 1959. In 1964, he went to the mission at Biringi in the Democratic Republic of the Congo. After the assassination of President Patrice Lumumba his supporters started a persecution of all white people, and the missioners were forced to go into hiding. However, Bl Francis was discovered, beaten and shot, dying as a result sixteen days later after expressing forgiveness. He was beatified in 2007.

Francis Stryjas (Bl) {2}

31 July
1882–1944. A layman and father of a family, he died of ill-treatment by the Nazis in a prison at Kalisz in Poland. Cf. **Poland, Martyrs of the Nazi Occupation of**.

Francis Takea (Bl) {2}

11 September
d. 1622. A Japanese twelve-year-old, the son of Bl Thomas Takea, he was beheaded at Nagasaki with Bl Caspar Koteda. Cf. **Japan, Martyrs of**.

Francis Taylor (Bl) {2}

20 June
d. 1584. A Dublin alderman, married with a family, he was imprisoned for his faith for seven years. He died in prison from neglect and was beatified as a martyr in 1992 Cf. **Ireland, Martyrs of**.

Francis Takea (Bl) {2}

11 September
d. 1622. A Japanese twelve-year-old, the son of Bl Thomas Takea, he was beheaded at Nagasaki with Bl Caspar Koteda. Cf. **Japan, Martyrs of**.

Francis Trần Văn Trung (St) {1 –group}

6 October
1825–58. From Phan Xa in Vietnam, he became the equivalent of a corporal in the army until his faith was discovered. Then he was vigorously urged to apostatize, and on his refusal was beheaded at An Hòa in central Vietnam on the personal orders of Emperor Tự Đức. Cf. **Vietnam, Martyrs of**.

Francis-of-Jesus Terrero Ortega (Bl) {2}

3 September
d. 1632. From Villamediana near Palencia (Spain), he became an Augustinian friar at Valladolid in 1614, went to Mexico in 1622 and thence to Japan with Bl Vincent Carvalho by way of Manila. He was burnt at Nagasaki. Cf. **Anthony Ishida and Comps** and **Japan, Martyrs of**.

Francis Tōyama Jintarō (Bl) {2 –add}

16 February
d. 1624. He was a young layman martyred at Hiroshima and beatified in 2008. Cf. **Japan, Martyrs of**.

Francis-of-Fabriano Venimbeni (Bl) {2}

22 April
1251–1322. From Fabriano (Italy), the son of a doctor of medicine, he became a Franciscan in 1267 and a disciple of St Bonaventure. He founded the first Franciscan library near his native city, and his cultus was confirmed for there in 1775.

Francis Xavier (St) {1, 3}

3 December
1506–52. Born at the family castle at Xavier in the Kingdom of Navarre (now in Spain), as his father was a courtier he was sent to study at Paris University. There he became a companion of St Ignatius Loyola and was with him in taking vows as the first Jesuits at Montmartre in 1534. He was sent as a missionary to Goa (India) in 1541, and worked in south India and Ceylon (Sri Lanka) until 1545. Then he was in Malaya, the East Indies and south Vietnam until 1548, whereupon he went to Japan. There he made c.2000 converts (the start of Christianity in Japan) in Kyushu and especially on Hirado-jima. The number of Japanese Christians reached six figures in a generation. In 1552, he set out on a journey to China but never got there, dying on the island of Shangchuan near Hong Kong. He is arguably the most successful missionary that the church of the second millennium has had.

He was canonized in 1602 and is joint patron of foreign missions with St Teresa of Lisieux.

Francis Zanfredini (St) {2}

5 August
d 1350. He was a Franciscan tertiary at Monte Granario near Pesaro (Italy) and lived an austere life as a hermit there for fifty years. His cultus was confirmed for Pesaro in 1859.

Francis Zhang Rong (St) {1 –group}

9 July
Cf. **Gregory Grassi and Comps**.

Francis Zirano (Bl) {2 –add}

25 January
1564–1603. Born at Sassari in Sardinia, he became a Franciscan at Porto Torres at a time when the island was ruled by Spain. When a cousin was captured by Algerian pirates and sold as a slave, he collected a ransom and went to Algiers. Unfortunately, the region of Kabylia to the east of the city was in rebellion and Bl Francis became involved in intrigues between it, the Spanish king and the government at Algiers. As a result, he himself was arrested and, after a huge ransom for his release was not forthcoming, he was flayed alive. He was beatified as a martyr in 2014.

Franco of Assergi (St) {2}

5 June
C12th. From near Assergi in the Abruzzi (Italy), he was a Benedictine at Colimento for twenty years before becoming a hermit near Assergi for the last fifteen years of his life.

Franco Lippi (Bl) {2}

11 December
d. 1292. From near Siena (Italy), when young he became the leader of a group of troublemakers but had to flee retribution and then joined a gang of robbers in the mountains. He was a brigand until the age of fifty but then he was blinded in a fight, repented, went on a penitential pilgrimage to Compostella and received papal absolution as well as getting his sight back. Then he became a Carmelite lay brother at Siena. He was already aged over sixty-five but gained a reputation for holiness before he died.

Fraternus of Auxerre (St) {2, 4}

29 September
d. p450. A bishop of Auxerre (France), by tradition he was killed by invading barbarians on the day of his consecration. He is not listed as a martyr.

Fredald (St) {2}

4 September
C9th. He was bishop of Mende (France), was killed by a nephew and is listed as a martyr. His shrine is at a place called Saint-Frézal after him.

Fredegand (Fregaut) (St) {2}

17 July
C8th. Possibly an Irish companion of St Foillan and a fellow missionary with St Willibrord, he was the first abbot of Kerkelodor near Antwerp (Belgium).

Frederick Albert (Bl) {2}

30 September
1820–76. Born at Turin (Italy), he became priest of the parish of St Charles there and proved a model pastor. He founded the 'Sisters of St Vincent de Paul of the Immaculate Conception' in order to help the children left roaming the streets by working parents or through being abandoned. He refused to become a bishop out of humility. He was beatified in 1984.

Frederick of Hallum (Bl) {2}

3 March
d. 1175. He was parish priest of Hallum in Friesland (Netherlands) when he founded the Premonstratensian abbey of Mariengaarden (Garden of Mary) nearby and became its first abbot.

Frederick Janssoone (Bl) {2}

4 August
1838–1916. Born near Dunkirk (France), he joined the Franciscans at Amiens in 1864. Ordained in 1870, he immediately had to serve as chaplain in the Franco-Prussian War and then was vicar-superior in the Holy Land from 1875 to 1888. Then he went to Canada for twenty-eight years, where he was on mission in all parts of the country and succeeded to such an extent that he has been called one of its apostles. He died at Montreal and was beatified in 1988.

Frederick Ozanam (Bl) {2}

8 September
1813–53. From Milan (Italy), he was brought up in Lyons (France) and went to Paris to study law in 1831. Two years later, he started a lay society for practical work among the poor, which became the 'Society of St Vincent de Paul'. As well as law, he studied literature and became a Sorbonne professor in 1844, specializing in Dante. He was involved in many contemporary Catholic causes, and denounced both economic liberalism and socialism. He died at Marseilles and was beatified in 1997.

Frederick of Regensburg (Bl) {2}

30 November
d. 1329. From a poor family of Regensburg in Bavaria (Germany), he became a lay brother at the Augustinian friary there and was the carpenter and chopper of firewood. His cultus was approved for Regensburg in 1909.

Frederick (Fridrich) of Utrecht (St) {2, 4}

18 July
d. 838. Grandson of a king of the Frisians, he became bishop of Utrecht (Netherlands) in 820. He was especially keen to prohibit those marriages between near relatives which were forbidden by the church, and was murdered as a result in a church at Maastricht. He is not listed as a martyr.

Frediano cf. **Frigidian**.

French Revolution (Martyrs of)

1792–4. The 'Ancien Regime' of the French monarchy was overthrown in May 1789. The Catholic Church was established by law before then in France, but had had its life perverted by the corruptions inherent in the determination to maintain a feudally structured society in the face of accelerating social change. Especially, the higher clergy and monastic religious enjoyed excessive income as being of noble status while the ordinary parish clergy were often poorly supported in all ways, material and spiritual. The initial reaction of the revolutionaries was to reform the church, but this quickly involved demands that priests, clerics and consecrated religious subscribe by oath to the new arrangements. Resistance to this and other measures led to a massacre by the mob in Paris in September 1792, and several other massacres during the 'Terror' in 1794 when the aim had changed to the de-Christianization of the country. Cf. lists of national martyrs in the appendix.

Friard and Secundel (SS) {2}

1 August
C6th. They were hermits on an island in the Loire near Nantes (France) who evangelized the surrounding area.

Frideswide (St) {2, 4}

19 October

C8th. According to her C12th biography she was the daughter of a Saxon ruler in the middle Thames valley (England) who founded a nunnery on the site of what is now Christ Church in Oxford. Before the Reformation this was an Augustinian priory named after her, and the church (the present Anglican cathedral) contains fragments of her shrine. She has a holy well at Binsey, and is the patron of the city and university of Oxford.

Fridigand cf. **Fredegand**.

Fridolin (St) {2}

6 March

C8th. An Irish missionary monk, he founded an abbey at Säckingen (Germany), on the right bank of the Rhine east of Basel, and is venerated as the apostle of the Upper Rhine region.

Frigidian (Frediano, Frigidanus) of Lucca (St) {2, 4}

18 March

d. ?588. According to his questionable C11th biography, he was an Irishman who went on pilgrimage to Rome, became a hermit on Monte Pisano and was then made bishop of Lucca (Italy). He allegedly formed the city's clergy into a community of Canons Regular and rebuilt the cathedral after it had been burnt by the Lombards. His veneration is very popular in Lucca.

Froilán (St) {2, 4}

5 October

d. 905. From Lugo in Galicia (Spain), when aged eighteen he teamed up with St Attilanus in restoring monastic life at Moreruela near León. He founded other monasteries in the region, at a time when most of Spain was still Muslim, and went on to become bishop of León.

Fromund (St) {2}

24 October

End C7th. He was abbot of a monastery at Coutances (France) before becoming bishop there.

Fronto of Nitria (St) {2, 4}

14 April

? He is listed as a monk of Nitria in Egypt, but his period is uncertain.

Fronto of Périgueux (SS) {2, 4}

25 October

? He is venerated as the first missionary to Périgueux (France). His unreliable legend mentions a companion named George who has been deleted from the Roman Martyrology.

Fructuosus of Braga (St) {2, 4}

16 April

d. 665. He was of the reigning Visigothic nobility in Spain but went off to be a hermit in the mountains near Astorga. There he founded the Complutum monastery, for which he wrote a rule, and was abbot until going back to being a hermit. He also founded nine other monasteries for his disciples. Against his will, he was made archbishop of Braga (Portugal) in 656.

Fructuosus of Tarragona and Comps (SS) {2, 4}

21 January

d. 259. The bishop of Tarragona (Spain) and two deacons, Augurius and Eulogius, they were burnt at the stake in the reign of Valerian. Their acta seem to be genuine.

Fructus (Frutos) (St) {2}

25 October
d. ?715. He was a hermit near Segovia (Spain).
His story is that he was one of three siblings
who were living as religious at Sepúlveda
near Segovia when the Arabs invaded. Valentine and Engratia were killed, but Fructus
escaped. These other two have been deleted
from the Roman Martyrology.

Frumentius and Aedisius (SS) {2, 4}

20 July
End C4th. They were probably brothers and
the former, at least, was from Tyre (Lebanon). They were wrecked on the Eritrean
coast while on a voyage on the Red Sea and
were taken to Axum inland (now Tigre, Ethiopia), which was the capital of a powerful
kingdom. They became courtiers of influence, and St Frumentius applied to St Athanasius, patriarch of Alexandria, for a bishop
for the country. He was the one chosen,
while St Aedisius was ordained priest. They
firmly established the church in Axum, and
the present Ethiopian Orthodox Church
is the direct descendant. Thus they are
venerated as the apostles of Ethiopia. The
Roman Martyrology lists Aedisius on
25 October.

Fulbert (St) {2}

10 April
d. 1029. From Italy, he studied at the abbey of
Rheims under Gerbert (the future Pope Sylvester II, and was the headmaster of the cathedral school of Chartres (one of the few centres
of learning in Western Europe at the time)
before becoming the city's bishop in 1007. He
was a great scholar as well as an outstanding
bishop and monastic reformer, being especially favourable to the Cluniacs.

Fulcran (St) {2}

13 February
d. 1006. He became bishop of Lodève near
Montpellier (France) in 949 and was known
for his public firmness. A casual remark of his
that a bishop who had converted to Judaism
deserved to be burnt resulted in just that, so he
undertook serious penances in expiation.

Fulgentius of Ecija (St) {2}

14 January
d. ?632. Brother of SS Isidore, Leander of
Seville and Florentina, he became bishop of
Ecija in Andalusia (Spain). He has been confused with St Fulgentius of Ruspe.

Fulgentius of Ruspe (St) {2, 4}

1 January
468–533. A Roman African nobleman of
Carthage, he became abbot of the monastery
of Byzacene but fled the Vandal invasion
and went to Rome. On his return he became
bishop of Ruspe in 502 or 507, and was exiled
twice again by the Arian Vandals to Sardinia.
There he was a prolific author. As a result of
his writings he is regarded as one of the most
important theologians in the Western church
in the C6th, being a disciple of St Augustine
in his thought. He also wrote on the history
of the Vandal persecutions. He died at Ruspe.

Fulk of Castrofuli (St)

22 May
d. p600. According to his dubious legend, he
was an English pilgrim who died as a result of
nursing sufferers of an epidemic at Castrofuli
near Arpino in western Lazio (Italy). He is
patron of Castrofuli and his cultus was confirmed in 1572. However, he is not listed in
the Roman Martyrology.

Fulk Scotti (St) {2, 4}

26 October
1164–1229. Born at Piacenza (Italy) of Scottish parents, he became an Augustinian canon there and was made bishop in 1210. He was transferred to Pavia in 1216.

Fursey (St) {2, 4}

16 January
d. c.650. An Irish monk, he founded a monastery on an island in Lough Corrib called Rathnat before emigrating to England and founding another in the abandoned Roman fort at Burgh Castle near Great Yarmouth (Norfolk). Then he went to France and founded a third at Lagny near Paris. He died at Forsheim in Picardy. His spiritual ecstasies were famous and were mentioned by St Bede.

(Fusca and Maura) *(SS) {4 –deleted}*

13 February
Mid C3rd? They were listed as a fifteen-year-old girl of Ravenna (Italy) and her nurse, martyred there in the reign of Decius.

G

Gabriel-Mary Allegra (Bl) {2 –add}

26 January
1907–76. From San Giovanni la Punta in Catania (Italy), he joined the Franciscans in 1918. Ten years later, before his ordination, he was inspired to begin a translation of the entire Bible into Chinese as his life's work despite not knowing the language. He was a missionary in China until he died, initially in Hunan, then at Beijing and finally at Hong Kong after the Communist takeover. He was beatified in 2012, the only biblical scholar of the twentieth century to be so honoured.

Gabriel of Ise (St) {1 –group}

6 February
d. 1597. He was a Japanese Franciscan tertiary crucified with SS Paul Miki and Comps. Cf. **Japan, Martyrs of**.

Gabriel-of-St-Mary-Magdalen of Fonseca (Bl) {2}

3 September
d. 1632. A Spanish Franciscan lay brother, in 1612 he was sent to Manila (Philippines) and, after studying medicine there, went to Japan secretly. He worked among the persecuted Christian community as a doctor until he was captured and burnt alive at Nagasaki with BB Anthony Ishida and Comps. Cf. **Japan, Martyrs of**.

Gabriel-John Taurin Dufresse (St) {1 –group}

14 September
1750–1815. From near Clermont-Ferrand (France), he joined the Paris Society for Foreign Missions in 1774 and went to Sichuan province in China in 1777. In 1800 he was made titular bishop of Tabraca and apostolic administrator of the area, while being in continual danger of arrest as an enemy alien. He

was finally betrayed by a native Christian and beheaded at Chengdu. Cf. **China, Martyrs of**.

(Gabinus) (St) {4 –deleted}

19 February
d. ?295. Listed as a Roman martyr, he was allegedly from Dalamatia (now part of Croatia) and a relative of the Emperor Diocletian as well as a brother of Pope St Gaius and father of St Susanna. His acta are unreliable, however.

Gabinus of Sardinia (SS) {2, 4}

30 May
C4th? He was martyred at Porto Torres near Sassari (Sardinia). His legend is unreliable; he was not martyred in the reign of Hadrian, and his companion Crispulus has been deleted from the Roman Martyrology.

Gabriel the Archangel (St) {1, 3}

29 September
The 'Angel of the Annunciation' is mentioned in the Bible at Daniel 8:16, 9:21 and Luke 1:26-38 and is venerated together with SS Michael and Raphael.

Gabriel Ferretti (Bl) {2}

9 November
1385–1456. From Ancona (Italy), a relative of the counts of Ferretti, he became a Franciscan there, founded several new friaries and served as provincial of the Marches. His cultus was confirmed for Ancona in 1753. He was responsible for promoting the 'Franciscan Crown', a type of rosary.

Gabriel Lalement (Bl) {2}

17 March
1610–49. A Frenchman, he joined the Jesuits in 1630 and taught and studied theology at Moulins and Bourges before going to Quebec

in Canada (then a French colony) in 1646. In 1648 he went as a missionary to the Huron nation in what is now Ontario (Canada), east of Lake Huron, and joined St John Brébeuf in his missionary activities. The two were captured together at St Ignace by an Iroquois raiding party and slowly tortured to death, St Gabriel taking longer to die and lingering to the day after St John died. He was canonized in 1930. Cf. **John Brébeuf and Comps**.

Gabriel-Mary Nicolas (Bl) {2}

27 August
1463–1532. From near Clermont-Ferrand (France), he tried to become a Franciscan Observant but was refused admission to several friaries before being accepted at Notre-Dame-de-la-Fon near La Rochelle. He became the confessor of St Jane of Valois and helped her to found the order of the Annonciades in 1532. His cultus was approved in 1647.

Gabriel Perboyre cf. **John-Gabriel Perboyre**.

Gabriel-of-Our-Lady-of-Sorrows Possenti (St) {2, 3}

27 February
1838–62. From Assisi (Italy), he was educated at Spoleto by the Jesuits and received a religious vocation after two serious illnesses. He joined the Passionists at Morovalle near Macerata in 1856 but only lived for another six years. He died at Isola in the Abruzzi, was remembered for heroic self-denial in small things and was canonized in 1920 after many miracles at his tomb. His cultus was confined to local or particular calendars in 1969.

Gaius, Pope (St) {4 –deleted} {2, 4}

22 April
d. 296. Nothing is known about him. He features in the acta of St Susanna and of St Sebastian, both of which are unreliable, and

he is not listed as a martyr in the early records. Fragments of the Greek epitaph on his tomb in the cemetery of Callistus are extant. His cultus was suppressed in 1969.

Gaius and Alexander (SS) {2, 4}

10 March
d. p171. They had been opponents of Montanism in Phrygia (Asia Minor) before being martyred at Apamea (now Dinar in Turkey) in the reign of Marcus Aurelius.

Gaius and Crementius (SS) {2, 4}

16 April
C4th. They were listed by the old Roman Martyrology as two of the martyrs of Zaragoza (Spain), but they died in peace after a long imprisonment in the reign of Diocletian.

(Gaius and Leo) (SS) {4 –deleted}

30 June
? They are listed as a priest and subdeacon, respectively, and were martyred either in Rome or in Roman Africa.

Gaius Jinyemon (Bl) {2}

27 August
d. 1627. A Japanese (or Korean) born of Christian parents on the island of Amakusa near Nagasaki, he became a Dominican tertiary and was martyred with BB Francis-of-St-Mary of Mancha and Comps. Cf. **Japan, Martyrs of**.

Gaius of Korea (Bl) {2}

15 November
d. 1624. Originally a Korean Buddhist monk, he migrated to Japan as a Christian, helped the Dominican missionaries in Kyushu as a catechist and became a Dominican tertiary. He was burnt at Nagasaki. Cf. **Japan, Martyrs of**.

Gaius of Milan (St) {2, 4}

27 September
C3rd. He was alleged to have succeeded
St Barnabas as second bishop of Milan (Italy)
in the second century, and to have baptized
St Vitalis with his sons, SS Gervase and Protase. There is no evidence of a diocese at Milan
before 200, and so his dates were subsequent.
St Charles Borromeo enshrined his relics
in 1571.

*(Gaius of Nicomedia and Comps) (SS)
{4 –deleted}*

4 March
? They were listed as twenty-eight (or thirty-
eight) soldiers drowned in the Sea of Marmara
near Nicomedia (Asia Minor).

Galactorius (St) {2}

27 July
C6th. He was a bishop of Lescar near Bayonne (France), and was allegedly tortured and
killed by the invading Arian Visigoths.

(Galation and Epistemis) (SS) {4 –deleted}

5 November
d. ?251. According to legend, the former was
a Christian who converted his pagan wife
whereupon both entered monasteries and
were martyred in the reign of Decius at Emesa
(now Homs in Syria). They never existed, and
their story was a Christianization of the pagan
fable of Clitophon and Leucippe.

Galdinus della Sala (St) {2, 4}

18 April
c.1100–76. A nobleman of Milan (Italy), he
became a diocesan priest and then archdeacon.
In 1161 he fled the city at the approach of the
army of Emperor Frederick Barbarossa, but
was made cardinal-archbishop in 1165 in his
absence .On his return he found the city mostly

in ruins and was instrumental in encouraging
its rebuilding. He was a great preacher and
peacemaker, and died immediately after
preaching a homily. He is the third most highly
venerated saint of the Milanese church after SS
Ambrose and Charles Borromeo.

Galganus Guidotti (St) {2, 4}

30 November
d. 1181. From Siena (Italy), he was a worldly
young man but converted and became a hermit on Monte Siepe nearby. He was popular in
the city, and a church was built on the site of
his cell. This became a Cistercian monastery
in 1201, which probably explains the false
claim that he had been a Cistercian monk.

Gall (St) {2, 4}

16 October
c.550–?645. A monk of Bangor (Ireland),
he went with St Columban to England and
France and helped him to found the abbey of
Luxeuil in Burgundy. When his master was
exiled to Italy he withdrew to be a hermit at
a site in Switzerland where the great abbey
of St Gall was founded after his death. The
territory of this was an independent principality of the Holy Roman Empire, and survives as the Swiss canton of St Gall. The
canton of Apenzell ('Abbot's Cell') was the
abbot's private territory around his summer
palace. The abbey's library was of very great
importance.

Gall of Clermont (St) {2, 4}

14 May
d. 551. From Clermont-Ferrand (France), he
became a monk and chief cantor in the Frankish Austrasian palace chapel. In 527 he succeeded St Quinctian as bishop of his native
city. He taught St Gregory of Tours, his
nephew.

Galla (St) {2, 4}

6 April
C6th. A Roman noblewoman, she was the sister-in-law of Boethius. Being widowed one year after her marriage, she became a hermit at the Vatican and practised severe austerities before dying of breast cancer. She is briefly described by St Gregory the Great. Her ancient church in Rome, north of the Bocca della Verità, was demolished on the orders of Mussolini.

(Gallicanus Avinius) (St) {4 –deleted}

25 June
d. ?362. A Roman consul and commander of the campaign against the Persians in the reign of Constantine, he converted in 330, retired to Ostia and built a church and hospital there. The old Roman Martyrology described him as later being exiled to Alexandria and being martyred there in the reign of Julian, but this is false.

Galmier cf. **Baldomer**.
Galnutius cf. **Winwaloe**.

(Gamaliel) *(St) {4 –deleted}*

3 August
C1st. He was the Jewish lawyer who taught St Paul (cf. Acts 22:3) and who intervened in favour of SS Peter and John (cf. Acts 5:34-9). A worthless tradition makes him a convert, and his spurious relics were allegedly found near Jerusalem in 415.

Gamelbert (Bl) {2}

17 January
d. ?502. From a rich family at Michelsbuch near Augsburg in Bavaria (Germany), he was a soldier in the Frankish army before he became parish priest of his native village. He was remembered for his severe asceticism and his effective missionary activity. His cultus was confirmed for Augsburg in 1909.

Gandulf Sacchi (Bl) {2}

3 April
d. c.1260. From Binasco near Milan (Italy), he was one of the earliest Franciscans and spent his life preaching in Sicily. He died as a hermit at Polizzi Generosa near Palermo and his cultus was confirmed in 1621.

Garembert cf. **Warembert**.
Garmier cf. **Baldomer**.
Garmon cf. **Germanus**.
Garnet cf. **Gervadius**.
Gaspar cf. **Caspar**.
Gaston cf. **Vedast**.

Gatian of Tours (St) {2, 4}

18 December
C3rd. He was allegedly a disciple of St Dionysius of Paris and the first bishop of Tours (France).

Gaucherius (Gaultier, Walter) de Meulan (St) {2}

9 April
d. 1140. The abbot-founder of the monastery of Augustinian canons at St John of Aureil near Limoges (France), he also helped his friend St Stephen Muret with the latter's new foundation at Grandmont. He died after falling off his horse.

(Gaudentia and Three Comps) *(SS) {4 –deleted}*

30 August
? They are listed in the old Roman Martyrology as having been Roman martyrs, but more ancient sources do not list them as martyrs, and nothing is known about them.

(Gaudentius and Culmatius) *(SS)* {4 –deleted}

19 June

d. 364. They were listed by the old Roman Martyrology as a bishop of Arezzo (Italy) and his deacon, late martyrs in the reign of Valentinian I.

Gaudentius of Brescia (St) {2, 4}

25 October

c.360–c.410. He was adopted and educated by St Philastrius of Brescia and became a monk at Caesarea in Cappodocia (Asia Minor) but was forced to return and become bishop of Brescia (Italy) on his foster father's death in 387. He went to Constantinople in 405 to plead the cause of St John Chrysostom but was harshly received, imprisoned and deported. He is chiefly remembered for his paschal sermons.

Gaudentius (Radzim) of Gniezno (St) {2}

11 October

d. ?1011. He was the younger brother of St Adalbert of Prague, and the two were monks together at St Alexius's abbey at Rome. They went on mission to Prussia, where St Adalbert died in a massacre which St Gaudentius escaped. He was later made bishop of Gniezno in Poland by Emperor Otto III.

Gaudentius of Novara (St) {2, 4}

22 January

d. ?418. From Ivrea near Turin (Italy) and a refugee from his city, he was sheltered by St Laurence of Novara and became a disciple of St Eusebius of Vercelli. After administering the dioceses of Novara and Vercelli while the former was in exile, he became bishop of Novara in 379. The Canons Regular of the Lateran venerated him as the first organizer of community life among cathedral clergy.

Gaudentius of Rimini (St) {2, 4}

14 October

C4th. Apparently from Ephesus, he became a priest at Rome in 332 and first bishop of Rimini (Italy) in 346. He opposed the Arians at the Council of Sirmium in 357. The Roman Martyrology has rejected the story that he was killed by them shortly afterwards.

(Gaudentius of Verona) *(St)* {4 –deleted}

12 February

C5th? He was listed as a bishop of Verona (Italy).

Gauderic (St) {2}

16 October

d. c.900. He was a peasant, apparently at Mirepoix to the southwest of Carcasonne (France) where some of his relics are enshrined. He was famous for his devotion to Our Lady.

Gaudiosus of Brescia (St) {2}

7 March

C5th. He was a bishop of Brescia (Italy) and has his shrine there.

Gaudiosus of Naples (St) {2, 4}

27 October

C5–6th. A bishop of Abitina in Roman Africa (and hence nicknamed 'the African'), he was exiled by the Arian Vandals in 440 and founded a monastery at Naples.

Gaugeric (Gau, Géry) (St) {2, 4}

11 August

d. ?625. From near Trier (Germany), he was ordained priest there and became bishop of Cambrai (France) in ?586. He was bishop for about four decades.

Gausbert (St) {2}

27 May
d. 1079. He had been a parish priest when he became a hermit at Montsalvy near Saint-Flour (France). His disciples founded a monastery here.

Gauzelin of Toul (St) {2}

7 September
d. 962. A Frankish noble, he became bishop of Toul (France) in 922 and supported the contemporary monastic reform movements.

Gelasius I, Pope (St) {2, 4}

21 November
d. 496. Born at Rome of Roman African parents, he became pope in 492. He was a vigorous pope, fighting the Pelagians and Manichaeans and upholding the Roman position as regards the continuing Acacian schism with Constantinople concerning Monophysitism. Some letters and treatises of his survive, but he was not the author of the 'Leonine Sacramentary' named after him.

Gemellus of Ancyra (St) {2, 4}

10 December
C4th? His story is that for publicly rebuking Emperor Julian he was flayed and crucified at Ancyra (Asia Minor, now Ankara in Turkey), and was the last Roman martyr to be crucified. The Roman Martyrology merely lists him as a martyr of Ancyra.

Geminian of Modena (St) {2, 4}

31 January
C4th. From near Modena (Italy), he became that city's bishop after 341 and had St Athanasius as a guest when the latter was on his way to exile in Gaul. He is the principal patron of the city.

Gemma Galgani (St) {2}

11 April
1878–1905. From Camigliano near Lucca (Italy), she lost her mother when she was seven and spent the rest of her short life at Lucca in intense suffering, both mental and physical. She never married and was under the spiritual care of the Passionists, although her desire to become a Passionist nun was frustrated by her physical ailments. She enjoyed spiritual peace in the face of her difficulties and was the subject of extraordinary supernatural phenomena, including the stigmata which recurred between 1899 and 1901. These phenomena caused adverse comment, but she was canonized in 1940.

Gemma of Goriano Sicoli (Bl) {2}

13 May
d. 1465. Initially a shepherdess, she was a hermit at Goriano Sicoli near Sulmona in the Abruzzi (Italy) for forty-two years. Her cultus was approved for Sulmona and Valva in 1890.

Genebrard cf. **Gerebern**.

(Generosus of Tivoli) (St) {4 –deleted}

17 July
? His shrine is under the high altar of the cathedral at Tivoli near Rome, but nothing is known about him.

Genesius (Genès) of Arles (St) {2, 4}

25 August
d. ?303. Formerly a soldier, he was appointed notary by the magistrates of Arles (France). As a catechumen he refused to copy an edict of persecution against the Christians and fled, but was caught and beheaded. He probably died in the reign of Maximian Herculius.

Genesius of Clermont (St) {2}

3 June
d. c.650. Bishop of Clermont-Ferrand (France), he was exceptionally popular, and his people thwarted his wish to retire and become a hermit.

(Genesius the Comedian) (St) {4 –deleted}

25 August
d. ?300. He is probably the same as St Gelasinus of Heliopolis (q.v.). His story is identical except that it is set in Rome, and is told of at least three other alleged martyrs.

Genesius of Thiers (St) {2}

28 October
Early C4th? He was martyred and enshrined at Thiers near Clermont-Ferrand (France).

Genevieve of Paris (St) {2, 4}

3 January
d. c.500. She is the patron of Paris (France), but the details of her life are controversial. According to the traditional version she was from Nanterre near Paris and became a friend of St Germanus of Auxerre when aged seven. Then she became a consecrated virgin when aged fifteen, moved to Paris and encouraged its people in the face of danger from the Huns and the Franks. She is depicted as a shepherdess holding a candle with a coin hanging from her neck. The Devil may be shown trying to extinguish the former, and an angel preventing him. Her shrine at Paris was in, what is now, the Pantheon, and was destroyed during the French Revolution.

Genevieve Torres Morales (St) {2}

5 January
1870–1956. Born in Almenara in Castile (Spain), she was orphaned when aged eight and lost a leg five years later. She lived in a 'Mercy Home' run by the Carmelites of Charity, where she learnt self-abandonment to the will of God and also sewing. Lack of a leg precluded a vocation to an existing congregation, so in 1911 she founded 'Religious of the Sacred Heart of Jesus and the Holy Angels' to help poor women unable to live on their own. This spread from Valencia throughout Spain. She was canonized in 2003.

Gengulf of Varennes (St) {2, 4}

11 May
C8th. A nobleman from Varennes-sur-Amance in Burgundy (France), according to his story he was a courtier and soldier until his wife's adultery persuaded him to become a hermit on his home estate. His wife's lover killed him, and the miracles at his tomb led him to be venerated as a martyr.

Gennadius of Astorga (St) {2}

25 May
d. ?925. A monk at Argeo near Astorga (Spain), he became the abbot-restorer of San Pedro de Montes and was a propagator of the Benedictine rule in León and Galicia. In ?895 he became bishop of Astorga for six years before retiring to be a hermit at San Pedro.

Gennaro cf. **Januarius**.
Gennys cf. **Germanus of Auxerre**.
Genovefa cf. **Genevieve**.
Geoffrey cf. **Ceolfred** or **Godfrey**.

George, Aurelius, Sabigotha, Felix and Liliosa (SS) {2, 4}

27 July
d. 852. George was from Bethlehem, a monk of Mar Saba who went to Spain to collect funds for his monastery. At Cordoba, ruled by the Umayyad emir Abd-er-Rahman II, he was seized on a charge of speaking against Islam, together with two married couples, Aurelius

and Sabigotha and Felix and Liliosa. He was offered his freedom as an alien, but chose to be executed with the others.

George of Antioch (St) {2, 4}

19 April
d. 818. A monk, he became bishop of Antioch in Pisidia (Asia Minor) and attended the second ecumenical council of Nicaea, which condemned iconoclasm in 787. He was banished by Emperor Leo V, who was trying to reverse that decision, died in exile and was venerated as a martyr.

George Beesley (Bl) {2}

1 July
1563–91. From Goosnargh, (Lancs), he was ordained at Rheims in 1587 and was arrested at Croydon races after being seen dressed up and wearing a pistol. He was viciously tortured and executed at Tyburn with Bl Montford Scott, and was beatified in 1987. Cf. **England, Martyrs of**.

George of Chozeba (St) {2}

8 January
d. ?614. From Cyprus, he journeyed to the Holy Land and became a monk and recluse at the monastery of Chozeba in a wadi near Jericho. He used to stay in solitude for the week, and on Sunday would worship with the brethren and give them spiritual direction. His monastery survives, and is named after him.

George Douglas (Bl) {2}

9 September
d. 1587. A teacher from Edinburgh, he was converted and ordained in Paris in 1574. He was a priest in York until his execution there, and was beatified in 1987. Cf. **England, Martyrs of**.

George Errington (Bl) {2}

29 November
1554–96. Born in Hirst Castle near Ashington (Northumberland), he was educated at Oxford and was repeatedly arrested for helping with the importation of priests and Catholic books. He was finally condemned for this and executed at York, being beatified in 1987. Cf. **England, Martyrs of**.

George Gervase (Bl) {2}

11 April
d. 1608. From Bosham (Sussex), when young he went privateering with Francis Drake in the West Indies but turned to priesthood, was educated at Douai and ordained there in 1603. There he also became a Benedictine monk. When he was on mission in England he was condemned and executed at Tyburn (London). He was beatified in 1929. Cf. **England, Martyrs of**.

George the Great (St) {1, 3}

23 April
d. c.300. One of the most popular saints in Christendom, he was fairly certainly a martyr at Diospolis (Lydda or Lod) in the Holy Land, possibly in the reign of Diocletian. All the other legends attached to his name are fictitious. His cultus as a soldier-saint, always popular in the East, spread to the West by the C7th and was greatly encouraged by the Crusaders. For obscure reasons he displaced St Edward the Confessor as major patron of England and is also a patron of Aragon, Portugal, Germany, Genoa, Venice and Ferrara. His shrine at Lod survives in the custody of the Greek Orthodox. He is familiarly depicted as a knight mounted on a white horse and killing a dragon with a lance. (If the horse is red, the depiction is of St Demetrius.)

George Häfner (Bl) {2 –add}

20 August
1900–42. From a working-class family of Würzburg (Germany), he became a diocesan priest there in 1924. He was assigned to the parish of Oberschwarzach, and as such manifested his total opposition for everything the Nazis stood for. After being repeatedly interrogated by the Gestapo he was arrested and taken to Dachau for reconciling a Nazi party member on his deathbed. He died there of malnutrition and abuse, and was beatified as a martyr in 2011.

George Haydock (Bl) {2}

12 February
1527–84. From Cottam Hall near Preston (Lancs), he studied at Douai and was ordained at Rheims. Being betrayed soon after his arrival at London, he was executed at Tyburn with BB James Fenn, Thomas Hemerford, John Nutter and John Munden. He was beatified in 1987. Cf. **England, Martyrs of**.

George Kaszyra (Bl) {2}

18 February
1910–43. Cf. A Marian, he was burnt to death by the Nazis at Rosica in Poland. **Poland, Martyrs of the Nazi Occupation of**.

George of Lodève (St) {2}

11 November
d. c.870. He was a bishop of Lodève (France).

George Limniotes (St) {2, 4}

24 August
d. c.730. An iconodule hermit on the Bithynian Olympus (a great monastic centre in Asia Minor near Constantinople), he was allegedly aged ninety-five when he had his hands and nose cut off in the reign of the iconoclast emperor Leo III.

George Matulewicz (Bl) {2}

27 January
1871–1927. From near Kaunas in Lithuania (then in the Russian Empire), after his ordination he taught at Kielce (Poland) and at St Petersburg. In 1909 he joined the Marian Clerks Regular, which the Russian government was suppressing, and re-formed them in secret. In 1911 he became the superior-general and opened noviciate houses in Poland, Lithuania, Switzerland and the United States of America for Poles and Lithuanians. He became bishop of Vilnius in 1918, but Poland annexed the city in 1920, and he resigned to become the apostolic visitor of newly independent Lithuania. After organizing the national church, he died at Kaunas and was beatified in 1987.

George of Mitylene (SS) {2}

7 April; 1 February; 1 February
There are three bishops of Mitylene on Lesbos, one of the Aegean islands, who are venerated as saints. 'The Elder' was bishop from 763 to 816, and died in exile for opposing iconoclasm. 'The Younger' succeeded him, and 'the Third', a brother of the latter, was bishop for a year, 843–4. Only the first is listed in the Roman Martyrology.

George Napper (Bl) {2}

9 November
d. 1610. From Holywell, then just outside Oxford, he was at Corpus Christi College in Oxford before his conversion. He then studied at Douai, was ordained there in 1596 and worked in Oxfordshire until he was condemned and executed at Oxford. He was beatified in 1929. Cf. **England, Martyrs of**.

George Nichols (Bl) {2}

5 July
d. 1589. A convert graduate of Oxford, he was ordained at Rheims in 1581 and was a priest

in Oxfordshire. Being seized at the Catherine Wheel Inn with BB Humphrey Pritchard, Thomas Belson and Richard Yaxley, he was executed with them at Oxford and was beatified in 1987. Cf. **England, Martyrs of**.

George Popiełuszko (Bl) {2 –add}

19 October

1947–84. Born at Okopy near Suchowola (Poland), he was ordained as a diocesan priest of Warsaw in 1972. He became associated with the Solidarity movement as Communism in eastern Europe entered its death throes in the 1980s. As a result, he openly criticized the political system in his sermons, and the authorities found it impossible to silence him. Finally, the secret police kidnapped him and beat him to death at Wloclawek and dumped his body in a reservoir. This act caused an uproar, and those responsible were convicted of murder. However, his martyrdom is widely recognized as the beginning of the definitive collapse of Communism. He was beatified in 2010.

George Preca (St) {2}

26 July

1880–1962. Born at Valletta, Malta, he was ordained in 1906 and quickly gathered a group of young disciples which led to the foundation of the 'Society of Christian Doctrine'. This is a lay society dedicated to catechesis which has spread worldwide. He became a Carmelite tertiary in 1918 and was canonized in 2007.

George of Suelli (St) {2}

23 April

d. 1117. He was a bishop of Suelli near Oristano in Sardinia, and was famous as a thaumaturge.

George Swallowell (Bl) {2}

26 July

d. 1594. From near Durham, he became an Anglican minister and a schoolmaster before

his conversion. As a result he was condemned and executed at Darlington, and was beatified in 1929. Cf. **England, Martyrs of**.

George of Vabres (St) {2}

19 February

d. ?879. From near Rodez (France), he became a Benedictine at Conques, but his monastery was destroyed by the Norse in 862, and he became a monk at Vabres near Rodez instead.

George and Raymund Vargas González (BB) {2 –add}

1 April

d. 1927. They were brothers, the first born in 1899 and the second in 1905 at Ahualco de Mercado in Jalisco, Mexico. Bl George was a hydroelectric engineer, and Bl Raymund was studying medicine. They were both active members of Catholic Youth, and helped the local priest in his secret ministry during the persecution leading to the Cristero War. The family home became known as a place of refuge for priests and seminarians, so the secret police mounted a raid in the early morning and arrested everyone they found. The two brothers were regarded as the organizers of clandestine Christian activity, so they were interrogated and tortured before being shot. They were beatified in 2005. Cf. **Mexico, Martyrs of**.

George of Vienne (St) {2, 4}

2 November

d. c.670. He was a bishop of Vienne (France) whose relics were discovered in 1251.

Georgia (St) {2, 4}

15 February

d. c.500. A young woman, she became a hermit at Clermont-Auvergne (France).

Gerald of Aurillac (St) {2}

13 October

855–909. Count of Aurillac in the Massif Central (France), he had a long illness when he was young and this gave him a taste for a life of prayer. He remained a layman instead of taking vows (exceptional for someone with such a disposition at the time) but did not marry and used his wealth for charity. He founded a Benedictine abbey on his estate at Aurillac, where he was buried.

Gerald of Béziers (St) {2}

5 November

d. 1123. An Augustinian canon regular, he became bishop of Béziers near Montpellier (France) and was remembered for spending most of his income on the poor.

Gerald of Braga (St) {2}

5 December

d. 1108. From near Cahors in Gascony (France), he became a Benedictine monk at Moissac. In time he became chief cantor at Toledo cathedral (Spain) and was made archbishop of Braga in Portugal in 1096, thus re-establishing the church hierarchy in Portugal after the period of Muslim rule.

Gerald Edwards (Bl) {2}

1 October

d. 1588. From Ludlow (Shrops), he studied at Jesus College at Oxford but converted, studied at Rheims and was ordained in 1587. He was executed at Canterbury with BB Robert Wilcox and Robert Widmerpool and was beatified in 1929. He is also known as 'Edward Campion', and is listed in the revised Roman Martyrology as a saint in error. Cf. **England, Martyrs of**.

Gerald of Ostia (St)

6 February

d. 1077. He was Benedictine prior of Cluny before being made bishop of Ostia near Rome by Pope Alexander II in succession to St Peter Damian. He served as papal legate, and was imprisoned by Emperor Henry V in the investiture controversy. He is the patron saint of Velletri, but is not listed in the Roman Martyrology.

Gerald de Salis (Bl) {2}

20 April

d. 1120. From Sales in Périgord (France), he became a canon regular of Saint Avitus. Then he was a penitential hermit, but was elected abbot of Chaseliers which was part of the Fontevrault congregation. He founded several other Augustinian monasteries for the disciples that he attracted.

Gerald of Sauve-Majeure (St) {2}

5 April

d. 1095. From Corbie in Picardy (France), he became a monk at the Benedictine abbey there and after pilgrimages to Rome and Palestine, became abbot of St Vincent at Laon in 1074. He was expelled by an usurper and founded the abbey of Sauve-Majeure near Bordeaux, which became the centre of a group of reformed monasteries. He introduced the Benedictine custom of saying Mass for a deceased monk for thirty successive days after the death.

Gerard of Brogne (St) {2, 4}

3 October

d. 959. From Brogne near Namur (Belgium), he became a soldier and a courtier of the count of Namur. Being sent on an embassy to the French king in 918, he stayed in Paris and became a monk at the Benedictine abbey of St Denis. He returned home to his own estate at Brogne in 914 and became abbot-founder of a monastery there (now the village of St Gérard), which became the centre of a monastic reform movement in the Low Countries and northern France during his twenty-two years as abbot. He was known for his equable disposition.

Gerard Cagnoli (Bl) {2}

29 December
1270–1342. A nobleman from near Pavia in Lombardy (Italy), he became a hermit on Mount Etna in Sicily and then a Franciscan lay brother. He worked as a cook, and was the recipient of many supernatural graces. His cultus was confirmed for Palermo in 1908.

(Gerard of Clairvaux 1) (Bl) {2}

13 June
d. 1138. One of the brothers of St Bernard of Clairvaux and apparently the favourite one, he was a soldier when St Bernard became a monk but was wounded and decided to become a monk himself. He entered Cîteaux, went to Clairvaux when his brother was made abbot there and became the cellarer. He died before St Bernard, who preached an extant panegyric in his honour.

(Gerard of Clairvaux 2) (Bl) {2}

16 October
d. 1177. From Lombardy, he became a Cistercian monk at Fossanova in the Roman Campagna and went on to be abbot. In 1170 he became abbot of Clairvaux, and was killed at the abbey of Igny by a rebellious monk while on a canonical visitation.

Gerard of Mâcon (St) {2}

29 May
d. 940. He was a monk before being elected bishop of Mâcon (France), and later retired to be a hermit in a forest.

Gerard Majella (St) {2, 4}

16 October
1725–55. From Muro Lucano in Basilicata (Italy), he trained and worked as a tailor before joining the Redemptorist noviciate at Deliceto as a lay brother. Initially it was thought that he was not much use except in tailoring, but his amazing austerity and virtue were soon recognized, and St Alphonsus ordered that he be professed early. The rest of his short life before his death of tuberculosis at Caposele contained a well-authenticated series of supernatural events including prophecies, the reading of consciences, bilocations and multiplication of food. He was canonized in 1904.

Gerard Mecatti (Bl) {4}

25 May
1174–1245. From a poor family at Villamagna near Florence (Italy), he was a knight's equerry on crusade on the Holy Land and was captured. Being ransomed, he became a penitential hermit back home in Villamagna with (apparently) a period serving as a Knight Hospitaller at Jerusalem. His cultus was approved for Florence and the Knights in 1833.

Gerard of Potenza (St) {2, 4}

30 October
d. 1122. From Piacenza (Italy), he became a diocesan priest and then bishop of Potenza in Basilicata.

Gerard (Collert) Sagredo (St) {2, 4}

24 September
d. 1046. The 'Apostle of Hungary' was from Venice, and was a Benedictine monk at St George's abbey in that city. He was passing through Hungary on a pilgrimage to the Holy Land when he was detained by King St Stephen, who was in the process of Christianizing his kingdom. He became the

tutor of the king's son, St Emeric (who died young), and was made the first bishop of Csanad in 1035. After the king's death there was a pagan reaction during which St Gerard was killed at what is now Budapest, and his body thrown into the Danube.

Gerard Tintorio *(Bl)*

6 June
d. 1207. A wealthy young merchant citizen of Monza in Lombardy (Italy), he used his wealth in founding a hospital where he served as a nurse. His cultus was approved for Monza in 1582, but he is not listed in the Roman Martyrology.

Gerard of Toul (St) {2, 4}

23 April
d. 994. From Cologne, he became bishop of Toul (France) in 963. He rebuilt the cathedral and founded monasteries which attracted Greek and Irish monk scholars, thus much improving the standard of religion in the diocese. His successor went on to become Pope St Leo IX, and canonized him.

Gerasimus of the Jordan (St) {2}

5 March
d. 475. From Lycia (Asia Minor), he became a monk in the Holy Land and a disciple of St Euthymius the Great. He founded a great monastery on the Jordan on the traditional site of Christ's baptism near Jericho. The story about a lion becoming the companion of St Jerome after being done a kindness really refers to him, as ignorant Western pilgrims confused the two names in the Middle Ages.

Geremar (Germer) (St) {2, 4}

30 December
d. ?658. From Beauvais (France), he was a Frankish courtier but retired to the abbey of Pentale on the Seine with his wife's consent. There he became abbot, but some of the monks thought him too severe and tried to kill him, whereupon he resigned to be a hermit in a cave nearby. In 655, however, he founded an abbey between Beauvais and Rouen which was afterwards named Saint-Germer after him.

Gereon and Comps (St) {2, 4}

10 October
C4th? They were martyred with the sword at Cologne (Germany). The extremely confused medieval legend amplifies them to a legion of 678 soldiers, and is merely a version of the story of the Theban Legion.

Gerin (St) {2, 4}

2 October
d. 676. Brother of St Leodegar, he was arrested with him by order of Ebroin, the mayor of the palace of the Merovingian kingdom, and was stoned to death near Arras (France) on suspicion of conspiracy against the king. This occurred two years before the martyrdom of his brother.

Gerius de Lunel (St) {2}

25 May
d. c.1270. Allegedly a French pilgrim, he died as a hermit and Franciscan tertiary at Monte Santo near Ancona (Italy) on his way back from the Holy Land. His cultus was approved for Fermo in 1742.

Gerlac (St) {2}

5 January
d. 1165. A knight of Valkenburg east of Maastricht (Netherlands), he was shocked into a life as a penitential hermit by the unexpected death of his wife. After serving in a hospital at Jerusalem for seven years, he settled as a

hermit in a hollow tree at Houtheim near his birthplace. This became the site of a Premonstratensian nunnery after his death.

Gerland of Caltagirone (St) {2}

19 June
d. ?1271. Allegedly a German knight of one of the military orders (Templars or Hospitallers), he has his shrine at Caltagirone in Sicily.

Gerland of Girgenti (St) {2}

25 February
d. 1100. Allegedly born at Besançon (France) and a relative of Robert Guiscard the Norman adventurer, he became bishop of Girgenti in Sicily after the Normans had conquered that island from the Muslims, and worked to restore Christianity there.

German cf. **Jermyn**.

Germana (Germaine) Cousin (St) {2}

15 June
1579–1601. From Pibrac near Toulouse (France), she was a daughter of a labourer who lost his wife and remarried. Her stepmother despised her, and used the excuse of a serious skin disease to banish her from the house and to force her to sleep in a barn with the sheep for which she had to care. Despite the hardship, dirt and neglect, she developed a full prayer life and was charitable to those in a similar state. Her stepmother eventually relented and allowed her back into the house, but she preferred to continue sleeping with the sheep and died alone with them. She was canonized in 1867.

Germanicus of Smyrna (St) {2, 4}

19 January
d. ?167. A young man of Smyrna (now Izmir in Turkey), he was thrown to the wild animals in the amphitheatre at the same games as featured in the *Martyrdom of St Polycarp*. The circular letter by the local church describing their martyrdoms survives.

Germanus and Randoald (SS) {2}

21 February
d. ?677. The former was from Trier (Germany) and became a monk near Remiremont in the Vosges (France) and then at Luxeuil under St Waldebert. He later became abbot of Grandval near Moutier in the Jura canton (Switzerland), and had St Randoald as his prior. They were killed by a local ruler for defending the peasantry against unjust extortion.

Germanus, Theophilus and Cyril (SS) {2, 4}

3 November
? They were martyred at Caesarea in Cappodocia (Asia Minor). The old Roman Martyrology listed Caesarius and Vitalis instead of Cyril.

Germanus of Auxerre (St) {2, 4}

31 July
?378–448. A nobleman from Auxerre (France), he studied law at Rome and was made governor of his native province by the Emperor Honorius. In 418 he seems to have had a spiritual conversion and became bishop of his native city, and as such he visited Britain twice (in 429 and 447) to help defeat the Pelagian heresy. He died at the imperial capital of Ravenna while appeasing the emperor for a rebellion that had occurred in Brittany.

(Germanus of Besançon) (St) {4 –deleted}

11 October
d. c.390. The successor of St Desideratus as bishop of Besançon (France), he was allegedly martyred by Arian heretics.

Germanus of Capua (St) {2, 4}

30 October
d. c.540. Bishop of Capua (Italy), he was sent to Constantinople by Pope Hormisdas to try and resolve the Acacian schism, and apparently met with ill-treatment.

Germanus of Constantinople (St) {2}

12 May
d. 733. From a patrician family, he became a priest at Constantinople and then bishop of Cyzicus on the Sea of Marmara (Asia Minor). In 715 he became patriarch of Constantinople, and energetically defended the dogmatic validity of icons against the iconoclast policy of Emperor Leo III. He was forced to resign and died in exile on his family estate. Some of his writings survive.

Germanus of Montfort (St) {2}

28 October
C11th. From Montfort near Malines (France), he studied at Paris, became a priest and then joined the reformed Benedictine monastery of Savigny. He was made prior of Talloires near Annecy in Savoy but ended his life as a hermit nearby. His relics were enshrined by St Francis de Sales in 1621, and his cultus was confirmed for Annecy in 1889.

Germanus of Paris (St) {2, 4}

28 May
?496–576. From near Autun (France), he became a priest there and was abbot of a local monastery before becoming bishop of Paris and royal chaplain in 555. He had a good influence on the violent and immoral Merovingian royal family, and King Childebert I was impressed enough to found an abbey for him later known as Saint-Germain-des-Près. He was remembered for his charity to the poor.

Germerius of Toulouse (St) {2}

16 May
End C7th. From Angoulême (France), he was a bishop of Toulouse.

Gerold of Einsiedeln (St) {2}

19 April
d. 978. A nobleman of the Voralberg (Austria), he gave his lands to the Swiss abbey of Einsiedeln (where his sons, BB Cuno and Ulric, were monks) and became a hermit nearby, where there is a village named after him.

Gertrude of Altenberg (Bl) {2}

13 August
1227–97. Daughter of Ludovic IV, landgrave of Thuringia (Germany) and of St Elizabeth of Hungary, she was educated at the Premonstratensian nunnery at Altenberg in Thuringia and became abbess there in 1248. She was abbess for half a century.

Gertrude Comensoli (St) {2}

18 February
1847–1903. From near Brescia (Italy), she tried to join the Sisters of Charity when aged fifteen, but her health quickly broke down. Then she lived in poverty for twenty years, doing domestic work and hoping to found a congregation of adorers of the Blessed Sacrament. This she did at Bergamo. They were called the 'Sacramentines' and supported themselves by teaching, moving to Lodi in 1891. She died at Bergamo and was canonized in 2009.

Gertrude the Great (St) {2, 3}

16 November
?1256–1302. Allegedly from Eisleben near Halle (Germany), when aged five she became a child-oblate at the nunnery of Helfta nearby

and went on to become a nun there. (The Roman Martyrology now describes this nunnery as Cistercian, dismissing a rival claim that it was Benedictine). From 1281 she had a continuous succession of mystical experiences and visions of Christ, especially during the Divine Office, and her writings derived from them helped to establish the devotion to the Sacred Heart. Her cultus was confirmed in 1677, and she is the patron of the West Indies. Her attribute is a flaming heart (she may be depicted with a mouse mistaken for Gertrude of Nivelles).

Gertrude of Nivelles (St) {2}

17 March
626–59. Daughter of Pepin of Landen and Bl Ida, when aged twenty she was made first abbess of the nunnery founded at Nivelles (Belgium) by her mother. She was known for her knowledge and charity at a time when both were in short supply, and became one of the most popular saints of the Middle Ages. Her attribute is a mouse, against which animal she is invoked.

Gerulf (St) {2}

21 September
?732–?750. According to the legend, he was the teenage son of the mayor of Merendree near Ghent (Belgium) and was killed by his godfather (who hoped to acquire his inheritance) on their way home from his confirmation. These circumstances led him to be venerated as a martyr, and he is so listed in the Roman Martyrology.

Geruntius of Cervia (St) {2}

10 May
d. ?501. Bishop of Cervia near Ravenna (Italy), he was on his way back home from a synod at Rome when he was ambushed by robbers at Cagli and killed.

Geruntius of Italica (St) {2, 4}

25 August
C4th? According to the unreliable local tradition, he was a bishop of Italica near Seville (Spain) who was martyred in the apostolic age and is commemorated in the Mozarabic rite. He was probably of the fourth century, and not a martyr.

Geruntius of Milan (St) {2, 4}

5 May
d. ?472. He succeeded St Eusebius as bishop of Milan (Italy) in ?465.

Gervase and Protase (SS) {2, 3}

19 June
? The relics of these supposed martyrs were discovered in Milan (Italy) in 386, during the episcopacy of St Ambrose. He mentioned the discovery in his letters, writing that the bloodstains were still visible on the bones, and proclaimed them to be the protomartyrs of Milan. Almost nothing was remembered of them at the time, and their traditional acta are spurious. There is a suspicion that what was actually discovered was a stone-age burial dressed with red ochre. Their cultus was confined to local calendars in 1969.

Géry cf. **Gaugeric.**

(Getulius, Amantius, Caerealis and Primitivus) (SS) {4 –deleted}

10 June
C2nd? According to their story, Getulius was the husband of St Symphorosa and Amantius was his brother. The other two were army officers sent to arrest them who were converted by them instead, and the four were beaten to death at Tivoli near Rome in the reign of Hadrian.

Ghebre Michael cf. **Michael Ghebre.**

Gherardesca (Bl) {2}

29 May
d. 1261. A noblewoman of Pisa (Italy), she married but persuaded her husband to become a Camaldolese monk at San Salvio there. She then lived as a hermit in a hut outside the monastery gate, being under the obedience of the monastic superior. Her cultus was confirmed for Pisa and the Camaldolese in 1856.

Ghislain (Gislenus, Guislain) (St) {2, 4}

9 October
d. betw. 681–5. A hermit in a forest near Mons (Belgium), he became the abbot-founder of a monastery which became known as St Ghislain. For it he wrote a rule which was not replaced by that of St Benedict until 930.

Gibrian (St) {2}

8 May
d. c.515. He was an Irish monk and priest who migrated to Brittany and then to the region of Châlons-sur-Marne (France) where he became a hermit. The legend gives him four brothers and three sisters who allegedly accompanied him: Tressan, Helan, Germanus, Petran, Franca, Promptia and Possenna. They are not in the Roman Martyrology.

Gideon (St) {2, 4}

1 September
He features in the Book of Judges in the Old Testament.

Gilbert of Dornoch (St) {2}

1 April
d. ?1245. Bishop of Caithness (Scotland) from 1225, he built the cathedral at Dornoch and was also of great service to the Scottish kings in their struggle to preserve the integrity of their nation. He is the most recent pre-Reformation Scotsman to have been canonized.

Gilbert of Cîteaux (Bl) {2}

17 October
d. 1167. He was an English abbot of Cîteaux (France), famous for his scholarship. He gave hospitality to the exiled St Thomas Becket, and died at Toulouse.

Gilbert of Neuffontaines (St) {2}

6 June
d. 1152. A nobleman from the Auvergne (France), after coming back from the Second Crusade, he and his wife became Premonstratensians and he became the abbot-founder of Neuffontaines near Clermont-Ferrand in 1151.

Gilbert of Sempringham (St) {2}

4 February
1083–1189. Son of a Norman knight from Sempringham in Lincolnshire (England), he became parish priest there in 1123. He organized a group of seven women of the village into a religious community and thus founded the Gilbertines, the only religious order to have been founded in England. It was based on the pattern of a double monastery of nuns following the Benedictine rule and of canons following that of St Augustine, sharing a church. Twenty-two of these were founded in eastern England (not all with nuns), and he was the master-general until he went blind. He died in extreme old age, and his shrine was a focus of pilgrimage at the great double monastery with its vast church (of which only crop marks remain) near the surviving parish church at Sempringham.

Gildard (Godard) (St) {2, 4}

8 June
d. p511. He was bishop of Rouen (France) for about fifteen years. He died about five years before St Medard was consecrated as bishop, yet the old Roman Martyrology repeated a

worthless story that the two shared the same birthday, day of consecration and day of death.

Gildas the Wise 'Badonicus' (St) {2}

29 January
d. 570. A Strathclyde Briton, he went to Wales as a refugee and became a monk under St Illtyd. Later he was a hermit on Flat Holm in the Bristol Channel and then emigrated to Brittany (France) and became a hermit on the peninsula of Rhuis near Vannes. He wrote 'De Excidiis Britanniae' concerning the tribulations afflicting his fellow Britons as a result of the Saxon invasions, and how these were justified given their immoral way of life. This work is a unique survival of, and witness to, post-Roman Christian British culture.

Gilduin (St) {2}

27 January
1052–77. A son of the count of Dol in Brittany (France), he was made a canon of St Samson's Church there when very young and was elected bishop in 1076. He refused out of humility, persuaded Pope St Gregory VII at Rome to accept his refusal and died on the journey back, at Chartres.

Giles

This is the English form of the Latin Aegidius, Italian Egidio, French Gilles and Spanish and Portuguese Gil.

Giles (St) {2, 3}

1 September
C8th. Very little is certainly known about him, yet he became one of the most popular saints of the Middle Ages (as witnessed by about 160 churches being dedicated to him in England), and many spurious legends were invented about him. He was possibly a Provençal who became a hermit and founded a monastery where the town of Saint-Gilles near Nîmes (France) now stands. This became a famous pilgrimage site. He is a patron saint of cripples, beggars and blacksmiths, has a deer or a crutch as an attribute and may be depicted with an arrow embedded in him. His cultus was confined to local calendars in 1969.

Giles of Assisi (Bl) {2}

23 April
d. 1262. He became the third disciple of St Francis of Assisi in 1209 and preached unsuccessfully to the Muslims of Tunis (the very early Franciscans thought that they could evangelize the Muslims). Then he became a hermit in Italy and died at Perugia.

Giles-of-Laurenzana de Bello (Bl) {2}

28 January
?1443–1518. From Laurenzana in Basilicata (Italy), he was a farm worker before becoming a Franciscan lay brother there and living as a hermit in the grounds of the friary. He was known for his love of animals. His cultus was approved for Matera in 1880.

Giles-Mary-of-St-Joseph Pontillo (St) {2}

7 February
1729–1812. Born in poverty at Taranto (Italy), he joined the Alcantarene Franciscans as a lay brother in 1754 and was at St Pascal's Hospice in Naples as a cook, mendicant and porter for fifty-three years. Although illiterate, he was an advanced contemplative and his nights of prayer before the Blessed Sacrament enabled him to inspire even the noble and learned who talked with him. He was canonized in 1996.

Giles of Vaozéla (Bl) {2}

14 May
1185–1265. A Portuguese, he studied medicine at Coïmbra, Paris and Toledo and was

reputed to have practised black magic. He converted, however, joined the Dominicans at Palencia (Spain), became the provincial superior for Spain and was based at Santarem (near Lisbon) when he died. His cultus was confirmed for Lisbon in 1748.

Giovanna, Giovanni cf. **Jane, John**.

Giovannina Franks (Bl) {2 –add}

23 February
1807–72. From a wealthy family of Como, Italy, she was concerned for the welfare of sick people in the primitive hospitals of the time and fairly late in life began a pious union of volunteer nurses called the Infirmaries Sisters of Charity. This developed into the Congregation of the Infirmarian Sisters of the Sorrowful Mother, of which she is considered the foundress. She died of smallpox in Como while nursing sufferers, and was beatified in 2014. Her name means 'Little Jane'.

Gisella (Gizella, Gisele) (Bl) {2}

7 May
d. 1060. Wife of King St Stephen and thus the first queen of Hungary, she may have been a sister of Emperor St Henry II. She helped the king in his policy of Christianizing Hungary, so she was ill-treated and imprisoned in the pagan reaction after his death in 1038. She allegedly became a nun at Niedernburg near Passau in Bavaria (Germany) in 1042 and died as abbess.

Gistilian (Gistlian) *(St)*

2 March
C5th–C6th. An uncle of St David, he was a monk at Menevia when that monastery was transferred to the site of the present St David's (Wales).

Giuseppe cf. **Joseph**
Giuseppina cf. **Josepha, Mary Catanea**.

(Glaphyra) *(St)* *{4 –deleted}*

13 January
d. ?324. According to the story, she was a slave in domestic service to Constantia, wife of Emperor Licinius but fled to St Basil, bishop of Amasea, when the emperor tried to seduce her. They were seized, but she died on the way to her execution.

Glodesind of Metz (St) {2}

25 July
C6th. A noblewoman from Metz (France), she overcame her father's opposition to become a nun at Trier (Germany) and founded a nunnery there.

Glyceria (St) {2, 4}

8 June
? According to her story, she was a young woman who broke a statue of Zeus at Heraclea on the Sea of Marmara (European Turkey) during a pagan festival and was thrown to the wild animals during the games.

Glycerius of Antioch (St) {2}

14 January
? He was a deacon martyred at Antioch in Syria. The old Roman Martyrology listed him as 'Clerus' on 7 January.

(Glycerius of Nicomedia) *(St)* *{4 –deleted}*

21 December
Early C4th? He was listed as a priest at Nicomedia (Asia Minor) who was burnt at the stake in the reign of Diocletian.

Goar (St) {2, 4}

6 July
Late C6th. A secular priest from Aquitaine, he became a hermit on the Rhine between Koblenz and Bingen (Germany). Charlemagne

built a pilgrimage church on the site of his cell. His C8th biography is fictitious.

Goban (Gobain) (St) {2}

20 June
d. c.670. From Ireland and a disciple of St Fursey, he was a monk under him at Burgh Castle in Suffolk (England) before both fled to France in the face of a Mercian incursion. He became a hermit on the river Oise near Laon, where the village of Saint-Gobain now stands.

Godard cf. **Godehard**.

Godehard (Godard, Gothard) (St) {2, 4}

5 May
961–1038. From near Passau in Bavaria (Germany), his father was a servant of the canons at the secularized monastery of Niederaltaich, so he joined them. In 996 he became their superior and reintroduced the Benedictine monastic life there and in other monasteries in a similar state in several German dioceses, being asked to do so by Emperor St Henry II. He became bishop of Hildesheim in 1022. The famous St Gothard's Pass in the Alps seems to be named after him.

Godeleva (Godliva) (St) {2}

6 July
1040–70. From near Boulogne (France), she married Bertulf van Gistel, a Flemish nobleman, and was viciously treated by him and his mother. She put up with it with patience, prayer and works of charity until he had her strangled. Later he did penance for this, went on crusade and became a monk. His castle at Gistel near Ostend (Belgium) became a nunnery.

Godfrey

The Latin Godefridus has many vernacular variants: Godefrid, Geoffrey, Jeffrey, Gotfrid, Goffry, Gottfried, Geoffroy, Gioffredo, Gaufrid, Geofroi, Goffredo, Gofrido, etc.

Godfrey of Amiens (St) {2, 4}

8 November
?1066–1115. From near Soissons (France), he became a child-oblate at the Benedictine abbey of Mont-Saint-Quentin when aged five, was made abbot of Nogent-sous-Coucy in 1096 and bishop of Amiens in 1104. He was a great enemy of simony and clerical concubinage and was known to be austere with himself and others. His people would not allow him to resign to become a Carthusian.

Godfrey van Dunyen (St) {2}

9 July
d. 1572. A secular priest and a former headmaster of a school at Paris, he was one of the **Gorinchem** martyrs (q.v.).

Godfrey of Kappenberg (Bl) {2}

13 January
1097–1127. Count of Kappenberg in Westphalia (Germany) and a substantial landowner, he was inspired by St Norbert to become a Premonstratensian monk and to convert his castles at Kappenberg, Ilmenstadt and Varlar into abbeys of the order. This was despite the violent opposition of his family, although his wife, brother and two sisters followed his example.

Godfrey of Merville (St) {2}

9 July
d. 1572. Custodian of the Franciscan friary at Gorinchem, he was one of the **Gorinchem** martyrs (q.v.).

Godric (St)

21 May
?1069–1170. From Walpole in Norfolk (England), he had an adventurous life as a

seafarer and pilgrim before settling down as a hermit at Finchale (pronounced 'Finkle') on the Wear, being under the obedience of the Benedictine cathedral priory at Durham. He was there for sixty years, becoming famous for his familiarity with wild animals as well as for his austerity and supernatural gifts and thus resembling the later Russian hermit saints. His biography was written by Reginald of Durham, and some of his poems survive. His veneration was popular in northern England in the Middle Ages, but he is not in the Roman Martyrology.

Gohard (St) {2}

24 June
d. 843. Bishop of Nantes (France) from 838, he was killed during a Norse raid on the city while he was celebrating Mass. Many of his congregation, as well as other monks and priests, died in the attack.

Golvin (Golwen) (St) {2}

1 July
C6th. Born near Brest in Brittany (France) of poor British immigrants, he became a hermit and later bishop of León. He died at Rennes, where his shrine was established.

Gomer cf. **Gummarus**.

Gomidas Keumurjian (Bl) {2}

5 November
?1656–1707. From Constantinople, he was an Armenian and became a priest of the Armenian patriarchate in that city. He and his family were reconciled to the Catholic Church in 1696, which caused him to be regarded as a schismatic by his fellow Armenians. The Ottoman authorities were informed that he was an agent of hostile Christian powers, and he was beheaded outside Constantinople, being beatified in 1929. His name is Armenian for 'Cosmas the Charcoal-Burner'.

Gonsalvo cf. **Gundesalvus**.
Gontram cf. **Gunthamnus**.
Gonzaga Gonza cf. **Aloysius-Gonzaga Gonza**.

Good Thief, The (St) {2}

25 March
d. ?33. The repentant crucified thief described in the Passion narrative of St Luke's Gospel is traditionally given the name of Dismas, but this is not in the Roman Martyrology. A number of fictitious legends feature him.

Gordian of Rome (St) {2, 3}

10 May
d. c.300. He was allegedly martyred at Rome in the reign of Julian, and his relics were placed in the same tomb as those of St Epimachus. This gave rise to their spurious acta and an erroneous entry in the old Roman Martyrology. He was actually a martyr of the persecution of Diocletian. Their cultus was confined to local calendars in 1969.

Gordius (St) {2}

3 January
d. 304. A centurion in the Roman army at Caesarea in Cappodocia (Asia Minor), he refused to take part in pagan sacrifice and was cashiered. Then he proclaimed Christ during a festival in honour of Mars and was martyred in the reign of Diocletian. St Basil preached a panegyric in his honour.

Gorgonia (St) {2, 4}

9 December
d. c.370. Sister of St Gregory Nazianzen and daughter of SS Gregory Nazianzen the Elder and Nonna, she married and had three children, being remembered as a model wife and mother. Her brother gave an extant oration at her funeral, which is the only source of information concerning her life.

Gorgonius (St) {2, 3}

9 September
d. p203. He was martyred on the Via Labicana outside Rome, and buried there. He is the patron of Minden (Germany), where some of his alleged relics were enshrined.

(Gorgonius and Firmus) (SS) *{4 –deleted}*

11 March
C3rd? They were martyred either at Nicaea in Bithynia (Asia Minor) or at Antioch (Syria).

Gorinchem (Gorkum) (Martyrs of) (SS) {2}

9 July
d. 1572. Nineteen priests and religious, they were hanged by Calvinists at the ruined Augustinian monastery of Briel at Gorinchem near Dordrecht (Netherlands). Eleven were Franciscan Observants from the friary at Gorinchem, two were Premonstratensians, one was a Dominican, one was an Augustinian canon and four were secular priests. The town had been captured by Calvinist forces in rebellion against the Spanish government and the nineteen were imprisoned, harshly treated and interrogated in order to obtain their apostasy. They were offered their liberty in exchange for denying the Papal primacy and the Real Presence in the Eucharist, and were executed when they refused. This was despite the objections of the Prince of Orange, leader of the rebellion. They were canonized in 1867. Cf. **Netherlands** in lists of national martyrs in appendix.

Gosbert (St) {2}

13 February
d. 874. A monastic disciple of St Ansgar, he became bishop of Osnabrück in Lower Saxony (Germany). He had trouble from the Danes and from the resentments caused by the forced conversion of the local Saxons, but he was not a martyr.

Gothard cf. **Godehard**.

Govan (St)

20 June
C6th. A hermit, probably a disciple of St Ailbe, he had a stone cell halfway down the cliff at St Govan's Head near Pembroke (Wales). After his death this was converted into a chapel, which survives and is one of the most evocative survivals of British eremitic monasticism. His name in Welsh is Cofen.

(Gracilian and Felicissima) (SS) *{4 –deleted}*

12 August
d. ?304. According to their untrustworthy legend, the former was in prison awaiting martyrdom at Falerna near Rome when he healed the latter, a blind girl, and hence converted her to Christianity. They were beheaded on the same day.

(Grata) (St) *{4 –deleted}*

1 May
C4th or C8th? She is venerated at Bergamo (Italy), but the traditional details of her life are incoherent. There may have been two of the same name.

Gratia of Kotor (Bl) {2}

9 November
1438–1508. From Cattaro in Venetian Dalmatia (now Kotor in Montenegro), he fished in the Adriatic Sea for thirty years before becoming an Augustinian lay friar. He had the charism of infused knowledge. He died at Murano near Venice and his cultus was confirmed for Kotor in 1889.

Gratian cf. **Gatian**.

Gratus of Aosta (St) {2}

7 September
C5th. A bishop of Aosta in the Alps (Italy), he is patron of that place.

Gratus of Oléron (St) {2}

19 October
d. p506. He was the first bishop of the extinct diocese of Oléron in the Pyrenees (France).

Great Martyrdom at Nagasaki (BB) {2}

10 September
d. 1622. On this date twenty-three missionaries and native Christians were burnt alive at Nagasaki in Japan, and twenty-nine were beheaded. Those burnt were eight Jesuits, six Dominicans, three Franciscans and five housekeepers of the missionaries, while those beheaded were two Dominicans, a Jesuit and twenty-six relatives of other martyrs. Two struggled from the fire only to be thrown back on it, and these were not beatified.

Gregory I 'the Great', Pope (St) {1, 3}

3 September
c.540–604. Born in Rome of a wealthy patrician family, he was prefect of Rome from 571 but converted the family mansion into a monastery (St Andrew on the Coelian Hill) after his father's death and became a monk there in 575. Then he became archdeacon of the Roman church and was its representative at Constantinople from 579 to 585. (The Byzantine Eucharistic liturgy of the pre-sanctified bears his name). He became pope in 590, and proved to be one of the greatest. The city of Rome had lost its economic and political reasons for existence, and he became the de facto local ruler, supporting the population from the landed patrimony of the papacy, especially in Sicily. He revised the Roman liturgy and wrote voluminously, especially on pastoral matters (being later declared a doctor of the Church), but as the first monk-pope he favoured his fellow monks at the expense of the secular clergy, and this was resented. He had to pay off the Arian Lombards but oversaw the conversion of the Arian Visigoths and is especially famous for instigating the mission to the Anglo-Saxons through St Augustine and his successors at Canterbury (England). A medieval legend that he received his doctrine directly from the Holy Spirit led him to be depicted with a dove near his ear. The famous 'Dialogues' may not be by him.

Gregory II, Pope (St) {2, 4}

13 February
669–731. A Roman, he was educated at the Lateran and was the archivist of the Roman church before he was elected pope in 715. He had to resist the religious policies of Emperor Leo III, who enforced iconoclasm in the Byzantine Empire in 726. For the German missions he consecrated SS Boniface and Corbinian, and he fostered monastic life everywhere in the West. For this reason it used to be falsely claimed that he was a Benedictine monk.

Gregory III, Pope (St) {2, 4}

28 November
d. 741. A Syrian, he became pope in 731 and immediately had to resist the strongly implemented iconoclastic policies of the Emperor Leo III. Also the Lombards took Ravenna, the capital of the local imperial province, in 734 and threatened finally to conquer Rome. He appealed for help to Charles Martel, thus forming the historically important link between the Papacy and the Frankish kingdom which led to the Carolingian Empire.

Gregory VII, Pope (St) {1, 3}

25 May
?1021–85. Hildebrand was from Soana in Tuscany (Italy), and was educated at the Roman Cluniac monastery of St Mary on the Aventine where his uncle was superior. In time he became a Benedictine monk and was made abbot of St Paul-outside-the-Walls in

1059. He was one of the leading figures in the reform movement in the Roman church, serving five popes as archdeacon before becoming pope himself in 1073. The thrust of his reform was against lay investiture, simony and clerical concubinage, but this conflicted with the way the church had been financed in other countries, especially in Germany, and he came into bitter conflict with Emperor Henry IV. Despite the famous penance by the latter at Canossa, in 1077 Gregory was finally driven into exile and died at Salerno. His work made possible the power of the medieval Papacy, and he was canonized in 1606.

Gregory X, Pope (Bl) {2, 4}

10 January
1210–76. Theobald Visconti was from Piacenza (Italy) but became archdeacon at Liege (Belgium). He helped preach a crusade to try to save the remnant Latin Christian outposts in the Holy Land, and was elected pope in 1271 while at Acre there. He was not yet a priest. He convened the second ecumenical council of Lyons, which resulted in the brief reunification of the Latin and Byzantine churches. His cultus was confirmed for Arezzo (where he had died) and Piacenza in 1713.

Gregory of Auxerre (St) {2, 4}

19 December
C6th. He was a bishop of Auxerre (France).

Gregory Barbarigo (St) {2, 3}

18 June
1625–97. A nobleman from Venice, he became bishop of Bergamo (Italy) in 1657, cardinal in 1660 and was transferred to Padua in 1664. He reformed his diocese as directed by the Council of Trent, was famous for the scale of his charity and was zealous for the reunification of the Eastern and Western churches and

for the support of Christians under Muslim rule. He was canonized in 1960 but his cultus was confined to local calendars in 1969.

Gregory-of-Verucchio Celli (Bl) {2}

4 May
d. 1343. From Verucchio near Rimini (Italy), he became an Augustinian friar at a friary founded in his hometown by his mother. He was expelled for some unknown but unjust reason and was hospitably received at the Franciscan friary at Monte Carnerio near Rieti. His cultus was confirmed for Rieti in 1769.

Gregory Decapolites (St) {2, 4}

20 November
d. 842. From the Isaurian Decapolis in central Asia Minor, he was in turn a monk, a bishop and a pilgrim but was remembered for going to Constantinople to oppose the iconoclast policy of Emperor Leo III. He had to suffer much as a result.

Gregory of Elvira (St) {2, 4}

24 April
C4th. Bishop of Elvira, the diocese of which was the precursor of Granada (Spain), he was a forceful opponent of Arianism and was one of the few bishops who refused the compromise of the council of Rimini in 359. He allegedly allied himself with the schism of Lucifer of Cagliari, but without himself lapsing from communion with Rome. No Luciferian influence is detectable in his surviving writings.

Gregory Frąckowiak (Bl) {2}

5 May
1911–43. A Polish priest and member of the Society of the Divine Word, he was guillotined in prison at Dresden in Germany. Cf. **Poland, Martyrs of the Nazi Occupation of**.

Gregory of Girgenti (St) {2, 4}

23 November
d. p603. A monk of the Byzantine rite from Girgenti (Sicily), for a long time he was a monk in the lauras of the Levant before being made bishop of his hometown by St Gregory the Great. A commentary on Ecclesiastes by him survives.

Gregory Grassi and Comps (SS) {1 –group}

9 July
d. 1900. He was the vicar-apostolic of northern Shanxi in China. During the Boxer Rebellion, he and twenty-five of his people were executed at Taiyuan at the orders of the governor of the province. The others were Francis Fogolla OFM, his coadjutor and vicar-general for Tianjin; two priests, Elias Facchini and Theodoric Balat, OFM; a lay brother, Andrew Bauer; seven Franciscan Missionaries of Mary: Mary-Adolphine Dierk, Mary-of-Peace Giuliani, Mary-Ermellina-of-Jesus Grivot, Mary-Amandina Jeuris, Mary-of-the-Holy-Birth Kerguin, Mary-of-St-Justus Moreau and Mary-Clare Nanetti; five Franciscan tertiary seminarians: John Zhang Huan, Patrick Dong Bodi, John Wang Rui, Philip Zhang Zhihe and John Zhang Jingguang; five other tertiaries: Thomas Shen Jihe (a manservant), Simon Chen Ximan (a lay catechist), Peter Wu Anpeng (a servant), Francis Zhang Rong (a farmer) and Matthias Feng De (a night watchman at the cathedral). Peter Zhang Banniu (a servant at the cathedral), James Yan Guodong (a cook), James Zhao Quanxin (a manservant) and Peter Wang Erman (a cook) were also killed. Cf. **China, Martyrs of**.

Gregory the Illuminator (St) {2, 4}

30 September
d. ?326. The details of the life of the 'Apostle of Armenia' are not well established, but it seems certain that he was a missionary to the independent kingdom of Armenia who converted Tiridat, the king, and became the first bishop of the new Armenian church at Ashtishat (now Etchmiadzin). The Armenian legends concerning him are numerous and fanciful.

Gregory Khomyšin (Bl) {2}

28 December
1867–1945. Bishop of Stanislav, he died in prison at Kiev in the Soviet Union, now Ukraine. Cf. **Nicholas Čarneckyj and 24 Comps**.

Gregory Lakota (Bl) {2}

5 November
1883–1950. He was auxiliary bishop of Przemysl in what had been Poland before the Second World War, and died in a gulag at Abez in Siberia, Soviet Union. Cf. **Nicholas Čarneckyj and 24 Comps**.

Gregory of Langres (St) {2}

4 January
d. 539. As the governor of the district around his native city of Autun (France) he was feared for his severity. He lost his wife, was ordained and made bishop of Langres and then became known for his gentleness and understanding. He was the father of St Tetricius and a great-uncle of St Gregory of Tours.

Gregory of Narek (St) {2}

27 February
d. c.1005. A monk of Narek in Armenia, he is one of the Doctors of the Armenian church and composed many liturgical hymns and prayers. His insertion into the revised Roman Martyrology is significant, since it was previously thought that the Armenian church was out of communion with Rome at the time.

Gregory Nazianzen 'the Theologian' (St) {1, 3}

2 January
d. ?389. The elder son of St Gregory Nazianzen the Elder, he studied law for ten years in Athens, during which he formed a close friendship with St Basil. They were briefly together at the latter's monastery on the Iris in Pontus, but then he went to Nazianzos to be a diocesan priest under his father, the bishop there, in 361. St Basil mistakenly consecrated him bishop of a hamlet called Sasima in 372 as a political move, but St Gregory did not accept this (his temperament was not suited for public office), and he became coadjutor to his father instead. In 380 he was made patriarch of Constantinople in order to restore the church there after the Arian ascendancy at court, but he resigned after only one month and went home to retirement. In that time he preached his 'Theological Orations' which, together with his other writings, show him to be one of the most important of the Eastern Fathers and have given him the status of doctor of the Church. His feast day was 9 May before 1969, but he is now celebrated with St Basil.

Gregory of Nyssa (St) {2, 4}

10 January
d. a.400. A younger brother of St Basil, he married and was a teacher of rhetoric before becoming a priest. In 372 he was consecrated bishop of Nyssa in Cappodocia by his brother for political reasons (St Basil, as metropolitan of Caesarea, wanted as many suffragan bishops as possible to help him in his struggle with the Arian court). As such he was initially not a success and was exiled, as the Arians were dominant in his diocese, and he was not temperamentally suited to public life, but he was able to return in 379 and became the mainstay of orthodoxy in the region after St Basil's death. His theological writings are lucid and profound, and he is one of the three 'Cappodocian Fathers' with SS Basil and Gregory Nazianzen but has not been declared a doctor of the Church, possibly because he accepted certain of Origen's speculations which were later condemned.

(Gregory of Spoleto) *(St) {4 –deleted}*

24 December
d. ?303. He was allegedly a priest martyred in the reign of Diocletian at Spoleto (Italy), but his acta are unreliable, and his existence is not certain.

Gregory Thaumaturgus (St) {2, 3}

17 November
d. ?270. From Pontus (Asia Minor), he was a disciple of Origen and became bishop of Neocaesarea in that province in 240. The story is that there were seventeen Christians in the town then and only seventeen pagans left when he died. His surname means 'the Wonderworker'. One of his close disciples was St Macrina the Elder, St Basil the Great's paternal grandmother. A little of his writings survives. His cultus was confined to particular calendars in 1969.

Gregory of Tours (St) {2}

17 November
540–94. From Clermont-Ferrand (France), he was educated by his uncle St Gall who was bishop there, and became bishop of Tours in 573. He was one of the most influential men in the Merovingian kingdom, and his chronological and hagiographical writings are important historical sources for the period.

Gregory of Utrecht (St) {2, 4}

25 August
d. 775. From Trier (Germany), he met St Boniface as a child and became a monk

under him. They were friends, and St Boniface made him abbot of St Martin's at Utrecht (Netherlands). He was administrator of the Utrecht diocese for twenty-two years, although he was never consecrated bishop. His abbey became a great missionary centre in his time.

(Grimwald of Pontecorvo) (St) {4 –deleted}

29 September
C12th? This alleged archpriest of Pontecorvo in eastern Lazio (Italy) was traditionally an Englishman.

Grimwald-of-the-Purification Santamaria (Bl) {2}

18 November
1883–1902. Born in Pontecorvo (Italy), he joined the Passionists there in 1889. His short religious life was outwardly ordinary, and he was never ordained, but he had a developed sense of God's presence and was heroically virtuous. He died of meningitis, and he was beatified in 1995.

Guala Roni (Bl) {2}

3 September
d. 1244. From Bergamo (Italy), he became one of St Dominic's first disciples there and was the founding superior of the friaries at Brescia and Bologna. He became bishop of Brescia in 1228, but resigned in 1242 because of civil disturbances and retired to the Vallumbrosan monastery at Astino, where he died. His cultus was confirmed for Bergamo and Brescia in 1868.

Gualfard (Wolfhard) (St) {2}

11 May
d. 1127. From Augsburg (Germany), he was a saddler and migrated to Verona (Italy) in 1096. The citizens started treating him as a holy man so he fled and became a hermit in a marsh by

the river until he was discovered, whereupon he became a recluse at the church of the Camaldolese monastery of San Salvatore.

Gualterius cf. **Walter**.

Guardian Angels (St) {2}

2 October
The teaching of the Catholic Church is that each person has an angel assigned to him as a guardian, and these angels are celebrated together liturgically on this date.

Guarin (Warin) of Corvey (Bl)

26 September
d. 856. Apparently a son of St Ida of Herzfeld and brother of the duke of Saxony, he became abbot of Corvey near Paderborn (Germany) in 826.

Guarin (Warin) of Palestrina (St) {2}

6 February
d. 1159. From Bologna (Italy), he became an Augustinian canon regular at Mortara in 1104 and was elected bishop of Pavia in 1144. He absolutely refused to accept, but was forced to become cardinal bishop of Palestrina by the pope instead.

Guarin (Guerin) of Sion (St) {2}

6 January
1065–1150. Originally a monk at Molesmes, he became abbot of Aulps near Geneva (Switzerland) and arranged that monastery's affiliation to Clairvaux. Later he became bishop of Sion in the Swiss canton of Valais. He died at Aulps and was buried there.

(Gudelia) (St) {4 –deleted}

29 September
Mid C4th? She is listed as a young woman who was scalped and nailed to a tree by order of Shah Shapur II of Persia.

Gudila (Goule) (St) {2}

8 January
d. ?712. Daughter of St Amelberga, she was educated by St Gertrude at Nivelles (Belgium) and, after the latter died, lived a life of prayerful seclusion near her parents' home at Merchtem near Brussels. She is the patron of Brussels. Her attribute is a lantern.

Guenhael (St) {2}

3 November
C6th. Born in Brittany (France), he was educated at Landevenec under St Winwaloe and became abbot there himself in due course. His name means 'White Angel'.

Guerric of Igny (Bl) {2}

19 August
d. betw. 1151–7. From Tournai (Belgium), he studied at the cathedral school there and went on to be a canon and headmaster. On a visit to St Bernard at Clairvaux, he was inspired to stay and to become a Cistercian, and was sent by the latter to be the first abbot of Igny near Rheims (France). His many writings on monastic spirituality are still popular.

Guethenoc (St) {2}

5 November
C6th. A son of SS Fragan and Gwen and a brother of SS Jacut and Winwaloe, he was a disciple of St Budoc and fled with him from Britain to Brittany (France) to escape the Saxons.

Guibert (St) {2}

23 May
d. 962. A noble of Lorraine, he was a soldier before becoming a hermit on an estate of his at Gembloux near Brussels (Belgium). He turned this into a monastery but became a monk at Gorze near Metz (France), which he had to leave several times in order to defend his foundation in lawsuits. He died at Gorze, but his shrine is at Gembloux.

Guido cf. **Guy**.
Guigner cf. **Fingar**.
Guingaloc (Guignole, Guinvaloeus) cf. **Winwaloe**.
Guislain cf. **Ghislain**.

Gulstan (Gustan, Constans) (St) {2}

27 November
d. 1040. He was a Benedictine monk at the abbey of St Gildas at Rhuys in Brittany (France) under St Felix.

Gumbert of Ansbach (St) {2}

15 July
d. c.790. A nobleman of Germany, he became abbot-founder of the monastery of Ansbach.

Gumesind (Gomez) and Servusdei (Servideus) (SS) {2, 4}

13 January
d. 852. The former was a parish priest, the latter a monk, and they were beheaded at Cordoba (Spain) in the reign of Abd-er-Rahman II.

Gummar (Gomer) (St) {2, 4}

Oct 11
d. ?775. A military officer at the Frankish court, he had a wife who was extravagant and malicious, and he separated from her after a long period of endurance in order to become a hermit. The present town of Lier near Antwerp (Belgium) grew up around his hermitage.

Guddenes (St) {2, 4}

18 July
d. 203. She was a young woman martyred at Carthage (Roman Africa) in the reign of

Septimus Severus after being imprisoned and seriously tortured several times.

Gundisalvus of Amarante (Bl) {2}

10 January
d. ?1259. From the Vizela valley near Braga (Portugal), he became parish priest at Rivas de Vizela but went on pilgrimage for fourteen years and was rejected by his vicar when he returned. Then he became a hermit at Amarante near Oporto, and later joined the Dominicans while remaining a hermit. His cultus was approved in 1560.

Gundisalvus Fusai (Bl) {2}

10 September
1582–1622. A Japanese, he held a high office at the court of his daimyo but attached himself to the Jesuit missionaries in Kyushu after his baptism{2} He was imprisoned at Omura and there received into the Society of Jesus by Bl Charles Spinola, with whom he was burnt alive in the 'Great Martyrdom' at Nagasaki. Cf. **Japan, Martyrs of** and **Great Martyrdom at Nagasaki**.

Gundisalvus Garcia (St) {1 –group}

6 February
1556–97. Born at Bassein (Burma) of a Portuguese father and Canarese mother, he was first a catechist for the Jesuits, then he ran a flourishing business in Japan and finally he joined the Franciscans at Manila as a lay brother in 1591. He returned to Japan as a translator for St Peter Baptist, with whom he was crucified at Nagasaki together with **Paul Miki and Comps**. Cf. **Japan, Martyrs of**.

Gundisalvus of Lagos (Bl) {2}

15 October
d. 1422. From Lagos in Portugal, he became an Augustinian friar and was famous as a great preacher throughout Portugal. He died at Torres Vedras, and his cultus was approved for Lisbon in 1778.

(Gundulf of Bourges) (St) {4 –deleted}

17 June
C6th? He had a cultus at Bourges (France) as an alleged bishop of Milan who had died there, and may have been a bishop somewhere in Gaul.

(Gunifort of Pavia) (St) {4 –deleted}

22 August
? He was allegedly from the British Isles and was martyred at Pavia (Italy). His legend resembles that of St Richard the King.

Gunther (Bl) {2}

9 October
955–1045. A cousin of St Stephen of Hungary and ancestor of the princes of Schwarzburg in Thuringia (Germany), he began life as an ambitious nobleman but was reformed by St Godehard of Hildesheim and became a Benedictine monk at Niederaltaich in Bavaria. His ambitious nature reasserted itself, however, and he had made himself abbot of Göllingen, but proved a failure and returned to Niederaltaich. Then he lived as a hermit for twenty-eight years in the mountains of Bakony in Hungary.

Gunthram (Gontram), King (St) {2, 4}

28 March
d. 593. King of Burgundy (France), he divorced his wife and over-hastily ordered the execution of his physician. Then he was overcome with remorse and lamented these sins for the rest of his life. He was also a good and popular king, and on his death was the object of popular veneration.

Gurias and Samonas (SS) {2, 4}

15 November
d. 306. They were beheaded at Edessa in Syria (now Turkey) in the reign of Diocletian.

Guthlac (St)

11 April
673–714. He had been a soldier in the Mercian army before joining the double monastery of Repton in Derbyshire (England). Then he became a hermit at Crowland, an island in the Lincolnshire Fens, where he apparently made a cell out of a sarcophagus excavated from a tumulus by treasure hunters. There he spent the last fifteen years of his life. At a later period the abbey of Crowland was erected nearby, but this was not on the site of his cell, the remains of which were wantonly destroyed in the C19th.

Guy

This is the English form of the Latin Vitus, and also of Guido. Variants in other languages are: Gui, Gwin, Guidone, Viton, Wido, Witen, Wit, Wye and Wyden.

Guy of Acqui (Bl) {2}

2 June
d. 1070. He was bishop of Acqui in Monferrato, Piedmont (Italy) from 1034. His cultus was confirmed for Acqui in 1853.

Guy of Anderlecht (St) {2, 4}

12 September
d. ?1012. Surnamed 'the Poor Man of Anderlecht' he was a labourer from near Anderlecht (Belgium) who served as sacristan at Laeken before going on pilgrimage to Rome and the Holy Land. On his return, sick and exhausted, he was admitted to the public hospital at Anderlecht and died there. His extant biography is late and unreliable.

Guy-Mary Conforti (St) {2}

5 November
1865–1931. Born near Parma (Italy), he was influenced by the life of St Francis Xavier and, after becoming a cathedral canon, founded the 'Xavieran Missionaries' in 1895 in order to send missionaries to China. He took vows himself in 1902 and became bishop of Parma in 1907, founding the Pontifical Missionary Union in 1916 and finally visiting China in 1928. He died exhausted, beloved by his city, and was beatified in 1996. He was canonized in October 2011.

Guy de Gherardesca (Bl) {2}

20 May
d. 1134. From Pisa (Italy), he became a hermit at Castagneto near Massa Maritima. His relics were eventually divided between Pisa and Castagneto.

Guy Maramaldi (Bl)

25 June
d. 1391. A nobleman from Naples, he became a Dominican, taught philosophy and theology, established a friary at Ragusa (now Dubrovnik in Croatia) and died as the inquisitor-general for the Kingdom of Naples. His cultus was confirmed in 1612, but he is not in the Roman Martyrology.

Guy of Pomposa (St) {2}

31 March
d. 1046. From Ravenna (Italy), he was a hermit before he became a Benedictine monk at the abbey of Pomposa near Ferrara. Then he was made prior of St Severus at Ravenna and abbot of Pomposa. He loved the study of

sacred subjects, and St Peter Damian gave lectures on the Bible to his monks for two years at his request. Towards the end of his life, he was fiercely, though unjustly, persecuted by the bishop of Ravenna.

Guy Vignotelli (Bl) {2}

16 June

d. ?1245. A rich citizen of Cortona (Italy), he gave up his wealth on hearing a sermon by St Francis of Assisi and was received as a Franciscan tertiary by the latter. He became a priest and lived the rest of his life as a hermit near Cortona.

Gwendolen cf. **Gundelind**.
Gwenhael cf. **Guenhael**.

Gyavira (St) {1 –group}

3 June

d. 1886. Known as the 'good runner of messages', he was killed by order of King Mwanga of Buganda (Uganda). Cf. **Charles Lwanga and Comps**.

H

H~ This initial letter became silent in later Latin, hence many saints' names with it have an alternative spelling without.

Habbakuk cf. **Abachum**.

Habbakuk the Prophet (St) {2}

2 December
He is one of the Minor Prophets of the Old Testament.

Habib (St) {2}

1 September
d. 322. He was a deacon at Edessa (Syria, now Urfa in Turkey), and was burnt to death at the end of the reign of Emperor Licinius. He was one of the last of the Christians martyred in the Roman Empire.

Hadrian cf. **Adrian**. (The Roman Martyrology prefers the former, but traditionally in English a distinction has been made between the Christian name Adrian and the pagan, Hadrian.)

Hadulf (St) {2}

19 May
d. ?728. He was simultaneously the abbot of Saint-Vaast and bishop of Arras-Cambrai in Flanders (France).

Haggai (Aggaeus) (St) {2}

15 December
He is the tenth of the Minor Prophets of the Old Testament.

Haimo cf. **Aimo**.

Hannibal-Mary de Francia (St) {2}

1 June
1851–1927. A nobleman born in Messina (Sicily), he was ordained in 1878 and was parish priest at Case Avignone (a very poor place), where he founded orphanages for boys and girls. He became a cathedral canon and the seminary's spiritual director in 1882, and went on to found the 'Daughters of Divine Zeal' (1887) and the 'Rogationists of the Heart of Jesus' (1897). To spread the work of 'Rogare' (petitioning the Sacred Heart), he also founded secular institutes for clerics and laypeople. He was canonized in 2004.

Harmon cf. **Germanus of Auxerre**.

Hartmann (Bl) {2}

23 December
d. 1164. From near Passau (Austria), he was educated at the Augustinian monastery there and became the superior of the cathedral chapter of Salzburg in 1122, when it was reorganized under the Augustinian rule. He was superior of two other Augustinian houses before becoming bishop of Brixen in South Tyrol in 1140. He had the respect of Emperor Frederick Barbarossa and of the pope as well as of the poor people of his diocese. He founded the famous Augustinian monastery of Neustift near Brixen, and his cultus was confirmed for the latter place in 1784.

Hedda of Winchester (St) {2, 4}

7 July
d. 705. An Anglo-Saxon monk and abbot, probably of Whitby, he was made bishop of Dorchester-on-Thames near Oxford (England) in 676 and transferred the see to Winchester. He was a great benefactor of the abbey of Malmesbury and the chief adviser of the king of Wessex.

Hedistius (St) {2, 4}

12 October
? He was martyred at Rome, on the Via Laurentina. The reference to Ravenna in the old Roman Martyrology was erroneous.

Hedwig

The ancient Germanic name of *Hadewig* meaning 'war battle' somehow became a girl's name in the Middle Ages, and has given rise to Hedda and Hadewych (a famous Dutch mystic). Two saints in Poland have the name, which in Polish is Jadwiga, but the Roman Martyrology has preferred the German version of Hedwig.

Hedwig (Jadwiga) of Poland (St) {2}

17 July
1373–99. Being the younger daughter of King Louis I of Hungary and thus a descendent of Charles of Anjou, she was elected and crowned Queen of Poland in 1384 when aged ten. In 1386 she was married to Jogaila, Grand Duke of Lithuania, thus uniting the two countries under one rule. Lithuania was still pagan, the last country in Europe to be so, and Jogaila's baptism before his marriage started its conversion. St Hedwig, a woman of extraordinary piety and kindness, encouraged this by her patronage of religion and scholarship and her work established the Polish–Lithuanian state as a power in Europe under her successors, the Jagiełłonian dynasty. She was also the founder of the Jagiełłonian University at Cracow, which became a major repository of Polish culture. She died at Cracow and was canonized in 1997.

Hedwig (Jadwiga) of Silesia (St) {1, 3}

16 October
?1174–1243. Born at Andechs in Bavaria (Germany) but of Moravian descent, she was a daughter of the duke of Croatia and an aunt of St Elizabeth of Hungary. She was educated at the Benedictine nunnery of Kitzingen and married the Piast prince of Silesia, head of the Polish royal family, at the age of twelve. She bore him seven children who later caused great anxiety to their parents. The couple

fostered religious life in Silesia, bringing in the orders of friars and founding the Cistercian nunnery at Trzebnica as the first nunnery in the country. Under their rule, the imposition of German culture in Silesia was well advanced. She retired to Trzebnica in her widowhood but never took vows as a nun. She was canonized in 1267.

Hegesippus (St) {2, 4}

7 April
d. c.180. A Jewish convert from Jerusalem, he spent twenty years in Rome. Reputed the father of ecclesiastical history, he was the first to trace the succession of bishops of Rome from St Peter to his own day. Only a few chapters of his work survive. It was commended by Eusebius and by St Jerome, who knew it well and made use of it.

Heimerad (St) {2}

28 June
d. 1019. From Messkirch in Baden (Germany), he was a serf who became a priest and was chaplain to the lady of his manor before becoming a wandering pilgrim. He eventually settled at Hasungenberg near Kassel as a hermit, and became famous for his miracles, asceticism and odd behaviour.

(Helan) (St) {4 –deleted}

7 October
C6th? He was allegedly an Irish monk who emigrated to France with six brothers and three sisters and settled near Rheims as a missionary priest during the episcopate of St Remigius.

Helen Aiello (Bl) {2 –add}

19 June
1895–1961. From Montalto Uffugo in the province of Cosenza (Italy), she joined the Sisters of the Precious Blood in 1920, but had to leave

because of a necrotic shoulder and stomach cancer. These conditions healed spontaneously in 1921, and from then she was the recipient of an amazing series of supernatural events. From 1923 until just before her death at Rome, she experienced the stigmata every Good Friday, and also saw apparitions of Our Lady from 1947 which allowed her to foretell future events. She founded a new religious order, the Sisters, Minims of the Passion of Our Lord Jesus Christ, in 1928 although this was only approved in 1949. She was beatified in 2011.

Helen Dall'Olio (Bl) {2}

23 September
1472–1520. From Bologna (Italy), she married against her own inclinations in order to please her mother, yet lived a happy married life for thirty years. After her husband's death she occupied herself completely with works of charity. Already revered during her life, she was the object of a popular cultus after her death, which was confirmed for Bologna in 1828.

Helen the Empress (St) {2, 4}

18 August
c.250–330. From Bithynia in Asia Minor (certainly not from Britain), she became the wife of Constantius Chlorus (who divorced her) and the mother of the Emperor Constantine. She became a Christian after the Edict of Milan in 313 and afterwards lived mostly at Rome. She helped to build many churches there and in the Holy Land and made a famous visit to Jerusalem during which (according to a later tradition) she found the True Cross. Her porphyry sarcophagus is still extant in the Vatican Museum.

Helen Enselmini (Bl) {2}

4 November
d. 1231. From Padua (Italy), when aged twelve she became a Poor Clare nun at Arcella near her native city. It was alleged that her only food for months on end was the Eucharist. Before her death she became blind and dumb. Her cultus was approved for Padua in 1695.

Helen Guerra (Bl) {2}

11 April
1835–1914. The founder of the 'Sisters of St Zita', also called the 'Handmaids of the Holy Spirit', she was born and died at Lucca in Tuscany (Italy). She had a strong devotion to the Holy Spirit and to the propagation of the faith, and taught St Gemma Galgani. Her congregation is prominent in mission territories.

Helen (Jolenta) of Poland (Bl) {2}

11 June
d. 1298. A daughter of the king of Hungary and a niece of St Elizabeth, she married King Boleslas V of Poland in 1256, after whose death in 1279 she lived as a Poor Clare at Gniezno. Her cultus was approved for Gniezno in 1827.

Helen of Skövde (St) {2}

31 July
d. c.1160. A Swedish noblewoman, when she was widowed she spent her fortune on the poor and on the church, still in the process of being established in Sweden. In a family feud connected with a pagan reaction she was waylaid on her way to the church at Skövde and murdered.

Helen Valentini (Bl) {2}

23 April
d. 1458. Married to a knight of Udine near Venice (Italy), she was known in her city both for her devotion to her husband and large family for twenty-five years and for her charity and austerities as an Augustinian tertiary after her husband's death. Her cultus was confirmed for Udine in 1848.

Helconides (St) {2, 4}

28 May
C3rd. A woman from Thessalonica, she was seized at Corinth (Greece) and beheaded in the reign of Gordian after prolonged torture.

Heliena (St) {2}

20 April
C7th. From Laureana near Paestum (Italy), she was persecuted by her parents for her piety so she ran away from home and lived in a cave. She was famous for her strict asceticism, and also for her concern for poor and sick people.

Helier (St) {2}

16 July
C6th. From Tongeren near Liege (Belgium), he went to live as a hermit on the island of Jersey and was murdered by robbers whom he was endeavouring to convert.

Helinand (Bl) {2}

3 February
d. p1230. He was a wandering minstrel and lute player who had performed at the court of the king of France, but converted and became a Cistercian monk at Froidmont.

(Heliodorus, Venustus and Comps) (SS) {4 –deleted}

6 May
C3rd. They are listed as seventy-seven who were martyred in the reign of Diocletian. Heliodorus and seven others seem to have been martyred in Africa, and St Ambrose claimed the greater part of the rest for Milan.

Heliodorus of Altinum (St) {2, 4}

3 July
d. c.400. A Dalmatian, when young he became a close friend of St Jerome whom he followed

to the Holy Land and helped in the preparation of the Vulgate, financially and otherwise. Later he settled in Aquileia (Italy) and was made bishop of Altinum near Venice, a small town since destroyed. He was a great bishop and a brave opponent of Arianism.

(Heliodorus of Magidus and Comps) (SS) {4 –deleted}

21 November
d. c.270. They were listed as martyred at Magidus in Pamphylia (Asia Minor) in the reign of Aurelian.

Helladius of Auxerre (St) {2, 4}

8 May
d. ?388. Bishop of Auxerre (France) for thirty years, he converted St Amator, his eventual successor, to a devout life.

Helladius of Toledo (St) {2, 4}

18 February
d. 632. From Toledo (Spain), he was a military officer at the Visigothic court before joining the abbey of Agali (Agallia) near Toledo, going on to become its abbot in 605. He was made archbishop of Toledo in 615.

Hemma cf. **Gemma**.

Hemma of Gurk (St) {2}

29 June
d. ?1045. Closely related to Emperor St Henry II, as a widow she founded a double Benedictine monastery at Gurk in Carinthia (Austria) and became a nun there. Her cultus was confirmed for Gurk in 1938.

Hemming (Bl) {2}

21 May
d. 1366. From Bälinge (Sweden), he became bishop of Turku in Finland (then Åbo, the

capital of Swedish-ruled Finland). He and St Brigid held each other in esteem.

Henrietta Alfieri (Bl) {2 –add}

23 November
1891–1951. From Borgovercelli near Vercelli (Italy), she joined the Daughters of Charity of St Jean Antida Thouret in 1911 but fell ill of Pott's disease in 1917. In 1923, after a trip to Lourdes, she experienced a spontaneous cure and went to work at San Vittore prison at Milan. There she gained the nickname of 'Angel of San Vittore', especially after the Nazis during the Second World War used it as a holding prison for Jews destined for the gas chambers. Her efforts to help led to her imprisonment and she was due to be shot, but Mussolini intervened to have her released after an appeal by Bl Albert-Ildephonsus Schuster. She died at Milan, and was beatified in 2011.

Henry

Originally *Heimirich,* a Germanic name meaning 'home ruler', it was rendered into Henricus in Latin and common vernacular variants are: German, Heinrich; French, Henri; Danish, Eric; Spanish and Portuguese, Enrique; Hungarian, Emeric; Italian, Enrico, Arrigo or Amerigo (whence America).

Henry II, Emperor (St) {1, 3}

13 July
973–1024. The last emperor of the Saxon dynasty was born in Bavaria, educated by St Wolfgang of Regensburg and, as duke of Bavaria, was elected emperor in 1002 on the death of Otto III. He was crowned by the pope in 1014. With his wife St Cunegund he tried hard to establish peace and prosperity in the empire through the proper establishment of the Ottonian system of administration, which gave an important role to bishops and monasteries. He was genuinely interested in the welfare of the church, was determined in the imposition of ecclesiastical discipline where needed and favoured the Benedictine reform movements, especially of Gorze. His grants to the imperial bishops enabled them to function as secular rulers, and he founded the see of Bamberg out of his own patrimony (his marriage was childless, which led to the legend that it had not been consummated). His justice, tempered with mercy, made him a popular ruler. Much legendary material was added to his biography after his death and before he was canonized in 1146, including the story that he had tried to become a Benedictine (which led to his being declared patron of Benedictine oblates by Pope St Pius X).

Henry Abbot (Bl) {2}

4 July
d. 1597. From Howden (Yorks), he was a layman who converted and was hanged at York for this reason with BB Edward Fulthrop, Thomas Bosgrave and William Andleby. He was beatified in 1929. Cf. **England, Martyrs of.**

Henry (Rigo) of Bozen (Bl) {2}

10 June
d. 1315. From Bozen (Bolzano) in South Tyrol, he moved to Treviso near Venice (Italy) and worked as a labourer and woodcutter after his family died. When old he lived on alms, which he shared with his fellow beggars. His cultus was confirmed for Treviso in 1750.

Henry Heath cf. **Paul-of-St-Mary-Magdalen Heath.**

Henry Hlebowicz (Bl) {2}

9 November
1904–41. A Polish priest, he was shot at Borysów in Poland by the Nazis. Cf. **Poland, Martyrs of the Nazi Occupation of.**

Henry Kaczorowski (Bl) {2}

6 May

1888–1942. A Polish priest, he was gassed at the concentration camp at Dachau with Bl Casimir Gostyński. Cf. **Poland, Martyrs of the Nazi Occupation of**.

Henry Krzystztofik (Bl) {2}

4 August

1908–42. He was the rector of the seminary at Wloclawek when the Nazis invaded Poland. Immediately arrested, he survived almost three years in concentration camps before being gassed at Dachau. Cf. **Poland, Martyrs of the Nazi Occupation of**.

Henry Morse (St) {2}

1 February

1549–1645. A convert from Brome in Suffolk, after working as a lawyer in London he studied for the priesthood at Douai and in Rome. Returning to England in 1624, he became a Jesuit in a prison at York in 1626 and then worked in London and as a military chaplain in the Low Countries. He was selfless in caring for victims of the plague in London of 1636, catching it and then recovering. Imprisoned in 1638 on the testimony of an informer, he was released, worked in various parts of the country, re-arrested nine years later and executed at Tyburn. An attractive character, he was canonized in 1970. Cf. **England, Martyrs of**.

Henry de Ossó y Cervelló (Bl) {2}

27 January

1840–96. Born near Tortosa (Spain), as a priest of that diocese he was inspired by St Teresa of Avila and became a proponent of her teaching on prayer. He founded the 'Society of St Teresa of Jesus' in order to catechize young women and girls and was also involved in other foundations and in publication. He was beatified in 1979.

Henry Rebuschini (Bl) {2}

10 May

1860–1938. From the shores of Lake Como (Italy), his family was wealthy and initially opposed his vocation to the priesthood. So he went to university, and then served in the army and in a family silk factory as an accountant. Finally he had the freedom to study for the diocesan priesthood, but illness prevented this. Then he joined the Camillans in 1887 at Verona, was ordained by the future Pope St Pius X in 1889 and settled at the Cremona community from 1899 until his death, being superior for eleven years. He was a true contemplative as well as a server of sick people, and was beatified in 1997.

Henry Suso (Bl) {2}

25 January

?1295–1366. From Constance (Germany), he became a Dominican when young, was prior in several friaries and was an excellent spiritual director. He was one of the greatest Dominican mystics and his 'Book of the Eternal Wisdom', a classic of German mysticism, is still read. He died at Ulm and his cultus was approved for the Dominicans in 1831.

Henry of Uppsala (St) {2}

19 January

d. ?1157. The details of the career of the English 'Apostle of Finland' are obscure. One manuscript connects him with a trip that Nicholas Brakspear (the future Pope Adrian IV) made to Scandinavia. Made bishop of Uppsala in Sweden in ?1152, he was helped in his missionary activity by King St Eric IX. He then went to Finland as a member of a colonizing expedition led by the same king and was murdered by a Finn in unclear circumstances. He was regarded as a martyr and was canonized in 1158.

Henry Walpole (St) {2}

7 April
1558–95. From Docking (Norfolk), before his conversion he was educated at Norwich, Cambridge (Peterhouse) and Gray's Inn. Then he studied for the priesthood at the English College at Rome, where he became a Jesuit in 1584 before his ordination in 1588. He was an army chaplain in the Netherlands and a seminary teacher in Spain before he went to England, but was arrested the day after his arrival at Bridlington in Yorkshire. He was executed at York and was canonized in 1970. Cf. **England, Martyrs of**.

Henry Webley (Bl) {2}

28 August
d. 1588. A layman from Gloucestershire, he was arrested at Chichester in Sussex for harbouring a priest and executed at Mile End Green in East London with Bl William Dean. He was beatified in 1987. Cf. **England, Martyrs of**.

Heraclas (St) {2, 4}

4 December
d. ?247. Brother of St Plutarch the martyr, he was a philosophy student at Alexandria (Egypt), was converted by Origen and succeeded him as head of the catechetical school there. He became patriarch in 231.

Heraclea, Martyrs of (SS) {2}

19 November
Early C4th. They were forty virgins, widows and holy women martyred at Heraclea in Thrace (now European Turkey).

(Heraclius and Zosimus) *(SS)* *{4 –deleted}*

11 March
C3rd?. They were listed as martyred at Carthage (Roman Africa) in the reign of Valerian and Gallienus.

(Heraclius of Sens) *(St)* *{4 –deleted}*

8 June
d. ?515. From Sens (France), he became bishop there and was one of those present in the cathedral of Rheims at the baptism of Clovis in 496. He was buried at his monastic foundation of St John the Evangelist at Sens.

Heraclius and Paul (SS) {2, 4}

17 May
Early C4th? They were martyred near Galaţi in Romania. The Latin name of the place 'Nivedunum' was erroneously transcribed as 'Noviodunum', and the number of martyrs increased to seven including one Aquilinus. The false tradition emerged that they had been martyred at Nyon on the lake of Geneva (Switzerland).

Herbert of Derwentwater *(St)*

20 March
d. 687. A hermit on an island (later named after him) in Derwentwater in the Lake District (England), he was a friend of St Cuthbert and traditionally died on the same day as him. Despite his obscurity, his name was fairly popular for boys until recently.

Herculanus of Brescia (St) {2, 4}

12 August
C6th. He was a bishop of Brescia in Lombardy (Italy).

Herculanus of Piegare (Bl) {2}

1 June
d. 1451. From Piegare near Perugia (Italy), he became a Franciscan at Sarteano and was famous as a preacher throughout Italy. He died near Lucca and his cultus was confirmed for Massa de Carrara in 1860.

Herculanus of Perugia (St) {2, 4}

7 November
d. 548. He was a bishop and martyr of Perugia (Italy) who was beheaded by a soldier on the orders of the Ostrogothic leader Totilla. The old Roman Martyrology listed him twice, also on 1 March, and the false tradition grew up that the entry for 7 November referred to a separate person, martyred in the reign of Domitian.

(Herculanus of Rome) (St) {4 –deleted}

25 September
C2nd. He is mentioned in the untrustworthy acta of Pope St Alexander I as a Roman soldier who was converted by that pope and martyred shortly afterwards.

Heribert (St) {2, 4}

16 March
d. 1021. From Worms (Germany), he was educated at the monastic school of Gorze, became the chancellor of Emperor Otto III and was made archbishop of Cologne in 998. A great churchman, well informed and enterprising, he was buried at the abbey he founded at Deutz on the Rhine. His extant bull of canonization is a forgery.

Herman cf. **Germanus**.

Herman 'Contractus' of Reichenau (Bl)

24 September
1013–54. A nobleman's son who was severely crippled (hence his nickname), when aged seven he became a child-oblate at the Benedictine abbey of Reichenau on the Rhine (Germany), above Basel. He became a polymath and a famous religious poet, knowing Greek and Arabic and writing on theology, astronomy, mathematics and history. His cultus was confirmed in 1863, but he is not in the Roman Martyrology.

Herman 'Joseph' of Steinfeld (St) {2}

7 April
d. betw. 1241–52. From Cologne, when aged seven he began to have mystical experiences which made him famous throughout Germany. Joining the Premonstratensians at Steinfeld in the Eifel, he served as sacristan, gained his nickname through a mystical marriage to Our Lady and helped propagate the spurious legend of St Ursula. He has left some mystical writings, and his cultus was confirmed in 1958.

Herman Stepień (Bl) {2}

19 July
1910–43. A Franciscan Conventual friar, he was shot with Bl Achilles Puchala at Borowikowszczyzna during the Nazi occupation of Poland. Cf. **Poland, Martyrs of the Nazi Occupation of**.

Hermas (St) {2, 4}

9 May
C1st. A Roman, he was mentioned by St Paul in his Letter to the Romans (16:14). A Byzantine tradition, not accepted by the Roman Martyrology, makes him a bishop of Philippi and a martyr.

(Hermas, Serapion and Polyaenus) (SS) {4 –deleted}

18 August
? They were listed as Roman martyrs who were dragged by their feet over rough ground by a pagan mob until they died. However Hermas seems to be a duplication of Hermes of Rome, and the other two to have been martyrs of Alexandria (Egypt).

Hermeland (Herblain, Erblon) (St) {2, 4}

25 March
d. c.720. He had been a cup-bearer at the Frankish royal court before he became a monk

at Fontenelle in Normandy (France) under St Lambert. Then he became the first abbot of a daughter foundation on the island of Aindre in the estuary of the Loire near Nantes, where the suburb of St Herblain now stands.

Hermellus of Constantinople (St) {4 –deleted}

3 August

? This alleged martyr was listed in the old Roman Martyrology but was unknown to the Byzantines. He either did not exist, or the name of the city was a copyist's error.

Hermenegild the Goth (St) {2, 3}.

13 April

d. 586. Son of Leovigild, the Visigothic king of Spain, he married a Frankish Catholic princess and was a subsidiary ruler at Seville. He became a Catholic and rebelled against his father, but was captured and executed. St Gregory the Great alleged that this was as a result of his conversion, but this is not confirmed by other contemporary authors. His cultus was confined to local calendars in 1969.

Hermenegild-of-the-Assumption Iza y Aregita and Comps (BB) {2 –add}

27 August

d. 1936. They are the six Trinitarian martyrs of Ciudad Real in Spain, who were part of a religious group rounded up at Alcázar de San Juan on 20 August in the context of vicious local public hostility during the Spanish Civil War. The others in the group were Franciscans and a Dominican novice. After being imprisoned in an abandoned hermitage on the outskirts of the town, they were shot in two groups at midnight six days later. The Trinitarians only were beatified in 2013. Cf. **Spanish Civil War, Martyrs of** and list in appendix.

(Hermes and Adrian) (SS) {4 –deleted}

1 March

End C3rd? According to the old Roman Martyrology, they were martyred at Marseilles in the reign of Maximian Herculius. They are now generally identified with the Massylitan martyrs on whose feast day St Augustine delivered a discourse. The original reading of the martyrology was Massylis (Marula) in Numidia (Roman Africa), the spelling of which is very similar to the Latin Massilia (Marseilles).

Hermes and Gaius (SS) {2, 4}

4 January

Early C4th. They were martyred in two towns on the Danube, in what is now Bulgaria. Hermes died at Retaria, and Gaius at Bononia. A false tradition grew up that the latter place was Bologna in Italy, and the former feast in their honour there was abolished in 1914. The old Roman Martyrology added a companion Haggai, who has been deleted.

Hermes of Rome (St) {2, 3}

28 August

C3rd. According to Pope St Damasus, he was a Greek expatriate martyred and buried at the Catacombs of Basilla on the Salarian Way outside Rome. The very dubious acta of Pope St Alexander described Hermes as a Roman martyred with him and several companions in the reign of Hadrian. Their cultus (which was confined to local calendars in 1969) was both ancient and widespread. The companions have been deleted from the Roman Martyrology.

Hermes of Bononia (St) {2, 4}

31 December

d. c.300. Listed as a Roman exorcist, he was actually martyred at Bononia in Moesia, on the Danube (the same place as in the entry for Hermes and Gaius, above).

Hermias (St) {2, 4}

31 May
C3rd. He was martyred at Comana in Pontus, Asia Minor.

(Hermogenes, Donatus and Comps) *(SS)*
{4 –deleted}

12 December
? Twenty-four martyrs, they are merely listed as having been driven into a marsh and there left to perish of cold and exhaustion. No other details are known.

Hermogenes and Elpidius (SS) {2, 4}

18 April
? They were martyred at Melitene in Roman Armenia, Asia Minor (although they have no cultus in the East). In the old Roman Martyrology, Elpidius became Expeditus and Gaius, Aristonicus, Rufus and Galata were added. These have been deleted. The cultus of St Expeditus as a patron against procrastination dates from C17th Germany.

(Hermolaus, Hermippus and Hermocrates) *(SS) {4 –deleted}*

27 July
Early C4th? According to the legend Hermolaus, an old priest of Nicomedia (Asia Minor), converted St Pantaleon the imperial physician and was martyred with him and with the two brothers Hermippus and Hermocrates.

Hermylius and Stratonicus (SS) {2, 4}

13 January
d. c.310. Hermylus, a deacon of Singidunum (near Belgrade, Yugoslavia), and Stratonicus, his servant, were drowned in the Danube in

the reign of Licinius. Their acta are, however, unreliable.

Herodion, Asyncritus and Phlegon (SS) {2, 4}.

8 April
C1st. St Paul refers to them in his Letter to the Romans (Rom. 16:11), the first as his relative.

Heron, Ateus, Isidore and Dioscorus (SS) {2, 4}

14 December
d. 250. The first three were burnt to death at Alexandria (Egypt) in the reign of Decius. Dioscorus, a boy, was merely whipped and set free.

(Heron of Antioch) *(St) {4 –deleted}*

17 October
d. ?136. A disciple of St Ignatius of Antioch (Syria), he succeeded him as bishop in ?116. He is doubtfully listed as a martyr.

Hervey the Blind (St) {2}

17 June
C6th. The son of a Welsh minstrel at the Frankish court at Paris and blind from birth, he was taken as a child to Brittany (France), where he grew up to become a teacher and a minstrel himself. Though blind he became abbot of Plouvien, whence he migrated with part of his community to Lanhouarneau. He is still a popular saint in Brittany and is represented as a blind man being led about by a wolf.

Hesperus, Zoë, Cyriac and Theodolus (SS) {2, 4}

2 May
C2nd. A married Phrygian couple and their two sons, they were slaves of a rich pagan native of Attalia in Pamphylia (Asia Minor)

during the reign of Hadrian and were allegedly thrown into a furnace when they refused to take part in a thanksgiving sacrifice for the birth of a son to their master.

Hesychius of Antioch (St) {2, 4}

29 May
d. ?303. A Roman soldier and officer, master of the palace at Antioch (Syria), he threw away his military belt (part of his insignia) and proclaimed himself a Christian when the Emperor Maximian ordered a persecution. As a punishment for this he was dressed as a woman and drowned in the River Orontes.

Hesychius of Durostorum (St) {2, 4}

15 June
d. ?302. A Roman soldier, he was martyred at Durostorum (now Silistra in Bulgaria) with St Julian.

Hesychius of Gaza (St) {2, 4}

3 October
C4th. A disciple of St Hilarion, he became a monk under him at Majuma near Gaza in the Holy Land. He followed his master in the latter's attempts to find solitude and, when Hilarion fled to Sicily, Hesychius spent three years searching for him. At Hilarion's death in 311 he took the body back to Majuma, where he lived until his own death.

Hesychius of Vienne (St) {2}

12 November
d. p552. A senator, he became bishop of Vienne (France) and was the father of St Avitus, his successor.

Hewald cf. **Ewald**.
Hia cf. **Ia**.

Hidulf of Trier (St) {2}

11 July
d. 707. From Regensburg in Bavaria (Germany), he became a monk at Trier and was later ordained as a missionary bishop. In ?676 he resigned and became abbot-founder of Moyenmoutier in the Jura. When he died he was abbot both of this and of Bonmoutier (afterwards called Saint-Dié) nearby.

Hierlath cf. **Jarlath**.

Hieron and Comps (SS) {2, 4}

7 November
Early C4th. They were martyred at Mitilene in Roman Armenia (Asia Minor). The Roman Martyrology has deleted their number (thirty-three) and the names of Nicander and Hesychius.

(Hieronides, Leontius, Serapion and Comps) (SS) {4 –deleted}

12 September
Early C4th? According to the legend, Hieronides was a very old deacon and Leontius and Serapion were brothers. They were thrown into the sea at Alexandria (Egypt) in the reign of Diocletian with Seleucus (not, as listed in the old Roman Martyrology, Selesius), Valerian and Straton.

Hieronymus cf. **Jerome**.

(Hierotheus) (St) {4 –deleted}

4 October
? It is likely that the alleged teacher and friend of St Dionysius the Areopagite either never existed or was of the C4th or the C5th. He has been claimed as bishop of Athens, of Jerusalem or of Segovia in Spain (the last is certainly false).

(Hilaria, Digna, and Comps) *(SS) {4 –deleted}*

12 August
Early C4th? Hilaria, alleged to be the mother of St Afra of Augsburg, was described as having been seized with her three maids while visiting her daughter's tomb and burnt alive. The companions (Quiriacus, Euprepia, Eunomia, Quiriacus, Largio, Crescentian, Nimmia, Juliana and another twenty) were Roman martyrs buried on the Ostian Way who allegedly died on the same day.

(Hilarinus of Ostia) *(St) {4 –deleted}*

16 July
Early C4th? He was allegedly a monk martyred with St Donatus of Arezzo, whose body was transferred to Ostia near Rome. This is historically false, and if he existed he was a martyr of Ostia.

Hilarinus of Perse *(St)*

15 June
C8th. A secular priest and schoolmaster in the Frankish Empire, he was killed by marauders at his base at Perse on the Lot River (France). His cultus was confirmed for Rodez in 1883, but he is not listed in the Roman Martyrology.

Hilarion the Great (St) {2, 3}

21 October
d. ?371. From Gaza in the Holy Land, he became a Christian and a disciple of St Anthony the Great while studying at Alexandria (Egypt). On his return to Gaza he was the first local Christian hermit in the desert nearby, but attracted so many disciples that he was able to found several monasteries. The latter part of his life was occupied with escaping from the crowds who followed him on account of his miracles. He lived on Mt Sinai, also in Egypt, Sicily, Dalmatia and finally on Cyprus, where he died at Paphos. His cultus in the Latin rite was confined to particular calendars in 1969.

Hilarion the New (St) {2}

6 June
d. 845. He was abbot of the Dalmatian monastery at Constantinople, and was repeatedly ill-treated and sent into exile for defending the veneration of sacred images. He died in peace in his monastery.

Hilarion of Pelekete (St) {2}

28 March
C8th. He was abbot of the monastery of Pelekete on the Bithynian Olympus near Brusa (Asia Minor), and was persecuted for his defence of sacred images.

Hilary, Pope (St) {2, 4}

29 February
d. 468. From Sardinia, he held high office in the Roman curia under St Leo the Great, who sent him as papal legate to the 'Robber Synod of Ephesus' in 449 (from which he narrowly escaped with his life). He became pope in 461, and fought energetically against the Nestorian and Monophysite heresies. Under him the first recorded synod was held at Rome.

Hilary and Tatian (SS) {2, 4}

16 March
? Hilary was a bishop of Aquileia (Italy) who was beheaded with Tatian. The Roman Martyrology has deleted the companions Felix, Largus and Dionysius.

Hilary of Arles (St) {2}

5 May
c.400–49. From Lorraine (France), while still a pagan he held an important office in the local administration until St Honoratus, a relative, invited him to visit his monastery recently

founded at Lérins. He was baptized and became a monk there, and when St Honoratus became archbishop of Arles he accompanied him as his secretary. He succeeded to the bishopric and was zealous in trying to establish metropolitan authority over other bishops of Gaul, which led him to be rebuked by Pope St Leo the Great. However his personal sanctity led him to be venerated even before his death.

Hilary of Carcassonne (St) {2}

3 June
C6th. He was bishop of Carcassonne (France).

Hilary Januszewski (Bl) {2}

25 March
1907–45. A Polish Discalced Carmelite friar, he died of typhus at the concentration camp at Dachau after nursing sufferers who had been abandoned to die in an isolation building. Cf. **Poland, Martyrs of the Nazi Occupation of**.

Hilary of Mende (St) {2, 4}

25 October
C6th. From Mende in the Massif Central (France), he became a hermit under the influence of the monastery of Lérins (where he spent some time) and founded a monastery before being made bishop of his native city.

Hilary of Poitiers (St) {1, 3}

13 January
d. 367. Of a pagan patrician family at Poitiers (France), he studied rhetoric and philosophy and married young. Shortly afterwards he became a Christian and was elected bishop of Poitiers in 353. He fought energetically against the Arianism of Emperor Constantius and was exiled to Phrygia (Asia Minor) for four years in 356. There he was able to study the theology of the Eastern fathers and

to write his magisterial work on the Trinity. After his return he continued his powerful defence of the Nicene Creed as well as introducing into the West much of Eastern Trinitarian and Christological thought, including the explanation of the divinity of Christ. He was declared a doctor of the Church in 1851.

Hilary of Toulouse (St) {2}

20 May
d. c.400. He was a bishop of Toulouse (France).

Hilda (Hild) (St) {2}

17 November
614–80. From Northumbria (England) and a relative of King St Edwin, she was baptized as a child in 631 by St Paulinus and became a nun at Hartlepool when aged thirty-three under the guidance of St Aidan. She became abbess in 649, and went on to become the first abbess of the double monastery (with monks and nuns) at Whitby in 657. The monastery held to the Celtic rule and liturgy, and she herself was a determined opponent of the Romanizing policy of St Wilfrid. However the monastery was the venue of the Synod of Whitby, called by King Oswy in 664 in order to make a definitive choice between Roman and Celtic observances, and she and her community abided by its decision to prescribe the Roman rite. She died after a long illness.

Hildebrand cf. **Gregory VII, Pope**.

Hildegard of Bingen (St) {2}

17 September
1098–1179. The 'Sibyl of the Rhine' was from Bemersheim in the Palatinate (Germany) and became a child-oblate at a Benedictine nunnery at Disibodenberg when aged eight. As a young woman she was made superior there, and moved the community to Rupertsberg near Bingen in ?1147. She had mystical experiences

from childhood and started publishing these when aged forty, becoming the first great German mystic. She denounced the vices of society and of the famous with fearlessness and justice, and her writings (which are prophetic, doctrinal and speculative) led her to be accused by numerous enemies. However she was defended by St Bernard and by his disciple, Pope Bl Eugene III. There has been much modern interest in her writings, music and art, and several works have been translated into English (some tendentiously) and her music performed.

Hildegard Burjan (Bl) {2 –add}

11 June
1883–1933. From a liberal Jewish family at Görlitz (Germany), she studied philosophy and sociology at university level before marrying a rich Hungarian industrialist and settling with him at Vienna (Austria). In 1909 she converted after recovery from a major illness, and thereafter took a practical interest in the social teaching of the church. This led to her founding a religious sisterhood called *Caritas Socialis* to help women and children in adverse conditions and also terminally ill people. She was active in the hospice movement, and in 1919 was elected to the Austrian parliament as one of its first woman members. As such she was active in furthering the interest of poor and working-class people, and in promoting the social well-being of women. She was beatified in 2012.

Hilduard (Hilward, Garibald) (St) {2}

7 September
d. c.760. A missionary bishop in Flanders, he founded the abbey at Dikelvenne on the Schlede above Ghent (Belgium).

Hiltrude (St) {2, 4}

27 September
d. p800. Daughter of the count of Poitou (France), she became a hermit attached to the abbey of Liessies which her father had founded and which had her brother as abbot.

Himerius (Immer, Imier) (St) {2}

13 November
d. ?612. A missionary monk in the Jura, he has a town in Berne canton (Switzerland) named St Imier after him.

(Himerius of Amelia) (St) {4 –deleted}

17 June
d. c.560. A Calabrian hermit, he was made bishop of Ameila in Umbria (Italy). He was described as a very austere man, primarily with himself and also with others. His relics were taken to Cremona in 995, where he is venerated as a principal patron.

(Hippolytus of Antioch) (St) {4 –deleted}

30 January
? He was listed as martyred at Antioch (Syria), but the details given in the old Roman Martyrology are borrowed from the story of St Hippolytus of Rome.

Hippolytus of Belley (St) {2}

20 November
d. c.770. A monk at St Claude in the Jura (France), he became bishop of Belley in 755 but resigned and returned to his abbey.

Hippolytus Galantini (Bl) {2}

20 March
1565–1619. From Florence (Italy), he was a silk weaver. When eleven years old he started to help priests in catechizing children and was imitated in this by others, whom he formed into the congregation of Italian Doctrinarians. It soon spread throughout Italy. He died at Florence and was beatified in 1825.

(Hippolytus of Porto) *(St) {3 –deleted}*

22 August

He is a duplication of St Hippolytus of Rome, the confusion having arisen through the latter having a basilica dedicated to him at Porto. The old Roman Martyrology listed him as a bishop of Porto martyred by drowning in the reign of Alexander. This assertion is false, and his cultus was suppressed in 1969.

Hippolytus of Rome (St) {1, 3}

13 August

d. ?235. A native priest of Rome, he supported the rigourist faction over the question as to whether the church could absolve those guilty of serious sin. He was the bitter enemy of Pope St Callistus I, and caused himself to be elected anti-pope. With St Pontian he was exiled to the Sardinian mines and was probably reconciled to the church there before his martyrdom. He is one of the most important ecclesiastical writers of his time. His story has been overlaid by spurious legends, however, such as the one that connects him with the death of St Laurence. St Concordia (a genuine martyr about whom nothing is known) was also falsely linked with him and they (with companions) were celebrated with a common feast day before 1969. He is now celebrated with St Pontian.

Holy Land (Martyrs of) (SS)

There were five groups of anonymous martyrs of the Holy Land listed in the old Roman Martyrology. Two have been kept:

19 February

d. 507. There was a raid by Bedouins allied to Persia, and many hermits and monks were slaughtered.

16 May

d. 614. Forty-four monks of the laura of Mar Saba were massacred during the invasion by Shah Chosroes II of Persia.

Three have been deleted:

28 May

d. c.410. There was a massacre of monks by Bedouin early in the reign of the Emperor Theodosius II.

22 June

d. ?614. Allegedly 1480 were massacred at Samaria or in its neighbourhood during the same Persian invasion.

16 August

? A group of thirty-three martyrs has been mentioned, about whom no details are known.

Homobonus (St) {2, 4}

13 November

d. 1197. A merchant of Cremona (Italy), he was famous in his city for his scrupulous honesty, his model family life and his charity to the poor. He died during Mass and was canonized within two years.

Honorata (St) {2, 4}

11 January

C5th. The sister of St Epiphanius, bishop of Pavia (Italy), she was a nun at Pavia when the soldiers of Odoacer, the king of the Heruli, kidnapped her. She was ransomed by her brother and returned to Pavia.

(Honoratus, Fortunatus, Arontius and Sabinian) *(SS) {4 –deleted}*

27 August

d. 303. They were beheaded at Potenza (Italy) in the reign of Maximian, and are one of the groups commemorated under the title of 'The Twelve Brothers'.

Honoratus of Amiens (St) {2, 4}

16 May

d. c.600. From near Amiens (France), he became bishop there. The church and street of St Honoré in Paris take their name from him.

Honoratus of Arles (St) {2}

16 January
c.350–429. Born probably in Lorraine of a Roman consular family, he converted from paganism in his youth and went to the East to study monasticism. Returning to the West, he founded a famous monastery on the Mediterranean island of Lérins (France). He was forced to accept the archbishopric of Arles in 426, but died three years later.

Honoratus of Buzancais (Bl) {2}

9 January
d. 1250. From Buzancais in Berry (France), he was a rich and charitable cattle merchant. On his return from a journey he found that he had been robbed by his servants and, when he remonstrated with them, they killed him at Parthenay in Poitou. There he is venerated as a martyr.

(Honoratus of Fondi) (St) {4 –deleted}

16 January
C6th. The alleged abbot-founder of the monastery of Fondi on the border between Lazio and Campania (Italy), he had a biography in the 'Dialogues' attributed to St Gregory the Great.

Honoratus Koźmiński of Biała Podlaska (Bl) {2}

13 October
1829–1916. Born into a pious family near Lublin (Poland), he studied architecture at Warsaw but lost his faith in the secular atmosphere of the university. But then he was imprisoned for a few months in 1846 on suspicion of conspiracy against the Russian government and caught typhoid. The experience of nearly dying restored his faith. Once released, he joined the Capuchins in Warsaw and was ordained in 1852, becoming well known as a preacher, confessor and prison chaplain. His friary was suppressed after the Polish rebellion of 1863 and he ended up in a prison-friary at Nowa Miasto, where he died. He was beatified in 1988.

Honoratus of Milan (St) {2, 4}

8 February
d. c.570. He became bishop of Milan (Italy) in 567 but fled into exile when the Lombards captured the city in 569 and died at Genoa.

Honoratus of Subiaco (St) {2}

23 May
End C6th. He succeeded St Benedict as a monastic superior at Subiaco (Italy).

Honoratus of Vercelli (St) {2, 4}

29 October
C4–5th. From Vercelli (Italy), he was educated there by St Eusebius, became a monk and accompanied his master into exile at Scythopolis in the Holy Land in 355. In 396 he was elected bishop of his native city on the recommendation of St Ambrose, whom he assisted on his deathbed.

Honoré cf. **Honoratus of Amiens**.

Honorina (St) {2}

27 February
? She is an early martyr of Gaul but her acta have been lost. Her veneration is ancient at Rouen in Normandy (France).

(Honorius, Eutychius and Stephen) (SS) {4 –deleted}

21 November
d. c.300. They were listed as martyred at Asta in Andalucia (Spain), in the reign of Diocletian.

(Honorius of Brescia) (St) {4 –deleted}

24 April
d. ?586. A hermit near Brescia (Italy), he became bishop there in 577.

Honorius of Canterbury (St) {2}

30 September
d. 653. A Roman monk, he joined the mission of St Augustine in England in 601 and succeeded St Justus as archbishop of Canterbury in 627, being consecrated at Lincoln by St Paulinus. He himself ordained as bishops St Felix for East Anglia and St Ithamar (the first native bishop) for Rochester. His attribute is a baker's peel (shovel), often with loaves upon it.

Hormisdas, Pope (St) {2, 4}

6 August
d. 523. From Frosinone in Lazio (Italy), he succeeded St Symmachus as pope in 514. He is best remembered for the profession of faith called the *Formula of Hormisdas* which was accepted in the East in the reign of Justin I (519), thus ending the Acacian schism. His son, St Silverius, became pope in 536.

(Hormisdas the Persian) (St) {4 –deleted}

8 August
d. 420. A young Persian nobleman who held the office of satrap, he refused to apostatize and was degraded by Shah Bahram to the rank of army camel driver and subsequently either executed or exiled.

Horsiesius (Orsisius) (St)

15 June
d. c.380. A favourite disciple of St Pachomius in Egypt, after his master died in an epidemic he succeeded him as superior of the cenobites of Tabennesis. Meek and gentle, he oversaw the expansion of the congregation but lacked leadership qualities and resigned in favour of St Theodore after a revolt by some of the monks in 351. He became superior again when St Theodore himself died in 368. He is the author of an ascetical treatise which St Jerome translated into Latin. He is not in the Roman Martyrology.

Hosanna Andreasi (St) {2}

18 June
d. 1505. A noblewoman of Mantua (Italy), she became a penitential Dominican tertiary and combined works of active charity with an ascetic and poverty-inspired life at home.

Hosanna-Catherine Cosie (Bl) {2}

27 April
d. 1565. Catherine was the daughter of Orthodox parents in Montenegro but became a Catholic at Cattaro (then under Venetian rule, now Kotor in Montenegro) and became a Dominican tertiary, taking the name of Hosanna. Her cultus was confirmed for Kotor in 1928.

Hosea (Osee) (St) {2}

17 October
He is the first of the Minor Prophets of the Old Testament.

Hospicius (St) {2, 4}

21 May
d. ?581. From Nice (France), he became a hermit nearby at the place now named Cap-Saint-Hospice after him.

Hospitaller Martyrs of Spain (BB) {2}

d. 1936. In the year of the outbreak of the civil war in Spain, seventy-one Hospitallers of St John were shot by the Republicans. They were from Toledo, Tarragona, Barcelona, Madrid and Castile and also included seven

Colombians who had been studying at Ciempozuelos at Madrid and who were seized at Barcelona when trying to return home. They were beatified in 1992. Cf. **Spanish Civil War, Martyrs of** and list in appendix.

Hroznata (Bl) {2}

14 July
1160–1217. A Czech nobleman, he was a courtier of King Ottokar the Great of Bohemia before the death of his wife and baby son. Then he founded the Premonstratensian abbey of Teplá near the Bavarian border and became a monk there. He was seized by some local nobles who coveted the monastery's lands and died of starvation in a dungeon, being subsequently venerated as a martyr. His cultus was approved for Prague in 1897.

Hubert of Liege (St) {2, 4}

30 May
d. 727. A Frankish courtier, he was widowed and (according to his late biography) was converted while he was out hunting in circumstances similar to those narrated of St Eustace and others. Then he is alleged to have become a hermit in the Ardennes or a monk at Stavelot (Belgium). Eventually he succeeded St Lambert as bishop of Maastricht in about 706 and transferred the see to Liege in Belgium, being the first bishop there. He is venerated as the apostle of the Ardennes, which was a remaining stronghold of paganism.

Hugh de Actis (Bl) {2}

26 July
d. 1250. From Serra San Quirico near Camerino (Italy), after studying at Bologna he became a monk under St Sylvester, whose devoted disciple he was. He died at Sassoferrato, and his cultus was approved for Nocera in 1717.

Hugh of Bonnevaux (Bl) {2}

1 April
d. 1194. A nephew of St Hugh of Grenoble, he became a Cistercian at Mezières. He was made abbot of Leoncel in 1163, and transferred to Bonnevaux in the Jura (France) in 1169. He had unusual powers of divination and exorcism, but is chiefly remembered as the mediator between Pope Alexander III and Emperor Frederick Barbarossa.

Hugh Canefro (St) {2}

8 October
d. a.1233. He was a chaplain of the Knights of St John of Jerusalem at Genoa (Italy).

Hugh Faringdon (Bl) {2}

15 November
Cf. **Benedictine Martyrs of the Reformation**.

Hugh of Fosse (Bl) {2}

10 February
d. ?1163. From Fosse near Namur (Belgium), he was chaplain to the bishop of Cambrai before becoming a monk at Prémontre (north of Soissons, France) under St Norbert, whose companion and assistant he became and whom he succeeded as abbot of Prémontre and superior-general of the Premonstratensian order. His cultus was confirmed for Namur in 1927.

Hugh the Great (St) {2}

29 April
1024–1109. A nobleman from Samur (France), he became a Benedictine monk at Cluny in 1039 and was elected abbot in 1049 when aged twenty-five. He was abbot for sixty years, and during this period was the adviser of nine popes, was consulted and revered by all the sovereigns of western Europe and governed over 1000 monasteries and dependent

houses of the Cluniac congregation. The vast abbey church at Cluny, at 169m long the biggest in Europe until the new St Peter's in Rome, was consecrated in 1095. An extremely gifted man, he retained his humility and charity, founding a leper hospital at Marcigny at which he nursed the inmates himself. He was canonized in 1120.

Hugh Green (Bl) {2}

19 August
d. 1642. From London, he was educated at Peterhouse, Cambridge before his conversion. Then he studied for the priesthood at Douai, was ordained there in 1612 and worked in Dorset before being captured and hanged at Dorchester. Cf. **England, Martyrs of**.

Hugh of Grenoble (St) {2, 4}

1 April
1053–1132. From Châteauneuf d'Isère (France), when aged twenty-five he became a lay canon at Valence and was made bishop of Grenoble in 1080. Convinced of his own inefficiency in the struggle especially against simony and clerical concubinage, he resigned and became a Benedictine monk at the austere monastery of Chaise-Dieu. Pope St Gregory VII refused his resignation, however. He gave to St Bruno the land for his new monastery at Grande Chartreuse.

Hugh of Lincoln (St) {2, 4}

17 November
1140–1200. From near Grenoble (France), he became a canon regular locally but joined the Carthusians at Chartreuse in 1160. In 1175 he was invited by King Henry II of England to make the first English Carthusian foundation at Witham in Somerset, which he did in the face of many difficulties. He was made bishop of Lincoln in 1181, and governed justly and wisely. He began the present cathedral of Lincoln and defended and befriended the Jews of the city. He died at London while on an embassy to France, and the kings of England and Scotland helped to carry his body back to Lincoln. Canonized in 1220, he is usually depicted as a bishop but sometimes as a Carthusian, in either case accompanied by a pet swan (or with seven stars above him, in mistake for St Hugh of Grenoble).

Hugh dei Lippi-Uguccioni (St) {1 –group}

17 February
d. 1282. He accompanied St Philip Benizi to France and Germany and was vicar-general of the order in Germany for eight years. He died on Mt Senario in Italy. Cf. **Servites, Founders of**.

Hugh More (Bl) {2}

28 August
d. 1588. From Grantham in Lincolnshire, he was educated at Oxford and at Gray's Inn (London) before becoming a convert at Rheims. He was hanged as a result at Lincoln's Inn Fields in London and beatified in 1929. Cf. **England, Martyrs of**.

Hugh of Noara (St) {2}

17 November
C12th. He was the first abbot of the Cistercian abbey of Noara (Sicily).

Hugh of Rouen (St) {2, 4}

9 April
d. 730. A Frankish nobleman, when very young he apparently became a monk at Fontenelle. Then he became vicar-general of Metz (France) and was then made bishop of Rouen and of Paris, also abbot of Fontenelle and of Jumièges. Before his death, however, he resigned all these offices and died at Jumièges as a simple monk.

Hugh Taylor (Bl) {2}

26 November
1562–85. From Durham, he was ordained at Rheims and was seized and executed at York soon after his arrival there. He was the first victim of the law of 1585 which defined as treason the entry into England by those who had been ordained abroad. He was beatified in 1987. Cf. **England, Martyrs of**.

Hugolin of Gualdo (Bl) {2}

1 January
C14th. He was allegedly the founder and first prior of the Augustinian friary at Gualdo in Umbria (Italy) and his cultus was approved in 1919. There is evidence that he was a Benedictine and that his monastery became Augustinian after his death.

Hugolin Magalotti (Bl) {2}

11 December
d. 1373. From Camerino (Italy), he became a Franciscan tertiary and a hermit there. His cultus was confirmed for Camerino in 1856.

Hugolin Zefferini (Bl)

22 March
d. c.1470? An Augustinian friar who lived at Cortona (or perhaps Mantua), his cultus was confirmed for Cortona in 1804. He is not listed in the Roman Martyrology.

Humbeline (St) {2}

12 February
1092–1136 A younger sister of St Bernard of Clairvaux, she married a rich Burgundian nobleman and was leading a worldly life when a visit to her brother in Clairvaux resulted in her spiritual conversion. She obtained her husband's consent to become a nun, entered the Benedictine nunnery of Jully-les Nonnais near Troyes (France) and became abbess

there. She died in St Bernard's arms at Jully. Her cultus was approved in 1763.

Humbert III of Savoy (Bl) {2}

4 March
1136–88. A count of Savoy, he had Bl Amedius of Lausanne as a tutor and succeeded to the throne at the age of thirteen. Later he retired to the Cistercian abbey of Hautcombe, but left to return to power and to get married for state reasons (he was three, perhaps four times married). He returned to the monastery after an heir was born, however, and the Cistercians claimed that he became a monk. His cultus was confirmed for Turin (Italy) in 1838.

Humfrid of Thérouanne (St) {2}

8 March
d. 871. He was a monk at the Benedictine abbey of Prüm in the Eifel (Germany) at the time of its greatest splendour, and became bishop of Thérouanne near St Omer (France) as well as abbot of St Bertin. He was a source of strength and comfort to his people during the Norse invasions which devastated his diocese.

Humiliana de'Cerchi (Bl) {2}

19 May
1220–46. From Florence (Italy), she married at the age of sixteen. After the early death of her husband she became the first Franciscan tertiary at Florence, as her being the mother of two little girls prevented her from joining the Poor Clares. Her cultus was approved for Florence in 1694.

Humilis of Bisignano (St) {2}

26 November
1582–1637. From Bisignano in Calabria (Italy), he became a Franciscan lay brother

and was so widely known for his sanctity that he was called to Rome, where Popes Gregory XV and Urban VIII consulted him. He was canonized in 2002.

Humilitas (or Rosanna) (Bl) {2}

22 May
1226–1310. From Faenza in the Romagna (Italy), when aged fifteen she was compelled to marry a frivolous young man named Ugoletto. After nine years of marriage he became seriously ill, recovered, converted, became a monk and allowed Humilitas to become a nun. She first lived as a hermit near the Vallumbrosan monastery of St Apollinaris where her husband was a monk and later (persuaded by the Vallumbrosan superior-general) founded and governed the first two houses of Vallumbrosan nuns. Her cultus was confirmed for Faenza and Florence in 1720.

Humphrey cf. **Onuphrius**.

Humphrey Middlemore (Bl) {2}

19 June
d. 1535. A Carthusian monk of the London Charterhouse, he was hanged at Tyburn with two of his brethren, BB Sebastian Newdigate and William Exmew, for denying the royal supremacy in spiritual matters of King Henry VIII. He was beatified in 1886. Cf. **England, Martyrs of**.

Humphrey Pritchard (Bl) {2}

5 July
d. 1589. He was a Welsh employee at the Catherine Wheel Inn at Oxford, which was a local centre of Catholic activity. When the place was raided he was seized with BB Thomas Belson, George Nichols and Richard Yaxley and was executed at Oxford. He was beatified in 1987. Cf. **England, Martyrs of**.

Hunger (St) {2}

22 December
d. 866. Bishop of Utrecht (Netherlands) from 856, during the Norse invasions he fled to the abbey of Prüm in the Eifel (Germany) and died there.

Hyacinth of Amastris (St) {2, 4}

17 July
C3rd? He cut down a tree sacred to a pagan god, was tortured as a result and died in prison at Amastris in Paphlagonia (Asia Minor).

(Hyacinth of Caesarea) (St) {4 –deleted}

3 July
d. c.120. According to his legend, he was from Caesarea in Cappadocia (Asia Minor) and became a chamberlain of the Emperor Trajan. When his faith was discovered he was imprisoned and offered as sustenance only meat consecrated to idols. This he refused, and died in consequence of starvation.

Hyacinth Castañeda (St) {1 –group}

7 November
d. 1773. From Setavo near Valencia (Spain), he became a Dominican priest and was a missionary firstly in China and then in Vietnam. There he was beheaded at Ket Cho with St Vincent Lê Quang Liêm on the orders of King Trịnh Sâm, a local ruler. Cf. **Vietnam, Martyrs of**.

Hyacinth Cormier (Bl) {2}

17 December
1832–1916. From Orleans (France), he joined the Dominicans and became master-general in 1904. He oversaw the spread of his order, promoted Thomism and founded the Angelicum in Rome in 1908. A noted ascetic writer of gentleness, firmness and wisdom based on a charism of liturgical prayer and sacred study,

he faithfully interpreted the church's teaching during the Modernist crisis. He was beatified in 1994.

Hyacinth of Fara (St) {2, 4}

9 September
? His shrine is at Fara in the Sabine country, about thirty miles from Rome, and he was martyred somewhere nearby. The Roman Martyrology has deleted his companions Alexander and Tiburtius.

Hyacinth Odrowaz (St) {2, 3}

15 August
1185–1257. Nicknamed 'the Apostle of Poland', he was from Silesia and became a canon of Cracow (Poland) before becoming a Dominican in Rome under St Dominic. In three missionary journeys he is alleged to have travelled through Poland, Scandinavia, Russia and as far as Tibet and China. The details of his life are, however, very uncertain. He died at Cracow, was canonized in 1594 and his cultus was confined to particular calendars in 1969.

Hyacinth Orfanel (Bl) {2}

10 September
1578–1622. From near Valencia (Spain), he became a Dominican at Barcelona, was sent to Japan and was burnt alive at Nagasaki in the 'Great Martyrdom' after many years on mission there. Cf. **Charles Spinola and Comps**, **Great Martyrdom at Nagasaki** and **Japan, Martyrs of**.

(Hyacinth of Porto Romano) (St) {4 –deleted}

26 July
C2nd? His existence as a martyr in the reign of Trajan is probable, but his acta are thoroughly untrustworthy. He is connected with Porto Romano (Italy).

Hyacinth-of-the-Angels and John-Baptist of San Francisco Cajonos (BB) {2}

15 September
1660–1700. They were native Mexicans of the Zapoteca tribe in Oaxaca, Mexico. Both were married with children, and both held responsible positions in their town of San Francisco Cajonos. Their responsibility included the suppression of pagan ceremonies, but after they had broken up one such and confiscated the sacred artefacts being used they were attacked by a mob. They took refuge in the local Dominican friary at Xagacía, but had to be handed over and were killed after being tortured to obtain their apostasy. They were beatified in 2002.

Hyacinth Serrano López and Comps (BB) {2}

d. 1936. They were eighteen Dominicans of the province of Aragon in Spain, killed with two priests of the archdiocese of Zaragoza (BB Emmanuel Albert Ginés and Zosimus Izquierdo Gil) during the civil war and beatified together in 2001. Cf. **Spanish Civil War, Martyrs of** and list in appendix.

Hyacintha de Mariscotti (St) {2}

30 January
1585–1640. A noblewoman of Viterbo (Italy), when aged twenty she lost her lover, a marquis, who married her younger sister. In reaction she became such a nuisance that her family pressured her into entering the convent of Franciscan tertiaries at Viterbo. There she began by scandalously ignoring the rule, was converted to a better life but relapsed. Finally, over a period of twenty-four years, she gave herself up to a life of heroic humility, prayer, patience and incredible penances. She founded the 'Sacconi', an oblate nursing sisterhood now suppressed, and was canonized in 1807. She is liturgically celebrated as a virgin, which she was probably not. However, the Roman Martyrology has given her the benefit of the doubt.

Hyginus, Pope (St) {2, 3}

11 January

d. 142. He was traditionally pope from 138. The Roman Martyrology has deleted the reference to his martyrdom. His cultus was suppressed in 1969.

Hypatius, Asianus and Andrew (SS) {2, 4}

20 September

d. c.740. Allegedly from Lydia (Asia Minor), Hypatius and Asianus were bishops and Andrew a priest. At Constantinople they were tortured, strangled and burnt under a pile of icons by order of Emperor Leo III because of their opposition to his policy of iconoclasm.

Hypatius of Chalcedon (St) {2, 4}

17 June

d. 446. A Phrygian, when aged nineteen he became a hermit, first in Thrace and then at Chalcedon opposite Constantinople, where he became abbot of a flourishing laura. He was a determined opponent of Nestorianism.

Hypatius of Gangra (St) {2, 4}

14 November

C4th. A bishop of Gangra in Paphlagonia (Asia Minor), he attended the council of Nicaea and was a prominent defender of the divinity of Christ. When on his way home he was stoned to death by a mob of Novatian heretics.

I

Ia (Hia, Ives) (St)

3 February

d. 450. From Ireland, a sister of St Ercus, she allegedly accompanied SS Fingar, Piala and other missionaries to Cornwall (England) and was martyred on the Hayle estuary. St Ives in Cornwall is named after her, but not St Ives near Cambridge. She is also linked with Plouyé in Brittany (France).

Ia (St) {2, 4}

4 August

d. ?362. A Greek slave (the name means 'Violet'), she was martyred in Persia during the persecution of Shah Shapur II. The Roman Martyrology has deleted the reference to her 9000 fellow martyrs.

Iago cf. **James**. (This obsolete Spanish form is now found only in the form 'Santiago', meaning St James).

Ian cf. **John**

Ida of Boulogne (Bl) {2}

13 April

d. 1113. A noblewoman from Bouillon (Belgium), she was the wife of the count of Boulogne (France) and mother of the famous crusaders Godfrey de Bouillon and King Baldwin of Jerusalem. She was extremely generous to several monasteries in the Low Countries.

Ida of Herzfeld (St) {2}

4 September

d. 825. A great-granddaughter of Charles Martel, she was happily married but was widowed when still young. She then founded the nunnery of Herzfeld in Westphalia (Germany), where she died after a life of charity. She was the mother of St Guarin of Corvey.

Ida of Louvain (Bl) {2}

13 April

d. c.1290. From Louvain (Belgium), she became a Cistercian nun at Roosendael near Mecheln and, according to her dubious biography, was subject to extraordinary mystical phenomena.

Idda of Toggenburg (Bl) {2}

3 November

d. ?1226. She was a hermit attached to the Benedictine nunnery at Fischingen in Thurgau canton (Switzerland). According to her unreliable legend, she was the wife of a count of Toggenburg (otherwise unknown), was thrown by him through a castle window after suspicion of adultery and eventually obtained his permission to become a nun.

Idesbald (Bl) {2}

18 April

1100–67. From Flanders, as a young man he was at the court of the count before becoming a canon at Veurne near Ostend (Belgium) in 1135. He left to become a Cistercian at the abbey of Duenen nearby, where he was abbot for twelve years. His cultus was confirmed for Bruges in 1894.

Ignatius of Antioch (St) {1, 3}

17 October

d. ?107. Nicknamed Theophorus ('God-bearer'), he became bishop of Antioch (Syria) in ?69 but nothing is known about his career. In the reign of Trajan he was arrested, taken to Rome and thrown to the wild animals in the amphitheatre during public games. On the way there he wrote seven letters, which are still extant and are of great doctrinal value. His name is mentioned in the Roman canon of the Mass.

Ignatius de Azevedo and Comps (BB) {2}

15 July

d. 1570. A group of forty Portuguese and Spanish Jesuit missionaries, they were on their way to Brazil and the West Indies when their ship, the 'Sancto Jacobo', was boarded by Calvinist Huguenot pirates near the Canary Islands. Ignatius was the superior, from Coïmbra (Portugal) where he had joined the Jesuits in 1548. The leader of the pirates had them massacred with lances and swords. This took over a day, and the last of them, Simon da Costa, died on 16 July. Their cultus was confirmed for Brazil in 1854. Cf. **Brazil** in lists of national martyrs in appendix.

Ignatius-of-Santhiá Belvisotti (St) {2}

22 September

1686–1770. From near Vercelli, he became a secular priest there in 1710 and then joined the Capuchins in 1716, being attracted by the charism of obedience. He spent his life at the Turin friary, serving as novice-master and also as a military chaplain, and was known for performing miracles. He was canonized in 2002.

Ignatius-of-Láconi Cadello Peis (St) {2}

12 May

1701–81. From Láconi in Sardinia, his parents were poor but he had a remarkable religious devotion as a child. He became a Capuchin lay brother at Cagliari and was occupied throughout his life in domestic work and in begging for the maintenance of his friary. Being illiterate he loved to listen to the gospels, especially to the Passion of Christ, and received the charisms of prophecy and the working of miracles. He was canonized in 1951.

Ignatius of Constantinople (St) {2, 4}

23 October

?799–877. Son of the Byzantine Emperor Michael I, he was castrated and forced to become a monk when his father was deposed in 813. He founded three monasteries in the Prinkipio islands before being appointed patriarch of Constantinople in 846. Standing firm against corruption in high places, he openly refused Holy Communion to Bardas Caesar (brother of the empress) on account of his public incest. Abdicating in 858, he was replaced by Photius but reinstated after nine years, remaining patriarch until his death.

Ignatius Falzon (Bl) {2}

1 July

1813–65. Born at Valletta, Malta, he obtained a doctorate in civil and canon law but did not feel called to become a lawyer or a priest. Instead, he dedicated his life to catechetical instruction among the British armed forces stationed on the island. He was a pioneer and advocate of ecumenism and became a Franciscan tertiary. He was beatified in 2001.

Ignatius Jorjes (Bl) {2}

10 September

d. 1622. The four-year-old son of Dominic Jorjes and Isabel Fernandez, he was beheaded with his mother at Nagasaki (Japan) during the 'Great Persecution'. Cf. **Charles Spinola and Comps**, **Great Martyrdom at Nagasaki** and **Japan, Martyrs of**.

Ignatius Kłopotowski (Bl) {2}

7 September

1866–1931. From Korzeniówka in Poland (then part of Russia), he became a priest of the diocese of Lublin and started to found numerous charitable institutions in the face of the almost total lack of welfare provision by the secular authorities. He was persecuted by them for trying to establish schools for rural Polish peasants. In 1908 he moved to Warsaw and started to publish many works on the faith, founding the 'Sisters of the Blessed

Virgin Mary of Loreto' to help him in this. He died at Warsaw and was beatified in 2005.

Ignatius of Loyola (St) {1, 3}

31 July

1491–1556. Born on the family estate at Loyola in the Basque Country (Spain), he was a page at the Spanish court and then a soldier. He was seriously wounded in the siege of Pamplona in 1521 during the conquest of the kingdom of Navarre, and during his convalescence was converted to the idea of serving the church. Preparing himself by a retreat at Montserrat and Manresa, he wrote his classic work on spirituality 'The Book of Spiritual Exercises'. Wishing to found a religious confraternity, he gathered a few companions while in Paris and they took their first vows together at the church of Montmartre in 1534. This was the start of the Society of Jesus, the aim of which was to work for the greater glory of God under the obedience of the pope. He was elected the first superior-general in 1541, which he remained until his death at Rome. By then his Society had over 100 houses in twelve provinces throughout the world. He was canonized in 1622.

Ignatius Maloyan (Bl) {2}

11 June

1869–1915. An Armenian Catholic from Mardin, Turkey, he became a monk and priest of Bzommar monastery in Lebanon and ministered to the small Catholic Armenian population in Egypt from 1897 to 1910. In 1911 he was made archbishop of his hometown and re-evangelized a decayed diocese. In 1915 he and most of the Armenian population of Mardin were rounded up by the Turkish authorities and offered the choice of conversion to Islam or death (contrary to Shahira law). On his refusal, after being tortured he was deported with 440 Armenians and some other

Christians. They were massacred at a place called Karakenpru near Amida; Bl Ignatius (alone) was beatified in 2001.

Ignatius Mangin and Comps (SS) {1 –group}

20 July

d. 1900. The Boxer Rebellion in China caused the deaths of about 5,000 Catholics in south-eastern Hebei. Notable among the massacres was that at Zhoujiahe, a walled town near Yingxian and Catholic centre where many refugees had gathered. The parish priest there was St Ignatius, from Verny (France) who was born in 1857 and became a Jesuit in 1875. He was sent to China in 1882. St Paul Denn from Lille (France), who had become a Jesuit in 1872 when aged twenty-five, joined him at Zhoujiahe with many of his people from Gucheng. A government army, sympathetic to the Boxers, helped to besiege and capture the town in the morning. The Boxers massacred the congregation at the church before setting fire to it, killing both priests there and over 2000 laypeople there and elsewhere. St Mary Zhu Wuzhi, a fifty-year-old housewife, was notable in being shot while shielding St Ignatius. Fifty-one survivors of the church massacre, including nineteen-year-old St Peter Zhu Rixin, were killed in the afternoon. He had refused to deny his faith before the prefect at Lujiazhuang nearby and was ordered to be beheaded as a result. Cf. **China, Martyrs of**.

Ignatius Rice (Bl) {2}

5 May

1762–1844. A businessman of Waterford (Ireland), he lost his wife when aged twenty-seven and was left with a small daughter, and thereupon devoted himself to charitable works. The Protestant government had a policy of repressing Catholic education so he sold his business, opened a school and founded the 'Congregation of Christian Brothers' on

Salesian principles in 1820. He was beatified in 1996.

Ignatius Uchibori (Bl) {2 –add}

21 February
Cf. **Balthasar Uchibori and Comps**.

Ildephonsus Schuster (Bl) {2}

30 August
1880–1954. A Roman, he became a Benedictine monk in 1896 at the local abbey of St Paul outside the Walls and was elected abbot in 1918. He served in the Curia, especially in liturgical matters, and became cardinal-archbishop of Milan in 1929. He denounced Fascism and proposed holiness as a good for all and the only way to human happiness. He was beatified in 1996.

Ildephonsus of Toledo (St) {2}

23 January
607–67. Nephew of St Eugene of Toledo (Spain), he was born in that city and studied at Seville under St Isidore. Then he joined the monastery at Agli on the Tagus near Toledo, becoming the abbot there, and was made archbishop of Toledo in 657. He revised the Spanish liturgy and was a capable writer, chiefly on the subject of Our Lady.

Illidius (Allyre) (St) {2, 4}

7 July
d. 384. The fourth bishop of Clermont-Ferrand (France), he was much admired by St Gregory of Tours.

Illtyd (St) {2}

6 November
d. c.540. He is one of the most famous of the saints of Wales, but his extant biography contains much legendary material. Becoming a monk under St Cadoc, he went on to found the influential monastery of Llanilltyd Fawr (Llantwit Major) near Cardiff. This was the source of many Welsh saints of the period. He is alleged to have died near Dol in Brittany.

Illuminata (St) {2, 4}

29 November
C4th. She has a cultus as a virgin at Todi in Umbria (Italy).

*(**Illuminatus of Sanseverino**) (St) {4 –deleted}*

11 May
d. c.1000. From Sanseverino in the Marches (Italy), he became a Benedictine monk at the abbey of San Mariano there.

Imelda Lambertini (Bl) {2}

12 May
d. 1333. Allegedly from the noble family of Lambertini at Bologna (Italy), she was educated at the Dominican nunnery at Valdipietra there and seems to have joined the community. Her story is that she received her first Holy Communion in a miraculous manner at the age of eleven (under the canonical age for communion at the time) and died enraptured as a result the same day. Her cultus was confirmed for Bologna in 1826.

Imelin cf. **Emilian**.
Inan cf. **Evan**.

*(**Indes, Domna, Agape and Theophila**) (SS) {4 –deleted}*

28 December
d. 303. They were listed as martyred at Nicomedia (Asia Minor) in the reign of Diocletian.

*(**India, Martyrs of**) (SS) {4 –deleted}*

3 August
? The old Roman Martyrology had an entry describing the martyrdom of monks and

laity by 'King Abenner', 'among the Indians bordering on Persia'.

Inés, Inez cf. **Agnes**.

Inés de Beniganim cf. **Josephine-Mary-of-St-Agnes Albiñana**.

Ingenuinus and Albinus (SS) {2}

5 February

d. ?605, and C11th resp. The former was the first bishop of Sabion (which no longer exists) near Brixen in South Tyrol (Italy), while the latter transferred the see to Brixen. They have a joint local cultus.

Ingrid Elofsdotter (St) {2}

2 September

d. 1282. She was a widow noted for good works before she went on pilgrimage to the Holy Land, and on her return she became a Dominican nun at Skene (Sweden).

Iñigo cf. **Eneco**.

Innocent I, Pope (St) {2, 3}

12 March

d. 417. From Albano near Rome, he succeeded his father Anastasius I as pope in 402. The outstanding event of his pontificate was the sack of Rome by Alaric the Goth in 410. He confirmed the acts of two African synods against the Pelagians and supported the deposed St John Chrysostom. His cultus was suppressed in 1969.

Innocent V, Pope (Bl) {2, 4}

22 June

1245–76. From Tarentaise in Burgundy (France), he became a Dominican and was well known as a theologian and as a preacher. He was made archbishop of Lyons in 1272, and during his episcopate, the second ecumenical council of Lyons was held, in which he took a prominent part. As cardinal of Ostia

he was made pope in 1276, but died only a few months later. His cultus was confirmed in 1898.

Innocent XI, Pope (Bl) {2, 4}

12 August

1611–89. From Como (Italy), he was elected pope in 1676. Outstanding for his charity, evangelical simplicity and poverty, he withstood the autocracy of King Louis XIV of France, struggled to stop nepotism, encouraged an exemplary life among the clergy and furthered catechetical instruction. He condemned Jansenism, Quietism and corrected the teaching of Molinos on grace. He was beatified in 1956.

(Innocent, Sebastia and Comps) (SS) {4 –deleted}

4 July

? A group of thirty-two, they were listed as martyred at Sirmium (now Srem Mitrovica in Serbia).

Innocent-of-Mary-Immaculate Canoura Arnau and Comps (SS) {2}

9 October

d. 1934. The Brothers of the Christian Schools had a school at Turón in Spain, south of the Sierra Nevada, and on 8 October Innocent-of-Mary-Immaculate Canoura Arnau, a Passionist priest, had come to hear confession and to say Mass. While assembled to celebrate Mass he and eight Brothers were seized by Republicans, taken to the cemetery where graves had been dug, and shot. Cyril-Bertrand Sanz Tejedor had been rector for two years; Marcian-Joseph López López was the sacristan and cook; Julian-Alfred Fernández Zapico prepared the pupils for First Communion; Victorianus-Pius Bernabé Cano was the choirmaster; Benjamin-Julian Alfonsus Andrés had just made final vows, and there were three juniors: Augustus-Andrew Martín Fernández, Benedict-of-Jesus Valdivieso Sáez and Anicetus-Adolf Seco Gutiérrez. They were canonized in 1999. Cf. **Spanish Civil War, Martyrs of**.

Innocent Guz (Bl) {2}

6 June
1890–1940. A Polish Franciscan Conventual friar, he was beaten to death by guards at the Sachsenhausen concentration camp. Cf. **Poland, Martyrs of the Nazi Occupation of**.

Innocent-of-Berzo Scalvinoni (Bl) {2}

3 March
1844–90. Raised as a child at Berzo near Brescia (Italy), he became a secular priest and curate for his hometown in 1867. Then he joined the Capuchins in 1874, becoming assistant novice-master and public preacher and confessor. His body was returned to Berzo after he died, and he was beatified in 1964.

Innocent of Tortona (St) {2, 4}

17 April
C4th. From Tortona (Italy), he was imprisoned and whipped in the reign of Diocletian, barely escaping death. The Edict of Milan, issued by the emperor Constantine in 313, put an end to persecution. St Innocent was then ordained became bishop of his native city in ?326.

Innocents, The Holy (SS) {1, 3}

28 December
C1st. The male children in Bethlehem and the area around it whose massacre was ordered by Herod (Matt. 2:1-18) have been liturgically venerated as martyrs from a very early date. The Gospel does not specify their number and this has led to the multiplication of their relics in many churches. They are depicted as a large number of small boys being killed by soldiers in various ways while their mothers utter protest.

(Iphigenia) (St) {4 –deleted}

21 September
C1st. According to an apocryphal work, she was a young woman of Ethiopia (now Nubia in northern Sudan, not the present country of that name) who was converted by St Matthew the apostle.

(Irais) (St) {4 –deleted}

22 September
d. c.300. A maiden of Alexandria or of Antinoe (Egypt), she was listed as beheaded in the reign of Diocletian.

Ireland (Martyrs of) (BB)

20 June
d. 1579–1654. After the nadir of English fortunes in Ireland in the reign of Henry VIII, the policy of conquest that followed assumed that English culture and the Protestant church would be imposed on the native Irish. The number of the resultant victims of massacre, starvation and dispossession runs into seven figures, but the number of those martyred strictly for the faith is relatively low and 282 have been identified. The main periods of persecution were under Queen Elizabeth I and by Oliver Cromwell. Seventeen martyrs were beatified in 1992, comprising four bishops, two secular priests, five religious and six laypeople. They are listed individually in the Roman Martyrology. Cf. lists of national martyrs in appendix.

(Irenaeus, Anthony and Comps) (SS) {4 –deleted}

15 December
C3rd? A group of twenty-two Romans, they were listed as martyred in the reign of

Valerian. Theodore, Saturninus and Victor were also named.

(Irenaeus, Peregrine and Irene) (SS) {4 –deleted}

5 May
Early C4th? They were listed as burnt at the stake at Thessalonica (Greece) in the reign of Diocletian.

Irenaeus of Lyons (St) {1, 3}

28 June
d. ?202 From Asia Minor and a disciple of St Polycarp (himself a pupil of St John the apostle), he migrated to Gaul and became bishop of Lyons in ?178. According to tradition he was a martyr, but there is no evidence of this. He is the first of the Western Fathers (although he wrote in Greek), and his writings (especially his work 'Against the Heretics') are a very early testimony to the teachings of the apostles and the traditions of the early church. His theological writings emphasize the importance of both Old and New Testaments, the unity of the gospels and the idea of the recapitulation of human nature in Christ.

Irenaeus of Sirmium (St) {2, 4}

6 April
Early C4th. A bishop in Pannonia, he was martyred in the reign of Diocletian at Sirmium (Srem Mitrovica in Serbia). His acta are authentic.

Irenarchus (St) {2, 4}

28 November
Early C4th. According to the legend, Acacius, a priest, was martyred with seven women at Sebaste in Armenia (Asia Minor). Irenarchus was a hostile pagan who was converted by witnessing their courage and was martyred with them. The revised Roman Martyrology describes him as a pagan enforcing the requirement to offer sacrifice, who was converted by the constancy of some Christian women and so was martyred himself. Acacius and the seven women martyrs have been deleted.

(Irene of Santarém) (St) {4 –deleted}

20 October
? According to her legend she was a C7th nun near the city named Santarém after her in Portugal, but it seems that she is a duplicate of the St Irene in 'Agape, Chionia and Irene'.

Irene Stefani (Bl) {2 –add}

31 October
1891–1930. From a large family at Anfo near Brescia, she joined the recently founded Consolata Missionary Sisters in 1914 and was sent to east Africa. There, she assisted those affected by the serious disruption caused by the conquest of German East Africa (now Tanzania) by Britain. After the war, she served as a missionary in central Kenya and died of bubonic plague at Gikondi. She was due to be beatified in 2015.

(Irenion) (St) {4 –deleted}

16 December
d. 389. He was bishop of Gaza in the Holy Land in the reign of Theodosius I.

Irmengard (Bl) {2}

17 July
d. 866. Daughter of Emperor Louis the German, she was appointed by her father as first Benedictine abbess of Frauenwörth in the Chiemsee, Bavaria (Germany). Her cultus was confirmed for Munich and Freising in 1928.

Irmgard (Bl) {2}

4 September
d. ?1089 She was a noblewoman who became a hermit at Süchteln (Germany) and later at Cologne, where she died.

Irmina (St) {2, 4}

24 December

d. c.710. Her unreliable C12th biography alleges the following. She was a daughter of King Dagobert II of Frankish Austrasia, and when aged fifteen she was engaged to marry but on the day of her wedding her betrothed died. She then persuaded her father to build the nunnery of Ohren near Trier for her. She was generous to both Celtic and Saxon missionary monks and built Echternach for St Willibrord in 698. She died at the monastery of Weissenburg, also founded by her father.

(Isaac of Cyprus) *(St)* *{4 –deleted}*

21 September

? He was listed by the old Roman Martyrology as a bishop of Cyprus who was martyred.

(Isaac the Great 1) (St) {2}

9 September

d. 438. Son of St Nerses the Great, he succeeded his father as Armenian Katholikos of Etchmiadzin and was the real founder of the Armenian national church, obtaining independence from the metropolitan of Caesarea. He translated a large part of the Bible with St Mesrop, founded monasteries and was practically the only ruler of the Armenians after the Persians had deposed their king.

(Isaac the Great 2) *(St)*

13 May

d. c.460. From Amida in Syria, he became abbot of a monastery near Antioch. He is the traditional author of a set of ascetical writings which remain popular in monastic circles, especially in the East. However the author of these seems to have been a Nestorian bishop of Nineveh who died in ?595. For this reason perhaps he was never listed in the Roman Martyrology.

Isaac Jogues (St) {2}

18 October

1607–46. From Orleans (France), he joined the Jesuits in 1624 and went as a missionary to Quebec in 1636. He was travelling by canoe to the Huron missionary territory on Lake Huron when he was captured by a Mohawk Iroquois raiding party with several companions. They tortured and enslaved him, cutting off several fingers. The Mohawk territory was in what is now upstate New York (USA), and St Isaac managed to escape with the help of some Dutch merchants from what is now New York City. Back in France, he was granted papal permission to say Mass despite his mutilated hands. In 1646 he went back to the Mohawk country as a missionary, but without any success. He was killed by a tomahawk blow at Ossernenon near present-day Auriesville in New York State (USA) together with his Jesuit companion St John de la Lande, and was canonized in 1930. Cf. **John de Brébeuf and Comps**.

Isaac of Monteluco (St) {2, 4}

11 April

d. c.550. A Syrian monk, he fled from the Monophysites and founded a laura at Monteluco near Spoleto in Umbria (Italy). He was one of the restorers of eremitical life in C6th Italy.

Isaac of Tabanos (St) {2, 4}

3 June

d. 851. From Cordoba (Spain), he became very proficient in Arabic and was made a notary under the Muslim government there. He resigned in order to become a monk at Tabanos nearby, but in a public debate at Cordoba he denounced Muhammed and was executed.

Isabella cf. **Elizabeth**.

Isabella Fernandez (Bl) {2}

10 September
d. 1622. A Spanish lady, widow of Dominic Jorjes, she was beheaded with her son Ignatius at Nagasaki in the 'Great Martyrdom' for having given shelter to Bl Charles Spinola. Cf. **Japan, Martyrs of** and **Great Martyrdom at Nagasaki**.

Isabella of France (Bl) {2}

22 February
d. 1270 The only sister of King St Louis of France, she refused to marry the emperor of Germany and, after the death of her mother Blanche of Castile, founded the convent of Poor Clares at Longchamps near Paris. There she lived under the rule without, however, taking vows. She was beatified in 1520.

Isaias (Isaiah) the Prophet (St) {2, 4}

9 May
He is the first of the Major Prophets of the Old Testament.

Isarnus (Ysarn) of Toulouse (St) {2}

24 September
d. 1043. From near Toulouse (France), he joined the Augustinian monastery of St Victor at Marseilles, going on to become abbot. His reform of the monastery was imitated by other houses. He was famous for his charity, especially towards criminals.

Isaurus and Comps (SS) {2, 4}

17 June
? From Athens, they hid in a cave at Apollonia in Macedonia (Greece) during one of the persecutions. On being discovered they were beheaded. The companions were Innocent, Felix, Jeremias, Basil and Peregrine.

Ischyrion the Egyptian (St) {2, 4}

22 December
d. c.250. He was the procurator of an Egyptian official (possibly in Alexandria), who had him castrated and impaled for the faith in the reign of Decius.

Ischyrion of Lycopolis and Comps (SS) {2, 4}

1 June
d. c.250. He was an army officer who was martyred at Lycopolis in Egypt with five other soldiers in the reign of Decius.

Isfried (Bl) {2}

15 June
d. 1204. He was a Premonstratensian at Kappenberg before being made bishop of Ratzeburg (Germany) in 1180, and was influential in support of the German drive to colonize the Slav lands east of the Elbe. His cultus was approved for the Premonstratensians in 1725.

(Isidore of Alexandria) *(St)* *{4 –deleted}*

5 February
? The old Roman Martyrology placed him at Alexandria (Egypt), but he is probably to be identified with St Isidore of Chios.

(Isidore of Antioch) *(St)* *{4 –deleted}*

2 January
? When Cardinal Baronius revised the old Roman Martyrology he included a listing for this alleged saint because of a note in the Hieronomian Martyrology which read: 'In Antiochia Siridoni episcopi eiusdem loci'. No such martyred bishop of Antioch is known.

Isidore Bakanja (Bl) {2}

12 August
c.1887–1909. Born in northeast Belgian Congo, now Congo (Kinshasa), he became a Christian

in his native village but was the only one to do so, so in order to make contact with other Christians he went to work on a rubber plantation. He was devoted to the scapular and the Rosary and, when refusing to desist from these, was ordered flogged by an atheist Belgian planter. He died six months later as a result, aged about twenty-one and after thirty months as a Christian. He was beatified in 1994.

Isidore of Chios (St) {2, 4}

15 May
C3rd. He was martyred on Chios in the Aegean (Greece) in the reign of Decius.

Isidore the Farmer (St) {2}

15 May
d. c.1130. A native of Madrid (Spain), married to St Mary Toribia de la Cabeza, he spent his whole life working in the fields on an estate just outside the city. Canonized in 1622, he is the patron of Madrid.

His feast day is given as 10 May in error in the old Roman Martyrology.

Isidore Gagelin (St) {1 –group}

17 October
1799–1833. From near Besançon (France), he joined the Paris Foreign Mission Society and was sent to Vietnam in 1822, being ordained priest on his arrival. He worked there until the persecution ordered by Emperor Minh Mạng, upon which he gave himself up to the governor of Bong Son and was strangled at Hué. Cf. **Vietnam, Martyrs of**.

Isidore the Hospitaller (St) {2, 4}

15 January
d. 404. An Egyptian priest, he was in charge of the hospice for pilgrims at Alexandria. In defending St Athanasius he suffered much at the hands of the Arians. Accused of Origenism by St Jerome and others, he fled

to Constantinople where he was befriended by St John Chrysostom.

Isidore-of-St-Joseph de Loor (Bl) {2}

6 October
1881–1916. Born near Ghent (Belgium), he was a very pious child with a devotion to the Passion. Joining the Passionists at Ere near Tournai, he was such a faithful religious that he was called an exemplar of the Passionist rule and of charity. He died in tranquil agony of pleurisy and was beatified in 1984.

(Isidore of Nitria) *(St)* *{4 –deleted}*

2 January
C4th. Mentioned by St Jerome as 'a holy venerable bishop' who had welcomed him to Egypt, he may have been identical with St Isidore of Pelusium.

Isidore of Pelusium (St) {2, 4}

4 February
d. ?449. A famous Egyptian abbot of a monastery at Pelusium (east of Port Said), he was much admired by St Cyril of Alexandria. A great number of his letters are still extant.

Isidore of Seville (St) {1, 3}

4 April
c.560–636. From Cartagena (Spain) and brother of SS Leander, Fulgentius and Florentina, he was educated by St Leander and succeeded him as bishop of Seville in 600. He presided over several synods, reorganized the Spanish church, encouraged monastic life (he wrote an influential rule), completed the Mozarabic liturgical rite, was responsible for the decree of the council of Toledo in 633 and was himself an encyclopaedic writer on theology, scripture, biography, history, geography, astronomy and grammar. He was declared a doctor of the Church in 1722, and his attribute is a swarm of bees or a hive.

Ismidon (St) {2}

30 September
d. 1115. He was a canon at the cathedral
of Lyons before he became bishop of Die
(France). He went on crusade to the Holy Land
twice, and brought back many holy relics.

Isnard (Bl) {2}

22 March
d. 1244. From Chiampo near Vicenza (Italy),
he was professed as a Dominican by St Dominic in 1219 and was the founder and first prior
of the friary at Pavia. It is written of him that,
in spite of his ascetic life, he was excessively
fat and people used to ridicule him about it
when he was preaching. His cultus was confirmed for Pavia in 1919.

Israel (St) {2}

12 December
d. 1014. He was a canon regular at le Dorat,
near Limoges (France), and was famous in the
diocese for his preaching on Scripture.

Issell cf. **Teilo**.
Issey cf. **Teilo**; perhaps also a Cornish variant
of **Ita**.
István cf. **Stephen**.

Ita (Ytha, Meda) (St) {2}

15 January
d. 570. From Drum in Co. Waterford (Ireland),
she founded the nunnery at Killeedy in Co.
Limerick, attracted a large number of disciples and taught several saints as children
(St Brendan, for example). Her extant biographies are full of incredible anecdotes.

Ithamar (St) {2}

10 June
d. ?666. A native of Kent (England), he was
the first Anglo-Saxon to be made bishop when
he succeeded St Paulinus at Rochester.

Itta cf. **Ida of Nivelles**.

Ivan Ziatyk (Bl) {2}

17 March
1900–52. A Redemptorist, he was vicar-general
of the Greek-Catholic Church in Ukraine and
died in the gulag at Oserlag near Irkutsk in the
Soviet Union. His name is Slavic for 'John'.
Cf. **Nicholas Čarneckyj and 24 Comps**.

Ives cf. **Ia** or **Ivo**.

Ivo (St)

24 April
? According to his medieval legend, he was
a Persian bishop who migrated to England in
the Saxon period. There he settled as a hermit at a location now marked by the town of
St Ives in Cambridgeshire.

Ivo of Chartres (St) {2, 4}

23 December
d. 1116. The provost of the Augustinian Canons Regular of Saint-Quentin, he was made
bishop of Chartres (France) in 1091. He was
renowned for his knowledge of canon law,
on which he wrote much, and was consulted
by the king on difficult canonical questions.
Upright and just, he opposed the rapacity of
contemporary ecclesiastical dignitaries.

Ivo (Yvo) Hélory (St) {2}

19 May
1253–1303. From near Tréguier in Brittany
(France), he studied at Paris and Orleans and
practised law in his native city and at Rennes,
both in the ecclesiastical and in the civil
courts. He defended the poor and unprotected
as well as the rich and was called 'the Advocate of the Poor'. He was canonized in 1347
and is patron of lawyers.

Ivor cf. **Ibar**.

J

Jacob cf. **James**.

Jacobinus de'Canepaci (Bl) {2}

3 March
1438–1508. From Vercelli (Italy), he was a Carmelite lay brother there and his cultus was approved for Vercelli and the Carmelites in 1845.

Jacques cf. **James**.

Jacut (St) {2}

8 February
C6th. A son of SS Fragan and Gwen and a brother of SS Guetenoc and Winwaloe, he was a disciple of St Budoc and fled with him from Britain to Brittany (France) to escape the Saxons.

Jadwiga cf. **Hedwig**.

James

This is the English form of Jacob, which is notably corrupted in other vernaculars also: Giacomo in Italian; Jacques in French; Jaume in Catalan; Iago in Portuguese; Jaime, Iago or **Diego** in Spanish. (The last is listed separately.)

James Alberione (Bl) {2 –add}

26 November
1884–1971. From a farming family of San Lorenzo de Fossano in Italy, he was ordained a diocesan priest of Alba in 1907. As well as teaching in the seminary, he became a famous preacher and realized how important the use of modern media was in spreading the Gospel. In 1914, he founded the 'Pious Society of St Paul' and (in 1915) the 'Congregation of the Daughters of St Paul', these together being nicknamed the 'Pauline Family'. He founded a second congregation for women, the 'Pious Disciples of the Divine Master' in 1924, and a third, the 'Sisters of the Good Shepherd', in 1938, as well as several secular institutes. He also founded several periodicals. He died at Rome and was beatified in 2003.

James-Hilary Barbal Cosán (St) {2}

28 July
1898–1937. From near Urgell in Catalonia (Spain), he joined the 'Brothers of the Christian Schools' at Mollensa in 1916 and taught Spanish and primary catechesis at Pibrac in France from 1926 (despite being deaf). In 1934, he went back to Calat in Spain as a cook and then moved to Tarragona. He was seized and imprisoned there in August 1936 at the start of the Spanish Civil War and was executed six months later. He was canonized in 1990. Cf. **Spanish Civil War, Martyrs of**.

James Bell (Bl) {2}

20 April
1521–84. From Warrington (Cheshire), he was educated at Oxford and was ordained in the reign of Queen Mary. Initially conforming to the state church under Elizabeth, he repented and was reconciled to the Catholic Church. For this, he was hanged at Lancaster with Bl John Finch and was beatified in 1929. Other documentary sources have their execution on the 10th of April, rather than the 20th. Cf. **England, Martyrs of**.

James Benfatti (Bl) {2}

19 November
d. 1332. From Mantua (Italy), he became a Dominican, a teacher of theology and a great preacher. He became bishop of Mantua in 1303, and as such was nicknamed 'Father of the Poor'. His cultus was confirmed for Mantua and the Dominicans in 1859.

James Berthieu (St) {2}

8 June
1838–96. From near St Flour (France), he was a parish priest there from 1864 until he

joined the Jesuits in 1873 and was sent to Madagascar. He was a missionary first on Nosy Borah off the east coast and then on the main island. The French conquered the island and overthrew the monarchy and government in 1895, but the following year there was a rebellion which proved anti-Christian. St James was seized at Ambohibernasoandro immediately after saying Mass, stripped, beaten to death and his body thrown into a river. He was canonized in 2012.

James-Philip Bertoni (Bl) {2}

25 May
?1444–83. From Faenza (Italy), when aged nine he joined the Servites there and was procurator of the friary from the time of his ordination until his death. His cultus was confirmed for Faenza in 1761.

James Bianconi of Mevania (Bl) {2}

23 August
d. 1301. From Mevania (now Bevagna) near Spoleto (Italy), he was the founder and first prior of the Dominican friary in his native city. His cultus was confirmed for Spoleto in 1674.

James Bird (Bl) {2}

25 March
1573–92. From Winchester, when aged nineteen he was hanged there for being reconciled to the church and was beatified in 1929. Cf. **England, Martyrs of**.

James of Bitetto (Bl) {2}

27 April
d. ?1485. Surnamed alternatively 'of Slavonia', 'of Illyricum', 'of Zara' or 'of Dalmatia', he was from Šibenik in Dalmatia (Croatia) and became a Franciscan lay brother at Zadar. Most of his life was spent at the friary of Bitetto near Bari (Italy). His cultus was approved for Bitetto in 1700.

James Buzabaliawo (St) {1 –group}

3 June
d. 1886. A soldier of King Mwanga of Buganda (Uganda) and a son of the royal bark-cloth maker, he was baptized in 1885 and burnt alive at Namuyongo in the following year. Cf. **Charles Lwanga and Comps**.

James Capocci (Bl) {2}

14 March
d. 1308. From Viterbo (Italy), he became an Augustinian friar there and taught theology with considerable success, being nicknamed 'Doctor Speculativus'. He became bishop of Benevento in 1302 and was transferred to Naples in 1303. His cultus was confirmed for Naples in 1911.

James Cinti of Cerqueto (Bl) {2}

17 April
d. 1367. From Cerqueto near Perugia (Italy), he joined the Augustinian friars at the latter city. His cultus was approved for Perugia in 1895.

James Chastan (St) {1 –group}

21 September
Cf. **Laurence Imbert and Comps**.

James of Citta della Pieve (Bl) {2}

15 January
d. 1304. A Servite friar from Chiusi near Montepulciano (Italy), he restored a ruined hospital near Citta della Pieve and was nicknamed 'Almsgiver'. The hospital's revenue was appropriated by the bishop of Chiusi, who had Bl James killed when the latter won an appeal to Rome. His cultus was confirmed for Citta della Pieve in 1806.

James Claxton (Bl) {2}

28 August

d. 1588. A Yorkshireman, he was educated at Rheims and ordained there in 1582. He was hanged at Isleworth (Middlesex), and was beatified in 1929. Cf. **England, Martyrs of**.

James the Confessor (St) {2}

21 March

d. ?874. He was martyred at Constantinople for defending the veneration of images. He is a minor patron of Catania in Sicily, and used to be considered a former bishop of that place.

James Cusmano (Bl) {2}

14 March

1834–88. Born in Palermo (Sicily), he became a physician at Palermo University and set out to use his skills to treat bodies and souls together. He treated the poor without charge, and was ordained to the diocese in 1883. In 1883, he founded the 'Sisters, Servants of the Poor' and in 1888 the 'Brothers, Missionary Servants of the Poor', with a charism of genuine humility in helping orphans and poor and derelict people. He was beatified in 1983.

James Đỗ May Năm and Comps (St) {1 –group}

12 August

d. 1838. A Vietnamese priest attached to the Paris Mission Society, he worked in secret in north Vietnam until he found shelter in a house belonging to St Anthony Nguyễn Đích, a wealthy farmer and benefactor of the Society's missionaries. With them was arrested St Michael Nguyễn Huy Mỹ, a married doctor of medicine and mayor of Ke Vinh. They were tortured in prison and beheaded during the persecution ordered by Emperor Minh Mạng. Cf. **Vietnam, Martyrs of**.

James Duckett (Bl) {2}

19 April

d. 1602. From Skelsmergh near Kendal in Cumbria, he became a convert and settled as a bookseller in London where he specialized in printing and selling Catholic books. He was regularly imprisoned for this, for nine years in total, until priestly vestments were found on his premises and he was hanged at Tyburn. He was beatified in 1929. Cf. **England, Martyrs of**.

James Fenn (Bl) {2}

12 February

d. 1584. From Montacute near Yeovil in Somerset, he was educated at Oxford, became a schoolmaster and got married. After his wife's death, he studied at Rheims and was ordained priest in 1580. Four years later, he was martyred at Tyburn with BB George Haydock, John Munden, John Nutter and Thomas Hemerford, and was beatified in 1929. Cf. **England, Martyrs of**.

James Gangala of the Marches (St) {2, 4}

28 November

1394–1476. From a poor family of the Marches (Italy), he studied law but became a Franciscan instead at Assisi. His penances were extreme. A companion missionary of St John Capistrano in the countries of the Holy Roman Empire and a fellow supporter of Franciscan reform, it is alleged that he preached daily for forty years. He was canonized in 1726.

James Gapp (Bl) {2}

23 August

1897–1943. Born in Tyrol (Austria) of the working class, he entered the Marianists in 1921 and worked as a priest in their schools, also helping unemployed people. A strong opponent of the Nazis, after 1938 he went into exile in France and then in Spain, whence he was abducted, taken to Berlin and guillotined. He was beatified in 1996.

James Gengoro (Bl) {2}

18 August
d. 1620. A Japanese toddler aged two, son of BB Thomas and Mary Gengoro, he was crucified with his parents and Bl Simon Kiyota Bokusai at Kokura and was beatified in 1867. Cf. **Japan, Martyrs of**.

James Ghazir Haddad (Bl) {2 –add}
1875–1954. From Ghazir in Lebanon, he became a Franciscan Capuchin at Khashbau in 1893. After his ordination in 1901, he became an itinerant preacher and walked all over the Lebanon in the process. In 1919, he erected a great cross at Jall-Eddib near Beirut, and this became the geographical focal point of his works of charity. To help him in these he founded the 'Sisters of the Holy Cross of Lebanon'. He opened several hospitals, schools, orphanages and asylums in and around Lebanon, including the best psychiatric hospital in the region at the Cross in 1950. He died, worn out, of leukaemia and was beatified in 2008.

James the Great (St) {1, 3}

25 July
d. 44. A son of Zebedee and Salome, he was the brother of St John the Evangelist and was called with him to the apostolate by Christ. He was quickly martyred after the Resurrection by order of King Herod Agrippa (Acts 12:2), the only apostle whose martyrdom is mentioned in the New Testament. A C9th legend, developed under Cluniac influence, makes him apostle of Spain and specifies Compostella in Galicia as the place where his body is enshrined. This legend spread throughout western Europe, so that Compostella became

the most famous place of pilgrimage in Christendom after Jerusalem and Rome. He is the patron saint of Spain, and his attribute is a scallop shell.

James Griesinger (Bl) {2}

11 October
1407–91. From Ulm (Germany), he was a soldier before he became a Dominican lay brother at Bologna (Italy) in 1441. The rest of his life was spent in painting on glass, for which he had a great talent. His cultus was confirmed for Bologna in 1825.

James Hayashida (Bl) {2}

8 September
d. 1628. A Japanese Dominican tertiary, he was beheaded at Nagasaki with **Dominic Castellet and Comps**. Cf. **Japan, Martyrs of**.

James Intercisus (St) {2, 4}

27 November
d. 421. A Persian Christian courtier of high rank, he apostatized to keep the favour of Shah Yezdegird but repented and was martyred by having his extremities slowly cut off in over twenty pieces in the reign of the next shah, Bahram V. Then he was beheaded, along with many others. His surname means 'cut up'.

James Kern (Bl) {2}

20 October
1897–1924. A Viennese, he entered the archdiocesan minor seminary in 1908 but was drafted into the Austrian army in 1915 and was very seriously wounded in the chest on the Italian front. After the war, he continued his seminary studies but decided to replace a Norbertine who had apostatized and so entered the abbey of Geras in 1920. He was allowed to be ordained while still a junior in 1922, but his old war wound became infected

and he died during surgery on the day fixed for his solemn profession. He was beatified in 1998.

James Kisai (St) {1 –group}

6 February
d. 1597. A Japanese Jesuit lay brother, he worked for the Jesuit missionaries at Osaka as catechist and domestic servant, and was crucified at Nagasaki with SS Paul Miki and Comps. Cf. **Japan, Martyrs of**.

James Kyuhei Gorobiyoye Tomonaga (St) {1 –group}

17 August
d. 1633. A Japanese born near Omura, he became a Dominican missionary priest in Taiwan and Manila (Philippines) before being martyred at Nagasaki with his assistant, St Michael Kurobioye. He was canonized in 1987 with **Laurence Ruiz and Comps**. Cf. **Japan, Martyrs of**.

James Lacops (St) {2}

9 July
d. 1572. A native of Oudenaarde near Ghent (Belgium), he became a Premonstratensian canon at Middelburg but apostatized in 1566, subsequently writing and preaching against the church. However, he repented, returned to his abbey and was martyred by Calvinists with the group at **Gorinchem**.

James-Desiderius Laval (Bl) {2}

9 September
1803–64. Born in Normandy (France), he became a doctor of medicine and a village practitioner but was then ordained when aged thirty-five. He went as a missionary to Mauritius, where he was for twenty-three years, being called a 'second Peter Claver' because of his work among the employees of the sugar

industry there. He became a Holy Ghost Father and was beatified in 1979.

James the Less (St) {1, 3}

3 May
d. ?62. Alternatively surnamed 'the Younger' or 'the Just', he was related to Christ and was one of the Twelve. After the Resurrection, he became the first bishop of Jerusalem, being mentioned by Eusebius, and is the putative author of one of the canonical letters. According to tradition, he was martyred at Jerusalem by being thrown from a pinnacle of the temple, stoned and then finally killed with the fuller's club which is his attribute.

James Matsuo Denshi (Bl) {2}

19 August
d. 1622. A Japanese sailor on board the ship of Bl Joachim Hirayama Diaz, he was beheaded at Nagasaki with BB Louis Flores and Comps. Cf. **Japan, Martyrs of**.

James of Nisibis (St) {2, 4}

15 July
C4th. He ranks second to St Ephrem among the Syrian Fathers, but not much is known about him except that he took part in the first ecumenical council of Nicaea in 325 as bishop of Nisibis.

James the Penitent (St) {2, 4}

28 January
C6th. He was a penitential hermit who lived shut into a tomb in the Holy Land, either on Mount Carmel or near Samaria. According to the legend, this is because he had murdered a girl when already a hermit.

James Puig Mirosa and Comps (BB) {2 –add}

d. 1936–7. They are the martyrs of the Congregation of the Sons of the Holy Family, who were martyred in and around Barcelona during the Spanish Civil War. Four of them were massacred at Villa Rodona on 25 August 1936. Some were killed in April 1937, which was late in the persecution that the church was suffering at the time. One member of the group was a lay helper. They were beatified in 2013. Cf. **Spanish Civil War, Martyrs of** and list in appendix.

James Salès and William Saltemouche (BB) {2}

7 February

d. 1593. A Jesuit priest and lay brother respectively, they conducted a mission at Aubenas in the Cévennes (France). Bl James attacked Protestant teaching in his sermons, with such success that a company of Huguenot raiders kidnapped them and took them before a kangaroo court of Calvinist ministers. After a heated theological discussion, Bl James was shot and Bl William was stabbed to death. They were beatified in 1926.

James Salomoni (Bl) {2}

31 May

1231–1314. A nobleman from Venice (Italy), he became a Dominican there and was at several friaries of the order until he died of cancer at Forli. His cultus was approved in 1526.

James of Sarugh (St) {2}

29 November

d. 521. He is a doctor of the Syriac-speaking Christians in the Middle East, and has been nicknamed the 'Harp of the Holy Spirit'. He was from Kurtam on the river Euphrates, in the district of Sarugh or Osrhoene in northern Syria (mostly now in Turkey), and was made bishop of Batnan, the chief city, in 519 (now Tell Batnan near Suruç in Turkey). He has left many homilies (allegedly numbering 763), and the text of a Syriac liturgy is ascribed

to him. Before his insertion into the revised Roman Martyology it was held that he was a Monophysite. Some of his writings have been translated into English, and in the literature, he is usually referred to as 'Jacob'.

James of Strepa (Bl) {2}

20 October

c.1350–?1409. A Pole from Galicia, he became a Franciscan and worked very successfully as vicar-general of the Franciscan missions among the Orthodox and pagans of what is now the western Ukraine. In 1392, he became archbishop of Halicz, based at Lemberg (now Lviv). His cultus was approved for Lviv in 1791.

(James the Syrian) (St) {4 –deleted}

6 August

Early C7th?. He was listed as a Syrian hermit at Amida (now Diyarbakir in Turkey).

James of Tarantaise (St) {2}

16 January

C5th. From Syria, he became a monk at Lérins (France) under St Honoratus and was a missionary in Savoy, becoming the first bishop of Tarentaise.

James Thomson (alias Hudson) (Bl) {2}

28 November

d. 1582. From York, he was educated for the priesthood at Rheims, ordained in 1581 and hanged the following year at York. He was beatified in 1895. His name is also spelt 'Thompson'. Cf. **England, Martyrs of**.

James of Voragine (Bl) {2}

13 July

c.1230–98. From Varezze (Voragine) near Savona (Italy), he became a Dominican in 1244, was provincial superior of Lombardy from 1267 to 1286 and became archbishop of Genoa in 1292. He is famous as the author of 'The Golden Legend', a major sourcebook for study of the medieval mind and its interests. His cultus was confirmed for Genoa and Savona in 1816.

James Walworth (Bl) {2}

11 May
d. 1537. A monk of the London Charterhouse, he was hanged in chains at York in the reign of Henry VIII and was beatified in 1886. Cf. **England, Martyrs of.**

James Yan Guodong and James Zhao Quanxin (SS) {1 –group}

9 July
Cf. **Gregory Grassi and Comps**.

Jane

Many feminine versions of 'John' have developed independently in the various vernaculars. For the purpose of this book, they are listed under 'Jane', although 'Joan' and 'Jean' are English alternatives (and the former is invariably used for St Joan of Arc). Other forms are: in Italian, Giovanna; in French, Jeanne; in Spanish, Juana; in Portuguese and Catalan, Joana.

Jane Antida Thouret (St) {2}

24 August
1765–1826. From near Besançon (France), the daughter of a tanner, she joined the 'Sisters of Charity of St Vincent de Paul' in 1787 but was forced to return home on the outbreak of the French Revolution. Then she started a school of her own for poor girls at Besançon, and attracted so many helpers in this and in other works of charity that she formed them into a new 'Institute of Sisters of Charity'. She died at Naples and was canonized in 1934.

Jane de Aza de Guzman (Bl) {2}

2 August
Early C13th. The mother of St Dominic was born at the family castle of Aza south of Burgos (Spain). She married Felix de Guzman, had two sons and a daughter and then conceived the future founder of the Dominicans after praying before the shrine of St Dominic of Silos. Her cultus was confirmed for Palencia, Osma and the Dominicans in 1828.

Jane of Bagno (Bl) {2}

16 January
d. 1105. From Fontechiuso in Tuscany (Italy), she became a Camaldolese lay sister at Santa Lucia near Bagno. Her cultus as patron of Bagno was approved for Borgo San Sepolcro in 1823.

Jane Beretta Molla (St) {2}

28 April
1922–62. Born near Milan (Italy), she became a doctor and specialized in paediatrics at the University of Milan from 1952, considering the practice of medicine to be a missionary vocation. Married in 1955, she developed a fibroma of the uterus during her third pregnancy and insisted that the life of the child should be saved rather than hers if a choice were necessary. This was done, and she died seven days after the birth of a healthy baby. She was canonized in 2004.

Jane-Elizabeth Bichier des Ages (St) {2}

26 August
1773–1838. A noblewoman born at the Château des Ages near Poitiers (France), she became a disciple of St Andrew Fournet at Saint-Pierre-de-Maillé after the Revolution and (in spite of grave difficulties at the outset) founded the 'Congregation of the Daughters of the Cross of St Andrew' for teaching and

nursing in hospitals. She died at Paris and was canonized in 1947.

Jane-Mary Bonomo (Bl) {2}

1 March

1616–70. Born at Asiago, near Vicenza (Italy) she was educated by the Poor Clares at Trent (Austria, now Trento in Italy), became a Benedictine nun at Bassano in 1622 and fell into supernatural ecstasy for the first time at the ceremony of profession. She was novice-mistress and was abbess three times, but was bitterly persecuted by some members of her own community. She was beatified in 1783.

Jane-Mary Condesa Lluch (Bl) {2 –add}

16 January

1862–1916. From a wealthy family of Valencia in Spain, she was touched by the sufferings of people who migrated from the countryside in order to work in factories in the city and who were often badly exploited. So, in 1884 she opened a refuge and school for such workers and their children, and was joined by several companions. This was the start of the 'Handmaids of the Immaculate Conception, Protectress of Workers', which received approval from the bishop in 1892. She died at Valencia and was beatified in 2003; her congregation received papal approval in 1947.

Jane-of-the-Cross Delanoue (St) {2}

16 August

1666–1736. The twelfth child of a man who ran a small business in the village of Fenet near Angers (France), she had a pious childhood but her father died and she took over the business. This left little time for piety and she became avaricious, but after an extraordinary supernatural vision, she began to help poor women and sick persons. For their care, she founded and joined the institute of the 'Sisters of St Anne'. She died at Fenet and was canonized in 1982.

Jane-Frances Frémiot de Chantal (St) {1, 3}

12 August

1572–1641. From Dijon (France), she married the Baron de Chantal in 1592. They were happily married for eight years and had four children before he died as the result of a hunting accident. Then she became the disciple and friend of St Francis de Sales, who described her as 'the perfect woman'. Under his guidance she founded the new order of the Visitation, chiefly for widows and for women unsuited to the austerities of the older religious orders. Sixty-six nunneries were established during her lifetime, the last years of which were a period of intense suffering in body and in mind. She died at Moulins, her shrine was established at Annecy and she was canonized in 1767.

Jane de Lestonnac (St) {2}

2 February

1556–1640. A noblewoman from Bordeaux (France) with a Calvinist mother, she married and had a family but her husband died when she was forty-six. Then she tried and failed to join a nunnery affiliated to the Cistercians, whereupon she set about founding a new religious institute for the education of girls in order to combat Calvinism. This was approved in 1607, and the first house of the 'Daughters of Our Lady of Bordeaux' was opened at Bordeaux. The order spread rapidly, some thirty houses being founded, and she was the superior-general. But as the result of a calumny and intrigue on the part of one of the sisters she was deposed and spent some years in seclusion but was vindicated before she died. She was canonized in 1949.

Jane-Mary de Maillé (Bl) {2}

28 March
1331–1414. A noblewoman born near Tours (France), she married the Baron de Sillé with whom she lived in virginity for sixteen years. After his death in 1362, she joined the Franciscan tertiaries and retired to Tours, where she spent the rest of her life in poverty and deprivation owing to persecution by her husband's relatives. Her cultus was confirmed in 1871.

Jane-Frances-of-the-Visitation Michelotti (Bl) {2}

1 February
1843–88. Born at Annecy, Savoy (now in France), from an early age she dedicated herself to caring for poor sick people in their homes, especially after she moved to Turin in 1871 and came under the influence of St John Bosco. In 1875, she founded the 'Little Servants of the Sacred Heart', whose fourth vow is to serve sick poor people without charge. She was beatified in 1975.

Jane (Vanna) of Orvieto (Bl) {2}

23 July
d. 1306. From near Orvieto (Italy), she entered the convent of Dominican tertiaries there. She is usually referred to as 'Vanna', which is a diminutive of 'Giovanna' the Italian version of 'Jane'. Her cultus was approved for Orvieto in 1754.

Jane of Portugal (Bl) {2}

12 May
1452–90. Born at Lisbon, a daughter of King Alphonsus V of Portugal, she entered the Dominican nunnery at Aveiro near Oporto in 1473. The king prevented her from taking vows, however, until a male heir was born in 1485. She had much trouble because of this. Her cultus was confirmed for Coïmbra in 1693.

Jane Scopelli (Bl) {2}

9 July
?1428–91. From Reggio d'Emilia (Italy), she founded the Carmelite nunnery there and was the first superior. She refused all endowments except those freely given to the nuns as alms. Her cultus was confirmed for Reggio and the Carmelites in 1771.

Jane of Signa (Bl) {2}

17 November
d. 1307. From Signa near Florence (Italy), she was a poor sheep-farmer's daughter and a shepherdess herself before she became a hermit for forty years near her home village. Several religious orders claimed her as a tertiary, but there is no evidence that she was linked to any of them. Her cultus was approved for Florence in 1798.

Jane Soderini (Bl) {2}

1 September
d. ?1367. From Florence (Italy), she was educated by St Juliana Falconieri and became a Servite tertiary through his guidance. Her cultus was confirmed for Florence in 1827.

Jane of Toulouse (Bl) {2}

31 March
Early C14th. A noblewoman of Toulouse (France), she was affiliated to the Carmelite order by St Simon Stock while continuing to live with her parents and is thus considered the first Carmelite tertiary. She spent her time and resources in training young candidates for the Carmelite friars. Her cultus was confirmed for Toulouse in 1895.

Jane of Valois (St) {2}

4 February
1464–1505. She was a daughter of King Louis XI of France, who despised her for her

bodily deformity and married her off to the duke of Orleans (afterwards King Louis XII). Her husband obtained a decree of nullity of marriage on the grounds of constraint, so she retired to her castle at Bourges. There, with her confessor Bl Gabriel-Mary Nicolas, she founded the order of nuns of the Annunciation ('Annunciades') which were more involved in works of active charity than the Poor Clares. She took vows but did not live in community. She was canonized in 1949.

Jane-Emily de Villeneuve (Bl) {2 –add}

2 October
1811–54. From a noble family she was born at Toulouse (France) and brought up at the Château d'Hauterive near Castres. As a girl, she was impressed by the social problems occurring as the Industrial Revolution took hold in France, and as a result tried to join the Sisters of Charity. Her father told her to wait, but instead she founded a new congregation, the Sisters of the Immaculate Conception of Castres, in 1836 when only aged twenty-five. This started in a modest building at Castres, but had spread throughout France and into French Africa while she was still alive. She retired as superior before she died of cholera, aged forty-three. She was beatified in 2009.

Januarius and Marinus, (SS) {2, 4}

10 July
? Nothing is known about these Roman African martyrs. Two others formerly listed with them, Nabor and Felix, have been deleted from the Roman Martyrology.

(Januarius, Maxima and Macaria) (SS) {4 –deleted}

8 April
? Nothing is known about these Roman African martyrs. Their names are sometimes given as 'Januarius, Maximus and Macarius' (three men instead of a man and two women).

(Januarius and Pelagia) (SS) {4 –deleted}

11 July
d. 320? They were listed as beheaded at Nicopolis in Lesser Armenia (Asia Minor) in the reign of Licinius.

Januarius (Gennaro) of Benevento (St) {1, 3}

19 September
Early C4th. Bishop of Benevento (Italy), he was beheaded at Pozzuoli near Naples in the reign of Diocletian and his body was eventually enshrined at Naples, of which city he is the patron. The yearly liquefaction of a solid kept in two vials and alleged to be his blood is a phenomenon well-attested since the C15th. A credible scientific explanation now exists, and the reference to the phenomenon has been deleted from the Roman Martyrology. A legend, now discredited but popular in the Middle Ages, linked him with the following: Festus and Desiderius; Sosius of Misenum; Proculus, Eutyches and Acurius. These are now listed separately in the Roman Martyrology, and the joint cultus was suppressed in 1969.

Januarius Sánchez Delgadillo (St) {1 –group}

17 January
1886–1927. From Zapopan, he became a diocesan priest of Guadalajara in Mexico in 1911. After the government suppressed church activities, he continued his work in secret, but was recognized by a squad of soldiers during the Cristero War and arrested near Tcolotlán. His body was found the next day, so mutilated as to be unrecognizable. Cf. **Mexico, Martyrs of**.

Januarius-Mary Sarnelli (Bl) {2}

30 June

1702–44. A nobleman of Naples (Italy), he met St Alphonsus Liguori while nursing in a hospital and they became life-long friends. As a parish priest, he tried to help young prostitutes. He became a Redemptorist in 1733, preached popular missions and helped the spread of the Congregation. He was beatified in 1996.

Japan (Martyrs of) (SS and BB)

6 February

d. 1597–1637. The start of the Catholic Church in Japan was marked by the arrival of St Francis Xavier in 1549. Missionary activity was successfully carried on by the Portuguese and Spanish, especially in the island of Kyushu (which became the centre of Japanese Christianity), and this was helped by the chaotic state of the country at the time and the lack of an effective central government. Many local rulers ('daimyos', sometimes incorrectly referred to as 'kings') converted, and inspired their subjects to do so. There was predictable hostility from the established religions of Buddhism and Shinto, and Japanese suspicion of the motivations of the foreign missionaries and their overseas sponsors. The first edict of persecution was in 1587, and the first mass execution in 1597 (cf. **Paul Miki and Comps**). A period of peace followed the establishment of strong central government with the Tokugawa shogunate in 1600, but persecution returned in 1612 and was violent from 1617, especially in Nagasaki. The complete suppression of the church became government policy, and this was successful after the Shimabara Uprising was crushed in 1638. The country was completely isolated from foreign influence until the C19th, and the only Christians remaining by then were about 15,000 secret worshippers in Kyushu. Cf. lists of national martyrs in appendix.

Jarlath of Tuam (St) {2}

6 June

d. c.550. The founder and first abbot-bishop of Tuam in Co. Galway (Ireland), he established a monastic school there which became famous. St Brendan the Voyager and St Colman of Cloyne were pupils. He is the principal patron of the diocese of Tuam.

Jarman cf. **Germanus**.

(Jason) (St) {4 –deleted}

12 July

C1st. The Acts of the Apostles (17:5-9) refer to St Paul staying at his house in Thessalonika (Greece), and he is also mentioned in the letter to the Romans (16:21). The Byzantine Martyrology describes him as a bishop of Tarsus in Cilicia (Asia Minor) who evangelized Corfu and died there. The old Roman Martyrology mistakenly confused him with Mnason the Cypriot mentioned in Acts (21:16).

Jean, Jeanne cf. **John**, **Jane**

Jeremias-of-Wallachia Kostistik (Bl) {2} {2, 4}

25 March

1556–1625. Born in Wallachia (now Romania), he went on pilgrimage to Italy when aged twenty-one but was robbed on the way and could only continue by begging and casual farm-work. Arriving at Bari, he went to Naples where he became a Capuchin lay brother in 1578. He used to nurse the sick and obtained the power to heal by signing with the cross; he also had the charisms of prophecy and the reading of consciences. Despite his illiteracy, he was sought out by the well educated. He was beatified in 1983.

Jeremias (Jeremiah) the Prophet (St) {2, 4}

1 May
He is the second of the major prophets of the Old Testament.

Jermyn Gardiner (Bl) {2}

7 March
d.1544. Educated at Cambridge, he became secretary to Stephen Gardiner, bishop of Winchester, and was executed at Tyburn with BB John Larke and John Ireland for denying the royal supremacy. His name is a medieval vernacular version of Germanus. He was beatified in 1886. Cf. **England, Martyrs of**.

Jero (St) {2}

17 August
d. 856. He was a priest killed by Vikings at Noordwijk near The Hague (Netherlands), and his shrine was established at Egmond near Alkmaar.

Jerome (St) {1, 3}

30 September
?341–420. Eusebius Hieronymus Sophronius was born at Stridon (near Ljubljana in Slovenia), studied in Rome (where he acquired a passion for classical literature) and was baptized there in 366. He was then with an ascetic community of friends (including Rufinus) at Aquila before going to the East in 373, travelling to Antioch (where he learn Greek, Hebrew and the practice of Biblical exegesis) and spending two years at the Syrian monastic colony at Chalcis. Returning to Rome in 382, he became secretary to Pope St Damasus, who entrusted to him the task of revising the Latin text of the New Testament. This eventually resulted in the Vulgate edition of the Bible, translated from the original Hebrew and Greek. He made enemies, and left with SS Paula and Eustochium to found a Latin monastery at Bethlehem in 386, where he died. Continually involved in controversy, he was a fierce polemicist and an unforgiving opponent (as is revealed in his surviving letters). He was the greatest biblical scholar after Origen, being unusual among the Fathers for his knowledge of Hebrew, and has been venerated as a doctor of the Church since the C8th. In the Western artistic tradition, he is often shown with a lion in mistake for St Gerasimus. He did not compile the martyrology named after him.

Jerome de Angelis (Bl) {2}

4 December
d. 1623. From Castrogiovanni in Sicily, he became a Jesuit at Messina and went with Bl Charles Spinola to Japan. He worked for twenty-two years in various parts of Japan and was finally betrayed and burnt alive at what is now Tokyo together with BB Francis Galvez and Simon Yempo. Cf. **Japan, Martyrs of**.

Jerome Emiliani (St) {1, 3}

8 February
1481–1537. From Venice (Italy), as a young man he was an army officer and served in the city's campaign of conquest of its hinterland. Being taken prisoner, he was set free after praying to Our Lady and became a priest as a result in 1518. He was fervent in wishing to help the poor, sick and orphans of Venice and elsewhere and so founded several orphanages and hospitals in northern Italy and started a religious society (the 'Servants of the Poor') to look after them. The first house of this was at Somascha near Milan, and it was raised to the status of a religious congregation (the 'Clerks Regular of Somascha') after his death. He died of an infection contracted while nursing at Bergamo, was canonized in 1767 and was declared the patron of orphans and street children in 1928.

Jerome Gherarducci (Bl) {2}

3 March
d. 1369. From Rencanati near Ancona (Italy), he became an Augustinian friar and a peacemaker between rival factions in and around his native town. His cultus was confirmed for the Augustinians in 1804.

Jerome Hermosilla (St) {1 –group}

1 November
d. 1861. From La Calzada near Ciudad Real (Spain), he became a Dominican and went to Manila, Philippines where he was ordained priest and sent to the mission of Vietnam in 1828. He succeeded St Ignatius Delgado as vicar-apostolic of 'East Tonkin' and was himself arrested, tortured and beheaded with SS Peter Almató Ribeira and Valentine Berrio Ochoa during the persecution ordered by Emperor Tự Đức. This was at Hải Dương in north Vietnam. Cf. **Vietnam, Martyrs of**.

Jerome-of-the-Cross Jo (Bl) {2}

3 September
d. 1632. A Japanese Franciscan priest, he had been educated in the seminary of Arima and ordained at Manila. Returning to Japan in 1628, he was burnt alive with BB Anthony Ishida and Comps. Cf. **Japan, Martyrs of**.

Jerome Lu Tingmei (St) {1 –group}

28 January
Cf. **Agatha Lin Zhao and Comps**.

Jerome of Nevers (St) {2}

5 October
d. 816. He was a bishop of Nevers (France), and was noted for his solicitude and generosity.

Jerome of Pavia (St) {2}

22 July
C8th. He was an obscure bishop of Pavia (Italy) whose cultus was confirmed for there in 1888.

Jerome Ranuzzi (Bl) {2}

11 December
d. ?1468. From Sant' Angelo in Vado near Urbino (Italy), he became a Servite and superior of the friary at his home town. As the personal adviser of the duke of Urbino he was nicknamed 'the Angel of Good Counsel'. His cultus was approved for Sant' Angelo in Vado in 1775.

Jerome de Weert (St) {2}

9 July
1522–72. From Weert in the Netherlands, he was a Franciscan missionary in the Holy Land for several years before becoming the vicar of the friary at Gorinchem under St Nicholas Pieck. He was a powerful preacher against Calvinism, and was one of the **Gorinchem** martyrs.

Jesus Méndez Montoya (St) {1 –group}

5 February
1880–1928. From Tarímbaro near Micoacán in Morelia, Mexico, he became a diocesan priest of the latter place and was later parish priest of Valtiervilla. During the Cristero War, in which he had no involvement, there was a government raid on the town and he was arrested while carrying the Blessed Sacrament. He managed to consume it in order to prevent its profanation, whereupon the soldiers sat him on a stump and shot him dead. Cf. **Mexico, Martyrs of**.

Joachim (St) {1, 3}

26 July
C1st. This is the name given to the father of Our Lady in the apocryphal gospel of James, although other sources name him as Heli, Cleopas, Eliacim, Jonachir or Sadoc. Nothing specific is known about him. He has been commemorated liturgically in the East from early times but in the West only since the C16th.

Joachim He Kaizhi (St) {1 –group}

9 July
1782–1839. A craftsman of Guizhou (China), he was converted in Guiyang and exiled to Mongolia for eighteen years. After assisting the authorities during a Mongol rebellion, he was allowed to return to Guiyang, but was later arrested, tortured and executed. Cf. **China, Martyrs of**.

Joachim Hirayama-Díaz (Bl) {2}

19 August
d. 1622. A Japanese ship's captain, he was hired to take BB Louis Flores (q.v.) and Peter Zuñiga to Japan. The ship was captured by Dutch privateers, brought to Hirado and her company taken to Nagasaki. Bl Joachim was burnt with the two missionaries while the rest were beheaded. Cf. **Japan, Martyrs of**.

Joachim Jovani Marín and Comps (BB) {2 –add}
d. 1936–8. These are the fifteen martyred Worker Priests of the Sacred Heart of Jesus, killed in hatred of the faith by Marxists in the diocese of Tortosa, Spain during the Spanish Civil War. They were beatified in 2013. Cf. **Spanish Civil War, Martyrs of** and list in appendix.

Joachim Kurōemon (Bl) {2 –add}

8 March
d. 1624. He was a catechist of Hiroshima, martyred in that city. He was beatified in 2008. Cf. **Japan, Martyrs of**.

Joachim Mine Sukedayū and Comps (BB) {2 –add}

17 May
d. 1627. He was married to Bl Mary Mine, who had already been martyred on 28 February. With him at Unzen near Nagasaki were martyred nine other laypeople of the Nagasaki diocese: Paul Nishida Kyūhachi, Mary of Fukae, John Matsutake Chōzaburō, Bartholomew Baba Han'emon, Louis Furue Sukeemon, Paul Onizuka Magoemon, Louis Hayashida Sōka, Mary-Magdalen Hayashida and Paul Hayashida Mohyōe. They were beatified in 2008. Cf. **Japan, Martyrs of**.

Joachim Piccolomini (Bl) {2, 4}

16 April
d. 1305. From Siena (Italy), he became a Servite lay brother when aged fourteen and was noted for his simple devotion to Our Lady as well as his concern for destitute people.

Joachim Royo Péréz (St) {1 –group}

28 October
1691–1748. From Teruel (Spain), he became a Dominican at Valencia and was sent to China in 1715. He worked in secret in Jiangxi and Zhejiang, but was captured and executed after two years in prison. Cf. **Francis Serrano and Comps**.

Joachim Sakakibara (St) {1 –group}

6 February
d. 1597. A Japanese doctor, he worked with the Franciscan missionaries as a catechist and was crucified at Nagasaki with SS Paul Miki and Comps. Cf. **Japan, Martyrs of**.

Joachim Senkivskyj (Bl) {2}

30 June
1897–1941. A monk and priest of the Basilian Order of St Josaphat, he died in prison at Drohobych after eastern Poland was annexed by the Soviet Union. Cf. **Nicholas Čarneckyj and 24 Comps**.

Joachim-of-St-Anne Wall (St) {2}

22 August
d. 1679. From a recusant family near Preston (Lancs), John Wall was educated at Douai and

in Rome and became a Franciscan at Douai in 1651. In 1656, he returned to England and worked in Warwickshire and Worcestershire until he was arrested and executed as a result of the Oates plot. He was canonized in 1970, and is listed in the Roman Martyrology under his baptismal name of 'John'. Cf. **England, Martyrs of**.

Joachima de Vedruna de Mas (St) {2}

28 August
1783–1854. A Spanish noblewoman, she was widowed in the Napoleonic wars and went to live at Vich in Catalonia where she founded the 'Carmelite Sisters of Charity'. They spread throughout Spain and South America. She died of cholera at Barcelona and was canonized in 1959.

Joan of Arc (St) {2, 4}

30 May
1412–31. Nicknamed 'the Maid of Orleans' or 'La Pucelle', she was the daughter of a peasant born at Domrémy in the Champagne (France). When aged seventeen, while keeping her father's sheep, she heard supernatural voices commanding her to take up arms and lead the French army against the English invaders then besieging Orleans. She left home disguised as a man, convinced the Dauphin of her sincerity and enabled him to be crowned as King Charles VII by her rapid military successes. As she herself had predicted, however, she was captured by the Burgundians and handed over to the English. Then she was tried by an ecclesiastical court, condemned as a heretic and burnt at the stake at Rouen. The case was re-tried in 1456 and she was declared innocent. She was canonized in 1920 and declared patroness of France in 1922. Problems exist, however, as to the 'heavenly' inspiration of her military career. She claimed that St Margaret of Antioch and St Catherine of Alexandria spoke to her but these persons never existed. She is usually depicted as a young woman in contemporary plate armour.

Joan, Joanna (others) cf. **Jane**.

Joanna (St) {2, 4}

24 May
C1st. The wife of Chuza, steward of the tetrarch Herod Antipas, she is mentioned by the Gospel of St Luke (8:3) as one of the women followers who ministered to the needs of Christ.

Joannicius the Great (St) {2, 4}

4 November
750–846. From Bithynia (Asia Minor), he was a soldier in the imperial bodyguards of emperors Leo III and Constantine V and supported their iconoclast policies. He converted, however, became a hermit on the Bithynian Olympus when aged forty and was thenceforth an energetic defender of icons. He was also known as a prophet and thaumaturge.

Joanninus de San Juan (Bl) {2}

15 July
d. 1570. A nephew of the captain of the ship which carried **Ignatius de Azevedo and Comps**, he volunteered to join them in their martyrdom and was thrown into the sea.

Job the Patriarch (St) {2, 4}

10 May
He is the principal character in the book of the Old Testament named after him, and has been kept in the revised Roman Martyrology despite serious scholarly doubts as to his historical existence.

Jodoc cf. **Judoc**.

Joel (St) {2}

19 October
He is the second of the Minor Prophets in the Old Testament.

John

This is the most popular name in Christendom, although its popularity has suffered a collapse in English-speaking countries. The original Hebrew Yokhanan has been Hellenized and Latinized into Joannes, whence the numerous variants in all languages. Examples are: Italian, Giovanni; French, Jean; Spanish, Juan; Portuguese, Joan; Dutch, Jan; German, Johann; Russian, Ivan. There are also numerous diminutive forms, for example, Italian, Giovannino, Nanino; Spanish, Juanito; French, Jeanin; Old English, Johnikin. The name is often used in combination with others, especially in the Latin countries, for example, Gianpier, Gianluigi, Jean-Benoît, Jean-François, Juan-José, Juan-Maria.

John I, Pope (St) {1, 3}

18 May
d. 526. A Tuscan, he became a priest at Rome and was made pope in 523. The city was then part of the Ostrogothic kingdom of Italy and was ruled by Therodoric, an Arian. It was known, however, that the Empire was planning a reconquest of Italy, and Pope John was ordered to go on an embassy to the emperor Justin I in 526 in order to try and forestall this and to ask for an end to imperial sanctions against Arians. On his return, Theodoric imprisoned him on suspicion of having conspired with the emperor and he died of ill-treatment in custody.

John XXIII, Pope (St) {2}

11 October
1881–1963. Angelo Roncalli was born at Sotto il Monte near Bergamo (Italy) of a peasant family, entered the seminary in 1892 and was ordained in 1904. In 1925, he was made Apostolic Visitor to Bulgaria, and to Turkey and Greece in 1935. In 1944 he became Nuncio in France, and was made Cardinal Patriarch of Venice in 1953. He was elected Pope in 1958, and the way he performed his duties earned him the nickname of 'Good Pope John'. He initiated the revision of the code of Canon Law but is most famous for his convening of the Second Vatican Council. He died when the council was still in session, and was canonized in 2014.

John-Paul II, Pope (St) {2 –add}

2 April
1920–2005. Born as Karol Woytiła at Wadowice (Poland), he was at university at Cracow when the Second World War started and he was indentured as a labourer in strategic industries. He was ordained as a diocesan priest of Cracow in 1946, and was consecrated as auxiliary bishop in 1958. In this capacity he attended the Second Vatican Council, became archbishop in 1964 and cardinal in 1967. He was elected pope in 1978, and served for twenty-six years. His was the second-longest pontificate in church history. He travelled widely on pastoral visits, and wrote much on church teachings especially as regards the dignity of the human person in the context of a just society. His experience of two vicious totalitarian systems gave him an uncompromising stance against political repression, and he is credited with an active part in the collapse of Communism. He also fostered ecumenical links with other Christian denominations and non-Christian religions, without dissembling on fundamental issues of difference. He continued his public duties almost to the end, despite suffering from Parkinson's disease. He died of septic shock caused by a bladder infection, and was canonized in 2014.

(John and Crispus) *(SS)* *{4 –deleted}*

18 August
? According to the old Roman Martyrology they were Roman priests who used to bury the bodies of martyred Christians, because of which they themselves suffered martyrdom. Their names are taken from the untrustworthy acta of SS Simplicius, Faustinus and Beatrix.

John and Festus (SS) {2, 4}

24 June
? They are listed in the old Roman Martyrology as having been martyred in Tuscany (Italy), but the revision places their martyrdom at a locality called 'Septem Palumbas' on the old Salarian Way outside Rome.

John and James (SS) {2, 4}

23 October
d. 344. They were Persian martyrs of the reign of Shah Shapur II. John is listed as a bishop.

John and Paul (SS) {2, 3}

26 June
Early C4th. They were martyred at Rome but not (as asserted in their spurious acta) in the reign of Julian. Their names occur in the Roman canon of the Mass and there is a basilica dedicated to them on the Coelian Hill, to which their cultus has been confined since 1969.

John Adams (Bl) {2}

8 October
d. 1586. A convert from Dorset, he was ordained at Rheims and seized at Winchester on his third missionary journey to England. He was executed at Tyburn with BB Robert Dibdale and John Lowe and was beatified in 1987. Cf. **England, Martyrs of**.

John of Afusia (St) {2}

27 April
C9th. He was the abbot of a monastery on the island of Afusia in the Sea of Marmara, and suffered much for his defence of the veneration of sacred images against the emperor Leo the Armenian.

John-Joseph Alcide Lataste (Bl) {2 –add}

10 March
1832–69. From Cadillac (France), after working at a tax office in Paris he joined the Dominicans at Flavigny in 1857. While exercising a preaching ministry around the convent at Bordeaux he became aware of the call to found a new congregation of sisters which would include repentant former prison inmates. The first convent of his new Dominican Sisters of Bethany was founded at Frasne-le-Château, where he died of pleurisy. He was beatified in 2012.

John Alcober Figuera (St) {1 –group}

28 October
1694–1748. From Gerona (Spain), he became a Dominican at Granada and was sent to China in 1728. For sixteen years, he worked in the province of Fujian but was arrested in 1746 and strangled in prison at Fuzhou. Cf. **Francis Serrano and Comps**.

John Almond (St) {2}

5 December
?1577–1612. From Allerton near Liverpool, he was educated for the priesthood at Rheims and Rome. Ordained in 1598, he worked on the English mission from 1602 and was highly regarded. Executed at Tyburn (London), he was canonized in 1970. Cf. **England, Martyrs of**.

John the Almsgiver (St) {2}

11 November
d. 620. Son of a governor of Cyprus, he lost his family, became a monk and went on to

become Melkite patriarch of Alexandria in 608. At this time, the Egyptian church was completely split between the majority Monophysite Copts and the minority Orthodox Melkites. He gained the admiration of both factions by his policy of liberal and systematic almsgiving and by his personal integrity (it being rumoured that he never spoke an idle word). He was exiled just before his death by the Persian conquest of Egypt.

John Amias (alias Anne) (B1) {2}

15 March
d. 1589. From near Wakefield (Yorks), he was a clothes-seller but his wife died and he went on to study at Rheims for the priesthood. Ordained in 1581, he was executed at York with Bl Robert Dalby. He was beatified in 1929. Cf. **England, Martyrs of.**

John-Juvenal Ancina (Bl) {2}

30 August
1545–1604. From Fossano in Piedmont (Italy), he became professor of medicine at the University of Turin and was posted to the Savoyard Embassy at Rome. There he came under the influence of St Philip Neri, joined the Oratory in 1575 and was sent to Naples to open a new oratory there. He was noted especially for his work for the poor. Finally he was made bishop of Saluzzo in 1602 and set out on his first episcopal visitation. On his return to Saluzzo, he was poisoned by a friar whose immorality he had rebuked. He was beatified in 1869.

John of Ávila (St) {2}

10 May
d. 1569. The 'Apostle of Andalucia' was born at Almodóvar del Pinar near Cuenca (Spain) and studied law at Salamanca and theology at Alcalá. He was about to leave for the New World after being ordained, but was detained by the archbishop of Seville and spent the forty years of his priestly career evangelizing Andalucia. He was a famous preacher, writer (his ascetical writings, especially his letters, are among the classics of Spanish literature) and spiritual director (he directed SS Teresa of Avila, Francis Borgia, John of God and Louis of Granada). He died at Montilla and was made a Doctor of the Church in 2012.

John-Adalbert Balicki (Bl) {2 –add}

24 October
1869–1948. A Pole from Staromieście (now in Ukraine), he became a diocesan priest of Przemisl and a seminary professor. He was famous as a confessor. He died of tuberculosis, and he was beatified in 2002.

John the Baptist (St) {1, 3}

24 June
C1st. The career of the last of the prophets and the forerunner of Christ is described in the four Gospels, where he is presented as modelled on Elijah (in his clothing, for example). He is also mentioned by Josephus. There has been much scholarly speculation on the wider context of his ministry in contemporary Jewish society, and on a possible link with the Essenes of Qumran. Patristic tradition maintained that St John was freed from original sin and sanctified in his mother's womb, hence his birthday is liturgically celebrated with a higher dignity than the day of his beheading (29 August). The fate of his relics, especially of his head, is confused by conflicting traditions after the destruction of his alleged tomb at Samaria in the reign of Julian. The earliest of these describes his head being found at Emesa (now Homs) in Syria and being venerated at the great basilica at Damascus, which is now the Umayyad mosque there. His attribute is a lamb.

John of Báculo (Bl) {2}

24 March
d. 1290. He was one of the first monk-disciples of St Sylvester at Montefano and his cultus was confirmed for Fabriano (Italy) in 1772.

John and Peter Becchetti (BB) {2}

2 July
d. c.1420. When St Thomas Becket was exiled by King Henry II he also banished other members of his family, and one branch allegedly became the Becchetti of Fabriano (Italy). These two Augustinian friars were descended therefrom. Bl John allegedly taught at Oxford. Their cultus was approved for the Augustinian friars in 1835.

John Beche (Bl) {2}

2 December
Cf. **Benedictine Martyrs of the Reformation**.

John Berchmans (St) {2}

13 August
1599–1621. From Diest in Brabant (Belgium), the son of a shoemaker, he studied at Mechelen and entered the Jesuits there at the age of seventeen, being sent to Rome for his novitiate. His short life of twenty-two years was remarkable for the heroic fidelity with which he kept even the most trivial points of regular observance, and yet he had great serenity. He was canonized in 1888 and is the patron of young altar-servers.

(John of Bergamo) (St) {4 –deleted}

11 July
d. c.690. Bishop of Bergamo (Italy) from ?656, he was famous for his scholarship and his success in resisting Arianism. The letters BM for 'Bonae Memoriae' ('of good memory') were added to his name in an early list and these were later misread as 'Beati Martyris' ('of the Blessed Martyr'), hence the spurious tradition of his martyrdom.

John of Beverley (St) {2}

7 May
d. 721. From Harpham near Driffield in Yorkshire (England), he studied at Canterbury under SS Adrian and Theodore before becoming a monk at Whitby. Eventually he was ordained bishop of Hexham, whence he was transferred to York. He ordained St Bede to the priesthood and was the founder of Beverley Abbey, to which he retired in 717. This abbey did not survive the Viking period as a monastery, but the Minster is its descendant.

John Beyzym (Bl) {2 –add}

1850–1912. From Beyzymy Wielkie in what is now the Ukraine and was then in the Hapsburg Empire, he became a Jesuit in 1872 and taught at the Jesuit colleges of Tanopol and Chyrów after ordination. In 1898, he went to Madagascar to work in the leprosarium at Ambahivoraka near Antananarivo, where 150 sick people lived in complete isolation from the wider society. Then the disease was incurable, but he did everything in his power to alleviate its effects. In 1903, he left Ambahivoraka to go to build a hospital at Marana near Fianarantsoa. Fr Beyzym's inner life was marked by a profound bond with Christ and the Eucharist. The Mass was the centre of his life and he was greatly devoted to Mary, attributing his successes to her and seeing himself as her instrument. He died at Fianarantsoa and was beatified in 2002.

John-Mary Boccardo (Bl) {2}

30 December
1848–1913. From Turin (Italy), he became a diocesan priest there in 1871 and was a seminary spiritual director before being made

parish priest of Pancalieri in 1882. Two years later there was a cholera epidemic there which left many children and old people with no one to care for them, so he founded a hospice and a congregation of 'Poor Daughters of St Cajetan' which spread throughout Italy. He was both cheerful and devoted to arduous penance. He died at Pancalieri, was beatified in 1998.

John Bodey (Bl) {2}

2 November

d. 1583. From Wells (Somerset) and a fellow of New College, Oxford, he became a convert and studied law at Douai. Returning to England, he worked as a schoolmaster, was condemned for repudiating the royal supremacy in spiritual matters and was hanged at Andover (Hants). He was beatified in 1929. Cf. **England, Martyrs of**.

John-Louis Bonnard (St) {1 –group}

1 May

1824–52. A French missionary priest who belonged to the Paris Society of Foreign Missions, he was beheaded at Nam Định in north Vietnam after being arrested and condemned on the charge of baptizing children. Cf. **Vietnam, Martyrs of**.

John Bonus of Siponto (St) {2}

5 September

C12th. He founded the abbey of St Michael on the Dalmatian coast near Dubrovnik (Croatia)

John Bosco (St) {1, 3}

31 January

1815–88. The son of a peasant from near Castelnuovo d'Asti in Piedmont (Italy), he became a diocesan priest at Turin in 1841 and began his life's work of educating boys. From the first he had a clear programme of education, namely to educate through love and to induce the boys to love their teachers, their studies and all the conditions surrounding their education. He gathered disciples and founded a new institute which received papal approval in 1860. This was dedicated to Our Lady, Help of Christians and St Francis of Sales, hence the name of 'Salesians'. It grew rapidly and spread throughout Europe and the foreign missions. He also formed a new sisterhood on the same pattern for the education of girls, the 'Daughters of Mary Auxiliatrix'. He died at Turin and was canonized in 1934.

John Boste (St) {2}

24 July

1543–94. From Dufton near Appleby in Cumbria, he studied at the Queen's College, Oxford, converted in 1576 and then studied for the priesthood at Rheims. Ordained in 1581, he worked in northern England for twelve years until his execution at Durham. He was canonized in 1970. Cf. **England, Martyrs of**.

John de Brébeuf and Comps (SS) {2}

16 March

1596–1649. From Condé-en-Brie in Normandy (France), he joined the Jesuits at Rouen in 1617 and was a missionary priest in the French colony of Quebec from 1625. There he worked among the native Huron nation for thirty-four years, from a mission base at Sainte Marie au Pays des Hurons. This settlement, near the present Midland in Ontario (Canada) which is on Georgian Bay off Lake Huron, existed from 1639 to 1649. He was head of the mission until 1638, but only achieved great success in making converts after 1644, becoming known as the 'Apostle of the Hurons' and being fluent in their language. The Hurons were the target of a policy of extermination by the Iroquois, their mortal enemies, and he and

St Gabriel Lalement fell into the hands of the latter during a raid. They were very slowly tortured to death by cutting, scalding and burning (eyeballs were replaced by burning coals) over a period of seventeen hours at a village called St Ignace. Their courage astounded their captors, and they ate his heart so as to acquire this courage for themselves. The two martyrs are liturgically celebrated on 19 October together with six other Jesuits of the same mission who were also martyred by the Iroquois: Anthony Daniel, Charles Garnier, Isaac Jogues, John de la Lande, Natalis (Noel) Chabanel and Renatus Goupil 20/9. As a result of the martyrdoms and destruction, the mission centre was abandoned.

John Bretton (Bl) {2}

1 April

1529–98. A well-known recusant and family man of Sandal Magna (Yorks), he was condemned for 'using seditious words against the Queen'. However he was offered a reprieve in exchange for his apostasy, which he refused. He was executed at York, and was beatified in 1987. Cf. **England, Martyrs of**.

John of Bridlington cf. **John Thwing**.

John de Brito (St) {2}

4 February

1647–93. From Lisbon (Portugal), he became a Jesuit in 1662 and soon afterwards was sent to India. He worked in what is now Kerala and Tamil Nadu, modelling his behaviour on that of the Brahmin caste in an attempt to make contact with the nobility. His methods were unconventional and enlightened in many other respects. He was captured, tortured and expelled in 1687 but returned in 1689 as superior of the Jesuit mission in India. He persuaded the rajah of Siruvalli to abandon polygamy, but one of the dismissed wives persuaded her relative, the rajah of Marava, to initiate a persecution and John was martyred at Oriyur. He was canonized in 1947.

John-of-Rieti Bufalari (Bl) {2}

1 August

d. ?1336. From Castel Porziano near Rome, he became an Augustinian friar at Rieti. His cultus was approved for the Augustinian friars in 1832.

John-Baptist Bullaker (Bl) {2}

12 October

d. 1642. The son of a physician at Midhurst in Sussex, he was baptized as Thomas. Studying at Valladolid, he joined the Franciscans at Abroya, was ordained and sent to Plymouth. He was caught on his arrival but released and had a ministry of eleven years before being caught saying Mass in London by the Parliamentary authorities during the civil war. He was executed at Tyburn and was beatified in 1987. Cf. **England, Martyrs of**.

John Buoni (Bl) {2}

23 October

d. 1249. From Mantua (Italy), he was a travelling jester with a flair for obscenity who was popular at various Italian courts, but converted in 1208 after a severe illness and became a penitential hermit near Cesena. Disciples gathered to him, and these were given the Augustinian rule by the pope. His group united with others to form the Order of Augustinian friars, often referred to as 'hermits' as a result of their origins. His cultus was approved in 1483.

John-of-Parma Buralli (Bl) {2}

19 March

1209–89. From Parma (Italy), he became a Franciscan and taught theology at Bologna and Naples. He was seventh minister-general of the Franciscans from 1247 to 1257 and visited the Franciscan provinces of various countries (including England). He also went to Constantinople as papal legate. He died in retirement at Greccio, and his cultus was confirmed for Camerino and the Franciscans in 1777.

John Cacciafronte (Bl) {2}

16 March
d. 1181. From Cremona (Italy), he became a Benedictine monk at the abbey of St Laurence there and was made abbot in 1155. He sided with the pope against the emperor Frederick I Barbarossa, by whom he was banished from his abbey. Then he lived as a hermit near Mantua until he was made bishop there in 1174, transferring to Vicenza in 1177. He was killed by a man whom he had excommunicated for embezzling episcopal revenues, and his cultus was confirmed for Vicenza in 1824.

John Calabria (St) {2}

4 December
1873–1954. Born at Verona (Italy) of a poor family, he was ordained there in 1901 and founded a refuge for poor and derelict children in 1907 which became known as the 'Opus Dei'. This moved to San Zenone in Monte the next year, and he organized his helpers as the 'Poor Servants and Handmaids of Divine Providence' in 1914. He also organized a corresponding extern society in 1944. He died at Verona and was canonized in 1999.

John Calabytes (St) {2, 4}

15 January
C5th. His romantic legend, probably the source of the similar one concerning St Alexis, is as follows. From Constantinople, the twelve-year-old child of a nobleman, he ran away from home to be a monk at Gomon on the Bosporus. After six years he returned home incognito, so changed in appearance that his parents did not recognize him. He then lived on their charity in a small hut (his surname is Greek for 'hut dweller') outside the gate of their mansion, and only revealed himself to them as their son just before he died.

John-Joseph-of-the-Cross Calosinti (St) {2}

5 March
1654–1734. From the island of Ischia near Naples (Italy), he became an Alcantarine Franciscan in 1670. He was superior of the new friary at Piedimonte di Alife before becoming superior of the new Italian branch of the Alcantarines in 1702. Dying at Naples, he was canonized in 1839.

John Camillus 'the Good' (St) {2, 4}

2 January
d. c.660. A friend of St Gregory the Great, he became bishop of Milan (Italy) in 649 and resided there, the first bishop to do so since the invasion of the Arian Lombards seventy years previously. He fought the Arian and Monothelite heresies.

John of Capistrano (St) {1, 3}

23 October
1386–1456. From Capistrano in the Abruzzi (Italy), he became a lawyer and was governor of Perugia in the Papal States. When aged thirty he separated from his wife, joined the Franciscans and (influenced by St Bernardine of Siena) became a famous preacher. He was made papal inquisitor in 1426 and prompted a reform of his order. In 1431, he became minister-general of the Observants, and was papal legate to many European states and in the Holy Land. He took measures against the Czech Hussites and the Jews (for which he has been criticized), and led a crusade to help the Hungarians against the Turks in

1455. He died near Belgrade and was canonized in 1724.

John Carey (Bl) {2}

4 July

d. 1594. He was the Irish servant of Bl Thomas Bosgrave and was martyred at Dorchester (Dorset) with him and with BB John Cornelius and Patrick Salmon. They were beatified in 1929. Cf. **England, Martyrs of.**

John Cassian (St) {2}

23 July

d. ?435. From Scythia (probably Dobruja in Romania), when young he became a monk at Jerusalem with his friend Germanus but they then went to stay in Egypt from 386, visiting the various monastic centres. Thus he was able to gather the material for his two seminal works on monastic spirituality, the 'Institutes' and the 'Conferences', which had a profound influence on Western monasticism (St Benedict recommended them in his rule). They were at Constantinople in 400, where St John was ordained deacon by St John Chrysostom, and were sent to Rome to seek help when the latter was exiled. In 414, St John founded two monasteries for men and women at Marseilles, where he died. He attacked St Augustine's teaching on grace on the basis that it denied free will, and hence has historically been regarded with a little suspicion by the church.

John of Cetina and Peter de Dueñas (BB) {2}

19 May

d. 1397. Franciscans of Spain, they were sent to the Muslim kingdom of Granada in order to try and evangelize the inhabitants and were predictably killed.

John Chen Xianheng (St) {1 –group}

18 February

1820–62. From Chengdu in Sichuan (China), he moved to Guiyang to help a destitute sister and was converted there. As a lay catechist he helped St John-Peter Néel and was seized and beheaded with him and SS John Zhang Tianshen, and Martin Wu Xuesheng at Kaiyang. Cf. **China, Martyrs of.**

John of Chinon (St) {2, 4}

27 June

C6th. A Breton, he became a hermit at Chinon near Tours (France) and was the spiritual adviser of Queen St Radegund.

John-Baptist Chŏn Chang-un (St) {1 –group}

9 March

Cf. **Peter Ch'oe Hyŏng and John-Baptist Chŏn Chang-un.**

John Chrysostom (St) {1, 3}

13 September

?347–407. From Antioch (Syria), he was a hermit-monk in his youth but the austerity ruined his digestion and he became a priest of the city in 386. The sermons that he gave in the great basilica there made him famous, and are the best extant examples of the Antiochian school of biblical exegesis. They gave him his surname 'Golden Mouth'. In 398, he was made patriarch of Constantinople and was zealous in reforming church life there, but this made enemies at the Imperial court and he was deposed and exiled at the 'Synod of the Oak' in 403 at the instigation of Theophilus, Patriarch of Alexandria. Returning by popular acclaim two months later, he was finally exiled to Armenia after he had offended the Empress and died at Pityus in Colchis (Georgia). He allegedly revised the Byzantine liturgy that now bears his name and was the most prolific of the Eastern doctors of the Church. His iconic representation shows him with a weak, wispy beard and is possibly based on his real appearance.

John-Nepomucene Chrzan (Bl) {2}

1 July
1885–1942. A Polish priest, he died of ill-treatment at the concentration camp at Dachau. Cf. **Poland, Martyrs of the Nazi Occupation of**.

John Chugoku (Bl). {2}

10 September
d. 1622. From Yamaguchi in Japan, he worked with Bl Charles Spinola as a cathechist and was received by him as a Jesuit in the prison at Omura. He was the only Jesuit beheaded at Nagasaki in the 'Great Martyrdom'. Cf. **Japan, Martyrs of** and **Great Martyrdom at Nagasaki**.

John Cini 'Soldato' or 'Stipendario' or 'della Pace' (Bl) {2}

12 November
d. 1435. A nobleman of Pisa (Italy), as a soldier he was one of a gang that attacked a group of priests. Afterwards, remorseful, he became a Franciscan tertiary in 1396 and founded several charitable organizations as well as a confraternity of flagellants. His cultus was approved for Pisa in 1856.

John Climacus (St) {2, 4}

30 March
570–649. From the Holy Land, he became a monk at St Catherine's monastery at Sinai and spent some time as a hermit before becoming abbot when aged seventy-five. He went back to being a hermit four years later. His fame, and his surname, derive from his popular ascetical work 'The Ladder of Perfection', which is still prescribed reading for monks of the Byzantine rite during Lent.

John of Cologne (St) {2}

9 July
d. 1572. From Cologne, he became a Dominican and parish priest of Hoornaer in the

Netherlands and was one of the **Gorinchem** martyrs.

John Colombini (Bl) {2}

31 July
c.1300–67. From Siena (Italy), he became an important figure in that city and was its first magistrate, being described as ambitious, avaricious and bad-tempered. While reading the story of St Mary of Egypt he was suddenly converted and eventually formed a small society of laypeople called Jesuati devoted to penance and deeds of charity. He has left a collection of letters.

John-Baptist Cơn (St) {1 –group}

8 November
Cf. **Joseph Nguyễn Đình Nghi and Comps**.

(John of Constantinople) (St) {4 –deleted}

27 April
d. 813. Abbot of the monastery of the Cathares at Nicaea near Constantinople, he was a firm opponent of the iconoclast emperor Leo III, by whom he was imprisoned and exiled.

John-Charles Cornay (St) {1 –group}

20 September
1809–37. From Loudun near Poitiers (France), he joined the Paris Society of Foreign Missions and worked in Vietnam. He was seized at Ban No, kept in a cage for three months at the castle of Sơn Tây and brutally treated during the persecution ordered by Emperor Minh Mạng. He finally had his limbs cut off before being beheaded. Cf. **Vietnam, Martyrs of**.

John Cornelius (Bl) {2}

4 July
d. 1594. Born at Bodmin (Cornwall) of Irish parents, he was a fellow of Exeter College,

Oxford before studying for the priesthood at Rheims and then at Rome, where he was ordained in 1583. He worked for ten years on mission at Lanherne in Cornwall, became a Jesuit in 1594 and was martyred at Dorchester (Dorset) with BB John Carey, Patrick Salmon and Thomas Bosgrave. They were beatified in 1929. Cf. **England, Martyrs of**.

John de Craticula (St) {2}

1 February

1098–1163. From Châtillon in Brittany (France), he was supposedly an Augustinian canon at Bourgmoyen in Blois and a friend of St Bernard. He became bishop of Aleth, and also abbot of the Augustinian abbey of Guingamp. He transferred his cathedral from Aleth to St Malo. His surname, 'of the Grating', derives from the metal railings that surrounded his shrine. He was not a Cistercian monk at Clairvaux under St Bernard and abbot-founder of Buzay and Bégard, as this was a separate person.

John of the Cross cf. **John-of-the-Cross de Yepes**.

John Damascene (St) {1, 3}

4 December

?676–749. Born in Damascus when that city was the capital of the Umayyad caliphate and where his father was the representative of the Christians at the court of the caliph, he was educated by a Sicilian monk who had been brought to Syria as a slave. After succeeding his father at court he became a monk at the laura of St Sabas in the Judaean Desert, where his writings made him the last of the Eastern fathers, influential in the medieval West as well as in the Byzantine East. He was the author of the first real compendium of theology, the 'Fountain of Wisdom' as well as of numerous liturgical hymns and of effective

polemic against the iconoclast policy of Emperor Leo III. He was proclaimed a doctor of the Church in 1890.

John Đạt (St) {1 –group}

28 October

1764–98. From north Vietnam, he was ordained in 1798 and beheaded that same year at Chợ Rạ after three months' imprisonment. Cf. **Vietnam, Martyrs of**.

John Davy (Bl) {2}

8 June

d. 1537. A Carthusian monk at the London Charterhouse, he was starved to death with six others of his community at Newgate Prison where they were imprisoned for resisting the claims to spiritual supremacy of King Henry VIII. Cf. **England, Martyrs of**.

John Diego Cuauhtlatoatzin (St) {1}

9 December

d. 1548. Born at Cuahtitlán near Mexico City, he was a married native Mexican but the couple had taken a vow of celibacy before the wife died in 1529. He saw a vision of Our Lady on a hill called Tepeyac (Guadalupe) in 1531, who told him to tell the bishop to build a church on the site. Three days later, in a second vision, she told him to pick wildflowers for the bishop which became roses on delivery. His cloak had developed an image of Our Lady on it, which is venerated at the shrine at Guadalupe. He became a hermit at the shrine, and he was canonized in 2002.

John Baptist Đinh văn Thành (St) {1 –group}

28 April
Cf. **Paul Phạm Khắc Khoan and Comps**.

John Đoàn Trinh Hoan (St) {1 –group}

26 May

?1789–1861. From Kim Long in central Vietnam, he was ordained priest and worked zealously as a missionary until he was arrested, tortured and beheaded near Đồng Hới with St Matthew Nguyễn Văn Phượng, who had aided him. This was during the persecution ordered by Emperor Tự Đức. Cf. **Vietnam, Martyrs of**.

John Dominici (Bl) {2}

10 June

?1356–1419. From Florence (Italy), he became a Dominican there in ?1373 and was involved in a contemporary restoration of discipline in his order. He was made vicar-general of the reformed friaries of Italy, and was made cardinal archbishop of Ragusa (now Dubrovnik in Croatia) in 1408, serving as papal legate in Bohemia and Hungary and converting many Hussites. He was also a leader in the healing of the Great Schism in the Western church. He died at Buda (Hungary) and his cultus was confirmed for Florence and the Dominicans in 1832.

John Duckett (Bl) {2}

7 September

d. 1644. From near Sedbergh (Yorks), a relative of Bl James Duckett, he was educated for the priesthood at Douai and ordained in 1639. He was on mission at Durham, and was executed at Tyburn (London) with Bl Ralph Corby. He was beatified in 1929. Cf. **England, Martyrs of**.

John of Dukla (St) {2}

29 September

1414–84. From a bourgeois family at Dukla near Tarnow (Poland), when young he was a hermit there before joining the Conventual Franciscans at Lemberg (now Lviv in Ukraine) in 1440. He was a preacher and local superior until he transferred to the Observants in 1463, and then spent the rest of his life ministering and preaching to the Germans in Lviv, where he died. His relics were taken from there back to Dukla after 1945, and he was canonized in 1997.

John Duns Scotus (Bl) {2}

8 November

1266–1308. Born in Duns, Berwickshire (Scotland), he became a Franciscan when aged fifteen and went to Oxford and Paris to study. He lectured on the 'Sentences of Lombard' and became the last of the great medieval scholastics (he is nicknamed 'Doctor Subtilis'). He became regent master in Paris in 1305 and went to lecture in Cologne before he died. His cultus was confirmed for the Franciscans in 1993.

(John of Emesa) (St) {4 –deleted}

21 July

C6th. From Emesa (now Homs) in Syria, as a monk he went with St Simeon Salus to Jerusalem and ended up as a disciple of St Gerasimus.

John Eudes (St) {1, 3}

19 August

1601–80. From Ri near Falaise (France), he became a priest at Caen and entered the Oratory there in 1625. In 1633, he started his enormously successful career as a parish missionary, but soon appreciated the need for properly educated priests and tried to found a seminary at Caen. This was opposed, so he left the Oratory and founded the secular 'Society of Jesus and Mary' in 1643 in order to found and run seminaries. In 1641, he also founded the 'Sisterhood of our Lady of Charity of the Refuge' to care for repentant former prostitutes.

A fervent propagator of the devotion to the Sacred Heart, the liturgical celebration and doctrinal foundations of which he helped to establish, he was well known as an ascetic writer on this and other topics. He died at Caen and was canonized in 1925.

John the Evangelist (St) {1, 3}

27 December
d. c.100. From Galilee, the son of Zebedee and brother of St James the Great, he was a fisherman until called to be an apostle. The author of the fourth gospel, he is usually identified with 'the Disciple whom Jesus loved' mentioned therein and also wrote three canonical letters. The tradition that he was 'John the Elder' of Patmos, author of the book of Revelation, has been disputed since patristic times. By tradition also he was based at Ephesus after the Resurrection and died there of natural causes. One legend holds that he survived being boiled in oil at Rome before his exile to Patmos, and this event was sometimes depicted in the Middle Ages. His attribute is an eagle, also a chalice with a serpent crawling out of it.

John Eynon (Bl) {2}

15 November
Cf. **Benedictine Martyrs of the Reformation**.

John-Anthony Farina (St) {2}

4 March
1803–88. From Gambellara in Italy, he was ordained at Vicenza in 1827 and served as a teacher and spiritual director in the seminary and schools there. In 1831, he founded the 'Sisters, Teachers of St Dorothy and Daughters of the Sacred Hearts' for teaching and nursing, and in 1850 he was made bishop of Treviso. In 1860, he was transferred back to Vicenza, where his compassion for poor people and his enlightened views concerning

education made him one of the outstanding bishops of the C19th. He died of a stroke and was canonized in 2014.

John Felton (Bl) {2}

8 August
d. 1570. Born at Bermondsey in London of a Norfolk family, he was living at Southwark when the Bull of Pope St Pius V excommunicating Queen Elizabeth reached London. He attached a copy to the door of the bishop of London's house, for which act he was executed in the churchyard of St Paul's Cathedral. He was beatified in 1886. Cf. **England, Martyrs of**.

John Fenwick (Bl) {2}

20 June
d. 1679. From Durham, he was educated at Saint-Omer and became a Jesuit in 1656. He was martyred at Tyburn (London) with **Thomas Whitbread and Comps**. Cf. **England, Martyrs of**.

John of Fermo (Bl) {2}

13 August
1259–1322. From Fermo (Italy), he became a Franciscan in 1272 and thereafter lived a semi-eremitical life at La Verna, his base for evangelizing the surrounding district. He was famous for his gift of infused knowledge. His cultus was approved for Arezzo and the Franciscans in 1880.

John of Fiesole (St) {2}

18 February
1387–1455. He is universally nicknamed 'Fra Angelico' (meaning 'angelic friar'). Born near Florence (Italy), he became a Dominican at Fiesole in 1407, was at San Marco in Florence and died at La Minerva at Rome. His fame rests on his talent for religious painting,

considered to be one of the greatest known in Western Europe. He was declared patron of artists in 1984, thus being effectively canonized.

John Finch (Bl) {2}

20 April

d. 1584. He farmed at Eccleston in Lancashire before being executed at Lancaster with Bl James Bell for being reconciled to the church and for sheltering priests. He was beatified in 1929. Other sources have their execution on the 10th. Cf. **England, Martyrs of**.

John Fingley (Bl) {2}

8 August

d 1586. From Barmby near Howden (Yorks), he studied at Cambridge and Douai, was ordained at Rheims and spent four years as a priest at York before his execution there. He was beatified in 1987. Cf. **England, Martyrs of**.

John Fisher (St) {2}

22 June

1469–1535. From Beverley (Yorks), the son of a draper, he went to Cambridge University and eventually became its chancellor, doing much to further its growth and development. In 1504, he became bishop of Rochester and was the only one of the English hierarchy seriously to oppose King Henry VIII's wish to divorce Queen Catherine of Aragon. He also refused to take the Oath of Supremacy. As a result, he was condemned for treason and beheaded on Tower Hill, having been created a cardinal shortly beforehand. He was canonized in 1969. His portrait is extant. Cf. **England, Martyrs of**.

John Forest (Bl) {2}

22 May

d. 1538. Apparently from Oxford and educated there, he became a Franciscan Observant at Greenwich in 1491 and was chosen as the confessor of Queen Catherine of Aragon, first wife of King Henry VIII. He opposed the queen's divorce and the king's supremacy in spiritual matters, so was gradually burnt to death at Smithfield. He was beatified in 1886. Cf. **England, Martyrs of**.

John-of-Vercelli Garbella (Bl) {2}

30 November

d. 1283. From Mosso Santa Maria near Vercelli (Italy), he studied at Paris and taught law there and at Vercelli. He then joined the Dominicans and eventually became their master-general in 1264. He was commissioned by the pope to draw up the schema for the second ecumenical council of Lyons. His cultus was confirmed for Vercelli and the Dominicans in 1903.

John-Baptist-of-the-Conception García (St) {2}

14 February

1561–1613. From near Toledo (Spain), he became a Trinitarian there in 1580 and founded a reformed house of that order at Valdepeñas in 1597. This was the start of the 'Discalced Trinitarians', which reform received papal approval in 1636. He had to endure the bitter opposition of the 'unreformed', but 34 monasteries had adopted his rule at the time of his death. He died at Cordoba and was canonized in 1975.

John-Mary-of-the-Cross García Méndez (Bl) {2}

23 August

1891–1936. From a peasant family near Avila in Spain, he initially was ordained as a diocesan priest in 1916 but joined the 'Congregation of Priests of the Sacred Heart of Jesus' after an abortive attempt to become a Carmelite (hence his name). He was based at the congregation's house at Puente la Reina at Valencia, but was picked up by anticlerical Republicans during the civil war and was shot with eleven others after a period of imprisonment. He was beatified in 2001. Cf. **Spanish Civil War, Martyrs of.**

John Gavan (Bl) {2}

20 June

d. 1679. A Londoner, he was educated at Saint-Omer and became a Jesuit in 1660. He was martyred at Tyburn (London) with BB Thomas Whitbread and Comps (q.v.). Cf. **England, Martyrs of**.

John of God (St) {1, 3}

8 March

1495–1550. From Montemor-o-Novo near Evora (Portugal), he became a mercenary soldier in 1522 and fought for Spain in Europe, lapsing from his faith in the process. Then he was a shepherd before re-converting in about 1535 and working as a pedlar of religious items and books. He opened a shop in Granada but suffered a nervous breakdown through guilt about his past. Bl John of Avila calmed him and inspired him to look after deprived people, so he founded a hospital at Granada in 1540 where he nursed the sick and which was the beginning of the new Order of Brothers Hospitallers (Brothers of St John of God), which was approved in 1572 after his death. He was canonized in 1690 and declared patron of sick people and of hospitals in 1886.

John-of-Sahagún González de Castrillo (St) {2, 3}

12 June

1419–79. From Sahagún near León (Spain), he studied at Salamanca and Burgos and was ordained in 1445, becoming a cathedral canon at Burgos. He initially held several benefices but his conscience led him to resign all but one, that of a chapel at Salamanca where he worked as a priest. He became an Augustinian friar in 1463, serving as novice-master and prior. His preaching and example, especially against sexual relations outside marriage, caused a great change in the social life of Salamanca but he was eventually poisoned by a woman who blamed him for the loss of her lover. He was canonized in 1690, but his cultus was confined to local calendars in 1969.

John de Goto Soan (St) {1 –group}

6 February

d. 1597. A Japanese Jesuit lay brother, he was a catechist at Osaka and was crucified at Nagasaki when aged eighteen. Cf. **Paul Miki and Comps** and **Japan, Martyrs of**.

John Grande (St) {2}

3 June

1546–1600. From Carmona near Seville (Spain), he dealt in linen before he became a hermit at Marcena nearby. Later he left his cell to work in the prisons and hospitals at Xeres, where a recently opened hospital was entrusted to his care. This he handed over to St John of God, joining the latter's new order at Granada, and he continued to care for prisoners and sick people until he died at Xeres. He used to call himself 'Grande Pecador' ('Great Sinner') as a pun on his name. He was canonized in 1996.

John Grove (Bl) {2}

24 January

d. 1679. He was a servant of Bl William Ireland, with whom he was martyred at Tyburn for alleged complicity in the Oates Plot. Cf. **England, Martyrs of**.

John Gualbert (St) {2, 3}

12 July

d. 1073. A nobleman of Florence (Italy), as a young man he spent his time in worldly amusements until one Good Friday when he forgave his brother's murderer and then saw the image of Christ on a crucifix miraculously bow its head in acknowledgement of his charity. Thereupon he became a monk at San Miniato del Monte at Florence, but left in order to avoid being made abbot and founded the monastery of Vallombrosa ('Shady Valley') near Fiesole. This grew into a powerful Benedictine congregation which survives, based chiefly in Tuscany and Lombardy. He died at Passignano, one of his own foundations, was canonized in 1193 and his cultus was confined to local or particular calendars in 1969.

John Haile (Bl) {2}

4 May

d. 1535. The vicar of Isleworth in Middlesex, he was martyred at Tyburn with St John Houghton and Comps. Cf. **England, Martyrs of**.

John Hambley (Bl) {2}

29 March

d. 1587. Born near Bodmin in Cornwall, he was ordained at Laon and worked in Dorset before being captured. He promised to conform and was released, but continued as a priest in Wiltshire until his recapture and execution on an uncertain day in late March at Salisbury. He was beatified in 1987. Cf. **England, Martyrs of**.

John Hara Mondo (Bl) {2 –add}

4 December

d. 1623. He was a Japanese Franciscan tertiary, and was martyred at Tokyō. He was beatified in 2008. Cf. **Japan, Martyrs of**.

John Hashimoto Tahyōe and Comps (BB) {2 –add}

6 October

d. 1619. He was a family man, martyred at the Japanese imperial capital of Kyōto with a group of fifty-one others. His family was martyred with him, being his wife Thecla Hashimoto and five children: Catherine, Thomas, Francis, Peter and Louis. Another family suffered: John Kyūsaku with his wife Mary-Magdalen and daughter Regina. Married mothers martyred with their children were Mary of Yamashiro with her daughter Monica; Martha of Kawachi with her son Benedict and Mary of Tanba with her son Sixtus. Widows martyred with their children were: Rufina of Owara with her daughter Martha; Anne Kajiya and her son Thomas Kajiya Yoemon and Mencia of Ōmi with her daughter Lucy. A father, Cosmas Shizaburo, was martyred with his son Francis. John Sakurai was martyred with his daughter-in-law Ursula. Couples martyred were: Linus and Mary Rihyōe, Thomas and Mary Koshima Shinshirō, Jerome and Lucy Sōruku, Thomas and Lucy Tōemon and Leo and Martha Kyūsuke. Married women martyred were Monica of Mino, Monica of Ōmi and Mary Chūjō. Single people who suffered were: Thomas Kian, Thomas Ikegami, Anthony Dōmi, Joachim Ogawa, Gabriel of Owari, Emmanuel Kosaburō, Agatha of Ōmi, Mancius Kyūjirō, Louis Matagorō, Mary-Magdalen of Owari, Diego Tzūzu, Francis of Kyōto and Mary of Tanba. They were beatified in 2008. Cf. **Japan, Martyrs of**.

John Hattori Jingorō and Comps (BB) {2 –add}

11 January

d. 1609. He was a married layperson from Muro in Nara, and was martyred at Yatsushiro in Kumamoto together with his son Peter Hattori, Michael Mitsuishi Hikoemon who was another married layperson and his son Thomas Mitsuishi. They were beatified in 2008. Cf. **Japan, Martyrs of**.

John the Hesychast (St) {2, 4}

7 December
454–558. Born at Nicopolis in Armenia, when aged nineteen he became a monk in a monastery that he founded there and was chosen bishop of Colonia when aged twenty-eight. He resigned after nine or ten years and anonymously entered the laura of St Sabas in the Judaean Desert (Holy Land). There he spent the rest of his life, part of it as a hermit walled up in his cell.

John Hewitt (alias Savell or Weldon) (Bl) {2}

5 October
d. 1588. A Yorkshireman, he was educated at Gonville and Caius College, Cambridge and studied for the priesthood at Rheims. Ordained in 1586, he was hanged at Mile End Green in London with BB William Hartley and Robert Sutton and beatified in 1929. Cf. **England, Martyrs of**.

John Hogg (Bl) {2}

27 March
Cf. **Edmund Duke and Comps**.

John Holiday cf. **Richard Holiday**.

John Houghton (St) {2}

4 May
d. 1535. From Essex, he was a secular priest before he became a Carthusian and prior of the London Charterhouse. He and his community were unusual among English-consecrated religious in refusing to assent to the Acts of Succession and Supremacy of King Henry VIII, and he was executed at Tyburn in his religious habit together with SS Augustine Webster and Robert Lawrence (fellow Carthusians) and with St Richard Reynolds and Bl John Haile. These were the protomartyrs of the English reformation. He was canonized in 1970. Cf. **England, Martyrs of**.

John Huguet Cardona (Bl) {2 –add}

23 July
1913–36. From the island of Menorca, Spain, he was ordained as a diocesan priest there and celebrated his first Mass as parish priest of Ferrerías on 21 June 1936. Just over a month later, he was picked up by a marauding group of Communist militia and, after a show trial, was shot in the face. It was clear that this was done simply because he was a priest, and after he refused to spit on a devotional object. He was beatified in 2013. Cf. **Spanish Civil War, Martyrs of** and list in appendix.

John Imamura (Bl) {2}

8 September
d. 1628. He was a Japanese tertiary burnt at Nagasaki. Cf. **Dominic Castellet and Comps** and **Japan, Martyrs of**.

John Ingram (Bl) {2}

26 July
d. 1594. From Stoke Edith in Herefordshire, he studied at New College, Oxford, and then (as a convert) at Rheims and at Rome. After his ordination in 1589, he worked in Scotland until his execution at Gateshead. Cf. **England, Martyrs of**.

John Ireland (BB) {2}

7 March
d. 1544. He was chaplain to St Thomas More before being made rector of Eltham, Kent. He was executed at Tyburn with BB Jermyn Gardiner and John Larke, and was beatified in 1929. Cf. **England, Martyrs of**.

John the Isaurian (St) {2}

18 April
d. p842. A monk-disciple of St Gregory Decapolites, he strenuously campaigned against the iconoclast policy of the emperor Leo the Armenian.

John Iwanaga (Bl) {v2}

27 November
d. 1619. He was of the family of the daimyos of Hirado-jima and was beheaded at Nagasaki (Japan). Cf. **Anthony Kimura and Comps** and **Japan, Martyrs of**.

John of Jerusalem (St) {2}

10 January
d. 417. A bishop of Jerusalem, he strenuously worked for true doctrine and for the peace of the church.

John Jones (alias Buckley) (St) {2}

12 July
1559–98. From Clynog Fawr in Gwynedd (Wales), he became a Franciscan Observant at Pontoise (France), was ordained at Rome and worked on the London mission from 1592 until 1597. He was martyred at Southwark and canonized in 1970. Cf. **England, Martyrs of**.

John Kemble (St) {2}

Aug 22
1599–1679. From near Hereford, he studied for the priesthood at Douai, was ordained there and worked on the missions of Monmouthshire and Herefordshire for fifty-three years. When aged eighty, he was hanged, drawn and quartered at Hereford as a result of the Oates plot. He was canonized in 1970. Cf. **England, Martyrs of**.

John Kearney (Bl) {2}

11 March
d.1653. A Franciscan priest, he was initially seized and condemned to death in England while journeying to Ireland from France. However, he escaped before the sentence could be carried out. This was remembered, and while Oliver Cromwell was campaigning in Ireland he was seized and hanged at Clonmel in contravention of Irish law. He was beatified in 1992. Cf. **Ireland, Martyrs of**.

John of Kenty cf. **John Wacienga**.

John Kinuya (St) {1 –group}

6 February
d. 1597. A Japanese silk-weaver from Miyako, he was baptized and became a Franciscan tertiary at Nagasaki shortly before his martyrdom there with SS Paul Miki and Companions. His name is also recorded as 'Leo'. Cf. **Japan, Martyrs of**.

John Kisaku (Bl) {2}

20 June
d. 1626. A Japanese Jesuit novice, he was burnt alive at Nagasaki with BB Francis Pacheco and Comps. Cf. **Japan, Martyrs of**.

John Kolobos ('the Short') (St)

15 September
C5th. From Basta in Lower Egypt, he became a disciple of St Poemen at Scetis and was one of the most attractive characters among the desert fathers, being described as short-tempered and proud by nature but gentle and humble by grace. He was also famous for his absent-mindedness. In obedience to his master, he regularly watered a walking-stick which, when it sprouted, was called 'the tree of obedience'. He is not in the Roman Martyrology.

John de la Lande (Bl) {2}

18 October

d. 1646. He was a Jesuit missionary accompanying St Isaac Jogues, and was killed with him by the Mohawk Iroquois at Ossernenon in New York State (USA). He was canonized in 1930. Cf. **John Brébeuf and Comps**.

John-of-Triora Lantrua (St) {1 –group}

7 February

1760–1816.From Triora in Liguria (Italy), when aged seventeen he became a Franciscan and went on to be guardian of the friary at Velletri near Rome. Then he volunteered to go to China. At that time, the church was being persecuted there, and he worked successfully in Shanxi and Hubei in the face of many dangers and hardships after his arrival in 1799. Eventually he was seized and executed by strangulation at Changsha in Hubei, and was beatified in 1900. Cf. **China, Martyrs of**.

John Larke (Bl) {2}

7 March

d. 1544. He was rector of St Ethelburga's, Bishopsgate (London), then of Woodford, Essex, and finally of Chelsea, to which parish he was nominated by St Thomas More. He was executed at Tyburn with BB John Ireland and Jermyn Gardiner and was beatified in 1886. Cf. **England, Martyrs of**.

John Lenaerts of Oosterwijk (St) {2}

9 July

d. 1572. A Dutchman, he became an Augustinian canon regular at Briel near Gorinchem and was director and confessor of a local community of Augustinian nuns. When the town was captured by Calvinist rebels, he was hanged with the **Gorinchem** martyrs in the ruins of his sacked monastery.

John-of-the-Mother-of-God Leonardi (St) {1, 3}

9 October

1542–1609. From near Lucca (Italy), he became a pharmacist's apprentice there but also studied for the priesthood and was ordained in 1571. He worked with great zeal in prisons and in hospitals and founded the 'Clerks Regular of the Mother of God' (approved in 1593) with the help of two laymen and some priests. He is also considered one of the founders also of the College of Propaganda Fide for Foreign Missions in Rome, and was appointed Visitor of the Vallumbrosan and Monteverginian monks when these needed reform. He died at Rome and was canonized in 1938.

John Licci (Bl) {2}

14 November

1400–1511. From Caccamo near Palermo (Sicily), he became a Dominican at Palermo and died at the age of 111. His cultus was confirmed for Palermo in 1753.

John Lloyd (St) {2}

22 July

d. 1679. From Brecon in Powys (Wales), he was educated for the priesthood at Valladolid, was ordained in 1653 and was then on mission in Wales. He was executed at Cardiff with Bl Philip Evans as a result of the Oates plot and was canonized in 1970. Cf. **Wales, Martyrs of**.

John Lockwood (alias Lascelles) (Bl) {2}

13 April

1561–1642. From Sowerby (Yorks), he studied for the priesthood at Rome, was ordained in 1597 and was on the English missions from 1598. He was aged eighty-one when he was hanged, drawn and quartered at York with Bl

Edward Catherick, and was beatified in 1929. Cf. **England, Martyrs of**.

John of Lodi (St) {2}

7 September
d. 1106. From Lodi Vecchio in Lombardy (Italy), after being a hermit for some years he became a monk at the abbey of Fontavellana under St Peter Damian, whose biography he wrote. He became prior of the abbey in 1072 and bishop of Gubbio in 1105.

John Lowe (Bl) {2}

8 October
d. 1586. He was born on London Bridge and was ordained at the English College at Rome. He then spent thirty months in London as a priest before being captured and executed at Tyburn with BB Robert Dibdale and John Adams. He was beatified in 1987. Cf. **England, Martyrs of**.

John-Baptist Luo Tingying (St) {1 –group}

29 July
1825–61. A prosperous farmer at Qingyan in Guizhou (China), he was converted and moved to Yaojiaguan. There he administered the finances of the new seminary. He was imprisoned with SS Joseph Zhang Wenlan, Paul Chen Changpin and Martha Wang Luozhi in a hot and humid cave at Qingyan, where they were tortured before being beheaded. Cf. **China, Martyrs of**.

John of Lycopolis (St) {2, 4}

17 October
C4th. One of the most famous of the Egyptian desert fathers, he was born near Asyut and was a carpenter before becoming a hermit when aged twenty-five in a cave in the cliffs overlooking the valley of the Nile at Lycopolis. He was there for forty years and became famous as a prophet, being consulted by the emperor Theodosius I as well as by many other people of all kinds, and his fame spread throughout the Roman Empire.

John-Baptist Machado (Bl) {2}

22 May
1580–1617. From Terceira, one of the Azores, he became a Jesuit at Coïmbra (Portugal) and went to Japan in 1609. He was beheaded at Nagasaki with Bl Peter of the Assumption and was beatified in 1867. Cf. **Japan, Martyrs of**.

John Macias (St) {2}

16 September
1585–1645. From Ribera del Fresno in Extremadura (Spain), he emigrated to the New World as a servant, worked on a cattle ranch and gained a fortune which he gave to the poor when he became a Dominican lay brother at Lima (Peru). He was the doorkeeper there for the rest of his life, and was canonized in 1975.

John Maki (Bl) {2}

7 September
d. 1627. An adopted son of Bl Louis Maki, he was burnt alive at Nagasaki (Japan) with his father and Bl Thomas Tsuji. Cf. **Japan, Martyrs of**.

John Marinoni (Bl) {2}

13 December
1490–1562. From Venice (Italy), he was a canon of St Mark's cathedral there but resigned to join the Theatines under St Cajetan in 1530. He was a ubiquitous preacher, the exclusive theme of his sermons being Christ crucified. He refused the archbishopric of Naples, the city in which he died. His cultus was confirmed for Naples and the Theatines in 1764.

(John Mark) (St) {4 –deleted}

27 September
C1st. The old Roman Martyrology listed him as a bishop of Byblos (Lebanon), but the consensus of biblical scholars identifies him with St Mark the evangelist. Cf. Acts 12:25.

John-of-St-Dominic Martínez (Bl) {2}

19 May
1619. A martyr of the Dominican mission in Japan, he died in prison at Omura. Cf. **Japan, Martyrs of**.

John Mason (Bl) {2}

10 December
d. 1591. A layman from Kendal in Cumbria, he was condemned for sheltering priests and was hanged at Tyburn with SS Eustace White and Comps. He was beatified in 1929. Cf. **England, Martyrs of**.

John of Matera (St) {2}

20 June
d. 1139. From Matera in Basilicata (Italy), when young he was a monk in a Benedictine monastery but his austerity was not popular. He next went to the monastery at Montevergine under St William, the founder, but left to become a popular preacher at Bari. Finally he settled at Pulsano near Monte Gargano where he established an abbey, the first of a series of foundations which became the new Benedictine Congregation of Pulsano (now extinct). He died at Pulsano.

John of Matha (St) {2, 3}

17 December
1160–1213. From Provence (France), he studied at Paris and later founded the Order of Trinitarians for the redemption of Christian captives enslaved by Muslims. This was approved in 1209. There are no trustworthy records of his life, and the story that he ransomed many captives himself at Tunis is unsupported by any evidence. He died at Rome and his cultus was approved in 1666, but was confined to local calendars in 1969.

John-Baptist Mazzuconi (Bl) {2}

7 September
1826–55. From near Milan, he was ordained in 1852 and was one of the first graduates of the new Pontifical Institute for Overseas Missions. His group was sent to Woodlark Island in Melanesia off New Guinea, where they had a very difficult time (the natives threatened to eat them). In 1855, he was so badly affected by an ulcerative disease that he was sent to Sydney to recuperate for six months. On his return, he found that his fellows had themselves left for Sydney. His ship struck coral off the island and a gang of natives boarded with an initial show of friendship, but they killed Bl John-Baptist with an axe before killing everybody else on board and plundering the ship. He was beatified in 1984.

John Merz (Bl) {2 –add}

10 May
1896–1928. From Banja Luka in Bosnia (then soon to become part of the Habsburg Empire), he went to the University of Vienna before fighting on the Italian front. The horror of this inspired a religious conversion. He obtained a doctorate in philosophy at Paris in 1923, and as a lay Catholic intellectual went on to found several Croatian youth movements in order to foster faith and holiness. He was also a pioneer of liturgical renewal in the Croatian church. He died at Zagreb, and was beatified in 2003.

John Minami Gorōzaemon (Bl) {2 –add}

8 December
d. 1603. He was a married Japanese layperson, born at Yamato in Kagoshima and martyred

at Kumamoto. He was beatified in 2008. Cf. **Japan, Martyrs of**.

John of Montemarano (St) {2}

14 April
d. c.1100. From near Montemarano in Campagna (Italy), he probably became a monk of Montecassino before being made bishop of Montemarano in 1074 by Pope St Gregory VII. His cultus was approved for Nusco in 1906.

John de Montmirail (Bl) {2}

29 September
1165–1217. The lord of Montmirail near Châlons-sur-Marne (France), he was a married soldier with a family but obtained his wife's consent to become a Cistercian at Longpoint, where he died. He has a cultus, approved in 1891, among the Cistercians and in several French dioceses.

John Motoyama (Bl) {2}

27 November
d. 1619. He was of the family of the daimyos of Hirado-jima and was beheaded at Nagasaki (Japan). Cf. **Anthony Kimura and Comps** and **Japan, Martyrs of**.

John-Martin Moyë (Bl) {2}

4 May
1730–93. From Lorraine (France), he became a diocesan priest of Metz in 1754 and founded the 'Sisters of Divine Providence' in 1762 in order to catechize in rural areas. In 1773, he joined the Paris Society of Missions and went to Chengdu in Sichuan (China) for eleven years. He baptized over 20,000 in the region and founded an institute of Chinese Christian virgins for nursing and catechesis. He returned exhausted, moved his earlier congregation to Trier and died there of typhus, being beatified in 1955.

John Munden (Bl) {2}

12 February
d. 1584. From Maperton (Dorset), he studied at New College, Oxford, became a schoolmaster, went to Rheims and to Rome for his seminary studies and was ordained in 1582. He was martyred at Tyburn with BB George Haydock, James Fenn, John Nutter and Thomas Hemerford, and was beatified in 1929 Cf. **England, Martyrs of**.

John-Mary Muzeyi (St) {1 –group}

27 January
d. 1887. A native of Buganda (Uganda), he baptized many who were about to die and was beheaded in the persecution of Mwanga. Cf. **Charles Lwanga and Comps**.

John Nagai Naizen (Bl) {2}

12 July
d. 1626. He was a wealthy Japanese layman from Arima. When the persecutors threatened him with the prostitution of his wife, Bl Monica Naizen, he apostatized for a while but repented and was burnt alive at Nagasaki. His wife and child, Bl Louis Naizen, were beheaded. Cf. **Mancius Araki and Comps** and **Japan, Martyrs of**.

John Nagata Matakichi (Bl) {2}

19 August
d. 1662. He was a sailor on the ship carrying BB Louis Flores and Comps. Cf. **Japan, Martyrs of**.

John-Baptist Nam Chong-sam (St) {1 –group}

7 March
d. 1866. A mandarin of Seoul in Korea and a royal chamberlain, he was a humble man and highly regarded by the people. However, he was charged with apostasy from the

national religion, tortured for information on other Christians and executed. Cf. **Korea, Martyrs of**.

John I of Naples (St) {2}

3 April

d. 432. Bishop of Naples (Italy), he transferred the body of St Januarius from Puteoli to Naples.

(John IV of Naples) (St) {4 –deleted}

22 June

d. 835. Bishop of Naples (Italy), he is locally known as 'the Peacemaker'.

John-Peter Néel (St) {1 –group}

18 February

1832–62. A French missionary priest of the Paris Foreign Missions Society, he was working in Guizhou province in China when he was arrested with SS John Chen Xianheng, John Zhang Tianshen and Martin Wu Xuesheng. He was tied to a horse's tail by his hair and dragged about before being beheaded with them at Kaiyang. Cf. **China, Martyrs of**.

John Nelson (Bl) {2}

3 February

d. 1578. From Skelton near York, he entered the seminary at Douai when aged forty and was ordained in 1575. He was sent to London but was quickly arrested and executed at Tyburn, becoming a Jesuit beforehand. Cf. **England, Martyrs of**.

John Nepomucene (St) {2}

20 March

d. 1393. From Nepomuk near Plzen in Bohemia (now the Czech Republic), he became a canon of Prague and eventually court chaplain and confessor to Queen Sophie, second wife of the dissolute King Wenceslaus IV. He

was of a retiring disposition, and repeatedly refused bishoprics which were offered to him. By order of the king, he was drowned in the river at Prague, by tradition because he refused to reveal to the king what he had heard from the queen in sacramental confession. He was canonized in 1729.

John-Nepomucene Neumann (St) {2}

5 January

1811–60. From Prachatice near Plzen (Czech Republic), he became a missionary priest in the Buffalo district of New York State, USA in 1836. In 1840, he became a Redemptorist at Baltimore and was made bishop of Philadelphia in 1852. He had great care for the proper establishment of the church in a developing society through the ministry of preaching, the education of youth (he increased the number of pupils at parish schools twentyfold), the building of churches (eighty, plus the cathedral), the fostering of good liturgy and, above all, care of orphans and the poor. He also founded the 'Sisters of the Third Order of St Francis' and brought in many teaching orders. He was canonized in 1977.

John-Henry Newman (Bl) {2 –add}

1801–90. Born in the City of London (England) to a middle-class family, when aged fifteen he became a fervent evangelical Protestant in the Anglican communion. He studied at Oxford, and became a fellow of Oriel College in 1822. In 1825, he was ordained as an Anglican minister, and became one of the leading religious controversialists in the university as a leading member of the Oxford Movement. However, study of the dogmatic foundations of the Anglican communion, especially with reference to patristic teaching, led him to convert in 1845. He was ordained as a priest in the following year, and joined the Oratorians. He founded Oratories at London and at Birmingham, spending the rest of his life at the latter and writing many apologetical works. He was made a cardinal in 1879. He died at Birmingham, and was beatified in 2010.

John Norton (Bl) {2}

8 September
Cf. **Thomas Palaser and Comps**.

John Nutter (Bl) {2}

12 February
d. 1584. From near Burnley, Lancs, he was a fellow of St John's College, Cambridge before converting, studying for the priesthood at Rheims and being ordained in 1581. He was executed at Tyburn (London) with BB George Haydock, James Fenn, John Munden and Thomas Hemerford. Cf. **England, Martyrs of**.

John Ogilvie (St) {2}

10 March
c.1580–1615. He is the only canonized martyr of the Scottish Reformation. Apparently from the farmstead of Drum near Keith, southeast of Elgin, Scotland, he was a Calvinist before converting while attending the Scottish College at Louvain in 1596. He became a Jesuit at Brno in 1599 and worked in the Czech lands and in France until 1613. Then he returned to Scotland, worked in and around Edinburgh and Glasgow and was captured at the latter place. For eight days and nights on end, he was tortured and forcibly kept from sleep so that he should reveal the names of other Catholics. He was also offered his freedom and preferment in exchange for reverting to Protestantism, but refused and was hanged at Glasgow. He was canonized in 1976.

John Paine (St) {2}

20 April
d. 1582. A convert from near Peterborough, he was educated for the priesthood at Douai where he was ordained in 1576. He was based at Ingatestone in Essex until his was betrayed, and was executed at Chelmsford. He was canonized in 1970. Cf. **England, Martyrs of**.

John Pak Hu-jae and Comps (SS) {1 –group}

3 September
d. 1839. They were a group of six who were tortured and beheaded at Seoul in Korea during a campaign of extirpation of Christianity ordered by the government. The others were Agnes Kim Hyo-ju, Barbara Kwŏn-hŭi the sister of St Augustine Yi Kwang-hŏn, Barbara Yi Chŏng-hŭi, Mary Pak Kun-a-gi Hui-sun the sister of St Lucy Pak Hŭi-sun and Mary Yi Yŏn-hŭi the sister of Damian Nam Myŏng-hyŏg. Cf. **Korea, Martyrs of**.

John de Palafox y Mendoza (Bl) {2 –add}

1 October
1600–59. From Fitero (Spain), he was the illegitimate son of a nobleman who was claimed by his father when aged ten, after being brought up by a family of millers. After a good if late education he became a senior civil servant to the Spanish crown, and after ordination was the chaplain of King Philip IV's sister. In 1639, he was consecrated as bishop of Puebla in Mexico, where he founded the Dominican convent, several schools, a major library and also completed the cathedral. He made the city the musical centre of Mexico, and was a prolific author. He incurred the enmity of the Jesuits, who refused to recognize his jurisdiction and succeeded in having him transferred back to Spain to the diocese of Osma in 1655. He died at Osma, and was beatified in 2011 after the initial petition for his cause in 1694 was blocked at Rome by the Jesuits.

John of Parma (St) {2}

22 May

C10th. From Parma (Italy), he became a cathedral canon there when young and allegedly made six pilgrimages to Jerusalem, where he became a monk. Then he became abbot of the Cluniac Benedictine monastery of St John's at Parma in 973.

John of Parrano (St) {2, 4}

19 March

C6th. He was a Syrian monk who settled at Parrano near Spoleto (Italy), where he was abbot of a large monastic colony for forty-four years. It is possible that he was a refugee from Monophysite persecution.

John of Pavia (St) {2, 4}

27 August

d. ?825. He was bishop of Pavia near Milan (Italy) from 801.

John Pelingotto (Bl) {2}

1 June

1240–1304. From Urbino (Italy), the son of a merchant, he became a Franciscan tertiary and spent his whole life in prayer and works of charity. His cultus was approved for Urbino in 1918.

John of Penna (Bl) {2}

3 April

d. 1275. From Penna San Giovanni near Fermo (Italy), he became a Franciscan at Recanati near Ancona, where he died after founding several friaries in Provence (France) over a period of twenty-five years. His cultus was confirmed for Fermo and the Franciscan Conventuals in 1806.

John-Gabriel Perboyre (St) {1 –group}

11 September

1802–40. From near Montauban (France), he joined the Vincentians there in 1818 and, after being ordained in 1825, was rector of the seminary at St Flour for ten years. Then he heard that his brother had died on mission in China and offered to replace him. He worked in Henan province until he was seized, imprisoned, given 110 strokes of a bamboo cane (which should have killed him) and strangled while tied to a cross at Wuchang. He was canonized in 1996. Cf. **China, Martyrs of**.

John of Perugia and Peter of Sassoferrato (BB) {2}

29 August

d. 1231. These two Franciscan friars were sent by St Francis of Assisi in 1216 to preach to the Muslims in Spain. They worked in the district between Teruel and Valencia until they were seized in a mosque at Valencia and, on refusing to apostatize, were beheaded. Their cultus was approved for Valencia and Teruel in 1783.

John-Baptist Piamarta (St) {2}

25 April

1841–1913. From a poor family in Brescia (Italy), he was ordained as a diocesan priest there in 1865. The state of the local proletariat inspired him to found the 'Istituto Artigianelli' in order to give boys (especially destitute ones) a Christian and professional training appropriate to the new industrial society. Also, noting the desperate poverty of the peasantry in assets and in knowledge, he helped found an agricultural colony at Remedello in order to propagate more effective agricultural techniques. To propagate these works he founded the 'Congregation of the Holy Family of Nazareth' and (with his mother) the 'Humble Servants of the Lord' for women. He died at Remedello and was canonized in 2012.

John Pibush (Bl) {2}

18 February

d. 1601. From Thirsk (Yorks), he studied at Rheims and was ordained in 1587. Most of his time in England subsequently was spent in prison, and he was executed at Southwark. He was beatified in 1929. Cf. **England, Martyrs of**.

John Plessington (St) {2}

July 19
d. 1679. From near Garstang (Lancs), he was educated for the priesthood at Valladolid and was ordained at Segovia in 1662. He worked at Holywell in Clwyd (Wales) and then in the Wirral, but was hanged at Chester as a result of the Oates plot. He was canonized in 1970. Cf. **England, Martyrs of**.

John-Angelus Porro (Bl) {2}

23 October
d. 1506. From Milan (Italy), he became a Servite and, after some time spent at Monte Senario, worked in Milan until the end of his life. His cultus was confirmed for Milan in 1737.

John del Prado (Bl) {2}

24 May
d. 1631. From near León (Spain), he joined the Franciscan Observants at Salamanca while studying theology there. Being sent to Morocco in order to minister to Christian slaves he was seized, tortured, burnt and killed with a heavy stone along with two other Franciscans at Marrakesh. He was beatified in 1728.

John-of-Saint-Martha of Prados (Bl) {2}

16 August
1578–1618. From near Tarragona (Spain), he became a Franciscan priest and was sent to Japan in 1606 where he became fluent in Japanese. Arrested at Omura in 1615, he was imprisoned for three years before being beheaded at Miyako He was beatified in 1867. Cf. **Japan, Martyrs of**.

John Prassek and Comps (BB) {2 –add}

d. 1943. They were martyred at Hamburg (Germany), but are generally known as the Lübeck martyrs. Bl John was from Hamburg; Bl Edward Müller was from Neumünster, and Bl Herman Lange was from Leer. They were based at the Herz-Jesu Church in Lübeck, and were close friends with a Lutheran pastor named Karl Stellbrink. On Palm Sunday 1942 the latter preached a sermon interpreting an air-raid as God's judgement on the Nazi regime, and the four were immediately arrested together with eighteen lay associates. They were tried for treason and sedition the following year, and sentenced to death. Whereas their bishop tried to obtain clemency for his priest, the Lutheran was dismissed from the ministry because of his conviction. They were beheaded in quick succession at Hamburg, and beatified in 2011. All four are commemorated together liturgically.

John of Ravenna (St) {2, 4}

19 January
d. 495. Bishop of Ravenna (Italy) from 452, he allegedly saved his city from destruction by Attila the Hun and mitigated its misery when it was captured by Theodoric, king of the Ostrogoths.

John-Francis Regis (St) {2, 4}

31 December
1597–1640. From Fontcouverte near Narbonne (France), at the age of eighteen he became a Jesuit and was ordained in 1631. He was an indefatigable missionary among the rural population of Languedoc and Auvergne, making numerous conversions among the Huguenots. He also worked to help prisoners and prostitutes and established many confraternities of the Blessed Sacrament. He died while preaching a mission at La Louvesc and was canonized in 1737.

John of Réôme (St) {2, 4}

28 January

d. ?554. From Dijon (France), when aged twenty he became a hermit at Réôme (now Ménétreux) but attracted disciples and, when these became too many, fled secretly and became a monk at Lérins. When he was exposed and recalled to Réôme, he regulated his monastery according to the customs of Lérins and thus became one of the pioneers of monastic life in the West.

John de Ribera (St) {2}

6 January

1532–1611. From Seville (Spain), he was a son of the duke of Alcala, viceroy of Naples. Educated at the university of Salamanca, he was ordained priest in 1557 and remained at the university as professor of theology. His talents became widely known and gained him the respect of Pope Pius V and of King Philip II of Spain. He became bishop of Badajoz, but was quickly transferred to Valencia as titular Latin Patriarch of Antioch (in effect, a missionary bishop) and was made viceroy of that province. His life's work was to convert the Muslims remaining there.

John Rigby (St) {2}

21 June

d. 1600. Born at Harrock Hall near Wigan (Lancs), he went into domestic service for a recusant family at Sawston Hall in Cambridgeshire. There he was converted, but was arrested when testifying in favour of his employer and was condemned for being reconciled to the church. He was executed at Southwark and canonized in 1970. Cf. **England, Martyrs of**.

John-Baptist-of-Fabriano Righi (Bl) {2}

11 March

1469–1539. From Fabriano in the Marches (Italy), he became a Franciscan and lived as a hermit at Massaccio. His cultus was approved for Iesi in 1903.

John Roberts (St) {2}

10 December

?1577–1610. From Trawsfynydd in Gwynedd (Wales), he was brought up nominally a Protestant but (like many contemporary Welshmen) had little identification with the Anglican communion. He studied at St John's College, Oxford and was about to become a student of law in 1598. He was received into the church in Paris while on holiday, however, and went to Valladolid to study for the priesthood. There he joined the Benedictines and was professed as a monk at Compostella in 1600. In 1602, after his ordination, he started work on the English mission. Six or seven times he was imprisoned and released, and during the plague of 1603 his services to the sick in London made him famous. Meanwhile he helped Dom Augustine Bradshaw in the founding of St Gregory's at Douai (now Downside abbey). He was captured while saying Mass, executed at Tyburn (London) and canonized in 1970. Cf. **England, Martyrs of**.

John Robinson (Bl) {2}

1 October

d. 1588. From Ferrensby near Knaresborough (Yorks), after losing his wife he went to Rheims to study for the priesthood and was ordained there in 1585. He was executed at Ipswich and was beatified in 1929. Cf. **England, Martyrs of**.

John Roche (alias Neale) (Bl) {2}

30 August

d. 1588. An Irish waterman on the Thames, he who was condemned to death for rescuing a fugitive priest and was executed at Tyburn (London) with St Margaret Ward and BB Edward Shelley, Richard Lloyd, Richard

Leigh and Richard Martin. He was beatified in 1929. As depicted, he always wears Elizabethan working man's dress and carries an oar or a small boat. Cf. **England, Martyrs of**.

John Rochester (Bl) {2}

11 May

d. 1537. From Terling near Witham (Essex), he became a Carthusian at the London Charterhouse and was executed at York with Bl James Walworth. He was beatified in 1886. Cf. **England, Martyrs of**.

(John of Rome) (St) {4 –deleted}

23 June

d. 362. A Roman priest, he was listed as beheaded in the reign of Julian. The relic venerated as the head of John the Baptist at the English church in Rome of San Silvestro in Capite has been claimed as his.

John-Baptist de Rossi (St) {2}

23 May

1698–1764. From Voltaggio near Genoa (Italy), he became a Roman priest in 1721 and canon of Santa Maria in Cosmedin in 1737. His main work as missionary and catechist was among the teamsters, farmers and herdsmen of the Campagna, and among the sick and prisoners of the city. He died at Remo and was canonized in 1881.

John Rugg (Bl) {2}

15 November

Cf. **Benedictine Martyrs of the Reformation**.

John of Sahagún cf. **John González of Sahagún**.

John van Ruysbroeck (Bl) {2}

2 December

1293–1381. From Ruysbroeck near Brussels (Belgium), he became a priest and a canon of Saint Gudule at Brussels and founder and first prior of the Augustinian monastery of Groenendael in 1343. His fame rests on his spiritual writings, which show him to be an important medieval mystic. His cultus was confirmed for Mechelen in 1908.

John of Salerno (Bl) {2}

29 August

d. ?1242. From Salerno (Italy), he became a Dominican under St Dominic and founded the friary of Santa Maria Novella at Florence in 1221. His cultus was approved for Florence in 1783.

John-Baptist de la Salle (St) {1, 3}

7 April

1651–1719. From Rheims (France), he was made a cathedral canon in 1667 and was ordained in 1678, after which he became chaplain to the 'Sisters of the Holy Infant'. These ran schools for girls, and he decided to devote his life to founding a similar institute for teaching boys. His ideas were original enough to meet serious opposition (no member of the institute was to be ordained, for example) but he started the noviciate of the 'Brothers of the Christian Schools' in 1691 and opened the first school at Paris in 1698. He died in retirement at the noviciate at St Yon and was canonized in 1900.

John-Baptist of San Francisco Cajonos (Bl) {2}

15 September

Cf. **Hyacinth-of-the-Angels and John-Baptist of San Francisco Cajonos**.

John Sandys (Bl) {2}

11 August

d. 1586. A Lancastrian convert and Oxford graduate, he was ordained at Rheims and worked in Gloucester. While visiting the Anglican Dean of Lydney (an old friend who did not know of his conversion) he was seized and suffered a botched execution at Gloucester. He was beatified in 1987. Cf. **England, Martyrs of**.

John Sarkander (St) {2}

17 March
1576–1620. From Skoczów near Katowice, Poland (but then in Austrian Silesia), he became a diocesan priest of Olomouc in the Czech lands and was attached to the church at Holešov, which was on an estate owned by a Catholic but surrounded by lands of Protestant nobles. He converted many Hussites and other Protestants but was unjustly accused as a result by the said nobles of conspiring to bring Polish troops into the country at the start of the Thirty Years' War. He was ordered to reveal what he heard in confession from the patron of his church and, on refusing, was racked, tortured with burning pitch and left to die in prison. He was canonized in 1995.

John Saziari (Bl) {2}

21 April
d. 1371. He was a Franciscan tertiary of Cagli near Urbino (Italy).

John-Baptist Scalabrini (Bl) {2}

1 June
1839–1905. From near Como (Italy), he became a diocesan priest there in 1863 and was a parish priest and seminary rector before being made bishop of Piacenza in 1876. He was zealous for all aspects of his responsibility as bishop, especially as regards catechesis and the implementation of the church's social teaching. Noting that Italian emigrants to the New World were in danger of losing their faith, he founded two congregations of 'Missionaries of St Charles' (the Scalabrinians) to care for them there and also inspired St Francis-Xavier Cabrini in her similar work. He died at Piacenza and was beatified in 1997.

John Scheffler (Bl) {2 –add}

25 March
1887–1952. From Kálmánd in Hapsburg Hungary (now in Romania), he was ordained a diocesan priest of Szatmár in 1910. This became Satu Mare in Romania in 1919. He became bishop of Satu Mare in 1942, but was arrested by the Communist regime and martyred in prison at Bucharest by being put into a boiling-hot shower. He was beatified in 2011.

John Shert (Bl) {2}

28 May
d. 1582. From near Macclesfield (Cheshire), he was at Brasenose College, Oxford before his conversion and later studied at Douai and Rome. He was ordained in 1576, went back to England in 1579 and was executed at Tyburn (London) with BB Thomas Ford and Robert Johnstone. He was beatified in 1886. Cf. **England, Martyrs of**.

John Shoun (Bl) {2}

18 November
d. 1619. A Japanese from Miyako, he was baptized by the Jesuits at Nagasaki and was a member of the confraternity of the Holy Rosary. He was burnt alive at Nagasaki. Cf. **Leonard Kimura and Comps** and **Japan, Martyrs of**.

John Shozaburo and Comps (BB) {2}

29 September
d. 1630. He was beheaded at Nagasaki with BB Laurence Hachizo, Mancius Ichizayemon, Michael Taiemon Kinoshi, Peter Terai

Kuhioye and Thomas Terai Kahioye. Cf. **Japan, Martyrs of**.

John Slade (Bl) {2}

30 October

d. 1583. Possibly from Manston (Dorset), he studied at New College, Oxford, became a schoolmaster and was martyred at Winchester for denying the royal supremacy in spiritual matters. He was beatified in 1929. Cf. **England, Martyrs of**.

John Slezyuk (Bl) {2}

2 December

1897–1973. He was a clandestine bishop of the Greek-Catholic Church in the Ukraine, which had been officially suppressed by the Soviet Union. He was imprisoned at Ivanovo-Frankivsk and died as a result of maltreatment. Cf. **Nicholas Čarneckyj and 24 Comps**.

John Soreth (Bl) {2}

25 July

c.1420–71 From Caen in Normandy (France), he became a Carmelite and was their prior-general from 1451. He was a forerunner of St Teresa in trying to reform his order and to admit nunneries, but with scant success. He was supposed to have died at Angers from eating unripe mulberries, and his cultus was confirmed for the Carmelites in 1865.

John Southworth (St) {2}

28 June

d. 1654. From Lancashire, he studied for the priesthood at Douai, was ordained in 1619 and went to England, working firstly in Lancashire and then in London. He was imprisoned in 1627 but subsequently released. The way he helped sufferers of the London plague epidemic of 1636 made him popular, but he was still executed at Tyburn during the

Commonwealth. He was canonized in 1970 and his shrine was established in Westminster Cathedral. Cf. **England, Martyrs of**.

John-Baptist de Souzy and Comps (BB) {2}

27 August

d. 1794 (one in 1795). During the French Revolution the 'Constitutive Assembly' required all priests to take an oath to the Civil Constitution, and those who refused (the 'non-jurors') were treated as enemies of the state. In 1794, 829 priests and religious were concentrated on two former slave ships in the mouth of the Charente River with the eventual intention of taking them to Guiana. Bl John-Baptist, a priest of La Rochelle, was appointed their vicar-general. They were packed together so that they had to stand most of the time and were starved and brutally treated. After ten months, 547 had died, mostly from disease. John-Baptist was beatified in 1995, together with a selection of sixty-three companions from thirteen other dioceses besides La Rochelle and twelve religious institutes. They are listed in the Roman Martyrology on the dates that they died. Cf. **French Revolution, Martyrs of**.

John Soyemon (Bl) {2}

19 August

d. 1662. He was a scribe on the ship carrying BB Louis Flores and Comps. Cf. **Japan, Martyrs of**.

John the Spaniard (Bl) {2}

25 June

1123–60. From Almanza near León (Spain), as a boy he travelled to France and studied at Arles. Then he became a Carthusian at Montrieu, was transferred to the Grande Chartreuse under St Anthelmus and finally became first prior of the new foundation at Reposoir near Lake Geneva. He drew up the first constitutions for the Carthusian nuns. His cultus was approved for the Carthusians in 1864.

John Speed (alias Spence) (Bl) {2}

4 February
d.1594. From Durham, he was martyred there for sheltering priests and was beatified in 1929. Cf. **England, Martyrs of**.

John-Henry-Charles Steeb (Bl) {2}

15 December
1775–1856. From a wealthy Lutheran family of Tübingen (Germany), he went to Verona in Italy to study. There he was reconciled to the church, was ordained and led a life involved in helping sick people, in catechesis and in education. To these ends, he founded the 'Sisters of Mercy' with Sr Luiga Poloni. He died at Verona, and was beatified in 1975.

John Stone (St) {2}

23 December
d. 1538. An Augustinian friar at Canterbury, he was executed there for denying the royal supremacy in spiritual matters of King Henry VIII and was canonized in 1970. Cf. **England, Martyrs of**.

John Storey (Bl) {2}

1 June
?1504–71. From the North, he became a doctor of law at Oxford University, was the principal of a hall of studies there, married after 1547 and became a member of parliament and vicar-general of the London diocese in 1553. During the reign of Edward VI, he went abroad but returned on the accession of Queen Mary, only to be imprisoned on the accession of Queen Elizabeth. He escaped to the Low Countries but was followed by Elizabeth's secret agents, kidnapped, brought back to England and executed at Tyburn for alleged treason. He was beatified in 1886. Cf. **England, Martyrs of**.

John Sugar and Robert Grissold (BB) {2}

16 July
d. 1604. From Wimbourne near Wolverhampton, Bl John had been an Anglican catechist before studying at Oxford and becoming a vicar at Cannock. After his conversion, he was ordained at Rheims in 1601 and was a priest for the poor Catholics around what is now West Midlands, being sheltered by Bl Robert (a gentleman-retainer at a Broadway household). They were seized near the latter's home at Rowington and were executed at Warwick, being beatified in 1987. Cf. **England, Martyrs of**.

John of Syracuse (St) {2}

23 October
d. ?609. He was bishop of Syracuse (Sicily) from 595.

John Talbot (Bl) {2}

8 September
Cf. **Thomas Palaser and Comps**.

John Tanaka (Bl) {2}

12 July
d. 1626. A Japanese layman, he sheltered Bl Balthasar de Torres, was seized with his wife, Bl Catherine Tanaka, as a result and, after a long imprisonment at Omura, was burnt alive at Nagasaki. Cf. **Mancius Araki and Comps** and **Japan, Martyrs of**.

John Tavelli (Bl) {2}

24 July
d. 1446. From Tossignano near Imola (Italy), he studied at the university of Bologna, joined

the Order of the Gesuati and became bishop of Ferrara in 1431. He produced an Italian translation of the Bible.

John the Thaumaturge (St) {2, 4}

4 December
C9th. Bishop of Polyboton in Phrygia (Asia Minor), he was one of the most strenuous champions of orthodoxy against the iconoclast emperor Leo III and his fame as a wonder-worker was such that the emperor did not dare to persecute him.

John Theristus (St) {2, 4}

24 February
1049–1129. He was born in Palermo (Sicily) after his mother had been captured and enslaved in a raid on Calabria by the Sicilian Muslims. When aged fourteen he escaped to Calabria and became a Basilian monk at Stilo, going on to be abbot. His surname ('Mower') refers to his allegedly having miraculously cut a large hay field in a short time.

John Thorne (Bl) {2}

15 November
Cf. **Benedictine Martyrs of the Reformation**.

John Thules and Roger Wrenn (Bl) {2}

18 March
d. 1616. The son of a schoolmaster at Whalley (Lancs), the former studied at Rheims and Rome and was ordained at Rome in 1592. Arrested soon after his return to England, he escaped and was a priest in Lancashire until his recapture. He escaped briefly again from Lancaster Castle with the latter (a recusant weaver from Chorley) but they got lost outside the town, were picked up and then executed together at Lancaster. They were beatified in 1987. Cf. **England, Martyrs of**.

John-of-Bridlington Thwing (St) {2}

11 October
d. 1379. He had been a student at Oxford University before he joined the Augustinian canons at Bridlington in Yorkshire (England) and was prior there for seventeen years. Little else is known about him. He was canonized in 1401.

John Tomachi (Bl) {2}

8 September
d. 1628. A Japanese married layman with four sons, he was a very active Christian and was a Dominican tertiary. He was burnt alive at Nagasaki while his sons were beheaded. Cf. **Dominic Castellet and Comps** and **Japan, Martyrs of**.

John of Trogir (St) {2}

14 November
d. ?1111. He was bishop of Trogir in Croatia, having been a Camaldolese monk at Absoritano on the Istrian peninsula. He bravely defended his city in a siege by King Coloman of Hungary, who subsequently granted the city a charter.

John-Nepomuk von Tschinderer und von Gleifheim (Bl) {2}

3 December
1777–1860. From Bozen in Tyrol, Austria (now in Italy), he became in turn a priest of Innsbruck, a canon of Trent (1827), auxiliary bishop of Voralberg (1832) and bishop of Trent (now Trento) in 1835. A model bishop in all aspects of his ministry, he built or restored over sixty churches, showed great interest in the seminary, was attentive to social problems and to the needs of the disadvantaged and had a great love for the pope and the church's magisterium. He was beatified in 1995.

John of Tupharia (Bl) {2}

14 November
d. 1170. He was a hermit attached to the abbey of Santa Maria di Gualdo Mazocca at Campobasso (Italy)

John of Valence (St) {2}

26 April
d. 1145. From Lyons (France), he was a canon there and became a Cistercian monk at Clairvaux after a pilgrimage to Compostella. Then he became first abbot of Bonnevaux on the Loire and was made bishop of Valence in 1141, despite his extreme reluctance. His cultus was approved in 1901.

John-Theophanes Vénard (St) {1 –group}

2 February
1829–61. From near Poitiers (France), he joined the Paris Society for Foreign Missions, was ordained in 1852 and went to Vietnam two years later. After teaching in a seminary, he secretly worked in the west of Hanoi for six years during the persecution ordered by Emperor Tự Đức that started in 1857, but was captured and beheaded. Cf. **Vietnam, Martyrs of**.

(John of Verona) *(St)* *{4 –deleted}*

6 June
C7th. He succeeded St Maurus as bishop of Verona (Italy).

John of Vespignano (Bl) {2}

4 July
C12–13th. From Vespignano near Florence (Italy), during the local armed conflicts of the period he cared for the refugees who had fled to Florence. His cultus was approved for there in 1800.

John-Mary Vianney (St) {1, 3}

4 August
1786–1859. From near Lyons (France), as a teenager he was a farmhand but he began studying for the priesthood when aged nineteen. This he found extremely difficult, but he managed to be ordained in 1815 and was made parish priest of Ars in 1818. This was a near-derelict rural parish of a sort common in post-revolutionary France, and he was there for the rest of his life. He restored the life of the parish to full vigour and became famous for prophecy, reading of consciences and supernatural knowledge as well as for being the target of diabolical manifestations. All kinds of people from all over the world asked him to hear their confessions, and during the last ten years of his life he had to spend from sixteen to eighteen hours a day in the confessional. He was canonized in 1925, being declared the patron of parish priests. He is commonly known as the 'Curé d'Ars' (priest of Ars).

John-of-Jesus Vilaregut Farré and Comps (BB) {2 –add}

d. 1936. Four Discalced Carmelites were massacred in two separate incidents in the diocese of Lerida during the Spanish Civil War. Two were killed at Almacelles on 25 June, and two at Lerida itself on 20 August. The latter had a companion martyr, Bl Paul Segalà who was a diocesan priest of Urgell. The five were beatified together in 2013. Cf. **Spanish Civil War, Martyrs of** and list in appendix.

John-of-Kęty Wacienga (St) {1, 3}

23 December
1390–1473. From Kęty in Silesia (Poland), he graduated from the University of Cracow and was appointed professor of theology there. For some time he took charge of a parish but, fearing the responsibility, returned to his biblical teaching and continued with this until his

death. He habitually shared his earnings with the poor. He was canonized in 1767.

John Wall cf. **Joachim-of-St-Anne Wall**.

John Wang Guixin (St) {1 –group}

14 July
Cf. **Joseph Wang Guiji and John Wang Guixin**.

John Wang Rui (St) {1 –group}

9 July
Cf. **Gregory Grassi and Comps**.

John of Warneton (Bl) {2}

27 January
d. 1130. From Warneton near Ypres (Belgium), he was a disciple of St Ivo of Chartres and became a canon regular at Mont-Saint-Eloi near Arras. Eventually he was appointed bishop of Thérouanne and accepted only when directed to do so by the pope. He founded eight monasteries of Canons Regular. Though he had a reputation for strictness he was noticeably merciful in dealing with a group of troublemakers who had conspired against his life as a result of his campaign against simony.

John Watanabe Jirōzaemon (Bl) {2 –add}

26 August
d. 1606. He was a married Japanese layperson from Yatsushiro in Kumamoto, and was martyred at Yatsushiro in Kumamoto. He was beatified in 2008. Cf. **Japan, Martyrs of**.

John-Baptist Wu Mantang (St) {1 –group}

29 June
Cf. **Paul Wu Juan and Comps**.

John Wu Wenyin (St) {1 –group}

8 July
1850–1900. From Dongertou in Hebei (China), he was a leader in his village and a catechist

until an attack by Boxers. He was taken before the magistrate, tortured to induce apostasy and executed. Cf. **China, Martyrs of**.

John Xenius (St) {2}

Oct 6
C11th. He was the propagator of a monastic reform on the island of Crete, and died at a place called Azogyrea.

John Yago (Bl) {2}

19 August
d. 1662. He was a sailor on the ship carrying **Louis Flores and Comps**.

John-of-the-Cross de Yepes (St) {1, 3}

14 December
1542–91. Born at Fontiveros near Avila (Spain), he was apprenticed to a silk-weaver but became a Carmelite at Medina in 1562. From 1564, he studied theology at Salamanca, where he fell under the influence of St Teresa of Avila. As a result, he opened the first house of the Discalced reform for men at Duruelo in 1568. From 1572 to 1577, he was her confessor but was then seized, imprisoned and viciously treated by Carmelite opponents of the reform at Toledo. This led to the definitive separation of the Discalced from the 'Calced' Carmelites in 1578. He was then made prior successively of several houses and visitor of the Andalusian province in 1585. The last years of his life were again a period of humiliation, misunderstanding and physical suffering. He died in obscurity at Ubeda. His fame rests on his mystical writings which contain a thorough exposition of empirical mysticism, besides being classics of Spanish literature. He was canonized in 1726 and declared a doctor of the Church in 1926.

John-Baptist Yi Kwang-nyol (St) {1 –group}

20 July
Cf. **Mary-Magdalen Yi Yŏn-hŭi and Comps**.

John Yi Mun-u (St) {1 –group}

1 February
Cf. **Paul Hong Yŏng-ju and Comps**.

John Yi Yun-il (St) {1 –group}

21 January
d. 1867. He was a farmer, family man and catechist at Daegu in Korea. He was arrested, tortured and had his limbs broken before being
beheaded, and is the latest canonized martyr of
the Korean persecution. Cf. **Korea, Martyrs of**.

John-Nepomucene Zegrí y Moreno (Bl) {2}

17 March
1831–1905. From Granada in Spain, he became
a diocesan priest and held several important
posts in the diocese, including those of cathedral
canon and chaplain to the queen. In 1878, he
founded the congregation of 'Sisters of Charity
of the Blessed Virgin Mary of Mercy' in order to
work for poor people, and this spread throughout Spain. In 1888, he was deposed as superior
after false accusations were made by some of
the sisters. His innocence was acknowledged
in 1894, but his congregation did not want him
back and only accepted him as founder after his
death. He was beatified in 2003.

**John Zhang Huan and John Zhang
Jingguang** (SS) {1 –group}

9 July
Cf. **Gregory Grassi and Comps**.

John Zhang Tianshen (St) {1 –group}

18 February
1805–62. From Kaiyang in Guizhou (China),
he was a married carpenter and lay catechist

who helped St John-Peter Néel and was
beheaded at Kaiyang with him and SS John
Chen Xianheng and Martin Wu Xuesheng. Cf.
China, Martyrs of.

John-Baptist Zhao Mingxi (St) {1 –group}

3 July
Cf. **Peter Zhao Mingzhen and John-Baptist
Zhao Mingxi**.

John-Baptist Zhou Wurui (St) {1 –group}

19 July
1883–1900. An adolescent from Lujiazhuang
in Qin County, Hebei (China), the same
county where SS Ignatius Mangin and Companions were massacred, he escaped his village when it was besieged by the Boxers
but was caught by government troops who
handed him over to the rebels to be beheaded.
He freely admitted his faith and was hence
tortured by mutilation before being executed.
Cf. **China, Martyrs of**.

John-Baptist Zola (Bl) {2}

Jun 15
1576–1626. From Brescia (Italy), he became
a Jesuit in 1595, went to India in 1602 and
then to Japan in 1606. Banished to China in
1614, he returned, was seized and then burnt
alive at Nagasaki. He was beatified in 1867.
Cf. **Francis Pacheco and Comps** and **Japan,
Martyrs of**.

Jolenta cf. **Helen of Poland**.

(Jonas, Barachisius and Comps) *(SS)*
{4 –deleted}

29 March
d. 327. Brothers from Beth-Asja in Persia, they were martyred in the reign of Shah
Shapur II for refusing to convert to Zoroastrianism. There is an extant eye-witness account

of the tortures that they suffered, which were examples of the contemporary Persian inventiveness in such matters. There were nine companions.

(Jonas the Gardener) *(St)* *{4 –deleted}*

11 February
C4th. A monk of Demeskenyanos in Egypt under St Pachomius, he was the gardener of the community for eighty-five years, working during the day and plaiting ropes and singing psalms at night. He lived on raw vegetables and vinegar.

(Jonas of Paris) *(St)* *{4 –deleted}*

22 September
C3rd. An alleged companion or disciple of St Dionysius of Paris (France), according to his story he preached in the area around the city and was martyred.

Jonas (Jonah) the Prophet (St) {2}

21 September
He is the fifth of the Minor Prophets in the Old Testament.

Jonatus (St) {2}

1 August
d. c.690. A monk at Elnone near Tournai (Belgium) under St Amandus, he was abbot first of Marchiennes from ?643 and then of Elnone from ?652.

Jordan-of -St-Stephen Ansalone (St) {1 –group}

28 September
1598–1634. Born near Agrigento (Italy), he became a Dominican missionary in the Philippines and was two years in Japan before being martyred at Nagasaki with St Thomas Hioji Rokuzayemon Nishi. They were left to die in narrow pits. He was canonized with SS Laurence Ruiz and Comps in 1987. Cf. **Japan, Martyrs of**.

Jordan Forzaté (Bl) {2}

7 August
d. ?1248. From Padua (Italy), he became a monk and then abbot of the Benedictine abbey of St Justina there and was appointed governor of the city by Emperor Frederick II. A local tyrant then imprisoned him for two years. He died at Venice and is venerated in the region.

Jordan of Pisa (Bl) {2}

19 August
d. 1311. He became a Dominican at Pisa (Italy) in 1280, studied at Paris and then became a famous preacher at Florence. He started using the local vernacular in his sermons instead of Latin and is thus reckoned as one of the founders of the Italian language. His cultus was approved for Pisa and the Dominicans in 1833.

Jordan of Saxony (Bl) {2}

14 February
d. 1237. A German nobleman, he became a Dominican under St Dominic himself in 1220, attending the first general chapter of the order at Bologna while still a novice. He was later elected second master-general and oversaw the rapid expansion of the new order throughout Germany and into Denmark. He was a powerful preacher, and one of his sermons persuaded St Albert the Great to become a Dominican. He was shipwrecked and drowned when on a voyage to the Holy Land. His cultus was confirmed for the Dominicans in 1828.

Josaphat Kocylovskyj (Bl) {2}

17 November
1876–1947. A monk of the Basilian Order of St Josaphat, he was the Greek-Catholic

bishop of Przemysl in Poland before the area was annexed by the Soviet Union. He died in a gulag near Kiev. Cf. **Nicholas Čarneckyj and 24 Comps**.

Josaphat Kuncewicz (St) {1, 3}

12 November
1584–1623. From Wołodimir in Poland, he became a monk of the Byzantine rite when aged twenty and abbot of Vilnius in 1614. He devoted himself to the work of promoting the unity of the local Orthodox with the Catholic Church, which had been arranged in the Union of Brest-Litovsk in 1596. He became archbishop of Polatsk in Bielarus in 1618 where he continued his work, defending the rights of the Byzantine-rite Catholics against the Latin-rite Polish clergy. There was an Orthodox reaction and the setting up of a rival hierarchy sponsored by Russia, and he was murdered at Vitebsk by a mob of Cossacks. He was the first Eastern-rite Catholic to be formally canonized in 1867, and his cultus was extended to the Latin rite in 1882.

Josaphata-Michaelina Hordáshevska (Bl) {2}

25 March
1869–1919. A Ukrainian Greek Catholic, she was born near Lviv, Ukraine and became a Basilian nun. However, there were no institutes established at the time in the Greek-Catholic Church for active women religious, and Bl Josephata was chosen to be the superior of the first, the 'Servants of Mary Immaculate'. The charism she established for her new institute was to 'serve your people where the need is greatest'. She died at Rome of bone cancer and was beatified in 2001.

José, Josemaria cf. **Joseph**.

Joseph

The spelling is similar in most modern languages except the Italian Giuseppe and the Spanish José. In both Italy and Spain, the name is frequently joined to that of Our Lady: Giuseppe-Maria, José-Maria. The feminine form takes the following variants: Italian: Giuseppa, Giuseppina; Spanish: Josefa, Josefina; French: Josephine, Josepha. The last two are used in this book.

Joseph Allemano (Bl) {2}

16 February
1851–1926. From near Turin (Italy), he became a diocesan priest there in 1873 and worked in the junior seminary of Our Lady of Consolation, which he made into a special centre of Marian devotion. He gave the students the example of his uncle, St Joseph Cafasso, to follow and later founded the 'Missionaries of Our Lady of Consolation' for both sexes (male in 1901, female in 1910). He was canonized in 1990.

Joseph de Anchieta (St) {2}

9 June
1534–97. Born in the Canary Islands, he went to Portugal in order to join the Jesuits and was sent to Brazil in 1553. He became the 'Apostle of Brazil', baptizing an enormous number of native Americans and serving as Provincial for the Jesuits of the entire colony for ten years. The city where he died, near Rio de Janeiro, is named Anchieta after him. He was canonized in 2014.

(Joseph of Antioch) (St) {4 –deleted}

15 February
? He is listed as a deacon martyred at Antioch (Syria).

Joseph Aparicio Sanz and Comps (BB) {2}

d. 1936. During the Spanish Civil War, a total of thirty-seven priests of the Archdiocese of Valencia were killed out of hatred of the faith by Republican forces, together with thirty-seven members of Catholic Action of both sexes. They were beatified as a group in 2001. Cf. **Spanish Civil War, Martyrs of** and list in appendix.

Joseph of Arimathea (St) {2, 4}

31 August
C1st. A member of the Jerusalem Sanhedrin, he is presented in the Gospels as a secret disciple who arranged Christ's burial. Later spurious legends concerning him are numerous. At the church of St Laurence in Genoa is kept the 'Sacro Catino' in which he is alleged to have caught Christ's blood at the crucifixion, and he is also connected with the foundation of the church at Glastonbury (the 'Holy Thorn' there allegedly being his staff which took root).

Joseph Baldo (Bl) {2}

24 October
1843–1915. From near Verona, he became a diocesan priest there, was deputy rector of the seminary for eleven years and then became parish priest of Ronchi. This was a rustic place, poor and ignorant, but he improved all aspects of parish life for the thirty-eight years he was there. In 1894, he founded the 'Poor Daughters of St Joseph' to take care of the elderly and children. He died slowly over two years, as he had prayed for, and was beatified in 1989.

Joseph Barsabas 'the Just' (St) {2, 4}

20 July
C1st. He was the losing candidate when St Matthias was chosen as an apostle in order to replace Judas Iscariot (Acts 1:23). A dubious tradition describes him as a martyr and a bishop of Eleutheropolis near Gaza. He is sometimes depicted as a child holding stones or loaves, or blowing soap bubbles.

Joseph Bilczewski (St) {2 –add}

20 March
1860–1923. From Wilamowice in Austrian Galicia (now Poland), he was ordained as a diocesan priest in Cracow in 1884 and was made Latin bishop of Lemberg (now Lviv in Ukraine) in 1910. He did much to build up the church in his diocese and was faithful to the church's doctrinal and social teaching. He was canonized in 2005.

Joseph-Gabriel-of-the-Rosary Brochero (Bl) {2 –add}

26 January
1840–1914. From Villa Santa Rosa in the province of Córdoba, Argentina, he was ordained as a diocesan priest in 1866 and was made pastor of Villa del Tránsito east of Cordoba (the town has recently been renamed Villa Cura Brochero after him). There he spent the rest of his life, ministering to the impoverished and scattered population of the parish of two hundred square kilometres. He was nicknamed the 'gaucho priest' owing to continually travelling on his mule to visit people. He was fearless in attending to those with leprosy, and caught the disease himself. This left him deaf and blind before he died, but he continued to say Mass. He was beatified in 2013.

Joseph Cafasso (St) {2}

23 June
1811–60. From Castelnuovo d'Asti (Italy), he was ordained in 1833 and three years later became professor of moral theology at the ecclesiastical college at Turin. In 1846, he was appointed superior of the college, which he remained until his death. He led a very penitential life and was famed for his skill in hearing confessions. He was canonized in 1947.

Joseph de Calasanz (St) {1, 3}

25 August
1557–1648. A nobleman from Peralta de la Sal near Barbastro (Spain), he was ordained a diocesan priest of Urguel and was engaged in pastoral work until he was directed to go to Rome in 1592 by a supernatural vision. There he joined the Confraternity of Christian Doctrine for the free education of poor and homeless children, and gradually organized it into a religious society called Le Scuole Pie (Clerks Regular of Religious Schools) whose members became known as Scolopi or Piarists. The new congregation had to pass through a period of violent persecution, mainly from other religious engaged in similar work. When old, he was unjustly accused of maladministration and removed as superior for a period. He died at Rome and was canonized in 1767.

Joseph-Mary Cassant (Bl) {2 –add}

17 June
1878–1903. From Casseneuil in Lot-et-Garonne, France, he was a frail boy with a poor memory and this prevented him from studying for the secular priesthood as was his wish. However, he became a Trappist monk at Saint-Marie-du-Désert near Toulouse in 1894, and was noted for his docility and happiness despite showing symptoms of neurosis that he bore with fortitude. He found his priestly studies extremely difficult, but passed and was ordained in 1902. Immediately afterwards he contracted tuberculosis, and died in six months. He was beatified in 2004.

Joseph Cebula (Bl) {2}

28 April
1902–41. A Polish member of the Congregation of the Missionary Oblates of the Immaculate Virgin, he died of ill-treatment at the concentration camp of Mauthausen in Austria. Cf. **Poland, Martyrs of the Nazi Occupation of.**

Joseph Chang Chu-gi (St) {1 –group}

30 March
Cf. **Anthony Daveluy and Comps.**

Joseph Chang Sŏng-jib (St) {1 –group}

26 May
d. 1839. He was a pharmacist at Seoul in Korea, and died of torture in prison. Cf. **Korea, Martyrs of.**

Joseph Cho Yun-ho (St) {1 –group}

23 December
d. 1866. He was the teenage son of St Peter Cho Hwa-sŏ, and was shot at Tjyentiyon in Korea. Cf. **Korea, Martyrs of.**

Joseph-Benedict Cottolengo (St) {2}

30 April
1786–1842. From Bra near Turin (Italy), he became a canon of Corpus Domini at Turin. In 1827 he opened a small shelter near his church for sick and derelict people, and in 1832 he transferred this to Valdocco, calling it the 'Little House of Divine Providence'. The 'Piccola Casa' soon grew into an extensive settlement, comprising asylums, orphanages, hospitals, schools, workshops and almshouses of all descriptions and catering for all needs. To meet the large daily expenditure needed to maintain all these institutions he relied almost entirely on alms, keeping no books of accounts and making no investments, and his trust in Divine Providence never failed him once. Throughout his life he was primarily a man of prayer. Dying at Chieri, he was canonized in 1934.

Joseph Czempiel (Bl) {2}

19 May

1883–1942. A Polish priest, he was gassed at the concentration camp at Dachau. Cf. **Poland, Martyrs of the Nazi Occupation of**.

Joseph Đặng Đình Viên (St) {1 –group}

21 August

1786–1838. A Vietnamese priest, he was beheaded at Hưng Yên in north Vietnam during the persecution ordered by Emperor Minh Mạng. Cf. **Vietnam, Martyrs of**.

Joseph-of-Cupertino Desa (St) {1, 3}

18 September

1602–63. From Cupertino near Brindisi (Italy), he tried his vocation as a religious at several places but failed because of his poor intelligence. Finally he became a lay-tertiary of the Conventual Franciscans at Grotella and worked as a stablehand until his spiritual charisms became manifest and he was professed and ordained. Thenceforward his life was marked by a series of frequent, remarkable and well-authenticated praeternatural incidents, such as the public manifestations of his power of levitation (he would fly from the church door to the altar over the heads of the worshippers. Once he flew to an olive tree and remained kneeling on a branch for half an hour). However he remained humble, gentle and cheerful. The publicity embarrassed his brethren and raised suspicions, and he was examined by the Inquisition and kept in remote friaries until he died at Osimo. He was canonized in 1767 and his cultus was confined to particular calendars in 1969.

Joseph-of-Leonessa Desideri (St) {2}

4 February

1556–1612. From Leonessa near Rieti (Italy), he became a Capuchin at Assisi in 1574 and was sent to Constantinople to minister to Christian slaves there. After two years, having already been imprisoned for preaching to Turks, he tried to enter the palace to preach to the Sultan and was almost tortured to death before returning to Italy in 1589. Then he spent twenty years as a missionary among poor people before dying of cancer at Amatrice. He was canonized in 1745.

Joseph-Mary Díaz Sanjurjo (St) {1 –group}

20 July

1857. He was a Spanish Dominican, and the vicar-apostolic of Central Tonkin in north Vietnam. During the persecution ordered by Emperor Tự Đức, he was arrested and beheaded at Nam Định. Cf. **Vietnam, Martyrs of**.

Joseph Đỗ Quang Hiển (St) {1 –group}

9 May

d. 1840. A Vietnamese Dominican priest, he was imprisoned during a persecution ordered by a local ruler of north Vietnam named Thiệu Trị. He encouraged fellow Christians in prison, and converted several pagans before being beheaded at Nam Định. Cf. **Vietnam, Martyrs of**.

Joseph-Benedict Dusmet (Bl) {2}

4 April

1818–94. A nobleman born in Palermo, Sicily (his father was from the Low Countries), he entered the Benedictine abbey of La Scala in 1833. After becoming abbot of Caltanisetta in 1852 and of St Nicholas at Catania in 1858, he was made archbishop of Catania in 1867 and Apostolic administrator of Caltagirone in 1885. He implemented Pope Leo XIII's scheme to re-found the Benedictine college of St Anselm's at Rome and was made a cardinal in 1888. Dying at Catania, he was beatified in 1988.

Joseph-Mary Escrivá de Balaguer (St) {2}

26 June

1902–75. Born in Barbastro (Spain), he became a secular priest in Zaragoza in 1925. In 1928 he founded in Madrid 'Opus Dei', a secular institute dedicated to offering a way of sanctification to laypeople through the exercise of one's ordinary work in the world and through exercising one's family, social and personal obligations. He also founded the Society of the Cross for priests in 1943. He died in Rome and was canonized in 2002.

Joseph Fernández (St) {1 –group}

24 July

1775–1838. A Spanish Dominican, he was sent to Vietnam in 1805 and became vicar-provincial in Tonkin (north Vietnam), where he was beheaded at Nam Định during the persecution ordered by Emperor Minh Mạng. Cf. **Vietnam, Martyrs of**.

Joseph-Isabel Flores Varela (St) {1 –group}

21 June

1866–1927. From San Juan Bautista de Teúl in Jalisco, Mexico, he became a diocesan priest of Guadalajara and was lately at the parish of Tonala. During the Cristero War he was arrested and ordered to sign a document agreeing to the government's anti-religious policies. When he refused, he was taken to the cemetery of Zapotlanejo and shot. Cf. **Mexico, Martyrs of**.

Joseph Freinademetz (St) {2}

28 January

1851–1908. Born near Brixen, Tyrol (now in Italy), he was ordained in 1875 and joined the Society of the Divine Word at its foundation by Bl Arnold Janssen. In 1879 he went to China and spent twenty-eight years there, first in Hong Kong and then in the new vicariate of

South Shandong. He was canonized in 2003. Cf. **China, Martyrs of**.

Joseph-Mary Gambaro (St) {1 –group}

7 July

Cf. **Antoninus Fantosati and Joseph-Mary Gamboro**.

Joseph Gérard (Bl) {2}

29 May

1831–1914. Born at Bouxières-aux-Chênes in Lorraine (France), he joined the Oblates of Mary Immaculate in 1851 and went to South Africa two years later. He was ordained at Pietermaritzburg in 1854 and worked with the Irish and Xhosas. Then, from 1864, he became the 'Apostle of the Basutos' and worked in Lesotho until he died at a mission there called Roma. He was beatified in 1988.

Joseph Girotti (Bl) {2 –add}

1 April

1905–45. From Alba near Cuneo in Italy, he joined the Dominicans and was ordained in 1930. He studied and taught Scripture at Rome and Jerusalem, and was opposed to the Fascist government of Mussolini as professor of theology at Turin. After the Germans occupied Italy in 1943 and started to deport Jews, he saved many by arranging escape routes and hiding places. For this he was arrested and sent to the concentration camp at Dachau, where he died. His beatification as a martyr was in 2014.

Joseph-Xavier Gorrosterratzu Jauranena and Comps (BB) {2 –add}

d. 1936–8. They are the Redemptorist martyrs of Cuenca, who were killed during the Spanish Civil War.

They were beatified in 2013. Cf. **Spanish Civil War, Martyrs of** and list in appendix.

Joseph Guardiet Pujol (Bl) {2 –add}

3 August
1879–1936. From Manlleu near Vic in Catalonia, Spain, he became a diocesan priest of
Barcelona in 1902, as well as a Doctor of Theology. In 1917 he was appointed parish priest
at the ancient church of *Sant Pere* in the town
of Rubí near Barcelona. After the outbreak
of the Spanish Civil War he refused to flee.
First his church was burnt by Communists,
then he was imprisoned and finally shot with
two other prisoners at a place called Pi Bessó
outside the town. He was beatified in 2013.
Cf. **Spanish Civil War, Martyrs of** and list
in appendix.

Joseph-Peter Han Chae-kwon (St) {1 –group}

13 December
Cf. **Peter Cho Hua-sŏ and Comps**.

Joseph Hoàng Lưởng Cành (St) {1 –group}

5 September
1765–1838. A Vietnamese doctor of medicine
and a Dominican tertiary, he was beheaded in
1838 at Ninh Tai in north Vietnam. With him
was martyred St Peter Nguyễn Văn Tuự, a
priest. Cf. **Vietnam, Martyrs of**.

**Joseph-Lucian-Ezekiel and Salvador
Huerta Gutiérrez** (Bl) {2 –add}

3 April
d. 1927. They were two brothers of Magda-
lena in Jalisco, Mexico. The former was an
organist and church singer, while the latter
was a mechanic. They both had large families, of ten and twelve children respectively.
Bl Joseph was spotted paying his respects to
the recently martyred corpse of Bl Anacletus
González Flores during the Cristero War, and
was viciously beaten and tortured for a day in
order to elicit information of the whereabouts
of his two priest brothers. Bl Salvador was

arrested at his garage in the same operation
and also tortured. Their captors obtained no
information from either of them, so the following day they took them to the cemetery of
Mezquitán and shot them. They were beatified
in 2005. Cf. **Mexico, Martyrs of**.

Joseph the Hymnographer (St) {2}

3 April
c 810–886. From Syracuse in Sicily, he was
a refugee from the invading Muslims and
became a monk at Thessalonika. Moving to
Constantinople, he then served as treasurer of
Hagia Sofia and is famous for the writing of
hymns for the Byzantine liturgy and office.

Joseph Im Ch'i-baeg (St) {1 –group}

20 September
Cf. **Laurence Han I-hyŏng and Comps**.

Joseph Jankowski (Bl) {2}

16 October
1910–41. A Polish priest and a member of the
Society of the Catholic Apostolate, he was
beaten to death by a camp guard at Auschwitz
on the same day as Bl Anicetus Kopliński was
gassed there. Cf. **Poland, Martyrs of the
Nazi Occupation of**.

Joseph Kowalski (Bl) {2}

4 July
1911–42. Born at Siedlinska in Poland, he was
educated by the Salesians at Oświęcim (later
notorious as Auschwitz), and joined them in
1927. He became famous for his ministry to
young people at Cracow, and was arrested
there by the Nazis as a result in 1941. Initially
he was intended for Dachau, but was sent to
Auschwitz instead for refusing to stamp on his
rosary and ministered as a priest to other prisoners there. The guards picked on him, and
eventually amused themselves by drowning

him in a latrine pit. Cf. **Poland, Martyrs of the Nazi Occupation of**.

Joseph Kurzawa (Bl) {2}

23 May
1910–40. A Polish priest, he was killed by the Nazis at Witowo in Poland together with Bl Vincent Matuszewski. Cf. **Poland, Martyrs of the Nazi Occupation of**.

Joseph Kut (Bl) {2}

18 September
1905–42. A Polish priest, he died of ill-treatment at the concentration camp at Dachau. Cf. **Poland, Martyrs of the Nazi Occupation of**.

Joseph Lambton (Bl) {2}

24 July
1568–92. A Yorkshire landowner from Malton, he was ordained at Rome and returned to England with five other priests, arriving at Newcastle. Such an arrival could not be concealed and he was quickly captured and executed. Other sources list the date as the 31st. He was beatified in 1987. Cf. **England, Martyrs of**.

Joseph Lê Đăng Thị (St) {1 –group}

24 October
d. 1860. A captain in the imperial Vietnamese army, he was imprisoned for his faith during the persecution ordered by Emperor Tự Đức. He was severely tortured before being garrotted at Hué. Cf. **Vietnam, Martyrs of**.

Joseph Ma Taishun (St) {1 –group}

26 June
1840–1900. He was a doctor and catechist of the village of Qianshengzhuang near Liushuitao in Hebei (China). During the Boxer uprising he was caught by a gang hiding in the fields, taken to Wanglajia and tied to a tree. He was invited to apostatize and, on his refusal despite other family members apostatizing, was beheaded. Cf. **China, Martyrs of**.

Joseph Manyanet y Vives (St) {2}

17 December
1833–1901. From Tremp near Urgell in Catalonia (Spain), after his ordination he gathered priests and clerics at Tremp as the 'Sons of the Holy Family' in order to teach and catechize. They opened schools throughout Catalonia. He also founded the 'Daughters of the Holy Family'. He was canonized in 2004.

Joseph Marchand (St) {1 –group}

30 November
1803–35. From Passavant near Besançon (France), he joined the Paris Society for Foreign Missions and was sent to Vietnam. He was seized at Hué during the persecution ordered by Emperor Minh Mạng, and died while bits of his flesh were being torn off with red-hot pincers. Cf. **Vietnam, Martyrs of**.

Joseph Marello (St) {2}

30 May
1844–95. From Turin (Italy), he was ordained a diocesan priest of Asti in 1868. He attended the First Vatican Council in 1869, and the proclamation of St Joseph as the patron of the universal church led him to found the Oblates of St Joseph in 1878. These were lay brothers who did domestic work, taught catechism to children and assisted with the liturgy in parish churches. (Priests were received from 1883.) In 1888 he became the bishop of Acqui, and died in 1895. He was canonized in 2001.

Joseph-de-Calasanz Marqués and Comps (BB) {2}

d. 1936. From Spain, they were Salesians and members of the province of Tarragona. Some were based at Barcelona, and some at Valencia. Twenty-six were priests, six clerical students and seven were coadjutors. Together with them were two sisters of the Congregation of Sisters of Mary Auxiliatrix and one layman (Bl Alexander Planas Saurí). They were killed by Republican soldiers in the Spanish Civil War and were beatified in 2001. Cf. **Spanish Civil War, Martyrs of**.

Joseph Mkasa Balikuddembe (St) {1 –group}

15 November
d. 1885. Major-domo to King Mwanga of Buganda (Uganda), he reproached him for ordering the killing of the newly arrived Anglican missionary bishop James Hannington. He was executed as a result. Cf. **Charles Lwanga and Comps**.

Joseph-Maximus Moro Briz and Comps (BB) {2 –add}
d. 1936. Five priests of the diocese of Ávila in Spain were killed in separate incidents by anarchists, in hatred of the faith during the Spanish Civil War. They were beatified in 2013. Cf. **Spanish Civil War, Martyrs of** and list in appendix.

Joseph Moscati (St) {2}

12 April
d. 1927. From Benevento (Italy), he became a famous doctor of medicine at Naples and a professor at the university there. Famous for his medical research, he also spent much of his time and resources in caring for poor people in the slums of the city. He was canonized in 1987.

Joseph Nadal Guiu and Joseph Jordán Blecua (BB) {2 –add}

12 August
d.1936. They were two diocesan priests in charge of the parish of Monzón near Lérida, Spain, who were shot by the local Republican militia after a court hearing which concluded that their being priests was enough justification for their execution. They are known as Los Curetas de Monzón, and were beatified in 2013. Cf. **Spanish Civil War, Martyrs of** and list in appendix.

Joseph Nascimbeni (Bl) {2}

22 January
1851–1922. Born on the shore of Lake Garda (Italy), he became a diocesan priest of Verona in 1874 and took on the parish of Castelleto (c.900 people) in 1884. He was there for forty-five years, fostering the apostolate of the laity, renewing the liturgical life and founding the 'Little Sisters of the Holy Family' (Franciscan tertiaries) with Bl Mary-Dominica Mantovani. By his death this had 1,200 members. He died of a stroke and was beatified in 1988.

Joseph Nguyễn Đình Nghi and Comps (SS) {1 –group}

8 November
d. 1840. He was a Vietnamese priest beheaded at Nam Định in north Vietnam with two other priests, SS Martin Tạ Đức Thịnh (who was an octogenarian) and Paul Nguyễn Ngân. With them were martyred two farmers, St John-Baptist Cơn who was a family man and St Martin Thọ who was also a tax collector. This occurred on the orders of Emperor Thiệu Trị. Cf. **Vietnam, Martyrs of**.

Joseph Nguyễn Duy Khang (St) {1 –group}

6 December
1832–61. From Tra-vi in the province of Nam-Dinh, Vietnam, he was a servant of St Jerome Hermosilla whom he tried to rescue from prison during the persecution ordered by Emperor Tự Đức. Caught in the attempt, he was punished with one hundred and twenty lashes and, after other tortures, was beheaded at Hải Dương. Cf. **Vietnam, Martyrs of**.

Joseph Nguyễn Đinh Uyển (St) {1 –group}

3 July

1778–1838. A Vietnamese catechist, he died in prison at Hưng Yên in north Vietnam during the persecution ordered by Emperor Minh Mạng. Cf. **Vietnam, Martyrs of**.

Joseph Nguyễn Văn Lựu (St) {1 –group}

2 May

d. 1854. He was a farmer and catechist of Vĩnh Long in the Mekong delta of Vietnam. When soldiers came searching for St Peter Nguyễn Văn Lựu during the persecution ordered by Emperor Tự Đức, he gave himself up voluntarily and died in chains in prison. Cf. **Vietnam, Martyrs of**.

Joseph Olallo Valdés (Bl) {2 –add}

1820–89. He was a foundling brought up in an orphanage at Havana in Cuba, and joined the Hospitaller Order of St John of God as a young teenager. In 1835 he was transferred to Camagüey, and remained in the hospital there first as a nurse, and then as superior from 1856, for the rest of his life. The order was suppressed by the anticlerical Spanish colonial government, and from 1876 he worked alone. He was especially famous for his care of the dying, and for saving his city from massacre in a time of insurrection by the respect for him on the part of the military authorities. He was beatified in 2008.

Joseph Oriol (St) {2, 4}

23 March

1650–1702. From a poor family of Barcelona (Spain), he managed to become a priest and a doctor of theology despite his poverty and was made a canon of Santa Maria del Pino in his native city. He lived on bread and water for twenty-six years while maintaining a very active apostolate, being particularly successful with soldiers and children. He was canonized in 1909.

Joseph-Dionysius-Louis Padilla Gómez (Bl) {2 –add}

1 April

1899–1927. From Guadalajara in Jalisco, Mexico, he was an active member of Catholic Youth and had a special devotion to helping poor people. During the Cristero War there was a special purge of active Christians in the Guadalajara area at the start of April 1927, and Bl Joseph was arrested, beaten and shot. He was beatified in 2005. Cf. **Mexico, Martyrs of**.

(Joseph of Palestine 'the Count') *(St)* *{4 –deleted}*

22 July

d. ?356. A Jewish disciple of Rabbi Hillel at Tiberias in the Holy Land, he was ruler of the synagogue there before being baptized at Tarsus in 326. Being made an imperial official by Emperor Constantine, he lived at Scythopolis and built many churches. His name was inserted into the old Roman Martyrology by Cardinal Baronius, but he has never had a cultus.

Joseph the Patriarch (St) {1, 3}

19 March

C1st. The foster father of Christ and the husband of Our Lady is only known from the gospels of Matthew and Luke. Since he is not mentioned in the narratives of Christ's passion it is believed that he was then already dead. His veneration was widespread in the East from early times, and grew in the West from the C14th. He was declared patron of the universal church in 1870 and is also patron of workers (as such he has a subsidiary feast on 1 May) and of those seeking a holy death. His attribute is a lily, and he is also depicted with carpenter's tools.

Joseph Pawlowski (Bl) {2}

9 January
1890–1942. A Polish priest, he was gassed at the concentration camp at Dachau with Bl Casimir Grelewski. Cf. **Poland, Martyrs of the Nazi Occupation of**.

Joseph-Sebastian Pelczar (St) {2}

28 March
1842–1924. Born in Korczyna in Austrian Galicia (now Poland), he became a diocesan priest of Przemysl in 1864. He was a professor at the seminary and Rector of the Jagiełłonian University at Cracow before being made auxiliary bishop of his diocese in 1890, and was made diocesan bishop the following year. He was especially careful in the formation of his priests, believing that only holy priests could produce lasting apostolic fruit. He was canonized in 2003.

Joseph Phạm Trọng Tả (St) {1 –group}

13 January
Cf. **Dominic Phạm Trọng Khảm and Comps**.

Joseph-Mary Pignatelli (St) {2}

15 November
1737–1811. A nobleman of Italian descent from Zaragoza (Spain), he became a Jesuit at Tarragona when aged fifteen and went on to teach at Manresa, Bilbao and Zaragoza. After the Jesuits were expelled from Spain he was in charge of the juniors in exile on Corsica and then at Ferrara (Italy). Finally, after the suppression of the Society in 1773, he was at Bologna for twenty years, helping with the livelihoods of his secularized brethren and counselling them. At the same time he worked hard for the restoration of the Society, and was allowed to open a quasi-novitiate in 1799. In 1804 he became the first Italian provincial of

the restored Jesuits: 'the link between the old and the new'. He died at Rome and was canonized in 1954.

Joseph Puglisi (Bl) {2 –add}

15 September
1937–93. From the working-class, Mafia-dominated neighbourhood of Brancaccio in Palermo, Sicily, Italy, he became a diocesan priest and was eventually put in charge of the parish of *San Gaetano* in his old neighbourhood in 1990. As a priest he was determined in his opposition to the Mafia, and witnessed publicly against them. It is thought that his refusal to employ a Mafia-sponsored builder to repair the roof of his church was the reason he was shot dead in front of his house on his birthday. He was beatified as a martyr to justice in 2013.

Joseph-Trinity Rangel Montaño (Bl) {2 –add}

25 April
1887–1927. From Dolores Hidalgo in Guanajuato, Mexico, he became a diocesan priest and latterly was based at the parish of Silao. He refused to register as a priest with the government during the Cristero War in 1927, and was forced into hiding. He celebrated Easter with the Minim friars at San Francisco del Rincón, but was discovered. After interrogation and torture he was shot with BB Andrew Sola y Molist and Leonard Pérez Larios. He was beatified in 2005. Cf. **Mexico, Martyrs of**.

Joseph-Mary Robles Hurtado (St) {1 –group}

26 June
1888–1927. From Mascota, he became a diocesan priest of Guadalajara in Mexico in 1900. He served in various parishes, and founded a female congregation the 'Sisters of the Heart of Jesus in the Eucharist'. During the Cristero War he continued his ministry in secret, but

was arrested while celebrating Mass and hanged from a tree at Jalisco near Guadalajara. The soldiers responsible dumped his body at the convent he had founded. Cf. **Mexico, Martyrs of**.

Joseph-Mary Rubio Peralta (St) {2}

2 May
1864–1929. Born near Granada (Spain), he became a parish priest there, then a teacher in the seminary and a member of the diocesan curia. He joined the Jesuits in 1906 and stayed at Matáro near Barcelona until his death. He was a model religious, and very charitable, being canonized in 2003.

Joseph-Mary Ruiz Cano and Comps (BB) {2 –add}

d. 1936. They were sixteen Claretians, martyred during the Spanish Civil War. Bl Joseph-Mary was abducted by Communist militia and shot at El Otero near Sigüenza, and the others were massacred at Fernán Caballero near Ciudad Real. They were beatified in 2013. Cf. **Spanish Civil War, Martyrs of** and list in appendix.

Joseph-of-St-Hyacinth de Salvanés (Bl) {2}

10 September
d. 1622. From near Jaén (Spain), he was provincial vicar of the Dominican missions in Japan and was fluent in Japanese. He was burnt alive in the 'Great Martyrdom' at Nagasaki. Cf. **Charles Spinola and Comps, Japan, Martyrs of** and **Great Martyrdom at Nagasaki**.

Joseph Samsó y Elias (Bl) {2 –add}

1 September
1887–1936. from Castellbisbal near Barcelona (Spain), he became a diocesan priest of Barcelona in 1910. After serving in several

parishes, and becoming known for his devotion to catechesis, he was transferred to Mataro where he also gained a reputation as a spiritual director. However, he became a target of anticlerical agitation, and was first attacked in 1934 when he refused to divulge the identities of his assailants to the police. After the outbreak of the Spanish Civil War he was imprisoned as a priest, and was shot without trial in the cemetery at Mataro. He was beatified in 2010. Cf. **Spanish Civil War, Martyrs of**.

Joseph Sanchez del Río (Bl) {2 –add}

10 February
1913–28. From Sahuayo in Michoacan, Mexico, as a teenager he joined the Cristero rebellion against the anti-Christian Calles government and was one of a group led by General Prudencio Mendoza at Cotija. The village was seized by government forces, who arrested him, removed the skin from the soles of his feet and forced him to walk to the cemetery while continually urging him to deny Christ. He was shot there while shouting 'Long live Christ the king' and was beatified in 2005. Cf. **Mexico, Martyrs of**.

Joseph Stanek (Bl) {2}

23 September
1916–44. A Polish priest, and a member of the Society of the Catholic Apostolate, he was hanged by the Nazis at Warsaw. Cf. **Poland, Martyrs of the Nazi Occupation of**.

Joseph Straszewski (Bl) {2}

12 August
1885–1942. A Polish priest, he was gassed at the concentration camp at Dachau with Bl Florian Stępniak. Cf. **Poland, Martyrs of the Nazi Occupation of**.

Joseph ot Thessalonica (St) {2}

15 July
d. 832. He was the brother of St Theodore Studites, and as a monk was famous for composing liturgical hymns. When he was made bishop of Thessalonica, he adamantly opposed the iconoclast policy of the imperial government at Constantinople, and as a result was persecuted and finally exiled to Thessaly. There he died of hunger.

Joseph-Mary Tomasi (St) {2}

3 January
1649–1713. Born at Licata in Sicily, a son of the duke of Palermo, he joined the Theatines and was based at Rome, where he devoted his scholarly talents to the methodical study of the liturgy and produced several very valuable works on the subject. He was the confessor of the future Pope Clement XI, and after the papal election ordered him to accept under pain of mortal sin. The new pope thereupon made Joseph a cardinal. He was in the habit of teaching the catechism to the children in his titular church's parish. He died at Rome and was canonized in 1986.

Joseph Toniolo (Bl) {2 –add}

7 October
1845–1918. From Treviso (Italy), the son of an engineer, he became a university scholar and ended up holding the chair of Political Economy at the University of Pisa from 1883 until his death. He was an outstanding example of the reconciliation of Catholic faith with the demands of modern Italian society after the reunification of the country in 1870, at a time when many educated people had become agnostic. He was involved in Social Action (the practical promotion of the church's social teaching), and was a member of the Society of St Vincent de Paul. He died at Pisa, and was beatified in 2012.

Joseph Tous y Soler (Bl) {2 –add}

27 February
1811–71. From Igualada near Barcelona (Spain), he became a Franciscan Capuchin at Sarria in 1827 and was assigned to the friary of San Madrone at Barcelona after being ordained in 1834. That year, the anticlerical government suppressed the friary and he was forced into exile in France. In 1843 he returned to Spain, but religious community life was still an impossibility so he served as a parish priest in Barcelona while maintaining the Capuchin charism in his private life. He was the founder of the Capuchin Sisters of the Mother of the Divine Shepherd for the pastoral care of young people. He died while saying Mass, and was beatified in 2010.

Joseph-Anthony Tovini (Bl) {2}

16 January
1841–97. From Cividate Camuno near Brescia (Italy), he studied law at the University of Padua and worked at Brescia where he married (the couple had ten children). He became mayor of his home town in 1871 and was later a councillor for Brescia. As such he made positive efforts to promote the church's witness in lay life at a period when anticlericalism was fashionable. He was involved in many social, charitable and especially educational projects and was also a Franciscan tertiary. He died at Brescia and was beatified in 1998.

Joseph Tuân (St) {1 –group}

7 January
d. 1862. He was a farmer and family man of An Bái in north Vietnam, and during the persecution ordered by Emperor Tự Đức was ordered to trample on a crucifix. He genuflected to it instead, and was beheaded. Cf. **Vietnam, Martyrs of.**

Joseph Tuấn (St) {1 –group}

30 April

d. 1861. He was Vietnamese priest from An Bái in north Vietnam. During the persecution ordered by Emperor Tự Đức he was betrayed while taking Holy Communion to his sick mother, and was immediately seized and beheaded. Cf. **Vietnam, Martyrs of**.

Joseph Túc (St) {1 –group}

6 January

1862. He was a young farmer at Hung Yén in north Vietnam, and refused to trample on a crucifix during the persecution ordered by Emperor Tự Đức. As a result he was imprisoned several times, tortured and finally beheaded. Cf. **Vietnam, Martyrs of**.

Joseph Vaz (St) {2}

16 January

1651–1711. The 'Apostle of Ceylon (Sri Lanka) was born in Portuguese Goa (India) and became a missionary priest there. In 1687 he went to Jaffna. The Portuguese had been expelled from Ceylon fifty years previously by the Calvinist Dutch and the resident Catholic population had had no priest since then. He soon had to flee to the inland kingdom of Kandy (then still independent) and was imprisoned, but won a rain competition with the local Buddhist clergy and won permission from the king to work as a priest in 1696. Then he was appointed vicar-general, organized the missions, translated religious works into Sinhalese and negotiated terms with the Dutch government. He was canonized in 2015.

Joseph Wang Guiji and John Wang Guixin (SS) {1 –group}

13 July

1875 and 1863–1900. First cousins of the Double-Tomb Village in Hebei (China), during the Boxer Uprising they were in an inn while on a journey when they were recognized as Catholics. St Joseph was killed at once at Nangong, but St John was taken before the county prefect there. The latter was sympathetic and promised him his freedom if he would apostatize by a simple verbal denial of his faith, but he refused and was handed over to the Boxers to be killed. This was done on the following day. Cf. **China, Martyrs of**.

Joseph Wang Yumei and Comps (SS) {1 –group}

21 July

d. 1900. He was the 77-year-old leader of the Catholic community at Majiazhuang near Daining in Hebei (China), and was seized by a Boxer gang at the entrance to his village with SS Anne Wang and Lucy Wang (Wang) with her nine-year-old son, St Andrew Wang Tianqing. He was killed on the road near his village on this date, while the other three were killed in the village on the following day. Cf. **China, Martyrs of**.

Joseph-Mary de Yermo y Parres (St) {2}

20 September

1851–1904. Born in Mexico City of wealthy parents, he became a diocesan priest at León in Guanajuato in 1879. Taking over 'El Calvario', a poor chapel in the suburbs, he turned it into a centre of perpetual adoration and evangelical charity. In 1885 he founded 'Servants of the Sacred Heart and the Poor' to help destitute people after finding two dead babies half-eaten by animals while walking by the river. He also founded a school for the Tarahumara nation in the north of Mexico and a refuge for destitute women in Los Angeles, where he died. He was canonized in 2000.

Joseph Yuan Gengyin (St) {1 –group}

30 July
1853–1900. From Hui in Hebei (China), he was on his way to the market town of Daying near Zaoqiang when he met a gang of Boxers who tried to make him worship in the town temple. On his refusal he was killed. Cf. **China, Martyrs of**.

Joseph Yuan Zaide (St) {1 –group}

24 June
1766–1817. From a Catholic family of the Peng district of Sichuan (China), he was ordained in 1795 and worked in the northeastern part of Sichuan until he was betrayed by an adulterous woman whom he had rebuked. He was executed at Hezhou after prolonged tortures in prison.

Joseph Zapłata (Bl) {2}

19 February
1904–45. A Polish priest of the Congregation of the Sacred Heart of Jesus, he died of ill-treatment at the concentration camp at Dachau. Cf. **Poland, Martyrs of the Nazi Occupation of**.

Joseph Zhang Dapeng (St) {1 –group}

12 March
1754–1815. From Duyun in Guizhou (China), he became a silk merchant at Guiyang and was baptized in 1800. He worked as a lay catechist, and became famous for his charitable activities. However, he was betrayed by his brother-in-law during a persecution and crucified at Xijiaotang. Cf. **China, Martyrs of**.

Joseph Zhang Wenlan (St) {1 –group}

29 July
1831–61. From a Catholic family of Sichuan, he was admitted to the seminary at Qingyan in the province of Guizhou but was arrested a year later with SS Paul Chen Changpin, John-Baptist Luo Tingyin and Martha Wang Louzhi. They were imprisoned in a hot and humid cave, where they were tortured before being beheaded. Cf. **China, Martyrs of**.

Josepha-Mary-of-St-Agnes Albiñana (Bl) {2}

21 January
1625–96. From near Valencia (Spain), she became an Augustinian nun at Benigamin. She was beatified in 1888, and is commonly known as 'Inés de Benigamin'.

Josepha Martínez Pérez and Comps (BB) {2 –add}

d. 1936. They are thirteen Martyrs of the Sisters of Charity of Valencia, attached to a hospital in that city who were massacred by Communists in six separate incidents during the Spanish Civil War. They were beatified in 2013. Cf. **Spanish Civil War, Martyrs of** and list in appendix.

Josepha-of-St-John-of-God Ruano García and Mary-of-Sorrows-of-St-Eulalia Puig Bonany (BB) {2}

8 September
d. 1936. They were sisters of the 'Congregation of Little Sisters of Abandoned Old People', the former the superior of the nursing-home at Requena near Valencia and the latter the doorkeeper. Together with another sister (who survived), they were seized by Republican soldiers while on the way to the railway station, taken to a nearby village called Buñol and shot. They were beatified in 2001. Cf. **Spanish Civil War, Martyrs of**.

Josepha Naval Girbés (Bl) {2}

24 February
1820–93. From Algemesí near Valencia (Spain), she lived and died there. Her mother

died when she was thirteen, so she turned to Our Lady and became a model of the 'parish lady', always helping in the life of the parish and basing her own life of prayer on the liturgical cycle. She ran a free needlework school at her home. Her beatification was in 1988.

Josephine Bakhita (St) {2}

8 February
1869–1947. Born in the Sudan, she was kidnapped when aged six and sold as a slave five times before being bought in Khartoum by the Italian consul. She went back to Italy with him and became the governess of a friend's daughter. They were both entrusted to the Canossian Sisters in Venice, where Josephine was baptized in 1890 and took vows in 1896. She worked in Schio as cook, seamstress and porter and died there after dictating her memoirs. She was canonized in 2000.

Josephine-Gabrielle Bonino (Bl) {2}

8 February
1843–1906. Born in Savigliano in Piedmont (Italy), she tried her vocation twice in cloistered orders before founding the 'Sisters of the Holy Family' in 1880 to catechize orphans and to nurse poor sick people. Her charism was based on the Holy Family of Nazareth. She was beatified in 1995.

Josephine Hendrina Stenmanns (Bl) {2 –add}

1852–1903. From Issum in Germany, she wished to become a religious but the German anti-Catholic 'Kulturkampf' of the time made this impossible. So she became a kitchen maid at the 'Mission House' at Steyl in the Netherlands founded by Bl Arnold Janssen. After five years of this she founded the 'Missionary Sisters, Servants of the Holy Spirit' as a female branch of the Mission House in 1894. The new congregation was an immediate success. She died at Steyl and was beatified in 2008.

Josephine Nicoli (Bl) {2 –add}

1863–1924. From Casatisma near Pavia in Italy, she joined the Daughters of Charity of St Vincent de Paul at Turin in 1883 and was sent to Sardinia. She remained there most of her life and worked at Cagliari and Sassari, founding many charitable institutes. She was beatified in 2008.

Josephine ('Pina') Suriano (Bl) {2 –add}

19 May
1915–50. From Partinico near Palermo in Sicily, in her early teens she joined Catholic Action and led a full spiritual life despite the opposition of her family, who wanted her to marry. This opposition prevented her from becoming a nun, but she made a private vow of chastity. She did try to become a Daughter of St Anne in 1940, but only lasted a week because a heart problem became manifest. In 1948 she offered herself in prayer as a sacrifice for the sanctification of priests, and the same year suffered the onset of acute rheumatoid arthritis. She died of a heart attack, and was beatified in 2004.

Josephine Vannini (Bl) {2, 4}

23 February
1859–1911. Born in Rome, she was orphaned and tried to join the Daughters of Charity but her health prevented this. In 1891 she met Bl Louis Tezza, procurator general of the Camillans, who encouraged her to found a female branch of his order. This she did, adding a fourth vow of service to the sick even at risk to one's life. The 'Daughters of St Camillus' had spread to France, Belgium and Argentina before she died. She was beatified in 1994.

Josse cf. **Judoc**.

Joshua (St) {2}

1 September
He features in the Old Testament, in the Pentateuch and the book named after him.

Jovinian (St) {2, 4}

5 May
C4th. He was with St Peregrinus of Auxerre on mission, was a church reader at Auxerre (France) when the latter was bishop there, survived him and is believed to have been martyred.

Jovinus and Basileus (SS) {2, 4}

25 December
C3rd–4th. They were martyred at Rome and were buried on the Latin Way.

Juan, Juanna cf. **John**, **Jane**.

(Jucunda of Reggio) *(St)* *{4 –deleted}*

25 November
d. 466. A consecrated virgin of Reggio-Emilia (Italy), she was a disciple of St Prosper, bishop of that city.

Jucundian (St) {2, 4}

4 July
? He is listed as a Roman African who was martyred by being thrown into the sea.

Jucundus of Aosta (St) {2}

30 December
d. p502. He was a bishop of Aosta in the Italian Alps.

(Jucundus of Bologna) *(St)* *{4 –deleted}*

14 November
d. 485. He was a bishop of Bologna (Italy).

Jude (Thaddeus) (St) {1, 3}

28 October
C1st. One of the twelve apostles, he was brother of St James the Less and therefore related to Christ. One of the canonical letters is attributed to him. The traditions concerning his later career are confused and unreliable, including the one that he was martyred in Persia with St Simon the Zealot. This legend has led to the two apostles sharing a feast-day. He is the patron of difficult or hopeless cases or problems.

Judicael, King of Brittany (St) {2}

17 December
d. c.650. As a royal prince he became a monk at the monastery of St Meen near Rennes (France), but was elected king of Brittany and married in 630. He retired to become a monk again in 642 after a successful reign.

Judoc (Jodoc, Josse), King of Brittany (St) {2, 4}

13 December
d. ?669. Brother of St Judicael, king of Brittany, when the latter abdicated he was the successor for a few months. Then he fled with twelve companions and ended up as a hermit at St Josse (named after him) near Boulogne-sur-Mer (France). His veneration was popular in medieval England and some relics were enshrined at Winchester.

(Julia) *(St)* *{4 –deleted}*

7 October
d. c.300. She was listed as martyred in the reign of Diocletian, either in Egypt or in Syria.

Julia Billiart (St) {2}

8 April
1751–1816. From Cuvilly in Picardy (France), the daughter of a shopkeeper, she

took a vow of chastity when aged fourteen and worked in helping and teaching the poor. In 1774 she saw an assault on her father and became bedridden by hysterical paralysis. However she became a mystic, attracted disciples and supported the 'non-juring' clergy during the French Revolution. Moving to Amiens to escape persecution, she formed a sisterhood for the education of girls in 1803 (later to become the 'Institute of Notre Dame of Namur'), and was cured of her paralysis in 1804. She moved the mother house of her institution to Namur in Belgium, died there and was canonized in 1970.

Julia della Rena (Bl) {2}

9 January

1319–67. From Certaldo near Florence (Italy), as a teenager she was a domestic servant but became an Augustinian tertiary at Florence when aged eighteen. Returning to her native town, she lived as a hermit in a cell next to the church of SS Michael and James. Her cultus was confirmed for Florence in 1819.

Julia of Corsica (St) {2, 4}

22 May

? Her story is that she was a young noblewoman of Carthage in Roman Africa who was sold as a slave by the Vandals when they captured that city. The ship on which she was being taken to Gaul was wrecked on Corsica while a pagan festival was taking place and, after being rescued, she refused to join in the festivities and was crucified on the northern tip of the island. She is the patron of Corsica.

(Julia of Mérida) (St) {4 –deleted}

10 December

Early C4th? She was listed as martyred with St Eulalia at Mérida (Spain) in the reign of Diocletian.

Julia Rodzińska (Bl) {2}

20 February

1899–1945. A Domincaness nun, she was sent to the concentration camp at Stutthof near Gdynia in Poland by the Nazis, and volunteered to nurse sufferers of typhoid there. She died herself of the disease. Cf. **Poland, Martyrs of the Nazi Occupation of.**

Julia Salzano (St) {2 –add}

17 May

1846–1929. From Santa Maria Capua Vetere in Italy, she was in an orphanage from age four to fifteen but did well and became a teacher at Casoria near Naples. In her spare time she taught catechism, based on the Scriptures, at home. In 1905 she founded the 'Cathechist Sisters of the Sacred Heart' for this work. She died at Casoria and was canonized in 2010.

(Julia of Troyes) (St) {4 –deleted}

21 July

C3rd? According to her story she was a young woman of Troyes (France) who was beheaded there in the reign of Aurelian. Her acta are a forgery.

Julian and Basilissa (SS) {2, 4}

6 January

Early C4th. They were martyred at Antinoe in the Thebaid of Egypt. Their story is that they were a married couple who took vows of celibacy and turned their house into a refuge for the poor and homeless. As a widower Julian was martyred in the reign of Diocletian with four named companions: Anthony, a priest; Anastasius, a new convert; Marcionilla, a married woman and Celsus, her little son together with his seven anonymous brothers and many others. The legend is a romantic story with a possible foundation in fact. These others have been deleted from the Roman Martyrology.

Julian, Eunus and Besas (SS) {2, 4}

27 February
C3rd. Julian, a citizen of Alexandria (Egypt), was accused of being a Christian and, having gout, was carried to the law-court by his two Christian slaves. One apostatized through fear but the other, Eunus, was martyred with his master. They were paraded on camels through Alexandria, whipped and burnt to death. Besas, a sympathetic soldier, was killed by the mob for having tried to help them. These details were preserved by St Dionysius of Alexandria.

(Julian, Eunus, Macarius and Comps) (SS) *{4 –deleted}*

30 October
They are listed in the old Roman Martyrology as martyrs of Alexandria in Egypt, but SS Julian and Eunus are duplicated on 27 February and St Macarius on 8 December. The duplication was caused by the insertion of a group of sixteen including those mentioned above.

Julian of Anazarbus (St) {2, 4}

16 March
Early C4th. A senator of Anazarbus in Cilicia (Asia Minor), in the reign of Diocletian he was tortured, sewn up in a sack with scorpions and vipers and thrown into the sea at Aegae. His body was recovered and enshrined at Antioch (Syria), where St John Chrysostom gave a sermon in his honour.

Julian of Ancyra (St) {2}

13 September
Early C4th. He was a priest of Ancyra in Asia Minor (now Ankara, Turkey) who was martyred in the reign of the emperor Licinius.

(Julian of Apamea) (St) *{4 –deleted}*

9 December
C3rd. Bishop of Apamea in Syria, he took part in the Montanist controversy.

Julian of Brioude (St) {2, 4}

28 August
C3rd? From Vienne (France), he was an imperial army officer and a secret Christian disciple of St Ferreolus of Vienne. On the outbreak of persecution he fled, but surrendered to his pursuers and had his throat cut near Brioude. His shrine became the most famous one in Auvergne.

(Julian of Caesarea -1) (St) *{4 –deleted}*

25 August
? Cardinal Baronius listed him as a Syrian priest martyred at 'Caesarea', but on poor evidence.

(Julian of Caesarea -2) (St) *{4 –deleted}*

23 March
? The old Roman Martyrology listed him as a confessor. Nothing more is known about him.

(Julian of Cagliari) (St) *{4 –deleted}*

7 January
? His alleged relics were discovered and enshrined at Cagliari (Sardinia) in 1615 and he was equated with the Julian mentioned in the old Roman Martyrology on this date.

Julian Cesarello de Valle (Bl) {2}

11 May
d. ?1349 He was born and died at Valle in Istria (near Rovinj in Croatia), where his tomb is venerated. Nothing is known about him. His cultus was approved in 1910.

Julian of Cuenca (St) {2, 4}

28 January
d. ?1207. From Burgos (Spain), he was appointed bishop of Cuenca in 1196 after that city was taken from the Muslims by the kingdom of Castile in 1177. He allegedly spent all

his spare time earning money for poor people by the work of his hands, and is the principal patron of the diocese of Cuenca.

(Julian of Edessa) (St) *{4 –deleted}*

9 June

d. c.370. A captive from Italy, he was sold into slavery at Baalbek in Lebanon and led an immoral life with his master while the latter was alive. On regaining his freedom he entered a monastery near Edessa (now Urfa, Turkey) under St Ephraem, who wrote his biography.

(Julian of Egypt and Comps) (SS) *{4 –deleted}*

16 February

? It is alleged that he was the leader of 5000 martyrs in Egypt, but nothing is known for certain. One source-text substitutes 'militibus' for 'millibus', that is, 'five soldiers' not 'five thousand persons'.

Julian-Alfred Fernández Zapico (St) {2}

9 October

Cf. **Innocent-of-Mary-Immaculate Canoura Arnau and Comps**.

Julian the Hospitaller (St)

12 February

? His legend, which was very popular in the Middle Ages, is as follows: Julian killed his own parents in error, went to Rome with his wife to obtain absolution and, on their return home, built a hospice on a riverbank where they looked after the poor and the sick and ferried travellers across the river. He is for this reason a patron of boatmen, innkeepers and travellers. The story is fictitious, and seems to be a variant of that of SS Julian and Basilissa. He is not in the Roman Martyrology, but has had churches dedicated to him at Rome.

Julian of Le Mans (St) {2, 4}

27 January

C3rd? He is traditionally the first bishop of Le Mans (France) and is patron of several churches in England. The reference in the old Roman Martyrology to his having been sent by St Peter is a Gallican delusion.

(Julian of Lyons) (St) *{4 –deleted}*

13 February

? He is listed in the old Roman Martyrology as having been martyred at Lyons, although Nicomedia in Asia Minor is a possible alternative.

Julian-of-St-Augustine Martinet (Bl) {2}

8 April

d. 1606. From Medinaceli near Soria (Spain), after being twice rejected by the Franciscans he was finally admitted as a lay brother near Segovia. He accompanied the Franciscan preachers on their home missions, and used to ring a handbell through the streets of the places visited in order to summon people to the public sermon. He died at Alcalá de Henares and was beatified in 1825.

Julian Maunoir (Bl) {2}

28 January

1606–83. From near Avranches (France), he became a Jesuit in 1625 and hoped to go to Canada. However he became a missionary in Brittany for forty years instead, learning the Breton language well enough to preach in it and allegedly reconciling 30,000 people to the faith in two years. Previously the Bretons had been neglected by the French-speaking clergy, but he was joined by several secular priests in his work. He died exhausted at Plévin and was beatified in 1951.

Julian Nakaura (Bl) {2 –add}

21 October

d. 1633. He was a Jesuit priest from Nakaura near Nagasaki, and was martyred at Nishizaka. He was beatified in 2008. Cf. **Japan, Martyrs of**.

Julian of Norwich

13 May
d. ?1416. The famous mystic of Norwich (England), the author of 'Revelations of Divine Love', had formerly been listed as a beata in Roman Catholic publications. However, she has been quoted in the Catholic Catechism with an attribution referring to her as 'Dame', which is a definitive indication that she has no approved cultus. The church at Norwich where she lived is now referred to as 'St Julian's'.

Julian Sabas (St) {2, 4}

17 January
d. 377. From Baalbek (Lebanon), he became a hermit near Edessa (now Urfa in Turkey). He visited Antioch to help the church there after the expulsion of St Meletius and also spent some time at Sinai. St John Chrysostom and Theodoret of Cyrrhus have left accounts of his life.

Julian of Sora (St) {2, 4}

27 January
C2nd? He was seized at Atina in eastern Lazio (Italy) while on a journey, then tortured and beheaded. His shrine is at Sora.

Julian of Toledo (St) {2, 4}

6 March
d. 690. He was a monk at Zaragoza under St Eugene, whom he succeeded as abbot in the same monastery and then as archbishop of Toledo in 680. He was the first archbishop to exercise primacy over the whole Iberian peninsula. Besides presiding over several national councils and revising and developing the Mozarabic liturgy, he was a voluminous writer (little of his writings survive).

Juliana and Sempronia (SS)

27 July
d. 303? They are principal patrons of Matarone in Catalonia (Spain), and their legend alleges that they buried St Cucuphas. Despite doubts as to their having existed, their cultus was confirmed in 1850 for Barcelona. They are not listed in the Roman Martyrology.

Juliana of Collalto (Bl) {2}

1 September
d. 1262. A noblewoman from near Treviso (Italy), when aged ten she entered the Benedictine nunnery at Salarola but transferred to Gemmola in 1222 with Bl Beatrix of Este. In 1226 she founded the nunnery of SS Biagio and Cataldo at Venice, and was the first superior. Her cultus was approved for Venice in 1753.

Juliana of Cornillon (Bl) {2}

5 April
1192–1258. From Rutten near Liege (Belgium), she became an Augustinian nun and prioress at Cornillon. As such she successfully promoted the institution of the feast of Corpus Christi, her greatest achievement, but was slandered as a false visionary and driven from her nunnery. Recalled by the bishop of Liege, she was expelled permanently in 1248. She took refuge at the Cistercian nunnery of Salzinnes and, when this place was burnt, became a hermit at Fosses. Her cultus was confirmed locally in 1869.

Juliana Falconieri (St) {2, 3}

19 June
1270–1341. A noblewoman of Florence (Italy), her uncle St Alexis Falconieri was a co-founder of the Servite Friars and she became a tertiary when aged sixteen. In 1304 the community of Servite tertiaries known as

the 'Mantellate', of which she was the first superior, was formally established and admitted into the order by St Philip Benizi. She was canonized in 1737 and her cultus was confined to local calendars in 1969.

Juliana of Florence (St) {2, 4}

7 February

C4th. She is described by St Ambrose of Milan as a married woman of Bologna (Italy) who gave permission for her husband to leave her and become a priest, and who then devoted herself to bringing up her four children and to the service of the church and the poor.

Juliana the Martyr (St) {2, 4}

16 February

? The old Roman Martyrology listed her as having been martyred at Nicomedia (Asia Minor), but she was actually martyred near Naples (perhaps at Cumae, where her relics are allegedly enshrined). The details are seriously confused.

Juliana Puricelli (Bl) {2}

14 August

1427–1501. From Busto Arsizio near Milan (Italy), she became an Augustinian nun and the first companion of Bl Catherine da Pallanza at the Sacro Monte sopra Varese, where she died. Her cultus was approved for Milan in 1769.

Julitta of Caesarea (St) {2, 4}

30 July

d. ?303. A rich citizen of Caesarea in Cappadocia (Asia Minor), she was cheated out of her property by a pagan and, on her appealing to the magistrates, was denounced as a Christian and burnt.

Julitta Kim (St) {1 –group}

26 September

Cf. **Sebastian Nam I-gwan and Comps**.

Julius I, Pope (St) {2, 4}

12 April

d. 352. A Roman, he was pope from 337 and supported the exiled St Athanasius, whom he defended against his Arian accusers. The letter he wrote to the East on this occasion is one of the most important dogmatic statements of the Roman see. He also built several churches in Rome.

Julius, Aaron and Comps (SS) {2, 4}

22 June

Early C4th? According to tradition they were martyred at Caerleon in Gwent (Wales) in the reign of Diocletian. They are included in St Bede's Martyrology and (with St Alban) are the only martyrs known of the Romano-British church.

(Julius, Potamia and Comps) (SS) {4 –deleted}

5 December

d. 302. Twelve Roman Africans, they were listed as martyred at Thagura in Numidia in the reign of Diocletian. Crispin, Felix and Gratus were also named.

Julius Álvarez Mendoza (St) {1 –group}

30 March

1866–1927. He was a native of Guadalajara in Mexico, and became a diocesan priest there in 1894. During the Cristero War he was parish priest of Mechocanejo, and was known for his kindness and gentleness during his secret ministry. He was surprised by a squad of soldiers while on the way to say Mass at a ranch, and ordered to be shot by their commanding officer at San Julio near Guadalajara. Cf. **Mexico, Martyrs of**.

Julius of Durostorum (St) {2, 4}

27 May
d. ?302. A veteran Roman soldier, he was martyred at Durostorum on the Danube (now Silistra in Bulgaria) in the reign of Diocletian, together with other soldiers.

(Julius of Gelduba) *(St) {4 –deleted}*

20 December
? He is listed as having been martyred at 'Gelduba' in Thrace (possibly in Bulgaria).

Julius of Novara (St) {2, 4}

31 January
Early C4th? He was a priest from Aegina (Greece) and, with his brother Julian (a deacon), was authorized by the emperor Theodosius I to convert the pagan temples around Lake Maggiore (Italy) into churches.

(Julius of Rome) *(St) {4 –deleted}*

19 August
d. ?190. An alleged Roman senator, he is mentioned in the unreliable acta of SS Eusebius, Pontian and Comps. There is no historical evidence for his existence.

Juniper Serra (Bl) {2}

28 August
1713–84. Born in Majorca, he joined the Franciscans at Palma in 1730 and went to Mexico in 1749 to teach in the Apostolic College there and to go on mission. In 1769 Spain started the conquest of California, then inhabited by many different nations mostly living as hunter-gatherers. He went with the army and founded nine missions, including San Francisco and San Diego (around which the namesake cities grew). He had a great devotion to the well-being of the natives but shared the contemporary views of their culture, which

has been unfairly held against him. He died at Carmel and was beatified in 1988.

Justa and Henredina (SS) {2, 4}

14 May
C3rd–4th. They are alleged to have been martyred somewhere on Sardinia in the reign of Hadrian, and are venerated on that island. A third martyr, Justina, arose from a dittography and has been deleted from the Roman Martyrology.

Justa and Rufina (SS) {2, 4}

19 July
d. ?287. According to their unreliable acta, they were two sisters of Seville (Spain) who worked as potters and who were martyred in the reign of Diocletian. They are the principal patrons of Seville. Early sources list them as 'Justus and Rufina' (i.e. as a man and woman).

Justin and Crescentio (SS) {2}

4 August
d. 258. They were martyred on the Via Tiburtina near Rome.

Justin of Chieti (St) {2}

1 January
d.?540. He has an ancient cultus as a bishop at Chieti near Pescara (Italy).

Justin de Jacobis (St) {2}

31 July
1800–60. From San Fele in Basilicata (Italy), he became a Vincentian and was superior of various communities in central Italy. In 1839 he was made prefect-apostolic of his congregation's mission in Ethiopia, and adapted his way of life to that of the country. This won him the respect of much of the native Monophysite church, but the government suspected him

to be a foreign agent and he was imprisoned twice. In 1848 he was made bishop and vicar-apostolic at Massawa. He founded many missions, established a native Catholic clergy and allegedly converted about 12,000, among them Bl Michael Ghebre. He died at Halai in Eritrea and was canonized in 1975.

(Justin of Louvre) (St) {4 –deleted}

1 August
C3rd? He is alleged to have been a little boy martyred at Louvre near Paris (France). He may be identical with St Justus of Beauvais, for their two stories seem to have a common source.

Justin Orona Madrigal and Atilanus Cruz Alvarado (SS) {1 –group}

1 July
d. 1928. They were two priests, massacred at Rancho del Los Cruces, Cuquio near Guadalajara in Mexico. Bl Atilano was born at Teocaltice in 1901, was ordained in 1927 and made parish priest of Cuquio. They were shot by a visiting platoon of soldiers who had heard that there were two priests at the ranch. Cf. **Mexico, Martyrs of**.

Justin Martyr (St) {1, 3}

1 June
d. ?165. The first Christian philosopher was from a pagan family of Nablus in the Holy Land and studied philosophy at Ephesus in Asia Minor. The great philosophical systems of the time failed to convince, however, and he was eventually converted to Christianity when aged about thirty. He was subsequently at Rome, where he was martyred. His acta are genuine. Of his many writings only two 'Apologies for the Christian Religion' and his 'Dialogue with Trypho' survive. Listed with him in the Roman Martyrology, but

not celebrated liturgically with him, are six disciples who were martyred with him. They are: Chariton, Charitus, Evelpistus, Jerax, Poeon and Liberianus.

(Justin of Rome) (St) {4 –deleted}

17 September
d. 259. He was allegedly a Roman priest who buried the bodies of martyrs such as St Laurence and was martyred himself. His relics were transferred to Freising in Germany.

Justin-Mary Russolillo (Bl) {2 –add}

2 August
1891–1955. From a working-class family of Pianura (Italy), now a suburb of Naples, he was ordained as a diocesan priest of Pozzuoli in 1913. He was assigned to the parish of San Giorgio in Pianura, and became interested in the work of fostering vocations to the priesthood and religious life. There, he founded the Society of Divine Vocations for priests (the 'Vocationist Fathers'), the Vocationist Sisters and the Apostolate of Universal Sanctification, a lay movement. The first two were approved in the early 1920s, the last in 1965. He died at Naples, and was beatified in 2011.

Justina Francucci Bezzoli (Bl) {2}

12 March
d. 1319. From Arezzo (Italy), when aged thirteen she became a Benedictine nun at St Mark's nunnery there but transferred to that of All Saints, also Benedictine. Later she lived as a hermit at Civitella, and finally returned to community life at All Saints. Her cultus was confirmed for Arezzo in 1890.

(Justina of Byzantium) (St) {4 –deleted}

30 November
? She is listed as having been martyred at Byzantium.

Justina of Padua (St) {2, 4}

7 October
d. c.300. She was a virgin martyr of Padua (Italy) in the reign of Diocletian. Her acta (a medieval forgery) linked her with St Prosdocimus, the alleged disciple of St Peter. Her veneration spread throughout Italy on account of the famous Benedictine abbey dedicated to her at Padua. She is depicted as a young woman with both breasts pierced by one sword.

(Justus) (St) {4 –deleted}

14 July
? He is listed as a Roman soldier martyred at Rome (or perhaps at 'New Rome', meaning Constantinople).

(Justus and Abundius) (SS) {4 –deleted}

14 December
d. 283. They were listed as beheaded at Baeza near Jaén (Spain) in the reign of Numerian, allegedly after a futile attempt to burn them.

Justus and Pastor (SS) {2, 4}

6 August
d. 304. They were two brothers, aged respectively thirteen and nine, who were whipped and beheaded at Alcalá (Spain) in the reign of Diocletian.

(Justus of Beauvais) (St) {4 –deleted}

18 October
C3rd? A child aged nine, he is alleged to have been martyred at Beauvais (France) but his acta are fictional and he is probably derived from another saint of the same name.

Justus of Canterbury (St) {2, 4}

10 November
d. ?627. A Roman monk, he was one of those sent by St Gregory the Great in 601 to reinforce the mission to the Anglo-Saxons.

He became bishop of Rochester (England) in 604 and he succeeded St Mellitus at Canterbury in 624.

Justus of Condat (St) {2}

6 July
? He was a monk of Condat in the Jura mountains (France), but his dates are unknown.

Justus of Lyons (St) {2}

2 September
d. 390. A deacon of Vienne (France), he became bishop of Lyons in 350. In 381 he fled secretly to Egypt and became a monk, refusing to return when his whereabouts were discovered by his people and preferring to die there.

Justus Ranfer de Bretenières (St) {1 –group}

7 March
Cf. **Simeon Berneaux and Comps**.

Justus of Susa (St)

17 October
C10th? He is the principal patron of Susa in Piedmont (Italy), where his body was found in 1087. A monastery was built around his shrine. His dubious legend states that he was a monk killed by marauders at Oulx nearby. His cultus was confirmed in 1903, but he is not listed in the Roman Martyrology.

Justus of Trieste (St) {2, 4}

2 November
Early C4th? From Trieste (Italy), he was martyred in the reign of Diocletian by being drowned in the sea.

Justus of Urgell (St) {2, 4}

28 May
C6th. He is the first recorded bishop of Urgell in Catalonia (Spain). St Isidore wrote about

him, and he himself wrote a commentary on the *Song of Songs*.

Jutta of Huy (St) {2}

13 January
d. 1228. She was a widow and hermit at Huy near Liege (Belgium), who lived near a leper colony in order to care for them.

Juvenal of Narni (St) {2, 3}

3 May
C4th. First bishop of Narni in central Italy, he was allegedly ordained by Pope St Damasus. His biographers have confused him with other saints of the same name and so there is no certainty as to the details of his career. His cultus was confined to local calendars in 1969.

(Juvenal II of Narni) *(St) {4 –deleted}*

7 May
C6th? Allegedly a bishop of Narni (Italy), he may be identical with his namesake. His reputed shrine is at Benevento.

Juvenal Aneina cf. **John-Juvenal Aneina**.

Juventinus and Maximinus (SS) {2, 4}

29 January
d. 363. They were officers in the army of Emperor Julian and, when they criticized the laws against Christians and refused to sacrifice to idols, were degraded, imprisoned, whipped and finally beheaded at Antioch (Syria).

(Juventius) *(St) {4 –deleted}*

1 June
? The relics of this alleged Roman martyr were transferred in the C16th to the Benedictine abbey of Chaise-Dieu, Evreux (France).

Juventius of Pavia (St) {2, 4}

8 February
d. 397. He was a bishop of Pavia (Italy). The worthless tradition is that St Hermagoras, bishop of Aquileia and disciple of St Mark, sent SS Syrus and Juventius to evangelize that place, of which city the former became the first bishop. The old Roman Martyrology listed him a second time with St Syrus on 12 September.

K

Karantoc cf. **Carantoc**.
Kateri Tekákwitha cf. **Catherine Tekákwitha**.
Katherine cf. **Catherine**.
Kebius cf. **Cuby**.
Kellach cf. **Ceallach**.

Kenelm (St) {2}

17 July
d. ?812. Historically he was a son of King Coenwulf of Mercia (d. 821) who appears to have died before his father, possibly in battle. The abbey at Winchcombe (then Mercia's capital) contained his shrine and inspired the entirely spurious medieval legend that he had succeeded his father as king when aged seven and was murdered in the forest of Clent in the Black Country by order of his sister. He was venerated as a martyr, but this veneration did not survive the suppression of the abbey (east of the present parish church) except for a passing interest among certain Victorian romantic medievalists. The Roman Martyrology describes him as 'having been reputed as a martyr'.

Kenneth cf. **Canice**.

Kentigern Mungo (St) {2}

13 January
d. betw. 603–12. The surname Mungo means 'darling'. The late sources assert that he settled as a missionary monk on the Clyde, on the site of the present city of Glasgow, and was ordained first bishop of the Strathclyde Britons in ?540. Driven into exile, he preached around Carlisle and then went to Wales to stay with St David at Menevia. Tradition alleges that he founded the monastery of Llanelwy (St Asaph), but if anything he was only its abbot for a time. In ?573 he was able to return to Scotland, initially to near Dumfries but then back to Glasgow where he died.

Kerrier cf. **Kieran**.
Kester cf. **Christopher**.

Ketill (Kjeld) (St) {2}

11 July
d. ?1151. He was a canon regular and provost of the cathedral at Viborg (Denmark), and was responsible for a famous cathedral school. He had to appeal to Rome against persecution by some of his brethren.

Kevin (Coemgen, Caoimhghin) (St) {2}

3 June
d. 622. From the ruling family of Leinster (Ireland), he was educated by St Petroc of Cornwall (who was then in Ireland) and became the abbot-founder of Glendalough in Co. Wicklow. This is perhaps the most famous and beautiful of the ancient Irish monastic sites. His extant biographies are full of untrustworthy legends (which may be based on actual facts, however). He is the principal patron of Dublin, and his attribute is a blackbird which allegedly nested in his hand.

Kieran (Kiernan, Kyran, Ciaran) (St) {2}

5 March
d. 530. Styled 'the first-born of the saints of Ireland', he was from Ossory (Co. Offaly) and was probably ordained bishop by St Patrick. He is wrongly identified with St Piran of Cornwall, but the tradition that he was the first bishop of Ossory and the founder of the monastery of Saighir is ancient. He is the principal patron of the diocese of Ossory.

Kilda (St)

The famously isolated Scottish island is named after a wholly unknown saint.

Kilian (St) {2, 4}

8 July
End C7th. He left Ireland as a missionary monk and settled near Würzburg in Franconia (Germany) where he converted the duke.

He became that city's first bishop, but was martyred on the orders of the duke's former wife whom he had had to divorce because she was his brother's widow. Two companions, Colman and Totnan, have been deleted from the Roman Martyrology.

Kinga cf. **Cunegund**.
Kitt cf. **Christopher**.

Kizito (St) {1 –group}

3 June
d. 1886. At fourteen he was the youngest of those martyred by King Mwanga of Buganda (Uganda). Cf. SS **Charles Lwanga and Comps**.

Klaus cf. **Nicholas**.

Korea (Martyrs of) (SS) {1 –group}

20 September
The church in Korea was not initially set up by missionaries but by native laypeople who had become familiar with the Jesuit mission at the court of the Ming emperor at Beijing (China). Many scholars of the Silhak (or 'practical wisdom') school of Korean philosophy at Seoul, the capital, took to Christianity in the C18th because of the obvious superiority of Western technology as a product of Christian belief. But Christianity was incompatible with State Confucianism, and the first persecution was in 1801. In 1837 the first missionaries, of the Paris Society of Foreign Missions, entered the country to organize the church which had slowly spread from Seoul. A formal edict of persecution was issued in response in 1839, and St Laurence Imbert and two priest companions were seized, imprisoned, tortured and solemnly beheaded near Seoul. Thousands of native Korean Catholics were killed then and during a second persecution after 1866, of all ages and social classes, priests as well as laypeople.

A hundred and three of these were canonized in 1984, and a further 124 were beatified in 2014. Cf. **Korea, Martyrs of** in the lists of national martyrs in the appendix.

Košice (Martyrs of) (SS) {2}

7 September
d. 1619. Mark Körösy was a Croatian nobleman, born at Krif'in in 1582 and, as a priest, becoming a member of the cathedral chapter of Esztergom. He was sent to Kassa in Imperial Hungary (now Košice in Slovakia) in order to administer the property of a defunct Benedictine abbey.

Stephen Pongrácz was a Transylvanian nobleman, born in 1582, who entered the Jesuit noviciate at Brno in 1602 and was sent to Kassa as chaplain to the imperial Hungarian troops and to the few Magyar Catholics in the town.

Melchior Grodziecky was a Polish nobleman from Silesia, born in 1584, who entered the Brno noviciate in 1603 and was sent to Kassa as chaplain to the Czech and Polish soldiers and to the Slovak civilians.

Kassa as a town was solidly Calvinist, and when the Calvinist prince of Transylvania rebelled against the Emperor in 1619 and besieged it, the townsfolk betrayed the garrison. The town council asked for the death of the three priests, and they were tortured first in order to induce their apostasy. SS. Mark and Stephen were beheaded, but St Melchior was castrated, roasted upside-down until his abdomen burst and then thrown alive into a ditch with the bodies of the other two, where he lingered for twenty hours. They were canonized in 1995.

Kuriakose cf. **Cyriac**.
Kybi cf. **Cuby**.
Kyran cf. **Kieran**.
Kyrin cf. **Boniface**.

L

Ladislas Batthyány-Strattmann (Bl) {2 –add}

22 January

1870–1931. From a noble family of Dunakiliti in Hungary, he initially studied agriculture at the University of Vienna with a view to managing the family estates, but his primary interest was medicine and he qualified as a doctor in 1900. He later became a well-known specialist in ophthalmology, and was noted for his consideration for the spiritual well-being of his patients as well as for waiving his fees for poor people. He married in 1898 and the couple had thirteen children; in 1915 he inherited the title of Prince. After a happy life, he contracted cancer of the bladder and died at Vienna after fourteen months of intense suffering which he bore with tranquillity. He was beatified in 2003.

Ladislas Błądziński (Bl) {2}

8 September

1908–44. A Polish priest of the Congregation of St Michael, he was deported to Germany to work as a slave in a quarry at Grossrosen and was there killed. Cf. **Poland, Martyrs of the Nazi Occupation of**.

Ladislas Demski (Bl) {2}

28 May

1884–1940. A Polish priest, he died of ill-treatment at the concentration camp at Sachsenhausen. Cf. **Poland, Martyrs of the Nazi Occupation of**.

Ladislas Findysz (Bl) {2 –add}

21 August

1907–64. From Krościenko Niżne in Poland, he was ordained for the diocese of Przemyśl in 1932 and was made parish priest of Nowy Żmigród in 1942. His zeal in performing his duties offended the Communist authorities, and he was sentenced to two and a half years in prison in 1963 for 'coercing' his parishioners into practising their faith. He was already suffering from thyroid cancer, and proper treatment for this was withheld. After his release he returned to his parish but soon died, and was beatified as a martyr in 2005.

Ladislas of Gielniów (Bl) {2}

4 May

1440–1505. A Pole, he joined the Franciscan Observants at Warsaw and eventually became their provincial superior. As such he sent Franciscan missionaries to Lithuania and occupied himself in preaching throughout Poland. He died at Warsaw and his cultus was confirmed for Poznan in 1750.

Ladislas Goral (Bl) {2}

26 April

1898–1942. The auxiliary bishop of Lublin in Poland, he died of ill-treatment at the concentration camp at Sachsenhausen on an unknown date. The RM lists him on this day. Cf. **Poland, Martyrs of the Nazi Occupation of**.

Ladislas-Aloysius Grozde (Bl) {2 –add}

1 January

1923–43. Layman martyr. Born at Tržišce near Moknorog (Slovenia), he was an illegitimate child whose mother married when he was aged four. The couple initially rejected him, but an aunt brought him up and arranged his schooling. He was an outstanding and devout school pupil, ending up at a boarding lyceum at Ljubljana when the Second World War broke out. On New Year's Day he tried to visit his family, but the journey was fraught because of damaged railways and he ended up walking. He was picked up by a group of Communist partisans at Mirna, and when they found devotional literature on him he was interrogated, tortured and shot. He was beatified as a martyr in 2010.

Ladislas (Lancelot, Laszlo) of Hungary, King (St) {2, 4}

30 June
1040–95. King of Hungary, he annexed Dalmatia and Croatia from the Byzantine Empire and thus helped to establish the borders that his country had until the First World War. His enlightened government with regard to the affairs of both church and state made him one of the great national heroes of Hungary. He fought successful wars against the Poles, Russians and Cumans and died while preparing to take part in the First Crusade as supreme commander. He was canonized in 1192.

Ladislas Maćkowiak (Bl) {2}

4 March
1910–42. A Polish priest, he was shot at Berezwecz near Głębokie by the Nazis together with BB Miechislav Bohatkiewicz and Ladislas Maćkowiak. Cf. **Poland, Martyrs of the Nazi Occupation of**.

Ladislas Mączkowski (Bl) {2}

20 August
1911–42. A Polish priest, he was hanged at the concentration camp at Dachau. Cf. **Poland, Martyrs of the Nazi Occupation of**.

Ladislas Miegoń (Bl) {2}

15 September
1892–1942. A Polish priest, he died of ill-treatment at the concentration camp at Dachau. Cf. **Poland, Martyrs of the Nazi Occupation of**.

(Laetus) *(St)* {4 –deleted}

5 November
d. 533. He was a hermit north of Orleans (France) at the place now called St Lié after him.

Lambert of Lyons (St) {2, 4}

14 April
d. ?688. From Flanders, he was a Frankish courtier before becoming a monk at Fontenelle in Normandy (France) under St Wandrille, whom he succeeded as abbot in 666. He became bishop of Lyons in 678.

Lambert of Maastricht (St) {2, 4}

17 September
d. ?705. From Maastricht (Netherlands), he became bishop of that city in 670 but was exiled by Ebroin, mayor of the Frankish palace, in 675. He lived at the abbey of Stavelot (Belgium) for seven years, allegedly as a monk, before being recalled by Pepin the Short. He helped St Willibrord with his missionary work, and was murdered at the altar of the church at Liege (then a village) because of a vendetta.

Lambert Péloguin (St) {2}

26 May
c.1080–1154. From Bauduen in north Provence (France), he became a Benedictine monk at Lérins and was made bishop of Vence near Nice in 1114.

Lambert of Zaragoza (St) {2, 4}

19 June
C8th? He was allegedly a servant killed somewhere near Zaragoza (Spain) by his Muslim master when the Moors ruled there.

Landelin of Ettenheimmünster (St) {2}

21 September
C7th. He was a monk at the monastery of Ettenheim, now a village called Ettenheimmünster, near Freiburg-in-Breisgau (Germany). The legend was that he became a hermit, and was killed by a hunter. His relics are enshrined at the village.

Landelin of Lobbes (St) {2, 4}

15 June
d. 686. A Frankish nobleman from Bapaume near Arras (France), he was educated by St Aubert of Cambrai but became a brigand. Repenting, he became the abbot-founder of Lobbes near Charleroi (Belgium) in 654 and then founded three other abbeys, the last being Crépy near Laon (France) where he died.

Landeric of Paris (St) {2}

10 June
d. ?656. Bishop of Paris (France) from 650, he founded the 'Hôtel-Dieu', the first hospital in Paris.

Landrada (St) {2}

8 July
d. 690. She was the abbess-founder of the nunnery at Munsterbilzen near Tongeren (Belgium).

Lanfranc of Canterbury (Bl) {2}

28 May
d. 1089. He was a monk of Bec in Normandy (France), and while there headed a famous monastic school and engaged in controversial disputation concerning the Real Presence in the Eucharist with Berengarius. After the conquest of England by the Normans by King William I, he was made archbishop of Canterbury and undertook a very necessary reform of the life of the church there.

Lanfranc of Pavia (Bl) {2}

23 June
d. 1194. He was a bishop of Pavia near Milan (Italy), and was remembered as a peaceful man who suffered much while trying to reconcile those at enmity in his city.

Lang Yangzhi and Paul Lang Fu (SS) {1 –group}

16 July
d. 1900. A woman catechumen, she was a villager of Lujiapo near Qinghe in southeastern Hebei, China. During the Boxer uprising she professed her faith when questioned, whereupon she was burnt alive in her house with her son, Paul Lang Fu (who had been baptized). Cf. **China, Martyrs of**.

Lantbert (St) {2}

19 September
d. 957. He was a bishop of Freising in Bavaria (Germany).

Lanuin (Bl) {2}

11 April
d. 1119. A disciple of St Bruno, he went with his master to Calabria (Italy) and succeeded him as prior of the Carthusian monastery which they founded at Torre near Squillace. He was also appointed visitor-apostolic of all the monastic houses in Calabria. His cultus was confirmed for Squillace in 1893.

Laserian (Molaise) (St) {2}

18 April
d. 638. He was the founder of the monastery and diocese of Leighlin in Co. Carlow (Ireland) as well as Inishmurray in Co. Sligo, and was allegedly appointed as apostolic legate to Ireland by the pope. He promoted the Roman observance of the date of Easter in place of the traditional Celtic one. He is the principal patron of the diocese of Leighlin.

Laszlo cf. **Ladislas**.

(Latinus of Brescia) *(St)* {4 –deleted}

24 March
C2nd? He is alleged to have succeeded St Viator as third bishop of Brescia (Italy) and

to have been imprisoned and tortured in the persecution of Domitian, but this tradition is unreliable.

Laudo (Lô) of Coutances (St) {2, 4}

22 September
d. p549. He was bishop of Coutances in Normandy (France) from 528, and his family estate is now the village of St-Lô.

Launomar (St) {2}

19 January
d. ?593. From Chartres (France), he was a diocesan priest before becoming a hermit and founding the abbeys of Corbion and Bellomer for his disciples. His shrine was at Blois until it was destroyed by the Huguenots.

Laura-of-St-Catherine-of-Siena Montoya y Upeguí (St) {2 –add}

21 October
1874–1949. From the province of Antioquia in Colombia, she was only a toddler when her father was killed and her family left destitute in civil disturbances. Despite a lack of formal education, she trained to be a schoolteacher aged sixteen but was early aware of a religious vocation. Being drawn to work among and for the Native American population, in 1914 she founded the 'Missionaries of Mary Immaculate and St Catherine of Siena' at Dalbeiba with some companions. This was at a time when the Native American population of South America mostly suffered vicious prejudice and persecution. She died at Medellín and was canonized in 2013. Her congregation is now international.

Laura Vicuña (Bl) {2}

22 January
1891–1904. Born at Santiago in Chile, her father died in 1893 and the family eventually settled at Junín de los Andes in Argentina in 1900. She failed to join the Sisters of Mary Auxililatrix which ran her school, but she took private vows and consecrated her life to God in 1903 in exchange for the conversion of her mother. Sickness followed and she died the next year aged twelve. She was beatified in 1988.

Laurence Bai Xiaoman (St) {1 –group}

25 February
1821–56. A labourer from a very poor family of Guizhou (China), he moved to Xilinxian in Guangxi in 1851 and was converted by St Augustine Chapdelaine. He was given the choice of denying his faith before being flogged and beheaded. Cf. **China, Martyrs of**.

Laurence of Brindisi cf. **Laurence-of-Brindisi Russo**.

Laurence of Belém (Bl) {2}

12 April
C14th. He was a Hieronomite monk at the monastery at Belém near Lisbon (Portugal), and had the gift of reconciling many penitents to the church.

Laurence of Canterbury (St) {2, 4}

2 February
d. 619. One of the monks sent on the English mission with St Augustine by Pope St Gregory the Great, he was sent back to Rome to report to St Gregory on progress and to bring back reinforcements. Becoming St Augustine's successor as archbishop of Canterbury in 604, he had to face the pagan reaction in Kent under Eadbald and thought of escaping to France but was allegedly rebuked by St Peter in a dream and eventually converted Eadbald. He is depicted as a bishop holding a whip or displaying the marks of a whipping.

Laurence of Frazanone (St) {2}

30 December
d. ?1162. He was a Byzantine-rite monk at Frazanone on Sicily, famous for his austerities and his preaching.

Laurence Giustiniani (St) {2, 3}

8 January
1381–1455. A nobleman of Venice (Italy), when aged nineteen he became a secular canon at San Giorgio in Alga, which he made into the centre of a congregation. In 1433 he was made bishop of Castello. This diocese was united with the patriarchate of Grado and the see transferred to Venice in 1451, thus making him the first patriarch of that city. His writings on mystical contemplation were popular. He was canonized in 1690 and his cultus was confined to local calendars in 1969.

Laurence-of-St-Nicholas Hachizo (Bl) {2}

28 September
d. 1630. A Japanese Augustinian tertiary, he was condemned for having sheltered the Augustinian missionaries and was beheaded at Nagasaki with BB John Chozaburo and Comps. Cf. **Japan, Martyrs of**.

Laurence Humphrey (Bl) {2}

7 July
1571–91. A native of Hampshire and a convert, he was only twenty years of age when he was hanged, drawn and quartered at Winchester with BB Roger Dickinson and Ralph Milner for becoming a Catholic. He was beatified in 1929. Cf. **England, Martyrs of**.

Laurence Han I-hyŏng and Comps (SS) {1 –group}

20 September
d. 1837. They were a group of seven who were ordered to be strangled in various prisons at Seoul in Korea on this day. St Laurence was a catechist, and the others were Agatha Yi Kan-nan a widow, Catherine Chŏng Ch'ŏr-yŏm and Joseph Im Ch'i-baeg who were baptized in prison, Peter Nam Kyŏng-mun also a catechist, Susanna U Surim a widow and Teresa Kim Im-i a virgin. Cf. **Korea, Martyrs of**.

Laurence Imbert and Comps (SS) {1 –group}

21 September
d. 1839. From Aix-en-Provence (France), he joined the Paris Society of Foreign Missions and worked as a priest in China before being consecrated missionary bishop for Korea. He was tortured and beheaded in public with Peter Maubant and James Chastan, priests of the same society. Cf. **Korea, Martyrs of**.

Laurence Johnson (alias Richardson) (Bl) {2}

30 May
d. 1582. From Great Crosby (Lancs), he was educated at Brasenose College, Oxford and, after his conversion, studied for the priesthood at Douai. Ordained in 1577, he worked in Lancashire, was martyred at Tyburn (London) with St Luke Kirby and BB Thomas Cottam and William Filby and was beatified in 1886. Cf. **England, Martyrs of**.

Laurence Loricatus (Bl) {2}

16 August
d. 1243. From Apulia (Italy), he became a soldier but accidentally killed a man and made a pilgrimage to Compostella in reparation. Then he settled as a penitential hermit in a cave near the Benedictine abbey at Subiaco in 1209. His surname derives from the coat of mail which he wore next to his skin. His shrine is at Sacro Speco (Subiaco) and his cultus was confirmed in 1778.

Laurence Majoranus (St) {2}

7 February

d. ?545. Bishop of Siponto (Italy) from 492, he founded the famous sanctuary of St Michael on Monte Gargano. His city is now replaced by Manfredonia, of which place he is the patron.

Laurence dei Mascoli (Bl) {2}

6 June

1476–1535. A nobleman from Villamagna in the Abruzzi (Italy), he became a Franciscan and was a very successful preacher. He died at Ortona and his cultus was confirmed for there in 1923.

Laurence Nguyễn Văn Hưởng (St) {1 –group}

27 April

?1802–56. A Vietnamese priest, he was arrested near Ninh Bình in north Vietnam while visiting a sick person at night. He was ordered to trample on a crucifix and, on his refusal, was flogged and beheaded during the persecution ordered by Emperor Tự Đức. Cf. **Vietnam, Martyrs of**.

Laurence of Novara and Comps (SS) {2, 4}

30 April

C4th. He is described as having migrated from the West (Spain or France?) to Piedmont (Italy) and to have become a diocesan priest under St Gaudentius, bishop of Novara. He was massacred with a group of children whom he was instructing.

Laurence O'Toole (Lorcan Ua Tuathail) (St) {2, 4}

14 November

1128–80. From Co. Kildare (Ireland), when young he became a monk at Glendalough and was made abbot at the age of twenty-five. In 1162 he became archbishop of Dublin and was faced with the English invasion in 1170, being much involved in negotiating on behalf of the Irish with King Henry II of England. He attended the Third Lateran Council at Rome in 1179, was made papal legate in Ireland and carried out many reforms in his diocese, where he introduced the Arrouasian Canons Regular (following their rule himself). He died at the Augustinian abbey of Eu in Normandy while on an embassy to the English king and was canonized in 1226.

Laurence of Rippafratta (Bl) {2}

27 September

d. 1456. From Rippafratta in Tuscany (Italy), he became a Dominican at Pisa under Bl John Dominic and was made novice-master at Cortona. SS Antoninus of Pierozzi and 'Fra Angelico' were among his novices, also Bl Benedict of Mugello. His cultus was approved for the Dominicans in 1851.

Laurence Rokuyemon (Bl) {2}

19 August

d. 1622. He was a Japanese merchant on the ship carrying BB Louis Flores and Comps. Cf. **Japan, Martyrs of**.

Laurence of Rome (St) {1, 3}

10 August

d. 258. In the patristic era he was probably the most famous of the Roman martyrs, as is evidenced by the writings of SS Ambrose, Leo the Great, Augustine and Prudentius. His martyrdom must have deeply impressed the contemporary Roman Christians, and Prudentius described it as the death of idolatry in Rome (which from that time began to decline). His acta are unreliable, however, having been written at least a century after his death. They claim that he was one of the deacons of Pope St Sixtus II when that pope was beheaded, and was himself martyred three days later by being roasted alive on a gridiron. It is more likely that he was beheaded. He was buried on the Via Tiburtina, where his basilica now stands, and is mentioned in the Roman canon of the Mass. His attribute is a gridiron.

Laurence Ruiz and Comps (SS) {1 –group}

28 September (d.n. 29)
d. 1637. Three Dominican priests and two lay-men, they went on a secret missionary expe-dition to Japan from Manila (Philippines) in 1636. The Japanese had closed their country and were in the process of extirpating the native Christians, and the group were captured immediately on arrival, tortured in prison and executed by being hanged head-down in pits and left to die. St William Courtet was born at Sérignan (France) in 1590; St Michael de Aozaraza was born at Oñate (Spain) in 1637 and died in prison on the 24 September; St Vincent-of-the-Cross Shiowozuka was a native Japanese who lapsed in prison but subse-quently repented. The laymen were St Lau-rence Ruiz, a family man from Manila, and St Lazarus of Kyoto, a Japanese translator who also lapsed briefly under torture. They were canonized in 1987, with ten other martyrs of the same period and are celebrated liturgically on this date. Cf. **Japan, Martyrs of**.

Laurence-of-Brindisi Russo (St) {1, 3}

21 July
1559–1619. From Brindisi (Italy), he joined the Capuchins at Venice, was ordained in 1582 and became a famous preacher in north Italy, south Germany and the lands of the Habsburgs. There he fought militant Prot-estantism from 1599 until 1602, when he became the Capuchin vicar-general. Then he was appointed the military chaplain of the imperial army fighting against the Turks in Hungary, and contributed to its success by his prayers and shrewd military advice. In 1606

he was sent back to Germany to establish the Capuchins there, was greatly favoured by the Catholic courts of central Europe and was entrusted with important diplomatic missions. He died at Lisbon during one of these, was canonized in 1881 and was declared a doctor of the Church (arguably the least famous) in 1959, mainly because of his contributions to Mariology.

Laurence-Mary-of-St-Francis-Xavier Salvi (Bl) {2}

12 June
1782–1856. Born at Rome, he joined the Pas-sionists at Monte Argentario in 1801 and had a fruitful apostolate of retreats and missions in central Italy, being also a member of the Passionist curia at Rome. His preaching was inspired by a great devotion to the Infant Jesus, and he held a series of prayer-meetings to him at Viterbo to free the city from cholera. He then died of a stroke at Vetralla nearby, where his shrine is, and was beatified in 1989.

Laurence Yamada (Bl) {2}

8 September
d. 1628. A Japanese Dominican tertiary, son of Bl Michael Yamada, he was beheaded at Nagasaki with BB Dominic Castellet and Comps. Cf. **Japan, Martyrs of**.

Laurentia Harasymiv (Bl) {2}

26 August
1912–52. A Sister of St Joseph, she died in the gulag at Kharsk near Tomsk in the Soviet Union (now Russia). Cf. **Nicholas Čarneckyj and 24 Comps**.

Laurentinus Sossius (Bl)

15 April
d. 1485. A boy aged five, he was allegedly killed by renegade Jews on Good Friday at

Valrovina near Vicenza (Italy) and his cultus was approved for Vicenza in 1867. He is not listed in the Roman Martyrology, and his cultus has been suppressed owing to scandal.

Laurianus (St) {2, 4}

4 July

C3rd–4th. He was martyred near Bourges (France). The Roman Martyrology has deleted the assertion that he was an archbishop of Seville (Spain), where his head was enshrined.

Laval (Martyrs of) (BB) {2}

19 June

d. 1794. They were nineteen martyrs of the French Revolution. At Laval, on 21 January, thirteen secular priests and one conventual Franciscan were guillotined for refusing to subscribe to the Civil Constitution of the Clergy. Frances Mézière was a teacher guillotined at Laval on 5 February; Frances Tréhet and Jane Véron were Sisters of Charity executed at Ernée on 13 and 20 March, respectively; Mary-of-St-Monica Lhuilier was a lay sister of the Sisters Hospitaller of the Mercy of Jesus and was executed at Laval on 25 June, and James Burin was a priest shot in an ambush at Champgeneteux on 17 October. They were beatified together in 1955. Cf. **French Revolution, Martyrs of**.

Laverius (St) {2}

27 November

Early C4th. He was martyred at a place called Grumentum, now destroyed, in Basilicata (Italy) and is a patron of the tiny cathedral city of Acerenza.

Lazarus (St) {2, 4}

29 July

C1st. He was the disciple and friend who was raised from the dead by Christ (Jn 11).

According to a Greek tradition he became bishop of Kition in Cyprus. The French legend which connects him with Marseilles is traceable only to the C11th, and has no historical foundation whatsoever. It probably arose from confusion with an early bishop of Aix-en-Provence with the same name.

Lazarus of Kyoto (St) {1 –group}

29 September
Cf. **Laurence Ruiz and Comps**.

Lazarus of Milan (St) {2, 4}

14 March
C5th. He was the archbishop of Milan (Italy) when the Ostrogoths took the city. His liturgical feast-day on 11 February is an example of the old Milanese tradition of not keeping saints' day in Lent, which practice is now generally followed by the Roman rite.

Lazarus the Stylite (St) {2}

7 November
d. 1054. He was allegedly from Magnesia (Asia Minor), and had been a monk at Mar Saba in the Holy Land when he founded a monastery on Mount Galesius near Ephesus. He lived on a pillar, subsisted on bread and water and wore heavy chains, with the result that he was the object of pilgrimage during his lifetime.

Lazarus Zographus (St) {2, 4}

17 November
d. ?867. From Armenia, he became a monk at Constantinople. A talented painter (hence his Greek surname, 'the Painter'), he used to restore defaced icons in the reign of the iconoclast emperor Theophilus. For this he was allegedly tortured, but after the final abandonment of iconoclasm he became an ambassador to Rome, dying on Cyprus on his way there.

Lea (St) {2, 4}

22 March

d. ?383. A wealthy Roman widow, she joined the community of St Marcella and was later elected abbess. In her humility she used to perform various menial domestic duties for her nuns (that this was considered worthy of note indicates the class structure of contemporary Roman monasticism).

Leafwine cf. **Lebuin**.

Leander (St) {2, 4}

27 February

d. c.600. The elder brother of SS Fulgentius, Isidore and Florentina, when young he became a monk at Seville (Spain) and was later sent to Constantinople on a diplomatic mission. There he met St Gregory the Great, whose close friend he became and whose *Moralia* were published at his request. On his return to Spain he became archbishop of Seville in 579, and proved to be a great pastor. He revised the Spanish liturgy, converted St Hermenegild (and thus started the conversion of the Visigoths from Arianism) and was responsible for convening two national synods at Toledo in 589 and 590. He also founded the episcopal school of Seville and wrote a monastic rule. His attribute is a flaming heart.

Lebuin (Leafwine) (St) {2}

November 12

d. ?775. A monk of Ripon (England), he went to the Netherlands on mission in 754 and was sent by St Gregory of Utrecht to the dangerous borderlands between the Franks and Saxons, where he founded the church at Deventer. His personal bravery won him the respect of the Saxons (although they preferred to stay pagan). Cf. **Livin**.

Leger cf. **Leodegar**.

Lelia (St) {2}

11 August

C5th. She lived as a nun at a very early period and has given her name to several places in Ireland, such as Killeely near Limerick.

(Leo) *(St) {4 –deleted}*

14 March

? The old Roman Martyrology listed him as a bishop martyred in the Agro Verano, Rome. Nothing else is known about him. He may have been a victim of the Arians.

Leo I, Pope 'the Great' (St) {1, 3}

10 November

d. 461. Probably from Tuscany (Italy), he became a priest at Rome and was archdeacon under two popes. He was made pope himself in 440 and emphasized his jurisdiction and responsibility as the successor of St Peter by fighting heretical tendencies in other churches, especially Nestorianism and Monophysitism in the East. His celebrated 'Tome' or dogmatic letter, which he sent to Flavian the patriarch of Constantinople, was acclaimed as the teaching of the church at the council of Chalcedon in 451. It summarized the exact Catholic position concerning the twofold nature and one person in Christ, as against the extreme positions of these two heresies, but was rejected especially by the church in Egypt which went into schism. He negotiated with Attila the Hun outside Rome in 452, apparently persuading him not to besiege the city, but had to endure its sack by Genseric the Vandal in 455. He was proclaimed a doctor of the Church in 1754.

Leo II, Pope (St) {2, 3}

3 July

d. 683. A Sicilian, he became pope in 681. He governed the church for only two years, and the outstanding event of his pontificate was his acceptance of the decrees of sixth ecumenical council of Constantinople which condemned Monothelitism and Pope Honorius I for accepting it.

Leo III, Pope (St) {2, 4}

12 June
d. 816. A Roman, he became pope in 795 but was attacked by a mob, imprisoned and maltreated in 799. He escaped and asked for help from Charlemagne, who re-established order in Rome. Subsequently he crowned Charlemagne as emperor of the West in St Peter's on Christmas Day, 800, thereby founding the Holy Roman Empire and ushering in the Middle Ages. Leo refused to add the 'filioque' to the Nicene creed. He was canonized in 1673.

Leo IV, Pope (St) {2, 4}

17 July
d. 855. A Roman and a monk of the Benedictine abbey of San Martino, he was chosen pope in 847. In response to the Muslim threat he finished enclosing the Vatican with a wall, thus creating the 'Leonine city'. Through his prayers and exhortations to the city militia, the Muslim raiders from Calabria were utterly routed at Ostia. His benefactions to churches take up many pages in the 'Liber Pontificalis'. The English king Alfred visited Rome in 853, and Leo was his sponsor at his confirmation.

Leo IX, Pope (St) {2, 4}

19 April
1002–54. Bruno of Dagsburg was from Alsace, a cousin of the emperor Conrad, and was made bishop of Toul (France) in 1026. In 1048 he was elected pope and immediately started the reform of the Roman curia with the help of his spiritual adviser Hildebrand, the future Pope St Gregory VII. He fought simony, lay investiture and clerical concubinage and condemned Berengar and his Eucharistic

doctrine. He went to war with the Normans in southern Italy, was taken prisoner at Benevento and released but shortly afterwards died before the high altar in St Peter's. One of his advisers was Humbert who overreached his authority as papal legate at Constantinople and precipitated the definitive schism with the patriarch, Michael Cerularius, in 1054.

(Leo, Donatus and Comps) (SS) {4 –deleted}

1 March
? They were listed as a group of thirteen martyrs. Abundantius and Nicephorus were also named.

Leo Aybara (Bl) {2}

8 September
d. 1628. A Japanese catechist and Dominican tertiary, he was beheaded at Nagasaki with BB Dominic Castellet and Comps. Cf. **Japan, Martyrs of**.

Leo of Bova (St) {2}

5 May
C12th. He was a Byzantine-rite monk of Calabria (Italy) and is the principal patron of Bova near Reggio Calabria, which is a cathedral city despite being very small.

Leo Carentanus (St) {2}

1 March
C9th. According to his story, he was from Carentan in Normandy (France) and was bishop of Rouen before becoming a missionary in the Basque Country. He was martyred by pirates near Bayonne, of which city he is now the patron.

Leo of Catania 'the Thaumaturge' (St) {2, 4}

20 February
d. ?787. A priest of Ravenna (Italy), he became bishop of Catania (Sicily) and was respected

by the emperors at Constantinople for his learning. His biography has been embellished with many unreliable anecdotes.

Leo I of Cava (St) {2}

12 July
d. 1079 From Lucca (Italy), he became a Benedictine monk at the abbey of La Cava near Naples under its founder St Alferius, and succeeded him as abbot in 1050. His cultus was approved for La Cava in 1893.

Leo II of Cava (Bl) {2}

19 August
1239–95. He became the fifteenth abbot of the Benedictine abbey of La Cava near Naples, in 1268. His cultus was approved for there in 1928.

Leo Karasuma (St) {1 –group}

5 February
d. 1597. From Korea, he was a Shinto priest before his conversion and became the first Franciscan tertiary in Japan. He helped the Franciscan missionaries as a catechist and was crucified at Nagasaki. Cf. **Paul Miki and Comps** and **Japan, Martyrs of**.

Leo Luke (St) {2}

1 March
d. c.900. He became abbot of a Byzantine-rite monastery at Corleone (Sicily), and also has a cultus in Calabria. He died a centenarian after eighty years of monastic life.

Leo of Mantenay (St) {2}

25 May
d. c.550. He succeeded St Romanus as abbot of the monastery of Mantenay near Troyes (France). He was enshrined at a place now known as Saint-Lyé.

Leo of Melun (St) {4 –deleted}

10 November
? The subject of an ancient cultus at Melun near Paris (France), he is now considered to be identical with Pope St Leo I.

Leo of Myra (St) {2, 4}

18 August
C3rd–4th. He was martyred at Myra in Lycia (Asia Minor). The Roman Martyrology has deleted a companion, Juliana.

Leo Nakanishi (Bl) {2}

27 November
d. 1619. A Japanese layman, he was related to the daimyos of Hirado-jima and was beheaded at Nagasaki with BB Thomas Koteda and Comps. Cf. **Japan, Martyrs of**.

Leo Nowakowski (Bl) {2}

31 October
1913–39. A Polish priest, he was shot by the Nazis at Piotrków Kujawski. Cf. **Poland, Martyrs of the Nazi Occupation of**.

Leo Saisho Shichiemon (Bl) {2 –add}

17 November
d. 1627. He was a Japanese layman, a member of the Confraternity of the Rosary of the diocese of Kagoshima, who was from Jōnai in Miyazaki and was martyred at Sendai in Kagoshima. He was beatified in 2008. Cf. **Japan, Martyrs of**.

Leo of Satsuma (Bl) {2}

10 September
d. 1622. A Japanese Franciscan tertiary, he was a catechist and was burnt alive in the 'Great Martyrdom' at Nagasaki with Bl Charles Spinola and Comps. Cf. **Japan, Martyrs of** and **Great Martyrdom at Nagasaki**.

Leo of Sens (St) {2, 4}

22 April

C6th. Bishop of Sens (France) for twenty-three years, he was the patron of St Aspasius.

Leo Sukeyemon (Bl) {2}

19 August

d. 1622. He was the Japanese pilot of the ship carrying BB Louis Flores and Comps. Cf. **Japan, Martyrs of**.

Leo Tanaka (St) {2}

1 June

d.1617. He worked with the Jesuit missionaries as a catechist and was beheaded at Nagasaki with Bl Alphonsus Navarete. Cf. **Japan, Martyrs of**.

Leo Wetmański (Bl) {2}

10 October

1886–1941. An auxiliary bishop of Plock, he died of ill-treatment at the concentration camp of Dzałdowo. Cf. **Poland, Martyrs of the Nazi Occupation of**.

Leobard (Liberd) (St) {2, 4}

18 March

d. ?593. A hermit at Tours (France), he was affiliated to the abbey of Marmoutier and lived in a cell nearby for twenty-two years as a disciple of St Gregory of Tours.

Leobat (St) {2}

16 January

C5th. He was a disciple of St Ursus of Loches and founded the abbey of Sennevières near Tours, where he died.

Leobin (Lubin) (St) {2, 4}

14 March

d. ?557. His family were peasants from Poitiers (France) and he became a hermit when young. Then he became a priest, then abbot of Brou and finally bishop of Chartres.

Leobonus (St) {2}

13 October

? He was a hermit allegedly from Fursac near Limoges (France), who settled at Salignac in the Dordogne.

Leocadia (Locaie) (St) {2, 4}

9 December

d. ?304. She was a young woman of Toledo (Spain) who was condemned to death and died in prison in the reign of Diocletian. Her cultus there is older than the C6th.

Leocadius and Lusor (SS) {2}

16 November

C4th. The former was a senator at Bourges (France), one of the first in the city to become a Christian. The latter was his son, who died just after his baptism. Their shrine is at Déols.

Leocritia (Lucretia) (St) {2, 4}

15 March

d. 859. A young woman of Cordoba (Spain), she was driven from home by her Muslim parents when she converted to Christianity and was sheltered by St Eulogius. Both were flogged and beheaded.

Leodegar (Leger) (St) {2, 4}

2 October

d. 679. He was educated at the Frankish court and then by his uncle, the bishop of Poitiers. In 653 he was made abbot of a monastery in that city, where he introduced the Benedictine rule. Chosen as bishop of Autun in 659 by St Bathilde the queen regent, he reformed his diocese but was also involved in secular matters, especially at court. This led him to incur the enmity of Ebroin, mayor (comptroller) of the palace, who had him degraded, imprisoned in the monasteries of Luxeuil and Fécamp, blinded and finally murdered. He is popularly venerated in France as St Leger, but the famous horse-race at Doncaster (England) has no connection with him. He is depicted with the instruments of his martyrdom (drill, bodkin, fish-hook) or with his eyes, tongue and other parts of his face on a plate.

Leonard-of-Port-Maurice Casanova (St) {2, 4}

26 November
1676–1751. From Imperia-Porto-Maurízio on the Riviera (Italy), he was a brilliant student at Rome and became a Franciscan Observant there. Soon after his ordination he began his career as a home missionary especially in Tuscany, spreading the devotions to the Blessed Sacrament, to the Sacred Heart, to the Immaculate Conception and especially to the Stations of the Cross. He is alleged to have established the last in five hundred and seventy-two places, including the Colosseum in Rome. He was a prolific ascetical writer and his works filled thirteen volumes. In 1744 he was sent to restore the discipline of the Franciscans in Corsica, was recalled to Rome in 1751 but died on the night after his arrival. He was canonized in 1867.

Leonard of Cava (Bl) {2}

18 August
d. 1255. He became eleventh Benedictine abbot of La Cava near Salerno (Italy), in 1232. His cultus was confirmed for there in 1928.

Leonard Kimura and Comps (BB) {2}

18 November
d. 1619. A Japanese nobleman, and convert, he became a Jesuit tertiary and was burnt alive at Nagasaki with BB Andrew Tokuan, Cosmas Takeya, Dominic Jorge and John Shoun. Cf. **Japan, Martyrs of**.

Leonard Murialdo (St) {2}

30 March
1828–1900. From Turin (Italy), after obtaining his doctorate at the university there and being ordained he devoted himself to the education of poor boys. In this he was an associate of St John Bosco, and was also a contemporary of SS Joseph Cafasso and Joseph Cottolengo. He founded the 'Pious Society of St Joseph' to care for young apprentices in 1873, and became heavily involved in the emergent Catholic worker movement. In many ways he sought to implement the church's social teaching as later summarized in the encyclical *Rerum Novarum* of 1891. He died at Turin and was canonized in 1970.

Leonard of Noblac (St) {2, 4}

6 November
C6th? According to his legend, for which no evidence exists before the C11th, he was a Frankish courtier converted by St Remigius of Rheims. He became a monk at Micy near Orleans and later a hermit in the forest of Noblac nearby. His veneration was very popular in the West during the Middle Ages, and the town and forest of St Leonard's in Sussex (England) are named after him. His attribute is a set of fetters or a lock.

Leonard Olivera Buera and Comps (BB) {2}

d. 1936. He was parish priest of the village of Movera en Puente Gallego near Zaragoza in Spain, and also of the school of Domina Nostra de la Bonanova which was run by the Brothers of the Christian Schools. He was killed in the Civil War, with three of the brethren who worked there and two others from Cambrils near Barcelona. They were beatified with twenty-four sisters of the Congregation of Carmelite Sisters of Charity, also martyred, in 2001. Cf. **Spanish Civil War, Martyrs of**.

Leonard Pérez Larios (Bl) {2 –add}

25 April

1883–1927. From Lagos di Moreno in Jalisco, Mexico, he wished to become a priest but responsibility to other family members prevented this. However, he made a private vow of chastity and never married. During the Cristero War he was attending a Mass and Holy Hour celebrated by Bl Andrew Sola y Molist when there was an army raid. The soldiers mistook him for a priest because of his dress and demeanour, and despite his denial he was shot with BB Andrew and Joseph-Trinity Rangel Montaño. He was beatified in 2005. Cf. **Mexico, Martyrs of**.

Leonard Vechel (St) {2}

9 July

d. 1572. From 's-Hertogenbosch (Netherlands), he studied at Louvain and became parish priest of Gorinchem, where he was noted for his opposition to Calvinism. He was one of the **Gorinchem** martyrs.

Leonian (St) {2}

13 November

d. ?518. From what is now Hungary, he was taken as a captive to Gaul and, on regaining his freedom, became a hermit near Autun (France). Later he joined the abbey of St Symphorian there. His cultus was approved in 1907.

(Leonidas of Antinoë and Comps) *(SS)* *{4 –deleted}*

28 January

Early C4th? They were listed as martyred at Antinoë in Egypt in the reign of Diocletian.

Leonidas of Corinth and Comps (SS) {2}

16 April

C3rd–4th. He was martyred with seven women at Corinth in Greece. They were: Carissa, Galina, Theodora, Nica, Nunecia, Callis and Basilissa.

Leonidas Fedorov (Bl) {2}

7 March

1880–1935. He was the exarch of the Catholic Church of the Russian Rite and a Studite monk. From St Petersburg, he initially entered a seminary to become a Russian Orthodox priest but converted to the Catholic Church and had to go into exile at Rome in 1902 (such a conversion was illegal in Tsarist Russia). He was ordained in the Russian rite, and was arrested and imprisoned during a secret visit to Russian in 1914. Released during the Russian Revolution in 1917, he was again imprisoned by the Bolsheviks in 1926 at Solovetski and died in exile at Vyatka. Cf. **Nicholas Čarneckyj and 24 Comps**.

Leonides of Alexandria (St) {2, 4}

22 April

d. 202. The father of the famous exegete Origen and himself a distinguished philosopher, he was martyred at his native city of Alexandria (Egypt) in the reign of Septimus Severus.

Leonius (St) {2}

3 February

C4th. He was a priest-disciple of St Hilary of Poitiers, and accompanied him into exile.

(Leontius, Attius, Alexander and Comps) *(SS) {4 –deleted}*

1 August

d. c.300. Three citizens of Perga in Pamphylia (Asia Minor), with six farm labourers (Cindeus, Mnesitheus, Cyriacus, Menaeus, Catunus and Eucleus) they set about destroying the altar of Artemis there and were executed as a result in the reign of Diocletian.

Leontius, Maurice and Comps (SS) {2, 4}

10 July
d. c.320. Numbering forty-five, they were martyred at Nicopolis in Armenia under the emperor Licinius and were among the last martyrs of the great persecution. Also named are Daniel, Anthony, Anicetus and Sisinnus.

(Leontius of Caesarea) (St) {4 –deleted}

13 January
d. 337. Bishop of Caesarea in Cappadocia (Asia Minor), he was at the council of Nicaea in 325 and was zealous against Arianism, being commended by St Athanasius.

Leontius of Fréjus (St) {2}

1 December
d. ?433. St John Cassian dedicated his first ten *Conferences* to him. He became bishop of Fréjus (France) in ?419.

Leontius of Tripoli (St) {2, 4}

18 June
Early C4th. He was imprisoned and martyred at Tripoli (Lebanon). The Roman Martyrology has deleted references to his worthless legend, which had him martyred in the C2nd with two companions, Hypatius and Theodulus.

Leontius the Younger (St) {2}

11 July
d. c.570. A soldier, he fought the Visigoths and then married and settled at Bordeaux (France). However he was forced to become bishop and governor of that city, his wife becoming a nun.

(Leopardus) (St) {4 –deleted}

30 September
d. 362. He was listed as a servant or slave in the household of the emperor Julian who was executed at Rome. His shrine was established at Aachen (Germany).

Leopold-of-Gaiche Croci (Bl) {2}

2 April
1732–1815. From Gaiche near Perugia (Italy), he became a Franciscan and was professor of philosophy and theology and apostolic missionary for the Papal States. During the Napoleonic period he was compelled to abandon his Franciscan habit when aged seventy-seven and become a parish priest. He died at Monteluco and was beatified in 1893.

Leopold II 'the Good', Margrave of Austria (St) {2, 4}

15 November
1073–1136. Born at Melk (Austria) and a grandson of Emperor Henry III, he became fourth Margrave of Austria in 1096. Austria at that time was a German borderland flanked by the non-German kingdoms of Bohemia and Hungary, and his successful reign of forty years helped to establish it as a power-base which was later built upon by the Hapsburgs. He founded many religious houses as a part of his plan to establish German culture on a secure foundation there, of the Benedictines and Cistercians as well as of the new friars.

Leopold Mandić (St) {2}

30 June
1866–1942. Born at Castelnovo (Italy) of Croat parents, he joined the Capuchins when aged eighteen and especially exercised his priestly vocation in Padua through the sacrament of penance. He was also involved in fostering unity between the Catholic Church and the Orthodox Slavs. He was canonized in 1983.

Leopold-of-Alpandeire Sánchez Márquez (Bl) {2 –add}

9 February
1864–1956. Born into a peasant family at Alpandeire near Málaga (Spain), he was a

peasant himself until he became a Capuchin lay brother at Seville in 1900. He transferred permanently to Granada in 1914, and never left the city. There, his major task was begging for supplies for his friary from the city's people, which entailed much walking around and meeting people. He became very popular, and was nicknamed 'the humble beggar of the three Hail Marys' because of the prayer he made for anybody who asked him. He died aged ninety-two, and was beatified in 2010.

Leothad of Auch (St) {2}

23 October
C7th. A Frankish nobleman, he became a monk and then abbot of Moissac near Montauban (France) before being made bishop of Auch.

Leovigild and Christopher (SS) {2, 4}

20 August
d. 852. They were two monks of monasteries near Cordoba (Spain), and were beheaded at that city by the Muslim authorities.

(Lesbos, Martyrs of) {4 –deleted}

April 5
? Five virgins were listed in the old Roman Martyrology as having been martyred on the Aegean island of Lesbos.

Lesmes cf. **Adelelm**.
Letard cf. **Liudhard**.
Leu cf. **Lupus of Sens**.

Leucius of Brindisi (St) {2, 4}

11 January
C4th. He was the first bishop of Brindisi (Italy).

Leutfrid (Leufroy) (St) {2, 4}

21 June
d. 738. From Évreux (France), he founded a monastery near there later called La-Croix-St-Leufroy and was allegedly abbot for

forty-eight years. He is usually depicted surrounded by the poor children whom he liked to befriend.

Lezin cf. **Lucinius**.

Liberalis of Rome (St) {2}

20 December
? He was a martyr, and apparently once a consul, who was buried at the catacombs of Septem Palumbae on the old Salarian Way north of Rome.

Liberalis of Treviso (St) {2}

27 April
d. c.400. A priest of the district around Ancona (Italy), he fought Arianism and was persecuted as a result. His shrine is at Treviso.

Liberata and Faustina (SS) {2, 4}

19 January
d. 580. Two sisters of Como (Italy), they founded a nunnery in that city and their shrine is at the cathedral.

(Liberatus and Bajulus) (SS) {4 –deleted}

20 December
? Nothing is known about these alleged Roman martyrs.

Liberatus, Boniface and Comps (SS) {2, 4}

2 July
d. 484. Liberatus was abbot of Capsa in Roman Africa and was martyred with several of his community at Carthage on the orders of King Hunneric the Vandal. Boniface was a deacon, Servus and Rusticus were subdeacons, Rogatus and Septimus were monks and Maximus was a child being educated in the monastery.

Liberatus da Lauro Brumforti (Bl)

6 September
d. 1258. From San Liberato in the Marches (Italy), he became a Franciscan at Suffiano

and introduced a reform there which set out to restore the initial austerity of his order. His cultus was approved for Camerino in 1731, but he is not in the Roman Martyrology.

Liberatus Weiss and Comps (BB) {2}

3 March
d. 1716. Liberatus was from Austria, Samuel Marzorati was from Piedmont and Michael-Pius Fasoli da Zerbo was from Lombardy. The three Franciscan friars went on mission to Ethiopia, meeting up in Cairo and travelling to Gondar (then the capital). They were initially welcomed, but the Negus was overthrown in a coup shortly after their arrival and the new regime arrested them on doctrinal grounds. They were questioned on the two natures of Christ (the Ethiopian church is Monophysite), the value of circumcision (traditional in Ethiopia), and the use of unleavened bread in the Eucharist (considered heretical there) and, on giving the Catholic position on these, were stoned to death. They were beatified in 1988.

(Liberius of Ravenna) *(St)* *{4 –deleted}*

30 December
d. c.200. He was allegedly one of the first bishops of the diocese of Ravenna (Italy).

Liberius Wagner (Bl) {2}

9 December
1593–1631. From Mühlhausen near Gotha (Germany), he was initially a Protestant but was converted by the Jesuits at Würzburg (Bavaria) and went on to become parish priest at Altenmünster nearby. His successful attempts to convert the local Protestants incurred enmity, which motivated his being betrayed to the invading Swedes in the Thirty Years' War. He was imprisoned and tortured for five days before his execution at Schonungen, and was beatified in 1974.

Libertinus (St) {2}

3 November
C3rd–4th. He was a martyred bishop of Agrigento in Sicily.

Liborius (St) {2, 3}

9 April
C4th. Bishop of Le Mans (France) from 348, he is the patron of Paderborn (Germany) as his relics were transferred there in 836. His cultus was confined to local calendars in 1969.

Libosus of Vaga (St) {2}

29 December
d. p258. He was bishop of Vaga in Roman Africa (now Baga in Algeria) and, at the council held at Carthage to decide the question of the validity of heretical baptism, declared: 'Christ said "I am the truth" and not "I am custom".'

Licerius (Lizier) (St) {2, 4}

27 August
d. c.560. A Spaniard, he migrated to France and became bishop of the Conserans region of the Pyrenees in 506.

Licinius (Lézin) of Angers (St) {2, 4}

1 November
d. ?606. A Frankish courtier and count of Anjou, he became a monk near Angers (France) and was chosen bishop of that city in 586. He was consecrated by St Gregory of Tours. Later he tried to resign but his people would not let him.

Lidanus (St) {2}

2 July
1026–1118. From the Abruzzi (Italy), he became the abbot-founder of the Benedictine abbey of Sezze on the Pontine Marshes,

of which place he is the patron. His was one of many attempts to drain the marshes, which task was only accomplished in the C20th. When old he retired to Montecassino.

Lidwina cf. **Lydwina**.
Lié cf. **Laetus** or **Leo**.

Lifard (St) {2}

3 June
d. ?550. An alleged brother of St Leonard of Noblac, he had been a judge at Orleans (France) before becoming a hermit when aged fifty and eventually the abbot-founder of the monastery of Meung-sur-Loire.

(Ligorius) *(St) {4 –deleted}*

13 September
? He is listed in the Roman Martyrology as an Eastern hermit who was killed by a pagan mob, but no details are known. His shrine is at Venice (Italy).

Lindalva Justo de Oliveira (Bl) {2 –add}

1953–93. She was born in Rio Grande do Norte, a very poor part of Brazil. The family made great sacrifices to move to Açu so that the children could attend school, and there she demonstrated a natural affinity for poorer children. From 1978 to 1988 she worked as a retail assistant, and then joined the 'Daughters of Charity'. She was assigned to a municipal nursing home for men at Salvador da Bahia in 1991, and encouraged the inmates to receive the sacraments as well as attending to their material well-being. However, a forty-six-year-old man managed to be admitted as a result of bribery, and he became besotted with her. She put him off, so he decided to kill her on Good Friday, which he did by stabbing her forty-four times. She was beatified as a martyr in 2007.

Linus, Pope (St) {2, 4}

23 September
d. ?79. Traditionally (according to St Irenaeus) he succeeded St Peter as pope in 67. There is no historical evidence that he was a martyr, and his cultus was suppressed in 1969. He continues to be mentioned in the Roman canon of the Mass, however.

Lioba (St) {2, 4}

28 September
d. ?782. A relative of St Boniface, she became a nun at Wimborne in Dorset (England) under St Tetta, entered into correspondence with him in Germany and, at his request, collected a group of nuns and went to join him on mission in 748. He made her abbess of a new nunnery at Tauberbischofsheim and also supervisor of the daughter houses founded therefrom. Thus she was an important source of the Benedictine contribution to the foundation of German Christian culture and civilization. She had been abbess for thirty-eight years before she resigned just before her death.

Litiphrid (St) {2}

8 March
d. 874. He was a bishop of Pavia near Milan (Italy).

Litorius (St) {2}

13 September
d. 371. He was bishop of Tours (France), and was the first to build a church inside the city walls.

Liudger (Ludger) (St) {2, 4}

26 March
d. 809. A Frisian from near Utrecht (Netherlands), he was educated under St Gregory there and under Alcuin at York (England).

After his ordination at Cologne in 777 he was a missionary in Friesland (Netherlands) and in what his now Lower Saxony and Westphalia (Germany) under the imperial patronage of Charlemagne. He spent some time as a refugee from the Saxons at the abbey of Montecassino in Italy but did not take vows as a monk. In 804 he became first bishop of Münster, and is hence called the apostle of Westphalia.

Liudwin (Leodewin) (St) {2}

29 September

d. 717. Educated under St Basinus, his uncle and bishop of Trier (Germany), he married when young but his wife died so he then founded the abbey of Mettlach and became a monk there. Later he became bishop of Trier himself.

Liutwin (St) {2}

29 September

d. ?717. He had been founder and monk of a monastery at Mettlach near Trier (Germany) before becoming bishop of the latter place.

(Livin) (St) {4 –deleted}

12 November

d. c.650. His extant biography is a forgery, and it is suspected that he is the same person as Lebuin of Deventer. According to his traditional story he was an Irishman, ordained by St Augustine of Canterbury, who crossed over to Flanders to become a successful missionary and to be martyred near Aalst (Belgium).

Lizier cf. **Licerius**.
Lô cf. **Lauto**.
Locaie cf. **Leocadia**.

(Lombards, Martyrs under the) (SS) {4 –deleted}

2 March

C6th? A group of eighty, they were killed by the invading Lombards in Campania (Italy) for 'refusing to adore the head of a goat', according to the old Roman Martyrology.

Longinus (St) {2, 4}

15 March.

C1st. The soldier who pierced the side of Christ hanging on the cross (Jn 19:34) is traditionally referred to by this name, and is alleged to have been from Cappadocia and to have been martyred there. He is depicted with his spear, the head of which became a famous relic in the Middle Ages. The centurion who acknowledged Christ crucified to be the son of God is also called Longinus (Matt. 27:54).

Lothar (Loyer) (St) {2}

15 June

d. 756. From Lorraine, he founded a monastery near Argentan (France) at a place later called St-Loyer-des-Champs. Afterwards he was bishop of Sées for thirty-two years.

Louis

The original Frankish name of Khlodovekh (Clovis in Latin) has given rise to two distinctive modern forms: Louis in French and Ludwig in German. The former is more familiar in English and has been preferred in this book (the traditional English form of Lewis is obsolescent). The modern Latin form is Ludovicus, and **Aloysius** is also a derivative (but listed separately). In Italian, both forms can occur: Lodovico and Luigi.

Louis Aleman (Bl) {2}

16 September

d. 1450. From the upper Rhône valley, he was made archbishop of Arles (France) in 1423 and cardinal shortly afterwards. He was leader of the anti-papal party at the council of Basel which had gathered to try to end the Western Schism, and consecrated the antipope Felix V.

As a result he was deprived of the cardinalate and excommunicated by Pope Eugenius IV, but Pope Nicholas V restored him and for the rest of his life he involved himself only with his duties as a bishop. He was austere in his private life. Dying near Arles, he was beatified in 1527.

Louis Amagasu Iemon and Comps (BB) {2 –add}

12 January
d. 1629. He was martyred with forty-two other laypeople of the Niigata diocese at Oksunbara near Yonezawa in Yamagata. With him suffered his son Vincent Kurogane Ichibiyōe, daughter-in-law Thecla Kurogane and granddaughter Lucy Kurogane. Other families martyred were: Michael Amagasu Tayemon, his wife Dominica Amagasu and daughter Justa Amagasu; Mary Itō and her children Marina Itō Chōbo, Peter Itō Yahyōe and Matthias Itō Hikosuke; John Banzai Kazue with his wife Aurea Banzai, son Anthony Banzai Orusu and daughter Rufina Banzai with her husband Paul Sanjūro and children Paul Sanjūro II and Martha Sanjūro; Simon Takahashi Seizaemon with his daughter Thecla Takahashi; Anthony Anazawa Han'emon and his son Paul Anzawa Juzaburō (for his wife Crescentia Anazawa and other two sons Cf. **Lucy Iida and Comps**); John Arie Kiemon and his son Peter Arie Jinzō (for his wife Mary-Magdalen Arie Cf. **Lucy Iida and Comps**); Alexis Satō Seisuke with his wife Lucy Satō, daughter Elizabeth Satō and brother Paul Satō Matagorō; and 'N. Shichizaemon' with his wife Mary-Magdalen Shichizaemon and two daughters whose names are unknown. Couples martyred were: Timothy Ōbasama and his wife Lucy Ōbasama; Louis Jin'emon and his wife Anna Jin'emon and Mancius Yoshino Han'emon with his wife Julia Yoshino. Married people martyred on their own were: John Gorōbyōe, Joachim Saburōyōe, Paul Nishihori Shikibu,

Andrew Yamamoto Shichiemon (for his wife Mary Yamamoto and daughter Ursula Cf. **Lucy Iida and Comps**) and Ignatius Iida Soemon (for his wife Lucy Iida Cf. **Lucy Iida and Comps**). They were beatified in 2008. Cf. **Japan, Martyrs of**.

Louis Baba (Bl) {2}

25 August
d. 1624. A Japanese catechist, he accompanied Bl Louis Sotelo to Spain when the latter was deported. Returning to Japan, he was arrested and became a Franciscan in prison at Omura before being burnt alive at Shimabara with BB Michael Carvalho and Comps. Cf. **Japan, Martyrs of**.

Louis Batis Sainz and Comps (SS) {1 –group}

15 August
1870–1926. From San Miguel del Mezquital in Durango, Mexico. As a diocesan priest he was in charge of the parish at Chalchihuites as well as being the spiritual director of the seminary. He had great devotion to Catholic Action. He was falsely denounced as plotting to rebel against the government, and so was arrested with SS Emmanuel Morales a family man, David Roldán Lara and Salvator Lara Puente. They were driven to Zacatecas and summarily shot. Cf. **Mexico, Martyrs of**.

Louis Beaulieu (St) {1 –group}

7 March
Cf. **Simeon Berneaux and Comps**.

Louis and Mary Beltrame Quattrocchi (BB) {2}

9 November
1880–1951 and 1884–1965, respectively. Louis was born in Catania, Sicily, grew up in Urbano, obtained a degree in law at Rome and became a senior civil servant. He married

Mary, a Florentine of the noble Corsini family, in 1905. The couple had two sons, one who became a diocesan priest and the other a Trappist monk, and two daughters, one who became a Benedictine nun. Louis died of a heart attack and Mary of old age. The God-centred witness of their family life led them to be chosen as the first married couple to be beatified together, in 2001.

Louis Bertrán (1) (St) {2, 4}

9 October

1526–81. From Valencia (Spain), a relative of St Vincent Ferrer, he became a Dominican in 1544 and was master of novices at Valencia before being sent to South America in 1562. There he was a missionary among the native peoples of what are now Colombia and Panama and also on the Leeward Islands. He was alleged to have the gift of tongues when preaching to them. After seven years of great success he was recalled to Valencia, where he died. He was canonized in 1671 and is the patron of Colombia.

Louis Bertrán (2) and Comps (BB) {2}

29 July

d. 1627. From Barcelona (Spain), a relative of the St Louis Bertrán who went to Colombia, he became a Dominican, was sent to the Philippines in 1618 and then to Japan. He was burnt alive with BB Mancius-of-the-Holy-Cross of Omura and Peter-of-the-Holy-Mother-of-God of Arima at Omura, and they were beatified in 1867. Cf. **Japan, Martyrs of**.

Louis Biraghi (Bl) {2 –add}

1801–79. From Vignate near Milan in Italy, he was ordained as a diocesan priest of the latter place in 1825. He became a seminary teacher, and the spiritual director of the major seminary at Milan in 1833. He was versed in patrology and archaeology, and became vice-rector of the Biblioteca Ambrosiana in 1864. He was devoted to the cult of St Ambrose, and founded the 'Sisters, Religious of St Marcellina' as a modern revival of the primitive ideal of the consecrated virgin (St Marcellina was a sister of St Ambrose who had this vocation). He died at Milan and was beatified in 2006.

Louis Boccardo (Bl) {2 –add}

1861–1936. From a peasant family of Moncalieri in Italy, he was ordained as a diocesan priest of Milan in 1884, following an elder brother in this regard. In 1886 he became the vice-rector and spiritual rector of the school for further priestly studies in the diocese, a place where Bl Joseph Allamano was the rector. In 1914 he was made superior-general of the Congregation of the Poor Sisters, and also of the Institute for the Blind at Turin. In the latter capacity he founded the 'Sisters of Christ the King' at the shrine of Christ the King that he had founded in the city, which was for blind women who could not exercise a contemplative vocation elsewhere. He died at Turin, beloved by the city, and was beatified in 2007.

Louis Bonnard cf. **John-Louis Bonnard**.

Louis Bordino (Bl) {2 –add}

25 July

1922–77. From Castellinaldo near Cuneo in the Piedmont, Italy, he enlisted in the Italian army and was sent to the Eastern Front in 1942. Captured in the following year, he was in a prisoner-of-war hospital in Siberia where he was noted for his assistance of sufferers until he caught typhus himself. The Soviets treated their Italian prisoners better than the Germans, and in 1945 he was repatriated. Then he joined the Brothers of St Joseph Cottolengo at the Little House of Divine

Providence at Turin, and nursed physically and mentally infirm people there until his death of leukaemia in 1977. He was due to be beatified in 2015.

Louis Brisson (Bl) {2 –add}

2 February
1817–1908. From Plancy-l'Abbaye near Aube (France), he was ordained as a diocesan priest of Troyes in 1840. In the same year he was appointed chaplain of the Visitation convent there, and taught in the junior seminary as well as furthering his interest in the natural sciences especially astronomy. Being struck by the moral as well as the physical deprivations of the young male and female workers in the city's new textile mills, he founded two new religious orders dedicated to their help and education. The 'Oblate Sisters of St Francis de Sales' in he founded in 1868 as a joint venture with St Frances Aviat, and the 'Oblates of St Francis de Sales' (for priests and laymen) he founded in 1872. The two orders spread through France despite opposition. But they were suppressed by an anticlerical government in 1903, so he went into exile at Rome before returning to die at his birthplace. He was beatified in 2012.

Louis Caburlotto (Bl) {2 –add}

9 July
1817–97. A native of Venice, Italy, he became a diocesan priest in 1842 and was allotted the parish of *San Giacomo d'Orio*. There, in 1850 he founded a school to help educate poor girls. This was run by two catechists of the parish, and proved to be the first house of a new congregation of teaching sisters, the Daughters of St Joseph. Bl Louis remained parish priest until 1872, when he resigned to devote himself to the affairs of his growing congregation. He spent the last few years of his life in prayerful seclusion, and the future Pope St Pius X was at his deathbed. He was due to be beatified in 2015, the first Venetian priest to receive that honour.

Louis-Edward Cestac (Bl) {2 –add}

31 October
1801–68. From Bayonne in France, he became a diocesan priest of his native city in 1825 and was later attached to the cathedral. He was struck by the number of poor homeless girls in the city whose only hope of a livelihood was prostitution, and for them he opened a refuge in a house donated to him by the city council. This was in 1836, and its success led him to by a farm at Anglet and open a centre for derelict young people called *Notre Dame du Refuge*. The volunteer helpers whom he attracted he organized into a new congregation, the Servants of Mary, in 1842. He died at Anglet and was due to be beatified in 2015.

Louis Flores and Comps (BB) {2}

19 August
1570–1622. From Antwerp (Belgium), he emigrated with his parents to Mexico, joined the Dominicans and became novice-master. In 1602 he went to the Philippines, and set out for Japan in 1620 with Bl Peter Zuñiga, an Augustinian missionary, on a ship captained by Bl Joachim Hirayama Diaz. This was captured by Dutch privateers en route and handed over to the Japanese authorities. The ship's company were tortured, imprisoned for two years and finally executed at Nagasaki. The three mentioned were burnt. Beheaded were eleven Japanese crew and passengers: Anthony Yamada, Bartholomew Mohoye, James Matsuo Denshi, John Matakichi Nagata, John Soyemon, John Yago, Laurence Rokuyemon, Leo Sukeyemon, Mark Takenoshima Shinyemon, Paul Sankichi, Thomas Koyanagi and a Spanish passenger, Michael Díaz Hori. Cf. **Japan, Martyrs of**.

Louis IX of France, King (St) {1, 3}

25 August

1214–70. Born at Poissy near Paris, he became king of France under the regency of his mother, Blanche of Castile, in 1226. He reigned for forty-four years and was successful in subverting the previous arbitrary and corrupt feudal system of local courts of law by establishing the Crown as the administrator of proper justice (especially for the poor and weak). He supported and implemented measures of church reform, was especially generous to the mendicant orders and founded many ecclesiastical institutions, the most famous being the Saint-Chapelle in Paris built for his large collection of relics. He was a devoted husband and father of eleven children, and was famously austere and prayerful in his private life. His domestic military campaigns had some success, but he led two crusades which were disasters. He was captured and ransomed during the first, to Damietta in Egypt, and died of dysentery during the second, to Tunis. He was canonized in 1297, and is usually depicted with a cross, crown of thorns or other emblems of Christ's Passion and with the royal fleur-de-lis as his emblem.

Louis-Roche Gietyngier (Bl) {2}

30 November
1904–41. He was a Polish priest who died of ill-treatment at the concentration camp of Dachau. Cf. **Poland, Martyrs of the Nazi Occupation of**.

Louis-Mary Grignion de Montfort (St) P. T(OP).

28 April
1673–1716. From a poor Breton family, he completed his priestly studies with the aid of a benefactor and was ordained in 1700. In 1705 he became a home missionary in north-western France and was known for his childlike devotion to Our Lady and to the Rosary (he was a Dominican tertiary) as well as for his fervent opposition to Jansenism. He became hospital chaplain at Nantes in 1715, and founded there the 'Sisters of Divine Wisdom' for teaching and nursing and the 'Company of Mary' for missionary work. He died at St-Laurent-sur-Sèvre and was canonized in 1947. His mariological writings, especially his 'True Devotion to the Blessed Virgin', remain influential and controversial.

Louis Higashi (Bl) {2}

8 September
d. 1628. A Japanese Dominican tertiary, he was beheaded at Nagasaki with his two sons, Francis and Dominic, for having given shelter to missionaries. Cf. **Dominic Castellet and Comps** and **Japan, Martyrs of**.

Louis Ibaraki (St) {1 –group}

5 February
1585–97. A Japanese boy aged twelve, he served at Mass for the Franciscan missionaries in Kyushu and was crucified at Nagasaki. Cf. **Paul Miki and Comps** and **Japan, Martyrs of**.

Louis Kawara (Bl) {2}

10 September
d. 1622. He was a page at the court of Michael, the Christian daimyo of Arima (Japan), but was exiled when the latter apostatized. He became a Jesuit under Bl Charles Spinola and was burnt alive with him at the 'Great Martyrdom' at Nagasaki. Cf. **Japan, Martyrs of** and **Great Martyrdom at Nagasaki**.

Louis Magaña Servín (Bl) {2 –add}

9 February
1902–28. From Arandas in Jalisco, Mexico, he became a family man running a tannery

and an active member of the parish at Los Cabos. During the Cristero rebellion the town was occupied by government forces and the officer in charge ordered practising Christians to be arrested. Bl Louis gave himself up in exchange for his younger brother, proclaimed his faith while denying involvement in active rebellion and was immediately ordered to be shot in the doorway of the church. He was beatified in 2005. Cf. **Mexico, Martyrs of**.

Louis Maki (Bl) {2}

7 September
d. 1627. He was burnt alive at Nagasaki (Japan) with his adopted son, Bl John Maki, and Bl Thomas Tsuji for allowing the latter to celebrate Mass in his house. Cf. **Japan, Martyrs of**.

Louis and Celia Martin (BB) {2 –add}

They are the parents of St Teresa of the Child Jesus. Bl Louis was born at Burdeos in France in 1823, the son of an army officer, but his family moved to Alençon when he was eight. When he was twenty, he tried his vocation with the Augustinian canons of Great St Bernard, but his Latin was insufficient and he married Celia Guerin instead in 1858. Meanwhile he had opened a shop selling clocks at Alençon. However, his mental health was fragile and he had to give up his business and go into social seclusion before his wife died.

She was born at Gandelin in 1831 and had also tried her vocation, with the 'Sisters of Charity of St Vincent de Paul'. The couple had nine children, of whom five daughters survived infancy and became nuns. (St Teresa was the youngest.) She died of breast cancer in 1877, and he died completely insane in 1894. They were beatified together, as a married couple, in 2008.

Louis Matsuo Soyemon (Bl) {2}

27 August
d. 1627. He was a Japanese Franciscan tertiary beheaded at Nagasaki. Cf. **Francis-of-St-Mary of Mancha and Comps** and **Japan, Martyrs of**.

Louis Morbioli (Bl) {2}

9 November
1439–85. From Bologna (Italy), as a young man he led an immoral life but was converted by sickness at Venice, became a Carmelite tertiary and lived as a wayfarer, teaching Christian doctrine to the young and begging alms which he gave to the poor. He died at Bologna and his cultus was confirmed for there in 1842.

Louis-Mary Monti (Bl) {2 –add}

1825–1900. From Bovisio near Milan, he was aged twelve when his father died and he became a woodworker with his own shop. This became a meeting-place of pious young craftsmen and farmers, who set out to help poor and sick people and to win back lapsed Catholics. He took private vows in 1846, and joined the 'Sons of Mary Immaculate' founded by Bl Ludovic Pavoni for six years. As the result of a vision he founded the 'Sons of the Immaculate Conception' (initially a lay congregation but later including priests) in order to nurse sick people, and he was made superior-general of this by the Pope in 1877. He died at Rome and was beatified in 2003.

Louis Monza (Bl) {2 –add}

1898–1954. From a peasant family at Cislago near Varese in Italy, he was ordained as a diocesan priest of Milan in 1925. He served as parish priest before being attached to the miraculous shrine of Our Lady of Saronno, where he took an especial interest in catechizing young people. In 1936 he was made parish priest of Lecco, where he founded the 'Little Apostles of Love' to help in the implementation of the church's social teaching among poor people and in their catechesis. He was beatified in 2006.

Louis-Zepherinus Moreau (Bl) {2}

24 May

1824–1901. From Beçancour in Quebec (Canada), one of a large peasant family, as a priest he became the cathedral master of ceremonies and chancellor of the diocesan curia. In 1852 he moved to the new diocese of St Hyacinth, and became its bishop in 1876. He fostered all aspects of church life with great loyalty to the magisterium and devotion to the Sacred Heart, and founded the 'Sisters of St Martha' in 1890 to work as domestics in seminaries and schools. He wrote about 20,000 letters as bishop. He was beatified in 1987.

Louis Mzyk (Bl) {2}

23 February

1905–42. A Polish priest and a member of the Society of the Divine Word, he was beaten to death by guards in a prison at Poznan. Cf. **Poland, Martyrs of the Nazi Occupation of**.

Louis Naizen (Bl) {2}

12 July

1619–26. A Japanese boy aged seven, son of BB John and Monica Naizen, he was beheaded with them at Nagasaki. Cf. **Mancius Araki and Comps** and **Japan, Martyrs of**.

Louis (Luigi) Novarese (Bl) {2 –add}

20 July

1914–84. From Casale Monferrato, Italy, he was a sickly child and almost died of tuberculosis before being unexpectedly healed of it when aged seventeen. He was ordained to the secular priesthood in 1938, and was employed

by the Vatican Secretariat of State from 1941 to 1970 and then the Italian episcopal conference until 1977. He was convinced of the value of suffering in the context of Christ's passion, and became well-known for his concern for sick and disabled people. He founded various associations for their spiritual and bodily care, notably the Silent Workers of the Cross. He died at Rocca Priora and was beatified in 2013.

Louis-of-Casoria Palmentieri (St) {2}

30 March

1814–85. From near Naples (Italy), he joined the Franciscans in 1832 and became a priest and teacher. In 1887 he had a mystical experience (his 'cleansing') and dedicated himself to caring for the poor and infirm after it. He established a friary of strict observance in Naples, and his co-workers became the 'Brothers of Charity' (1859) and the 'Sisters of St Elizabeth' (1862). He was canonized in 2014.

Louis Pavoni (Bl) {2}

1 April

1784–1848. From Brescia (Italy), he spent his entire life there, becoming a diocesan priest in 1807. His concern for young people led him to found the institute of the 'Sons of Mary Immaculate' to help care for them. He was beatified in 1947.

Louis Sasada (Bl) {2}

25 August

d. 1624. Son of Bl Michael Sasada, he accompanied Bl Louis Sotelo to Mexico when the latter was deported from Japan, became a Franciscan there and was ordained at Manila in the Philippines in 1622. He then returned to Japan and was burnt alive with **Michael Carvalho and Comps**.

Louis Sotelo (Bl) {2}

25 August
d. 1624. A nobleman from Seville (Spain), he became a Franciscan at Salamanca, was sent to Manila in the Philippines in 1601 and to Japan in 1603. He was deported in 1613 and went back to Spain but returned in 1622, was arrested at Nagasaki and burnt alive with Michael Carvalho and Comps. Cf. **Japan, Martyrs of**.

Louis Talamoni (Bl) {2}

31 January
1848–1926. From Monza in Italy, he became a diocesan priest of Milan in 1871 and became a teacher at the diocesan seminary for the rest of his life. He was famous as a confessor and a parish missioner, and was especially concerned with visiting housebound sick people. He founded the 'Misericordines of St Gerard' to help nurse such people so that their family carers could get some rest. He died at Milan and was beatified in 2004.

Louis Tezza (Bl) {2}

26 September
1841–1923. From Conegliano near Treviso, Italy, he early recognized a vocation to serve sick people and joined the Camillans at Verona in 1850. In 1871 he was sent to make a new province of his congregation in France, and in 1891 he became the vicar-general of the Camillans. He helped Bl Josephine Vannini found the 'Daughters of St Camillus' as the female branch of the Camillans. In 1900 he went to refound the Camillans at Lima in Peru, where he stayed until his death. He was beatified in 2001.

Louis of Toulouse (St) {2, 4}

19 August
1274–97. Son of Charles II of Anjou, king of Naples, he was great-nephew of St Louis of France and of St Elizabeth of Hungary. Probably born at Nocera (Italy), he grew up in Provence and was sent as a hostage to Aragon in 1288, spending seven years at Barcelona. He was appointed bishop of Toulouse (France) just before his release, reluctantly accepted but became a Franciscan just before his ordination and consecration. He died six months later at Brignoles and was canonized in 1317.

Louis Yakichi (Bl) {2}

2 October
d. 1622. A Japanese, he tried to rescue Bl Louis Flores from prison on Hirado-jima and was burnt alive at Nagasaki with his wife, Lucy, and his two sons, Andrew and Francis. He was beatified in 1867. Cf. **Japan, Martyrs of**.

Louise degl' Albertoni (Bl) {2, 4}

31 January
1474–1533. A Roman noblewoman, as a widow with three children she became a Franciscan tertiary and spent the rest of her life in works of charity. Her cultus was approved locally for Rome in 1671.

Louise-Elizabeth de Lamoygnon (Bl) {2 –add}

4 March
1763–1825. She was born in Paris (France) into a family of the highest nobility, her father being the Keeper of the Seals at the French court. She married Edward Molé, count of Champlâtreux, in 1779 and the couple had five children before he was guillotined during the French Revolution. This led to a religious conversion, and in 1804 she founded a new congregation of sisters at Vannes dedicated to charitable works especially among poor people. This, the Sisters of Charity of St Louis, has since become international in scope. She died at Vannes, and was beatified in 2012.

Louise de Marillac (St) {2}

15 March
1591–1660. Born in Paris, she wanted to become a nun but married instead on the advice of her confessor. Being widowed in 1625, she spent the rest of her life in working with St Vincent de Paul in founding the 'Sisters of Charity'. The sisters took their vows for the first time in 1638, and she was their superior until she died at Paris. She was canonized in 1934.

Louise-Teresa de Montaignac de Chauvence (Bl) {2}

27 June
1820–85. Born at Le Havre (France) of an old noble family, when aged eighteen she consecrated herself to the Hearts of Jesus and Mary and set out to further devotion thereto. Setting up house at Montluçon, she founded the 'Pious Union of Oblates of the Sacred Heart of Jesus' (approved 1874) which taught girls, ran orphanages, helped in poor parishes and fostered devotion to the Sacred Heart. She was beatified in 1990.

Louise of Savoy (Bl) {2}

24 July
1462–1503. Daughter of Bl Amadeus IX, Duke of Savoy, and cousin of Bl Joan of Valois, she was married when aged seventeen and widowed at twenty-seven. Then she joined the Poor Clares at Orbe, Switzerland and was employed in collecting food for the community, which she did with a cheerful spirit (a noblewoman doing such a thing was a wonder in those days). Her cultus was approved for Turin in 1839.

Loup cf. **Lupus of Troyes**.

Lua (Moloch) (St) {2}

25 June
d. ?592. Allegedly from Limerick (Ireland), he became a disciple of St Comgall and founder of many monasteries (the legendary number is 120), notably that at Killaloe in Co. Clare where St Flannan was his disciple. His rule was extremely austere but he had great tenderness for people and animals.

Lubentius (St) {2}

13 October
C4th. He was a missionary priest who evangelized the Moselle valley near Trier (Germany) and has a church and shrine at Dietkirchen.

Lubin cf. **Leobin**.

(Lucanus of Gascony) *(St) {4 –deleted}*

30 October
C5th. He was alleged to have been martyred at Lagny near Paris (France), where his relics were enshrined.

Luchesius (Bl) {2}

28 April
d. 1260. From Poggibonsi near Siena (Italy), he was married and in business as a grocer, money-changer and corn merchant. However, with his wife Bonadonna (not listed in the Roman Martyrology) he became a Franciscan tertiary in ?1221. They then led penitential lives as hospital nurses. It is not certain that they were the first such tertiaries, as has been claimed.

Lucian and Marcian (SS) {2, 4}

26 October
d. c.250. They were martyred at Nicomedia (Asia Minor) in the reign of Decius. The old Roman Martyrology listed them as 'Lucian, Florius and Companions', relying on their unreliable acta.

Lucian, Maximian and Julian (SS) {2, 4}

8 January
d. c.290. They were Roman missionaries martyred at Beauvais (France).

(Lucian, Metrobius and Comps) *(SS)*
{4 –deleted}

24 December
? They were listed as martyred at Tripoli (Libya). The companions were Paul, Zenobius, Theotimus and Drusus.

Lucian of Antioch (St) {2, 4}

7 January
d. 312. Possibly from Edessa (now Urfa, Turkey), where he was educated as a scripture scholar, he became a priest and teacher of exegesis at Antioch (Syria). He especially opposed the allegorizing tendencies of Alexandrian exegesis, and the leaders of the Arian heresy in the C4th regarded him as their greatest master. In 304 he was seized, taken to Nicomedia and put in prison, where he died of torture after nine years. He was highly regarded by St John Chrysostom and St Jerome.

Lucian of Lentini (St) {2}

3 January
C8–9th. He was a bishop of Lentini in Sicily.

(Lucidius) *(St)* *{4 –deleted}*

26 April
C4th? A bishop of Verona (Italy), he was listed as being famous for a life of prayer and study.

Lucidus (St) {2}

5 December
d. ?938. A Benedictine monk of Aquara in the Valley of Diano near Salerno (Italy), he became a hermit at Santa Maria dell' Albaneta and his cultus was confirmed for Diano and Aquara in 1880.

Lucifer of Cagliari (St) {2}

20 May
d. 370. Bishop of Cagliari in Sardinia, he was an energetic defender of the Nicene creed against the Arian sympathies of the emperor Constantius. As a result he was exiled to Egypt, and when released when to Antioch and schismatically consecrated Paulinus as patriarch. His adherents refused any communion with former Arians. He returned home before his death, and the revised Roman Martyrology has given him the benefit of the doubt by including him.

(Lucilla, Flora, Eugene, Antoninus, Theodore and Comps) *(SS)* *{4 –deleted}*

29 July
d. c.260. According to their unreliable acta they were a group of twenty-three who were martyred at Rome in the reign of Gallienus, but seem rather to have been confused duplications of the following: Faustus of Rome and Comps; Lucy, Antoninus and Comps; Lucy of Rome and Comps. Ancient records seem to have been badly muddled.

(Lucillian, Claudius, Hypatius, Paul and Dionysius) *(SS)* *{4 –deleted}*

3 June
d. 273. The first was allegedly a convert in his old age at Byzantium who was crucified there with four young men. An embellishment alleges that he was their father and that Paula of Byzantium was their mother. They were probably martyred elsewhere and their relics brought to Constantinople (as Byzantium later became).

(Lucina) *(St)* *{4 –deleted}*

30 June
C1st? She was mentioned in the spurious acta of SS Processus and Martinianus as a disciple of the apostles who was martyred at Rome.

Lucinus (Lezin) of Angers *(St)*

13 February
d. ?618. A Frankish courtier, he became bishop of Angers (France).

(Lucius, Absalon and Lorgius) *(SS)*
{4 –deleted}

2 March
? The old Roman Martyrology listed these as having been martyred at Caesarea in Cappadocia (Asia Minor).

Lucius, Montanus and Comps (SS) {2, 4}

23 May
d. ?259. Disciples of St Cyprian of Carthage (Roman Africa), they were martyred in that city in the reign of Valerian. Their acta are authentic, as the story of their imprisonment was related by themselves and that of their martyrdom by eye-witnesses. The companions were Julian, Victoricus, Victor and Donatian.

(Lucius, Rogatus, Cassian and Candida) *(SS) {4 –deleted}*

1 December
? They were listed as martyrs of Rome.

(Lucius, Silvanus, Rutilus, Classicus, Secundinus, Fructulus and Maximus) *(SS)* *{4 –deleted}*

18 February
? They were allegedly Roman African martyrs. When Cardinal Baronius revised the old Roman Martyrology, he stated that he inserted them on the evidence of reliable manuscripts. Such have not survived.

Lucius I, Pope (St) {2, 4}

4 March
d. 254. He succeeded St Cornelius as pope in 253, but was immediately exiled and died at Rome on his return after eight months. St Cyprian referred to him as a martyr, but this is false and his cultus was suppressed in 1969.

(Lucius of Adrianople and Comps) *(SS) {4 –deleted}*

11 February
d. 350. Bishop of Adrianople near Constantinople, he was a vigorous opponent of Arianism and was twice exiled by Emperor Constantius before being restored by the council of Sardica in 347. Then he was imprisoned during a purge of supporters of St Athanasius ordered by the emperor and died in prison. Some of his people were killed in the disturbances.

Lucius of Chur (St) {2, 4}

3 December
C6–7th. He was a hermit at Chur in Switzerland. According to his fantastic legend, he was a king of Britain who asked Pope St Eleutherius to send missionaries to Britain. He then founded the dioceses of London and Llandaff, and eventually went as a missionary himself to Switzerland at the end of the C2nd. This story is romantic fiction, based on the story of King Agbar IX of Edessa (now Urfa, Turkey). The latter was also known as Lucius, and he also asked Pope St Eleutherius for missionaries to be sent to his country.

(Lucius of Cyprus and Comps) *(SS) {4 –deleted}*

20 August
? According to the unreliable story in the old Roman Martyrology he went from Cyrene in Libya to Cyprus, and this implies an identity with Lucius of Cyrene.

Lucius of Cyrene (St) {2, 4}

6 May
C1st. He was one of the prophets and teachers mentioned in Acts 13:1 as being in the church at Antioch when Paul and Barnabas were set apart for their apostolate. His cognomen led

to the tradition that he was the first bishop of Cyrene in Libya.

Lucretia cf. **Leocritia**.

Lucretia of Mérida (St) {2, 4}

23 November
Early C4th? She was martyred at Mérida (Spain).

(Lucy, Antoninus, Severinus, Diodore, Dion and Comps) (SS) {4 –deleted}

6 July
They result from an apparent duplication in the old Roman Martyrology of Lucilla, Flora and Comps.

(Lucy and Geminian) (SS) {4 –deleted}

16 September
d. c.300. According to their untrustworthy acta they were a 75-year-old Roman widow and a catechumen martyred together in the reign of Diocletian. Their cultus was suppressed in 1969.

Lucy Broccadelli (Bl) {2}

15 November
1476–1544. From Narni in Umbria (Italy), after three years of unconsummated marriage to a Milanese nobleman she became a Dominican regular tertiary at Viterbo. In 1494 she became the first prioress of the new nunnery at Ferrara and received the stigmata two years later, but she was hopeless as a superior and was deposed. Then she was treated with serious cruelty by her successor, and lived on in uncomplaining obscurity for thirty-nine years. Her cultus was confirmed for the Dominicans, Ferrara, Narni and Viterbo in 1710.

Lucy Bufalari (Bl) {2}

27 July
d. ?1350. From Castel Ponziano near Rome, a sister of Bl John Bufalari of Rieti, she became

an Augustinian nun at Amelia and went on to be prioress. She is a patron against demonic possession. Her cultus was confirmed for the Augustinians in 1832.

Lucy of Caltagirone (Bl) {2}

26 September
d. 1400. From Caltagirone (Sicily), she became a Poor Clare at Salerno, Italy and had her cultus approved for that place in 1514.

Lucy Filippini (St) {2}

25 March
1672–1732. From Tarquinia in Latium (Italy), when aged sixteen she became a consecrated religious under the guidance of the bishop of Montefiascone near Viterbo. In 1692 she started helping Bl Rosa Venerini in her work of teaching poor girls, but took over the enterprise in the diocese of Montefiascone and founded her own community in 1704. This was summoned to Rome, where it became the Pontifical Institute of Religious Teachers or 'Filippinini'. She died at Montefiascone and was canonized in 1930.

Lucy de Freitas (Bl) {2}

10 September
d. 1622. A Japanese woman married to a Portuguese, she gave shelter to missionaries and was hence burnt alive in the 'Great Martyrdom' at Nagasaki (Japan). Cf. **Japan, Martyrs of** and **Great Martyrdom at Nagasaki**.

Lucy Iida and Comps (BB) {2 –add}

12 January
d. 1629. Some relatives of 'Louis Amagasu Iemon and Comps' were martyred on the same day but in a different place, at Nukayama at Yonezawa near Yamagata. They were Lucy Iida, wife of Ignatius Iida Soemon; Crescentia

Anazawa, Romanus Anazawa Matsujiro and Michael Anazawa Osamu, the wife and two sons of Anthony Anazawa Han'emon; Mary and Ursula Yamamoto, the wife and daughter of Andrew Yamamoto Shichiemon; and Mary-Magdalen Arie, the wife of John Arie Kiemon. They were beatified in 2008. Cf. **Japan, Martyrs of**.

Lucy Kim (1) (St) {1 –group}

20 July
Cf. **Mary-Magdalen Yi Yŏn-hŭi and Comps**.

Lucy Kim (2) (St) {1 –group}

26 September
Cf. **Sebastian Nam I-gwan and Comps**.

Lucy-Louise of Omura (Bl) {2}

8 September
d. 1628. She was the eighty-year-old Japanese housekeeper of Bl Dominic Castellet and was burnt with him at Nagasaki. Cf. **Japan, Martyrs of**.

Lucy Pak Hŭi-sun (St) {1 –group}

24 May
Cf. **Augustine Yi Kwang-hŏn and Comps**.

(Lucy of Rome and Comps) (SS) {4 –deleted}

25 June
They are an apparent duplication in the old Roman Martyrology of Lucilla, Flora and Comps.

Lucy of Syracuse (St) {1, 3}

13 December
d. 304–5. She is one of the most famous of the Western virgin martyrs and her name is in the Roman canon of the Mass, but her acta are not reliable (despite antedating the C6th). She

was martyred at Syracuse (Sicily) in the reign of Diocletian but her shrine is at Venice. Her attribute is her pair of gouged-out eyes.

Lucy Wang Cheng and Comps (SS)
{1 –group}

28 June
d. 1900. She was born in 1882 at Laochuntan in Hebei (China), but was orphaned and was brought up at the Catholic orphanage at Wanglajia near Dongguanxian. The village was invaded by a gang of Boxers and all the Catholics massacred, but she and three other orphan girls were initially kept alive. The others were Mary Fan Kun, aged sixteen from Daji, Mary Qi Yu, aged fifteen from the same place and Mary Zheng Xu aged eleven from Kou. The Boxers spent four days trying to persuade them to apostatize and to marry, but they refused and were massacred together. Cf. **China, Martyrs of**.

Lucy Wang Wang (St) {1 –group}

22 July
Cf. **Joseph Wang Yumei and Comps**.

Lucy Yi Zhenmei (St) {1 –group}

19 February
1813–62. From a Catholic family of Mianyiang in Sichuan (China), when young she took a private vow of virginity and worked as a schoolteacher and lay catechist. She moved to Guiyang and taught at a convent there, but was seized upon meeting St John-Peter Néel and companions as prisoners on the road near Kaiyang and greeting them. She was beheaded the next day. Cf. **China, Martyrs of**.

Ludan (St) {2}

12 February
d. 1202. He was a 'Scot' (Scots or Irish) pilgrim who died at Northeim in Alsace (France) on pilgrimage to the Holy Land.

Ludmilla (St) {2}

16 September
d. 921. The wife of the first Christian duke of Bohemia, she was entrusted with the education of St Wenceslas, her grandson. The latter's mother, her daughter-in-law, resented her influence and had her strangled by hired assassins at Tetin, her private estate. Her shrine was at Prague (Czech Republic).

Ludolf of Ratzeburg (St) {2}

29 March
d. 1250. A Premonstratensian canon, he became bishop of Ratzeburg near Lübeck (Germany) and imposed the rule of his order on his cathedral chapter. He was imprisoned and badly treated by the secular ruler, dying as a result. He is listed as a martyr.

Ludovic (others) cf. **Louis**.

Ludovic Pavoni (Bl) {2}

18 May
1784–1849. From Brescia in Italy, he was ordained in 1807 and made his life's work the education of neglected boys. He founded his first school and orphanage in 1821, and went on to found the 'Congregation of the Sons of Mary Immaculate' (the 'Pavoniani') to work in this field. He died near Brescia while the city was being sacked by the Austrian army, and was beatified in 2002.

Luigi cf. **Louis** or **Aloysius**.

Luke the Archimandrite (St) {2}

5 February
d. 995. He was a Basilian monk and abbot of the Byzantine-rite monastery of San Salvatore dei Greci at Messina in Sicily. Owing to the incursions of the Muslims he moved to Lucania in Italy, and died at the monastery of SS Elias and Anastasius of the Charcoal Burners near Armento.

Luke Banabakintu (St) {1 –group}

3 June
d. 1886. A native of Buganda (Uganda), he was baptized in 1881 and burnt alive at Namuyongo. Cf. **Charles Lwanga and Comps**.

Luke Belludi (Bl) {2}

17 February
1200–86. He became a Franciscan at Padua (Italy) under St Francis himself, and was the intimate associate of St Anthony of Padua. On his own death he was laid in the empty tomb from which the body of St Anthony had been transferred. His cultus was confirmed for Padua in 1927.

Luke Casali de Nicosia (St) {2}

2 March
C9th. He was the Byzantine-rite abbot of the monastery of San Filippo d'Argira in Sicily, reputed to have been from Nicosia in Cyprus.

Luke the Evangelist (St) {1, 3}

18 October
C1st. A Greek doctor of medicine at Antioch (Syria), he wrote the third gospel and the Acts of the Apostles. The autobiographical passages in the latter describe how he accompanied St Paul on some of the latter's missionary journeys, and he is referred to in St Paul's letter to the Colossians (4:14). Nothing is known about his life after the ending of Acts, and there is no evidence that he was martyred. A C6th legend asserts that he painted the original of the *Hodegetria* icon of Our Lady, and several surviving Byzantine icons have been traditionally claimed as his work. In 2001 his alleged relics at Padua, Italy were DNA-tested and found to be probably genuine. His attribute is an ox.

Luke-Alphonsus Gorda (St) {1 –group}

19 October

1594–1633. From Asturias (Spain), he became a Dominican missionary in the Philippines and was ten years in the north of Honsu (Japan) before being martyred at Nagasaki with his assistant, St Matthew Kohioye. He was canonized in 1987 with SS Laurence Ruiz and Comps. Cf. **Japan, Martyrs of**.

Luke Hwang Sŏk-tu (St) {1 –group}

30 March

Cf. **Anthony Daveluy and Comps**.

Luke of Isola (St) {2}

10 December

d. 1114. He was a Byzantine-rite monk of Melicuccà in Calabria (Italy), and became the bishop of Isola di Capo Rizzuto. He worked hard for the good of poor people and the propagation of the monastic life, and died at the monastery of San Nicola di Viotorito.

Luke Kirby (St) {2}

30 May

?1548–82. From Richmond in Yorkshire, he was probably educated at Cambridge. After his conversion he studied for the priesthood at Rome and Douai, returned to England in 1580 and was immediately arrested on landing at Dover. He was seriously tortured in the Tower of London before being executed at Tyburn with BB Laurence Richardson, Thomas Cottam and William Filby. He was canonized in 1970. Cf. **England, Martyrs of**.

Luke Kiyemon (Bl) {2}

27 August

d. 1627. A Japanese Franciscan tertiary, he was beheaded at Nagasaki with BB Francis-of-St-Mary of Mancha and Comps. Cf. **Japan, Martyrs of**.

Luke of Messina (St) {2}

27 February

d. 1149. He was an abbot of the Byzantine-rite monastery of San Salvatore die Greci at Messina in Sicily.

Luke Passi (Bl) {2 –add}

18 April

1789–1816. A nobleman of Bergamo in Italy, he was ordained in 1813 and was a member of an informal group of Italian diocesan priests interested in missionary activity called the 'Apostolic College'. Pope Gregory XVI gave him the status of an apostolic missionary, thus removing him from diocesan control, and as such he preached parish missions throughout Italy. He also founded the Institute of the Teaching Sisters of St Dorothy to educate girls, and a supporting lay association called the Pious Work of St Dorothy. He died at Venice and was beatified in 2013.

Luke Thìn (St) {1 –group}

13 January

Cf. **Dominic Phạm Trọng Khảm and Comps**.

Luke Vũ Bà Loan (St) {1 –group}

5 June

1756–1840. An elderly priest of Hanoi in north Vietnam, he was beheaded during the persecution ordered by Emperor Minh Mạng. Cf. **Vietnam, Martyrs of**.

Luke the Younger (St) {2}

7 February

d. 955. From a peasant family of Aegina (Greece), he became a monk at Athens and a hermit near Corinth before dying on a mountain in Phocis which was later called 'Soterion' after the miracles that he worked. These also gave him the nickname 'the Thaumaturge'.

Lull (St) {2, 4}

16 October
?710–86. A monk of Malmesbury (England), he was a relative of St Boniface and joined him in Germany in 725, becoming his archdeacon and chief assistant. He was sent to Rome in 751, and on his return Boniface ordained him as his coadjutor at Mainz. He took over as bishop when Boniface left for Frisia and his murder, and founded the monastery of Hersfeld where his shrine is now located.

Lunaire cf. **Leonorius**.

Lupentius (St) {2}

22 October
d. ?684. He was abbot of Saint-Privat-de-Javols near Châlons-sur-Marne (France), and had to go to the Frankish court to answer to a false charge of treason. He was acquitted, but on his return the local count had him imprisoned, tortured and beheaded anyway.

(Luperius) (St) {4 –deleted}

15 November
C6th or C8th. Nothing is known about this alleged bishop of Verona (Italy).

Lupicinus of Lyons (St) {2, 4}

3 February
End C5th. He was bishop of Lyons (France) when the Vandals passed through. The Roman Martyrology has deleted another bishop of Lyons listed with him, one Felix.

Lupicinus of Condat (St) {2, 4}

21 March
d. 480. Brother of St Romanus of Condat, with him he founded two monasteries in the Jura (France), Condat (now the town of St Claude) and Lauconne.

(Lupicinus of Verona) (St) {4 –deleted}

3 May
C5th. He was a bishop of Verona (Italy).

Luppus of Novae (St) {2, 4}

23 August
? He was listed as being a slave of St Demetrius of Thessalonika and a martyr in that city, but this is false. He had a basilica at Novae near Svishtov in Bulgaria, and was probably martyred in the area.

Lupulus (St) {2}

14 October
? He was martyred at Capua (Italy).

Lupus of Limoges (St) {2}

22 May
d. 637. Bishop of Limoges (France), he helped with the foundation of the famous abbey of Solignac.

Lupus of Lyons (St) {2, 4}

24 September
d. p528. A monk of a monastery near Lyons (France), he became archbishop of that city and had to cope with the annexation of the Kingdom of Burgundy by the Franks in 534.

Lupus of Sens (St) {2, 4}

1 September
d. ?623. A monk of Lérins, he became bishop of Sens (France) in 609.

Lupus of Troyes (St) {2, 4}

29 July
d. ?478. From Toul (France), he married a sister of St Hilary of Arles but they separated by mutual consent after seven years and he became a monk at Lérins. He was made

bishop of Troyes in 426. He allegedly accompanied St Germanus of Auxerre to Britain to help combat Pelagianism, and allegedly saved his city from being sacked by Attila the Hun. Both of these assertions are probably false.

(Lupus of Verona) (St) *{4 –deleted}*

2 December
? Nothing is known about this bishop of Verona (Italy).

Lutgard (St) {2, 4}

16 June
1182–1246. From Tongeren (Belgium), she became a Benedictine nun there when aged twenty, and transferred to the Cistercian nunnery of Aywières in 1208 in order to escape being made abbess. She was favoured with apparitions of Christ, Our Lady and of many saints and is outstanding among the women mystics of the Middle Ages. She went blind eleven years before her death.

Luxorius (St) {2, 4}

21 August
d. ?303. He was martyred at a locality called Forum Traiani in Sardinia (now Fordongianus), and his shrine is at Pisa. His legend alleged that he was a soldier beheaded with two boys named Cisellus and Camerinus. These have been deleted from the Roman Martyrology.

(Lybe, Leonis and Eutropia) (SS) *{4 –deleted}*

15 June
d. 303. The first two were sisters who were beheaded and burnt alive, respectively, and the last was a girl aged twelve who was used as an archery target. They were martyred at Palmyra (Syria) in the reign of Diocletian.

(Lycarion) (St) *{4 –deleted}*

7 June
? He is listed as an Egyptian martyr.

Lydia Purpuraria (St) {2, 4}

20 May
C1st. From Thyatira (Asia Minor, now Akhisar in Turkey), a city famous for its dye-works, she was a dealer in Tyrian purple dye (hence her surname). While at Philippi in Greek Macedonia she became St Paul's first convert in Europe (Acts 16:14-15).

Lydwina (St) {2}

14 April
1380–1433. The daughter of a labourer from Schiedam (Netherlands), she was a pretty girl but prayed that she would be disfigured in order to avoid marriage. So she broke a rib while skating when aged sixteen and suffered complications which left her bedridden, gangrenous and in agony for the rest of her life (over forty years). She had mystical visions and ecstasies, allegedly took no food except the Eucharist and reached a high level of contemplative prayer. Her cultus was confirmed for Haarlem (Netherlands) in 1890.

Lydwina Meneguzzi (Bl) {2}

2 December
1901–41. From near Padua in Italy, she joined the 'Sisters of St Francis de Sales' at that city in 1926 and was sent to a new mission at Dire Dawa in Ethiopia in 1937 after the Italian conquest. She was based at the city hospital, and became well-known and liked for her joy and serenity despite the local tradition of despising foreigners. She died of abdominal cancer, and was beatified in 2002.

Lyé cf. **Leo** or **Laetus**.

M

(Macarius and Julian) (SS) *{4 –deleted}*

12 August
? They are listed by the old Roman Martyrology as martyrs of Syria, but earlier martyrologies list them as confessors.

(Macarius, Rufinus and Comps) (SS) *{4 –deleted}*

28 February
d. 250? These alleged potters were listed as martyred in Rome in the reign of Decius. The companions were Justus and Theophilus.

Macarius of Alexandria (St) {2, 4}

8 December
d. 250. He was burnt alive at Alexandria (Egypt) in the reign of Decius after successfully resisting much persuasion to apostasy from the judge of his case.

Macarius the Alexandrian (St) {2, 4}

19 January
c.300–90. He was a sweet maker in Alexandria (Egypt) before his conversion in c.340, and became one of the great desert fathers of Nitria on the western edge of the Nile Delta. A famous athletic ascetic, he became the priest and superior of the hermit colony situated in the desert of the Cells nearby. He was a friend of his namesake of Scetis. He was allegedly also a monk under St Pachomius for a while, but the other Tabennesiote brethren disapproved of his asceticism.

Macarius of Collesano (St) {2}

16 December
d. 1005. He was one of the two sons of St Christopher of Collesano (the other was St Sabas the Younger), and with his family founded several cenobitic Byzantine-rite monasteries on Monte Mercurion in Calabria and Monte Latinion in Basilicata (Italy).

Macarius of Ghent (St) {2, 4}

10 April
d. 1012. He was a pilgrim who died in a hospice at Ghent (Belgium) during an epidemic. His biography is a forgery, hence the detail that he was formerly a bishop of Antioch in Pisidia (Asia Minor) has been deleted from the Roman Martyrology.

Macarius the Great (St) {2, 4}

19 January
d. c.390. The founder of the monastic colony at Scetis (now the Wadi-el-Natrun) in Egypt was apparently a native Egyptian camel driver associated with the natron trade before he settled as a monk in this rift valley in the desert when aged about thirty. He was there for about sixty years, and attracted thousands of disciples. Scetis became the stronghold of Coptic monasticism, as distinct from the more intellectual Greek monasticism at Nitria, and the site of his cell is still marked by a functioning monastery. A collection of ascetical homilies have been traditionally attributed to him, although he is not the author. With Macarius the Alexandrian, he was banished for a while by the Arians after the death of St Athanasius.

Macarius of Jerusalem (St) {2, 4}

10 March
d. ?335. Bishop of Jerusalem from 314, he oversaw the construction of the Anastasis and Martyrion at the site of Calvary. According to legend this involved his identifying the True Cross found by St Helen. He was present at the first Council of Nicaea.

Macarius of Petra cf. **Arius**.

Macarius the Scot (Bl) {2}

6 January
d. 1153. From Scotland (or Ireland), he migrated to Germany and became first Benedictine abbot of St James's monastery at Würzburg.

Macarius the Thaumaturge (St) {2, 4}

18 April
d. 850. Abbot of Pelecetes near Constantinople, he upheld the validity of icons and was hence persecuted by the iconoclast emperors Leo V and Michael II. After several years in prison he died in exile.

Macartan (Aedh mac Cairthinn) (St) {2}

24 March
C5th. He was an early disciple of St Patrick, by whom he is alleged to have been ordained bishop of Clogher (Ireland). He is the principal patron of the diocese of Clogher.

Maccabean Martyrs (SS) {2, 3}

1 August
d. ?168 BC. Apart from the archangels, these were the only persons in the Old Testament (2 Mac 6 & 7) who had a liturgical cultus in the Western Church, being the elder Eleazar and the mother with her seven sons. Their alleged relics were in the church of St Peter ad Vincula in Rome, but in the 1930s they were discovered to be dogs' bones and were removed. Their cultus was confined to local calendars in 1969.

Macedonius, Patricia and Modesta (SS) {2, 4}

13 March
? They were a married couple and their daughter, who were martyred at Nicomedia (Asia Minor).

Macedonius, Theodulus and Tatian (SS) {2, 4}

12 September
d. ?362. When the Emperor Julian restored paganism as the state religion, the temple at Meros in Phrygia (Asia Minor) was reopened and its idols restored. These three broke into the temple, destroyed the idols and were consequently slowly roasted to death on gridirons.

Machar (Mochumna) (St) {2}

12 November
C6th. An Irish nobleman, he was baptized by St Colman and became a disciple of St Columba at Iona (Scotland). Then he was sent with twelve companions to convert the Picts, and allegedly founded the church at Old Aberdeen.

MacNissi (St) {2}

3 September
d. 514. He was allegedly baptized as an infant by St Patrick, who then ordained him bishop when he grew up. He was the abbot-founder of a monastery (probably at Kells) which was the progenitor of the diocese of Connor in Co. Antrim (Ireland). He is the principal patron of the diocese.

Machutus cf. **Malo**.

(Macra) (St) {4 –deleted}

6 January
C3rd? According to her distasteful legend, she was a virgin of Rheims (France) who was martyred at Fismes nearby after the usual tortures and mutilations.

Macrina cf. **Margaret**.

Macrina the Elder (St)

14 January
d. c.340. The paternal grandmother of SS Basil and Gregory of Nyssa, she was a native of Neocaesarea in Pontus (Asia Minor) and as a young woman was a disciple of St Gregory Thaumaturgus, the bishop there. During the persecution ordered by Diocletian, she and her husband hid for over seven years in a forest on their land near the shore of the Black Sea. They returned home in 311, but were further persecuted under Licinius. She taught St Basil as a boy. The Roman Martyrology does not list her.

Macrina the Younger (St) {2}

19 July
?327–79. Granddaughter of St Macrina the Elder, she was the eldest daughter of SS Basil the Elder and Emmelia and sister of SS Basil the Great and Gregory of Nyssa. She helped her parents to educate her younger brothers and sisters, and then became a nun with her mother at a nunnery they founded on the Iris River.

(Macrobius and Julian) *(SS) {4 –deleted}*

13 September
Early C4th? The old Roman Martyrology had a confused entry for these two, who were martyred in the reign of Licinius. The first was apparently a Cappadocian martyred at Tomi on the Black Sea (Romania), and the latter was apparently martyred in Galatia (Asia Minor). They seem to be duplicated in **Valerian, Macrinus and Gordian**.

Madeleine cf. **Mary-Magdalen**.
Maedoc (Modoc, Aedan, Edan, Aidus) cf. **Aidan**.

Maelruain (St) {2}

7 July
d. 789. Abbot-founder of the monastery of Tallaght near Dublin (Ireland), he helped to compile the martyrologies of Tallaght and Oengus. Other writings of his are extant.

Maelrubha (St) {2}

21 April
d. 722. A monk of St Comgall's monastery at Bangor in Co. Down (Ireland), he migrated to Iona (Scotland) and later founded a church at Applecross on the western coast of Ross in the Highlands. His cultus was confirmed in 1898.

Mafalda (Bl) {2}

1 May
1184–1257. Daughter of King Sancho I of Portugal, when aged twelve she was married to King Henry I of Castile, but the marriage was later nullified on account of consanguinity. She then became a nun at Arouca near Oporto in 1216, the nunnery of which became Cistercian in 1222. Her cultus was confirmed for Portugal in 1792.

Magdalen cf. **Mary-Magdalen**.
Magenulf cf. **Meinulf**.

Magi (SS)

24 July
C1st. The story in Matthew's gospel (Matt. 2) concerning the visit of some Persian wise men to Christ as a baby in Bethlehem does not specify their number. That they were three is an ancient tradition, probably deriving from the three gifts. The tradition that they were kings is from the C6th, probably from Psalm 72:10, and the names Balthasar, Caspar and Melchior are from the C8th. Their alleged shrine is at Cologne (Germany), where they were enshrined on this date, and they are usually depicted as being of different races and ages so as to represent all of humanity.

Maginus (Magí) (St) {2, 4}

19 August
? From Tarragona (Spain), he was a missionary in the hills behind that city and was beheaded.

Maglorius (Maelor, Magloire) (St) {2, 4}

24 October
d. ?605. From Glamorgan (Wales), he was educated under St Illtyd and emigrated to Brittany with St Sampson, his relative. There he became abbot of Lammeur, while Samson

became abbot and then bishop of Dol. Maglorius succeeded him as bishop, but later resigned and founded a monastery on Sark in the Channel Islands. He died there.

Magneric of Trier (St) {2, 4}

25 July
d. ?596. A Frank, he succeeded St Nicetius as bishop of Trier (Germany) in ?566 and was a friend of St Gregory of Tours.

Magnoaldus cf. **Magnus**.

(Magnus) (St) {4 –deleted}

1 January
? He is listed as a martyr in the old Roman Martyrology, but with no details.

(Magnus, Castus and Maximus) (SS) *{4 –deleted}*

4 September
? They probably belong with SS Rufinus, Silvanus and Comps of Ancyra, and have been separated in error.

(Magnus of Anagni) (St) {4 –deleted}

19 August
The old Roman Martyrology listed him as a bishop martyred in the reign of Decius, but he is a mistaken duplication of St Andrew the Tribune. The original entry for the latter was 'Andreas Tribunus Magnus Martyr (the Great Martyr)', but an early scribe inserted a comma after 'Tribunus' and thus created a fictitious entry. The fiction was later padded out with worthless acta.

Magnus of Ceccano (St) {2}

19 August
? He was martyred at Ceccano in Lazio (Italy).

Magnus of Eraclea (St) {2, 4}

6 October
d. c.670. A Venetian, he became bishop of Oderzo near Treviso (Italy) but the Lombards destroyed his city in 638, and he moved the bishopric to the new city of Eraclea, nearer the Adriatic and named after the Emperor Heraclius. This in turn is now only a village.

Magnus (Maginold, Mang) of Füssen (St) {2}

6 September
C8th. Nothing is known for certain about the abbot-founder of Füssen in the Bavarian Alps (Germany), although he has been falsely described as a fellow missionary with SS Columbanus and Gall.

Magnus of Milan (St) {2, 4}

1 November
C6th. Not much is known about him, except that he became archbishop of Milan in c.520.

Magnus of Orkney (St) {2}

16 April
?1076–1116. Son of an earl of the Orkneys (Scotland) when they were part of Norway, he was forced by the king to go raiding but refused to fight and fled to the court of Scotland. There he lived a life of penance, but later returned to share the government of the earldom with Haakon, his cousin. The latter had him murdered. The motive was political, but he was regarded as a martyr and his shrine is in the Kirkwall cathedral. His attribute is an axe or club.

Maguil cf. **Madelgisilus**.

Maimbod (St) {2}

23 January
C8th. An Irish missionary monk, while on his way to Rome he was allegedly killed by

robbers near Besançon (France). He is not listed as a martyr.

Mainchin (St) {2}

2 January

C7th. The principal patron of the city and diocese of Limerick (Ireland) may have been the first bishop there, or a monastic founder in the vicinity.

Maine (Mewan, Méen) (St) {2}

21 June

C6th. He was a Welsh or Cornish disciple of St Samson, whom he accompanied to Brittany (France). There he founded a monastery at the place now called St Méen near Rennes.

Majolus of Adrumetum (St) {2}

11 May

d. c.200. He was thrown to the wild animals in the amphitheatre at Adrumetum, now Sousa in Tunisia.

Majolus (Maieul) of Cluny (St) {2}

11 May

?906–94. The fourth abbot of Cluny was from Avignon (France) and became archdeacon of Mâcon after being educated at Lyons and while still very young. To escape being made bishop of Besançon he became a monk at Cluny, and was shortly afterwards made coadjutor to the blind Abbot Aymard. In 965 he succeeded as abbot, and under him the Cluniac congregation spread throughout western Europe. He was the friend of Emperors Otto I and II, and several times refused the papacy. He died at Souvigny.

Malachi the Prophet (St) {2}

18 December

He is the twelfth of the Minor Prophets of the Old Testament.

Malachy O'More (Maolmhaodhog ua Morgain) (St) {2, 4}

2 November

1094–1148. From Armagh (Ireland), he was ordained by St Cellach and was successively vicar-general to the latter, abbot of Bangor, bishop of Connor and Down and archbishop of Armagh from 1132. In 1137 he resigned and made a pilgrimage to Rome, visiting St Bernard at Clairvaux. The pope made him apostolic legate for Ireland with powers to correct abuses. He was a great restorer of the Church in Ireland, finished the replacement of the Celtic liturgy by the Roman and founded Mellifont (the first Cistercian abbey in Ireland) in 1142. He died at Clairvaux on his way back from another visit to Rome, allegedly in St Bernard's arms, and was canonized in 1190. The spurious 'prophecies of the popes' attributed to him were first found in Rome four centuries later.

Malard (St) {2}

15 January

d. c.650. This bishop of Chartres (France) was present at the council of Châlons-sur-Saône in 650.

Malchus of Chalcis (St) {2, 4}

21 October

C4th. A Syrian monk at Chalcis near Antioch, after about twenty years of monastic life he was kidnapped by the Bedouin and sold as a slave. His master gave him another captive, already married, to be his wife, but they lived in continence until they managed to escape after seven years. He returned to Chalcis, where St Jerome knew him and wrote his biography.

Malo (Machutis, Maclou) (St) {2, 4}

15 November

d. c.640. Possibly from Wales, he became a monk under St Brendan and eventually migrated to Brittany (France) with a group of missionaries. He settled near the site of the town of St Malo, of which he is recognized as the first bishop. He resided at Saintes during his banishment.

Mallo (St) {2, 4}

22 October
Early C4th. The tradition alleges that the first bishop of Rouen (France) was a missionary from near Cardiff (Wales), where there is now a village named St Mellons after him.

Mamas (Mammas, Mamans) (St) {2, 4}

17 August
d. ?274. A shepherd of Caesarea in Cappadocia (Asia Minor), he was martyred in the reign of Aurelian. His cultus is popular in the East, but his acta are not reliable.

(Mamelta) (St) {4 –deleted}

17 October
C4th? Her story is that she was a Zoroastrian priestess at Bethfarme in Persia who was converted and baptized, but was recognized as a Christian by her white baptismal garment. A mob stoned her and drowned her in a lake.

Mamertus of Vienne (St) {2, 4}

11 May
d. ?475. He was archbishop of Vienne (France) from 461, and introduced the Rogation Days before the Ascension as liturgical acts of supplication in times of great difficulty for his city. These were taken up by the Roman rite, but have now been abolished.

(Mamilian) (St) {4 –deleted}

12 March
? Nothing is known for certain about this Roman martyr.

Mamlacha (St) {2}

5 October
d. ?343. She was a virgin martyred at a place called Beth Garma during the persecution ordered by Shapur II, Shah of Persia.

Mammea cf. **Mannea**.

Manahen (St) {2, 4}

24 May
C1st. He is mentioned in the Acts of the Apostles (13:1) as a courtier of King Herod Antipas and as a prophet. He is alleged to have died at Antioch (Syria).

Mancius Araki and Comps (Bl) {2}

8 July
d. 1626. A Japanese layman, he was seized with eight others for giving shelter to missionaries working in Kyushu and was imprisoned at Omura. There he died of tuberculosis, but his body was burnt with the other men of the group, including his brother Matthias Araki and cousin Peter Arakiyori Chobioye, as well as John Tanaka and John Naizen Nagai. Susanna Chobioye (Peter's wife), Catherine Tanaka (John Tanaka's wife) and Monica and Louis Naizen (John Naizen's family) were beheaded. Cf. **Japan, Martyrs of**.

Mancius of Évora (St) {2, 4}

21 March
C6th. From Rome, he appears to have been bought as a slave by Jewish traders and taken to Évora (Portugal), where he was tortured and killed by his masters.

Mancius Ichizayemon (Bl) {2}

28 September
d. 1630. A Japanese Augustinian tertiary, he was beheaded at Nagasaki with BB John Chozaburo and Comps. Cf. **Japan, Martyrs of**.

Mancius-of-the-Holy-Cross of Omura (Bl) {2}

29 July
d. 1627. An old Japanese catechist, he was burnt alive at Omura and became a Dominican just beforehand. Cf. 'Louis Bertrán and Comps' and **Japan, Martyrs of**.

Manechild (Ménéhould) (St) {2}

14 October
C6th. She was the youngest of seven sisters, all of whom are honoured as saints in different parts of Champagne (France), and is the patron of the town of Ste Ménéhould.

Manettus (Manetto) dell' Antella (St) {1 –group}

17 February
d. 1268. Cf. **Servites, Founders of**. He became provincial of Tuscany and then fourth general of the order. He attended the council of Lyons in 1246, and at the request of St Louis introduced the order into France. He resigned in favour of St Philip Benizi and retired to Mt Senario in the year before he died.

Manez (Mannes, Manes) de Guzmán (Bl) {2}

30 July
d. 1230. An elder brother of St Dominic, he was born at Calaruega in Old Castile (Spain). He joined the original sixteen Dominicans in 1216, was later the prior at Paris and founded a Dominican nunnery at Madrid. His cultus was approved for the Dominicans in 1834.

Mannus cf. **Magnus**.

(Mansuetus, Severus, Appian, Donatus, Honorius and Five Comps) *(SS) {4 –deleted}*

30 December
C5th? The old Roman Martyrology lists them as having been martyred at Alexandria (Egypt) during the Monophysite reaction against the council of Chalcedon.

Mansuetus of Milan (St) {2, 4}

19 February
d. c.680. From Rome, he became archbishop of Milan (Italy) in ?672. He was one of the leaders of the Western campaign against Monothelitism.

Mansuetus (Mansuy) of Toul (St) {2}

3 September
C4th. He allegedly became the first bishop of Toul (France) in 338, but his extant biography is fictitious.

Manuel cf. **Emmanuel**.

(Manuel, Sabel and Ismael) *(SS) {4 –deleted}*

17 June
d. 362. Persian noblemen, they were sent by the Shah to Emperor Julian at Chalcedon to negotiate for peace. The tradition is that Julian, finding that they were Christians, had them beheaded, and this was one of the immediate causes of the war that led to the emperor's death in battle.

Mappalicus and Comps (SS) {2, 4}

19 April
d. 250. Protomartyrs of the Decian persecution in Roman Africa, they suffered at Carthage and were commended by St Cyprian. Mappalicus was martyred after his mother and sisters had apostatized. Named among the companions are Bassus, Fortunio, Paul, Fortunata, Victorinus, Victor, Heremius, Credula, Hereda, Donatus, Firmus, Venustus, Fructus, Julia, Martial and Ariston. The first was stoned, the second killed in prison, the third executed at the tribunal and the rest were starved to death in prison.

Marana and Cyra (SS) {2, 4}

28 February
C5th. Two women of Beroea (Syria), they became hermits together and allegedly only spoke on the day of Pentecost. They have no cultus in the East.

Marcella of Rome (St) {2, 4}

31 January
325–410. A Roman noblewoman, she was widowed when young. Under the direction of St Jerome, who was her guest for three years, she then devoted herself to the study of the Bible, to prayer and to works of charity. Her house became a centre of activity for several like-minded ladies of the Roman nobility. She had given away her wealth by the time Alaric the Goth sacked Rome, but the invaders thought that she had hidden it and whipped her. This caused her death shortly afterwards.

Marcellina (St) {2, 4}

17 July
End C4th. She was the elder sister of St Ambrose of Milan, and he dedicated several of his writings to her, notably his treatise 'On Virginity'. Pope Liberius heard her vows as a consecrated virgin at Rome in 353, but she later lived with her brothers at Milan (Italy), where her shrine is.

Marcellina Darowska (Bl) {2}

5 January
1827–1911. Born in the Ukraine, she was of the 'kresy' (borderland) Polish gentry. Her father forced her to marry, but she was early widowed and helped found the 'Sisters of the Immaculate Conception' at Jazlowiec (near Lviv, now in the Ukraine) in 1860. She was convinced that a morally healthy society depended on the regeneration of the family, helped by the education of women. In fifty years as superior she opened seven other convents with schools, but her work and her ancestral culture were destroyed by the Second World War and by the Soviets. She was beatified in 1996.

Marcellinus, Pope (St) {3 –deleted}

26 April
d. 304. Virtually nothing certain is known about his life, most of which was spent in a period when the Church was not being persecuted. He allegedly complied with the order of the Emperor Diocletian in 303 to worship pagan gods, together with several prominent members of his clergy, and had his name left out of the list of popes compiled by Pope St Damasus. Later apologists over-compensated and invented the story of his remorse and subsequent martyrdom, for which there is no contemporary evidence. His cultus was suppressed in 1969 and, unusually, he has also been deleted from the Roman Martyrology.

(Marcellinus, Claudius, Cyrinus and Antoninus) (SS) {4 –deleted}

25 October
d. 304. The spurious legend of the martyrdom of Pope St Marcellinus lists these as his fellow martyrs.

Marcellinus, Mannea, John, Serapion and Peter (SS) {2, 4}

27 August
Early C4th?. According to their authentic acta, this family comprising a tribune, his wife and three sons were arrested with a bishop, three priests, eight laymen and another woman. They together formed the entire Christian population of a small place now thought to be Oxyrinchus in Egypt, and were taken to Thmuis and beheaded.

Marcellinus and Peter (SS) {1, 3}

2 June
d. 304. Marcellinus was a priest and Peter probably an exorcist, both of the Roman clergy. Their extant acta are unreliable, but they were certainly greatly venerated by the contemporary Romans since they are commemorated in the Roman canon of the Mass and Emperor Constantine built a basilica (remains of which survive) over their tombs in the catacomb at Duas Lauros.

Marcellinus of Ancona (St) {2, 4}

9 January
C6th. From Ancona (Italy), he became bishop there in c.550.

Marcellinus-Joseph-Benedict Champagnat (St) {2}

6 June
1789–1840. Born in the Loire valley (France), the son of a miller, while studying in the Lyons seminary (in company with SS John Vianney and Peter Chanel) he was involved in the discussions over the foundation of the Marist Fathers. He was ordained in 1816, and founded the Marist Brothers after giving the last rites to a dying boy who was completely ignorant of Church teaching. He himself became a Marist Father when that institute was approved in 1836. He was canonized in 1999.

Marcellinus of Embrun (St) {2, 4}

20 April
d. ?374. He was ordained first bishop of Embrun near Gap (France) by St Eusebius of Vercelli. Vincent and Domninus, early bishops of Digne, were listed with him but have been deleted by the Roman Martyrology.

(Marcellinus of Ravenna) (St) {4 –deleted}

5 October
Late C3rd? Traditionally the second or third bishop of Ravenna (Italy), he allegedly succeeded St Agapitus.

Marcellinus the Tribune (St) {2, 4}

13 September
d. 413. Tribune and secretary of state of Emperor Honorius, he was sent by the latter to Africa to resolve the Donatist schism. He tried to enforce with severity the decisions of a synod at Carthage against the Donatists, but they intrigued against him and managed to have him executed without trial. St Augustine was his friend, and dedicated his work *De Civitate Dei* to him.

Marcellus cf. **Marcellinus**.

Marcellus I, Pope (St) {2, 3}

16 January
d. 309. He was pope for only one year and was exiled by the usurper Maxentius, but there is no proof that he was a martyr. An unreliable legend alleges that he was forced to work in the stables of the public post service. His cultus was confined to local calendars in 1969.

(Marcellus and Anastasius) (SS) {4 –deleted}

29 June
C3rd? They were listed as Roman missionaries martyred at Argenton-sur-Creuse near Châteauroux (France) in the reign of Aurelian. Marcellus was beheaded, and Anastasius whipped to death.

(Marcellus, Castus, Emilius and Saturninus) (SS) {4 –deleted}

6 October
? The shrine of these martyrs was at Capua (Italy).

Marcellus Akimetes (St) {2, 4}

29 December
d. c.480. From Apamea (Syria), he joined the monks who were called the Akimetes ('non-sleepers') because they recited the divine office in relays non-stop, day and night. He became the third abbot of their chief abbey at Constantinople, and under his rule they grew in numbers and influence. He was present at the council of Chalcedon.

Marcellus of Apamea (St) {2, 4}

14 August
d. c.390. From Cyprus, where he was governor, he was made bishop of Apamea (Syria) after the death of his wife in 381. He had to enforce the decree of Emperor Theodosius I prohibiting paganism and was overseeing the burning of the temple at Aulona when he was thrown into the flames by its infuriated congregation.

Marcellus of Capua (St) {2, 4}

7 October
C3rd–4th. He was martyred at Capua (Italy). The Roman Martyrology has deleted a companion Apuleius.

Marcellus Callo (Bl) {2}

19 March
1921–45. Born in Rennes (France), he joined the 'Young Christian Workers' in 1936 and worked for a printing company. He was a model Christian working man. In 1943 he shared the fate of many in occupied Europe when he was seized and deported to Thuringia in Germany as a forced worker for the German war effort. He gave witness to his faith there which led the Nazis to send him to the concentration camp at Mauthausen, where he died. He was beatified as a martyr in 1987.

Marcellus of Die (St) {2, 4}

17 January
d. 510. From Avignon (France), he was educated by his brother St Petronius, bishop of Die near Valence (not of Saint-Dié) and succeeded him as bishop. He had much difficulty with the Arians, and died after a long episcopate.

Marcellus of Lyons (St) {2, 4}

4 September
C3rd–4th. A priest of Lyons (France), he was imprisoned but escaped, was recaptured and then buried up to his waist on the banks of the Saône and left to die. It is alleged that he survived three days.

(Marcellus of Nicomedia) (St) {4 –deleted}

26 November
d. 349. He was listed as a priest of Nicomedia (Asia Minor) who was seized by Arians and thrown over a precipice during the reign of the Emperor Constantius.

Marcellus of Paris (St) {2, 4}

1 November
End C4th. A bishop of Paris (France), he was buried in the old Christian cemetery outside the walls of the city; the locality is now called St Marceau.

Marcellus Spinola y Mestre (Bl) {2}

19 January
1835–1906. After a childhood spent in various Spanish ports he became a parish priest at Seville in 1866, going on to become a cathedral canon and then auxiliary bishop. He became bishop of Malaga in 1886 and then archbishop of Seville in 1896. He worked to put the Church's social teaching into practice, as had been set out in the encyclical *Rerum Novarum*, and founded the 'Handmaids of the Immaculate Virgin and the Divine Heart'. He

was made a cardinal just over a month before he died. He was beatified in 1987.

Marcellus of Tangier (St) {2, 4}

30 October
d. 298. A centurion of the Roman army stationed at Tangier (Roman Africa), he refused to join in the celebration of the emperor's birthday because this involved a pagan sacrifice. He discarded his weapons and insignia, declared himself a Christian and was then tried and executed. His acta are genuine. The notary was St Cassian, who refused to write the official report of the case and who was also martyred in consequence. His alleged relics were enshrined at Léon (Spain) in the late C15th, and the unreliable Spanish tradition makes him the father of twelve martyrs: Claudius, Lupercius, Victoricus, Facundus, Primitivus, Faustus, Januarius, Martial, Hemeterius, Chelidonius, Servandus and Germanus.

(Marcellus of Trier) (St) {4 –deleted}

4 September
? This alleged martyr-bishop of Trier in Germany (or of Tongeren in Belgium) was listed in the old Roman Martyrology despite being seemingly a C10th invention.

Marchelm of Deventer (St) {2, 4}

14 July
d. 775. An Anglo-Saxon, he followed St Willibrord to the Netherlands and was a missionary in Overijssel together with St Lebuin. In 738 he accompanied St Boniface to Rome. He died at Oldenzaal, but his shrine was established at Deventer.

Marcian, Nicanor, Apollonius and Comps (SS) {2, 4}

5 June
C3rd. They were martyred in Egypt by being shut into an open walled enclosure and left to die of thirst and sunstroke.

Marcian of Auxerre (St) {2, 4}

20 April
d. ?488. A peasant from Bourges (France), he became a lay brother at the abbey of SS Cosmas and Damian at Auxerre and looked after the cows.

Marcian of Constantinople (St) {2, 4}

10 January
d. 471. Born in Rome, he was brought up in Constantinople where he was ordained. He was appointed treasurer of the church of Hagia Sofia and as such he arranged for the building of several lesser churches, notably that of the Anastasis. He was wrongly suspected of Novatianism and was persecuted as a result.

Marcian of Cyrrhus (St) {2, 4}

2 November
End C4th. He left the emperor's court at Constantinople and gave up a brilliant military career in order to become a hermit in the desert of Chalcis in Syria. He had several well-known disciples.

Marcian of Iconium (St) {2, 4}

11 July
C3rd–4th. He was a young man martyred at Iconium in Lycaonia (Asia Minor), and his tongue was cut out before his execution in order to stop him from praying aloud.

Marcian-Joseph López López (St) {2}

9 October
Cf. **Innocent-of-Mary-Immaculate Canoura Arnau and Comps**.

Marcian of Syracuse (St) {2, 4}

30 October
C2nd. According to the Sicilian legend, 'the first bishop of the West' was sent to Syracuse by St Peter himself and was thrown from a

tower by a Jewish mob. It is more likely that he was a bishop of the C3rd.

Marcian of Tortona (St) {2, 4}

6 March
? He was a martyred bishop of Tortona in Piedmont (Italy). The worthless legend is that he was a disciple of St Barnabas, and was the first bishop of that city for forty-five years before being martyred in the reign of Trajan.

Marciana of Caesarea (St) {2, 4}

11 July
d. ?303. She was a consecrated virgin of Caesarea in Mauritania (now Cherchel in Morocco), was accused of having shattered a statue of the goddess Diana and was thrown to the wild animals in the amphitheatre. There she was gored to death by a bull. Her relics were transferred to Toledo (Spain), where she has been falsely claimed as a native.

(Marciana of Toledo) (St) {4 –deleted}

12 July
The old Roman Martyrology listed her as having been martyred at Toledo (Spain), but she is identical with St Marciana of Caesarea.

Marcolinus Ammani (Bl) {2}

2 January
1317–97. From Forli (Italy), he became a Dominican there when very young and was a model religious, but it was only after his death that his brethren realized how heroic his sanctity was. His cultus was confirmed for Forli in 1750.

Marculf (St) {2}

1 May
d. ?558. From Bayeux (France), he was the abbot-founder of a monastery of hermit-monks on the Egyptian model at Nanteuil. His relics

were enshrined at Corbigny near Nevers in 898, and after the French kings were crowned at Rheims they used to go there and touch the relics. They were then themselves allegedly able to heal by touch those suffering from scrofula ('the king's evil'). The shrine was predictably destroyed in the French Revolution.

Marculus (St) {2}

25 November
d. 347. He was a bishop of some city in Numidia in Roman Africa (now Algeria) who was martyred in the reign of the Arian Emperor Constantius by being thrown from the top of a cliff.

Mard cf. **Medard**.

(Mardonius, Musonius, Eugene and Metellus) (SS) {4 –deleted}

24 January
? They were listed as burnt at the stake somewhere in Asia Minor.

Maryahb (St) {2, 4}

22 April
d. 342. A Persian chorepiscopus, he was martyred during the Easter Octave in the reign of Shah Shapur II. With him died twenty-one other bishops, nearly two hundred and fifty priests, many monks and nuns and a large number of laypeople. The church of Persia was brought to the verge of extinction by this persecution, which was motivated by the suspicion that Christians were fifth-columnists loyal to the Roman Empire.

Margaret d'Youville cf. **Mary-Margaret d'Youville**.

Margaret-Mary Alacoque (St) {1, 3}

16 October
1647–90. From L'Hautecourt in Burgundy (France), she became a Visitation nun at

Paray-le-Monial in 1671 and then had a series of visions of Christ which led her to start work at the spreading of public and liturgical devotion to the Sacred Heart in 1675. This led to violent opposition from members of her own community, and also from clerics influenced by Jansenist teachings. However, her humility prevailed over the persecution and also over serious problems that she had with her mental health. Her autobiography witnesses to the latter in a disarming way. The modern popularity of the devotion to the Sacred Heart derives from her. She was canonized in 1920, and has a flaming heart as her attribute.

Margaret of Antioch (St) {2, 3}

20 July
? She was a virgin martyr of Antioch in Pisidia (Asia Minor). Her acta are worthless, being exaggerated legend, but she is one of the most popular of virgin martyrs, and her cultus is very ancient. In the East she is known as Pelagia. Part of her legend involves her being swallowed and regurgitated by a dragon before being beheaded, and she is often depicted with such. Her feast was dropped from the General Calendar of the Latin rite in 1969.

Margaret Ball (Bl) {2}

20 June
d. 1584. An Irish widow in her seventies, she sheltered some fugitive priests. However, she was betrayed by her son and spent three years being maltreated in prison before dying of hardship on an unknown date. She was beatified in 1992. Cf. **Ireland, Martyrs of.**

Margaret the Barefooted (St) {2, 4}

5 August
d. 1395. A peasant girl of Sanseverino near Ancona (Italy), when aged fifteen she married a fairly prosperous man of that town. She had great sympathy for the poor, and in solidarity with them always went barefoot whatever the weather. Her husband regarded this as an insult to his dignity, and treated her with contempt and cruelty for years.

Margaret-of-Cortona di Bartolomeo (St) {2}

22 February
1247–97. From Laviano in Tuscany (Italy), a farmer's daughter, she was the mistress of a young nobleman for nine years, but he was murdered, and she repented after seeing his decomposing corpse. After publicly confessing her sins in the church of Cortona she placed herself under the direction of the Franciscans there and became a penitential tertiary, founding a hospital where she (and a community of other tertiaries that she had founded) nursed. She was involved in the city's political affairs and was much slandered, but was nevertheless in receipt of supernatural charismata. She was canonized in 1728.

Margaret Bays (Bl) {2}

26 June
1815–79. Born at Siviriez in Fribourg (Switzerland), she lived there all her life as a dressmaker, being involved in the social works of mercy and in evangelization through the media. She was miraculously cured of intestinal cancer at the moment that the dogma of the Immaculate Conception was pronounced in 1854, and thereupon received the stigmata and a mystical experience of the Passion every Friday. Being centred on God made her profoundly humble, however, and she was beatified in 1995.

Margaret Bourgeoys (St) {2}

12 January
1620–1700. From Troyes (France), she went to Canada (then a French colony) as tutor to the children of the French garrison of Montreal. In 1688 she founded the congregation of the 'Sisters of Notre Dame de Montreal' in order

to teach in the colony, for which work she obtained royal approval. Her congregation subsequently spread to the United States of America, receiving papal approval in 1889. She was canonized in 1982.

Margaret of Città-di-Castello (Bl) {2}

13 April
1287–1320. Born to a noble family at Méldola near Forli (Italy), she was blind and deformed and her shamed parents kept her locked up until she was aged twenty. Then they took her to the shrine at Città-di-Castello hoping for a cure, and abandoned her there when this was not forthcoming. She was rescued by a charitable family, and looked after by a series of well-wishers whom she repaid by serving as a child-sitter. On reaching maturity, she became a Dominican tertiary. She is the earliest person formally beatified (in 1609) who has not yet been canonized.

Margaret Clitherow (St) {2}

25 March
1556–86. Born in York, she became a Catholic shortly after she married and was imprisoned for two years as a consequence. On her release she began to shelter priests in her house. This caused her to be arrested again and put on trial, but she refused to plead in order to protect those she had helped. The legal penalty imposed on her at York, and which was specified for this, was to be laid down on the ground and pressed with heavy weights,. She died as a result. She was canonized in 1970, and is depicted as an Elizabethan housewife kneeling or standing on the heavy door on which the weights had been piled. Cf. **England, Martyrs of**.

Margaret Colonna (Bl) {2}

30 December
d. 1280. Daughter of Prince Odo Colonna of Palestrina (Italy), she turned the family

castle on a mountainside above the city into a Poor Clare nunnery which she joined, and for which her brother, Cardinal James Colonna, wrote a mitigated version of the Franciscan rule. Her cultus was confirmed locally for Rome in 1847.

Margaret Ebner (Bl) {2}

20 June
1291–1351. Born at Donauwörth in Bavaria (Germany), she became a Dominican nun and died at Medingen. Her cultus was confirmed for Augsburg in 1979.

Margaret of Hungary (St) {2}

18 January
1252–70. Daughter of Bela IV, king of Hungary, she founded a Dominican nunnery on an island in the Danube near Budapest and herself joined it. Her life there was famously penitential, and she was canonized in 1943.

Margaret-Mary López de Maturana (Bl) {2 –add}

23 July
1884–1934. From Bilbao in the Basque Country, Spain, she became a boarder in a Mercedarian school and joined that order, working at the same school for twenty years. The nunnery had papal enclosure, but Bl Margarita inspired her community to become an active missionary congregation. Sisters were sent to China and Micronesia, and the 'Mercedarian Missionaries of Berriz' was officially founded in 1931 with Bl Margarita as first superior. She died of cancer in Spain after lengthy missionary journeys, and was beatified in 2006.

Margaret of Lorraine (Bl) {2}

6 November
1463–1521. A daughter of a duke of Lorraine, she married the duke of Alençon (France) in

1488 and had three children, but he died in 1492. After she had brought up her children she founded a Poor Clare nunnery at Argentan and became a nun there herself in 1519. Her cultus was confirmed for Sées in 1921.

Margaret Pole (Bl) {2}

28 May

1471–1541. She was a Plantagenet, a niece of Edward IV and Richard III, and married Sir Reginald Pole. They had five children before she was widowed. Then she was created Countess of Salisbury in her own right and appointed governess to Princess Mary, daughter of King Henry VIII. When her son Cardinal Pole opposed the royal supremacy in spiritual matters and refused to return to England, Henry revenged himself on her, holding her in the Tower of London for two years. Finally she was condemned for high treason by 'Bill of Attainder', beheaded on Tower Hill and beatified in 1886. Cf. **England, Martyrs of**.

Margaret of Savoy (Bl) {2}

23 November

d. 1464. A daughter of Duke Amadeus II of Savoy, she was born at Pinerolo near Turin (Italy) and married the marquis of Montferrat in 1403. In 1418 she was widowed and, influenced by St Vincent Ferrer, became a Dominican tertiary. She founded a nunnery at Alba in Liguria in 1426 and became first prioress there. Her cultus was confirmed for Alba and Savoy in 1669.

Margaret of Scotland (St) {1, 3}

16 November

1046–93. Her father was a son of King Edmund Ironside of England and her mother was a Hungarian princess reputed to be related to St Stephen of Hungary. She was born in Hungary but grew up in the court of St Edward the Confessor. At the Norman Conquest she tried to flee back to Hungary, but her ship was wrecked off Scotland, and she became the queen-consort of King Malcolm III of Scotland instead in 1070. The eldest son of her large family became King David I, one of Scotland's greatest kings. She was pious, charitable and just and, among other good works, founded the great Benedictine abbey of Dunfermline as a royal mausoleum. She was canonized in 1251.

Margaret-Lucy Szewczyk (Bl) {2 –add}

5 June

1828–1905. She was of the *Kresy* or 'borderland' Polish nobility in what is now western Ukraine, and was orphaned when young. After escaping a storm on the voyage home from a long pilgrimage to the Holy Land when aged forty-five, she made a vow to be of service to poor people. The result was that she founded, and was first superior of, the Congregation of the Daughters of the Sorrowful Mother of God – the Seraphic Sisters. She died at Nieszawa near Torun in Poland, and was beatified in 2013.

Margaret Ward (St) {2}

30 August

d. 1588. A laywoman from Congleton in Cheshire, she was in domestic service with a recusant family in London. She helped to arrange the escape of a priest from the Bridewell prison, but a rope used was traced to her, and she was severely tortured before being hanged at Tyburn with BB Richard Leigh, Edward Shelley, Richard Lloyd, Richard Martin and John Roche. She was canonized in 1970. Cf. **England, Martyrs of**.

Margaritus Flores García (St) {1 –group}

12 November

d. 1927. From Taxco in Guerrero, Mexico, he became a diocesan priest of Chilapa and was appointed parish priest of Atenango del Rio three years after his ordination. He was arrested and shot for his priesthood at Tulimán in Chilpancingo, Mexico. Cf. **Mexico, Martyrs of**.

Maria cf. **Mary**.
Mariana cf. **Mary-Anne**.

Marianne Cope (St) {2 –add}

23 January
1838–1918. She was born in Hesse in Germany, but her family emigrated to the United States of America when she was a baby and settled near Syracuse in New York State. She joined the Sisters of St Francis there in 1862, and became the head of the province in 1883. However, she received a request for help in nursing sufferers of leprosy in Hawaii in the same year, and moved to Honolulu with six sisters. She was associated with Bl Damian de Veuster in this apostolate. She died at Honolulu and was canonized in 2012.

Marianus, James and Comps (SS) {2, 4}

6 May
d. 259. They were martyred at Lambesa in Numidia (Roman Africa, now Algeria). Marianus was a reader and James a deacon, and their acta are authentic.

Marianus Alcalá Pérez and Comps (BB) {2 –add}

d. 1936. They are the nineteen Mercedarian martyrs of the diocese of Lérida, Spain who were killed during the Spanish Civil War. They were beatified in 2013. Cf. **Spanish Civil War, Martyrs of** and list in appendix.

Marianus Arciero (Bl) {2 –add}

16 February
1707–88. From a peasant family of Contursi Terme near Salerno (Italy), he became a diocesan priest of Naples in 1731and immediately became famous for his spiritual erudition. He spent twenty years in the new diocese of Cassano allo Ionio in Calabria, founding churches and devoting himself to catechesis. On his return to Naples, he became a famous confessor and spiritual director to all ranks of people and was well known for his devotion to the Eucharist and to Our Lady. He lived very simply, and gave most of his income away in charity. He was beatified in 2012.

Marianus-of-Roccacasale di Nicolantonio (Bl) {2}

30 May
1778–1866. From Roccacasale near L'Aquila (Italy), he was a shepherd before becoming a Franciscan at Arischia for twelve years from 1802. Then he transferred to Bellegra and was the receptionist there for the rest of his life, manifesting a special love for poor people. He was beatified in 1999.

Marianus of Entreaigues (St) {2, 4}

19 September
C6th. A biography of this hermit, who lived in the forest of Entreaigues near Evaux-les-Bains (France), was written by St Gregory of Tours.

Marianus-of-Jesus Euse Hoyos (Bl) {2}

13 July
1845–1926. From a peasant family of Yarumal in Colombia, he was ordained at Medellín in 1872 and became parish priest of Angostura in 1878. He proved an exemplary pastor, his ministry being based on continuous prayer and asceticism. He was beatified in 2000.

Marianus Górecki (Bl) {2}

22 May
1903–40. A Polish priest, he was shot by the Nazis at the concentration camp of Stutthof

near Gdynia in Poland together with Bl Bronislav Komorowski. Cf. **Poland, Martyrs of the Nazi Occupation of**.

Marianus Konopiński (Bl) {2}

1 January
1907–43. A Polish priest, he died as a result of medical experimentation at Dachau. Cf. **Poland, Martyrs of the Nazi Occupation of**.

Marianus de la Mata Aparicio (Bl) {2 –add}

5 April
1905–83. From Puebla deValdavia in Spain, he became an Augustinian in 1921 and was sent to Brazil as a missionary in 1931 after being ordained. He was initially curate at Taquaritinga in São Paulo State, but then taught at his Order's college in São Paulo and was parish priest of St Augustine's church there. He had great zeal for the education and support of poor and sick people, and was a conspicuous success in balancing his apostolic and community responsibilities as a religious. He was also enamoured by the beauty of God's creation in living things, and was a fervent stamp collector. He died of cancer and was beatified in 2006.

Marianus Skrzypczak (Bl) {2}

5 October
1909–39. A Polish priest, he was shot by the Nazis at Płonkowo in Poland. Cf. **Poland, Martyrs of the Nazi Occupation of**.

Marie cf. **Mary**.
Marie-Celine cf. **Mary-Celine-of-the-Presentation Castang**.

Marina

This is the Latin form of the Greek name Pelagia, a fact which has caused a few duplicates in extant martyrologies.

(Marina) (St) {4 –deleted}

18 June
? In the ancient martyrologies she is listed also as Mary, Marina or even Marinus (which would make her a male). She is moreover listed simply as a consecrated virgin, not as a martyr. She has been identified with St Margaret or with St Pelagia the Penitent, and her legend served as a model for those of SS Euphrosyne, Theodora and others. The old Roman Martyrology listed her as a martyr at Alexandria (Egypt).

Marina of Omura (St) {1 –group}

11 November
d 1634. A Japanese Dominican tertiary and a consecrated virgin, she was imprisoned, ridiculed in public and burnt alive at Nagasaki. Her surname is not known. She was canonized in 1987 with SS Laurence Ruiz and Comps. Cf. **Japan, Martyrs of**.

(Marina of Orense) (St) {4 –deleted}

18 July
? Her relics are at Orense in Galicia (Spain), but nothing is known about her. Cardinal Baronius added her to the old Roman Martyrology.

Marinus and Anianus (SS) {2}

15 November
C7–8th. They were hermits on the Irschenberg in the district of Miesbach in southern Bavaria (Germany), and were killed by barbarians. The former had been a bishop.

Marinus and Asterius (SS) {2, 4}

3 March
d. c.260. Marinus was a Roman soldier stationed at Caesarea in the Holy Land who was about to be promoted to the rank of centurion, but he was denounced as a Christian by a jealous rival and immediately martyred. Asterius

(or Astyrius) was a senator who buried the body and hence also martyred.

(Marinus, Theodotus and Sedopha) *(SS)* *{4 –deleted}*

5 July
? They were listed as martyred at Tomi on the Black Sea coast of Romania.

Marinus of Anazarbus (St) {2, 4}

8 August
d. 303–11. An old man, he was martyred at Anazarbus in Cilicia (Asia Minor) in the reign of Diocletian.

Marinus of Cava (Bl) {2}

15 December
d. 1170. A Benedictine monk of La Cava near Salerno (Italy), he became abbot there in 1146. He was a friend both of several popes and of the kings of Sicily, and he acted as mediator between pope and king in 1156. His cultus was confirmed for La Cava in 1928.

***(Marinus* of Rome)** *(St)* *{4 –deleted}*

26 December
Late C3rd? His legend describes him as the son of a Roman senator, beheaded under Numerian after having been miraculously delivered from various tortures and other means of death. His acta are romantic fiction, and his existence is questionable as there was no persecution in the period concerned.

Marinus of San Marino (St) {2, 4}

3 September
C4–5th. According to the tradition, he was a stonemason from an island off the coast of Dalmatia (Croatia) who was ordained deacon by St Gaudentius of Rimini and who died as a hermit on the site of the capital of the tiny

Republic of San Marino, which is named after him.

Marius cf. **Maurus**.

Marius, Martha, Audifax and Abachum (SS) {2, 3}

19 January
Early C4th? All that is known of them are their names and place of martyrdom and burial (the cemetery 'Ad Nymphas' on the Via Cornelia near Rome). According to their fictional legend, they were a Persian nobleman, his wife and their two sons. Travelling to Rome on pilgrimage, when they got there they started to bury the bodies of those who were being martyred in the persecution of Claudius II. They were seized, the three men were beheaded and St Martha was drowned. Their cultus was suppressed in 1969.

Marius of Bodon (St) {2, 4}

27 January
d. ?555. He was abbot-founder of Bodon near Sisteron in upper Provence (France), not Bobbio as the old Roman Martyrology had it.

Marius of Lausanne (St) {2}

31 December
d. 594. He was made bishop of Avenches on the Lake of Geneva (Switzerland) in 574, and in 590 moved his cathedral to Lausanne. He built many churches.

Marius Vergara and Isidore Ngei Ko Lat (BB) {2 –add}

25 May
d. 1950. Bl Marius was born at Fratamaggiore near Aversa, Italy in 1910 and was ordained as a priest of the Pontifical Institute for Foreign Missions in 1934 and was sent to Burma. The locality for his activity was the Karen region, in the east of the country. As an enemy

national he was interned by the British (who then ruled Burma), and taken to India in 1940. There he ministered to Italian prisoners-of-war, but went back to Burma in 1946. There he teamed with Bl Isidore, a Karenni catechist who could read English and Latin. However, the Karenni, not being Burmese, rebelled when Burma became independent and the guerrilla fighters adopted an anti-Christian stance. The two missionaries were killed on the bank of the Salween River near Loikaw, and beatified as martyrs in 2014.

Mark cf. **John Mark**.
Mark cf. **Marcius**.

Mark and Marcellian (SS) {2, 4}

18 June
d. ?304. The legend concerning these Roman martyrs describes them as twins, both deacons, who were martyred in the reign of Maximian Herculeus. Their underground basilica on the Via Ardeatina was rediscovered in 1902. Their cultus was confined to local calendars in 1969.

(Mark, Marcian and Comps) (SS) {4 –deleted}

4 October
Early C4th? The old Roman Martyrology had a confused entry for these Egyptian martyrs, describing them as two brothers and their companions as 'innumerable' and 'of all ages and both sexes'. **Marcian** seems to be a duplication of one of a pair of martyrs listed as **Nicander and Marcian**. The companions are thought to be those martyred Egyptian during the persecution ordered by Diocletian, and mentioned by Eusebius.

Mark and Mocian (SS) {2, 4}

3 July
Early C4th? They were martyred in Moesia (modern Bulgaria) by beheading after refusing to sacrifice to idols. The old Roman

Martyrology listed two onlookers who were encouraging them, one an unnamed little boy and the other called Paul, and who were also martyred. These have been deleted.

(Mark and Stephen) (SS) {4 –deleted}

22 November
Early C4th? They were listed as martyred at Antioch in Pisidia (Asia Minor) in the reign of Galerius.

(Mark and Timothy) (SS) {4 –deleted}

24 March
C2nd? These alleged Roman martyrs are mentioned by Pope St Pius I in a letter to a bishop of Vienne. They are patrons of Orte in Tuscany (Italy).

Mark I, Pope (St) {2, 3}

7 October
d. 336. A Roman, he died in the year that he was elected pope. His cultus was confined to local calendars in 1969.

Mark of Arethusa (St) {2}

29 March
d. 364. Bishop of Arethusa in Lebanon, he attended the synod of Sirmium in 351 and drew up a creed for which he was unjustly accused of Arianism by Baronius, who excluded his name from the old Roman Martyrology. He has since been vindicated by the Bollandists. He died shortly after he destroyed a pagan temple in his city, which action led to its congregation giving him a thorough beating.

Mark Barkworth (alias Lambert) (Bl) {2}

27 February
d. 1601. From Lincolnshire, he was educated at Oxford before his conversion and then studied for the priesthood at Rome and Valladolid (Spain) in order to go on the English mission.

While at Valladolid he became a Benedictine monk at the abbey of Hirache near Estella in Spanish Navarra. He was executed at Tyburn (London) with Bl Roger Filcock. Cf. **England, Martyrs of**.

Mark Chŏng Ui-bae and Alexis U Se-yŏng (SS) {1 –group}

11 March
d. 1866. Mark was the royal master of games in Korea before his conversion and execution as a catechist when aged seventy. He was accompanied by Alexis, who was a convert aged nineteen whose parents had tried to make him abandon his faith by force. They were subjected to scorn and beating by members of their families before being martyred at Sainamhte in Korea. Cf. **Korea, Martyrs of**.

Mark Criado (Bl) {2}

25 September
1522–69. From Andújar near Cordoba (Spain), he became a Trinitarian in 1536 but was tortured and killed at Almería by a group of Muslims. His cultus was approved for Guadix and the Trinitarians in 1899.

Mark-of-Aviano Cristofori (Bl) {2}

13 August
1631–99. From Aviano in Italy, he became a Franciscan Capuchin friar at Conegliano Veneto in 1648 and was appointed an itinerant preacher for Italy in 1664. He became famous in many European countries, became an adviser of Leopold I of Austria in 1680 and papal legate in Vienna. As such, he participated in the military campaigns against the Ottomans after their siege of Vienna in 1683, which led to the liberation of Hungary. He died of cancer at Vienna, and was beatified in 2003. The type of coffee named 'Cappuccino' was allegedly invented by him.

Mark-Anthony Durando (Bl) {2}

10 December
1801–80. From a well-known family of Mondovi in Italy, he joined the 'Congregation of the Mission of St Vincent de Paul' and was ordained in 1824. He was made superior at Turin in 1831, and stayed there all his life. As well as preaching popular missions, he introduced the 'Daughters of Charity' into northern Italy and helped in the foundation of the 'Nazarene Sisters'. He was beatified in 2002.

Mark the Evangelist (St) {1, 3}

25 April
d. ?75. He is probably the young man who ran away when Christ was arrested (Mk 14:51-2), and the 'John whose other name was Mark' of Acts 12:25. He accompanied SS Paul and Barnabas on their first missionary journey but turned back after Cyprus. By Roman tradition (possibly derived from the reference to 'my son Mark' in 1 Pet. 5:13) he was St Peter's disciple and interpreter at Rome and wrote his gospel as a summary of the apostle's preaching. The Egyptian tradition is that he founded the church at Alexandria and was martyred there, but there is no historical evidence for this. His alleged relics were taken from Alexandria to Venice in the C9th and are in the cathedral there. His attribute is a winged lion.

Mark Fantucci (Bl) {2}

10 April
1405–79. From Bologna (Italy), he was a law student before becoming a Franciscan Observant in 1430. He went on to become vicar-general and preached throughout Italy and the Croatian coast, also visiting the friars in Austria, Poland, Russia and the Middle East. He died at Piacenza, and his cultus was approved for the Friars Minor in 1868.

(Mark of Galilee) (St) {4 –deleted}

28 April
He was allegedly a Galilean by descent and the first bishop of Atina in Lazio (Italy), a missionary in the Abruzzi and a martyr in his city. The traditional claim that he died in the year 92 is grossly anachronistic.

Mark of Jerusalem (St) {2, 4}

22 October
C2nd. He was the first bishop of Jerusalem not to be of Jewish extraction, and was allegedly bishop for twenty years before being martyred. The Roman Martyrology has deleted the reference to his martyrdom.

Mark Ji Tianxiang (St) {1 –group}

7 July
1834–1900. From Yanzhuangtou in Hebei (China), he was the leader of the Catholics in his village and worked as a doctor. However, he became addicted to opium and was excommunicated as a result for thirty years. The local magistrate was sympathetic to the Boxers, and allowed them to behead eleven of St Mark's family before his eyes. He was offered his life in exchange for his faith, and was beheaded when he refused. Cf. **China, Martyrs of**.

Mark-of-Montegallo de Marchio (Bl) {2}

20 March
1426–97. From Montegallo near Ascoli Piceno (Italy), he was a doctor of medicine and happily married, but he and his wife parted by mutual consent to become Franciscans. Ordained at Fabriano, he became a famous home missionary in Italy and established a chain of charitable pawnshops for the poor, known in Italy as 'Monti di Pietà'. His cultus was confirmed for Vicenza in 1839.

Mark dei Marconi (Bl) {2}

24 February
1480–1510. From a poor family at Milliarino near Mantua (Italy), he joined the Hieronymite monastery of Bl Peter of Pisa at Mantua. His order is now extinct. His cultus was approved for Mantua in 1906.

Mark-of-Modena Scalabrini (Bl) {2}

23 September
d. 1498. From Modena (Italy), he became a Dominican and was a very successful preacher in north and central Italy. He died at his reform friary at Pesaro and his cultus was confirmed for there and for the Dominicans in 1857.

Mark Takenoshima Shinyemon (Bl) {2}

19 August
d. 1622. A Japanese merchant, he joined the expedition to Japan of BB Louis Flores and Comps and shared their fate. Cf. **Japan, Martyrs of**.

Mark of Troia (St) {2}

5 November
C4th? He was an early bishop of Troia near Foggia (Italy), but his extant biography is unreliable.

Marmaduke Bowes (Bl) {2}

27 November
d. 1585. A farmer at Ingram Grange at Welbury, Yorks, he had sheltered Bl Hugh Taylor and had gone to York to help him after he had heard of his arrest. He was seized and executed without proper trial, and was beatified in 1987. Cf. **England, Martyrs of**.

Maro (St) {2}

9 February
d. ?423. A Syrian hermit, he lived on the bank of the Orontes River between Emesa

(Homs) and Apamea and was admired by St John Chrysostom and by Theodoret of Cyrrhus. The monastery of Beit-Marun was built around his shrine and became the focus of a Monothelite sect in the C7th. They fled to Lebanon to escape persecution, and later became the Catholics of the Maronite rite.

Maro of Monte Aureo (SS) {2, 4}

15 April
? He was martyred on Monte Aureo near Novana in Piceno (Italy). According to the worthless legend of SS Nereus and Achilleus, he was one of three of the household of St Flavia Domitilla who went with her into exile. The other two were Eutyches and Victorinus. Then they returned to Rome, and were martyred in the reign of Trajan. The old Roman Martyrology listed Victorinus again on 5 September as a bishop, but it is not clear why. The two companions have been deleted.

Marolus (St) {2, 4}

23 April
C5th. From Syria, he became bishop of Milan (Italy) in 408. The Christian poet Ennodius wrote a poem in his honour.

Marsica, Deacon of *(St) {4 –deleted}*

14 March
C6th? This anonymous deacon of Marsica (Italy) was listed as martyred during the Lombard invasion.

Mar Saba, Martyrs of (SS) {2}

20 March
d. 797. Twenty monks of the monastery of Mar Saba in the Judaean Desert were suffocated by smoke in the church of the Theotokos by Bedouin raiders. The Byzantine menology preserves the names of six: Anastasius,

Cosmas, John, Patricius, Sergius and Theoctistus. A survivor of the raid named Stephen the Poet wrote an account of the event.

Martha (St) {1, 3}

29 July
d. ?80. Sister of St Lazarus and of St Mary of Bethany (often identified in the West with St Mary Magdalen), she was Christ's hostess in their house at Bethany (Lk. 10:38; Jn 11:2) and was 'anxious and troubled about many things'. Hence she is the patron of housewives, and is depicted with an attribute of housework such as a distaff or a bunch of keys. The legend of her subsequent journey to the south of France is worthless.

(Martha, Saula and Comps) *(SS) {4 –deleted}*

20 October
? The old Roman Martyrology listed them as having been martyred at Cologne (Germany), but they seem to be part of the worthless legend of St Ursula and Comps.

(Martha of Astorga) *(St) {4 –deleted}*

23 February
C3rd? She was listed as beheaded in the reign of Decius at Astorga (Spain), and is the patron of that city.

Martha of Ctesiphon (St) {2, 4}

19 April
d. 241. She was the unmarried daughter of St Pusicius, and was martyred herself at Ctesiphon, the capital of the Persian Empire, on Easter Sunday.

Martha Kim Sŏng-im (St) {1 –group}

20 July
Cf. **Mary-Magdalen Yi Yŏn-hŭi and Comps**.

473

Martha Le Bouteiller (Bl) {2}

18 March
1806–83. From near Coutances (France), in 1841 she joined the 'Sisters of Mercy of the Christian Schools' at Saint-Sauver-le-Vicomte, being received by St Mary-Magdalen Postel and having Bl Placida Viel as novice-mistress. She spent forty years there as cook, gardener and cellarer, doing the domestic work and receiving guests with joy. Extremely charitable, she lived a fervent prayer life centred on the Eucharist and Our Lady. She was beatified in 1990.

Martha the Syrian (St) {2}

5 July
d. 551. She was the mother of St Simon Stylites the Younger, and was buried near his column on the 'Wonderful Mountain' near Antioch in Syria.

Martha Wang Louzhi (St) {1 –group}

29 July
1802–61. From Zunyi in Guizhou (China), she was a widow running an inn at Qingyian before her conversion. She was appointed chef at the newly founded seminary at Yaojiaguan in 1857 and took letters from the imprisoned seminarians SS Joseph Zhang Wenlan and Paul Chen Changpin to their bishop. She was arrested and beheaded with them and St John-Baptist Luo Tingyin. Cf. **China, Martyrs of**.

Martha-Mary Wiecka (Bl) {2 –add}

1874–1904. From a wealthy Polish family of Nowy Wieck near Chelmo in Prussia, she went to Cracow in the Hapsburg Empire to join the Daughters of Charity of St Vincent de Paul in 1892. Her first posting was at the hospital in Lemberg (now Lviv in the Ukraine), and she was then at those in Bochnia and Sniatyn. At the latter place she volunteered to clean the room of a typhoid patient and caught the disease herself, dying in ecstasy. Her shrine at Sniatyn has become a place of ecumenical prayer. She was beatified in 2008.

(Martial, Laurence and Comps) (SS) {4 –deleted}

28 September
? They are listed as twenty-two Roman African martyrs of Numidia (Algeria).
(Martial, Saturninus, Epictetus,

Maprilis, Felix and Comps) (SS) {4 –deleted}

22 August
d. ?300. They are mentioned in the unreliable acta of St Aurea of Ostia, and are otherwise unknown.

Martial of Limoges (St) {2, 4}

30 June
d. ?250. He was the alleged first bishop of Limoges (France) and apostle of the Limousin (where his veneration is popular) and (according to St Gregory of Tours) was one of seven missionary bishops sent from Rome to Gaul. His extant biography is a worthless medieval forgery. Alpinian and Austriclinian were his assistant priests therein, and have been deleted from the Roman Martyrology.

Martin cf. **Marcius**.

Martin I, Pope (St) {1, 3}

13 April
d. 656. From Todi in Umbria (Italy), he was elected pope in 649. At once he condemned the Monothelite doctrine being promulgated by the reigning Emperor Constans II, and was deported as a result to the Aegean island of Naxos in 653. The following year he was tried and condemned to death at Constantinople, but was exiled to the Crimea instead. There

he died of starvation some months after his successor at Rome had been elected as pope.

Martin-of-the-Ascension Aguirre (St) {1 –group}

6 February

d. 1597. From near Pamplona in Navarra (Spain), he became a Franciscan in 1586 and was a missionary in Mexico, at Manila and finally in Japan. He was crucified at Nagasaki with SS Paul Miki and Comps. Cf. **Japan, Martyrs of**.

Martin of Braga (St) {2, 4}

20 March

d. ?579. From Pannonia (now Hungary), he became a monk in the Holy Land and somehow ended up in northwest Spain as a missionary to the barbarian Suevi, whom he helped to convert from Arianism in 560. He was bishop first of Mondoñedo and then of Braga in Portugal, and introduced monasticism in the area. Several of his writings are still extant, and he seems to be responsible for the days of the week in modern Portuguese being numbered instead of having pagan names.

Martin Cid (St) {2}

7 October

d. 1152. From Zamora (Spain), he became the abbot-founder of the Cistercian abbey of Valparaiso which was staffed by a community of monks sent from Clairvaux by St Bernard. His veneration is popular in Zamora.

Martin Gómez (Bl) {2}

27 August

d. 1627. He was a Japanese of Portuguese descent, beheaded at Nagasaki with BB Francis-of-St-Mary of Mancha and Comps. Cf. **Japan, Martyrs of**.

Martin-Luke Huin (St) {1 –group}

30 March

Cf. **Anthony Daveluy and Comps**.

Martin-of-St-Nicholas Lumberes Peralta & Melchior-of-St-Augustine Sánchez Pérez (BB) {2}

11 December

d. 1632. Martin was born in 1599 at Zaragoza (Spain) and joined the Augustinian Recollects in 1619. Melchior was born in Granada (Spain) in 1598 and became a Recollect in 1617. They were missionaries in Mexico and at Manila in the Philippines and travelled together to Nagasaki (Japan) in September 1632. Arrested two months later, they were burnt alive in public, and their ashes were thrown into the sea. They were beatified in 1989. Cf. **Japan, Martyrs of**.

Martin of Montemassico (St) {2}

3 August

d. 580. He was a hermit at Montemassico in Campania (Italy). A late and false tradition associated him with the Benedictine abbey of Montecassino.

Martin Oprządek (Bl) {2}

18 May

1884–1942. A Franciscan friar, he died of ill-treatment at Hartheim near Linz in Austria while being deported to the concentration camp at Dachau. Cf. **Poland, Martyrs of the Nazi Occupation of**.

Martin de Porres (St) {1, 3}

3 November

1569–1639. Born at Lima (Peru), his parents were a Spanish knight of Alcantara and a Negro or native American woman from Panama. He became a barber and studied surgery before becoming a Dominican lay brother at Lima. There he nursed the sick and soon became a friend of stray animals, maltreated slaves and the destitute and marginalized people of what was then one of the richest cities in the world. When he was dying the Spanish viceroy came to kneel by his bed and asked for his blessing. He was canonized in 1962.

Martin-of-León de Sancta Cruce (St) {2}

12 January
d. 1203. From León (Spain), he became an Augustinian canon regular at the monastery of St Marcellus there before it was suppressed, and then at that of St Isidore. He was a prolific ascetical writer.

Martin of Saujon (St) {2, 4}

8 May
C6th. He was an abbot of the monastery of Saujon near Saintes (France). He was not a disciple of St Martin of Tours at Marmoutier, as alleged.

Martin Tạ Đức Thịnh (St) {1 –group}

8 November
Cf. **Joseph Nguyễn Đình Nghi and Comps.**

Martin Thọ (St) {1 –group}

8 November
Cf. **Joseph Nguyễn Đình Nghi and Comps.**

(Martin of Tongeren) (St) {4 –deleted}

21 June
C4th? He is alleged to have been an early missionary bishop of Tongeren (Belgium), but was possibly a bishop of Trier (Germany) instead.

Martin of Tours (St) {1, 3}

11 November
?316–97. From what is now Szombathely in Hungary, he was the son of a pagan Roman officer and was educated at Pavia, Italy before joining the imperial cavalry himself at the age of fifteen. He was baptized five years later (according to legend, this was the result of his sharing his cloak with a poor beggar and a subsequent vision of Christ as the same beggar). Leaving the army, he became a disciple of St Hilary of Poitiers, France and later founded a community of monk-hermits at Ligugé, allegedly the first monastery in Gaul. In 372 he reluctantly became bishop of Tours and founded another monastery near that city at Marmoutier as a base for himself. He was a zealous and charismatic bishop, to the extent that relations with his aristocratic and urbane fellow bishops of Gaul were never easy. He fought both heretics and the use of the secular authorities against them. His biography was written by Sulpicius Severus, who presented him as the West's answer to the great monastic fathers of the East. Around his popular pilgrimage shrine at Tours was built a vast Romanesque basilica, but this was destroyed in the French Revolution.

(Martin of Trier) (St) {4 –deleted}

19 July
C3rd? He is listed as the tenth bishop of Trier (Germany), but there is no evidence for the tradition that he was martyred.

Martin of Vertou (St) {2, 4}

24 October
C6th. The abbot-founder of Vertou near Nantes (France), he also founded several other monasteries in Poitou. His extant biography is mostly legendary.

Martin of Vienne (St) {2, 4}

1 July
End C3rd. He was anachronistically alleged to have been sent to Vienne (France) as its third

bishop by Pope St Alexander, about 170 years before his actual time.

Martin-of-St-Felix Woodcock (Bl) {2}

7 August
1603–46. From near Preston and baptized as John, he was educated at Douai and Rome before joining the Franciscans at Douai in 1631. He went to England in 1644 and was immediately seized near Clayton-le-Woods (Lancs), imprisoned for two years at Lancaster and executed with BB Edward Bamber and Thomas Whitaker. They were beatified in 1987. Cf. **England, Martyrs of**.

Martin Wu Xuesheng (St) {1 –group}

18 February
1817–62. A farmer from Chuchangbo in Guizhou (China), he became a lay catechist and was imprisoned twice. He was then seized with SS John-Peter Néel, John Zhang Tianshen and John Chen Xianheng, and was beheaded with them at Kaiyang. Cf. **China, Martyrs of**.

Martina (St) {2, 3}

30 January
? Nothing is known about her except her name and the existence of an early cultus at Rome. There is a basilica dedicated to her in the Forum, consecrated in 677, where a sarcophagus containing her remains was found in 1634 and to which her cultus was confined in 1969. She is alleged to have been martyred in the reign of Alexander Severus, but her acta are a worthless forgery based on those of SS Prisca and Tatiana.

Martinian, Saturian and Comps (SS) {2, 4}

16 October
C5th. Four Roman African brothers, with a young woman called Maxima they were made slaves in the house of an Arian Vandal in what is now Algeria. By the command of King Genseric they were dragged to death by horses, but Maxima died in peace in a nunnery.

Martinian of Caesarea (St) {2}

13 February
d.?398. He was a hermit living near Caesarea in the Holy Land, who migrated to Athens and died there. According to his dubious story he was the target of an attempt at seduction by Zoë, a promiscuous woman, whom he persuaded to become a nun at Bethlehem instead.

Martinian of Milan (St) {2}

29 December
d. p431. He was bishop of Milan (Italy) from 423, was at the council of Ephesus in 431 and wrote against Nestorianism.

(Martyrius) (St) {4 –deleted}

23 January
C6th. A hermit in the Abruzzi (Italy), he was mentioned in the 'Dialogues' attributed to St Gregory the Great.

Martyrius and Marcian (SS) {2, 4}

25 October
d. ?351. A subdeacon and a chorister of Constantinople, they were executed there on a charge of sedition for preaching against Arianism in the reign of Valens.

Marutha (St) {2, 4}

16 February
d. a.420. One of the great Syrian fathers, he was bishop of Maiferkat (Martyropolis) in Persian Armenia (now Hazro in Turkey) and reorganized the church in the western Sassanid Empire after the vicious persecution of Shah Shapur II. He collected the relics of

many martyrs (hence the name of his city), transcribed their acta and wrote liturgical hymns in their honour. St John Chrysostom was his friend.

Mary (St) {1, 3}

15 August

C1st. The Virgin Mother of God features in the infancy narratives of the gospels of Matthew and Luke, and is referred to as having been present at the Crucifixion and at the descent of the Holy Spirit at Pentecost. There are two conflicting traditions concerning her subsequent life. One depends on John 29:25 in linking her with St John the Evangelist and thus indicating her place of death as Ephesus in Asia Minor. The other describes her death ('dormition') on the site of the Dormition Abbey at Jerusalem, her burial in the tomb now venerated in the Kidron Valley and her being taken from there bodily into heaven (her 'assumption'). She has always had a special cultus, in Greek called 'hyperdulia' (extreme veneration) to distinguish it from the veneration paid to saints ('dulia') and the worship given to God ('latria'). The intensity of this cultus is Christological in basis, as witnessed at the ecumenical council of Ephesus in 351 when the teaching that Christ was fully God and fully human led her to be declared 'Mother of God' ('Theotokos'). The dogmatic implications of this have been developed through the Church's history, and the present situation is that her conception free from original sin, her lifelong physical virginity and her assumption into heaven are all integral parts of the deposit of Catholic faith. The first recorded of her apparitions was to St Gregory Thaumaturgus in c.250, and these have featured in the Church's life ever since. Many of these (such as that at Lourdes) are celebrated with special feast days, as are the principal events of her life, certain aspects of her special status and many of the varied representations of her.

Individual apparitions notwithstanding, she is traditionally depicted in both East and West with head covered, shoes on and holding the Christ-Child.

Mary-Magdalen Albrizzi (Bl) {2}

13 May

d. 1465. From Como (Italy), she entered a nunnery at Brunate near there, became prioress and affiliated it with the Augustinian friars. She advocated frequent communion for her community in an era when this was unusual. Her cultus was approved for Como in 1907.

Mary-of-the-Hope-of-Jesus Alhama y Valera (Bl) {2 –add}

8 February

1893–1983. From Santomera in Murcia, Spain, she entered the Daughters of Calvary when aged twenty-one and founded the Handmaids of Merciful Love at Madrid in 1930. She moved to Collevanlenza near Todi in Italy, and founded the Sons of Merciful Love as a priestly society in 1951. Also, she founded there a sanctuary of Merciful Love, which has prospered. She was a noted mystic for the remaining part of her life (thirty-two years) at the sanctuary (she died aged ninety). She was beatified in 2014.

Mary-of-St-Joseph Alvarado Cardozo (Bl) {2}

2 April

1875–1967. Born at Choroní in Venezuela, she made a private vow of virginity at her first communion, identifying with Our Lady's love for the Eucharist. When young she started instructing children at home in Maracay and in the hospital founded by Fr Vincent López Aveledo, the parish priest. They founded the 'Augustinian Recollects of the Heart of Jesus' in 1901 to care for the sick, elderly and orphans: 'Those no-one wants to take are ours'. She founded thirty-seven houses in Venezuela, and was beatified in 1995.

Mary An Guozhi and Mary An Lihua (SS) {1 –group}

11 July
Cf. **Anne An Xinzhi and Comps**.

Mary-Ludovica de Angelis (Bl) {2 –add}

25 February
1880–1962. From Cassant in the Abruzzi, Italy, she joined the Daughters of Our Lady of Mercy in 1904 and was sent to Buenos Aires in Argentina, where she became superior of the community running a children's hospital. She became famous in the city as a source of counsel and comfort for people in distress and was beatified in 2004, thirty-two years after her death.

Mary-Agnes-Teresa-of-the-Blessed-Sacrament Arias Espinosa (Bl) {2 –add}

22 July
1904–81. From Ixtlán del Rio in the state of Nayarit, Mexico, as a young laywoman she attended the Mexican National Eucharistic Congress in 1924 and was inspired by the life and teaching of St Teresa of the Child Jesus to dedicate her own life as a contemplative nun fostering missionary activity. Because of anti-Christian persecution she had to leave Mexico and entered a Poor Clare convent in Los Angeles, United States of America in 1929. She founded the Poor Clare Missionaries of the Blessed Sacrament, and for men the Missionaries of Christ for the Universal Church. She died at Rome and was beatified in 2012.

Mary-Angela Astorch (Bl) {2}

2 December
1592–1665. From Barcelona (Spain), she joined the Capuchin nuns there when aged sixteen and became abbess and novice-mistress.

She drew up the constitutions for the Spanish Capuchinesses and founded the nunnery at Murcia, where she died. She was known for mystical graces, and was beatified in 1982.

Mary-of-the-Incarnation Avrillot Acarie (St) {2}

18 April
1566–1618. A Parisian married to a French government official, when young she was nicknamed 'the beautiful Acarie' but her husband was imprisoned and their property confiscated. She arranged the introduction of the Discalced Carmelite nuns of St Teresa into France (at Paris) and became a lay sister at Amiens when widowed in 1613. She died at Pontoise and was canonized in 2014.

Mary-Bartholomea Bagnesi (Bl) {2}

28 May
1511–77. From Florence (Italy), she became a Dominican nun there in 1544 and was famous for the variety of her sufferings, including demonic obsessions. Her cultus was confirmed for Florence in 1804.

Mary Baldillou y Bullit and Comps (BB) {2}

d. 1936. They were six members of the Institute of Daughters of Mary, Religious of Pious Schools, who were martyred during the Spanish Civil War. BB Mary Baldillou, Presentation Gallén, Mary-Aloysia Girón, Carmel Gómez and Clementia Riba worked at the institute's college at Valencia and were killed on the beach at Saler di Valencia on 8 August. Bl Mary de la Yglesia was headmistress of Carabanchal College in Madrid, and was killed in a suburb together with two alumni of the college, BB Mary-of-Sorrows Aguiar-Mella and Consolata Aguiar-Mella, whose family was originally from Uruguay. They were beatified in 2001. Cf. **Spanish Civil War, Martyrs of**.

Mary-Antonia Bandrés y Elósegui (Bl) {2}

27 April
1898–1919. Born in the Basque Country (Spain) of a very large family, when young she helped female factory workers with their problems. She joined the 'Daughters of Jesus' in Salamanca in 1915, and died while singing to Our Lady three years later. She was beatified in 1996.

Mary-Magdalen-Sophia Barat (St) {2}

25 May
1779–1865. From Joigny in Burgundy (France), she was the daughter of a vintner and received a vocation while studying in Paris. She founded the first house of her new congregation, the 'Society of the Sacred Heart of Jesus', at Amiens in 1801. A woman of great charm and enterprise, before her death she had established 105 houses running schools for girls throughout Europe, America and Africa. She died at Paris and was canonized in 1925.

Mary-Candida-of-the-Eucharist Barba (Bl) {2 –add}

12 June
1884–1949. From Catanzaro in Italy of a wealthy family, she was brought up in Palermo and was a carefree girl until she had a conversion experience in her teens. She wanted to become a nun, but her family was totally opposed and she only joined the Carmelites at Ragusa in 1920. As prioress and disciple of St Teresa of Lisieux, she revitalized and extended the Carmelites in Sicily, also managing to re-introduce the male friars to the island. She died of liver cancer and was beatified in 2004.

Mary-of-Jesus-Crucified Bawardy (Bl) {2}

26 August
1846–78. From Abellin near Nazareth in the Holy Land, her family were Catholics of the Melkite rite. She was orphaned when aged three and taken to Alexandria, where she avoided marriage by cropping her hair in response to a private vow. She went to Marseilles (France) and joined the Carmelites in 1867, being sent to a new foundation at Mangalore (India) in 1870. She had to return after problems with her health, and went back to the Holy Land where she founded a Carmel at Bethlehem in 1875. She died of a fall while working in the garden, and was beatified in 1983.

Mary-of-St-Cecilia Bélanger (Bl) {2}

4 September
1897–1929. From Quebec City (Canada), she was a talented girl, especially at the piano. In 1921 she joined the 'Religious of Jesus and Mary' at Sillery (founded by Bl Claudia Thévenet) and taught music to the community, but had very poor health and died after only eight years of religious life. Her spiritual life was extremely rich, however, and she was granted mystical marriage and a mystical share in the Passion. She was beatified in 1993.

Mary Beltrame Quattrocchi (St) {2}

26 August
Cf. **Louis and Mary Beltrame Quattrocchi**. She died in 1965.

Mary-Anne Biernacka (Bl) {2}

13 June
1888–1943. A Polish married woman with a family at Naumowice near Hrodno (now in Bielarus), she offered herself as a hostage in exchange for her pregnant daughter-in-law and was shot by the Nazis. Cf. **Poland, Martyrs of the Nazi Occupation of**.

Mary Bolognesi (Bl) {2 –add}

30 January
1924–80. She was an illegitimate child at Rovigo in between Padua and Ferrara in

Italy, and never left that town. Her mother married another man who was a seasonal agricultural labourer, and she grew up in an extremely poor and abusive family environment with only two years in school. Despite the complete lack of religious practice at home, she was a pious child although also rejected by neighbouring children. She suffered serious illnesses all her life, and was the subject of demonic attacks and possession. On the other hand, she achieved a high level of mystical prayer and received the stigmata. She also spent her time in serving other poor and sick people. She was beatified in 2013, only twenty-three years after her death.

Mary-Teresa Bonzel (Bl) {2 –add}

6 February
1830–1905. From Olpe near Dortmund in Germany, she became a secular Franciscan tertiary at aged twenty despite family pressure to marry. In 1865 she founded the Poor Franciscan Sisters of Perpetual Adoration, with the twofold mission of perpetual Eucharistic adoration and the care of orphaned children. The social policy of 'Kulturkampf' advocated by Otto von Bismarck persuaded her to extend activities to the United States of America, and she founded the first convent of her congregation there at Lafayette in Indiana in 1876. By the time she died she was in charge of 1500 sisters in Germany and the United States of America. She was beatified in 2013.

Mary-Bertilla Boscardin (St) {2}

20 October
1888–1922. From Vicenza (Italy), she joined the 'Teaching Sisters of St Dorothy and the Sacred Hearts' and lived a life of obedience in the care of sick people and of children. She died at Treviso and was canonized in 1961.

Mary-of-Charity Brader (Bl) {2}

27 February
1860–1943. From Kaltbrunn in the canton of St Gall, Switzerland, she joined the enclosed Franciscan convent at Maria Hilf in 1881. After a change in canon law it became possible for sisters from such convents to volunteer for mission work, and she went with a group from Maria Hilf to Chone in Ecuador in 1888. Later she was based at Tùquerres in Colombia, where she founded the 'Congregation of the Franciscan Sisters of Mary Immaculate' in order to recruit helpers. These were initially mostly Swiss, but the congregation is now well established in South America. She died at Pasto in Colombia and was beatified in 2003.

Mary-Christine-of-the-Immaculate-Conception Brando (Bl) {2}

20 January
1856–1906. From Naples in Italy, she tried her vocation with the Poor Clares and the Sacramentine nuns, but became ill both times and had to leave. So, in 1878 she moved to Torre del Greco to live communally with a sister and a few others, and this was the start of the 'Sisters, Expiatory Victims of Jesus in the Blessed Sacrament' which was established at Casoria. The charism was to combine perpetual adoration of the Blessed Sacrament with the education of girls. She died at Casoria and was beatified in 2003.

Mary-Dominica Brun Barbatini (Bl) {2}

12 May
1789–1868. From Lucca (Italy), she was widowed at the age of twenty-two when she had a son and took up her husband's business by day while helping derelict people by night. When her son died she worked wherever needed in Catholic activity. A Camillan priest taught her the charism of service to the

sick, and she founded the 'Sisters, Servants of St Camillus'. She was beatified in 1995.

Mary-Bernarda Bütler (St) {2}

19 May

1848–1924. Born in Aargau (Switzerland), she became a Poor Clare at Atstätten in 1869 and went on to be superior. Then she and six others obtained papal authorization in 1888 to go to Ecuador, and they founded the 'Franciscan Missionaries of Mary Help of Christians' at Chone. They had to leave that place in 1895 and move to Cartagena in Colombia, but other houses were founded in Austria and Brazil. She was canonized in 2008.

Mary-of-the-Transitus Cabanillas (Bl) {2}

25 August

1821–85. From Cordoba in Argentina, where she lived all her life, she became a Franciscan tertiary in 1858 and followed a vocation to educate and care for poor and neglected children. To this end she founded the 'Congregation of Third Order Franciscan Missionaries of Argentina' in 1878. This was successful, and has spread to neighbouring countries. She was beatified in 2002.

Mary de la Cabeza (Bl) {2}

9 September

C12th. From Torrejon (Spain), she was the wife of **Isidore the Farmer**. Her cultus was confirmed for Toledo in 1697.

Mary-Margaret Caiani (Bl) {2}

8 August

1863–1921. From near Pistoia (Italy), she tried to become a Benedictine nun there but left when she realized that her vocation was outside the cloister. Opening a school at Podi a Caiano, her native village, she formed a community there in 1896 which became the

'Franciscan Tertiaries of the Sacred Heart'. When she died at Florence there were twenty-one houses. She was beatified in 1989.

Mary-Magdalen of Canossa (St) {2}

10 April

1774–1835. From Verona (Italy), she was a daughter of the marquis of Canossa but he died when she was a child and her mother remarried, abandoning her children. She managed her late father's household till she was thirty-three. Then, after a brief period of hospital nursing in Venice in 1808, she founded the first house of the 'Daughters of Charity' at Verona for educating poor girls, nursing in hospitals and teaching the catechism in parishes. When she died at Verona several houses had been founded in north Italy, and the congregation is now worldwide. She was canonized in 1988.

Mary-Celine-of-the-Presentation Castang (Bl) {2 –add}

1878–97. She was from Nojals near Bergerac de Périgord in France, where her father was a storekeeper. She contracted poliomyelitis when aged four, and her father's business went bankrupt leaving the family having to beg for food. She was taken in by the Sisters of Nazareth at Bordeaux, where she became aware of her vocation. Her handicap (she had a bad limp) led to rejections, but the Poor Clares at Talence accepted her in 1896. But the hardship of her childhood had damaged her health, and she died of tuberculosis in the bones of her paralysed leg only a year later. She made her final vows on her deathbed. Her love for God, the Church and her community left such an impression that her grave became a place of pilgrimage, and her memory is revered as one who overcame physical handicap in order to reach holiness. She was beatified in 2007.

Mary-Josephine-of-Jesus-Crucified ('Giuseppina') Catanea (Bl) {2 –add}

1894–1948. From a noble family of Naples, she joined the Third Order Carmelite community at Ponti Rossi in 1918. However, she contracted tuberculosis of the spine which left her paralysed until her miraculous cure at the intercession of St Francis Xavier. As a result she became famous and proved a great spiritual director. Her community became an enclosed nunnery in 1932, and she was elected prioress in 1934, a post she held until her death. She wrote her autobiography under obedience. She was beatified in 2008.

Mary de Cerevelló (St) {2, 4}

19 September
d. 1290. From Barcelona, she became one of the first Mercedarian nuns at the new community there in 1264 and served as superior. She was especially famous for her charity, and was nicknamed 'Mary of Help'. Her cultus was confirmed for Barcelona in 1692.

Mary-of-the-Passion de Chappotin de Neuville (Bl) {2}

15 November
1839–1904. From Nantes in France, she joined the Poor Clares in 1860 but had to leave after a serious illness. Then she joined the 'Society of Mary Reparatrix' in 1864 and was sent to Madurai in India in 1865. Serious dissensions caused her to leave the Society, with some others, and this led her to found a new missionary institute, based at St Brieuc in France, in 1877. An awareness of her old Franciscan charism influenced her spirituality in doing this, and resulted in the 'Franciscan Missionaries of Mary' being definitively approved in 1896. Members of this have been sent as missionaries worldwide, including the most dangerous places such as Imperial China. She died at San Remo in Italy and was beatified in 2002.

Mary-Vincenza-of-St-Dorothy Chávez Orosco (Bl) {2}

30 July
1867–1949. From Cotija in Michoacán state, Mexico, she was treated at the parish hospital for pleurisy in 1892 and received a vocation to serve sick people. Starting at the same hospital, she went on to found the 'Servants of the Holy Trinity and the Poor' in 1905 and became the superior-general in 1913. The congregation spread in and around Guadalajara, but the anti-clerical Mexican Revolution in 1911 raised a serious danger. This the sisters ignored, successfully continuing their religious life and work as usual. She died at Guadalajara and was beatified in 1997.

Mary-Teresa Chiramel Mankidiyan (Bl) {2}

8 June
1876–1926. From Puthenchira in Kerala, India, she was from a family which had once been wealthy but had become impoverished through paying dowries. After taking a private vow of chastity when aged ten she became a visionary and penitent. In 1913 she was allowed by her bishop to build a prayer house, and soon attracted companions to her life of eremitic prayer and penance with service to needy people regardless of caste. This was the beginning of the 'Congregation of the Holy Family', which is now international. She died of complications caused by her diabetes and was beatified in 2000.

Mary-Magdalen Cho (St) {1 –group}

26 September
Cf. **Sebastian Nam I-gwan and Comps**.

Mary-Raphaela Cimatti (Bl) {2}

23 June {2} {2, 3}
1861–1945. From Ravenna (Italy), when little she taught her brothers and catechized in

her parish, and went on to join the 'Hospitaller Sisters of Mercy' in 1890. She settled at Alatri near Rome as the superior, but ended up as an ordinary nun who nursed wounded soldiers in the Second World War when aged 83. She was beatified in 1996.

Mary Clopas (St) {2, 4}

9 April

C1st. The wife of Clopas or Alpheus (cf. Jn 19:25) and the mother of St James the Less, she was one of the 'three Marys' who followed Christ in his final journey to Jerusalem and who witnessed the Crucifixion. The legends about her subsequent life are worthless. She is depicted carrying a pot of ointment or a jar of spices.

Mary-Crucified Curcio (Bl) {2 –add}

4 July

1877–1957. From a large family of Ispica in Sicily, as a child she was inspired by the life of St Teresa of Avila and joined the Carmelite Third Order in 1890. She was inspired by the idea of a missionary Carmel, uniting the contemplative life with an apostolic outreach, and ended up settling at Santa Marinella north of Rome with some disciples in 1925. This was the start of the 'Carmelite Missionary Sisters of St Teresa of the Child Jesus', which spread to Brazil in her lifetime. She died at the mother house and was beatified in 2005.

Mary-Alphonsa Danil Ghattas (Bl) {2 –add}

25 March

1843–1927. She was born into a wealthy Latin Catholic Palestinian family of Jerusalem, and when aged fourteen joined the French congregation of Sisters of St Joseph. As a result of supernatural visions that she received, she joined in the foundation of the Dominican

Sisters of the Holy Rosary of Jerusalem. This is the only religious order that has arisen in the Latin Patriarchate of Jerusalem, and has spread among Latin Catholic Arabs in the Middle East. It is especially interested in the education of girls. She was beatified in 2009.

Mary-of-Jesus Deluil-Martiny (Bl) {2}

27 February

1841–84. From Marseilles, she founded the 'Daughters of the Heart of Jesus' to give consolation to the Sacred Heart of Jesus for the wrongs done to it. The congregation's headquarters was at Berchem-Anvers near Mecheln, Belgium and the Rule was based on that of the Jesuits. She was killed by a gardener whom she had sacked for negligence, and was beatified in 1989.

Mary-Michaela-of-the-Blessed-Sacrament Desmaisières (St) {2}

24 August

1809–65. The Viscountess of Jorbalán was born at Madrid (Spain), educated by the Ursulines and then lived with her family at Guadalajara. There she helped prostitutes and sufferers of epidemic disease, and to further her work for the former she founded the institute of 'Handmaids of the Blessed Sacrament and of Charity' in 1848. She died of cholera at Valencia after nursing her own nuns during an epidemic, and was canonized in 1934.

Mary-Adolphine Dierk (St) {1 –group}

9 July

Cf. **Gregory Grassi and Comps**.

Mary-Henrietta Dominici (Bl) {2}

21 February

1829–94. From near Turin (Italy), she joined the 'Sisters of St Anne and of Providence' in 1850 and became the superior in 1861, which she remained until death. A confidante of

St John Bosco, she wrote an autobiography and was beatified in 1978.

Mary-of-the-Divine-Heart Droste zu Vischering (Bl) {2}

8 June

1863–99. A noblewoman born at Münster (Germany), she lacked the health to enter religious life until she recognized a vocation to help destitute and unchaste girls. She became a 'Good Shepherd Sister' at Münster when aged twenty-four, and was made superior at Oporto (Portugal) when aged thirty. Her visions of the Sacred Heart led Pope Leo XIII to consecrate the world to it in the year of her early death. She was a very beautiful woman. She was beatified in 1975.

Mary-Rose Durocher (Bl) {2}

6 October

1811–49. Born at Saint-Antoine-sur-Richelieu in Quebec (Canada), she helped her brother, a priest, in his parish work despite not having good health. She set up the first Marian sodality in Canada and founded the 'Sisters of the Sacred Name of Jesus' at Longueil, chiefly to care for girls. She was beatified in 1982.

Mary Du Tianshi and Mary-Magdalen Du Fengju (St) {1 –group}

29 June

1858 and 1881–1900. They were mother and daughter, from Dujiadun near Shenxian in Hebei (China). During a Boxer raid they hid in a small marsh near their village with two sons and another daughter of the family, but were discovered. The daughters ran away, but St Mary-Magdalen was caught and shot. St Mary and her two sons were killed in the marsh. The villagers buried them, including St Mary-Magdalen who was still alive but who volunteered to be buried in order to go to heaven. Cf. **China, Martyrs of**.

Mary Du Zhaozhi (St) {1 –group}

28 June

1849–1900. From a Catholic family of Qifengzhuang in Hebei (China), she married and moved to Dujiatun. Her son became a priest. While visiting a cousin and his wife in Wangjiatian she was killed with them by a gang of Boxers at Jieshuiwang near Shenxian. Cf. **China, Martyrs of**.

Mary of Egypt (St) {2}

1 April

C5th. According to her story, she was an Egyptian actress and high-class prostitute at Alexandria. She was converted at the Holy Sepulchre at Jerusalem (where there is a chapel dedicated to her) and then fled into the desert beyond the Jordan to spend the rest of her life doing penance. She was discovered living in a pit by St Zosimus, but on his second visit he found her dead. He then buried her with the help of a lion which dug the grave. She is depicted naked but covered with her long hair and holding loaves, or with the lion that dug her grave, or kneeling before a skull.

Mary-of-the-Sacred-Heart Encarnación Rosal (Bl) {2}

27 October

1820–86. Born at Quetzaltenango in Guatemala, in 1837 she joined the Bethlemite congregation founded there by Bl Peter de Betancur but discovered that the founder's charism was being lost. She became prioress in 1855 and revised the constitutions to restore the charism, but the older sisters refused to accept the changes and she left to found a new house in 1861. (This reformed 'Institute of Bethlemite Sisters' is now in thirteen countries.) She had a special devotion to the sorrows of the Sacred Heart and to reparation for humanity's sins, and was beatified in 1997.

Mary Fan Kun (St) {1 –group}

28 June
Cf. **Lucy Wang Cheng and Comps**.

Mary-Teresa Fasce (Bl) {2}

18 June
1881–1947. From near Genoa (Italy), she entered the Augustinian nunnery of St Rita in Cascia in 1906. She became abbess in 1920, and was repeatedly re-elected until her death. Her life's work was the propagation of devotion to St Rita of Cascia, and she built up a great pilgrimage centre. Also around the shrine she founded an orphanage, a seminary, a hospital and a retreat house. Her health was very poor long before she died. She was beatified in 1997.

Mary-of-the-Angels Fontanella (Bl) {2}

16 December
1661–1717. A noblewoman born at Baldinero near Turin (Italy), she became a Carmelite at Turin in 1616. For fourteen years she was tormented by violent temptations to blasphemy. She founded the Carmel of Moncaglieri (which still exists) and was beatified in 1865.

Mary-Victoria Fornari Strata (Bl) {2}

15 December
1562–1617. A noblewoman of Genoa (Italy), she was married with six children but was widowed in 1589. After she had brought up her children she founded a congregation of contemplative nuns called the 'Blue Annunciades'. They have a charism based on the hidden life of Our Lady at Nazareth and part of their otherwise white habit is sky-blue in her honour(hence the name). She was superior of the first house at Genoa, died there and was beatified in 1828.

Mary-Assumption González Trujilano and Comps (BB) {2 –add}
d. 1936. Three members of the Franciscan Missionaries of the Mother of the Divine Shepherd were martyred in Madrid during the Spanish Civil War. The actual dates of their martyrdoms are unclear, as two of them were imprisoned and killed secretly, while the third was killed after a riot when she was dragged out of a hospital where she was being treated. They were beatified in 2013. Cf. **Spanish Civil War, Martyrs of** and list in appendix.

Mary Fu Guilin (St) {1 –group}

20 July
1863–1900. From Luopo in Hebei (China), she took a private vow of virginity and taught in the parish school at Daliucun near Wuyi. During a Boxer raid she was beheaded. Cf. **China, Martyrs of**.

Mary-Frances-of-the-Wounds-of-Our-Lord Gallo (St) {2}

6 October
1715–91. From a bourgeois family of Naples (Italy), she had a father who was brutal and avaricious and who was especially cruel when she refused to marry the man he had chosen for her. In 1731 he let her become a Franciscan tertiary, and she lived with her parents until she found a priest who would employ her as his housekeeper. This she was for thirty-eight years before her death at Naples. She was favoured with extraordinary graces, including mystical marriage and the stigmata. She was canonized in 1867.

Mary-Clare Galvão Meixa de Moura Telles (Bl) {2 –add}

1 December
1843–99. From Amadora near Lisbon (Portugal), she initially became a Capuchiness in

France in 1869 but left the following year to found a new congregation in Portugal. The Franciscan Hospitallers of the Immaculate Conception began in Lisbon in 1871. She died at Lisbon, and was beatified in 2011.

Mary-of-Montserrat García Solanas and Comps (BB) {2 –add}

23 July

d. 1936. During the Spanish Civil War, the twenty-five members of the convent of Minim nuns at Barcelona were arrested and imprisoned by the Republican authorities. Ten of them were shot, including the superior Bl Mary-of-Montserrat and a laywoman helper who was her blood sister. This was an especially disgusting atrocity even by the standards of the time, since five of the nuns were aged over sixty. They were beatified in 2013. Cf. **Spanish Civil War, Martyrs of** and list in appendix.

Mary-of-Guadalupe García Zavala (St) {2 –add}

1878–1963. From Zapopan in Jalisco, Mexico, she became aware of a religious vocation when in her twenties and founded the 'Handmaids of St Margaret Mary and the Poor' with the help of her spiritual director. The charism was one of exterior and interior poverty while nursing poor sick people in their hospital. After the Mexican Revolution in 1911, when the government tried to suppress the Church, she, her sisters and their hospital were left alone because of the witness to charity that they gave. Eleven other foundations were made in her lifetime, and the congregation is now international. She was canonized in 2013.

Mary Gengoro (Bl) {2}

16 August

d. 1620. A Japanese, she was the wife of Bl Thomas Gengoro and mother of Bl James. The whole family was crucified at Kokura.

Cf. **Simon Kiyota and Comps** and **Japan, Martyrs of**.

Mary-Teresa-of-Jesus Gerhardinger (Bl) {2}

9 May

1797–1879. Born near Regensburg (Bavaria), she trained as a teacher and, when aged eighteen, was told by her bishop that she would be useful helping to found a community of teaching sisters not confined to monasteries but making the rounds of poor villages. This resulted in the 'School Sisters of Notre Dame'. She died at Munich after forty-six years in vows, and was beatified in 1985.

Mary-of-St-John Giner Gomis (Bl) {2}

13 November

1874–1936. From Tortosa in Spain, she became a Claretian Sister at Valencia in 1893 and became superior of a new school and community at Puerto de Saguno near the city in 1925. In 1931 the foundation was suppressed by the anti-clerical Republican government, and she went to live at Carcagente. However, she was picked up and shot during the Civil War. She was beatified in 2001. Cf. **Spanish Civil War, Martyrs of**.

Mary-of-Peace Giuliani (St) {1 –group}

9 July

Cf. **Gregory Grassi and Comps**.

Mary Goretti (St) {1}

6 July

1890–1902. Born at Corinaldo near Ancona, Italy, she showed clear signs of youthful holiness despite being illiterate. She was being harassed by a youth who was sexually obsessed with her, and one day they were left alone in their village of Nettuno while the rest of the population were working in the fields. He tried to rape her, she resisted successfully and he stabbed her to death. About forty miracles were ascribed to her intercession, and her canonization in 1950 was attended by her mother, family and repentant murderer.

Mary-of-the-Passion-of-Our-Lord-Jesus-Christ Grazia Tarallo (Bl) {2 –add}

27 July
1866–1912. From Barra near Naples in Italy, she made a private vow of virginity when aged five and entered the local nunnery of the 'Sisters, Crucified Adorers of the Eucharist' in 1891. She performed many different tasks in the nunnery, and was always edifying in her life of charity and prayer. This was especially the case in her following the community's charism of adoration of the Blessed Sacrament. She was beatified in 2006.

Mary-Antonia Grillo Michel (Bl) {2}

26 January
1855–1944. She was from a well-placed family (her father was head physician of the hospital) of Alessandria in Piedmont (Italy). In 1877 she married an army officer, but was widowed in 1891 and became prey to depression which only lifted when she decided to spend her life in helping the poor. In 1893 she founded the 'Little Shelter of Divine Providence' at Alessandria, and became founder-superior of the 'Little Sisters of Divine Providence' in 1899. By the time she died these had twenty-five houses in Italy, nineteen in Brazil and seven in Argentina. She was beatified in 1998.

Mary-Ermellina-of-Jesus Grivot (St) {1 –group}

9 July
Cf. **Gregory Grassi and Comps**.

Mary Guo Lizhi (St) {1 –group}

7 July
1835–1900. From Hujiacun near Shenxian in Hebei (China), she had many children and grandchildren whom she brought up to be Catholics. She was beheaded with two of her daughters-in-law, two grandsons and two granddaughters by a gang of Boxers. Cf. **China, Martyrs of**.

Mary-of-the-Incarnation Guyart-Martin (Bl) {2}

30 April
1599–1672. Born in Tours (France), when aged nineteen she was left a widow with a small son. After involvement in business she joined the Ursulines in 1630 and went to Canada for the rest of her life nine years later. (The Ursulines were the first religious foundation in the colony, which was then French.) She was a noted mystic, and her autobiography and letters were published by her son (who became a Benedictine). She was beatified in 1980.

Mary-Magdalen Han Yŏng-i (St) {1 –group}

29 December
Cf. **Benedicta Hyŏn Kyŏng-nyŏn and Comps**.

Mary-Teresa-of-the-Sacred-Heart Haze (Bl) {2}

7 January
1782–1876. From Liege (Belgium), her family was rich and she had a happy childhood broken off by chaos and exile in the Revolution. She wanted to become a religious but the new civil law prevented this when she returned home, so she opened a free school instead. In 1832 she finally founded the 'Daughters of the Cross', which spread worldwide to help orphans and women in prison and also to work in education and nursing. She died at Liege and was beatified in 1991.

Mary-Elizabeth Hesselblad (Bl) {2}

24 April
1870–1957. From Fåglavik in Västergötland, Sweden, she was raised as a Lutheran and was a housemaid before migrating to the United States of America in 1888. As a nurse in New York she came into contact with Catholic patients and chaplains, her first contact with Catholics. A period as a house-nurse in a convent led eventually to her conversion in 1902 and she moved back to Sweden to become a Brigittine in 1906. She founded houses of her order in Rome and Sweden, and was active in the ecumenical movement after the Second World War. She was beatified in 2000.

Mary-Refuge de Hinojosa Naveros and Comps (Bl) {2}

18 November
d. 1936. When the Spanish Civil War broke out in early 1936 the community of the Visitation at Madrid moved out of the city, leaving a group of six nuns in her charge. They tried to live unobtrusively but were noticed and harassed. Finally their apartment was raided by a patrol of anarchists and they were taken by van to a vacant site to be shot. The bullets missed Mary-Cecilia Cendoya Araquistan, who ran away but immediately gave herself up and was shot five days later. They were beatified in 1998. Cf. **Spanish Civil War, Martyrs of** and list in appendix.

Mary-Magdalen Hŏ Kye-im (St) {1 –group}

26 September
Cf. **Sebastian Nam I-gwan and Comps**.

Mary-Crescentia Höss (St) {2}

5 April
1682–1744. From Kaufbeuren in Bavaria (Germany), she had mystical experiences from an early age and was admitted to the Mayerhof convent of Franciscan tertiaries without a dowry in 1703 at the request of the Protestant mayor. This did not make her popular there, but her holiness overcame the resentment and she became novice-mistress and superior. She became famous for her sanctity, and was canonized in 2001.

Mary-Julia Ivanišević and Comps (BB) {2 –add}

15 December
d. 1941. They were five Daughters of Divine Charity of Drina, who were martyred at Goražde in Bosnia-Herzegovina. The others were: Catherine Ivanišević, Josephine Bojanc, Josephine Fabjan and Teresa Banja. They belonged to a convent at Pale near Sarajevo, where they were noted for caring for anybody in need regardless of religious affiliation. In December 1941 they were driven out of their convent by Communist partisans, who forced them to march through deep snow without proper clothing to Gorazde. There they were locked in a barracks, and the same evening their captors tried to rape them. They jumped from a window, were picked up, stabbed and thrown into a river the Drina after which their congregation was named. They were beatified in 2011.

Mary-Pillar Izquierdo Albero (Bl) {2}

27 August
1906–45. From a poor family of Zaragoza in Spain, she became a worker in a shoe factory but fractured her pelvis by falling off a tram in 1926. Complications set in, leaving her blind and paralysed, yet she became known for her spiritual discernment. In 1939 her health suddenly improved and she set about founding a missionary congregation. The first attempt was a failure; the second was in 1942 but she was forced out of the nascent congregation and was in the process of making a third attempt at

Madrid when she died at San Sebastiano. Her disciples became the 'Missionary Workers of Jesus and Mary' in 1948, and she was beatified in 2001.

Mary-Bernardina Jabłońska (Bl) {2}

23 September
1878–1940. From near Zamość in Poland, when young she joined a youth group founded by St Albert Chmielowski to help very poor people and became his chief helper in this work at Cracow. She was the first superior-general of the 'Albertine Sisters', an institute of Franciscan tertiaries founded by her spiritual father to bring together his female disciples. She died at Cracow and was beatified in 1997.

Mary-Amandina Jeuris (St) {1 –group}

9 July
Cf. **Gregory Grassi and Comps**.

Mary-of-the-Cross Jugan (St) {2}

29 August
1792–1879. From St Malo (France) and baptized as Joanne, she joined the 'Eudist Third Order' and worked as a domestic and hospital servant in St Servan. With two others she set up an old peoples' home in 1839 and supported it by begging. Thus began the 'Little Sisters of the Poor'. She was initially the superior but proved incompetent in administration and was deposed, but her congregation had 177 houses at her death. She was canonized in 2009.

Mary-Restituta Kafka (Bl) {2}

30 March
1894–1943. A shoemaker's daughter of what is now Brno in the Czech Republic, she grew up in Vienna (Austria) and joined the 'Franciscan Sisters of Christian Charity' in 1914, becoming a surgical nurse. After the 'Anschluss' she made her rejection of Nazism quite clear, and when she hung crucifixes in every room of a new wing of the hospital she was arrested. Charged with this and with writing a poem mocking Hitler, she was beheaded in 1942 and beatified in 1998.

Mary Karłowska (Bl) {2}

24 March
1865–1935. From Słupówka near Poznan in Poland (then Posen in Germany), she wished to help the prostitutes for which Posen was notorious by running refuges where they could experience God's love and learn a respectable trade. This led to her founding the 'Good Shepherd Sisters of Divine Providence' for that work, and these spread throughout Poland. She died near Toruń and was beatified in 1997.

Mary-Catherine Kasper (Bl) {2}

2 February
1820–98. Born at Dernbach near Limburg (Germany), she collected a few companions in her home village to look after poor sick people and orphans. At the time of her death these had become the 'Poor Handmaids of Jesus Christ', an international congregation numbering in thousands. Her charism was personal humility in service. She was beatified in 1978.

Mary-of-the-Holy-Birth Kerguin (St) {1 –group}

9 July
Cf. **Gregory Grassi and Comps**.

Mary-Magdalen Kim Ŏ-bi (St) {1 –group}

24 May
Cf. **Augustine Yi Kwang-hŏn and Comps**.

Mary-Magdalen Kiyota (Bl) {2}

27 August
d. 1620. Wife of Bl Simon Kiyota, she was crucified with him and his companions at Kokura in Japan. Cf. **Japan, Martyrs of**.

Mary of Korea (Bl) {2}

10 September
1622. Wife of Bl Anthony, she was beheaded at the 'Great Martyrdom' at Nagasaki (Japan) with her family. Cf. **Japan, Martyrs of** and **Great Martyrdom at Nagasaki**.

Mary-Faustina Kowalska (St) {2}

5 October
1905–38. Born in Glogowiec (Poland) of poor but devout peasants, she worked as a housemaid after leaving school at sixteen until she joined the 'Sisters of Our Lady of Mercy' in 1925. She lived in various Polish houses of her order, and had many private revelations leading her to promote the devotion to the Divine Mercy. She died of tuberculosis at Cracow and was canonized in 2000.

Mary-Teresa Kowalska (Bl) {2}

25 July
1902–41. A Capuchiness, she died of ill-treatment at the concentration camp of Dzałdowo. Cf. **Poland, Martyrs of the Nazi Occupation of**.

Mary-Antonina Kratochwil (Bl) {2}

2 October
1881–1942. A 'School Sister of Our Lady', she died of ill-treatment at Stanisławów in Poland. Cf. **Poland, Martyrs of the Nazi Occupation of**.

Mary-Teresa-of-Jesus Le Clerc (Bl) {2}

9 January
1576–1622. From a wealthy family of Remiremont, Lorraine (now in France), when young she was hedonistic but then became a religious under the guidance of St Peter Fourier and founded the 'Congregation of Our Lady, Canonesses of St Augustine' in order to educate girls ('rich and poor alike'). Called 'a woman of profound silence', she was a noted mystic. Dying at Nancy, she was beatified in 1947. She is usually referred to as 'Alix', her baptismal name.

Mary Teresa Ledochowska (Bl) {2}

6 June
1863–1922. Born at Loosdorf (Austria) of a famous noble family of the Hapsburg Empire, she dedicated herself to the abolition of slavery and the evangelization of Africa and founded the 'Sodality of St Peter Claver for African Missions' in 1894 to the latter end. She was also much involved in publishing work for African catechesis. She was beatified in 1975.

Mary-of- Jesus López de Rivas (Bl) {2}

13 September
1560–1640. Born near Segovia (Spain), she became a disciple of St Teresa of Jesus and entered the reformed convent at Toledo where she stayed for sixty-three years, serving as prioress and novice-mistress. She was beatified in 1976.

Mary-of-the-Cross Mackillop (St) {2}

8 August
1842–1909. From Melbourne (Australia), she started work as a governess when young in order to support her family and went to Penola, South Australia. Finding that the Catholic children of the vast parish had no schooling whatsoever, she started the 'Sisters of St Joseph of the Sacred Heart' in 1866 in order to 'destroy the secular spirit of education among our schools'. The order multiplied in Australia and New Zealand, running schools,

orphanages and nursing homes and relying entirely on donations. She suffered a lot of human opposition and poor health. She was canonized in 2010.

Mary Magdalen (St) {1, 3}

22 July

C1st. One of the Galilean women who ministered to Christ, she had had 'seven devils' expelled from her (Mk 16:9) and was one of the first witnesses of Christ's Resurrection. The Western Church used to follow the opinion of St Gregory the Great in identifying her with the unnamed sinner in Luke 7:37; 8:2 and with Mary of Bethany, the sister of Martha and Lazarus. This led her to be depicted in the West as having long, unbound hair (usually blonde) and carrying a jar of unguent. The Eastern tradition never accepted this identification, and it is now discredited. The legend connecting her with France is worthless.

Mary-Barbara-of-the-Holy-Trinity Maix (Bl) {2 –add}

17 March

1818–73. From Vienna (Austria), as a young woman she became interested in the religious education of young workers and wished to emigrate to North American as a missionary. However, she could only arrange a sea passage to Brazil, and ended up in Porto Allegre. There she founded the Sisters of the Immaculate Heart of Mary. She died at Rio de Janeiro, and was beatified in 2010.

Mary Mancini of Pisa (Bl) {2}

22 December

d. 1431. A noblewoman of Pisa (Italy), she received extraordinary mystical graces from childhood, for example the visibility of her Guardian Angel. She married when aged twelve and was left a widow with two children at sixteen. She married again, but lost her second

husband eight years later. Then she became a Dominican tertiary and joined Bl Clare Gambacorta at her reformed foundation, succeeding her as prioress. Her cultus was confirmed for Pisa and the Dominicans in 1855.

Mary-Dominica Mantovani (Bl) {2}

3 February

1862–1934. She was from a farming family of Castelletto di Brensone in Italy, and remained there all her life. When a teenager she became a disciple of Bl Joseph Nascimbeni. In 1892 she helped him in the foundation of the 'Little Sisters of the Holy Family' and became the first superior, a position she held until death. She was beatified in 2003.

Mary Mardosewicz and Comps (BB) {2}

4 September

d. 1943. They were eleven sisters of the Holy Family of Nazareth at Nowogródek in eastern Poland, now Navahradak in Bielarus. Their convent had been founded in 1929, but the town was overrun by the Soviet Union in 1939 and by the Third Reich in 1941. The German policy was to destroy all aspects of Polish culture, and the sisters were summoned to Gestapo headquarters, driven to a wood near the town and shot. They were beatified in 2000. See list in appendix.

Mary-Magdalen Martinengo (Bl) {2}

27 July

1687–1737. From Brescia (Italy), she became a Capuchin nun there and was a capable novice-mistress and prioress. She was beatified in 1900.

Mary-of-the-Pillar-of-St-Francis-Borgia Martínez García and Comps (BB) {2}

24 July

d. 1936. The city of Guadalajara (Spain) was captured in 1936 by the Republican militia during the Civil War, and the Carmelite community there dispersed to private houses in secular dress. Three of them together were recognized as religious by a militiaman they met on the road, and he took them at gunpoint to his comrades and said that they were nuns and should be shot. His comrades obliged. Mary-of-the-Angels-of St-Joseph Valtierra Tordesillas died instantly, Mary-of-the-Pillar-of-St-Francis-Borgia Martínez García was mortally wounded and died clutching a crucifix, and Teresa-of-the-Child-Jesus García García was told to say 'Success to Communism' but replied 'Success to Jesus Christ' and was shot with a revolver. They were beatified in 1987. Cf. **Spanish Civil War, Martyrs of**.

Mary-Pia Mastena (Bl) {2 –add}

28 June
1880–1951. From Bovolone near Verona, Italy, she joined the 'Sisters of Mercy' at Verona in 1901, qualified as a teacher and became the superior of a new foundation at Miane near Treviso in 1908. Being called to a more contemplative life, she tried the Cistercian nunnery of San Giacomo di Veglia in 1927 but could not abandon the vocation to teach and left. In 1930 she started a new institute, the 'Sisters of the Holy Face', at San Flor, with a charism of 'propagating, repairing and renewing Jesus' gentle image in souls'. She died on a visit to Rome and was beatified in 2005.

Mary de Mattias (St) {2}

20 August
1805–66. From Vallecorsa near Frosenone (Italy), when aged seventeen she was inspired by St Caspar del Bufalo to found a congregation of sisters teaching girls corresponding to that which he was founding for teaching boys. In 1834 she opened her first school at Acuto, and this was the beginning of the 'Sisters, Adorers of the Precious Blood'. When she

died they were running about seventy schools. She was canonized in 2003.

Mary-Dominica Mazzarello (St) {2}

14 May
1837–81. From a peasant family of Mornese near Acqui (Italy), she helped on the farm as a child and then joined the 'Pious Union of Mary Immaculate' to lead a life of charity. She attracted companions and thus her institute, the 'Daughters of Mary Auxiliatrix', came into being. Under the direction of St John Bosco it received full canonical formation and status, and undertook for girls what the Salesians were doing for boys. She reluctantly became the first superior-general in 1874, died after a long illness at Nizza Monferrato and was canonized in 1951.

Mary-Louise Merkert (Bl) {2 –add}
1817–72. From Nysa in Silesia (now in Poland, then part of Prussia), she looked after her widowed mother until 1842 then joined a small group of laywomen who devoted themselves to nursing sick people in their homes. They were advised to join the 'Sisters of Mercy of St Charles Borromeo' at Prague in 1846, where they received a religious formation. In 1850, she and one other left to found the 'Grey Sisters of St Elizabeth' at Nysa, following their original charism. The mother house of the new congregation was established there in 1865, and she became the first superior. In her twenty-two years of service in this post she oversaw the foundation of ninety houses staffed by about 500 sisters. She was beatified in 2007.

Mary-Seraphina-of-the-Sacred-Heart Micheli (Bl) {2 –add}

24 March
1849–1911. She was from Imer near Trentino (Italy, then in Austria) and when a teenager

received a vision of Our Lady instructing her to found a new congregation with special devotions to the Holy Trinity, Our Lady and the angels. This was not easy, as she fled pressure to marry and spent seven years working as a nurse in Germany. She only returned when her parents died, and then wandered through Italy until she gathered a group of disciples at Caserta in 1891. This was the beginning of the Sisters of the Angels, who managed an orphanage. She died at another foundation at Facchio near Benevento, and was beatified in 2011.

Mary-Eugenia-of-Jesus Milleret de Brou
(St) {2}

10 March
1817–98. From Metz (France), her home was irreligious and her family broke up in her teens. She received faith when aged seventeen and founded her 'Congregation of Our Lady of the Assumption' five years later. Her charism was summarized in the latter's motto: 'Pray and Teach'. She was canonized in 2007.

Mary-Anne Mogas Fontcuberta (Bl) {2}

3 July
1827–86. An orphan girl, she was brought up in Barcelona (Spain) where she met three exclaustrated Capuchins trying to start a school. She joined them at Ripoll where the school was set up, and the 'Capuchins of the Divine Shepherdess' were thus founded. She died at her other foundation in Madrid after a monastic career inspired by love of Our Lady and was beatified in 1996.

Mary-of the-Sanctuary-of-St-Aloysius-Gonzaga Moragas Cantarero (Bl) {2}

16 August
1881–1936. Her father was the royal purveyor of pharmaceuticals at Madrid (Spain) and she qualified as a pharmacist herself. In 1915 she entered the Carmel at Madrid and served as prioress and as novice-mistress. She was prioress for a second term when the convent was attacked by an anti-clerical mob on 20 July 1936 on the outbreak of the Spanish Civil War, and the community dispersed for safety. On 14 August she was arrested, interrogated and shot the following day. She was beatified in 1998. Cf. **Spanish Civil War, Martyrs of**.

Mary-Magdalen-Catherine Morano
(Bl) {2}

26 March
1847–1908. Born near Turin (Italy), she had to start to earning when she was eight years old at the death of her father, and she went on to become a teacher and a catechist. In 1878 she entered the congregation of 'Daughters of Mary Auxiliatrix' founded six years previously by St John Bosco, and was sent to Sicily in 1881. She was a catechist in Catania diocese until her death, believing that the formation of a Christian conscience was the basis of personal maturity and of social improvement. She was beatified in 1994.

Mary-of-St-Justus Moreau (St) {1 –group}

9 July
Cf. **Gregory Grassi and Comps**.

(Mary, Mother of John Mark) (St)
{4 –deleted}

29 June
C1st. She is mentioned in the Acts of the Apostles (12:12) as the mother of John, surnamed Mark. From the text it appears that her house in Jerusalem was a place of assembly for the apostles and the faithful generally. Subsequent traditions about her are conflicting.

(Mary-Magdalen of Nagasaki 1) (St)
{1 –group}

15 October
1610–34. A Japanese consecrated virgin, she was martyred at Nagasaki by being hung up by the hands and left to die. This took thirteen days. She was canonized in 1987 with SS Laurence Ruiz and Comps. Cf. **Japan, Martyrs of**.

(Mary-Magdalen of Nagasaki 2) (Bl) {2}

15 October
d. 1627. A Japanese Dominican tertiary and a relative of the daimyos of Bungo, she was burnt at Nagasaki with BB Francis-of-St-Mary of Mancha and Comps for having received missionaries as guests. Cf. **Japan, Martyrs of**.

Mary-Clare Nanetti (St) {1 –group}

9 July
Cf. **Gregory Grassi and Comps**.

Mary-Anne-of-Jesus Navarro de Guevara (Bl) {2}

27 April
1565–1624. Nicknamed the 'Lily of Madrid', she was born in that city in Spain, became a Discalced Mercedarian there and was famous for her life of penance. She was beatified in 1783.

Mary-Eve-of-Providence Noisezewska (Bl) {2}

19 December
1885–1942. A Sister of the Immaculate Conception, she was shot by the Nazis at Słonim in Poland with Bl Mary-Martha-of-Jesus Wołowska. Cf. **Poland, Martyrs of the Nazi Occupation of**.

Mary of Oignies (Bl) {2}

23 June
d. 1213. From Nivelles (Belgium), she married when young but persuaded her husband not to consummate the marriage. They turned their house into a leper hospital where they nursed, and when she was widowed she became a hermit attached to the church at Oignies.

Mary-of-Jesus d'Oultremont d'Hooghvorst (Bl) {2}

22 February
1818–78. A noblewoman from near Liege (Belgium), she was married with four children but was widowed in 1847 and refused to remarry, choosing instead to found a new religious congregation. The 'Sisters of Mary Reparatrix' thus began at Strasbourg in 1887, with the aim of making the name of Jesus better known and loved in the world. They spread through western Europe and were established in India and on the Mascarene Islands in the Indian Ocean. She died at Florence and was beatified in 1997.

Mary Pak Kun-a-gi Hui-sun (St) {1 –group}

3 September
Cf. **John Pak Hu-jae and Comps**.

Mary-Magdalen Pak Pong-sŏn (St)
{1 –group}

26 September
Cf. **Sebastian Nam I-gwan and Comps**.

Mary-Assumpta Pallotta (Bl) {2}

7 April
1878–1905. From a poor family living at Force near Ancona (Italy), in 1898 she joined the Franciscan Missionaries of Mary after the pope dispensed her from the obligation of a dowry. She was at Grottaferrata and Florence

before leaving with a group of sisters for China in 1904. They established themselves in the province of Shanxi, at a place called Dongerkou where they founded an orphanage. She died there of typhus. She was humble, given to hard work, simple and uneducated yet very prayerful and faithful. She was beatified in 1954.

Mary-Magdalen dei Panatieri (Bl) {2}

13 October
1443–1503. From Trino near Vercelli (Italy), she modelled herself on St Catherine of Siena, becoming a Dominican tertiary in her own home and being occupied with charitable works among her neighbours. Her cultus was approved for Trino in 1827

Mary-Leonia Paradis (Bl) {2}

4 May
1840–1912. Born in Quebec (Canada), she joined the 'Marian Sisters of the Holy Cross' when she was fourteen and was a priests' housekeeper in Canada and the United States of America. In 1867 her congregation gave up housekeeping for priests, with the result that she founded the 'Poor Sisters of the Holy Family' at Côtes des Neiges (Quebec) for this work alone. She died at the convent at Sherbrook, and was beatified in 1984.

Mary-Anne-of-Jesus Paredes y Flores (St) {2}

26 May
1618–45. Nicknamed the 'Lily of Quito', she was of Spanish descent and was born at Quito (Ecuador). She tried her vocation as a consecrated religious, but failed and then lived as a hermit in the house of her brother-in-law. Her penitential practices were extreme, but she received mystical graces. During the earthquakes at Quito in 1645 she offered herself as a sacrificial victim in reparation for the city and

died shortly afterwards. She was canonized in 1950.

Mary-Magdalen de' Pazzi (St) {1, 3}

25 May
1566–1607. From Florence (Italy), when aged sixteen she became a Carmelite there. Throughout her life she was subject to remarkable mystical experiences (which she described in writing) and suffered both spiritually and physically. This did not prevent her being a capable worker and administrator at her nunnery. She was canonized in 1669.

Mary-Rose Pellesi (Bl) {2 –add}

1917–72. From Prignano sulla Secchia, she had a happy childhood until her late teens when two of her sisters-in-laws died and left six children aged four or under. She willingly undertook their care, but obeyed a vocation to join the 'Franciscan Missionary Sisters of Christ' in 1940. She worked in education for three years, but contracted tuberculosis in 1945. Her lungs rotted and she died twenty-seven years later, being bedridden in a sanatorium at Bologna, although she managed to undertake three pilgrimages to Lourdes with this health condition. Her tranquillity was evident from the broad smile for which she became famous. She was taken to the house where she was first a teacher at Sassuolo just before she died. She was beatified in 2007.

Mary-of-St-Euphrasia Pelletier (St) {2}

24 April
1796–1868. From Noirmoutier in the Vendée (France), when aged eighteen she joined the 'Sisters of Our Lady of Charity' founded by St John Eudes and herself founded the first house of the 'Sisters of the Good Shepherd' at Angers in 1829 in order to re-educate delinquent girls and young women whose only

future otherwise would be in prostitution. She died there and was canonized in 1940.

Mary-Crescentia Pérez (Bl) {2 –add}

20 May

1897–1932. From a family of modest means at San Martín near Buenos Aires (Argentina), as a child she went to a school run by the Daughters of Our Lady of the Garden, an Italian sisterhood founded by St Anthony Gianelli. She joined the congregation in 1916, and worked as a teacher in Buenos Aires and as a nurse in Mar del Plata. She was inspired by St Teresa of the Child Jesus, and her motto was: 'Do, want and be where God what God wants you to be'. She contracted tuberculosis, and for her health she was sent to Vallenar in Chile, where she died. She was beatified in 2012.

Mary-of-the-Crucified-Jesus Petković (Bl) {2}

9 July

1892–1956. She was born into a wealthy family on the island of Korčula near Blato in what is now Croatia (then the Habsburg Empire), and was educated by the 'Servants of Charity', an Italian congregation of sisters. She joined it in 1919, but the Italian sisters had to leave after the formation of Yugoslavia and she was left with one companion. This was the start of the Croatian 'Daughters of Mercy', which she founded in 1920 and of which she was superior until 1952. The congregation had become international when she died. She was beatified in 2003.

Mary-Miracles-of-Jesus Pidal y Chico de Guzmán (St) {2}

11 December

1891–1974. Born at Madrid (Spain) to a devout family in diplomatic service, she joined the Carmel at El Escorial in 1920 and was a founder member of the Carmel at Cerro de los Ángeles in 1924. This was the founding house of several others in India. After the destruction of the Spanish Civil War she oversaw the foundation and restoration of thirteen Carmels, and was a great proponent of the Carmelite charism. She died at La Aldehuela and was canonized in 2003.

Mary Pierina (Bl) {2 –add}

26 July

1890–1945. Born in Milan (Italy), she joined the Daughters of the Immaculate Conception of Buenos Aires in 1914. She subsequently experienced several visions of Christ and Our Lady which inspired her to propagate the devotion for the Holy Face of Jesus. This work included the manufacture and distribution of the Holy Face Medal, bearing a reproduction of the image on the Shroud of Turin. From 1919 to 1921 she was at her congregation's mother house at Buenos Aires, but she returned to Milan and died there. She was beatified in 2010.

Mary-Adeodata Pisani (Bl) {2}

25 February

1806–55. Born in Naples of a noble Maltese family, she suffered the breakup of her family when her father was sentenced to exile and went back to Malta. In 1825 she and her mother also went to Malta, but the family did not get back together. She joined the Benedictine nuns at Medina in 1828 and served as novice-mistress and abbess before her early death of heart disease. She was beatified in 2001.

Mary-Magdalen Postel (St) {2}

16 July

1756–1846. From Barfleur (France), when young she opened a school for girls but this was suppressed by the French Revolution. During the period of persecution she administered the Blessed Sacrament to the dying. In 1805 she reopened her school at

Cherbourg, and this proved to be the origin of the 'Sisterhood of Christian Schools' which spread throughout the world after serious difficulties. She died at St-Sauveur-le-Vîcomte and was canonized in 1925.

Mary Poussepin (Bl) {2}

24 January
1652–1744. Born at Dourdin near Paris (France), her family ran a stocking factory and she took this over in 1680. In 1691 she entered the Dominican Third Order and moved to Sainville nearby to help in nursing sufferers from repeated epidemics there. She founded the 'Dominican Sisters of Charity of the Presentation of the Blessed Virgin' in 1697 to help in teaching, nursing and catechesis. She hoped that the sisters would not be confined to an enclosed convent, but this freedom did not happen in her lifetime. She was beatified in 1994.

Mary-of-Mercy Prat y Prat (Bl) {2}

24 July
1880–1936. Born in Barcelona (Spain), she joined the 'Society of St Teresa of Jesus' at Tortosa in 1904 and was at the mother house at Barcelona from 1920. When the Civil War broke out the community decided to disperse and to meet up in a safer place. She was sent with a companion to stay with her sister, but they met a group of armed militia on the way. Being questioned, they declared themselves to be consecrated religious and so were seized, driven to a lonely place and shot. She died after some hours, praying for her executors, but her companion survived and gave witness. The beatification was in 1990. Cf. **Spanish Civil War, Martyrs of**.

Mary-Louise Prosperi (Bl) {2 –add}

12 September
1779–1847. From 'Flogiano' (a small locality near Sarteano?) in the diocese of Norcia in Italy, in 1820 she entered the Benedictine nunnery of Santa Lucia at Trevi. She quickly became known for the strength of her spiritual life, and for her fidelity to her religious vows. She was in receipt of mystical gifts, as well as of physical and mental suffering. In 1837 she was elected abbess of her monastery, and implemented a thorough renewal of the consecrated life there. She died at her monastery at Trevi, and was beatified in 2012.

Mary Qi Yu (St) {1 –group}

28 June
Cf. **Lucy Wang Cheng and Comps**.

Mary Rafols (Bl) {2}

30 August
1781–1853. Born near Barcelona (Spain), she joined a group of young women at Zaragoza who were dedicated to serving the most helpless people at a hospital there. They took vows in 1825 as the 'Sisters of Charity of St Anne', and cared for the wounded and mentally ill during the Napoleonic and Carlist wars (she was imprisoned during the latter). Then she ran a home for foundlings, where she died. She was beatified in 1994.

Mary Repetto (Bl) {2}

5 January
1807–90. Born at Voltaggio near Genoa (Italy), when aged twenty-two she joined the 'Daughters of Our Lady of Refuge on Mount Calvary' at Brignolini. She was gatekeeper there for sixty-one years, and stepped out of the convent only to nurse cholera sufferers, and impressed all sorts of people with her holiness and by the help she gave in advice and prayer. She was beatified in 1981.

Mary-of-Guadalupe Ricart Olmos (Bl) {2}

2 October
1881–1936. From Abal near Valencia, she became a Servite nun at Pié de la Cruz at

Valencia in 1900 and served as prioress, procurator and novice-mistress. The monastery had to close as a result of the anti-clerical policies of the Republican government in 1936, and she took refuge with a relative but was arrested as a religious, molested and shot. She was beatified in 2001. Cf. **Spanish Civil War, Martyrs of**.

Mary-Anne Rivier (Bl) {2}

3 February
1768–1838. Born a cripple at Montpezat near Viviers (France), when aged eleven she was healed after praying to Our Lady and thus began her vocation. When aged twenty-two she started to teach and catechize the women and girls of her parish, and led the people in prayer and pious activity when the Revolution left the area bereft of priests and sacraments. To assist in this she gathered a group of helpers which became the 'Congregation of the Presentation of the Blessed Virgin Mary'. This had 137 houses when she died. She was beatified in 1982.

Mary-Emily de Rodat (St) {2}

19 September
1787–1852. From near Rodat in the Massif Central (France), she tried her vocation with three different congregations before starting a new teaching order in Villefranche in 1816 called the 'Congregation of the Holy Family'. This was to make up for the suppression of the Ursuline schools. She was helped by Fr Anthony Marty, who wrote the rule. She died at Villefranche and was canonized in 1950.

Mary-of-the-Immaculate-Conception Salvat y Romero (Bl) {2 –add}

1926–98. She was the superior-general of the Sisters of the Company of the Cross. Born at Madrid (Spain), she died at Seville and was beatified in 2010.

Mary-of-Sorrows Rodríguez Sopeña (Bl) {2}

10 January
1848–1918. From a family of high social standing near Almería in Spain (her father became the city judge), she started to help poor and sick people when a teenager. Her family moved to Madrid and to Puerto Rico, where she started to open schools for neglected children. Then she went to Cuba, doing the same, and back to Madrid. She was a pioneer in being a laywoman prepared to do social work in poor neighbourhoods and founding centres for this purpose. She also founded several sodalities and secular institutes, rather than any religious congregations because of prevailing anti-clerical sentiment in Spain. These are now known collectively as the 'Sopeño Family', and also work in Latin America. She died at Madrid and was beatified in 2003.

Mary Romero Meneses (Bl) {2}

7 July
1902–77. From a rich family of Granada in Nicaragua, she received a strong devotion to Our Lady after a serious bout of rheumatic fever and joined the Salesian Sisters in 1920. In 1931 she was sent to San José in Costa Rica, where her work made her famous as a social apostle. She died at Leon in Nicaragua during a rest break, and was beatified in 2002.

Mary-Crucifixa di Rosa (St) {2}

15 December
1813–55. A noblewoman from Brescia (Italy), from childhood she showed a lively piety and sympathy with the poor while running her father's household after her mother died. When cholera broke out in 1836 she was enthusiastic in nursing its sufferers, and in the course of this gathered the first companions of her institute, the 'Handmaids of Charity',

which was founded in 1840. She died at Brescia and was canonized in 1954.

Mary-Joseph Rossello (St) {2}

7 December

1811–80. From a poor family at Albisola near Savona (Italy), she wished to become a religious, but her poor health and lack of a dowry prevented her, and she became a Franciscan tertiary. In 1837 she founded a new institute, the 'Daughters of Our Lady of Mercy', which spread through Italy and South America. As superior she suffered from constant illness, but ruled her institute with heroic courage amid many difficulties until her death at Savona. She was canonized in 1949.

Mary-Frances-of-Jesus Rubatto (Bl) {2}

6 August

1844–1904. From Carmagnola in Piedmont (Italy), she moved with her widowed mother to Turin and, while on holiday in Loano in Liguria, helped a workman injured while working on a new convent. The edification she gave led her to be persuaded to join it, and she became the superior and formation director. Thus started the 'Capuchin Sisters of Mother Rubatto', which spread to Argentina and Uruguay. As superior-general, she died while visiting the house at Montevideo and was beatified in 1993.

Mary-Gabrielle Sagheddu (Bl) {2}

22 April

1914–39. From Dorgali in Sardinia, she became a Trappestine at the nunnery at Grottaferrata (now moved to Viterbo), making profession in 1937. Supported by her community (who were influenced by the Abbé Couturier) she offered her life as a mystical sacrifice for church unity, especially between Catholics and Orthodox. Immediately she started suffering painful illnesses and severe spiritual trials,

which only ended with her early death. She was beatified in 1983.

Mary-Anne Sala (Bl) {2}

24 November

1829–91. Born in Lombardy (Italy), she joined the 'Sisters of St Marcellina' (a teaching order) in 1848. She was a very good teacher, based mainly in Milan, where she died and where her body was found to be incorrupt in 1921. She was beatified in 1980.

Mary-of-Mt-Carmel Sallés y Barangueras (St) {2}

6 December

1848–1911. From a prosperous family at Vich in Catalonia (Spain), when young she was aware of the urgent need to help prostitutes and realized that their lack of education was a factor in their plight. So she devoted her life to educating women, and founded the 'Sisters of the Immaculate Conception' for that purpose. She died at Madrid and was canonized in 2012.

Mary Salome (St) {2, 4}

24 April

C1st. One of the 'three Marys' (the others being Our Lady and Mary Cleophas), she was the wife of Zebedee and the mother of St James the Great and St John the Evangelist. One of the women who ministered to Christ during his public ministry, she also witnessed his crucifixion, burial and resurrection. She is depicted carrying a pot of ointment, a cruse or a pair of cruets.

Mary-of-the-Heart-of-Jesus Sancho de Guerra (St) {2}

20 March

1842–1912. Born at Vitoria in the Basque Country (Spain), in 1864 she joined the

'Sisters, Servants of Mary for the Sick' which had just been founded by St Mary Torres Acosta. In 1871 she founded the 'Sisters, Servants of Jesus' at Bilbao under the bishop of Vitoria. She died after a long illness, and was canonized in 2000.

Mary-Crucified Satellico (Bl) {2}

8 November
1706–45. Born in Venice (Italy), when aged nineteen she became a Poor Clare at Ostra Vetere. Working to become more like Jesus crucified, she enjoyed extraordinary mystical graces and took her authority as superior as being one of loving service to her community and of charity to poor people, as all were redeemed by the Cross. She was beatified in 1993.

Mary-Christine of Savoy, Queen of the Two Sicilies (Bl) {2 –add}

31 January
1812–36. Born at Cagliari in Sardinia, she was the daughter of Victor Emanuel I, king of Sardinia, and Maria Teresa who was a niece of Emperor Joseph II of Austria. She married King Ferdinand II of the Two Sicilies in 1832, and died of complications arising from the birth of her first child, the future King Francis II. She was queen only for four years, but became famous for her piety and charity in that time. The process for her canonization was introduced in 1859, but was stalled by political events. Her husband reacted violently to the revolutions of 1848, and left a very bad reputation. The queen was only formally beatified in 2014, despite having had an informal cultus for well over a century.

Mary-Teresa Scherer (Bl) {2}

16 June
1825–88. Born near Lucerne (Switzerland), in 1854 she joined Fr Theodosius Florentini (OFMCap) in his new foundation, the

'Sisters of Schools and the Care of the Poor', which was to educate poor girls. However he extended his concern to the social works of mercy and opened a hospital at Ingenbohl, which she ran. This was not acceptable to all in the congregation and it split, Bl Mary becoming the superior of the 'Sisters of Mercy of the Holy Cross'. She was beatified in 1995.

Mary-of-the-Sacred-Heart-of-Jesus Schininà (Bl) {2}

11 June
1844–1910. Born at Ragusa (Sicily), she was a rich noblewoman, but she changed her life when aged twenty-five and started to help the poor, sick and aged, to catechize and to propagate devotion to the Sacred Heart. This caused some scandal in the town. In 1889 she founded the 'Institute of the Sacred Heart of Jesus' to help in her work, and she sometimes went begging for its support. She died in her hometown and was beatified in 1990.

Mary-Teresa-of-Jesus Scrilli (Bl) {2 –add}

1825–89. From Montevarchi in Arezzo, Italy, she tried to become a Carmelite nun as a teenager but failed and opened a school at her home instead. In 1854 she founded the 'Sisters of Our Lady of Carmel' for the education of children, but anti-clerical persecution caused this to fail in 1862. In 1878 she re-established her institution with a boarding school at Florence, but the austere life and unhealthy living conditions caused the death of most of the sisters, including the foundress. The institute only started to flourish after the First World War, and it is now international in scope. She was beatified in 2006.

Mary-of-Jesus-the-Good-Shepherd de Siedliska (Bl) {2}

21 November
1842–1902. A Polish aristocrat, she was born near Warsaw but contracted tuberculosis as a

girl and spent 1866–70 in Tyrol and Provence. She almost died in 1872, but unexpectedly recovered and went to Rome the next year to set about founding a new congregation, away from the Russians who were suppressing Latin consecrated life in Poland. The 'Sisters of the Holy Family of Nazareth', originally contemplative with the Augustinian rule but later with various apostolates, received many vocations from expatriate Poles and the mother house was founded at Cracow (under the Austrians) in 1880. She founded twenty-nine other houses in Europe and the United States of America, died at Rome and was beatified in 1989.

(Mary the Slave) (St) {4 –deleted}

1 November
d. c.300. Her story is that she was a slave girl in the household of a Roman patrician in the reign of Diocletian who, because she fasted against her mistress's will, was whipped and given to a soldier to be sexually abused. He let her escape instead, and she died in peace. She was mistakenly listed as a martyr.

Mary-of-Providence Smet (Bl) {2}

7 February
1825–71. From Lille (France), she took the advice of St John Vianney to found the congregation of the 'Helpers of the Holy Souls' in order to make atonement on behalf of the souls in purgatory by works of charity. This she did in Paris after 1856, writing a rule modelled on that of the Jesuits. The new and little congregation initially shared the material destitution of the people it helped but is now worldwide, being active in mission territories. She was noteworthy for her great patience in various difficulties, especially when she contracted terminal cancer. She died at Paris and was beatified in 1957.

Mary-Magdalen Son So-byŏg (St) {1 –group}

31 December
Cf. **Augustine Pak Chŏng-wŏn and Comps**.

Mary-Magdalen-of-the-Incarnation Sordini (Bl) {2 –add}

1770–1824. From Grosseto in Italy, she defied her father by entering the Franciscan Third Order convent at Ischia di Castro on the eve of her wedding in 1788. In 1802 she was elected abbess, but wished to found a new congregation devoted to perpetual, solemn and public adoration of the Blessed Sacrament. This was as a result of a vision. In 1807 she opened her first house at Rome, which was eventually established at Sant'Anna al Quirinale after a period of exile. As the founder of the 'Perpetual Adorers of the Blessed Sacrament' she was beatified in 2007.

Mary-Teresa de Soubiran La Louvière (Bl) {2}

20 October
1834–89. A noblewoman from Castel-naudary near Carcassonne (France), she wanted to become a Carmelite nun but was advised to join to Beguines of Ghent and to found a house in her home village. This she did in 1855, and in 1864 she transferred the community to Toulouse and founded the 'Institute of Mary Auxiliatrix', which ran an orphanage and practised perpetual adoration of the Blessed Sacrament. As superior she was advised by her deputy to undertake a disastrous expansion of the institute, and through the machinations of the latter was then deposed and expelled. In 1868 she joined the 'Institute of Our Lady of Charity' and died as a member thereof. The truth then emerged and her treacherous deputy, who had become superior, was herself expelled. She was beatified in 1946.

Mary-Bernarda Soubirous (St) {2}

16 April
1844–79. Universally known as 'Bernardette', she was the daughter of a destitute miller at Lourdes (France) and experienced a series of apparitions of Our Lady by the river just outside the town when aged fourteen. This experience led to the establishment of the famous shrine there. Eight years later she joined the 'Sisters of Charity of Our Lady' at Nevers, where she lived in obscurity until her death from tuberculosis. She was canonized in 1933.

Mary-Anne Soureau-Blondin (Bl) {2}

(2 January)
1809–90. From a family in humble circumstances at Terrebonne in Quebec, Canada, in her twenties she became a domestic servant in a convent situated in her village. As such she managed to overcome her illiteracy, became a teacher and noticed that a high level of illiteracy among the Catholics of Quebec was a result of insisting on separate schools for boys and girls in the face of inadequate educational resources. As a result she founded the coeducational Sisters of St Anne at Vaudreuil in 1850. Her congregation flourished, but in 1858 she was permanently excluded from any position of authority on the pretext that she was a poor administrator. She was beatified in 2001.

Mary-Magdalen-of-the-Passion Starace (Bl) {2 –add}

1845–1921. From Castellamare di Stabia near Naples in Italy, in 1867 she joined the 'Third Order of the Servants of Mary' and taught catechism to local children. The experience of teaching and the suffering resulting from a cholera epidemic led her to found the 'Compassionist Sisters, Servants of Mary' in 1869. This was an active order, but based on a charism of the primacy of prayer inspired by the compassion of Jesus Christ and the sorrows of Our Lady. She died of pneumonia and was beatified in 2007.

Mary-Clementina Staszewska (Bl) {2 –add}

27 July
1890–1943. A Polish Ursuline, she died of ill-treatment at Auschwitz. Cf. **Poland, Martyrs of the Nazi Occupation of**.

Mary-Helen Stollenwerk (Bl) {2 –add}

28 November
1852–1900. Born in the Eifel (Germany) and early wishing to go to China as a missionary, she was employed aged twenty-nine as a mission-house domestic by Bl Arnold Janssen at Steyr (Netherlands). He was the founder of the 'Society of the Divine Word,' and he also founded the 'Servants of the Holy Spirit' in 1889. In 1892 she joined the latter and became a contemplative in the cloistered branch in 1898, contracting tubercular meningitis three years later. She was beatified in 1995.

Mary-Catherine-of-St-Augustine Symon de Longpré (Bl) {2}

8 May
1623–68. Born at Saint-Sauveur-le-Vicomte in Normandy (France), she joined the Augustinian Hospitaller nuns at the 'Hôtel-Dieu' at Bayonne when aged twelve. In 1648 she emigrated to their foundation in Quebec City (Canada) and (despite her youth) became noted for her prudence and intellect. Totally devoted to caring for sick people, she served as bursar and novice-mistress and was beatified in 1989.

Mary-of-the-Passion Tarallo (Bl) {2 –add}

1866–1912. From Barra near Naples, in 1891 she entered the nunnery of the 'Sisters Crucified, Adorers of the Eucharist' in her hometown. She lived the ordinary life of a contemplative nun, serving as novice-mistress, but became famous for her exemplary life of prayer and charity. She was especially fervent for her congregation's charism of Eucharistic adoration. She was beatified in 2006.

Mary-Teresa-of-St-Joseph Tauscher van den Bosch (Bl) {2 –add}

1855–1938. She was born at Sandow in East Prussia (then in Germany, now in Poland), and her father was a Lutheran pastor. As a young Lutheran she was fervent, but converted at Cologne in 1888 and set about founding an active religious congregation based on the life of St Teresa of Jesus. This became the 'Carmelites of the Sacred Heart', dedicated to helping homeless and marginalized people of all kinds. As a result she was estranged from her family and exiled from Germany, finally establishing the mother house of the new congregation at Roca di Papa near Rome. She died at Sittard in the Netherlands, and was beatified in 2006. Her congregation has spread worldwide.

Mary-Emily Tavernier Gamelin (Bl) {2}

23 September
1800–51. From Montreal, Canada, when aged twenty-three she married and had three children, but her entire family was dead by the time she was twenty-seven. Then she dedicated herself to alleviating human misery in all its forms, and gathered many disciples. In 1844 these became the 'Sisters of Providence' with herself as superior, and this congregation has become international in scope after her death. She died of cholera. She was beatified in 2001.

Mary-of-the-Incarnation Thévenet (St) {2}

3 February

1774–1837. From Lyons (France), she was educated at a Benedictine convent school, but

her family was disrupted by the Revolution. Helping the victims of the 'Terror' led her to renounce marriage for the Church's sake, and this resulted in her founding the 'Religious of Jesus and Mary' in 1818. Her charism derived from the union of the Hearts of Jesus {2} and Mary. She died at the mother house at Fourvière and was canonized in 1993.

Mary-Desolata Torres Acosta (St) {2}

11 October
1826–87. From a poor family of Madrid (Spain), she tried unsuccessfully to become a Dominican nun before founding an institute, the 'Handmaids of Mary, Ministers to the Sick' in 1848 to care for sick people in their own homes. A subsequent priest-director of the new institute removed her and appointed another superior, with the result that the institute nearly failed. But she was reappointed after inquiry by the bishop and went on to found forty-six houses before dying in Madrid. She was canonized in 1970.

Mary-Louise of Jesus Trichet (Bl) {2}

28 April
1684–1759. From Poitiers (France), when aged seventeen she became a disciple of St Louis Grignon de Montfort in that city. She entered the hospital for the poor in which he worked in 1703 and became the first of the 'Daughters of Wisdom'. This congregation received the approval of the bishop in 1715, just before St Louis died. She founded a number of houses between 1725 and 1748 and died at the mother house at St Laurent sur Sevre in 1759. She was beatified in 1993.

Mary-Catherine-of-St-Rose Troiani (Bl) {2}

6 May
1813–87. An orphan, she was brought up in the Poor Clare convent at Ferentino near Rome and became a nun there in 1829. In 1859 she

was one of a group who got permission to go to Cairo (Egypt) and to open a school. There they also cared for abandoned children. This foundation became the 'Franciscan Missionary Sisters of the Immaculate Heart of Mary', which had her as its first superior. She also opened a house in Jerusalem before dying in Cairo, being beatified in 1985.

Mary Troncatti (Bl) {2 –add}

25 August
1883–1969. Born at Corteno Golgi near Brescia (Italy), she joined the Salesian Sisters in 1907 and was a Red Cross nurse during the First World War. In 1922 she went to Ecuador as a missionary, and three years later was sent to work among the Shuar people in the Amazon rainforest. She remained with them for the rest of her life as a catechist and medical practitioner, learning their language in order to do so. She died in an aeroplane crash at Sucúa near Morona Santiago, and was beatified in 2012.

Mary-Elizabeth Turgeon (Bl) {2 –add}

17 August
1840–81. From a farming family of Saint-Étienne-de-Beaumont of Quebec, Canada, she trained as a teacher and graduated in 1862. Her experiences of the poverty and ignorance of those settling the southeastern part of Quebec, where the diocese of Rimouski was established, led her to found the Sisters of Our Lady of the Rosary as a French teaching order in Quebec. This was approved in 1879. Only two years later, she died of acute tuberculosis. Her beatification was due in 2015.

Mary-Christine of the Two Sicilies cf. **Mary-Christine of Savoy**.

Mary-Euthymia Üffing (Bl) {2}

9 September
1914–55. From Halver in Westphalia, Germany, she came from a large farming family and joined the Sisters of Charity of Münster in 1934. Her work was in nursing, and during the Second World War she nursed a large number of prisoners of war and indentured foreign workers with spiritual concern. After the war she ran the laundry at the central convent at Münster before dying of cancer. The memory of her kindliness and devotion to prayer led her to be beatified in 2001.

Mary Vaz (Bl) {2}

27 August
d. 1627. A Japanese Franciscan tertiary, wife of Bl Caspar Vas, she was beheaded at Nagasaki with him and BB Francis-of-St-Mary of Mancha and Comps. Cf. **Japan, Martyrs of**.

Mary-of-Jesus-in-the-Sacrament Venegas de la Torre (St) {2}

30 July
1868–1959. From a middle-class family of Zaplotanejo in Jalisco (Mexico), in 1905 with three companions she joined a group of pious women running a hospital. In 1910 she took religious vows and established the group as a new religious congregation, the 'Daughters of the Sacred Heart', in 1921. She was canonized in 2000.

Mary Wang Lizhi (St) {1 –group}

22 July
1851–1900. From Wei county in Hebei (China), she met a gang of Boxers on the road near Daining while trying to flee with her two children and was beheaded. Cf. **China, Martyrs of**.

Mary-Martha-of-Jesus Wołowska (Bl) {2}

19 December
1879–1942. A Sister of the Immaculate Conception, she was shot by the Nazis at Słonim in Poland with Bl Mary-Eve-of-Providence Noisezewska. Cf. **Poland, Martyrs of the Nazi Occupation of**.

Mary Wŏn Kwi-im (St) {1 –group}

20 July
Cf. **Mary-Magdalen Yi Yŏn-hŭi and Comps**.

Mary-of-the-Apostles von Wüllenweber
(Bl) {2}

25 December
1838–1907. A German baroness born near Gladbach, she had a pious upbringing but had difficulty in discerning the form of her religious vocation. She bought a house in Neuwerk in order to set up a community of Franciscan tertiaries dedicated to missionary work among women, but had trouble keeping it going at the time of the 'Kulturkampf'. Inspired by Fr John Jordan, the founder of the Salvatorians, she and five others moved to Rome and settled at Tivoli, despite not knowing the Italian language and customs. Thus began the 'Salvatorian Sisters', which had twenty-five other mission houses by the time she died. She was beatified in 1968.

Mary Yi In-dŏg (St) {1 –group}

31 January
Cf. **Augustine Pak Chŏng-wŏn and Comps**.

Mary Yi Yŏn-hŭi (St) {1 –group}

3 September
Cf. **John Pak Hu-jae and Comps**.

Mary-Magdalen Yi Yŏn-hŭi and Comps
(St) {1 –group}

20 July
d. 1839. They were a group of eight martyred at Seoul in Korea. The others were Anne Kim Chang-gŭm, John-Baptist Yi Kwang-nyol, Lucy Kim (1), Martha Kim Sŏng-im, Mary Wŏn Kwi-im, Rose Kim and Teresa Yi Mae-im. The women were virgins. Cf. **Korea, Martyrs of**.

Mary-Magdalen Yi Yŏng-dŏg (St) {1 –group}

29 December
Cf. **Benedicta Hyŏn Kyŏng-nyŏn and Comps**.

Mary-Margaret d'Youville (St) {2}

23 December
1701–71. Born at Varennes in French Canada, she married a government agent who was a swindling merchant but was widowed after eleven years and six children (two survived infancy). She ran a shop to pay her husband's debts and performed works of charity with some companions. Thus started the congregation of the 'Grey Nuns', who later ran hospitals and orphanages but who initially suffered vicious persecution because people refused to believe that the widow of such a worthless man as her husband could herself do any good. She died at Montreal and was canonized in 1990.

Mary Zhao Guozhi and Comps (St)
{1 –group}

20 July
d. 1900. She was a sixty-year-old woman of Wuqiao Zhaojia in Hebei (China) with two unmarried daughters, SS Mary and Rose Zhao. They hid in a well from a gang of Boxers, but were discovered and told to deny their faith. They refused and were beheaded. Cf. **China, Martyrs of**.

Mary Zheng Xu (St) {1 –group}

28 June
Cf. **Lucy Wang Cheng and Comps**.

Mary Zhu Wuzhi (St) {1 –group}

20 July
Cf. **Ignatius Mangin and Comps**.

Massa Candida (SS) {2}

18 August
d. c.260. Meaning 'white mass', this name denotes a large group who were martyred

at Utica (Roman Africa) in the reign of Gallienus and Valerian. The old Roman Martyrology asserted that they numbered 300 and that the name referred to what was left of them after they had been thrown into a pit of quicklime. St Augustine, however, mentioned in a sermon that they numbered 153, and the name appears rather to refer to a locality near Utica.

Maternian cf. **Martinian.**

Maternus of Cologne (St) {2, 4}

14 September
d. p334. He is the first bishop of Cologne mentioned in historical sources (in connection with the Donatist controversy). A medieval myth, invented to enhance the reputation of the diocese, identified him with the son of the widow of Naim and made him a disciple of St Peter.

Maternus of Milan (St) {2, 4}

18 July
C4th. Elected by popular acclamation as bishop of Milan (Italy) in 295, he was imprisoned and tortured in the persecution of Diocletian but survived and died in peace.

Matilda (Mathild, Maud) of Germany, Queen (St) {2}

14 March
d. 968. Wife of the German king Henry I and mother of Emperor Otto I and Duke Henry I of Bavaria, she was of a generous disposition and founded many monasteries. She was a widow for thirty years and had much trouble from her two sons, who relieved her of most of her possessions. She died at the Quedlinburg nunnery, one of her foundations, and hence has been claimed as a Benedictine oblate.

Matilda-of-the-Sacred-Heart Téllez Robles (Bl) {2}

17 December
1841–1902. From Robedillo de la Vera in Spain but brought up in Béjar, she was early aware of a religious vocation but was discouraged by her middle-class family who wished her to marry. However, her father changed his mind and allowed her to found a new congregation devoted to Eucharistic adoration and to helping poor people at Béjar in 1875. This initially grew slowly, but was approved by the bishop of Plasencia and had seven convents by the time she died of a stroke. She was beatified in 2004.

Matrona (St) {2, 4}

15 March
? She was a serving maid of a rich Jewish woman of Thessalonika (Greece) who ordered her to be whipped to death on discovering that she was a Christian.

(Matronian) (St) {4 –deleted}

14 December
? Nothing is known about this alleged hermit of Milan (Italy).

Matthew (St) {1, 3}

21 September
C1st. Matthew, or Levi, was a tax collector at Capernaum before being called as an apostle, and is the author of the first gospel in the New Testament. The gospels provide the only trustworthy data concerning him. His career subsequent to Pentecost is unclear, as is whether or not he died a martyr, and the various traditions are unreliable. His attribute is a winged man (not an angel), and he may be depicted holding money, a bag of coins or a money box.

Matthew Alonso de Leziniana (St) {1 –group}

22 January

d. 1745. A Dominican priest from Navas del Rey near Valladolid (Spain), he was martyred in north Vietnam with St Francis Gil de Frederich on the orders of Emperor Trịnh Doanh. Cf. **Vietnam, Martyrs of**.

Matthew Alvarez (Bl) {2}

8 September

d. 1628. A Japanese catechist and Dominican tertiary, he was burnt alive at Nagasaki with BB Dominic Castellet and Comps. Cf. **Japan, Martyrs of**.

Matthew Carreri (Bl) {2}

7 October

d. 1470. From Mantua (Italy), he became a Dominican and spent his life in preaching throughout Italy. He died at Vigevano in Piedmont, and his cultus was confirmed for there in 1625.

Matthew-of-St-Thomas Chiwiato (Bl) {2}

12 September

d. 1622. A Japanese catechist, he was burnt alive with **Thomas Zumarraga and Comps**, and became a Dominican in prison beforehand. Cf. **Japan, Martyrs of**.

Matthew Correa Magallanes (St) {1 –group}

6 February

1866–1927. From a poor family of Tepechitlán, he became a diocesan priest of Zacatecas in 1893 and served in several parishes. He knew the family of Bl Michael Pro at Concepción del Oro. In 1926 he was appointed to the parish at Valparaiso. During the Cristero War he was arrested by the military, taken to Durango and ordered to hear the confessions of those about to be shot. After he refused to divulge the contents of these confessions, he was ordered to be shot as well. His relics are enshrined at the cathedral at Durango. Cf. **Mexico, Martyrs of**.

Matthew Flathers (Bl) {2}

21 March

d. 1608. A farmer's son from Weston near Otley (Yorks), he was a graduate of Oxford and was ordained at Arras. He was a priest in Yorkshire (being banished once) until he was captured and executed at York. He was beatified in 1987. Cf. **England, Martyrs of**.

Matthew-of-Girgenti Guimerá (Bl) {2}

7 January

d. 1450. From Girgenti (Sicily), he became a Conventual Franciscan but transferred to the Observants as a disciple of St Bernardine of Siena. He was forced by the pope to become bishop of Girgenti, but was not popular there. So he resigned and died in the Conventual friary at Palermo. His cultus was confirmed for Palermo and Girgenti in 1767.

Matthew-of-the-Rosary Kohioye (St) {1 –group}

19 October

d. 1633. A Japanese Dominican novice aged eighteen, he was a helper of St Luke-Alphonsus Gorda and was martyred with him at Nagasaki. He was canonized in 1987 with SS Laurence Ruiz and Comps. Cf. **Japan, Martyrs of**.

Matthew Lambert and Comps (BB) {2}

5 July

d. 1581. He was a baker, and was condemned with three sailor companions, BB Robert Mayler, Edward Cheevers and Patrick Cavenagh, for arranging the transport of priests to and from France. For this they were hanged, drawn and quartered at Wexford and were beatified in 1992. Cf. **Ireland, Martyrs of**.

Matthew Lê Văn Gẫm (St) {1 –group}

11 May
1812–47. A Vietnamese shipowner, he used to ferry missionaries of the Paris Society from Singapore to Vietnam in his ship. He was imprisoned at Saigon in 1846, tortured and beheaded on the orders of Emperor Thiệu Trị. Cf. **Vietnam, Martyrs of**.

Matthew Nguyễn Văn Phượng (St) {1 –group}

26 May
?1801–61. Born at Ke Lav in Vietnam, he became a catechist and a family man and was beheaded near Đồng Hới with St John Đoàn Trinh Hoan whom he had aided. Cf. **Vietnam, Martyrs of**.

Matthia del Nazarei (Bl) {2}

28 December
d. 1326. From Metalica in the Marches (Italy), she entered the Poor Clare nunnery of St Mary Magdalen there and went on to serve as abbess for forty years. Her cultus was confirmed for Camerino and Metalica in 1765.

Matthias (St) {1, 3}

14 May
C1st. He was chosen by lot to take the place of Judas Iscariot among the apostles (Acts 1:21-22). The traditions concerning his later life are conflicting, but his relics were allegedly removed by St Helena from Jerusalem to what is now St Matthias' Abbey at Trier (Germany). He is depicted as an elderly man holding (or being pierced by) a halberd.

Matthias Araki-Hyozaemon (Bl) {2}

12 July
d. 1626. Brother of **Mancius Araki-Kyuz-aburo**, he was burnt alive at Nagasaki (Japan) for having accommodated European missionaries at his house. Cf. **Japan, Martyrs of**.

Matthias of Arima (Bl) {2}

22 May
d. 1622. A Japanese, he worked with the Jesuit missionaries in Japan as a catechist and was the provincial's servant. He refused to betray his master when interrogated in prison, was subjected to the water torture and died as a result. He was beatified in 1867. Cf. **Japan, Martyrs of**.

Matthias Feng De (St) {1 –group}

9 July
Cf. **Gregory Grassi & Comps**.

Matthias of Jerusalem (St) {2, 4}

30 January
d. ?120. Of Jewish descent, he was bishop of Jerusalem after that city's destruction by the Romans and probably had few people left in his diocese.

Matthias of Miyako (St) {1 –group}

6 February
d. 1597. From Miyako in Japan, he became a Franciscan tertiary and was crucified at Nagasaki with SS Paul Miki and Comps. Cf. **Japan, Martyrs of**.

Matthias Mulumba (St) {1 –group}

3 June
d. 1886. He was the chief of several villages in Buganda (Uganda), and had been a Muslim and then a Protestant before becoming a Catholic. He was executed on the orders of King Mwanga. Cf. **Charles Lwanga and Comps**.

Matthias Nakano (Bl) {2}

27 November
Cf. **Thomas Koteda and Comps**.

Matthias Shōbara Ichizaemon (Bl) {2 –add}

17 February
d. 1624. He was a layman martyred at Hiroshima. He was beatified in 2008. Cf. **Japan, Martyrs of**.

Maturin (St) {2, 4}

1 November
C7th? He was a priest of Montargis near Sens (France). According to his romantic legend he was converted and ordained by Polycarp, bishop of that city. Then he converted his parents and was a successful missionary in the area.

Maud cf. **Mechtilde**, **Matilda** or **Mary-Magdalen**.

(Maura of Byzantium) *(St)* *{4 –deleted}*

30 November
? She was listed as martyred at Byzantium (Constantinople), but no details are extant. Her cultus was extremely popular in the patristic era.

Maura of Troyes (St) {2}

21 September
?827–50. From Troyes (France) and sister of a bishop there, she lived as a consecrated virgin in her parents' house.

Maurice of Carnoët (St) {2}

29 September
?1114–91. From Brittany (France), he became a Cistercian at Langonel and went on to be abbot-founder of Carnoët near Morlaix in 1177. He was an adviser to the dukes of Brittany.

Maurice Iñiguez de Heredia and Comps (BB) {2 –add}

1936–7. They were the Hospitallers of St John of God who were martyred during the Spanish Civil War. Eight were massacred at Malaga on 17 August 1936 and nine at La Malvarrosa near Valencia on 9 October. A further seven were killed in separate incidents elsewhere, making a total of twenty-four. They were beatified in 2013. Cf. **Spanish Civil War, Martyrs of** and list in appendix.

Maurice McKenraghty (Bl) {2}

20 April
d. 1585. A diocesan priest, he was hanged at Clonmel after being imprisoned for denying the spiritual supremacy of Queen Elizabeth I of England. He was beatified in 1992. Cf. **Ireland, Martyrs of**.

Maurice Tornay (Bl) {2}

11 August
1910–49. Born in Valais (Switzerland), he joined the 'Canons Regular of St Bernard' in 1931 and was sent to Yunnan in China in 1936. In 1945 he was appointed priest to Yerkalo, the only parish in Tibet (then autonomous). The local lamas expelled him and forced his people to apostatize. Going to Lhasa to intercede for them, he was ambushed and killed with his servant. He was beatified in 1993.

Maurilius of Angers (St) {2, 4}

13 September
d. 453. From Milan, he migrated to France, became a disciple of St Martin of Tours and was made bishop of Angers in 407.

Maurinus of Agen (St) {2}

25 November
C6th. He was a rural missionary based at Agen (France), and was beheaded by pagan peasants. His shrine formed the nucleus of the monastery and village of Saint-Maurin east of Agen.

(Maurinus of Cologne) *(St)* {4 –deleted}

10 June
? The rebuilding of the church of St Pantaleon's Abbey at Cologne in 966 allegedly uncovered his tomb with an epitaph describing him as abbot and martyr. There is no historical record of him.

Mauritius cf. **Maurice**.

Maurontus of Douai (St) {2}

5 May
d. 702. Eldest son of SS Adalbald and Rictrude, he was educated at the Frankish court and succeeded his father as lord of Douai (France). About to marry, he suddenly chose to become a monk at Marchiennes instead and was later the abbot-founder of Breuil-sur-Lys near Douai. He is the patron of Douai.

Maurontus of Marseilles (St) {2}

21 October
d. c.780. Abbot of St Victor at Marseilles (France), he was made bishop of the city in ?767.

(Maurus, Panteleimon and Sergius) *(SS)* {4 –deleted}

27 July
d. ?117. They are alleged by their worthless acta to have been martyred at Bisceglie near Bari (Italy). Maurus is said to have been from Bethlehem and to have been sent by St Peter to be the first bishop of Bisceglia, but they were probably Roman martyrs whose relics were transferred.

(Maurus the African) *(St)* {4 –deleted}

22 November
d. c.280. From a Christian family in Roman Africa, he travelled to Rome and was martyred there in the reign of Numerian. About ten different cities in Italy and France claimed to possess his relics as a result of his story being applied to various local saints.

(Maurus of Cesena 1) (St) {2}

21 November
C4th? He was an early bishop of Cesena (Italy).

(Maurus of Cesena 2) (St) {2, 4}

21 November
d. 946. A Roman, he was ordained by Pope John IX, his uncle, and became a monk and abbot of Classe at Ravenna in 926. In 934 he was made bishop of Cesena, and the cell on a hill near the city which he built as a retreat for himself later grew into the Benedictine abbey of Santa Maria del Monte.

Maurus of Glanfeuil (St) {2}

15 January
C6–7th. He was the founder of the abbey of Glanfeuil, near Angers (France), and was maliciously confused with St Maurus of Subiaco in the Middle Ages in order to increase the abbey's prestige. His relics were at St Germain, Paris until destroyed during the French Revolution.

Maurus Palazuelos Maruri and Comps (BB) {2 –add}

28 August
d. 1936. The entire community of the Benedictine priory of El Pueyo, numbering eighteen, was massacred at Barbastro during the Spanish Civil War after imprisonment and ill-treatment. Three of the number had been killed earlier. They were beatified in 2013. Cf. **Spanish Civil War, Martyrs of** and list in appendix.

Maurus of Pećs (Bl) {2}

25 October
d. p1070. A Benedictine abbot, he was invited to Hungary by King St Stephen and

joined the royal foundation of Pannonhalma before becoming bishop of Pécs in 1036. He wrote biographies of SS Benedict Zorard and Andrew Szkalka. His cultus was confirmed for Pécs in 1848.

(Maurus of Rheims and Comps) (SS) {4 –deleted}

22 August
? They were listed by the old Roman Martyrology as a priest and forty-nine others who were martyred at Rheims (France).

Maurus of Rome (St) {2}

10 December
Early C4th? He was a martyr buried at the catacomb of Traso on the new Salarian Way outside Rome. Pope St Damasus composed an epitaph, describing him as a child who was steadfast under tortures designed to make him abandon his faith.

Maurus (William) Scott (Bl) {2}

30 May
d. 1612. Born at Chigwell (Essex) and baptized as William, he studied law at Cambridge but was converted by reading Catholic literature and received into the Church by Bl John Roberts, who sent him to the Benedictine abbey at Sahagún in Spain. He became a monk there in 1604, and after his ordination was sent back to England as a missionary. Shortly after his arrival he witnessed the martyrdom of his mentor, and shortly afterwards was captured and himself martyred at Tyburn with Bl Richard Newport. He was beatified in 1929. The Roman Martyrology lists him under his baptismal name. Cf. **England, Martyrs of**.

(Maurus of Subiaco) (St) {4 –deleted}

15 January
C6th? He features in the second of the 'Dialogues' attributed to St Gregory the Great as a young disciple of St Benedict at Subiaco. Apart from this reference, nothing is known about him. Odo, an early medieval abbot of Glanfeuil, maliciously concocted a foundation legend for his abbey, alleging that Maurus migrated to found that monastery near Angers (France). Maurus and Placid, his companion at Subiaco, are patrons of Benedictine novices and still have a cultus in the Order of St Benedict, but only Placid is now listed in the Roman Martyrology.

(Maurus of Verdun) (St) {4 –deleted}

8 November
d. 383. He allegedly became second bishop of Verdun (France) in 353, and his shrine was especially famous for miracles in the Dark Ages.

(Maurus of Verona) (St) {4 –deleted}

21 November
d. c.600. This bishop of Verona (Italy) apparently resigned when old to become a hermit.

(Mavilus) (St) {4 –deleted}

4 January
C3rd? He was allegedly thrown to the wild animals in the arena at Adrumetum in Roman Africa.

Mawes (Maudez) (St) {2}

18 November
C5th. He was a Welsh hermit, based firstly across the estuary from Falmouth in Cornwall (England) where a small town is named after him, and then on the island of Modez in Brittany (France), where many churches are dedicated to him as St Maudez.

Mawgan (Magald, Morgan) (St) {2}

27 April
C6th. He appears to have been a disciple of St Illtyd, to have lived as a hermit in several

places and to have died on the island of Bardsey (Wales). Several churches in Wales and Cornwall are dedicated to him. The Roman Martyrology lists him as a bishop.

Maxellend (St) {2}

13 November
d. 670. She was stabbed to death near Cambrai (France) by the lord of Solesmes because she wished to be a nun and refused to marry him.

(Maxentius, Constantius and Comps) (SS) {4 –deleted}

12 December
Late C3rd?. They were martyred at Trier (Germany) at the beginning of the reign of Diocletian. Crescentius and Justin are also named.

Maxentius (Maixent) of Agde (St) {2, 4}

26 June
d. ?515. From Agde near Béziers (France), he was educated by St Severus and then became a monk and abbot of a monastery in Poitou. The place is now called Saint-Maixent-l'Ecole after him. He allegedly provided the local inhabitants with miraculous protection against the marauding Visigoths.

Maxima, Donatilla and Secunda (SS) {2, 4}

30 July
d. 304. Three young women (Secunda was aged twelve), they were martyred at Tebourba in Roman Africa in the reign of Diocletian.

(Maxima of Caillon) (St) {4 –deleted}

16 May
? She is venerated in the diocese of Fréjus (France), but nothing is known about her.

(Maxima of Rome) (St) {4 –deleted}

2 September
d. 304. A Roman slave, she was described as having been whipped with St Ansanus. She died as a result, but he survived and escaped.

Maximian of Bagae (St) {2, 4}

3 October
d.?410. A Roman African convert from Donatism, he was made bishop of Bagae in Numidia (Algeria) but the people there did not want him. When he took an important church from the Donatists, he was attacked by them, seriously beaten and thrown from a tower. He recovered, migrated to Italy (where he gained the sympathy of the Emperor Honorius) and died in peace.

Maximian of Ravenna (St) {2, 4}

22 February
d. 556. He became bishop of Ravenna (Italy) in 546, built the basilica of St Vitalis and is depicted on a mosaic therein.

Maximian of Syracuse (St) {2, 4}

9 June
d. 594. A Sicilian, he became a monk of St Andrew's abbey on the Coelian Hill in Rome under St Gregory the Great. He represented him and his predecessor, Pope Pelagius, at Constantinople, and was made bishop of Syracuse and apostolic legate in Sicily in 591. This was an important responsibility, as the city of Rome as well as the papacy depended on food and revenue from the Sicilian estates of the pope.

Maximilian Binkiewicz (Bl) {2}

24 August
1913–42. A Polish priest, he died of a beating at the concentration camp at Dachau. Cf. **Poland, Martyrs of the Nazi Occupation of.**

Maximilian-Mary Kolbe (St) {1}

14 August

1894–1941. Born at Zdunska-Wola in Poland (then in Russia), when young he became a Franciscan Conventual and worked hard as a missionary in Japan and in the newly independent Poland. He considered that the life of the Church depended on right devotion to Our Lady. During the German occupation after 1939 he sheltered over 2000 Jews and refugees and was at length sent to Auschwitz concentration camp. There he volunteered to take the place of a family man among a group selected to die of starvation in a punishment bunker, and was heard encouraging his fellow victims with hymns and prayers during the fortnight that starved to death. He was canonized in 1982.

Maximilian of Lorch (St) {2, 4}

12 October

Before C7th. The 'Apostle of Noricum' (roughly modern Austria) was born at Celje in Slovenia and became a missionary bishop with a base at Lorch near Passau in Bavaria, Germany. He was martyred at his home city in the reign of Numerian. His extant biography is unreliable, and the old Roman Martyrology duplicates him on 29 October.

Maximilian of Rome (St) {2}

26 August

? He was a martyr buried at the catacomb of Basilla on the old Salarian Way north of Rome.

Maximilian (Mamilian) of Thebeste (St) {2, 4}

12 March

d. 295. He was conscripted into the army at Thebeste in Numidia (Africa), but refused to join because of the pagan ceremonies that were an integral part of army life. As a result he was executed. His acta are genuine. The old Roman Martyrology is erroneous in listing him as a martyr of Rome.

Maximinus of Aix (St) {2, 4}

8 June

? The Roman Martyrology lists him as the first missionary of Aix in Provence (France). He features in the worthless legend concerning the journey of St Mary Magdalen to Marseilles as the city's first bishop. Further, he was imaginatively identified with the man born blind in the gospel of John, Ch. 9.

Maximinus (Mesmin) of Micy (St) {2, 4}

15 December

C6th. From Verdun (France), he followed his uncle St Euspicius to Micy near Orleans and succeeded him as abbot there. He allegedly suppressed the local paganism which had survived two centuries of state Christianity (which apparently did not evangelize rural Gaul very well).

Maximinus of Trier (St) {2, 4}

29 May

d. ?346. From near Poitiers (France) (his brother was St Maxentius of Poitiers), he succeeded St Agrecius, his teacher, as bishop of Trier (Germany) in 333 and was a powerful opponent of imperial Arianism. He sheltered and defended St Athanasius of Alexandria and St Paul of Constantinople when they were exiled to Trier, and was mentioned with approbation by St Jerome.

Maximus cf. **Maginus**.
Maximus cf. **Maximinus**.

(Maximus) (St) {4 –deleted}

28 September

Mid C3rd? He was listed by the old Roman Martyrology as a martyr in the reign of the Emperor Decius.

(Maximus, Bassus and Fabius) (SS)
{4 –deleted}

11 May
Early C4th? They were listed as martyrs of Rome in the reign of Diocletian.

(Maximus, Claudius and Comps) (SS)
{4 –deleted}

18 February
Late C3rd? They were allegedly martyred at Ostia near Rome in the reign of Diocletian, but their legend is worthless. Praepedigna, Alexander and Cutias are also named.

Maximus, Dadas and Quintilian (SS) {2, 4}

28 April
Early C4th. Three brothers of Durostorum (now Silistra on the Danube in Bulgaria), they were beheaded at Ozobia in the reign of Diocletian.

(Maximus and Olympiades) (SS) *{4 –deleted}*

15 April
Mid C3rd? They are listed as Persian noblemen who were beaten to death with iron bars in the reign of Decius.

Maximus, Theodore and Asclepiodotus (SS) {4 –deleted}

15 September
d. c.310. They were from Marcianopolis in what is now Bulgaria, and were martyred at Adrianopolis (in European Turkey).

Maximus of Alexandria (St) {2, 4}

9 April
d. 282. A priest of Alexandria (Egypt), he administered the patriarchate while St Dionysius was in exile from 261 and succeeded him in 282. He excommunicated Paul of Samosata for his adoptionist Christology.

Maximus of Apamea cf. **Maximus of Cuma**.

Maximus of Chinon (St) {2, 4}

20 August
C5th. A disciple of St Martin, he became a hermit and then abbot-founder of Chinon near Tours (France).

Maximus the Chorepiscopus (St) {2}

19 November
Early C3rd? He was a regionary bishop of Caesarea in Cappadocia (Asia Minor) who was martyred.

Maximus the Confessor and Comps (SS) {2, 4}

13 August
580–662. A nobleman of Constantinople, he became a monk at Chrysopolis across the Bosporus with a disciple named Anastasius in 613. They migrated to Africa in 628, where he publicly opposed the imperial Monothelite doctrine being promulgated for political reasons. In 649 he visited Rome and supported the stand of Pope St Martin I against the same doctrine, but was seized with the pope in 653, tried at Constantinople and exiled. He refused to keep silence on the controversial subject and had his tongue and right hand amputated before a final exile to what is now Batum in Georgia with Anastasius (22 July) and another disciple of the same name (not in the Roman Martyrology). He was a prolific and profound theological and spiritual writer, and is arguably the most important Church father not to have been declared a doctor.

Maximus of Cuma (St) {2, 4}

30 October
d.?303. He was martyred at Cuma in Campania (Italy), but the old Roman Martyrology

erroneously listed him as having been martyred at Apamea in Phrygia (Asia Minor).

Maximus of Ephesus (St) {2, 4}

14 May

d. c.250. A merchant of Asia, possibly of Ephesus (Asia Minor), when the edict of Decius against the Christians was published in 250 he voluntarily gave himself up to the judge as a Christian and was martyred. His acta are extant.

Maximus of Jerusalem (St) {2, 4}

5 May

d. c.350. As a priest of Jerusalem he was blinded in one eye and lamed in one foot in the persecution of Diocletian. He succeeded St Macarius as bishop of Jerusalem in 333, but was persuaded by the Arian faction to join them against St Athanasius. This he repented of later, but he has never been venerated in the East.

(Maximus of L'Aquila) (St) {4 –deleted}

20 October

Mid C3rd? This patron of L'Aquila in the Abruzzi (Italy) was described as a deacon there who was martyred in the reign of Decius by being thrown over a precipice.

(Maximus of Mainz)(St) {4 –deleted}

18 November

d. 378. He became bishop of Mainz (Germany) in ?354, and as a bishop had a continual struggle against the Arian heresy. He wrote on the subject.

Maximus of Naples (St) {2, 4}

11 June

C4th. He became the tenth bishop of Naples (Italy) in 359 but died in exile, allegedly as a martyr. His cultus was confirmed for Naples in 1872.

Maximus of Nola (St) {2, 4}

7 February

C3rd. Bishop of Nola (Italy), he ordained St Felix. During the persecution of Decius in 250 he took to the hills and nearly died there of exposure and hunger. Being rescued by St Felix, he died at Nola shortly afterwards.

Maximus of Padua (St) {2, 4}

2 August

C3rd–4th. He was the successor of St Prosdocimus as bishop of Padua (Italy), and his alleged relics were found and enshrined in 1053 by Pope St Leo IX.

Maximus of Pavia (St) {2}

8 January

Pavia in Italy had two bishops of this name venerated as saints, one who succeeded St Crispin I in 270 and the other who succeeded St Epiphanius in 496 and who died in 514. The latter is the one listed in the Roman Martyrology.

Maximus of Riez (St) {2, 4}

27 November

d. p455. A monk of Lérins (France), he became abbot there in 426 and bishop of Riez in Provence reluctantly in 434. He was a prominent bishop of the time, and was allegedly a missionary in the area around Calais.

(Maximus of Rome) (St) {4 –deleted}

19 November

C3rd? He was listed as martyred at Rome in the reign of Valerian.

Maximus of Turin (St) {2, 4}

25 June

d. 408–23. Bishop of Turin (Italy), he has left 110 extant homilies which have been published in a critical edition and are of value.

He has been confused with a namesake bishop of Turin who died about fifty years later.

(Maximus of Verona) (St) {4 –deleted}

29 May
C6th? He was a bishop of Verona (Italy).

Mbaya-Tuzinde (St) {1 –group}

3 June
d. 1886. A page at the court of King Mwanga of Buganda and adopted son of the chief executioner, he was burnt alive at Namuyongo and had to resist the pleas of his family to apostatize up to the time of his death. Cf. **Charles Lwanga and Comps**.

Mechtild of Hackeborn (St) {2}

19 November
d. 1298. A noblewoman from Eisleben near Halle (Germany), she was a Benedictine child-oblate and ended up at the Cistercian nunnery of Helfta where her sister was abbess. She was a noted mystic, and her experiences were recorded after her death by St Gertrude the Great (her former novice) in the 'Book of Special Grace'. There was another mystic at Helfta with the same name at the same period, Mechtild of Magdeburg, who has not been canonized.

Mechtild of Spanheim cf. **Matilda of Spanheim**.
Meda cf. **Ita**.

Medard (St) {2, 4}

8 June
d. 561. A nobleman from Picardy (France), he became bishop of Vermand in 530 and transferred the see to Noyon as the latter place was easier to defend. Later he also became bishop of Tournai, which remained united with Noyon until 1146. A legend similar to that of St Swithin is told about him.

Mederic (Merry) (St) {2, 4}

29 August
d. c.700. From Autun (France), when aged thirteen he became a child-oblate at the abbey of St Martin there and went on to be abbot. Later he resigned and became a hermit locally and then near Paris, where the church of St Merry is now situated.

Meen cf. **Maine**.
Meginrat cf. **Meinrad**.

Meinhard (Bl) {2}

11 October
d. 1196. A Dutch Augustinian canon regular, he went to Livonia as a missionary, was made bishop in 1184 and lived at Ikškile on the Dvina. The see was moved to Riga (Latvia) in 1201 when that city was founded by the Knights of the Sword.

Meinrad (St) {2}

21 January
d. ?861 A nobleman from near Tübingen (Germany), allegedly of the Hohenzollern family, he was a schoolboy and then a Benedictine monk at Reichenau on the Rhine above Basel. Then he became a hermit for twenty-five years at the place in Switzerland later occupied by the abbey of Einsiedeln ('Hermitage'), but was murdered by robbers hoping to find hidden treasure in his cell. He is not listed as a martyr.

Meinulf (St) {2}

5 October
d. ?857. A Westphalian nobleman, he became a cathedral canon at Paderborn (Germany) and founded the abbey of Bödeken, where he died.

Mel (Melchno) (St) {2}

6 February
d. 488. According to the tradition he was one of the four nephews (Mel, Melchu, Munis

and Rioch) of St Patrick, sons of Darerca (St Patrick's sister) and Conis. They accompanied St Patrick to Ireland as missionaries, Mel becoming the first abbot-bishop of Ardagh. The historical evidence concerning him and his brothers is hopelessly entangled and conflicting, however. He is the principal patron of the diocese of Ardagh, with its cathedral at Longford.

Melania the Elder *(St)*

8 June

?342–?410. Of a Roman patrician family and a relative of St Paulinus of Nola, she was one of those caught up in the surge of interest in the ascetical life at Rome caused by the visit of the exiled St Athanasius and his companion monks in 340. Widowed when aged twenty-two, she was one of the first Roman women to visit the Holy Land and Egypt and founded a double monastery at Jerusalem in 378 with Rufinus of Aquilea. She incurred the enmity of St Jerome in the Origenist controversy, which is perhaps why she is not listed in the Roman Martyrology.

Melania the Younger and Pinian (SS) {2, 4}

31 December

A granddaughter of St Melania the Elder, she was born in Rome and received a vast inheritance. Marrying Pinian, a cousin, she had (and lost) two children before the couple decided to live in continence, turning their home into a pilgrim's hostel and giving their wealth to the poor. In ?406 they joined Rufinus in Sicily, from 410 they were in Roman Africa (where they got to know St Augustine) and finally settled in Jerusalem in 417. Pinian died in 431, and Melania founded a nunnery on the Mount of Olives in the following year. She died there in 439.

Melanius of Rennes (St) {2}

6 November

d. p511. From Brittany (France), he was bishop of Rennes when the Franks were conquering Gaul and won the friendship of King Clovis. He is alleged to have almost completely succeeded in extirpating rural paganism from his diocese (in contrast to the Gallic church in general), and tried to persuade his Breton countrymen to abandon the Celtic church customs that they had brought from Britain when they emigrated.

Melas (Melantius) (St) {2, 4}

16 January

d. c.390. An Egyptian monk, he was made bishop of Rhinocolura (now El-Arish) on the coast of Egypt east of Port Said. He was imprisoned and banished on the orders of Emperor Valens for opposing Arianism.

Melasippus cf. **Meleusippus**.

(Melasippus, Carina and Anthony) (SS) *{4 –deleted}*

7 November

d. 360. They were allegedly a couple with a son (or daughter) who were martyred at Ancyra (Asia Minor, now Ankara in Turkey) in the reign of Julian. The parents died under torture, and the child was beheaded. This story conflicts with the declared policy of that emperor in not directly persecuting Christians.

Melchiades cf. **Miltiades**.

Melchior García Sampedro (St) {1 –group}

28 July

d. 1858. He was the Dominican coadjutor of St Joseph Diaz Sanjurjo in central Tonkin, north Vietnam, and was beheaded the year after him at Nan Định during the persecution ordered by Emperor Tự Đức. Cf. **Vietnam, Martyrs of**.

Melchior Kumagai Motonao (Bl) {2 –add}

16 August
d. 1605. He was a married Japanese layperson, from Miiri in Kōchi, who was martyred at Hagi in Yamaguchi. He was beatified in 2008. Cf. **Japan, Martyrs of**.

Melchior-of-St-Augustine Sánchez Pérez (Bl) {2}

11 December
Cf. **Martin of St Nicholas**.

Melchiora-of-the-Adoration Cortés Bueno and Comps (BB) {2 –add}

d. 1936. They are the fifteen martyred Daughters of Charity of St Vincent de Paul, who were killed in several separate incidents in the diocese of Madrid, Spain during the Spanish Civil War (Bl Gaudentia died in hospital as a result of ill-treatment in prison, but is counted as a martyr). They were beatified in 2013. Cf. **Spanish Civil War, Martyrs of** and list in appendix.

Melchisedech (St) {2}

26 August
He was the priest who blessed Abraham in the Book of Genesis in the Old Testament, and is also presented as an exemplar of Christ in the Letter to the Hebrews in the New Testament.

Meletius of Antioch (St) {2, 4}

12 February
d. 381. From Melitene in Armenia, he became bishop of Sebaste in Armenia in 358 and was exiled by Emperor Julian before being elected patriarch of Antioch (Syria) in 360. The church there had been in schism between a semi-Arian majority with its own bishop whom he replaced when he was elected and an orthodox minority whose bishop, St Eustathius, had been deposed. Meletius tried to reconcile the former group, but was himself exiled by Emperor Valens and replaced by another semi-Arian. The priest Paulinus was then consecrated for the Eustathian party, and this caused a schism between the Meletian and Eustathian factions in the city which lasted until 418 and which disturbed the entire Eastern church. Meletius returned in 378 and died while attending the first ecumenical council of Constantinople.

(Meletius the Elect) (St) {4 –deleted}

21 September
? The martyrology of St Basil associates him with an alleged martyr called Isacius, and both are described as bishops in Cyprus.

Meletius of Sebastopolis (St) {2, 4}

4 December
Early C4th. A bishop in Pontus (Asia Minor), he took refuge in the Holy Land during the persecution of Diocletian and became acquainted with Eusebius. The latter wrote that his name derived from 'Mel Atticum' (Attic honey), and was a description of his preaching style. If so, his real name is unknown.

(Meletius Stratelates and Comps) (SS) {4 –deleted}

24 May
C2nd? They are listed in the old Roman Martyrology as a general of the Roman army who was martyred with 252 companions. There is no other information about them, and their acta are fictitious.

(Melitina) (St) {4 –deleted}

15 September
C2nd? She was listed as a virgin martyred at Marcianopolis (near Varna, Bulgaria) in the reign of Antoninus Pius.

Melito of Sardis (St)

1 April
d. c.180. He was a bishop of Sardis in Lydia (Asia Minor), but biographical details are scanty. He was a well-known ecclesiastical writer of the period of the Apologists, but little of his work is extant apart from his famous paschal homily. He is not listed in the Roman Martyrology.

Mellitus (St) {2, 4}

24 April
d. 624. A Roman abbot, presumably from St Andrew's monastery on the Coelian Hill, he was sent to England in 601 by St Gregory the Great as the head of a group of monks intended as reinforcements for St Augustine. He spent three years in Kent before becoming a missionary bishop for the East Saxons based at London, but was exiled to France for excommunicating the apostate sons of their king. In 619 he succeeded St Laurence as archbishop of Canterbury.

Memmius (Menge, Meinge) (St) {2, 4}

5 August
C3rd–4th. The traditional first bishop of Châlons-sur-Marne (France) was alleged to have been a disciple of St Peter in a typical pretence at apostolicity by the medieval French church, but the diocese was founded in the late C3rd at the earliest.

Memnon (St) {2, 4}

3 July
Early C4th? He was a centurion in the Roman army, and was converted by St Severus of Bizya in Thrace (European Turkey). He was martyred there after severe tortures.

Memorius (Mesmin) and Comps (SS) {2, 4}

7 September
C5th. According to the tradition, he was a deacon of Troyes (France) when St Lupus was bishop and was sent with five companions on an embassy to Attila the Hun to ask that the city be spared. They were beheaded. Attila has been traditionally blamed for the killing of Christians by various barbarians at this time. The old Roman Martyrology misspells his name as 'Nemorius'.

(Menas, Hermogenes and Eugraphus) (SS) {4 –deleted}

10 December
Early C4th?. They were listed as beheaded at Alexandria (Egypt) in the reign of Diocletian. Their acta are worthless, and were falsely attributed to St Athanasius.

Menas of Constantinople (St) {2, 4}

25 August
d. 552. From Alexandria (Egypt), he became superior of the hospice of St Samson at Constantinople and was made patriarch in 536. He condemned Origenism but endorsed the decrees of the Emperor Justinian condemning 'the Three Chapters' at a time when the Western Church strongly opposed this policy, and was excommunicated by Pope Vigilius in 551. He withdrew his endorsement and was reconciled just before his death. The chapters were eventually condemned at the fifth ecumenical council, which caused a schism in the West.

Meneleus (Ménelé, Mauvier) (St) {2, 4}

22 July
d. c.700. He was the abbot-founder of Menat near Clermont-Ferrard (France).

(Meneus and Capito) (SS) {4 –deleted}

24 July
? They are listed in both the Roman and Byzantine Martyrologies, but nothing is known about them.

Menignus (St) {2, 4}

15 March

d. c.250. From Parium on the Hellespont (Asia Minor), he was a dyer who tore down the town's publicly displayed copy of the imperial edict against the Christians. His fingers were cut off and he was later beheaded.

Mennas of Egypt (St) {2, 3}

11 November

d. c.300. He was alleged to have been an Egyptian officer in the imperial army martyred at Alexandria, and his cultus became extremely popular during the Christian era of Egypt. He had a shrine at Kotyaeum in Phrygia, Asia Minor, which led to the erroneous tradition that he was martyred there. His main shrine was in the desert south of Alexandria at Abu-Mîna, and was a large complex including a basilica and monastery. The Coptic Church ascribed the victory of the Allies at El Alamein during the Second World War to his intercession, and in thanksgiving his ruined shrine has been restored and is now a functioning pilgrimage centre.

Mennas of Santomena (St) {2, 4}

11 November

C6th. A Greek from Asia Minor, he became a hermit in the Abruzzi (Italy), probably at Santomena (of which place he is patron and which is named after him).

Mennas cf. **Menas.**

(Menodora, Metrodora and Nymphodora) *(SS)* *{4 –deleted}*

10 September

d. 306. Three sisters, they were listed as martyred under Galerius near the Pythian hot springs in Bithynia (Asia Minor). Their acta are worthless.

Mercedes-Mary-of-Jesus Molina (Bl) {2}

12 June

1828–83. Born in Los Rios (Ecuador), she made a private vow of chastity in 1849. While living in her sister's house she tried to help the poor, and in 1867 she went to work in an orphanage and was involved in missionary work in the Andes with two companions. After several journeys they ended up at Rivibamba in 1872. There she founded the 'Congregation of Mary and Anne, Progenitors of Jesus' in order to help poor girls and lapsed women. She was beatified in 1985. Her first name means 'Mercies'.

Mercurialis (St) {2}

30 April

C4th. Allegedly from what is now Azerbaijan, he was the first bishop of Forli (Italy). His cultus is ancient but has inspired many fanciful legends.

Mercurius of Caesarea (St) {2, 4}

25 November

? He was martyred at Caesarea in Cappadocia (Asia Minor). According to his untrustworthy acta, he was a Scythian officer in the imperial army and died in the reign of Decius. He is popular in the East as one of the great soldier-martyrs.

(Mercurius of Lentini and Comps) *(SS)* *{4 –deleted}*

10 December

Early C4th? According to their story, they were a group of twenty soldiers who were detailed to escort some Christian prisoners to their place of execution at Lentini (Sicily) They were so impressed with the behaviour of the prisoners that they declared themselves to be Christians also, and were thus also beheaded.

Merry cf. **Mederic**.

Mesme cf. **Maximus**.

Mesmin cf. **Memorius** or **Maximinus**.

Mesopotamia (Martyrs of) (SS) {2, 4}

23 May

d. ?307. This group was martyred in the region of Edessa (now Urfa in Turkey) in the reign of Galerius by being hanged head-downwards over slow fires.

Mesrop the Teacher (St) {2}

17 February

d. c.440. He was a monk and disciple of St Nerses the Great, Catholicos of Armenia, and was an auxiliary bishop under St Isaac the Great, his successor. He became Catholicos himself only six months before he died. The Armenians attribute to him the invention of their alphabet and the translation of the New Testament into Armenian, and he founded many schools and monasteries. This activity was in the context of Armenia having been annexed by the Persian Empire, and arguably saved the Armenians from extinction as a nation.

Methodius the Confessor (St) {2, 4}

14 June

d. 847. From Syracuse (Sicily), he was a civil servant at Constantinople before founding and joining a monastery on the Aegean island of Chios (Greece). When iconoclasm was re-introduced as imperial policy in 814 he joined the opposition and was imprisoned for seven years from 821. Finally the Empress Theodora designated him patriarch of Constantinople in 842 in place of the deposed iconoclast John the Grammarian, and the synod that he then convoked marked the final end of iconoclasm.

Methodius of Olympus (St) {2}

20 June

d. 312. He was bishop of Olympus in Lycia (Asia Minor), and possibly then of Tyre in Lebanon (if St Jerome's assertion is correct). He is alleged to have been martyred at Chalcis. An eminent theologian, he is known for his 'Banquet of the Ten Virgins' (a Christian version of Plato's Symposium) and for his treatise on the resurrection against Origen.

Methodius-Dominic Trkča (Bl) {2}

23 March

1886–1959. From near Ostravici, Czech Republic, he became a Redemptorist in 1902. He then went to work with the Greek Catholics of the Ukrainian and Ruthenian rites in what was then the northeastern part of the Hapsburg Empire. (The Ruthenians are Slavs living southwest of the Carpathian mountains.) In 1921 he founded a mixed-rite Redemptorist community at Stropkov in Slovakia and a Ruthenian-rite community at Michalovce where he became the superior. In 1949 the Communist government of Czechoslovakia suppressed his foundations; he was accused of collaboration with Bl Paul Gojdič and imprisoned. He eventually died of pneumonia after ill-treatment and was beatified as a martyr in 2001.

Metranus (Metras) (St) {2, 4}

31 January

d. ?249. From Alexandria (Egypt), he was martyred in the reign of Decius. St Dionysius of Alexandria, his bishop and contemporary, left an account of the martyrdom.

Metro (St) {2}

8 May

C8th. He was a hermit at Verona (Italy), noted for his penitential life.

Metrophanes (St) {2, 4}

4 June

d. ?325. Bishop of Byzantium from 313, he was apparently that city's first, but very little is known about him. The town was previously in the diocese of Heraclea. It became Constantinople five years after his death.

(Meuris and Thea) *(SS) {4 –deleted}*

19 December

d. ?307. They were listed as martyred at Gaza in the Holy Land, and are probably identical with SS Valentina and Comps.

Mewan cf. **Maine**.

Mexico (Martyrs of) (SS) {1 –group}

25 May

d. 1915–37. The Mexican Revolution of 1911 gave rise to the 'Constitution of Querétaro', which aimed at eliminating the Church from all aspects of the country's secular life. The period in office of President Calles (1924–8) saw an attempt at its enforcement, and all Catholic organizations and institutions were suppressed. The 'Cristero' rebellion in favour of the Church was defeated, and many priests as well as laypeople were killed. Twenty-six were beatified in 1992, all of them priests except Bl Michael de la Mora (a cleric) and three lay companions of Bl Aloysius Batis: BB Emmanuel Morales, Salvator Lara and David Roldán. All but one were canonized in 2000. A further thirteen were beatified in 2005, comprising two priests and eleven laypeople. Cf. lists of national martyrs in appendix.

Mgagga (St) {1 –group}

3 June

d. 1886. He was an apprentice of the royal cloth maker at the court of King Mwanga of Buganda, and was martyred on the latter's orders. Cf. **Charles Lwanga and Comps**.

Micah (Michaeas) (St) {2}

21 December

He is the sixth of the Minor Prophets of the Old Testament.

Michael the Archangel (St) {1, 3}

29 September

He is described in the Bible as 'one of the chief princes' of the angels (Dan. 10:13) and as the leader of the heavenly armies in their battle against the forces of evil (Rev. 12:7). He is mentioned also in the letter of Jude as 'rebuking the devil'. His veneration in both East and West is ancient, and his feast day is probably the anniversary of the dedication of a church in his honour on the Salarian Way at Rome in the C6th. His most famous shrine is at Monte Gargano on the Adriatic coast of Italy. In northern Europe, there were often churches dedicated to him on hilltops (e.g. at Glastonbury), apparently in order to supplant worship of the pagan god Wotan. He is depicted as an angel in full armour with a sword and a pair of scales, or piercing a dragon or devil with his lance. Since 1969 his feast day on this date has been combined with those of SS Gabriel and Raphael.

Michael de Aozaraza (St) {1 –group}

24 September
Cf. **Laurence Ruiz and Comps**.

Michael-of-the-Saints Argemir (St) {2}

10 April
1591–1625. Born at Vich in Catalonia (Spain), he joined the Calced Trinitarians at Barcelona in 1603 and took his vows at Zaragoza in 1607. The same year he transferred to the

Discalced Trinitarians and renewed his vows at Alcalá. After his ordination he was twice superior at Valladolid, where he died. He was canonized in 1862.

Michael Carvalho and Comps (Bl) {2}

25 August
1577–1624. From Braga (Portugal), he became a Jesuit in 1597, taught theology at Goa for fifteen years and then went to Japan. He was burnt to death at Shimabara with BB Louis Baba, Louis Sasada, Louis Sotelo and Peter Vasquez. They were beatified in 1867. Cf. **Japan, Martyrs of**.

Michael Czartoryski (Bl) {2}

6 September
1897–1944. A Polish Dominican, he was shot by the Nazis at Warsaw. Cf. **Poland, Martyrs of the Nazi Occupation of**.

Michael Febres-Cordero Muñoz (St) {2}

9 February
1854–1910. From Ecuador, he became a de la Salle Brother and was their first indigenous vocation. A gifted teacher and author, he was much loved by his pupils, and his literary and poetic works earned him membership of the 'Academie Française'. A person full of charity and good humour, he led an intense life of personal prayer. He died near Barcelona (Spain), and owing to anti-clerical hostility his body was taken back to Ecuador in 1936. He was canonized in 1984.

Michael Díaz Hori (Bl) {2}

19 August
d. 1622. He was a Spanish merchant accompanying **Louis Flores and Comps** and was beheaded at Nagasaki (Japan) with them. Cf. **Japan, Martyrs of**.

Michael Garicoïts (St) {2}

14 May
1797–1863. From a Basque peasant family of Ibarre near Bayonne (France), he became a domestic servant of his parish priest and then of the bishop of Bayonne in exchange for their educating him for the priesthood. He was ordained in 1823 and was appointed professor of philosophy at the diocesan seminary. He went on to become rector there, and as such he founded at Betharram in 1838 the congregation of 'Auxiliary Priests of the Sacred Heart' (the 'Betharram Fathers') for home mission work. After many initial difficulties the congregation became international in scope, being established in America. He was canonized in 1947.

Michael Ghebre (Bl) {2}

14 July
1791–1855. From Mertule Maryam near the Blue Nile in Ethiopia, he became a monk of the native Ethiopian church and was a noted theologian. He met Bl Justin de Jacobis while in Cairo in 1841, which led to a visit to Rome and his conversion in 1844. With the help of the Vincentians he established a seminary at Gaula to train a native Catholic clergy, and translated many Catholic writings into the native languages. In 1851 he joined the Vincentians and was secretly ordained, but a persecution against the Ethiopian Catholics was started in 1855 by Theodore II, an usurper of the throne. Michael was arrested and died from ill-treatment while in custody. He was beatified in 1926.

Michael Gómez Loza (Bl) {2 –add}

21 March
1888–1927. From Tepatitlán in Jalisco, Mexico, he became a lawyer at Arandas and was involved in Catholic Youth. In 1919 he established a national congress of Catholic workers, and was tireless in protesting against

the oppression of poor people. As a result he was arrested fifty-nine times for organizing protests against the government. During the Cristero War he advocated non-violent resistance to the official persecution, and was appointed as governor of Jalisco by the rebels. As a result he was placed on a government death list, and when federal forces discovered him at a ranch near Atotonilco he was immediately shot by a firing squad. He was beatified in 2005. Cf. **Mexico, Martyrs of**.

Michael Hồ Đinh Hy (St) {1 –group}

22 May
?1808–57. From a Christian family of Nhu-Lam in south Vietnam, he became a great mandarin and superintendent of the royal silk mills in the reign of Tu-Duc. As a young man he was an agnostic, but converted and used his position to try and protect his fellow Christians. He was for this reason beheaded at An Hoa near Hué after vicious tortures. Cf. **Vietnam, Martyrs of**.

Michael Ichinose (Bl) {2}

28 September
d.1630. A Japanese Augustinian tertiary, he was beheaded at Nagasaki with BB John Chozaburo and Comps for having given shelter to the Augustinian missionaries. Cf. **Japan, Martyrs of**.

Michael Kizayemon (Bl) {2}

27 August
d. 1627. He was a Japanese Franciscan tertiary beheaded at Nagasaki with BB Francis-of-St-Mary of Mancha and Comps. Cf. **Japan, Martyrs of**.

Michael Kozaki (St) {1 –group}

6 February
d. 1597. A Japanese catechist and hospital nurse, he worked with the Franciscan missionaries in Kyushu and was crucified at Nagasaki with SS Paul Miki and Comps (including his own son, St Thomas Kosaki). Cf. **Japan, Martyrs of**.

Michael Kozal (Bl) {2}

16 January
1893–1943. A Pole, when he was born his hometown was Gniesen in Germany, but it became Gniezno in Poland in 1919. He became a priest there, taught in the diocesan seminary and became auxiliary bishop in 1939. Two months later the Germans invaded Poland and re-annexed the area. They set out to destroy all manifestations of the Polish Church and culture there and sent him to the concentration camp at Dachau, where he used to celebrate the Mass in secret for his fellow inmates before his death. He was beatified as a martyr in 1987.

Michael Kurobioye (St) {1 –group}

17 August
d. 1633. He was the secular assistant of St James Gorobioye, was martyred with him at Nagasaki (Japan) and was canonized in 1987 with SS Laurence Ruiz and Comps. Cf. **Japan, Martyrs of**.

Michael Kusuriya (Bl) {2 –add}

28 July
1633. A single layperson, a Nagasaki native, he was martyred in that city and beatified in 2008. Cf. **Japan, Martyrs of**.

Michael de la Mora (St) {1 –group}

7 August
d. 1927. He was born into a peasant family of Tecalitlán in Colima, Mexico, and initially worked on the family farm until he discovered his priestly vocation. After ordination he served in several parishes, but was urged to flee during the Cristero War. He was captured

at Cardona, taken back to Colima and shot in a stable while saying the Rosary. His relics are enshrined at the cathedral at Colima. Cf. **Mexico, Martyrs of**.

Michael Nakashima (Bl) {2}

25 December
d. 1628. From near Nagasaki, he concealed missionaries in his house for years and became a Jesuit. In 1627 he was placed under house arrest, and in the following year was taken to Shimabara and tortured. Then he was finally taken to Unzen-dake, a volcano above the town, and had boiling water from the hot springs there poured upon him until he died. He was beatified in 1867. Cf. **Japan, Martyrs of**.

Michael Nguyễn Huy Mỹ (St) {1 –group}

12 August
Cf. **James Đỗ May Năm and Comps**.

Michael Oziębłowski(Bl) {2}

31 July
1900–42. A Polish priest, he died of ill-treatment at the concentration camp at Dachau. Cf. **Poland, Martyrs of the Nazi Occupation of**.

Michael Piaszczyński (Bl) {2}

20 December
1885–1940. A Polish priest, he died of ill-treatment at the concentration camp at Sachsenhausen. Cf. **Poland, Martyrs of the Nazi Occupation of**.

Michael-Augustine Pro (Bl) {2}

23 November
1894–1927. Born of a wealthy family at Guadalupe near Zacatecas (Mexico), he joined the Jesuits in 1911, just in time for the viciously anti-clerical Mexican Revolution. He was in exile in Belgium from 1912 to 1926 and was ordained despite having serious health issues. On his return, he worked very hard in the persecuted Church until he was seized and executed on suspicion of plotting against President Obregón. He was beatified in 1988. Cf. **Mexico, Martyrs of**.

Michael Rua (Bl) {2}

6 April
1837–1910. From Turin (Italy), he was an early disciple of St John Bosco and succeeded him as superior-general of the Salesians in 1888. Nearly 300 new houses of the institute were opened under him. He was beatified in 1972.

Michael Sopoćko (Bl) {2 –add}

1888–1975. From a noble Polish family of Nowosady in Lithuania (then part of the Russian Empire), he became a diocesan priest of Vilnius in 1914. Initially a parish priest, he became an army chaplain when Poland became independent and conquered Vilinius. In 1927 he became spiritual director of the seminary, but resigned most of his pastoral duties to concentrate on theological studies at the university. As confessor to several congregations of nuns he became spiritual director to St Faustina Kowalska, and it was on his advice that she promulgated her visions concerning the Divine Mercy. This doctrine became his inspiration, and as a result he founded the 'Sisters of Divine Mercy' and published works on the subject in many languages. Under the Soviet Union he was a professor at the seminary. He was beatified in 2008.

Michael Shumpo (Bl) {2}

10 September
1589–1622. A Japanese, he started helping the Jesuit missionaries when only eight years

old. He made his profession as a Jesuit to Bl Charles Spinola in prison at Omura just before they were burnt in the 'Great Martyrdom' at Nagasaki. Cf. **Japan, Martyrs of** and **Great Martyrdom at Nagasaki**.

Michael of Synnada (St) {2}

23 May
d. 826. He was a disciple of St Tarasius, patriarch of Constantinople, and was appointed by him bishop of Synnada in Phrygia (Asia Minor) in 787. He was a fearless opponent of iconoclasm, and when this heresy became imperial policy again under Emperor Leo IV he was exiled to Galatia, where he died.

Michael Takeshita (Bl) {2}

27 November
1594–1619. A Japanese layman, he was related to the daimyos of Hirado-jima and was described as a very amiable man. He was beheaded at Nagasaki with **Thomas Koteda and Comps**. Cf. **Japan, Martyrs of**.

Michael Timoyona (Bl) {2}

28 September
d. 1628. A Japanese catechist and Dominican tertiary, he was beheaded at Nagasaki with his son, Bl Paul, and Bl Dominic Shobyoye. Cf. **Japan, Martyrs of**.

Michael Tomachi (Bl) {2}

8 September
1613–28. A Japanese teenager, he was beheaded at Nagasaki with his father, John, and his three brothers: Dominic, Paul and Thomas. Cf. **Dominic Castellet and Comps** and **Japan, Martyrs of**.

Michael Tozo (Bl) {2}

20 June
d. 1626. He was a Japanese catechist who worked with Bl Balthasar Torres and became

a Jesuit just before his execution. Cf. **Francis Pacheco and Comps** and **Japan, Martyrs of**.

Michael Woźniak (Bl) {2}

16 May
1875–1942. A Polish priest, he died of ill-treatment at the concentration camp at Dachau. Cf. **Poland, Martyrs of the Nazi Occupation of**.

Michael Yamada (Bl) {2}

8 September
d. 1628. A Japanese Dominican tertiary, he was beheaded at Nagasaki with **Dominic Castellet and Comps**. Cf. **Japan, Martyrs of**.

Michael Yamichi (Bl) {2}

10 September
1617–22. The five-year-old-son of Bl Damian Yamiki, he was beheaded at Nagasaki with his father in the 'Great Martyrdom'. Cf. **Japan, Martyrs of** and **Great Martyrdom at Nagasaki**.

Michaela cf. **Mary-Michaela**.

Michelina-of-Pesaro Metelli (Bl) {2}

20 June
1300–56. A noblewoman from Pesaro (Italy), when aged twelve she married the duke of Malatesta but was widowed when she was twenty. Then her only child died and she became a Franciscan tertiary. Her disgusted parents treated her as a madwoman and imprisoned her for a while. On being released she gave her property to the poor and lived in asceticism for the rest of her life. Her cultus for Gubbio was confirmed in 1737.

Mida cf. **Ita**.

Miechislav Bohatkiewicz (Bl) {2}

4 March
1904–42. A Polish priest, he was shot at Berezwecz near Głębokie by the Nazis together

with BB Ladislas Maćkowiak and Stanislaus Pyrtek. Cf. **Poland, Martyrs of the Nazi Occupation of**.

Miguel cf. **Michael**.

Milburga (St) {2, 4}

23 February
d. ?722. Eldest daughter of St Ermenburga and sister of SS Mildred and Mildgyth, she became second abbess of the nunnery of Wenlock in Shropshire (England) founded by her father, the king of Mercia. St Theodore consecrated her as a nun, and the nunnery apparently flourished under her. (It became extinct in the Viking era and was re-founded after the Norman Conquest as a Cluniac priory, whereupon her alleged relics were discovered.) She was a thaumaturge, and had a peculiar rapport with birds.

Mildred of Thanet *(St)*

13 July
d. c.700. The second of the three daughters of St Ermenburga, she was sent to be educated in the French nunnery of Chelles and, on her return, was consecrated as a nun by St Theodore at Minster in Thanet (Kent, England). She eventually succeeded her mother as abbess. The monks of St Augustine's Abbey in Canterbury stole her relics for their own monastery in 1030 (an account of the escapade survives), and they were taken to Deventer in the Netherlands after the Reformation. Part has now been returned to Minster. Her cultus was popular in the Middle Ages, and is approved for the district of Thanet despite her not being listed in the Roman Martyrology. Her attribute is a white deer.

Miles Gerard (alias William Richardson) (Bl) {2}

13 April
d. 1590. From near Wigan (Lancs), he became a schoolteacher before studying for the priesthood at Rheims. He was ordained in 1583,

executed at Rochester (Kent) with Bl Francis Dickenson and beatified in 1929. Other sources have their execution on the 30th. Cf. **England, Martyrs of**.

Miltiades, Pope (St) {2, 3}

10 January
d. 314. Perhaps a Roman African, he became pope in 311. He was reigning when the Edict of Milan was promulgated by Emperor Constantine, and was asked to arbitrate in the Donatist controversy in Africa by him. His name was wrongly spelt 'Melchiades' in the old Roman Martyrology. His cultus was confined to local calendars in 1969.

(Minervius, Eleazar and Comps) *(SS)* *{4 –deleted}*

23 August
C3rd? Their surviving acta are worthless, but it seems that they were martyred at Lyons (France). They have been alleged to have been a married couple with eight children, or two men with the children belonging to one or the other. Eleazar is the one with uncertain gender.

Minias (Miniato) (St) {2, 4}

25 October
C3rd. A Roman soldier at Florence (Italy), he tried to evangelize his comrades and was beheaded in the reign of Decius. A famous abbey grew around his shrine.

Mirocles (St) {2, 4}

30 November
d. p314. An archbishop of Milan (Italy), he was one of the authors of the Ambrosian liturgy used in that diocese.

Miroslav Bulešić (Bl) {2 –add}

24 August
1920–47. From Čabrunići in Croatia (then in Istria, Italy), he was ordained to the diocese

of Pula in 1943. At the end of the Second World War the territory of Istria was annexed by Yugoslavia, and that country taken over by Communists. After preventing a Communist gang from desecrating his parish church at Lanišće, he was stabbed in the throat at home the following day. He was beatified in 2013.

Mirren of Paisley (St)

15 September
d. c.620. Allegedly a disciple of St Comgall at Bangor (Ireland), he became a missionary bishop based at Paisley (Scotland), of which place he is the patron. The local soccer club is named after him.

Mitrias (Mitre, Metre, Merre) (St) {2, 4}

13 November
C4th. A Greek slave at Aix-en-Provence (France), because he was a Christian he was savagely ill-treated by his master and his fellow slaves and ended up being beheaded.

Minason cf. **Jason**.

Mocius (St) {2}

11 May
? He was a priest martyred at Byzantium, which later became Constantinople. His acta are spurious.

Moderan (Moderamnus, Moran) (St) {2}

22 October
d. c.720. From Rennes (France), he became bishop there in 703. In c.720 he made a pilgrimage to Rome, resigned as bishop and became a monk-hermit in the abbey of Berceto near Parma.

Modesta of Ohren (St) {2, 4}

4 November
C7th. She was the niece of St Modoald, who appointed her first abbess of the nunnery of Ohren which he had founded at Trier (Germany).

Modestinus-of-Jesus-and-Mary Mazzarella (Bl) {2}

24 July
1802–54. From near Naples, he became a Franciscan there in 1822, serving as a preacher and confessor and as the guardian of two friaries. In 1839 he transferred to a friary in a Neapolitan slum, where he helped the poor and sick, defended newborn babies against neglect and spread devotion to Our Lady of Good Counsel in what was a post-Christian environment. He died of cholera while nursing victims of an epidemic, and was beatified in 1995.

(Modestus and Ammonius) (SS) {4 –deleted}

12 February
? They were listed as children having been martyred at Alexandria (Egypt), but nothing is known about them.

(Modestus and Julian) (SS) {4 –deleted}

12 February
? Modestus was listed as martyred at Carthage, Julian at Alexandria (in 160). The former is the patron of Cartagena (Spain). They were arbitrarily listed together in the old Roman Martyrology.

Modestus Andlauer (St) {1 –group}

19 June
Cf. **Remigius Isoré and Modestus Andlauer**.

(Modestus of Benevento) (St) {4 –deleted}

12 February
d. ?304. Allegedly a Sardinian deacon, he was martyred at an uncertain place in the reign of Diocletian. His shrine was established at Benevento (Italy).

Modestus of Jerusalem (St) {2}

17 December
d. 634. He was Patriarch of Jerusalem after the Persians had captured it and burnt the Holy Places. He organized much rebuilding, and also arranged the repopulation of abandoned monasteries.

Modestus of Trier (St) {2, 4}

24 February
d. c.480. He was bishop of Trier (Germany) from 486, when the city was being rebuilt under the rule of the Franks.

Modoald (St) {2, 4}

12 May
d. /647. From Gascony, he was either a relative or a friend of most of the saints of the contemporary Merovingian church. He was an adviser to King Dagobert I before he became bishop of Trier (Germany) in 622.

Modoc cf. **Aidan of Ferns**.
Molaisse cf. **Laserian**.
Molua cf. **Lua**.
Mommolinus cf. **Mummolinus**.
Mommolus cf. **Mummolus**.
Monacella cf. **Melangell**.

Mona (St) {2, 4}

25 March
d. c.300. He was bishop of Milan (Italy) from 193 and was noted as a philosopher.

Monegund (St) {2, 4}

2 July
d. p557. A married woman of Chartres (France), when her two daughters died she became a hermit with the consent of her husband. To escape attention she migrated to Tours and lived in a cell near the tomb of St Martin, where she died and where her disciples founded a nunnery.

Monenna (St) {2}

6 July
d. 517. By tradition she was the founder of the nunnery at Killeevy in Co. Armagh (Ireland), and was associated with SS Patrick and Brigid. She has been confused with St Modwenna.

Monica (St) {1, 3}

27 August
332–87. From a Christian family of Carthage (Roman Africa), she married a pagan and had three children. The eldest of these was St Augustine, who did not imitate his mother's faith as a young man. Her patience converted her husband, and after his death she followed St Augustine to Italy. Her prayers contributed to her son being baptized a Catholic, which event took place in Milan in 387. She died the same year at Ostia near Rome, on the way back to Africa with him, and her shrine is in his church at Rome.

Monica Naizen (Bl) {2}

12 July
d. 1626. A Japanese laywoman, she was beheaded at Nagasaki with her husband, Bl John Naizen, and her son, Bl Louis, for having sheltered Bl John-Baptist Zola. Cf. **Mancius Araki and Comps** and **Japan, Martyrs of**.

(Monitor) (St) {4 –deleted}

10 November
d. c.490. Nothing is known about this bishop of Orleans (France).

Mono (St) {2}

18 October
d. 630–40. A Scottish (or Irish) pilgrim, he settled as a hermit at Nassogne in the

Ardennes (Belgium) and was murdered by some malefactors whom he had rebuked.

Montanus and Maxima (SS) {2, 4}

26 March
d. 304. A priest and his wife, they were martyred by being drowned in the river Save at Sirmium (now Srem Mitrovica in Serbia).

(Montanus of Gaeta) (St) *{4 –deleted}*

17 June
Early C4th? The story is that he was a Roman soldier exiled to the island of Ponza off Gaeta (Italy) and later thrown into the sea with a stone tied to his neck. His body was recovered and enshrined at Gaeta.

Montford Scott (Bl) {2}

1 July
d. 1591. A Suffolk landowner, he studied at Douai in the 1570s, started work in East Anglia while still a deacon and was ordained at Brussels in 1577. In 1584 he was captured at York while about to leave the country, imprisoned for seven years and executed at Tyburn with Bl George Beesley. He was beatified in 1987. Cf. **England, Martyrs of.**

Monulf and Gandulf (SS) {2}

16 July
C6–7th. The first was bishop of Maastricht, who transferred his cathedral to Tongeren (Belgium). The latter was his successor.

Morand (St) {2}

3 June
d. ?1115. A nobleman from near Worms (Germany), he became a monk at Cluny under St Hugh the Great after a pilgrimage to Comopstella. Eventually he became the first superior of the new Cluniac Benedictine foundation at Altkirch near Mulhouse (France).

Moses (St) {2}

4 September
He is the great leader of Israel in the Pentateuch of the Old Testament.

(Moses of Africa) (St) *{4 –deleted}*

18 December
C3rd? He was listed as a Roman African martyr.

Moses the Arab (St) {2, 4}

7 February
d. ?389. He was an Arab hermit at what is now El-Arish on the Mediterranean coast of the Sinai Peninsula, and became a missionary bishop among his fellow Bedouin of the region.

Moses the Ethiopian (St) {2}

28 August
d. c.400. A black Cushite of enormous stature, he was born in slavery in Egypt and turned out to have such a nasty character that his master drove him from the household and he became the leader of a gang of robbers. As a fugitive from justice he took refuge among the hermits of Scetis (now the Wadi Natrun), was converted and joined them. He was ordained and became one of the most famous of the second generation of Egyptian desert fathers. When old he was murdered by barbarian raiders after refusing either to flee or to defend himself.

Moses of Rome (St) {2, 4}

25 November
d. 251. A Roman priest, noted for his zeal against Novatianist rigorism, he was martyred in the reign of Decius.

Moses Tovini (Bl) {2 –add}

28 January
1877–1930. From near Brescia (Italy), he was ordained as a diocesan priest for that

city in 1899 and was made a professor at the seminary in 1904, a position he held all his life. He became its rector in 1926. He was constantly vigilant over the souls of the seminarians, with combined severity and benevolence as circumstances required, forming their priestly vocations around the Eucharist, the Blessed Virgin and loyalty to the pope. He died of pneumonia and was beatified in 2006.

(Moseus and Ammonius) (SS) {4 –deleted}

18 January
d. 250. The story is that for being Christians these two soldiers were sentenced to forced labour for life in the mines and later burnt alive at Astas in Bithynia (Asia Minor).

Mucian-Mary Wiaux (Bl) {2}

30 January
1841–1917. From Mellet (Belgium), as a teenager he joined the Brothers of the Christian Schools with difficulty since he had little natural aptitude for teaching. But he then spent fifty-five years at a school in Malonne as a prefect and primary music teacher, with no great success but with such personal holiness that he was canonized in 1989.

Muirchu (Maccutinus) (St)

8 June
C7th. From Ireland, he wrote biographies of SS Brigid and St Patrick. Nothing is known about his own life.

Mukasa Kiriwanvu (St) {1 –group}

3 June
d. 1886. He waited at the table of King Mwanga of Buganda (Uganda) and was martyred on his orders. Cf. **Charles Lwanga and Comps**.

Mullion cf. **Melanius**.

Mummolin (Mommolin) (St) {2}

16 October
d. ?686. From Constance (Germany), he became a monk at Luxeuil and then superior of the Old Monastery (later named St Mommolin after him) at St Omer (France). Then he transferred to Sithiu nearby, which had been founded by (and later named after) his friend St Bertinus. Finally he was made bishop of Noyon-Tournai in 660.

Mummolus (Mommolus, Mommolenus) (St) {2}

8 August
d. 678. He was the second abbot of Fleury near Orleans (France). During his abbacy there was an alleged transfer of the relics of SS Benedict and Scholastica from Montecassino to Fleury (that this event took place is denied by the former monastery). Thus Fleury is now known as Saint-Benoît-sur-Loire.

Mungo cf. **Kentigern**.
Munnu cf. **Fintan**.

Muredach (Murtagh) (St) {2}

12 August
C5th? Allegedly a disciple of St Patrick and the first bishop of Killala in Co. Mayo (Ireland), he either became a hermit on the island of Inishmurray in Donegal Bay or became involved with St Columba at Iona. Both traditions together cannot be correct. He is the principal patron of the diocese of Killala.

Muredhae cf. **Marianus Scotus**.

Mustiola (St) {2, 4}

3 July
? She was martyred at Chiusi in Tuscany (Italy). Her legend pairs her with a deacon Irenaeus, and has them martyred in the reign of Aurelian for ministering to other martyrs and having buried their bodies. He has been deleted from the Roman Martyrology.

Mygdon and Comps (SS) {2, 4}

23 December

d. 303. When the Emperor Diocletian instigated his persecution in 303, the imperial court at Nicomedia in Asia Minor was purged of Christian officials. This priest with six other faithful refused to apostatize, and so were imprisoned and martyred. Also named are Eugenius, Maximus, Domna, Mardonius, Smaragdus and Hilary.

Mylor cf. **Melor**.

(Myron the Wonderworker) (St) {4 –deleted}

8 August

C4th? He allegedly became a bishop somewhere in Crete and died a centenarian.

Myron of Cyzicus (St) {2, 4}

17 August

C3rd. He was martyred at Cyzicus on the Asian shore of the Sea of Marmara after having confronted some imperial officers directed to destroy his church by decree of the Emperor Decius.

Myrope (St) {2, 4}

13 July

C3rd–4th. A native of Chios in the Aegean Sea (Greece), she buried some martyrs of the Decian persecution, including St Isidore. Because of this she was whipped and died in prison as a result.

N

Nabor and Felix (SS) {2, 4}

12 July
d. ?304. They were beheaded at Milan (Italy) in the reign of Diocletian and had their relics enshrined by St Ambrose almost a century later. Their cultus was confined to local calendars in 1969.

Nahum the Prophet (St) {2}

1 December
He was the prophet who advised King David in the Old Testament.

Najran (Martyrs of) (SS) {2, 4}

24 October
d. 523. A large group of martyrs (numbering 340, according to the Roman Martyrology), they were massacred at Najran in southwest Arabia by Jews and pagan Arabs at the instigation of the Jewish leader of the Homerites, Dū Nuwās (Dun`an). The head of the group was the chief of the Beni Harith, Abdullah ibn Kaab (the 'Arethas' of the Roman Martyrology). Religion in Arabia before Muhammed was an eclectic mixture of paganism and orthodox and heterodox versions of both Judaism and Christianity. This massacre left such a deep contemporary impression that Muhammed later mentioned it in the Koran (Sura 85).

Namatius (Namace) of Clermont (St) {2}

27 October
d. c.460. He was a bishop of Clermont-Ferrand (France).

Namatius (Namat) of Vienne (St) {2}

17 November
d. 599. He was a bishop of Vienne (France) whose cultus was confirmed in 1903.

Namphamo and Comps (SS) {2, 4}

18 December
? A Roman African of Carthaginian descent, he was martyred with several companions (named are Miggi, Sanam and Lucita) at Madaura in Numidia (Algeria). Patristic African writers referred to him as 'the Archmartyr', implying that he was the province's first.

Napoleon cf. **Neopolus**.

Narcissa-of-Jesus Martillo Morán (St) {2}

8 December
1832–69. Born at a little village near Guayaquil (Ecuador), when both her parents died, she went to that city to work as a cook, sharing her wages with the poor. She saw her vocation as one of reparative expiation to the Sacred Heart on behalf of the world and lived for a time with Bl Mercedes Molina. In 1868 she went to the monastery of Our Lady of Protection at Lima (Peru), but died before she could join. She was canonized in 2008.

(Narcissus and Crescentio) *(SS)* *{4 –deleted}*

17 September
C3rd? They are mentioned in the unreliable acta of St Laurence of Rome, who allegedly used to distribute alms to the poor in the house of Narcissus and there cured Crescentio of blindness. On the Salarian Way a cemetery bore the name of Crescentio, indicating his historical existence.

(Narcissus and Felix) *(SS)* *{4 –deleted}*

18 March
? A bishop and his deacon, they are venerated as martyrs at Gerona (Spain). Nothing else is known about them, as the story of their escape to, and their apostolate in, Germany and Switzerland (including their conversion of St Afra) is fictitious.

Narcissus of Jerusalem (St) {2, 4}

29 October
d. ?222. A Greek, he became bishop of Jerusalem when already very old and supported the Alexandrine mode of computation of the date of Easter (used at Rome) against the earlier one linking it to the Passover. As a result he was calumniated, had to resign and apparently became a hermit but later returned and died as bishop.

Narcissus Putz (Bl) {2}

5 December
1887–1942. A Polish priest, he died of ill-treatment at the concentration camp at Dachau. Cf. **Poland, Martyrs of the Nazi Occupation of**.

Narcissus Turchan (Bl) {2}

19 March
1879–1942. A Polish Franciscan friar, he died of ill-treatment at the concentration camp at Dachau. Cf. **Poland, Martyrs of the Nazi Occupation of**.

Narnus of Bergamo (St) {2, 4}

27 August
C4th. He was the first bishop of Bergamo (Italy). According to the spurious legend, he was consecrated by St Barnabas.

Narses and Joseph (St) {2}

10 November
d. 343. Narses was bishop of Subogord in Persia, and was martyred with his disciple Joseph (possibly in the persecution of Shah Shapur II).

(Natalia of Nicomedia) (St) {4 –deleted}

1 December
Early C4th? According to the story, she was the wife of St Adrian of Nicomedia (Asia Minor) who imitated her husband in helping those imprisoned during the persecution of Diocletian. Surviving the persecution, she died in peace at Constantinople.

Natalia Tułasiewicz (Bl) {2}

31 March
1906–45. A teacher from Poznan in Poland, she volunteered to move to Germany with a group of conscripted women workers in order to help them spiritually. When the Gestapo discovered this, they tortured and humiliated her in public before having her gassed on Easter Sunday at the concentration camp of Ravensbrück. Cf. '**Poland, Martyrs of the Nazi Occupation of**'.

Natalis (Noel) Chabanel (Bl) {2}

8 December
1613–49. From Toulouse (France), he joined the Jesuits in 1630 and became a professor of rhetoric at several Jesuit colleges in France. In 1643 he went as a missionary to the Huron nation in what is now Ontario (Canada), east of Lake Huron. Despite the efforts of St John Brébeuf and his fellow missionaries, the Huron nation was then deeply divided between the Christian converts and those who wished to keep to the old ways. St Natalis was killed by a renegade Huron just before the collapse of the mission as a result of Iroquois raids. He was canonized in 1930. Cf. **John Brébeuf and Comps**.

Natalis (Noel) Pinot (Bl) {2}

21 February
1747–94. From Angers (France), he was ordained as a diocesan priest there in 1771 and was parish priest of Louroux-Beconnais until the outbreak of the French Revolution. When he refused to take the oath recognizing the civil constitution of the clergy he was expelled from his parish but continued to

minister to it, at first in secret and afterwards openly. In 1794 he was captured when about to say Mass and immediately guillotined, still wearing his vestments. He was beatified in 1926. Cf. **French Revolution, Martyrs of**.

Nathalan (St) {2}

8 January
d. ?678. According to his legend he was a wealthy man who became a hermit near Aberdeen (Scotland) and supported himself by cultivating his smallholding 'which work approaches nearest to divine contemplation'. He became a missionary bishop based at Old Meldrum, and his cultus was confirmed in 1898.

Nathanael cf. **Bartholomew**.

Nathy (David) (St) {2}

9 August
C6th. Disciple of St Finian of Clonard, he became the founder and abbot-bishop of a monastery at Achonry in Co. Sligo (Ireland), of which diocese he is the principal patron. His cultus was confirmed in 1903.

Nazaria-Ignatia-of-St-Teresa-of-Jesus March Mesa (Bl) {2}

6 July
1889–1943. From Madrid (Spain), she migrated with her family to Mexico when aged twenty and joined the 'Sisters of Forsaken Old People'. After her noviciate in Spain she joined a group making a new foundation at Oruro in Bolivia and was extremely enthusiastic, despite knowing little about Bolivian culture. She was asked to found the first Bolivian religious congregation, the 'Crucified Missionaries of the Church', with an Ignatian spirituality and a special vow of obedience to the pope. They spread to Argentina, Uruguay and Spain. She died at Buenos Aires and was beatified in 1992.

Nazarius and Celsus (SS) {2, 4}

28 July
? According to their worthless acta, they were beheaded at Milan (Italy) in the reign of Nero. St Ambrose discovered their relics at Milan in 395. The cultus was confined to local calendars in 1969.

Nectan (St)

17 June
C6th. Allegedly a son of St Brychan, he became a hermit at Hartland in Devon (England). He was later venerated as a martyr, for unknown reasons (the extant legend is untrustworthy). His shrine was in an Augustinian monastery and was a focus of pilgrimage in north Devon until the Reformation.

Nemesia Valle (Bl) {2}

18 December
1847–1916. From a middle-class family of Aosta in Italy, she attended a boarding school run by the Sisters of Charity at Besançon in France and was thus inspired to join them in 1866. Initially she was at Tortona, but she was novice-mistress at the new foundation at Borgono from 1903. She was beatified in 2004.

Nemesian and Comps (SS) {2, 4}

10 September
d. 257–8. Nine Roman African bishops of Numidia (Algeria), they were sentenced to slavery in the marble quarries of Sigum with many priests and laypeople. There they were worked to death. The other bishops were: two named Felix, Lucius, Litteus, Polyanus, Victor, Jader and Dativus. A letter by St Cyprian to them survives.

(Nemesius and Lucilla) (SS) {4 –deleted}

25 August
d. c 260. According to their untrustworthy acta they were a Roman deacon and his

daughter and were martyred at Rome in the reign of Valerian.

Nemesius of Alexandria (St) {2, 4}

10 September
d. 251. He was burnt at the stake between two thieves at Alexandria (Egypt) in the reign of Decius.

(Nemesius of Liewen) (St) {4 –deleted}

1 August
? He is venerated around Lisieux (France), but nothing is known about him.

Nemorius cf. **Memorius**.

Neophytus of Nicaea (St) {2}

20 January
Early C4th. He was a teenager martyred at Nicaea (Asia Minor) in the reign of Galerius.

Neopolus (Neapolysus, Napoleon) of Alexandria (St)

15 August
d. c.300. He was tortured at Alexandria (Egypt) in the reign of Diocletian and died immediately afterwards. The French emperor was named after him, but he is not in the Roman Martyrology.

Neot (St)

31 July
d. c.880. According to his tradition he was a monk of Glastonbury, England (insofar as any monastic life survived there at the time) and became a hermit near Liskeard in Cornwall at the place now called St Neot. Apparently his relics were taken to a monastery in Cambridgeshire in the C10th, and this led to his name being given to the town of St Neot's there. There may have been two saints of the same name.

Nereus and Achilles (SS) {1, 3}

12 May
End C3rd. They were soldiers of the Praetorian Guard, according to the epitaph written by Pope St Damasus. Their acta are worthless and anachronistic, alleging that they were baptized by St Peter and were exiled with St Flavia Domitilla to the island of Ponza and later to Terracina, where they were beheaded.

(Nerses of Sahgerd and Comps) (SS) {4 –deleted}

20 November
d. 343. A group of at least twelve Persian martyrs, including Nerses bishop of Sahgerd and four other bishops, they were killed by strangling, stoning, and beheading in the persecution of Shah Shapur II.

Nestor of Magydos (St) {2, 4}

25 February
d. c.250. Bishop of Magydos in Pamphylia (Asia Minor), he was crucified at Perga in the reign of Decius.

(Nestor of Thessalonika) (St) {4 –deleted}

8 October
d. ?304. He was listed as martyred at Thessalonika (Greece) in the reign of Diocletian. His acta are worthless.

Nevolo (Bl) {2}

27 July
d. 1280. A married shoemaker of Faenza (Italy), he lived a frivolous life until a conversion when aged twenty-four, whereupon he became a penitential pilgrim hermit. He has been claimed as a tertiary or lay brother by both the Franciscans and Camaldolese, but the Roman Martyrology admits neither. His cultus was approved for Faenza in 1817, and is kept by both orders.

(Nicaeas and Paul) (SS) {4 –deleted}

29 August
? They are listed as having been martyred at Antioch (Syria).

Nicander and Hermes (SS) {2, 4}

4 November
C4th? They were a bishop and a priest who were martyred at Myra in Lycia (Asia Minor).

Nicander and Marcian (SS) {2, 4}

17 June
d. ?297. They were two officers in the imperial army who refused to sacrifice to idols and were martyred at Silistra in Bulgaria in the reign of Diocletian.

(Nicander of Egypt) (St) {4 –deleted}

15 March
Early C4th? He is listed as an Egyptian physician who ministered to Christians in prison and buried those martyred in the persecution of Diocletian. He was beheaded himself as a result.

(Nicanor the Deacon) (St) {4 –deleted}

10 January
C1st. A Jew, he was one of the seven deacons of Jerusalem chosen by the apostles (Acts 6:5). The tradition is that he eventually went to Cyprus and was martyred there in the reign of Vespasian, but there is no historical evidence for this.

(Nicarete) (St) {4 –deleted}

27 December
d. ?405. She was a noblewoman of Nicomedia, living at Constantinople. As a loyal supporter of St John Chrysostom, she was sent into exile with him.

Nicasius Jonson van Hees (St) {2}

9 July
?1522–72. Born in the castle of Hees in Brabant, Belgium, he became a Franciscan licentiate of theology and was the author of several polemical works against Protestantism. He was based at the friary at Gorinchem when he was hanged with the other **Gorinchem** martyrs (q.v.).

Nicasius of Rheims and Comps (SS) {2, 4}

14 December
d. 407. He was a bishop of Rheims (France) and was killed at the door of his cathedral by invading barbarian Vandals with his sister Eutropia, a consecrated virgin, a deacon Florentius and Jucundus, a layman.

Nicasius of Rouen and Comps (SS) {2, 4}

11 October
? He was martyred at Rouen (France) with Quirinus, Scubiculus and Pienta. According to his unreliable legend, he was a bishop of the city who was killed on the way home from Paris with a priest, a deacon and a consecrated virgin. There was no such bishop of the city, and the story is derived from Nicasius of Rheims.

(Nicephorus of Antioch) (St) {4 –deleted}

9 February
d. 260. The story of this alleged martyr of Antioch (Syria) in the reign of Valerian is probably a pious fiction, written to teach the necessity of forgiving one's enemies.

Nicephorus of Constantinople (St) {2, 4}

2 June
758–829. He had been imperial secretary at the court of Constantinople before retiring to a monastery for a while (without becoming

a monk) and then running the city's largest alms-house. He was chosen patriarch in 806, despite still being a layman. Initially opposed by St Theodore Studites, he proved himself by standing firm against the revival of iconoclasm by Emperor Leo V in 815. He died in exile at a monastery which he had founded on the Bosporus.

Nicephorus-of-Jesus-and-Mary Díez Tejerina and Comps (BB) {2}

d. 1936. They were the superior and brethren (mostly clerics studying philosophy) of the Passionist community at Daímiel near Ciudad Real in Spain. During the Civil War the retreat was raided by a couple of hundred Republican soldiers on the night of 21 June, and Bl Nicephorus and twenty-five out of thirty of the others were taken away in four groups and shot at various times and in various places nearby. They were beatified in 1989. Cf. **Spanish Civil War, Martyrs of** and list in appendix.

(Niceta and Aquilina) (SS) {4 –deleted}

24 July

? These names were originally Nicetas and Aquila, and were of two mythical soldier-martyrs. In the fictional acta of St Christopher the names were feminized and given to two prostitutes converted by him, and executed with him.

Nicetas of Appolonias (St) {2, 4}

20 March
d. 733. Bishop of Apollonias in Bithynia (Asia Minor), he died in exile for opposing the iconoclast policy of Emperor Leo III.

Nicetas Budka (Bl) {2}

28 September
1877–1949. He was the exarch for Ukrainian Catholics in Canada, and was arrested by the Soviet authorities after the annexation of eastern Poland by the Soviet Union. He died in a gulag at Karaganda in what is now Kazakhstan. Cf. **Nicholas Čarneckyj and 24 Comps**.

Nicetas the Great (St) {2, 4}

15 September
d. c.370. An Ostrogoth nobleman, he was converted with many of his nation (in what is now the Ukraine) by the Arian missionary Ulfilas, who probably also ordained him priest. A Gothic leader started a persecution of Christianity in 377, and Nicetas was burnt at the stake somewhere in Bessarabia (roughly present-day Moldova). His shrine was established at Mopsuestia near Antioch (Syria), and his veneration became popular in the East. It is virtually certain that he was an Arian, however.

Nicetas of Medikion (St) {2, 4}

3 April
d. 824. He was abbot of Medikion, one of the monasteries of the great monastic colony on the Bithynian Olympus near Nicaea (Asia Minor), and stood out against the iconoclastic policy of Emperor Leo V. As a result he was imprisoned for six years on an island in the Sea of Marmara, but after the emperor's death was set free and died as a hermit near Constantinople.

Nicetas of Remesiana (St) {2, 4}

22 June
d. ?414. He was a missionary bishop working among the barbarians on the Empire's Danube frontier, and seems to have been based at what is now Biela Palanka near Niš (Serbia). He was a distinguished church author, although his authorship of the ancient hymn called the *Te Deum* is doubtful.

Nicetius (Nizier) of Besançon (St) {2}

8 February
d. c.610. Bishop of Nyon on the Lake of Geneva, he re-established his see at Besançon (France) whence it had been transferred after the city's destruction by the Huns. He was a friend and supporter of St Columbanus and dedicated the abbey church at Luxeuil. His cultus was confirmed for Besançon in 1900.

Nicetius (Nizier) of Lyons (St) {2, 4}

2 April
d. 573. He became bishop of Lyons (France) in 553 and was noted for his solicitude for ordinary people, especially poor ones. He also regularized the psalmody in his cathedral.

Nicetius of Trier (St) {2, 4}

1 October
d. 566. A monk and abbot of Auvergne, he became bishop of Trier (Germany) in 532 and was the last who was a Gallo-Roman rather than a Frank. He withstood the cruelty of the new Frankish rulers, excommunicated two kings for disgusting behaviour and was exiled for a year as a result. He also founded a school of clerical studies and rebuilt the cathedral.

Nicetius (St) {2, 4}

5 May
C5th. He was a bishop of Vienne (France).

Nicholas and Tranus (SS) {2}

4 June
Before C12th. The revised Roman Martyrology lists them as hermits of Sardinia, without any further details.

Nicholas I, Pope 'the Great' (St) {2, 4}

13 November
d. 867. A native priest of Rome, he was elected pope in 858 at a time when the Dark Ages in the West were taking a turn for the worse. His energy and courage in office, especially in dealing with bad bishops and rulers, led him to be the last of the popes to be nicknamed 'the Great'. He had to cope with the schism of Photius, patriarch of Constantinople, and tried to extend the influence of the Latin church in Scandinavia under St Ansgar as legate and in Bulgaria, where Khan Boris wished to convert his country to Christianity. His replies to a long list of questions by the Khan survive. Both of these initiatives lacked success (Bulgaria opted for the Eastern church).

Nicholas Albergati (Bl) {2}

10 May
1375–1443. From Bologna (Italy), he became a Carthusian in 1394 but was made bishop of Bologna (against his will) in 1418 and cardinal in 1426. He served as papal legate to France and Germany and also at the council of Basel, and was a generous benefactor of many Renaissance scholars. His cultus was confirmed for Bologna in 1744.

Nicholas Barré (Bl) {2}

31 May
1621–86. From Amiens (France), he became a Minim friar and settled at Rouen, where he began a movement offering education to ordinary people. This led to the foundation of the 'Charitable Teachers', a secular institution for both sexes, and he also influenced St John-Baptist de la Salle. He was beatified in 1999.

Nicholas Bùi Việt Thể (St) {1 –group}

13 June
d. 1839. A Vietnamese soldier, he was sawn in half with Bl Augustine Phan Viết Huy at Hué during the persecution ordered by Emperor Minh Mạng. Cf. **Vietnam, Martyrs of.**

Nicholas Bunkerd Kitbamrung (Bl) {2}

12 January

1895–1956. From a native Catholic family of Nakhon Pathom near Bangkok, Thailand, he was ordained priest at Bangkok in 1926 and served in several parishes in Thailand. However, there was a strong anti-Catholic sentiment in Thailand arising partly from hostility to French interests in the area and partly from the identification of Thai nationalism with Buddhism. As a result, Bl Nicholas was arrested in 1941, accused of having the bells of his church rung in violation of an official ban and sentenced to fifteen years in prison. He continued his priestly work in prison, but died of tuberculosis before his sentence was finished. He was beatified in 2000.

Nicholas Čarneckyi and Comps (BB) {2}

June 27

1885–1959. Before 1902, the official religion of the Russian Empire was the Russian Orthodox Church, and other Christian denominations, including the Roman Catholic Church, were subject to persecution. Conversion from Orthodoxy to the Catholic Church was especially regarded as a serious crime. Toleration was granted by the Tsar in 1905. However, after the foundation of the Soviet Union in 1917, the Communist Party there carried out a policy of systematic and gradual suppression of the public manifestations of all organized religions. This was especially vicious during the Stalinist terror of the 1930s, when almost all priests and religious of both Catholic and Orthodox churches were killed or sent to the gulags as well as many brave enough to witness to their faith. After the Soviet annexation of eastern Poland in 1945, the Communist government set out to extirpate the Catholic Church in these areas, paying special attention to the Byzantine rite, and many of the clergy died in captivity. Nicholas Čarneckyi was the apostolic exarch of the Byzantine rite for Volhynia and Podlasia, and he died in prison at Lvov (now Lviv in Ukraine) after vicious ill-treatment. He, and twenty-four other representative martyrs of the Soviet Union, were beatified in 2001.

Nicholas Cehelskyj (Bl) {2}

25 May

1897–1951. A diocesan priest of Lwow (now Lviv in Ukraine), he was imprisoned after the Soviet Union annexed that part of Poland and died in a gulag in Mordovia. The Polish population of Lwow was deported to the German territories transferred to Poland. Cf. **Nicholas Čarneckyj and 24 Comps**.

Nicholas Factor (Bl) {2}

23 December

1520–83. Born at Valencia (Spain), he became a Franciscan there in 1537 and was an itinerant preacher of extreme asceticism, whipping himself before every sermon. He died at Valencia and was beatified in 1786.

Nicholas von Flüe (St) {2}

21 March

1417–87. From a peasant family near Sarnen in Unterwalden canton, Switzerland, he married and had ten children. He became a judge and councillor for his canton as well as a soldier in its army, but when aged fifty he obtained the consent of his family to become a hermit at Ranft. It is alleged that he then went without any food except Holy Communion for nineteen years. Many sought his advice, especially civil magistrates. He was canonized in 1947 and is the patron of Switzerland, being nicknamed 'Bruder Klaus'.

Nicholas of Forca-Palena (Bl) {2}

29 September

1349–1449. From Palena near Sulmona (Italy), he founded the 'Hermits of St Jerome' and established houses at Naples, Rome (St Onufrius) and Florence. Afterwards he amalgamated these with the Hieronymites founded by Bl Peter of Pisa (and not connected with the Spanish order of the same name). His cultus was approved for Rome locally and Sulmona in 1771.

Nicholas Fukunaga Keian (Bl) {2 –add}

31 July
d. 1633. He was an unordained Jesuit from Nagawara near Nagasaki, and was martyred at Nishizaka. He was beatified in 2008. Cf. **Japan, Martyrs of**.

Nicholas Garlick (Bl) {2}

24 June
1555–88. Born at Dinting in Derbyshire, he was ordained at Châlons-sur-Marne in 1582 and was a priest in Hampshire, Dorset and then Derbyshire. Being captured at Padley Hall with Bl Robert Ludlum, he was executed at Derby with him and Bl Richard Simpson. He was beatified in 1987. Cf. **England, Martyrs of**.

Nicholas Gross (Bl) {2}

15 January
1898–1945. From Niederwenigern near Essen, Germany, as a young coal miner he joined the 'St Anthony's Miners' Association', an influential union for Catholic miners, and went on to become the editor of the union's newspaper. Settling at Bochum in the Ruhr, he married and had seven children. His religious convictions led him to oppose Nazism totally, and his newspaper was banned in 1938. But he continued to publish pamphlets aiming at strengthening the Christian faith among manual workers, and was eventually arrested on a false suspicion of involvement in the plot to assassinate Hitler. He was hanged in Berlin and was beatified in 2001.

Nicholas Hermanssön (Bl) {2}

2 May
1331–91. A Swede, he was educated at Paris and Orleans before being ordained and appointed tutor to the sons of St Brigid of Sweden. Eventually he became bishop of Linköping. He was a great Swedish liturgist and poet. That he was formally canonized in 1414 is not now provable.

Nicholas Horner (Bl) {2}

3 March
d. 1590. Born in Ripon, he was a tailor in London. He was imprisoned in Newgate and lost a leg through gangrene. He was bought out but was re-arrested and executed on Ash Wednesday with Bl Alexander Blake on the charge of aiding Bl Christopher Bales, a priest. He was beatified in 1987. Cf. **England, Martyrs of**.

Nicholas Janssen-Poppel (St) {2}

9 July
d. 1572. He was the curate of St Leonard Vechel, and both were among the **Gorinchem** martyrs.

Nicholas Konrad (Bl) {2}

26 June
1877–1941. A diocesan priest of Lwow (now Lviv in Ukraine), he was killed by a detachment of the Red Army in a wood at Birok, near Stradch together with Bl Vladimir Pryjma. Cf. **Nicholas Čarneckyj and 24 Comps**.

Nicholas-of-Gesturi Medda (Bl) {2}

8 June
1882–1958. From Gesturi on Sardinia (Italy), he became a Capuchin at Cagliari in 1911 and spent most of his life begging alms for the friary there. He was beatified in 1999.

Nicholas of Myra (St) {1, 3}

6 December

Early C4th. All that is known about him is that he was a bishop of Myra in Lycia (Asia Minor) and that his relics were stolen by Italian merchants in 1087, being now enshrined at Bari. His veneration as one of the most popular saints in Christendom is based mainly on his accumulated legends, especially as narrated by Simon Metaphrastes in the C10th. These include the story of his revivifying three children killed and pickled in brine, which has led to his being a patron of children and is the remote cause of the legend of 'Santa Claus'. He is also a patron of prisoners, sailors and pawnbrokers and is a principal patron of Russia. The three golden balls which are the sign of a pawnbroker derive from a legend about him. In this, he provides three bags of gold as dowries for three poor sisters. He is often depicted with the aforesaid children or balls, or with a ship or anchor.

Nicholas Owen ('Little John') (St) {2}

22 March

d. 1606. The details of his early life are unknown, although he is alleged to have been a servant of St Edmund Campion before being on record as a Jesuit lay brother imprisoned in London in 1582. After his release he constructed priests' hiding places in mansions throughout England with amazing ingenuity. He was finally captured just after hiding in one of these with Bl Ralph Ashley at Hinlip Hall near Worcester. The Gunpowder Plot had just taken place, and he was racked for information at London with such severity that his abdomen burst and he died. He was canonized in 1970. The Roman Martyrology lists his death on this date, but other sources give the 2nd March. Cf. **England, Martyrs of**.

Nicholas Paglia (Bl) {2}

16 February

1197–1256. From near Bari (Italy), after hearing St Dominic preach at Bologna he became a Dominican and founded friaries at Perugia in 1233 and at Trani in 1254. He was also twice superior of the Roman province. He had died at Perugia, and his cultus was confirmed for there and for the Dominicans in 1828.

Nicholas Peregrinus (St) {2, 4}

2 June

1075–94. Historically he appears as a teenage Greek immigrant in Apulia (Italy) who wandered about shouting 'Kyrie eleison' (Lord, have mercy). Crowds of people (especially children) followed and imitated him, and he was understandably regarded as mad. He died at Trani (of which place he is the patron), and so many miracles were alleged to have taken place at his tomb that he was canonized in 1098.

Nicholas Pieck (St) {2}

9 July

d. 1572. A Dutchman and a former student at Louvain, he was the Franciscan guardian of the friary at Gorinchem. He had made the conversion of Calvinists his life's work, and was one of the **Gorinchem** martyrs (q.v.).

Nicholas Politi (St) {2}

17 August

1117–67. From Adernò near Patti (Sicily), he allegedly abandoned his wife on his wedding night to become a hermit on Mt Etna. He has a cultus in the diocese of Patti.

Nicholas Postgate (Bl) {2}

7 August

1604–79. Ordained at Douai, he had been a priest in Yorkshire for nearly fifty years when he was seized while baptizing a baby at Littlebeck and executed at York during the agitation caused by Titus Oates. He was beatified in 1987. Cf. **England, Martyrs of**.

Nicholas Roland (Bl) {2}

27 April

1642–78. Born at Reims (France), he abandoned the prospect of a successful business career in order to become a priest, hoping to set up free schools for girls. Inspired by Nicholas Barré (a Minim of Rouen) and the ideals of spiritual childhood, he founded the 'Sisters of the Infant Jesus'. He died worn out at the age of thirty-five and was beatified in 1994. His disciple, St John-Baptist de la Salle, did the equivalent work for boys.

Nicholas Rusca (Bl) {2 –add}

4 September

1563–1618. From Bedano in the canton of Ticino in Switzerland, he was ordained as a diocesan priest of Como in Italy (in the territory of which the canton was located) in 1587. In 1571 he was appointed as parish priest of Sondrio in the Valtellina, which at the time belonged to the Swiss canton of Graubünden (it is now in Italy). The area was being strongly evangelized by Calvinists, and serious persecution began in 1608. He was seized and put under trial by his Protestant enemies at Thusis near Chur, and died as a result of torture. He was beatified as a martyr in 2013.

Nicholas Saggio of Longobardi (St) {2}

12 February

d. 1709. From a poor family at Longobardi in Calabria (Italy), he became a Minim lay brother and was already famous in his local area as a catechist before moving to Rome. From his base at the Minim convent of San Francesco di Paola in the city he continued his catechetical outreach and became beloved by

the local Roman. He died in that convent and was canonized in 2014.

Nicholas Stensen (Bl) {2}

5 December

1638–83. He was from Copenhagen (Denmark), and his family had contained many Lutheran pastors. One of the most important pioneer anatomists of all time, he studied at Leyden (1660), Paris (1665) and Florence (1666) and also made discoveries in geology and palaeontology. In 1667 he became a Catholic, then was the royal anatomist in Denmark from 1672 and was ordained in Florence in 1675. He was quickly made vicar-apostolic for the Nordic missions and became auxiliary bishop of Münster, Germany in 1681. As a bishop he was a Tridentine reformer who strived for personal sanctification, but he left in protest of diocesan corruption. The last part of his life was spent as a missionary in Protestant areas around Schwerin in Germany. He was beatified in 1988.

Nicholas Studites (St) {2}

4 February

d. 860. From Kydonia in Crete, when young he became a monk at the Studion at Constantinople under St Theodore. During the iconoclastic persecution he accompanied the latter into exile and, after their return, succeeded him as abbot in 884. He was exiled again by the Emperor Michael III for refusing to recognize Photius as patriarch and for condemning the emperor's morals, but was restored by the Emperor Basil I. Thereupon he lived as an ordinary monk at the Studion.

Nicholas Tavelić and Comps (SS) {2}

5 December

d. 1391. A Croat from Sibenik in Dalmatia (Croatia), he became a Franciscan near

Assisi and was on mission in Bohemia (Czech Republic) before being sent to the Holy Land with BB Deodatus Anibert, Peter of Narbonnne and Stephen of Cuneo. For preaching to Muslims they were imprisoned and dismembered. They were canonized in 1970.

Nicholas of Tolentino (St) {2, 3}

10 September
1245–1305. From Sant' Angelo near Fermo in the Marches (Italy), he became an Augustinian friar at Cingoli in 1263 and, after his ordination, made a resolution to preach daily to the people. This he did, first at Cingoli and then for thirty years at Tolentino, where he was an enormous success. He was canonized in 1446, and his cultus was confined to local calendars in 1969.

Nicholas Wheeler (alias Woodfen) (Bl) {2}

21 January
d. 1586. Born in Leominster (Herefordshire), he studied at Douai and worked for St Swithin Wells in London after being ordained. He then ran a school in Wiltshire before being seized and executed at Tyburn with Bl Richard Stransham. He was beatified in 1987. Cf. **England, Martyrs of**.

Nicodemus (St) {2, 4}

31 August
C1st. He is mentioned in the gospel of St John (3 & 7) as a secret follower of Christ, and helped St Joseph of Arimathaea in the entombing of Christ's body. There was an apocryphal gospel circulated under his name. By tradition he was martyred, and his alleged relics were found with those of SS Stephen, Gamaliel and Abibas. These two assertions are not in the Roman Martyrology.

Nicodemus of Mammola (St) {2}

25 March
d. 990. He was a Byzantine-rite monk who founded a monastery at Mammola in Calabria (Italy) and was famous for his austerity.

Nicolino Magalotti (Bl)

29 November
d. 1370. A Franciscan tertiary, he was a hermit near Camerino (Italy) for thirty years and his cultus was confirmed in 1856. He is not in the Roman Martyrology.

Nicomedes (St) {2, 3}

15 September
? He was a Roman martyr buried on the Via Nomentana. According to his legend, he was a priest connected with SS Nereus, Achilleus and Petronilla who was martyred in the reign of Domitian. His cultus was confined to local calendars in 1969.

Nicomedia, Martyrs of (SS) {2, 4}

23 June
d. 303. During the persecution by the Emperor Domitian many Christians of Nicomedia (Asia Minor), his seat of government, fled to the hills and hid in caves. They were hunted down and martyred.

The old Roman Martyrology listed four other anonymous groups of martyrs at Nicomedia, which as the residence of the Emperor Diocletian seems to have been the locality of especially intense persecution. The figures of thousands traditionally quoted are wildly exaggerated, and these entries have been deleted.

18 March
Allegedly 10,000 were massacred following a fire in the imperial palace.

23 December
A group of twenty martyrs was separately listed in the old Roman Martyrology.

25 December
Allegedly many thousands were burnt alive in the great basilica by order of the emperor while they were celebrating Christmas. (Christmas was not celebrated in the East on this date at the time).

(Nicon and Comps) *(SS)* *{4 –deleted}*

23 March
d. c.250. Their legend is that Nicon was a pagan imperial soldier from Naples (Italy) who travelled to the East, became a Christian and then was a monk in the Holy Land. He became superior of about two hundred disciples, and when persecution broke out in the reign of Decius they fled to Sicily and were martyred there. The old Roman Martyrology wrongly assigned them to Caesarea in the Holy Land, and the whole story is dubious.

Nicon Metanoite (St) {2, 4}

26 November
d. 998. He was an Armenian monk at Khrysopetro in Pontus (Asia Minor) and became an itinerant preacher throughout present-day Greece, where his theme of 'metanoite!' (repent!) gave him his surname. He died near Sparta.

(Nicostratus, Antiochus and Comps) *(SS)* *{4 –deleted}*

21 May
d. 303. A cohort of Roman soldiers, according to the unreliable acta of St Procopius they were martyred at Caesarea Philippi in the Holy Land in the reign of Diocletian. Nicostratus was their tribune.

Nidan cf. **Midan**.
Nighton cf. **Nectan**.

(Nilammon) *(St)* *{4 –deleted}*

6 January
C5th. His story is that he was an Egyptian monk who was chosen to become a bishop and who barricaded his cell and died in prayer while the bishops due to ordain him were waiting outside. Forced ordination was a feature of the early Egyptian church, as was a strong opposition among monks to being ordained for pastoral duties among the laity.

Nilus the Elder (St) {2, 4}

12 November
d. c.430. His worthless tradition describes him as a courtier at Constantinople who became a monk on Mt Sinai with his son, but he was actually a bishop of Ancyra (Asia Minor, now Ankara in Turkey) and a friend of St John Chrysostom. He was a prolific spiritual writer, and under his name some important treatises by Evagrius Ponticus survive. The tradition may have been invented to help preserve these writings on monastic spirituality after Evagrius's speculative theology had been condemned.

Nilus the Younger (St) {2, 4}

26 September
d. 1004–5. A Greek of Rossano in Calabria (Italy), he became a hermit after losing his wife and other members of his family, but Muslim raids drove him into the relative safety of the Byzantine-rite monastery of St Adrian near his home village. He became abbot there, but the community fled as refugees from further Muslim incursions and eventually settled near Gaeta. Just before he died he designated the permanent site of the new monastery to be at Grottaferrata near Frascati, which still survives as an abbey of the Italo-Greek rite using the rule of St Basil.

Nimatullah-Joseph Kassab Al-Hardini
(St) {2}

14 December
1808–58. From Hardin in the Lebanon, he became a Maronite monk at Qozhaya in 1828 and transferred to Kfifan as director of the house of studies there. In 1845 he became assistant-general, but refused to be appointed abbot-general. He was remembered for saying 'A monk's first concern should be not to hurt or trouble his brethren' and for his devotion to Our Lady. He died of pneumonia at Kfifan, Lebanon and was canonized in 2004.

Ninian (St) {2}

16 September
d. ?432. According to St Bede, he was a Briton educated in Rome who founded a church at Whithorn ('Candida Casa' or the White House, so called because the church was built of white-painted stone) at Galloway (Scotland). The monastery attached to it became a missionary centre for evangelizing the northern Britons and the Picts. The connection with Rome is historically very dubious. Archaeological investigations have, however, revealed an early Christian settlement on the site. He is depicted with heavy chains about him or hanging from his arm.

Nino (St) {2, 4}

14 January
d. c.320. According to tradition, Christianity was brought to Georgia by a captive from Cappodocia who was a slave-girl in the royal household. She converted the royal family and built the first church in the country at Mtskhet near Tbilisi. She is a historic personage and is regarded as the apostle of Georgia, but her extant biography has many contradictory legends. The original compilers of the old Roman Martyrology did not know her name, and listed her as 'Christiana'.

Nizier cf. **Nicetius**.

Noah Mawaggali (St) {1 –group}

31 May
d. 1886. He was a potter at the court of King Mwanga of Buganda, at whose orders he was executed. Cf. **Charles Lwanga and Comps**.

Noel cf. **Natalis**.

Nonius Alvarez Pereira (St) {2}

1 November
1360–1431. A Portuguese nobleman, he became major-general in 1383 of the Portuguese forces successfully fighting to break their country's union with Spain. After the death of his wife in 1422 he became a Carmelite lay brother at Lisbon. He was canonized in 2009.

Nonna (St) {2, 4}

5 August
d. 374. She was the wife of St Gregory Nazianzen the Elder, whom she converted. Their three children, Gorgonia, Gregory and Caesarius, are also saints.

Nonnosus (St) {2, 4}

2 September
d. c.570. He was prior at the monastery of Monte Soracte near Rome, and his miracles were recounted by St Gregory the Great in his 'Dialogues'. He has been claimed to be a Benedictine. His shrine was established at Freising (Germany).

(Nonnus) (St) {4 –deleted}

2 December
C5th? A Tabennesiote monk of Egypt, he was made bishop of Edessa (now Urfa in Turkey) in 448 but also seems to have been connected with the former pagan stronghold of Baalbek

(Lebanon), where his missionary efforts had some success. He also features in the story of St Pelagia the Penitent.

Norbert (St) {1, 3}

6 June

c.1080–1134. Born into a princely family at Xanten near Cleves (Germany), he was at the courts of the emperor and the prince-bishop of Cologne, and became a subdeacon and canon of Xanten so as to enjoy the benefice. Then he almost died in 1115 when he fell off his horse, and this caused a radical conversion. He tried to reform the chapter of canons at Xanten but was treated with contempt, so he became an itinerant preacher and founded a community of reformed Canons Regular under the rule of St Augustine at Prémontré near Laon (France) in 1121. This was the first house of the Premonstratensians (now usually called Norbertines), and the new order became very popular in Western Europe as it combined the priesthood with an austere common life. He was compelled to become archbishop of Magdeburg, where he reformed the clergy by force and where he died.

Nostrianus (St) {2, 4}

14 February

d. c.450. This bishop of Naples (Italy) opposed Arianism and Pelagianism and his cultus was confirmed for Naples in 1878.

Notburga of Eben (St) {2}

14 September

d. 1313. She was born at Rottenburg near Innsbruck in the Tyrol (Austria) and was a serving maid in the castle there most of her life, except for a period when she worked for a peasant at Eben (where her shrine is now established). She was remembered for her hard work, charity and piety and had her cultus confirmed for Brixen in the South Tyrol in 1862.

Notker Balbulus (Bl) {2}

6 April

c.840–912. His surname means 'the Stammerer'. Born at Elgg in the canton of Zurich (Switzerland), he became a child-oblate and then a monk at the Benedictine abbey of St Gall. There he spent his life, serving as librarian, guest-master and precentor. An excellent musician, he was famous as a composer of liturgical sequences. His cultus was confirmed in 1512.

(Novatus) (St) {4 –deleted}

20 June

C2nd? He was alleged to have been a brother of SS Praxedes and Pudentiana (q.v.), but this is false and he probably never existed.

Novellone cf. **Nevolo**.

(Numerian) (St) {4 –deleted}

5 July

d. ?666. A nobleman of Trier (Germany), he became a monk at Remiremont under St Arnulf, then transferred to Luxeuil under St Waldebert and finally became bishop of his native city.

(Numidicus and Comps) (SS) {4 –deleted}

9 August

C3rd? Roman Africans, they were burnt at the stake at Carthage in the reign of Decius (not in that of Valerian, pace the old Roman Martyrology). Numidicus is alleged to have been dragged from the pyre while still alive and to have survived to be ordained priest by St Cyprian. The latter mentions a priest of that name in his letters, but this group of martyrs is not listed in the earliest sources.

Nunilo and Alodia (SS) {2, 4}

22 October

d. 851. Two sisters from near Huesca (Spain) when most of Spain was under Arab rule, they had a Muslim father and a Christian mother and were raised as Christians. After the death of their father their mother married another Muslim, who brutally persecuted them and had them imprisoned. They were finally beheaded at Huesca.

Nuntius Sulprizio (Bl) {2}

5 May

1817–36. From the Abruzzi (Italy), he became an apprentice blacksmith at Naples and died when only nineteen. However he was remembered for his patience and chastity and was beatified in 1963.

(Obdulia) (St) {*4 –deleted*}

5 September
? She has a cultus as a virgin at Toledo (Spain), but nothing is known about her.

Obediah (Abdias) (St) {2}

19 November
He is the fourth of the Minor Prophets of the Old Testament.

Obitius (St) {2}

6 December
d. 1204. A knight of Brescia (Italy), he almost drowned in a river during a battle and had a vision of hell in the process. This led him to live the rest of his life in austere penance while working for the Benedictine nuns of St Julia at Brescia. His cultus was approved for Brescia in 1900.

Oceanus (St) {2}

18 September
? He was a martyr of Nicomedia (Asia Minor).

(Octavian and Comps) (SS) {*4 –deleted*}

22 March
d. 484. He was archdeacon at Carthage (Roman Africa) and was martyred with many others (allegedly several thousand) at the instigation of the Arian Vandal king, Hunneric.

Octavian of Savona (Bl) {2}

6 August
c.1060–1132. A Burgundian nobleman, he became a Benedictine monk at the abbey of St Peter in Ciel d'Oro, Pavia (Italy) and was made bishop of Savona in 1129. His cultus was confirmed in 1793.

Octavius, Solutor and Adventor (SS) {2, 4}

20 November
C3rd. They were martyred at Turin (Italy), of which place they are patrons. Later they were connected with the legend of the Theban Legion.

Oddinus Barrotti (Bl) {2}

7 July
1324–1400. From Fossano in Piedmont (Italy), he became parish priest there and a Franciscan tertiary. Later he resigned and turned his house into a hospital. His cultus was locally approved in 1808.

Odilia cf. **Ottilia**.

Odilo of Cluny (St) {2, 4}

1 January
?962–1049. A nobleman of the Auvergne (France), he was a canon at Brioude before becoming a monk at Cluny in 991. He was made coadjutor to the abbot, St Majolus, the following year and became abbot himself in 994. An affable and gentle man, he was also a great organizer and under his government the Cluniac congregation increased from thirty-seven to sixty-five houses. He was personally acquainted with most of those in high office in western Europe, secular and ecclesiastical. The commemoration of the faithful dead (All Soul's Day) was initially introduced by him for Cluny but soon spread to the entire church.

Odo of Cluny (St) {2, 4}

19 November
?879–942. A nobleman from Maine (France), he was educated at the cathedral school of Tours before becoming a Benedictine monk at Baume under Berno, the abbot-founder of Cluny, in 909. He became abbot of Baume in 924 and of Cluny in 927. A great abbot and monastic reformer, he arranged for Cluny to be free from any secular control and thus secured the monastery's rapid growth and flourishing life for the next few centuries.

Under him Cluny began to exert its influence in France and Italy (including Rome, where he restored the abbey of St Paul-outside-the-Walls). He died at Tours, by the tomb of St Martin.

Odo of Novara (Bl) {2}

14 January
d. c.1200. From Novara in Piedmont (Italy), he became a Carthusian and was made prior of Geyrach in Slavonia (Croatia). Owing to difficulties with the bishop he resigned, and then became chaplain to a nunnery at Tagliacozzo in the Abruzzi (Italy). His cultus was confirmed for the Carthusians in 1859.

Odo of Urgell (St) {2, 4}

7 July
d. 1122. A relative of the counts of Barcelona (Spain), he fought in the petty wars of Catalonia as a soldier before becoming a priest and archdeacon of Urgell. He was made bishop there in 1095, and was remembered as a reformer of a rundown diocese.

Odoard Focherin (Bl) {2 –add}

27 December
1907–44. He was an insurance agent at Carpi near Modena in Italy, as well as being a father of seven children and a member of Catholic Action. During the Second World War he set up a network to help Jews escape being rounded up for the gas chambers, and was responsible for sending over a hundred to safety in Switzerland. For this he was arrested by the Germans, and executed at the concentration camp of Hersbruck in Germany. He was beatified as a martyr in 2013.

Odoric-of-Pordenone Mattiuzzi (Bl) {2}

14 January
1285–1331. From near Pordenone in Friuli (Italy), he became a Franciscan at Udine and spent some time as a hermit. Then he set out on an amazing missionary journey, from Trebizond (now Trabzon, Turkey) on the Black Sea along the Silk Road as far as Beijing and even into Tibet. This was possible after the great conquests of the Mongols had imposed an imperial peace on much of Asia. After sixteen years he returned to Europe to report to the pope at Avignon, but died at Udine and his cultus was confirmed for there in 1775.

Odrada (St) {2}

3 November
C11th? All that is known is that she was a consecrated virgin associated with Haelen near Roermond (Netherlands). Her shrine was at the Carthusian monastery at Antwerp.

Odulf (St) {2}

12 June
d. ?865. From North Brabant (Netherlands), he was made a canon of Utrecht by St Frederick, whom he assisted in the evangelization of Friesland. He allegedly founded a monastery of Augustinian canons at Stavoren on the Ijsselmeer, but this was probably a house of secular canons at first. His relics were allegedly stolen in 1034 and taken to England, firstly to London and then to Evesham Abbey near Worcester.

Oengus cf. **Angus**.

Ogasawara family (BB) {2 –add}

30 January
d. 1636. The Ogasawara family, numbering eleven with four servants, were from Buzen near Fukuoka and were martyred at Kumamoto. Their Christian names are unknown. In the traditional Japanese nomenclature, the family name Ogasawara precedes the traditional given names as follows. Yosaburō

Gen'ya was the head of the family, and Miya Luisa was his wife. Their sons were: Genpachi, Sasaemon, Sayuemon, Shiro, Goro and Gonnosuke. Their daughters were: Mari, Kuri and Tsuchi. The names of the four servants are unknown, and it is an innovation for anonymous persons to be beatified. The family received their beatification together in 2008. Cf. **Japan, Martyrs of**.

Ogler (Bl) {2}

10 September
d. 1214. From Trino near Vercelli (Italy), he became a Cistercian and then abbot of Locedio nearby. He is famous for a series of sermons defending the doctrine of the Immaculate Conception. His cultus was confirmed for Vercelli and Trino in 1875.

Ogmund (St)

8 March
d. 1121. He was first bishop of Holar in Iceland, and is counted as one of the apostles of that nation. He was locally canonized in 1201, but is not listed in the Roman Martyrology.

Olalla cf. **Eulalia of Merida**.

Olav of Norway, King (St) {2}

29 July
995–1030. Son of King Harald of Norway, as a young man he was a raider in western Europe. The contact with Christianity led him to be baptized at Rouen (France) in 1010, and he helped King Ethelred of England against the Danes in 1013. In 1015 he became king of Norway and summoned missionaries (chiefly from England) to complete the Christianization of his country. He succeeded to some extent, but his harshness led to his deposition and exile. In an attempt to recover power he led an invasion which was defeated at the battle at Stiklestad, during which he was killed. His opponents were also Christians, but he was regarded as a martyr, and his veneration was popular in northern Europe (the city of London had four churches dedicated to him). In Norway he is regarded as a patron of national independence.

Olga (St) {2}

11 July
?879–969. She married Igor I, prince of Kiev (Ukraine) in 903, and when he was assassinated in 945 she became regent for Svyatoslav, their infant son. In 958 she was baptized at Constantinople but had little success in introducing Christianity into Kievan Rus (apart from the settlements of Byzantine merchants at Kiev). The conversion of the country was achieved by St Vladimir, her grandson.

Oliva of Anagni (St) {2, 4}

3 June
C6–7th. She is venerated as a nun at Anagni near Rome, but nothing is known about her.

Oliver Plunket (St) {2}

11 July
1629–81. From Loughcrew in Co. Meath (Ireland), he studied for the priesthood and was ordained in Rome in 1654. There he remained as professor of theology in the college 'de Propaganda Fide' until he was made archbishop of Armagh in 1669, whereupon he set about renewing the persecuted church in Ireland. He was arrested on a patently false charge of treason and was brought for trial to London because the Irish judges refused to convict him. There the first trial collapsed for lack of evidence, but on a second trial he was found guilty of treason 'for propagating the Catholic religion'. While in prison with the president of the English Benedictines he became a Benedictine oblate, which is why his body is now enshrined at Downside abbey in

Somerset (his head is enshrined at Drogheda). He was the last Catholic to be martyred at Tyburn, and was canonized in 1975.

Ollegarius (Oldegar, Olegari) (St) {2}

6 March

1060–1137. From Barcelona (Spain), he became an Augustinian canon regular and was prior in several houses in France before being made bishop of Barcelona in 1115. The following year he was transferred to the archbishopric of Tarragona, which city had just been conquered from the Muslims. He successfully restored church life there. His cultus was confirmed for Barcelona in 1675.

(Olympiades of Amelia) (St) {4 –deleted}

1 December

Early C4th? He was allegedly consular prefect at Amelia in Umbria (Italy) and was martyred in the reign of Diocletian.

Olympias (St) {2, 4}

25 June

d. 408. A noblewoman of Constantinople, she was the widow of a prefect of the city and became a deaconess (rather akin to a modern active female religious, but not in vows). She worked in the service of the church with a community of like-minded women living with her. She was a loyal supporter of St John Chrysostom, and as a result was deprived of her property and exiled, her house being sold and her community disbanded. She died in exile at Nicomedia.

Olympias Bidà (Bl) {2}

28 January

1903–52. A Sister of St Joseph, she died in the gulag at Kharsk near Tomsk in Siberia, Soviet Union. Cf. **Nicholas Čarneckyj and 24 Comps**.

(Olympius of Aenos) (St) {4 –deleted}

12 June

d. p343. Bishop of Aenos (now Enez, at the western extremity of European Turkey), he was in solidarity with St Athanasius in opposing Arianism and was exiled as a result by the Emperor Constantius.

Omer cf. **Audomar**.

Onesimus (St) {1, 3}

16 February

C1st. A runaway slave, he was the reason for St Paul's letter to Philemon. The old Roman Martyrology wrongly alleged that he was bishop of Ephesus after St Timothy and was martyred (this seems to refer to another person).

Onesiphorus (St)

6 September

C1st. Onesiphorus is mentioned by St Paul in his second letter to Timothy (4:19). According to his legend, he accompanied St Paul to Spain and then back to the East, where he was tied to wild horses and torn to pieces somewhere on the Hellespont in the reign of Domitian. Porphyry was allegedly his servant who was martyred with him, and who has been deleted from the Roman Martyrology.

Onuphrius (Humphrey) (St) {2, 4}

12 June

d. c.400. According to his story, he was an Egyptian hermit for seventy years in the Thebaid (Upper Egypt). He was a very popular saint in the Middle Ages, both in East and in West, but his existence has been questioned. He is the patron saint of weavers, possibly because 'he was dressed only in his own abundant hair and a loincloth of leaves', and is depicted nude with his long beard protecting his modesty.

Onuphrius of Panaia (St) {2}

4 August
d. 995. He was a hermit living in the forest of Panaia near Catanzaro in Calabria (Italy), and was famous for his fasting and austerity. He is the patron of Centrache.

Opilio (St) {2}

12 October
C5th? He was a deacon of Piacenza (Italy).

Opportuna (St) {2}

22 April
d. c.770. From Exmes near Argentan (Normandy), she was a sister of St Chrodegang, bishop of Sées, and when young became a nun at Montreuil near her home. She went on to be abbess, and was described as 'a true mother to all her nuns'. Her veneration is popular in France.

Optatian of Brescia (St) {2, 4}

14 July
d. ?505. He became bishop of Brescia (Italy) in ?451.

(Optatus of Auxerre) (St) {4 –deleted}

31 August
C6th. He was listed as bishop of Auxerre (France) in c.530.

Optatus of Milevis (St) {2}

4 June
C4th. Bishop of Milevis in Numidia (Roman Africa, now Algeria), he wrote six treatises against the native Donatist schismatics and is the principal authority on the history of Donatism. Nothing is known about his life.

Orange (Martyrs of) (BB) {2}

d. 1794. Thirty-two consecrated religious women, they were imprisoned at Orange (France) in October 1793 for refusing to take the civil oath demanded during the French Revolution. Two were Cistercians from Avignon, while the others were from Bollène north of Orange: sixteen Ursulines, thirteen Sacramentines and one Benedictine (Mary-Rose Deloye). They formed an impromptu religious community in prison, trying to lead a life of prayer as far as possible, until they were guillotined during the following July on different days. Cf. **French Revolution, Martyrs of.**

(Orentius, Heros, Pharnacius, Firminus, Firmus, Cyriac and Longinus) (SS) {4 –deleted}

24 June
Early C4th? According to the old Roman Martyrology, they were seven brothers who were soldiers in western Asia Minor but who were dismissed from the army by Maximian, sent into exile and died of hardship or were killed in various places.

(Orentius and Patientia) (SS) {4 –deleted}

1 May
C3rd?. According to a Spanish tradition they were the parents of St Laurence of Rome and lived at Loret near Huesca (Spain).

Orentius-Louis Solá Garriga and Comps (BB) {2 –add}

d. 1936. Numbering twenty-one, they were the superior and community of Brothers of the Christian Schools at the noviciate at Griñon in Madrid, Spain. On 28 July the institution was attacked by Communist militia, and several of the brethren massacred together with one lay employee. Others were killed later, one at Torrejon de Ardoz in August and eight at Paracuellos de Jarama in the course of November. The chaplain of the noviciate, a diocesan priest, was killed at Torrejón de la

Calzada in August but is counted in this group. They were beatified in 2013. Cf. **Spanish Civil War, Martyrs of** and list in appendix.

Orestes of Tyana (St) {2, 4}

10 November
d. c.300. From Tyana in Cappadocia (Asia Minor), he was tortured to death there in the reign of Diocletian.

Orgonne cf. **Aldegund**.
Oria cf. **Aurea**.

(Oriculus and Comps) *(SS)* *{4 –deleted}*

18 November
C5th? They were listed as martyred by the Arian Vandals in the province of Carthage (Roman Africa).

Orientius of Auch (St) {2}

1 May
d. ?439. A nobleman, he became a hermit in the Lavedan valley near Tarbes (France) but was made bishop of Auch in 419 and proved an effective pastor, allegedly eliminating paganism from his diocese.

Orsisius cf. **Horsiesius**.

Ortarius (St) {2}

15 April
C11th. He was abbot of Landelle near Coûtences (France), and was noted for his austerity and charity. His extant biography is full of legendary material.

Osanna cf. **Hosanna**.

Osburga (St) {2}

30 March
d. ?1018. She was the first abbess of the nunnery founded by King Canute at Coventry (England). This later failed and was replaced by a Benedictine monastery after the Norman Conquest, which itself became a cathedral priory. Her shrine there became a focus of pilgrimage, and her cultus was confirmed for Coventry in 1410. The cathedral with shrine was destroyed in the Reformation (the only English cathedral to be lost), and the present modern Anglican cathedral and its bombed-out predecessor (formerly a parish church) are on adjacent sites.

Oscar cf. **Ansgar**.
Osith cf. **Osyth**.

Osmund (St) {2, 4}

4 December
d. 1099. A Norman nobleman, he accompanied his relative William the Conqueror on his expedition to England and became chancellor of the kingdom after the conquest. He was made bishop of Sarum in 1078, his diocese having been formed by uniting those of Sherborne and Ramsbury. He completed the cathedral at the city now known as Old Sarum, but this was later abandoned when a new city and cathedral were built at Salisbury. He was formerly credited with a compilation of liturgical services for his diocese, now known as the *Sarum Rite*. His hobby was copying books and binding them. He was canonized in 1457.

(Ostia, Martyrs of) *(SS)* *{4 –deleted}*

8 July
Fifty soldiers, disciples of St Bonosa, were allegedly martyred at Ostia near Rome in the reign of Aurelian.

(Ostianus) *(St)* *{4 –deleted}*

30 June
? He is venerated as a priest at Viviers (France). Nothing is known about him.

Oswald of Northumbria, King (St) {2}

5 August

604–42. The son of King Ethelfrith of Northumbria (England), he fled to Scotland after his father's death in battle and the seizure of the throne by St Edwin. He was baptized at Iona, and after St Edwin was overthrown and killed in battle by the Cymric King Cadwalladr he returned, defeated the latter near Hexham and started his reign. His policy was the Christianization of his kingdom, and he was the patron of St Aidan in this. In 642 he was killed in battle against Penda, the pagan king of Mercia, and the dismemberment of his body led to his having a popular cultus in various places as a martyr. His head is still in St Cuthbert's coffin at Durham, and his attribute is a raven with a ring in its beak.

Oswald of Worcester (St)

28 February

d. 992. A Danish nobleman born in England, he was educated under his uncle St Odo of Canterbury and became dean of Winchester. Having a monastic vocation at a time when the monastic life did not exist in England, he went to Fleury on the Loire (France) to become a monk and was made bishop of Worcester on his return in 961. He allied himself with St Dunstan and with St Ethelwold in their efforts to revive monastic life and ecclesiastical discipline in England, and founded the Benedictine abbey of Ramsey in the Fens and the cathedral priory at Worcester. In 972 he became archbishop of York while remaining the bishop of Worcester, and died while still on his knees after having finished his daily practice of washing the feet of twelve poor men. He is not listed in the Roman Martyrology, despite having an active cultus in England.

Osyth (St)

7 October

d. c.700. A minor Saxon princess, she married a sub-king of East Anglia (England) and apparently founded a nunnery at what is now St Osyth in Essex. According to her unreliable biography she was killed by robbers. Her nunnery died out, but was re-founded as an Augustinian monastery containing her shrine in the early C12th. Her attribute is a white stag.

Othmar (Otmar, Audemar) (St) {2, 4}

16 November

d. 759. A German priest, he was made superior of the then dilapidated monastery of St Gall (Switzerland) in 720. He introduced the Benedictine rule (the Columbanian rule had been used before), and the abbey began to grow in prosperity. Some donations of land were disputed, however, so he was seized and imprisoned by two neighbouring noblemen and died in prison.

Otteran (Odran) of Iona (St) {2}

27 October

C6th. Superior of a monastery at Tyfarnham in West Meath (Ireland), he emigrated to Iona with St Columba and was the first to die there. He is the principal patron of the diocese of Waterford.

Ottilia (Odilia, Ottilien, Adilia) (St) {2}

13 December

C7th. According to her story, she was a noblewoman of Alsace (France) who had been born blind. Rejected by her family, she was taken in as a child-oblate by a nunnery. Miraculously recovering her sight, she eventually became abbess-founder of the nunneries of Odilienberg and Niedermünster in Alsace. Her shrine is at the former.

Otto of Ariano Irpino (St) {2}

23 March
d. c.1120. He was a hermit of Ariano Irpino near Benevento (Italy), and was allegedly originally a soldier belonging to the Frangipani family of Rome.

Otto of Bamberg (St) {2}

30 June
?1062–1139. A nobleman of south Germany, he became chancellor of Emperor Henry IV in 1101 and was made bishop of Bamberg (Bavaria) in 1106. He tried hard to achieve reconciliation of the investiture controversy, but was more successful in his missionary activities among the Pomeranian Slavs and is regarded as their apostle. He was canonized in 1189.

Otto of Freising (Bl) {2}

22 September
d. 1158. He was a bishop of Freising (Germany) who died as a Cistercian monk at Morimond (France).

Otto Neururer (Bl) {2}

30 May
1882–1940. Born to a peasant family of Piller (Austria), he became a priest and an active member of the 'Christian Social Movement'. As parish priest at Götzens in the Tyrol after the 'Anschlüss' in 1938, he advised a girl not to marry an immoral friend of the local Nazi gauleiter. As a result he was sent to Büchenwald and later hanged upside down until he died. He was the first priest to die in a Nazi concentration camp, and was beatified in 1996.

Oudoceus (Eddogwy) *(St)*

2 July
d. ?615. His biography as found in later Welsh chronicles may contain some truth. His family were apparently Breton emigrants to Wales, and he became a bishop with jurisdiction over an area roughly corresponding to the present Anglican diocese of Llandaff. His shrine was at Llandaff Cathedral until the Reformation.

Ouen cf. **Audöenus**.

Our Lady of the Snows, Martyrs of (BB) {2 –add}

15 February
d. 1611. They were a group of fourteen Franciscans, martyred at the church of the friary of Our Lady of the Snows at Prague (now Czech Republic, then part of the Habsburg Empire). The community had been formed to minister to the small Catholic population of a city which was then militantly Protestant. In 1611, a mercenary raid on the city was instigated by the Bishop of Passau, and in response the citizens rioted and attacked all Catholic institutions. At the friary, all the friars except one were tortured and beaten to death by a mob.

They were: Frederick (Bedřich) Bachstein and John Martinez, Czech priests; Simon, a French priest; Bartholomew Dalmasoni, an Italian priest; Jerome of Arezzo, an Italian deacon; Caspar Daverio, James and Clement who were non-ordained brethren from Italy, Germany and Slovakia, respectively; Christopher Zeld and John Rode, lay brothers from the Netherlands and Italy, respectively; Didacus Jan and Emmanuel, lay brothers who were probably Czech; and John and Anthony who were novices also probably Czech. They were beatified in 2012.

Owen (Owin, Ouini) (St) {2}

4 March

d. c.670. After having been steward in the household of St Etheldreda he became a monk at Lastingham in Yorkshire (England) under St Chad and was known for his devotion to manual work. The latter became missionary bishop of Mercia and established a monastery at his base at Lichfield, where St Owen was one of the founder members. There was a church dedicated to him at Gloucester.

Oyand cf. **Eugendus**.
Oye cf. **Authaire** or **Eutychius**.

P

Pachomius (St) {2, 4}

9 May
d. 346–7. From the Upper Thebaid in Egypt, he became a Christian after a period of military conscription in 313 and became a hermit three years later. In 320 he built his first monastery at Tabennesi north of Thebes on the east bank of the Nile, and subsequently founded several others. He governed them all rather like a superior-general nowadays, and wrote for them a rule for life under obedience in a monastic community. In this he was an innovator, as previous Egyptian consecrated life was eremitic. When he died in an epidemic he ruled at least eleven monasteries (two of them nunneries) allegedly containing thousands of monastics. His rule was translated into Latin by St Jerome and influenced later monastic founders.

Pacian (St) {2, 4}

9 March
d. c.390. He became bishop of Barcelona (Spain) in 365 and wrote much on ecclesiastical discipline, but most of his work is lost. His treatise on penance survives, as do three letters against Novatian. The first of these contains the famous tag: 'My name is Christian, my surname is Catholic'.

Pacificus-of-San-Severino Divini (St) {2}

24 September
1653–1721. From San Severino near Ancona (Italy), he became a Franciscan at Forano and was a popular preacher in the badly-evangelized rural districts of the Apennines. However, a serious illness in 1688 left him deaf, blind and severely disabled, and the rest of his life involved intense suffering and the receipt of supernatural charismata. He died at his home town and was canonized in 1839.

Pacificus-of-Cerano Ramoati (Bl) {2}

8 June
1424–82. From Cerano near Novara (Italy), he became a Franciscan at the latter place in 1445 and proved a popular preacher in country districts. He wrote the 'Summa Pacifica' as a popular guide for priests hearing confessions. His cultus was approved for Novara in 1745.

Padarn cf. **Paternus**.
Padre Pio cf. **Pius-of-Pietrelcina Forgione**.

Palaemon (St) {2, 4}

25 January
C4th. A hermit in the Thebaid (Egypt), he taught St Pachomius about the eremitic life and eventually followed him to Tabennesi, where he died.

(Palatias and Laurentia) (SS) {4 –deleted}

8 October
d. 302. According to their story, they were a noblewoman of Ancona (Italy) and her slave. The latter converted the former and both were exiled to Fermo near Ancona in the reign of Diocletian, where they died of hardship.

Palestine, Martyrs of cf. **Holy Land, Martyrs of**.

Palladius of Auxerre (St) {2}

10 April
d. 658. He was abbot of St Germanus's Abbey at Auxerre (France) before he was made bishop of that city in 622. He founded several monasteries.

Palladius of Ireland (St) {2}

6 July
d. 432. According to St Prosper of Aquitaine, he was sent by Pope St Celestine I to Ireland

in 430 as first bishop of the Christians there. He was either a deacon of Rome or (more probably) one from Auxerre who had accompanied St Germanus on his first visit to Britain. He seems to have landed and worked mainly in Co. Wicklow, but apparently soon left for Scotland and died at Fordoun (north of Montrose).

Palladius of Saintes (St) {2}

7 October
d. p596. He became bishop of Saintes (France) in 570 and was locally venerated, although he seems to have been unworthy of this. The Roman Martyrology has kept his listing.

(Palmatius of Trier and Comps) (SS) {4 –deleted}

5 October
C3rd? They were alleged to have been martyred at Trier (Germany) in the reign of Maximian Herculius, but their existence is doubtful as their cultus dates only from the C11th.

Pammachius (St) {2, 4}

30 August
c.340–410. A Roman senator, he was proconsul in 370. He was a friend of SS Jerome and Paulinus of Nola, married one of the daughters of St Paula but was left a widower in 395. Then he spent the rest of his life and his wealth in the personal service of the sick and the poor, meanwhile living an ascetic life. Remains of his house survive beneath the Roman church of SS John and Paul.

Pamphilus of Caesarea and Comps (St) {2, 4}

16 February
d. 309. From Beirut (Lebanon), he studied at Alexandria (Egypt) under Pierius, a disciple of Origen. Later he became a priest at Caesarea in the Holy Land, was head of the theological school and catalogued Origen's library there. He was one of the greatest biblical scholars of his day, and while in prison awaiting martyrdom wrote an 'Apology' to defend Origen's memory against charges of heresy. His disciple was Eusebius, who took the surname 'Pamphili' in admiration. With him were martyred Valens a deacon of Jerusalem, Paul from Jamnia who had spent two years in prison, Porphyry, Pamphilus a slave, Seleucus an army officer from Cappadocia and Theodulus an old man from the household of the judge. d. 309. Julian the Cappadocian was visiting Caesarea when the martyrdom took place. He was observed venerating the corpses of the martyrs, and as a result was himself roasted to death over a slow fire.

(Pamphilus of Capua) (St) {4 –deleted}

7 September
d. c.400. From Greece, he was consecrated bishop of Capua (Italy) by Pope St Siricius.

Pamphilus of Sulmona (St) {2, 4}

28 April
d. c.700 Bishop of Sulmona (a diocese later merged with Valva) in the Abruzzi (Italy), he was accused before Pope St Sergius of being an Arian, allegedly because he celebrated Mass before daybreak on Sundays. He completely vindicated himself.

Pamphilus of Rome (St) {2, 4}

21 September
? Nothing is known about this Roman martyr.

Panacea de'Muzzi (St) {2}

27 March
d. 1383. Born at Quarona near Novara (Italy), when aged fifteen she was killed with a

spindle by her stepmother while praying. Her cultus as a virgin martyr was confirmed for Novara in 1867.

(Pancharius of Nicomedia) (St) {4 –deleted}

19 March
d. 303. According to his story, he was a Roman senator and was secretary to the emperor Maximian. When Christianity was proscribed he denied (or at any rate concealed) his faith but was then edified by a letter from his mother and sister. Thereupon he proclaimed his faith and was beheaded at Nicomedia (Asia Minor).

Pancras of Rome (St) {1, 3}

12 May
Early C4th. Beyond the fact of his martyrdom at Rome and the antiquity of his cultus, nothing is known about him (his extant acta are worthless). A church was dedicated to him at Canterbury by St Augustine, and relics of him were sent to the king of Northumbria in 664. Subsequently his cultus in England was very popular. The railway station in London is named after a nearby church dedicated to him.

Pancras of Taormina (St) {2, 4}

3 April
? He was a martyred bishop of Taormina (Sicily), and according to tradition was the first bishop there. His worthless legend was that he was from Antioch (Syria) and was consecrated bishop of by St Peter, only to be stoned to death by pagans.

Pantaenus (St) {2, 4}

7 July
C3rd. A Sicilian convert from Stoicism, he became the head of the catechetical school of Alexandria (Egypt) and made it the intellectual centre of the Christian East. His most famous pupil was Clement of Alexandria. He

went on a journey as a missionary to 'India' (more probably somewhere around the southern Red Sea), and died in peace after his return.

Pantagathus (St) {2, 4}

17 April
475–540. He had been at the Frankish court of King Clovis before he became bishop of Vienne (France).

Panteleimon (Pantaleon) (St) {1, 3}

27 July
d. ?305. His name is Greek for 'the all-compassionate', and this may have given rise to the untrustworthy legend that he was a doctor of medicine who did not charge for his services and who was martyred at Nicomedia (Asia Minor) in the reign of Diocletian. His cultus was confined to local calendars in 1969.

Papas (St) {2, 4}

16 March
Early C4th. He was martyred in Lycaonia (Asia Minor) in the reign of Diocletian.

(Paphnutius of Dendara and Comps) (SS) {4 –deleted}

24 September
Early C4th? They were martyred in Egypt in the reign of Diocletian, at Dendera near Thebes according to their unreliable acta.

Paphnutius the Great (St) {2, 4}

11 September
C4th. An Egyptian, during the persecution under Maximinus Daza he had one eye gouged out and one leg hamstrung. He became a disciple of St Anthony in 311, but shortly afterwards was ordained bishop of an unknown town in the Upper Thebaid. Highly respected by the emperor Constantine, he attended the first council of Nicaea in 325,

where he successfully moved that married priests should not have to divorce their wives. He was a strenuous opponent of Arianism.

(Paphnutius of Jerusalem) (St) *{4 –deleted}*

19 April
? He was listed as a priest martyred at Jerusalem.

Papias, Diodore and Claudian (SS) {2, 4}

26 February
C3rd. They were tortured and martyred at Perga in Pamphylia (Asia Minor). The Roman Martyrology has deleted a fourth named Conon.

Papias and Maurus (SS) {2, 4}

29 January
d. ?303. They were Roman soldiers martyred at Rome in the reign of Maximian.

Papias of Hierapolis (St) {2, 4}

22 February
C2nd. Bishop of Hierapolis in the valley of the Lycus in Phrygia (Asia Minor), he wrote the 'Explanation of the Sayings of the Lord', a lost work which was referred to by St Irenaeus and by Eusebius (who wrote a cutting comment about his intelligence). It is the source of the traditions that St Matthew wrote his gospel in Aramaic and that St Mark wrote his as a summary of St Peter's preaching. He is described as having heard St John preach and as being acquainted with St Polycarp, but no details are known about his life.

Papinianus, Mansuetus and Comps (SS) {2, 4}

28 November
d. 453–60. They were Roman African bishops martyred under the Arian Vandal king Genseric by being burnt with red-hot plates. The former was bishop of Vita, the latter of Urusi. In the same persecution the following bishops were also martyred: Urbanus of Girba, Crescens of Byzaciena, Habetdeus of Teudala, Eustratius of Sufes, Cresconius of Oëa, Vicis of Sabrata and Felix of Hadrumetum. Subsequently, under Hunneric son of Genseric, Hortulanus of Bennefa and Florentianus of Midila were also martyred.

(Papius) (St) *{4 –deleted}*

28 June
d. c.303. He was listed as martyred in the reign of Diocletian.

Papolenus cf. **Babolenus**.
Pappus cf. **Papias**.

Papulus (Papoul) (St) {2}

3 November
d. c.300. A missionary priest, he worked with St Saturninus around Toulouse (France) and the two were martyred in the reign of Diocletian. His shrine is at Toulouse.

Paraguay (Martyrs of) (SS) {2}

15 November
d. 1628. Three Spanish Jesuits – Roch (Roque) Gonzalez (born at Asunción, Paraguay), Alphonsus Rodriguez and John de Castillo – they founded the 'reduction' or mission of the Assumption at Itapúa on the Jiuhi River in Paraguay. In 1628 they established the new mission of All Saints at Caaró near the Uruguay River (now in Brazil), where they were murdered at the instigation of a local chief. John de Castillo was martyred two days after the other two, on the 17th. They were canonized in 1988.

(Paramon and Comps) (SS) *{4 –deleted}*

29 November
d. 250. A group of three hundred and seventy-six, they were alleged to have martyred in

Bithynia (Asia Minor) on the same day during the Decian persecution. Their veneration is popular in the East.

Pardulf (Pardoux) (St) {2}

6 October
d. 737. A blind boy from near Guéret near Limoges (France), he was a hermit before becoming a monk and then abbot at Guéret. At the time of the Arab incursion which was defeated by Charles Martel he remained alone in the abbey, which he allegedly saved by prayer.

Paris (St) {2, 4}

5 August
C4th. He was a Greek bishop of Teano near Naples (Italy).

Parisius (St) {2, 4}

11 June
1152–1267. Probably from Treviso (Italy), when aged twelve he became a Camaldolese monk and went on to be the chaplain of the Camaldolese nuns of St Christina there for seventy-seven years. His shrine is in the cathedral.

(Parmenas) (St) {4 –deleted}

23 January
C1st. He was one of the original seven deacons (Acts 6:5). According to tradition he was a missionary in Asia Minor and was martyred at Philippi in Greek Macedonia in the reign of Trajan.

(Parmenius and Comps) (SS) {4 –deleted}

22 April
d. c 250. The priests Parmenius, Helimenas and Chrysotelus and the deacons Luke and Mucius were allegedly beheaded near Babylon during the fictitious invasion of Persian Mesopotamia (now Iraq) by the emperor Decius. Cf. **Abdon and Sennen**.

Parthenius and Calogerus (SS) {2, 4}

19 May
d. 304. They were martyred in the reign of Diocletian. The old Roman Martyrology mistakenly listed them as Roman brothers who were eunuchs in the palace of Tryphonia, wife of Emperor Decius.

Parthenius Thaumaturgus (St) {2}

7 February
C4th. He was bishop of Lampsacus on the Hellespont during the reign of the emperor Constantine, and destroyed the pagan shrines in his diocese with the permission of the emperor.

Paschal I, Pope (St) {2, 4}

14 May
d. 824. A Roman, he became abbot of the Benedictine monastery of St Stephen near the Vatican and was elected pope in 817. He protested against the revival of iconoclasm in the Byzantine Empire and helped the victims of the resulting persecution, as well as restoring many Roman churches and transferring many relics of martyrs.

Paschal Baylon (St) {2, 3}

17 May
1540–92. A peasant from Torre Hermosa in Aragon (Spain), he was a shepherd before becoming a Franciscan lay brother of the Alcantarine reform in 1564. He spent his life mainly as a doorkeeper in various Spanish friaries, except for one journey through France in 1570. During this his intense love for the Eucharist led him to defend the Real Presence in polemical debate with Protestants, with such success that he was declared patron of

all Eucharistic confraternities and congresses in 1897. Canonized in 1690, his cultus was confined to local calendars in 1969.

Paschal Fortuño Almela and Comps (BB) {2}

d. 1936. They were four Franciscans who were killed in the Spanish Civil War. They took refuge with relatives, but were tracked down and killed after torture. BB Paschal Fortuño and Placid García were from the province of Alicante, while BB Salvator Mollar and Alfred Pellicer were from that of Valencia. Cf. **Spanish Civil War, Martyrs of**.

Pascharius (Pasquier) (St) {2}

10 July
d. c.680. Bishop of Nantes (France), he founded the abbey of Aindre and made St Hermenland its first abbot.

Paschasius Radbert (St) {2}

26 April
c.790–865. From near Soissons (France), he became a monk at Corbie in Flanders (France) under St Adalard and was novice-master and headmaster of the abbey school for many years, both at Corbie and at New Corvey near Paderborn (Germany) whither he accompanied his abbot in 822. He was made abbot of Corbie in 844, but was not suited to the post and resigned in 849. A noted scholar, he wrote much on biblical studies but his most famous book is on the Eucharist: *De Corpore et Sanguine Domini*.

(Paschasius of Rome) (St) *{4 –deleted}*

31 May
d. ?512. A Roman deacon and church author, he violently opposed the election of Pope Symmachus and sided with an antipope. His noted work on the Holy Spirit has been lost.

Paschasius of Vienne (St) {2, 4}

22 February
C4th. He was a bishop of Vienne (France).

Pasicrates and Valentio (SS) {2, 4}

25 April
d. ?302. They were martyred at Silistra (Bulgaria). The Roman Martyrology has deleted two anonymous companions.

(Pastor, Victorinus and Comps) (SS) *{4 –deleted}*

29 March
Early C4th? They were listed as a group of seven martyred at Nicomedia (Asia Minor) in the reign of Galerius.

(Pastor of Orléans) (St) *{4 –deleted}*

30 March
C6th? This alleged bishop of Orléans (France) does not appear in the ancient lists.

(Pastor of Rome) (St) *{4 –deleted}*

26 July
C2nd? He was allegedly a Roman priest and a brother of Pope St Pius I who founded the church of St Pudentiana in Rome.

Patapius (St) {2, 4}

8 December
C5–6th. An Egyptian monk from the Thebaid, he migrated to Constantinople and became a hermit in the Blachernae suburb of that city. His veneration is popular in the East.

(Paterius) (St) *{4 –deleted}*

21 February
d. 606. A Roman monk, he was a disciple and friend of St Gregory the Great and was the

notary of the Roman church before becoming bishop of Brescia in Lombardy (Italy). He was a prolific commentator on the Bible.

(Patermuthius, Copres and Alexander) (SS) *{4 –deleted}*

9 July

C4th. What is known is that Copres was an Egyptian hermit who converted Patermuthius, a notorious robber who then became a hermit also. The old Roman Martyrology listed them as having been martyred with Alexander (a converted soldier) at the orders of the emperor Julian, but this is fiction (Julian was never in Egypt).

(Paternian of Bologna) (St) *{4 –deleted}*

12 July

C5th? He was allegedly a bishop of Bologna (Italy) from c.450, but was probably identical with Paternian of Fano.

Paternian of Fano (St) {2}

12 July

C4th. He was a fugitive in the Apennines (Italy) during the persecution of Diocletian, and later became bishop of Fano on the Adriatic coast.

Paternus (Pair) of Avranches (St) {2}

21 May

d. c.460–90. From Poitiers (France), he became a monk with St Scubilio at Saint-Jouin-de-Marnes south of Saumur, and later a hermit near Coutances. Eventually he became the first bishop of Avranches in Normandy, and was consecrated without warning by St Perpetuus of Tours during a synod. He died as a hermit at a place now called Saint-Pair after him. He is often confused with St Paternus of Wales.

(Paternus the Breton) (St) *{4 –deleted}*

12 November

C8th. Born in Brittany (France), he was a monk first at Cessier near Avranches and then at Saint-Pierre-le-Vif near Sens. He was murdered by robbers, allegedly because he had admonished them.

(Paternus of Fondi) (St) *{4 –deleted}*

21 August

C3rd? According to his unreliable acta, he was an Alexandrian returning from a pilgrimage to Rome who was arrested at Fondi (Italy) and died in prison there.

Paternus (Pern) of Vannes (St) {2}

15 April

d. ?565. He was a monk who founded many monasteries in Brittany (France), and who became bishop of Vannes when a septuagenarian. He retired to be a hermit again. He is often confused with St Paternus of Wales.

Paternus (Padarn) of Wales (St)

15 April

C5–6th. A Welsh missionary monk, he founded Llanbadarn Fawr ('the great monastery of Padarn') near Aberystwyth and was bishop for the region. His veneration was very popular in Wales in the Middle Ages.

Patiens of Lyons (St) {2, 4}

11 September

d. c.480. Archbishop of Lyons (France), he gave his revenues to the poor during a famine and the invasion of the Visigoths and was commended by St Sidonius Apollinaris, his contemporary.

Patiens of Metz (St) {2}

8 January

C4th. He was the fourth bishop of Metz (France).

(Patricia of Naples) *(St) {4 –deleted}*

25 August
C7th? According to her legend she was a relative of the emperor Constans II and, in order to avoid marriage, went on a pilgrimage from Constantinople to Jerusalem and then to Rome where she became a nun. She is believed to have died at Naples (Italy) and her shrine is located there.

Patrick (St) {1, 3}

17 March
d. 461. A Roman Briton, when aged sixteen he was abducted by Irish slave-raiders from his home (the location of this is uncertain) and was a shepherd during his six years of slavery in Antrim (Ireland). Then he escaped and obtained a monastic education in Gaul. In ?432 he returned to Ireland as a missionary bishop and thoroughly established the Church there, to the extent that he is regarded as Ireland's apostle. His main base was apparently at Armagh, which became the primatial see. The extant biographies contain much contradictory and legendary material, but the wealth of this is a testimony of the impact that he had and his veneration has always been central to Irish nationality and culture throughout the world. He has one of the largest modern bibliographies of any saint, with works ranging from the scholarly to the demented. He is often depicted getting rid of snakes, and the shamrock is his attribute.

(Patrick, Acacius and Comps) *(SS) {4 –deleted}*

28 April
? They were martyred at Brusa, Asia Minor after being tortured with water from the hot springs there. The acta of Patrick are possibly authentic, and the names of the others were added in early martyrologies. The other two are Menander and Polyaenus.

(Patrick of Auvergne) *(St) {4 –deleted}*

16 March
? He is listed in the old Roman Martyrology as a bishop of Auvergne (France), but his name is not in the lists of bishops of that region and he is probably a duplicate of St Patrick of Ireland created by an ignorant copyist reading 'Arvernia' for 'Hibernia' (Ireland). A further dubious tradition claims that he was previously a bishop of Malaga (Spain) who fled to the Auvergne in the reign of Diocletian.

Patrick Cavenagh (Bl) {2}

5 July
Cf. **Matthew Lambert and Comps**.

Patrick Dong Bodi (St) {1 –group}

9 July
Cf. **Gregory Grassi and Comps**.

(Patrick of Nevers) *(St) {4 –deleted}*

24 August
He was listed in the old Roman Martyrology as an abbot of Nevers, France, but the data concerning these and other saints of the same name is hopelessly confused.

Patrick O'Healey and Comps (BB) {2}

20 June
d. 1579. The Franciscan bishop of Mayo, he was hanged at Killmalloch with Bl Conrad O'Rourke, a fellow Franciscan priest. They were beatified in 1992. Cf. **Ireland, Martyrs of**.

Patrick O'Loughlan (Bl) {2}

1 February
Cf. **Conor O'Devany and Comp**.

Patrick Salmon (Bl) {2}

4 July
d. 1594. A servant of Bl Thomas Bosgrave, he was seized with him and Bl John Craven for sheltering priests and executed with them and Bl John Cornelius at Dorchester. Cf. **England, Martyrs of.**

Patroclus of Colombiers (St) {2}

18 November
d. ?576. He was a priest who became a hermit at Colombiers in Berry (France), and who founded a monastery there for his numerous disciples.

Patroclus of Troyes (St) {2, 4}

21 January
C3rd? He was a wealthy and charitable citizen of Troyes (France), and was martyred there. His relics were translated in 960 to Soest near Dortmund (Germany), which became a great pilgrimage shrine.

Paul

In Latin this name is Paulus; in Italian and Portuguese, Paolo; in Spanish, Pablo; in Catalan, Pau.

Paul (St) {1, 3}

29 June
c.3–65. Most of his career as an apostle (the 'apostle to the Gentiles') is familiar in outline from the Acts of the Apostles, and forms the greater part of that work. The thirteen letters by him in the New Testament give a good presentation of his theology, and attempts to dispute his authorship of many of them are not conclusive. (The letter to the Hebrews is, however, not by him). His conversion near Damascus was about the year 34, and his apostolic journeys were from 47 until his arrest in Jerusalem in 58. He was in Rome in 61.

There is no evidence of his career apart from the New Testament, but it is noticeable that the areas in Asia Minor and modern Greece described as having been evangelized by him were strongholds of Christianity during the Roman persecutions. The year of his martyrdom at Rome is uncertain (he was traditionally beheaded near the Ostian Way where the church of Tre Fontane now stands), and nothing is known of his activities after his first visit to Rome. Some have postulated further missionary journeys.

A very ancient iconographic tradition, possibly based on his real appearance, shows him as a small, balding, thin-faced old man with a long, pointed dark beard.

Paul I, Pope (St) {2, 4}

28 June
d. 767. A native Roman priest, he succeeded Stephen II (his brother) as pope in 757 and continued the policy of relying on the Frankish ruler as patron to protect the independence of the Papacy against threats from the Lombard kingdom. He also sheltered refugees from the iconoclast persecution of emperor Constantine V.

Paul VI, Pope (Bl) {2 –add}

6 August
1897–1978. Giovanni Battista Montini was from Concesio near Brescia, Italy and was ordained as a diocesan priest of the latter city in 1920 but joined the Papal Secretariat of State two years later. He had a fruitful career at the Vatican under Pope Pius XII until he became archbishop of Milan in 1954. He was elected as pope in 1963, and re-convened the Second Vatican Council after its interruption by the death of Pope St John XXIII. Then he was immediately faced with massive problems of re-adjustment in the Church which followed, notably the revision of the Latin-rite liturgy

which was concluded with his promulgation of a revised Missal (the 'Mass of Paul VI') in 1970. His major encyclical against artificial birth control, *Humanae vitae*, was issued in 1968. He died in 1978, and was beatified in 2014.

(Paul and Cyriac) (SS) {4 –deleted}

20 June
? They were listed as martyred at Tomi on the Black Sea coast of Romania.

Paul and Cyril (SS) {2, 4}

20 March
? They were martyred in Syria. The Roman Martyrology has deleted Eugene and four anonymous companions.

(Paul, Gerontius and Comps) (SS) {4 –deleted}

19 January
C2nd? They were listed as having been martyred in Numidia (Roman Africa, now Algeria), but with no details. The companions were Januarius, Saturninus, Successus, Julius, Catus, Pia and Germana. Of these, SS Successus, Paul and Lucius did exist as martyrs of Carthage and are listed in the revised Roman Martyrology.

(Paul, Heraclius and Comps) (SS) {4 –deleted}

2 March
Early C4th? They were listed as martyred in the reign of Diocletian at Porto Romano at the mouth of the Tiber (Italy). The companions were Secundilla and Januaria.

(Paul and Juliana) (SS) {4 –deleted}

17 August
C3rd? According to their unreliable acta they were a brother and sister beheaded at Ptolemais (Acre) in the Holy Land in the reign of Aurelian.

(Paul, Lucius and Cyriac) (SS) {4 –deleted}

8 February
? They were martyred at Rome.

Paul, Tatta and Comps (SS) {2, 4}

25 September
C4th? A married couple with their four sons Sabinian, Maximus, Rufus and Eugene; they were tortured to death at their native city of Damascus (Syria).

Paul Aurelian (St) {2}

12 March
C6th. Born in Wales, he was educated at Llantwit Major under St Illtyd with many other famous saints (e.g. David, Samson and Gildas). After spending some time on Caldey Island he migrated to Brittany (France) with twelve companions and founded a monastery on the island of Ushant. Later he moved to what is now Saint-Pol-de-Leon and became bishop there.

Paul of Brusa (St) {2}

7 March
d. 850. Bishop of Brusa in Bithynia (Asia Minor), he opposed the iconoclast policy of the emperor Leo VI and died in exile. He had no connection with Egypt (pace the old Roman Martyrology), which was under Muslim rule.

Paul Burali d'Arezzo (Bl) {2}

17 June
1511–78. From Itri near Gaeta (Italy), he was a lawyer for ten years at Naples before becoming a royal counsellor in 1549. In 1558 he became a Theatine and was superior of the houses at Naples and Rome before being made cardinal and bishop of Piacenza. Finally he was transferred as bishop to Naples. He was beatified in 1772.

Paul Chen Changpin (St) {1 –group}

29 July

1838–61. From Xingren in Guizhou (China), he was brought up by a priest after his family broke up and became a seminarian at Yao-jiaguan. He was beheaded with SS Joseph Zhang Wenlan, John-Baptist Lou Ting-yin and Martha Wang Louzhi. Cf. **China, Martyrs of**.

Paul Chŏng Ha-sang and Augustine Yu Chin-gil (SS) {1 –group}

22 September

d. 1839. They were two catechists of Seoul in Korea. The former had directed a worship-ping congregation for twenty years without a priest during a period of persecution. The lat-ter had written to the pope in Rome in order to appeal for priests to be sent to Korea. They were arrested, tortured and beheaded together. Cf. **Korea, Martyrs of**.

Paul of Constantinople (St) {2, 4}

6 November

d. ?351. From Thessalonika, he was elected bishop of Constantinople in 336 but was exiled to Pontus in Asia Minor in 337 by Emperor Constantine for opposing a concil-iatory policy towards the Arians. Returning after the emperor's death, he was exiled to Trier by the Arian emperor Constantius until 340, to Mesopotamia from 342 to 344 and finally to Cucusus in Armenia, where he was allegedly locked up without food for six days and then strangled.

Paul of Cordoba (St) {2, 4}

20 July

d. 851. A deacon of Cordoba (Spain), he was involved in the "martyr movement" there and ministered to those imprisoned by the Muslim rulers. He was himself beheaded, and his remains enshrined in the church of St Zoilus.

Paul of the Cross cf. **Paul-of-the-Cross Danei**.

Paul of Cyprus (St) {2, 4}

17 March

d. c.770. A monk of Cyprus, during the icono-clast persecution of the emperor Constantine V he refused to trample on a crucifix and was hence hanged head downwards over a slow fire until he died.

Paul-of-the-Cross Danei (St) {1, 3}

19 October

1694–1775. Born at Ovada near Genoa (Italy) of an impoverished noble family, he was a pious youth and initially tried to join the Venetian army in order to fight the Turks. Then he had a series of visions in 1720 which inspired him to write the rule of a religious order (the Passionists) dedicated to propagat-ing devotion to the passion of Christ espe-cially by conducting missions, and this was approved by the bishop of Alessandria. The first 'retreat' (house) was at Monte Argentaro near Orbitello, and eleven other houses were founded in his lifetime throughout Italy. He also founded the congregation of the Passion-ist nuns. A great mystic, he died at Rome and was canonized in 1867.

Paul Denn (St) {1 –group}

20 July
Cf. **Ignatius Mangin and Comps**.

(Paul of Gaza) *(St)* *{4 –deleted}*

25 July

d. 308. He was listed as beheaded at Gaza in the Holy Land in the reign of Galerius.

Paul Gojdič (Bl) {2}

(17 July)
1888–1960. He was a son of a Catholic parish priest of the Ruthenian rite near Prešov in eastern Slovakia, and followed his father's vocation to the priesthood. (The Ruthenians are Slavs living in that part of the Ukraine south-west of the Carpathian mountains.) He was ordained at Prešov in 1911 and became a Basilian monk in 1922. In 1926 he was appointed apostolic administrator of the diocese there, and was made bishop in 1940. He had to contend with the upheavals of the Second World War and with the suppression of the Greek Catholic Church of the Ruthenian rite by the Communists in 1950. He was imprisoned for continuing his pastoral ministry, died of cancer in prison and was beatified as a martyr in 2001.

Paul Hạnh (St) {1 –group}

28 May
d. 1859. A native of the Mekong delta of Vietnam, he was a lapsed Christian who joined a gang of brigands. After his arrest, however, he returned to the faith and was beheaded at his home town of Chợ Quán near Saigon after being viciously tortured. Cf. **Vietnam, Martyrs of**.

Paul-of-St-Mary-Magdalen Heath (Bl) {2}

17 April
d. 1643. Born in Peterborough, he was baptized as Henry. Educated at Cambridge, he became an Anglican minister but was converted by reading the Fathers and went to Douai. There he joined the new English province of the Franciscans at their friary of St Bonaventure, and served as guardian of the friary and superior of the province. Wanting to go on mission in England, he arrived penniless in London and was immediately arrested as a vagrant, but it was then realized that he was a priest and so he was executed at Tyburn. He was beatified in 1987. Cf. **England, Martyrs of**.

Paul the Hermit (St) {2, 3}

10 January
C4th. He is listed by the Roman Martyrology as a hermit during the period of the emergence of the monastic life. His biography by St Jerome is the sole source, and there is a scholarly suspicion that he never existed. The story is that he was a well-educated Egyptian who fled into the desert of Thebes to escape the persecution under Decius when aged twenty-two, and remained there as a hermit for ninety years. He was eventually found by St Anthony, who found him dead on a second visit and buried him. He is depicted dressed in rough garments made from leaves or skins with a bird bringing him food or a lion digging his grave. His cultus was confined to local or particular calendars in 1969.

Paul Hŏ Hyŏb (St) {1 –group}

30 January
d. 1840. He was a soldier at Seoul in Korea. After being arrested, imprisoned and tortured for his faith he lapsed, but immediately repented of this and stood before the magistrate to re-affirm his belief in Christ. For this he was imprisoned again, and after some time died of the beatings that he regularly received. Cf. **Korea, Martyrs of**.

Paul Hong Yŏng-ju and Comps (SS) {1 –group}

1 February
d. 1840. He was a catechist beheaded at Seoul in Korea with two others, John Yi Mun-u who was noted for ministering to poor people and burying the bodies of martyrs, and Barbara Ch'oe Yŏng-i. Cf. **Korea, Martyrs of**.

Paul Ibaraki (St) {1 –group}

6 February
d. 1597. He was a Japanese layman crucified at Nagasaki with SS Paul Miki and Companions. Cf. **Japan, Martyrs of**.

Paul Ke Tingzhu (St) {1 –group}

8 August
1839–1900. A peasant and a leader of the Catholics of Xixiaodun near Xinhexian in Hebei (China), he was going to work at sunrise when he was seized by a gang of Boxers, tied to a tree and disembowelled. Cf. **China, Martyrs of**.

Paul Kinsuke (Bl) {2}

20 June
d. 1626. A Japanese catechist, he worked with Bl Paul Navarro and became a Jesuit in prison just before he was burnt alive at Nagasaki with Francis Pacheco and Comps. Cf. **Japan, Martyrs of**.

Paul Lang Fu (St) {1 –group}

16 July
Cf. **Lang Yangzhi and Paul Lang Fu**.

Paul Lê Bảo Tịnh (St) {1 –group}

6 April
d. 1857. A native of north Vietnam, he suffered imprisonment for his faith while studying for the priesthood. After his ordination he became the seminary rector, and wrote and preached much on Christian doctrine. He was beheaded at Vĩnh Trị during the persecution ordered by Emperor Tự Đức. Cf. **Vietnam, Martyrs of**.

Paul Lê Văn Lộc (St) {1 –group}

13 February
1831–59. A Vietnamese priest, he was beheaded at the gate of the town of Thị Nghè near Saigon shortly after his ordination. This was during the persecution ordered by Emperor Tự Đức. Cf. **Vietnam, Martyrs of**.

Paul Liu Hanzhuo (St) {1 –group}

13 February
1778–1819. From a poor Catholic family of Lezhi in Sichuan (China), he was a shepherd before being accepted into the seminary and was ordained in 1813. He was betrayed while staying at Dongjiaochang, arrested while saying Mass and hanged. Cf. **China, Martyrs of**.

Paul Liu Jinde (St) {1 –group}

13 July
1821–1900. An old peasant of Langziqiao near Hengshui in southeastern Hebei (China), he was the only one of his locality who remained true to his faith during the Boxer uprising. He was killed at home by a gang of Boxers after proclaiming himself a Christian while holding the Rosary. Cf. **China, Martyrs of**.

Paul Manna (Bl) {2}

(15 September)
1872–1952. From Avellino in Italy, he was ordained as a missionary priest at Milan in 1894 and went to Burma but had to return owing to ill-health. But his passion for missionary activity overseas led him to organize support for the foreign missions in various ways and to direct the formation of missionary priests. In 1916 he founded the Pontifical Missionary Union, and in 1926 was made superior of the pontifical missionary seminaries in Italy. He died at Naples and was beatified in 2001.

Paul Miki and Comps (SS) {1 –group}

6 February
1562–97. From the Tsunokuni district of Kyushu (Japan), the son of a samurai, he

was educated by the Jesuits and became one himself in 1580. He was famed as an orator and controversialist and was able to continue missionary activity even after the decree of banishment of foreign missionaries by the shogun Toyotomi Hideyoshi in 1587. Sharper measures followed in reaction to the activities of Spanish Franciscans from the Philippines in Kyushu, and the shogun ordered the execution of Paul, two other Japanese Jesuits, six Spanish Franciscans and seventeen Japanese laymen (including interpreters, cathechists and tertiaries) on the Nishizaka at Nagasaki. They were tied to crosses and stabbed to death on 5 February, and were canonized as a group in 1862. Cf. **Japan, Martyrs of**.

Paul Nagaishi (BB) {2}

10 September
d. 1622. He was a Japanese burnt in the 'Great Martyrdom' at Nagasaki. Cf. **Charles Spinola and Comps**, **Great Martyrdom at Nagasaki** and **Japan, Martyrs of**.

Paul of Narbonne (St) {2, 4}

22 March
C3rd. According to St Gregory of Tours, he was a missionary priest from Rome who worked around Narbonne (France) and was martyred. A late and worthless legend identifies him with the Roman proconsul Sergius Paulus converted by St Paul the Apostle (Acts 13).

Paul-Joseph Nardini (Bl) {2 –add}

27 January
1821–62. From Germersheim on the Rhine in Germany, he became a diocesan priest of Speyer and served as parish priest of Pirmasens until his death. He obtained a reputation for both holiness and effectiveness, and was especially concerned for neglected children and old people. To help he founded the 'Sisters

of the Holy Family of Mallersdorf'. He died of typhus contracted on a visit to a dying parishioner and was beatified in 2006.

Paul Nguyễn Ngân (St) {1 –group}

8 November
Cf. **Joseph Nguyễn Đình Nghi and Comps**.

Paul Nguyễn Văn Mỹ and Comps (SS) {1 –group}

18 December
d. 1838. They were three Vietnamese catechists and associates of the Paris Society of Foreign Missions, who were martyred by strangulation during the persecution ordered by Emperor Minh Mạng. The other two were SS Peter Trương Văn Dường and Peter Vũ Văn Truật. Cf. **Vietnam, Martyrs of**.

Paul Phạm Khắc Khoan and Comps (SS) {1 –group}

28 April
d. 1840. From north Vietnam, he was a priest of the Paris Society for Foreign Missions for forty years and was imprisoned for two years before being beheaded at Ninh Bình during the persecution ordered by Emperor Minh Mạng. With him were martyred two catechists, John Baptist Đinh văn Thành and Peter Nguyễn Văn Hiếu. Cf. **Vietnam, Martyrs of**.

Paul Sadayu Aybara (Bl) {2}

8 September
d. 1628. A Japanese catechist and Dominican tertiary, he was beheaded with Dominic Castellet and Comps at Nagasaki. Cf. **Japan, Martyrs of**.

Paul Sankichi (Bl) {2}

19 August
d. 1622. He was a Japanese sailor on board the ship carrying Bl Louis Flores and Comps

and was beheaded with them at Nagasaki. Cf. **Japan, Martyrs of**.

Paul the Simple (St) {2}

7 March
C4th. An Egyptian farmer of the Thebaid, when aged sixty he discovered his wife in bed with a neighbour and immediately left home to become a hermit in the desert. A disciple of St Anthony, he became famous for his prompt obedience and the childlike disposition which gave him his nickname. He is mentioned by Rufinus and Palladius.

Paul Suzuki (St) {1 –group}

6 February
d. 1597. He was a Japanese layman crucified at Nagasaki with SS Paul Miki and Companions. Cf. **Japan, Martyrs of**.

Paul Tanaka (Bl) {2}

10 September
d. 1622. He was the Japanese host of Bl Joseph of St Hyacinth and was burnt with him in the 'Great Martyrdom' at Nagasaki. Cf. **Charles Spinola and Comps**, **Great Martyrdom at Nagasaki** and **Japan, Martyrs of**.

Paul Timonoya (Bl) {2}

16 September
d. 1628. He was beheaded at Nagasaki with Bl Michael Himonoya, his father, and Bl Dominic Shobyoye. Cf. **Japan, Martyrs of**.

Paul Tomachi (Bl) {2}

8 September
d. 1628. A seven-year-old, he was beheaded with Bl John Tomachi, his father, at Nagasaki (Japan). Cf. **Dominic Castellet and Comps** and **Japan, Martyrs of**.

Paul Tống Viết Bường (St) {1 –group}

23 October
d. 1833. A soldier of the Vietnamese army, he was captain of the bodyguard of Emperor Minh Mạng and was an associate of the Paris Society of Foreign Missions. He was arrested in 1832, degraded and beheaded. Cf. **Vietnam, Martyrs of**.

Paul of Trois-Chateaux (St) {2}

1 February
C4th. From Rheims (France), as a refugee from the barbarians he became a hermit near Arles and eventually bishop of Trois-Chateaux (a diocese now extinct) in Dauphiné.

Paul Uchibori Sakuemon and Comps (BB) {2 –add}

28 February
d. 1627. They were fifteen laymen and one laywoman of the diocese of Nagasaki who were martyred together at Unzen near that city. The others were Caspar Kizaemon, Mary Mine (wife of Bl Joachim Mine Sukedayū), Caspar Nagai Sōhan, Louis Shinzaburō, Dionysius Saeki Zenka and his son Louis Saeki Kizō, Damian Ichiyata, Leo Nakajima Sōkan and his son Paul Nakajima, John Kisaki Kyūhaachi, John Heisaku, Thomas Uzumi Shingoro, Alexis Sugi Shōhachi, Thomas Kondō Hyōemo and John Araki Kanshichi. They were beatified in 2008. Cf. **Japan, Martyrs of**.

Paul of Verdun (St) {2, 4}

8 February
d. ?647. Formerly a Frankish courtier from Autun, he was a hermit on the Paulsberg near Trier (Germany) before becoming a monk at Tholey in Saarland, where he was headmaster of the monastic school. He was made bishop of Verdun, c.630.

Paul Wu Juan and Comps (SS) {1 –group}

29 June
1900. The sixty-two-year-old head of a Catholic family of Xihetou in Hebei (China), he fled with nine of his relatives to Xiaoluyi near Shenxian during the Boxer uprising. They were, however, discovered hiding in some bushes by a gang and killed on the spot. St Paul has been canonized, with two of his grandsons: Paul Wu Wanshu and John-Baptist Wu Mantang. Cf. **China, Martyrs of.**

Paul Yun Ji-chung and Comps (BB) {2 –add}

When Pope Francis visited Korea in 2014, he beatified a total of 124 martyrs in addition to those already canonized. These comprise people of all classes and occupations, the earliest being martyred in 1791 and the latest in 1888.

Bl Paul Yun Ji-chung and his cousin Bl James Gwon Sang-yeon were high-status noblemen from Jinsan who converted to Christianity after studying for the civil service examinations. In 1790 Bl Paul burnt his family's ancestral record, which was an act equivalent to treason under the Confucian system by which the country was governed. As a result, the two went into hiding but gave themselves up when other family members were targeted. After severe but unsuccessful torture in order to obtain names of other Catholics, they were beheaded on the orders of the king. Cf. **Korea, Martyrs of** and list in appendix.

Paula (St) {2, 4}

26 January
347–404. A Roman noblewoman, in 380 she was left a widow with five children, two of which were SS Eustochium and Blesilla. She became a disciple of St Jerome, and when he left for the Holy Land after his enemies had questioned their relationship she followed

suit and founded a nunnery and hospice near his monastery in Bethlehem. He wrote her biography.

Paula-Elizabeth Cerioli (St) {2}

24 December
1816–65. A noblewoman from Soncino near Cremona (Italy), she was educated by the Visitation nuns and wished to become a consecrated religious but her parents wanted her to marry and she did so. She had three children, but they and her husband had all died by 1854 and she then started to lodge and care for orphan girls at her house at Como. She educated these as farm workers. Companions started to gather, and thus was founded the institute of the 'Sisters of the Holy Family', of which she was made superior. She founded a similar orphanage for boys in 1863. Dying early of heart disease at Comonte, she was canonized in 2004.

Paula Frassinetti (St) {2}

11 June
1809–82. From Genoa (Italy), she lived with her brother who was parish priest of the suburb of Quinto. There she taught poor children at their home, and this led to her founding the 'Congregation of St Dorothy' (Dorotheans) for the education of poor girls, which spread throughout Italy and to the New World in her lifetime. She died at Rome and was canonized in 1984.

Paula Gambara-Costa (Bl) {2}

24 January
1473–1515. A noblewoman of Brescia (Italy), when aged twelve she married a young nobleman who proved a bad husband, habitually adulterous. He also objected to her lavish charitable donations. By her heroic patience she won him over, and they passed the rest of

their married life in peaceful wedlock with an austere lifestyle. She died worn-out by self-imposed penances, and her cultus was confirmed for Monreale in 1867.

Paula-of-St-Joseph-Calasantz Montal Fornés (St) {2}

26 February
1779–1889. Born near Barcelona, she had to leave school early in order to support her family as a lace-maker. However she became active in her parish as a catechist and, inspired by St Joseph Calasantz, she founded the 'Daughters of Mary of Religious Schools' in 1847. She never took high office, but remained an ordinary sister until her death. She was canonized in 2001.

Paula of Montaldo (Bl) {2}

18 August
1443–1514. From Montaldo near Mantua (Italy), when aged fifteen she joined the Poor Clares at the nunnery of St Lucy in Mantua, where she was later elected abbess three times. She was a noted mystic. Her cultus was approved for Mantua in 1866.

(Paula of Nicomedia) (St) {4 –deleted}

3 June
C3rd? According to one late and unreliable legend, she was the wife of St Lucillian and the mother of his four sons, all of whom were martyred at Byzantium. She is also described as a young woman of Nicomedia (Asia Minor) who visited the five mentioned above in prison where she was seized, tortured and beheaded. Probably none of these was martyred at Byzantium.

Paulina von Mallinckrodt (Bl) {2}

30 April
1817–81. Born near Paderborn (Germany), she lost her mother when she was a child and

she had to care for her family until her father died in 1842. This left her with a great compassion for sick, poor and blind children and she founded the 'Sisters of Christian Charity, Daughters of Our Lady of the Immaculate Conception' to help them in 1849. She served as superior for thirty-two years, and was beatified in 1985.

Paulina of Paulinzelle (St) {2}

14 March
d. 1107. She was a noblewoman of high status at the court of the Holy Roman Emperor, but retired to found a double monastery for monks and nuns at Paulinzelle (Paula's cell) in the principality of Schawarzburg-Rudolstadt in Thuringia (Germany). She died at Münster-schwarzach while on a journey.

Paulina-of-the-Heart-of-Jesus-in-Agony Wisenteiner (St) {2}

9 July
1865–1942. Born near Trent (then in Austria, now Trento in Italy), her family migrated to Brazil when she was ten and settled at Nova Trento in Santa Catarina state. She nursed at home and catechized children and went with a companion in 1890 to nurse a woman with cancer (who recovered) at her cottage. This was the start of the 'Poor Sisters of the Immaculate Conception', which institute moved to São Paolo in 1909. She died of diabetes as a simple sister after losing her eyesight and one arm, and was canonized in 2002. The Roman Martyrology lists her with the Brazilian spelling of 'Visintainer'.

(Paulinus of Antioch and Comps) (SS) {4 –deleted}

12 July
? According to his worthless C13th legend, the patron of Lucca in Tuscany (Italy) was a native of Antioch in Syria sent to Lucca by

St Peter to be its first bishop but who was martyred there with a priest, a deacon and a soldier. There was a bishop of the city with this name in the C4th.

Paulinus of Aquileia (St) {2}

11 January

?726–802. From near Cividale in Friuli (Italy), he was well educated and became a courtier of Charlemagne after the destruction of the Lombard kingdom in 774. The emperor appointed him patriarch of Aquileia in 787 (the bishop of that city had taken the title 'Patriarch' while in schism from Rome over the question of the 'Three Chapters'). He wrote against adoptionism, was a notable poet and a firm supporter of the 'Filioque' doctrine. He also carried on missionary work among the Avars before they were exterminated by the Franks.

(Paulinus of Brescia) (St) {4 –deleted}

29 April

C6th. He was listed as a bishop of Brescia (Italy).

(Paulinus of Capua) (St) {4 –deleted}

10 October

d. 843. According to his story he was an English pilgrim on his way to Jerusalem who stopped off at Capua (Italy) and was forced by the inhabitants to become their bishop in 835. He died as a refugee after the city was destroyed in a Muslim raid.

(Paulinus of Cologne) (St) {4 –deleted}

4 May

? Nothing is known about this martyr, whose relics are enshrined at Cologne (Germany).

Paulinus of Nola (St) {1, 3}

22 June

354–431. Born at Bordeaux (France), he was the son of a Roman patrician who was praetorian prefect in Gaul at the time. He was taught by the poet Ausonius and became prefect of Rome, but after the death of his only child in 390 he resigned and went to Spain, where the people of Barcelona compelled him to become a priest. Finally he settled as a hermit near Nola in Campania (Italy), and was made bishop there in 400. He proved to be very capable, especially during the invasion by the Goths under Alaric, and was friendly with most of the great teachers of the Church at that time, for example Ambrose, Jerome, Augustine, Martin of Tours. Most of his poems and a number of his letters are extant, showing him to have been a talented Christian poet and a fluent writer of Latin prose.

Paulinus of Trier (St) {2, 4}

31 August

d. 358. From Gascony (France), he accompanied St Maximinus to Trier (Germany) and succeeded him as bishop in 349. He supported St Athanasius and was hence exiled to Phrygia in Asia Minor by the Arian emperor Constantius in 355. He died in exile, but his relics were brought back to Trier in 396.

Paulinus of York (St) {2, 4}

10 October

d. 644. A Roman monk, he was sent to England in 601 with SS Mellitus and Justus by Pope St Gregory the Great in order to reinforce St Augustine's mission. He spent twenty-four years in Kent, but the princess St Ethelburga was sent to Northumbria in 625 to marry King St Edwin and he was consecrated as bishop of York and sent with her. The new mission was a success and the king was converted and baptized in 627, but was then killed in battle. In the pagan reaction that followed Ethelburga and Paulinus fled back to Kent, where he was appointed bishop of Rochester. St James the Deacon was left behind to minister to the

Christians left in Northumbria, but the mission there was later re-started from Iona.

Pega (St)

8 January
d. ?719. A sister of St Guthlac of Croyland, she imitated him in becoming a hermit in the Fens north of Peterborough (England) at a place now called Peakirk after her. She died at Rome while on a pilgrimage.

Pelagia of Antioch (St) {2, 4}

9 June
d. ?302. A girl of fifteen, she was a disciple of St Lucian at Antioch (Syria). When soldiers were sent to arrest her she killed herself by leaping from the roof of her house in order to avoid being raped. St John Chrysostom praised her courage and attributed her action to divine inspiration, but St Augustine later expounded the Church's teaching that suicide in such circumstances is not permissible.

(Pelagia the Penitent) (St) {4 –deleted}

8 October
According to her fictitious legend, she was an actress of Antioch (Syria) who was converted by St Nonnus and who spent the rest of her life disguised as a male hermit on the Mount of Olives at Jerusalem. There is a suspicion that the story was merely attached to the memory of St Pelagia of Antioch, but her cultus dates from the C6th at Jerusalem.

(Pelagia of Tarsus) (St) {4 –deleted}

4 May
According to her fictitious legend, she was a maiden of Tarsus in Cilicia (Asia Minor) who was roasted to death for refusing to marry one of the sons of the emperor Diocletian. She never existed.

Pelagius of Aemonia (St) {2, 4}

28 August
C3rd? He was allegedly martyred at Aemonia in Istria in the reign of Numerian, and after that town was destroyed his relics were taken to Citta Nuovo nearby (now Novigrad in Slovenia). A portion of them was apparently taken to Constance in Germany, of which place he is the patron.

Pelagius (Pelayo) of Cordoba (St) {2, 4}

26 June
d. 925. A boy of eleven from Asturias (Spain), he was left as a hostage with the dominant Muslim government at Cordoba. During his three years of imprisonment he was offered freedom and preferment if he would convert to Islam, but he refused and in the end he was tortured to death over a period of six hours. His relics were enshrined at Oviedo in Asturias in 985.

(Pelagius of Laodicea) (St) {4 –deleted}

25 March
d. p381. A bishop of Laodicea (Asia Minor), he opposed the Arian policy of the emperor Valens and was exiled to Bostra (Syria). Recalled by the emperor Gratian, he was present at the council of Constantinople in 381 but there is no later record of him.

Peleus, Nilus and Comps (SS) {2, 4}

19 September
d. 310. They were two Egyptian bishops who were sentenced to be worked as slaves in quarrying, probably at Phunon near Petra (Jordan), and who were finally burnt alive for celebrating Mass at their labour-camp with Elias, a priest, and a layman called Patermuthius. Many other anonymous clerics and faithful were martyred with them. Nilus and Elias were apparently duplicated under 'Tyranno and Comps' in the old Roman Martyrology.

(Pelinus) (St) {4 –deleted}

5 December
C4th? According to his legend he from Dur-rës (Albania), became bishop of Confinium, a town in the Abruzzi (Italy) now destroyed, and was martyred in the reign of Julian.

Pelusius (St) {2, 4}

7 April
? He was a martyred priest of Alexandria (Egypt).

(Peregrine, Lucian, Astius and Comps) (SS) {4 –deleted}

7 July
C2nd? According to the legend, Astius was bishop of Dyrrachium (Durrës in Albania) and was crucified there in the reign of Trajan. The others were Italian refugees from persecution who expressed sympathy for him and were seized, loaded with chains, taken out to sea and thrown overboard. The companions were Pompeius, Hesychius, Papias, Saturninus and Germanus.

Peregrine (Cetheus) of Aquila (St) {2, 4}

13 June
d. c.600. Bishop of L'Aquila in the Abruzzi (Italy), he was drowned in a river by Arian Lombards because he interceded for a condemned prisoner.

Peregrine of Auxerre (St) {2, 4}

16 May
C4–5th. He was a martyr at Bouhy near Nevers, where his shrine was initially established, and is traditionally regarded as the first bishop of Auxerre (France). According to his dubious legend, he was a Roman missionary sent by Pope Sixtus II and was martyred in the reign of Diocletian.

Peregrine of Falerone (Bl) {2}

27 March
d. 1232. From Falerone near Fermo (Italy), he was a disciple of St Francis of Assisi and became a lay brother at San Severino after a pilgrimage to the Holy Land. His cultus was confirmed for Fermo and San Severino in 1821.

Peregrine Laziosi (St) {2, 4}

1 May
?1265–1345. A native of Forli near Rimini (Italy), he was a worldly youth until he slapped St Philip Benizi across the face during a popular revolt. He was converted on the spot when Philip turned the other cheek, and joined the Servites at Siena. He was sent back to Forli, where he spent the rest of his long life. While waiting to have his leg amputated because of cancer of the foot he was instantaneously cured as a result of a vision, and is thus invoked against cancer. He was canonized in 1726.

(Peregrine of Lyons) (St) {4 –deleted}

28 July
C2nd? He was allegedly a priest of Lyons (France) contemporary with St Irenaeus, and lived as a hermit on an island in the Saône River during a persecution in the reign of Severus.

Perfectus (St) {2}

18 April
d. 850. A priest of Cordoba (Spain), he spoke publicly against Islam and was beheaded on Easter Sunday, being the first of the 'martyr movement' to die in this way.

(Pergentinus and Laurentinus) (SS) {4 –deleted}

3 June
C3rd? It is uncertain whether these two alleged brothers, martyred at Arezzo (Italy) in the reign of Decius, ever existed.

Perpetua, Felicity and Comps (SS) {1, 3}

7 March
d. 203. Vivia Perpetua was a young married noblewoman of Carthage (Roman Africa) and Felicity (also married) was a slave. They were catechumens together with Saturninus, Revocatus and Secundulus, while Saturus was possibly their instructor. All were imprisoned at Carthage under a law of Septimus Severus forbidding conversions to Christianity. Secundulus died in prison and the others were thrown to the wild animals in the amphitheatre during the games. Their acta are authentic, having been written by Saturus before his martyrdom and completed by an eyewitness (perhaps Tertullian). Perpetua and Felicity are mentioned in the Roman canon of the Mass.

Perpetua Hong Kŭm-ju (St) {1 –group}

26 September
Cf. **Sebastian Nam I-gwan and Comps**.

(Perpetua of Rome) (St) {4 –deleted}

4 August
According to her fictitious legend, she was a married woman of Rome who was baptized by St Peter and who converted her husband and her son, St Nazarius. (Cf. **Nazarius and Celsus**.) Her relics are at Milan and Cremona.

Perpetuus of Tours (St) {2, 4}

8 April
d. 491. He was bishop of Tours (France) from c.460. His alleged will is a C17th forgery.

Perpetuus of Utrecht (St) {2}

4 November
d. c.620. He was a bishop of Utrecht (Netherlands).

Perreux cf. **Petroc**.

(Perseveranda) (St) {4 –deleted}

26 June
C8th? According to her fictitious story, she was a Spanish maiden who emigrated with her two sisters to Poitiers (France) where they founded a nunnery. This was sacked by a brigand, so she fled and died of exhaustion at a place now named Sainte-Pezaine after her.

Persia, Martyrs of (SS) {2, 4}

In its first two centuries the only place where Christianity penetrated beyond the Roman Empire was into the Parthian Empire of Persia (roughly modern Iraq and Iran). Nothing is known historically of how it arrived in Mesopotamia (modern Iraq), although a large and prosperous Jewish population had lived there since the Exile. Christianity was tolerated by the Parthians but these were overthrown in 226 by the Sassanids, whose official policy was to hark back to the great days of Persia under the Achaemenids. This included the encouragement of Zoroastrianism as the state religion, and consequent suspicion of Christianity. The situation abruptly deteriorated when Christianity became the state religion of the Roman Empire under Constantine, as Persian Christians were then regarded as fifth-columnists. Persecution was especially vicious under Shah Shapur II (309–79) until the Persian church went into schism after the Council of Ephesus condemned Nestorianism, but it continued until a treaty of toleration in 422 and sporadically afterwards until the arrival of the Muslim Arabs. The old Roman Martyrology lists two anonymous groups of martyrs:

9 May
C4th? A group of three hundred and ten, about whom nothing is known.

5 April
d. ?342. A group of one hundred and twenty, including nine women, they were collected from various towns in the Persian Empire and

brought before Shah Shapur II. After refusing to worship fire as required by the Zoroastrian state religion, they were burnt alive.

The following three entries have been deleted from the Roman Martyrology:

10 March
? A group of forty-two, about which nothing is known.

22 April
d. 376. A very large number killed in the reign of Shah Shapur II on Good Friday. Among them were about twenty-five bishops, two hundred and fifty priests and deacons and many monastics.

8 February
C6th? 'Martyrs slain under Cabas'.

Peter

The name Petrus is the Latinized form of the Greek Petros, which means 'Rock'. In Italian it is Pietro; in Spanish and Portuguese, Pedro; in French, Pierre; in Catalan, Pere.

Peter (St) {1, 3}

29 June
d. ?64. A married fisherman of Galilee, he was a disciple of St John the Baptist before being called by Christ to be an apostle with St Andrew, his brother. As the chief of the apostles and one of Christ's 'inner council' with SS James and John, the early part of his career is familiar from the Gospels and the first part of the Acts of the Apostles. From his imprisonment by Herod Agrippa (and his miraculous release) until his martyrdom at Rome his career is virtually unknown, however. He made a decisive intervention at the Council of Jerusalem, and St Paul described a difference with him at Antioch (Syria) in his letter to the Galatians. This attested visit to Antioch may account for the early tradition that he was the first bishop of Antioch. The tradition that he was crucified upside-down in the reign of Nero derives from Tertullian. Excavations under his basilica at Rome strongly suggest that he was buried there, but some sloppiness in archaeological technique have left loopholes for doubt. His authorship of the first letter bearing his name is not conclusively doubted, and the reference found therein to his being at Babylon is generally accepted to be a euphemism for Rome (this usage occurs in Jewish apocalyptic). The second letter is probably not by him, as it deals with themes apparently post-dating his martyrdom and depends on the letter of Jude. An ancient iconographic tradition has him as a sturdy old man with curly hair and a curly, square-cut beard. His attribute is the familiar pair of keys, one gold and one silver.

Peter, Andrew, Paul and Dionysia (SS) {2, 4}

15 May
C3rd. Peter was a young man of Lampsacus on the Hellespont and martyred at Troas (Asia Minor) with the other three in the reign of Decius.

(Peter and Aphrodisius) (SS) {4 –deleted}

14 March
C5th? They were allegedly martyred by the Arian Vandals in Roman Africa, but no details are known.

Peter and Hermogenes (SS) {2, 4}

17 April
Early C4th? A deacon and his servant, they were martyred at Melitene in Roman Armenia (Asia Minor).

(Peter, Julian and Comps) (SS) {4 –deleted}

7 August
C3rd? They were listed as twenty or more Roman martyrs of the reign of Valerian and Gallienus.

(Peter, Marcian and Comps) (SS) *{4 –deleted}*

26 March
? Nothing is known about these alleged Roman martyrs. Also listed were Jovinus, Thecla (or Theodula) and Cassian.

(Peter, Severus and Leucius) (SS) *{4 –deleted}*

11 January
? Peter and Leucius are listed in the Hieronomian Martyrology as confessors. To them the old Roman Martyrology added Severus and described all three as martyrs of Alexandria (Egypt).

(Peter, Successus and Comps) (SS) *{4 –deleted}*

9 December
? Nothing is known about these alleged Roman African martyrs. Bassian and Primitivus were also named.

Peter Acotanto (Bl) {2}

23 September
d. c.1187. He was a nobleman of Venice who became a hermit and recluse in a cell attached to the abbey of San Giorgio Maggiore. He refused to be made abbot out of humility.

Peter Almató Ribera (St) {1 –group}

1 November
d. 1861. From near Vich (Spain), he became a Dominican, was sent to the Philippine Islands and thence to north Vietnam to assist St Jerome Hermosilla, with whom he was beheaded at Hải Dương during the persecution ordered by Emperor Tự Đức. Cf. **Vietnam, Martyrs of**.

Peter of Alcántara (St) {2, 3}

19 October
1499–1562. From Alcántara in Extremadura (Spain), at the age of sixteen he became a Franciscan Observant at Manjarates and was made provincial in 1524. In 1555 he received papal approval to found a reform friary at Pedrosa, the first house of the Discalced or Alcantarene Franciscans. This was marked by an intense austerity in imitation of the first Franciscans, forbidding the eating of meat, wearing of sandals (hence 'discalced') and keeping of libraries. He was a great mystic who wrote a famous treatise on prayer and was the confessor of St Teresa, whom he encouraged and defended. The latter admired him and described his austerities as 'incomprehensible to the human mind', having reduced him to looking 'as if he were made from the roots of trees'. He was canonized in 1669, is the patron of Brazil and his cultus was confined to local and particular calendars in 1969. His congregation was amalgamated to the Friars Minor in 1897.

Peter of Alexandria and Comps (St) {2, 3}

25 November
d. ?311. Born in Alexandria (Egypt), as a young man he witnessed to the faith during the persecution by the emperor Diocletian and afterwards became the head of the catechetical school. As such he opposed Origenistic speculative theology. In 300 he became patriarch and had to oppose the Meletian schism and the first manifestations of Arianism. He was martyred in the reign of Galerius, and the Coptic Church refers to him as 'the seal and completion of the martyrs' because he was the last to be executed as a Christian by public authority at Alexandria. With him were martyred three bishops, Hesychius, Pachomius and Theodore, and many others. His cultus was confined to particular calendars in 1969.

Peter of Anagni (St) {2, 4}

3 August
d. 1105. From Salerno (Italy), he became a Benedictine monk there and was made bishop

of Anagni in 1062 by Pope St Gregory VII. He built a new cathedral, took part in the First Crusade and was papal legate in Constantinople. He was canonized in 1109.

Peter Apselamus (St) {2, 4}

3 January
d. 309. Peter Apselamus (or Balsamus) was a young man who was burnt at Caesarea in the Holy Land in the reign of Maximinus.

Peter Arakiyori Chobioye (Bl) {2}

12 July
d. 1626. Cousin of Bl Mancius Araki (q.v.), he was burnt alive at Nagasaki for having accommodated European missionaries at his house. Cf. **Japan, Martyrs of**.

Peter de Arbués (St) {2}

17 September
1442–85. From Epila near Zaragoza (Spain), he was a student at Huesca and Bologna before becoming an Augustinian canon regular at Zaragoza in 1478. He was appointed inquisitor of Aragon by Torquemada in 1484. Allegations made about his cruelty are unsubstantiated, and not a single sentence of death or of torture can be ascribed to him. He was zealous, however, in investigating the persistence of non-Christian customs among those former Jews and Muslims who had been forcibly baptized or who had accepted baptism in order to avoid deportation, and this was resented. He was murdered in Zaragoza Cathedral and canonized in 1867.

Peter of Argos (St) {2}

3 May
d. ?922. He was bishop of Argos in Greece, and was strenuous in defence of poor and oppressed people. He received the nickname of 'Wonderworker'.

Peter-Paul-of-St-Clare of Arima (Bl) {2}

12 September
d. 1622. From Arima (Japan), he worked with Bl Apollinaris Franco as a catechist, became a Franciscan in prison and was burnt alive at Omura with Thomas Zumarraga and Comps. Cf. **Japan, Martyrs of**.

Peter-of-Assche van der Slagmolen (St) {2}

9 July
d. 1572. From Assche near Brussels, he became a Franciscan lay brother at **Gorinchem** (Netherlands) and was one of the martyrs there.

Peter Asúa Mendía (Bl) {2 –add}

29 August
1890–1936. From Balmaseda in the Basque Country, Spain, he became a noted architect specializing in ecclesiastical buildings such as schools, convents and churches. In 1924 he was ordained as a diocesan priest of Vittoria, apparently abandoning a promising career, and served in his home town for the next twelve years. However, he did design the new seminary in Vittoria. He was shot by Republican militia at Candina de Liendo, and was beatified in 2014. His martyrdom as a Basque priest was unusual, as the Basques did not join other parts of Spain which viciously persecuted the Church under the Republican government. C. **Spanish Civil War, Martyrs of**.

Peter Aumaître (St) {1 –group}

30 March
Cf. **Anthony Daveluy and Comps**.

Peter of Avila (Bl) {2}

10 September
1562–1622. From Palomares in Castile (Spain), he was sent to Manila with Bl Louis Sotelo in

1617 and thence to Japan. He was burnt alive at Nagasaki in the 'Great Martyrdom'. Cf. **Japan, Martyrs of** and **Great Martyrdom at Nagasaki**.

Peter Berna (Bl) {2}

25 July
d. 1583. From Ascona near Locarno in Ticino canton (Switzerland), he studied at the German college in Rome and joined the Jesuits. He went to Goa (India) with Bl Rudolf Acquaviva (q.v.) and was martyred with him.

Peter-of-St-Joseph de Betancur (St) {2}

25 April
?1619–67. A shepherd from Tenerife (Canary Islands), he went to Guatemala City hoping to be a missionary but became destitute and could not afford to study for the priesthood. As a casual worker on the margins of society he joined the Franciscan tertiaries, and started many institutions for poor people as well as catechizing them. His co-workers became, in time, the 'Congregation of Our Lady of Bethlehem' (the 'Bethlemites'). He was canonized in 2002.

Peter-Baptist Blázquez of San Esteban (St) {1 –group}

6 February
1545–97. From near Avila (Spain), he became a Franciscan in 1567 and was sent to the Philippines, arriving there in 1583 after three years in Mexico. In 1593 he was sent to Japan as one of a group of Franciscan missionaries sponsored by the governor of the colony. The mission was initially a success, but the government were led to believe that it was in preparation for a Spanish invasion and St Peter was one of the companions of St Paul Miki crucified at Nagasaki in consequence. Cf. **Japan, Martyrs of**.

Peter Bonhomme (Bl) {2}

9 September
1803–61. From Gramat near Cahors in France, he was ordained in 1818 at a time when the Church was still recovering from the difficulties of the Revolution and the Napoleonic period. He became parish priest of his native town, and undertook an extraordinary range of activities devoted to spiritual and material charity as well as being a gifted preacher. The sufferings caused by the neglect of vulnerable people such as the elderly, sick and disabled led him to found the 'Congregation of the Sisters of Our Lady of Calvary', and he also became a regional missioner. He lost his voice to disease before he died at Gramat, and he was beatified in 2003.

Peter Bonilli (Bl) {2}

5 January
1841–1935. From near Terni in Umbria (Italy), he became a priest there in 1863 and was appointed to a small and poor parish called Cannaiola. There he stayed until 1897. In 1887 he opened a girls' orphanage and founded the 'Sisters of the Holy Family' the following year to run it. Then he opened a hospital for deaf, dumb and blind girls in 1893, which he moved to Spoleto where he was appointed seminary rector. He died there, and was beatified in 1988.

(Peter of Braga) (St) {4 –deleted}

26 April
? According to the tradition he was associated with the apostolate of St James the Great in Spain, became the first bishop of Braga (Portugal) and was martyred. Historically he seems to have been a C5th or C6th bishop.

Peter Calungsod (St) {2}

2 April
d. 1672. He was a native of the Philippines, but it is wholly unknown as to from which

island. He received some basic training in the catechism and in spoken Spanish, before becoming an assistant catechist. As such, he accompanied Bl Diego-Aloysius de San Vitores to Guam in 1668 in order to evangelize the native Chamorros, a work which they undertook for four years. However, medicine men and other opponents of Christianity fomented a rumour that baptism poisoned babies. As a result, when the pair arrived at the village of Tumon and baptized the chief's infant daughter without permission, he had them martyred. St Peter (only) was canonized in 2012.

Peter Cambiani de Ruffi (Bl) {2}

2 February
d. 1365. A Dominican, he was made inquisitor general of Piedmont and Lombardy (Italy) in 1351 in response to the growth of the dualist heresy of the Waldenses. A group of these trapped and killed him at the Franciscan friary at Susa, and his cultus was approved for Turin and the Dominicans in 1856.

Peter Canisius (St) {1, 3}

21 December
1521–97. From Nijmegen (Netherlands), he became a Jesuit as a disciple of St Peter Faber at Mainz in 1543. He was the leader of the Catholic counter-Reformation in Germany, attending the Council of Trent in 1547 and subsequently being engaged in preaching, teaching, writing and instructing in Germany, Austria, Switzerland, Bohemia and Poland. His short catechism in Latin and German had passed through two hundred editions before his death at Fribourg (Switzerland), and was translated into twelve European languages. He also wrote theological, ascetical and historical treatises. He has been called 'the Second Apostle of Germany' but was hated by the Protestants, who called him 'the dog' (which is what his surname means). He was

canonized and declared a doctor of the Church in 1925.

Peter of Capitoliadus (St) {2}

13 January
d. 713. From Capitoliadus in Batanea (Syria), he was accused of preaching to Muslims and was ordered by Walid, the Arab caliph at Damascus, to have his tongue and extremities amputated and to be crucified.

Peter Capucci (Bl) {2}

21 October
1390–1445. From Città di Castello (Italy), he joined the Dominicans at Cortona and became known as 'the preacher of death' because he used to preach with a skull in his hands. His cultus was confirmed for the Dominicans in 1816.

Peter-of-the-Birth-of-Mary Casani (Bl) {2}

17 October
1572–1647. Born in Lucca (Italy), he joined the 'Congregation of the Mother of God' founded there by St John Leonardi. When the latter died, his disciples offered assistance to the 'Piarists' of St Joseph Calasanz and temporarily joined them 1614–17. When they left, Bl Peter stayed and eventually became assistant-general to St Joseph, dying just before him. Their charism together was a love of poverty combined with a preferential option for poor children. He was beatified in 1995.

Peter of Castelnau (Bl) {2}

15 January
d. 1208. Born near Montpellier (France), he became archdeacon of Maguelonne in 1199 and a Cistercian monk at Fontfroide in 1202. The following year Pope Innocent III appointed him apostolic legate and inquisitor in southern France in order to combat the Albigensian

heresy prevalent there. He excommunicated Count Raymond VI of Toulouse (their main patron) who submitted, but the day following the submission Bl Peter was killed by an official of the count at St Gilles near Nîmes. This act triggered the Albigensian Crusade.

Peter II of Cava (Bl) {2}

13 March
d. 1208. He became the ninth Benedictine abbot of Cava near Salerno (Italy) in 1195 and was described as 'an enemy of all litigation' which, for monks of that era, was praise indeed. His cultus was confirmed in 1928.

Peter Celestine (St) {2, 3}

19 May
?1215–96. From Isernia in Molise (Italy), he became a priest-hermit and joined the abbey of Faizola in 1246. Becoming a hermit again at Morone near Sulmona in 1251, he attracted numerous disciples and founded the new Benedictine congregation of the Celestines (which was suppressed in the C18th). In 1294 he was elected pope as Celestine V because factionalism prevented any more obvious candidate being acceptable, and was a disaster owing to his simplicity and lack of political knowledge. The Curia fell into complete disorder. He resigned after nine months, and Pope Boniface VIII (his successor) kept him imprisoned until his death. He was canonized (as Peter) in 1313 but his cultus was confined to local calendars in 1969. Pathological evidence of murder has been discounted.

Peter Chanel (St) {1}

28 April
1803–40. The protomartyr of Oceania was from a peasant family at Cluet near Belley (France) and was ordained as a diocesan priest of Belley in 1827. He was parish priest of Crozet before transferring to the Marist

Fathers in 1831, and was in the first group of missionaries sent to Oceania by that new society. He established himself on Futuna Island, north-east of Fiji, and was welcomed until he baptized the chief's son. Then he was killed. He was canonized in 1954.

Peter of Chavanon (St) {2}

8 September
d. c.1080. From Langeac in the Massif Central (France), he was a secular priest before becoming the prior-founder of an abbey of Augustinian Canons Regular at Pébrac in Auvergne.

Peter Cho Hwa-sŏ and Comps (SS) {1 –group}

13 December
d. 1866. He was the father of a family, and was brought before the magistrate at Tjyentiyou in Korea with five companions. After resisting torture and persuasion to abandon their faith they were beheaded. The others were Bartholomew Chŏng Mun-ho the head of a family, Joseph-Peter Han Chae-kwon formerly a cathechist, Peter Chŏng Won-ji a teenager, Peter Sŏn Sŏn-ji and Peter Yi Myŏng-sŏ also heads of families with the former also a catechist. Cf. **Korea, Martyrs of**.

Peter Ch'oe Ch'ang-hŭb (St) {1 –group}

29 December
Cf. **Benedicta Hyŏn Kyŏng-nyŏn and Comps**.

Peter Ch'oe Hyŏng and John-Baptist Chŏn Chang-un (SS) {1 –group}

9 March
d. 1866. They were family men in their fifties who helped St Simeon Berneaux in preparing candidates for baptism and distributing Christian literature. They were arrested and viciously tortured, gaining the admiration of their persecutors through

their endurance before their martyrdom. Cf. **Korea, Martyrs of**.

Peter Chŏng Won-ji (St) {1 –group}

13 December
Cf. **Peter Cho Hua-sŏ and Comps**.

Peter Chrysologus (St) {1, 3}

30 July
d. c.450. From Imola (Italy), he was archdeacon of Ravenna before becoming archbishop in ?433. The city was the capital of the western Roman Empire at the time. His skill in preaching earned him his surname, 'Golden Speech' (although a he was a Latin, the nickname is Greek in imitation of St John Chrysostom). He died at Imola, where his shrine is located. A large number of his sermons are extant, and he was declared a doctor of the Church in 1729.

Peter Claver (St) {1}

9 September
1581–1654. From a peasant family of Verdù near Barcelona (Spain), he became a Jesuit in 1601 and went to Majorca, where he was inspired by St Alphonsus Rodriguez to work in America. He was sent to Bogota (Colombia) in 1610 and to Cartagena in 1616, where he remained for forty years. The city was the central slave-market for the Caribbean area, and he made a special vow to minister to the enslaved blacks there. He was alleged to have baptized and cared for over 300,000 of them. During the last four years of his life he was an invalid, and was often neglected by his brethren. Canonized in 1888, he was declared patron of all missions of the church among black people in 1896.

Peter of Cordoba and Comps (SS) {2, 4}

7 June
d. 851. He was a priest at Cordoba (Spain) during the rule of the Umayyad emirs there, and was involved in the 'martyr movement'. With five companions (Wallabonsus, a deacon; Sabinian and Wistremund, monks of St Zoilus's; Habentius, a monk of St Christopher's and Jeremiah, the aged founder of the monastery of Tabanos near Cordoba) he publicly preached against Islam. They were beheaded, except Jeremiah who was whipped to death.

Peter-of-Mogliano Corradini (Bl) {2}

25 July
d. 1490. From Mogliano near Fermo (Italy), he studied law at Perugia and joined the Observant Franciscans there. Later he became a companion missionary of St James Gangala della Marca. His cultus was confirmed for Camerino in 1760.

Peter Criscus (Bl) {2}

19 July
d. c.1323. From Foligno (Italy), he gave all his positions to the poor and became a verger and recluse in the cathedral, living a penitential life in the bell-tower.

Peter-of-the-Assumption of Cuerva (Bl) {2}

22 May
d. 1617. From Cuerva near Toledo (Spain), he was one of fifty Franciscan missionaries sent to Japan in 1601 and was appointed guardian of the friary at Nagasaki. He was beheaded at Nagasaki with Bl John Machado, which martyrdom was the first in the great wave of persecution aimed at the Japanese church thereafter. Cf. **Japan, Martyrs of**.

(Peter of Damascus) (St) {4 –deleted}

4 October
d. c 750. A bishop of Damascus (Syria), according to the story he preached against Islam and so had his tongue cut out and

was exiled to Arabia. Later he was maimed, blinded, bound to a cross and beheaded.

Peter Damian (St) {1, 3}

21 February

1007–72. From Ravenna (Italy), the youngest of a large family, he was orphaned and allegedly left in the care of an elder brother who illtreated him and made him look after his pigs. Another brother, the archpriest of Ravenna, took pity on him and paid for his education at Faenza and Parma. Then he taught at Ravenna, but became a monk at Fontavellana in 1035 and went on to be elected prior in 1043. He made the monastery the centre of a very strict monastic reform with an eremitic character, but also became involved in the contemporary moves to reform the church and was in contact with the papal curia and the imperial German court. In 1057 he was forced to become cardinal-bishop of Ostia, and was papal representative in various capacities. His literary output was prodigious and varied, including very capable Latin verse as well as theological and ascetical works. He died exhausted at Faenza and was declared a doctor of the Church in 1828. His monastic congregation eventually decayed and was joined to the Camaldolese in 1569.

Peter-Edward Dańkowski (Bl) {2}

3 April

1908–42. A Polish priest, he died of illtreatment at the concentration camp at Auschwitz. Cf. **Poland, Martyrs of the Nazi Occupation of**.

Peter Đa (St) {1 –group}

17 June

1862. He was a carpenter and sacristan of Qua Linh in north Vietnam. During the persecution ordered by Emperor Tự Đức he was viciously tortured to induce his apostasy, and on remaining firm in his faith was beheaded. Cf. **Vietnam, Martyrs of**.

Peter the Deacon (St)

12 March

C7th? He appears in the 'Dialogues' attributed to St Gregory the Great as the disciple and secretary to whom the various stories comprising that work were told, and was probably a literary device rather than a real person. Other legends about him are derivative. He is patron of Salussola near Vercelli (Italy), but has never been in the Roman Martyrology.

Peter Đoàn Công Quý (St) {1 –group}

31 July

d. 1859. A priest of the Mekong delta in Vietnam, he was imprisoned for three months with St Emmanuel Phụng at Cây Mét near Saigon. They were beheaded together. Cf. **Vietnam, Martyrs of**.

Peter Đoàn Văn Vân (St) {1 –group}

25 May

c.1780–1857. A Vietnamese catechist of Bầu Nọ in north Vietnam, he was beheaded during the persecution ordered by Emperor Tự Đức when eighty years old. Cf. **Vietnam, Martyrs of**.

Peter Donders (Bl) {2}

14 January

1809–87. Born of a poor family at Tilburg (Netherlands), he tried his religious vocation without success before becoming a priest and going to Dutch Guiana (now Surinam) in 1842. There he was an outstanding success as a missionary, especially to lepers (he was nicknamed 'apostle of the lepers'). He joined the Redemptorists in 1867 after they had taken over the mission, and was beatified in 1982.

Peter-Henry Dorié (St) {1 –group}

7 March
Cf. **Simeon Berneaux and Comps**.

Peter Dumoulin-Borie and Comps (SS)
{1 –group}

24 November
1808–38. From Cors near Tulle (France), he joined the Paris Society for Foreign Missions in 1829 and was sent to north Vietnam after his ordination in 1832. In 1836 he was arrested, and while in prison was made vicar-apostolic of so-called 'West Tonkin' and titular bishop of Acanthus. He was beheaded at Đồng Hới, and with him were strangled two Vietnamese priests, SS Peter Võ Đăng Khoa and Vincent Nguyễn Thế Điểm. Cf. **Vietnam, Martyrs of**.

Peter Dũng and Comps (SS) {1 –group}

6 June
1862. He was a fisherman of Lương Mỹ in north Vietnam, and was arrested during the persecution ordered by Emperor Tự Đức together with St Peter Thuần, a fellow fisherman and St Vincent Dương, a farmer. After they together refused to trample on a crucifix they were burnt alive. Cf. **Vietnam, Martyrs of**.

Peter Ermengol (St) {2, 4}

27 April
1238–1304. A nobleman related to the counts of Urgell in Catalonia (Spain), as a young man he lived recklessly but repented and joined the Mercedarians in 1528 in order to help ransom Christians enslaved by Muslim raiders from Africa. He offered himself as a hostage for eighteen Christian children in the Maghrib, and when the ransom was not paid by the stipulated date he was hanged. A few hours later the money arrived so he was cut down, found to be still alive and was released. This is the reason for his cultus as a martyr, despite his having died in peace at Tarragona. His cultus was confirmed for there in 1686.

Peter Esqueda Ramírez (St) {1 –group}

22 November
1887–1927. He was born at San Juan de los Lagos in Jalisco, Mexico and as a priest was noted for his devotion to catechizing children. He was imprisoned for his priesthood, beaten in prison and then shot at Teocaltitlán near Guadalajara in Mexico. Cf. **Mexico, Martyrs of**.

Peter Julian Eymard (St) {2}

2 August
1811–64. He was born and died at La Mure d'Isère near Grenoble (France). Being ordained as a diocesan priest in 1834, he joined the 'Marist Fathers' five years later. He then tried to organize a group of priests dedicated to the adoration of the Blessed Sacrament within this congregation, but was told that this activity did not match their charism. So he was allowed to leave, and founded the 'Blessed Sacrament Fathers' in Paris in 1856, the 'Sisters, Servants of the Blessed Sacrament' in 1858 and then a confraternity for seculars. He was canonized in 1963.

Peter Faber (Lefèvre) (St) {2}

1 August
1506–46. From Villaret in Savoy (France), as a priest and a student at Paris he became one of the first disciples of St Ignatius of Loyola (by tradition the first) and said the Mass at Montmartre during which the first Jesuits took their vows. After 1540 he was mainly occupied in converting Protestants and reforming Catholics along the Rhine in Germany, especially at Cologne, and had St Peter Canisius as a disciple. He was an attractive character,

with great ability and untiring energy. He died in Rome when about to leave for the council of Trent, and his cultus was confirmed for Annecy in 1872. He was equivalently canonized in 2013.

Peter Fourier (St) {2}

9 December
1565–1640. From Mirecourt in Lorraine (France), he became an Augustinian canon regular at Chaumousey and served as procurator and parish priest of the monastery after his ordination in 1585. In 1597 he was appointed to the neglected parish of Mattaincourt. There he founded two congregations for the education of children: the 'Augustinian Canonesses of Our Lady' for girls and the 'Augustinian Canons of Our Saviour' for boys. He was superior of the latter from 1632 until he fled to Gray in Spanish Burgundy (now Franche Comté) to avoid taking an oath of allegiance to King Louis XIII in 1640, just before he died. He was canonized in 1897. His male congregation was first suppressed in the French Revolution, and then finally became extinct in 1919.

Peter-George Frassati (Bl) {2}

4 July
1901–25. From Turin (Italy), in 1918 he enrolled at Turin University to study engineering, specializing in tunnelling design. He aimed also at Christian perfection, joining several confraternities (including the Dominican tertiaries), and had a strong Marian piety. He had achieved his doctorate before dying of poliomyelitis, and was beatified in 1990.

Peter Friedhofen (Bl) {2}

21 December
1819–60. From Vallendar near Koblenz (Germany), he was orphaned as a child, became a municipal street-cleaner and was made the foreman of the gang in 1842. He helped many families in difficulties (including that of his deceased brother) and set up sodalities of St Aloysius in several parishes. He also started a nursing home for invalids in Weitersburg which became the 'Brothers of Mercy of Mary Auxiliatrix'. He was beatified in 1985.

Peter Gambacorta (Bl) {2}

17 June
1355–1435. Born at either Pisa or Lucca (Italy), a son of the ruler of these cities, he was a reckless young man but repented and became a hermit at Montebello near Urbino. According to the story he converted twelve robbers there and thus founded the Italian Hieronomites (the 'Poor Brothers of St Jerome'). When his father and two brothers were murdered he refused to leave his cell and forgave the assassins. His sister was Bl Clare Gambacorta. His cultus was confirmed for Pisa in 1693.

Peter Geremia (Bl) {2}

3 March
1381–1452. From Palermo (Sicily), he was a student of law at Bologna when he decided to join the Dominicans and became famous as a preacher and missionary in central and southern Italy. He was prior at Palermo where he died, and his cultus was confirmed for there in 1784.

Peter-of-Gubbio Ghisleni (Bl) {2}

23 March
d. ?1306. From Gubbio in Umbria (Italy), he became an Augustinian friar and provincial of a small congregation based at Fano. His shrine is at Gubbio, and his cultus was confirmed for there in 1847.

Peter González ('Telmo') (St) {2}

14 April

1190–1246. A nobleman from Astorga (Spain), he became a cathedral canon at Palencia before joining the Dominicans. He was the confessor and court-chaplain of King St Ferdinand III of Castile, and in that position was influential in fostering the 'Reconquista' and in obtaining a policy of tolerance of the kingdom's new Muslim subjects when Cordoba and Seville were conquered. He also worked among the sailors and peasants of Galicia. Spanish sailors mistakenly call him Telmo or Elmo, thought to be a corruption of 'St Erasmus' (another patron of sailors).

Peter Higgins (Bl) {2}

23 March

d. 1642. A Dominican priest, he was seized and hanged without trial at Naas during the reign of Charles I. He was beatified in 1992 Cf. **Ireland, Martyrs of.**

Peter Hong Pyŏng-ju (St) {1 –group}

31 January

Cf. **Augustine Pak Chŏng-wŏn and Comps**.

Peter Igneus (Bl) {2}

8 February

d. 1089. A nobleman of Florence (Italy), he became a monk at Vallombrosa under St John Gualbert. According to the story, shortly afterwards he accused the bishop of Florence of simony and submitted to trial by ordeal to prove his case, walking uninjured through a fire. This gave him his nickname of Igneus, 'of the fire'. Later he became cardinal-bishop of Albano and served as papal legate. His cultus was confirmed by his insertion into the revised Roman Martyrology.

Peter of Imola (Bl) {2}

5 October

d. 1320. He was a knight of the Hospitaller order of St John of Jerusalem, and was famous at Florence (Italy) for his attention to sick people.

Peter-Francis Jamet (Bl) {2}

12 January

1762–1845. From Fresnes in Normandy (France), he was ordained in 1787 and became the confessor in 1790 of the 'Daughters of the Good Saviour' at Caen, becoming the canonical superior in 1819. During the 'Terror' he was imprisoned but was released and ministered to the scattered sisters. Afterwards he helped them open schools, hospitals and dispensaries and is called their 'second founder'. He died at Caen and was beatified in 1987.

Peter Khanh (St) {1 –group}

12 July

c.1780–1842. A Vietnamese priest of Nghê An in central Vietnam, he was recognized as a Christian by tax-collectors and as a result imprisoned and tortured for six months during the persecution ordered by Emperor Thiêu Tri. He was finally beheaded. Cf. **Vietnam, Martyrs of.**

Peter Kibe Kasui (Bl) {2 –add}

4 July

d. 1639. He was a Jesuit priest from Kibe, Ōita who was martyred at Tokyo. He was beatified in 2008. Cf. **Japan, Martyrs of.**

Peter of Korea (Bl) {2}

10 September

d. 1622. He was only three years old when he was beheaded with his mother Mary and brother John in the 'Great Martyrdom' at

Nagasaki (Japan). His father Anthony was burnt. Cf. **Japan, Martyrs of** and **Great Martyrdom at Nagasaki**.

Peter Kwon Tŭ-gin (St) {1 –group}

24 May

Cf. **Augustine Yi Kwang-hŏn and Comps**.

Peter Lê Tùy (St) {1 –group}

11 October

1763–1833. A Vietnamese priest of Hanoi, he was beheaded in the persecution ordered by Emperor Minh Mạng. Cf. **Vietnam, Martyrs of**.

Peter Levita (Bl) {2}

30 April

d. 605. He was a monk of the monastery of St Gregory the Great on the Coelian Hill at Rome. When his abbot became pope he was ordained deacon, and wisely administered the patrimony of the Church of Rome. His cultus was confirmed for Biella (Italy) in 1866.

Peter Li Quanhui and Raymund Li Quanzhen (SS) {1 –group}

30 June

1837 and 1841–1900. Brothers, they were from Chendun near Jiaohe in Hebei (China). During the Boxer rebellion they were caught hiding in a marsh by a Boxer gang and taken to a local Buddhist temple as an invitation to apostasy. There they were tortured and killed. Cf. **China, Martyrs of**.

Peter Liu Wenyuan (St) {1 –group}

17 May

1760–1834. A vegetable farmer of Giuzhu county in Guizhou (China), he was converted when young and exiled as a result to Manchuria in 1800. After thirty years of slavery he was allowed to return home, but when his sons were imprisoned for the faith he tricked his way into prison at Guiyang to visit them, was apprehended and strangled. Cf. **China, Martyrs of**.

Peter Liu Ziyu (St) {1 –group}

17 July

1843–1900. From Zhujiaxiezhuang near Shenxian in Hebei (China), he was a worker in a pottery factory and refused to flee during the Boxer rebellion. He was seized on the orders of the local magistrate and, on declining to apostatize, was thrust through with a sword. Cf. **China, Martyrs of**.

Peter of Luxembourg (Bl) {2}

2 July

1369–87. A nobleman from Ligny-en-Baurrois in Lorraine (France), as a boy he was interested in religion and so (in accordance to a common contemporary abuse) he was given made a cathedral canon of Paris, Chartres and Cambrai and archdeacon of Dreux. When aged fourteen he was made bishop of Metz, and at sixteen was created cardinal by the antipope Clement VII at Avignon. A young man of great holiness, he retired to the Carthusian monastery of Villeneuve-les-Avignon and died there aged eighteen, being beatified in 1527.

Peter of Majuma *(St)* *{4 –deleted}*

21 February

C8th? His story is that he was a scribe working at the court of the Caliph at Damascus (Syria) who was a secret Christian. When on his deathbed he called in some imams, declared his faith and reviled Muhammad. The Caliph ordered his execution before he could die naturally.

Peter-of-Jesus Maldonado Lucero (St)

11 February

1892–1937. From Sacramento, he entered the seminary at Chihuahua in Mexico but the

Mexican Revolution prevented his ordination there and he was ordained instead at El Paso in Texas, USA in 1918. He worked in secret in Chihuahua state until he was expelled back to El Paso in 1934, but soon returned and continued work until seized by a drunken gang near Santa Isabel and imprisoned. He was beaten unconscious by the mayor and other politicians of the town, and died in hospital at Chihuahua city as a result. Cf. **Mexico, Martyrs of**.

(Peter Martinez of Mozonzo) (St) {4 –deleted}

10 September
d. c.1000. From Galicia (Spain), he became a Benedictine monk at the abbey of Mozonzo in 950. Later he was appointed abbot of St Martin de Antealtares at Compostella, and finally archbishop of that city in ?986. He is one of the heroes of the Spanish Reconquista, and also one of candidates for authorship of the *Salve Regina*.

Peter Martyr (St) {2, 3}

6 April
?1205–52. From Verona (Italy), his parents were Waldensian dualist heretics but he became a Dominican in 1221 and was appointed inquisitor of Lombardy, where Waldensians were then common. He preached successfully throughout northern and central Italy until he was ambushed and killed by two heretics on the road between Como and Milan. He was canonized in the following year as the first Dominican martyr. His attribute is the large knife used to kill him, often shown in his head. His cultus was confined to local or particular calendars in 1969.

Peter Maubant (St) {1 –group}

21 September
Cf. **Laurence Imbert and Comps**.

Peter Nam Kyŏng-mun (St) {1 –group}

20 September
Cf. **Laurence Han I-hyŏng and Comps**.

Peter Nagaishi (Bl) {2}

10 September
d. 1622. A seven-year-old Japanese boy, he was beheaded with his parents BB Paul and Thecla Nagaishi in the 'Great Martyrdom' at Nagasaki. Cf. Japan, Martyrs of and **Great Martyrdom at Nagasaki**.

Peter-Paul Navarro and Comps (BB) {2}

1 November
d. 1622. An Italian Jesuit, as a scholastic he was sent to Goa (India), ordained there and then sent to Japan. He had complete success in learning the language, was made superior of the college at Yamaguchi and was a missionary around Nagasaki. He was burnt alive at Shimabara with two Jesuit juniors, Peter Onizuka Sandayu and Dionysius Fujishima (who took vows in prison), and Clement Kyuyemon, a servant. Cf. **Japan, Martyrs of**.

Peter-Francis Néron (St) {1 –group}

3 November
1818–60. From Bornay in the Jura (France), he joined the Paris Society of Foreign Missions in 1846 and was ordained as a missionary priest two years later. He went to Vietnam via Hong-Kong, and was the director of the central seminary of north Vietnam until he was arrested during the persecution ordered by Emperor Tự Đức. He was then kept in a tiny cage for three months, after which he was viciously flogged and starved for three weeks. After his unexpected survival he was beheaded at Xã Đoài. Cf. **Vietnam, Martyrs of**.

Peter Nguyễn Bá Tuân (St) {1 –group}

15 July

1766–1838. A Vietnamese priest, he died of starvation in prison at Nam Định in north Vietnam during the persecution ordered by Emperor Minh Mạng. He had been sentenced to be beheaded. Cf. **Vietnam, Martyrs of**.

Peter Nguyễn Khắc Tự (St) {1 –group}

10 July

d. 1840. A Vietnamese catechist in central Vietnam, he was beheaded with St Anthony Nguyễn Hữu Quỳnh at Đồng Hới during the persecution ordered by Emperor Minh Mạng. Cf. **Vietnam, Martyrs of**.

Peter Nguyễn Văn Hiếu (St) {1 –group}

28 April

Cf. **Paul Phạm Khắc Khoan and Comps**.

Peter Nguyễn Văn Lựu (St) {1 –group}

7 April

1861. He was a Vietnamese secular priest, and was martyred at an unknown place in the Mekong delta during the persecution ordered by Emperor Tự Đức. Cf. **Vietnam, Martyrs of**.

Peter Nguyễn Văn Tự (St) {1 –group}

5 September

d. 1838. A Vietnamese Dominican priest, he was beheaded at Ninh Tai in north Vietnam together with St Joseph Hoàng Lưỡng Cành. Cf. **Vietnam, Martyrs of**.

Peter of Nicomedia and Comps (St) {2, 4}

12 March

d. 303. A chamberlain in the palace of Diocletian at Nicomedia (Asia Minor), he was one of the first victims of the persecution ordered by that emperor. Bits of his flesh were torn off,

salt and vinegar were applied to the wounds and he was finally roasted to death over a slow fire. Two other chamberlains, Dorotheus and Gorgonius, were martyred with him.

Peter Nolasco (St) {2, 3}

6 May

d. 1245. A native of Languedoc, he took part in the Albigensian crusade before becoming a courtier of King James I of Aragon at Barcelona (Spain). There he got to know St Raymund of Peñafort, and in about 1218 they reorganized a lay confraternity for ransoming captives from the Muslims with the help of the king. This became the Mercedarian order. He journeyed to the Maghrib twice, died at Barcelona and his cultus was confirmed for there in 1628. From 1664 to 1969 this was extended to the whole church.

Peter-of-the-Holy-Mother-of-God of Omura (Bl) {2}

29 July

d. 1629. A Japanese catechist and a Dominican lay brother, he was burnt alive at Omura with BB Louis Bertrán and Comps. Cf. **Japan, Martyrs of**.

Peter Onizuka Sandayu (Bl) {2}

1 November

d. 1622. A Japanese from Arima, he became a Jesuit in prison before being burnt alive with Bl Paul Navarro and Comps. Cf. **Japan, Martyrs of**.

Peter of Osma (St) {2}

2 August

d. 1109. From Berry (France), he became a Benedictine monk of Cluny and was one of the numerous Cluniac monks who settled in Spain from c.1050 to c.1130. He was archdeacon of Toledo before being made bishop of

Osma in Old Castile in 1101, of which diocese he is the principal patron.

Peter Pascual (St) {2, 4}

6 December
1227–1300. From Valencia (Spain), he became tutor to Sancho, archbishop of Toledo and the son of King James I of Aragon, and administered the diocese for him. In 1296 he became bishop of Jaén, which was still under Muslim rule. He was zealous in ransoming captives and in preaching and writing against Islam, for which he was executed at Granada. His cultus was confirmed for Granada and Jaén in 1673.

(Peter of Pavia) (St) {4 –deleted}

7 May
d. ?735. A relative of Luitprand, king of the Lombards, he was briefly bishop of Pavia (the Lombard capital in Italy).

Peter Pectinarius (Bl) {2}

4 December
d. 1249. He was a Franciscan tertiary at Siena (Italy), and was noted for his concern for poor and sick people as well as for his silence and humility.

Peter-James of Pesaro (Bl) {2}

23 June
d. ?1496. He was an Augustinian friar at Pesaro (Italy), and his cultus was confirmed for there in 1848.

Peter of Poitiers (St) {2}

4 April
d. 1115. He became bishop of Poitiers (France) in 1087, was a friend of Bl Robert Arbrissel and helped him in founding the double abbey of Fontrevault. He was unjustly deposed, and died in exile.

Peter Poveda Castroverde (St) {2}

28 July
1874–1936. From Linares (Spain), he became a priest of Guadix in 1897 before moving to Madrid and founding the 'Teresian Association' for the spiritual and pastoral formation of teachers. He taught in seminaries, started periodicals and was a royal chaplain. Marked by simplicity and a constant devotion to study, he was canonized in 2003.

Peter Regalado (St) {2}

30 March
1390–1456. A nobleman of Valladolid (Spain), he became a Franciscan there and instituted a reform movement starting at Aguilar, where he died. Many Spanish friaries joined this. He was canonized in 1746.

Peter Rinsei (Bl) {2}

20 June
1589–1626. A Japanese, he was educated at the Jesuit seminary of Arima and worked with Bl Francis Pacheco as a catechist. The latter received his vows as a Jesuit while they were in prison before being burnt together at Nagasaki. Cf. **Francis Pacheco and Comps** and **Japan, Martyrs of**.

Peter-Renatus Rogue (Bl) {2}

3 March
1758–96. From Vannes in Brittany (France), he became a Vincentian priest at Paris and refused to take the constitutional oath during the French Revolution. He returned home to minister in secret as one of the 'non-juring' clergy but was captured and guillotined outside the building where he had celebrated Mass. He was beatified in 1934. Cf. **French Revolution, Martyrs of**.

Peter Ruiz de los Paños y Angel and Comps (BB) {2}

1881–1936. From near Toledo (Spain), he was fervent for priestly vocations and worked in various seminaries after ordination, founding the sisterhood of 'Disciples of Jesus' to help him. He became general director in Toledo of the 'Diocesan Worker Priests', and was killed with eight of his fellow members at various dates in Toledo during the Civil War. They were beatified in 1995. Cf. **Spanish Civil War, Martyrs of** and list in appendix.

Peter Sampo (Bl) {2}

10 September
d. 1622. A Japanese catechist, he was received into the Jesuits by Bl Charles Spinola while they were in prison at Omura. They were burnt alive together at Nagasaki in the 'Great Martyrdom'. Cf. **Japan, Martyrs of** and **Great Martyrdom at Nagasaki**.

Peter Sanz i Jordá (St) {1 –group}

26 May
1680–1747. From Asco in Catalonia (Spain), he became a Dominican at Lerida in 1697 and was sent to China by way of the Philippines in 1713. In 1730 he was made vicar-apostolic of Fujian and titular bishop of Mauricastro, but in 1746 he was imprisoned and beheaded at Fuzhou after some years in hiding. Cf. **China, Martyrs of**.

Peter of Sebaste (St) {2}

26 March
d. ?391. The younger brother of SS Basil and Gregory of Nyssa, he succeeded St Basil as abbot of his monastic foundation on the Iris River, south of Samsun in Turkey. In 380 St Basil appointed him bishop of Sebaste in Armenia, and he attended the first ecumenical council of Constantinople in 381. (Not to be confused with another Peter who was bishop of Sebaste, who died c.320 and who was also listed as a saint.)

(Peter of Seville) (St) *{4 –deleted}*

8 October
? He has a cultus as a martyr at Seville (Spain), but nothing is known and the legends concerning him are worthless.

Peter Shichiemon (Bl) {2}

11 September
d. 1622. The seven-year-old son of Bl Bartholomew Shichiyemon, he was martyred with BB Caspar Koteda and Comps at Nagasaki (Japan) the day after his father. Cf. **Japan, Martyrs of.**

Peter Snow (Bl) {2}

15 June
d. 1598. From Ripon (Yorks), he was ordained at Soissons in 1591 and was caught celebrating Mass at Nidd Hall near Knaresborough, the residence of Bl Ralph Grimston. They were executed at York and were beatified in 1987. Cf. **England, Martyrs of.**

Peter Sŏn Sŏn-ji (St) {1 –group}

13 December
Cf. **Peter Cho Hua-sŏ and Comps.**

(Peter the Spaniard) (St) *{4 –deleted}*

11 March
? According to his story, he was a Spanish soldier who made a pilgrimage to Rome and then became a hermit at Babuco near Veroli (Italy). He wore a coat of mail next to his skin as a penance.

Peter Spanò (St) {2}

5 June
C12th. He was a hermit associated with the Byzantine-rite abbey of Ciana near Mileto on

Sardinia. His surname means 'thorn', because he was known to pray in a thorn-bush.

Peter Sukejiro (St) {1 –group}

6 February
d. 1597. He was a Japanese Franciscan tertiary, a catechist, domestic servant and sacristan to the Spanish Franciscan missionaries on Kyushu in Japan and was martyred with SS Paul Miki and Comps. Cf. **Japan, Martyrs of**.

Peter of Tarantaise (St) {2}

14 September
1102–74. From near Vienne in Dauphine (France), at the age of twelve he joined the Cistercians at Bonnevaux and was made first abbot of Tamiens in 1132. In 1142 he became archbishop of Tarantaise and was one of the most notable churchmen of his time, but according to the story he fled after thirteen years and was eventually found serving his novitiate as a lay brother in a remote Cistercian abbey in Switzerland. He was compelled to return, and died at Bellevaux while mediating between the kings of England and France. Pope St Innocent V had the same name before his election.

Peter Tarrés I Claret (Bl) {2 –add}

31 August
1905–50. From Manresa near Barcelona in Spain, he became a medical doctor at Barcelona. He was also involved in Catholic Action and did much as a lay missionary. After the traumatic experience of being drafted as a medical orderly into the Republican army during the Spanish Civil War, he was ordained in 1942. As such he assisted Catholic Action and helped religious congregations and sick people. He died of lymphatic cancer and was beatified in 2004.

Peter-of-Siena Tecelano *(Bl)*

10 December
d. 1289. From near Siena (Italy), he was initially a married comb-maker there but his wife died and he then joined the Franciscans as a lay brother and carried on his craft in his friary at Rome for the remainder of his long life. He reached a high degree of mystical prayer. His cultus was confirmed locally for Rome in 1802, bit he is not in the Roman Martyrology.

Peter Terai Kuhyoye (Bl) {2}

28 September
d. 1630. A Japanese Augustinian tertiary, he gave shelter to the Augustinian missionaries and was hence beheaded at Nagasaki with BB John Chozaburo and Comps. Cf. **Japan, Martyrs of**.

Peter Thomas (St) {2}

6 January
1305–66. From Breil in Gascony (France), he became a Carmelite at Condom in 1325 and was sent to Avignon as procurator of the order in 1342. There he entered the service of the papal curia and was sent on diplomatic missions to Italy, Serbia, Hungary and the Middle East, being appointed successively bishop of Patti-Lipari in 1354, of Coron in the Peloponnesus (Greece) in 1359, archbishop of Candia (Crete) in 1363 and titular Latin patriarch of Constantinople in 1364. With the support of King Peter I of Cyprus he led an unsuccessful crusade against Alexandria in Egypt, and died three months later at Cyprus (allegedly of wounds received). His cultus was confirmed in 1608.

Peter Thuần (St) {1 –group}

6 June
Cf. **Peter Dũng and Comps**.

Peter To Rot (Bl) {2}

7 July

1912–45. He was born at Rakunai on the Melanesian island of New Britain, which had been first evangelized by Methodists. His father was chief of the village and was one of several in the area who had asked to become the island's first Catholics in 1898. He became a catechist for Rakunai in 1933. Married with three children, he was left as the only spiritual guide for the district when the Japanese invaded and interned all the missionaries. The Japanese forbade Christian worship in 1942 and tried to enforce the old traditions, especially polygamy. He resisted this and was arrested, imprisoned and poisoned. He was beatified in 1995.

Peter-Adrian Toulorge (Bl) {2 –add}

12 October

1757–93. From Muneville-le Bingard on the Contentin peninsula (France), he was ordained as a diocesan priest of Coutences in 1782. However, he experienced the call to enter monastic life as well as to evangelize the rural population, and so joined the Premonstratensian (Norbertine) canons at Blanchelande in 1788. This abbey was suppressed after the French Revolution, and Bl Peter-Adrian went into exile on Jersey after the revolutionary authorities required all clergy to swear an oath of loyalty to the Civil Constitution. Returning, he ministered as a priest in hiding in the countryside around Coutences until captured. His stay on Jersey made him subject to the law that prescribed death to all returning exiles, and he chose to tell the truth on this point rather than remain silent (which would have saved his life). He was executed at Coutences as a result, and was beatified in 2012.

Peter of Tréia (Bl)

20 February

d. 1304. From near Tréia in the Abruzzi (Italy), he was an early Franciscan and a disciple and fellow worker of Bl Conrad of Offida at Forano. He died at Sirolo near Ancona, and his cultus was confirmed locally in 1793, but is not in the Roman Martyrology.

Peter of Trevi (St) {2}

30 August

d. c.1050. From Carsoli in the Abruzzi (Italy), he became a diocesan priest of Marsi and preached successfully to the peasants around Tivoli, Anagni and Subiaco. He died while still young at Trevi, near Subiaco, and was canonized in 1215.

Peter Trương Văn Dường (St) {1 –group}

18 December

Cf. **Paul Nguyễn Văn Mỹ and Comps**.

Peter Trương Văn Thi (St) {1 –group}

21 December

1763–1839. A Vietnamese priest, he was beheaded with St Andrew Dũng Lạc at Hanoi after refusing to trample on a crucifix. Cf. **Vietnam, Martyrs of**.

Peter Vasquez (Bl) {2}

25 August

d. 1624. From Galicia (Spain), he joined the Dominicans in Madrid, was sent to Japan and burnt alive at Shimabara with BB Michael Carvalho and Comps. Cf. **Japan, Martyrs of**.

Peter the Venerable (Bl) {2}

11 May

?1092–1156. A nobleman from the Auvergne (France), he became a monk at Cluny in 1109, prior of Vézelay in 1102 and abbot of Cluny in 1109. The abbey had experienced a period of setback, but during his long tenure of office he regulated the finances, raised the standard of scholarship (he was himself a poet and a theologian and had the

Koran translated into Latin) and restored its position as the church's greatest and most influential monastery. He gave shelter to Abelard at the end of the latter's tempestuous career and was a contrast in many ways to his contemporary, friend and rival, St Bernard of Clairvaux. He has a cultus at Arras and in the Benedictine order.

Peter Verhun (Bl) {2}

7 February
1890–1957. He was a diocesan priest of Lwow (now Lviv in Ukraine) and Apostolic Visitor for the Ukrainian Catholics in Germany. He died in the gulag at Angarsk near Krasnoyarsk, in Siberia in the Soviet Union. Cf. **Nicholas Čarneckyj and 24 Comps**.

Peter Vičev, Paul Džidžov and Josaphat Šiškov (BB) {2}

13 November
d. 1952. Born in 1893, from Srem in Bulgaria, Peter Vičev was an Eastern-Rite Catholic and joined the Assumptionists at Gemp in 1910, being ordained in 1921. From 1930 he was rector and lecturer in philosophy at St Augustine's College in Plovdiv, being noted for his ecumenical attitude. In 1948 the college was closed by the Communist government, and he became the superior of the seminary and of the Bulgarian Assumptionists.

Born in 1919, Paul Džidžov was a Latin-rite Catholic of Plovdiv. He emigrated to France in order to become an Assumptionist in 1938 but returned to his home city and was ordained in 1945. He worked in Varna, and was also treasurer of the college where Bl Kamen Vitchev was rector. He was arrested with him.

Born in 1884, Josaphat Šiškov was a Latin-rite Catholic of Plovdiv. He joined the Assumptionists at Kara-Agatch and, after his ordination in 1909, he was a college teacher and parish priest of Yambol as well as the superior of the seminary there. In 1949 he became parish priest at Varna, until his arrest. The three were tried and secretly executed at Sofia, being beatified in 2002. Cf. **Eugene Bossilkov**.

Peter Vigne (Bl) {2}

1670–1740. From Privas in France, he became a diocesan priest of Viviers but joined the Vincentians at Lyons in 1700 in order to work as a missionary among poor people. Six years later he left in order to help those living in the countryside, who were very badly served by the contemporary church in France, and spent thirty years touring Viverais and Dauphiné. Then he settled at Boucieu-le-Roi and constructed a 'Via Dolorosa' in the landscape there. This became a focus of pilgrimage, some young women joined him to help them and in 1715 he founded the congregation of 'Sisters of the Blessed Sacrament' for perpetual adoration. He also founded several schools. He died on tour at Rencorel and was beatified in 2004.

Peter Vincioli (St) {2}

10 July
d. 1007. A nobleman from near Perugia (Italy), he was the abbot-restorer of the Benedictine monastery of St Peter at Perugia.

Peter Võ Đăng Khoa (St) {1 –group}

24 November
Cf. **Peter Dumoulin-Bori and Comps**.

Peter Vũ Văn Truật (St) {1 –group}

18 December
Cf. **Paul Nguyễn Văn Mỹ and Comps**.

Peter Wang Erman (St) {1 –group}

9 July
Cf. **Gregory Grassi and Comps**.

Peter Wang Zuolong (St) {1 –group}

6 July
1842–1900. From a Catholic family of Shuangzhong near Jixian in Hebei (China), he was captured by a Boxer gang in his village, hanged by his pigtail from a temple flagpole and tortured to induce apostasy. Failing, they killed him and left his body to be eaten by dogs. Cf. **China, Martyrs of**.

Peter Wright (Bl) {2}

19 May
d. 1651. From Slipton near Thrapston (Northants), he was a convert who studied for the priesthood at Ghent and at Rome. In 1629 he became a Jesuit and was a chaplain in the royalist army during the Civil War. He was executed at Tyburn (London). Cf. **England, Martyrs of**.

Peter Wu Anpeng (St) {1 –group}

9 July
Cf. **Gregory Grassi and Comps**.

Peter Wu Gusheng (St) {1 –group}

7 November
1768–1814. Originally an innkeeper of Longping in Guizhou (China), on his conversion he became a catechist in his home town and instructed about six hundred people before being strangled at Zunyi. He was canonized in 2000. Cf. **China, Martyrs of**.

Peter Yi Ho-yŏng (St) {1 –group}

25 November
d. 1838. A brother of St Agatha Yi So-sa, he was arrested with her and, after refusing to apostatize, had bones broken three times before being imprisoned for four years. He died in prison, and is reckoned as the first of the Korean martyrs. Cf. **Korea, Martyrs of**.

Peter Yi Myŏng-sŏ (St) {1 –group}

13 December
Cf. **Peter Cho Hua-sŏ and Comps**.

Peter Yu Tae-ch'ol (St) {1 –group}

21 October
d. 1839. He was thirty years old when imprisoned with other Christians at Seoul in Korea. He was detected encouraging his fellow prisoners in the faith, and as a result was flogged and strangled. Cf. **Korea, Martyrs of**.

Peter Yu Chŏng-nyul (St) {1 –group}

17 February
d. 1866. He was a family man of Pyongyang in Korea, and was arrested while reading the Gospels to an assembly at his house. He was then flogged to death. Cf. **Korea, Martyrs of**.

Peter Zhang Banniu (St) {1 –group}

9 July
Cf. **Gregory Grassi and Comps**.

Peter Zhao Mingzhen and John-Baptist Zhao Mingxi (SS {1 –group}

3 July
1839 and 1844–1900. They were brothers of a Catholic family of Dongyangtai near Shenxian in Hebei (China). During the Boxer uprising they took refuge in a marsh, but were discovered and massacred by Boxers together with sixteen relatives and friends.

Peter Zhu Rixin (St) {1 –group}

20 July
Cf. **Ignatius Mangin and Comps**.

Peter de Zuñiga (Bl) {2}

19 August
1585–1622. From Seville (Spain), he spent his youth in Mexico where his father was viceroy.

On his return to Spain became an Augustinian at Seville and volunteered to be sent to Japan as a missionary. He arrived at Manila in 1610, set out for Japan in 1620 but his ship was captured and two years later he was burnt alive at Nagasaki with Bl Louis Flores and Comps. Cf. **Japan, Martyrs of.**

Petra-of-St-Joseph Pérez Florido (Bl) {2}

16 August

1845–1906. From Malaga (Spain), she had a great devotion to St Joseph and begged on behalf of the destitute when young. Being joined in this by three companions, she started the 'Congregation of the Mothers of the Helpless and of St Joseph of the Holy Mountain' in 1880. The sanctuary of the latter she founded at Barcelona in 1895. She was beatified in 1994.

Petrina Morosini (Bl) {2}

6 April

1931–57. Born into a large family near Bergamo (Italy), she wanted to become a missionary but her family needed her earnings, so she learned dressmaking and started work in a factory some distance from home when she was fifteen. She continued her domestic and religious duties, made private vows when she was seventeen and joined several sodalities. She was walking back home one lunch-time when she was waylaid by a youth in a wood who wanted to have sexual intercourse. She reminded him of the requirements of moral behaviour, he tried to rape her and broke her neck in the struggle. She died two days later, and was beatified as a virgin martyr in 1987.

Petroc (Pedrog, Perreux) (St) {2}

4 June

C6th. Allegedly the son of a Welsh prince, he studied in Ireland, settled in Cornwall (England) and was evidently very active as a missionary. He founded a monastery at a place later called Petrocston (Padstow) after him and another at Bodmin, where he died. In Brittany he is called Perreux. His attribute is a stag, and he is sometimes shown as a bishop holding a church.

Petronilla of Moncel (Bl) {2}

1 May

d. 1355. She was the first abbess of the nunnery founded by King Philip the Fair at Moncel near Beauvais (France).

Petronilla of Rome (St) {2, 3}

31 May

? She has an ancient cultus as a consecrated virgin at Rome, being buried in the Catacomb of Domitilla on the Via Ardeatina. Her worthless legend alleged that she helped look after St Peter there, and the old Roman Martyrology described her as the daughter of the apostle (which she certainly was not). Her cultus was confined to local calendars in 1969. Her attribute is a bunch of keys.

Petronius of Bologna (St) {2, 4}

4 October

d. c.450. Probably the son of a praetorian prefect in Gaul, as a young man he visited the monks and shrines in Egypt and the Holy Land. While in Italy on a mission from the emperor he was made bishop of Bologna in 432 and allegedly built the monastery of St Stephen there, modelled on the buildings of the holy places at Jerusalem. A fictitious biography increased his popularity in the Middle Ages.

Petronius of Die (St) {2}

10 January

d. p463. The son of a senator of Avignon (France), he became a monk at Lérins and was bishop of Die in the Dauphiné from ?456.

(Petronius of Verona) *(St) {4 –deleted}*

6 September
d. c.450. He was a bishop of Verona (Italy).

Phaganus cf. **Fugatius**.
Phal cf. **Fidolus**.
Phara cf. **Burgundofara**.

Pharaildis (Varede, Verylde, Veerle) (St) {2}

4 January
d. ?745. Details concerning this patron of Ghent (Belgium) differ. Apparently a native of that city, she suffered abuse on the part of her husband either because he objected to her nocturnal visits to churches or because she refused to consummate the marriage, having been married against her will after making a private vow of virginity. The latter story has caused her to be venerated as a virgin.

Pharo cf. **Faro**.

Pherbutha (St) {2}

5 April
d. ?342. She was a widow and the sister of St Simeon Barsabae, being martyred in the same persecution as him in the reign of Shah Shapur of Persia. This took place at Seleucia on the Tigris.

Philaretus (St) {2}

6 April
d. 1076. From Palermo in Sicily, he fled with his family to Calabria for some reason and when aged fifty became a lay brother at the Byzantine-rite monastery of San Elia di Aulino near Palmi.

Philastrius (St) {2, 4}

18 July
d. a.397. A Spaniard, he became bishop of Brescia (Italy) in 379 and wrote an extant work against the Arian heresy. St Gaudentius, his successor, praised him for his 'modesty, quietness and gentleness towards all'.

Phileas and Comps (SS) {2, 4}

4 February
C4th. Their martyrdom was described by the historian Eusebius, their contemporary. Phileas, a bishop of Thmuis in the Nile Delta (Egypt), was seized, imprisoned at Alexandria and beheaded with a Roman tribune named Philoromus and a number of other Christians from Thmuis. While in prison he wrote a letter to his church describing the sufferings of his fellow Christian prisoners.

Philemon and Apphia (SS) {2, 4}

22 November
d. ?70. Philemon was the Christian of Colossae (Asia Minor) who owned the runaway slave Onesimus and to whom St Paul addressed a letter concerning the latter. Apphia is presumed to have been Philemon's wife. Their alleged martyrdom by stoning at their home has been deleted from the Roman Martyrology.

(Philemon and Domninus) *(SS) {4 –deleted}*

21 March
? They were listed as Roman missionaries who worked in various parts of Italy and martyred somewhere.

(Philetus, Lydia and Comps) *(SS) {4 –deleted}*

27 March
C2nd? They were allegedly martyred in present-day Bosnia in the reign of Hadrian. The old Roman Martyrology described Philetus as a senator, Lydia as his wife, Macedo and Theoprepius as their sons, Amphilochius as a captain and Cronidas as a notary. Their acta are not reliable.

Philibert (St) {2}

20 August

d. ?684. From Gascony (France), he was educated at the Merovingian court and became a monk when aged twenty at Rebais near Paris under St Agilus. Shortly afterwards he was made the abbot, but his inexperience led to a revolt and he left, visited several famous Columbanian houses (which were at that time starting to use the rule of St Benedict in their customaries) and then became the abbot-founder of Jumièges in Normandy. He opposed Ebroin (the mayor of the palace) and so was imprisoned and then exiled to Poitiers, where he founded Noirmoutier and restored Quinçay. He died at the former.

Philip

This is the English form of the Latin Philippus. The French is Philippe; the Italian, Filippo; the Spanish, Felipe.

Philip and Severus (SS) {2, 4}

22 October

d. 303. Philip was bishop of Heraclea near Byzantium, Severus was his apparently his deacon and Hermes was a priest. During the persecution by Diocletian they were arrested, put on trial and instructed to hand over the sacred books of their church to be burnt in accordance with the emperor's edict. On their refusal they were taken to Adrianople (European Turkey) and burnt at the stake. Their acta appear to be genuine. The old Roman Martyrology included priests named Eusebius and Hermes, and these have been deleted.

Philip of Agirone (St) {2, 4}

12 May

C5th. He has a cultus at the little hill town of Agirone in Sicily as a missionary priest from Thrace.

(Philip of Alexandria -1) and Comps (SS) {2, 4}

15 July

Early C4th? He was martyred at Alexandria (Egypt) with ten small children. The Roman Martyrology has deleted two adult companions, Zeno and Narseus.

(Philip of Alexandria -2) (St) {4 –deleted}

13 September

C3rd? His existence is doubtful, since it depends on the witness of the worthless acta of St Eugenia in which he is described as her father.

Philip the Apostle (St) {1, 3}

3 May

d. c.80. From Bethsaida in Galilee, he is listed as fifth among the Twelve and is mentioned three times as a confidant of Christ in St John's gospel. His career after the Resurrection is obscure, and the traditions are late and conflicting. He has been confused with St Philip the Deacon in them. His attributes are a basket of loaves and a cross, sometimes T-shaped.

Philip Benizi (St) {2, 3}

22 August

1233–85. A nobleman of Florence (Italy), he studied medicine at Paris and Padua and became a physician at Florence. In 1253 he became a Servite lay brother by pretending to be ignorant, but was found out and was then compelled by his superiors to be ordained in 1259. He became known as one of the most able preachers in Italy. After being superior of several friaries he became the fifth superior-general of the order in 1267 and oversaw its rapid spread into Poland, Hungary and Germany. He was also influential in his attempts to maintain concord between the

Guelfs and Ghibellines in northern Italy and took part in the council of Lyons in 1274. He died at Todi in Italy, was canonized in 1671 and his cultus was confined to local calendars in 1969.

Philip-of-Jesus de las Casas Martínez (St) {1 –group}

6 February
d. 1597. Born into a Spanish family at Mexico City, he became a Franciscan at Puebla but left in 1589 and went to the Philippines as a merchant. He rejoined at Manila in 1590, and was on his way back to Mexico to be ordained when his ship was driven by a storm to Japan in 1596. He was arrested with St Peter-Baptist of San Esteban and crucified at Nagasaki. Cf. **Paul Miki and Comps** and **Japan, Martyrs of**.

Philip the Deacon (St) {2, 4}

11 October
C1st. One of the first seven deacons ordained by the apostles (Acts 6:5), he worked in Samaria in the Holy Land, baptized the Ethiopian eunuch (Acts 6:8) and (with his four daughters who were prophets) was the host of St Paul at Caesarea in the Holy Land (Acts 21:9). Traditions concerning his subsequent career are unreliable, and he has been confused with St Philip the Apostle.

Philip Evans (St) {2}

22 July
1645–79. From Gwent (Wales), he was educated at Saint-Omer, joined the Jesuits in 1665 and worked on the Welsh mission from 1675. He was a skilled harpist and a good real-tennis player. In consequence of the Oates plot he was imprisoned and executed at Cardiff, and was canonized in 1970. Cf. **Wales, Martyrs of**.

(Philip of Fermo) (St) {4 –deleted}

22 October
C3rd? The shrine of this alleged martyred bishop is at the cathedral at Fermo (Italy).

Philip of Gortyna (St) {2, 4}

11 April
d. c.180. A bishop of Gortyna in Crete, he wrote a lost treatise against the Marcionite Gnostics.

Philip Howard (St) {2}

19 October
1557–95. The Earl of Arundel and Surrey was of a recusant family but was initially rather indifferent to religious matters. He converted, however, and became a conscientious Catholic, which led to his arrest and imprisonment in the Tower of London in 1585. Four years later he was sentenced to death, but this was not implemented and he died in the Tower after another six years. His shrine is at Arundel Cathedral in Sussex. He was canonized in 1970, and his attribute is a greyhound. Cf. **England, Martyrs of**.

Philip-of-Jesus Munárriz Azcona and Comps (BB) {2}

d. 1936. At the start of the Spanish Civil War the superiors of the Claretian noviciate and seminary at Barbastro and all their charges, a total of fifty-one, were seized on 20 June and massacred by Republican forces after being kept in prison for three weeks. The superior, Bl Philip, and his two deputies, BB John Díaz Nosti and Leontius Pérez Ramos, were shot first in the cemetery, while the rest were shot over four days during the middle of August at a place called Berbegal nearby. They were beatified in 1992. Cf. **Spanish Civil War, Martyrs of** and list in appendix.

Philip Neri (St) {1, 3}

26 May

1515–95. The son of a lawyer of Florence (Italy), he was educated by the Dominicans before being apprenticed to his uncle's mercantile business when aged seventeen. Rejecting this in 1533, he migrated to Rome, became a tutor in the house of a Florentine nobleman there and studied for the priesthood, but abandoned this in turn and spent several years on his own as a layman among those of the city whom the corrupt and indifferent institutional clergy of the era were neglecting. In 1548 he gathered fourteen companions, the start of the 'Congregation of the Oratory', and was ordained in 1551. For thirty-three years he ran a popular mission centre (virtually the centre of local Roman church life) at the presbytery of S. Girolamo della Carità before moving to the Chiesa Nuova in 1583, which latter church he had rebuilt and where he had established his infant congregation of secular priests. He was cheerful and very friendly, was acquainted with most of the great saints of the counter-Reformation and was nicknamed the 'Second Apostle of Rome'. His congregation was already spreading through Italy by the time of his death at Rome, and he was canonized in 1622. A portrait from life by Guido Reni is the basis for all other representations, and his attribute is a lily.

Philip Phan Văn Minh (St) {1 –group}

3 July

1815–53. A Vietnamese born at Cai Mong, he became a priest of the Paris Society for Foreign Missions. He was beheaded at Vĩnh Long in the Mekong delta during the persecution ordered by Emperor Tự Đức. Cf. **Vietnam, Martyrs of**.

Philip Powell (Bl) {2}

30 June

d. 1646. From Gwent (Wales), he was educated at Abergavenny grammar school before joining the Benedictines of St Gregory's at Douai (the community later moved to Downside) in 1614, being ordained in 1621. In the following year he went on mission to England and worked chiefly in Devon (but also in Somerset and Cornwall) for twenty years. He was executed at Tyburn (London) and was beatified in 1929. Cf. **England, Martyrs of**.

Philip Rinaldi (Bl) {2}

5 December

1866–1931. Born at Lu Monferratone near Casale (Italy), as a boy he had St John Bosco as a spiritual director and so joined the Salesians. After his final vows in 1880 he was sent to Spain and became inspector of the Iberian houses, returning to become vicar-general under Bl Michael Rua at Turin in 1901. He became the superior of the Salesians in 1922, and took care to foster the charism as laid down by the founder. He died suddenly in Turin and was beatified in 1990.

Philip Ripoll Morata (Bl) {2}

7 February
Cf. **Anselm Polanco Fontecha and Philip Ripoll Morata**.

Philip Smaldone (St) {2}

4 June

1848–1923. Born in Naples (Italy), he early started his life's work of helping deaf-mutes and, as a priest in Lecce, founded the 'Salesian Sisters of the Sacred Heart' to this end. He became a cathedral canon there and a well-known spiritual director, being canonized in 2006.

Philip Suzanni (Bl) {2}

24 May

d. 1306. From Piacenza (Italy), he became an Augustinian friar there and was famous for his spirit of prayer and compunction. His cultus was approved for Piacenza in 1766.

Philip Zhang Zhihe (St) {1 –group}

9 July
Cf. **Gregory Grassi and Comps**.

Philippa Mareri (Bl) {2}

16 February
d. 1236. A noblewoman of the Abruzzi (Italy), she met St Francis of Assisi at her parents' home and was inspired to become a hermit on a mountain above Mareri. Eventually she founded a Franciscan nunnery at Rieti with the help of Bl Roger of Todi, and became its first superior.

Philippine Duchesne (St) {2}

18 November
1769–1852. From Grenoble (France), she became a Visitation nun there but the community were scattered in the French Revolution and she returned to her family home. After attracting disciples she took the advice of St Mary-Magdalen-Sophia Barat to join the new community to the 'Society of the Sacred Heart' and then emigrated to what was then French Louisiana in 1818. Arriving at New Orleans, she founded her first mission station at St Charles near St Louis in Missouri and went on to found six others. She died at St Charles and was canonized in 1988.

Philippopolis, Martyrs of (St) {2}

24 May
d. ?304. Numbering thirty-eight, they were beheaded at Philippopolis (now Plovdiv in Bulgaria).

(Philo and Agathopodes) (SS) {4 –deleted}

25 April
C2nd? Two deacons of Antioch (Syria), they allegedly accompanied their bishop St Ignatius on his journey to martyrdom at Rome in ?107, and returned to Antioch with such relics of him that they were able to recover. They are believed to have written his acta also. Their subsequent careers are unknown.

Philogonius (St) {2, 4}

20 December
d. 324. A lawyer at Antioch (Syria), he was a confessor in the persecution of Licinius and later (after the death of his wife) became bishop of the city. As such he was one of the first to denounce Arianism. St John Chrysostom preached an extant panegyric in his honour.

(Philologus and Patrobas) (SS) {4 –deleted}

4 November
C1st. They were Roman Christians saluted by St Paul in his letter to the Romans (16:14-18).

Philomena

In 1802 the bones of a young woman were discovered in a niche in the catacomb of St Priscilla on the Via Salaria at Rome in the course of an excavation for supposed relics of martyrs. The niche was closed by three tiles bearing the description 'LUMENA' 'PAX TECUM' 'FI'. Reading 'Filumena pax tecum' (Philomena, peace be with you), the conclusion was drawn that here was buried a martyr called St Philomena, and a shrine was set up at Mugnano near Nola (Italy). The cultus proved extremely popular, helped by a completely fictitious biography written by the parish priest, and spread throughout the world. Further archaeological investigation indicated, however, that the muddling of the tiles of the epitaph was a regular practice of the C4th whenever materials already engraved were being re-used, and this so as to indicate that they did not belonging to the interment concerned. The shrine was dismantled and the cultus forbidden by a decree of the Magisterium in 1961, although some private veneration continues.

(Philomena of San Severino) (St) {4 –deleted}

5 July
Her relics were found and enshrined in the C16th at San Severino near Ancona (Italy), but nothing is known about her. By default she has a cultus as a virgin martyr.

Philomenus of Ancyra (St) {2, 4}

29 November
C3rd. He was martyred at Ancyra (Asia Minor, now Ankara in Turkey) in the reign of Aurelian.

(Philoterius) (St) {4 –deleted}

19 May
Early C4th? He was listed as a nobleman of Nicomedia (Asia Minor), martyred there in the reign of Diocletian. His acta are unreliable.

Phocas the Gardener (St) {2, 4}

5 March
Early C4th. A smallholder near Sinope on the Black Sea coast of Asia Minor, he was martyred in the reign of Diocletian. His existence, martyrdom and the antiquity of his cultus (which remains popular in the East) are established facts.

(Phocas of Sinope) (St) {4 –deleted}

14 July
C2nd? He was allegedly a bishop of Sinope who was martyred in the reign of Trajan, and is not identified with Phocas the Gardener in the Byzantine Martyrology.

Phoebad of Agen (St) {2}

25 April
d. ?393. He was bishop of Agen (France), and was a strong opponent of Arianism.

Phoebe (St) {2, 4}

3 September
C1st. A married deaconess of Cenchreae near Corinth (Greece), she was the bearer of St Paul's letter to the Romans and was commended by him therein (Rom. 16:1-3).

(Photina and Comps) (SS) {4 –deleted}

20 March
? According to the old Roman Martyrology as revised by Baronius, she was the Samaritan woman in the fourth chapter of St John's gospel and was martyred with her sons Joseph and Victor, together with Sebastian, Anatolius, Photius, Photis (Photides), Parasceve and Cyriaca. Their legend is both obscure and unreliable, and Baronius may have inserted them because he believed that the head of St Photina was preserved at St Paul's basilica at Rome.

Piaton (Piato, Piat) (St) {2}

1 October
C3rd–4th. According to his C10th biography he was from Benevento (Italy), became a missionary priest in the districts around Tournai and Chartres (France) and was martyred at the former place in the reign of Maximian.

Pientius of Poitiers (St) {2}

13 March
C6th. He was a bishop of Poitiers (France), and helped Queen St Radegund with the foundation of several monasteries.

Pierius (St) {2, 4}

4 November
Early C4th. A priest of Alexandria (Egypt), he taught at the catechetical school there. His scholarship (he wrote several philosophical and theological treatises) and his voluntary poverty led him to be compared with Origen.

Piety-of-the-Cross Ortiz Real (Bl) {2 –add}

26 February

1842–1916. From a middle-class family near Valencia in Spain, she was aware of a religious vocation but poor health and family opposition prevented her from following this (anti-clericalism was fashionable at the time). In 1884 she and three companions began a new congregation which grew to two convents, but there was a quarrel and all but one of the sisters decamped. Then she founded another congregation, the 'Salesian Sisters of the Sacred Heart of Jesus', which grew rapidly under the patronage of St Francis de Sales. She was beatified in 2004.

(Pigmenius) (St) {4 –deleted}

24 March

d. 362. A priest at Rome, he was listed as thrown into the Tiber by a pagan mob in the reign of Julian.

Pimen cf. **Poemen**.

Pimenius (St) {2}

2 December

C3rd–4th. He was a priest who was martyred and buried in the catacomb of Pontian on the Via Portuense outside Rome.

Pinnock (St)

6 November

? He is the putative patron of St Pinnock near Liskeard in Cornwall (England), but it is probable that Pinnock is a corruption of Winoc.

Pinytus (St) {2, 4}

10 October

d. c.180. A bishop of Knossos in Crete, he was praised by the historian Eusebius.

Pionius (St) {2, 4}

1 February

d. c.250. A priest of Smyrna (Asia Minor) in the reign of Decius, he was seized while celebrating the anniversary of the martyrdom of St Polycarp. Then he was burnt at the stake after a long cross-examination and after having been severely tortured. There is an extant eyewitness account of his death, which document was known to Eusebius. His fifteen companions have been deleted from the Roman Martyrology.

Piran (St)

5 March

d. c.480. A hermit near Padstow in Cornwall (England), he has Perranporth named after him and is the patron of Cornish tin-miners. His flag, a vertical white cross on a black background, is now the national flag of Cornwall and is based on a fictitious legend wherein he discovered tin-smelting by finding the white metal in the ashes of his fire after he had used bits of ore to build a surround for it. He has been identified with St Kieran of Ossory, but this is unlikely.

Pirmin (St) {2, 4}

3 November

d. ?755. Apparently a Visigothic refugee from the Arab invasion of Spain, he founded several monasteries in southern Germany (notably Reichenau near Constance) and restored several others (notably Disentis). He was also a regionary bishop, but was never bishop of Metz nor of Meaux.

Pistis cf. **Faith**.

Pius I, Pope (St) {2, 3}

11 July

d. 155. He was listed as pope from ?142, and may have been a brother of that Hermas who was the author of 'The Shepherd'. If so, they were born into a family of slaves. His was a period of opposition to popular Gnosticism. He is first listed as a saint by the forger St Ado, and his cultus was suppressed in 1969.

Pius V, Pope (St) {1, 3}

30 April

1504–72. Anthony Ghislieri was born at Bosco in Piedmont (Italy), joined the Dominicans in 1518, was ordained in 1540, taught philosophy and theology for sixteen years and became bishop of Sutri and inquisitor for Lombardy in 1556. In 1557 he was made a cardinal, was transferred to the see of Mondovi in 1559 and was elected pope in 1565. Of an austere character, he was well suited to the necessary task of fighting the corruption endemic in many aspects of church life at that time, including the Roman curia. He insisted (where he could) on the implementation of the decrees of the council of Trent, organized the Holy League against the Ottoman Turks which resulted in the victory of Lepanto in 1570, promoted ecclesiastical learning, reformed the liturgy (the Tridentine missal and breviary were promulgated in his time) and excommunicated Queen Elizabeth of England. He was canonized in 1712.

Pius IX, Pope (Bl) {2}

7 February

1792–1878. John-Mary Mastai Ferretti was born into a noble family of Senigallia (Italy), and after studying at Rome was ordained in 1819. His qualities as a pastor and his life of prayer were early recognized, and he was made archbishop of Spoleto in 1827. Transferring to Mastai in 1832, he was made cardinal in 1840 and was elected Pope in 1846. At that time, the popes still ruled central Italy (the 'Papal States') and the policy since the Napoleonic Wars had been one of strict adherence to the status quo ante. This had entailed to incompetent and reactionary government by clerics, so Bl Pius was welcomed as a modernizer before the revolutions of 1848. He defined the dogma of the Immaculate Conception in 1854, convened the First Vatican Council in 1869 and lost his temporal power with the annexation of Rome by Italy in 1870. He did not accept this (the situation was only regularized in 1923). His pontificate was the longest in history.

Pius X, Pope (St) {1, 3}

21 August

1835–1914. Joseph Sarto was born in 1835 at Riese near Venice, then part of the Austrian empire. His father was a postman and the family was poor, but he was accepted at the diocesan junior seminary at Treviso in 1850. After his ordination he became parish priest of Salzano in 1867, bishop of Mantua in 1884 and cardinal-patriarch of Venice in 1893. To his own surprise he was elected pope in 1903, and as such he made his principle 'to restore all things in Christ'. He encouraged early and frequent communion, liturgical reform and the teaching of the Catechism and also reorganized the Curia and started the very necessary codification of canon law. He was most famous for the condemnation of Modernism, which was a heterogeneous collection of ideas alleged to make the deposit of faith subordinate to the conclusions of secular scholarship and fashionable thought. His will read: 'I was born poor, I lived poor, I wish to die poor'. He was canonized in 1954.

Pius Bartosik (Bl) {2}

12 December

1909–41. A Polish Franciscan Conventual friar, together with Bl Anthony Bajewski he had been a colleague of St Maximilian Kolbe before the Nazi invasion, and they supported each other in the camp. He died of ill-treatment. Cf. **Poland, Martyrs of the Nazi Occupation of**.

Pius-of-St-Aloysius Campidelli (Bl) {2}

2 November

1868–89. Born near Rimini (Italy), his peasant father died when he was a child and left the family in serious poverty, which frustrated his wish to enter the junior seminary. In 1882 he joined the Passionists at S. Maria de Casale and reached minor orders, but he died before he could be ordained as deacon. He was beatified in 1985.

Pius-Albert Del Corona (Bl) {2 –add}

15 August

1837–1912. From Livorno in Italy, he joined the Dominicans at Florence in 1859. As a Dominican priest in 1872 he helped to found the Dominican Sisters of the Holy Spirit to care for and teach young children in the city. In 1874 he was made coadjutor bishop of San Miniato, and succeeded to the bishopric in 1897. He died in retirement in Florence, and was due to be beatified in 2015.

Pius-of-Pietrelcina Forgione (Bl) {1}

23 September

1887–1968. From Pietrelcina near Benevento (Italy), he became a Franciscan at Morcone in 1903. In 1916, after his ordination, he went to San Giovanni Rotondo where he remained all his life. The Mass as the recapitulation of the sacrificial passion of Christ was central to his ministry as a priest, the effectiveness of which was shown by the number of people who sought his help. He was in receipt of extraordinary mystical phenomena, most famously the stigmata, and has been the subject of worldwide popular devotion as 'Padre Pio' since his death. He was canonized in 2002.

Placid and Sigisbert (SS) {2}

11 July

C7th. The latter was a disciple of St Columba and the abbot-founder of the abbey of Disentis in Graubünden (Switzerland). This had been built on land donated by the former, a wealthy landowner who then became a monk there and was martyred for being outspoken in defence of the abbey's privileges. Their cultus was approved for the Benedictines in 1905.

Placid Riccardi (Bl) {2}

25 March

1844–1915. Born near Spoleto (Italy), he joined the Benedictine abbey of St Paul's outside the Walls at Rome in 1864. He was thirteen years there, then ten years as chaplain to the Benedictine nuns at Amelia and finally the rest of his life he spent in charge of the shrine at Farfa. He had no special charism, but his prayer, penance and humility were such that he was beatified in 1955.

Placid of Rodi (Bl) {2}

12 June

d. 1248. From working-class family of Rodi on the Gargano promontory (Italy), he became a Cistercian monk at Corno, then a hermit at Ocre in the Abruzzi and finally the abbot-founder of the monastery of Santo Spirito nearby. It was alleged that he slept in a standing posture for thirty-seven years.

Placid of Subiaco (St) {2, 3}

5 October

C6th. The Roman Martyrology lists him as a young disciple of St Benedict, and by tradition he was at Subiaco. The Roman Martyrology has deleted his companion, Maurus.

He was confused with Placid, Eutychius, Victorinus, Flavia and companions, who were apparently martyred at Messina in Sicily in the reign of Diocletian. A refugee Greek priest at Montecassino in 1115 produced a maliciously forged document alleging that Placid was the disciple of St Benedict at Subiaco, that the others were his siblings, that they had been sent by St Benedict to Messina to found a monastery and that they had been killed by pirate raiders in c.540. In 1588 'relics' were conveniently found in a Roman cemetery at Messina. The unjustifiable cultus was suppressed in 1969.

Placida Viel (Bl) {2}

4 March
1815–77. Born on a farm in Normandy (France), through a family connection she got to know St Mary-Magdalen Postel, the first mother-general of the 'Sisters of the Christian Schools'. She joined them in 1833 and became assistant-general when aged twenty-six, which caused some resentment against her. Nevertheless on the death of St Mary-Magdalen in 1846 she succeeded her, and in 1859 obtained papal approval of the institute. Her work during the Franco-Prussian war was heroic and probably hastened her death at St Sauveur-le-Vicomte. She was beatified in 1951.

(Placidia of Verona) (St) {4 –deleted}

11 October
d. c.460. She is venerated as a virgin at Verona (Italy), and has been erroneously identified with Galla Placidia the daughter of the emperor Valentinian III.

Plato of Ancyra (St) {2, 4}

22 July
d. c.300. He was a rich young man martyred at Ancyra (Asia Minor, now Ankara in Turkey).

Plato of Constantinople (St) {2, 4}

4 April
d. 814. From a rich family of Constantinople, he became a monk and abbot at Symboleon on the Bithynian Olympus and then at Sakkudion near Constantinople. He was prominent in opposing iconoclasm, being present at the second ecumenical council of Nicaea in 787, and appointed St Theodore Studites his successor before retiring in 794. He was subsequently imprisoned and exiled both by the emperor Constantine VI Porphyrogenitus for opposing his divorce and remarriage and by the emperor Nicephorus I for opposing the reconciliation of the priest who officiated at his predecessor's second marriage. However he died in peace at Constantinople.

(Plato of Tournai) (St) {4 –deleted}

1 October
Early C4th? He was allegedly a Roman missionary, a companion of St Quentin who was martyred at Tournai (France) in the reign of Maximian.

(Platonides and Comps) (SS) {4 –deleted}

6 April
Early C4th? She apparently derives from a deaconess who founded a nunnery at Nisibis, now on the border of Turkey with Syria. The old Roman Martyrology listed her as a martyr of Ascalon in error and added two companions.

(Plautilla) (St) {4 –deleted}

20 May
The alleged widowed mother of St Flavia Domitilla was, according to legend, baptized by St Peter and present at the martyrdom of St Paul. She never existed.

Plechelm (St) {2}

15 July
d. ?713. Cf. **Wiro and Comps**.

Plutarch of Alexandria and Comps (SS) {2, 4}

28 June
d. ?202. They were pupils of Origen at the catechetical school of Alexandria (Egypt) and were martyred there in the reign of Septimius Severus. The companions were a young woman called Potamioena (who was lowered slowly into a cauldron of boiling pitch), her mother Marcella, two named Serenus, Heraclides, Heron and Herais.

(Podius) *(St)* *{4 –deleted}*

28 May
d. 1002. A son of the margrave of Tuscany, he became a canon regular and then bishop of Florence (Italy) in 990.

Podlasia (Martyrs of) (BB) {2}

23 January
d. 1874. In the C19th the Imperial Russian government's policy was to forcibly convert all Byzantine-rite Catholics under its rule to Russian Orthodoxy, so the hierarchy of the remaining Polish ecclesiastical province of Chelm was deported to Siberia in 1874 and the churches were seized. In Pratulin in Podlasia (now eastern Poland) the congregation blockaded their church when an army detachment came to seize it, so they were fired upon and thirteen of them killed. They were ordinary laymen aged between nineteen and fifty, mostly married with families: Vincent Lewoniuk, Daniel Karmasz, Luke Bojko, Constantius Bojko, Bartholomew Osypiuk, Michael-Nicephorus Hryeiuk, Philip Geryluk, Ignatius Franczuk, John Andrzejuk, Maxim Hawryluk and Onuphrius Wasyluk; Consantius Lubaszuk and Michael Wawrzyszuk died the next day. They were beatified in 1996.

Poemen (Pimen, Pastor) (St) {2}

27 August
C4–5th. His name means 'Shepherd'. Together with two of his brothers he was a monk at Scetis (Egypt), but they were driven out by barbarians in 407 and settled for a while at the abandoned pagan temple at Tereneuthis, the nearest point on the Nile. A substantial section of the *Apophthegmata Patrum* is in his name, and his disciples may have initiated that collection of sayings.

Pol de Leon cf. **Paul Aurelian**.

Poland, Martyrs of the Nazi Occupation of (BB) {2}
1939–45. Of the people killed in hatred of the faith in Nazi-occupied Poland during the Second World War, one hundred and eight were beatified in 1999. They comprise three bishops, fifty-two diocesan priests, twenty-nine male religious, eight female religious, three seminarians and nine laypeople. They are listed in the Roman Martyrology under their various dates of martyrdom. See list in appendix.

Pollio (St) {2, 4}

7 April
d. ?303. A reader in the church at Cybalae (now Vinkovci in Croatia), he was burnt alive in the reign of Diocletian.

(Polycarp and Theodore) *(SS)* *{4 –deleted}*

7 December
? They were listed as martyred at Antioch (Syria).

(Polycarp of Rome) *(St)* *{4 –deleted}*

23 February
Early C4th? He is mentioned in the acta of SS Mark and Marcellian and of St Sebastian as a Roman priest who ministered to those

imprisoned for their faith. His existence is dubious.

Polycarp of Smyrna (SS) {1, 3}

23 February
d. ?155. According to St Ireneaus (who knew him) he had been a disciple of St John the Evangelist and became bishop of Smyrna (now Izmir in Turkey) in about the year 96. He opposed Gnosticism, had a letter written to him by St Ignatius of Antioch and wrote an extant letter to the church at Philippi which was read liturgically for three centuries. He was burnt alive in the amphitheatre at the instigation of the pagans in the reign of Marcus Aurelius. The authentic contemporary account of this is the earliest surviving acta of any martyr. The Roman Martyrology has deleted a reference to twelve companion martyrs from Philadelphia.

(Polychronius) (St) {4 –deleted}

17 February
C3rd? According to the old Roman Martyrology, he was bishop of Babylon in the Persian Empire and was martyred on the orders of the emperor Decius. The difficulty with this is that Decius never invaded Persia. He may be a duplicate of St Polychronius of Nicaea.

(Polychronius of Nicaea) (St) {4 –deleted}

6 December
C4th. He was present at the council of Nicaea in Asia Minor in 325 as a reader, became a priest and was killed by Arians in the reign of the emperor Constantius while he was celebrating Mass.

Polydore Plasden (Oliver Palmer) (St) {2}

10 December
1563–91. A Londoner, he was educated for the priesthood at Rheims and in Rome and was ordained at Rome in 1588. He worked in London and Sussex before being captured with St Edmund Genings at the house of St Swithun Wells, and was executed at Tyburn with St Eustace White and Comps. He was canonized in 1970. Cf. **England, Martyrs of.**

Polyeuctus of Caesarea (St) {2, 4}

21 May
? He was martyred at Caesarea in Cappadocia (Asia Minor). The Roman Martyrology has deleted two companions, Victorius and Donatus

Polyeuctus of Melitene (St) {2, 4}

7 January
d. c.250. A Roman officer, he was martyred at Melitene in Armenia in the reign of Valerian, allegedly after having destroyed some pagan idols.

Pompey of Pavia (St) {2, 4}

14 December
C4th. He was a bishop of Pavia (Italy).

Pompilius-Mary-of-St-Nicholas Pirotti (St) {2}

15 July
1710–66. From Montecalvo near Benevento (Italy), he joined the Piarist Fathers at Naples in 1727 and taught in schools run by them in Apulia, Naples and Ancona. He died near Lecce in Apulia and was canonized in 1934.

Pomponius (St) {2, 4}

30 April
C6th. Bishop of Naples from 508, he strongly opposed the court Arianism of Theodoric, the Ostrogothic king of Italy (which was more than the papacy did).

Pomposa (St) {2, 4}

19 September
d. 853. A nun of Peñamelaria near Cordoba
(Spain), she was involved in the 'martyr
movement' and was beheaded by the Muslims
at Cordoba.

Pons cf. **Pontius**.

Pontian, Pope (St) {1, 3}

13 August
d. 235. He succeeded St Urban I as pope in
230 but was exiled by the emperor Maximinus
Thrax as a slave to the mines of Sardinia about
five years later, where the working conditions
are thought to have killed him. He shares a
feast day with St Hippolytus, his fellow exile.

Pontian Ngondwe (St) {1 –group}

26 May
d. 1886. He was one of the royal guard of
King Mwanga of Buganda (Uganda) by whose
orders he was executed. Cf. **Charles Lwanga
and Comps**.

*(Pontian of Rome and Comps) (SS) {4
–deleted}*

2 December
C3rd? They were listed as five Romans martyred in the reign of Valerian.

Pontian of Spoleto (St) {2, 4}

19 January
C2nd. He was martyred at Spoleto (Italy) in
the reign of Marcus Aurelius. His acta are
authentic in outline, although embellished.

Pontius of Carthage (St) {2, 4}

8 March
C3rd. A deacon under St Cyprian at Carthage
(Roman Africa), he was his attendant in exile

and at his trial and execution and wrote a
graphic account of his life and martyrdom.

Pontius of Cimiez (St) {2, 4}

14 May
C3rd? Apparently he was martyred at Cimiez
near Nice (France) and had his relics transferred to St Pons (named after him) near
Béziers. His acta are unreliable.

Pontius of Faucigny (Bl) {2}

26 November
d. 1178. A Savoyard nobleman, at the age of
twenty he became an Augustinian canon regular at Abondance in the Chablais (France) and
was abbot there after being abbot-founder of
St Sixtus. He was held in great veneration by
St Francis of Sales and his cultus was confirmed for Annecy in 1896.

Pontus, Martyrs of (SS) {2}

5 February
End C3rd. The early church author Rufinus described how many martyrs of Pontus
on the Black Sea coast of Asia Minor were
subjected to atrocious tortures in the persecution ordered by the emperor Maximian.
These included sprinkling with molten lead
and having sharp reeds driven under the
fingernails.

Poppo (St) {2, 4}

25 January
978–1048. He was initially a soldier without much thought for religion but converted,
made a penitential pilgrimage to Jerusalem
and Rome and then joined the Benedictine
abbey of St Theodoric at Rheims in 1006.
Two years later he migrated to St Vitonius's
Abbey at Verdun and helped Bl Richard of
Verdun in the revival of monastic discipline
there. Then he was provost of St Vedast

at Arras, became an adviser of Emperor St Henry II and was appointed by him abbot of Stavelot-Malmédy (Belgium) with responsibility for sixteen other abbeys of the Empire. Into some of these he introduced the Cluniac reform.

Porcarius and Comps (SS) {2, 4}

12 August
C8th. Abbot of Lérins, on its island off the coast of Provence (France), he was massacred with his entire community by Muslim pirates who also burnt the abbey and remained in occupation for the next two centuries. The total number of dead, including lay employees, was reckoned as five hundred and only some boys and young monks previously sent to the mainland for safety escaped.

(Porphyry) (St) {4 –deleted}

15 September
d. 362. According to his legend he was a horse-dealer and an actor who, while taking part in a parody of Christian baptism in the presence of the emperor Julian, suddenly declared himself a believer and was at once killed. The story is repeated of several alleged martyrs and seems to be a fiction.

(Porphyry of Camerino) (St) {4 –deleted}

4 May
C3rd? He never existed, as his name was transferred from the unreliable acta of St Agapitus of Palestrina to the equally fictitious acta of St Venantius. He was alleged to have been a priest martyred at Camerino in Umbria (Italy) in the reign of Decius.

(Porphyry of Ephesus) (St) {4 –deleted}

4 November
C3rd? He was listed as martyred at Ephesus (Asia Minor) in the reign of Aurelian.

Porphyry of Gaza (St) {2, 4}

26 February
d. 420. From Thessalonika (Greece), he was wealthy but gave everything away and was a monk in Scetis (Egypt) and by the Jordan in the Holy Land before becoming cross-warden in Jerusalem. In 395 he was made bishop of Gaza, a stronghold of prosperous and aggressive paganism where Christianity had made little impact. His zeal and ability resulted in a flow of conversions, however. This caused persecution and attempts to kill him, so he appealed to the emperor Arcadius and the temples were eventually destroyed by imperial troops. His extant biography was written by his deacon, Mark.

(Porphyry of Palestrina) (St) {4 –deleted}

20 August
? He features in the unreliable acta of St Agapitus of Palestrina (Italy).

Portianus (St) {2, 4}

24 November
d. p532. He was a slave before becoming a monk and then abbot of Miranda in Auvergne (France) and was remembered for his courage in obtaining the release of his compatriots taken prisoner by the Merovingian king.

Possidius (St) {2, 4}

16 May
d. p437. A friend and disciple of St Augustine of Hippo (whose biography he wrote), he became bishop of Calama in Numidia (Roman Africa, now Algeria) but was exiled by the Vandal invasion and died in Apulia (Italy). He was one of the most talented polemicists of his time against Donatism and Pelagianism.

(Potamius and Nemesius) *(SS)* *{4 –deleted}*

20 February

? Nothing is known about them. The old Roman Martyrology listed them as martyred in Cyprus, but Eusebius associated them with Alexandria (Egypt).

Potamon, Ortasius, Serapion and Comps (SS) {2, 4}

18 May

Early C4th. They were three priests and some laymen who were martyred together at Alexandria (Egypt).

(Potamon of Heraclea) *(St)* *{4 –deleted}*

18 May

d. c.340. Bishop of Heraclea in Upper Egypt, during the persecution of Maximinus Daza he was lamed in one leg, deprived of one eye and sent as a slave to the mines. Released after Constantine's edict of toleration, he was at the council of Nicaea and was a strong supporter of St Athanasius. As a result he was fiercely persecuted by the Arians, who eventually arranged his murder.

Potentiana cf. **Pudentiana**.

Potentinus, Simplicius and Felicius *(BB)*

18 June

C4th. Their relics were brought to Steinfeld monastery (Germany) in 920, and their cultus was confirmed for Cologne in 1908. Their legend states that they were Gascon pilgrims going to the Holy Land who settled instead with St Castor on the Moselle. They are not in the Roman Martyrology.

Pothmius cf. **Potamius**.

Pothinus and Comps (SS) {2, 4}

2 June

d. 177. They were martyred at Lyons (France), and the graphic details are preserved in an authentic letter (possibly written by St Irenaeus) sent by the churches of Vienne and Lyons to those of Asia. They were firstly attacked by a pagan lynch-mob in the reign of Marcus Aurelius, but were rescued and put on trial. Pothinus was the bishop, aged ninety, and he died in prison from the beating he had received. Blandina was killed by the sword after torture, and the other forty-two were thrown to the wild animals in the amphitheatre at the next public games. Their names were: Zacharias the priest, Vetius Epagatus, Macarius, Asclibiades, Silvius, Primus, Ulpius, Vitalis, Comminus, October, Philomenus, Geminus, Julia, Albina, Grata, Aemilia, Potamia, Pompeia, Rodana, Biblis, Quartia, Materna, Helpis, Sanctus the deacon, Maturus the neophyte, Attalus of Pergamum, Alexander the Phrygian, Ponticus, Justus, Aristeus, Cornelius, Zosimus, Titus, Julius, Zoticus, Apollonius, Geminianus, another Julia, Ausonia, another Aemilia, Jamnica, another Pompeia, Domna, Justa, Trophima and Antonia.

Potitus (St) {2, 4}

13 January

? He is venerated as a boy-martyr at Naples (Italy), but his acta are legendary. The Roman Martyrology lists him as a martyr of Sardica in Dacia.

Praejectus (Prix) and Amerinus (SS) {2, 4}

25 January

d. 676. From Auvergne (France), Praejectus was an abbot before becoming bishop of Clermont-Ferrand in 666. A great administrator and patron of monasticism, he had cause to complain in person about a nobleman of Marseilles to the king and was assassinated as a result on his return at Volvic near Clermont, together with a hermit Amarinus. They are not listed as martyrs.

(Praetextatus of Rouen) (St) *{4 –deleted}*

24 February
d. 586. He was bishop of Rouen (France) from 550, but became involved in politics, was accused of treason and was exiled in 577. He was restored in 584, against the wishes of Queen Fredegonda whose crimes he publicly denounced. As a result she had him assassinated in his cathedral on Easter Sunday.

Pragmatius (St) {2, 4}

22 November
d. ?517. He was a bishop of Autun (France).

Prague (Martyrs of) *(BB)*

11 August
d. 1420. Four Servite friars from the nobility of Siena (Italy), Augustine Cennini, Bartholomew Sonati, John Baptist Petrucci and Laurence Nerucci, they were sent by the pope to Bohemia to help combat the Hussite heresy. With sixty other Servites they were burnt in their church at Prague while singing the *Te Deum*. Their cultus was approved for Prague (Czech Republic) in 1918, but they are not listed in the Roman Martyrology.

Praxedes (St) {2, 4}

21 July
d. a.491. A church in Rome is dedicated to her, and probably stands on the site of her house. According to her unreliable legend she was a consecrated virgin, daughter of the Roman senator St Pudens and sister of St Pudentiana. Her cultus was confined to her church in 1969.

(Primitiva) *(St)* *{4 –deleted}*

24 February
? She was an early martyr, probably of Rome. Some old martyrologies list her as 'Primitivus', which would make her a he.

(Primitiva) *(St)* *{4 –deleted}*

23 July
? She was an early martyr, probably of Rome and very probably identical with the above. She is also listed as 'Primitia' and 'Privata'.

Primitivus (St) {2}

26 April
? He was martyred on the Via Prenestina near Rome by being thrown into a lake at a place called Gabii.

(Primus, Cyril and Secundarius) *(SS)* *{4 –deleted}*

2 October
? They are listed as having been martyred at Antioch (Syria) during an early persecution.

Primus and Donatus (SS) {2, 4}

9 February
d. ?361. They were two deacons in Roman Africa, killed in an attempt by the local Donatist schismatics to take over the Catholic Church at Lavallum during the reign of Julian.

Primus and Felician (SS) {2, 3}

9 June
? Two old brothers of Rome, they were beheaded on the Via Nomentana and had a basilica built over their tomb. Their acta are not entirely reliable, but seem to be based on original sources. Their cultus was confined to local calendars in 1969.

Principius (St) {2, 4}

25 September
C6th. The elder brother of St Remigius of Rheims, he became bishop of Soissons (France).

Prisca (St) {2, 3}

18 January
d. a.449. Formerly listed as a Roman virgin martyr, her cultus is ancient and she has a church dedicated to her on the Aventine, but nothing is known about her. In 1969 her cultus was confined to her church.

(Priscilla) (St) {4 –deleted}

16 January
C1st. According to the legend, she was the widowed mother of St Pudens and was the hostess in Rome of St Peter, whose headquarters were at her villa near the Roman catacombs which are named after her.

Priscus and Comps (SS) {2, 4}

26 May
? They were martyred near Auxerre (France) after fleeing persecution.

(Priscus, Crescens and Evagrius) (SS) {4 –deleted}

1 October
? They were listed as martyred at Tomi, on the Black Sea coast of Romania.

Priscus, Malchus and Alexander (SS) {2, 4}

28 March
d. 260. They were thrown to the wild animals during some public games at Caesarea in the Holy Land in the reign of Valerian.

(Priscus, Priscillian and Benedicta) (SS) {4 –deleted}

4 January
C4th? Their existence depends upon the untrustworthy acta of St Bibiana, which state that they were Christians buried by her father. The forger St Ado was responsible for listing them as martyrs.

Priscus I of Capua (St) {2, 4}

1 September
C4th? He is venerated as the first bishop of Capua (Italy). According to the fictitious legend, he was a native of Jerusalem and a disciple of Christ who was sent to Capua by St Peter and who was martyred in the reign of Nero.

(Priscus II of Capua and Comps) (SS) {4 –deleted}

1 September
C5th? The legend is that Priscus, a Roman African bishop, and his priests were set adrift in a rudderless boat by the Arian Vandals invaders. They reached Italy, where eventually Priscus became bishop of Capua and several of the others also became bishops. The acta are untrustworthy, however, and it seems that the companions of St Priscus (Castrensis, Tammarus, Rosius, Heraclius, Secundinus, Adjutor, Mark, Augustus, Elpidius, Canion and Vindonius) are Campanian saints unconnected with the story. It may be that the listing 'Priscus Castrensis' means 'Priscus, formerly Bishop of Castra in Africa'.

Priscus of Nocera (St) {2}

16 September
Early C4th? He was a martyred bishop of Nocera in Campania (Italy) who was extolled in verse by St Paulinus of Nola.

Privatus of Gevaudan (St) {2, 4}

21 August
d. 260. A bishop of the region of Gevaudan in the southern Massif Central (France), he was beaten to death by invading Vandal barbarians for refusing to tell them the place where some of his people were hiding.

(Privatus of Rome) (St) *{4 –deleted}*

28 September
d. 223. A Roman, he was listed as whipped to death in the reign of Alexander Severus.

Prix cf. **Praejectus** or **Praetextatus**.

Probus of Ravenna (St) {2, 4}

10 November
C3rd–4th. A Roman, he was allegedly the sixth bishop of Ravenna (Italy) and his shrine is in the cathedral there. The tradition that he was of the second century is anachronistic.

Probus of Rieti (St) {2, 4}

January 15
d. c.570. He was bishop of Rieti (Italy) and his deathbed visions feature in the 'Dialogues' attributed to St Gregory the Great.

(Probus of Verona) (St) *{4 –deleted}*

12 January
d. p591. Nothing is known about this bishop of Verona (Italy).

Processus and Martinian (SS) {2, 3}

2 July
? Martyrs of Rome, they have an ancient cultus (confined to local calendars in 1969). Apparently originally buried on the Aurelian Way, they had their relics transferred to St Peter's in the C9th. Nothing is known about them, and the story associating them with SS Peter and Paul in the Mamertine prison is legendary.

Prochorus and Comps (St) {2, 4}

9 April
C1st. They were five of the seven deacons ordained by the apostles, the names of the others being Nicanor, Timon, Parmenas and Nicolaus of Antioch. Philip and Stephen the Protomartyr, the remaining two, are venerated on other dates.

Proclus and Hilarion (SS) {2, 4}

12 July
C2nd. They were martyred at Ancyra (Asia Minor, now Ankara in Turkey) in the reign of Trajan.

Proclus of Bisignano (St) {2}

19 February
d. c.970. He was a monk of Bisignano in Calabria (Italy) who was famous for his spiritual and monastic doctrine.

Proclus of Constantinople (St) {2, 4}

24 October
d. 446. A priest of Constantinople and a disciple of St John Chrysostom, he became patriarch in 434. He was a zealous supporter of St Cyril in the campaign against Nestorianism, but tempered zeal with gentleness. According to tradition he introduced the *Trisagion* into the liturgy. Some of his homilies and letters are extant, notably his famous homily on the Mother of God.

Procopius the Great (St) {2, 4}

8 July
d. ?303. According to Eusebius he was from Jerusalem, was a reader in the church of Scythopolis and was beheaded at Caesarea in the Holy Land. He was the first local martyr of the persecution of Diocletian. His cultus is extremely popular in the East, and his story has attracted much later legend.

Procopius of Sázava (St) {2}

25 March
c.980–1053. Born in Bohemia, he was educated at a Basilian monastery at Prague (Czech

Republic), married and was then ordained in the Byzantine rite and became a cathedral canon. Later he became a hermit and finally abbot-founder of the Basilian abbey of Sázava near Prague. He was canonized in 1804.

Proculus, Eutyches and Acutius (St) {2, 3 –group}

18 October

Early C4th. They were martyred at Pozzuoli (Italy). Proculus was a deacon. Formerly they were included in the worthless legend of St Januarius of Benevento, and liturgically celebrated with him.

(Proculus, Ephebus and Apollonius) (SS) {4 –deleted}

14 February

C3rd? They are mentioned in the untrustworthy Acts of St Valentine of Terni (Italy) as having been martyred there, but Proclus seems to be a duplicate of the alleged bishop of Terni and the other two belong elsewhere.

(Proculus of Autun) (St) {4 –deleted}

4 November

C8th? This bishop of Autun (France) was alleged to have been killed in the invasion of the Huns in the C5th, but seems to be of later date.

Proculus of Bologna (St) {2, 4}

1 June

d. c.300. According to his unreliable acta he was a Roman officer martyred at Bologna (Italy) in the reign of Diocletian. His cultus is ancient.

(Proculus of Narni) (St) {4 –deleted}

1 December

C6th? He was allegedly either a bishop of Narni or of Terni in Umbria (Italy) who was killed by order of Totila, leader of the Ostrogoths.

(Proculus of Teramo) (St) {4 –deleted}

14 April

? He was allegedly a martyr-bishop in the reign of Maxentius, but his details are seriously confused. There are suspicious similarities with the Proculus of 'Proculus, Ephebus and Apollonius', also with Proculus of Bologna 2) and Proculus of Narni.

(Proculus of Verona) (St) {4 –deleted}

9 December

d. c.320. A bishop of Verona (Italy), he was a confessor during the persecution of Diocletian but died in peace.

Projectus cf. **Praejectus**.

Prosdocimus (St) {2, 4}

7 November

C3rd. He is listed as the first bishop of Padua (Italy), but the story that he was sent there from Antioch by St Peter is unhistorical.

Prosper of Aquitaine (St) {2, 4}

7 July

d. 463. From Aquitaine (France), he was a layman, probably married and apparently lived in Provence. He was a capable theologian, a prolific writer and an enthusiastic disciple of St Augustine, becoming heavily involved in controversy with the local opponents of the latter's teaching on grace (the so-called semi-Pelagians).

Prosper of Orléans (St) {2, 4}

29 July

C5th. A bishop of Orleans (France), he has been confused with the Prospers of Aquitaine and Reggio.

Prosper of Reggio (St) {2}

25 June
C5–6th. He was a bishop of Reggio in Emilia (Italy) and is that city's principal patron, but little is known about him.

Prosper of Tarragona (St) {2}

2 September
C4th or C5th. He is the third known bishop of Tarragona (Spain), and has a cultus in Genoa (Italy) which was confirmed in 1854.

(Protase of Cologne) (St) {4 –deleted}

4 August
? He has a cultus as a martyr at Cologne (Germany), but is probably identical with the companion of St Gervase.

Protase Chong Kuk-bo (St) {1 –group}

20 May
d. 1839. From Seoul in Korea, he apostatized during the persecution ordered by the government, but repented and publicly proclaimed his faith. As a result he was tortured to death in prison. Cf. **Korea, Martyrs of**.

Protase of Lausanne (St) {2}

6 November
C7th. He is venerated at Saint-Prex on the shore of the Lake of Geneva (Switzerland), and is thought to have been a bishop of Lausanne.

Protase of Milan (St) {2, 4}

24 November
d. ?356. He was bishop of Milan (Italy) from 331, and was one of the defenders of St Athanasius against the Arians.

Proterius (St) {2}

28 February
d. 454. After Dioscorus, patriarch of Alexandria, was deposed and disgraced at the council of Chalcedon in 451 for Monophysite leanings, Proterius was selected to succeed him from the few clergy in the city who accepted the council's decisions. The vast majority of the people were, however, violent in rejection and he had to rely on imperial troops for protection. After the death of the emperor Maurice he was killed by a lynch-mob on Good Friday, his body was dismembered and burnt and his place taken by the Monophysite called Timothy the Cat.

Prothadius (Protagius) (St) {2}

10 February
d. ?624. The son of a Frankish courtier, he succeeded St Nicetius as bishop of Bresançon (France) in 613 and was influential at the Merovingian court.

(Protogenes) (St) {4 –deleted}

6 May
C4th. A priest of Carrhae in Syria (the Harran where Abraham stayed, now Altinbasak near Urfa in Turkey), he was exiled by the Arian emperor Valens but recalled by Theodosius I and ordained bishop. His city remained a stronghold of paganism until after the Muslim conquest.

Protomartyrs of Rome (SS) {1, 3}

30 June
d. 64. When a large part of the city of Rome was burnt in June 64, the emperor Nero accused the local Christians of starting the fire and ordered a pogrom. Some of them were sewn up in animal skins and had dogs set upon them, while others were covered in pitch, tied to poles and used as living torches in the public gardens after sunset. It is not certain whether Nero started the fire himself to clear the ground for his palace, the 'Domus Aurea', and there is no evidence that the persecution spread outside the city.

Protomartyrs of the West (SS)

22 July

C1st? They are venerated at Nepi in Tuscany (Italy) as a group of thirty-eight who were thrown over a precipice there before the persecution by Nero in Rome, but their existence is unhistorical and seems to depend on ecclesiastical one-upmanship.

Protus and Hyacinth (SS) {2, 3}

11 September

C3rd. According to their fictitious acta they were Roman brothers who were servants in the house of St Philip of Rome and who were martyred in the reign of Valerian. The genuine relics of St Hyacinth were, however, apparently discovered in the cemetery of St Basilla at Rome in 1845. There is apparently one church in Britain dedicated to them, at Blisland in Cornwall. Their cultus was confined to local calendars in 1969.

(Protus and Januarius) (SS) {4 –deleted}

25 October

d. 303. They were listed as Roman missionaries, a priest and a deacon, in Sardinia and were beheaded at Porto Torres in the north of the island in the reign of Diocletian.

Protus of Aquileia (St) {2}

14 June

? He was martyred at Aquileia (Italy).

Provinus of Como (St) {2}

8 March

d. c.420. From Gaul, he became a disciple of St Ambrose at Milan and then coadjutor to St Felix, bishop of Como. He became bishop himself in 391.

Prudentius Galindo (St) {2}

6 April

d. 861. A Spanish nobleman, he was a refugee from the Arabs at the court of France, became bishop of Troyes in 846 and played a prominent part in a controversy concerning predestination. He wrote works against Gottschalk and John Scotus Erigena, but his defence of double predestination (to damnation as well as salvation) was suspect. He had a cultus, not approved, at Troyes.

Prudentius of Tarazona (St) {2}

28 April

C5–6th. From the Basque province of Alava (Spain), he was a hermit for several years before becoming a priest of Tarazona (not Tarragona) in Aragon and then bishop there. He is patron of the diocese.

Psalmodius (Psalmet, Sauman) (St) {2}

14 June

C7th. A 'Scot' (Irish or Scottish), he was a disciple of St Brendan of Clonfert who emigrated to France and lived as a hermit near Limoges.

Ptolemy, Lucius and Companion (SS) {2, 4}

19 October

d. c.160. Ptolemy was a Roman sentenced to death for catechizing a woman in the reign of Antoninus Pius. Lucius and an unnamed man protested against the injustice of the sentence and were also martyred. St Justin Martyr, their contemporary, wrote an extant account of the event.

(Ptolemy of Nepi) (St) {4 –deleted}

24 August

C1st? He was allegedly a disciple of St Peter and a martyr-bishop of Nepi in Tuscany (Italy).

Publia (St) {2, 4}

9 October

C4th. According to the story she was a widow of Antioch (Syria) who founded a community of consecrated virgins in her house.

The emperor Julian happened to pass by on his way to the Persian front while they were singing Psalm 115:4: 'Their idols are silver and gold, the work of human hands'. This he took as a personal insult, his bodyguard beat up the singers and he promised their deaths when he returned. He was killed in battle.

(Publius, Julian and Comps) (SS) {4 –deleted}

19 February
? They are listed merely as Roman African martyrs. The companions were: Marcellus, Manubius, another Julian, Baraceus, Tullius, Lampasius, Majolus, Julius, Paul and Maximilla.

(Publius, Victor, Hermes and Papias) (SS) {4 –deleted}

2 November
? They were listed as Roman African martyrs.

Publius of Athens (St) {2, 4}

21 January
C2nd. He was an early bishop of Athens (Greece) who was martyred. By tradition, not accepted by the Roman Martyrology, he was also the Publius who was 'chief man of the island' of Malta and who befriended the castaways including St Paul (Acts 28:7). Other sources merely listed him as the first bishop of Malta. Three separate people seem to have been conflated here.

(Pudens) (St) {4 –deleted}

19 May
C3rd. It is thought that he was a wealthy Roman Christian who founded a church in his house known as the *titulus Pudentiana*. From this title was erroneously inferred the existence of a St Pudentiana, and spurious acta were written for her. Pudens was then identified as her father, a C1st senator baptized by the apostles, and also falsely identified with the Pudens mentioned by St Paul in 2 Timothy 4:21.

(Pudentiana) (St) {4 –deleted}

19 May
? She is a mythical Roman virgin, daughter of St Pudens (q.v.). Her name does not occur in any ancient martyrology, and her cultus was suppressed as unhistorical in 1969 (except for her church in Rome).

Pulcheria, Empress (St) {2, 4}

10 September
399–453. Daughter of the Eastern emperor Arcadius, she was regent during the minority of her brother Theodosius II and influenced the condemnation of Nestorianism in 431. However a Monophysite clique centred on the dowager empress Eudocia caused her withdrawal from court life until after the emperor's death in a hunting accident. Then she married the elderly senator Marcian, who thus became emperor, but apparently refused to consummate the marriage because of a private vow of virginity. Together they arranged the holding of the council of Chalcedon to condemn Monophysitism in 451.

Pusicius (St) {2, 4}

18 April
d. 341. He was the overseer of works at the palace of the Persian Shah Shapur II at Ctesiphon, the capital. The day after the massacre of St Simon Barsabae and his companions on Good Friday, he was seized and had his throat cut.

Pyran cf. **Piran**.

Q

(Quadragesimus) (St) {4 –deleted}

26 October
d. c.590. He features in the 'Dialogues' attributed to St Gregory the Great as a shepherd and subdeacon who resurrected a dead man at Policastro south of Naples (Italy).

(Quadratus) (St) {4 –deleted}

26 May
? St Augustine preached an extant panegyric in honour of this Roman African martyr at a church dedicated to him at what is now Bizerte (Tunisia), but without giving any historical details.

Quadratus the Apologist (St) {2, 4}

21 September
C2nd. He is the first known to have written a defence ('apology') of Christianity, which he addressed to the emperor Hadrian in ?124. He used to be confused with an early bishop of Athens.

(Quadratus of Hermopolis) (St) {4 –deleted}

7 May
d. 257. He was allegedly imprisoned for years at Nicomedia and Nicaea (Asia Minor) and Apamea (Syria) before being martyred at Hermopolis (Egypt) in the reign of Valerian. Possibly several martyrs have been conflated.

Quadratus of Utica (St) {2, 4}

21 August
C3rd–4th. Bishop of Utica in Roman Africa, he was highly praised by St Augustine: 'He taught his whole people, clergy and laity, to confess Christ'. His cultus was widespread in Africa.

(Quartus) (St) {4 –deleted}

3 November
C1st. He was a Corinthian whom St Paul mentioned in his letter to the Romans (Rom. 16:23) as 'greeting the Christians of Rome'. One tradition described him as one of the seventy-two disciples and others, which contradict, that he was a bishop.

Quartus and Quintus (SS) {2, 4}

10 May
C4th? Two Roman citizens of Capua (Italy), they were arrested and (because of their status) condemned and executed in Rome. Their relics were enshrined at Capua.

Quentin (St) {2, 4}

31 October
C3rd. He was of senatorial rank, and was martyred at the town on the Somme (France) now called St Quentin. According to his unreliable acta (which contain fanciful legendary material) he was a Roman who went as a missionary to the district round Amiens. He is variously and erroneously depicted either as a bishop or as a Roman soldier, and his attribute is a roasting-spit or two.

Quentin of Tours (St) {2}

4 October
C6th. From Tours (France), he was a Frankish courtier who fended off an attempted seduction by a powerful woman (apparently the queen). Spurned, she had him assassinated on the Indrois River near Montrésor.

Queranus cf. **Kieran**.

Quinidius (St) {2, 4}

15 February
d. ?578. He was a hermit at Aix-en-Provence (France) before becoming bishop of Vaison near Orange.

Quinta cf. **Cointha**.

(Quintian) *(St)* *{4 –deleted}*

14 June
? He was listed in the old Roman Martyrology as a bishop of Rodez (France), but this is mistaken.

(Quintian and Irenaeus) *(SS)* *{4 –deleted}*

1 April
? Nothing is known about these alleged martyrs of Roman Armenia.

(Quintian, Lucius, Julian and Comps) *(SS)* *{4 –deleted}*

23 May
d. c.430. They were allegedly nineteen Roman Africans (including several women) martyred in the reign of the Arian Vandal King Hunneric.

Quintian of Clermont (St) {2, 4}

13 November
d. ?525. A Roman African refugee from the Arian Vandals, he became bishop of Rodez (France) but was again exiled, this time by the Arian Visigoths. Then St Euphrasius made him his successor as bishop of Clermont-Ferrand.

(Quintilis and Capitolinus) *(St)* *{4 –deleted}*

8 March
? He was originally listed with one Capitolinus as martyrs of Nicomedia (Asia Minor). Capitolinus was then not listed by the old Roman Martyrology, which listed Quintilis as a bishop.

(Quintus, Quintilla and Comps) (St) *{4 –deleted}*

19 March
? They are martyrs venerated at Sorrento near Naples (Italy). The companions were listed as Quartilla, Mark and nine others.

(Quintus, Simplicius and Comps) *(SS)* *{4 –deleted}*

18 December
C3rd? They were listed as martyred in various places in Roman Africa in the reigns of Decius and Valerian.

Quintus of Capua (SS) {2, 4}

5 September
? He was martyred at Capua (Italy). The Roman Martyrology has deleted two companions, Arcontius and Donatus.

Quiriacus cf. **Cyriac**.

Quiriacus of Trier (St) {2}

6 March
Early C4th. He was a priest of Trier (Germany), and was remembered for his zeal. He is a patron of sick children.

Quiricus and Julitta (SS) {2, 4}

16 June
? They were martyred somewhere in Asia Minor. According to their fictitious acta, they were a widowed noblewoman from Iconium and her three-year-old son. He was beaten to death before her eyes because he had scratched the face of the examining magistrate at Tarsus, just before she herself was executed. She has been confused with Juliot, a Cornish saint.

(Quirinus of Rome 1) (St) {2, 4}

25 March
? He was a martyr of Rome who was buried in the catacomb of Pontian on the Portuensian Way. He features in the dubious acta of SS Marius, Martha and Companions, but did exist.

(Quirinus of Rome 2) (St) {2, 4}

30 April
C3rd? He was a tribune at Rome who was martyred and buried in the catacomb of Praetextatus on the Appian Way. According to the fictitious acta of Pope St Alexander I, he was his jailer and was converted with his daughter, St Balbina before his execution.

Quirinus of Sisak (St) {2, 4}

4 June
d. 309. Bishop of what is now Sisak (Croatia), according to his story he fled from his city to escape the persecution of Galerius, was captured, brought back and ordered to sacrifice to the gods. He refused, was thoroughly beaten and handed over to the provincial governor at Sabaria (now Szombathely in Hungary). There, on his continued refusal to apostatize, he was drowned in the river.

(Quirinus of Tivoli) *(St) {4 –deleted}*

4 June
? He was listed as martyred at Tivoli near Rome.

Quiteria (St) {2}

22 May
? She has a cultus as a virgin martyr in the Basque regions straddling the Franco-Spanish border, but nothing is known about her and her traditional story is completely unreliable.

Quodvultdeus (St) {2, 4}

19 February
d. 439. A bishop of Carthage (Roman Africa), he was exiled by the Arian King Genseric of the Vandals after the capture of the city in 439. He died at Naples.

R

Rabanus Maurus (St) {2}

4 February
?776–856. From Mainz (Germany), he was a child-oblate at the abbey of Fulda but studied under Alcuin at Tours for two years. He was appointed headmaster of the abbey school in 799, was abbot from 822 to 847, then resigned and was immediately made arch-bishop of Mainz. An outstanding scholar for the time, he tried to improve the education of his clergy and was a prolific writer, producing many homilies and poems and being noted for works on biblical exegesis and hagiography.

Radbod (St) {2}

29 November
d. 917. The great-grandson of the last pagan king of Friesland, he was raised in the house-hold of an uncle who was archbishop of Cologne, Germany and studied at the imperial court and at Tours, France. In 900 he became bishop of Utrecht (Netherlands) but had to move the see to Deventer in the face of Norse raids. His cathedral at Utrecht was a Benedic-tine monastery of which he was nominally abbot, hence the false tradition that he became a monk when made bishop.

Radegund, Queen (St) {2, 4}

13 August
518–87. Daughter of a pagan king of Thur-ingia, when aged twelve she was abducted by the Frankish king Clotaire I who had her baptized and educated before marrying her in 536. He was an unfaithful and cruel husband, so she left him in 542, took vows at Noyon under the authority of St Medard and went on to found the monastery of the Holy Cross at Poitiers (France), using the rule of St Cae-sarius. During the thirty years she was there as a nun; the nunnery became a noted centre of scholarship and initiated the fashion for royal

Frankish patronage of monasticism. She was a friend of St Venantius Fortunatus.

Radingus cf. **Roding**.
Radulphus cf. **Ralph**.

Ragenfred (St) {2}

8 October
C8th. She was the founder and first abbess of an Augustinian nunnery at Denais near Valen-ciennes (France).

Ragnebert (St) {2}

13 June
d. 680. He was a nobleman at the court of the Merovingian French king Theodoric III, and made an enemy of Ebroin, the mayor of the palace. He was exiled, and finally assassi-nated near the abbey of Saint-Domitian in the Jura. He was enshrined as a martyr at a place named Saint-Rambert after him.

Raithu and Sinai, Martyrs of (SS) {2}

14 January
The revised Roman Martyrology commemo-rates those monks massacred by Bedouin raid-ers at Sinai and at Raithu on the Red Sea in the C4th. The former were recorded elsewhere as dying in 309 and as numbering thirty-eight monks, with Isaias and Sabas named. The lat-ter were killed in 371.

22 December
There was another massacre at Raithu possi-bly in the C4th, involving forty-three monks.

Ralph

This is the English form of Radulf, which is Raoul in French. There are many other variants, for example, Radult, Raul, Radolph, Randulph, Rodolfo, Rodolphe, Rollon, Ruph. The German form Rudolf is listed separately.

Ralph Ashley (Bl) {2}

7 April

d. 1606. A Jesuit lay brother, he was seized with Bl Edward Oldcorne and executed with him at Worcester. He was beatified in 1929. Cf. **England, Martyrs of**.

Ralph of Bourges (St) {2}

21 June

d. 866. A child-oblate at the abbey of Solignac near Limoges (France), he possibly became a monk there. He was abbot of several monasteries (notably that of St Medard at Soissons) before becoming bishop of Bourges in 840.

Ralph Corby (alias Corbington) (Bl) {2}

7 September

d. 1644. Born in Dublin, he was educated at St Omer and then studied for the priesthood at Seville and Valladolid. In 1631 he became a Jesuit, was sent on mission to England and worked as a priest in Co. Durham. He was executed at Tyburn (London) and was beatified in 1929. Cf. **England, Martyrs of**.

Ralph Crockett (Bl) {2}

1 October

d. 1588. From Cheshire, he was educated at Cambridge and at Oxford before becoming a schoolmaster in East Anglia. After his conversion he studied for the priesthood at Rheims, where he was ordained in 1586. He went on the English mission, was executed at Chichester (Sussex) and was beatified in1929. Cf. **England, Martyrs of**.

Ralph de la Futaye (de Flageio) (Bl) {2}

16 August

d. 1129. A Benedictine monk of St-Jouin-de-Marne (France), he helped Bl Robert of Arbrissel to found the great double monastery and congregation of Fontevrault and

was himself the abbot-founder in 1092 of the double monastery (for monks and nuns) of St Sulpice near Rennes.

Ralph Grimston (Bl) {2}

15 June

d. 1598. He lived at Nidd Hall near Knaresborough (Yorks) and was known for sheltering priests. His house was raided on the feast day of SS Philip and James while Bl Peter Snow was celebrating Mass there, and the two of them were executed at York. He was beatified in 1987. Cf. **England, Martyrs of**.

Ralph of Gubbio (St) {2}

26 June

d. 1064. He was a bishop of Gubbio in Umbria (Italy) who was remembered for his preaching, and for giving away so much of his income to poor people that he had little left to live on.

Ralph Milner (Bl) {2}

7 July

d. 1591. A Hampshire small-holder, he was convicted of sheltering Bl Roger Dickinson and executed with him at Winchester. He was beatified in 1929. Cf. **England, Martyrs of**.

Ralph Sherwin (St) {2}

1 December

1550–81. From Rodsley near Ashbourne in Derbyshire, he gained a fellowship as a classical scholar of distinction at Oxford University. After his conversion he studied for the priesthood at Douai and Rome, was ordained in 1577, returned to England in 1580 and was quickly arrested. Despite torture and an offer of preferment by Queen Elizabeth if would become a Protestant, he held on to his faith and was executed at Tyburn (London). He is the protomartyr of the English College

at Rome, and was canonized in 1970. Cf.
England, Martyrs of.

(Rambert) *(St)* *{4 –deleted}*

13 June
d. c.680. A Frankish nobleman, he was influential at the court of King Thierry III of Austrasia but Ebroin, mayor of the palace, had
him exiled and then ambushed and murdered
in the Jura mountains (France). He was (with
little justification) venerated as a martyr.

Ramón cf. **Raymund.**

(Ranulf) *(St)* *{4 –deleted}*

27 May
d. c.700. The father of St Hadulph, bishop of
Arras-Cambrai, he was killed at Thélus near
Arras (France) and venerated as a martyr.

Raphael the Archangel (St) {1 –group}

29 September
The three archangels Michael, Gabriel and
Raphael are liturgically venerated together.
The last-named, 'the Healer of God', features
in the deuterocanonical book of Tobit and is
the only one of the three not to be mentioned
in the New Testament. Because of his name,
however, he has been traditionally identified
with the angel of the sheep-pool in the Gospel
of John 5:1-4.

Raphael Arnáiz Barón (St) {2}

26 April
1911–38. Born at Burgos (Spain), to wealthy
parents, he went to Madrid University to study
architecture. He loved beauty in nature, music
and painting. Giving up a promising secular
career, he joined the Trappists at Dueñas near
Palencia in 1934. His health forced him to
return home for two years after a few months
there, but with no damage to his vocation.

He considered his bad health to be a purgation
of his soul, and he died at the monastery. He
was canonized in 2009.

Raphael Chylinski (Bl) {2}

2 December
1694–1741. Born near Poznan (Poland), he
joined the Capuchins at Cracow in 1715. In
1728 he moved to Łagiewniki near Łódz where
he stayed until death, apart from two years spent
nursing sufferers of an epidemic at Cracow. He
was known for his preaching, moral catechesis
and hearing of confessions, and he subjected
himself to severe penances for the sins of the
world. However he was joyful in the liturgy, in
the care of the poor and in his chastity and love
for Our Lady. He was beatified in 1991.

Raphael Guizar Valencia (St) {2}

24 October
1878–1938. Born in Michoacán, Mexico, he
became a priest of the diocese of Zamorra
but persecution of the church drove him
underground and into exile. He returned and
became bishop of Veracruz in 1919, re-found-
ing the seminary there, but the government
set out to destroy the church and he went into
exile again, assisting the hierarchies in neighbouring countries and keeping in touch with
the underground church in Mexico by letter.
He was allowed to return just before he died,
and was canonized in 2006.

Raphael-of-St-Joseph Kalinowski (St) {2}

15 November
d. 1907. Born of Polish parents in Lithuania
when this was part of the Russian Empire, he
served in the army and civil service. But he
took part in the Polish rebellion of 1863, was
exiled to Siberia for ten years and became
a Carmelite priest in Poland on his return.
He had such success as a spiritual director

that he became known as the 'martyr of the confessional'. He died at Wadowice and was canonized in 1991.

Raphaela-Mary-of-the-Sacred-Heart Porras Ayllón (St) {2}

6 January

1850–1925. From Pedro Abad near Cordoba (Spain), with her sister she joined the 'Society of Mary Auxiliatrix' at the latter place in 1875, but stayed behind when the society had to leave the city. In 1877 she founded the 'Handmaids of the Sacred Heart' at Madrid, and became the first superior-general in 1887. The charism involved teaching and also adoration of the Blessed Sacrament in reparation for outrages against it. Six years later she resigned, and then lived a busy but anonymous life until her death in Rome. She was canonized in 1977.

Raphaela de Villalonga Ybarra (Bl) {2}

23 February

1843–98. Born in Bilbao, she married and had seven children (five survived). In 1885 she took religious vows in private with the consent of her husband, and became known as a 'mother of charity' through her benefactions. She had especial care for derelict young people, and founded the 'Sisters of the Guardian Angels' in order to help teenage girls facing the choice between prostitution and starvation. She was beatified in 1984.

(Rasyphus) (St) {4 –deleted}

23 July

? He has an ancient cultus as a martyr at Rome, and may be identical with a St Rasius whose relics are enshrined in the Pantheon there.

Raymund of Barbastro (St) {2}

21 June

d. 1126. From Durban south of Toulouse (France), he became an Augustinian canon regular at Pamiers and second bishop of Barbastro in Aragon (Spain) in 1104. The city had been recently conquered from the Muslims. He is its principal patron.

Raymund-Joachim Castaño González and Joseph-Mary González Solis (BB) {2 –add}

25 September

d. 1936. They were two Dominican friars, in charge of the friary at Quejana near Bilbao, Spain which had been emptied as a result of the Spanish Civil War. On 25 August 1936 they were arrested and imprisoned at Bilbao by Communist militia, and executed a month later after being badly treated in prison. They were beatified in 2013. Cf. **Spanish Civil War, Martyrs of** and list in appendix.

Raymund of Fitero (St) {2}

1 February

d. c.1160. An Aragonese cathedral-canon of Tarazona (Spain), he became a Cistercian at the French abbey of Scala Dei and was sent to be the abbot-founder of Fitero in Navarre (now in Spain). In 1158 the city of Calatrava in New Castile was abandoned by the Knights Templar and threatened by the Muslims, so he founded the military order of Calatrava for its defence. This utilized the Benedictine rule and the Cistercian customary and played a notable part in the 'Reconquista'. He died near Toledo and his cultus as a saint was confirmed in 1719.

Raymund Gayrard (St) {2}

3 July

d. 1118. He had been a cantor in the church of St Sernin at Toulouse (France) before his wife died, whereupon he became a secular canon there and founded a hospice in the city later named after him. He was noted for his generosity to the poor and for his personal austerity.

Raymund Li Quanzhen (St) {1 –group}

30 June
Cf. **Peter Li Quanhui and Raymund Li Quanzhen**.

Raymund Lull (Bl) {2}

29 June
d. 1316. From Palma on Majorca (Spain), he married young and was seneschal at the court of Aragon. When aged about thirty he was converted by a vision of Christ crucified, became a Franciscan tertiary and devoted his whole life to the conversion of the Muslims. To this end he travelled extensively in Italy, France, England and Germany, wrote copiously in Latin, Arabic (which he learnt) and Catalan, and encouraged the study of oriental religion and culture. He was, however, unsuccessful in his attempts to interest the Holy See and the courts of Western Europe in his objective. He made three journeys to preach the gospel to the Muslims of Tunis and was allegedly stoned to death there, but there is no contemporary proof of this. He was a philosopher, a poet, an alchemist and a chemist as well as a theologian (nicknamed 'Doctor Illuminatus'), but he had no formal training in the scholastic theology of his age and invented his own method, which had a small but enthusiastic following in his time.

Raymund Nonnatus (St) {2, 3}

31 August
d. 1240. According to his unreliable biography he was from an impoverished noble family of Catalonia and was cut out of his dead mother's womb (hence his surname, 'Unborn'). He joined the Mercedarian order, which had been recently founded in Spain for the ransoming of Christian captives from the Muslims of North Africa, and succeeded St Peter Nolasco

as its second master-general. He surrendered himself as a hostage in exchange for a Christian slave when he was out of funds, and was very badly treated until ransomed in turn. He was created a cardinal in 1239 but died on his way to Rome. His cultus was confined to local calendars in 1969.

Raymund Palmerio (Bl) {2}

27 July
d. 1200. He was a layman of Picenza (Italy), and when his wife and children died he founded a hospital and took care of poor people.

Raymund of Peñafort (St) {1, 3}

7 January
c.1180–1275. Related to the royal family of Aragon, he was born at Villafranca in Catalonia (Spain) and studied and taught at Barcelona, where he became a priest and archdeacon of the cathedral. In 1222 he became a Dominican and worked among the Muslims and the Albigenses until summoned to Rome by Pope Gregory IX. He became the pope's confessor, and was given the task of systematizing and codifying the contemporary canon law. This resulted in his five books of the 'Decretals', finished in 1234, which remained the most authoritative codification of ecclesiastical legislation until 1917. He became master-general of the Dominicans in 1238 and encouraged St Thomas Aquinas to write his *Contra Gentiles*. In later life he lived on Majorca, but died at Barcelona. He is alleged to have helped in the foundation of the Mercedarians, but this is debatable. He was canonized in 1601.

Raymund Vargas González (Bl) {2 –add}

1 April
Cf. **George and Raymund Vargas González**.

Raymund-of-Capua delle Vigne (Bl) {2}

5 October

d. 1399. From Capua (Italy), he joined the Dominicans and taught at Bologna, Rome and (from 1374) at Siena, where he was the spiritual director of St Catherine of Siena. Later he became master-general of the Dominicans and restored discipline with such success that he has been called the second founder of the order. He wrote biographies of St Catherine and of St Agnes of Montepulciano. His cultus was confirmed for the Dominicans and locally for Rome in 1899.

Raynald Concorrezzo (Bl) {2}

18 August

d. 1321. From Milan (Italy), he became a canon of Lodi, then bishop of Vicenza in 1296 and archbishop of Ravenna in 1303. He was a friend and defender of the Knights Templar. His cultus was confirmed for Ravenna in 1852.

Raynald of Nocera (St) {2}

9 February

d. 1222. Of German ancestry, he was born near Nocera in Umbria (Italy), became a monk at Fontavellana and was made bishop of Nocera in 1222, of which city he is the principal patron.

Raynerius of Aquila (St) {2, 4}

30 December

d. 1077. He was a bishop of Aquila in the Abruzzi (Italy).

Raynerius-of-Arezzo Mariani (Bl) {2}

3 November

d. 1304. From Arezzo (Italy), he became a Franciscan lay brother and died at Borgo San Sepolcro. His cultus was confirmed for there in 1802.

Raynerius (Raniero, Rainerius) Scacceri (St) {2, 4}

17 June

d. 1160. From Pisa (Italy), after a dissipated youth he undertook several penitential pilgrimages to Jerusalem and afterwards lived as a conventual oblate in the Benedictine abbey of St Andrew at Pisa and then in that of St Vitus in the same city, where he died.

Raynerius of Split (St) {2}

4 August

d. 1180. A Camaldolese monk of Fontavellana, he was made bishop of Cagli (Italy) in 1156 and archbishop of Split in Dalmatia (Croatia) in 1175. His attempts to reclaim property alienated from his diocese led to his murder.

Rebecca Ar Rayès de Himlaya (St) {2}

23 March

1832–1914. Born at Himlaya in the Lebanon, she joined the 'Religious of Our Lady' ('Marianettes') in 1853 and taught girls. There was a persecution by the Turks and her congregation had to leave the country, so she joined the 'Maronite Order of St Anthony' at Al-Qarn in 1871. She spent twenty-six years there, then went blind and moved to Ad-Dahr where she became paralysed as well before her death. She was beatified in 1985 and canonized in 2001.

(Redemptus of Ferentini) *(St)* *{4 –deleted}*

8 April

d. 586. Bishop of Ferentini south of Rome, he was a friend of St Gregory the Great.

Regina (Regnia, Reine) (St) {2, 4}

7 September

? She has an ancient cultus as a virgin martyr in the diocese of Autun (France), but no reliable information about her survives.

Regina Protmann (Bl) {2}

18 January
1552–1613. From a bourgeois family of Braniewo in Warmia (Poland), she had an ordinary life appropriate to her background until the spread of Protestantism and the plague suddenly inspired her to leave her family in 1571 and found the Sisters of St Catherine of Alexandria for prayer, nursing and teaching without an enclosure (an innovation at the time). She died at her home town and was beatified in 1999.

Reginald of Picardy (St) {2}

17 September
d. 1104. He was a canon regular at Soissons (France) before becoming a hermit at Melinais near La Flèche. King Henry II of England had an abbey built over his tomb. His cultus was confirmed for Angers in 1868.

Reginald of St Gilles (Bl) {2}

1 February
1183–1220. From St Gilles near Nîmes (France), he taught canon law at the university of Paris from 1206 and was dean of the collegiate church of St Agnan in Orleans from 1211. He met St Dominic in Rome, became his disciple and helped to establish the Dominicans at Bologna and at Paris. His cultus was confirmed for Paris and the Dominicans in 1885.

(Regulus of Lucca) (St) {4 –deleted}

1 September
d. ?545. A Roman African, possibly a bishop, he was exiled by the Arian Vandals and settled as a hermit on the coast of Tuscany (Italy). He appears to have been killed by order of the Ostrogothic leader Totila, and his relics were enshrined at Lucca.

Regulus (Rieul) of Senlis (St) {2, 4}

30 March
C4th. Allegedly a Greek and the first bishop of Senlis (France), he is also linked with Arles.

Regulus (Rule) of St Andrew's (St)

17 October
C4th? According to the C9th legend, he was a Greek abbot who brought some relics of St Andrew to Scotland and founded the church at St Andrew's in Fife. He was more likely a later Irish missionary, whose monastery later became the most important church in Scotland.

Reine cf. **Regina**.

Reineldis de Contich and Comps (SS) {2, 4}

16 July
d. c.680. According to her dubious C11th biography she was a daughter of St Amelberga of Maubeuge, became a nun at Saintes near Brussels (Belgium) and was killed with a subdeacon Grimwald and her servant Gondulf by invading barbarians.

Reinild (Renula) (St) {2}

6 February
C8th. She was appointed by St Boniface abbess of a nunnery called Eyck, at the town now called Maaseyk in Belgium north of Maastricht. She was a noted embroiderer.

Rembert (St) {2}

11 June
d. 888. From Torhout near Bruges, Belgium, he was educated at the monastery founded there by St Ansgar, accompanied the latter on his missionary journeys and succeeded him as archbishop of Hamburg-Bremen in 865. He died at Bremen (Germany), and is

remembered for a biography that he wrote of St Ansgar.

Rémy cf. **Remigius**.

Remigius Isoré and Modestus Andlauer (St) {1 –group}

19 June
d. 1900. Two French Jesuits, they were missionaries around the city of Xian in Hebei (China). St Modestus was pastor of Wuyi, while St Remigius was that of Zhoujiazhuang. The latter came to Wuyi on a journey, and the two were beaten to death in the church by Boxers. Cf. **China, Martyrs of**.

Remigius of Rheims (St) {2, 3}

13 January
d. c.530. The 'Apostle of the Franks' was a Gallo-Roman nobleman who was elected bishop of Rheims (France) in 459 when still a layman. He was the most influential bishop of Gaul during the seventy-four years of his episcopate, and was instrumental in the conversion to Catholicism of Clovis, king of the Franks. He baptized him at Rheims during the Easter vigil of 496. His cultus was confined to particular calendars in 1969.

Remigius of Rouen (St) {2}

19 January
d. ?762. An illegitimate son of Charles Martel, he became bishop of Rouen (France) in 755 and was successful in introducing the Roman rite and liturgical chant into France.

Remo cf. **Romulus**.

Renatus Goupil (Bl) {2}

23 September
1608–42. From near Angers (France), he joined the Jesuits and went to Quebec (Canada) as a missionary. He was one of the companions of St Isaac Jogues on the trip to the Huron nation when they were captured and enslaved by the Mohawk Iroquois. St Isaac eventually escaped, but St Renatus was killed by a thrown spear when he was spotted teaching the sign of the Cross to children at Ossernenon near present-day Auriesville in New York State (USA). He was canonized in 1930. Cf. **John Brébeuf and Comps**.

Renatus of Sorrento (St) {2}

12 November
C5th. He was an early bishop at Sorrento (Italy).

Reol cf. **Regulus**.

Reparata (St) {2, 4}

8 October
Early C4th? She was a virgin martyr of Caesarea in the Holy Land in the reign of Decius. Her acta are spurious.

Restituta (St) {2, 4}

17 May
d. 304. A Roman African maiden, she was martyred at Carthage in the reign of Diocletian. Her alleged relics are in the cathedral of Naples (Italy).

(Restituta and Comps) (SS) *{4 –deleted}*

27 May
d. 272. According to her story she was a patrician maiden of Rome who fled to Sora in Campania (Italy) to escape persecution in the reign of Aurelian and who was martyred there with several companions.

(Restitutus, Donatus and Comp)s (SS) *{4 –deleted}*

23 August
d. ?305. They were listed by Florus of Lyons in c.850 as a group of sixteen Syrians martyred at Antioch. Valerian and Fructuosa were also named.

Restitutus of Carthage (St) {2, 4}

28 August
d. c.360. He was a martyred bishop of Carthage (Roman Africa) in whose honour St Augustine preached a sermon which is now lost.

Restitutus of Rome (St) {2, 4}

2 May
Early C4th? He was a Roman martyr of the reign of Diocletian. His acta are unreliable.

(Reverianus, Paul and Comps) *(SS)*
{4 –deleted}

1 June
C3rd? They were described as an Italian missionary bishop and priest who worked in the region around Autun (France) and were martyred with several companions in the reign of Aurelian.

Reyne cf. **Regina**.
Rhais cf. **Irais**.

Rheticus (Rheticius, Rhetice) (St) {2}

15 May
C4th. A Gallo-Roman nobleman, he became bishop of Autun (France) about three years before he attended the Roman synod which condemned Donatism in 313.

Rhipsime, Gaiana and Comps (SS) {2, 4}

29 September
Early C4th. A group of virgin martyrs, they have an ancient cultus as the first martyrs of the Armenian Church. Their existence is certain but their acta are unreliable.

Riccerius (Bl) {2}

7 February
d. 1236. From near Camerino in the Marches (Italy), he was a student at Bologna when he heard St Francis preaching. He at once became his disciple and friend and was present at his death. He later became Franciscan provincial of the Marches. His cultus was confirmed for Camerino in 1838.

Richard of Andria (St) {2}

9 June
End C12th. He was an English bishop of Andria near Bari (Italy). The assertion that he was of the C5th is erroneous.

Richard Bere (Bl) {2}

9 August
d. 1537. From Glastonbury (Somerset), he was educated at Oxford and the Inns of Court in London before becoming a Carthusian at the London Charterhouse. He was among those of that community starved to death in Newgate prison for refusing the spiritual supremacy of Henry VIII. Cf. **England, Martyrs of**.

Richard-of-St-Anne of Brussels (Bl) {2}

10 September
1585–1622. Born of Spanish parents in Flanders, he was a tailor at Brussels before becoming a Franciscan lay brother. He was sent as a missionary firstly to Mexico and then to the Philippines in 1611, where he was ordained on Cebu. In 1613 he went to Japan and was martyred at Nagasaki on the day of the 'Great Martyrdom'. Cf. **Charles Spinola and Comps**, **Great Martyrdom at Nagasaki** and **Japan, Martyrs of**.

Richard Featherstone (Bl) {2}

30 July
d. 1540. Educated at Cambridge, he was appointed archdeacon of Brecon, tutor to Princess Mary and was one of the chaplains of Queen Catherine of Aragon. He defended the validity of her marriage to King Henry

VIII, refused the latter's oath of supremacy and was executed at Smithfield (London) with BB Edward Powell and Thomas Abel. He was beatified in 1929. Cf. **England, Martyrs of**.

Richard Gil Barcelón and Anthony Arrué Peiró (BB) {2 –add}

3 August
d. 1936. Bl Richard Gil Barcelón was from a rich Spanish noble family, and served in the war between the United States and Spain in 1898. He converted in a moment of great danger, joined the Dominicans and was ordained in 1904. However, he transferred to the newly founded congregation of the Little Work of Divine Providence after meeting the founder Don Orione in Rome in 1910. After service at Rome and in Sicily he went to Spain to establish the congregation in Valencia and to work among the poor people of that city. He was kidnapped by Anarchist militia and shot at Saler de Valencia. Bl Anthony Arrué Peiró volunteered to accompany him, and had his skull fractured by a rifle butt. They were beatified in 2013. Cf. **Spanish Civil War, Martyrs of** and list in appendix.

Richard Gwyn (alias White) (St) {2}

17 October
1537–84. From Llanidloes in Powys (Wales), he was educated at St John's College, Cambridge before converting, marrying and working as a schoolteacher at Overton in Clwyd. He was imprisoned for four years (during which he wrote many religious poems in Welsh) before he was executed at Wrexham. He is the protomartyr of the Reformation in Wales, and was canonized in 1970. Cf. **Wales, Martyrs of**.

Richard Herst (Hurst, Hayhurst) (Bl) {2}

29 August
d. 1618. From near Preston (Lancs), he was a farmer there and, because he was a Catholic,

was falsely found guilty and hanged at Lancaster for murder. He was beatified in 1929. Cf. **England, Martyrs of**.

Richard Hill & Richard Holliday (BB) {2}

27 May
Cf. **Edmund Duke and Comps**.

Richard Kirkman (Bl) {2}

22 August
d. 1582. From Addingham near Skipton (Yorks), he was educated at Douai, ordained in 1579 and was a tutor at Scrivelsby Manor near Hornchurch (Lincs). He was executed at York with Bl William Lacey and was beatified in 1886. Cf. **England, Martyrs of**.

Richard Langhorne (Bl) {2}

14 July
d. 1679. From Bedfordshire, he was a law student at the Inner Temple in London and became a barrister in 1654. He was executed at Tyburn for alleged involvement in the Oates plot and was beatified in 1929. Cf. **England, Martyrs of**.

Richard 'the King' (St) {2}

7 February
d. ?720. He was the Anglo-Saxon father of SS Willibald, Winebald and Walburga, and died at Lucca on a pilgrimage to Rome. The earlier Italian legend describes him as a prince of Wessex (England), and the later one as a duke of Swabia (Germany). Both are fictitious.

Richard Langley (Bl) {2}

1 December
d. 1586. A landowner at Ousethorpe near Pocklington (Yorks), he was hanged at York for sheltering priests in his house. He was beatified in 1929. Cf. **England, Martyrs of**.

Richard Leigh (alias Garth or Earth) (Bl) {2}

30 August

d. 1588. A Londoner, he was educated at Rheims and Rome, was ordained in 1586 and was executed at Tyburn together with St Margaret Ward and BB Edward Shelley, John Roche, Richard Lloyd and Richard Martin. He was beatified in 1929. Cf. **England, Martyrs of**.

Richard Lloyd (alias Flower) (Bl) {2}

30 August

d. 1588. He was born on Anglesey (Wales) of a Catholic family called Lloyd (of which 'Flower' was an English mispronunciation). His brother Owen was a priest. Condemned for giving shelter to priests, he was executed at Tyburn with St Margaret Ward and BB Richard Leigh, Edward Shelley, Richard Martin and John Roche. He was beatified in 1987. Cf. **England, Martyrs of**.

Richard Martin (BB) {2}

30 August

d. 1588. He was a Shropshire landowner and was executed at Tyburn for sheltering priests together with St Margaret Ward and BB Edward Shelley, John Roche, Richard Lloyd and Richard Leigh. He was beatified in 1929. Cf. **England, Martyrs of**.

Richard Newport (alias Smith) (Bl) {2}

30 May

d. 1612. From Harringworth in Northamptonshire, he was educated for the priesthood at Rome, ordained in 1597 and worked in the London district until his execution at Tyburn. Cf. **England, Martyrs of**.

Richard Pampuri (St) {2}

1 March

1897–1928. Born at Trivolzio near Pavia (Italy), he studied medicine before the First World War and was a paramedic during it. Afterwards he qualified as a surgeon and, wishing to combine the vocations of ministering to sick bodies and to needy souls, he helped poor people and catechized in his spare time. He was led to join the 'Hospitaller Order of St John of God' in 1927. He was canonized in 1989.

Richard Reynolds (St) {2}

4 May

?1492–1535. From Devon, he studied at Cambridge, became a fellow of Corpus Christi College and was appointed university preacher in 1513. In the same year he became a Bridgettine monk at Syon Abbey near Isleworth (Middlesex), a recently founded double house for nuns and monks famous for its spiritual and intellectual fervour. He refused to take the oath of spiritual supremacy demanded by King Henry VIII and was executed at Tyburn with three Carthusians. He was canonized in 1970. His community fled into exile, and is now in Devon. Cf. **England, Martyrs of**.

Richard Sargeant (alias Lee or Long) (Bl) {2}

20 April

d. 1586. Born in Gloucestershire, he was ordained at Douai and was a priest in London. He was executed at Tyburn with Bl William Thompson, and was beatified in 1987. Cf. **England, Martyrs of**.

Richard Simpson (Bl) {2}

24 June

d. 1588. Born near Ripon (Yorks), he was a convert Anglican minister who was probably an Oxford graduate. Ordained in Brussels in 1577, he was a priest in the North for three years and was caught travelling between Lancashire and Derbyshire. He was executed at Derby with BB Nicholas Garlick and Robert Ludlum, and was beatified in 1987. Cf. **England, Martyrs of**.

Richard Thirkeld (Thirkild) (Bl) {2}

29 May
d. 1583. From Co. Durham, he was educated at the Queen's College, Oxford and as an old man completed his studies for the priesthood at Douai and Rheims, being ordained in 1579. He worked in Yorkshire and was executed at York, being beatified in 1886. Cf. **England, Martyrs of**.

Richard Whiting (Bl) {2}

15 November
Cf. **Benedictine Martyrs of the Reformation**.

Richard de Wych (St) {2}

3 April
1197–1253. From Droitwich near Worcester (England), he studied at Oxford, Paris and Bologna before becoming chancellor of Oxford University in 1235. Then he was legal adviser to two archbishops of Canterbury, St Edmund Rich (with whom he shared exile in France) and St Boniface of Savoy. Having been ordained in France, he became bishop of Chichester in 1244 (although King Henry III sequestered his revenues for two years because the election was disputed). He died at Dover while preaching a crusade. Being remembered as a model pastor, he was canonized in 1262 and his pilgrimage shrine was at Chichester Cathedral until the Reformation. His attribute is a chalice lying on its side on the ground at his feet.

Richard Yaxley (Bl) {2}

7 July
1560–89. Born at Boston (Lincs), he was ordained at Rheims in 1586, went to Oxford and was seized on his arrival with BB Humphrey Pritchard, Thomas Belson and George Nichols. They were executed together in Oxford and were beatified in 1987. Cf. **England, Martyrs of**.

Richardis, Empress (St) {2}

18 September
d. ?895. Daughter of a count of Alsace (France), in 862 she married the emperor Charles the Fat but nineteen years later was accused of adultery with the chancellor. She was vindicated but retired to the nunnery of Andlau which she had founded near Strasbourg, and died there. She has been claimed as a Benedictine oblate.

Richarius (Riquier) (St) {2, 4}

26 April
d. 645. From Celles near Amiens (France), he became a priest and was at the Frankish court and in England before founding an abbey in his native village. He was famous for ransoming those kidnapped by invading barbarians. After some years as abbot he resigned and spent the rest of his life as a hermit. His shrine was at St-Riquier-sur-Somme.

Rictrude (St) {2}

12 May
d. ?688. A Gascon noblewoman, she married St Adalbald d'Ostrevant and had four children who all became saints (Maurontius, Eusebia, Clotsindis and Adalsindis). After her husband's murder she founded the nunnery of Marchiennes near Douai (France) with the help of St Amandus of Elnone, and was abbess there for forty years.

Rieul cf. **Regulus**.

Rigobert (St) {2}

4 January

d. ?743. He was abbot of Orbais near Rheims (France) before he became archbishop of the latter place in 696. In 721 he was ejected by Charles Martel for opposing the sequestration of church lands and returned to his abbey. Later he became a hermit, and died near Soissons.

Rigomer of Meaux (St) {2}

4 January

C6th. He was a bishop of Meaux (France), and his shrine was at the cathedral there until it was destroyed by Huguenots in the sixteenth century.

Rimagilus (St) {2}

3 September

d. 671–9. From Aquitaine (France), he was a courtier before becoming a monk-disciple of St Sulpicius at Bourges. He was the first abbot of Solignac near Limoges and then of Cougnon in Luxembourg before founding the twin abbeys of Stavelot-Malmédy in the Ardennes, Belgium in 648. In 652 he allegedly became bishop of Maastricht, Netherlands but resigned in 663 and died at Stavelot. His extant biographies are unreliable.

Ringan cf. **Ninian**.
Riquier cf. **Richarius**.

Rita of Cascia (St) {1}

22 May

1381–a.1457. From Roccaporena near Cascia in Umbria (Italy), she married a brutal man who ended up being murdered. Her two sons swore a vendetta against the killers, but she prayed that they would not persevere and they died shortly afterwards having expressed forgiveness. Then she entered an Augustinian nunnery at Cascia, where she suffered from a permanent maggoty ulcer on her forehead after a vision of Christ crowned with thorns. She was canonized in 1900, and is the patron of desperate or impossible problems as well as of abused wives. Her name is a diminutive of 'Margaret'.

Rita-Beloved-of-Jesus Lopez (Bl) {2 –add}

6 January

1848–1913. From Ribafelta in Portugal, she grew up in a very devout family and wished to become a consecrated religious, but all religious houses in the country had been closed by an anti-clerical government in the 1830s. So she became an itinerant preacher on the theme of the Rosary and the Eucharist until she joined the Sisters of Charity in 1877. Not being satisfied with their charism, she founded the 'Sisters of Jesus, Mary and Joseph' in 1880 and opened a school in her home parish. The spread of the new institute was hindered by anti-clericalism and it was confined to her parents' home for several years, but she sent several sisters to Brazil which ensured the institute's survival. She died at Ribafelta and was beatified in 2006.

Rita-of-the-Sorrows Pujalte Sánchez and Frances-of-the-Sacred-Heart Aldea Araujo (BB) {2}

20 July

d. 1936. The former, from near Alicante (Spain), joined the 'Sisters of Charity of the Sacred Heart of Jesus' in 1888 and was their superior-general from 1900 to 1928. Then she retired to St Susanna's College at Madrid. The latter was an orphan brought up at the same college who took vows in 1903 and became Bl Rita's general secretary. During the Spanish Civil War the college was attacked by an anti-clerical mob, and the two sick religious were misguidedly advised to take refuge in a nearby flat. Two hours after they did so they were seized, driven out of the city and shot. They were beatified in 1998. Cf. **Spanish Civil War, Martyrs of**.

Ro cf. **Maelrubha**.
Robert also cf. **Rupert**.

Robert Anderton (Bl) {2}

25 April
d. 1586. From Chorley (Lancs), he was educated at Brasenose College in Oxford before his conversion. Then he studied at Rheims, was ordained in 1585 and was executed on the Isle of Wight in the following year. He was beatified in 1929. Cf. **England, Martyrs of**.

Robert of Arbrissel (Bl) {2}

24 February
d. 1116. From Arbrissel in Brittany (France), the son of a priest, he studied at the University of Paris and then became vicar-general at Rennes in 1085, but his preaching and attempts at reform were so unpopular there that he had to flee Brittany. In 1092 he became a hermit in the forest of Craon near Angers, and he founded the Augustinian monastery of La Roë there. However, Pope Urban II visited Angers in 1096 and commissioned him as an itinerant preacher. In 1099 he founded a Benedictine double monastery for monks and nuns at Fontevrault near Saumur, and this was the first house of a new congregation over which the abbess of Fontevrault had supreme jurisdiction. He died there.

Robert Bellarmine (St) {1, 3}

17 September
1542–1621. From Montepulciano in Tuscany (Italy), he was educated by the Jesuits and joined them in 1560. From 1570 he taught Greek, Hebrew and theology at Louvain (Belgium) and became famous there as an effective polemicist against Protestantism. His opponents in the Netherlands hated him to the extent that his name was later given to a style of pot-bellied pottery wine jug. From 1576 he taught in Rome, and was the provincial superior at Naples before being made cardinal in 1598 and archbishop of Capua in 1602. Recalled to Rome in 1605, he became head of the Vatican library and theological adviser to the pope. His interventions against Galileo were disastrously mistaken. He was canonized in 1930, and declared a doctor of the Church in the following year.

Robert Bickendyke (Bl) {2}

8 August
d. 1586. Born near Knaresborough (Yorks), while apprenticed at York he was spotted drinking in a pub with a known priest and paying for the beer. This was regarded as "harbouring a priest" and, after three trials, he was executed at York on an uncertain date in August. He was beatified in 1987 Cf. **England, Martyrs of**.

Robert Dalby (Bl) {2}

15 March
d. 1589. From Hemingborough near Selby (Yorks), he became an Anglican minister but converted and was ordained priest at Rheims in 1588. He was hanged at York in the following year. Cf. **England, Martyrs of**.

Robert Dibdale (Bl) {2}

10 August
d. 1586. Born at Stratford-upon-Avon, he was ordained at Rheims and became chaplain at Denham to Sir George Peckham. He was executed at Tyburn with BB John Adams and John Lowe and was beatified in 1987. Cf. **England, Martyrs of**.

Robert Drury (Bl) {2}

26 February

1568–1607. A Buckinghamshire landowner, he studied at Rheims and at the new college at Valladolid (Spain), being ordained there in 1595. He was a priest in London, was arrested near Fleet Street and was executed at Tyburn. He was beatified in 1987. Cf. **England, Martyrs of.**

Robert Grissold (Bl) {2}

16 July

Cf. **John Sugar and Robert Grissold.**

Robert Hardesty (Bl) {2}

24 September

d. 1589. From York, possibly a clothier, he was seized while acting as a guide to Bl Robert Dibdale on the road to Ripon. Since they were not caught together he was charged with having previously aided Catholic prisoners at York Castle and was executed at York. He was beatified in 1987. Cf. **England, Martyrs of.**

Robert Johnson (Bl) {2}

28 May

d. 1582. From Shropshire, he was educated at Rome and Douai, was ordained in 1576 and was able to work in London for two years before being executed at Tyburn. He was beatified in 1886. Cf. **England, Martyrs of.**

Robert Lawrence (St) {2}

4 May

d. 1535. Prior of the Carthusian monastery at Beauvale (Notts), he was executed at Tyburn (London) with SS Augustine Webster and John Houghton (fellow Carthusian priors) and with St Richard Reynolds and Bl John Haile. He was canonized in 1970. Cf. **England, Martyrs of.**

Robert Ludlum (Bl). {2}

24 June

d. 1588. Born in Derbyshire, he studied at Oxford and was ordained at Rheims in 1581. After being on the mission for six years in the North he was captured at Padley Hall with Bl Nicholas Garlick and executed at Derby with him and Bl Robert Dibdale. He was beatified in 1987. Cf. **England, Martyrs of.**

Robert Mayler (Bl) {2}

5 July

Cf. **Matthew Lambert and Comps**.

Robert Middleton (Bl) {2}

3 April

1571–1601. Born in York (a relative of St Margaret Clitherow), he converted when he was eighteen and was ordained at Rome in 1598. He was captured in the Fylde (near what is now Blackpool), and there followed an attempt to free him by ambush in which Bl Thurstan Hunt was also captured. They were executed together at Lancaster. He became a Jesuit in prison and was beatified in 1987. Cf. **England, Martyrs of**.

Robert of Molesmes (St) {2}

17 April

1027–1111. From near Troyes in Champagne (France), he became a Benedictine monk at Moutier-la-Celle and was made abbot of Tonnerre. He left this monastery to become the superior of some hermits in the forest of Collan, and founded with them the monastery of Molesmes near Tonnerre in 1075. As the community grew he became dissatisfied with the standard of observance and withdrew to a hermitage at Or. He was recalled but left again, this time in the company of SS Stephen Harding and Alberic. In 1098 they founded at Cîteaux a new monastery which corresponded more with their monastic ideals and he was the first superior, but the monks of Molesmes appealed to Rome and obtained his recall as their abbot, which he remained until his death. He is counted as one of the founders of the Cistercians.

Robert Morton (Bl) {2}

28 August
d. 1588. From Bawtry (Yorks), he studied for the priesthood at Rheims and Rome, was ordained in 1587 but was quickly apprehended on his return to England and executed at Lincoln's Inn Fields, London. He was beatified in 1929. Cf. **England, Martyrs of**.

Robert of Newminster (St) {2}

7 June
1100–59. He was a parish priest in north Yorkshire before becoming a Benedictine monk at Whitby, but in 1132 he joined the new reformed monastery at Fountains, founded from St Mary's Abbey at York. This quickly became Cistercian. Newminster Abbey at Morpeth (Northumberland) was founded from it in 1137, and he became the first abbot. His shrine there was a centre of pilgrimage and his abbey became important, but few remnants survive.

Robert Nutter (Bl) {2}

26 July
d. 1600. From Burnley (Lancs), the brother of Bl John Nutter, he was ordained at Rheims in 1582, was in the Tower of London by 1584 and was deported back to France. Then he acted as an escort for priests crossing the Channel to England, but was captured on board ship off Gravesend and sent to the prison camp for English Catholic priests at Wisbech. He joined the Dominicans there before escaping and going back to Burnley.

Re-captured, he was executed at Lancaster with Bl Edward Thwing. He was beatified in 1987. Cf. **England, Martyrs of**.

Robert Salt (Bl) {2}

9 June
d. 1537. A Carthusian lay brother at the London Charterhouse, he was starved to death with six of his brethren in Newgate prison at the instigation of King Henry VIII. He was beatified in 1886. Cf. **England, Martyrs of** and **Carthusian Martyrs**.

Robert Southwell (St) {2}

21 February
1561–95. From Horsham St Faith's in Norfolk, when aged seventeen he became a Jesuit at Rome and worked as a priest in London from 1584 to 1592. He was betrayed and spent three years in prison (being tortured thirteen times) before being executed at Tyburn. He was a notable religious poet. He was canonized in 1970. Cf. **England, Martyrs of**.

(Robert Sutton 1) (Bl) {2}

27 July
d. 1588. Born in Burton-upon-Trent, he studied at Oxford and became the Anglican rector of Lutterworth (Leics). He was converted in 1577, was ordained at Rheims and was a priest in Staffordshire. He was executed at Stafford and was beatified in 1987. Cf. **England, Martyrs of**.

(Robert Sutton 2) (Bl) {2}

5 October
d. 1588. From Kegworth (Leics), he was a schoolmaster in London and was hanged at Clerkenwell for having converted to the Catholic Church. He was beatified in 1929. Cf. **England, Martyrs of**.

Robert Thorpe (Bl) {2}

31 May

1591. A Yorkshireman who was ordained at Rheims, he was a priest in his native county for six years before his capture while saying a Palm Sunday Mass at Menthorp. A servant was spotted collecting flowering sallow for use as palm, and this tipped off the pursuivants. He was executed at York with Bl Thomas Watkinson and was beatified in 1987. Cf. **England, Martyrs of**.

Robert de Turlande (St) {2}

17 April

d. 1067. From the Auvergne (France), he became a priest and canon at Brioude where he founded a hospice. After spending some time at Cluny under St Odilo he made a pilgrimage to Rome and then became a hermit near Brioude, where he was joined by many disciples. Thus was founded the great Benedictine abbey of Chaise-Dieu (housing some three hundred monks) and this became the mother house of a Benedictine congregation of some three hundred monasteries.

Robert Watkinson (Bl) {2}

20 April

1579–1602. From Hemingborough (Yorks), he studied for the priesthood at Douai and Rome and was ordained in 1602. He was immediately captured on his return to England and executed at Tyburn (London). Cf. **England, Martyrs of**.

Robert Widmerpool and Robert Wilcox (BB) {2}

1 October

d. 1588. The former was from a Nottinghamshire landowning family and was a schoolmaster in Kent after having been educated at Oxford. The former was from Chester,

studied for the priesthood at Rheims and was ordained there in 1585. They were executed together at Canterbury with Gerald Edwards and were beatified in 1929. Cf. **England, Martyrs of**.

(Robustian) *(St) {4 –deleted}*

24 May

? Nothing is known about this alleged early martyr of Milan (Italy), who is possibly a duplicate of the Robustian of the next entry.

(Robustian and Mark) *(SS) {4 –deleted}*

31 August

? They had an early cultus at Milan (Italy), but nothing is known about them.

Roch (St) {2}

16 August

d. ?1379. According to his legendary biography he was from Montpellier (France) and went to Italy as a pilgrim. There he nursed those suffering from plague in various places before dying at Angera on Lake Maggiore (he did not return home to die in prison under suspicion of being a spy, as alleged). He is invoked against epidemic diseases. In Italy he is Rocco; in Spain, Roque; in Scotland Rollock, Rollox or Seemirookie. He is depicted dressed as a pilgrim with a plague bubo (boil) on his thigh, sometimes with a dog licking it.

Roderick cf. **Ruderic**.

Roding (Rouin) (St) {2}

17 September

Early C8th. An Irish missionary monk, he preached in Germany and joined the abbey of Tholey near Trier. Disturbed by the visits of his converts, he left and became a hermit in the forest of Argonne, France where he became the abbot-founder of Beaulieu.

Rodolf cf. **Rudolf**.

Rodrigo cf. **Ruderic**.

Rogatian and Felicissimus (SS) {2, 4}

26 October

C3rd. They were a priest and layman at Carthage (Roman Africa), and were described by St Cyprian as having 'witnessed a good confession for Christ'. This was taken by the old Roman Martyrology as referring to their martyrdom, but the revision refers to their sufferings in prison instead.

(Rogatus, Successus and Comps) *(SS)* *{4 –deleted}*

28 March

? They are listed as eighteen martyrs of Roman Africa.

Rogellus and Servusdei (SS) {2, 4}

16 September

d. 852. A monk of Cordoba (Spain) and his young disciple, they belonged to the 'martyr movement' and were executed for invading the city's Friday Mosque and denouncing Islam.

Roger Cadwallador (Bl) {2}

27 August

d. 1610. A farmer's son from Stretton Sugwas (Herefordshire), he studied at Rheims and Valladolid and was ordained at the latter place in 1593. He was a priest in Herefordshire and Powys for sixteen years before being seized near Hereford and executed at Leominster. He was beatified in 1987. Cf. **England, Martyrs of**.

Roger of Canna (St) {2}

30 December

C12th. He was a bishop of Canna in Apulia, and was allegedly from Normandy. When his city was destroyed by Muslim raiders his relics were moved to Barletta.

Roger Dickinson (Bl) {2}

7 July

d. 1591. From Lincoln, he was educated for the priesthood at Rheims and ordained there in 1583. He was hanged at Winchester with Bl Ralph Milner, a layman who had sheltered him, and was beatified in 1929. Cf. **England, Martyrs of**.

Roger Filcock (Bl) {2}

27 February

d. 1601. From Sandwich in Kent, he studied at Rheims and was ordained at Valladolid in 1597. After being a priest in London for two years he was about to leave for the Jesuit noviciate when he was arrested, but he became a Jesuit in prison. He was executed at Tyburn with St Anne Line and Bl Mark Barkworth and was beatified in 1987. Cf. **England, Martyrs of**.

Roger James (Bl) {2}

15 November

Cf. **Benedictine Martyrs of the Reformation**.

Roger of Todi (Bl) {2}

5 January

d. 1237. St Francis of Assisi praised this disciple of his for the charity that he showed. He died at Todi (Italy), but was only confirmed as a beatus by his insertion into the new Roman Martyrology.

Roger Wrenn (Bl) {2}

18 March

Cf. **John Thules and Roger Wrenn**.

Roland de' Medici (Bl) {2}

15 September

d. 1386. Related to the famous ruling family of Florence, he lived without any shelter for twenty-six years in the forests around Parma

(Italy). He died at Borgone and his cultus was confirmed for Borgo San Donnino in 1852.

Roland-Mary Rivi (Bl) {2 –add}

13 April
1931–45. From the village of San Valentino near Modena, Italy, he entered the diocesan junior seminary in 1942 but was sent home two years later when the seminary was closed by the German occupiers. However, he continued to wear his seminary cassock at all times, which made him identifiable by Communist partisans. While walking and studying in a forest near Monchio, he was abducted by a band of Communists who tortured him for three days before shooting him. He was beatified as a martyr in 2013, the first seminarian to be so honoured.

Rollock cf. **Roch**.

Romacharius (St) {2}

18 November
C6th. He was a bishop of Coutences (France).

(Romana) (St) {4 –deleted}

23 February
C4th? According to the legendary biography of Pope St Sylvester, she was a Roman maiden who lived as a hermit in a cave (or ruined cellar) on the banks of the Tiber.

Romanus and David cf. **Boris and Gleb**.

Romanus Adame Rosales (St) {1 –group}

21 April
1859–1927. From Teocaltiche, he became a diocesan priest of Guadalajara in 1890 and founded several rural Mass centres and schools During the Cristero War he was arrested, tortured and deprived of food and drink before being shot for his priesthood at Nochistlán near Guadalajara in Mexico. Cf. **Mexico, Martyrs of**.

Romanus of Antioch (St) {2, 4}

18 November
d. 304. The former was a young deacon martyred at Antioch (Syria) in the reign of Diocletian. A companion Barulas was listed in the old Roman Martyrology as a young boy, but has been deleted.

Romanus Archutowski (Bl) {2}

18 April
1882–1943. A Polish priest, he died of illtreatment at the concentration camp at Majdanek. Cf. **Poland, Martyrs of the Nazi Occupation of**.

Romanus of Auxerre (St) {2, 4}

6 October
d. ?564. He was a bishop of Auxerre (France).

Romanus Aybara (Bl) {2}

8 September
d. 1628. A Japanese Dominican tertiary, he was beheaded at Nagasaki with his father Paul and brother Leo. Cf. **Dominic Castellet and Comps** and **Japan, Martyrs of**.

Romanus of Condat (St) {2}

28 February
d. 463. A Gallo-Roman, when aged thirty-five he went to live as a hermit in the Jura mountains (France) and was joined by St Lupicinus, his brother. They attracted disciples and thus were founded the abbeys of Condat (later known as St-Oyend) and Leuconne. They were joint superiors of these, and also founded the nunnery of La Beaume (afterwards St-Romain-de-la-Roche) where their sister was superior.

Romanus Lysko (Bl) {2}

14 October
1914–49. A diocesan priest of the Polish city of Lwow (now Lviv in Ukraine), he died in prison there after the area had been annexed by the Soviet Union. Cf. **Nicholas Čarneckyj and 24 Comps**.

Romanus of Le Mans (St) {2, 4}

24 November
d. c.380. A Gallo-Roman missionary priest, he worked along the estuary of the Gironde north of Bordeaux (France) and died at Blaye. He is a patron of sailors.

Romanus Matsuka Miota (Bl) {2}

27 November
d. 1619. A Japanese layman related to the rulers of Hirado-jima, he was born at Omura and beheaded at Nagasaki. Cf. **Thomas Koteda and Comps** and **Japan, Martyrs of**.

Romanus the Melodist (St) {2}

1 October
d. 555–65. From Syria, he was a deacon at Beirut before becoming a priest at Constantinople. He was the greatest Byzantine hymnographer, and allegedly wrote a thousand hymns. Some eighty of these are extant, and some may be misattributed. Their literary quality is very high.

(Romanus of Nepi) (St) {4 –deleted}

24 August
C1st? He was allegedly a disciple of St Ptolemy of Nepi, succeeded him as bishop of that place in Tuscany (Italy) and was himself martyred.

Romanus Ostiarius (St) {2, 3}

9 August
d. ?258. There are no reliable data concerning him. He was martyred at about the same time as St Laurence, and one legend describes him as a soldier converted by the latter. He was probably a Roman church doorkeeper, as is indicated by his surname. His cultus was confined to local calendars in 1969.

Romanus of Rouen (St) {2, 4}

23 October
d. ?644. A Frankish nobleman and courtier, he became bishop of Rouen (France) in ?629 and had a special concern for prisoners. He also set about eliminating paganism from his diocese, especially in rural areas (a task not seriously attempted by his Gallo-Roman predecessors).

Romanus Sitko (Bl) {2}

12 October
1880–1942. A Polish priest, he died of ill-treatment at the concentration camp at Auschwitz. Cf. **Poland, Martyrs of the Nazi Occupation of**.

Romaric (St) {2, 4}

8 December
d. 653. A Merovingian nobleman and courtier, he became a monk and disciple of St Amatus at Luxeuil (France) and founded the double monastery on his estate on the river Moselle later named Remiremont after him. St Amatus was the first abbot and St Romaric the second. The Divine Office was celebrated there continuously, the monastics taking turns in choir in seven shifts.

Rome (Martyrs of) (SS)

Despite its importance in the church as a whole, the church at Rome was marginal to the general life of the city for much of the imperial period. Rome was a stronghold of paganism until the C5th, and Christianity was probably regarded with suspicion and contempt by most of the population there as well as by the imperial government before 313. Thus the church was especially vulnerable to persecution. Apart from the **Protomartyrs of Rome**, the Roman Martyrology lists one anonymous group of martyrs:

22 December

? A group of thirty were martyred in the reign of Diocletian and buried on the Via Lavicana 'between the two laurels' (ad Duas Lauros).

Another fifteen such entries have been deleted:

25 March

? A group of two hundred and sixty-two martyrs, they were probably identical with those on 1 March.

17 June

? A group of two hundred and sixty-two, they were alleged to have been martyred in the reign of Diocletian and to have been buried on the Via Salaria but were apparently identical with the above and with those of the year 269.

14 March

C1st? According to the unreliable acta of SS Processus and Martinian, forty-seven were baptized by St Peter and martyred the same day in the reign of Nero.

2 July

C1st? Three soldiers, according to the legend they were converted during the execution of St Paul and were themselves martyred.

10 April

Early C2nd? According to the probably fictional narrative, several criminals imprisoned with Pope St Alexander were baptized by him and were subsequently taken to Ostia and put on board an old boat which was then taken out to sea and scuttled.

2 March

Early C3rd? A large number were martyred in the reign of Alexander Severus by the prefect Ulpian.

13 January

Mid C3rd? Forty soldiers were martyred on the Via Lavicana in the reign of Gallienus.

10 February

Mid C3rd? Ten soldiers were martyred on the Via Lavicana.

1 March

Mid C3rd? Two hundred and sixty were put to work as slaves in sand-pits on the Salarian Way and then used for archery practice in the amphitheatre in the reign of Claudius II.

4 March

Mid C3rd? Nine hundred martyrs were buried in the catacombs of Callistus on the Appian Way, concerning whom no details are extant.

25 October

Mid C3rd? Forty-six soldiers and one hundred and twenty-one civilians were martyred in the reign of Claudius II.

10 August

Late C3rd? One hundred and sixty-five were martyred in the reign of Aurelian.

1 January

Early C4th? Thirty soldiers were martyred in the reign of Diocletian.

2 January

Early C4th? Many were martyred in the reign of Diocletian for refusing to hand over sacred texts.

5 August

Early C4th? Twenty-three were martyred on the Salarian Way in the reign of Diocletian.

Romedius (St) {2}

15 January

C8th? He was a hermit at Tavo near Trento (Italy), where his shrine is now established. His cultus was confirmed for Trento in 1907.

Romeo (Romaeus) *(Bl)*

4 March

d. 1380. An Italian Carmelite lay brother, he accompanied St Avertanus on pilgrimage to the Holy Land from Limoges (France) but they both apparently died of plague at Lucca (Italy). His cultus was confirmed for the Carmelites in 1842, but he is not in the Roman Martyrology. His name is the origin of that of the famous Shakespearean lover.

Romuald (St) {1, 3}

19 June

?951–1027. A nobleman of Ravenna (Italy), in his youth he saw his father commit a murder and resolved to make vicarious atonement by becoming a monk at the Benedictine abbey of Classe near Ravenna. In 996 he was elected abbot, but he resigned in 999 and thereupon led a wandering life in northern Italy and southern France, founding hermitages and monasteries. The best known of these is Camaldoli near Arezzo (Italy), founded in 1009, which became the mother house of a Benedictine congregation combining the eremitic life of an Eastern laura with the cenobitic monachism of the West. He made repeated attempts to undertake missionary work among the Magyars and Slavs. He died at Val di Castro near Camaldoli.

(Romula, Redempta and Herundo) *(SS)* {4 –deleted}

23 July

d. c.580. They were allegedly three Roman maidens who lived an austere life of prayer and solitude near the church of St Mary Major in Rome.

(Romulus) *(St)* {4 –deleted}

5 September

C2nd? He was allegedly a court official of the emperor Trajan, and was whipped and beheaded after rebuking him for persecuting Christians while on campaign at Melitene in Armenia. This story is fictional.

(Romulus and Secundus) *(SS)* {4 –deleted}

24 March

? They were listed as two brothers who were martyred in Roman Africa. Secundus also appears as Secundulus.

Romulus of Fiesole *(St)* {2, 4}

6 July

? He was a deacon martyred Fiesole near Florence (Italy). According to his fictitious acta, he was consecrated first bishop of the place by St Peter and was martyred with several companions in the reign of Domitian. This is typical of several such malicious stories invented to further the prestige of old-established bishoprics in Italy and France.

Romulus (Remo) of Genoa *(St)* {2}

13 October

C5th. There is no reliable evidence concerning this bishop of Genoa (Italy). He died at the Riviera town later named San Remo after him.

Romulus of Saissy *(St)* {2}

1 November

C5th. He was abbot of St Baudilius's Abbey near Nîmes (France) but Arab raids drove the community away and they settled in a ruined monastery at Saissy-les-Bois near Nevers.

Ronald *(St)*

20 August

d. 1158. An earl of Orkney (Scotland), he built the cathedral of St Magnus at Kirkwall but was assassinated by rebels and was then venerated as a martyr. His name is still fairly popular for boys.

Ronan (St) {2}

1 June
C7–8th. He was a missionary bishop from Ireland who settled in a forest in Brittany (France). There are about a dozen other Celtic saints listed of this name, involving Cornwall (England) also, and the evidence is very confused. Cf. **Rumon**.

Roque cf. **Roch**.

Rosalia of Palermo (St) {2, 4}

4 September
C12th. According to her tomb inscription, discovered with her relics in 1624, she was a hermit in a cave on Mt Coschina near Bivona and later in another cave on Mt Pellegrino near Palermo. She is a patron of the latter place. The old Roman Martyrology listed her twice in error, also on 15 July.

Rosalia Rendu (Bl) {2}

7 February
1786–1856. Of a rural family near Gex in France, she was aged three when the French Revolution broke out. Her household became a refuge for priests refusing to take the revolutionary oath, which helped foster the faith which led her to join the Sisters of Charity of St Vincent de Paul in 1802. She was sent to the Mouffetard district of Paris, alleged to have been one of the poorest in the city, and became superior of the convent there in 1815. Her charitable work among poor people and her intense life of prayer led her to be awarded the Legion of Honour by Napoleon III in 1852. Despite always being in fragile health, she lived until almost seventy. She was beatified in 2003.

Rosaria Quintana Argos and Comps (BB) {2}

d. 1936. They were three Third Order Capuchin Sisters of the Holy Family, martyred during the Spanish Civil War. BB Rosaria and Seraphina Fernández Ibero were killed at Puzol near Valencia on 23 August, and Bl Frances-Xavier Fenollosa Alcaina was killed at Gilet on 27 September. Cf. **Spanish Civil War, Martyrs of**.

Rose Chen Anxie (St) {1 –group}

5 July
Cf. **Teresa Chen Jinjie and Rose Chen Aixie**.

Rose-Philippine Duchesne cf. **Philippine Duchesne**.

Rose Fan Hui (St) {1 –group}

16 August
1855–1900. From Fanjiazhuang near Wujiao in Hebei (China), she became a schoolteacher but her school was closed during the Boxer Uprising and she hid in the village's fields. She was betrayed, however, and a gang of Boxers slashed her with knives and threw her into a river to drown. Cf. **China, Martyrs of**.

Rose-Margaret Flesch (Bl) {2 –add}

1826–1906. She was born into a poor working-class family near Koblenz in Germany, and had to work as a labourer to help support her family when her father died when she was aged sixteen. Despite this she was solicitous for poor and sick people elsewhere, and she and one of her sisters started a small orphanage at Waldbreitbach in 1851 while still working as labourers. Later two others joined her, and this was the beginning of the 'Franciscan Sisters of the Blessed Virgin Mary of the Angels'. When she died there were 900 sisters in 72 houses. She was beatified in 2008.

Rose-of-Lima Flores (St) {1, 3}

23 August
1586–1617. Born of Spanish parents at Lima in Peru, from childhood she set out to imitate

St Catherine of Siena while living at her family home as a Dominican tertiary. Her physical austerities were such as to amount to self-torture, and she suffered from mental as well as physical sickness. She was, however, favoured with extraordinary mystical graces. She was the first American to be canonized (in 1671) and is the patron of South America. Her attribute is a thorny rose or roses, and she is sometimes depicted with the Holy Infant.

Rose Kim (St) {1 –group}

20 July
Cf. **Mary-Magdalen Yi Yŏn-hŭi and Comps**.

Rose-Frances-Mary-of-Sorrows Molas y Vallvé (St) {2}

11 June
1815–76. From Reus near Tarragona (Spain), she saw her vocation as being in hospital work and ran away from home to join a sodality at the local hospital. She soon became their leader, and they also started teaching in local schools. In 1858 she founded the 'Sisters of Our Lady of Consolation' at Tortosa. She was canonized in 1988.

Rose of Viterbo (Bl) {2}

6 March
1234–52. She was born at Viterbo (Italy) into a poor family. Even as a little girl she received mystical graces, and used to speak out in the streets against the Ghibellines (the anti-papal faction) and in favour of the pope. This caused her and her family to be expelled from the city for a time. She tried to join the Poor Clare nunnery in the city and was repeatedly refused, but she was buried there after her death by order of the pope. She has been listed as a beatus and as a Franciscan tertiary by the Roman Martyrology.

Rose Venerini (St) {2}

7 May
1656–1728. After her fiancé died she had to start caring for her widowed mother, so she began to teach religion to women and girls at her home in Verona (Italy) and opened a free school there in 1685 with three companions. This was the beginning of the 'Verona Sisters', which had forty houses by the time she died at Rome. Their special charism is in maintaining liaison between school, child and parents. She was canonized in 2006.

Rose Zhao (St) {1 –group}

20 June
Cf. **Mary Zhao Guozhi and Comps**.
Rosendo cf. **Rudesind**.

Rosseline de Villeneuve (Bl) {2}

17 January
d. 1329. A noblewoman from near Fréjus in Provence (France), she became a Carthusian nun at Bertrand and then prioress of Celle-Roubaud. She had frequent visions and other mystical graces, and her cultus was confirmed in 1851.

Rotobald (St) {2}

12 October
d. 1254. He was a bishop of Pavia (Italy), noted for his abstinent life and for his zeal for the liturgy and for obtaining sacred relics.

Rouin cf. **Rodingus**.

Ruderic (Roderick) and Solomon (Salomon) (SS) {2, 4}

13 March
d. 857. The former was a priest at Cordoba (Spain) who was accused by his brother of apostasy from Islam. In prison he met the

latter, accused of the same charge, and they were executed together.

Ruderic Aguilar Alemán (St) {1 –group}

28 October
1875–1928. From Sayula, he became a diocesan priest of Guzmán in Mexico in 1905. When the Cristero War broke out he was parish priest of Tula, and continued his ministry in secret. However, he was betrayed by one of his parishioners and killed for his priesthood at Ejutla near Guadalajara by being hanged from a tree in the town square by soldiers. Cf. **Mexico, Martyrs of.**

Rudesind (Rosendo) (St) {2}

1 March
907–77. A nobleman of Galicia (Spain), he became bishop of Mondoñedo when aged eighteen but was transferred to Compostella after the deposition of an unworthy bishop there. He had to organize resistance to raids by Norsemen and Muslims before being ejected in turn by the one deposed, after which he founded the Benedictine abbey of Celanova, became a monk there and founded other monasteries. He died as second abbot of Celanova and was canonized in 1195.

Rudolf Aquaviva and Comps (BB) {2}

25 July
d. 1583. Born at Atri near Pescara (Italy) in 1550, a nephew of a Jesuit general, he became a Jesuit himself and taught philosophy at Goa in India from 1578 to 1580. Goa was the centre of the Portuguese mercantile empire in the Far East and of corresponding missionary activity. He was at the court of the Mughal emperor Akbar from 1580, and was killed with four fellow missionaries on the island of Salsette next to Bombay, which the Portuguese were trying to bring under their rule. The others were Alphonsus Pacheco, Anthony Francisco, Francis Aranha and Peter Berna. They were beatified in 1893.

Rufillus (Ruffilius) (St) {2, 4}

18 July
C5th. He was the alleged first bishop of Forlimpopoli near Forli in Emilia (Italy).

Rufina and Secunda (SS) {2, 4}

10 July
? They were martyred and buried at a locality called Selva Candida to the west of Rome, which in their time was a wood but is now a suburb. On the site (now lost) was built a basilica, which became one of the two ancient cathedrals of the later see of Porto Santa Rufina.

(Rufinus, Mark, Valerius and Comps) (SS) *{4 –deleted}*

16 November
? They were listed as martyrs of Rom an Africa.

(Rufinus and Martia) (SS) *{4 –deleted}*

21 June
? They were listed as early martyrs at Syracuse (Sicily).

(Rufinus and Rufinian) (SS) *{4 –deleted}*

9 September
? They are listed as brothers who were martyred together, but nothing else is known.

Rufinus and Secundus (SS) {2, 3}

10 July
? These Roman martyrs were buried on the Via Cornelia and had their relics transferred to the Lateran basilica in the C12th. Nothing is known about them. Since 1969 their cultus has been confined to local calendars.

(Rufinus, Silvanus and Vitalicus) (SS)
{4 –deleted}

4 September
? They are listed as three children who were among a large group of martyrs at Ancyra (Asia Minor, now Ankara in Turkey).

Rufinus of Assisi (St) {2, 4}

11 August
C4th? He was by tradition the first bishop of Assisi (Italy) and a martyr.

(Rufinus of Capua) (St) {4 –deleted}

27 August
C5th. He was allegedly a bishop of Capua (Italy), and his shrine is in the cathedral there.

(Rufinus of Mantua) (St) {4 –deleted}

19 August
? He has an ancient cultus at Mantua (Italy), but nothing is known about him except that he may have been a priest.

(Rufinus of the Marsi and Comps) (SS) {4 –deleted}

11 August
? He was listed in the old Roman Martyrology as 'bishop of the Marsi', but may be the same as St Rufinus of Assisi. Nothing is recorded about his companions.

(Rufus and Carpophorus) (SS) {4 –deleted}

27 August
Early C3rd? They were listed as martyrs of the reign of Diocletian. Their acta are unreliable, and nothing is known about them.

Rufus and Zosimus (SS) {2, 4}

17 October
d. 107. From Philippi in Macedonia (Greece), they were taken to Rome with St Ignatius of Antioch and thrown to the wild animals in the amphitheatre two days before the latter's own martyrdom.

Rufus of Avignon (St) {2}

14 November
C4th. Venerated as the first bishop of Avignon (France), he certainly existed but the extant biographies are unhistorical and anachronistic.

Rufus of Capua (St) {2, 4}

27 August
? He was a martyr Capua (Italy). The old Roman Martyrology listed him as a bishop of that place and a disciple of St Apollinaris of Ravenna, but in this confused him with Rufinus of Capua.

Rufus of Glendalough (St)

2 April
C6th? He was a hermit at Glendalough in Co. Wicklow (Ireland) where he was buried, and may have been a bishop.

Rufus Ishimoto (Bl) {2}

10 September
1622. A Japanese layman, he was beheaded at Nagasaki in the 'Great Martyrdom'. Cf. **Charles Spinola and Comps**, **Great Martyrdom at Nagasaki** and **Japan, Martyrs of**.

(Rufus of Metz) (St) {4 –deleted}

7 November
d. c.400. He was bishop of Metz (France) for about twenty-nine years, and is perhaps identical with the Rufus of Metz mentioned in 386 in connection within the Priscillianist controversy.

Rufus of Rome (St) {2, 4}

21 November
d. c.90. He is mentioned by St Paul in his letter to the Romans, 16:13, and a guess is that

he was the son of Simon of Cyrene mentioned in the Gospel of Mark 15:21. A later tradition, not accepted by the Roman Martyrology, made him a bishop in the East.

(Rufus of Rome and Comps) (SS) {4 –deleted}

28 November
d. 304. A Roman, he was listed as martyred with his entire household in the reign of Diocletian.

Rule cf. **Regulus**.

Rumold (Rumbold, Rombauld) (St) {2, 4}

24 June
d. 775. As far as can be ascertained from his unreliable biography he was a monk, probably an Anglo-Saxon, who became a missionary bishop and worked under St Willibrord in Holland and Brabant. He was murdered near Mechelen near Brussels (Belgium) and is patron of the cathedral there. The old Roman Martyrology alleged that he was an Irish bishop of Dublin, who in reality was a different person.

Rumwold (St)

28 August
d. ?650. According to his weird legend, he was a three-day-old baby prince of Northumbria who, immediately after baptism, spoke like an adult in making a profession of faith and then died at King's Sutton in Northants (England). He had a popular cultus centred on Brackley (Northants) and Buckingham before the Reformation, but the story is possibly a fictional tale in defence of infant baptism.

Rupert of Bingen (St) {2}

15 May
C9th. A young nobleman, he became a hermit on a hill near Bingen (Germany) later named Rupertsberg after him, and founded several churches. St Hildegard fostered his cultus, together with his mother Bertha who allegedly accompanied him and who has been deleted from the Roman Martyrology.

Rupert Mayer (Bl) {2}

3 November
1876–1945. Born in Stuttgart (Germany), he became a priest at Rottenburg in 1899 but joined the Jesuits a year later. From 1906 to 1912 he worked in various parts of Germany, noting the social effects of rapid industrialization, and became the chaplain for new immigrants to Munich in danger of losing touch with the church. In 1939 the Nazis sent him to Sachsenhausen but did not want him to become a martyr and put him in isolation in the Benedictine abbey of Ettal instead. He died there of a stroke and was beatified in 1987.

Rupert (Hrodbert, Robert) of Salzburg (St) {2, 4}

27 March
d. ?718. Apparently from France, he became missionary bishop at Worms (Germany) and worked at Regensburg and down the Danube. The Duke of Bavaria gave him the ruined town of Iuvavum which he rebuilt as Salzburg (Austria), becoming the first archbishop and founding St Peter's Abbey (with school and church attached) and the nunnery of Nonnberg, for which he made his niece St Erentrude abbess. He is venerated as an apostle of Bavaria and Austria.

Rusticola of Arles (St) {2}

11 August
d. 632. She was abbess of the nunnery at Arles (France) for about sixty years.

Rusticus of Clermont (St) {2, 4}

24 September
C5th. He became bishop of Clermont-Auvergne (France) in 426.

Rusticus of Narbonne (St) {2, 4}

26 October
d. ?461. A monk of Lérins, he became bishop of Narbonne (France) and was present at the council of Ephesus in 431.

(Rusticus of Trier) *(St) {4 –deleted}*

14 October
d. 574. Bishop of Trier (Germany), he was allegedly accused of sexual impurity by St Goar so resigned and retired to the latter's hermitage. This is probably a fable.

Rutilius (St) {2, 4}

2 August
d. a.212. A Roman African in what is now Algeria, during a persecution he became a fugitive and paid money to obtain exemption from sacrifice but was at length arrested and bravely witnessed to his faith. The story was given by Tertullian in his *De Fuga in Persecutione*.

(Rutilus and Comps) *(SS) {4 –deleted}*

4 June
? They were listed as martyrs of Sabaria, now Szombathely (Hungary).

S

(Sabas the Goth and Comps -1) *(SS)*
{4 –deleted}

24 April
C3rd? A Christian officer of Gothic descent, he was allegedly martyred with seventy companions at Rome in the reign of Aurelian. They may be a duplicate of those in the next entry.

Sabas the Goth -2 (SS) {2, 4}

12 April
d. 372. A Visigoth and a church reader in what is now Romania, he was captured by pagan soldiers and refused to eat food which had been sacrificed to idols. Then he was tortured to death and thrown into the river Mussovo near Tirgovişti, upstream from Bucharest. Several others allegedly died with him, but the Roman Martyrology has deleted them.

Sabas the Great (St) {1, 3}

5 December
439–532. A Cappadocian, when young he fled a family quarrel and became a monk at various places in the Judaean Desert in the Holy Land. He eventually founded a famous laura (eremitic monastery) there, which was named Mar Saba after him and which has been a functioning monastery from his time to the present. It has been a major source of Eastern monastic custom. He was appointed archimandrite over all the monasteries of the Holy Land, and as such was important in the local campaign against Monophysitism. His incorrupt body, which had been stolen by the Venetians, was returned to his monastery (now Orthodox) in 1965 as an ecumenical gesture. His cultus was confined to local calendars in 1969.

Sabas Reyes Salazar (St) {1 –group}

13 April
1879–1927. From Cocula near Guadalajara in Mexico, he became a diocesan priest of Tamaulipas in 1911 but fled back to Guadalajara during the Mexican Revolution. There he worked in various parishes, and continued his ministry in secret after persecution broke out. During the Cristero War he was picked up on the orders of a high-ranking officer of the government forces, tortured to reveal the whereabouts of other priests and finally shot at Totoclán near Guadlajara. Cf. **Mexico, Martyrs of**.

Sabas the Younger (St) {2}

5 February
d. 995. He was one of the two sons of St Christopher of Collesano (the other was St Macarius of Collesano), and followed the family's fortunes as a Byzantine-rite monk in Sicily, Calabria and Basilicata but eventually ended up in Rome where he died at the monastery of St Caesarius.

(Sabina of Milan) *(St)* *{4 –deleted}*

30 January
Early C4th? The legend is that she was a married woman of Milan (Italy) who, during the persecution of Diocletian, visited the martyrs in prison and buried their bodies after execution. Then she died while praying at the tomb of SS Nabor and Felix.

Sabina Petrilli (Bl) {2}

18 April
1851–1923. From Siena (Italy), she had to help to educate and catechize her younger siblings, and this helped to give her a precocious vocation to help poor girls. She founded the 'Sisters of St Catherine of Siena' in 1874 when aged twenty-three, although they only took formal vows in 1900. She developed cancer in 1890, and from this year onwards, it was a long battle for her, and she died eventually. She was beatified in 1988.

Sabina of Rome (St) {2, 3}

29 August
? A famous basilica on the Aventine in Rome is dedicated to her, and she was probably a rich noblewoman who founded it in the fourth century and not (as her unreliable acta assert) a martyr. Nothing is known about her, and her cultus was confined to her basilica in 1969.

(Sabina of Troyes) (St) {4 –deleted}

29 August
C3rd? Alleged to have been the sister of St Sabinian of Troyes (France), she has a cultus as a virgin at that place, but nothing is known about her.

Sabinian and Potentian (SS) {2, 4}

19 October
C4th? According to tradition they were the first and second bishops of Sens (France) and were martyred. The legend that they were disciples of St Peter is worthless. They are patrons of the diocese.

Sabinian (Savinien) of Troyes (St) {2, 4}

24 January
C3rd. He was allegedly martyred at Troyes (France) in one of the early persecutions. The local tradition is that he and St Sabina, his sister, were refugees from Samos in the Aegean Sea.

(Sabinus and Cyprian) (SS) {4 –deleted}

11 July
? They are listed in the old Roman Martyrology as brothers who were martyred at 'Brixia'. This was taken to be either Brescia (Italy) or La Bresse in Poitou (France), and they were venerated in both places.

Sabinus of Spoleto (St) {2, 4}

7 December
d. c.300. He was a bishop of Spoleto (Italy) who was martyred. His unreliable legend mentions companion martyrs, who have been deleted from the Roman Martyrology. These are described as two deacons, Exuperantius and Marcellus, and a called Venustian with his family.

(Sabinus, Julian and Comps) (SS) {4 –deleted}

20 July
? They were listed as sixteen Syrians martyred at Damascus. Maximus, Macrobius, Cassia and Paula are also listed.

Sabinus of Canosa (St) {2, 4}

9 February
d. ?566. Bishop of Canosa in Apulia (Italy), he was papal legate of Pope St Agapitus I at the court of Emperor Justinian I for a year from 535. When his city was destroyed his relics were taken to Bari, of which place he is the patron.

Sabinus of Hermopolis (St) {2, 4}

13 March
Early C4th. A nobleman of Egypt, he was drowned in the Nile at Antinoë in the reign of Diocletian.

Sabinus of Piacenza (St) {2, 4}

11 December
End C4th. While a deacon at Milan he was sent by Pope St Damasus to help resolve the Meletian schism at Antioch (Syria). Then he became bishop of Piacenza (Italy) and a friend of St Ambrose, who used to send him his writings for revision.

(Sabinus of Poitiers) (St) {4 –deleted}

11 July
C5th. Allegedly a disciple of St Germanus of Auxerre at Poitiers (France), he is venerated locally.

Sabinus (Savin) of Tarbes (St) {2}

9 October
C5th. According to the dubious tradition he was born at Barcelona, educated at Poitiers, became a monk at Ligugé and died as a hermit at Tarbes in the Pyrenees (France). The Roman Martyrology accepts the last assertion.

Sacerdos (Sardot, Serdot) of Limoges (St) {2, 4}

5 May
C8th. From Périgord (France), he became a monk and eventually the abbot-founder of Calabre before being made bishop of Limoges.

Sacerdos of Lyons (St) {2, 4}

11 September
d. 552. He became bishop of Lyons (France) in 544 and was an adviser of King Childebert. He presided at the council of Orleans in 549.

Sadoc of Sandomir and Comps (BB) {2}

2 June
d. 1250. He was a disciple of St Dominic, who sent him to Hungary. Later he moved to Poland where he founded a Dominican friary at Sandomir and became its prior. The town was destroyed in a Mongol raid and he and the other forty-eight brethren were massacred in their church while singing the *Salve Regina*. Their cultus was confirmed for the Dominicans in 1807. Cf. 'Poland' in lists of national martyrs in appendix.

Sadoc of Seleucia and Comps (SS) {2, 4}

20 February
d. 345 or 342. The metropolitan of Seleucia-Ctesiphon in Persian Mesopotamia (modern Iraq) and head of the Persian church, he was arrested in the persecution of Shah Shapur II with one hundred and twenty-eight others. Most of these were martyred at once, but he was kept with eight companions for five months in a filthy prison at Bei-Lapat before being executed.

Sagar (St) {2, 4}

6 October
d. c.175. Bishop of Laodicea in Phrygia (Asia Minor), he was martyred in the reign of Marcus Aurelius. The tradition that he was a disciple of St Paul is false.

Salaberga (St) {2, 4}

22 September
d. ?664. From near Langres (France), as a young widow she married St Blandinus and had five children, including SS Anstrudis and Baldwin of Laon. The couple separated to become consecrated religious, and she founded the great double monastery of St John the Baptist at Laon, dying there as abbess.

(Sallustian) (St) {4 –deleted}

8 June
? He has an ancient cultus in Sardinia, but the sources differ as to whether he was a martyr or a hermit.

Salome cf. **Mary Salome**.

Salome of Galicia (Bl) {2}

17 November
?1219–68. Daughter of Prince Lesko of Poland, when aged three she was betrothed to Prince Coloman of Galicia (in what is now the

western Ukraine). In 1241 her husband was killed in the Mongol incursion, whereupon she founded a Poor Clare nunnery at Strala and died as a nun there. Her shrine is at the Poor Clare nunnery at Cracow, and her cultus was confirmed for there and Galicia in 1673.

Salomon cf. **Solomon**.

Salonius of Geneva (St) {2, 4}

28 September
d. p450. He was a bishop of Geneva (Switzerland) after having been a monk at Lérins. An early scribal error led him to be listed as 'Solomon of Genoa' in the old Roman Martyrology.

Salvator-of-Horta Grionesos (St) {2}

18 March
1520–67. From Santa Coloma de Farnés near Gerona (Spain), he was a shoemaker before becoming a Franciscan lay brother at Barcelona. He spent most of his life as cook at the friary of Horta near Tortosa, Spain, but died at the friary of Cagliari in Sardinia. He was canonized in 1940.

Salvator Huerta Gutiérrez (Bl) {2 –add}

3 April
Cf. **Joseph-Lucian-Ezekiel and Salvator Huerta Gutiérrez**.

Salvator Lara Puente (St) {1 –group}

15 August
Cf. **Aloysius Batis Sainz and Comps**.

Salvator Lilli and Comps (BB) {2}

22 November
1853–95. Born in the Abruzzi (Italy), he became a Franciscan in 1870 and went to the Holy Land. Then he was sent to the region of Kahramurasc in Turkey (northeast of Aleppo) and became pastor at the mission of Mujuk-Deresi, where his people were mostly Armenian. Starting in 1894, the Ottoman government carried out a systematic policy of massacre and repression of the native Christians of eastern Anatolia. In 1895 a detachment of Turkish soldiers arrived at the mission, offered Bl Salvator and some others the choice between conversion to Islam or death and, on their refusal, shot them and burnt their bodies. They were beatified in 1982. The government policy culminated in the Armenian genocide in the First World War, and led to the deaths of between one and three million Christians. The companions were: John Balžinian, K'adir Xodianian, Cerun K'uražinian, Vardavar Dimbalacian, Paul Ieremianinian, David Davidian and Theodore Davidian. The last two were brothers.

Salvinus of Verona (St) {4 –deleted}

12 October
C6th? He was allegedly a bishop of Verona.

Salvius and his disciple (SS) {2, 4}

26 June
C8th. Salvius was a missionary bishop in the district of Angoulême (France) who went to Valenciennes to evangelize the Flemish. He was seized, imprisoned, killed and buried with an anonymous companion by a relative of the local count, and when the bodies were exhumed the latter was on top. He was hence given the nickname Superius, 'one on top', but this has been deleted from the Roman Martyrology.

Salvius of Albi (St) {2, 4}

10 September
d. 584. He was in turn a lawyer, a monk, an abbot and a hermit before becoming bishop of Albi (France) in 574. He allegedly died as a result of nursing sufferers of an epidemic.

Salvius (Salve, Sauve) of Amiens (St) {2, 4}

28 October
d. ?625. He was a bishop of Amiens (France) and had his shrine at Montreuil sur Mer near Boulogne. The old Roman Martyrology listed him as a martyr in error, and he has been confused with the others of the same name.

Salvius of Carthage (St) {2, 4}

11 January
C3rd? A Roman African martyr, he had his shrine at Carthage, and St Augustine preached in his honour.

Salvius Huix Miralpeix (Bl) {2 –add}

5 August
1877–1936. From near Gerona in Spain, he became a diocesan priest in 1903 and then joined the Oratorians at Vic. In 1927 he was made bishop of Ibiza, and in 1935 that of Lérida. At the start of the Spanish Civil War he initially hid, but gave himself up and was imprisoned. Then he was massacred with twenty other prisoners during a journey to Barcelona with the connivance of the Republican authorities at Lérida. He was beatified in 2013. Cf. **Spanish Civil War, Martyrs of** and list.

Samson of Caldey (St) {2, 4}

28 July
c.490–?565. Born in Wales, he was a disciple of St Illtyd before becoming a monk and then abbot of the monastery on Caldey Island. After a visit to Ireland he was ordained as a missionary bishop by St Dubricius, spent some time in Cornwall and finally went to Brittany (France). There he spent the rest of life, fixing his missionary headquarters at a monastery at Dol (although no permanent diocese was established there for many centuries to come). His veneration is very popular in Brittany and Wales.

Samson Xenodochius (St) {2, 4}

27 June
d. 560. A rich citizen of Constantinople, he was ordained and studied medicine in order to devote his life to the spiritual and physical care of the sick and destitute (his surname means 'the Hospitable'). He founded a hospital near Hagia Sophia.

Samuel the Prophet (St) {2}

20 August
He features as the last of the great judges of Israel in the First Book of Samuel in the Old Testament.

Sancius (St) {2, 4}

5 June
d. 851. From Albi (France), he was captured in a Muslim raid and brought to Cordoba (Spain) as a prisoner of war. There he was educated at the court of the Umayyad emir and was enrolled into his bodyguard, but refused to convert to Islam and was impaled (an act contrary to Muslim law).

Sanctes of Cori (Bl) {2}

5 October
d. 1392. From Cori, near Velletri (Italy), he became an Augustinian friar and was famous as a home missionary. His cultus was confirmed for Cori and Velletri in 1888.

Sanctia of Portugal (St) {2}

11 April
c.1180–1229. Daughter of King Sancho I of Portugal and sister of BB Teresa and Mafalda, she helped the Franciscans and Dominicans establish themselves in Portugal and herself became a Cistercian nun at Cellas in 1223. Her cultus was approved for Portugal in 1705.

Sanctia Szymkowiak (Bl) {2}

18 August
1910–42. From Możdżanóv in Poland, she became a Seraphic Sister at Poznan in 1936 and was sent to an orphanage at Naramowice. She had to return to the convent at Poznan during the Nazi occupation. She became famous for her holiness before her death due to tuberculosis. She was beatified in 2002.

Sanctinus (St) {2}

11 October
C4th. He is traditionally venerated as the first bishop of Verdun (France). The Roman Martyrology has not admitted the rival claim of Meaux.

Sanctus Brancasino (Bl) {2}

14 August
d. 1390. From Monte Fabri near Urbino (Italy), he became a Franciscan lay brother at Scotamento, where he spent most of his life. His cultus was approved for Urbino in 1770.

Sandalius (St) {2, 4}

3 September
C3rd? He was martyred at Cordoba (Spain).

Sándor cf. **Alexander**.
Santiago cf. **James the Great**.
Sapientia cf. **Sophia**.
Sapor cf. **Shapur**.
Saragossa cf. **Zaragoza**.

Sarah Salkaházi (Bl) {2 –add}

27 December
1899–1944. From a rich family of Kassa in Imperial Hungary (now Košice in Slovakia), she became a teacher but was inspired by the Christian Socialist movement to work as a bookbinder and shop assistant before becoming a journalist. In 1929 she became a member of the new congregation of 'Sisters of Social Service' founded in Budapest. She worked at many assignments and was director of the Catholic Working Girls' Movement. During the war she helped many refugees, including Jews and, perhaps as a result, was shot by Nazi sympathizers. She was beatified as a martyr in 2006.

Sardon cf. **Sacerdos**.

Sarmata (St) {2, 4}

11 October
d. 357. An Egyptian disciple of St Anthony, he was killed in his monastery during a raid by barbarian nomads. He is not listed as a martyr.

Saturius (St) {2}

2 October
d. 606. He was a hermit at a place called Numancia near Soria (Spain).

(Saturnina) (St) {4 –deleted}

4 June
? According to her legend she was a young German woman who fled from her impending marriage to near Arras (France), but was pursued by her betrothed and killed. She probably never existed.

Saturninus, Castulus and Comps (SS) {4 –deleted}

15 February
d. ?273. They were allegedly martyred at Terni (Italy) when St Valentine was bishop there. Magnus and Lucius were the companions.

Saturninus, Dativus, Felix and Comps (SS) {2, 4}

12 February
d. 304. A group of forty-six from Albitina in Roman Africa, they were seized while

celebrating Mass and were taken to Carthage for interrogation, and apparently all died in prison. Saturninus was the priest and had with him his four children: Saturninus and Felix (readers), Mary and Hilarion (a young boy). Dativus and another Felix were senators, and the others were listed as: Felix, Ampelius and Emeritus, readers; Rogatian, Quintus, Maximian, Telica, Rogatian, Rogatus, Januarius, Cassian, Victorian, Vincent, Cecilian, Restituta, Prima, Eve, Rogatian, Givalius, Rogatus, Pomponius, Secunda, Januaria, Saturnina, Martin, Clautus, Felix, Margaret, Major, Honorata, Regiola, Victorinus, Pelusius, Faustus, Dacian, Matron, Cecilia, Victoria, Berectina, Secunda, Matrona and Januaria. The child Hilarion, when threatened by the magistrates while his companions were being tortured, replied: 'Yes, torture me too; anyway, I am a Christian'. Their acta are genuine.

(Saturninus and Lupus) (SS) {4 –deleted}

14 October
? They were listed as martyrs of Caesarea in Cappadocia (Asia Minor).

(Saturninus, Neopolus and Comps) (SS) {4 –deleted}

2 May
d. 304. Saturninus was martyred at Alexandria (Egypt) in the reign of Diocletian, not at Rome as stated in the old Roman Martyrology. Nothing is known about the other three, including Germanus and Celestine.

(Saturninus, Nereus and Comps) (SS) {4 –deleted}

16 October
d. c.450. They are listed as some three hundred and sixty-five who were martyred in Roman Africa in the reign of the Vandal King Genseric, but they may be a duplicate of **Martinian, Saturian and Comps**.

(Saturninus, Theophilus and Revocata) (SS) {4 –deleted}

6 February
? Nothing is known about these martyrs.

(Saturninus, Thyrsus and Victor) (SS) {4 –deleted}

31 January
d. c.250. They were listed as martyrs of Alexandria (Egypt).

(Saturninus of Cagliari) (St) {4 –deleted}

30 October
d. 303. He was allegedly martyred at Cagliari (Sardinia) in the reign of Diocletian. According to his untrustworthy acta this was during a festival of Jupiter.

Saturninus of Carthage (St) {2, 4}

29 November
d. c.250. He was from Carthage (Roman Africa), and in the reign of Emperor Decius was tortured in his home city before being sent to Rome. There he was further tormented before being beheaded and buried on the Salarian Way. A companion named Sisinnius has been deleted from the Roman Martyrology.

(Saturninus of Numidia and Comps) (SS) {4 –deleted}

22 March
? They were listed as a group of ten Roman African martyrs in what is now Algeria.

Saturninus (Sernin) of Toulouse (St) {2, 3}

29 November
d. c.250. A Roman missionary, he worked in the district around Pamplona (Spain), and then in and around Toulouse (France), of which city he was apparently the first bishop. He was allegedly martyred in the persecution

of Valerian by being tied behind a wild bull which dragged him about until his body disintegrated.

(Saturninus of Verona) (St) {4 –deleted}

7 April

C4th. Nothing is known about this alleged bishop of Verona (Italy).

(Satyrus) (St) {4 –deleted}

12 January

? He was allegedly an Arab who was martyred in Achaia (Greece) for insulting an idol. Another version of the legend alleges that the idol fell to the ground when he made the sign of the cross over it. The sources are extremely confused.

Satyrus of Milan (St) {2, 4}

17 September

d. ?377. The elder brother of St Ambrose of Milan, he was a lawyer and then prefect of Liguria (Italy) before taking over the administration of his brother's property on the latter's election as bishop of Milan. The sermon preached by St Ambrose at his funeral, 'On the death of a brother', survives.

Sauman cf. Psalmodius.
Sauve cf. **Salvius**.
Savina cf. **Sabina**.
Savinian cf. **Sabinian**.
Savinus cf. **Sabinus**.

Schecelin (St) {2}

6 August

d. 1138. A hermit at Schlebusch near Cologne (Germany), he allegedly worked as a builder for the Cistercian abbey of Himmerod and imitated some early Syrian monks in never sleeping under a roof. He had his shrine at Luxembourg.

Scholastica (St) {1, 3}

10 February

d. ?547. The 'Dialogues' attributed to St Gregory the Great are the only source concerning her, and describe her as a sister (according to later tradition, the twin) of St Benedict who followed him to Montecassino (Italy) and lived a life of prayer nearby. The tradition that she was the first Benedictine nun dates from the C11th, and she is usually depicted as an abbess. Her attribute is a dove flying from her mouth. Her alleged relics are at Montecassino, with a rival set at Le Mans (France).

Scillitan Martyrs (SS) {2, 4}

17 July

d. 180. A group of seven men and five women, they were martyred at Scillium in Roman Africa in the reign of Septimius Severus. Their names were Speratus, Nartzales, Sittinus, Veturius, Felix, Aquilinus, Laetantius, Januaria, Generosa, Vestia, Donata and Secunda. The official record of the proceedings is extant, and is an important historical source. St Augustine preached three sermons in their honour at their tomb.

Scubilio Rousseau (Bl) {2}

20 December

1797–1867. Born at Annay-le-Côte in Burgundy (France), his father was a mason and he was a great help to a new parish priest when young, especially in the parish school. This led to his joining the 'Brothers of the Christian Schools' in 1822, and he went to Réunion in the Indian Ocean in 1833. He was there for twenty-three years until his death, and was beatified in 1987.

Sebald (St) {2, 4}

19 August

C9–10th. Apparently an Anglo-Saxon missionary, he became a hermit in the Reichswald near Nuremberg (Bavaria), of which city he is a patron.

Sebaste (Martyrs of) cf. **Forty Armenian Martyrs**.

Sebastian Aparicio (Bl) {2}

25 February
1502–1600. From Galicia (Spain), he was a farm worker and then a gentleman's valet before migrating to Mexico, where he was contracted by the government to maintain roads and run the postal service between Mexico City and Zacateca. After the death of his second wife, when he was seventy-two years old, he became a Franciscan lay brother at Puebla. He lived for another twenty-six years, his chief occupation being to beg for alms for the community. He was beatified in 1789.

Sebastian Kimura (Bl) {2}

10 September
d. 1622. A grandson of the first Japanese to be baptized by St Francis Xavier, when aged eighteen he became a Jesuit and worked as a catechist at Miyako before becoming the first Japanese to be ordained. After two years imprisonment at Omura he was burnt alive with Bl Charles Spinola and Comps in the Great Martyrdom and was beatified in 1867. Cf. **Japan, Martyrs of** and **Great Martyrdom at Nagasaki**.

Sebastian Maggi (Bl) {2}

16 December
d. 1496. From Brescia (Italy), he became a Dominican and was famous for his penitential sermons and for his zeal in reform. He was vicar of the Lombard province twice, and was Savonarola's confessor for a time. He died at Genoa, and his cultus was confirmed for there in 1760.

Sebastian Nam I-gwan and Comps (SS) {1 –group}

26 September
d. 1839. They were a group of twelve who were martyred at Seoul in Korea. Nine of them were beheaded after being tortured in prison, namely SS Sebastian, Agatha Chŏn Kyŏng-hyŏb, Charles Cho Shin-ch'ŏl, Columba Kim Hyo-im a virgin, Ignatius Kim Che-jun, Julitta Kim, Mary-Magdalen Hŏ Kye-im, Mary-Magdalen Pak Pong-sŏn a widow and Perpetua Hong Kŭm-ju a widow. Three died beforehand in prison on uncertain dates, namely Catherine Yi a widow, her daughter Mary-Magdalen Cho who was a virgin and Lucy Kim (the second of that name among the Korean martyrs). Cf. **Korea, Martyrs of**.

Sebastian Newdigate (Bl) {2}

19 June
d. 1535. From Harefield near Uxbridge (Mx), he was educated at Cambridge and became a Carthusian monk at the London Charterhouse. He was executed at Tyburn with two brethren, BB Humphrey Middlemore and William Exmew, for denying the royal supremacy of King Henry VIII and was beatified in 1886. Cf. **England, Martyrs of**.

Sebastian of Rome (St) {1, 3}

20 January
Early C4th. He is one of the most famous of the Roman martyrs with a cultus dating from the C4th, but his C5th acta are not reliable. According to them he was a favourite army officer of the Emperor Diocletian until his Christianity was discovered. Then he was tied to a tree, used for archery practice and finally clubbed to death. Pope St Damasus built a basilica over his tomb on the Appian Way in 367. His attribute is a bundle of arrows, or he is depicted as a naked youth tied to a tree and pierced with arrows.

Sebastian-of-Jesus Sillero *(Bl)*

15 October
1665–1734. From Montalban near Teruel (Spain), he became a Franciscan lay brother at Seville and his cultus was confirmed for there in 1776. However, he is not listed in the Roman Martyrology.

Sebastian Valfré *(Bl)* {2}

30 January
1629–1710. From Verduno near Alba (Italy), he joined the Oratorians at Turin after his ordination and spent the rest of his life there, becoming prefect of the Oratory and a famous spiritual director. He was beatified in 1834.

Sebastiana (St) {4 –delete}

16 September
C1st? She was allegedly converted by St Paul at Heraclea in Thrace (now European Turkey), and martyred there.

Sebbi *(St)* {2, 4}

29 August
d. ?693. He was king of Essex at the time of the Heptarchy in England. After a peaceful reign lasting thirty years he became a monk at London and died shortly afterwards, being buried in old St Paul's Cathedral. There was no cultus, and his name was inserted in the old Roman Martyrology by Baronius on the grounds of St Bede's description of him. Unlike most of Baronius's insertions, he has been kept in the revision of the martyrology.

(Secundian, Marcellian and Verian) (SS) {4 –deleted}

9 August
d. 250. They were listed as martyred near Civitavecchia in Tuscany (Italy) in the reign of Decius. Secundian was described as a prominent government official and the others were listed as 'scholastics'.

Secundina *(St)* {2, 4}

15 January
? She was a virgin martyr whipped to death at Anagni near Rome.

Secundinus of Cordoba *(St)* {2}

20 May
Early C4th. He was martyred at Cordoba (Spain) in the reign of Diocletian.

Secundinus of Troia *(St)* {2}

11 February
C5–6th. He was a bishop in Apulia (Italy), perhaps of Troia where he is enshrined.

Secundulus *(St)* {2}

24 March
? He was a martyr of Mauretania (now Morocco).

Secundus of Asti *(St)* {2, 4}

30 March
? A patrician of Asti in Piedmont (Italy) and a subaltern officer in the imperial army, he was beheaded at Asti. He is depicted as a soldier-martyr, often with a horse.

(Secundus of Amelia) (St) {4 –deleted}

1 June
d. 304. He was an alleged martyr of Amelia in Umbria (Italy) who was drowned in the Tiber in the reign of Diocletian. He is the patron of several places in central Italy, but his historical existence cannot be proved.

Secundus Pollo *(Bl)* {2}

26 December
1908–41. From Caresanablot near Vercelli (Italy), he entered the minor seminary of the archdiocese of Vercelli and became a diocesan priest in due course. He served as a curate

and parish priest, as a professor of theology and philosophy, as the spiritual director at the major seminary, as prison chaplain and as chaplain to the youth of Catholic Action. In 1941 he was conscripted as an army chaplain and sent to Montenegro but was quickly killed in battle. He was beatified in 1998.

Secundinus of Rome (St) {2}

1 August
? He was martyred on the Via Prenestina, thirty miles from Rome.

(Secundus of Ventimiglia) *(St)* *{4 –deleted}*

26 August
C3rd. According to the legend he was an officer of the **Theban Legion** who fled its massacre but was captured and executed near Ventimiglia (Italy).

Seduinus cf. **Swithin**.
Seemie-Rookie cf. **Roch**.
Seine cf. **Sequanus**.

Seiriol *(St)*

1 February
C6th. He founded monasteries (remains of which are extant) at Penmon on Anglesey (Wales) and on the island named Ynys-Seiriol after him, off the eastern tip of Anglesey.

(Seleucus) *(St)* *{4 –deleted}*

24 March
? He was merely listed as a Syrian. Nothing else is known, not even whether he was a martyr.

Senan of Scattery (St) {2}

8 March
C6th. A monk of Kilmanagh in Co. Kilkenny (Ireland), he apparently founded a monastery at Enniscorthy in Co. Wexford, then went on pilgrimage to Rome and stayed with St David

in Wales on his way back. Then he founded several more monasteries, notably one at Inishcarra near Cork, before settling on Scattery Island in the Shannon estuary. He died and was buried there. There are at least a dozen other Irish saints with the same name and yet others with similar names, and there is serious confusion between them.

Senarius (St) {2}

18 September
C6th. He was a bishop of Avranches (France).

Senator of Albanum (St) {2, 4}

26 September
? He was martyred at Albano near Rome. The alternative claim of Apt (the ancient Alba Helvetiorum) in the south of France is now not accepted.

Senator of Milan (St) {2, 4}

29 May
d. c.480. When still a young priest of Milan (Italy) he attended the council of Chalcedon as a legate of Pope St Leo the Great, and became archbishop in 477.

Senoch (St) {2}

24 October
d. 576. From Poitiers (France), he became a priest of Tours and founded a small monastery called Tiffauges in some ancient Roman ruins. He became famous for his austerity and charity.

Señorina (St) {2}

22 April
d. 980. A relative of St Rudesind of Mondonedo, she was educated at the nunnery of Vieyra where her aunt was abbess, became abbess herself and moved the community to Basto near Braga (Portugal).

September (Martyrs of) (BB) {2}

2 September
d. 1792. One hundred and ninety-one martyrs were massacred by the mob in Paris on 2 and 3 September after having been imprisoned by the Legislative Assembly of the French Revolution for refusing the oath to support the civil constitution of the clergy. They were three bishops, one hundred and twenty-four secular priests, twenty-three former Jesuits, twelve Sulpicians, eighteen other religious (including Ambrose Chevreaux, the superior-general of the Maurist Benedictines), five deacons, a cleric and five laymen. Ninety-five died at the Carmelite church in the rue de Rennes on the 2nd, seventy-two at the Vincentian seminary of St Firman on the 3rd, twenty-one at the Abbey of St Germain des Prés on the 2nd and three at the prison of La Force on the 3rd. They were beatified in 1926. Cf. **French Revolution, Martyrs of**.

Sepulchre

Old churches in England called 'St Sepulchre's' are commemorating Christ's tomb and not any saint of that name.

Sequanus (Seine, Sigo) (St) {2, 4}

19 September
C6th. He was the abbot-founder of a monastery near Dijon (France) which was later named St Seine after him.

Seraphia cf. **Serapia**.

Seraphim Morazzone (Bl) {2 –add}

13 April
1747–1822. From Milan, he became a diocesan priest there and died at Chiuso where he was in charge of the parish. He was described as a 'second St John-Mary Vianney', and was beatified in 2011.

(Seraphina) (St) {4 –deleted}

29 July
? The old Roman Martyrology placed her at 'Civitas Mamiensis', which is unknown. Armenia, Spain and Italy have been suggestions.

Seraphina Sforza (Bl) {2}

8 September
1434–78. From Urbino (Italy), the daughter of the count there, she married Alexander Sforza, Duke of Pesaro in 1448, but the marriage was a disaster. He treated her with cruelty before ejecting her from their home at Pesaro, whereupon she took refuge at a local Poor Clare nunnery. She eventually became a nun there, and was later abbess. Her cultus was confirmed for Pesaro in 1754.

Seraphinus de Nicola (St) {2}

12 October
1540–1604. A shepherd from Montegranaro in the Marches (Italy), he became a Capuchin lay brother at Ascoli Piceno in 1556 and spent an outwardly uneventful life there. However he became a thaumaturge and, despite being illiterate, was allegedly the spiritual director of important people in church and society. He was canonized in 1767.

(Serapia) (St) {4 –deleted}

29 July
C2nd? She features in the legendary acta of St Sabina as a Syrian slave who converted her to the faith and was beheaded in the reign of Hadrian.

(Serapion of Alexandria -1) (St) {2, 4}

13 July
d. ?212. He was martyred at Alexandria (Egypt) in the reign of Caracalla.

(Serapion of Alexandria -2) (St) {2, 4}

20 February
d. ?248. A citizen of Alexandria (Egypt), he died after his house was sacked in an anti-Christian riot. He was thrown from the roof after being tortured.

Serapion of Antioch (St) {2, 4}

30 October
d. 211. A bishop of Antioch (Syria), he was praised by Eusebius and St Jerome for his theological writings, but only small fragments of these survive.

Serapion of Arsinoe (St) {2, 4}

21 March
? According to the old Roman Martyrology, he was a bishop of Thmuis who was exiled by the Arians in 359. This person existed, and wrote an extant Sacramentary. The revision merely describes him as an anchorite, and not the same person.

Serapion the Mercedarian (St) {2, 4}

14 November
d. 1240. Allegedly an English soldier, he served in the army of Castile in Spain before joining the Mercedarian order in order to help ransom Christians taken captive by the Muslims. He surrendered himself as a hostage to this end at Algiers, but was crucified for preaching to Muslims while awaiting his ransom. His cultus as a saint was confirmed for Gerona and Barcelona in 1728.

Serdot cf. **Sacerdos**.

(Serena) (St) {4 –deleted}

16 August
C3rd? According to the old Roman Martyrology she was a wife of the Emperor Diocletian and a secret Christian who died of a fever at Rome, but this information derives from the spurious acta of St Cyriac and is unhistorical.

Serenus of Marseilles (St) {2}

2 August
d. p601. As bishop of Marseilles (France) he was the recipient of several letters from St Gregory the Great, who commended to his care the Roman missionaries travelling to England and who twice reprimanded him for his iconoclastic tendencies.

Serf cf. **Servan**.

Sergius I, Pope (St) {2, 4}

8 September
d. 701. He was born at Palermo in Sicily of refugee Syrian parents, became a priest at Rome and was made pope in 687. He was one of the Greek-speaking clergy who dominated Roman church life at the period, but was adamantly opposed to the imposition of Eastern church customs by the Empire and refused to sign the decrees of the 'Quinisext' council at Constantinople in 692. One of these prohibited the representation of Christ as a lamb, so he introduced the 'Agnus Dei' into the Roman Eucharistic rite. He supported the English missionary monks in Friesland and Germany and baptized King St Ceadwalla of Wessex in 689.

Sergius and Bacchus (SS) {2, 3}

7 October
d. ?303. According to the story, they were senior Roman army officers in Syria who refused to join in pagan sacrifices. As a result they were dressed in women's clothes and paraded through the streets of Arabissus in Cappadocia (Asia Minor). Then Bacchus was beaten to death and Sergius was beheaded a week later. Their cultus was suppressed in 1969. The revised Roman Martyrology merely lists them as martyrs of Bethsaloe in Syria.

(Sergius of Caesarea) *(St)* *{4 –deleted}*

24 February

d. 304. He was allegedly a hermit near Caesarea in Cappadocia (Asia Minor) who was martyred in the reign of Diocletian. His alleged relics are at Ubeda near Tarragona (Spain).

Sergius of Radonezh (St) {2}

25 September

1313–92. From Rostov near Yaroslavl (Russia), after his parents died he gave his property to the poor and became a hermit in a forest near Radonezh. He attracted disciples, and thus he founded the Trinity Laura which became the most important and influential monastery in Russia and has remained so to the present day. It was the only monastery of monks allowed to stay open during Stalin's terror in the 1930s. The saint was enshrined there, and gave his name to both monastery (Troitsa-Sergeievskaya Laura) and to the town adjacent (Sergeievsk).

Serlo of Savigny *(Bl)*

10 September

d. 1158. A Benedictine monk of Cherisy near Chartres (France), he became abbot of Savigny in 1140. This was the mother house of a reform Benedictine congregation, which he arranged to be united to the Cistercians in 1147. This involved the latter accepting the Savignac nunneries as Cistercian as well as the appropriation of tithes and the ownership of manors with feudal rights, all of which involved a mitigation of the original Cistercian ideals. His cultus became extinct in the French Revolution.

Sernin cf. **Saturninus**.

Servandus and Germanus (SS) {2, 4}

23 October

Early C4th. They were martyred at Cadiz (Spain) in the reign of Diocletian.

Servatius (Servais) (St) {2, 4}

13 May

d. /384. He was bishop of Tongeren near Liege (Belgium), and showed hospitality to St Athanasius when the latter was an exile in the West.

Servulus of Rome (St) {2, 4}

23 December

d. c.590. A tetraplegiac beggar in Rome based at the door of the church of St Clement in Rome, he shared what he received with other beggars. St Gregory the Great, who probably knew him personally, described his edifying death in an extant homily.

Servulus of Trieste (St) {2}

24 May

? He was martyred at Trieste in Istria (now in Italy).

(Servus of Tuburbum) *(St)* *{4 –deleted}*

7 December

C5th? He was described as a Roman African nobleman of what is now Algeria, seized and tortured to death in the reign of the Arian Vandal King Hunneric.

Servites, Founders of (SS) {1, 3 –group}

17 February

Noblemen of Florence (Italy) and members of the 'Confraternity of Our Lady', they withdrew to a hermitage on Mt Senario in revolt against the materialism and moral laxity of their city and founded there the Order of the 'Servants of Mary'. These became known as the Servite Friars, with a rule based on those of St Augustine and of the Dominicans, and were approved in 1304. Bonfilius Monaldi was the first superior-general, Bonajuncta Manetti the second and Manettus dell' Antella the fourth. Bartholomew degli' Amidei was first prior of Carfaggio. Hugh dei Lippi-Uguccioni and Sosthenes Sostegni established the order in France and Germany, respectively. Alexis Falconieri was a lay brother and was the last to die, in 1310. They were canonized together in 1887.

Seven Archangels (SS)

20 April
As well as SS Michael, Gabriel and Raphael, four other archangels have traditionally been given names derived from apocryphal writings. They are Uriel, Shealtiel, Jehudiel and Berachiel. The seven together have a local cultus at Palermo (Sicily).

Seven Brothers (SS) {2, 3}

10 July
d. ?150. The old Roman Martyrology alleges that they were the seven sons of St Felicity of Rome, martyred in the reign of Antoninus Pius in the following ways: Januarius, Felix and Philip, scourged to death; Silvanus, thrown over a precipice; Alexander, Vitalis and Martial, beheaded. This is fiction. They are seven early martyrs, not brothers and probably unconnected, about whom nothing definite is known except for their places of burial. That they shared the same feast day was the probable motivation for the writing of the legend. Their cultus was suppressed in 1969, but they are listed in the revised Roman Martyrology.

Seven Robbers cf. **Corfu, Martyrs of**.

Seven Sleepers (SS) {2, 3}

27 July

? They were martyred at Ephesus (Asia Minor). Their fantastic legend is that they were seven young men who were walled up in a cave where they had taken refuge from the persecution of Decius in 250 and were found there alive in 362, having been sleeping in the meantime. There are several different lists of names (the old Roman Martyrology giving them as John,

Maximian, Constantine, Mortian, Malchus, Serapion and Dionysius) and various versions of the legend. Cardinal Baronius left their entry in the old Roman Martyrology, despite his having expressed doubts about the story, but the cultus is now suppressed although they continue to be listed as martyrs.

(Severa of Oehren) (St) {4 –deleted}

20 July
d. c.750. She was abbess of Oehren nunnery at Trier (Germany).

Severian and Aquila (SS) {2, 4}

23 January
C3rd. A husband and wife, Roman Africans, they were martyred at Julia Caesarea in what is now Morocco.

Severian Baranyk (Bl) {2}

1890–1941. A monk and priest of the Basilian Order of St Josaphat of the Greek-Catholic rite, he died in prison at Drohobych after eastern Poland had been occupied by the Soviet Union. The day of his death is unknown. Cf. **Nicholas Čarneckyj and 24 Comps**.

(Severian of Scythopolis) (St) {4 –deleted}

21 February
C5th. A bishop of Scythopolis (now Bet Shean) in the Holy Land, he attended the council of Chalcedon in 451 and supported its decrees against Monophysitism. For this he was killed on his return by partisans of Theophilus, the Monophysite who intruded as bishop of Jerusalem in place of Juvenal.

(Severian of Sebaste) (St) {4 –deleted}

9 September
Early C4th? According to his legend, he was a senator at Sebaste in Armenia, who witnessed the martyrdom of the Forty Martyrs

of Sebaste, openly professed his Christianity and was torn with iron rakes until he died.

Severinus, Exsuperius and Felician (SS) {2, 4}

19 November
C3rd? They were martyred near Vienne (France).

Severinus of Agaunum (St) {2, 4}

11 February
C6th. A Burgundian, he was abbot of Agaunum (now St Maurice in Valais, Switzerland).

Severinus Boethius cf. **Boethius**.

Severinus (Seurin) of Bordeaux (St) {2}

21 October
C5th. Allegedly from the East, he became bishop of Bordeaux (France).

Severinus of Cologne (St) {2, 4}

10 October
d. c.400. He was a bishop of Cologne (Germany) and a prominent opponent of Arianism. The Roman Martyrology has deleted his alleged connection with Bordeaux (France).

(Severinus of Naples) (St) {4 –deleted}

8 January
? The old Roman Martyrology listed him as a bishop of Naples (Italy), but he is a result of the confusion between his namesakes of Noricum and Septempeda and never existed.

Severinus of Noricum (St) {2, 4}

8 January
d. 482. Apparently a monk from the East, he settled on the Danube in what is now Austria and founded several monasteries including at Passau and at Favianae near Vienna, which was his base and where he died. He organized

help for the local people being harassed by the invasions of the Huns and other barbarians, but six years after his death these incursions escalated, and his community fled with his relics. These were eventually enshrined at the abbey named after him at Naples.

Severinus of Paris (St) {2, 4}

23 November
C6th. He was a hermit at Paris (France) whose cell was where the church dedicated to him now stands.

Severinus of Septempeda (St) {2, 4}

15 May
? He was bishop of Septempeda in the Marches in 540, which place is now named Sanseverino after him. According to the unreliable legend, he and his brother, St Victorinus of Camerino, were noblemen who distributed their wealth among the poor and became hermits at Montenero near Livorno, Italy. However, Pope Vigilius then forced St Severinus to become bishop of Septempeda.

Severinus of Tivoli (St) {2}

1 November
C6th. He was a hermit at Tivoli near Rome and has his shrine in the church of St Laurence there.

(Severinus of Trier) (St) {4 –deleted}

23 October
d. c.300. He was allegedly a bishop of Trier (Germany) who transferred to Bordeaux (France) and died there.

(Severus, Securus, Januarius and Victorinus) (SS) {4 –deleted}

2 December
d. c.450. They were listed as Roman Africans martyred by the Arian Vandals.

Severus of Barcelona (St) {2, 4}

6 November
C7th? Bishop of Barcelona (Spain), he was killed by the Arian Visigoths who hammered nails into his head. He is a minor patron of Barcelona.

Severus of Bizya (St) {2, 4}

23 July
d. c.304. He converted the centurion St Memnon at Bizya in Thrace (European Turkey), and as a result was himself martyred after him in the reign of Diocletian.

Severus of Catania (St) {2}

24 March
d. 814. He was a bishop of Catania in Sicily.

Severus of Münstermaifeld (St) {2, 4}

15 February
C6th. St Gregory the Great described this parish priest of Interocrea (Androcca) in the Abruzzi (Italy) as having neglected to ensure that he was present to administer viaticum to a dying man, and so brought him back to life so that he might do so. His relics were transferred to Münstermaifeld near Koblenz (Germany) in the C10th.

Severus of Naples (St) {2, 4}

29 April
d.? 409. Bishop of Naples (Italy), he was a famous thaumaturge and (according to the legend) revived a dead man so that he could bear witness for his persecuted widow.

(Severus of Orvieto) *(St) {4 –deleted}*

1 October
? He is listed by the old Roman Martyrology as a priest at Orvieto (Italy), but seems to be a duplicate of St Severus of Münstermaifeld.

Severus of Ravenna (St) {2, 4}

1 February
d. p342. A weaver of Ravenna (Italy), he was made bishop there in 283 and was assistant papal legate at the synod of Sardica in 344. His relics ended up at Erfurt in Thuringia (Germany), and he is a patron of weavers.

Severus of Rustan (St) {2}

1 August
d. c.500. A nobleman who became a priest, he has an ancient cultus at the village near Tarbes (France) named St Sever de Rustan after him.

Severus of Trier (St) {2, 4}

15 October
C5th. A Gallo-Roman, he was a disciple of St Lupus of Troyes and of St Germanus of Auxerre and allegedly accompanied the latter to Britain to oppose the Pelagian heresy. He was a missionary among the Germans on the lower Moselle and became bishop of Trier (Germany) in 446.

Severus of Vienne (St) {2, 4}

8 August
C5th? He was a missionary priest based in Vienne (Gaul) who had migrated from the East (allegedly from 'India', meaning perhaps the Yemen).

Shadost cf. **Sadoc**.

Sharbel and Bebaia (SS) {2, 4}

29 January
d. c.250. They were martyred at Edessa (Syria, now Urfa in Turkey). According to the legend, they were brother and sister, and he had been a pagan high priest there before their conversion. They were tortured with red-hot irons before having nails hammered into their heads.

Sharbel Mafkhlouf (St) {1}

24 December
1828–98. A Maronite of Lebanon born at Beqa Kafra, he became a monk at Annaya in 1848 and was then a hermit for twenty-three years. He was greatly devoted to the Eucharist, and became revered in the region by Muslims as well as Christians. He was canonized in 1977.

Shenoute (St)

1 July
d. c.450. A native Egyptian, he became a monk at the White Monastery at Sohag in 370 and was made abbot in ?388. According to ancient sources he had charge of 2200 monks and 1800 nuns in several houses. His rule was very strict, featuring beatings and imprisonment even for minor offences. He seems to have been the first monastic superior to have used a written charter of profession for his monastics and this practice (as well as that of encouraging experienced monastics to live as hermits) influenced the rule of St Benedict. He attended the council of Ephesus in 431. He is a pioneer figure in early monasticism, but many of the writings formerly attributed to him seem to be spurious. He is not in the Roman Martyrology.

Siagrius cf. **Syagrius**.

Siard (St) {2}

14 November
d. 1230. He became Premonstratensian abbot of Mariengaarden in Friesland (Netherlands) in 1196.

Sibyllina Biscossi (Bl) {2}

19 March
1287–1367. An orphan of Pavia (Italy), when aged twelve she became blind and was adopted by a community of Dominican tertiaries. In 1302 she retired to a cell near the Dominican friary and lived as a hermit there for the rest of her long and penitential life, becoming famous as a thaumaturge. Her cultus was approved for Pavia and the Dominicans in 1853.

(Sicily, Martyrs of) (SS) {4 –deleted}

21 February
Early C4th? They were listed as seventy-nine Christians martyred in Sicily during the reign of Diocletian.

Sidney Hodgson (Bl) {2}

10 December
d. 1591. A convert layman, he was hanged at Tyburn with St Eustace White and Comps for sheltering priests. He was beatified in 1929. His name is a medieval English corruption of 'St Denis'. Cf. **England, Martyrs of**.

Sidonius Apollinaris (St) {2, 4}

21 August
d. ?479. Gaius Sollius Apollinaris Sidonius, a Gallo-Roman aristocrat from Lyons (France), was at first a soldier and married the daughter of Avitus, emperor of the West, in 455. He was prefect of Rome 468–9 and then retired to his estate, but was made bishop of Clermont while still a layman in 472. As bishop he had to deal with the Gothic invasion under Alaric, using diplomacy and also a cycle of public prayers called 'Rogation Days' (his invention). His main fame derives from his twenty-four Latin poems and his collected letters. He is one of the last examples in the West of an intellectual formed in the classic Roman culture which was in the process of alteration by the barbarian invasions.

Sidonius (Saëns) of Jumièges (St) {2}

14 November
d. c.690. From Ireland, he became a monk at Jumièges in Normandy (France) under St Philibert in 644. Later he became first abbot

of a monastery founded by St Ouen near Rouen, at the place later named St Saëns after him.

(Sidronius) *(St) {4 –deleted}*

11 July

C3rd? He was allegedly a Roman martyr of the reign of Aurelian venerated at Mesen south of Ypres (Belgium) in the Middle Ages, and also at Sens in France. There may have been two persons concerned, and the traditions involved are untrustworthy.

Siffred (Siffrein, Syffroy) (St) {2}

27 November

C6th. From Albano near Rome, he became a monk at Lérins and later bishop of Carpentras near Avignon (France), of which diocese he is the principal patron.

Sigebald (St) {2}

26 October

d. 741. He became bishop of Metz (France) in 716, and as such promoted scholarship and founded schools and the abbeys of Neuweiter and Saint Avold. He died at the latter.

Sigfrid of Växjö (St) {2}

15 February

d. ?1045. A monk of England (probably of Glastonbury), he went to Norway as a missionary at the invitation of King St Olav and passed over to Sweden, where he became a bishop based at Växjö in the south of the country. He died there. His work was successful, and he baptized the Swedish king who was also called Olav. He was allegedly canonized in 1158, but documentary proof is lacking.

Sigiran (Cyran, Siran, Sigram) (St) {2}

4 December

C7th. A Frankish nobleman, he was at first cup-bearer at the Merovingian court and then archdeacon of Tours (France), of which city his father was bishop. Later he became a monk and abbot-founder of Méobecq near Châteauroux and of Lonrey near Bourges. The abbey of Lonrey was later named Saint Cyran after him.

Sigisbert III of Austrasia, King (St) {2}

1 February

631–56. A son of King Dagobert I of the Franks, when aged three he was made king of Austrasia (straddling the present French–German border, with a capital at Metz). He was baptized by St Amandus of Elnone and had St Cunibert of Cologne and Bl Pepin of Landen as regents. His reign is not well documented, but he was venerated as the founder of various religious institutions and for his justice and moral probity, even though he was a failure as a warrior and was later to be known as the first of the Merovingian 'rois fainéants' (incapable kings).

Sigismund of Burgundy, King (St) {2, 4}

1 May

d. 523. A Vandal by descent, he was converted from Arianism by St Avitus of Vienne just before he became king of Burgundy (France) in 515. He founded the great abbey of Agaunun (now St Maurice) in Valais (Switzerland) and did penance there after having his son strangled at the instigation of his second wife. He was defeated by the Franks, and the story is that he then fled, disguised himself as a monk and hid in a cell near the above abbey, only to be taken prisoner and killed. He is not listed as a martyr.

Sigismund-Felix Feliński (St) {2}

17 September

1822–95. From a noble family of Wojutyn in a Polish region of Russia (now in Ukraine), he was ordained for the Latin-rite Polish

Catholics in St Petersburg in 1855. In 1857 he founded the 'Franciscan Sisters of the Family of Mary' to help alleviate the desperate poverty among the workers in the city. In 1862 he was nominated as bishop of Warsaw, but in the subsequent year he was exiled to Yaroslavl for twenty years because of an anti-Russian rebellion in Poland. In 1883 he was made titular archbishop of Tarsus (he was forbidden from entering Warsaw). He spent the last twelve years of his life in pastoral work in Galicia (then part of the Hapsburg Empire), and died at Cracow. He was canonized in 2009.

Sigismumd Gorazdowski (St) {2}

1 January
1845–1920. A Pole from Sanok (Ukraine), he became a diocesan priest of Lviv in 1871 and served in several parishes in the diocese. At this time the city was known as Lwow and was predominantly Polish. He established several charitable and educational institutions in the city, and founded the 'Sisters of St Joseph' to help run them. He died at Lviv and was canonized in 2005. The entire Polish population of his city was deported by the Soviets after the Second World War.

Sigismund Horazdowsky (Bl) {2}

1845–1920. From Lviv, Ukraine, he became a Latin-rite priest there in 1871 and founded several charitable institutions in the city. In 1884 he founded the 'Sisters of Mercy of St Joseph' to help run these; he also wrote many catechetical works. He was beatified in 2001.

Sigismund Pisarski (Bl) {2}

30 January
1902–43. A Polish priest, he was shot by the Nazis for refusing to leave his parish at Gdeszyn in Poland. Cf. **Poland, Martyrs of the Nazi Occupation of**.

Sigismund Sajna (Bl) {2}

17 September
1897–1940. A Polish priest, he was shot by the Nazis in a forest called Palmiry near Warsaw. Cf. **Poland, Martyrs of the Nazi Occupation of**.

Sigolena (Segouleme) (St) {2}

24 July
C6th. A noblewoman of Aquitaine (France), she was widowed when young and became a nun and later abbess at Troclar near Albi. She is a patron of the latter place.

Silas (St) {2, 4}

13 July
C1st. He is mentioned in the Acts of the Apostles as a disciple from Jerusalem who accompanied St Paul on his second missionary journey as far as Corinth (15:22; 18:5). According to legend he was the first bishop of that city, but the Roman Martyrology neither accepts this nor the identification with the Silvanus mentioned in the New Testament: 2 Cor. 1:19; 1 Thess. 1:1-2; 2 Thess. 1:1; 1 Pet. 5:12.

Silvanus, Luke and Mocius (SS) {2, 4}

6 February
d. 235–8. They were bishop, deacon and reader, respectively, at Emesa (now Homs) in Syria and were martyred after a long imprisonment. The old Roman Martyrology listed Silvanus again with St Tyrannio in error.

Silvanus of Gaza and Comps (SS) {2, 4}

4 May
d. ?304. Bishop of Gaza, he was sentenced to work as a slave in the copper mines of Phaeno in the Holy Land but proved too old for the purpose and was beheaded instead. Thirty-nine others from Egypt and the Holy Land

who also proved incapable were killed with him, and Eusebius left an account of their martyrdom.

Silvanus of Levroux (St) {2, 4}

22 September
C5th? He has an ancient cultus at Levroux near Châteauroux (France) as a hermit. His worthless legend identified him with the Zacchaeus of the gospel account set in Jericho.

(Silvanus of Rome) (St) {4 –deleted}

5 May
? He was listed as a martyr of Rome.

Silvanus of Terracina (St) {2, 4}

10 February
Early C4th. Bishop of Terracina (Italy), he is listed as a 'confessor' with the original meaning of someone who had survived imprisonment or torture during a persecution.

(Silvanus of Troas) (St) {4 –deleted}

2 December
d. c.450. He was a rhetorician at Constantinople before becoming an ascetic and being made bishop of Philippopolis (now Plovdiv in Bulgaria). But he could not endure the cold weather there so was made bishop of Troas on the Dardanelles instead.

Silverius, Pope (St) {2, 3}

2 December
d. 537. Born at Frosinone in Campania (Italy), a son of Pope St Hormisdas, he was only a subdeacon when the Ostrogothic king appointed him pope. But Vigilius, the papal ambassador at Constantinople, promised the Empress Theodora that he would rehabilitate Anthimos, the excommunicated Monophysite patriarch of Constantinople, if he were made pope instead. Silverius was accused of treason and deported to Anatolia after Belisarius, the imperial general, had captured Rome from the Ostrogoths, and Vigilius became pope in 537. Emperor Justinian repented, however, and sent Silverius back to Rome for a proper trial, only for Vigilius to arrange his imprisonment on the island of Ponza (off Gaeta) where he died of malnutrition. His cultus was confined to local calendars in 1969.

Silvester cf. **Sylvester**.

(Silvinus of Brescia) (St) {4 –deleted}

28 September
d. 444. He became bishop of Brescia (Italy) in 440 in extreme old age.

Silvinus of Thérouanne (St) {2, 4}

17 February
C8th. A Frankish courtier, he was consecrated as a missionary bishop at Rome and evangelized the district round Thérouanne in Picardy (France) for forty years, being active in ransoming those enslaved in barbarian raids. At the end of his life he became a monk at Auchy-les-Moines near Arras.

(Silvinus of Verona) (St) {4 –deleted}

12 September
C6th? Nothing is known about this alleged bishop of Verona (Italy).

Silvius of Toulouse (St) {2}

31 May
d. c.400. He was a bishop of Tours, and began the construction of the basilica over the shrine of St Saturninus there.

Simbert (Simpert, Sintbert) (St) {2, 4}

13 October
d. ?807. He was educated at the abbey of Murbach near Colmar in Alsace (France), became

a monk there and was made abbot. In 778 he was made bishop of Augsburg by Charlemagne (remaining abbot of Murbach) and was a notable restorer of church life. He was canonized in 1468.

Simeon Barsabae and Comps (SS) {2, 4}

17 April

d. 341. He was bishop of Seleucia-Ctesiphon, the patriarchal see of the Persian church situated in central Mesopotamia (modern Iraq). In the reign of Shah Shapur II he was arrested in the capital city of Ctesiphon by order of the Shah and ordered to worship the sun. On his refusal, he was chained in a prison for slaves with over a hundred others, including bishops, priests and clerics. On Good Friday they were massacred before his eyes while he shouted encouragement, and at the end he was himself beheaded.

Simeon Berneaux and Comps (St) {1 –group}

20 September

d. 1866. Born near Le Mans (France), he became a priest of the Paris Foreign Mission Society and went to Manchuria in 1840. He was coadjutor to the vicar-apostolic there before becoming vicar-apostolic of Korea. He was seized in Seoul with three fellow priests, accused of corrupting Korean customs, imprisoned, tortured and beheaded. His companions were Justus Ranfer de Bretenières, who was a twenty-eight-year-old nobleman from Châlon-sur-Saône; Louis Beaulieu of the same age from Bordeaux; and Peter-Henry Dorié from Luçon, aged twenty-seven. They were canonized in 1984. Cf. **Korea, Martyrs of**.

Simeon of Cava (Bl) {2}

16 November

d. 1141. Abbot of the great Benedictine abbey of La Cava near Salerno (Italy) from 1124, he was highly regarded by Pope Innocent II and by King Roger II of Sicily. During his abbacy Cava reached the peak of its splendour. His cultus was confirmed for there in 1928.

Simeon of Jerusalem (St) {2, 3}

27 April

d. 107. He was the son of Clopas and relative of Christ mentioned in Matthew 13:55, Mark 6:3 and John I9:25. The tradition is that he succeeded St James the Less as bishop of Jerusalem and was crucified in extreme old age in the reign of Trajan. His attribute is a fish. His cultus was confined to local calendars in 1969.

Simeon Lukač (Bl) {2}

22 August

1893–1964. He was a clandestine bishop to the Greek-Catholic Church of Ukraine in the Soviet Union, which had been officially suppressed after the Second World War. He died in prison of ill-treatment in Starunya near Stanislav. Cf. **Nicholas Čarneckyj and 24 Comps**.

Simeon the New Theologian (St)

12 March

949–1022. A Studite monk at Constantinople, he became abbot of St Mamas there in 981. His spiritual teachings caused controversy, so he resigned and was later exiled. Although he was pardoned he remained away from the city. He is one of the greatest Byzantine mystics and wrote much on the divine light manifested at the Transfiguration, thus being influential in the development of hesychastic prayer in the East. Modern Catholic liturgical documents refer to him as a saint, but he is not in the Roman Martyrology.

Simeon of Polirone (St) {2, 4}

26 July

d. 1016. Allegedly an Armenian hermit, he went on pilgrimage to Jerusalem, Rome,

Compostela and Tours and became famous as a thaumaturge. Finally he settled at the Cluniac abbey of Polirone near Padua (Italy), where he died.

Simeon Salus (St) {2, 4}

21 July

C6th. Apparently from Emesa (now Homs) in Syria, he was at the monastery of St Gerasimus on the Jordan for twenty-eight years before returning to Emesa. There he pretended to be subnormal in order not to be praised, hence his surname which means 'fool'. He was alive when an earthquake destroyed the city, but nothing is known about him afterwards.

Simeon Senex (St) {2, 4}

3 February

C1st. The prophecy which he made when the infant Jesus was presented at the Temple in Jerusalem is described in Luke 2:25-35. His traditional surname means 'Elder', although the text of the Gospel merely describes him as a righteous and devout man without indication of age. The legends concerning him are worthless.

Simeon Stylites the Elder (St) {2}

27 July

c.390–459. From Sisan near Aleppo (Syria), he was a shepherd like his father until he became a monk at the Syrian monastery of Tel Ada. He was ejected because of his excessive austerities and became a hermit at Telanissos in the hills west of Aleppo, attaching himself by chains to a rock, but many visitors disturbed his solitude so he started living on a platform mounted on a pillar. He gradually raised the height of this until it reached sixty-six feet and he spent the remaining thirty-seven years of his life on the platform, about a yard in width. His surname means 'on a pillar', and he was imitated by many in Syria and elsewhere. He became famous throughout the Roman Empire, being consulted by all sorts of people from emperors to the local nomads, and he was influential in support of the council of Chalcedon. After his death his pillar became the focus of a pilgrimage centre containing four basilicas, and the ruins of this form the most important Christian monument in Syria.

Simeon Stylites the Younger (St) {2}

24 May

521–92. From Antioch (Syria), as a child he became a monk and as a young man became a stylite like his elder namesake. He was on a pillar situated on the 'Wonderful Mountain' (near the pagan shrine of Daphne) for forty-five years, and while he was still alive a great basilica was built around him there. The ruins of this survive near Antioch, which is now in Turkey.

Simeon of Trier (St) {2, 4}

1 June

d. 1035. A Greek from Syracuse (Sicily), he studied at Constantinople and was in turn a hermit by the Jordan and a monk at Bethlehem. Then he migrated to St Catherine's on Sinai and again became a hermit, first in a cave near the Red Sea and then on the summit of Sinai. But he was chosen to go on a trip to Europe to collect alms, and after a series of adventures he settled at Trier (Germany) as a hermit affiliated to the Benedictine abbey of St Martin. The abbot of this monastery was at his deathbed and wrote his biography. He was canonized in 1042.

Simetrius (St) {2, 4}

26 May

? He was a martyr of Rome, buried in the catacomb of Priscilla on the Salarian Way. The Roman Martyrology has deleted the reference to his twenty companions.

Similian (Sambin) (St) {2, 4}

16 June
C4th. This bishop of Nantes (France) was highly regarded by St Gregory of Tours.

Simon Ballachi (Bl) {2}

3 November
d. 1319. A nobleman from near Rimini (Italy), he was a nephew of two archbishops of that city. When aged twenty-seven he became a Dominican lay brother at Rimini and was famous for his extraordinary austerities. His cultus was confirmed for there in 1820.

Simon Chen Ximan (St) {1 –group}

9 July
Cf. **Gregory Grassi and Comps**.

Simon of Créspy (St) {2}

30 September
d. 1082. Count of Créspy in Valois (France), he was a descendant of Charlemagne and was brought up at the court of William the Conqueror. The sight of his father's decomposing body caused a conversion and he went on pilgrimage to Rome but stopped off on the way at the Benedictine abbey of St Claude in the Jura. He became a monk there in 1070, but was called to Rome by Pope St Gregory VII in 1080 to act as a papal ambassador. He died at Rome.

Simon-of-Cascia Fidati (Bl) {2}

2 February
d. 1348. From Cascia in Umbria (Italy), he became an Augustinian friar and was a prominent figure as a writer, preacher and spiritual director in the life of most of the cities of central Italy. Scholars have claimed to find in his book 'De Gestis Domini Salvatoris' a source of several of Luther's doctrines. His cultus was confirmed for the Augustinian friars in 1883.

Simon Kiyota Bokusai and Comps (BB) {2}

16 August
d. 1620. An army officer from Bungo in Japan, he became a catechist and was crucified at Kokura on Kyushu when aged sixty together with his wife, Mary-Magdalen Kiyota, and a family of three who had been his servants: Thomas and Mary Gengoro and their son, James. They were beatified in 1867. Cf. **Japan, Martyrs of**.

Simon of Lipnicza (St) {2}

20 July
d. 1482. From Lipnicza in Poland, he was inspired to become a Franciscan after hearing a sermon by St John de Capistrano and was a famous preacher of the Holy Name. He died of the plague while nursing those suffering at Cracow during an epidemic, and was canonized in 2007.

Simon of Montemercurio (St) {2}

19 November
C10th. He was a hermit at the monastery of Montemercurio in Calabria (Italy).

Simon Phan Đắc Hòa (St) {1 –group}

12 December
d. 1840. A Vietnamese physician and family man in the Mekong Delta and also mayor of his village, he was affiliated to the Paris Foreign Mission Society. He was known for his care for poor people As a result of his assisting missionary priests he was imprisoned, viciously tortured and beheaded at Hué. Cf. **Vietnam, Martyrs of**.

Simon Qin Qunfu (St) {1 –group}

19 July
Cf. **Elizabeth Qin Bianzhi and Simon Qin Qunfu**.

Simon Rinalducci (Bl) {2}

20 April
d. 1322. From Todi (Italy), he became an Augustinian friar and a famous preacher and was provincial superior of Umbria for a time. He kept silence in face of an unjust accusation rather than cause scandal among his brethren. He died at Bologna and his cultus was confirmed for the Augustinian friars in 1833.

Simon de Rojas (St) {2}

28 September
1522–1624. From Valladolid (Spain), he became a Trinitarian and was superior-general as well as a famous missionary. Later he was confessor at the court of King Philip III of Spain and tutor to the royal family. Dying at Madrid, he was canonized in 1988.

Simon Stock (Bl) {2}

16 May
d. 1265. An English superior-general of the Carmelites, he was elected in ?1234, had a reputation for sanctity and died at Bordeaux (France). Nothing more is known about him from contemporary sources. He was not responsible for converting the Carmelites from hermits to friars, as that had been done before he was elected. The famous legend wherein he is alleged to have been given the scapular (his attribute) by Our Lady is based on a C17th forgery. He is venerated as a saint by the Carmelites and at Bordeaux, but has only been listed as a beatus by the Roman Martyrology.

Simon Takeda Gohyōe and Comps (BB) {2 –add}

9 December
d. 1603. He was a married Japanese layperson from Kyōto, who was martyred at Yatsushiro in Kumamoto. With him were martyred Agnes Takeda his wife, Jane Takeda his mother, Mary-Magdalen Minami the wife of Bl John Minami Gorōzaemon and their adopted son Louis Minami. They were beatified in 2008. Cf. **Japan, Martyrs of**.

(Simon of Trent) (St) {4 –deleted}

24 March
d. 1474. A child aged two of Trent in Austria (now Trento in Italy), he was allegedly ritually tortured to death by Jews on Good Friday. The confessions of those accused were obtained under torture and the actual events are uncertain, but the trial was reviewed by the pope in 1478 and no objections were raised. In 1588 Simon became the only alleged victim of Jewish ritual murder to be inserted into the Roman Martyrology as a saint after several miracles were reported at his shrine, but the cultus was suppressed in 1965 as being scandalous.

Simon Yempo (Bl) {2}

4 December
d. 1623. A Japanese Buddhist bonze, he converted to Christianity with the rest of his community and became a lay catechist. He was burnt alive at Edo (now Tokyo) with BB Francis Galvez and Jerome de Angelis. He was beatified in 1867. Cf. **Japan, Martyrs of**.

Simon the Zealot (St) {1, 3}

28 October
C1st. In the New Testament he is only referred to in the lists of the apostles with the surname 'Cananean' meaning 'Zealot' (not a 'native of Cana', pace St Jerome and later tradition in the West). The traditions concerning his career after the Resurrection are conflicting and nothing is known about his life. He has various attributes: a fish or two, a boat, an oar or a saw. He is also depicted being sawn in half lengthwise.

Simplician of Milan (St) {2, 4}

15 August
d. 401. A friend and adviser of St Ambrose, he succeeded him as archbishop of Milan (Italy) but was elderly and died three years later. He played a leading part in the conversion of St Augustine, by whom he was remembered with gratitude.

Simplicius, Pope (St) {2, 4}

10 March
d. 483. From Tivoli near Rome, he became pope in 468 and upheld the council of Chalcedon against three successive Eastern emperors who sought a modus vivendi with the Monophysites in Egypt and Syria. The last Western emperor was deposed during his reign in 476 by the Arian King Odoacer.

(Simplicius, Constantius and Victorian) (SS) {4 –deleted}

26 August
? According to the old Roman Martyrology they were a father and his two sons who were martyred 'among the Marsi'. However they seem to be a mistaken grouping of Simplicius of Rome, Victorianus of Amiternum and Constantius of Perugia.

Simplicius, Faustinus, Beatrice and Rufus (SS) {2, 3}

29 July
d. c.300. They were martyred at Rome in the reign of Diocletian and buried in the catacomb of Generosa. Their acta are untrustworthy, and their cultus was confined to local calendars in 1969.

Simplicius of Autun (St) {2, 4}

24 June
d. ?375. He was married but was allegedly abstaining from sexual relations when he became bishop of Autun (France). He worked zealously and successfully for the conversion of pagans.

Simplicius of Tempio Pausania (St) {2, 4}

15 May
d. c.300. He used to be claimed as a bishop in the north of Sardinia who was buried alive in the reign of Diocletian. The Roman Martyrology merely lists him as a priest, not as a martyr.

(Simplicius of Verona) (St) {4 –deleted}

20 November
C6th? He was allegedly a bishop of Verona (Italy).

Sindonia (Zdenka) Schelingová (Bl) {2 –add}

31 July
1916–55. From Krivá in northeastern Slovakia, she joined the 'Sisters of Charity of the Holy Cross' at Podunajské Biskupice in 1937 and became a radiologist and nurse at Bratislava. After the Second World War the Communist government in Czechoslovakia began to persecute the church, and in 1952 she tried to help six clerics to escape who were at her hospital awaiting deportation to Siberia. She was arrested, tortured and imprisoned for three years, only being released because she was dying of cancer possibly engendered by the torture. Her congregation refused to accept her out of fear, and she died at Trnava. She was beatified as a martyr in 2004.

Sindulf of Rheims (St) {2, 4}

20 October
d. c.600. From Gascony, he became a hermit at Aussonce near Rheims (France).

(Sindulf of Vienne) (St) {4 –deleted}

10 December
C6th. He was a bishop of Vienne (France).

Sinope, Martyrs of (SS) {2, 4}

7 April
Early C4th. Two hundred soldiers were martyred in a massacre at Sinope on the Black Sea coast of Asia Minor.

Siran cf. **Sigiran.**

Siricius, Pope (St) {2, 4}

26 November
d. 399. A Roman, he succeeded St Damasus as pope in 384. A collection of his letters are regarded as the first papal decretals, and the consolidation of papal authority was also manifest in the foundation of a vicariate at Thessalonica (Greece) in opposition to the patriarchate of Constantinople.

(Siridion) *(St)* *{4 –deleted}*

2 January
? This entry in the old Roman Martyrology is probably a copyist's error for 'Isidore of Antioch'.

Sirenus (Sinerus) of Sirmium (St) {2, 4}

23 February
d. ?307. He was from Greece but fled to Sirmium (now Srem Mitrovica in Serbia) during the persecution of Diocletian and became a gardener. But he became involved in a dispute with a pagan woman, admitted to being a Christian in court and was martyred.

(Sirmium, Martyrs of) *(SS)* *{4 –deleted}*

23 February, 9 April
Early C4th? The old Roman Martyrology listed two anonymous groups of martyrs at Sirmium (now Srem Mitrovica in Serbia) in the rule of Diocletian. One numbered seventy-two, and the other comprised seven virgins. The place was an imperial seat of government at the time.

Sisebut (St) {2}

15 March
d. 1087. He was abbot of the Benedictine monastery of Cardena near Burgos (Spain), which was an important centre of contemporary ecclesiastical and civil life. He gave shelter to El Cid, the famous hero of the 'Reconquista', when the latter was exiled by the king.

Sisenand (St) {2, 4}

16 July
d. 851. Allegedly from Badajoz in Extremadura (Spain), he was a deacon at Cordoba and was beheaded in the reign of Emir Abderrahman II.

Sisinnius, Martyrius and Alexander (SS) {2, 4}

29 May
d. 397. According to their story, they were missionaries from Cappadocia (Asia Minor) who were welcomed by St Vigilius of Trent (now Trento in Italy) on the recommendation of St Ambrose and sent to evangelize the Tyrol. They were lynched by a mob during a pagan festival in the Val di Non.

Sisinnius of Cyzicus (St) {2, 4}

23 November
Early C4th. Bishop of Cyzicus on the south shore of the Sea of Marmara (Asia Minor), he was martyred by the sword during the persecution of Diocletian. He has been confused with a namesake who attended the council of Nicaea in 325.

Sisoes the Great (St) {2}

4 July
d. ?429. He was one of the desert fathers of Egypt and was initially a hermit at Scetis. Finding this monastic settlement becoming

too crowded, he went off and settled at St Anthony's 'Interior Mountain' in the desert east of the Nile, which he found deserted and where he remained for over seventy years.

Sithian cf. **Swithin**.

Siviard (St) {2}

1 March
d. c.680. A monk at Saint-Calais near Le Mans (France), he succeeded his own father as abbot and wrote a biography of St Carilefus, founder of the monastery.

Sixtus cf. **Xystus**.

Sixtus of Rheims (St) {2, 4}

1 September
C3rd. He was a Roman missionary who became first bishop of Rheims (France) in c.290. He had previously established his base at Soissons before moving to Rheims.

(Socrates and Dionysius) *(SS)* {4 –deleted}

19 April
d. 275. They were listed as killed with lances at Perga in Pamphylia (Asia Minor) in the reign of Aurelian.

(Socrates and Stephen) *(SS)* {4 –deleted}

17 September
? The old Roman Martyrology listed them as martyrs of Britain in the reign of Diocletian, but it is probable that 'Britain' is a copyist's error either for Abretania or for Bithynia, both in Asia Minor.

Sola (Sol, Suolo) (St) {2}

4 December
d. 794. An Anglo-Saxon missionary monk, he followed St Boniface to Germany and lived as a hermit near the abbey of Fulda. Then

Charlemagne gave him some land near Eich-stätt on which he founded a monastery later named Solnhofen after him.

Solemnis (Soleine) (St) {2, 4}

25 September
d. a.511. He was made bishop of Chartres (France) in c.490 and assisted in the baptism of Clovis, king of the Franks.

Solomon cf. **Salonius**.

Solomon (Selyf) III of Brittany (St) {2}

25 June
d. 874. King of Brittany (France), he was a brave (though at times brutal) warrior who fought the Franks, Norse and his own rebellious subjects. He did penance for the crimes that he had committed when he was a youth, and when he was assassinated, he was counted as a martyr. The Bretons regard him as a national hero.

Solongia (Solange) (St) {2}

10 May
C9th? A peasant's daughter of Villemont near Bourges (France), when shepherding her father's sheep she was sexually assaulted by a local nobleman and murdered when she resisted. She is listed as a virgin martyr.

Sophia

The famous church in Constantinople has often been referred to in the West as St Sophia's. This does not commemorate a saint but is a corruption of the Greek words 'Hagia Sofia' or Holy Wisdom.

(Sophia and Irene) *(SS)* {4 –deleted}

18 September
Early C3rd? They were listed as beheaded in Egypt.

Sophia Czeska-Maciejowska (Bl) {2 –add}

1 April
1584–1650. From a middle-class family of Cracow in Poland, she married aged sixteen but was widowed six years later without having had any children. She spent the rest of her long life in caring for orphaned girls, and opened a school and orphanage for them in the city. This was actually the first public school for girls in Poland. She attracted helpers, whom she formed into the Congregation of the Virgins of the Presentation of the Blessed Virgin Mary, one of the first active religious sisterhoods in the country. She was the first superior, dying at the mother house at Cracow. She was beatified in 2013.

Sophia of Fermo (St) {2, 4}

30 April
? She was a virgin martyred at Fermo (Italy).

(Sophia of Rome) *(St) {4 –deleted}*

30 September
C2nd? According to the legend she was the widowed mother of the three unmarried sisters Faith, Hope and Charity who were martyred at Rome in the reign of Hadrian. Three days later she visited their tomb and died there. The story is apparently a fictional Eastern allegory of God's wisdom ('sophia') from which come the virtues of faith, hope and charity.

(Sophronius of Cyprus) *(St) {4 –deleted}*

8 December
C6th. The old Roman Martyrology alleged that he was a bishop of Cyprus, but there is no evidence supporting this.

Sophronius of Jerusalem (St) {2}

11 March
d. 639. From Damascus (Syria), as a monk he accompanied John Moschus on his journeys to the various monastic sites in the Middle East. (The latter wrote a description of them, the extant 'Spiritual Meadow'.) He was at the monastery of St Theodosius near Bethlehem from 616 and became patriarch of Jerusalem in 634. A noted ecclesiastical writer, he was in the forefront of the struggle against the Monothelite policy of the imperial government. The Muslims took Jerusalem in 637, and he fled to Alexandria, where he died.

(Sosipater) *(St) {4 –deleted}*

25 June
C2nd. The relative that St Paul mentioned in Romans 16:21 has been hypothetically identified with the Sosipater of Beroea who accompanied him on the initial stage of his final return to Jerusalem from Greece (Acts 20:4). Conflicting traditions allege that he either became bishop of Iconium in Asia Minor or evangelized Corfu with St Jason.

Sossius of Misenum (St) {2, 3 –group}

23 September
d. 305. He was a martyred deacon of Misenum in the Campagna (Italy). Formerly he was included in the worthless legend of St Januarius of Benevento, and liturgically celebrated with him.

(Sosthenes and Victor) *(SS) {4 –deleted}*

10 September
C4th? They were listed as martyred at Chalcedon on the Bosporus in the reign of Maximian. In the unreliable acta of St Euphemia they featured among the executioners appointed to torture her, being converted through her prayers and example.

(Sosthenes of Corinth) *(St) {4 –deleted}*

28 November
C1st. He is the ruler of the synagogue at Corinth mentioned in Acts 18:17 who

became a disciple of St Paul and is possibly the 'brother' mentioned in 1 Corinthians 1:1. Byzantine tradition made him the first bishop of Colophon in Ionia.

Sosthenes Sostegni (St) {1, 3 –group}

17 February
Cf. **Servites, Founders of**.

Soter, Pope (St) {2, 3}

22 April
d. 175. An Italian, he is eleventh in St Irenaeus's list of early popes and Eusebius referred to his correspondence with the church of Corinth. In his time Easter was fixed as an annual festival, to be celebrated on the Sunday following the Jewish Passover. There is no evidence that he was a martyr, and his cultus was suppressed in 1969.

Soteris (St) {2, 4}

10 February
d. ?304. A Roman maiden, she was martyred in the reign of Diocletian and seems to have been a sister of the great-grandmother of St Ambrose. The latter mentioned her in writing several times.

Sozon (St) {2, 4}

7 September
? According to the legend he was a shepherd of Cilicia (Asia Minor) who pulled a hand off an idol made of gold being displayed at a pagan festival, broke it up and distributed the pieces among the poor. He was burnt at the stake.

Spanish Civil War (Martyrs of)

1934–9. The election of a Republican government in Spain in 1931 initiated a policy of government hostility towards the church that was a consequence of the radical anti-clericalism that had been a feature of Spanish politics in the C19th. Persecution soon grew vicious, especially in areas controlled by Communist or Anarchist factions, and this was a factor leading to the rebellion by Nationalist forces under General Franco and the consequent civil war which saw the defeat of the Republicans. Many victims of massacre have been beatified. In total, 4,184 priests, 283 female and 2,365 male consecrated religious were reported to have been killed in cold blood, along with many lay members of the church. Up to 2001, 17 had been canonized and 212 beatified; a further 233 were beatified in that year, and another 522 in 2013. Cf. lists of national martyrs in the appendix.

(Speciosus) (St) {4 –deleted}

15 March
C6th? According to the second 'Dialogue' attributed to St Gregory the Great, he was from Rome and became a disciple of St Benedict at Montecassino with his brother, Gregory. They were then sent to found a monastery at Terracina, but he died at Capua while on an errand connected with this. The story is probably fictional.

Sperandea (Sperandia) (St)

11 September
d. 1276. A relative of St Ubald Baldassini, she became a Benedictine nun at Cingoli in the Marches (Italy), going on to become abbess. She is the patron of Cingoli, but is not in the Roman Martyrology.

Spes (St) {2}

23 May
d. ?517. He was the abbot-founder of a monastery at Campi near Norcia (Italy) and was totally blind for forty years, but fifteen days before his death his eyesight returned. This was considered remarkable but is medically explicable.

Speusippus, Elasippus, Melasippus and Leonilla (SS) {2, 4}

17 January
? They were triplet brothers of Cappadocia (Asia Minor) who were martyred with their grandmother in the reign of Marcus Aurelius. Their alleged relics were taken to Langres (France) in the C6th.

Spiridion (St) {2, 4}

12 December
d. ?348. He was a shepherd before becoming bishop of Tremithus on his native Cyprus. In the persecution of Diocletian he had one eye removed and was made a slave in the copper mines, but survived. He was allegedly one of the 'confessors of the Faith' present at the council of Nicaea and a strong opponent of Arianism there, although his name is not among the list of signatories. He was, however, definitely present at the council of Sardica in 343.

(Stachys) (St) {4 –deleted}

31 October
C1st. St Paul referred to him as 'my beloved Stachys' in Romans 16:9. The unreliable tradition concerning the apostolic foundation of the church at Constantinople makes him the first bishop of Byzantium, ordained by St Andrew.

(Stacteus of Rome) (St) {4 –deleted}

28 September
? Nothing is known about this alleged martyr of Rome.

Stanislaus Kazimierczyk (St) {2}

3 May
1433–89. Born near Cracow (Poland), he studied in the Jagełłonian University there and became a canon regular in 1456. He was a well-known preacher who stressed the centrality of the Eucharist in the Christian life and has left many spiritual writings. His was canonized in 2010.

Stanislaus Kostka (St) {2}

15 August
1550–68. A young nobleman from Rostkóv in Poland, in 1563 he went to study at the Jesuit College at Vienna and (despite the fierce opposition of his family) fled to St Peter Canisius at Augsburg (Bavaria) in order to become a Jesuit himself. He was received into the noviciate at Rome by St Francis Borgia in 1567 and died as a novice after having quickly acquired a reputation for moral purity. He was canonized in 1726.

Stanislaus Kubista (Bl) {2}

26 April
1898–1942. A Polish priest, he died of ill-treatment at the concentration camp at Sachsenhausen. Cf. **Poland, Martyrs of the Nazi Occupation of**.

Stanislaus Kubski (Bl) {2}

18 May
1876–1942. A Polish priest, he was gassed at the concentration camp at Dachau. Cf. **Poland, Martyrs of the Nazi Occupation of**.

Stanislaus Mysakowski (Bl) {2}

14 October
1896–1942. A Polish priest, he was gassed at the concentration camp at Dachau with Bl Francis Rosłaniec. Cf. **Poland, Martyrs of the Nazi Occupation of**.

Stanislaus-of-Jesus-and-Mary Papczyński (Bl) {2 –add}

1631–1701. From Podegrodzie in Poland, he joined the 'Clerks Regular of the Mother of

God' (Piarists) in 1654. He became famous for his academic and pastoral success, but wished to found a new Order of 'Marian Clerks of the Immaculate Conception'. This was to be the first native Polish religious order. In 1673 he opened the first house at Skierniewice, initially with an eremitic charism but later with more emphasis on catechesis. The Marians became a full religious order in 1701. He died at Gora Kalwaria and was beatified in 2007.

Stanislaus Pyrtek (Bl) {2}

4 March
1913–42. A Polish priest, he was shot at Bere-zwecz near Głębokie by the Nazis together with BB Ladislas Maćkowiak and Miechislav Bohatkiewicz. Cf. **Poland, Martyrs of the Nazi Occupation of**.

Stanislaus Starowieyski (Bl) {2}

4 June
1895–1942. A Polish priest, he was beaten to death at the concentration camp at Dachau with Bl Anthony Zawistowski. Cf. **Poland, Martyrs of the Nazi Occupation of**.

Stanislaus Szczepanowsky (St) {1, 3}

11 April
1030–79. From near Cracow (Poland), he was educated at Gniezno and Paris and became bishop of Cracow in 1072. He excommunicated King Boleslaus II for his evil life, and the king killed him with a sword as a result while he was celebrating Mass. Pope St Gregory VII laid an interdict upon Poland, the king fled to Hungary and died in exile. Stanislaus was canonized in 1253, although there is a disputed theory that the assassination was as a result of his plotting to dethrone the king. He is often depicted being hacked in pieces at the foot of the altar.

Stephana Quinzani (Bl) {2}

2 January
1457–1530. From Brescia (Italy), she became a Dominican tertiary when aged fifteen and lived at the family home for many years. Then she founded, and was first superior of, a monastery at Soncino near Cremona, where she died. She was noted for her ecstasies and for having the stigmata, which were attested by many eyewitnesses. Her cultus was confirmed for Cremona in 1740.

Stephen

Deviant vernacular forms of the original Greek 'Stefanos' (meaning 'crowned') are: French, Etienne; Spanish, Esteban; Hungarian, István.

Stephen I, Pope (St) {2, 3}

2 August
d. 257. A nobleman of Rome, he was made pope in 254 and maintained the validity of baptism by heretics against the rigorist position held by St Cyprian of Carthage and others. According to the unreliable legend (contradicted by early evidence and now discarded) he was beheaded while seated in his chair during the celebration of Mass in the catacombs. His cultus was confined to local calendars in 1969.

(Stephen, Pontian and Comps) (SS) *{4 –deleted}*

31 December
? They are listed as martyrs of Catania (Sicily). Also named are Attalus, Fabian, Cornelius, Sextus, Flos, Quintian, Minervinus and Simplician.

Stephen of Antioch (St) {2, 4}

25 April
d. 479. He was elected patriarch of Antioch (Syria) in 478 after the Monophysite Peter the

Fuller had been exiled. The partisans of the latter refused to accept him, and eventually assassinated him in one of the city's churches and threw his body into the river.

Stephen of Apt (St) {2}

6 November
975–1046. From Agde near Montpellier (France), he became bishop of Apt in 1010 and rebuilt the cathedral there.

Stephen Bandelli (Bl) {2}

11 June
d. 1450. From Castelnuovo near Piacenza (Italy), he became a Dominican at the latter place and was famous as a preacher and reformer. He died at Saluzzo, and his cultus was confirmed for there and for the Dominicans in 1856.

Stephen Bellesini (Bl) {2}

2 February
1774–1840. From Trent (Austria, now Trento in Italy), he became an Augustinian friar at Bologna (Italy) and studied there and at Rome. When the French Revolution brought war he fled back to Trent and became the government inspector of schools after the religious orders were suppressed. As soon as it was possible he became a friar again and was novice-master at Rome and parish priest at the shrine of our Lady at Genazzano, where he died as a result of nursing cholera sufferers. He was beatified in 1904.

Stephen of Caiazzo (St)

29 October
935–1023. From Macerata near Ancona (Italy), he was Benedictine abbot of San Salvatore Maggiore before becoming bishop of Caiazzo near Naples in 979. He is the principal patron of the city and diocese, but is not listed in the Roman Martyrology.

(Stephen of Cardeña and Comps) (SS) {4 –deleted}

6 August
d. ?872. He was allegedly abbot of Cardena near Burgos (Spain) and was massacred with his community of two hundred by Muslim raiders. The cultus was approved in 1603, but the earliest evidence for their existence is an inscription of the C13th which does not give the name of the abbot.

Stephen of Chatillon (St) {2}

7 September
d. 1208. A nobleman from Lyons (France), he became a Carthusian at Portes and was made prior in 1196. In 1203 he became bishop of Dié, where he died. His cultus was approved in 1907.

Stephen-Theodore Cuénot (St) {1 –group}

14 November
1802–61. From Beaulieu in Franche Comté (France), he joined the Paris Society for Foreign Missions and was sent to Vietnam. In 1833 he was appointed vicar-apostolic of 'East Cochin-China' (the area around Saigon). He was one of the first to be arrested on the outbreak of persecution in 1861, and died of hardship in captivity, chained up with the imperial elephants, shortly before the date fixed for his execution. This was during the persecution ordered by Emperor Tự Đức. Cf. **Vietnam, Martyrs of**.

Stephen Grelewski (Bl) {2}

9 May
1899–1941. A Polish priest, he died of ill-treatment at the concentration camp at Dachau. Cf. **Poland, Martyrs of the Nazi Occupation of**.

Stephen Harding (St) {2}

28 March
d. 1134. A monk (or student) of Sherborne Abbey (England), after a pilgrimage to

Rome he joined St Robert at Molesmes and migrated to Cîteaux with him. There he was successively sub-prior under St Robert, prior under St Alberic and third abbot from 1109. He initiated the unified congregational structure of the Cistercians but was not the author of the original constitutions (as previously thought). He received St Bernard as a novice at Cîteaux and sent him to become the abbot-founder of Clairvaux two years later, thus starting the spectacular success of the Cistercians in Europe. He was canonized in 1623.

Stephen of Hungary, King (St) {1, 3}

16 August
d. ?935–1038. Born at Esztergom (Hungary), he was baptized when young, succeeded as duke of the Magyars in 997 and made his life's work the Christianization of his people. In this he was aided by the connections made by his marriage to Gisela, a sister of Emperor St Henry II, and he obtained the title of king from the pope in 1000 (the original crown used in his coronation survives). He organized dioceses and founded several abbeys (the greatest being Pannonhalma, which survives), successfully suppressed revolts motivated by pagan reaction and gave his kingdom the civil organization which survived until the incursion of the Ottomans. His son, St Emeric, predeceased him and the later years of his reign were very difficult. He was canonized in 1083 and is the patron of Hungary and the Magyar people.

Stephen of Lyons (St) {2, 4}

13 February
d. ?515. He was a bishop of Lyons (France) who was instrumental in converting the Arian Burgundians to orthodoxy.

Stephen Min Kŭk-ka (St) {1 –group}

20 January
d. 1840. He was a catechist at Seoul in Korea, and was strangled in prison. Cf. **Korea, Martyrs of**.

Stephen of Muret (St) {2}

8 February
1046–1124. A son of a nobleman of the Auvergne (France), when aged twelve he went on pilgrimage with his father to Bari (Italy) but fell ill at Benevento and had to stay behind. Then he lived with hermits in Calabria before returning to France and becoming a hermit himself at Muret in the Limousin in 1076. He attracted many hermit-disciples, and he became their informal superior, dying as such but apparently not having formally taken religious vows. The brethren then moved to Grandmont and became the nucleus of a new monastic order, the Grandmontines. This was not Benedictine, as their 'Rule of St Stephen' was written from reminiscences of his teachings. The order was suppressed before (not by) the French Revolution.

Stephen Nehmé (Bl) {2 –add}

3 August
1889–1938. Born at Lehfed (Lebanon), he became a Maronite monk at Kfifane in 1905. He was placed in various monasteries, working as a gardener, carpenter and builder and becoming known for his life of intense prayer and fidelity to the rules and spirituality of his monastic order. He died at Kfifane, having received the nickname of the 'disciple of the earth'. He was beatified in 2010.

Stephen Nguyễn Văn Vinh (St) {1 –group}

19 December
Cf. **Francis-Xavier Hà Trọng Mậu and Comps**.

Stephen of Obazine (St) {2}

8 March
d. 1159. With another priest he withdrew into the forest of Obazine near Tulle (France) to be a hermit, but disciples joined them and they built a monastery. This became a congregation (which included a nunnery), and he arranged for its affiliation to the Cistercian order in 1147. He died at Bonaigne, one of his foundations.

Stephen of Perm (St) {2}

26 April
d. 1396. From Veliky Ustyug in the oblast of Vologda, Russia, he was a monk at Rostov for thirteen years before migrating in 1379 to the territory of the Komi. These are a Finno-Ugric people then living around Perm as well as north of it, and for their evangelization he translated the Bible and the Church's liturgical texts into the Komi language. To do so he used an alphabet that he invented himself. He also founded schools and seminaries for the region. In 1383 he was consecrated as first bishop of Perm, and died at Moscow. The Komi used to be called Zyrians. His insertion into the revised Roman Martyrology is significant, as it was not previously considered that the medieval Russian church had any communion with Rome.

Stephen the Protomartyr (St) {1, 3}

26 December
d. ?35. He was one of the first seven deacons of the infant church in Jerusalem and was stoned to death by a lynch mob after being interrogated by the Sanhedrin (Acts 6,7). His attribute is a number of stones.

Stephen of Reggio (St) {2}

5 July
d. 78? According to a C10th Byzantine tradition he was consecrated as first bishop of Reggio in Calabria and was martyred in the reign of Nero. There was no such tradition in the city itself until the C17th, but the Roman Martyrology has accepted the story.

Stephen of Rieti (St) {2, 4}

13 February
C6th. He was an abbot at Rieti (Italy) whom St Gregory the Great described as 'rough in speech but cultured in life'.

Stephen de Rossano (St) {2}

26 September
d. 1001. He was a Byzantine-rite monk and companion of St Nilus the Younger at Gaeta near Rome (Italy).

Stephen Rowsham (Bl) {2}

11 August
d. 1587. Born in Oxfordshire, he was an Oxford graduate and vicar of St Mary's Church there before his conversion. Ordained in 1881 at Soissons, he was captured immediately on his return to England and kept for eighteen months in 'Little Ease' (reputedly a cell of sixty-four cubic feet) in the Tower of London before being deported. Returning, he was executed at Gloucester on an uncertain date and was beatified in 1987. Cf. **England, Martyrs of.**

Stephen Sándor (Bl) {2 –add}

8 June
1914–53. From a working-class family at Szolnok, Hungary, he went to Budapest aged twenty-two in order to be trained as a priest by the Salesians. His subsequent wish to join that order was interrupted by the Second World War, during which he served on the Eastern Front, and he only made final vows as a Salesian in 1946 when Hungary had been taken over by the Communists. They banned

the Salesians in 1950, but he continued with clandestine work with young people and as a result he was arrested and hanged in 1953. He was beatified as a martyr in 2013.

Stephen the Younger (St) {2, 4}

28 November

714–64. A native of Constantinople, he became a monk at St Auxentius's Abbey there in 730 and was made abbot in 744. He resigned and became a hermit on the outbreak of the iconoclast controversy, but his opposition to the imperial policy led to his monastery being destroyed by the Emperor Constantine V, and he was exiled in 754. Later he was brought back and imprisoned, but was dragged from prison and lynched by a mob. The old Roman Martyrology alleged that he died with Andrew, Basil, Peter and 339 other monks, but these have been deleted.

Stilla (Bl) {2}

19 July

d. c.1140. A relative of the counts of Abenberg near Nuremberg (Bavaria), as a hermit she founded a chapel near her home and was buried there. Nothing else is known. Her cultus was confirmed for Eichstätt in 1927.

(Strato) *(St)* *{4 –deleted}*

9 September

? He is listed as having been martyred by having his ankles tied to two young trees which were bent towards each other and then let go. Nothing else is known.

Strato, Philip and Eutychian (SS) {2, 4}

15 August

? They were martyred at Nicomedia (Asia Minor). Most sources add a fourth martyr, Cyprian, but he is not in the Roman Martyrology.

Strato, Valerius, Macrinus and Gordian (SS) {2, 4}

15 September

C4th. They are listed as having been martyred at 'Noviodunum', which is Tomi near the Danube delta in Romania. The rival claims of Nyon in Bern canton (Switzerland), at Nevers and at Noyon (France) are not accepted by the Roman Martyrology.

Sturmi (St) {2, 4}

17 December

d. 779. The first native German to be a monk in Germany was born to Christian parents, educated by St Wigbert in the abbey of Fritzlar and became one of the favourite disciples of St Boniface. As a missionary he worked in Hesse and founded the abbey of Fulda for St Boniface as a central mission base there in 744. For a year from 747 he was at Montecassino to learn the monastic observance there before becoming abbot of Fulda. He was with Charlemagne on the latter's campaign against the Saxons in the year that he died. He was canonized in 1139.

(Stylianos) *(St)* *{4 –deleted}*

28 November

Late C4th? He was allegedly a hermit near Adrianople in Paphlagonia (Asia Minor), but his extant biography is legendary. He is probably identical with Alypius the Stylite.

Suairlech *(St)*

27 March

d. c.750. He was the first bishop of Fore in Co. Westmeath, Ireland. Another of the same name was abbot at Magheralin in Co. Down.

Successus, Paul and Lucius (SS) {2}

18 January

d. 259. They were bishops of the Roman province of Africa (now Tunisia), and were martyred at Carthage in the reign of Decius. Cf. **Paul, Gerontius and Comps**.

Sulinus cf. **Silin**.

Sulpicius and Servitian (SS) {2, 4}

20 April

? They were Roman martyrs buried on the Via Latina. According to the worthless tradition, they were associated with St Flavia Domitilla and beheaded in the reign of Trajan.

Sulpicius I of Bourges 'Severus' (St) {2}

29 January

d. 591. He became archbishop of Bourges (France) in 584 and has been confused with the writer Sulpicius Severus. This resulted in the latter being inserted in the old Roman Martyrology.

Sulpicius II of Bourges 'Pius' (St) {2}

17 January

d. 647. A nobleman from near Béziers (France), he became archbishop of Bourges in 624. He is commemorated by the church and seminary of St Sulpice in Paris.

(Suranus) (St) {4 –deleted}

24 January

C6th? According to the 'Dialogues' attributed to St Gregory the Great, he was the abbot of a monastery at Sora in Umbria (Italy). When the Lombards invaded, he distributed all the possessions of the monastery among the refugees so that the invaders had nothing to plunder when they arrived. They killed him as soon as they realized this. The story is probably fictional.

(Susanna, Marciana, Palladia and Comps) (SS) {4 –deleted}

24 May

C2nd? According to their legendary acta, they were the wives and children of certain soldiers belonging to the military unit commanded by St Meletius Stratelates and were killed with other Christians in Galatia (Asia Minor).

Susanna Chobioye (Bl) {2}

12 July

d. 1628. The wife of Bl Peter Arakiyori Chobioye, she was beheaded with her husband at Nagasaki. Six months earlier she had been hanged naked by her hair from a tree for eight hours. Cf. **Mancius Araki and Comps** and **Japan, Martyrs of**.

Susanna of Eleutheropolis (St) {4 –deleted}

19 September

C4th? According to the old Roman Martyrology she was the daughter of a pagan priest and a Jewish woman. Being converted after their deaths, she became a deaconess at Eleutheropolis between Jerusalem and Gaza and was martyred there in the reign of Julian. This story is considered to be fictional.

Susanna of Rome (St) {2, 3}

11 August

? Her acta are worthless, but there probably was a Roman martyr of this name, and the Roman church of St Susanna is dedicated to her. She had no connection with St Tiburtius who is commemorated on the same day. Since 1969 her cultus has been confined to her basilica in Rome.

Susanna U Sur-im (St) {1 –group}

20 September

Cf. **Laurence Han I-hyŏng and Comps**.

Swithbert (St) {2}

1 March

?647–713. A Northumbrian, he was one of twelve missionary monks who went with

St Willibrord to Friesland in 690. Three years later he returned to be consecrated as a regionary bishop by St Wilfrid and was then active around what is now the Ruhr (Germany). Saxon incursions destroyed his work, and he retired to the small island of Kaiserswerth in the Rhine, near Düsseldorf, where he founded a monastery and where he died.

Swithin (Swithun) of Winchester (St) {2}

2 July

d. 862. From Wessex (England), he was educated at the cathedral at Winchester and, after being ordained, was chaplain to King Egbert of Wessex and tutor to the crown prince. In 852 he was appointed bishop of Winchester, and during the decade for which he was bishop of the Kingdom of Wessex attained the height of its power and influence. On his death, at his request, he was buried in the cemetery outside the cathedral, but his body was moved into the cathedral in 971. According to legend his disapproval was shown by a downpour, which gave rise to the absurd but popular saying 'If it rains on St Swithin's day it will rain for the following forty days'. His shrine was destroyed at the Reformation.

Swithin Wells (St) {2}

10 December

d. 1591. From a landowning family at Brambridge (Hants), he ran a Catholic school in Wiltshire until 1582 and then was involved with his wife in helping priests working in secret. He was arrested at his house in Gray's Inn Road (London) together with St Edmund Genings and was hanged, drawn and quartered with him at Gray's Inn Fields. His wife died in prison. He was canonized in 1970. Cf. **England, Martyrs of**.

Syagrius (Siacre) of Autun (St) {2, 4}

2 September

d. 599–600. A Gallo-Roman nobleman, he became bishop of Autun (France) in c.560 and was one of the most influential men in the contemporary Gallic church. He showed hospitality to St Augustine and his companions on their way to England.

Syagrius (Siacre) of Nice (St) {2}

23 May

d. ?787. A relative of Charlemagne, he became a monk at Lérins and then abbot-founder of the monastery of St Pons at Cimiez in Provence (France). In 777 he was made bishop of Nice.

(Sycus and Palatinus) (SS) *{4 –deleted}*

30 May

? They are listed as two martyrs of Antioch (Syria) but the original entry was probably 'Hesychius Palatinus' (one person).

Sylvanus cf. **Silvanus**.

Sylvester, Pope (St) {1, 3}

31 December

d. 335. A Roman, he became pope in 314, just after the Emperor Constantine had granted imperial toleration to Christianity in the edict of Milan in 313. Very little that is historically certain is known about his life, though there are various unreliable legends connecting him with Constantine. He did not baptize the emperor, which event only took place after his death. During his pontificate the first ecumenical council of Nicaea was convened to deal with the Arian heresy, and he was represented by bishop Hosius of Cordoba. Most of his relics are at San Silvestro in Capite, Rome. His attribute is a small dragon in his hand or on a chain.

Sylvester of Châlons-sur-Saône (St) {2, 4}

20 November
d. 520–30. Bishop of Châlons-sur-Saône (France) from ?484, he was praised by St Gregory of Tours.

Sylvester Gozzolini (St) {2, 3}

26 November
1177–1267. From Osimo near Ancona (Italy), he studied law at Padua and Bologna before becoming a secular priest and canon at Osimo. Later he became a hermit at Montefano near Fabriano. There he had a vision of St Benedict in 1231, which led him to found a new reformed Benedictine congregation initially known as the Blue Benedictines (from the colour of their habits) and later as the Silvestrines. This had a centralized structure, was approved in 1247 and had eleven monasteries by the time of his death as abbot-general. He was listed in the Roman Martyrology as a saint in 1598, but his cultus was confined to particular calendars in 1969.

Sylvester of Troina (St) {2}

2 January
C12th. He was from Troina in Sicily, and became a Byzantine-rite monk at San Michele before living the life of a hermit in a forest near Troina, of which place he is the patron.

Sylvia (St) {2, 4}

3 November
C7th. She was the mother of Pope St Gregory the Great and had a chapel dedicated to her on the site of her house on the Coelian Hill at Rome. The assertion that she persuaded her husband, Gordianus, to donate his lands to the abbey of Montecassino is false and was possibly maliciously invented there in furtherance of legal claims.

Symmachus, Pope (St) {2, 4}

19 July
d. 514. A pagan convert from Sardinia, he was elected pope in 498 by the Roman clerical faction determined not to grant any concessions to the patriarchate of Constantinople in order to end the Acacian schism. The aristocratic opponents of this policy, wanting reconciliation with the emperor, elected an anti-pope called Laurence. Both factions were violently competing in Rome until Theodoric, the Arian king of the Ostrogoths, was appealed to and made judgement in favour of Symmachus in 506. He was not listed in any martyrology before the C16th.

Symphorian of Autun (St) {2, 4}

22 August
C3rd–4th. A nobleman of Autun (France), he was martyred for refusing to sacrifice to the goddess Cybele. He is one of the most famous martyrs of Gaul.

Symphorian Ducki (Bl) {2}

11 April
1888–1942. A Polish Franciscan Capuchin friar, he died of ill-treatment at the concentration camp at Auschwitz. Cf. **Poland, Martyrs of the Nazi Occupation of**.

Symphorosa of Tivoli and Comps (SS) {2, 3}

18 July
C2nd? She was martyred on the Via Tiburtina (the road to Tivoli) outside Rome with seven companions: Crescens, Julian, Nemesius, Primitivus, Justin, Stacteus and Eugene. According to their worthless acta (an adaptation of the story of the mother with seven sons in the second book of the Maccabees) she was the widow of the martyr St Getulius and the mother of seven brothers. Their cultus was suppressed in 1969.

(Symphronius of Rome and Comps) (SS)
{4 –deleted}

26 July
C3rd? According to the legend, he was a Roman slave who converted the tribune Olympius, the latter's wife Exuperia and their son Theodulus before they were all burnt to death in the reign of Valerian.

Syncletica of Alexandria (St) {2}

5 January
C4th. A wealthy inhabitant of Alexandria (Egypt), she fled the city to live as a hermit in a tomb until her eighty-fourth year. For a long time she suffered from temptations and spiritual aridity, and in her later years from cancer and tuberculosis. She is one of the famous 'desert mothers' in whom much interest has been shown recently.

Synesius and Theopompus (SS) {4 –deleted}

May
They were an erroneous duplication of SS Theopemptus and Theonas in the old Roman Martyrology.

(Synesius of Rome) (St) {4 –deleted}

12 December
d. 275. He was listed as a Roman church reader martyred in the reign of Aurelian.

(Syntyche of Philippi) (St) {4 –deleted}

22 July
C1st. She is referred to by St Paul in Philippians 4:2-3.

(Syrian Monks) (SS) {4 –deleted}

31 July
Early C6th? They were listed as a group of 350 monks of Syria massacred by Monophysites

for defending the decrees of the council of Chalcedon.

(Syrian Women) (SS) {4 –deleted}

14 November
C8th. They were listed as a large number of women viciously killed at Emesa (now Homs) in Syria by Muslim invaders.

Syrus of Genoa (St) {2}

29 June
d. c.330. He was bishop of Genoa (Italy) and is the principal patron of the city and diocese.

Syrus of Pavia (St) {2}

9 December
C4th. The first bishop of Pavia (Italy), he is the city's principal patron. Worthless legends attempt to place him in the C1st and to make him a companion of St Juventius of Pavia.

Sytha cf. **Osyth**.

Szilárd Bogdánffy (Bl) {2 –add}

3 October
1911–53. A Magyar from what is now Crna Bara in Vojvodina (Serbia) but was then in Hapsburg Hungary, he moved with his family to Timişoara (now in Romania), and became a priest of the Latin-rite diocese of Oradea in 1934. When the area was annexed by Romania in 1919, he came under suspicion from the government as a Hungarian priest. This turned to hostility after the Communists took over in 1945, and his consecration as auxiliary bishop of Satu Mare in 1949 had to be in secret. He was imprisoned two months later, suffering torture and ill-treatment, and was kept in custody until he died of pneumonia at Aiud. He had been refused medical care. He was beatified as a martyr in 2010.

T

Tancha (St) {2}

10 October
C6–7th. The daughter of Syrian refugees, she was killed when she resisted an attempt at rape at Arcis, north of Troyes (France). She is venerated as a virgin martyr at the latter place.

Taracus cf. **Tharacus**.

Tarasius (St) {2, 4}

18 February
d. 806. A nobleman of Constantinople, he was the secretary of Empress Irene during her regency for her son, Emperor Constantine VI. He was chosen to be patriarch in 784 while still a layman, and he accepted on condition that a general council be convened to end iconoclasm. The second council of Nicaea took place in 787. Shortly after, however, Constantine VI divorced his wife and remarried, and St Theodore the Studite and his followers condemned Tarasios of being too lenient in the resultant 'Moechian controversy'.

Tarsicia (Tarsitia) (St) {2, 4}

15 January
C6–7th Allegedly of royal descent, she was a sister of St Ferreolus of Uzès and was a hermit near Rodez (France). Her shrine is in the cathedral there.

Tarsicia Mackiv (Bl) {2}

18 July
1919–44. A young religious of the Sisters, Handmaids of Mary Immaculate, she was killed by a Red Army soldier at Krystonopil in what became the western part of the Soviet republic of Ukraine. Cf. **Nicholas Čarneckyj and 24 Comps**.

(Tarsicius, Zoticus, Cyriac and Comps) *(SS)* {4 –deleted}

31 January
? They are listed as martyrs at Alexandria (Egypt).

Tarsicius of Rome (St) {2, 4}

15 August
d. ?257. According to the inscription upon his tomb, written by Pope St Damasus, he was carrying the Blessed Sacrament (perhaps to Christians in prison) when he was ambushed by a pagan mob. He chose to die rather than let the sacred elements be profaned. He was probably a deacon.

Tarsilla (St) {2, 4}

24 December
d. a.593. She was an aunt of Pope St Gregory the Great and sister of St Emiliana, and lived a life of seclusion and mortification in her family home.

(Tarsus, Martyrs of) *(SS)* {4 –deleted}

6 June
C3rd? The listing in the old Roman Martyrology of twenty martyrs at Tarsus in Cilicia (Asia Minor) in the reign of Diocletian seems to depend on the fictitious acta of St Boniface of Tarsus.

Tate cf. **Ethelburga**.

(Tatiana) *(St)* {4 –deleted}

12 January
d. c.230. According to the old Roman Martyrology she was martyred at Rome in the reign of Alexander Severus. The Byzantine Martyrology has added Euthasia and Mertius as companions. Her acta are worthless.

Tation (St) {2, 4}

24 August
? He was beheaded at Claudipolis in Bithynia (Asia Minor).

Taurinus (St) {2, 4}

11 August
C5th. He was a bishop of Evreux in Normandy (France). The legend connecting him with St Dionysius of Paris is a worthless medieval forgery.

Teilo (St) {2}

9 February
C6th. Born probably at Penally near Tenby (Wales), according to his C12th biography he was educated by St Dyfrig and was a companion of SS David and Samson. He became the founder and abbot-bishop of a monastery at Llandeilo Fawr in Dyfed and was buried in Llandaff cathedral. There are many variants of his name: Teilio, Teiliavus, Teilus, Thelian, Teilan, Teilou, Teliou, Dillo, Dillon, etc.

Telchild (Theodichild) (St) {2}

28 June
d. p660. A nun of Faremoutier, she became the first abbess of the great double monastery of Jouarre near Meaux (France).

Telemachus cf. **Almachius**.

Telesphorus, Pope (St) {2, 3}

5 January
d. ?136. A Calabrian Greek, he was pope for ten years. According to a discredited tradition he was martyred in the reign of Hadrian. His cultus was suppressed in 1969.

Terence, Africanus and Comps (SS) {2, 4}

10 April
d. c.250. A group of forty-five Roman Africans, they were beheaded at Carthage in the reign of Decius. Beforehand they had been imprisoned with a number of snakes and scorpions which did not harm them, a fact which was regarded as miraculous by those ignorant of how those creatures actually behave when unmolested. Also named are Maximus, Pompeius, Alexander and Theodore.

(Terence of Iconium) *(St) {4 –deleted}*

21 June
C1st? He was allegedly a very early bishop of Iconium (Asia Minor, now Konya in Turkey). His identification with the Tertius mentioned by St Paul in Romans 16:22 is based on a presumption.

Terence-Albert O'Brien (Bl) {2}

30 October
d. 1651. He was a Dominican and the bishop of Emly in Co. Tipperary, and is noted for his care of victims of the bubonic plague. He was hanged after the siege of Limerick by Cromwell's forces and was beatified in 1992. Cf. **Ireland, Martyrs of**.

Terentian (St) {2, 4}

1 September
C4th. He was a bishop of Todi in Umbria (Italy). The Roman Martyrology has deleted the reference to his martyrdom.

Teresa Bracco (Bl) {2}

30 August
1924–44. Of a pious peasant family at Santa Giulia near Acqui (Italy), she was known for her piety and modesty when she was a schoolgirl. After Italy was invaded by the Allies in 1943 during the Second World War, guerilla warfare against the Germans broke out behind the front line. Santa Giulia was suspected of being a partisan stronghold and so the Germans raided it. A soldier seized her

and took her into the woods in order to rape her, but her resistance was so vigorous that he strangled and shot her instead. She was beatified in 1998.

Teresa Bojaxhiu of Calcutta (Bl) {2}

5 September
1910–97. She is universally known as 'Teresa of Calcutta', partly because of problems pronouncing her surname ('Boyajiw'). An Albanian from Skopje in Macedonia, she joined the 'Sisters of Loreto' in Ireland and was sent as a missionary to Calcutta in 1929. She taught at a school there, but in 1946 she received a call to found a new religious congregation devoted to serving the 'poorest of the poor'. Calcutta had many completely destitute people even then. She started in 1948, and her congregation, the 'Missionaries of Charity', received diocesan approval in 1950. She oversaw its spread to other parts of India from the 1960s, and had founded 610 convents in 123 countries by her death. One of the most famous persons to have been beatified in recent centuries, she received the Nobel Peace Prize in 1979. She was beatified in 2003, and her beatification was noted as having the shortest period between death and formal beatification in the church's history.

Teresa-of-Jesus Cepeda de Ahumada (St) {1, 3}

15 October
1515–82. From Avila near Madrid (Spain), she entered the local Carmelite nunnery when aged eighteen and found that the observance there had grown lax. This, together with a series of profound spiritual experiences, led her to undertake the reform of the Carmelite order and she opened her first reformed nunnery of St Joseph at Avila in 1562. From then on until her death, she was always travelling and opening new houses (fifteen directly

and seventeen through others). She had to ameliorate difficulties for her nuns and placate those in authority (both clerical and lay), who often opposed her and called her the 'roving nun'. During all this her remarkable mystical experiences continued and these she described (under obedience) in treatises which led her to be declared a doctor of the Church in 1970. She was a woman of sound common sense, of sane good humour and of generous ideals. She died at Alba de Tormes and was canonized in 1622. She is often depicted with her heart being pierced by an arrow held by an angel, as in the famous sculpture of her at Rome by Bernini.

Teresa Chen Jinjie and Rose Chen Aixie (SS) {1 –group}

5 July
1875 and 1878–1900. They were sisters at Feng in Hebei (China), and tried to flee the Boxers with a group of relatives and friends. They were, however, caught and three of the party were killed and two wounded. St Teresa was also killed, but St Rose survived being stabbed for a few hours. Cf. **China, Martyrs of**.

Teresa Couderc (St) {2}

26 September
1805–85. From Sablières in Ardèche (France), when aged twenty she joined a new teaching congregation at Apt. Then she was sent to open a hostel for women pilgrims at La Louvesc near Valence. Thus was founded the 'Society of Our Lady of the Cenacle', which became a separate congregation in 1836. Her intention was to attract pilgrims to the tomb of St John Francis Regis there and to help them to spend time in recollection. The institute developed as one of the retreat houses for women and rapidly spread throughout Europe and to America. She had to resign as superior

in 1835 owing to illness, but lived for another fifty years under superiors whose incompetence almost destroyed the congregation. She was canonized in 1970.

Teresa Demjanovich (Bl) {2 –add}

8 May

1901–27. She was born to a Ruthenian immigrant family in Bayonne, New Jersey, United States of America and was of the Byzantine rite. She became aware of a religious vocation when studying at the College of St Elizabeth at Convent Station, New Jersey but delayed making a choice until 1925 owing to health problems and the death of her parents. She then chose the Sisters of Charity of St Elizabeth, the teaching congregation running the school, which was Latin rite (she remained Byzantine rite, however). Her health quickly broke down, and she died of appendicitis with complications in hospital at Newark. Her evident holiness and piety led to her beatification in 2014. She has left a collection of spiritual conferences.

Teresa-of-Jesus Fernández Solar of Los Andes (St) {2}

12 April

1900–20. Born in Santiago (Chile), she was a very pious child who loved Our Lady. Being influenced by St Teresa of the Child Jesus and Bl Elizabeth of the Trinity, she entered the Carmel at Los Andes in 1919 but died of typhus the following year, being allowed to make her profession beforehand. She was canonized in 1993.

Teresa-of-Jesus Jornet Ibars (St) {2}

26 August

1843–97. She was brought up on a farm at Aytona near Lérida (Spain) but managed to qualify as a teacher at the latter place. Trying

her vocation at several religious institutions and failing, she then took the advice of her spiritual director and started one of her own at Barbastro in 1872. Her deep spiritual insight, firmness of spirit, unflagging energy and endurance were responsible for the foundation of fifty-eight houses of the 'Little Sisters of the Poor' in her lifetime. She died at Liria near Valencia and was canonized in 1974.

Teresa Kim (St) {1 –group}

9 January
Cf. **Agatha Yi and Teresa Kim**.

Teresa Kim Im-i (St) {1 –group}

20 September
Cf. **Laurence Han I-hyŏng and Comps**.

Teresa-Mary-of-the-Cross Manetti (Bl) {2}

23 April

1846–1910. Born near Florence (Italy), she started common life at home with two companions in 1868, and moved to St Justus in Florence in 1874. There they opened an orphanage, and became the 'Tertiary Sisters of the Order of Discalced Carmel' in 1885. Other houses were opened in Tuscany, also a house of perpetual adoration in Florence and a foundation at Carmel in the Holy Land. She suffered painfully from illness before she died, and was beatified in 1985.

Teresa Manganiello (Bl) {2 –add}

4 November

1849–76. From Montefusco (Italy), she belonged to a poor but pious peasant family. She never went to school and so was illiterate, but when she was aged twenty-two she became a Franciscan tertiary in her hometown in response to the efforts of Fr Giovanni Acernese towards the evangelization of rural areas. She herself became known as the 'Wise

Illiterate of Montefusco' as a result of her missionary work in the area. She wanted to found a regular congregation of sisters to help deprived people, but died before she could manage this. Her disciples founded the Franciscan Immaculatine Sisters at Pietradefusi in Avellino with the help of Fr Acernese. She was beatified in 2010.

Teresa-of-the-Child-Jesus Martin (St) {1, 3}

1 October

1873–97. Born at Alençon (France), she was one of five sisters in a pious bourgeois family which later moved to Lisieux. An initially happy childhood was marked by the death of her mother from cancer, the entry of her oldest sister into the local Carmel and the mental deterioration of her father (later to lead to complete insanity). She entered the Carmel herself in 1888 when aged only fifteen, despite serious opposition on account of her age. This initially seemed justified, as she died in agony of disseminated tuberculosis nine years later after having served as assistant novice-mistress. Her subsequent fame rests entirely on her spiritual autobiography, written under obedience and containing her doctrine of the 'Little Way' of spiritual childhood, which was published after her death. She was canonized in 1925, declared co-patron of foreign missions (with St Francis Xavier), co-patron of France (with St Joan of Arc) and finally doctor of the Church in 1997. Her attribute is a rose or rose petals. Photographs of her have survived, and the fact that many extant artistic representations of her do not much resemble these is owing to attempts at portraiture by one of her sisters.

Teresa (Tarasia) of Portugal (St) {2}

17 June

d. 1250. Daughter of King Sancho I of Portugal, she married her cousin Alphonsus IX,

king of Leon, but the marriage was annulled on the grounds of consanguinity. Returning to Portugal, she became a Cistercian nun at Lorvao near Coïmbra and died there. Her cultus as a saint was confirmed in 1705 for Portugal.

Teresa-Margaret-of-the-Sacred-Heart Redi (St) {2}

7 March

1747–70. From Arezzo (Italy), she became a Discalced Carmelite nun at Florence in 1765 and only lived another five years, but her witness of penance and prayer led her to be canonized in 1934.

Teresa-Benedicta-of-the-Cross Stein (St) {1}

9 August

1891–1942. Born in Breslau, Germany (now Wroclaw, Poland) of a rich and devout Jewish family, Edith Stein lost her faith early in life. She studied philosophy under Husserl at Göttingen University and became a noted philosopher in her own right, being converted to Catholicism by reading the works of St Teresa of Jesus. Baptized in 1922, she entered the Carmel at Cologne in 1933. Her main work was in synthesizing Thomism with modern philosophy (especially phenomenology). She moved to Echt (Netherlands) in 1938, but was taken from there to Auschwitz by the Nazis and gassed. She was canonized in 1998 and declared a patron of Europe in 2000.

Teresa-Eustochium Verzeri (St) {2}

3 March

1801–52. A noblewoman of Bergamo (Italy), she attempted three times to become a Benedictine nun but failed and took to teaching young girls at home instead. This led her to found the 'Daughters of the Sacred Heart' in 1831. Both the numbers and the scope of the institute grew so as to include a wide range of charitable works. The bishop of Bergamo, at first favourable, turned against her, but approval was given by Rome in 1841. She died comparatively young, worn out by her activities, at Brescia, was beatified in 1946 and canonized in 2001.

Teresa Yi Mae-im (St) {1 –group}

20 September
Cf. **Mary-Magdalen Yi Yŏn-hŭi and Comps**.

Teresa Zhang Hezhi (St) {1 –group}

16 July
1864–1900. From a Catholic family of Zhangji-aji near Ningjin in southeastern Hebei (China), she was seized while working in a vegetable garden by a Boxer gang and taken to the village temple. She refused to worship and she and her two sons were stabbed. Cf. **China, Martyrs of**.

Teridius and Remedius (SS) {2}

3 February
C4–5th. They were early bishops of Gap (France).

(Tertullian) (St) {4 –deleted}

27 April
Late C5th? He was listed as a bishop of Bologna (Italy). (His famous namesake among the Latin Fathers is not a saint, having died in heresy.)

Tertullinus (St) {2, 4}

31 July
Early C4th? A Roman priest, he was allegedly martyred two days after his ordination.

Thaddeus cf. **Jude**.

Thaddeus Dulny (Bl) {2}

6 August
1914–42. A Polish priest, he died of ill-treatment at the concentration camp at Dachau. Cf. **Poland, Martyrs of the Nazi Occupation of**.

Thaddeus Liu Ruiting (St) {1 –group}

30 November
1773–1823. From Qunglai county in Sichuan (China), he was a poor peasant until he became a priest's helper and was recommended for ordination. After this took place in 1807 he worked in northeast Sichuan until he was captured, imprisoned for two years and then hanged at Quxian. Cf. **China, Martyrs of**.

Thaddeus (Tadhg) McCarthy (Bl) {2}

25 October
d. 1492. He was made bishop of Ross in Co. Wexford (Ireland) in 1482 but was exiled in 1488. The pope then nominated him bishop of Cork and Cloyne, but he was not allowed into the diocese. So he returned to Rome to plead his cause personally, but died on his way home at Ivrea in Piedmont (Italy). His cultus was approved for Ivrea and Ireland in 1910.

Thalelaeus of Aegae (St) {2, 4}

20 May
C3rd. He was martyred at Aegae, a town on the coast near Anazarbus in Cilicia (Asia Minor). According to his dubious legend, he was a physician who treated his patients free of charge. The old Roman Martyrology listed with him Asterius and Alexander, two of his executioners, and others of the spectators who were converted by his example, but these companions have been deleted.

(Thamel and Comps) (SS) {4 –deleted}

4 September
C2nd? He is listed as a convert pagan priest who was martyred with four or five others (one of them his sister) somewhere in the East in the reign of Hadrian.

Tharacus, Probus and Andronicus (SS)
{2, 4}

11 October
d. ?304. They were beheaded at Anazarbus near Tarsus in Cilicia (Asia Minor) in the reign of Diocletian. According to their dubious acta, they were a retired Roman army officer and two civilians from Pamphilia and Ephesus, respectively.

Tharasius cf. **Tarasius**.
Thaw cf. **Lythan**.
Theau cf. **Tillo**.

Thebaid (Martyrs of) (SS) {2, 4}

28 July
d. c.250 During the reigns of Galerius and Valerian, there were a series of pogroms in the area in Upper Egypt around the old capital of Thebes. Some were killed by the sword, while others were hung up by their limbs and given the choice of apostasy or being left to a lingering death taking days.

The reference on 5 January in the old Roman Martyrology to a similar persecution in the reign of Diocletian has been deleted.

Theban Legion (SS) {2, 3}

22 September
d. ?302. In the reign of Maximian Herculius there was a massacre of soldiers at Agaunum (now St Maurice) on the Rhône in the Vallais (Switzerland). St Eucherius of Lyons is the earliest source for this, and he names Maurice, Exsuperius, Candidus and anonymous companions as soldiers and Victor as a retired veteran. According to the developed legend, the Theban was a legion of 6600 Christians recruited in Upper Egypt. When the emperor took his army across the Alps to suppress a revolt in Gaul, he camped at Agaunum and prepared for battle with public sacrifices. The Christian legion refused to attend (another version says that they refused to attack innocent people) and were in consequence twice decimated. When they persevered in their refusal they were massacred. Names added were Innocent, Vitalis, two Victors, Alexander (at Bergamo) and Gereon (at Cologne). A basilica was built on the site in the late C4th (where the town of St Maurice now is), which indicates that the story is based on truth. Perhaps a large number of soldiers were massacred there, but not a whole legion. Their cultus was confined to particular calendars in 1969.

(Thecla the Apostolic) (St) {3 –deleted}

23 September
C1st? According to the work of pious fiction entitled the 'Acts of Paul and Thecla', which contains extravagant legends and is not doctrinally sound, she was a maiden of Iconium (Asia Minor) who heard St Paul preaching while she sat at a window, became a Christian as a result and followed him dressed in boy's clothes. Several times she was viciously tortured, and finally died as a hermit at Seleucia. It is not possible to disentangle truth (if any) from fiction in her case. Her cultus was suppressed in 1969.

Thecla of Kitzingen (St) {2, 4}

15 October
d. c.790. A nun of Wimborne in Dorset (England) under St Tetta, she belonged to one of the groups that set out for the German missions under St Lioba. She was chosen by St Boniface as first abbess of Ochsenfurt near Würzburg and then of Kitzingen on the Main river, over which monastery she ruled for many years.

Thecla Nagaishi (Bl) {2}

10 September
d. 1622. A Japanese woman, she was beheaded at Nagasaki in the 'Great Martyrdom' with

her husband Paul and son Peter. Cf. **Charles Spinola and Comps**, **Great Martyrdom at Nagasaki** and **Japan, Martyrs of**.

Themistocles and Dioscorus (SS) {2, 4}

21 December

C3rd. The former was a shepherd of Myra in Lycia (Asia Minor) who was beheaded for refusing to reveal the hiding place of the latter. Their attribute is a set of caltrops (spikes used to cripple horses in battle).

Theobald of Dorat (St) {2}

6 November

d. 1070. He became a canon regular at le Dorat, near Limoges (France), under St Israel and went on to be prior. He never left the monastery except to perform his duties and to help poor people.

Theobald of Marly (St) {2}

8 December

d. 1247. A nobleman born at Marly near Laon (France), he was a knight at the court of King Philip Augustus before abandoning his career and becoming a Cistercian monk at Vaux-de-Cernay near Paris in 1220. He was made abbot there in 1235, and was esteemed by King St Louis IX.

Theobald (Thibaut) of Provins (St) {2, 4}

30 June

1017–66. A nobleman from Brie (France), he was a soldier as a teenager but converted and became a pilgrim with a companion, Walter, at the age of eighteen. After a time as hermits at Pettingen in Luxembourg they settled at Salanigo near Vicenza (Italy) and attracted disciples who settled around them. This was the start of a Camaldolese monastery. He was canonized in 1073.

Theobald Roggeri (Bl) {2}

1 June

d. 1150. From Vico in Liguria (Italy), allegedly of a wealthy family, he left home and worked as a cobbler at Alba in Piedmont. After a pilgrimage to Compostella he earned his living as a carrier and shared his wages with the poor. His shrine is at Alba.

Theobald (Thibaud) of Vienne (St) {2}

21 May

d. 1001. He was archbishop of Vienne (France) from 970 and his cultus was confirmed for Grenoble in 1903.

(Theoctista of Lesbos) (St) {4 –deleted}

10 November

C10th. She was allegedly a nun of Lesbos in the Aegean who became a hermit on Paros in the Cyclades after escaping a Muslim slave raid. The story of her last holy communion appears to be an adaptation from the biography of St Mary of Egypt.

Theodar (Chef) of Vienne (St) {2, 4}

29 October

d. ?575. A disciple of St Caesarius of Arles, he was abbot of one of the monasteries of Vienne (France) and founded several monasteries in the neighbourhood before dying as a hermit in the city.

Theodard of Maastricht (St) {2, 4}

10 September

d. c.670. He succeeded St Remaclus as abbot of Stavelot-Malmédy (Belgium) in 653 and became bishop of Maastricht in 663. He was on his way to the Frankish court to seek justice in a legal dispute when he was ambushed in the Bienwald near Speyer (Germany) and killed.

Theodard (Audard) of Narbonne (St) {2}

1 May

d. 893. From Montauban (France), he was educated at the Benedictine abbey of St Martin at Montauriol and became archbishop of Narbonne. He died at Montauroil (later named St Audard after him), allegedly having become a monk there just beforehand.

Theodgard (St) {2}

24 June

d. ?1065. He was an early priest-missionary in northwest Denmark, building one of the first churches in the area at Vestervig.

Theodemir of Carmona (St) {2, 4}

25 July

d. 851. A monk from Carmona near Cordoba (Spain), he was beheaded at the latter place in the reign of Emir Abd-er-Rahman II.

(Theodora and Didymus) (SS) {4 –deleted}

28 April

d. 304. Their legend is that the former was a maiden of Alexandria (Egypt) who was sentenced to be a sex slave in a brothel, but was rescued by the latter who was still a pagan. This led to his conversion, and the two were martyred together.

Theodora-Anne-Teresa Guérin (St) {2}

(14 May)

1798–1856. From Etables (France), she joined the 'Sisters of Providence' at Ruillé-sur-Loir in 1823 and became a noted teacher and nurse. In 1839 she was the head of a group of six sisters who were sent to the diocese of Vincennes in Indiana, United States of America to make a foundation at St Mary of the Woods. The area was then mostly still undeveloped and the new community had enormous problems establishing itself, but by the time of her death it had established schools throughout Indiana. She was canonized in 2006.

(Theodora the Penitent) (St) {4 –deleted}

11 September

d. 491. Her developed story is similar to that of St Pelagia of Antioch, but the old Roman Martyrology merely described her as a woman of Alexandria (Egypt) who sinned but repented and remained as a consecrated hermit until her death.

(Theodora of Rome -1) (St) {4 –deleted}

1 April

C2nd? According to the worthless acta of Pope St Alexander I, she was a sister of St Hermes of Rome and assisted him when he was in prison and being tortured. She was herself martyred some months later, and brother and sister were buried side by side.

(Theodora of Rome -2) (St) {4 –deleted}

17 September

Early C4th? She was allegedly a wealthy Roman noblewoman who assisted those being persecuted in the reign of Diocletian.

Theodora of Rossano (St) {2}

28 November

d. 980. She was a Byzantine-rite abbess of a nunnery near Rossano in Calabria (Italy), and was a disciple of St Nilus the Younger.

Theodora of Tyre (St) {2}

2 April

d. 307. She was a virgin of Tyre who shouted her support for Christians brought before the public tribunal in order to be condemned for their faith. For this she was herself seized by the soldiers and brought before the magistrate, who ordered her to be tortured and killed and her body to be thrown into the sea.

(Theodore, Oceanus, Ammianus and Julian) *(SS)* *{4 –deleted}*

4 September
They were listed as burnt at the stake some-where in the eastern Roman Empire.

Theodore and Pausilypus (SS) {2, 4}

15 April
d. 117–37. They were martyred near Byzan-tium (Constantinople) in the reign of Hadrian.

(Theodore of Bologna) *(St)* *{4 –deleted}*

5 May
d. c.550. He was listed as a bishop of Bologna (Italy).

Theodore of Canterbury (St) {2}

19 September
?602–90. An Asiatic Greek from Tarsus in Cilicia (Asia Minor), he spent some time at Athens and apparently became a monk at Rome. He was in his sixties when Pope Vital-ian chose him in 666 to be archbishop of Canterbury at the suggestion of St Adrian, who went to England with him as adviser. He is arguably the unifier of the Anglo-Saxon church, as he made the first visitation of most of the country as archbishop and held the first national council at Hatfield in 672. He tried to rationalize the boundaries of the extant dio-ceses and created several new ones, but this policy was opposed by St Wilfrid. The school that he opened at Canterbury with St Adrian became nationally important, and he was a noted scholar in his own right, but none of his writings survives.

(Theodore of Cyrene) *(St)* *{4 –deleted}*

4 July
Early C4th? He was allegedly a bishop of Cyrene in Libya, who was a skilled copy-ist and was tortured and martyred in the reign of Diocletian for refusing to surrender manuscripts of the Bible in his possession. There is confusion with St Theodore of Pentapolis.

(Theodore of Egypt) *(St)* *{4 –deleted}*

7 January
C4th. He was one of the disciples of St Ammon the Great at Nitria (Egypt).

Theodore Graptus *(and Theophanes Graptus)* (SS) {2, 4}

27 December
d. ?841. Brothers, they were monks at Mar Saba in the Holy Land and then at Constantinople. They were fervent opponents of the renewal of iconoclasm after the second ecumenical council of Nicaea, and the Emperor Theophilus ordered that they be whipped and their faces tattooed with insulting verses before being exiled (hence their nickname). Theodore died of ill-treatment in exile at Apamea in Syria, but Theophanes survived and was allegedly made bishop of Nicaea by Empress St Theodora. He has been deleted from the Roman Martyrology, while his brother is listed as a martyr.

Theodore of Marseilles (St) {2}

2 January
d. 594. He was zealous for the reform of church life, and as a result was exiled three times to Trier by the Burgundian kings Childebert and Guntram. He was eventually vindicated by a local synod of bishops which accepted his ideas.

Theodore of Pavia (St) {2, 4}

20 May
d. ?785. Bishop of Pavia near Milan (Italy) in 743, he was harassed and exiled by the Arian Lombard kings (whose capital it was) until the kingdom was conquered by Charlemagne.

Theodore of Pentapolis and Comps (SS) {2, 4}

7 April
Early C4th. He was described as a bishop of Pentapolis in Libya (this was actually a region, not a city) who had his tongue cut out in the reign of Gallienus with Irenaeus, his deacon, and Serapion and Ammonius, two church readers. They survived and died in peace, yet are listed as martyrs.

(*Theodore of Perga and* Comps) *(SS)* *{4 –deleted}*

20 September
d. 220. According to the legend, Theodore and Socrates were soldiers, Dionysius was a former pagan priest and Philippa was Theodore's mother. They were crucified at Perga in Pamphylia (Asia Minor) in the reign of Eliogabalus, and took three days to die.

Theodore Romzha (Bl) {2}

1911–47. From Nagybocso in Ruthenia, then part of the Hapsburg Empire and now in Ukraine, he was ordained as a priest of the Byzantine rite in 1936 and was made auxiliary bishop of Mukachievo in 1944. He was made apostolic administrator of his diocese two years later, by which time the Soviet policy of liquidating all non-Latin rites of the Catholic Church in Eastern Europe was being promulgated. Refusing to consider joining the Russian Orthodox Church, he was ambushed by soldiers while on a parish visitation and severely beaten. While recovering in hospital, he was murdered by being injected with a dose of curare and was beatified as a martyr in 2001.

(*Theodore the Sacristan*) *(St)* *{4 –deleted}*

26 December
C6th. He was sacristan at St Peter's in Rome and a contemporary of Pope St Gregory the Great.

Theodore of Sion (St) {2}

16 August
C4th. He was the first bishop of Sion in the Vallais (Switzerland), and a disciple of St Ambrose of Milan in his campaign against Arianism. He discovered and enshrined the relics of the Theban Legion at the place now named Saint-Maurice.

(*Theodore Stratelates*) *(St)* *{4 –deleted}*

7 February
C4th? He was allegedly a general ('stratelates') in the army of Emperor Licinius, by whose order he was tortured and crucified at Heraclea in Thrace (European Turkey). He is identical with St Theodore Tyro.

Theodore Studites (St) {2, 4}

11 November
759–826. From Constantinople, he became a monk at Saccudion where his uncle St Plato was abbot and succeeded him in 794. His community opposed Emperor Constantine VI in the 'moechian controversy' and they were dispersed and exiled, but he was recalled by Irene and re-founded his monastery at Studios in 799. This became a lasting source of monastic revival in the East, its influence reaching to Mt Athos and later to Russia, Rumania and Bulgaria, and was famous for its liturgical prayer, community life, enclosure, poverty, studies and manual work (the monks excelled in calligraphy). It was also a powerful centre of opposition to the revival of iconoclasm, and he was again exiled because of this before his death at Chalcis. His monastery church survived (latterly as a mosque) until its roof fell in during a snowfall in 1912.

Theodore of Sykeon (St) {2, 4}

22 April
d. 613. Born at Sykeon in Galatia (Asia Minor), where his parents ran a way station for the

imperial postal service, he became a monk at Jerusalem and was later the abbot-founder of several monasteries in his native province. About 590 he was made bishop of Anastasiopolis in Galatia but resigned before he died. He was a great promoter of the cultus of St George.

Theodore of Tabennesis (St) {2}

27 April
C4th. From near Thebes (Egypt), he joined the cenobites of Tabennesis and was a favourite disciple of St Pachomius. He had to replace St Horsiesius as superior in 351 when there was a revolt among the brethren, but he always regarded this as a temporary expedient. He oversaw, with sorrow, the growing wealth of the congregation. When he died St Horsiesius became superior again.

Theodore Trichinas (St) {2, 4}

20 April
C5th. From Constantinople, he became a hermit near his city and was nicknamed Trichinas, 'the hairy', because his only garment was a rough hair shirt.

Theodore Tyro (St) {2, 3}

9 November
d. 306–11. According to his story he was a recruit ('tyro') in the Roman army who set fire to the temple of Cybele at Euchaita near Amasea in Pontus (Asia Minor) and was himself burnt alive at the same place. He is almost certainly identical with St Theodore Stratelates. In the East he is venerated as one of the 'three soldier saints' (George, Demetrius and Theodore), but his cultus in the Roman rite was confined to local calendars in 1969.

Theodoret (Theodore) of Antioch (St) {2, 4}

23 October
d. 362. A priest of Antioch (Syria) and treasurer to the great church there, he was beheaded

in the reign of Julian for refusing to hand over church property formerly belonging to pagan institutions. He was highly regarded by St John Chrysostom.

Theodoric Balat (St) {1 –group}

9 July
Cf. **Gregory Grassi and Comps**.

Theodoric van der Eem (St) {2}

9 October
d. 1572. A Dutch Franciscan, he was confessor to the Franciscan nuns at **Gorinchem** and one of the martyrs there.

Theodoric (Thierry) of Mont d'Or (St) {2, 4}

1 July
d. 533. He was educated by St Remigius of Rheims (France), by whom he was appointed abbot of Mont d'Or near that city.

Theodoric II of Orleans (St) {2}

27 January
d. 1022. He was a Benedictine monk at Saint-Pierre-le-Vif at Sens (France) and was a royal counsellor before being made bishop of Orleans. He died at Tonnerre on his way to Rome.

(Theodosia of Caesarea Philippi and Comps) (SS) {4 –deleted}

29 May
d. ?303. According to the legend, probably a fabrication, she was the mother of St Procopius the Great and was martyred at Caesarea Philippi in the Holy Land with twelve other women in the reign of Diocletian.

Theodosia of Constantinople (St) {2}

18 July
C8th. A nun of the monastery of St Anastasia at Constantinople, she led a group of other

nuns in a violent attempt to prevent the destruction of the icon of Christ over the so-called Bronze Gate of the imperial palace by soldiers sent on the orders of the iconoclast emperor, Constantine V. She died of torture in prison.

(Theodosia of Tyre) (St) {4 –deleted}

2 April

Early C4th? According to her story, she was a teenager of Tyre (Lebanon) and was on a visit to Caesarea in the Holy Land when she asked some martyrs on their way to execution to pray for her. She was overheard, seized, tortured and finally thrown into the sea.

Theodosius of Auxerre (St) {2, 4}

17 July

C6th He was bishop of Auxerre (France) from ?507.

Theodosius the Cenobiarch (St) {2}

11 January

423–529. A Cappadocian, he went to Jerusalem to be a monk and joined a monastery on the road to Bethlehem, but then fled in order to avoid being made abbot and settled as a hermit in the desert east of Bethlehem in 479. He attracted disciples and founded the largest and most thoroughly organized of the Judaean monasteries with several hundred monks. He built a church for each of three language groups (Greeks, Armenians and Arabs), and made the monastery famous for its hospitality and charitable works. The patriarch of Jerusalem appointed him visitor to all the cenobitical communities in the Holy Land (St Sabas was responsible for the hermits), and as such he was forceful in support of the council of Chalcedon against the Monophysites. His monastery has been re-founded, but is now surrounded by a suburb.

Theodosius of Kiev (St) {2}

3 May

d. 1074. He is regarded as the father of monasticism in Russia. During the reign of the Grand Princes at Kiev, the centre of Slav culture at the time, he became a monk at the Pechera or Cave monastery at Kiev (Ukraine), named because it began as a group of hermits living in caves in the bluffs overlooking the Dneiper River. He was chosen as abbot in 1057 by the founder St Anthony, and introduced the cenobitic life to his monastery. The customary of St Theodore of Studion from Constantinople was used, and this was the definitive beginning of organized monastic life in Russia.

(Theodosius, Lucius, Mark and Peter) (SS) {4 –deleted}

25 October

C3rd? They were listed as among fifty soldiers martyred at Rome in the reign of Claudius II.

(Theodota of Constantinople) *(St)* {4 –deleted}

17 July

C8th. A noblewoman of Constantinople, she was executed for having hidden three icons to save them from destruction by the officials of the iconoclastic emperor Leo III.

Theodota of Nicaea and Comps (SS) {2, 4}

2 September

Early C4th. They were a mother and three sons (Evodius, Hermogenes and Callistus) who were martyred at Nicaea (Asia Minor).

Theodotus of Ancyra and Comps (SS) {2, 4}

18 May

d. ?303. He was martyred at Ancyra (Asia Minor, now Ankara in Turkey) with his aunt Thecusa and six virgins named Alexandra,

713

Claudia, Phaina, Euphrasia, Matrona and Julitta. The virgins were raped in a brothel, and then all eight had stones tied round their necks and were thrown into a marsh in the reign of Diocletian.

(Theodotus of Caesarea and Comps) *(SS)* *{4 –deleted}*

31 August
d. ?270. According to the unreliable acta of St Mamas (the only source) they were the martyr's father, mother (Rufina) and foster-mother (Ammia) and were themselves martyred at Caesarea in Cappodocia (Asia Minor) in the reign of Aurelian.

(Theodotus of Cyrenia) *(St)* *{4 –deleted}*

6 May
Early C4th. He was bishop of Cyrenia in Cyprus and suffered a long term of imprisonment in the reign of Licinius.

Theodotus of Heraclea (St) {2, 4}

14 November
? He was martyred at Heraclea in Thrace (European Turkey), but nothing is known about him. His companions, Clementinus and Philomenus, have been deleted from the Roman Martyrology.

(Theodotus of Laodicea) *(St)* *{4 –deleted}*

2 November
d. 334. A bishop of Laodicea (Latakia in Syria), he was an Arian and a friend of the historian Eusebius but signed the decrees of the council of Nicaea. Afterwards he sided with the Arian leader Eusebius of Nicomedia. His insertion in the Roman Martyrology was an error.

Theodula cf. **Dula.**

Theodulf (Thiou) of Lobbes (St) {2, 4}

24 June
d. 776. He was the third abbot-bishop of Lobbes near Liege (Belgium).

(Theodulus, Anesius and Comps) *(SS)* *{4 –deleted}*

31 March
? They were Roman African martyrs. Felix and Cornelia are also listed.

Theodulus, Saturninus and Comps (SS) {2, 4}

23 December
d. 250. They were ten martyrs who were tortured and beheaded at Gortyna in Crete in the reign of Decius after refusing to sacrifice to the goddess Fortune. The others were Euporus, Gelasius, Eunician, Zoticus, Pontius, Agathopus, Basilides and Evaristus.

(Theodulus of Antioch) *(St)* *{4 –deleted}*

23 March
? He was listed as a priest of Antioch (Syria), but with no further information.

Theofrid (Theofroy, Chaffre) of Carmery (St) {2}

18 November
d. ?752. From Orange (France), he joined the abbey of Carmery-en-Velay near Le Puy and became its abbot. He died as a result of injuries received in an Arab raid and is listed as a martyr. The abbey was renamed St Chaffre after him.

Theogenes of Cyzicus (St) {2, 4}

3 January
d. 320. He was a recruit to the army of the Emperor Licinius, and refused to serve as a soldier because of his faith. As a result he

was imprisoned and then thrown into the sea at Cyzicus on the Sea of Marmara (Turkey). The old Roman Martyrology added two companions, Cyrinus and Primus. But they came from a garbled rendering of 'At Cyzicus, at the entrance of the Hellespont', and hence have been deleted.

Theogenes of Hippo Regius (St) {2, 4}

26 January
d. ?257. He was a martyr of Hippo Regius in Roman Africa, and St Augustine preached in his honour. His thirty-six companions have been deleted from the Roman Martyrology.

Theonas of Alexandria (St) {2, 4}

28 December
d. 300. He became patriarch of Alexandria (Egypt) in 281, supported the famous catechetical school there and opposed Sabellianism (which denied any real distinctions between the persons of the Trinity).

Theonestus (St) {2, 4}

20 November
d. a.313. He was a martyr at Vercelli (Italy). According to his discredited and anachronistic legend, he was a refugee bishop of Philippi in Greek Macedonia in exile from the Arians and was sent by the pope with several companions (including St Alban of Mainz) as missionaries to Germany. They were at Mainz but had to flee the invading Vandals, and Theonestus was martyred at Altino near Venice. None of this is correct.

Theopemptus and Theonas (SS) {2, 4}

3 January
d. ?304. They were martyred at Nicomedia (Asia Minor) in the reign of Diocletian. According to their worthless acta they were the bishop and a magician, respectively. The

latter was converted by the martyrdom of the former, and was himself then martyred. The old Roman Martyrology listed them again in error on 21 May, as 'Theopompus and Synesius'.

(Theophanes, Papias, Strategius and Jacob) (SS) {4 –deleted}

4 December
d. ?815. Four officials at the court of Leo V at Constantinople, they were imprisoned and tortured for their opposition to iconoclasm. Theophanes died under torture, but the others survived and eventually became monks.

Theophanes the Chronographer (St) {2}

12 March
d. 818. From Constantinople, as an orphan he was educated at the imperial court and married young, but the couple separated to enter monastic life in 780. He became a monk at Polychronion and was later abbot-founder of Mt Sigriana near Cyzicus. He was a determined opponent of the revival of iconoclasm by Emperor Leo V and was exiled to the island of Samothrace, where he died from ill-treatment.

Theophilus and Helladius (SS) {2, 4}

8 January
C3rd? A deacon and a layman, they were tortured and thrown into a furnace in Libya (Roman Africa).

Theophilus the Apologist (St) {2, 4}

13 October
C2nd. An Eastern philosopher, he read the scriptures with the intention of rebutting them but was converted and became bishop of Antioch (Syria). He wrote an extant 'Apology' in three volumes, in which he contrasted the pagan myths of Greece with the Biblical

account of creation. His work developed the idea of the Logos or Word of God.

(Theophilus of Brescia) *(St)* *{4 –deleted}*

27 April
C5th. He succeeded St Gaudentius as bishop of Brescia (Italy).

Theophilus of Caesarea (St) {2, 4}

5 March
d. 195. Bishop of Caesarea in Palestine, he opposed the Quartodecimans, a sect which celebrated Easter on the Jewish Passover day regardless of whether it fell on a Sunday or not.

Theophilus Fernández de Legaria Goñi and Comps (BB) {2 –add}

11 August
d. 1936. Five members of the Congregation of the Sacred Hearts of Jesus and Mary based at that congregation's college at El Escorial in Madrid were shot by Communist militia after the start of the Spanish Civil War. They were beatified in 2013. Cf. **Spanish Civil War, Martyrs of** and list in appendix.

Theophilus the New Martyr (St) {2, 4}

30 January
d. 792. He was an officer of the imperial forces stationed in Cyprus when the Arabs invaded the island, was taken prisoner after battle and was executed after a year for refusing to become a Muslim.

Theophilus of Seleution (St) {2, 4}

2 October
d. c.795. A Bulgarian, he became a monk of a monastery on Mt Seleution in Asia Minor, which allegedly used the western European monastic rule of St Benedict. For opposing iconoclasm he was persecuted and exiled by the Emperor Leo IV.

Theophilus-of-Corte de Signori (St) {2, 4}

19 May
1676–1740. From Corte in Corsica, he became a Franciscan in 1693, was ordained at Naples and taught theology at Civitella near Rome. Later, he became a famous missioner in Italy and Corsica, and was zealous for Franciscan reform. He died at Fucecchio, and was canonized in 1930.

Theophilact (St) {2}

8 March
d. c.840. He was a monk from Asia Minor and became bishop of Nicomedia (Asia Minor) in 816. He helped in the opposition to the iconoclastic policy of Emperor Leo V and was exiled to Caria, where he died thirty years later. He was mistakenly listed as Theophilus in the old Roman Martyrology.

(Theotimus and Basilian) *(SS)* *{4 –deleted}*

18 December
? They were listed as martyrs of Laodicea (Latakia) in Syria.

(Theotimus of Tomi) *(St)* *{4 –deleted}*

20 April
d. 407. Bishop of Tomi (on the coast of Romania), he defended the writings of Origen against St Epiphanius of Salamis and evangelized the barbarian tribes of the Lower Danube then migrating into imperial territory.

Theotonius (St) {2}

18 February
d. 1162. From Galicia, he was educated at Coïmbra (Portugal) and became archpriest of Viseu but resigned to go on pilgrimage to the Holy Land. On returning he joined the Augustinian Canons Regular at Coïmbra and was highly regarded by the first ruler of the new Kingdom of Portugal.

Theresa cf. **Teresa**.

(Thespesius) *(St)* *{4 –deleted}*

1 June
C3rd? He was martyred in Cappadocia (Asia Minor) in the reign of Alexander Severus.

Theuderius cf. **Theodore**.

(Theusetas, Horres and Comps) *(SS)* *{4 –deleted}*

13 March
? According to the old Roman Martyrology, they were a father and his young son who were martyred at Nicaea (Asia Minor) together with Theodora, Nymphodora, Mark and Arabia. Earlier martyrologies have a much longer list of martyrs, and Horres is variantly given as Choris, a virgin.

Thierry cf. **Theodoric**.
Thillo cf. **Tillo**.
Thiou cf. **Theodulf**.

Thomais *(St)* *{2, 4}*

14 April
d. 476. The wife of a fisherman at Alexandria (Egypt), she was murdered by her father-in-law after she had rejected an indecent proposal that he had made.

Thomas Abel *(Bl)* *{2}*

30 July
d. 1540. He obtained a doctorate at Oxford University before becoming a chaplain to Queen Catharine of Aragon. As such he defended the validity of her marriage to King Henry VIII and was imprisoned in the Tower of London for six years before being executed at Smithfield with BB Edward Powell and Richard Featherstone for refusing to acknowledge the king's spiritual supremacy.

He was beatified in 1886. Cf. **England, Martyrs of**.

Thomas-of-Olera Acerbis *(Bl)* *{2 –add}*

3 May
1563–1631. From Olera, a village in a dead end valley in the hills north of Bergamo, Italy, he became a Capuchin at Verona when aged seventeen. In 1619 he was transferred to Innsbrück on the request of Archduke Leopold of Tyrol, who had heard of his sanctity. There he lived an austere life of penance while attending to poor and sick people in the city and, despite not being ordained, became a spiritual adviser to many at the highest levels of Austrian society. A collection of his writings has been published. He was beatified in 2013.

Thomas Akahoshi *(Bl)* *{2}*

10 September
d. 1622. A Japanese nobleman, he worked as a catechist with Bl Leonard Kimura and was burnt alive in the 'Great Martyrdom' at Nagasaki with BB Charles Spinola and Comps. Cf. **Japan, Martyrs of** and **Great Martyrdom at Nagasaki**.

Thomas Alfield *(Bl)* *{2}*

6 July
d. 1585. From Gloucester, he was educated at Eton and King's College, Cambridge before his conversion. Then he studied for the priesthood at Douai and Rheims and was ordained in 1581. After his return to England he was arrested while engaged in distributing copies of Dr Allen's 'True and Modest Defence', and was hanged at Tyburn for this. He was beatified in 1929. Cf. **England, Martyrs of**.

(Thomas of Antioch) *(St)* *{4 –deleted}*

18 November
d.782. He was a Syrian monk in a monastery near Antioch, and a patron against epidemics.

Thomas the Apostle (St) {1, 3}

3 July

C1st. He is surnamed 'Didymus', meaning 'the twin'. All that is known for certain about him is in the gospels, where he chiefly features in the episode concerning his unbelief and subsequent profession of faith in Christ's resurrection (Jn 20:24-9). According to an ancient tradition (important to the native churches but lacking proof) he went as a missionary to Kerala in south India and was martyred there. His name was later attached to apocryphal writings of the C2nd–4th such as the Gospel of Thomas. His attribute is a lance.

Thomas Aquinas (St) {1, 3}

28 January

?1225–74. Born at Roccasecca near Aquino in Campania (Italy), the son of a local nobleman, he was educated at Montecassino and then joined the recently founded Dominicans (despite the opposition of his family). After becoming doctor of theology at the University of Paris, he taught at Paris (1252–60), at Orvieto up to 1264, at Rome up to 1267, at Viterbo in 1268, at Paris again up to 1271 and finally at Naples up to 1274. He died at Fossanova near Rome while on his way to the council of Lyons. His systematic philosophical and theological writings, especially the 'Summa Theologiae', have had a profound influence up to the present day and were a successful synthesis of Christian and Aristotelian thought (western Christian philosophy having previously been Platonic, mediated through Augustine). As a person he was humble and prayerful, and very fat. He was canonized in 1323, declared a doctor of the Church in 1567 and patron of Catholic centres of study in 1880. His special attribute is a star or rays of light on his breast.

Thomas Atkinson (Bl) {2}

11 March

d. 1616. From the East Riding, he was ordained at Rheims in 1588 and was a priest in Yorkshire. He was very charitable, and travelled on foot until a leg broken by slipping on ice forced him to rely on a horse. He was captured at Willitoft, executed at York and beatified in 1987. Cf. **England, Martyrs of**.

Thomas Becket (St) {1, 3}

29 December

1118–70. His father was a Norman merchant in London and he studied at Paris before entering the service of the archbishop of Canterbury, who made him his archdeacon in 1154. He was a close friend of King Henry II, who made him royal chancellor in the following year and archbishop of Canterbury in 1162. Previously he had lived a rather worldly life, but as archbishop he concentrated on his pastoral duties and insisted on the independence of the church from the jurisdiction of the Crown. He went into exile in 1164, returned in 1170 and was assassinated in Canterbury Cathedral by four royal knights who thought they were acting on the king's wishes. He was canonized as a martyr in 1173, and his tomb became one of the foremost pilgrimage shrines in western Christendom until its destruction by King Henry VIII. He is often depicted with a wounded head, or holding an inverted sword or a crosier with a battleaxe head on it.

Thomas Bellacci (Bl) {2}

31 October

1370–1447. From Florence (Italy), he became a Conventual Franciscan lay brother at Fiesole and was novice-master there before successfully introducing reform measures to the Franciscans in Corsica and southern Italy and withstanding the heretical Fraticelli in Tuscany. When over seventy he went to preach in Syria, where (to his sorrow) he narrowly escaped being killed by the Muslims. He died at Rieti, Italy, and his cultus was approved for there and for the Conventual Franciscans in 1771.

Thomas Belson (Bl) {2}

5 July
1565–89. Born at Brill of a recusant Buckinghamshire landowning family, he studied at Oxford and Rheims and was seized when the Catherine Wheel Inn in Oxford (the city's centre of Catholic activity) was raided. He was executed at Oxford with those captured with him, namely BB Humphrey Pritchard, George Nichols and Richard Yaxley, and was beatified in 1987. Cf. **England, Martyrs of**.

Thomas Benstead (alias Hunt) (Bl) {2}

11 July
1577–1600. From Norfolk, he was among the first students of St Gregory's College at Seville and was ordained there in 1599. On his arrival at London he was captured and sent to the prison camp for English Catholic priests at Wisbech, but he escaped and was recaptured at the Saracen's Head Inn at Lincoln with Bl Thomas Sprott. They were executed together in that city, and were beatified in 1987. Cf. **England, Martyrs of**.

Thomas Bosgrave (Bl) {2}

4 July
d. 1594. A Dorset landowner, he was hanged at Dorchester with two of his servants, BB John Carey and Patrick Salmon, for aiding Catholic priests. Bl John Cornelius was executed with them. He was beatified in 1929. Cf. **England, Martyrs of**.

Thomas de Cantalupe (St) {2}

3 October
?1218–82. A nobleman from Hambleden near Great Marlow (Bucks), he studied at Oxford and Paris and became chancellor of Oxford University in 1261 (serving for a time as chancellor of England). He was made bishop of Hereford in 1275. The seven years of his episcopate he spent in continually fighting the mismanagement and neglect of his diocese (caused especially by civil war) and in untiring pastoral activities. He died at Montefiascone in Italy after setting out to appeal to the pope as he had quarrelled with John Peckham, archbishop of Canterbury, and had been excommunicated by him. Some relics were returned to Hereford and a popular cultus grew up based on his personal holiness and pastoral zeal and overlooking his irascibility and the fact that he died technically excommunicated. He was canonized in 1320.

Thomas Corsini (Bl) {2}

21 June
d. 1343. Born in Orvieto (Italy), he became a Servite lay brother there and spent his life collecting alms for his friary, where he died. He had many visions. His cultus was confirmed for Orvieto in 1768.

Thomas (Thomasius) of Costacciaro (Bl) {2}

25 March
d. 1337. From Costacciaro in Umbria (Italy), the son of poor peasants, he joined the Camaldolese at Sitria and then became a hermit on Monte Cupo. He has a cultus at Gubbio.

Thomas Cottam (Bl) {2}

30 May
1549–82. From Dilworth near Preston (Lancs), he came from a Protestant background, but

after his graduation at Oxford University he was converted and studied for the priesthood at Douai and Rome. At Rome he became a Jesuit and returned to England in 1580, but was arrested on landing at Dover and imprisoned in the Tower of London. Two years later he was hanged at Tyburn with St Luke Kirby and BB Laurence Richardson and William Filby, and was beatified in 1886. Cf. **England, Martyrs of**.

Thomas Dangi (St) {1 –group}

6 February

d. 1597. A Japanese Franciscan tertiary, he worked with the Franciscan missionaries in Kyushu (Japan) as a catechist and interpreter. He was crucified at Nagasaki with SS Paul Miki and Comps. Cf. **Japan, Martyrs of**.

Thomas Đinh Viết Dụ (St) {1 –group}

26 November

1774–1839. A Vietnamese priest and Dominican tertiary, he worked in the province of Nam Định before being arrested, tortured and beheaded with St Dominic Nguyễn Văn Xuyên during the persecution ordered by Emperor Minh Mạng. Cf. **Vietnam, Martyrs of**.

Thomas of Farfa (St)

10 December

d. c.720. From Maurienne in Savoy, he went on pilgrimage to the Holy Land and on his return became a hermit near Farfa (Italy). With the help of the Duke of Spoleto he restored the abbey there to its former splendour. His cultus was confirmed for Farfa in 1921, but he is not listed in the Roman Martyrology.

Thomas Felton (Bl) {2}

28 August

1568–88. From Bermondsey (London), son of Bl John Felton, he was educated at Rheims

and became a Minim Friar. He was hanged at Isleworth in his twentieth year and beatified in 1929. Cf. **England, Martyrs of**.

Thomas Ford (Bl) {2}

28 May

d. 1582. From Devon, he was at Trinity College, Oxford when he converted and then studied for the priesthood at Douai. After ordination in 1573 he worked in Oxfordshire and Berkshire until his arrest and execution at Tyburn with BB John Shert and Robert Johnson. He was beatified in 1886. Cf. **England, Martyrs of**.

Thomas-Mary Fusco (Bl) {2}

(24 February)

1831–91. From a middle-class family of Pagani near Salerno, Italy, he was orphaned as a child and was ordained priest in 1855. In 1857 he became an itinerant missionary in southern Italy and in 1860 he became chaplain at the Marian shrine at Pagani. There he founded the 'Daughters of Charity of the Precious Blood' in 1873 in order to run orphanages for poor girls. He died of liver failure and was beatified in 2001.

Thomas Garnet (St) {2}

23 June

?1575–1608. From Southwark, a nephew of the famous Fr Henry Garnet SJ, he was educated for the priesthood at St Omer and Valladolid. At first he was on the English mission as a secular priest but became a Jesuit in 1604. He was hanged at Tyburn as a result of returning after being exiled and was canonized in 1970. Cf. **England, Martyrs of**.

Thomas Gengoro (Bl) {2}

18 August

d. 1620. A Japanese layman, he was a servant of Bl Simon Kiyota Bokusai and had a wife, Mary, and a two-year-old son, James. They were crucified at Kokura and beatified in 1867. Cf. **Japan, Martyrs of**.

Thomas Green (alias Greenwood) (Bl) {2}

15 June
d. 1537. He was a fellow of St John's College, Cambridge before becoming a Carthusian monk at the London Charterhouse, and was one of the seven of that community who were starved to death at Newgate prison for refusing to take the oath of spiritual supremacy demanded by King Henry VIII. Cf. **England, Martyrs of**.

Thomas Green (alias Richard Reynolds) (Bl) {2}

31 January
d. 1642. From Oxford, he was educated for the priesthood at Rheims, Valladolid and Seville. After his ordination in 1592 he returned to England and was on mission for nearly fifty years. He must have been an octogenarian when he was hanged at Tyburn with Bl Alban-Bartholomew Roe. He was beatified in 1929. Cf. **England, Martyrs of**.

Thomas Hélye (Bl) {4}

19 October
d. 1259. From Biville in Normandy (France), he led an ascetic life in the house of his parents and spent some of his time teaching the catechism to the poor. He accepted ordination at the request of his bishop and became an itinerant preacher in Normandy before being made the royal almoner. He died at the castle of Vauville, Manche and his cultus for Coutances was confirmed in 1859.

Thomas Hemmerford (Bl) {2}

12 February
d. 1584. From Dorset, he was at the University of Oxford and studied for the priesthood at the English College, Rome, where he was

ordained in 1583. The following year he was hanged at Tyburn (London) with BB George Haydock, James Fenn, John Munden and John Nutter. He was beatified in 1929. Cf. **England, Martyrs of**.

Thomas of Hereford cf. **Thomas de Cantalupe**.

Thomas-of-St-Hyacinth Hioji Rokuzaymon Nishi (St) {1 –group}

17 November
d. 1634. A Japanese Dominican priest from Hirado, he worked in Taiwan before being martyred in Nagasaki with St Jordan Ansa-loneHio. He was left hanging in a pit to die (which took a week) and was canonized in 1987 with SS Laurence Ruiz and Comps. Cf. **Japan, Martyrs of**.

Thomas Holford (alias Acton, Bude) (Bl) {2}

28 August
d. 1588. From Acton near Nantwich (Cheshire), his family was Protestant and he became a schoolmaster in Herefordshire before his conversion. Then he studied for the priesthood and was ordained at Rheims in 1583. After being on mission in Cheshire he was hanged at Clerkenwell (London) and was beatified in 1929. Cf. **England, Martyrs of**.

Thomas Holland (alias Sanderson, Hammond) (Bl) {2}

12 December
d. 1642. From Sutton near Prescot (Lancs), he was educated at St Omer and Valladolid and became a Jesuit in 1624. He was hanged at Tyburn (London) and was beatified in 1929. Cf. **England, Martyrs of**.

Thomas Johnson (Bl) {2}

20 September
d. 1537. A Carthusian at the London Charterhouse, he was one of that community

which starved to death in Newgate prison for refusing to take the oath of spiritual supremacy demanded by King Henry VIII. Cf. **England, Martyrs of**.

Thomas Kozaki (St) {1 –group}

6 February
d. 1597. He was a Japanese teenager aged fifteen, the son of St Michael Cozaki, and served at Mass for the Franciscan missionaries in Kyushu (Japan). He was crucified at Nagasaki with his father and Paul Miki and Comps. Cf. **Japan, Martyrs of**.

Thomas Koteda Kiuni and Comps (BB) {2}

27 November
d. 1619. Related to the ruling family on the Japanese island of Hirado-jima, he was educated by the Jesuits and lived in exile at Nagasaki, where he was ultimately beheaded with ten companions: Alexis Nakamura, Anthony Kimura, Bartholomew Seki, John Iwanaga, John Motoyama, Leo Nakanishi, Matthias Kozaka, Matthias Nakano Miota, Michael Takeshita and Romanus Matsuoka Miota. They were beatified in 1867. Cf. **Japan, Martyrs of**.

Thomas Koyanagi (Bl) {2}

19 August
d. 1622. He was a Japanese passenger on the ship carrying BB Louis Flores and Comps and was beheaded with them at Nagasaki. Cf. **Japan, Martyrs of**.

Thomas Maxfield (Bl) {2}

1 July
d. 1616. A native of Enville near Stourbridge (Staffs), he was educated for the priesthood at Douai and ordained in 1615 but was captured and hanged at Tyburn (London) the year after. He was beatified in 1929. Cf. **England, Martyrs of**.

Thomas More (St) {2}

22 June (d.n. 7 July)
1478–1535. A Londoner, he studied at Oxford University and became a barrister in London in 1501. Married twice, he was a good husband, devoted to wife and children, devout, cheerful and charitable. In 1516 he published his 'Utopia', which earned him a European reputation as a scholar and humanist. He was highly regarded by King Henry VIII and Cardinal Wolsey, and succeeded the latter in 1529 as lord chancellor. He did not accept the king's wish to divorce Queen Catherine, however, so he resigned and, for refusing to take the oath of spiritual supremacy demanded by the king, he was imprisoned in the Tower of London for fifteen months. Then he was condemned for treason and beheaded on Tower Hill. He was canonized with St John Fisher in 1935. Cf. **England, Martyrs of**.

Thomas-of-the-Holy-Rosary of Nagasaki (Bl) {2}

10 September
d. 1622. A Japanese Dominican lay brother, he worked as a catechist before being beheaded in the 'Great Martyrdom' at Nagasaki with BB Charles Spinola and Comps. Cf. **Japan, Martyrs of** and **Great Martyrdom at Nagasaki**.

Thomas-of-St-Hyacinth of Nagasaki (Bl) {2}

8 September
d. 1628. A Japanese catechist and Dominican lay brother, he was burnt alive at Nagasaki with BB Dominic Castellet and Comps. Cf. **Japan, Martyrs of**.

Thomas Nguyễn Văn Đệ (St)

19 December
Cf. **Francis-Xavier Hà Trọng Mậu and Comps**.

Thomas Khuông (St) {2}

30 January

1861. He was a Vietnamese secular priest in north Vietnam, and when he was ordered to trample on a crucifix during the persecution ordered by Emperor Tự Đức, he genuflected to it instead. As a result he was immediately killed. Cf. **Vietnam, Martyrs of.**

Thomas-of-St-Augustine Ochia Jihyōe (Bl) {2 –add}

6 November

d. 1637. He was a priest of the Augustinian friars, from Ōmura near Nagasaki and martyred at Nishizaka. He was beatified in 2008. Cf. **Japan, Martyrs of.**

Thomas Palaser and Comps (Bl) {2}

8 September

d. 1600. Born at Ellerton on Swale, Yorks, he studied at Rheims and was ordained at Valladolid in 1596. He was a priest for three years in Yorkshire before being picked up on suspicion near Raven's Hall at Laymsley, a known recusant house. His vestments and books were then found there and he was executed at Durham with the owner of the house, Bl John Norton and his guest, Bl John Talbot from Thornton le Street. They were beatified in 1987. Cf. **England, Martyrs of.**

Thomas Percy (Bl) {2}

22 August

1528–72. As Earl of Northumberland he was leader of the Catholic gentry of the North of England, and was condemned to death and executed at York for his part in the insurrection in favour of Mary, Queen of Scots. He was in prison for nearly three years before being executed, and was repeatedly offered his freedom on condition of his apostasy to Protestantism. He was beatified in 1896. Cf. **England, Martyrs of.**

Thomas Pickering (Bl) {2}

9 May

d. 1679. From Westmoreland, he became a Benedictine lay brother at St Gregory's in Douai (the precursor of Downside Abbey) in 1660 and was sent to England to join the small community of Benedictine chaplains who served the Chapel Royal. He was falsely accused in the Oates plot, was hanged at Tyburn and beatified in 1929. Cf. **England, Martyrs of.**

Thomas Pilchard (Pilcher) (Bl) {2}

21 March

1557–87. Born in Battle in Sussex, he studied at Oxford and Rheims and was ordained at Laon. Then he was a priest in Dorset and Hampshire before being deported, but returned to Dorset. He was recognized and captured while on a visit to London and was executed at Dorchester by a butcher (no hangman being available). He was beatified in 1987. Cf. **England, Martyrs of.**

Thomas-of-Cori Placidi (St) {2}

11 January

1653–1729. From near Velletri (Italy), he was a shepherd in the Roman Campagna before becoming an Observant Franciscan in 1675. After his ordination he was at Civitella near Subiaco and spent the rest of his life ministering to the inhabitants of the mountains round about. He was beatified in 1786 and canonized in 1999.

Thomas Plumtree (Bl) {2}

4 January

d. 1570. From Lincolnshire, he was at the University of Oxford and became rector of Stubton in the reign of the Catholic Queen Mary I. After the Protestant Queen Elizabeth I succeeded to the throne he became chaplain to the insurgents of the North, and was executed in the marketplace at Durham after refusing an offer of clemency if he would become a Protestant. He was beatified in 1886. Cf. **England, Martyrs of**.

Thomas Pormont (Bl) {2}

21 February
1560–92. Born near Brocklesby, he was of the Lincolnshire gentry and his family were fervent Anglicans (John Whitgift, later arch-bishop of Canterbury, was his godfather). He converted, however, was ordained at Rome and taught at the Swiss College. His return to London was quickly followed by his capture and execution, and he was beatified in 1987. Cf. **England, Martyrs of**.

Thomas Reding (Bl) {2}

16 June
d. 1537. A Carthusian lay brother at the Lon-don Charterhouse, he was one of the seven of that community who were starved to death at Newgate prison for refusing to take the oath of spiritual supremacy demanded by King Henry VIII. Cf. **England, Martyrs of**.

Thomas Reggio (Bl) {2}

9 January
1818–1901. A nobleman from Genoa (Italy), he was ordained in 1841 despite the prom-ise of a brilliant secular career and became bishop of Ventimiglia in 1877. He revitalized that poor diocese and founded the 'Sisters of St Martha' in 1878. In 1892 he was made arch-bishop of his home city of Genoa and was one of the great C19th bishops seeking to imple-ment the social teaching of the church. He died at Ventimiglia and was beatified in 2000.

Thomas Scryven (Bl) {2}

15 June
d. 1537. A Carthusian lay brother at the Lon-don Charterhouse, he was one of the seven of

that community who were starved to death at Newgate prison for refusing to take the oath of spiritual supremacy demanded by King Henry VIII. Cf. **England, Martyrs of**.

Thomas Shen Jihe (St) {1 –group}

9 July
Cf. **Gregory Grassi and Comps**.

Thomas Sherwood (Bl) {2}

7 February
1551–78. A Londoner, he was preparing to go to Douai to study for the priesthood when he was betrayed, imprisoned and racked in the Tower of London in order to force him to reveal the place where he had been going to Mass. He was finally executed at Tyburn on the charge of denying the Queen's ecclesiasti-cal supremacy and was beatified in 1886. Cf. **England, Martyrs of**.

Thomas Shichiro (Bl) {2}

10 September
d. 1622. A seventy-year-old Japanese layman with a sound reputation, he was beheaded in the 'Great Martyrdom' at Nagasaki with BB Charles Spinola and Comps. Cf. **Japan, Mar-tyrs of** and **Great Martyrdom at Nagasaki**.

Thomas Sitjar Fortiá and Comps (BB) {2}

d. 1936. During the Spanish Civil War, twelve Jesuits in total were killed by anti-clerical Republican elements and were beatified in 2001. Cf. **Spanish Civil War, Martyrs of** and list in appendix.

Thomas Somers (alias Wilson) (Bl) {2}

10 December
d. 1610. From Skelsmergh near Kendal in Cumbria, he was a schoolmaster before study-ing and being ordained at Douai. He was on the London mission, was hanged at Tyburn

with Bl John Roberts and was beatified in 1929. Cf. **England, Martyrs of**.

Thomas Son Cha-sŏn (St) {1 –group}

30 March
Cf. **Anthony Daveluy and Comps**.

Thomas Sprott (Bl) {2}

11 July
d. 1600. Born near Kendal, he was ordained at Rheims in 1596 but was captured in Holland on his way to England and was forwarded by the Dutch to London. He escaped but was recaptured at the Saracen's Head Inn at Lincoln with Bl Thomas Bensted. They were executed together and were beatified in 1987. Cf. **England, Martyrs of**.

Thomas Terai Kahioye (Bl) {2}

28 September
d. 1630. A Japanese Augustinian tertiary, he was beheaded at Nagasaki with BB John Chozaburo and Comps. Cf. **Japan, Martyrs of**.

Thomas of Terreto (St) {2}

5 July
d. 1000. He was abbot of the Byzantine-rite monastery of Santa Maria de Terréto near Reggio di Calabria (Italy).

Thomas Thwing (Thweng) (Bl) {2}

23 October
d. 1680. From Heworth near York, he was educated for the priesthood at Douai, was ordained in 1665 and was on the Yorkshire mission for fifteen years. He was executed at York for alleged involvement in the Oates plot, and was beatified in 1929. Cf. **England, Martyrs of**.

Thomas Toán (St) {1 –group}

27 June
1767–1840. A Vietnamese Dominican tertiary, he worked at Truing Linh in north Vietnam.

After being arrested he initially apostatized but quickly repented and was in consequence whipped and exposed to the sun and insects without food or drink for twelve days until his death. This was at Nam Định during the persecution ordered by Emperor Minh Mạng. Cf. **Vietnam, Martyrs of**.

Thomas of Tolentino (St) {2}

9 April
d. 1321. From Tolentino (Italy), he became a Franciscan and travelled as a missionary to Armenia and Iran. He was on his way to Sri Lanka, intending eventually to go to China, when he was shipwrecked at Tana near Bombay with three companions: James of Padua and Peter of Siena, Franciscans, and Demetrius of Tbilisi, a layman. They were beheaded by native Muslims and had their cultus approved for Tolentino in 1894. The companions are not listed by the Roman Martyrology.

Thomas Tomachi (Bl) {2}

8 September
d. 1628. He was a ten-year-old Japanese boy, and when his father, Bl John Tomachi, was burnt with Bl Dominic Castellet, he was beheaded with his three brothers: Dominic, Michael and Pau Cf. **Japan, Martyrs of**.

Thomas Trần Văn Thiện (St) {1 –group}

21 September
1820–38. A Vietnamese catechist attached to the Paris Society for Foreign Missions in the Mekong delta, he was studying for the priesthood when he was viciously whipped and strangled with St Francis Jaccard at Quảng Trị during the persecution ordered by Emperor Minh Mạng. Cf. **Vietnam, Martyrs of**.

Thomas Tsuji (Bl) {2}

7 September
d. 1627. A Japanese, he was educated by the Jesuits at Arima and joined them in 1589,

becoming famous as a preacher. He was exiled to Macao in 1614, but returned to Japan in disguise. Becoming discouraged, he abandoned his vocation for one day but repented and was eventually captured and burnt alive at Nagasaki with his housekeeper and son, BB Louis and John Maki. He was beatified in 1867. Cf. **Japan, Martyrs of**.

Thomas Tunstal (alias Helmes) (Bl) {2}

13 July

d. 1616. From Whinfell near Kendal in Cumbria, he was educated for the priesthood at Douai, ordained there in 1609, sent to the English mission in 1610 and arrested almost at once. He spent six years in prison, becoming a Benedictine meanwhile, before being hanged at Norwich. He was beatified in 1929. Cf. **England, Martyrs of**.

Thomas of Villanueva (St) {2, 3}

22 September

1486–1555. From Fuellana near Villanueva (Spain), he was a miller's son who joined the Augustinian friars at Salamanca in 1516 and was prior successively of the Augustinian friars of Salamanca (where he taught moral theology in the university), Burgos and Valladolid. Later he was in turn provincial superior of Andalusia and Castile, court chaplain and finally archbishop of Valencia in 1544. As archbishop he was known as the 'grand almoner of the poor'. He has left a number of theological writings. Canonized in 1658, his cultus was confined to particular calendars in 1969.

Thomas Warcop (Bl) {2}

4 July

d. 1597. A Yorkshire landowner, he was hanged at York with BB Edward Fulthrop, Henry Abbot and William Andleby for sheltering Catholic priests. He was beatified in 1929. Cf. **England, Martyrs of**.

Thomas Watkinson (Bl) {2}

31 May

d. 1591. A widower living at Menthorp (Yorks), he was seized at home with Bl Robert Thorpe when the latter was saying Mass for Palm Sunday. They were executed together at York. He was beatified in 1987. Cf. **England, Martyrs of**.

Thomas Welbourne (Bl) {2}

1 August

d. 1605. From Hutton Bushel near Scarborough (Yorks), he was a schoolmaster who was hanged at York for proselytizing Protestants. He was beatified in 1929. Cf. **England, Martyrs of**.

Thomas Whitaker (Bl) {2}

7 August

d. 1646. The son of a Burnley schoolmaster, he studied at St Omer and Valladolid and was ordained in 1638. He was a priest in Lancashire until caught at Goosnargh and executed at Lancaster with BB Edward Bamber and Martin Woodcock. They were beatified in 1987. Cf. **England, Martyrs of**.

Thomas Whitbread (alias Harcourt) and Comps (Bl) {2}

20 June

d. 1679. From Essex, he was educated at St Omer (France) and became a Jesuit in 1635. He became provincial superior of the English mission, and at the time of the Oates Plot was convicted with four other Jesuits (BB Anthony Turner, John Fenwick, John Gavan and William Harcourt) on a bogus charge of conspiring to murder King Charles II. They were hanged at Tyburn and beatified in 1929. Cf. **England, Martyrs of**.

Thomas Wo Jinyemon (Bl) {2}

27 August
d. 1627. A Japanese layman, he was beheaded at Nagasaki with BB Francis-of-St-Mary of Mancha and Comps for sheltering missionaries. Cf. **Japan, Martyrs of**.

Thomas Woodhouse (Bl) {2}

19 June
d.1573. A secular priest in Lincolnshire, he was also a private tutor in Wales. In 1561 he was imprisoned in the Fleet prison in London for eleven years before being executed at Tyburn. During his imprisonment he was admitted by letter to the Society of Jesus. He was beatified in 1886. Cf. **England, Martyrs of**.

Thomas-of-the-Holy-Spirit Zumarraga and Comps (BB) {2}

12 September
1575–1622. From Vitoria in the Basque Country (Spain), he became a Dominican missionary in Japan and was imprisoned for three years at Omura before being burnt there with BB Matthew-of-St-Thomas Chiwiato and Dominic Magaoshichi de Hyuga (who became Dominicans in prison with him) and the Franciscans BB Apollinaris Franco, Francis-of-St-Bonventure of Musashino and Peter-Paul-of-St-Clare of Arima. They were beatified in 1867. Cf. **Japan, Martyrs of**.

Thomasius cf. **Thomas of Costacciaro**.

Thorlák Thórhallsson (St) {2}

23 December
1133–93. From Iceland, he was ordained priest when aged eighteen and studied at Paris before becoming a canon regular at Thykkvibaer, being made abbot there in 1172. In 1174 he became bishop of Sklholt and was vigorous

against simony and clerical concubinage. He was declared a saint in 1198 by the Althing (the Icelandic Parliament).

(Thrace, Martyrs of) (SS) {4 –deleted}

20 August
? They were listed as a group numbering thirty-seven who were thrown into a furnace somewhere in Thrace (southeastern Balkans) after having their hands and feet cut off. They seem to relate to the martyrs of Philippopolis.

Three Wise Men (SS) {2, 4}

24 July
They are the wise men 'from the East' who were prompted by a star to go to Bethlehem and venerate the Infant Jesus. The revised Roman Martyrology lists them on this day, when their alleged relics were enshrined at Cologne (Germany). It does not name them (the traditional names are Caspar, Melchior and Balthasar), nor refer to them as kings.

Thraseas (St) {2, 4}

25 October
d. 170–80. Bishop of Eumenia in Phrygia (Asia Minor) and an opponent of the Montanist heretics, he was martyred at Smyrna (now Izmir, Turkey).

Thrasilla cf. **Tarsilla**.

Thurstan Hunt (Bl) {2}

3 April
d. 1601. Born at Carlton Hall near Leeds, he had been a priest on mission for fifteen years when he heard that Bl Robert Middleton had been captured near Preston. With four laymen he ambushed the posse taking Bl Robert to Lancaster but was himself captured. They were executed together and were beatified in 1987. Cf. **England, Martyrs of**.

Thyrsus, Leucius, Callinicus and Comps (SS) {2, 4}

14 December
d. c.250. They were martyred at Apollonia in Bithynia (Asia Minor), and their alleged relics were taken to Constantinople and thence to Spain and France.

(Thyrsus and Projectus) (SS) {4 –deleted}

24 January
? Nothing is known about these martyrs.

(Tiberius, Modestus and Florentia) (SS) {4 –deleted}

10 November
d. ?303. They were listed as martyred in the reign of Diocletian at Agde near Montpellier (France).

Tiburtius, Valerian and Maximus (SS) {2, 3}

14 April
? They were martyred at Rome and buried in the catacomb of Praetextatus. Their names occur in the unreliable acta of St Cecilia as her brother-in-law, her husband and an official. Their cultus was confined to local calendars in 1969.

Tiburtius of Rome (St) {2, 3}

11 August
C3rd–4th. This Roman martyr had an ancient cultus based on his tomb on the Via Lavicana, but nothing is known about him, and the connection with St Sebastian was a later invention. His cultus was confined to local calendars in 1969.

(Tigides and Remedius) (SS) {4 –deleted}

3 February
C6th? They were listed as bishops of Gap (France), Remedius being the successor to Tigrides.

Tigris (St) {2}

25 June
C6th. She was a hermit in the valley of Maurienne in the Alps of Savoy (France) who helped pilgrims passing through before going on pilgrimage herself to the Holy Land. She brought back a finger-bone of St John the Baptist, and established the shrine and town of St Jean de Maurienne.

Tigrius and Eutropius (SS) {2, 4}

12 January
d. 406. A priest and reader, respectively, of Constantinople, they were disciples of St John Chrysostom. When the latter was banished they were falsely accused of setting fire to the cathedral and senate house of the city and were tortured. Eutropius died as a result, while Tigrius apparently survived and was exiled to Asia Minor.

Tillo (St) {2}

7 January
d. ?702. From Lower Saxony (Germany), he was kidnapped in a raid and sold as a slave in the Low Countries, where he was bought by St Eligius of Noyon. He became a monk at Solignac, France, and after his ordination evangelized the district round Tournai and Courtrai (Belgium). He returned to Solignac and died as a hermit nearby. His name has many variants: Thillo, Thielman, Theau, Tilloine, Tillon, Tilman, Hillonius etc.

Timolaus and Comps (SS) {2, 4}

24 March
d. 303. A group of eight, they were beheaded at Caesarea in the Holy Land in the reign of Diocletian. Eusebius listed the names of the others: Dionysius (two), Romulus, Pausdes, Alexander (two) and Agapius.

(Timon) (St) {4 –deleted}

19 April
C1st. He was one of the first seven deacons chosen by the apostles (Acts 6:5), but the traditions concerning his subsequent career conflict. The old Roman Martyrology listed him as martyred at Corinth.

Timothy (St) {1, 3}

26 January
d. ?97. He features in the Acts of the Apostles (16:1-3) as a companion of St Paul on the latter's missionary journeys, and two letters of St Paul are addressed to him. Eusebius wrote that he became bishop at Ephesus and an ancient tradition describes him as having been stoned to death for denouncing the worship of Dionysius.

Timothy, Diogenes, Macarius and Maximus (SS) {2, 4}

6 April
d. ?345. They were martyred at Antioch (Syria).

(Timothy and Faustus) (SS) {4 –deleted}

8 September
? They were listed as martyred at Antioch (Syria).

Timothy and Maura (SS) {2, 4}

3 May
d. 286. Husband and wife, they had been married for only three weeks when they were martyred at Antinoë in Egypt by being nailed to a wall. They lingered for nine days while consoling each other. Timothy (who was a church reader) had been condemned for refusing to hand over the sacred books for burning.

(Timothy, Polius and Eutychius) (SS) {4 –deleted}

21 May
? They were listed as three deacons martyred in the Roman African province of Mauretania (now Morocco) in the reign of Diocletian.

Timothy of Gaza (St) {2, 4}

19 August
d. c.305. He was bishop of Gaza in the Holy Land, and was burnt alive in that city. Formerly listed with him were Thecla, who was thrown to the wild animals at the games, and Agapius, who was mistakenly also listed with them, as he was thrown into the sea at Caesarea in the Holy Land in 306.

Timothy of Africa (St) {2, 4}

21 May
? He was a Roman African deacon burnt alive in Mauretania (present-day Morocco).

(Timothy of Brusa) (St) {4 –deleted}

10 June
C4th? He was listed as a bishop of Brusa (Asia Minor, now Bursa in Turkey) martyred in the reign of Julian.

Timothy Giaccardo (Bl) {2}

24 January
1896–1948. Born near Alba in Piedmont (Italy), he entered the seminary there but discerned his vocation to be in the apostolate of social communications and joined the 'Society of St Paul' (which had been newly founded at Alba for this work). He was ordained in 1919 and was their first priest, master of students and vicar-general. He founded the mother house in Rome and built the Society up to become international in scope. He died of leukaemia at Rome and was beatified in 1989.

Timothy of Montecchio (Bl) {2}

22 August
1414–1504. From Montecchio near Aquila (Italy), he became a Franciscan Observant and was known for his humility. He died at Fossa and his cultus was confirmed for Aquila in 1870.

Timothy of Rome (St) {1, 3} {2, 3}

22 August
d. 303. A Roman, he was martyred in the reign of Diocletian and had his shrine near St Paul's outside the Walls. His cultus was confined to local calendars in 1969.

Timothy Trojanowski (Bl) {2}

28 February
1908–42. A Polish Franciscan Conventual friar, he died of ill-treatment at the concentration camp at Auschwitz. Cf. **Poland, Martyrs of the Nazi Occupation of**.

Titian of Brescia (St) {2, 4}

3 March
d. ?526. Allegedly a German, he was bishop of Brescia (Italy).

Titian of Oderzo (St) {2, 4}

16 January
C5th. He was bishop for thirty years at Oderzo near Venice (Italy). His diocese is now extinct.

Titus (St) {1, 3}

26 January
C1st. He was a helper and disciple of St Paul, who addressed a letter to him concerning the organization of the church in Crete. Later he was sent to Dalmatia, but the tradition is that he returned to Crete and (according to Eusebius) died as a bishop there. His alleged relics were at the cathedral of Gortyna before the island was conquered by the Muslims.

Titus Brandsma (Bl) {2}

26 July
1881–1942. Born in Bolsward in Friesland (Netherlands), he joined the Carmelites when aged seventeen and taught in the Catholic University of Nijmegen, becoming rector there in 1923. When the Germans occupied the Netherlands in 1940 he adhered to the teaching of the church in refusing to dismiss Jewish pupils or to propagate the Nazi doctrine. He was arrested, taken to the concentration camp at Dachau and killed with an injection of phenol. He was beatified in 1985.

(Titus of Rome) (St) {4 –deleted}

16 August
C5th? According to the story, he was a Roman deacon who was killed by a barbarian soldier during one of the two sacks of Rome in the C5th while distributing aid to the starving population.

Tochumra (St)

11 June
? She was venerated as a virgin in the former diocese of Kilmore in Co. Cavan (Ireland) and was a patron of women in childbirth.

Tooley cf. **Olav**.

Torpes (St) {2, 4}

29 April
? He was martyred at Pisa (Italy). His extant acta are worthless.

Torquatus, Ctesiphon and Comps (SS) {2, 4}

15 May
? They were seven early bishops in the south of Spain: Torquatus at Guadix, near Granada;

Ctesiphon at Verga (Vierzoa); Secundus at Avila; Indaletius at Urci, near Almeria; Caecilius at Granada; Hesychius at Gibraltar; and Euphrasius at Andujar. The Mozarabic liturgy had a common feast day for all seven, but the Roman Martyrology has deleted the reference to their being first-century martyrs.

Tranquillinus Ubiarco Robles (St) {1 –group}

5 October
1899–1928. From a poor family of Zapotlán el Grande, he became a diocesan priest of Guadalajara in Mexico in 1923 and was appointed to the parish of Tepatitlán. During the Cristero War he continued to say Mass in secret, and was captured just after finishing one such celebration. He was hanged from a tree at Tepatitlán. Cf. **Mexico, Martyrs of**.

(Tranquillinus of Rome) *(St) {4 –deleted}*

6 July
C3rd? An alleged Roman martyr, he features in the legend of St Sebastian.

(Trason, Pontian and Praetextatus) (SS) {4 –deleted}

11 December
Early C4th? They were listed as Romans executed in the reign of Diocletian for ministering to the Christian prisoners awaiting martyrdom.

Trier, Martyrs of (SS) {2, 4}

5 October
d. 287. There was a pogrom of Christians at the Imperial capital of Trier (Germany) in the reign of Diocletian.

Triphyllius (St) {2, 4}

13 June
d. c.370. A convert lawyer, he was a disciple of St Spiridion and became bishop of what is now Nicosia in Cyprus. As a loyal supporter of St Athanasius he was seriously harassed by the Arians, and was at the council of Sardica in 347.

Triverius (St) {2}

16 January
d. c.550. From a Gallo-Roman family, he was apparently a hermit near the monastery of Thérouanne in the Pas de Calais (France) before he moved to the Pays de Dombes north of Lyons. Two villages named Saint Trivier commemorate him, and he is venerated locally at Lyons and in the diocese of Belley.

Troadius (St) {2, 4}

2 March
d. 251. He was martyred at Neocaesarea in Pontus (Asia Minor) in the reign of Decius.

Trojan (Troyen) (St) {2, 4}

10 November
d. c.550. He allegedly had a Jewish father and a Muslim mother and was a disciple of St Vivian of Saintes (France), whom he succeeded as bishop.

Trond cf. **Trudo**.

Trophimus and Eucarpius (SS) {2, 4}

18 March
d. ?304. Two pagan soldiers, they were employed in hunting out Christians but converted and were themselves burnt alive at Nicomedia (Asia Minor) in the reign of Diocletian.

Trophimus of Synnada (St) {2, 4}

19 September
? He was martyred at Synnada at Phrygia (Asia Minor). The Roman Martyrology has deleted a companion called Sabbatius.

Another companion called Dorymedon was martyred the following day.

Trophimus and Thalus (SS) {2, 4}

11 March
d. c.300. They were crucified at Laodicea (Latakia in Syria) in the reign of Diocletian.

(Trophimus and Theophilus) (SS) {4 –deleted}

23 July
Early C4th? They were listed as beheaded at Rome in the reign of Diocletian.

Trophimus of Arles (St) {2, 4}

29 December
C3rd. He is venerated as the first bishop of Arles. Since the C5th he had been falsely identified with St Trophimus the Ephesian, the disciple of St Paul, but this confusion of two persons has been deleted from the Roman Martyrology.

(Trophimus the Ephesian) (St) {4 –deleted}

29 December
C1st. He accompanied St Paul to Jerusalem, and his presence there was the motivation for the riot which caused the latter's arrest (Acts 21:29). By one tradition he was beheaded at Rome in the reign of Nero. The allegation in the old Roman Martyrology that he was the first bishop of Arles is false.

Trudo (Truiden, Trond) (St) {2, 4}

23 November
d. c.690. He was a monk at Stavelot-Malmédy under St Remaclus, was ordained by St Clodulf of Metz and eventually became the abbot-founder of a monastery on his family's estate where the town of St Truiden (Belgium) now is.

(Tryphaena of Cyzicus) (St) {4 –deleted}

31 January
? She was listed as a married woman of Cyzicus on the Sea of Marmara (Asia Minor), tortured and then thrown to a wild bull to be gored to death.

(Tryphenna and Tryphosa) (SS) {4 –deleted}

10 November
C1st. They are mentioned by St Paul in his letter to the Romans (16:12). The worthless legend of St Thecla describes them as converts of Iconium (Asia Minor).

(Tryphon of Alexandria and Comps) (SS) {4 –deleted}

3 July
? A group of thirteen, they were listed as martyred at Alexandria (Egypt).

Tryphon of Phrygia (St) {2, 3}

2 February
? He was a martyr of Phrygia in Asia Minor. According to his unreliable legend, he kept geese at Campsada near Apamea (Syria) and was martyred at Nicaea (Asia Minor) in the reign of Decius. His relics are in the church of St Augustine at Rome. Respicius and Nympha, his alleged companions, have been linked with him only since the C11th, and are otherwise unknown. Their feast day on 10 November was suppressed in 1969, and the companions have been deleted from the Roman Martyrology.

(Tryphonia) (St) {4 –deleted}

18 October
C3rd? An alleged Roman widow martyr, according to her worthless acta she was the wife either of the Emperor Decius or of his son.

Tude cf. **Antidius**.

Tudinus cf. **Tudy**.

Tudwal (Tugdual) (St) {2}

30 November
C6th. A British monk, he migrated to Brittany (France) and became bishop of Tréguier. Three places in the Lleyn Peninsula (Wales) are named after him.

Tudy (Tegwin, Thetgo) (St)

11 May
C5th. A Breton, possibly a disciple of St Brieuc, he was a hermit near Landevennec in Brittany (France) and then abbot there. He apparently spent some time in Cornwall (England), where a village is named after him.

Tugdual cf. **Tudwal**.

Turiaf (Turiav) (St) {2, 4}

13 July
C6–7th. From Brittany (France), he succeeded St Samson as bishop of Dol.

Turibius of Astorga (St) {2, 4}

16 April
d. c.460. Bishop of Astorga (Spain) at a time when that place was ruled by the barbarian Suevi, he was troubled by the Priscillianist heretics and obtained a condemnation of them from the pope.

Turibius de Mongrovejo (St) {2, 4}

23 March
1538–1606. From Mayorga de Campos in the province of León (Spain), he was professor of law at Salamanca and was made president of the Inquisition at Granada while still a layman. King Philip II made him archbishop of Lima in Peru in 1580, and he zealously set out to reform the corruptions and abuses prevalent in church life in what was then one of the richest cities in the world. He especially tried to protect the native Americans against exploitation by Spanish immigrants. He was canonized in 1726.

Turibius Romo González (Bl) {1 –group}

25 February
1900–28. From Jalostotitlàn, he became a diocesan priest of Guadalajara in 1922 and was committed to Catholic Action and the apostolate to workers. When the Cristero War broke out he was parish priest of Tequila, and continued his ministry in secret while hiding in an abandoned factory. However, his whereabouts were discovered, and he was arrested and shot at the Town Hall of Tequila. Cf. **Mexico, Martyrs of.**

Tuscana (St) {2}

14 July
d. 1343–4. She was a widow of Verona (Italy) and joined the Hospitaller Order of St John of Jerusalem in order to nurse sick people.

Twelve Brothers (SS) {3 –deleted}

1 September
Early C4th? The alleged relics of four groups of southern Italian martyrs were brought together and enshrined at Benevento in 760. A spurious legend subsequently grew up that they were the remains of the twelve sons of SS Boniface and Thecla and had been arrested in Africa and martyred in Italy. The four groups concerned are: (1) At Potenza in Basilicata on 27 August, Arontius (Orontius), Honoratus, Fortunatus and Sabinian. (2) At Venosa in Apulia on 28 August, Septiminus, Januarius and Felix. (3) At Velleianum in Apulia on 29 August, Vitalis, Sator (Satyrus) and Repositus. (4) At Sentianum in Apulia on 1 September, Donatus and another Felix. The cultus was suppressed in 1969.

Tychicus (St) {2, 4}

29 April
C1st. He was a disciple of St Paul (Acts 20:4; 21:29) and his fellow worker (Col. 4:7; Eph. 6:21). The tradition that he became bishop of Paphos in Cyprus is not in the Roman Martyrology.

Tychon (St) {2, 4}

16 June
C5th. Bishop of Amathus in Cyprus, he energetically fought against the surviving paganism in the island, especially the cult of Aphrodite based at Paphos.

Tydfil (St)

23 August
d. ?480. Allegedly of the clan of St Brychan, she was apparently killed by Pictish or Saxon invaders where the Welsh town of Merthyr Tydfil now stands. (The story may be based on a false etymology of 'Merthyr', taken to mean 'martyr' when it probably means 'shrine'.)

Typasius (St) {2}

11 January
d. 297–8. He was a Roman veteran who had become a hermit near Tigava in Mauretania, Roman Africa (now Morocco). When recalled to army duty he refused to serve or to sacrifice to idols, and as a result was beheaded. He was not included in the old Roman Martyrology, but has been inserted into the revised one since his surviving acta seem to be genuine.

Tyrannio and Zenobius (SS) {2, 4}

20 February
d. 311. They were a bishop and priest of Tyre, martyred at Antioch in Syria. The old Roman Martyrology mistakenly added three companions now deleted: Silvanus was martyred at Emesa in Syria, and Peleus and Nilus were (according to Eusebius) Egyptian bishops among those enslaved and martyred in the quarries of the Holy Land.

Tyre, Martyrs of (SS) {2, 4}

20 February
d. 303. They were five young men who were viciously flogged at Tyre (Lebanon) before being thrown to the wild animals in the amphitheatre to be mauled. They were finally killed with the sword. The old Roman Martyrology fictitiously made their number very large, and mistakenly included Tyrannio and the companions mentioned in the previous entry.

U

Ubald Adimari (Bl) {2, 4}

9 April

1246–1315. A nobleman of Florence (Italy), he was a leader of the anti-papal Ghibelline party and was notoriously dissolute. In 1276 he was converted by St Philip Benizi, however, then became a Servite and spent the rest of his life as a penitential hermit on Mt Senario. His cultus was confirmed for the Servites in 1821.

Ubald Baldassini (St) {2}

16 May

?1080–1160. From Gubbio near Ancona (Italy), as dean of the cathedral there he reorganized the chapter around a rule of common life. He became bishop in 1128 and was famous for being both gentle and brave (which helped him in dealing with Emperor Frederick Barbarossa). He was canonized in 1192, but his cultus was confined to local calendars in 1969.

Ubaldesca (St) {2}

28 May

d. 1206. From near Pisa (Italy), she joined the Hospitaller Sisters of the Holy Sepulchre when aged sixteen and served sick people in the hospital at Pisa until her death at the age of fifty-five.

Ubric cf. **Ulric**.
Uda cf. **Tudy**.

Udalric of Augsburg (St) {2}

4 July

c.890–973. From Augsburg (Bavaria), he was educated at the abbey of St Gall (Switzerland) and became bishop of his native city and its secular ruler in 923. He was the protector of his people against the invading Magyars and a friend and supporter of the Emperor Otto I.

When old he retired to St Gall and took one of his nephews as his coadjutor, but he does not seem to have taken religious vows. He was canonized in 993, the first formal canonization at Rome.

Uganda (Martyrs of) cf. **Charles Lwanga and Comps**.

Ukraine (Martyrs of) (BB)

C20th. At the start of the C20th, what is now the Ukrainian Republic was divided between the Hapsburg Empire to the West and Russia to the East. The western regions had originally belonged to Poland, and in these the majority of the Orthodox Christians with their clergy had joined the Roman Catholic Church in 1596. Thus was formed the 'Ukrainian Greek Catholic Church', accepting the authority of the Pope and using the Byzantine rite in worship. This was unacceptable to the Russian Orthodox Church and to the Russian government, and the policy of the latter before 1989 was one of suppression. After the Russian Revolution in 1917 all Christians in the Soviet Union were subjected to vicious persecution. In 1946, when the entire Ukraine fell under the rule of the Soviet Union, the Greek Catholic Church was proscribed and its clergy liquidated by being deported to prison camps, where many died. Twenty-five bishops, priests and religious with one layman who suffered in the persecution were beatified in 2001, along with one Latin-rite bishop (Bl Joseph Bilczewski) and one priest killed by the Nazis (Bl Emilian Kovch). Cf. list in the appendix.

Ulmar cf. **Wulmar**.

Ulpian (St) {2, 4}

3 April

d. 306. A Syrian, he was martyred at Tyre (Lebanon), allegedly by being sewn up in a leather sack with a dog and a snake before being thrown into the sea.

Ulric cf. **Wulfric**.

Ulrica Nisch (Bl) {2}

8 May
1882–1913. She was born in Württemberg (Germany), and her family was very poor. In 1898 she became a domestic servant and went to Rorschach in Switzerland, where she fell seriously ill in 1904. She had already been thinking about a religious vocation, and her being nursed by the 'Sisters of Charity of the Holy Cross' led her to join them at Baden in 1907. She was a model religious for six years despite her bad health, and treated her work in the kitchen as a holy exercise. She was beatified in 1987.

Urban I, Pope (St) {2, 3}

25 May
d. 230. A Roman, he succeeded St Callistus I as pope in 222. During his pontificate there was apparently no serious persecution of the church at Rome. His cultus was suppressed in 1969.

Urban II, Pope (Bl) {2}

29 July
1042–99. Odo of Lagery was a nobleman from Chatillon-sur-Marne (France) who studied at Rheims under St Bruno (the founder of the Carthusians) and became archdeacon there. In 1070 he became a monk at Cluny and was grand prior under St Hugh, then was made cardinal bishop of Ostia in 1080 and pope in 1088. A strong advocate of the Gregorian policy of ecclesiastical reform, he had St Bruno as an adviser and is remembered as the promoter of the first crusade at the council of Clermont in 1095. His cultus was confirmed for Rheims in 1881.

Urban V, Pope (Bl) {2, 4}

19 December
1309–70. William of Grimoard was from Languedoc (France) and was educated at the universities of Montpellier and Toulouse. He became a Benedictine monk at the priory of Chirac, was abbot of St Germanus at Auxerre from 1352 and of St Victor at Marseilles in 1361. Later that year he was sent as papal legate to Italy (the papacy then being at Avignon) and in the following year (although not a cardinal) was elected pope. He succeeded in transferring the papacy back to Rome, but was forced to return to Avignon in 1370 just before he died. His cultus was confirmed for Marseilles in 1870.

Urban, Theodore, Menedemus and Comps (SS) {2, 4}

5 September
d. 370. They were a group of eighty priests and clerics of Constantinople who, in the reign of the Arian Emperor Valens, were left to die in a burning ship for having appealed to the emperor against the persecution of Catholics.

(Urban of Langres) (St) *{4 –deleted}*

2 April
d. c.390. He became bishop of Langres in Burgundy (France) in 374, and is a local patron of vine-dressers.

Urban of Teano (St) {2, 4}

7 December
C4th. He was a bishop of Teano in Campania (Italy).

Urbitius of Metz (St) {2}

20 March
d. c.450. He was bishop of Metz (France).

Urbitius (Úrbez) of Nocito (St)

15 December
d. ?805. He was allegedly born at Bordeaux, became a monk in France and was taken prisoner in a Spanish Muslim raid. Escaping, he became a hermit in the valley of Nocito in the Pyrenees near Huesca (Spain). His extant biography is unreliable, but his local cultus is still popular. He is not included in the Roman Martyrology.

(Urciscenus) (St) *{4 –deleted}*

21 June
C3rd? He supposedly became the seventh bishop of Pavia (Italy) in 183, but his dates probably belonged to a much later period.

Ursacius cf. **Arsacius**.

(Ursicinus of Brescia) (St) *{4 –deleted}*

1 December
d. p347. A bishop of Brescia in Lombardy (Italy), he was at the council of Sardica in 347.

Ursicinus of Chur (St) *{2}*

2 October
C8th. He was abbot of Disentis in Graubünden, Switzerland before becoming bishop of Chur nearby in 754. In 758 he resigned and became a hermit.

Ursicinus of Luxeuil (St) *{2}*

20 December
d. c.620. An Irish monk at Luxeuil, he left that monastery with St Columban when the latter went into exile. Instead of going to Italy with him he settled as a hermit at the place later named St Ursanne, in Jura canton in Switzerland.

(Ursicinus of Ravenna) (St) *{4 –deleted}*

19 June
C2nd? According to his unreliable acta he was a physician at Ravenna (Italy) who wavered in his faith after being sentenced to death but repented and was martyred. He was probably martyred elsewhere and his relics transferred to Ravenna. Another saint of the same name was archbishop of the city in the C6th.

(Ursicinus of Sens) (St) *{4 –deleted}*

24 July
d. c.380.This bishop of Sens (France) was an opponent of Arianism and a friend of St Hilary of Poitiers.

Ursicinus (St) *{2, 4}*

14 August
Early C4th. An Illyrian tribune in the imperial army, he was beheaded somewhere in the Roman province of Illyricum in the reign of Diocletian.

Ursinus (St) *{2, 4}*

9 November
C3rd. Though once alleged to have been one of several disciples of Christ sent by the apostles to be bishops in Gaul, it is clear that he lived in the C3rd and was the first bishop of Bourges (France).

Ursmar (St) *{2, 4}*

18 April
d. 713. He was abbot and missionary bishop of the Benedictine abbey of Lobbes on the Sambre River (Belgium) and founder of the abbeys of Aulne and Wallers. His missionary work in Flanders was of great importance.

Ursula and Comps (SS) {2, 3}

21 October
C4th? They were a group of virgins martyred at Cologne (Germany). The fantastic legend, as fully developed, alleged that Ursula was a British young woman who was about to be married when a storm drove her and 11,000 virgin companions on board ship to the Low Countries. They visited Rome before returning to Cologne and were martyred by the Huns. The basis of this story is an inscription of c.400 recording the restoration of a church by Clematius in honour of some local early virgin martyrs whose number and names are not given. By the C9th they were claimed to have been a large number martyred in the reign of Maximian, and the discovery of an old cemetery at Cologne in 1155 provided a vast number of bones as spurious relics. The cultus was very popular in northern France, the Rhineland and the Low Countries in the Middle Ages but subsequently proved an embarrassment to the church and was suppressed in 1969. The medieval artistic legacy concerning her is rich; she is depicted as being shot with arrows while her companions are killed in various grotesque ways.

Ursula Ledochówska (St) {2}

29 May
1865–1939. She was born in Loosdorf (Austria) of a famous noble family of the Hapsburg Empire. In 1886 she joined the Ursulines in Cracow, became the superior and founded the first university college of theology for girls in the Polish lands. She moved to St Petersburg and did the same there in 1906, and then worked among the Lutherans of Finland and Scandinavia. In 1923 she founded the 'Ursuline Sisters of the Heart of Jesus in Agony' and worked in the Polish borderlands. She had great charity in ecumenical matters, and was canonized in 2003.

Ursus and Victor (SS) {2, 4}

30 September
d. ?286. They were alleged soldiers of the Theban Legion captured and executed at Solothurn in Switzerland.

Ursus of Aosta (St) {2}

1 February
Before C9th. According to his unreliable biography he was an Irish missionary who preached against the Arians in the South of France and became archdeacon of Aosta in the Alps (Italy).

Ursus of Auxerre (St) {2, 4}

30 July
C6th. He was a hermit at the church of St Amator of Auxerre, (France) and was made bishop of that city when aged seventy-five.

Ursus of Loches (St) {2}

27 July
C5–6th. From Cahors (France), he founded several monasteries in Berry and Touraine and died at Loches, one of them. He was a thaumaturge, noted for an abstinent way of life.

Ursus of Ravenna (St) {2, 4}

13 April
d. ?425. A pagan Sicilian nobleman, he became a convert and fled from his father's anger to Ravenna (Italy) where he became bishop in 378.

Usthazades and Comps (St) {2, 4}

17 April
d. 341. After the massacre of Christians at Ctesiphon ordered by the Persian Shah Shapur II (cf. **Simon Barsabae and Comps**),

the Shah ordered a pogrom throughout his empire. Usthazades was a eunuch in the palace of the Shah and had been nursed with him as a child, yet he was martyred at the palace of Artaxerxes, the Shah's brother, in the province of Adiabene on the Euphrates River.

Utto (Bl) {2}

3 October
d. 802. From Milan, he was abbot-founder of the Benedictine monastery of Metten in Bavaria (Germany). His cultus was confirmed for Regensburg in 1909.

V

Vaast cf. **Vedast**.

Valenciennes (Martyrs of) (BB) {2}

17 October
d. 1794. The Ursuline convent and school at Valenciennes in northern France were shut by the French Revolution in 1792, and the community moved to Mons in the Austrian Netherlands. The Austrians captured Valenciennes in 1793 and the sisters returned and reopened their school. When the revolutionary forces returned, Bl Mary-Clotilde-Anglea-of-St-Francis-Borgia Poillot (the superior) and seven of her community were condemned as returned emigrées and guillotined in two groups, one on the 17th and one on the 23rd. The latter included Bl Mary-Cordelia-Josepha-of-St-Dominic Barré, a lay sister who was overlooked when the tumbril was departing for the guillotine and who jumped on board herself. Two former Bridgettines and one former Poor Clare, who had joined the Ursulines when their own houses were suppressed, were also executed. Cf. **French Revolution, Martyrs of**.

(Valens of Auxerre and Comps) (SS) {4 –deleted}

21 May
? He is listed as a bishop martyred at Auxerre (France) with three boys.

(Valens of Verona) (St) {4 –deleted}

26 July
d. 531. He was bishop of Verona (Italy) from 524.

Valentina and Comps (SS) {2, 4}

25 July
d. 308. They were martyred at Caesarea in the Holy Land in the reign of Maximian. Valentina, a consecrated virgin, threw down and trampled an idol. As a result she was tortured and burnt alive with Thea, another virgin. Paul was beheaded at the same time.

(Valentine) (St) {4 –deleted}

29 October
? He is listed as a bishop in the old Roman Martyrology but nothing is known about him and he may be a duplicate of Valentine of Passau.

(Valentine, Concordius, Navalis and Agricola) (SS) {4 –deleted}

16 December
Early C4th? They were allegedly martyred at Ravenna (Italy) in the reign of Diocletian. St Peter Chrysologus (d. c.450) wrote, however, that St Apollinaris was the only martyr of Ravenna, which implies that they were martyred elsewhere and had their relics transferred to Ravenna.

(Valentine, Felician and Victorinus) (SS) {4 –deleted}

11 November
Early C4th? They are most probably duplicates of SS Valentine, Concordius and Comps.

Valentine and Hilary (SS) {2, 4}

3 November
? A priest and his deacon, they were beheaded at Viterbo near Rome.

(Valentine, Solutor and Victor) (SS) {4 –deleted}

13 November
Early C4th? They are most probably duplicates of SS Valentine, Concordius and Comps.

Valentine Berrio-Ochoa (St) {1 –group}

1 November
1827–61. From Ellorio near Vitoria (Spain), he became a Dominican and was a missionary

in the Philippines before going to Vietnam as vicar-apostolic of 'Central Tonkin' (the area around Hanoi). He was beheaded with SS Jerome Hermosilla and Peter Almató Ribeira during the persecution ordered by Emperor Tự Đức. This was at Hải Dương in north Vietnam. Cf. **Vietnam, Martyrs of**.

Valentine of Langres (St) {2}

4 July
C5th? He was a young courtier who gave up his career to become a diocesan priest at Langres (France), but then became a hermit and died relatively young.

Valentine Paquay (Bl) {2}

1 January
1828–1905. From Tongeren in Belgium, as a teenager he started to study for the secular priesthood but joined the Franciscans and became superior of the friary at Hasselt after his ordination in 1854. He remained there for the rest of his life, and was famous as a preacher and confessor and also for his spontaneous humility. He was beatified in 2003.

Valentine of Passau (St) {2}

7 January
d. c.450. He was a missionary bishop in the region around Passau (Austria), of which place he is the principal patron.

Valentine of Rome (St) {2, 3}

14 February
? According to his unreliable acta he was a priest and physician at Rome. He was possibly martyred in the reign of Claudius II and buried on the Flaminian Way, and a church was built over his tomb in 350. The custom of sending 'Valentines' on his feast-day is based on the medieval belief that perching birds

begin courtship then. His cultus was confined to local calendars in 1969.

(Valentine of Terni) *(St) {4 –deleted}*

14 February
C3rd? According to his unreliable acta he was a bishop of Terni near Rome who was martyred in the reign of Claudius II. It seems very probable that he is identical with Valentine of Rome.

(Valentine of Trier) *(St) {4 –deleted}*

16 July
Early C4th? He was a bishop allegedly martyred in the reign of Diocletian, listed as of Trier (Germany) but more probably of Tongeren (Belgium).

Valentinian of Chur (St) {2}

7 January
d. 548. He was a bishop of Chur (Switzerland), noted for his care for poor people and for the captives whom he ransomed.

(Valeria, Martyrs of) *(SS) {4 –deleted}*

14 March
C5th. The 'Dialogues' attributed to St Gregory the Great described them as two monks who were hanged by the invading Lombards in the Italian province of Valeria and who were heard singing psalms after they had died. The story is probably fictional.

Valerian of Abbenza (St) {2, 4}

15 December
d. p460. Bishop of Abbenza in Roman Africa, when aged over eighty he refused to hand over his church's sacred vessels to the Arians patronized by Genseric, king of the Vandals. As a result he was driven into the desert and left to die of exposure.

Valerian of Aquileia (St) {2, 4}

27 November
d. 388. He succeeded an Arian as bishop of Aquileia near Venice (Italy) and had to re-establish orthodoxy in his diocese.

Valerian of Cimiez (St) {2}

23 July
d. c.460. A monk of Lérins, he became bishop of Cimeiz near Nice (France). A collection of his homilies is extant.

Valerian of Lyons (St) {2, 4}

15 September
? He was with SS Photinus and Comps in prison at Lyons (France) but escaped to the mountains and was a missionary there. He was recaptured at Tournus near Autun and beheaded.

Valerius and Rufinus (SS) {2, 4}

14 June
Early C4th. Roman missionaries, they were martyred at Soissons (France).

Valerius of Langres (St) {2}

22 October
C4th. He was a deacon of Langres (France) who was killed by barbarians.

Valerius of Limoges (St) {2}

10 January
C6th. He was a hermit near Limoges (France).

Valerius of Trier (St) {2, 4}

29 January
End C3rd. According to legend he was the second bishop of Trier (Germany) and a disciple of St Peter, but this is anachronistic and he was bishop there about two hundred years later.

Valerius of Zaragoza (St) {2, 4}

22 January
d. 305–15. He was the bishop of Zaragoza (Spain) when St Vincent was a deacon there. Arrested and exiled in the reign of Diocletian, he survived the persecution and died in peace in his city.

Valéry cf. **Waleric**.
Vandrille cf. **Wandrille**.
Vanna cf. **Jane of Orvieto**.
Vanne cf. **Vitonus**.
Varelde cf. **Pharaildis**.

Varmund Arborio (Bl) {2}

13 November
d. 1010–14. Born at Vercelli (Italy), he became bishop of Ivrea in Piedmont in 969. His cultus was confirmed for there in 1857.

Varus (St) {2, 4}

19 October
d. 307. A Roman soldier in Upper Egypt, he was on guard at a prison containing some monks condemned to death. When he discovered that one of them had died he insisted on taking his place and was immediately hanged from a tree. The acta are genuine.

Vedast (Vaast, Vaat, Gaston, Foster) (St) {2, 4}

6 February
d. c.540. A fellow worker with St Remigius of Rheims in the conversion of the Franks, he was bishop of the combined dioceses of Arras-Cambrai for almost forty years. He renewed the church therein and instructed King Clovis the Frank for his baptism by St Remigius. Several churches in England are dedicated to him, notably the one in the City of London. He is depicted with a wolf and a goose, the latter of which he raises to life.

Venantius and Comps (St) {2, 4}

1 April
C3rd–4th. He was a bishop in Dalmatia (Croatia), but his era and diocese are uncertain. His body was taken from Split to the Lateran basilica in Rome in 641. He is commemorated with several other Dalmatian and Istrian martyrs: Anastasius, Maurus, Paulinian, Telius, Septimius, Antiochianus and Gaianus.

(Venantius of Camerino) *(St)* *{3 –deleted}*

18 May
C3rd? According to his spurious acta, written in the C13th, he was a teenager aged fifteen who was martyred at Camerino near Ancona (Italy) in the reign of Decius. He is not listed in the ancient martyrologies, and his cultus was confined to local calendars in 1969. He is now deleted from the Roman Martyrology.

Venantius Fortunatus (St) {2}

14 December
d. p610. From near Treviso (Italy), he migrated to Poitiers (France) when aged thirty, was ordained and became a friend of the Frankish Queen St Radegund. He became bishop of Poitiers in ?594. His fame is owing to his large number of extant hymns and poems, notably the *Vexilla Regis* and *Pange Lingua Gloriosi*, which had a major influence on later Christian hymnography and poetry.

Venantius of Luna (St) {2}

14 October
C4th. He was a bishop of Luna in Liguria (Italy), a now ruined city four miles south-east of Sarzana. He had great care for the welfare of priests and monks, and was a friend of Pope St Gregory the Great.

Venantius of Tours (St) {2, 4}

13 October
C5th. He was abbot of the monastery of St Martin at Tours (France).

Venantius of Viviers (St) {2}

5 August
d. p535. He became bishop of Viviers (France) in 517 and his cultus was popular, but his C12th biography is worthless.

(Veneranda) *(St)* *{4 –deleted}*

14 November
C2nd. She was listed in the old Roman Martyrology as a virgin martyr of Gaul, but apparently Veneranda is a corruption of Venera from 'dies veneris' (Friday), itself the Latin equivalent of 'Parasceves' in Greek. She is thus probably the same as the St Parasceve of Iconium found in the Byzantine Martyrology on 26 July.

(Venerandus of Troyes) *(St)* *{4 –deleted}*

14 November
d. 275. He was allegedly an influential citizen of Troyes (France), martyred in the reign of Aurelian.

Venerius of Milan (St) {2, 4}

6 May
d. 409. Ordained deacon by St Ambrose, he eventually became bishop of Milan (Italy). He was a loyal supporter of St John Chrysostom.

Venerius of Tino (St) {2, 4}

13 September
C7th. He was a hermit and then abbot-founder of a monastery on the island of Tino in the Gulf of Genoa (Italy). His extant biography is unreliable.

Veranus of Cavaillon (St) {2, 4}

19 October
d. p589. From near Avignon (France), he became bishop of the local town of Cavaillon.

(Veranus of Lyons) (St) {4 –deleted}

11 November
C5th? The old Roman Martyrology lists him as a bishop of Lyons (France), but he is probably a duplicate of St Veranus of Vence.

Veranus of Vence (St) {2}

11 November
C5th. Son of St Eucherius of Lyons, he was a monk at Lérins and then bishop of Vence near Nice (France).

(Verecundus of Verona) (St) {4 –deleted}

22 October
d. 522. He was a bishop of Verona (Italy).

Veremund of Hierache (St) {2}

8 March
d. 1092. A native of Navarre (now in Spain, then independent), he entered the Benedictine abbey of Hirache and became its abbot. Under him the monastery was the most influential religious centre of Navarre, and he was a royal adviser. He was famous for his charity towards the poor and for his zeal for the accurate recitation of the divine office, and he helped forestall the papal intention to suppress the local Mozarabic rite as part of the Gregorian reform.

Verena (St) {2, 4}

1 September
C4th. According to her legend she was an Egyptian maiden, related to a soldier of the Theban Legion, who travelled to Switzerland in search of him and settled as a hermit near Zurich. Her cultus is very ancient.

Vergil cf. **Virgil**.

Verissimus, Maxima and Julia (SS) {2, 4}

1 October
C3rd–4th. They were martyred at Lisbon (Portugal) in the reign of Diocletian.

Veronica (St)

12 July
The legend is that she was a woman (identified with several in the Gospels) who took pity on Christ on his way to crucifixion and wiped his face with a cloth, on which an image of his face was left imprinted. This story seems to have been supplied in the C14th as a background to a relic called the 'veil of Veronica' which has been enshrined at St Peter's at Rome since the C8th, and she was not listed in any of the ancient martyrologies nor in the old Roman Martyrology. There is now no trace of any image on the relic. She features in the 'Stations of the Cross', a devotion propagated by the Franciscans at Jerusalem only since the C18th.

Veronica Giuliani (St) {2}

9 July
1660–1727. From Mercatello near Urbino (Italy), she spent her life as a Capuchin nun at Città di Castello in Urbino, being novice-mistress for thirty-four years. Her amazing mystical experiences, including continual visions, revelations and the stigmata, were described by eyewitnesses and described in her extant diary but did not prevent her from having a practical and level-headed personality. She was canonized in 1839.

Veronica-of-Binasco Negroni (Bl) {2}

13 January
d. 1497. From Binasco near Milan (Italy), she was the daughter of poor peasants and a worker on their farm before becoming an

Augustinian lay sister at Milan. She spent her life collecting alms for her community in the streets of the city, and in the process became a great mystic. Her cultus was confirmed in 1517.

(Verulus, Secundinus and Comps) (SS) {4 –deleted}

21 February
C5th? According to the old Roman Martyrology they were twenty-six martyred at Hadrumetum in Roman Africa by the Vandals. They probably died in an earlier persecution. Also named are Siricius, Felix, Servulus, Saturninus and Fortunatus.

(Verus of Arles) (St) {4 –deleted}

1 August
d. p314. A bishop of Vienne (France), he was at the synod of Arles in 314.

(Verus of Salerno) (St) {4 –deleted}

23 October
C4th. He was the third bishop of Salerno (Italy).

Vial cf. **Vitalis**.

(Viator of Bergamo) (St) {4 –deleted}

14 December
C4th? The local tradition alleges that he was one of the first bishops of Brescia (Italy) and transferred to Bergamo during the C1st, but it seems that he was bishop of Bergamo only from 344.

Viator of Lyons (St) {2, 4}

21 October
d. p381. He was a disciple of St Justus, archbishop of Lyons (France), and went with him to Egypt to be a hermit.

Viator of Sologne (St) {2}

5 August
C6th. He was a hermit in the Sologne (France) whose relics were enshrined at Tremblay.

Vibiana (St)

1 September
? Her remains were brought from the Roman catacombs to the cathedral of Los Angeles (USA) by the bishop in 1858. She is the city's principal patron. The assertion that she was a virgin martyr is unsupported by any evidence, as is the case with all the alleged relics of 'martyrs' removed from the catacombs in the C19th, and the name was given to her arbitrarily.

Vicelin (St) {2}

12 December
1090–1154. From Hameln (Germany), he became a cathedral-canon at Bremen and a disciple of St Norbert. From 1126, he worked among the Wagrian Slavs of what is now Holstein, but his efforts were frustrated by the great rebellion of the Slavs against German colonization in 1147. In 1149, he was made bishop of Oldenburg (now Stargard, Poland). He died at Neumünster, an Augustinian monastery that he had founded.

Vicinius of Sarsina (St) {2}

28 August
C4–5th. He was the first bishop of Sarsina, a small place in the mountains south-west of Rimini (Italy). The legend is that he founded the cathedral church when he was a refugee from the persecution of Diocletian, but this seems to be too early.

Victor I, Pope (St) {2, 3}

28 July
d. 198. From Roman Africa, he became pope in 188 and excommunicated several Eastern

churches for not keeping the date of Easter according to the Roman practice (for which act he was rebuked by St Irenaeus). His cultus was suppressed in 1969.

Victor III, Pope (St) {2}

16 September
d.1087. From Benevento (Italy) and related to the Norman rulers there, Desiderius Danfari became a Benedictine monk in the face of his family's opposition and was at various monasteries before becoming abbot of Montecassino in 1057. The abbey flourished under his rule and he became one of the great churchmen of Italy. On the death of Pope St Gregory VII he was elected pope by the cardinals meeting at Montecassino in 1086. Initially he refused, was not consecrated for a year and died after another four months without having been able to stay at Rome (the city was occupied by an antipope). His cultus as a saint was confirmed in 1887.

(Victor, Alexander and Marianus) (SS) {4 –deleted}

17 October
d. 303. They were listed as martyred at Nicomedia (Asia Minor) in the reign of Diocletian.

Victor and Corona (SS) {2, 4}

14 May
C3rd? They were martyred together in Syria, but their acta are unreliable.

Victor, Felix and Comps (St) {2}

16 September
? They were martyred at a place called 'At the Goat' on the Via Nomentana outside Rome. The companions were Alexander and Papias.

Victor and Mallosus (SS) {2, 4}

10 October
Early C4th? According to the old Roman Martyrology, they were 330 soldiers of the Theban Legion martyred at Birten just south-east of Xanten on the Rhine (Germany). The revision has reduced the number to two, and put them in the following century.

Victor and Stephen (SS) {4 –deleted}

1 April
? They were listed as martyred in Egypt.

Victor, Stercatius and Antinogenes (SS) {4 –deleted}

24 July
d. 304. They were allegedly three brothers martyred at Mérida in Extremadura (Spain), but probably only Victor belonged there. The other two were probably among a group listed in the Hieronomian Martyrology as having been martyred at Sebaste in Armenia.

(Victor, Zoticus and Comps) (SS) {4 –deleted}

20 April
Early C4th? They were listed as martyred at Nicomedia (Asia Minor), and feature in the unreliable acta of St George. The others were Zeno, Acindynus, Caesareus, Severian, Chrysophorus, Theonas and Antoninus.

Victor the African (St) {2, 4}

10 March
? A Roman African, he was possibly martyred in the reign of Decius. He is mentioned in St Augustine's commentary on Psalm 116.

(Victor of Braga) (St) {4 –deleted}

12 April
d. c.300. A catechumen, he was allegedly martyred at Braga (Portugal) in the reign of

Diocletian and is an example of 'red baptism' (being baptized with one's own blood).

Victor of Cambon (St) {2}

29 August
C7th? He was a hermit at Cambon near Nantes (France), where he founded a little church in a 'good field' (campus bonus), hence the name.

Victor of Capua (St) {2, 4}

2 April
d. 554. Bishop of Capua (Italy), he was an ecclesiastical writer.

Victor of Cereso (St) {2, 4}

26 August
C3rd–4th. According to the acta written in the C15th, he was a priest at Cereso near Burgos (Spain) and was martyred in c.950 for converting Muslims. This is false; he was actually a Roman African martyred at Caesarea in Mauretania (now Morocco) in one of the early persecutions.

Victor of Marseilles (St) {2, 4}

21 July
d. ?292. He was martyred at Marseilles (France). According to the unreliable acta, he was a Roman army officer stationed there and was martyred there with three prison guards, Alexander, Felician and Longinus, whom he had converted. These have been deleted from the Roman Martyrology. In the C4th St John Cassian built a monastery over their tomb. His attribute is a windmill.

Victor the Moor (St) {2, 4}

8 May
d. ?304. A soldier from Mauritania (now Morocco) in Roman Africa, he was martyred at Milan (Italy) in the reign of Maximian. He

was associated by St Ambrose with SS Nabor and Felix.

Victor of Plancy (St) {2, 4}

26 February
C7th. From Troyes (France), he became a hermit at Arcis-sur-Aube in Champagne. St Bernard of Clairvaux wrote a hymn in his honour, but his extant acta are worthless.

Victor of Rome (St) {2}

17 May
Early C4th? He was martyred at the catacomb of Basilla near the old Salarian Way outside Rome.

(Victor of Vita) (St) *{4 –deleted}*

23 August
C6th? From Carthage (Roman Africa), he was bishop either there or (as stated in the old Roman Martyrology) at Utica. Baronius identified him (without proof) with the Victor of Vita who wrote an account of the persecution by King Hunneric.

(Victoria) (St) *{4 –deleted}*

23 December
C3rd? According to her worthless acta she was martyred at Rome for refusing to marry a pagan. The legend added a sister and fellow martyr Anatolia, but she was not listed in the old Roman Martyrology.

Victoria Diez y Bustos de Molina (Bl) {2}

11 August
1903–36. Born in Seville (Spain), she became a state teacher and was deeply influenced by the Teresian Association of Bl. Peter Poveda Castroverde, desiring to join holiness and apostolicity in her career. She worked at Hornachudos, where she was a great help to the parish

priest and was very charitable to her needier pupils. She was thrown down a mineshaft at Rincón during the Civil War along with seventeen other Catholics, and was beatified in 1993. Cf. **Spanish Civil War, Martyrs of**.

Victoria Rasoamanarivo (Bl) {2}

21 August

1848–94. Born in Antananarivo, the capital of the native Kingdom of Madagascar, she was a noblewoman of the highest rank. Her family was pagan but they sent her to be taught by the 'Sisters of St Joseph of Cluny' and she was baptized in 1863. Then she was married off to a drunken and vicious cousin, but she insisted on the marriage being solemnized and later refused divorce as being against church teaching. (Rather she prayed for his conversion, which took place after a drunken fall in 1887 which proved fatal.) In 1883 the government tried to suppress the church and expelled the missionaries. Bl Victoria's position enabled her to obtain many concessions and to support the laity, so that the missionaries found healthy churches on their return three years after. Then she retired into obscurity. She was beatified in 1989.

Victoria Valverde González (Bl) {2 –add}

12 January

1888–1937. From Vicálvaro near Madrid in Spain, she joined the Sisters of the Divine Shepherdess (a Calasanzian congregation) in 1917 and went on to be made the superior of the convent at Martos near Jaén in 1922. At the outbreak of the Spanish Civil War the sisters dispersed but she remained as caretaker of the convent until it was sacked by Republican militia. She was arrested together with two other local superiors, Bl Frances-of-the-Incarnation Espejo Martos and Isabel of San Rafael (not yet beatified). They were shot at the cemetery at Las Casillas, and she was beatified in 2013. Cf. **Spanish Civil War, Martyrs of** and list in appendix.

Victorian and Comps (SS) {2, 4}

23 March

d. 484. Victorian, a former pro-consul in Roman Africa, his two anonymous brothers and two wealthy merchants both named Frumentius were martyred at Adrumetum in the reign of the Vandal King Hunneric for refusing to become Arians.

Victorian-Pius Bernabé Cano (St) {2}

9 October

Cf. **Innocent-of-Mary-Immaculate Canoura Arnau and Comps**.

Victoricus and Fuscian (SS) {2, 4}

11 December

C3rd? They were martyred near Amiens (France). According to their unreliable legend, they were Roman missionaries. The Roman Martyrology has deleted an old man named Gentian who was allegedly killed while trying to protect them when they were arrested.

Victorinus, Victor and Comps (SS) {2, 4}

25 February

d. c.250. They were citizens of Corinth (Greece) martyred in the reign of Decius. The others were Nicephorus, Claudius, Diodorus, Serapion and Papias.

Victorinus of Amiternum (St) {2}

24 July

C4th? He was martyred at a place called Amiternum on the Via Salaria north of Rome. The locality is now called San Vittorino after him.

(Victorinus of Camerino) (St) {4 –deleted}

8 June

d. 543. Brother of St Severinus of Septempeda, he was a hermit with him at Montenero near Livorno (Italy) and apparently became bishop of Camerino, where he died.

Victorinus of Nicomedia (St) {2, 4}

6 March
? He was a martyr of Nicomedia (Asia Minor). The Roman Martyrology has deleted his companions Victor, Claudian and Bassa (a married couple).

Victorinus of Pettau (St) {2, 4}

2 November
d. ?303. Bishop of Pettau (now Ptuj in Slovenia), he is the earliest known biblical exegete of the Western church, his commentary on the Apocalypse being extant. He was martyred in the reign of Diocletian.

Victorius of Le Mans (St) {2, 4}

1 September
d. c.490. A disciple of St Martin of Tours, he became bishop of Le Mans (France) in ?453.

Victricius (St) {2, 4}

7 August
d. c.410. A Roman army officer, he resigned because he thought military service incompatible with Christianity. He was sentenced to death, but the sentence was commuted and he became a missionary among the northern tribes of Gaul, being made bishop of Rouen (France) while still a layman in 380.

(Victurus, Victor and Comps) (SS) {4 –deleted}

18 December
? Thirty-five Roman Africans, they were listed as martyred in what is now Morocco. Victorinus, Adjutor, Quartus were the companions

Vietnam (Martyrs of) (SS) {2}

24 November
1798–1862. The first missionaries arrived in Vietnam in the 1530s, but great success followed only after the foundation of the Jesuit mission at Hanoi in 1615. Christianity was not compatible with State Confucianism, and the first persecution was in 1698. The country was in chaos between 1772 and 1802, but persecution intensified on its reunification and foreign missionaries were killed, especially in the reigns of Kings Minh Mang (1820–41) and Tu Duc (1847–83). The country was then conquered by France. A hundred and seventeen of the martyrs (the total of whom is allegedly in six figures) were canonized in 1988, this being the largest mass canonization in the church's history. Another was beatified in 2000. (N.B. The names 'Tonkin', 'Annam' & 'Cochin China' were colonial names for the three main parts of the country, north to south, and were not used by the Vietnamese themselves.) Cf. lists of national martyrs in appendix.

(Vigilius of Brescia) (St) {4 –deleted}

26 September
d. p506. He was a bishop of Brescia in Lombardy (Italy).

Vigilius of Trent (St) {2, 4}

26 June
d. 405. A Roman nobleman, he studied at Athens and then emigrated with his family to Trent (now Trento in Italy). He became bishop and took effective measures against the local paganism until he was stoned to death for toppling a statue of Saturn in the Val di Rendena.

Vigor (St) {2, 4}

1 November
d. ?537. A disciple of St Vedast, he was a hermit and then a diocesan priest before becoming bishop of Bayeux (France). He was remembered for opposing the surviving paganism.

Viho (St) {2}

20 April

d. 804. He was originally from Friesland, and was a monk and abbot when sent by the emperor Charlemagne to evangelize the Saxons. He was made bishop of Osnabrück, and suffered much in establishing the church in the region.

Villana de' Botti (Bl) {2}

29 January

d. 1361. Daughter of a rich merchant of Florence (Italy), when young she wanted to become a nun but was opposed by her father, so she married and led a life of worldliness and pleasure. Then she converted completely and became a Dominican tertiary devoted to penance and charity, allegedly because she saw the face of a demon instead of her own face in a mirror one day. Her cultus was confirmed for Florence in 1824.

Vilmos cf. **William**.

(Vincent, Orontius and Victor) (SS)
{4 –deleted}

22 January

d. 305. According to the legend, the first two were brothers from Cimiez near Nice (France) and went as missionaries to the Spanish Pyrenees. They were martyred with St Victor at Puigcerda near Gerona and their shrine subsequently established at Embrun near Gap (France).

Vincent, Sabina and Christeta (SS) {2, 4}

28 October

d. ?305. They were martyred at Avila (Spain), but their acta are unreliable.

Vincent of Agen (St) {2, 4}

9 June

C4th. He was a deacon allegedly killed at Agen in Gascony (France) for having interrupted a feast of the Druids.

Vincent of Aquila (Bl) {2}

7 August

d. 1504. From Aquila (Italy), he became a Franciscan lay brother there and was famous for his mystical gifts. His cultus was approved for Aquila in 1785.

Vincent-of-St-Joseph of Ayamonte (Bl) {2}

10 September

1596–1622. From Ayamonte near Huelva (Spain), he emigrated to Mexico and became a Franciscan lay brother in 1615. In 1618 he accompanied Bl Louis Sotelo to Manila and was sent to Japan in 1619. He was arrested in 1620 and, after two years of inhuman imprisonment, was burnt alive in the 'Great Martyrdom' at Nagasaki with BB Charles Spinola and Comps. Cf. **Japan, Martyrs of** and **Great Martyrdom at Nagasaki**.

Vincent Cabanes Badenas and Comps (BB) {2}

d. 1936. Twenty Third Order Capuchins of Our Lady of Sorrows were martyred by Republican forces during the Spanish Civil War, and were beatified together in 2001. Cf. **Spanish Civil War, Martyrs of** and list in appendix.

Vincent Carvalho (Bl) {2}

3 September

d. 1632. From near Lisbon (Portugal), he became an Augustinian friar there, was sent to Mexico in 1621 and to Japan in 1623. He was burnt alive at Nagasaki with BB Anthony Ishida and Comps. Cf. **Japan, Martyrs of**.

(Vincent of Collioure) (St) {4 –deleted}

19 April

Early C4th? He was allegedly martyred at Collioure near Perpignan (France) in the reign of Diocletian, but his acta are worthless and he may be a duplicate of St Vincent the Deacon.

Vincent of Dax (St) {2, 4}

1 September
Early C4th. The old Roman Martyrology described him as a martyr of Spain with a companion Laetus, but the revision deletes the latter and describes Vincent as a martyred bishop of Dax in Gascony (France).

Vincent the Deacon (St) {1, 3}

22 January
d. 304. From Huesca (Spain), he became a deacon under St Valerius at Zaragoza and was martyred at Valencia in the reign of Diocletian. St Augustine, Pope St Leo I and Prudentius all wrote in his honour, but details of his martyrdom are lacking. He is a local patron of vine dressers and is depicted being torn with hooks, carrying his intestines or having ravens defending his body. His attributes are a set of cruets or a millstone.

Vincent Đỗ Yến (St) {1 –group}

30 June
?1765–1838. A Vietnamese, he became a Dominican in 1808. After his ordination he worked in north Vietnam for forty years, the last six in hiding after the edict of persecution in 1832 by Emperor Minh Mạng. He was betrayed, and was beheaded at Hải Dương. Cf. **Vietnam, Martyrs of**.

Vincent Đương (St) {1 –group}

6 June
Cf. **Peter Dũng and Comps**.

Vincent Ferrer (St) {2, 3}

5 April
d. 1419. Born in Valencia in Spain (his father was English), when young he joined the Dominicans and soon became the adviser of the king of Aragon and of the Avignon antipope, with whom he sided in good faith.

In 1399, he started travelling through Spain, France, Switzerland and Italy preaching penance (he was convinced that the end of the world was imminent), working miracles and converting thousands. He had an extraordinary gift for learning languages. He realized that the Avignon antipope needed to resign for the good of the church and played a vital role at the council of Constance in 1414. He died at Vannes in Britanny. His cultus was confined to particular calendars in 1969.

Vincent Frelichowski (Bl) {2}

23 February
1913–45. From Chełmża (Poland), he became a priest of the diocese of Pelplin in 1937 and served as curate at Toruń. Immediately after the German invasion of Poland in 1939, he was arrested and sent in turn to the concentration camps at Stuthoff, Sachsenhausen and Dachau. He engaged in clandestine pastoral work, and died of typhus at Dachau after nursing sufferers of that disease. He was beatified in 1999.

Vincent Grossi (Bl) {2}

7 November
1845–1917. Born near Cremona (Italy), he became a parish priest of that diocese and remained one all his life, being an exemplary pastor. In 1885 he founded the 'Daughters of the Oratory' to assist in catechizing young people according to the principles of St Philip Neri. He was beatified in 1975.

Vincent Kadlubek (Bl) {2}

8 March
d. 1223. A German from the Palatinate, he studied in France and Italy and was made provost at Sandomir in Poland. In 1208, he became bishop of Cracow, but resigned in 1218 and became a Cistercian monk at Jendrzejó. He is one of the earliest Polish chroniclers, and his cultus was approved for Cracow in 1764.

Vincent Kaun (Bl) {2}

20 June
d. 1626. From Seoul in Korea, he was taken to Japan as a prisoner of war in 1591. There he became a Christian and entered the Jesuit seminary at Arima, spending thirty years as a catechist in Japan and in China. He was burnt alive at Nagasaki with BB Francis Pacheco and Comps. Cf. **Japan, Martyrs of**.

Vincent Lê Quang Liêm (St) {1 –group}

7 November
d. 1773. A Vietnamese nobleman, he became a Dominican priest and worked with St Hyacinth Castañeda in north Vietnam until they were beheaded together at Ket Chợ. Cf. **Vietnam, Martyrs of**.

(Vincent of León) (St) {4 –deleted}

11 September
d. c.630. He was abbot of the monastery of St Claudius at León (Spain), and was ordered killed by the Arian Visigothic king Leovegild during a royal persecution of Catholic Christians.

Vincent of Lérins (St) {2}

24 May
d. c.450. Possibly a Gallo-Roman nobleman, he was a soldier before he became a monk on the island of Lérins off the Riviera coast (France). He is remembered as the author of the *Commonitorium* concerning the development of church doctrine, and in which is the famous precept (the 'Vincentian canon') that the only true doctrines are those adhered to 'everywhere, always and by all'.

Vincent Madelgar (St) {2}

14 July
d. ?677. A Frankish nobleman named Madelgar from Strepy near Mons (Belgium), he married and his wife Waldetrude and his four children, Aldetrude, Dentlin, Landeric and Madalberta, are saints also. In ?653 the couple separated to become consecrated religious and he took the name Vincent as a monk in the monastery of Haumont which he had founded. Later he founded another abbey at Soignies (Belgium), where he became abbot and where he died.

Vincent Matuszewski (Bl) {2}

23 May
1869–1940. A Polish priest, he was killed by the Nazis at Witowo in Poland together with Bl Joseph Kurzawa. Cf. **Poland, Martyrs of the Nazi Occupation of**.

Vincent Nguyễn Thế Điểm (St) {1 –group}

24 November
Cf. **Peter Dumoulin-Bori and Comps**.

Vincent Pallotti (St) {2}

22 January
1795–1850. A Roman, his father was a grocer and he became a secular priest in 1820. After a short period of theological teaching he took up pastoral work in Rome and became famous for his zeal (especially during the cholera epidemic of 1837) and his austerities. He founded his society of missionary priests, the 'Pallotines', in 1835 and a corresponding congregation of sisters in 1843. In 1836 he started the keeping of an octave of prayer after the Epiphany for the reunion of the Eastern churches with Rome, and was also very interested in the English mission. He died at Rome and was canonized in 1963.

Vincent de Paul (St) {1, 3}

27 September
1581–1660. From near Dax in the Landes, France, he studied at Toulouse and was ordained in 1600. According to legend he was

captured by Muslim pirates in 1605 and was sold as a slave at Tunis, but escaped in 1607. He was a court chaplain at Paris while carrying out his life's work of active charity for all sorts of deprived people, for example abandoned orphans, sick children, prostitutes, the destitute, the blind and the insane. He also preached missions and retreats, and enlisted a number of priests for this work who formed the nucleus of a new religious institute, the 'Lazarists' or 'Vincentian Fathers', in 1625. In 1633 he founded the congregation of the 'Sisters of Charity' who have become an integral feature of church life worldwide. Dying at Paris, he was canonized in 1737 and is the patron of organizations devoted to charitable works.

(Vincent of Porto) *(St)* *{4 –deleted}*

24 May
? He was listed as martyred at Porto Romano, the ancient port of Rome at the mouth of the Tiber.

Vincent Romano (Bl) {2}

20 December
1751–1831. He was born at Torre del Greco near Naples (Italy) and lived there all his life, being rather like St John Vianney in character. He had great care for orphans and deprived people, but was persecuted by the French in the Napoleonic period and by anti-clericals afterwards. He was beatified in 1963.

(Vincent of Rome) *(St)* *{4 –deleted}*

24 July
? He was listed as a Roman martyred outside the walls of the city on the road to Tivoli.

Vincent-of-the-Cross Shiwozuka (St) {1 –group}

29 September
Cf. **Laurence Ruiz and Comps**.

Vincent Soler and Comps (BB) {2}

d. 1936. They were seven Augustinian recollects (Vincent Soler, Deogratias Palacios, Leo Inchausti, Joseph Rada, Vincent Pinilla, Julian Moreno and Joseph-Richard Díez) and the parish priest (Emmanuel Martin Sierra) of Motril near Granada (Spain). After the Spanish Republican government came to power, there were violent popular demonstrations against the church in the town. On 25 July BB Deogracias, Leo, Joseph, Julian and Joseph-Richard were summarily seized and shot; the following day, Bl Manuel was machine-gunned at the door of his church with Bl Vincent Pinilla. Bl Vincent Soller went into hiding, but was betrayed and captured and was shot on 15 August with twenty-eight others. Cf. **Spanish Civil War, Martyrs of**.

Vincent-Mary Strambi (St) {2}

1 January
1745–1824. From Civitavecchia near Rome, he was ordained in 1767 and then joined the Passionists. He filled almost all the offices of his order and was also an effective home-missioner. He was made bishop of Macerata and Tolentino in 1801, but was exiled in 1808 for refusing to take the oath of allegiance to Napoleon. At the end of his life, he was appointed papal adviser to Pope Leo XII. Dying at Rome, he was canonized in 1950.

Vincent Tường (St) {1 –group}

16 June
Cf. **Dominic Nguyễn and Comps**.

Vincent Vilar David (Bl) {2}

14 February
1889–1937. Born near Valencia (Spain), he worked as an industrial engineer in his family's ceramics firm and held municipal office. As a Catholic he was involved in parish

activities and in youth and workers' groups, and tried to help persecuted priests and religious after the outbreak of the Civil War. He was shot as a result, and beatified in 1995. Cf. **Spanish Civil War, Martyrs of**.

Vincentia Gerosa (St) {2}

28 June

1784–1847. She was born and died at Lovere near Bergamo (Italy), and until her fortieth year led an undistinguished domestic life in the context of a wealthy but dysfunctional family. Then she became acquainted with St Bartolomea Capitanio and joined her work in founding the 'Sisters of Charity of Lovere' at Lovere. When St Bartolomea died in 1833 St Vincenza succeeded her as superior, and oversaw the massive growth of the institute. She was canonized in 1950.

Vincentia-Mary López Vicuña (St) {2}

26 December

1847–90. From a bourgeois family of Cascante in Navarra (Spain), she was sent to Madrid for her education and lodged with an aunt who ran a hostel for casually employed female domestic servants. The importance of this work impressed her, and she started living a life in common with her aunt and some others in 1871 (despite her family wanting her to get married). This was the start of the 'Daughters of Mary Immaculate' which taught domestic science and ran hospices for young women servants in danger of becoming prostitutes. She became the first superior, died at Madrid of overwork and was canonized in 1975.

Vincentia-Mary Poloni (Bl) {2 –add}

1802–55. From Verona in Italy, when young she was influenced by Bl Charles Steeb and also by the violent epidemic of cholera in 1832 to care for poor and neglected people. Thus she founded the 'Sisters of Charity of Verona' in 1848. She was beatified in 2008.

Vincentian (Viance, Viants) (St) {2}

2 January

d. 672. He was allegedly a disciple of St Menelaus who became a hermit near Tulle (France), but his extant biography is an C11th forgery.

Vindemialis and Longinus (SS) {2, 4}

2 May

d. 483. They were Roman African bishops executed on the orders of the Arian Vandal King Hunneric after having been viciously tortured. The Roman Martyrology has deleted a third, Eugene.

Vindician (St) {2}

11 March

d. ?712. A disciple of St Eligius, he became bishop of Arras-Cambrai (France) in 675. He protested at the crimes of the degenerate Merovingian kings and the powerful mayors of the palace (especially the murder of St Leodegar) with great courage. He died at Brussels.

Virgil of Arles (St) {2}

5 March

d. ?618. A monk of Lérins, he became archbishop of Arles (France) in 580 and was probably the consecrator of St Augustine as bishop of Canterbury at the request of Pope St Gregory the Great. The latter had to rebuke him for trying to convert Jews by force.

Virgil (Fergal) of Salzburg (St) {2, 4}

27 November

d. 784. An Irish monk, he was allegedly abbot of Aghadoe in Co. Kerry before going on pilgrimage and ending up in Bavaria in 745. He continued the work of St Rupert and was made bishop of Salzburg in Austria (where he consecrated the first cathedral) and abbot of St Peter's Abbey in that city in c.765. He was regarded as one of the foremost scholars of the period, but St Boniface complained to Rome about some of his ideas and this may have been a continuation of the friction between Celtic and Roman traditions. He is venerated as the apostle of Carinthia, Austria and was canonized in 1233.

Virginia Centurione Bracelli (St) {2}

15 December
1587–1651. Born in Genoa (Italy), she wanted to become a nun but her parents forced her to marry Gaspar Bracelli, a noble so addicted to vice that he ruined his health and left her a widow in 1607 (after she had helped him die in grace). Then she made private vows and performed the social works of mercy. After 1624, during social chaos caused by famine and war, she took in fifty young refugee girls and then opened four other houses in the city to cater for others like them. She was very much loved by her city, and was canonized in 2003.

Viridiana (St) {2, 4}

1 February
d. 1236–42. A maiden of Castelfiorentino in Tuscany (Italy), she went on pilgrimage to Compostella and was then walled up as a hermit in her native town, where she lived for thirty-four years as an affiliate of a Vallumbrosan abbey. Her cultus was approved in 1533.

Vissia (St) {2, 4}

12 April
? She was a virgin martyr of Fermo near Ancona (Italy).

Vitalian, Pope (St) {2, 4}

27 January
d. 672. He was pope from 657 and tried to resolve the Monothelite controversy. He sent St Theodore to England as archbishop of Canterbury in 668.

(Vitalian of Capua) (St) {4 –deleted}

16 July
? He was a bishop of Capua (Italy).

Vitalian of Catanzaro (St) {2}

3 September
C7–8th. He was a bishop who became a hermit at a place called Caudium in Campania (now Montesarchio) between Capua and Benevento. He was enshrined at Catanzaro in Calabria (Italy). The revised Roman Martyrology does not accept the tradition that he had been bishop of Capua.

Vitalis and Agricola (SS) {2, 3}

4 November
d. 304. According to the legend narrated by St Ambrose of Milan, they were martyred at Bologna (Italy) in the reign of Diocletian. Vitalis was a slave of Agricola, and was martyred in the presence of his master with such courage that the latter was inspired to accept death also. The cultus was confined to local calendars in 1969.

(Vitalis, Revocatus and Fortunatus) (SS) {4 –deleted}

9 January
? They were listed as martyred at Smyrna, (Asia Minor, now Izmir in Turkey).

(Vitalis, Sator and Repositus) (SS) {4 –deleted}

29 August
Early C4th? They were listed as martyred at Velleianum in Apulia (Italy) and were included in the legend of the **Twelve Brothers**.

Vitalis-Vladimir Bajrak (Bl) {2}

16 May
1907–46. A monk and priest of the Basilian Order of St Josaphat of the Greek-Catholic rite, he died in prison at Drohobych after eastern Poland had been occupied by the Soviet Union. Cf. **Nicholas Čarneckyj and 24 Comps**.

Vitalis of Castronovo (St) {2}

9 March
d. 993. He was a monk of Rapolla near Melfi in Basilicata (Italy).

Vitalis (Vial) of Noirmoutier (St) {2}

16 October
C8th. Apparently an Anglo-Saxon, he joined the monastery of Noirmoutier at the mouth of the Loire river (France) and later became a hermit on Mt Scobrit nearby.

Vitalis of Ravenna (St) {2, 3}

28 April
? He was martyred at Ravenna (Italy), but was later incorporated into the legend of SS Gervase and Protase as their alleged father and husband of St Valeria. His acta are spurious, and his cultus was suppressed in 1969.

Vitalis of Salzburg (St) {2}

20 October
d. c.730. He was St Rupert's successor as archbishop of Salzburg (Austria) and abbot of St Peter's Abbey in that city in 717.

Vitalis of Savigny (Bl) {2}

16 September
?1063–1122. From near Bayeaux in Normandy (France), when young he was chaplain to a relative of William the Conqueror but then became a hermit and itinerant preacher for seventeen years. Being acquainted with Bl Robert of Arbrissel he followed his example, settled in the forest of Savigny and founded a reformed Benedictine monastery in 1112. This became the nucleus of a new congregation which had spread through France and into England by the time of its incorporation into the Cistercians in 1147.

Vitalis of Spoleto (St) {2, 4}

14 February
Early C4th? He was martyred at Spoleto in Umbria (Italy), not at Rome as stated in the old Roman Martyrology. The revision has deleted two companions, Felicula and Zeno.

Vito (Vanne, Vaune) (St) {2}

9 November
d. c.530. He was bishop of Verdun (France) from c.500, and his shrine was in a monastery named after him, which became the motherhouse of the Benedictine congregation of St Vanne in 1600.

Vitus (St) {2, 3}

15 June
? He was martyred somewhere in Lucania, an ancient province of Italy north of Calabria. His cultus is ancient, but his acta (in various versions) are legendary. In them, he is described as a child, martyred in the reign of Diocletian with his nurse Crescentia and her husband Modestus. The latter two are fictional characters, however, and their cultus has been suppressed, while that of St Vitus has been confined to local calendars from 1969. St Vitus is a patron of epileptics, and the nervous disorder called St Vitus's dance is named after him.

Vivald (Ubaldo, Gualdo) (St) {2}

1 May
d. c.1320. He was a disciple and companion of Bl Bartholomew Buonpedoni and nursed him

as a leper for twenty years. Then he became a hermit in a hollow chestnut tree at Bosco-tondo near Montone in Tuscany (Italy), alleg-edly as a Franciscan tertiary. His cultus was approved for Volterra in 1908.

Viventiolus (St) {2}

12 July
d. ?523. He was a monk of St Oyend at Condat before becoming archbishop of Lyons (France), and was a friend of St Avitus of Vienne.

(Viventius of Poitiers) (St) {4 –deleted}

13 January
d. c.400. Allegedly a refugee born in Sama-ria who spent some time with St Martin of Tours on the Ligurian island of Gallinara, he became a disciple of St Hilary at Poit-iers (France) and died as a hermit at Sables d'Olonne in the Vendee. His C10th biogra-phy is unreliable.

Vivian cf. **Bibiana**.

Vivian of Saintes (St) {2, 4}

28 August
C5th. He succeeded St Ambrose as bishop of Saintes (France). His extant biography is spurious.

Vivina cf. **Wivina**.

Vladimir (St) {2}

15 July
956–1015. Of the princely house of Rurik ruling at Kiev (Ukraine) and a grandson of St Olga, he was a pagan when he became Grand Prince of Kievan Rus in 972 but was baptized before his marriage to the sister of the Byzantine emperor Basil II in 987. Previously licentious and immoral, he took

his new faith seriously, invited Byzantine missionaries to evangelize his country and is counted as the founder of the Russian Ortho-dox Church. His two sons SS Boris and Gleb were killed after his death and are venerated as martyrs.

Vladimir Ghika (Bl) {2 –add}

16 May
1873–1954. He was of the Romanian nobil-ity, and was born at Constantinople where his father was a diplomat. When young he was Romanian Orthodox, but was received into the Catholic Church when aged twenty-nine. He studied in Rome, went back to Romania and founded the first free hospital in the country. He was ordained in Paris in 1923, served the Romanian diaspora there until 1939 and then went to Romania again. When the Communists took power after the Second World War, the Catholic Church in the country was suppressed and he was arrested in 1952. He died from the effects of torture in 1954, and was beatified as a martyr in 2013.

Vladimir Laskowski (Bl) {2}

8 August
1886–1940. A Polish priest, he was killed by the Nazis at a concentration camp at Gusen in Germany. Cf. **Poland, Martyrs of the Nazi Occupation of**.

Vladimir Pryjma (Bl) {2}

26 June
1907–41. A layman, he was killed by a detach-ment of the Red Army in a wood at Birok, near Stradch together with Bl Nicholas Kon-rad after the Lwow area of Poland had been occupied by the Soviet Union. Cf. **Nicholas Čarneckyj and 24 Comps**.

Volusian (St) {2, 4}

18 January

d. ?498. A senator of Tours (France) who was married to a memorably bad-tempered wife, he was chosen to be bishop in 491 and shortly after exiled by the Arian Visigoths. He died at Toulouse.

Vulcherius cf. **Mochoemoc**.

Vulliermus de Leaval *(Bl)*

7 February

His cultus was confirmed for Aosta in 1877, but he is not in the Roman Martyrology.

W

Walburga (St) {2}

25 February
?710–79. Sister of SS Willibald and Wine-bald, she became a nun at Wimborne in Dorset (England) under St Tatta and followed St Lioba to Germany at the invitation of St Boniface. She died as abbess of Heidenheim in Württemberg (a double monastery) and her relics were taken to Eichstätt. A liquid that oozes from the rock beneath the shrine, known as 'St Walburga's oil', is reputed to have curative properties.

Walde (St) {2}

31 January
C7th. He was a bishop of Evreaux (France), and as a result of civil war retired to be a hermit near Coutences, where he died.

Waldebert (Walbert, Gaubert) (St) {2}

2 May
d. 665–70. A Frankish nobleman, he was a soldier before becoming a monk at the Columbanian monastery of Luxeuil in the Vosges (France). In ?628, he became abbot and introduced the Benedictine rule into the abbey's customary. Under him, the monastery reached the peak of its religious and cultural influence in western Europe. He helped St Salaberga to found her monastery at Laon.

Waldetrude (Valdetrudis, Vaudru) (St) {2, 4}

9 April
d. 688. She was daughter of SS Walbert and Bertilla, wife of St Vincent Madelgar and mother of SS Landeric, Dentelin, Madalberta and Aldetrude. When her husband became a monk she founded a nunnery at Mons in Belgium (around which the town grew up) and became a nun there.

Waleric (Valéry) (St) {2}

1 April
C7th. From the Auvergne (France), he was a monk under St Columban at Luxeuil before becoming a missionary in northern France, where he became the abbot-founder of Leuconay at the mouth of the Somme. Two settlements in that district are called Saint-Valéry after him.

Wales (Martyrs of)

The Reformation was a disaster for Christianity in Wales as well as for Welsh culture, because the Latin in the liturgy was replaced by English (which was a foreign language for the majority of the people). There was not much Catholic missionary activity in Wales in penal times compared to that in England, but six martyrs have been recognized. They are: Bl Charles Meehan, an Irish Franciscan executed at Ruthin in 1679 after being shipwrecked; St David Lewis, executed at Usk in the same year; SS John Lloyd and Philip Evans, executed together at Cardiff in the same year; St Richard Gwyn, executed at Wrexham in 1584 and Bl William Davies, executed at Beaumaris in 1593.

Walfrid (Gualfredo) della Gherardesca (St) {2}

15 February
d. ?765. A married nobleman of Pisa (Italy) with five sons and one daughter, in middle age he joined with two other married men in founding the abbey of Palazzuolo (between Volterra and Piombino) and a nunnery nearby for their wives and Walfrid's daughter. He was Palazzuolo's first abbot and was succeeded by one of his sons. His cultus was confirmed for Pisa and the Benedictines in 1861.

Walhere (St) {2}

23 June
d. 1199. His story is that he was from near Dinant (Belgium), became parish priest at Onhaye nearby and was killed by a nephew (priest of the neighbouring parish of Hastière) whom he had reproved for his immoral life. He is locally venerated as a martyr, but not listed as such.

Walpurgis cf. **Walburga**.

Walstan (St)

30 May
C11th? Possibly from Bawburgh in Norfolk (England), according to his legend he was a farm worker at Taverham and Costessey nearby and was famous for his charity. This may be historical, unlike the assertion that he was a prince who exiled himself to live with ordinary people. He had a locally popular shrine at Bawburgh before the Reformation, and is depicted as a king with scythe and sceptre and accompanied by calves.

Walter cf. **Gaucherius**.

Walter of L'Esterp (St) {2}

11 May
d. 1070. He was abbot of the Augustinian monastery of L'Esterp in the Limousin (France).

Walter of Lodi (St) {2}

22 July
d. 1224. He was a layman of Lodi (Italy) who founded a hospital there, and also in nearby towns of Lombardy.

Walter Pierson (Bl) {2}

10 June
d. 1537. A Carthusian lay brother of the London Charterhouse, he was one of seven of that community starved to death at the Newgate prison for refusing the oath of supremacy demanded by King Henry VIII. Cf. **England, Martyrs of**.

Walter of Pontoise (St) {2}

23 March
d. ?1095. From Picardy (France), he was a professor of philosophy and rhetoric but tired of his fame and became a Benedictine monk at Rebais. Against his will he was made abbot of Pontoise and fled the responsibility several times, once to Cluny and on the last occasion to Rome where the pope refused his resignation and ordered him to return.

Walter of Serviliano (St) {2}

4 June
C8th. A Roman, he became a hermit at Serviliano in the Marches (Italy) and founded a monastery there. His extant biography is spurious.

Wandrille (Wandregisilus) (St) {2}

22 July
d. ?668. From near Verdun (France), he was a royal courtier and became count of the palace of King Dagobert I. He married, but after a pilgrimage to Rome, the couple separated to become monastics, and he was a monk in various places before founding the monastery of Fontenelle in Normandy in 648. This became the missionary centre of the district as well as a school of arts and crafts, and it soon had a community of over three hundred monks. It survives as an abbey, now called St Wandrille, on the Seine below Rouen.

Warin cf. **Guarin**.

Wasnulf (St) {2}

1 October
C7th. He was abbot of a monastery at Conde near Cambrai (Belgium), and originally came from Scotland or Ireland.

Wenceslas (Vatslav) (St) {1, 3}

28 September
907–29. Born near Prague (Czech Republic), he was raised as a Christian by his grandmother St Ludmilla and became duke of Bohemia in 922 at the time of a pagan and anti-German reaction. He met this with patience and tolerance, but was eventually conspired against and assassinated at the door of the church at Stara-Boleslav by his brother Boleslav. He is the patron of the Czech Republic. The incidents recorded in the popular carol 'Good King Wenceslas looked out' are fictional.

Wendolin (Wendelin, Wendel) (St) {2}

21 October
C7th. All that is known is that he was a shepherd who had a shrine at St Wendel in the Saarland (Germany). An unreliable legend describes him as an Irish hermit who became abbot of Tholey nearby.

Werburga of Chester (St) {2}

3 February
d. c.700. Traditionally the daughter of St Ermenilda and of King Wulfhere of Mercia (England), she became a nun at Ely under St Etheldreda and later founded the nunneries of Hanbury near Tutbury (Staffs), Trentham (near Stoke-on-Trent) and Weedon (Northants). She died at Trentham but her body was transferred to the abbey (now Anglican cathedral) of Chester, of which city she is the patron.

Wiborada (Guiborat, Weibrath) (St) {2}

2 May
d. 926. A noblewoman from the Aargau (Switzerland), she became a hermit walled up in a cell near the Benedictine abbey of St Gall, to which she was affiliated. She worked as a bookbinder for the abbey library and was killed in a Magyar raid, being canonized in 1047 and listed as a martyr.

Widukind cf. **Wittikund**.

Wigbert of Fritzlar (St) {2, 4}

13 August
d. ?739. An Anglo-Saxon monk, he went to the missions in Germany under St Boniface and was appointed by the latter abbot of Fritzlar near Kassel. A few years later he transferred to Ohrdruf in Thuringia, Germany, but returned to Fritzlar before his death.

Wilfrid of York (St) {2, 4}

24 April
633–709. A Northumbrian nobleman from Ripon in Yorkshire (England), he was educated at Lindisfarne under the Celtic monastic observance before going to Rome in 653 to learn Roman church customs. Returning to Northumbria in 657, he founded the abbey of Ripon with a customary based exclusively on the rule of St Benedict (which he claimed as the first such in England) and played a leading part in the council of Whitby in 664 at which Roman usages were adopted for the English church. He was then consecrated bishop of York at Compiègne, but only started ruling his diocese in 669 when his rival St Chad had withdrawn. He exalted his position as bishop into one of great power, wealth and display and St Theodore divided his diocese into four as a result. He was eventually vindicated in appealing to Rome against this (the first such appeal in English history) after several periods of exile, and did missionary work in Sussex and among the Frisians in the Netherlands meanwhile. He died at Oundle (Northants) after apparently founding several monasteries in Mercia. His model of the secular dignity of bishops has been criticized as a corrupting influence within the church.

(Wilgefortis) (St) {4 –deleted}

20 July

? According to her legend she was one of sextuplet sisters and miraculously grew a beard in order to escape marriage. This strange story was possibly invented in the Middle Ages to explain earlier representations of Christ on the cross clothed in a tunic (a loincloth having become the usual garment depicted). She is depicted as a maiden with a long beard, carrying a T-shaped cross or crucified. Her name is derived from 'Virgo fortis', and she was known as Uncumber in England, Ontkommena in the Netherlands, Kümmernis in Germany, Livrade in Gascony and Librada in Spain. The old Roman Martyrology listed her as a virgin martyr of Portugal, but her cultus is extinct.

Willehad of Bremen (St) {2, 4}

8 November

d. 789. A Northumbrian monk educated at York (England), he went as a missionary to Friesland (Netherlands) in 766. Charlemagne sent him to Germany to evangelize the Saxons in 780, but was lucky to escape death in the Saxon revolt two years later. He was at the abbey of Echternacht during the bloody suppression of the revolt, and then became the first bishop of Bremen in 787. He died there.

Willehad of Denmark (St) {2}

9 July

1482–1572. A Danish Franciscan, he was exiled when Denmark became Lutheran and went to the friary at Gorinchem (q.v.) in the Netherlands. He was one of the martyrs there.

William

This is the English form of the Germanic Wilhelm, which has been Latinized into Gulielmus or Guilielmus whence in turn the Italian

Gulielmo, the French Guillaume and the Spanish Guillermo. In Hungarian, it is Vilmos.

William and Peregrinus (SS) {2}

26 April

C12th. They were hermits at Foggia in Apulia (Italy), and are the principal patrons of that place. Their legend asserts that they were father and son, officials of the Crusader Kingdom of Antioch who lost contact and found each other again at Jerusalem.

William of Aebelholt (St) {2, 4}

6 April

d. 1203. A French Augustinian canon regular at St Genevieve's in Paris, he was sent to Denmark in 1171 to reform the monastery at Eskilsø on Ise Fjord, Zealand, and then founded the abbey of Aebelholt on the same island. He was canonized in 1224.

William Andleby (Bl) {2}

4 July

d. 1597. From Etton near Beverley (Yorks), he was educated at St John's College, Cambridge before converting, studying for the priesthood and being ordained in 1577. He was on the Yorkshire mission for twenty years before being executed at York with BB Edward Fulthrop, Henry Abbot and Thomas Warcop. He was beatified in 1929. Cf. **England, Martyrs of.**

William Apor (Bl) {2}

2 April

1892–1945. A nobleman from Segesvár (Hungary), he was ordained for the Nagyvárad diocese in 1915 and was a successful parish priest at Gyula. In 1941, he was made bishop of Győr, and worked hard to alleviate the suffering caused by war. He also fought against the Nazi persecution of the Jews. When the

Red Army invaded Hungary many female refugees gathered at the bishop's palace for security from molestation. On Good Friday in 1945 a gang of drunken soldiers tried to abduct them but was confronted by the bishop. He was shot, the soldiers fled and he died on Easter Monday, being beatified in 1997.

William Arnaud and Comps (BB) {2}

29 May
d. 1242. A Dominican, he was chosen by the papal legate to be Inquisitor-General for southern France in order to suppress the Catharist heresy. In the year that the Count of Toulouse (the protector of the Cathars) broke with the French king, the Inquisitor's party went on a tour during which they stayed at the castle of Avignonet (between Toulouse and Carcasonne). The castle bailiff, with the probable connivance of the Count, arranged their massacre by enthusiastic knights and local people. The others killed were Stephen de Saint-Thibéry, OFM and assistant Inquisitor; Garcia d'Aure and Bernard de Roquefort, OP; Raymond Carbonier, the bishop's representative; Raymond Cortisan, archdeacon; Peter d'Arnaud, a lay notary; Fortanerius, a Franciscan and two Benedictines, the anonymous prior of Avignonet and Ademar, a monk of Chiusa. Their cultus was confirmed for Toulouse and the Dominicans in 1866.

William Browne (Bl) {2}

5 September
d. 1605. A layman from Northamptonshire, he was executed at Ripon (Yorks) and beatified in 1929. Cf. **England, Martyrs of**.

William Carter (Bl) {2}

11 January
1550–84. A Londoner, he ran a printing and bookbinding business and used this to disseminate Catholic publications. Being persecuted for this, he was finally condemned and executed at Tyburn for 'persuading to popery' after he was found to be holding sacred vessels and vestments in safe keeping. He was beatified in 1987. Cf. **England, Martyrs of**.

William-Joseph Chaminade (Bl) {2}

22 January
1761–1850. From Périgueux (France), he was ordained in 1785 and settled at Bordeaux for most of his life, apart from some time in exile during the French Revolution. He was committed to the re-Christianization of France under the guidance of Our Lady and attracted disciples who became a secular sodality (later to be called Marianists). He also helped to found the 'Daughters of Mary Immaculate' and the 'Society of Mary'. He was beatified in 2000.

William Courtet (St) {1 –group}

29 September
Cf. **Laurence Ruiz and Comps**.

William Cufitella (Bl) {2}

7 April
d. 1411. From Noto in Sicily, he was a hermit and a Franciscan tertiary at Sciacca for seventy years. His cultus was approved in 1537.

William Davies (Bl) {2}

27 July
d. 1593. Born near Colwyn Bay (Wales), he studied at Oxford and was ordained at Rheims in 1595. After being a priest for five years in north Wales he was captured in 1592 and imprisoned at Beaumaris for a year before execution. He was beatified in 1987. Cf. **Wales, Martyrs of**.

William Dean (St) {2}

28 August
d. 1588. From Linton in Craven (Yorks), he was a Protestant minister before his conversion and was ordained at Rheims in 1581. He was executed at Mile End Green, East London with seven companions and was beatified in 1929. Cf. **England, Martyrs of**.

William of Dijon (St) {2}

1 January
962–1031. A nobleman from Novara (Italy), he became a Benedictine monk at Locedio near Vercelli and transferred to Cluny in 987. Sent to restore the abbey of St Benignus at Dijon (France), he made this a centre from which he extended the Cluniac observance throughout Burgundy, Normandy, Lorraine and northern Italy. Gentle with the poor, he was remarkably firm in dealing with important people. Towards the end of his life he re-founded the abbey of Fécamp, where he died.

William de Donjeon (St) {2}

10 January
d. 1209. From Nevers (France), as a priest he was a canon at Soissons and at Paris before becoming a monk at Grandmont and transferring to the Cistercians of Pontigny. He was successively abbot of Fontaine-Jean near Sens, abbot of Châlis near Senlis and bishop of Bourges from 1200. He converted many Cathars. He was canonized in 1218.

William Exmew (Bl) {2}

19 June
d. 1535. Educated at Christ's College, Cambridge, he became a Carthusian at London and was sub-prior there. He was executed with BB Humphrey Middlemore and Sebastian Newdigate. Cf. **England, Martyrs of**.

William of Fenoli (Bl) {2}

19 December
d. c.1200. He was a Carthusian lay brother at Casotto in Lombardy (Italy). His cultus was confirmed for the Carthusians in 1860.

William Filby (Bl) {2}

30 May
d. 1582. From Oxfordshire, he was at the University of Oxford and, after his conversion, studied for the priesthood at Rheims where he was ordained in 1581. He was executed at Tyburn with St Luke Kirby and BB Laurence Richardson and Thomas Cottam, and was beatified in 1886. Cf. **England, Martyrs of**.

William Firmatus (St) {2}

24 April
d. 1103. From Tours (France), he became a canon at St Venance and practised medicine before receiving a divine warning against avarice. Then he gave his property to the poor and spent the rest of his life on pilgrimages and as a hermit at Savigny and at Mantilly near Le Mans, where he died.

William Fitzherbert (Thwayt) (St) {2}

8 June
d. 1154. A nephew of King Stephen, he became a canon of York (England) in 1130 and was appointed archbishop there in 1142 at the request of the king. The rival candidate was Murdac, a Cistercian monk, and powerful enemies (chiefly the Cistercians supported by St Bernard of Clairvaux) declared the appointment to be simoniacal. The pope initially found in his favour and he was consecrated in 1143, but his partisans burnt Fountains Abbey (Murdac's monastery), so he was deposed and his rival consecrated. He went into retirement at Winchester and lived a very penitential life of patience and resignation until he was

finally restored after the death of Murdac. He died, perhaps of poison, almost immediately and was canonized in 1226.

William Freeman (Mason) (Bl) {2}

13 August
d. 1595. From Yorkshire, he was at Magdalen College, Oxford before his conversion. He was ordained at Rheims in 1587 and worked in Worcestershire and Warwickshire until his execution at Warwick. He was beatified in 1929. Cf. **England, Martyrs of**.

William of Gellone (St) {2}

28 May
755–812. As the duke of Aquitaine and a knight at the court of Charlemagne he took part in campaigns against Muslim insurgency in the south of France. Afterwards he built a monastery near Montpellier as an offshoot of the nearby abbey of Aniane and joined the new community as a lay brother. Later the abbey was named Saint-Guilhem-du-Désert after him. He was canonized in 1066.

William Gibson (Bl) {2}

29 November
d 1596. From Ripon (Yorks), he was imprisoned for many years at York for recusancy before being executed with Bl William Knight. He was beatified in 1987. Cf. **England, Martyrs of**.

William Greenwood (Bl) {2}

6 June
d. 1537. A Carthusian lay brother of the London Charterhouse, he was one of the six of that community starved to death at Newgate prison for refusing the oath of supremacy demanded by King Henry VIII. Cf. **England, Martyrs of**.

William Gunter (Bl) {2}

28 August
d. 1588. From Raglan in Gwent, he was educated at Rheims and ordained there in 1587. He was hanged at Shoreditch (London) and was beatified in 1929. Cf. **England, Martyrs of**.

William Harcourt (Bl) {2}

20 June
d. 1679. A Lancastrian, he became a Jesuit at St Omer in 1632 and was on the English mission from 1645, chiefly in London. He was executed at Tyburn with BB Thomas Whitbread and Comps. Cf. **England, Martyrs of**.

William Harrington (Bl) {2}

18 February
1567–94. From Felixkirk near Thirsk (Yorks), he studied at Rheims, was ordained there in 1592 and was hanged, drawn and quartered at Tyburn. He was beatified in 1929. Cf. **England, Martyrs of**.

William Hart (Bl) {2}

15 March
d. 1583. From Wells (Somerset), he was educated the University of Oxford before converting and studying for the priesthood at Douai, Rheims and Rome. After his ordination in 1581, he returned to England, was betrayed by an apostate in the house of Bl Margaret Clitherow and was executed at York. He was beatified in 1886. Cf. **England, Martyrs of**.

William Hartley (Bl) {2}

5 October
d. 1588. From Church Wilne near Derby, he was educated at St John's College, Oxford and became an Anglican minister. After his conversion he studied for the priesthood at Rheims, was ordained there in 1580 and was

hanged at Shoreditch (London) with three companions. He was beatified in 1929. Cf. **England, Martyrs of**.

William Horne (Bl) {2}

4 August
d. 1540. A Carthusian lay brother of the London Charterhouse, he was executed at Tyburn with two companions. He was beatified in 1886, but his companions have not yet been. Cf. **England, Martyrs of**.

William Howard (Bl) {2}

29 December
1616–80. Grandson of St Philip Howard and viscount of Stafford, he was accused of being involved in the Oates Plot and was beheaded on Tower Hill after two years' imprisonment. He was beatified in 1929. Cf. **England, Martyrs of**.

William Ireland (Iremonger) (Bl) {2}

24 January
d. 1679. From Lincolnshire, he was educated at St Omer, became a Jesuit there in 1655 and was executed at Tyburn for alleged complicity in the Oates Plot, being beatified in 1929. His servant Bl John Grove was executed with him. Cf. **England, Martyrs of**.

William Knight (Bl) {2}

29 November
1573–96. From South Duffield (Yorks), he was the orphan of a yeoman farmer and was denounced for recusancy when he grew up by a relative who coveted his inheritance. While imprisoned at York, he was convicted of trying to convert a renegade Anglican minister imprisoned with him and was executed with Bl William Gibson. He was beatified in 1987. Cf. **England, Martyrs of**.

William Lacey (Bl) {2}

22 August
d. 1582. From Horton in Ribblesdale (Yorks), he was a wealthy recusant landowner. After fourteen years of his married life his second wife died, so he went to Rheims to study for the priesthood and was ordained at Rome. He worked around York and was secretly chaplain to the Catholics in York prison for two years until he was spotted, arrested and executed with Bl Richard Kirkman. He was beatified in 1886. Cf. **England, Martyrs of**.

William Lampley (Bl) {2}

11 August
d. 1588. A poor glove maker, he was condemned at Gloucester for 'persuading to Popery' and was offered a reprieve if he attended a Protestant service. He preferred to die, and was beatified in 1987. His date of execution is unknown; the Roman Martyrology places it on this date arbitrarily. Cf. **England, Martyrs of**.

William of Maleval (St) {2, 4}

10 February
d. 1157. Apparently a French soldier, he went on pilgrimage to the Holy Land and was made superior on his return of an abbey near Pisa (Italy). Failing to maintain discipline there (as well as at a foundation of his own on Monte Bruno), he became a hermit at Maleval near Siena in 1155 and attracted disciples. This was the beginning of the monastic order of the Williamites, which made use of the Benedictine rule but was later mostly absorbed by the Augustinian friars.

William Marsden (Bl) {2}

25 April
d. 1586. A Lancastrian, he was educated at St Mary Hall, Oxford, studied for the priesthood at Rheims and was ordained there in 1585.

The following year he was executed on the Isle of Wight. He was beatified in 1929. Cf. **England, Martyrs of.**

William of Montevergine (St) {2, 3}

25 June

1085–1142. From Vercelli (Italy), after a pilgrimage to Compostella he became a hermit on the summit of what is now Montevergine between Nola and Benevento. He attracted disciples, founded a monastery and gave it a rule based on that of St Benedict. Then he founded other monasteries and formed a new monastic congregation, which became definitively Benedictine under his successor. He died at the monastery of Guglieto near Nusco, one of his foundations. Only the monastery of Montevergine survives of his congregation, and this now belongs to the Subiaco Benedictines. His cultus was confined to local calendars in 1969.

William de Naurose (Bl) {2}

18 May

1297–1369. From Toulouse (France), he became an Augustinian friar and was famous as a home missioner specializing in preaching on purgatory. His cultus was confirmed for Toulouse in 1893.

William of Norwich (St)

26 March

d. 1144. A twelve-year-old apprentice tanner at Norwich, he was found murdered in Thorpe Wood just outside the city. Two Jews were accused of having killed him in a parody of the Crucifixion, which makes him the first case of alleged 'Jewish ritual murder'. His shrine at Norwich Cathedral (which lacked a proper saint) was popular in the Middle Ages, but his cultus was never approved. He is depicted as a boy crowned with thorns with a knife piercing his side, with wounded extremities and holding a cross and nails.

William Patenson (Bl) {2}

22 January

d. 1592. From Durham, he studied for the priesthood at Rheims and was ordained there in 1587. He was hanged, drawn and quartered at Tyburn in 1592 and beatified in 1929. Cf. **England, Martyrs of.**

William Pike (Bl) {2}

21 March

d. 1591. From Christchurch (Hants), he was a carpenter and a family man who was executed outside Dorchester for denying the Royal supremacy in spiritual matters. His date of execution is unknown; the Roman Martyrology places it on this date arbitrarily. He was beatified in 1987.

William Pinchon (St) {2, 4}

29 July

d. 1234. A Breton nobleman, he was a canon of Saint-Brieuc before becoming bishop there in 1220. He was exiled for a time to Poitiers by the Duke of Brittany for defending the independence of the church. He was canonized in 1253.

William of Pontoise (St) {2}

10 May

d. 1195. Apparently an English priest, he settled at Pontoise near Paris (France) and was highly regarded by King Philip Augustus. He died in the latter's palace at Pontoise. There is no proof that he was a monk.

William Repin and Comps (BB) {2}

d. 1793–4. The period known as the 'Terror' during the French Revolution saw an anti-Catholic pogrom in the Vendée around Angers, and about 2,000 people were guillotined, burnt or beaten to death. There were major massacres at Avrillé to the north-west of

Angers, with forty-seven killed on 1 February and twenty-five on 16 April. Ninety-nine of the total number of people who died were beatified in 1983, and they included William Repin, eleven other priests, three female religious, four laymen and the rest laywomen. Cf. **French Revolution, Martyrs of**.

William Richardson (Anderson) (Bl) {2}

27 February
d. 1603. From Wales near Sheffield in Yorkshire, he was educated for the priesthood at Valladolid and at Seville, where he was ordained in 1594. He was executed at Tyburn and beatified in 1929. Cf. **England, Martyrs of**.

William of Rochester (St)

23 May
d. 1201. Allegedly a baker or fisherman of Perth (Scotland), he was on his way to the Holy Land when he was robbed and murdered at Rochester (Kent) by his servant. Owing to miracles being reported he became the focus of popular veneration, and his shrine was at Rochester Cathedral before the Reformation.

William Scott cf. **Maurus Scott**.

William Southerne (Bl) {2}

30 April
d. 1618. From Ketton near Darlington, he was ordained at Valladolid and was a priest among the poor Catholics of Northumberland for fourteen years before being captured and executed at Newcastle. The date of his execution is uncertain. He was beatified in 1987. Cf. **England, Martyrs of**.

William Spencer (Bl) {2}

24 September
d. 1589. From Gisburgh (Yorks), he became a fellow of Trinity College, Oxford but converted, went to Rheims and was ordained in 1583. He was a priest at York but was seized on the road to Ripon with his guide, Bl Robert Hardesty, and was executed with him at York. He was beatified in 1987. Cf. **England, Martyrs of**.

William Tempier (St) {2}

29 March
d. 1197. He was bishop of Poitiers (France) after having been a canon regular, and firmly opposed simony in his diocese. This led to his being persecuted.

William Thomson (Bl) {2}

20 April
c.1560–86. From Blackburn (Lancs), he was ordained at Douai and was a priest in London before being seized at Harrow and executed at Tyburn with Bl Richard Sergeant. He was beatified in 1987. Cf. **England, Martyrs of**.

William Tirry (Bl) {2}

2 May
d. 1654. An Augustinian priest, he was hanged at Clonmel in the persecution by Cromwell and was beatified in 1992. Cf. **Ireland, Martyrs of**.

William Way (Bl) {2}

23 September
d. 1588. From Devon, he was educated for the priesthood at Rheims, ordained there in 1586 and executed at Kingston-on-Thames (Surrey). He was beatified in 1929. Cf. **England, Martyrs of**.

William Webster (Ward) (Bl) {2}

26 July
d. 1641. From Westmorland, he was educated at Douai and ordained there in 1608. He spent thirty-three years on the English

mission (twenty of them in prison) and was executed at Tyburn. He was beatified in 1929. Cf. **England, Martyrs of**.

Willibald (Willebald) (St) {2}

7 July
d. 787. From Wessex (England), he was a brother of SS Winebald and Walburga and a relative of St Boniface. When aged five he became a child-oblate at the monastery of Bishop's Waltham (Hants), and in 722 went with his brother on a long journey via Rome, the Holy Land, many famous monastic centres of the East and Constantinople. In 730 he settled at the newly re-founded Italian monastery of Montecassino under St Petronax for ten years, but the pope then sent him to Germany to help St Boniface. He was made bishop of Eichstätt (Germany) in 742 and founded the double abbey of Heidenheim with his brother St Winebald, making their sister St Walburga the first abbess. His shrine is at Eichstätt Cathedral. He was canonized in 938.

Willibrord (St) {2, 4}

7 November
?658–739. A Northumbrian, he was educated by St Wilfrid at Ripon (England) and also spent twelve years under St Egbert of Iona in Ireland. From there he went to Friesland with eleven other Anglo-Saxon monks in c.690, and became missionary archbishop of Utrecht in 696. His work in the Low Countries (he also went on mission to Denmark and the island of Heligoland) was of lasting success in the areas ruled by the Franks. He founded the monastery of Echternach in Luxembourg in 698, where he died and where his shrine is located.

Willigis (St) {2, 4}

23 February
d. 1011. The son of a wheelwright of Schöningen near Brunswick (Germany), he became a canon of Hildesheim and then chaplain to Emperor Otto III and chancellor of the Empire in 971. He was made archbishop of Mainz in 975 as well as papal vicar-apostolic for Germany. He campaigned for the election of Emperor St Henry II and crowned him in 1002. His attribute is a wheel, which he chose to adorn his shield in memory of his father.

Winebald (Winnibald) of Heidenheim (St) {2}

18 December
d. 761. Brother of SS Willibald and Walburga, he accompanied the former on his journey to the East but fell ill and remained at Rome, where he studied for seven years. Eventually he returned to England, collected some disciples and went to Germany at the invitation of St Boniface. Later he became the superior of the monks of Heidenheim, a double monastery founded by his brother (then bishop of Eichstätt) and where his sister was abbess. He died there.

Winebald (Vinebaud) of Troyes (St) {2}

6 April
d. c.620. At first a hermit near Noyon (France), he then joined the monastery of St Loup at Troyes and became abbot there.

Winefride (Gwenfrewi, Guinevra) (St) {2, 4}

3 November
C7th. According to her late legend, she was a niece of St Beuno from Holywell (Wales) and was beheaded by a suitor near there for refusing his amorous proposal. A spring of water emerged from the spot where her head fell, and this was the alleged origin of the famous Holy Well which has been an ancient focus of pilgrimage. A gloss on the legend adds that she was restored to life by St Beuno and became abbess of Gwytherin in Clwyd. She was a real

person, but historical details are obscure. Her shrine was at Shrewsbury Abbey.

Winin cf. **Finian**.

Winnoc (St) {2}

6 November
d. ?716. Probably from Wales, he became a monk of Sithiu at St Omer (France) under St Bertin and was sent to become abbot-founder of the monastery at Wormhoudt near Dunkirk. He was famously devoted to manual work. The Cornish village of St Winnow probably commemorates him (see below).

Winwaloe (St) {2}

3 March
d. 533. From Brittany (France), he became a disciple of St Budoc and abbot-founder of Landevennec near Brest. Several Cornish churches are dedicated to him, indicating a possible connection with Cornwall (they may have received portions of his relics after the Viking invasions). He is depicted as carrying a church on his shoulders or ringing a bell, and has many variants on his name: Guengaloeus, Gwenno, Wonnow, Wynwallow, Valois, etc.

Wiro and Comps (SS) {2}

8 May
d. c.700. A Northumbrian monk, he went to the Friesland mission and was made bishop of Utrecht by St Boniface in c.741. He and his two companions, Plechelm and Odger, founded a monastery at Odiliënberg near Roermond (Netherlands) and their shrine was established there.

Wistan (St) {2}

1 June
d. 849. According to his legend he was a prince of Mercia (England) who was murdered by a cousin for thwarting his wish to marry Wistan's mother, the Queen Regent. He was probably killed at Wistow (Leics) rather than at Wistanstow in Shropshire, and eventually his shrine was established at Evesham Abbey.

Witesind (St) {2}

15 May
d. 855. From Cordoba (Spain) when that place was ruled by the Moors, he was persuaded to become a Muslim but repented of this, publicly proclaimed his Christianity and was executed as a result.

Witta cf. **Albinus**.

Wivina (Vivina) (St) {2, 4}

17 December
d. 1170. A Flemish noblewoman, when aged twenty-two she secretly left the family home and became a hermit in a wood called Grand-Bigard near Brussels (Belgium). There she founded a nunnery, affiliated it to the Benedictine abbey of Affligem and became the first abbess.

Wolfgang (St) {2, 4}

31 October
924–94. From Swabia (Germany), he was educated at the abbey of Reichenau and, after being dean of the cathedral school at Trier, became a Benedictine monk at Einsiedeln in Switzerland in 964. He was headmaster of the abbey school and a missionary to the Magyars before being made bishop of Regensburg in Bavaria in 972. He restored abbeys (notably that of St Emmeram at Regensburg), improved the standard of education, reformed ecclesiastical discipline and was a great benefactor of the poor. He was canonized in 1052.

Wolfhard cf. **Gualfard**.

Wulfram (St) {2, 4}

20 March
C7th. From near Fontainebleu (France), he was one of the Merovingian court clergy and was made bishop of Sens in 683. In 685 he resigned, spent some time at the abbey of Fontenelle and went on mission to Friesland for many years with some of the monks. He died at Fontenelle and his shrine is at Abbeville.

Wulmar (St) {2, 4}

20 July
d. c.700. From near Boulogne (France), he married but the couple were forcibly separated and he then became a lay brother at the abbey of Haumont in Hainault (Belgium). Initially a cowherd and wood-chopper, he was later ordained and eventually became the abbot-founder of Samer near Boulogne, afterwards called St Vulmaire after him. He also founded the nunnery at Wierre-aux-Bois. His name has many variants: Ulmar, Ulmer, Vilmarus, Volmar, Vilmer, etc.

Wulstan (Wulfstan, Ulfstan, Wolstan) (St) {2}

19 January
d. 1095. From one of two villages named Itchington (Warwickshire, England), he studied at the abbeys of Evesham and Peterborough and became a Benedictine monk at the cathedral priory of Worcester where he was precentor and prior. Finally he was made bishop of Worcester in 1062, and his success was such that he was the only Anglo-Saxon bishop who was allowed to remain in place after the Norman Conquest. He rebuilt his cathedral and was the first English bishop to hold a regular visitation of his diocese. He was canonized in 1203.

X–Z

S. ZACHARIAS Græcus Polychronij
fil. creat. die 5. Dece mb. an., 741. Sedit
an. io. mens. 3. dies io. Obijt die 15.
Martij an. 752 Vac. Sed. dies 12.

(Xantippa and Polyxena) *(SS) {4 –deleted}*

23 September
C1st? The old Roman Martyrology listed them as virgins who were disciples of the Apostles, but nothing is known about them.

Xenophon and Comps (SS) {2}

26 January
C6th. They were a patrician family of Constantinople, being Xenophon and Mary and two sons, John and Arcadius. They all became monastics at Jerusalem, but their story has romantic details attached to it.

Xi Guizi (St) {1 –group}

20 July
1882–1900. From a peasant family of Dechao in Hebei (China), he became a catechumen but his parents objected when the Boxer Uprising took place. He fled to a Catholic area, where he initially failed to find acceptance because he was unbaptized, and worked as a servant. His parents ordered him to return home but he met a Boxer gang on the way who recognized him as a Christian. He was dismembered near his home village. Cf. **China, Martyrs of**.

Xystus I, Pope (St) {2, 4}

3 April
d. 128. He was pope from 117 and had a cultus as a martyr, but there are no acta and the list of popes by St Irenaeus makes no mention of martyrdom. The revised Roman Martyrology concurs.

Xystus II, Pope and Comps (St) {1, 3}

7 August
d. 258. A Greek, he was pope for one year. While preaching during Mass he was seized with four of his deacons and beheaded on the orders of the emperor Valerian. They were buried in the catacomb of Callistus. Another two deacons, Felicissimus and Agapitus, were martyred in a separate incident and buried in the catacomb of Praetextatus. A seventh one, St Laurence, was martyred later. The name of Xystus is in the Roman canon of the Mass, but rendered as 'Sixtus'. The old Roman Martyrology named the four deacons as Januarius, Magnus, Vincent and Stephen, and added one Quartus. The last owes his existence to a bad manuscript in which 'diaconus Quartus' was written for 'diacones quattuor'. The names have been deleted.

Xystus III, Pope (St) {2, 4}

19 August
d. 440. A Roman, he became pope in 432. He opposed Nestorianism and Pelagianism and restored the basilica of St Mary Major in thanksgiving for the declaration at the Council of Ephesus that Our Lady is the Mother of God.

Yolanda cf. **Helen of Poland**.
Yon cf. **Jonas**.
Yrieix cf. **Aredius**.
Yvo cf. **Ivo**.

Ywi (St) {2}

6 October
d. ?704. A monk of Lindisfarne in Northumberland (England), he was a disciple of St Cuthbert. According to his legend he migrated to Brittany (France) and died there but had his relics brought back to England c.950, where they were enshrined at Wilton near Salisbury.

Zacchaeus of Jerusalem (St) {2, 4}

23 August
C2nd. Patristic sources list him (variantly as Zacharias) as the fourth bishop of Jerusalem.

Zacharias, Pope (St) {2, 4}

15 March
d. 752. Born at San Severino in Calabria of a Greek family, he became pope in 741 and successfully negotiated a peace between the Lombards and the imperial exarchate at Ravenna. The iconoclastic policy of Emperor Constantine V led him to look to the Franks for support, however, and he permitted the coronation of Pepin. He also encouraged the German missions under of St Boniface and part of their correspondence is extant.

Zacharias Angelicus (St) {2}

21 January
d. c.950. He was abbot of a monastery at Montemercurio in Lucania (Italy).

(Zacharias of Nicomedia) (St) *{4 –deleted}*

June 10
? He is listed as a martyr of Nicomedia (Asia Minor).

Zacharias the Priest (St) {2, 4}

5 November
C1st. The only available information on the father of St John the Baptist is in the first chapter of the gospel of St Luke.

Zacharias (Zechariah) the Prophet (St) {2}

6 September
He is the eleventh of the Minor Prophets in the Old Testament.

(Zacharias of Vienne) (St) *{4 –deleted}*

26 May
C2nd? He was alleged to have been the second bishop of Vienne (France) and to have been martyred in the reign of Trajan.

Zama (St) {2, 4}

24 January
C4th. He is the first recorded bishop of Bologna (Italy).

(Zambdas) (St) *{4 –deleted}*

19 February
Early C4th? He was allegedly a bishop of Jerusalem and features in the legend of the Theban legion.

(Zanitas and Comps) (SS) *{4 –deleted}*

27 March
d. 326. He was martyred in the reign of the Persian Shah Shapur II with Abibos, Elias, Lazarus, Mares, Marotas, Narses, Sembeeth and Sabas.

Zaragoza (Eighteen Martyrs of) (SS) {2, 4}

16 April
Early C4th. They were martyred at Zaragoza (Spain) under the prefect Dacian in the reign of the emperor Diocletian. Prudentius (who lived at Zaragoza later in the century) described their martyrdom. Their names were Apodemius, Caecilian, Evodius, Felix, Fronto, Julia, Lupercus, Martial, Optatus, Primitivus, Publius, Quintilian, Successus, Urban and four named Saturninus.

(Zaragoza, Innumerable Martyrs of) (SS) *{4 –deleted}*

3 November
Early C4th. As well as the eighteen martyrs named by Prudentius, very many were killed at Zaragoza by the prefect Dacian who had been sent to Spain to enforce the decrees of Emperor Diocletian against Christianity. He published an edict expelling all Christians from the city, and while they were leaving he ordered the garrison to massacre them.

Zdenka cf. **Sindonia**.

Zdislava Berka (St) {2}

1 January
d. 1252. A Czech noblewoman born at Krizanov, she married and had four children. Her generosity to the poor was resented by her husband but she won him over by her heroic patience. She died as a Dominican tertiary in the priory of St Lawrence at Jabbone which she had founded and was canonized in 1995.

(Zenais, Cyria, Valeria and Marcia) (SS) {4 –deleted}

5 June
? Zenais was apparently martyred at Constantinople and was not connected with the other three, who were traditionally disciples of Christ martyred at Caesarea in the Holy Land.

(Zenais and Philonilla) (SS) {4 –deleted}

11 October
C1st? Their story is that they were two sisters of Tarsus related to St Paul who were stoned by pagans at Demetrias in Thessaly (Greece).

(Zeno) (St) {4 –deleted}

5 April
? He was listed as having been burnt alive, but not where or when.

(Zeno and Chariton) (SS) {4 –deleted}

3 September
Early C4th? They were listed as martyred somewhere in the East in the reign of Diocletian.

(Zeno and Zenas) (SS) {4 –deleted}

23 June
Early C4th? Their story is that Zeno was a wealthy citizen of Philadelphia near the Dead Sea who freed all his slaves and gave his property to the poor. Zenas, one of the former slaves, remained with him as a servant and both were beheaded in the reign of Diocletian.

Zeno Kovalyk (Bl) {2}
1904–41. A Redemptorist, he died in prison at Lwow (now Lviv in Ukraine) in 1941 after the Soviet Union invaded and annexed that part of Poland. The exact date of his death is not known. Cf. **Nicholas Čarneckyj and 24 Comps**.

Zeno of Maiuma (St) {2, 4}

26 December
d. p400. He was allegedly related to the Eusebius, Nestabus and Comps who destroyed the main temple at Gaza in the Holy Land and were lynched as a result. He himself became bishop of Maiuma, the port of Gaza.

(Zeno of Nicomedia -1) (St) {2, 4}

2 September
Early C4th. He was martyred at Nicomedia (Asia Minor) in the reign of Diocletian. His two sons and companion martyrs, Concordius and Theodore, have been deleted from the Roman Martyrology.

(Zeno of Nicomedia -2) (St) {4 –deleted}

22 December
Early C4th? A soldier based at the imperial capital of Nicomedia (Asia Minor), he laughed during the offering of a sacrifice to Ceres by the emperor Diocletian. As a result his jaw was broken and he was beheaded.

(Zeno of Rome -1) (St) {2}

14 February
? He was a Roman martyr of unknown date who was buried in the catacomb of Praetextatus on the Appian Way.

(Zeno of Rome -2 and Comps) *(SS)*
{4 –deleted}

9 July
Early C4th? He was apparently the spokes-man of the Christians enslaved to work on the public baths built at Rome on the orders of the emperor Diocletian, who ordered their massa-cre when the project was completed. The old Roman Martyrology asserted that they num-bered 10,204 (a gross exaggeration).

Zeno of Verona (St) {2, 4}

12 April
d. ?372. From Roman Africa, he was bishop of Verona (Italy) from 362 and was a fervent opponent of Arianism. He also corrected litur-gical abuses and supported consecrated vir-gins living at home. His attribute is a fish.

(Zenobius and Zenobia) *(SS) {4 –deleted}*

30 October
C3rd? He was allegedly bishop and physi-cian at Aegae (now Alexandretta on the Turk-ish coast near Syria) and is probably identical with St Zenobius of Antioch, in which case his martyrdom took place later than the year given. Zenobia was alleged to have been his sister.

Zenobius of Florence (St) {2, 4}

25 May
d. c.400. He was bishop of Florence (Italy) and a friend of St Ambrose and of Pope St Damasus, by whom he was sent as papal rep-resentative to Constantinople in connection with the Arian controversy. He is sometimes depicted raising a dead child to life.

Zenobius of Sidon (St) {2, 4}

29 October
Early C4th. A priest of Sidon (Lebanon), he martyred there in the reign of Diocletian.

Zephaniah (Sophonias) (St) {2}

3 December
He is the ninth of the Minor Prophets of the Old Testament.

Zephyrinus, Pope (St) {2, 4}

26 August
d. 217–18. He was pope from 198 and had to contend with an adoptionist heresy disturb-ing the church at Rome. His cultus was sup-pressed in 1969.

Zephyrinus Agostini (Bl) {2}

6 April
1813–96. From Verona (Italy), he was ordained as a diocesan priest there in 1837 and was appointed to the large and poor city parish of St Nazarius, where he remained all his life. He took a special interest in the moral and material poverty of the local young women, and set up a pious society on Ursuline principles to help them. This he established as the 'Ursuline Congregation of Daughters of Mary Immaculate' in 1869. He was beatified in 1998.

Zephyrinus Giménez Malla (Bl) {2}

2 August
1861–1938. A gypsy from Fraga in Huesca (Spain), he married and became a flourishing horse-dealer at Barbastro. He was a model Christian, honest in his business dealings and charitable, and was esteemed for his wisdom despite his illiteracy. He was arrested at the start of the Civil War for defending a priest who was being attacked in the street, and was offered his freedom on condition that he stop saying the Rosary. He refused, was shot on 8 August, 1936 and was beatified in 1997 (the first gypsy to be honoured thus). Cf. **Spanish Civil War, Martyrs of**.

Zephyrinus Namuncurá (Bl) {2 –add}

1886–1905. He was born at Chimpay in Argentina, and his father was the Mapuche Chief of the Araucanian Native Americans of the Pampas. The nation had just lost a war of conquest against Argentina, and the chief and his family had converted to Christianity. So Bl Zephyrinus was sent to the Salesian mission school at Buenos Aires. As an adolescent he had a well-rounded personality, enjoying studies, sport and friendship, and had a strong devotion to the Blessed Sacrament, Our Lady and the Rosary. Then he entered the junior seminary at Viedma, but quickly contracted tuberculosis. He was sent to Italy for his health, but died in hospital at Rome. He was beatified in 2007.

Zhang Huailu (St) {1 –group}

1 July
1843–1900. From Zhuhedian near Jieshui in Hebei (China), he was the first of his family to become a Catholic catechumen. When a gang of Boxers visited his village the Catholics fled but he was too old and infirm to keep up and was captured. He insisted that he was a Christian and was beheaded in consequence, witnessing to his faith by his death despite not being baptized. Cf. **China, Martyrs of**.

Zita (St) {2, 4}

27 April
1218–78. From Monsagrati near Lucca (Italy), when aged twelve she started work as a domestic servant at a household at Lucca and remained there all her life. She would give her food and clothing to the poor, and also her employer's when she had none. For this she was initially misunderstood and treated harshly, but she eventually became respected by the whole household. Her cultus was confirmed for Lucca in 1696 and she is the patron of domestic servants. Thus she is depicted in working clothes with a bag, keys, loaves or a rosary.

(Zoë of Rome) *(St) {4 –deleted}*

5 July
C3rd? She was allegedly a Roman martyr who was the wife of a high official of the imperial court, but she possibly never existed.

Zoëllus (St) {2, 4}

24 May
C2nd–3rd. He was martyred at Lystra in Lycaonia (Asia Minor). The old Roman Martyrology placed him in Istria in error, and added companions Servilius, Felix, Silvanus and Diocles. These have been deleted.

Zoerard cf. **Andrew Zoerard**.

Zoilus (St) {2, 4}

27 June
d. 303. He was martyred at Cordoba (Spain) in the reign of Diocletian. The Benedictine abbey of San Zoil de Carrión near León was founded to enshrine his relics, together with those of nineteen other dubious martyrs who have been deleted from the Roman Martyrology.

Zoltán Lajos Meszlényi (Bl) {2 –add}

11 January
1892–1953. From Hatvan near Budapest (Hungary), he was ordained as a diocesan priest of Esztergom in 1915 and worked in the archbishop's curia, being noted for his knowledge of canon law and of several languages. In 1937 he was consecrated as auxiliary bishop of Esztergom and was elected as the episcopal vicar after the death of the archbishop in 1950. The new Communist regime objected to his integrity, and he was seized and imprisoned several days later. His subsequent fate was

kept completely secret, but it transpired after the collapse of Communism that he had died in 1953 (or perhaps 1951) after continual and serious ill-treatment. His body was traced to a cemetery in Esztergom. He was beatified as a martyr in 2009. His first name is peculiar to Hungary, and means 'Sultan'.

(Zosimus) (St) {4 –deleted}

4 April
C5th. He features in the story of St Mary of Egypt as a hermit who lived on the banks of the River Jordan and who discovered her in the desert before she died.

Zosimus, Pope (St) {2, 4}

26 December
d. 418. A Greek, he was pope for a year and his short pontificate was marked by a high view of papal authority linked to tactlessness and personality clashes in which he seems to have been usually wrong.

(Zosimus and Athanasius) (SS) {4 –deleted}

3 January
Early C4th? One story describes them as martyrs of Cilicia (Asia Minor) in the reign of Diocletian, but another alleges that Zosimus was put to the torture and that Athanasius (a spectator) was converted and immediately tortured also, but that both survived and died in peace as hermits.

(Zosimus of Spoleto) (St) {4 –deleted}

19 June
C2nd? He was allegedly martyred at Spoleto in Umbria (Italy) in the reign of Trajan.

Zosimus of Syracuse (St) {2, 4}

30 March
d. c.600. A Sicilian, when aged seven he became a child-oblate at the monastery of St Lucia (of uncertain rite) near Syracuse. After being a monk for thirty years he became abbot and then bishop of the city.

(Zosimus the Thaumaturge) (St) {4 –deleted}

30 November
C6th. He was a hermit in the Holy Land, famous as a wonder-worker.

Zoticus and Amantius (SS) {2, 4}

10 February
C3rd–4th. They were martyred at Rome and buried at the tenth milestone on the Via Labicana outside the city. The Roman Martyrology has deleted Irenaeus, Hyacinth and six anonymous companions.

(Zoticus, Rogatus and Comps) (SS) {4 –deleted}

12 January
? They were listed as a group of forty-four soldiers, martyred in Roman Africa. Modestus and Castulus were also named.

(Zoticus of Comana) (St) {4 –deleted}

21 July
d. ?204. This alleged martyr-bishop of Comana in Cappodocia (Asia Minor) was inserted into the old Roman Martyrology by Baronius, on what authority is unclear.

Zoticus of Constantinople (St) {2, 4}

31 December
C4th. A Roman priest, he migrated to Constantinople when Constantine made that city the capital of the Empire and founded a hospital for the poor and for orphans.

(Zoticus of Tivoli) (St) {4 –deleted}

12 January
C2nd? This alleged martyr of Tivoli near Rome is an erroneous duplication of St Getulius.

Bibliography

'Acta Apostolicae Sedis' Vatican 1884 to date. (The Church's official record of the workings of the Magisterium, including canonizations and beatifications. In Latin.)

'Acta Sanctorum' 64 vv. Antwerp, 1643–. (This vast compendium of Bollandist scholarship is still valuable as a source, but is in Latin and will only be found in the greater libraries.)

'Bibliotheca Sanctorum' 12 vv. Vatican 1960–70. (The latest product of Bollandist scholarship is in Italian.)

Butler's 'Lives of the Saints' 12 vv. B&O 1995–. (This classic has been thoroughly revised and contains individual biographies of saints listed by feast-day.)

Chitty, D. 'The Desert a City' Mowbrays 1966. (The standard work on the history of the desert fathers.)

Catholic University of America 'New Catholic Encyclopaedia' 1967– with supplementary vols.

Congregatio Pro Causis Sanctorum 'Index ac Status Causarum' Vatican 1988. (Lists of canonizations, beatifications, confirmations of cultus and processes pending.)

Cross and Livingstone 'Oxford Dictionary of the Christian Church' Oxford 1978.

Ellwood Post, W:- 'Saints, Signs and Symbols' SPCK 1964 (The best short introduction to hagiographical symbols available.)

Farmer, D. H. 'The Oxford Dictionary of Saints' Oxford 1978. (Gives alphabetical entries for c.1000 saints known in the British Isles, each with an individual biography. Excellent, but with a few errors.)

Holweck, F. G. 'A Biographical Dictionary of the Saints' Herder 1924. (Almost eighty years old and containing many errors, this is still the only attempt at a full alphabetical listing of all saints, including those of the Eastern churches. It has been recently reprinted in the USA.)

Jedin, H. (ed.) 'History of the Church' 10 vv. B&O 1962–.

Kalberer, A. 'Lives of the Saints' Franciscan Herald 1983. (A useful alternative to the Roman Martyrology for reading in religious communities.)

Lawrence, C. H. 'Medieval Monasticism' Longman 1989. (A good modern introduction to the subject for Western Europe.)

Meinardus, O. 'The Saints of Greece' Athens 1970. (Contains many post-schism Greek Orthodox saints.)

Sacra Congregatio pro Sacramentis 'Notitiae' Vatican 1964 to date. (Official periodical including matters pertaining to liturgical veneration of saints. Has included useful biographies. In Latin.)

'Roman Martyrology' B&O 1937. (This is the 'old Roman Martyrology' as referred to in the text of this book. See also glossary entry.)

'Roman Martyrology' Libreria Editrice Vaticana 2001, revised 2004. (In Latin.)

'Sayings of the Desert Fathers' Mowbray 1981. (Alphabetically listed according to name.)

The Times 'Atlas of the World, Comprehensive Edition' 2014.

Velimirovic, N. 'Prologue from Ochrid' Lazarica 1985. (The Serbian Orthodox equivalent of 'Butler').

Glossary to *The Book of Saints*

Acta

When Christians were martyred in the days of the Roman Empire their brethren in the local church often wrote down what happened in order to inform other churches. These written 'acta' survive in several cases, for example, Polycarp, Perpetua and Felicity. Many must have been lost in later persecutions, and many were probably never written down. Later, after persecution ceased, the tendency was to provide spurious acta where genuine ones were lacking and many famous martyrs have them. These inventions vary from an embroidery on what seems actually to have happened to absurd pieces of fiction repeating stock themes. A common example of the latter is the martyr who proves invulnerable to various grotesque attempts at execution until he or she is beheaded.

Africa

In the martyrologies this refers to Roman Africa, which comprised what is now known as the Maghrib (Morocco, Algeria, Tunisia and Libya). The Church there (concerning the foundation of which absolutely nothing is known) was the first to use Latin in its liturgy. It suffered seriously in persecutions, especially during that of Diocletian, and disagreements about how to deal with apostates led to the Donatist schism. After the arrival of Islam in the C7th the African Church became extinct in circumstances which are obscure.

Apophthegmata Patrum

These are the collected sayings of the early desert fathers in Egypt. The most famous collection is the 'alphabetical' where the sayings are attributed to famous individuals, although there are also anonymous ones ordered according to subject.

Apostles

There are fourteen saints liturgically venerated as apostles: the Twelve (including St Matthias), St Paul and St Barnabas. Of these, St James the Great was martyred in New Testament times, St James the Less just afterwards and SS Peter, Paul, Andrew, John, Barnabas and Thomas have strong traditions associating them with certain local churches. St Matthew was an evangelist. The others (SS Philip, Bartholomew, Simon, Matthias and Jude) have left no old traditions of apostolic journeys or activity, which is probably significant since a claim to apostolic foundation was of advantage to any local church in later centuries. All five have late and conflicting traditions ascribed to them and all the apostles, except St John, are venerated as martyrs. They are usually depicted without shoes (cf. Mt. 10:10) and holding books.

Arianism

The Church in the C4th was especially concerned with the question of the divine nature of Christ, and an influential body of opinion held that he was entirely created by God ('there was a time when he was not'). This doctrine first came to cause controversy through the teachings of Arius of Alexandria, Egypt after 313 and was condemned at the first ecumenical council at Nicaea near Constantinople in 325. This proclaimed that Christ was fully God. However, Arianism subsequently became popular among those governing the Roman Empire and the controversy was only settled at the second ecumenical council at Constantinople in 381. This produced the present Christian creed, and since then Arianism has been held to be incompatible with Christianity. The Jehovah's Witnesses are a notable group of modern Arians.

Assyrian Church

This is the nickname of the 'Ancient Church of the East', the descendent of the church in the pre-Muslim Persian Empire. It went out of communion with the rest of Christianity after 431 when it did not accept the Council of Ephesus, and has been pejoratively referred to as 'Nestorian'. It has its own ancient calendar of saints. The corresponding Catholic rite is the Chaldean.

Attributes

After the art of portraiture was lost in the West in the Dark Ages, representations of saints were identified either by a personal characteristic or by some object or objects associated with the saint concerned. These latter are called attributes, and are either generic (e.g. palm branches for martyrs) or specific (e.g. stones for St Stephen).

Augustinians

The Rule of St Augustine, based on two letters written by him, emerged at the start of the Middle Ages as an alternative to the Rule of St Benedict. Various religious orders have used it, notably the Canons and Canonesses Regular (monastic) and the Augustinian Friars (apostolic). The official name of the latter is the 'Hermits of St Augustine', but this derives from their early history and not their charism.

Barefoot Saints

In much religious art saints are represented with bare feet, often inappropriately. Usually the symbolism intended is that of heavenly status, but this is properly shown by the halo. Apostles are traditionally represented with bare feet because of the apparent prohibition of footwear expressed to them by Christ in Matthew 10:10 (actually a ban on carrying a spare pair). Certain founders of apostolic congregations initially tried to imitate them, such as St Ignatius Loyola and St Paul-of-the-Cross Danei. Monks and hermits in patristic times often went barefoot as a sign of poverty, and this was imitated by the early Franciscans. Only the Poor Clares reformed by St Colette maintained the practice, however. It is to be noted that 'discalced' means 'without shoes' and not 'barefoot'. For example, the 'Discalced Carmelites' reformed by St Teresa of Jesus have worn straw sandals, as distinct from the 'Calced' Carmelites who wear shoes or boots. St Teresa disapproved of habitually going barefoot as a penitential practice; it is only so in cold weather and otherwise can become physically stimulating once the soles harden.

Beatification

By this act of the Magisterium a person is declared to be worthy of a local or particular public cultus (the latter usually being within a religious congregation). It is often an intermediate stage to canonization if this is considered of advantage to the Church as a whole. The act is permissive, not prescriptive, and is not infallible (although no beatification has ever been rescinded). In recent years the number of beatifications has been substantially in excess of canonizations, showing the

Church's recognition of the value of such local venerations.

Benedictines

From 817, when the Monastic Capitulary imposed the Benedictine Rule on all monasteries of the Carolingian Empire, until the rise of the Augustinian Canons Regular in the early Middle Ages (to be followed by the various orders of friars) virtually all Western European monasticism was Benedictine. Many saints before 817 have, however, been claimed for the Order.

The traditional position is as follows: When Montecassino was destroyed in c.570 and its monks took refuge in Rome, the Rule of St Benedict quickly took over Roman monasticism. This meant that St Gregory was a Benedictine, as were the missionaries he sent to England with St Augustine and, through them, all of Roman-rite Saxon monasticism with its saints. Further, the Benedictine rule replaced other rules in Europe as the seventh and eighth centuries progressed, so that all the monasteries were Benedictine by the time of Charlemagne.

The historical evidence is as follows: There is no evidence of a cultus of St Benedict at Rome before the C10th (except that three popes were named Benedict), and the writings of St Gregory the Great show no acquaintance with the Rule of St Benedict (the famous 'Dialogue' featuring St Benedict may not have been by him). No direct evidence survives that pre-Viking Saxon monasticism was exclusively Benedictine, although the Rule was in use (especially the houses associated with St Wilfrid, who claimed to have introduced the full observance of the Rule to England). Finally, rather than a process of one rule replacing another taking place, European monasticism before Charlemagne was eclectic with the tendency being for monastic customaries to make use of more than one rule. Especially popular was a conflation of the Benedictine and Columbanian rules known as the 'Mixed Rule'. The Benedictine rule gradually came to dominate, but the process was not complete by 817 as several abbeys resisted the imposition of the full rule even then.

Calced cf. Barefoot Saints.

Calendar (Revision of)

The general liturgical calendar of the Latin rite was thoroughly revised in 1969, and it is well known that several saints of ancient veneration (mostly martyrs of the Roman Empire) had their cultus suppressed then. This was not primarily a judgement on their existence, as is often alleged, although many of them are historically dubious and this was a factor in the suppression. Rather, the Church had decided that their veneration was no longer of any advantage, especially since the old calendar had been rather cluttered with the feast days of saints (especially of obscure martyrs). The Eastern rites have their own calendars in which many of these saints are still venerated. Other saints in the former general calendar had their veneration restricted to local or particular calendars at the same time. The cultus of Simon of Trent was unusual in being suppressed because of scandal.

Canons

These are priests who live a life in common. They can be secular (e.g. cathedral canons) or regular (e.g. Augustinians or Premonstratensians).

Canonization

By this act of the Magisterium a person is declared to be a saint and worthy of a cultus in the Church as a whole. The act is prescriptive, in that the cultus is mandatory. It is infallible, in that the person is declared without possibility of error to be in heaven and to be worthy of veneration. Such an act cannot be rescinded and a saint cannot be unmade.

Carmelites

This religious order was founded in the early C13th when the Latin-rite hermits on Mount Carmel were organized under a rule. Originally the order claimed the prophet Elijah as its historical founder, and several Biblical characters and early saints were claimed as Carmelites (e.g. St Cyril of Alexandria). This fiction was strenuously defended up to the C19th. The order was divided in 1580 and the Discalced Carmelite saints after then are separately noted.

Catacomb Saints

The necessity to build new churches to match the growth in world population in the C19th, especially in America, led to an increased demand for relics of saints to place under their altars. The catacombs in Rome, where Christians had been buried during the era of the Roman Empire, were considered to be a suitable source of these. This was so because it was thought that the graves of martyrs could be easily identified, for example by a burial being accompanied by a small glass bottle. Such confidence was misplaced, and 'St' Philomena is only the most notorious of the doubtful relics of martyrs which were excavated from the catacombs before the necessary archaeological knowledge was available to make a proper judgement of them.

Catholicos

Originally, this was a bishop of territorial jurisdiction subordinate to a patriarch (q.v.). The title was taken by the heads of the churches of Georgia and Armenia, and by a historical quirk the latter now has two independent catholicates of Etchmiadzin and Sis with three subordinate patriarchates at Constantinople, Jerusalem and Aghtamar (extinct).

Charism

This is a gift or talent granted by God to a recipient for the benefit of others, especially the Church. The recipients are usually individuals and the charisms need not be spectacular, but groups of people (especially consecrated religious) are also described as having charisms. In the latter case, these charisms are often considered to be a defining characteristic of the group.

Child-Oblate

It was an early tradition in Western monasticism (one accepted by St Benedict) to allow parents of young children to give their children to monasteries to be brought up as monks or nuns. Initially such a donation was regarded as being binding on the child as if the latter had taken vows, but the problems caused by oblates without vocations later led the Church to condemn this insistence as an abuse and to require the oblate to make a free choice of monastic life on reaching the age of discretion. This was done by a papal decretal of 1198.

Cistercians

They started out as a Benedictine reform movement but became a separate monastic order. In the Middle Ages several saintly churchmen retired to Cistercian monasteries to die, and claims that they became Cistercian monks need to be treated with caution. After many tribulations two separate orders were established in 1892, the Common Observance and the Strict Observance ('Trappists'), and saints and blesseds belonging to the latter are separately noted.

Confessor

In the old Roman Martyrology all male saints were listed either as martyrs or confessors. This latter category (so wide as to be useless) derived from the latter persecutions of the Roman Empire when those Christians who witnessed for their faith and suffered for it, but were not killed, were given great honour and accepted as equal to the martyrs so that they were listed in the martyrologies when they died.

Confirmation

An ancient local cultus (one claimed to date from before the reservation of the process of canonization to the Holy See) can be presented to the Magisterium for confirmation. This usually involves confirmation of beatification but sometimes of canonization. There are many local venerations which have not been so confirmed and these are tolerated, but cannot be regarded as approved by the Church and (in principle) are liable to suppression by the local Ordinary.

Cultus

This is the public liturgical veneration paid to saints and to those beatified (and has been rendered as 'cult' in English, although that now means something more pejorative). The latter is confined to local churches and congregations. It may be noted that 'veneration' is quite distinct from 'worship', which is something paid to God alone.

Desert Fathers

This is the generic term for the first hermit-monks in Egypt, as distinct from the cenobites founded by St Pachomius. The first of them was traditionally St Anthony, and the two great monastic centres were at Nitria on the edge of the Nile Delta (being near Alexandria, it was influenced by Greek thought and culture) and at Scetis, now known as the Wadi Natrun (this was, and is, the stronghold of native Coptic monasticism). Their importance in the early development of monastic theory and practice cannot be exaggerated, although the greatest systematizer of their doctrine on prayer, Evagrius Ponticus of Nitria, fell into disfavour because of his Origenist speculations.

Dies Natalis Cf. **Feast Day**.

Discalced cf. **Barefoot Saints**.

Doctors

Those pastors of the Church whose writings are especially important in the elucidation of the deposit of faith have been formally declared to be doctors (with the original meaning of 'teachers'). They can be of either sex. Such a declaration can be the equivalent of canonization if the person concerned was a blessed, for example, St Albert the Great was equivalently canonized when declared a doctor in 1931. The teaching in good faith of doctrines later condemned can prevent a Church father being declared a doctor, for example certain Origenist ideas that St Gregory of Nyssa accepted. The following are the doctors of the Church: Albert the Great, Alphonsus-Mary Liguori, Ambrose of Milan, Anselm of Canterbury, Anthony of Padua, Athanasius of Alexandria, Augustine of Hippo, Basil the Great, Bede the Venerable, Bernard of Clairvaux, Bonaventure, Catherine of Siena, Cyril of Alexandria, Cyril of Jerusalem, Ephraem the Syrian, Francis de Sales, Gregory I, Pope 'the Great', Gregory of Nazianzen, Hilary of Poitiers, Hildegard of Bingen, Isidore of Seville, Jerome, John of Ávila, John Chrysostom, John Damascene, John-of-the-Cross de Yepes, Laurence of Brindisi, Leo I Pope 'the Great', Peter Canisius, Peter Chrysologus, Peter Damian, Robert Bellarmine, Teresa-of-Jesus Cepeda de Ahumada, Teresa-of-the-Child-Jesus Martin and Thomas Aquinas.

Eastern Churches Cf. **Assyrians, Oriental Orthodox, Orthodox**.

Eastern Rites

The Latin rite is only one of nineteen rites of the Roman Catholic Church which are of equal dignity. Each of these has its own calendar. Most of them, apart from the Latin and the Maronite, are descended from Eastern churches out of communion with Rome and derive their calendars from them.

Enclosure

This is the part of a monastery which is closed to persons of the opposite sex. For some nunneries, the nuns are not allowed to leave this area except in an emergency.

Evangelists

These are the four authors of the Gospels: Matthew, Mark, Luke and John. Mark and Luke are not apostles but are given the same liturgical veneration.

Feast Day

Originally all saints were liturgically commemorated on the anniversaries of their deaths (each of these being referred to as the 'dies natalis' or 'birthday' into heaven). They are still listed under these in martyrologies. However, the inconvenience of having saints' days clashing with more important feasts or with penitential seasons such as Lent led to many feast days being transferred, sometimes to the nearest suitable day and sometimes to another date significant to the saint (e.g. anniversary of ordination or of transfer of relics).

Franciscans

The heroic charism of St Francis of Assisi has called for repeated revitalization among his followers throughout their history. In 1517 the Franciscan order split into Conventuals and Observants, and the Capuchins were founded in 1525. The Observants themselves split into various reform movements until they were finally reunited as the Friars Minor in 1897. Thus there are three male Franciscan orders today. The Conventuals after 1517 and the Capuchins are administered separately. The Franciscan nuns are usually known as 'Poor Clares', and there are many tertiary congregations.

Friar

This is a male religious whose vows are to a religious institute, rather than to a monastery as in the case of a monk. He does not have to be a priest.

General Calendar

This is the liturgical calendar for the Roman Catholic Church of the Latin Rite as a whole, ignoring local differences. It used to be known as the 'Universal Calendar'.

Gothic Revival

During the C19th it was fashionable to imitate medieval forms in church buildings and furnishings, and this activity has left many artistic representations of saints. These need to be regarded with caution, however. Some of the proponents of romantic medievalism had an uncritical attitude to medieval devotions and sought to revitalize the extinct veneration of dubious and unauthorized local saints. Further, it was sometimes pretended that a medieval person was a saint when there had never been any sort of veneration in the first place.

Hermit

This is a consecrated religious living in solitude, sometimes referred to as an anchorite or a solitary. For some reason the word has not been used in the past for women, who have been generally referred to as anchoresses.

Halo

This was originally meant to be the nimbus surrounding a holy person, and became stylized into the circular region around the head in iconography. When perspective was rediscovered in the West artists had difficulty with halos and they tended to mutate into pie-pans and the horizontal rings familiar in cartoon imagery.

Incorruptibility

From early days the refusal of a person's corpse to decay has been taken as an indication of that person's sanctity. This still tends to be the case in the Eastern churches, especially if a sweet odour is noticed. Forensic medicine has, however, noted many cases where incorruption has occurred naturally, and this is especially associated with the condition known as adipocere in which the body's fat turns to wax. Thus no conclusive importance is nowadays attached to the condition of the body of a candidate for canonization in the West.

Islam

Apart from certain civic disabilities, Shahira law actually forbids the active persecution of its Christian subjects by a Muslim government. Apart from those killed by corrupt and vicious Muslim rulers, martyrs under Islam mostly fall into two categories prescribed by this law. Publicly speaking against Islam ('blasphemy') and converting from Islam to Christianity ('apostasy') are both punishable by death, and in the latter case includes those considered to be Muslim because their fathers were.

Jewish Ritual Murders

There are at least thirteen cases in western Europe of children venerated as martyrs who were allegedly killed by Jews out of hatred for Christianity, in several cases in a parody of the Crucifixion on Good Friday. These allegations form part of the notorious 'Blood Libel' which has been a major feature of anti-Semitism, and it is certain that the liturgical veneration was an expression of such prejudice in most or all cases. It is possible that black magic involving human sacrifice lay behind some of the events. Only one of them, Simon of Trent, was canonized (his cultus was suppressed in 1965) but Andrew of Rinn, Christopher of Guardia and Laurentinus Sossius also had their veneration as beati confirmed.

Laura

This is a form of monastic settlement characterized by individual monks or nuns living in separate cells scattered around a central church. The word originally meant 'wadi', and the first lauras were series of caves along the sides of Palestinian wadis in which hermits lived, with a larger cave being used as a church. An alternative spelling is 'lavra'.

Liturgical Categories

The liturgical celebration of saints in the Latin rite maintained an extremely conservative categorization until the revision of the Roman rite in 1970, basically continuing that which pertained at the end of the Roman Empire. This categorization in the old Roman Martyrology was quite different for the two sexes. 'Martyrs' were of either sex, but other men were 'confessors', whereas women were 'virgins', 'widows' or 'matrons' according to their marital status at death. It may be noted that there was no separate category for consecrated religious.

The revised Roman Martyrology of 2001 has abandoned this categorization for a set of more descriptive appellations: 'martyr', 'pope', 'bishop', 'priest', 'religious', 'mother', 'father', 'layperson' or 'widow'.

Martyr

In the early Church, the only saints venerated were martyrs. The requirement for being one was to have been killed out of hatred for the faith, and this condition is now strictly applied (and distinguished from political motivations). In the early Middle Ages, however, many saints were accepted as martyrs who did not fit this condition (perhaps because there were few genuine martyrs in that period). There were those who chose the injustice of being killed rather than acquiesce in an injustice being done to others (cf. **Alphege**, **Boris** & **Gleb**). Others were ecclesiastical personages who were killed in the course of robbery (cf. **Boniface**).

Martyr Movement of Cordoba

During the C9th most of Spain was ruled by the Ummayad Arab emirate of Cordoba. Among Christian monastic circles in and around the capital arose the idea that it would be virtuous to seek martyrdom by publicly preaching against Islam, and several achieved that fate by doing so in the reign of Abderrahman II. These were (and are) locally venerated as martyrs. It may be noted that they did not die in the context of any persecution of the Church by the Muslim government, nor were they necessarily executed out of hatred of Christianity. Cf. **Islam**.

Matron

This was the category into which the old Roman Martyrology put married non-martyr women saints whose husbands were still alive when they died. There were not many of them.

Mental Illness

The traditional, and nowadays offensive, stigma attached to mental illness has caused a lack of proper attention to be paid to its occurrence among saints. Hagiographical works have tended either to ignore manifestations of mental illness among saints or to try to explain them away. On the other hand, polemical works by writers hostile to the veneration of saints have emphasized such manifestations as being a reproach. Neither approach is fitting. It is clear that many saints, for example St Margaret-Mary Alacoque and St Rose Flores of Lima, were seriously mentally ill. However this is no bar to sanctity, and may even be a means to it, as long as the subject has the capacity for moral behaviour presumed in the practice of heroic virtue.

Miracles

The process of canonization requires two miracles for confirmation, one before beatification and one before final canonization. These are usually (although not necessarily) ones of healing, and a process can be halted indefinitely for lack of them. They are not necessary in cases of martyrs. Unlike the Eastern churches the Catholic church does not accept miracles as sole proof of sanctity. It did so in past ages, until the scandals caused by 'miracles' occurring at the shrines of wholly unsuitable people (e.g. King Edward II of England).

Monk

This is a consecrated male religious who lives a community life in a monastery and who makes a vow of stability thereto. He does not have to be a priest, although for much of the Church's history most have been.

Monophysitism

Put crudely, this is the doctrine that Christ is one person with one, divine, nature. It over-emphasizes Christ's divinity at the expense of his humanity, and was condemned at the ecumenical council at Chalcedon in 451. The Church in Egypt (the Coptic Church), a large part of the Church in Syria (the Jacobite Church) and the Armenian Church did not accept this council and have since often been pejoratively referred to as Monophysite.

Nestorianism

Put crudely, this is the doctrine that Christ is two persons, one with a divine nature and one with a human one. It has serious difficulty in explaining how Christ is one entity, and was condemned at the ecumenical council at Ephesus in 431. The Church in the Persian Empire did not accept this council and has since often been pejoratively referred to as Nestorian.

Nun

This is a consecrated female religious who lives a community life in a monastery (a nunnery) and who makes a vow of stability thereto. Active female religious, whose stability is in the congregation, are called 'sisters'.

Oblates cf. Tertiaries or Child-Oblates.

Oriental Orthodox

These are the Eastern churches which refused to accept the Council of Chalcedon in 451 and have hence been called Monophysite. They are the Coptic, Syrian and Armenian churches. Apart from the Orthodox Syrian Church, recently established in India, each has its own ancient calendar of saints.

Origen

This Egyptian genius was head of the Alexandrian catechetical school in the C3rd and was the greatest biblical exegete of the patristic era if not of all time. His influence on subsequent church fathers was profound, but he was condemned posthumously because his theological speculations proved incompatible with Christianity and most of his vast opus has been lost.

Orthodox

These are the Eastern churches which went out of communion with Rome after 1056. There are generally accepted to be fifteen of them, each of which has its own calendar and can canonize its own saints. In theory at least, all the Orthodox churches accept each others' saints as well as those Western saints before the acceptance of the 'Filioque' into the Latin Creed (at different times in different places). The ancient calendars of saints are the Byzantine from Constantinople, the Russian, the Serbian and the Georgian. The rest are derivative.

Patriarch

By ancient tradition this is the title given to the bishops of the four great cities of the Roman Empire, namely Rome, Constantinople, Alexandria and Antioch. It implies territorial jurisdiction over a wide area. Jerusalem became a patriarchate also in 451. After the schism between Rome and the Eastern churches, Latin-rite patriarchates were set up for the four latter cities but only Jerusalem survives. As churches of various Eastern rites (q.v.) were set up in communion with Rome, some became patriarchates, and so also did many independent national Orthodox churches such as the Russian. There are patriarchates in the Western church at Lisbon, Venice and Goa but for these the title is an empty honorific.

Patrons

Local churches and settlements have always had their own patron saints. Since the Middle Ages many trades, crafts and states of life have also had their own patrons. The Church can declare a saint or a blessed to be a patron of any such, and for a blessed this is equivalent to canonization (e.g. 'Fra Angelico' or John Faesulanus was declared patron of artists in 1984 while still a beatus).

Persecutions

From AD100, when it broke from Judaism, until the edict of toleration in 313 Christianity was a proscribed religion in the Roman Empire. There was little attempt at any central co-ordination of persecution early on, however, when local pogroms could alternate with periods of toleration. The emperor Decius attempted to eliminate Christianity from the Empire in 250, but his reign ended before any lasting damage was done. The major persecution was by Diocletian, whose reordering of the social and economic structures of Empire had no place for Christianity and who ordered a determined campaign of extirpation from 303. This lasted longer in some places than in others, until 313. Then there was a vicious series of persecutions in the Persian Empire until the mid C5th. Active persecutions of Catholic Christianity by hostile governments wanting to destroy it have, since then, mostly been a feature of the post-medieval world. These have led to mass beatifications and canonizations for Imperial China, England and Wales, Revolutionary France, Republican Spain, Ireland, Japan, the Kingdom of Korea, revolutionary Mexico, Buganda in Uganda and the Kingdom of Vietnam. Notable recent persecutions awaiting such recognition have been in the Stalinist Soviet Union, Khmer-Rouge Cambodia, North Korea, Communist Albania and Equatorial Guinea (especially barbaric).

Process of Canonization

This seems to be extremely complex, but is fairly straightforward in outline. A local church or religious congregation proposes to the Magisterium at Rome that a person is fit to be canonized (or only beatified, if the cultus sought is local). The first stage is the discernment as to whether the person was either martyred in hatred of the faith or lived the Christian virtues in a heroic manner. If so, then he or she is declared 'Venerable'. Subsequent is an extremely painstaking investigation into the person's life, writings, reported sayings and actions, and all possible objections are entertained. For a non-martyr a verified miracle is also required before beatification. After beatification the investigation is repeated and another miracle required before canonization. The process can be aborted by unauthorized public veneration taking place.

Reformation

None of the various communions arising as a result of the Protestant Reformation has maintained the ability to canonize its own saints.

Relics

These are what remains of a saint, basically the body or bits of it. 'Second class relics' are things (usually bits of cloth) which have touched these. Cf. **Incorruptibility**.

Religious (Consecrated)

Apart from the martyr, the most common type of saint is the consecrated religious (monk, friar, nun, sister, hermit) nowadays defined as one making vows of poverty, chastity and obedience.

Religious Institutes

In the Eastern churches the tradition has been that consecrated religious are regarded as either hermits or cenobitic monks and nuns without any further categorization arising from different charisms and types of work undertaken. This state of affairs also obtained in the Western church until the onset of the Middle Ages, and no attempt is made in this book to categorize saints who were consecrated religious before 817 (when the Benedictine rule was imposed on the monasteries of the Carolingian Empire). In the late C11th there began a proliferation of different institutes mostly arising either from the wish to reform a form of religious life already existing or to create new institutes in response to perceived needs, usually apostolic. The older-established institutes, with a greater number of saints, are noted in the entries. One unfortunate past result of the pluralism has been a certain competitiveness as institutes claimed various saints as having belonged to them, with resulting distortions in the historical witness and some outright forgery. Institutes can be called 'orders', 'congregations' or 'societies' according to the descending gravity of obligation formerly incurred in their vows.

Roman Martyrology

A martyrology is a list of saints (initially only martyrs) in feast-day order, and the Roman Martyrology is the official list of all the saints recognized as such by the Roman Catholic Church of the Latin rite. Attempts at a historical listing of saints date back to St Bede and were initially apparently conscientious. However, St Ado of Vienne in 865 drew up a martyrology which he claimed was based on an ancient Roman one but which was forged by him and which contained many grave errors. This was utilized in the martyrology of Usuard, which was used by the Roman church until 1584. Then a new martyrology (unfortunately still containing errors, but a creditable attempt at historical accuracy for the time) was published (and amended by Cardinal Baronius in 1586), and this was the Roman Martyrology for the next 417 years. It was revised several times, lastly in 1924 but never thoroughly, and became obsolete when the church's calendar was revised in 1969. The new edition was finally published in October, 2001, with a revision in 2004.

Scots

Many saints of the Dark Ages and early Middle Ages are described as 'Scoti' in the contemporary records. This term is equivocal, meaning either Irish or Scottish, and it is often not now possible to discern which country is meant. Originally it referred to the Irish who settled in what is now Argyll in western Scotland and who founded the Kingdom of Dalriada in the C6th.

Sister

This is a female consecrated religious whose vows are to a religious institute with no fixed geographical location. In this she contrasts with a nun who is established in one place, in her monastery.

Subdeacon

This used to be a clerical rank below that of deacon before its suppression in the Latin rite after the Second Vatican Council. There are very few saints who were subdeacons only.

Tertiaries

These are people associated with monasteries or religious congregations by virtue of a promise of self or by temporary vows where no permanent vows are intended. They are not consecrated religious but usually live in the world while intending to share in the graces and to practise the particular virtues of the congregation concerned. In the past many congregations of sisters were tertiaries so as to avoid the necessity of the monastic enclosure and physical virginity which used to be required of female religious. They are also known as 'oblates'.

Translation

An obsolescent term concerning relics, meaning a transfer.

Venerable

This is the first stage in the process of canonization. It is when a person is declared either to have been martyred in hatred of the faith or to have practised the Christian virtues to a heroic degree. Private individuals can ask the intercession of any such, but public veneration is not permitted (and would abort the process).

Virgin

The consecrated virgin has an ancient history in the Roman church, and was a woman who chose and vowed to remain unmarried for love of God. The ceremony of receiving the veil on making such a vow existed by the C4th, paralleling the veiling of the bride in the contemporary rite of marriage. Such virgins either lived with relatives or together in communities and in the latter case the evolution to consecrated religious life as nowadays understood was straightforward, especially after Egyptian monachism became known in Rome in the C4th. The two states are not nowadays equivalent, however. Consecrated religious life requires three vows: poverty, chastity (not necessarily virginity) and obedience. Consecrated virginity merely requires a vow of chastity while in a state of virginity. Traditionally all unmarried women saints, including consecrated religious, have been liturgically celebrated as virgins.

Virgin Martyr

Some very popular Roman women martyrs are also venerated as virgins, especially if their wish to remain virgins had something to do with their martyrdom (cf. **Agnes**). In this category are included virgins who have resisted attempted rape at the cost of their lives, even if no vow of virginity was previously made (cf. **Mary Goretti**), and several such have been recently beatified. Suicide to avoid rape is, however, impermissible.

Widow

This was one of the three categories into which non-martyr women saints are put in the old Roman Martyrology.

Appendix to *The Book of Saints*: Lists of National Martyrs

BRAZIL

'Ignatius de Azevedo and Comps'

Alexis Delgado
Alphonsus de Baena
Alvarez Mendes
Andrew Goncalves
Anthony Correia
Anthony Fernandes
Anthony Soares
Benedict de Castro
Blaise Ribeiro
Caspar Alvares
Diego de Andrade
Diego Pérez
Dominic Fernandes
Emmanuel Alvares
Emmanuel Fernándes
Emmanuel Pacheco
Emmanuel Rodrígues
Ferdinand Sanchez
Francis Alvares
Francis de Magalhães
Francis Perez Godoy
Gregory Escrivano
Gundisalvus Hendriques
Ignatius de Azevedo
Joanninus de San Juan
John Fernandes of Braga
John Fernandes of Lisbon
John de Mayorga
John de San Martin
John de Zafra
Louis Correia
Louis Rodríguez
Mark Caldeira
Maurus Vaz
Nicholas Dinis
Peter de Fontura
Peter Nuñes
Simon de Costa
Simon Lópes
Stephen de Zuraire

'Andrew de Soveral and Comps'

(Note that the names of twelve of these are unknown.)

Ambrose-Francis Ferro
Andrew de Soveral
Anthony Baracho
Anthony Vilela, and his son
Anthony Vilela Cid
Dominic Carvalho
Emmanuel Moreira, and his wife
Francis de Bastos
Francis Mendes Pereira
James Pereira
John Lostau Navarro
John Martins, and seven young companions.
John da Silveira
Joseph do Porto
Matthew Moreira
Simon Correia
Stephen Machado de Miranda, and his two children.
Vincent de Souza Pereira
(First name unknown) Dias, son of Francis Dias (not martyred).

CHINA

Saints (121):-

Agatha Lin Zhao	28/01/1858
Agnes Cao Kuiying	01/03/1856
Alberic Crescitelli	21/07/1900
Aloysius Versiglia	25/02/1930
Andrew Bauer OFM	09/07/1900
Andrew Wang Tiangqing	22/07/1900
Anne An Jiaozhi	11/07/1900
Anne An Xinzhi	11/07/1900
Anne Wang	22/07/1900
Antoninus Fantosati	07/07/1900
Augustine Zhao Rong	21/03/1815
Augustus Chapdelaine	29/02/1856
Barbara Cui Lianzhi	15/06/1900
Caesidius Giacomantonio	04/07/1900

Callistus Caravario	25/02/1930	Mary Du Zhaozhi	28/06/1900
Elias Facchini OFM	09/07/1900	Mary-Magdalen Du Fengju	29/06/1900
Elizabeth Qin Bianzhi	19/07/1900	Mary Du Tianshi	29/06/1900
Francis-Ferdinand de Capillas	15/01/1648	Mary Fan Kun	28/06/1900
Francis Díaz del Rincón	28/10/1748	Mary Fu Guilin	20/06/1900
Francis Fogolla OFM	09/07/1900	Mary-of-Peace Giuliani	09/07/1900
Francis Regis Clet	18/02/1820	Mary-Ermellina-of-Jesus Grivot	09/07/1900
Francis Serrano Frias	28/10/1748	Mary Guo Lizhi	07/07/1900
Francis Zhang Rong	09/07/1900	Mary-Amandina Jeuris	09/07/1900
Gabriel-John Taurin Dufresse	14/09/1815	Mary-of-the-Holy-Birth Kerguin	09/07/1900
Gregory Grassi OFM	09/07/1900	Mary-of-St-Justus Moreau	09/07/1900
Ignatius Mangin	20/07/1900	Mary-Clare Nanetti	09/07/1900
James Zhao Quanxin	09/07/1900	Mary Qi Yu	28/06/1900
James Yan Guodong	09/07/1900	Mary Wang Lizhi	22/07/1900
Jerome Lu Tingmei	28/01/1857	Mary Zhao	28/07/1900
Joachim He Kaizhi	09/07/1839	Mary Zhao Guozhi	20/07/1900
Joachim Royo Péréz	28/10/1748	Mary Zheng Xu	28/06/1900
John Alcober Figuera	28/10/1748	Mary Zhu Wuzhi	20/07/1900
John Chen Xianheng	18/02/1862	Matthias Feng De	09/07/1900
John-of-Triora Lantrua	07/02/1816	Modestus Andlauer	19/07/1900
John-Baptist Luo Tingying	29/07/1861	Patrick Dong Bodi	09/07/1900
John-Peter Néel	18/02/1862	Paul Chen Changpin	29/07/1861
John-Gabriel Perboyre	11/09/1840	Paul Denn	20/07/1900
John Wang Guixin	14/07/1900	Paul Ke Tingzhu	08/08/1900
John Wang Rui	09/07/1900	Paul Lang Fu	16/07/1900
John-Baptist Wu Mantang	29/06/1900	Paul Liu Hanzhuo	13/02/1819
John Wu Wenyin	08/07/1900	Paul Liu Jinde	13/07/1900
John Zhang Huan	09/07/1900	Paul Wu Juan	29/06/1900
John Zhang Jingguang	09/07/1900	Paul Wu Wanshu	29/06/1900
John Zhang Tianshen	18/02/1862	Peter Li Quanhui	30/06/1900
John-Baptist Zhao Mingxi	03/07/1900	Peter Liu Wenyuan	17/05/1834
John-Baptist Zhu Wurui	19/08/1900	Peter Liu Ziyu	17/07/1900
Joseph-Mary Gambaro	07/07/1900	Peter Sanz i Jordá	26/05/1747
Joseph Ma Taishun	26/07/1900	Peter Wang Erman	09/07/1900
Joseph Wang Guiji	13/07/1900	Peter Wang Zuolong	06/07/1900
Joseph Wang Yumei	21/07/1900	Peter Wu Anpeng	09/07/1900
Joseph Yuan Gengyin	30/07/1900	Peter Wu Gusheng	07/11/1814
Joseph Yuan Zaide	24/06/1817	Peter Zhang Banniu	09/07/1900
Joseph Zhang Dapeng	12/03/1815	Peter Zhao Mingzhen	03/07/1900
Joseph Zhang Wenlan	29/07/1861	Peter Zhu Rixin	20/07/1900
Lang Yangzhi	16/07/1900	Philip Zhang Zhihe	09/07/1900
Laurence Bai Xiaoman	25/02/1856	Raymund Li Quanzhen	30/06/1900
Laurence Wang Bing	28/01/1857	Remigius Isoré	19/07/1900
Lucy Wang Cheng	28/06/1900	Rose Chen Anxie	05/07/1900
Lucy Wang Wang	22/07/1900	Rose Fan Hui	16/08/1900
Lucy Yi Zhenmei	19/02/1862	Rose Zhao	20/07/1900
Mark Ji Tianxiang	07/07/1900	Simon Chen Ximan	09/07/1900
Martha Wang Louzhi	29/07/1861	Simon Qin Qunfu	19/07/1900
Martin Wu Xuesheng	18/02/1862	Teresa Chen Jinjie	05/07/1900
Mary An Guozhi	11/07/1900	Teresa Zhang Hezhi	16/07/1900
Mary An Lihua	11/07/1900	Thaddeus Liu Ruiting	30/11/1823
Mary-Adolphine Dierk	09/07/1900	Theodoric Balat OFM	09/07/1900

Thomas Shen Jihe	09/07/1900
Xi Guizi	20/07/1900
Zhang Huailu	01/07/1900

ENGLAND

Saints (38):

Alban-Bartholomew Roe	21/01/1642
Ambrose-Edward Barlow	10/09/1641
Alexander Briant	01/12/1581
Anne Line	27/02/1601
Augustine Webster	04/05/1535
Cuthbert Mayne	30/11/1577
Edmund Arrowsmith	28/08/1628
Edmund Campion	01/12/1581
Edmund Gennings	10/12/1591
Eustace White	10/12/1591
Henry Morse	01/02/1645
Henry Walpole	07/04/1595
Joachim-of-St-Anne Wall (John Wall)	22/08/1679
John Almond	05/12/1612
John Boste	24/07/1594
John Fisher	22/06/1535
John Jones	12/07/1598
John Houghton	04/05/1535
John Kemble	22/08/1679
John Payne	02/04/1582
John Plessington	19/07/1679
John Rigby	21/06/1600
John Roberts	10/12/1610
John Southworth	28/06/1654
John Stone	23/12/1539
Luke Kirby	30/05/1582
Margaret Clitherow	25/03/1586
Margaret Ward	30/08/1588
Nicholas Owen	22/03/1606
Philip Howard	19/10/1595
Polydore Plasden	10/12/1591
Ralph Sherwin	01/12/1581
Richard Reynolds	04/05/1535
Robert Lawrence	04/05/1535
Robert Southwell	21/02/1595
Swithin Wells	10/12/1591
Thomas Garnet	23/06/1608
Thomas More	22/06/1535

Beati (240):

Adrian Fortescue	09/07/1539
Alexander Blake	04/03/1590*
Alexander Crow	30/11/1586*
Alexander Rawlins	07/04/1595

Anthony Middleton	06/05/1590
Anthony Page	20/04/1593*
Anthony Turner	20/06/1679
Brian Lacey	10/12/1591
Christopher Bales	04/03/1590
Christopher Buxton	01/10/1588
Christopher Robinson	31/03/1597*
Christopher Wharton	28/03/1600*
David Gunston	12/071541
Edmund Duke	27/05/1590*
Edmund Sykes	23/03/1588*
Edward Bamber	07/08/1646*
Edward Burden	29/11/1588*
Edward Catherick	13/04/1642
Edward Coleman	03/12/1678
Edward Fulthorp	04/07/1597
Edward James	01/10/1588
Edward Jones	06/05/1590
Edward Oldcorne	07/04/1606
Edward Osbaldeston	16/11/1594*
Edward Powell	30/06/1540
Edward Shelley	30/08/1588
Edward Stransham	21/01/1586
Edward Thwing	26/07/1600*
Edward Waterson	08/01/1593
Everard Hanse	31/07/1581
Francis Bell	11/12/1643*
Francis Dickenson	13/04/1590
Francis Ingleby	03/06/1586*
Francis Page	20/04/1602
George Beesley	01/07/1591*
George Douglas	09/09/1587*
George Errington	29/11/1596*
George Gervase	11/04/1608
George Haydock	12/02/1584*
George Napper	09/11/1610
George Nichols	05/07/1589*
George Swallowell	26/07/1594
Gerald Edwards	01/10/1588
Henry Abbot	04/07/1597
Henry Webley	28/08/1588*
Hugh Faringdon	15/11/1539
Hugh Green	19/08/1642
Hugh More	28/08/1588
Hugh Taylor	26/11/1585*
Humphrey Middlemore	19/06/1535
Humphrey Pritchard	05/07/1589*
James Bell	20/04/1584
James Bird	25/03/1593
James Claxton	28/08/1588
James Duckett	19/04/1602
James Fenn	12/02/1584

James Thomson	28/11/1582	Laurence Johnson	30/05/1582
James Walworth	11/05/1537	Margaret Pole	28/05/1541
Jermyn Gardiner	07/03/1544	Mark Barkworth	27/02/1601
John Adams	08/10/1586*	Marmaduke Bowes	27/11/1585*
John Amias	15/03/1589	Martin Woodcock	07/08/1646*
John Beche	01/12/1539	Matthew Flathers	21/03/1608*
John Bodey	02/11/1583	Montford Scott	01/07/1591*
John Bretton	01/04/1598*	Miles Gerard	13/04/1590
John Carey	04/07/1594	Nicholas Garlick	24/07/1588*
John Cornelius	04/07/1594	Nicholas Horner	04/03/1590*
John Davy	08/06/1537	Nicholas Postgate	07/08/1679*
John Duckett	07/09/1644	Nicholas Woodfen	27/01/1586*
John Eynon	15/11/1539	Patrick Salmon	04/07/1594
John Felton	08/08/1570	Paul Heath	17/04/1643*
John Fenwick	20/06/1679	Peter Snow	15/06/1598*
John Finch	20/04/1584	Peter Wright	19/05/1651
John Fingley	08/08/1586*	Philip Powel	30/06/1646
John Forest	22/05/1538	Ralph Ashley	07/04/1606
John Gavan	20/06/1679	Ralph Corby	07/09/1644
John Grove	24/01/1679	Ralph Crockett	01/10/1588
John Haile	04/05/1535	Ralph Grimston	15/06/1598*
John Hambley	29/03/1587*	Ralph Milner	07/07/1591
John Hewett	05/10/1588	Richard Bere	09/08/1537
John Hogg	27/03/1590*	Richard Fetherstone	30/07/1540
John Houghton	04/05/1535	Richard Herst	29/08/1628
John Ingram	26/07/1594	Richard Hill	27/05/1590*
John Ireland	07/03/1544	Richard Holiday	27/05/1590*
John Larke	07/03/1544	Richard Kirkman	22/08/1582
John Lockwood	13/04/1642	Richard Langhorne	14/07/1679
John Lowe	08/10/1586*	Richard Langley	10/12/1596
John Mason	10/12/1591	Richard Leigh	30/08/1588
John Munden	12/02/1584	Richard Lloyd	30/08/1588*
John Nelson	03/02/1578	Richard Martin	30/08/1588
John Norton	08/09/1600*	Richard Newport	30/05/1612
John Nutter	12/02/1584	Richard Sargeant	20/04/1586*
John Paine	02/04/1582	Richard Simpson	24/07/1588*
John Pibush	18/02/1601	Richard Thirkeld	29/05/1583
John Robinson	01/10/1588	Richard Whiting	15/11/1539
John Roche	30/08/1588	Richard Yaxley	05/07/1589*
John Rochester	11/05/1537	Robert Anderton	25/04/1586
John Rugg	15/11/1539	Robert Bickendyke	08/08/1586*
John Sandys	11/08/1586*	Robert Dalby	15/03/1589
John Shert	28/05/1582	Robert Dibdale	08/10/1586*
John Slade	30/10/1583	Robert Drury	26/02/1607*
John Speed	04/02/1594	Robert Grissold	16/07/1604*
John Storey	01/06/1571	Robert Hardesty	24/09/1589*
John Sugar	16/07/1604*	Robert Johnson	28/05/1582
John Talbot	08/09/1600*	Robert Ludlam	24/07/1588*
John Thorne	15/11/1539	Robert Middleton	03/04/1601*
John Thules	18/03/1616*	Robert Morton	28/08/1588
Joseph Lambton	24/07/1592*	Robert Nutter	26/07/1600*
Laurence Humphrey	07/07/1591	Robert Thorpe	31/05/1591

Robert Salt	09/06/1537
Robert Sutton (1)	27/07/1588*
Robert Sutton (2)	05/10/1588
Robert Watkinson	20/04/1602
Robert Widmerpool	01/10/1588
Robert Wilcox	01/10/1588
Roger Cadwallador	27/08/1610*
Roger Dickinson	07/07/1591*
Roger Filcock	27/02/1601*
Roger James	15/11/1539
Roger Wrenn	18/03/1616*
Sebastian Newdigate	19/06/1535
Sidney Hodgson	10/12/1591
Stephen Rowsham	11/08/1587
Thomas Abel	30/07/1540
Thomas Alfield	06/07/1585
Thomas Atkinson	11/03/1616*
Thomas Belson	05/07/1589*
Thomas Benstead	11/07/1600*
Thomas Bosgrave	04/07/1594
Thomas Bullaker	12/10/1642*
Thomas Cottam	30/05/1582
Thomas Felton	28/08/1588
Thomas Ford	28/05/1582
Thomas Green (1)	10/06/1537
Thomas Green (2)	21/01/1642
Thomas Hemerford	12/02/1584
Thomas Holford	28/08/1588
Thomas Holland	12/12/1642
Thomas Johnson	20/09/1537
Thomas Maxfield	01/07/1616
Thomas Palaser	08/09/1600*
Thomas Percy	22/08/1572
Thomas Pickering	09/05/1679
Thomas Pilchard	21/03/1587*
Thomas Plumtree	04/01/1570
Thomas Pormont	21/02/1592*
Thomas Reding	16/06/1537
Thomas Scryven	15/06/1537
Thomas Sherwood	07/02/1578
Thomas Somers	10/12/1610
Thomas Sprott	11/07/1600*
Thomas Thwing	23/10/1680
Thomas Tunstal	13/07/1616
Thomas Warcop	04/07/1597
Thomas Watkinson	31/05/1591*
Thomas Welbourne	01/08/1605
Thomas Whitaker	07/08/1646*
Thomas Whitbread	20/06/1679
Thomas Woodhouse	19/06/1573
Thurston Hunt	03/04/1601*
Walter Pierson	10/06/1537

William Andleby	04/07/1597
William Browne	05/09/1605
William Carter	11/01/1584*
William Dean	28/08/1588
William Exmew	19/06/1535
William Filby	30/05/1582
William Freeman	13/08/1595
William Gibson	29/11/1596*
William Greenwood	06/06/1537
William Gunter	28/08/1588
William Harcourt	20/06/1679
William Harrington	18/02/1594
William Hart	15/03/1583
William Hartley	05/10/1588
William Horne	04/08/1540
William Howard	29/12/1680
William Ireland	24/01/1679
William Knight	29/11/1596*
William Lacey	22/08/1582
William Lampley	11/08/1588*
William Marsden	25/04/1586*
William Patenson	22/01/1592
William Pike	21/03/1591*
William Richardson	27/02/1603
William Scott	30/05/1612
William Southerne	30/04/1618*
William Spenser	24/09/1589*
William Thomson	20/04/1586*
William Way	23/09/1588
William Webster	26/07/1641

* These were beatified in 1987.

FRENCH REVOLUTION

Beati (438):-

'Cambrai, Martyrs of' (26/06/1794):-

(Daughters of Charity of Arras)
Frances Lanel
Jane Gérard
Mary-Magdalen Fontaine
Teresa Fantou

'Valenciennes, Ursuline Martyrs of' (October 1794):-

Anne-Mary Erraux (Bridgettine)	23rd
Josephine Leroux (Poor Clare)	23rd
Mary-Cordula-Josepha-of-St-Dominic Barré	23rd
Mary-Ursula-of-St-Bernardine Bourla	17th
Mary-Augustina-of-the-Sacred-Heart Dejardin	17th
Mary-Louise-of-St-Francis-of-Assisi Ducrez	17th

Mary-Frances Lacroix (Bridgettine)	23rd
Mary-Scholastica-Josepha-of-St-James Leroux	23rd
Mary-Clotilde-Angela-of-St-Francis-Borgia Paillot	23rd
Mary-Laurentina-of-St-Stanislaus Prin	17th
Mary-Natalia-of-St-Louis Vanot	17th

'Compiègne, Carmelite Martyrs of' (17/07/1794):-

Catherine Soiron
Charlotte-of-the-Resurrection Thouret
Constance Meunier
Elizabeth-Julia-of-St-Francis Verolot
Euphrasia-of-the-Immaculate-Conception Brard
Henrietta-of-Jesus de Croissy
Julia-Louise-of-Jesus Chrétien de Neufville
Mary-Anne-of-St-Louis Brideau
Mary-of-St-Martha Dufour
Mary-Henrietta-of-Providence Pelras
Mary-of-Jesus-Crucified Piedcourt
Mary-of-the-Holy-Spirit Roussel
Teresa-of-the-Heart-of-Mary Hanisset
Teresa-of-St-Augustine Lidoine
Teresa Soiron
Teresa-of-St-Ignatius Trézelle

'John-Baptist Souzy and Comps' (1794):-

Anthony Auriel	16/06
Anthony Bannassat	18/08
Augustine-Joseph Desgardin OCist	06/07
Bartholomew Jarrige de la Morélie de Biars	13/07
Charles-Nicholas-Anthony Ancel	29/07
Charles-Renatus Collas de Bignon	03/06
Charles-Arnold Hanus	28/08
Claudius Béguignot OCart	16/07
Claudius Dumonet	13/09
Claudius-Joseph Jouffret de Bonnefont	10/08
Claudius Laplace	14/09
Claudius-Barnabas Laurent de Mascloux	07/09
Claudius Richard OSB	09/08
Elias Leymarie de Laroche	22/08
Florentius Dumontet de Cardaillac	05/09
Francis D'Oudinot de la Boissière	07/09
Francis François OFM Cap	10/08
Francis Hunot	06/10
Francis Mayaudon	11/09
Gabriel Pergaud CR	21/07
George-Edmund René	02/10
Gervase-Protase Brunel OCist	20/08
James Gagnot OCD	10/09

James Lombardie	22/07
James Morelle Dupas	21/06
James Retouret OC	26/08
John Bourdon OFM Cap	23/08
John-Baptist de Bruxelles	18/09
John-Nicholas Cordier SJ	30/09
John-Baptist Duverneuil OCD	01/07
John Hunot	07/10
John-Francis Jarrige de la Morélie du Breuil	31/07
John-Joseph Jugé de Saint Martin	07/07
John-Baptist Laborier du Vivier	26/09
John-Baptist Loir OFM Cap	19/05
John-Baptist Menestrel	16/08
John Mopinot	21/05
John-George Rehm OP	11/08
John-Baptist de Souzy	27/08
John-Baptist Vernoy de Montjournal	01/06
Joseph Imbert SJ	09/06
Joseph Marchandon	22/09
Lazarus Tiersot OCart	10/08
Louis-Armand-Joseph Adam OFM Conv	13/07
Louis-Francis Lebrun OSB	20/08
Louis Wulphy Huppy	29/08
Lupus-Sebastian Loup Hunot	17/11
Marcellus Gaucher Labigne de Reignefort	26/07
Michael-Louis Brulard OCD	25/07
Michael-Bernard Marchand	15/07
Natalis-Hilary Le Conte	17/08
Nicholas Savouret OFM Conv	16/07
Nicholas Tabouillot (1795)	23/02
Paul-John Charles OCist	25/08
Peter-Sulpicius-Christopher Faverge	12/09
Peter Gabilhaud	13/08
Peter Jarrige de la Morélie du Puyredon	10/08
Peter-Joseph Legroing de La Romagère	26/07
Peter-Michael Noël	05/08
Peter Yriex Labrouhe de Laborderie	01/07
Philip Papon	17/06
Raymund Petinaud de Jourgnac	26/06
Scipio-Jerome Brigéat de Lambert	04/09
Udalric Guillaume	27/08

'Laval, Martyrs of' (1794):-

(Secular Priests)	21/01
Andrew Duliou	21/01
Augustine-Emmanuel Philippot	21/01
Francis Duchesne	21/01
Francis Migoret Lambeardière	21/01
James André	21/01
James Burin	17/10
John-Mary Gallot	21/01

John-Baptist Turpin du Cormier	21/01
Joseph Pellé	21/01
Julian-Francis Morin de la Girardière	21/01
Julian Moulé	21/01
Louis Gastineau	21/01
Peter Thomas	21/01
Renatus-Louis Ambroise	21/01

(Religious)

Frances Mézière (private vows)	05/02
Frances Tréhet (OL of Charity, Evron)	13/03
Jane Véron (OL of Charity, Evron)	20/03
John-Baptist Triquerie OFM Conv	21/01
Mary-of-St-Monica Lhuilier (Hospitaller of Mercy of Jesus)	25/06

'Orange (Martyrs of)' (1794):-

(Benedictine)

Susanna-Agatha Deloye	06/07

(Cistercians)

Dorothy-of-the-Heart-of-Mary de Justamond	16/07
Mary-of-St-Henry de Justamond	12/07

(Sacramentines)

Amata-of-Jesus de Gordon	16/07
Anne-of-St-Alexis Minutte	13/07
Iphigenia-of-St-Matthew de Gaillard de la Valdène	07/07
Margaret-of-St-Augustine Bonnet	26/07
Martha-of-the-Good-Angel Cluse	12/07
Mary-Anne-of-St-Joachim Béguin-Royal	16/07
Mary-Clare-of-St-Martin Blanc	11/07
Mary-of-Jesus Charansol	16/07
Mary-Elizabeth-of-St-Theoctistus Pélissier	11/07
Mary-Magdalen-of-the-Mother-of-God Verchière	13/07
Rosalia-Clotilde-of-St-Pelagia Bès	11/07
Rose-of-St-Xavier Tallien	12/07
Teresa-Henrietta-of-the-Annunciation Faurie	13/07

(Ursulines)

Agnes-of-Jesus de Romillon	10/07
Anne-of-St-Basil Cartier	26/07
Catherine-of-Jesus de Jastamont	26/07
Clare-of-St-Rosalia du Bac	26/07
Elizabeth-Teresa-of-the-Heart-of-Jesus Consolin	26/07
Jane-Mary-of-St-Bernard de Romillon	12/07
Mary-Margaret-of-St-Sophia de Barbegie d'Albarède	11/07

Mary-Anne-of-St-Francis Depeyre	13/07
Mary-Anne-of-St Michael Doux	16/07
Mary-Magdalen-of-St-Melania de Guilhermirer	09/07
Mary-Magdalen-of-Blessed-Sacrament de Justamond	16/07
Mary-Anne-of-St-Francis Lambert	13/07
Mary-Rose-of-St-Andrew Laye	16/07
Mary-Gertrude-of-St-Sophia de Ripert d'Alauzier	10/07
Mary-Margaret-of-the-Angels du Rocher	09/07
Mary-Anastasia-of-St-Gervase de Roquard	13/07

'September (Martyrs of)' (02/09/1792 and 03/09/1792):-

(Bishops)

John-Mary du Lau d'Alleman, of Arles
(Carmelite friary, 2nd)

Francis-Joseph de la Rochefoucault, of Beauvais (Carmelite friary, 2nd)

Peter-Louis de la Rochefoucault, of Saintes (Carmelite friary, 2nd)

(Secular priests)

Andrew-Abel Alricy (Seminary of St Firman, 3rd)

Andrew Angar (Carmelite friary, 2nd)

Andrew Grasset de Saint-Sauveur
(Carmelite friary, 2nd)

Anthony-Charles-Octavian de Bouzet
(St Germain des Prés Abbey, 2nd)

Bertrand-Anthony de Caupenne
(Seminary of St Firman, 3rd)

Caspar-Claudius Maignien (Carmelite friary, 2nd)

Charles Carnus (Seminary of St Firman, 3rd)

Charles-Victor Veret (Seminary of St Firman, 3rd)

Claudius Chaudet (Carmelite friary, 2nd)

Claudius Colin (Carmelite friary, 2nd)

Claudius Fontaine
(St Germain des Prés Abbey, 2nd)

Claudius-Louis Marmotant de Savigny
(Seminary of St Firman, 3rd)

Claudius-Silvanus Mayneud de Bizefranc
(Seminary of St Firman, 3rd)

Daniel-Louis-Andrew des Pommerayes
(St Germain des Prés Abbey, 2nd)

Dionysius-Claudius Duval
(Seminary of St Firman, 3rd)

Francis Dardin (Carmelite friary, 2nd)

Francis Dumasrambaud de Calandelle
(Carmelite friary, 2nd)

Francis-Caesar Londiveau
(Carmelite friary, 2nd)

Francis-Louis Méallet de Fargues
          (Carmelite friary, 2nd)
Francis-Joseph Monnier
          (Seminary of St Firman, 3rd)
Francis-Joseph Pey
          (St Germain des Prés Abbey, 2nd)
Francis-Urban Salin de Niart
          (Carmelite friary, 2nd)
Gabriel Desprez de Roche   (Carmelite friary, 2nd)
George-Jerome Giroust
          (Seminary of St Firman, 3rd)
Gilbert-John Fautrel (Seminary of St Firman, 3rd)
Giles-Louis-Symphorian Lanchon
          (Seminary of St Firman, 3rd)
Henry-Hippolytus Ermès   (Carmelite friary, 2nd)
Henry-John Millet   (Seminary of St Firman, 3rd)
Ivo-Andrew Guillon de Keranrun
          (Seminary of St Firman, 3rd)
Ivo-John-Peter Rey de Kervizic
          (Seminary of St Firman, 3rd)
James Dufour   (Seminary of St Firman, 3rd)
James de la Lande   (Seminary of St Firman, 3rd)
James-Joseph Lejardinier-Deslandes
          (Carmelite friary, 2nd)
James-Francis de Lubersac (Carmelite friary, 2nd)
James-Alexander Menuret (Carmelite friary, 2nd)
James-John Lemeunier   (Carmelite friary, 2nd)
James Rabé   (Seminary of St Firman, 3rd)
James-Louis Schmid (Seminary of St Firman, 3rd)
John-Baptist-Claudius Aubert
          (Carmelite friary, 2nd)
John-Peter Bangue   (Carmelite friary, 2nd)
John-Baptist Bottex   (La Force, 3rd)
John-Anthony-Hyacinth Boucharène de
  Chaumeils   (Carmelite friary, 2nd)
John-Francis Bousquet   (Carmelite friary, 2nd)
John-Andrew Capeau
          (St Germain des Prés Abbey, 2nd)
John Goizet   (Carmelite friary, 2nd)
John-Anthony Guilleminet (Carmelite friary, 2nd)
John-Louis Guyard de Saint-Clair
          (St Germain des Prés Abbey, 2nd)
John-Baptist Jannin   (Carmelite friary, 2nd)
John Lacan   (Carmelite friary, 2nd)
John-Joseph de Lavèze Belay
          (Seminary of St Firman, 3rd)
John-Charles Legrand
          (Seminary of St Firman, 3rd)
John-Peter Le Laisant
          (Seminary of St Firman, 3rd)
John Lemaitre   (Seminary of St Firman, 3rd)
John-Thomas Leroy (Seminary of St Firman, 3rd)

John-Philip Marchand   (Carmelite friary, 2nd)
John-Baptist Nativelle   (Carmelite friary, 2nd)
John-Michael Phillippot
          (Seminary of St Firman, 3rd)
John-Robert Quéneau   (Carmelite friary, 2nd)
John-Joseph Rateau
          (St Germain des Prés Abbey, 2nd)
John-Henry-Louis Samson (Carmelite friary, 2nd)
John-Anthony de Savine   (Carmelite friary, 2nd)
John-Anthony-Barnabas Séguin
          (Carmelite friary, 2nd)
John-Peter Simon
          (St Germain des Prés Abbey, 2nd)
John-Baptist-Mary Tessier (Carmelite friary, 2nd)
Joseph Bécavin   (Carmelite friary, 2nd)
Joseph Falcoz   (Seminary of St Firman, 3rd)
Joseph-Mary Gros   (Seminary of St Firman, 3rd)
Joseph-Louis Oviefre (Seminary of St Firman, 3rd)
Joseph-Thomas Pazery de Thorame
          (Carmelite friary, 2nd)
Julian-Francis Hédouin
          (Seminary of St Firman, 3rd)
Julian Le Laisant   (Seminary of St Firman, 3rd)
Julian Poulain-Delaunay   (Carmelite friary, 2nd)
Julius-Honoratus-Cyprian Pazery
  de Thorame   (Carmelite friary, 2nd)
Laurence (? -surname unknown)
          (St Germain des Prés Abbey, 2nd)
Louis-Francis-Andrew Barret
          (Carmelite friary, 2nd)
Louis-Remigius Benoist
          (St Germain des Prés Abbey, 2nd)
Louis-Renatus-Nicholas Benoist
          (St Germain des Prés Abbey, 2nd)
Louis le Danois (St Germain des Prés Abbey, 2nd)
Louis-Laurence Gaultier   (Carmelite friary, 2nd)
Louis-John-Matthew Lanier
          (Seminary of St Firman, 3rd)
Louis Longuet   (Carmelite friary, 2nd)
Louis Maudit   (Carmelite friary, 2nd)
Mark-Louis Royer
          (St Germain des Prés Abbey, 2nd)
Martin-Francis-Alexis Loublier
          (Seminary of St Firman, 3rd)
Mary-Francis Mouffle
          (Seminary of St Firman, 3rd)
Maturinus-Victor Deruelle (Carmelite friary, 2nd)
Matthias-Augustine Nogier (Carmelite friary, 2nd)
Michael-Andrew-Silvester Binard
          (Seminary of St Firman, 3rd)
Michael-Mary-Francis de la Gardette
          (La Force, 3rd)

Michael Leber   (Seminary of St Firman, 3rd)
Nicholas Bize   (Seminary of St Firman, 3rd)
Nicholas Clairet   (Carmelite friary, 2nd)
Nicholas Gaudreau   (Seminary of St Firman, 3rd)
Nicholas-Claudius Roussel
                               (Seminary of St Firman, 3rd)
Oliver Lefebvre   (Carmelite friary, 2nd)
Ormond Chapt de Rastignac
                   (St Germain des Prés Abbey, 2nd)
Ormond de Foucauld de Pontbriand
                               (Carmelite friary, 2nd)
Peter-Paul Balzac   (Seminary of St Firman, 3rd)
Peter Bonzé   (Seminary of St Firman, 3rd)
Peter Briquet   (Seminary of St Firman, 3rd)
Peter Brisse   (Seminary of St Firman, 3rd)
Peter-John Garrigues   (Seminary of St Firman, 3rd)
Peter-Louis Gervais
                   (St Germain des Prés Abbey, 2nd)
Peter Hénocq   (Seminary of St Firman, 3rd)
Peter-Louis Joret   (Seminary of St Firman, 3rd)
Peter Landry   (Carmelite friary, 2nd)
Peter-Florentius Leclerq
                               (Seminary of St Firman, 3rd)
Peter-Francis Pazery de Thorame
                               (Carmelite friary, 2nd)
Peter Ploquin   (Carmelite friary, 2nd)
Peter-Robert Régnet (Seminary of St Firman, 3rd)
Peter Saint-James   (Seminary of St Firman, 3rd)
Peter-James de Turménies
                               (Seminary of St Firman, 3rd)
Peter-Louis-Joseph Verrier   (Carmelite friary, 2nd)
Peter-James-Mary Vitalis
                   (St Germain des Prés Abbey, 2nd)
Philibert Fougères   (Seminary of St Firman, 3rd)
Renatus Nativelle   (Carmelite friary, 2nd)
Renatus-Nicholas Poret   (Carmelite friary, 2nd)
Renatus-Joseph Urvoy
                               (Seminary of St Firman, 3rd)
Robert Le Bis   (Carmelite friary, 2nd)
Sanctus Huré   (St Germain des Prés Abbey, 2nd)
Stephen-Michael Gillet
                               (Seminary of St Firman, 3rd)
Thomas-Nicholas Dubray   (Carmelite friary, 2nd)
Thomas-Renatus Dubuisson (Carmelite friary, 2nd)
Thomas-John Monsaint
                   (St Germain des Prés Abbey, 2nd)
Vincent Abraham   (Carmelite friary, 2nd)

(Former Jesuits)
Alexander-Charles Lenfant
                   (St Germain des Prés Abbey, 2nd)
Charles-Francis Legué   (Carmelite friary, 2nd)

Claudius-Francis Cagnières des Granges
                               (Carmelite friary, 2nd)
Claudius Cayx-Dumas   (Carmelite friary, 2nd)
Claudius-Anthony-Ralph Laporte
                               (Carmelite friary, 2nd)
Eligius Herque du Roule
                               (Seminary of St Firman, 3rd)
Francis Balmain   (Carmelite friary, 2nd)
Francis-Hyacinth le Livec de Tresurin
                               (La Force, 3rd)
Francis Vareilhe-Duteil   (Carmelite friary, 2nd)
James-Julius Bonnaud   (Carmelite friary, 2nd)
James Friteyre-Durvé   (Carmelite friary, 2nd)
John-Francis-Mary Benoît-Vourlat
                               (Seminary of St Firman, 3rd)
John Charton de Millon   (Carmelite friary, 2nd)
John-Anthony Seconds
                               (Seminary of St Firman, 3rd)
Lupus Thomas-Bonnotte   (Carmelite friary, 2nd)
Maturin-Nichlas Le Bous de Villeneuve
   de la Villecrohain   (Carmelite friary, 2nd)
Nicholas-Mary Verron
                               (Seminary of St Firman, 3rd)
Peter Guérin du Rocher
                               (Seminary of St Firman, 3rd)
Renatus-Mary Andrieux
                               (Seminary of St Firman, 3rd)
Robert-Francis Guérin du Rocher
                               (Seminary of St Firman, 3rd)
Vincent-Joseph le Rousseau de Rosencoat
                               (Carmelite friary, 2nd)
William-Anthony Delfaut   (Carmelite friary, 2nd)

(Sulpicians)
Bernard-Francis de Cucsac (Carmelite friary, 2nd)
Claudius Rousseau   (Carmelite friary, 2nd)
Henry-Augustus Luzeau de la Mullonière
                               (Carmelite friary, 2nd)
James-Gabriel Galais   (Carmelite friary, 2nd)
James-Stephen-Philip Hourrier
                               (Carmelite friary, 2nd)
John-Baptist-Michael Pontus
                               (Carmelite friary, 2nd)
Peter Gaugain   (Carmelite friary, 2nd)
Peter-Michael Guérin   (Carmelite friary, 2nd)
Peter-Nicholas Psalmon   (Carmelite friary, 2nd)

(Other Religious)
Ambrose-Augustine Chevreaux
   (OSB Maur)   (Carmelite friary, 2nd)
Apollinaris Morel (OFM Cap)
                               (Carmelite friary, 2nd)

Charles-Louis Hurtel (Minim)
  (St Germain des Prés Abbey, 2nd)
Charles-Jeremiah Bérard de Pérou (Eudist)
  (Carmelite friary, 2nd)
Claudius Bochot (Doctrinarian)
  (Seminary of St Firman, 3rd)
Claudius Pons (CR)   (Seminary of St Firman, 3rd)
Cosmas Duval (OFM Cap)
  (Seminary of St Firman, 3rd)
Eustace Félix (Doctrinarian)
  (Seminary of St Firman, 3rd)
Francis-Louis Hébert (Eudist)
  (Carmelite friary, 2nd)
Francis Lefranc (Eudist)   (Carmelite friary, 2nd)
John-Charles-Mary Bernard du Cornillet (CR)
  (Seminary of St Firman, 3rd)
John-Francis Bonnel de Pradal (CR)
  (Seminary of St Firman, 3rd)
John-Francis Burté (OFM)   (Carmelite friary, 2nd)
John-Charles Caron (Vincentian)
  (Seminary of St Firman, 3rd)
John-Henry Gruyer (Vincentian)
  (Seminary of St Firman, 3rd)
Louis Barreau de la Touche (OSB Maur)
  (Carmelite friary, 2nd)
Louis-Joseph François (Vincentian)
  (Seminary of St Firman, 3rd)
Nicholas Colin (Vincentian)
  (Seminary of St Firman, 3rd)
Peter-Claudius Pottier (Eudist)
  (Seminary of St Firman, 3rd)
Renatus-Julian Massey (OSB Maur)
  (Carmelite friary, 2nd)
Severinus Girauld (Tertiary OSF)
  (Carmelite friary, 2nd)
Solomon Leclercq (Xn Brother)
  (Carmelite friary, 2nd)
Urban Lefebvre (Paris Society for Foreign
  Missions)   (Carmelite friary, 2nd)

(Deacons)
James-Augustine-Robert de Lézardières
  (Carmelite friary, 2nd)
Louis-Alexis-Matthias Boubert
  (Carmelite friary, 2nd)
Louis-Benjamin Hurtrel
  (St Germain des Prés Abbey, 2nd)
Stephen-Francis-Deusdedit de Ravinel
  (Carmelite friary, 2nd)

(Cleric)
Augustus Nézel   (Carmelite friary, 2nd)

(Laymen)
Charles-Regis-Matthew de la Calmette
  (Carmelite friary, 2nd)
Louis-Francis Rigot
  (Seminary of St Firman, 3rd)
John-Anthony-Joseph de Villette
  (Seminary of St Firman, 3rd)
Sebastian Desbrielles
  (Seminary of St Firman, 3rd)

'William Repin and Comps' (1794):-

Fr Andrew Fardeau	24/08
Anne Hamard	01/02
Anne Maugrin	16/04
Anne-Frances de Villeneuve	01/02
Anthony Fournier	12/01
Carol Davy	01/02
Caroline Lucas	18/01
Catherine Coltenceau	01/02
Catherine du Verdier de la Sorinière	10/02
Felicity Pricet	18/01
Frances Bellanger	01/02
Frances Bonneau	01/02
Frances Michau	01/02
Frances Michineau	16/04
Frances Pagis	01/02
Frances Suhard	16/04
Fr Francis-Louis Chartier	22/03
Fr Francis Peltier	05/01
Gabrielle Androuin	01/02
Jacobina Monnier	01/02
Fr James Laigneau de Langellerie	14/10
Fr James Ledoyen	05/01
Jane Bourigault	01/02
Jane Fouchard	01/02
Jane Gourdon	16/04
Jane Gruget	01/02
Jane-Mary Leduc	16/04
Jane Onillon	16/04
Jane-Mary Saillard d'Epinatz	01/02
Jane Thomas	16/04
Fr John-Michael Langevin	30/10/1793
Fr John-Baptist Lego	01/01
John Ménard	16/04
Fr Joseph Moreau	18/04
Fr Laurence Bâtard	02/01
Louise-Amata Déan de Luigné	01/02
Louise Bessay de la Voûte	10/02
Louise Poirier	10/02
Louise Raillier de la Tertinière	01/02
Margaret Rivière	01/02

Margaret Robin	16/04
Martha Poulin de la Forestrie	16/04
Mary-Magdalen Blond	01/02
Mary-Magdalen Cady	16/04
Mary Cassin	01/02
Mary-Jane Chauvigné	01/02
Mary de la Dive	25/01
Mary Fausseuse	01/02
Mary Forestier	16/04
Mary Gallard	01/02
Mary Gasnier	01/02
Mary Gingueneau	16/04
Mary Grillard	01/02
Mary-Anne Hacher du Bois	10/02
Mary Lardeux	16/04
Mary Lenée	01/02
Mary Leroy	01/02
Mary Leroy-Brevet	01/02
Mary-Magdalen Perrotin	01/02
Mary-Anne Pichery	01/02
Mary Piou	16/04
Mary-Genevieve Poulin de la Forestrie	16/04
Mary Rochard	16/04
Mary Roger	16/04
Mary Rouault	01/02
Mary-Magdalen Saillard d'Epinatz	01/02
Mary-Magdalen Sallé	16/04
Sr Mary-Anne Vaillot	01/02
Mary-Louise du Verdier de la Sorinière	10/02
Monica Pichery	18/01
Sr Ottilia Baumgarten	01/02
Peter Délepine	16/02
Peter Frémond	10/02
Fr Peter Tessier	05/01
Petra Androuin	01/02
Petra Besson	01/02
Petra Bourigault	16/04
Petra Grille	01/02
Petra Laurent	16/04
Petra Ledoyen	01/02
Petra Phélippeaux	01/02
Petra-Renata Potier	16/04
Petra-Jane Saillard d'Epinatz	01/02
Renata Bourgeais	16/04
Renata Cailleau	01/02
Renata-Mary Feillatreau	28/03
Renata Grillard	01/02
Renata Martin	01/02
Renata Rigault	16/04
Renata Séchet	16/04
Renata Valin	01/02
Fr Renatus Lego	01/01

Sr Rosalia du Verdier de la Sorinière	27/01
Rose Quenion	01/02
Simone Chauvigné	01/02
Susan Androuin	01/02
Victoria Bauduceau	01/02
Victoria Gusteau	
Fr William Repin	

(Others):-

Natalis Pinot	21/02/1794
Peter-Renatus Rogue	03/03/1796

IRELAND

Conor O'Devany	01/02/1611
Conrad O'Rourke	13/08/1579
Dermitius O'Hurley	20/06/1584
Dominic Collins	31/10/1602
Edward Cheevers	05/07/1581
Francis Taylor	30/01/1584
John Kearney	11/03/1653
Maurice MacKenraghty	20/04/1585
Margaret Ball	20/06/1584
Matthew Lambert	05/07/1581
Patrick Cavenagh	05/07/1581
Patrick O'Healey	13/08/1579
Patrick O'Loughlan	01/02/1611
Peter Higgins	23/03/1642
Robert Mayler	05/07/1581
Terence-Albert O'Brien	30/10/1651
William Tirry	02/05/1654

JAPAN

(OP Dominican, OFM Franciscan, SJ Jesuit, OSA
  Augustinian.)

Saints (42)

'St Paul Miki & Comps' 05/02/1597:-

Anthony Deynan
Bonaventure of Miyako
Cosmas Takeya
Francis Blanco OFM
Francis-of-Nagasaki Adauctus
Francis of Miyako
Francis-of-St-Michael of Parilla OFM
Gabriel of Ise
Gundisalvus Garcia OFM
James Kisai SJ
Joachim Sakakibara
John Kinuya
John de Goto Soan SJ

Leo Karasuma
Louis Ibaraki
Martin-of-the-Ascension Aguirre OFM
Matthias of Miyako
Michael Kozaki
Paul Ibaraki
Paul Miki SJ
Paul Suzuki
Peter-Baptist Blázquez OFM
Peter Sukejiro
Philip-of-Jesus de las Casas Martínez OFM
Thomas Dangi
Thomas Kozaki

'St Laurence Ruiz and Comps' :-

Anthony González OP	24/09/1637
Dominic Ibañez de Eriquicia OP	14/08/1633
Francis Shoyemon OP	14/08/1633
James Kyuhei Gorobiyoye	
Tomonaga OP	17/08/1633
Jordan-of-St-Stephen Ansalone OP	17/11/1634
Laurence Ruiz	29/09/1637
Lazarus of Kyoto	29/09/1637
Luke-Alphonsus Gorda OP	19/10/1633
Marina of Omura OP	11/11/1634
Mary-Magdalen of Nagasaki	15/10/1634
Matthew-of-the-Rosary Kohioye OP	19/10/1633
Michael de Aozaraza OP	24/09/1637
Michael Kurobioye	17/08/1637
Thomas-of-St-Hyacinth Hioji	
Rokuzayemon Nishi OP	17/11/1634
Vincent-of-the-Cross Shiwozuka OP	29/09/1637
William Courtet OP	29/09/1637

Beatified in 1867 (205):

Agnes Takeya	10/09/1622*
Alexis of Nagasaki OP	10/09/1622*
Alexis Nakamura	27/11/1619
Alphonsus de Mena OP	10/09/1622*
Alphonsus Navarete OP	01/06/1617
Ambrose Fernandez SJ	07/01/1620
Andrew Tokuan	18/11/1619
Andrew Yakichi	02/10/1622
Andrew Yoshida	01/10/1617
Angelus Orsucci OP	10/09/1622*
Anthony Ishida SJ	03/09/1632
Anthony Kimura	27/11/1619
Anthony Kiuni SJ	10/09/1622*
Anthony of Korea	10/09/1622*
Anthony-of-St-Dominic	
of Nagasaki OP	08/09/1628

Anthony-of-St-Francis of	
Nagasaki OFM	27/08/1627
Anthony-of-St-Bonaventure of	
Tuy OFM	08/09/1628
Anthony Sanga	10/09/1622*
Anthony Vom	10/09/1622*
Anthony Yamada	19/08/1622
Apollinaris Franco OFM	12/09/1622
Apollonia of Nagasaki	10/09/1622*
Augustine Ota SJ	10/08/1622
Balthasar de Torres SJ	20/06/1626
Bartholomew Gutiérez OSA	03/09/1632
Bartholomew Kawano Shichiyemon	10/09/1622*
Bartholomew Laurel OFM	27/08/1627
Bartholomew Mohioye	19/08/1622
Bartholomew Seki	27/11/1619
Camillus Costanzo SJ	15/10/1622
Caspar Hikojiro	01/10/1617
Caspar Koteda	11/10/1622
Caspar Sadamatsu SJ	20/06/1626
Caspar Vas	27/08/1627
Catherine of Nagasaki	10/09/1622*
Catherine Tanaka	12/07/1626
Charles Spinola SJ	10/09/1622*
Clare Yamada	10/09/1622*
Clement Kyuyemon	01/11/1622
Clement Vom	10/09/1622
Cosmas Takeya	18/11/1619
Damian Yamichi Tanda	10/09/1622*
Diego Carvalho SJ	22/02/1624
Dionysius Fujishima SJ	01/11/1622
Dominic Castellet OP	08/09/1628
Dominic Higashi	08/09/1628
Dominic Jorge	18/11/1619
Dominic Magoshichi de Hyuga OP	12/09/1622
Dominic of Nagasaki OFM	08/09/1628
Dominic-of-the-Holy-Rosary of	
Nagasaki OP	10/09/1622*
Dominic Nakano	10/09/1622*
Dominic Shobioye	16/09/1628
Dominic Tomachi	08/09/1628
Dominic Yamada	10/09/1622*
Dominica Ogata	10/09/1622*
Ferdinand-of-St-Joseph Ayala OSA	01/06/1617
Frances Bisoka	27/08/1627
Francis Galvez OSF	04/12/1623
Francis Higashi	08/09/1628
Francis Kuhioye	27/08/1627
Francis Kurobioye	27/08/1627
Francis-of-St-Mary of Mancha	
OFM	27/08/1627
Francis Morales OP	10/09/1622

Francis-of-St-Bonaventure of Musashino OFM	12/09/1622	Louis Flores OP	19/08/1622	
Francis Pacheco SJ	20/06/1626	Louis Kawara SJ	10/09/1622*	
Francis Takeya	11/09/1622	Louis Maki	07/09/1627	
Francis-of-Jesus Terrero Ortega OSA	03/09/1632	Louis Matsuo Soyemon	27/08/1627	
Francis Yakichi	02/10/1622	Louis Naizen	12/07/1626	
Gabriel-of-St-Mary-Magdalen of Fonseca OFM	03/09/1632	Louis Higashi	08/09/1628	
Gaius Jinyemon	27/08/1627	Louis Sasada OFM	25/08/1624	
Gaius of Korea	15/11/1624	Louis Sotelo OFM	25/08/1624	
Gundisalvus Fusai SJ	10/09/1622*	Louis Yakichi	02/10/1622	
Hyacinth Orfanel OP	10/09/1622*	Lucy de Freitas	10/09/1622*	
Ignatius Jorjes	10/09/1622*	Lucy-Louise of Omura	08/09/1628	
Isabella Fernandez	10/09/1622*	Lucy Yakichi	02/10/1622	
James Gengoro	16/08/1620	Luke Kiyemon	27/08/1627	
James Hayashida	08/09/1628	Mancius Araki	08/07/1626	
James Matsuo Denshi	19/08/1622	Mancius Ichizayemon OSA	28/09/1628	
Jerome de Angelis SJ	04/12/1623	Mancius-of-the-Holy-Cross of Omura	29/07/1627	
Jerome-of-the-Cross Jo	03/09/1632	Mark Takenoshima Shinyemon	19/08/1622	
Joachim Hirayama Díaz	19/08/1622	Martin Gómez	27/08/1627	
John Chozaburo OSA	28/09/1630	Mary Gengoro	16/08/1620	
John Chugoku	10/09/1622*	Mary-Magdalen Kiyota	27/08/1620	
John Imamura	08/09/1628	Mary-Magdalen of Nagasaki	15/10/1627	
John Iwanaga	27/11/1619	Mary of Korea	10/09/1622*	
John Kisaku SJ	20/06/1626	Mary-Magdalen Sanga	10/09/1622*	
John of Korea	10/09/1622*	Mary Shoun	10/09/1622*	
John-Baptist Machado SJ	22/05/1617	Mary Tanaka	10/09/1622*	
John Maki	07/09/1627	Mary Tanaura	10/09/1622*	
John-of-St-Dominic Martínez OP	19/05/1619	Mary Tokuan	10/09/1622*	
John Motoyama	27/11/1619	Mary Vaz	27/08/1627	
John Nagai Naizen	12/07/1626	Matthew Alvarez	08/09/1628	
John Nagata Matakichi	19/08/1622	Matthew-of-St-Thomas Chiwiato OP	12/09/1622	
John-of-St-Martha of Prados OFM	16/08/1618	Matthias Araki	12/07/1626	
John Shoun	18/11/1619	Matthias of Arima	22/05/1620	
John Soyemon	19/08/1622	Matthias Kozaka	27/11/1619	
John Tanaka	12/07/1626	Matthias Nakano Miota	27/11/1619	
John Tomachi	08/09/1628	Michael Carvalho SJ	25/08/1624	
John Yago	19/08/1622	Michael Díaz Hori	19/08/1622	
John-Baptist Zola SJ	20/06/1626	Michael Timonoya	16/09/1628	
Joseph-of-St-Hyacinth de Salvanés OP	10/09/1622*	Michael Kizayemon	27/08/1627	
Laurence Hachizo OSA	28/09/1628	Michael Nakashima SJ	25/12/1628	
Laurence Rokuyemon	19/08/1622	Michael Takeshita	27/11/1619	
Laurence Yamada	08/09/1628	Michael Shumpo SJ	10/09/1622*	
Leo Aybara	08/09/1628	Michael Timonoya	16/09/1628	
Leo Nakanishi	27/11/1619	Michael Tomachi	08/09/1628	
Leo of Satsuma	10/09/1622*	Michael Tozo SJ	20/06/1626	
Leo Sukeyemon	19/08/1622	Michael Yamada	08/09/1628	
Leo Tanaka	01/06/1617	Michael Yamichi	10/09/1622*	
Leonard Kimura SJ	18/11/1619	Monica Naizen	12/07/1626	
Louis Baba OFM	25/08/1624	Paul Kinsuke SJ	20/06/1626	
Louis Bertrán OP	29/07/1627	Paul Nagaishi	10/09/1622*	
		Paul Sankichi	19/08/1622	
		Paul Sadayu Aybara	08/09/1628	
		Paul Tanaka	10/09/1622*	

Paul Timonoya	16/09/1628
Paul Tomachi	08/09/1628
Peter Arakiyori Chobioye	12/07/1626
Peter-Paul-of-St-Clare of Arima	12/09/1622
Peter of Avila OFM	10/09/1622*
Peter-of-the-Assumption of Cuerva OFM	22/05/1617
Peter of Korea	10/09/1622*
Peter Nagaishi	10/09/1622*
Peter-Paul Navarro SJ	01/11/1622
Peter-of-the-Holy-Mother-of-God of Omura OP	29/07/1627
Peter Onizuka-Sandayu SJ	01/11/1622
Peter Rinsei SJ	20/06/1626
Peter Sampo SJ	10/09/1622*
Peter Shichiemon	11/09/1622
Peter Terai Kuhyoye OSA	28/09/1628
Peter Vasquez OP	25/08/1624
Peter de Zuñiga OSA	19/08/1622
Richard-of-St-Ann of Brussels OFM	10/09/1622*
Romanus Aybara	08/09/1628
Romanus Matsuka Miota	27/11/1619
Rufus Ishimoto	10/09/1622*
Sebastian Kimura SJ	10/09/1622*
Simon Kiyota Bokusai	16/08/1620
Simon Yempo SJ	04/12/1623
Susanna Chobyoye	12/07/1626
Thecla Nagaishi	10/09/1622*
Thomas Akahoshi SJ	10/09/1622*
Thomas Gengoro	16/08/1620
Thomas Koteda Kiuni	27/11/1619
Thomas Koyanagi	19/08/1622
Thomas-of-the-Holy-Rosary of Nagasaki OP	10/09/1622*
Thomas-of-St-Hyacinth of Nagasaki OP	08/09/1628
Thomas Shichiro	10/09/1622*
Thomas Terai Kahioye OSA	28/09/1628
Thomas Tomachi	08/09/1628
Thomas Tsuji SJ	07/09/1627
Thomas Wo Jinyemon	27/08/1627
Thomas Zumarraga OP	12/09/1622
Vincent-of-St-Joseph of Ayamonte OFM	10/09/1622*
Vincent Carvalho OSA	03/09/1632
Vincent Kaun SJ	20/06/1626

* These died in the 'Great Martyrdom'.

Beatified in 1989

Martin-of-St-Nicholas Lumberes Peralta	11/12/1632

Melchior-of-St-Augustine Sánchez Pérez	11/12/1632

Beatified in 2008 (188)

Adam Arakawa	05/06/1614
Adrian Takahashi Mondo	07/10/1613
Agatha of Ōmi	06/10/1619
Agnes Takeda	09/12/1603
Alexis Choemon	12/01/1629
Alexis Satō Seisuke	12/01/1629
Alexis Sugi Shōhachi	28/02/1627
Andrew Yamamoto Shichiemon	12/01/1629
Anne Jin'emon	12/01/1629
Anne Kajiya	06/10/1619
Anthony Anazawa Han'emon	12/01/1629
Anthony Banzai Kazue	12/01/1629
Anthony Dōmi	06/10/1619
Anthony Uchibori	21/02/1627
Aurea Banzai	12/01/1629
Balthasar Kagayama Hanzaemon	15/10/1619
Balthasar Uchibori	21/02/1627
Bartholomew Baba Han'emon	17/05/1627
Benedict of Kawachi	06/10/1619
Candidus 'Bōzu'	12/01/1629
Caspar Kizaemon	28/02/1627
Caspar Nagai Sohan	28/02/1627
Caspar Nishi Genka	14/11/1609
Catherine Hashimoto	06/10/1619
Cosmas Shizaburo	06/10/1619
Crescentia Anazawa	12/01/1629
Damian Ichiyata	28/02/1627
Damian of Sakai	19/08/1605
'Daughters of' Shichizaemon (2) *(full names unknown)*	12/01/1629
Diego Hayashida	07/10/1613
Diego Kagayama Haito	14/10/1619
Diego Tzūzu	06/10/1619
Diego Yūki Ryōsetsu	25/02/1636
Dionysius Saeki Zenka	28/02/1627
Dominica Amagasu	12/01/1629
Elizabeth Satō	12/01/1629
Emmanuel Kosaburō	06/10/1619
Francis Hashimoto	06/10/1619
Francis of Kyōto	06/10/1619
Francis Shizaburo	06/10/1619
Francis Tōyama Jintarō	16/02/1624
Gabriel of Owari	06/10/1619
Ignatius of Hanazawa	12/01/1629
Ignatius Iida Soemon	12/01/1629
Ignatius Uchibori	21/02/1627
James Kagayama	15/10/1619

Jane Takahashi	07/10/1613	Martha Kyūsuke	06/10/1619
Jane Takeda	09/12/1603	Martha of Owari	06/10/1619
Jerome Sōroku	06/10/1619	Martha Sanjūro	12/01/1629
Joachim Kurōemon	08/03/1624	Mary-Magdalen Arie	12/01/1629
Joachim Mine Sukedayū	17/05/1627	Mary Chūjo	06/10/1619
Joachim Ogawa	06/10/1619	Mary of Fukae	17/05/1627
Joachim Saburōbyōe	12/01/1629	Mary-Magdalen Hayashida (married)	17/05/1627
John Araki Kanshichi	28/02/1627	Mary-Magdalen Hayashida (single)	07/10/1613
John Arie Kiemon	12/01/1629	Mary Itō	12/01/1629
John Banzai Kazue	12/01/1629	Mary Koshima	06/10/1619
John Gorōbyōe	12/01/1629	Mary-Magdalen Kyūsaku	06/10/1619
John Hara Mondo	04/12/1623	Mary-Magdalen Minami	09/12/1603
John Hashimoto Tahyōe	06/10/1619	Mary Mine	28/02/1627
John Hattori Jingorō	11/01/1609	Mary-Magdalen of Owari	06/10/1619
John Heisaku	28/02/1627	Mary Rihyōe	06/10/1619
John Kisaki Kyūhachi	28/02/1627	Mary-Magdalen Shichizaemon	12/01/1629
John Kyūsaku	06/10/1619	Mary of Tanba (married)	06/10/1619
John Matsutake Chozaburō	17/05/1627	Mary of Tanba (single)	06/10/1619
John Minami Gorōzaemon	08/12/1603	Mary Yamamoto	12/01/1629
John Nishi Mataishi	14/11/1609	Mary of Yamashiro	06/10/1619
John Sakurai	06/10/1619	Matthias Itō Hikosuke	12/01/1629
John Watanabe Jirōzaemon	26/08/1606	Matthias Shōbara Ichizaemon	17/02/1624
Julia Yoshino	12/01/1629	Melchior Kumagai Motonao	16/08/1605
Julian Nakaura	21/10/1633	Mencia of Ōmi	06/10/1619
Justa Amagasu	12/01/1629	Michael Amagasu Tayemon	12/01/1629
Leo Hayashida Sukeemon	07/10/1613	Michael Anazawa Osamu	12/01/1629
Leo Kyūsuke	06/10/1619	Michael Kusuriya	28/07/1633
Leo Nakajima Sōkan	28/02/1627	Michael Mitsuishi Hikoemon	11/01/1609
Leo Saisho Shichiemon	17/11/1627	Monica of Mino	06/10/1619
Leo Takedomi Kan'emon	07/10/1613	Monica of Ōmi	06/10/1619
Linus Rihyōe	06/10/1619	Monica of Yamashiro	06/10/1619
Louis Amagasu Iemon	12/01/1629	'N.' *(full name unknown)*	
Louis Furue Sukeemon	17/05/1627	Shichizaemon	12/01/1629
Louis Hashimoto	06/10/1619	Nicholas Fukunaga Keian	31/07/1633
Louis Hayashida Sōka	17/05/1627	Ogasawara (anonymous servant 1)	30/01/1636
Louis Jin'emon	12/01/1629	Ogasawara (anonymous servant 2)	30/01/1636
Louis Matagorō	06/10/1619	Ogasawara (anonymous servant 3)	30/01/1636
Louis Minami	09/12/1603	Ogasawara (anonymous servant 4)	30/01/1636
Louis Saeki Kizō	28/02/1627	Ogasawara Genpachi	30/01/1636
Louis Shinzaburō	28/02/1627	Ogasawara Gonnosuke	30/01/1636
Lucy Iida	12/01/1629	Ogasawara Goro	30/01/1636
Lucy Kurogane	12/01/1629	Ogasawara Kuri	30/01/1636
Lucy Ōbasama	12/01/1629	Ogasawara Mari	30/01/1636
Lucy of Ōmi	06/10/1619	Ogasawara Miya Luisa	30/01/1636
Lucy Satō	12/01/1629	Ogasawara Sasaemon	30/01/1636
Lucy Sōroku	06/10/1619	Ogasawara Sayuemon	30/01/1636
Lucy Tōemon	06/10/1619	Ogasawara Shiro	30/01/1636
Mancius Kyūjirō	06/10/1619	Ogasawara Tsuchi	30/01/1636
Mancius Yoshino Han'emon	12/01/1629	Ogasawara Yosaburō Gen'ya	30/01/1636
Marina Itō Chōbo	12/01/1629	Paul Anazawa Juzaburō	12/01/1629
Martha Hayashida	07/10/1613	Paul Hayashida Mohyōe	17/05/1627
Martha of Kawachi	06/10/1619	Paul Nakajima	28/02/1627

Paul Nishida Kyūhachi	17/05/1627	Alexis U Se-yŏng	11/03/1866
Paul Nishihori Shikibu	12/01/1629	Andrew Chŏng Hwa-gyŏng	23/01/1840
Paul Onizuka Magoemon	17/05/1627	Andrew Kim Tae-gŏn	16/09/1846
Paul Sanjūro (Senior)	12/01/1629	Anne Kim Chang-gŭm	20/07/1839
Paul Sanjūro (Junior)	12/01/1629	Anne Pak A-gi	24/05/1839
Paul Satō Matagorō	12/01/1629	Anthony Daveluy	30/03/1866
Paul Takedomi Dan'emon	07/10/1613	Anthony Kim Sŏng-u	29/04/1841
Paul Uchibori Sakuemon	28/02/1627	Augustine Pak Chŏng-wŏn	31/01/1840
Peter Arie Jinzō	12/01/1629	Augustine Yi Kwang-hŏn	24/05/1839
Peter Hashimoto	06/10/1619	Augustine Yu Chin-gil	22/09/1839
Peter Hattori	11/01/1609	Barbara Cho Chŭng-i	29/12/1839
Peter Itō Yahyōe	12/01/1629	Barbara Ch'oe Yŏng-i	01/02/1840
Peter Kibe Kasui	04/07/1639	Barbara Han A-gi	24/05/1839
Regina Kyūsaku	06/10/1619	Barbara Kim	27/05/1839
Romanus Anazawa Matsujiro	12/01/1629	Barbara Ko Sun-i	29/12/1839
Rufina Banzai	12/01/1629	Barbara Kwŏn-hŭi	03/09/1839
Rufina of Owari	06/10/1619	Barbara Yi	27/05/1839
Simon Takahashi Seizaemon	12/01/1629	Barbara Yi Chŏng-hŭi	03/09/1839
Simon Takeda Gohyōe	09/12/1603	Bartholomew Chŏng Mun-ho	13/12/1866
Sixtus of Tanba	06/10/1619	Benedicta Hyŏn Kyŏng-nyŏn	29/12/1839
Thecla Hashimoto	12/01/1629	Catherine Chŏng Ch'ŏr-yŏm	20/09/1837
Thecla Kurogane	12/01/1629	Catherine Yi	26/09/1839
Thecla Takahashi	12/01/1629	Cecilia Yu So-sa	23/11/1839
Thomas Hashimoto	06/10/1619	Charles Cho Shin-ch'ŏl	26/09/1839
Thomas Ikegami	06/10/1619	Charles Hyon Sŏng-mun	19/09/1846
Thomas Kajiya Yoemon	06/10/1619	Columba Kim Hyo-im	26/09/1839
Thomas Kian	06/10/1619	Damian Nam Myŏng-hyŏg	24/05/1839
Thomas Kondō Hyōemon	28/02/1627	Elizabeth Chŏng Chŏng-hye	29/12/1839
Thomas Koshima Shinshirō	06/10/1619	Francis Ch'oe Kyŏng-hwan	12/09/1839
Thomas Mitsuishi	11/01/1609	Ignatius Kim Che-jun	26/09/1839
Thomas-of-St-Augustine Ochia Jihyōe	06/11/1637	James Chastan	21/09/1839
		John-Baptist Chŏn Chang-un	09/03/1866
Thomas Tōemon	06/10/1619	John-Baptist Nam Chong-sam	07/03/1866
Thomas Uzumi Shingoro	28/02/1627	John Pak Hu-jae	03/09/1839
Timothy Ōbasama Jirōbyōe	12/01/1629	John-Baptist Yi Kwang-nyol	20/07/1839
Ursula Nishi	14/11/1609	John Yi Mun-u	01/02/1840
Ursula Sakurai	06/10/1619	John Yi Yun-il	21/01/1867
Ursula Yamamoto	12/01/1629	Joseph Chang Chu-gi	30/03/1866
Vincent Kurogane Ichibiyōe	12/01/1629	Joseph Chang Sŏng-jib	26/05/1839
		Joseph Cho Yun-ho	23/12/1866
		Joseph-Peter Han Chae-kwon	13/12/1866
KOREA		Joseph Im Ch'i-baeg	20/09/1837
		Julitta Kim	26/09/1839
Saints (103):-		Justus Ranfer de Bretenières	07/03/1866
		Laurence Han I-hyŏng	20/09/1837
Agatha Chŏn Kyŏng-hyŏb	26/09/1839	Laurence Imbert	21/09/1839
Agatha Kim A-gi	24/05/1839	Louis Beaulieu	07/03/1866
Agatha Kwŏn Chin-i	31/01/1840	Lucy Kim (1)	20/07/1839
Agatha Yi	09/01/1840	Lucy Kim (2)	26/09/1839
Agatha Yi Kan-nan	20/09/1837	Lucy Pak Hŭi-sun	24/05/1839
Agatha Yi Kyŏng-i	31/01/1840	Luke Hwang Sŏk-tu	30/03/1866
Agatha Yi So-sa	24/05/1839	Mark Chŏng Ui-bae	11/03/1866
Agnes Kim Hyo-ju	03/09/1839		

Martha Kim Sŏng-im	20/07/1839	Paul Yun Yu-il	28/06/1795
Martin-Luke Huin	30/03/1866	Matthias Choe In-gil	28/06/1795
Mary-Magdalen Cho	26/09/1839	Sabas Ji Hwang	28/06/1795
Mary-Magdalen Han Yŏng-i	29/12/1839	Paul Yi Do-gi	24/07/1798
Mary-Magdalen Hŏ Kye-im	26/09/1839	Francis Bang	21/01/1799
Mary-Magdalen Kim Ŏ-bi	24/05/1839	Lawrence Pak Chwi-deuk	03/04/1799
Mary Pak Kun-a-gi Hui-sun	03/09/1839	James Won Si-bo	17/04/1799
Mary-Magdalen Pak Pong-sŏn	26/09/1839	Peter Jeong San-pil	??/??/1799
Mary-Magdalen Son So-byŏg	31/12/1840	Francis Bae Gwan-gyeom	07/01/1800
Mary Wŏn Kwi-im	20/07/1839	Martin In Eon-min	09/01/1800
Mary Yi In-dŏg	31/01/1840	Francis Yi Bo-hyeon	09/01/1800
Mary Yi Yŏn-hŭi	03/09/1839	Peter Jo Yong-sam	27/03/1801
Mary-Magdalen Yi Yŏn-hŭi	20/07/1839	John Choe Chang-hyeon	08/04/1801
Mary-Magdalen Yi Yŏng-dŏg	29/12/1839	Augustine Jeong Yak-jong	08/04/1801
Paul Chŏng Ha-sang	22/09/1839	Francis-Xavier Hong Gyo-man	08/04/1801
Paul Hŏ Hyŏb	30/01/1840	Thomas Choe Pil-gong	08/04/1801
Paul Hong Yŏng-ju	01/02/1840	Luke Hong Nak-min	08/04/1801
Perpetua Hong Kŭm-ju	26/09/1839	Marcellinus Choe Chang-ju	25/04/1801
Peter Aumaître	30/03/1866	Martin Yi Jung-bae	25/04/1801
Peter Cho Hwa-sŏ	13/12/1866	John Won Gyeong-do	25/04/1801
Peter Ch'oe Ch'ang-hŭb	29/12/1839	James Yun Yu-o	27/04/1801
Peter Ch'oe Hyŏng	09/03/1866	Peter Choe Pil-je	14/05/1801
Peter Chŏng Won-ji	13/12/1866	Lucy Yun Un-hye	14/05/1801
Peter-Henry Dorié	07/03/1866	Candida Jeong Bok-hye	14/05/1801
Peter Hong Pyŏng-ju	31/01/1840	Thaddeus Jeong In-hyeok	14/05/1801
Peter Kwon Tŭ-gin	24/05/1839	Charles Jeong Cheol-sang	14/05/1801
Peter Maubant	21/09/1839	Barbara Sim A-gi	??/04/1801
Peter Nam Kyŏng-mun	20/09/1837	Columba Kang Wan-suk	02/07/1801
Peter Sŏn Sŏn-ji	13/12/1866	Susanna Kang Gyeong-bok	02/07/1801
Peter Yi Ho-yŏng	25/11/1838	Matthew Kim Hyeon-u	02/07/1801
Peter Yi Myŏng-sŏ	13/12/1866	Bibiana Mun Yeong-in	02/07/1801
Peter Yu Tae-ch'ol	21/10/1839	Juliana Kim Yeon-i	02/07/1801
Peter Yu Chŏng-nyul	17/02/1866	Anthony Yi Hye-on	02/07/1801
Protase Chong Kuk-bo	20/05/1839	Ignatius Choe In-cheol	02/07/1801
Rose Kim	20/07/1839	Agatha Han Sin-ae	02/07/1801
Sebastian Nam I-gwan	26/09/1839	Agatha Yun Jeom-hye	04/07/1801
Simeon Berneaux	20/09/1866	Barbara Jeong Sun-mae	03/07/1801
Stephen Min Kŭk-ka	20/01/1840	Barnabas Kim I-u	??/05/1801
Susanna U Sur-im	20/09/1837	Paul Yi Guk-seung	??/05/1801
Teresa Kim	09/01/1840	Andrew Kim Gwang-ok	25/08/1801
Teresa Kim Im-i	20/09/1837	Peter Kim Jeong-deuk	25/08/1801
Teresa Yi Mae-im	20/09/1839	Stanislaus Han Jeong-heum	26/08/1801
Thomas Son Cha-sŏn	30/03/1866	Matthias Choe Yeo-gyeom	27/08/1801
		Francis Kim Jong-gyo	04/10/1801

Beati (124):

(This list is transcribed without editing from
www.koreanmartyrs.or.kr)

Paul Yun Ji-chung	08/12/1791
James Zhou Wen-mo	31/05/1801
James Gwon Sang-yeon	08/12/1791
Peter Won Si-jang	28/01/1793

Philip Hong Pil-ju	04/10/1801
Augustine Yu Hang-geom	24/08/1801
Francis Yun Ji-heon	24/08/1801
John Yu Jung-cheol	14/11/1801
John Yu Mun-seok	14/11/1801
Florus Hyeon Gye-heum	10/12/1801
Francis Kim Sa-jip	25/01/1801
Gervase Son Gyeong-yun	29/01/1802

Charles Yi Gyeong-do	29/01/1802
Simon Kim Gye-wan	29/01/1802
Barnabas Jeong Gwang-su	29/01/1802
Anthony Hong Ik-man	29/01/1802
Thomas Han Deok-un	30/01/1802
Simon Hwang Il-gwang	30/01/1802
Leo Hong In	30/01/1802
Sebastian Kwon Sang-mun	30/01/1802
Lutgard Yi Sun-i	31/01/1802
Matthew Yu Jung-seong	31/01/1802
Pius Kim Jin-hu	01/12/1814
Agatha-Magdalene Kim Yun-deok	??/05/1815
Alexis Kim Si-u	??/10/1816
Francis Choe Bong-han	??/05/1815
Andrew Seo Seok-bong	??/10/1816
Simon Kim Gan-gi	05/12/1816
Francis Kim Hui-seong	19/12/1816
Barbara Ku Seong-yeol	19/12/1816
Anne Yi Si-im	19/12/1816
Peter Ko Seong-dae	19/12/1816
Joseph Ko Seong-un	19/12/1816
Andrew Kim Jong-han	19/12/1816
James Kim Hwa-chun	19/12/1816
Peter Jo Suk	??/08/1819
Teresa Kwon Cheon-rye	??/08/1819
Paul Yi Gyeong-eon	27/06/1827
Paul Pak Gyeong-hwa	15/11/1827
Ambrose Kim Se-bak	03/12/1828
Richard An Gun-sim	??/??/1835
Andrew Yi Jae-haeng	26/05/1839
Andrew Pak Sa-ui	26/05/1839
Andrew Kim Sa-geon	26/05/1839
Job Yi Il-eon	29/05/1839
Peter Sin Tae-bo	29/05/1839
Peter Yi Tae-gwon	29/05/1839
Paul Jeong Tae-bong	29/05/1839
Peter Gim Dae-gwon	29/05/1839
John Cho Hae-song	06/09/1839
Anastasia Kim Jo-i	??/10/1839
Barbara Sim Jo-i	11/11/1839
Anastasia Yi Bong-geum	05/12/1839
Brigid Choe	08/12/1839
Protase Hong Jae-yeong	04/01/1840
Barbara Choe Jo-i	04/01/1840
Magdalen Yi Jo-i	04/01/1840
James Oh Jong-rye	04/01/1840
Mary Yi Seong-rye	31/01/1840
Paul Oh Ban-ji	27/03/1866
Mark Sin Seok-bok	31/03/1866
Stephen Kim Won-jung	16/12/1866
Thomas Jang	??/??/1866
Thaddeus Ku Han-seon	??/??/1866

Anthony Jeong Chan-mun	25/01/1867
Felix-Peter Kim Gi-ryang	??/01/1867
Matthias Pak Sang-geun	??/01/1867
Benedict Song	??/??/1867
Peter Song	??/??/1867
Anne Yi	??/??/1867
John Yi Jeong-sik	??/09/1868
Martin Yang Jae-hyeon	??/09/1868
Peter Yi Yang-deung	14/09/1868
Luke Kim Jong-ryun	14/09/1868
James Heo In-baek	14/09/1868
Francis Pak Gyeong-jin	28/09/1868
Margaret Oh	28/09/1868
Victorinus Pak Dae-sik	12/10/1868
Peter-Joseph Yun Bong-mun	01/04/1888

MEXICO

Saints (25):-

Atilanus Cruz Alvarado	01/07/28
Augustine Caloca Cortés	25/05/27
Christopher Magallanes Jara	25/05/27
David Galván Bermúdez	30/01/15
David Roldán Lara	15/08/26
David Uribe Velasco	12/04/27
Emmanuel Morales	15/08/26
Januarius Sánchez Delgadillo	17/01/27
Jesus Méndez Montoya	05/02/28
Joseph-Isabel Flores Varela	21/06/27
Joseph-Mary Robles Hurtado	26/06/27
Julius Álvarez Mendoza	30/03/27
Justin Orona Madrigal	01/07/28
Louis Batis Sainz	15/08/26
Margaritus Flores García	12/11/27
Matthew Correa Magallanes	06/02/27
Michael de la Mora	07/08/27
Peter Esqueda Ramírez	22/11/27
Peter-of-Jesus Maldonado Lucero	11/02/37
Romanus Adame Rosales	21/04/27
Ruderic Aguilar Alemán	28/10/28
Sabas Reyes Salazar	13/04/27
Salvator Lara Puente	15/08/26
Tranquillinus Ubiarco Robles	05/10/28
Turibius Romo González	25/02/28

Beati (15):-

Anacletus González Flores	01/04/27
Andrew Sola Molist	25/04/27
Angelus-Darius Acosta Zurita	25/07/31
Elias-del-Socorro Nieves OSA	10/03/28
George Vargas González	01/04/27

Joseph-Lucian-Ezekiel Huerta Gutiérrez	03/04/27
Joseph-Dionysius-Louis Padilla Gómez	01/04/27
Joseph-Trinity Rangel Montaño	25/04/27
Joseph Sanchez del Río	10/02/28
Leonard Pérez Larios	25/04/27
Louis Magaña Servín	09/02/28
Michael Gómez Loza	21/03/27
Michael-Augustine Pro SJ	23/11/27
Raymund Vargas González	01/04/27
Salvador Huerta Gutiérrez	03/04/27

NETHERLANDS (Gorinchem, Martyrs of)

Saints (19):-

Adrian van Hilvarenbeek OPrem
Andrew Wouters van Heynoert
Anthony van Hoornaert OFM
Anthony Weerden OFM
Cornelius van Wijk OFM
Francis van Rauga OFM
Godfrey van Duynen
Godfrey of Merville OFM
James Lacops OPrem
Jerome de Weert OFM
John of Cologne OP
John Lenaerts van Oosterwijk CR
Leonard Vechel
Nicasius Jonson van Hez OFM
Nicholas Janssen-Poppel
Nicholas Pieck OFM
Peter van Assche van der Slagmolen OFM
Theodoric van der Eem OFM
Willehad of Denmark OFM

POLAND

'Mary Mardosewicz and Comps'

Mary-Felicita Borowik
Mary-Canuta-of-Jesus-in-the-Garden Chrobot
Mary-Gwidona-of-the-Mercy-of-God Cierpka
Mary-Daniela-of-Jesus-and-Mary-Immaculate
    Jóźwik
Mary-Raymund-of-Jesus-and-Mary Koklowicz
Mary-Canisia Mackiewicz
Mary-Stella-of-the-Blessed-Sacrament
    Mardosewicz
Mary-Heliodora Matuszewska
Mary-Boromea Narmontowicz
Mary-Sergia-of-the-Sorrowful-Mother-of-God
    Rapiej
Mary-Imelda-of-Jesus-in-the-Host Żak

'Sadoc of Sandomir and Comps' (49):-

(Priests):-

Abel
Andrew
Barnabas
Bartholomew
Clement
Elias
James
John (1)
Luke
Malachy
Matthew
Paul
Peter
Philip
Sadoc
Simeon

(Deacons):-

Joachim
Joseph
Stephen

(Subdeacons):-

Abraham
Basil
Moses
Thaddeus

(Clerics):-

Aaron
Benedict
David
Dominic
Matthias
Michael
Onuphrius
Timothy

(Novices):-

Christopher
Daniel
Donatus
Felician
Gervase
Gordianus
Isaias
John (2)

Macarius		Francis Drzewiecki	10/08/42
Mark		Francis Kęsy	24/08/42
Maurus		Francis Rogaczewski	11/08/40
Medardus		Francis Rosłaniec	14/10/42
Raphael		Francis Stryjas	31/07/44
Tobias		George Kaszyra	18/02/43
Valentine		Gregory Frąckowiak	05/05/43
		Henry Hlebowicz	09/11/41
(Lay brothers):-		Henry Kaczorowski	06/05/42
		Henry Krzysztofik	04/08/42
Cyril		Herman Stepień	19/07/43
Jeremias		Hilary Januszewski	25/03/45
Thomas		Innocent Guz	06/06/40
		John-Nepomucene Chrzan	01/07/42
'Poland, Martyrs of the Nazi		Joseph Cebula	28/04/41
Occupation of'.		Joseph Czempiel	19/05/42
		Joseph Jankowski	16/10/41
Achilles Puchala	19/07/43	Joseph Kowalski	04/07/42
Adalbert Nierychlewski	07/02/42	Joseph Kurzawa	23/05/40
Adam Bargielski	08/09/42	Joseph Kut	18/09/42
Alexis Sobaszek	01/08/42	Joseph Pawlowski	09/01/42
Alice-Mary-Jadwiga Kotowska	11/11/39	Joseph Stanek	23/09/44
Aloysius Liguda	08/12/42	Joseph Straszewski	12/08/42
Alphonsus-Mary Mazurek	28/08/44	Joseph Zapłata	19/02/45
Anastasius-James Pankiewicz	20/04/42	Julia Rodzińska	20/02/45
Anicetus Kopliński	16/10/41	Ladislas Błądziąski	08/09/42
Anthony Bajewski	08/05/41	Ladislas Demski	28/05/40
Anthony Beszta-Borowski	15/07/43	Ladislas Goral	26/04/42
Anthony Leszczwicz	17/02/43	Ladislas Maćkowiak	04/03/42
Anthony-Julian Nowowiejski	28/05/41	Ladislas Mączkowski	20/08/42
Anthony Rewera	01/10/42	Ladislas Miegoń	15/09/42
Anthony Świadek	25/01/45	Leo Nowakowski	31/10/39
Anthony Zawistowski	04/06/42	Leo Wetmański	10/10/41
Boleslav Strzlecki	02/05/41	Louis-Roche Gietyngier	30/11/41
Boniface Żukowski	10/04/42	Louis Mzyk	23/02/42
Bronislav Komorowski	22/03/40	Marianus Górecki	22/05/40
Bronislav Kostkowski	27/11/42	Marianus Konopiński	01/01/43
Bruno Zembol	21/08/42	Marianus Skrzypczak	05/10/39
Casimir Gostyński	06/05/42	Martin Oprządek	18/05/42
Casimir Grelewski	09/01/42	Mary-Teresa Kowalska	25/07/41
Casimir Sykulski	01/12/41	Mary-Antonina Kratochwil	02/10/42
Celestina Faron	09/04/44	Mary-Eve-of-Providence Noisezewska	19/12/42
Cheslav Jóźwiak	24/08/42	Mary-Clementina Staszewska	27/07/43
Christinus Gondek	23/07/42	Mary-Anne Biernacka	13/06/43
Dominic Jędrzejewski	29/08/42	Mary-Martha-of-Jesus Wołowska	19/12/42
Edward Detkens	10/10/42	Maximilian Binkiewicz	24/08/42
Edward Grzymala	10/08/42	Michael Czartoryski	06/09/44
Edward Kaźmierski	24/08/42	Michael Oziębłowski	31/07/42
Edward Klinik	24/08/42	Michael Piaszczyński	20/12/40
Emilian Szramek	13/01/42	Michael Woźniak	16/05/42
Fidelis Chijnacki	09/07/42	Miechislav Bohatkiewicz	04/03/42
Florian Stępniak	12/08/42	Narcissus Putz	05/12/42
Francis Dachtera	23/08/44		

Narcissus Turchan	19/03/42
Natalia Tułasiewicz	31/03/45
Peter-Edward Dańkowski	03/04/42
Pius Bartosik	12/12/41
Romanus Archutowski	18/04/43
Romanus Sitko	12/10/42
Sigismund Pisarski	30/01/43
Sigismund Sajna	17/09/40
Stanislaus Kubista	26/04/42
Stanislaus Kubski	18/05/42
Stanislaus Mysakowski	14/10/42
Stanislaus Pyrtek	04/03/42
Stanislaus Starowieyski	04/06/42
Stephen Grelewski	09/05/41
Symphorian Ducki	11/04/42
Thaddeus Dulny	06/08/42
Timothy Trojanowski	28/02/42
Vincent Matuszewski	23/05/40
Vladimir Laskowski	08/08/40
Yarogniev Wojciechowski	24/08/42

SPANISH CIVIL WAR

Saints:-

James-Hilary Barbal Cosán	28/07/37

'Innocent-of-Mary-Immaculate Canoura Arnau and Comps' (09/10/34):-

Anicetus-Adolf Seco Gutiérrez
Augustus-Andrew Martín Fernández
Benedict-of-Jesus Valdivieso Sáez
Benjamin-Julian Alfonsus Andrés
Cyril- Bertrand Sanz Tejedor
Innocent-of-Mary-Immaculate Canoura Arnau
Julian-Alfred Fernández Zapico
Marcian-Joseph López López
Victorian-Pius Bernabé Cano

Beati:-

'Angela Lloret Martí and Comps' (20/11/36):-

Angela-of-St-Joseph Lloret Martí
Elizabeth Ferrer Sabría
Heart-of-Jesus Gómez Vives
Ignatia-of-the-Blessed-Sacrament
    Pascual Pallardó
Marcella-of-St-Thomas Navarro
Mary-of-the-Rosary Calpe Ibáñez
Mary-of-Succour Jiménez Baldoví
Mary-of-Sorrows Llimona Planas
Mary-of-Peace López García

Mary-of-the-Conception Martí Lacal
Mary-of-the-Assumption Mogoche Homs
Mary-of-Suffrage Orts Baldó

Mary-of-Calvary Romero Clariana	26/09/36
Mary-of-Refuge Rosat y Balasch	26/09/36

Mary-of-Grace de San Antonio
Mary-of-Sorrows Surís Brusola
Teresa-of-St-Joseph Duart Roig

'Aurelius-Mary Villalón Acebrón and Comps' (16/11/1936):-

Amalius Zariquiegui Mendoza	31/08/36
Aurelius-Mary Villalón Acebrón	13/09/36
Edmigius Primo Rodríguez	31/08/36
Evincius-Richard Alonso Uyarra	08/09/36
Joseph-Cecil Rodríguez Gonzalez	08/09/36
Theodemar-Joaquim Sainz Sainz	08/09/36
Valerius-Bernard Herrero Martínez	31/08/36

'Charles Eraña Guruceta and Comps'

Charles Eraña Guruceta	18/09/36
Jesus Hita Miranda	25/09/36
Fidelis Fuidio Rodríguez	17/10/36

'Dionysius Pamplona Polo and Comps':-

Alfred Parte Saiz	27/12/36
Charles Navarro Miquel	22/09/36
David Carlos Marañón	28/07/36
Dionysius Pamplona Polo	25/07/36
Emmanuel Segura López	28/07/36
Faustinus Oteiza Segura	09/08/36
Florentinus Felipe Naya	09/08/36
Francis Carceller Galindo	02/10/36
Henry Canadell Quintana	17/08/36
Ignatius Casanovas Perramon	16/09/36
John Agramunt Riera	13/08/36
Joseph Ferrer Esteve	09/12/36
Matthias Cardona Meseguer	20/08/36

'Hospitaller Martyrs':-

Talavera de la Reina, Toledo; 25/07/36:-

Frederick Rubio Alvarez
Jerome Ochoa Urdangarín
John-of-the-Cross Delgado Pastor
Primus Martínez de San Vicente Castillo

Calafell, Tarragona; 30/07/36:-

Anthony Llauradó Parisi
Anthony Sanchis Silvestre

Benedict-Joseph-Labre Mañoso González
Braulius-Mary Corres Díaz de Cerio
Constans Roca Huguet
Dominic Pitarch Gurrea
Emmanuel Jíménez Salado
Emmanuel López Orbara
Eusebius Forcades Ferraté
Henry Betrán Llorca
Ignatius Tejero Molina
Julian Carrasquer Fos
Raphael Flamarique Salinas
Thomas Urdánoz Aldaz
Vincent de Paul Canelles Vives

Columbians at Barcelona; 09/08/36:-

Arthur Ayala Niño
Caspar Páez Perdono
Eugene Ramirez Salazar
John-Baptist Velázquez Peláez
Melchiades Ramírez Zuluaga
Ruben-of Jesus López Aguilar
Stephen Maya Gutierrez

Carabanchal Alto, Madrid; 01/09/36:-

Benjamin Cobos Celada
Caesarius Niño Pérez
Caecilius López López
Canute Franco Gómez
Carmelus Gil Arano
Christinus Roca Huguet
Cosmas Brun Arará
Dositheus Rubio Alonso
Euthymius Aramendía García
Faustinus Villanueva Igual
Processus Ruiz Cascales
Rufinus Lasheras Aizcorbe

Ciemposuelos Hospital, Paracuellos del Jarama, Madrid; 28/11/36:-

Angelus Sastre Corporales
Clement Díez Sahagún
Edward Bautista Jímenez
Hilary Delgado Vílchez
Isidore Martínez Izquierdo
John-Jesus Adradas Gonzalo
John Alcalde Alcalde
Joseph Mora Velasco
Joseph Ruiz Cuesta
Julian Palazaola Artola
Lazarus Múgica Goiburu
Martinian Meléndez Sánchez

Peter-Mary Alcalde Negredo
Peter-of-Alcantara Bernalte Calzado
William Llop Gayá

Ciemposuelos Hospital, Paracuellos del Jarama, Madrid; 30/11/36:-

Anthony Martinez Gil-Leonis
Arthur Donoso Murillo
Diego-of-Cadiz García Molina
Jesus Gesta de Piquer
Michael Ruedas Megías
Nicephorus Salvador del Río
Romanus Touceda Fernández

Barcelona; killed on different dates:-

Acisclus Piña Piazuelo	10/11/36
Francis-Xavier Ponsa Casallach	28/09/36
John-Anthony Burró Más	05/11/36
John-Baptist Egozcuezábel Aldaz	29/07/36
Peter-of-Alcantara Villanueva Larráyoz	11/09/36
Protase Cubells Minguell	14/12/36

Castille; diffferent places and times:-

Flavius Argüeso González, *at Valle de Mauro.*	12/08/36
Francis Arias Martín, *at Valle de Mauro.*	18/08/36
Gundisalvus Gonzalo Gonzalo, *at Madrid.*	04/08/36
Hyacinth Hoyuelos González, *at Cienpozuelos.*	19/09/36
Tobias Borrás Romeau, *at Vinaroz.*	11/02/36

'Mary-Refuge de Hinojosa Naveros and Comps' (18/11/36):-

Josephine-Mary Barrera Izaguirre	
Mary-Cecilia Cendoya Araquistain	23/11/36
Mary-Refuge de Hinojosa Naveros	
Mary-Engratia Lecuona Aramburú	
Mary-Angela Olaizola Garagarza	
Mary-Agnes Zudaire Galdeano	
Teresa-Mary Cavestány Anduaga	

'Mary-of-the-Pillar-of-St-Francis-Borgia Martínez García and Comps' (24/07/36):-

Mary-of-the-Pillar-of-St-Francis-Borgia
    Martínez García
Mary-of-the-Angels-of-St-Joseph Voltierra
    Tordesillas
Teresa-of-the-Child-Jesus García García

'Nicephorus Díez Tejerina and Comps':-

At Manzanares, 23/07/36:

Abilius-of-the-Cross Ramos y Ramos
Epiphanius-of-St-Michael Sierra Conde
Fulgentius-of-the-Heart-of-Mary Calvo Sánchez
Joseph-of-the-Sacred-Heart Estalayo García
Nicephorus-of-Jesus-and-Mary Díez Tejerina
Zechariah-of-the-Blessed-Sacrament
    Fernández Crespo

At Carabanchel Bajo, 23/07/36:

Anacarius-of-the-Immaculate Benito Nozal
Germanus-of-Jesus-and-Mary Pérez Gímenez
Joseph-of-Jesus-and-Mary Osés Sainz
Joseph-Mary-of-Jesus-Dying Ruiz Martínez
Julius-of-the-Sacred-Heart Mediavilla Concejero
Laurinus-of-Jesus-Crucified Proaño Cuesta
Maurilius-of-the-Infant-Jesus Macho Ródriguez
Philip-of-St-Michael Ruiz Fraile
Philip-of-the-Sacred-Heart-of-Mary Valcabado
    Granado

At Urda near Toledo, 25/07/36:

Benedict-of-the-Virgin-del-Villar Solana Ruiz
Felix-of-the-Five-Wounds Ugalde Irurzun
Peter-of-the-Heart-of-Jesus Largo Redondo

*At Carrión de Calatrava near Ciudad Real,
25/09/36:*

John-Peter-of-St-Anthony Bengoa Aranguren
Paul-Mary-of-St-Joseph Leoz y Portillo

At Ciudad Real, 23/10/36:

Euphrasius-of-the-Merciful-Love de Celis Santos
Honorinus-of-the-Sorrowing-Virgin Carracedo
    Ramos
Ildephonsus-of-the-Cross Garcia Nozal
Joseph-Mary-of-Jesus Cuartero Gascón
Justinian-of-St-Gabriel-of-Our-Lady-of-Sorrows
    Cuesta Redondo
Thomas-of-the-Blessed-Sacrament Cuartero
    Gascón

Peter Ruiz de los Paños y Angel and Comps:-

Anthony Perulles Estíval	12/08/36
Isidore Bover Oliver	02/10/36
Joseph-Paschal Cada Saporta	04/09/36
Joseph-Mary Peris Polo	15/08/36
Joseph Sala Picó	23/06/36
Martin Martínez Pascual	18/08/36
Peter Ruiz de los Paños y Angel	23/06/36
Recared Centelles Abad	25/10/36
William Plaza Hernández	09/08/36

Philip-of-Jesus-Munárriz Azcona and Comps:-

At Barbastro, 02/08/36:-

John Díaz Nosti
Leontius Pérez Ramos
Philip-of-Jesus-Munárriz Azcona

At Barbastro, 12/08/36:-

Gregory Chirivás Lacambra
Joseph Pavón Bueno
Nicasius Sierra Ucar
Peter Cunill Padrós
Sebastian Calvo Martínez
Wenceslas-Mary Clarís Vilaregut

At Barbastro, 13/08/36:-

Alphonsus Miquel Garriga
Anthony-Mary Dalmau Rosich
Antoninus Calvo Calvo
Emmanuel Buil Lalueza
Emmanuel Torras Sais
Eusebius Codina Millá
Hilary-Mary Llorente Martín
John Codinachs Tuneu
John Echarri Vique
John Sánchez Munárriz
Joseph Brengaret Pujol
Joseph-Mary Ormo Seró
Peter García Bernal
Raymund Novich Rabionet
Salvator Pigem Serra
Secundinus-Mary Ortega García
Stephen Casadevall Puig
Theodore Ruiz de Larrinaga García
Thomas Capdevila Miró
Xavier-Aloysius Bandréz Jímenez

At Barbastro, 15/08/36:-

Alphonsus Sorribes Teixidó
Aloysius Escalé Binefa
Aloysius Lladó Teixidó
Aloysius Masferrer Vila
Edward Ripoll Diego
Emmanuel Martínez Jarauta
Faustinus Pérez García
Francis Castán Messeguer

Francis-Mary Roura Farró
Jesus-Augustine Viela Ezcurdia
John Baixeras Berenguer
Joseph-Mary Amorós Hernández
Joseph-Mary Badía Mateu
Joseph-Mary Blasco Juan
Joseph Figuero Beltrán
Joseph-Mary Ros Florensa
Michael Masip González
Raphael Briega Morales
Raymund Illa Salvía
Sebastian Riera Coromina

At Barbastro, 18/08/36:-

Athanasius Vidauretta Labra
James Falgarona Vilanova

'Vincent Soler and Comps':-

25/07/36:-
Deogratias Palacios
Leo Inchausti
Joseph-Richard Díez
Joseph Rada
Julian Moreno

26/07/36:-

Vincent Pinilla
Emmanuel Martin Sierra

15/08/36:-

Vincent Soler

Other individuals:-

Anselm Polanco Fontecha	07/02/39
Diego Ventaja Milán	30/08/36
Emmanuel Medina Olmos	30/08/36
Florentinus Asensio Barroso	09/08/36
Philip Ripoll Morata	07/02/39
Frances-of-the-Sacred-Heart Aldea Araujo	20/07/36
Frances-of-the-Incarnation Espejo Martos	12/01/37
Mary-of-the-Sanctuary-of-St-Aloysius-Gonzaga Moragas Cantarero	15/08/36
Mary-of-Mercies Prat y Prat	24/07/36
Peter Asúa Mendía	29/08/36
Rita-of-the-Sorrows Pujalte Sánchez	20/07/36
Victoria Diez y Bustos de Molina	11/08/36
Vincent Vilar David	14/02/36
Zephyrinus Giménez Malla	02/08/36

'Beatified in 2001' (233):-

'Alphonsus López López and Comps':-

Alphonsus López López	03/08/36
Dionysius Vicente Ramos	31/07/36
Francis Remón Játiva	31/07/36
Michael Remón Salvador	03/08/36
Modestus Vegas Vegas	27/07/36
Peter Rivera Rivera	01/09/36

'Aurelius Ample Alcaide and Comps':-

Franciscans, Capuchin:-

Ambrose Valls Matamales	26/08/36
Aurelius Ample Alcaide	28/08/36
Bernard Bieda Grau	04/09/36
Bonaventure Esteve Flors	26/09/36
Fidelis Climent Sanchés	27/09/36
Henry García Beltrán	16/08/36
Germanus Garrigues Hernández	09/08/36
James Mestre Iborra	29/09/36
Joachim Ferrer Adell	30/08/36
Modestus García Martí	13/08/36
Pacificus Salcedo Puchades	12/10/36
Peter Mas Ginester	26/08/36

Poor Clare Capuchinesses, at Alzira near Valencia:-

Elizabeth Calduch Rovira (at Cuevas de Vinromá)	14/04/37
Mary-Felicity Masía Ferragud	25/10/36
Mary-of-Jesus Masía Ferragud	25/10/36
Mary-Teresa Masía Ferragud	25/10/36
Mary-Veronica Masía Ferragud	25/10/36
Mary-of-Miracles Ortells Gimeno (at Picadero de Paterna)	20/11/36

Discalced Augustinian Nun, at Alzira near Valencia:-

Josepha-of-the-Purification Masía Ferragud	25/10/36

'Hyacinth Serrano López and Comps':-

Anthony López Couceiro	29/07/36
Constantine Fernández Álvarez	29/08/36
Emmanuel Albert Ginés *(secular priest)*	29/07/36
Felicissimus Díez González	29/07/36
Francis Calvo Burillo	02/08/36
Francis Monzón Romeo	29/08/36
Gumersind Soto Barros	29/07/36

Hyacinth Serrano López	25/11/36
James Meseguer Burillo	25/11/36
Joachim Prats Baltueña	30/07/36
Joseph-Mary Muro Sanmiguel	30/07/36
Joseph-Mary Vidal Segú	??/09/36
Lambert de Navascués y de Juan	29/07/36
Louis Urbano Lanaspa	25/08/36
Lucius Martínez Mancebo	29/07/36
Raphael Pardo Molina	26/09/36
Raymund Peiró Victori	21/08/36
Saturius Rey Robles	29/07/36
Thyrsus Manrique Melero	29/07/36
Zosimus Izquierdo Gil *(secular priest)*	30/07/36

'Joseph Aparicio Sanz and Comps':-

Diocesan priests:

Alphonsus Sebastiá Viñals	01/09/36
Anthony Silvestre Moya	08/08/36
Carmel Sastre Sastre	15/08/36
Diego Llorca Llopis	06/09/36
Elias Carbonell Mollá	02/10/36
Felix Yuste Cava	14/08/36
Ferdinand García Sendra	18/09/36
Ferdinand González Añón	27/12/36
Francis Ibáñez Ibáñez	19/08/36
Francis Sendra Ivars	04/09/36
Germanus Gozalvo Andreu	22/09/36
Gundesalvus Viñes Masip	10/12/36
Henry Juan Requena	29/12/36
Henry Morant Pellicer	03/10/36
Joachim Vilanova Camallonga	27/07/36
John Carbonell Mollá	02/10/36
John Ventura Solsona	17/09/36
Joseph Aparicio Sanz	29/12/36
Joseph Canet Giner	04/10/36
Joseph Fenellosa Alcayna	27/09/36
Joseph-Mary Ferrándiz Hernández	24/09/36
Joseph García Mas	18/09/36
Joseph González Huguet	12/10/36
Joseph Ruiz Bruixola	28/10/36
Joseph-Mary Segura Penadés	11/09/36
Joseph Toledo Pellicer	10/08/36
Paschal Ferrer Botella	24/09/36
Paschal Penadés Jornet	15/09/36
Raymund-Stephen Bou Pascual	17/10/36
Raymund Martí Soriano	27/08/36
Salvador Estrugo Solves	21/08/36
Salvador Ferrandis Seguí	03/08/36
Vincent Ballester Far	23/09/36
Vincent-Mary Izquierdo Alcón	18/08/36
Vincent Pelufo Corts	22/09/36

Vincent Rubiols Castelló	14/08/36
Vincent Sicluna Hernández	22/09/36

Members of Catholic Action:

Amelia Abad Casasempere	28/09/36
Anne-Mary Aranda Riera	14/10/36
Arthur Ros Montalt	28/08/36
Charles Díaz Gandía	11/08/36
Charles López Vidal	06/08/36
Crescentia Valls Espí	26/09/36
Emmanuel Torró García	21/09/36
Florence Caerols Martínez	02/10/36
Francisca Cualladó Baixauli	19/09/36
Herminia Martínez Amigó	27/09/36
Incarnation Gil Valls	24/09/36
Ishmael Escrihuela Esteve	08/09/36
Joseph-Raymund Ferragud Girbés	24/09/36
Joseph Medes Ferrís	12/11/36
Joseph Perpiñá Nácher	29/12/36
Joseph-Mary Zabal Blasco	08/12/36
John-Baptist Faubel Cano	28/08/36
John Gonga Martínez	13/11/36
Joseph-Mary Corbín Ferrer	27/12/36
Josephine Moscardó Montalvá	22/09/36
Louise-Mary Frías Cañizares	06/12/36
Marinus Blanes Giner	08/09/36
Mary Climent Mateau	20/08/36
Mary-Teresa Ferragud Roig	25/10/36
Mary Jordá Botella	26/09/36
Mary-Louise Montesinos Orduña	28/01/37
Mary-of-Oblivion Noguera Albelda	26/09/36
Mary-of-the-Purification Vidal Pastor	22/09/36
Mary-of-Carmel Viel Ferrando	05/11/36
Mary-of-the-Pillar Villalonga Villalba	11/12/36
Paschal Torres Lloret	06/09/36
Paul Meléndez Gonzalo	23/12/36
Raphael Alonso Gutiérrez	11/08/36
Salvador-Damian Enguix Garés	28/10/36
Sophia Ximénez Ximénez	23/09/36
Tarsilla Córdoba Belda	17/10/36
Vincent Galbis Gironés	21/09/36

'Joseph-Calasanz Marqués and Comps':-

Salesians:-

Alexander Planas Saurí *(lay associate)*	19/11/36
Alvarez Sanjuan Canet	01/10/36
Angelus Ramos Velázquez	11/10/36
Anthony Martín Hernández	10/12/36
Augustine García Calvo	10/12/36
Elisha García García	19/11/36
Felix Vivet Trabal	26/08/36

Francis Bandrés Sánchez	03/08/36		Consolata Cuñado González	24/11/36
Giles Gil Rodicio	04/08/36		Daria Campillo Paniagua	24/11/36
James Bonet Nadal	15/08/36		Elvira Torrentallé Paraire	19/08/36
James Buch Canals	29/07/36		Erundina Colino Vega	24/11/36
James Ortíz Alzueta	27/07/36		Feliciana de Uribe Orbe	24/11/36
John Martorell Soria	10/08/36		Francisca de Amezúa Ibaibarriaga	19/08/36
Joseph Batalla Parramón	04/08/36		Justa Maiza Goicoechea	24/11/36
Joseph Bonet Nadal	13/08/36		Mary Calaf Miracle	19/08/36
Joseph Calasanz Marqués	29/07/36		Mary-of-the-Snows Crespo López	19/08/36
Joseph Caselles Moncho	28/07/36		Mary-of-the-Helpless Giner Lister	19/08/36
Joseph Castell Camps	28/07/36		Mary-Josepha del Río Messa	23/09/36
Joseph Giménez López	09/12/36		Mary-of-Sorrows Vidal Cervera	19/08/36
Joseph Otín Aquilé	30/11/36		Mary-of-the-Purification Ximénez	
Joseph Rabasa Bentanachs	04/08/36		Ximénez	23/09/36
Julian Rodríguez Sánchez	09/12/36		Niceta Playa Xifra	24/11/36
Julius Junyer Padern	26/04/36		Paula Isla Alonso	24/11/36
Michael Domingo Cendra	12/08/36		Rose Pedret Rull	19/08/36
Peter Mesonero Rodríguez	10/08/36		Teresa Chambó Palés	19/08/36
Philip Hernández Martínez	27/07/36			
Richard de los Ríos Fabregat	09/12/36			

'Mary Baldillou y Bullit and Comps':-

Sergius Cid Paso	30/07/36
Xavier Bordás Piferer	24/07/36
Zacharias Abadía Buesa	27/07/36

Carmel-of-St-Philip-Neri Gómez Lezaun	08/08/36
Clementia-of-St-John-Baptist Riba	
Mestres	08/08/36
Consolata Aguiar-Mella Díaz *(school	
pupil)*	19/09/36
Mary-of-Sorrows Aguiar-Mella Díaz	
(school pupil)	19/09/36
Mary-of-the-Child-Jesus Baldillou	
Bullit	08/08/36
Mary-Aloysia-of-Jesus Girón Romera	08/08/36
Mary-of-Jesus de la Yglesia de Varo	19/09/36
Presentation-of-the-Holy-Family	
Gallén Martí	08/08/36

Daughters of Mary, Help of Christians-

Mary-of-Refuge Carbonell Muñoz	01/09/36
Mary-of-Carmel Moreno Benitez	01/09/36

Priest of the Sacred Heart:-

John-Mary-of-the-Cross García	
Méndez	23/08/36

'Leonard Olivera Buera and Comps':-

'Paschal Fortuño Almela and Comps':-

Brothers of the Christian Schools:-

Alfred Pellicer Muñoz	04/10/36
Paschal Fortuño Almela	08/09/36
Placid García Gilabert	16/08/36
Salvador Mollar Ventura	26/10/36

Ambrose-Leo Lorente Vicente	23/10/36
Bertrand-Francis Lahoz Moliner	14/12/36
Elias-Julian Torrijo Sánchez	22/11/36
Florentius-Martin Ibáñez Lázaro	23/10/36
Honoratus-Andrew Zorraquino Herrero	23/10/36
Leonard Olivera Buera *(priest chaplain)*	23/10/36

'Rosaria Quintana Argos and Comps':-

Frances-Xavier Fenollosa Alcaina	23/09/36
Rosaria Quintana Argos	23/08/36
Seraphina Fernández Ibero	23/08/36

Carmelite Sisters of Charity:-

'Thomas Sitjar Fortiá and Comps':-

Agatha Hernández Amorós	19/08/36
Antonia Gosens Sáez de Ibarra	24/11/36
Ascension Lloret Marco	07/09/36
Candida Cayuso González	24/11/36
Clare Ezcurra Urrutia	24/11/36
Concepta Odriozola Zabalia	24/11/36
Concepta Rodríguez Fernández	24/11/36

Alfred Simón Colomina	29/11/36
Aloysius Campos Górriz	28/11/36
Constantine Carbonell Sempere	23/08/36
Darius Hernández Morató	29/09/36

John-Baptist Ferreres Boluda	29/12/36
Joseph Tarrats Comaposada	28/09/36
Narcissus Basté Basté	15/10/36
Paul Bori Puig	29/09/36
Peter Gelabert Amer	23/08/36
Raymund Grimaltós Monllor	23/08/36
Thomas Sitjar Fortiá	19/08/36
Vincent Sales Genovés	29/09/36

'Vincent Cabanes Badenas and Comps':-

Ambrose Chuliá Ferrandis	18/09/36
Benedict Ferrer Jordá	16/09/36
Bernardine Martínez Robles	16/09/36
Bonaventure Arahal de Miguel	01/08/36
Carmen García Moyon	30/01/37
Crescentius García Pobo	03/10/36
Dominic Hurtado Soler	15/08/36
Florentinus Pérez Romero	23/08/36
Francis Lerman Martínez	18/09/36
Francis Tomás Serer	02/08/36
Gabriel Sanchís Monpó	16/08/36
Joseph Llosá Balaguer	07/10/36
Laureanus Ferrer Cardet	16/09/36
Leo Legua Martí	26/09/36
Modestus Gay Zarzo	18/09/36
Richard López Mora	18/09/36
Timothy Valero Pérez	17/09/36
Urban Gil Sáez	23/08/36
Valentine Jaunzarás Gómez	18/09/36
Vincent Cabanes Badenas	30/08/36

Other individuals:-

Francis-of-Paola Castelló y Aleu	29/09/36
Joseph Samsó y Elias (beatified 2010)	01/09/36
Josephine-of-St-John-of-God Ruano García	08/09/36
Mary-of-St-John Giner Gomis	13/11/36
Mary-of-Sorrows-of-St-Eulalia Puig Bonany	08/09/36
Mary-of-Guadalupe Ricart Olmos	02/10/36

'Beatified in 2013' (522):-

'Albert-Mary Marco Alemán and Comps'
(17/08/36)

Adalbert-Mary Vicente Muñoz	23/11/36
Albert-Mary Marco Alemán	
Angelus-Mary Reguilón Lobato	
Angelus-Mary Sánchez Rodríguez	
Aurelius-Mary García Antón	
Bartholomew-Infant-Mary Andrés Vecilla	

Daniel-Mary García Antón	
Francis-Mary Pérez Pérez	
Silvanus-Mary Villanueva González	

'Andrew-of-Palazuelo González-Díez González
Núñez and Comps'

Alexander-of-Sobradillo Barahona Martín	15/08/36
Alexis-of-Terradillos González Herrero	14/08/36
Ambrose-of-Santibáñez Pan López	27/12/36
Andrew-of-Palazuelo González-Díez González Núñez	31/07/36
Angelus-of-Cañete-La-Real González Ramos Campos	06/08/36
Archangelus-of-Valdavida de la Red Pérez	14/08/36
Aurelius-of-Ocejo Escanciano Tejerina	17/08/36
Berard-of-Visantoña Frade Eiras	14/08/36
Charles-of-Alcubilla-de-Nogales Merillas Fernández	14/01/37
Crispin-of-Cuevas-de-San-Marcos Pérez Ruano	06/08/36
Diego-of-Guadilla Gutiérrez Terciado	29/12/36
Domitillus-of-Ayoó Llamas Barrero	06/09/36
Eusebius-of-Saludes Prieto Otero	14/08/36
Erasmus (Elmo)-of-Orihuela Simón Gómez	07/11/36
Eustachius-of-Villaquite Cembranos Nistal	31/08/36
Ferdinand-of-Santiago Olmedo Reguera	02/08/36
Gabriel-of-Aróstegui Ilarregui Goñi	23/08/36
Giles-of-Puerto-de-Santa-María Soto Carrera	06/08/36
Gregory-of-La-Mata Díez del Blanco	27/08/36
Honorius-of-Orihuela Juan Costa	30/11/36
Ignatius-of-Galdácano Recalde Magúregui	06/08/36
Ildephonsus-of-Armellada Pérez Arias	14/08/36
John-Chrysostom-of-Gata-de-Gorgos Caselles García	24/12/36
Joseph-of-Chauchina Casare Menéndez	06/08/36
Joseph-Mary-of-Manila Sanz-Orozco Mortera	17/08/36
Louis-of-Valencina Limón Márquez	03/08/36
Michael-of-Grajal de Felipe González	??/??/36
Norbert Cembranos de la Verdura (oblate)	23/09/36
Pacificus-of-Ronda Rodríguez Navarro	07/08/36
Primitivus-of-Villamizar Fontanil Medina	19/08/37
Ramirus-of-Sobradillo Pérez González	27/08/36
Saturninus-of-Bilbao Serano Lizarralde	26/08/36

'Anthony Faúndez López and Comps'

Anthony Faúndez López	19/09/36
Bonaventure Muñoz Martínez	04/09/36
Fulgentius Martínez García	04/10/36
Peter Sánchez Barba	04/09/36

'Aurelia Arambarri Fuente and Comps'

Augustina Peña Rodríguez	05/12/36
Aurelia Arambarri Fuente	06/12/36
Aurora López González	06/12/36
Daria Andiarena Sagaseta	06/12/36

'Augustine-Mary García Tribaldos and Comps' (30/07/36)

Anastasius-Peter Bruch Cortecáns
Anselm-Paul Solas de Val
Augustine-Mary García Tribaldos
Braulius-Joseph González Blanco
Braulius-Charles Lucas Manzanares
Chrysologus Sanz y Palanca
Eleutherius-Romanus Mancho López
Hosea (Oseas) Álvarez Quernada
Irenaeus-Hyacinth Rodríguez Bueno
Junian-Albert Larzábal Michelena
Louis-Victor Angulo Ayala
Norbert-Joseph Díaz de Zárante y Ortiz de Zárante
Rogatian González Calzada
Stephen-Vincent Herrero Arnillas
Vidal-Ernest Frías García
Virginius-Peter López y López

'Carmel-Mary Moyano Linares and Comps'

Anthony-Mary Martín Povea	14/08/36
Carmel-Mary Moyano Linares	23/09/36
Elisha-Mary Carmago Montes	18/08/36
Elisha-Mary Durán Cintas	22/07/36
James-Mary Carretero Rojas	22/07/36
Joseph-Mary González Delgado	27/07/36
Joseph-Mary Mateos Carballido	22/07/36
Joseph-Mary Ruiz Cardeñosa	18/08/36
Peter Velasco Narbona	14/08/36
Raymund-Mary Pérez Sousa	22/07/36

'Chrysanthus González García and Comps'

Abdon Iglesias Bañuelos
Adrian Llop Plana
Alipius-Joseph Dronda Leoz
Anacletus-Louis Busto Pérez
Andrew-Joseph Donázar Goñi

Angelus-Hippolytus Pablos Carvajal
Aquilinus Baró Riera
Aurelian Ortigosa Oraá
Benedict-Andrew Andrés Monfort
Benedict-Joseph Galeron Parte
Benignus-Joseph Valencia Janices
Berard-Joseph Pampliega Santiago
Bruno-Joseph Ayape Remón
Camerinus Álvarez Palacín
Caspar Martínez Esteban
Chrysanthus González García
Columbanus-Paul Oza Motinot
Cyprian-Joseph Iglesias Bañuelos
Dominic-Cyriac Domínguez Martínez
Edward-Mary Alonso Fontaneda
Egbert Arce Ruiz
Eligius-Joseph Rodríguez Guttíerez
Emilian-Joseph Leyún Goñi
Eucherius Llanillo García
Eventius Pérez Moral
Fabian Pastor Marco
Felician Ruiz Báscones
Felix-Amantius Noriega Núñez
Felix-Lawrence Gutiérrez Rojo
Ferdinand-Mary Martínez Infantes
George-Camillus García García
George-Louis Lizasoáin Lizaso
Guzman Becerril Merino
Herminius-Paschal Jaunsarás Zabaleta
Jerome Tobar Calzada
John-Mary Gombert Olympe
Joseph-Zephyrinus Garet Ventejo
Joseph-Theophilus Mulet Velilla
Joseph-of-Arimathea Santiago Allende
Julian Aguilar Martín (layman)
Julian-Joseph Cabria Andrés
Julian-Marcellinus Rebollar Campo
Julius-Firminius Múzquiz Erdozáin
Justus-Pastor Aranda Modrego
Leo-Argimir García Sandoval
Ligurius-Peter de Santiago Paredes
Louis-Firiminius Huerta Lara
Louis-Alphonsus Moreno Aliende
Louis-Damian Sobraqués Glory
Louis-Daniel Viñuela Flecha
Lucian Álvarez Renedo
Marinus Alonso Ortega
Millan Llover Torrent
Narcissus Arribas Arnaiz
Nestor-Eugene Ortega Villamudrio
Paul-Daniel Altabella Gracia
Peter Cortas Monclús

Philip-Neri Zabaleta Armendáriz
Raymund-Emilian Horteleno Gómez (layman)
Roch Villareal Abaza
Severinus Ruiz Hidalgo
Peter-Jerome Serret Anglés
Theogenes Valls Piernau
Theophilus-Martin Erro Ripa
Timothy-Joseph Lisbona Royo
Valens-Joseph Delgado de la Fuente
Victoricus-Mary Artola Sorolla
Xavier-Benedict Alonso Fernández

'Emmaunel Basulto Jiménez and Comps'

Emmanuel Aranda Espejo (seminarian)	08/08/36
Emmaunel Basulto Jiménez (bishop)	12/08/36
Felix Pérez Portela (priest)	12/08/36
Francis López Navarrete (priest)	28/08/36
Francis Solís Pedrajas (priest)	03/04/36
Joseph-Mary Poyatos Ruiz (layman)	03/10/36

'Emmanuel Borrás Ferré and Comps, Martyrs of the Diocese of Tarragona'

(Bishop)

Emmanuel Borrás Ferré	12/08/36

(Diocesan priests)

Agapitus Gorgues Manresa
Alexis Miquel Rossell
Andrew Prats Barrufet
Anthony Nogués Martí
Anthony Pedro Minguella
Anthony Prenafeta Soler
Augustine Ibarra Anguela
Dalmas Llebaria Torné
Francis Company Torrelles
Francis Mercader Randé
Francis Vidal Sanuy
Francis Vives Antich
Helladius Peres Bori
Henry Gispert Domènech
Isidore Fábregas Gils
Isidore Torres Balsells
James Tarragó Iglesias
James Sanromà Solé
Jerome Fábregas Camí
Joachim Balcells Bosch
Jocundus Bonet Mercadé
John Ceró Cedó
John Farriol Sabaté
John Gilbert Galofré

John Montpeó Masip (seminarian)
John Roca Vilardell
John Rofes Sancho
John Tomàs Gibert
John Vernet Masip
Joseph Badía Minguella
Joseph Bru Boronat
Joseph-Mary Bru Ralduà
Joseph Civit Timoneda
Joseph Colom Alsina
Joseph Garriga Ferrer
Joseph Gassol Montseny (seminarian)
Joseph Gomis Martorell
Joseph Mañé March
Joseph Masquef Ferré
Joseph Mestre Escoda
Joseph-Mary Panadés Tarré
Joseph Pandrell Navarro
Joseph Roselló Sans
Joseph-Mary Sancho Toda
Louis Domingo Mariné
Louis Janer Riba
Louis Sans Viñas
Margaretus (Magín) Albaigés Escoda
Margaretus (Magín) Civit Roca
Michael Grau Antolí
Michael Rué Gené
Michael Saludes Ciuret
Michael Vilatimó Costa
Narcissus Feliu Costa
Paul Bertrán Mercadé
Paul Gili Pedrós
Paul Figuerola Rovira
Paul Roselló Borgueres
Paul Virgili Monfá
Peter Farrés Valls
Peter Rofes Llauradó
Pius Salvans Corominas
Raphael Martí Fugueras
Raymund Artiga Aragonés
Raymund Martí Amenós
Sebastian Tarragó Cabré
Stanislaus Sans Hortoneda
Thomas Capdevila Mique

(Benedictines of Montserrat)

Aloysius-Gonzaga Alesanco Maestro
Ambrose-Mary Busquets Creixell
Angelus-Mary Rodamilans Canals
Bernard Vendrell Olivella
Dominic González Millán
Emilian-Mary Guilà Ximenes

Eugene-Mary Erausquin Aramburu
Francis-Mary De Paula Sánchez Solé
Fulgentius Albareda Ramoneda
Hildebrand-Mary Casanovas Vila
Ildephonsus Civil Castellví
John Roca Bosch
Joseph-Mary Fontseré Masdeú
Joseph-Mary Jordá y Jordá
Louis Palacios Lozano
Narcissus-Mary Vilar Espona
Odilo-Mary Costa Canal
Peter Vallmitjana Abarca
Placid-Mary Feliu Soler
Robert Grau Bullich

(Brothers of the Christian Schools -Salesians)

Agapitus-Modestus Pamplona Falguera
Albert-Joachim Linares De La Pinta
Alexander-Anthony Arraya Caballero
Alexander-John Gellida Cornelles
Alphius-Barnabas Nuñez Alonso
Anastasius-Luke Martín Puente
Andrew-Sergius Pradas Lahoz
Angelus-Amandus Fierro Pérez
Anselm-Felix Godo Buscato
Anthony-Giles Gil Monforte
Aristides-Mark José Cano
Arnaud-Cyril Font Taulat
Augustus-Mary Merino Miguel
Benedict-John Urgell Coma
Benildus-Joseph Casademunt Ribas
Bonaventure-Pius Ruiz De La Torre
Claudius-Joseph Mateo Calvo
Clement-Faustinus Fernández Sáenz
Clement-Adolf Vea Balaguer
Daniel-Anthony Rueda Barriocanal
Elias-Paulinus Pradas Vidal
Erasmus (Elmo)-Michael Sisterna Torrent
Exuperius Alberto Flos
Faustus-Louis Tolaguera Oliva
Felix-Adrian Vicente Edo
Fulbert-James Jardí Vernet
Gilbert-of-Jesus Boschdemont Mitjavila
Heladius-Vincent España Ortiz
Honorius-Sebastian Obeso Alario
Hugh-Barnabas Trullen Gilisbarts
Hyacinth-Jordan Camprubí Corrubí
Janarius Navarro Blasco
Justus-Gabriel Albiol Plou
Leontius-Joachim Pallerola Feu
Louis-Albert Alberto Flos

Marcian-Paschal Escuin Ferrer
Nicholas-Adrian Pérez Rodrigo
Peter-Magi Salla Saltó
Raphael-Joseph Gellida Llorach

(Capuchin Franciscan)

Carmel-of-Colomers Salvà Menescal

(Carmelite Tertiaries of Teaching -this
    congregation is now extinct.)

Bonaventure Toldrà Rodon
Isidore Tarsá Giribets
Julius Alameda Camarero
Louis Domingo Oliva

(Claretians)

Andrew Felíu Bartomeu
Anthony Capdevilla Balsells
Anthony Vilamassana Carulla
Frederick Vila Bartolì
James Mir Vime
Paul Castellá Barbará
Sebastian Balcells Tonijuan

(Discalced Carmelites)

Angelus-of-St-Joseph Fort Rius
Charles-of-Jesus-and-Mary Barrufet Tost
Damian-of-the-Holy-Trinity Rodríguez Pablo
Elipius-of-St-Rose Arce Fernández
Joseph-Cecilius-of-Jesus-and-Mary
    Alberich Luch
Vincent-of-the-Cross Gallen Ibañez
Peter-of-St-Elias De Eriz Eguiluz

'Fortunatus Velasco Tobar and Comps'

Amandus García Sánchez	24/10/36
Andrew-of-Avellino Gutiérrez Moral	03/08/36
Anthony Carmaniú Mercader	17/08/36
Fortunatus Velasco Tobar	24/08/36
Gregory Cermeño Barceló	06/12/36
Irenaeus Rodríguez González	06/12/36
Leontius Pérez Nebreda	02/08/36
Louis Aguirre Bilbao	30/07/36
Narcissus Pascual y Pascual	06/12/36
Pelagius-Joseph Granado Prieto	27/08/36
Richard Atanes Castro	14/08/36
Salustian González Crespo	13/10/36
Thomas Pallarés Ibáñez	13/10/36
Vincent Vilumbrales Fuente	06/12/36

'Hermenegild-of-the-Assumption Iza y Aregita and Comps' (27/08/36)

Anthony-of-Jesus-and-Mary Salútregui
  Iribarren
Bonaventure-of-St Catalina Gabika-Etxebarria
  Gerrikabeitia
Francis-of-St-Lawrence Euba Gorroño
Heremenegild-of-the-Assumption Iza y Aregita
Placid-of-Jesus Camino Fernández
Stephen-of-St-Joseph Barrenechea Arriaga

'James Puig Mirosa and Comps'

Anthony Mascaró Colomina	27/01/37
Edward Cabanach Majem	25/08/36
Firminius Martorell Víes	25/08/36
Francis Llach Candell	25/08/36
James Llach Candell	19/04/37
James Puig Mirosa	30/07/36
John Cuscó Oliver	21/08/36
John Franquesa Costa	02/09/36
Joseph Vila Barri	21/09/36
Narcisus Sitjà Basté	09/08/36
Peter Roca Toscas	04/04/37
Peter Ruiz Ortega	04/04/37
Peter Sadurní Raventós	21/08/36
Peter Verdaguer Saurina	15/10/36
Raymund Cabanach Majem	25/08/36
Raymund Llach Candell	19/04/37
Raymund Oromí Sullà	26/04/37
Robert Montserrat Beliart	13/11/36
Sebastian Llorens Telarroja (layman)	30/07/36
Sigismund Sagalés Vilà	08/09/36

'Joachim Jovani Marín and Comps'

Amadeus Monje Altés	16/08/36
Christopher Baqués Almirall	20/08/36
Joachim Jovani Marín	05/12/36
John Vallés Anguera	09/08/36
Joseph-Emmanuel Claramonte Agut	10/06/38
Joseph Piquer Arnáu	11/09/36
Joseph Pla Arasa	11/09/36
Joseph Prats Sanjuán	01/08/36
Joseph-Mary Tarín Curto	29/08/36
Laurence Insa Celma	02/09/36
Matthew Despóns Tena	13/08/36
Michael Amaro Rodríguez	02/08/36
Sebastian Segarra Barberá	05/09/36
Thomas Cubells Miguel	10/09/36
Vincent Jovaní Ávila	05/12/36

'John-of-Jesus Vilaregut Farré and Comps'

Bartholomew-of-the-Passion Olivé Vivó	25/07/36
Francis-of-the-Assumption Segalà Solé	20/08/36
John-of-Jesus Vilaregut Farré	25/07/36
Paul Segalà Solé (diocesan priest)	20/08/36
Silverius-of-St-Aloysius-Gonzaga Perucho Fontarro	20/08/36

'Joseph-Xavier Gorrosterratzu Jauranena and Comps'

Cyriac Olarte Pérez
Joseph-Xavier Gorrosterratzu Jauranena
Julian Pozo Ruiz
Michael Goñi Áriz
Peter Romero Espejo
Victor Calvo Lozano

'Joseph-Maximus Moro Briz and Comps'

Augustine Bermejo Miranda	28/08/36
Damian Gómez Jiménez	19/08/36
John Mesonero Huerta	15/08/36
Joseph García Librán	14/08/36
Joseph-Maximus Moro Briz	24/07/36

'Joseph-Mary Ruiz Cano and Comps' (28/07/36)

Abelard García Palacios	
Angelus López Martínez	
Angelus Pérez Murillo	
Anthony Lasa Vidauretta	
Anthony Orrego Fuentes	
Candidus Catalán Lasala	
Claudius López Martínez	
Gabriel Barriopedro Tejedor	
Jesus-Hannibal Gómez y Gómez	
Joseph-Mary Ruiz Cano	27/07/36
Meletius Pardo Llorente	
Otilius del Amo Palomino	
Philip González de Heredia Barahona	02/10/36
Primitivus Berrocoso Maillo	
Thomas Cordero y Cordero	
Vincent Robles Gómez	

'Josepha Martínez Pérez and Comps'

Carmen Rodríguez Banazal	09/12/36
Dolores Broseta Bonet	09/12/36
Isidora Izquierdo García	09/12/36
Joaquina Rey Aguirre	29/08/36
Josepha Laborra Goyeneche	09/12/36

Josepha Martínez Pérez	15/10/36
Martina Vázquez Gordo	04/10/36
Mary-Louise Bermúdez Ruiz	18/08/36
Mary-Pillar Nalda Franco	09/12/36
Michaela Hernán Martínez	18/08/36
Rosary Ciércoles Gascón	18/08/36
Stephania Irisarri Irigaray	09/12/36
Victoria Arregui Guinea	29/10/36

'Marianus Alcalá Pérez and Comps'

Amantius Marín Mínguez	26/07/36
Anthony González Penín	10/08/36
Anthony Lahoz Gan	01/09/36
Emmanuel Sancho Aguilar	07/08/36
Francis Gargallo Gascón	07/08/36
Francis Llagostera Bonet	20/08/36
Francis Mitjá i Mitjá	??/01/37
Henry Morante Chic	25/07/36
James Codina Casellas	05/08/36
Jesus-Edward Massanet Flaquer	25/07/36
Joseph Reñé Prenafeta	16/08/36
Joseph Trallero Lou	05/08/36
Lawrence Moreno Nicolás	03/11/36
Marianus Alcalá Pérez	15/10/36
Marianus Pina Turón	08/08/36
Peter Esteban Hernández	01/09/36
Serapius Sanz Iranzo	20/08/36
Thomas Campo Marín	20/08/36
Thomas Carbonell Miquel	25/07/36

'Mary-of-Montserrat García Solanas and Comps'

Josepha-of-the-Coronation-of-Mary Panyella
    Doménech
Lucretia García Solanas (laywoman)
Margaret-of-Alacoque Ors Torrents
Mary-of-Montserrat García Solanas
Mary-of-Jesus Jordá Martí
Mary-of-Mercy Mestre Trinché
Mary-of-St-Henry Ors Molist
Mary-of-the-Assumption Vilaseca Gallego
Philomena-of-St-Francis-of-Paola Ballesta
    Gelmá
Trinity Rius Casas

'Mary-Assumption González Trujilano and Comps'

Elizabeth Remuiñan Carracedo	06/08/36
Gertrude Llamazares Fernández	13/08/36
Mary-Assumption González Trujilano	28/10/36

'Maurice Iñiguez de Heredia and Comps'

Avellinus Martínez de Arenzana Candela	04/10/36
Balthasar del Charco Horques	17/08/36
Christopher Barrios Pérez	04/10/36
Cross Ibáñez López	04/10/36
Felician Martínez Granero	04/10/36
Gaudentius Iñiguez de Heredia Alzola	01/08/36
Gumersind Sanz y Sanz	17/08/36
Honorius Ballesteros Rodríguez	17/08/36
James Óscar Valdés	11/08/36
John-Joseph Orayen Aizcorbe	04/10/36
Joseph-Michael Peñarroya Dolz	04/10/36
Leander Aloy Doménech	04/10/36
Leontius Rosell Laboria	11/08/36
Leopold de Francisco Pío	04/10/36
Matthias Morín Ramos	??/09/37
Maurice Iñiguez de Heredia Alzola	28/12/36
Publius Fernández González	04/10/36
Raymund García Moreno	17/08/36
Salustian Alonso Antonio	17/08/36
Secundus Pastor García	17/08/36
Louis-Beltran Solá Jiménez	28/08/36
Stanislaus-of-Jesus Valentín Peña Ojea	17/08/36
Sylvester Perez Laguna	17/08/36
Trinity Andrés Lanas	05/02/37

'Maurus Palazuelos Maruri and Comps' (28/08/36)

Angelus Fuertes Boira	
Anselm Palau Sin	
Aurelius Boix Cosials	
Dominic Caballé Bru	
Ferdinand Salinas Romero	
Honoratus Suárez Riu	
Ildephonsus Fernández Muñiz	
Laurence Ibañez Caballero	
Laurence Santolaria Ester	05/08/36
Laurence Sobrevia Cañardo	
Leander Cuesta Andrés	
Marianus Sierra Almázor	09/08/36
Maurus Palazuelos Maruri	
Ramirus Sanz de Galdeano Mañeru	
Raymund Lladós Salud	
Rosendus Donamaría Valencia	
Santiago Pardo López	
Vincent Burrel Enjuanes	26/07/36

'Melchiora-of-the-Adoration Cortés Bueno and Comps'

Andrea Calle González	03/09/36
Conception Pérez Giral	03/09/36

Dolores Barroso Villaseñor	12/08/36	Joseph Guardiet Pujol	03/08/36
Dolores-Ursula Caro Martín	03/09/36	Joseph-Mary González Solis	25/09/36
Gaudentia Benavides Herrero	11/02/37	Joseph Jordán Blecua	12/08/36
Joanna Pérez Abascal	12/08/36	Joseph Nadal Guiu	12/08/36
Laurentia Díaz Bolaños	17/11/36	Raymund-Joachim Castaño González	26/09/36
Mary-Severina Díaz-Pardo Gauna	12/08/36	Richard Gil Barcelón	03/08/36
Mary-Assumption Mayoral Peña	12/08/36	Salvius Huix Miralpeix	05/08/36
Melchiora-of-the-Adoration		Victoria Valverde González	12/01/37
Cortés Bueno	12/08/36		
Modesta Moro Briz	31/10/36		

UGANDA (Charles Lwanga and Comps)

Josepha Gironés Arteta	17/11/36
Pilar-Elizabeth Sánchez Suárez	31/10/36
Raymunda Cao Fernández	12/08/36
Stephanie Saldaña Mayoral	12/08/36

Saints (22):-

Achilles Kiwanuka	03/06/1886
Adolphus Ludigo Mkasa	03/06/1886

'Orentius-Louis Solá Garriga and Comps'

		Aloysius-Gonzaga Gonza	27/05/1886
Adalbert-John Angulo García	30/11/36	Ambrose Kibuka	03/06/1886
Alexis-Andrew Beobide Cendoya	03/08/36	Anatolius Kiriggwajjo	03/06/1886
Angelus-Gregory Arribas y Arribas	28/07/36	Andrew Kaggwa	26/05/1886
Anthony Mateo Salamero		Athanasius Bazzekuketta	27/05/1886
(diocesan priest)	09/08/36	Bruno Seronum	03/06/1886
Aquilinus-Xavier Ruiz Alegre	28/07/36	Charles Lwanga	03/06/1886
Arthur Oliveras Puljarás	28/07/36	Dionysius Ssebuggwawo	25/05/1886
Benjamin-Leo Ortega Narganes	28/07/36	Gyavira	03/06/1886
Chrysostom-Albinus Ruiz Peral	28/07/36	James Buzabaliawo	03/06/1886
Dacian de Bengoa Larriñaga	27/11/36	John-Mary Muzeyi	27/01/1887
Florian-Felix Santamaría Angulo	30/11/36	Joseph Mkasa Balikuddembe	15/11/1885
Ishmael-Richard Arbé Barrón	30/11/36	Kizito	03/06/1886
John-Paul Álvarez Fernández	27/11/36	Luke Banabakintu	03/06/1886
Joseph Gorastazu Labayen (layperson)	28/07/36	Matthias Mulumba Kalemba	30/05/1886
Joseph-Alphonsus Serrano Sáiz	08/11/36	Mbaya-Tuzinde	03/06/1886
Marianus-Paul Pérez Gómez	28/07/36	Mgagga	03/06/1886
Marius-Felix Sousa de Sousa	28/07/36	Mukasa Kiriwanvu	03/06/1886
Orentius-Louis Solá Garriga	28/07/36	Noah Mawaggali	31/05/1886
Paul-of-the-Cross Sanz y Sanz	30/11/36	Pontian Ngondwe	26/05/1886
Symphronius Miguel Sánchez	30/11/36		
Sixtus-Andrew Mereno Báscones	28/07/36		

UKRAINE

Xavier-Elisha Castellanos López	28/07/36

Bishops:-

Theophilus Fernández de Legaria Goñi and Comps (11/08/36):-

Basil Velyčkovskyj	30/06/73
Gregory Khomyšin	28/12/45
Gregory Lakota	05/11/50
John Slezyuk	02/12/73
Josaphat Kocylovskyj	17/11/47
Joseph Bilczewski	20/03/23
Nicholas Čarneckyj	02/04/59
Nicetas Budka	28/09/49
Simeon Lukač	22/08/64
Theodore Romzha	01/11/47

Gonsalvus Barrón Nanclares
Helladius López Ramos
Marius Ros Ezcurra
Isidore Iñiguez de Ciriano Abechuco
Theophilus Fernández de Legaria Goñi

Other individuals:-

Priests:-

Alexis Zaryckyj	30/10/63
Andrew Iščak	26/06/41
Emilian Kovch	25/03/44

Anthony Arrué Peiró	03/08/36
Emmanuel (Manuel)-of-the-Holy-	
Family Sanz Dominguez	08/11/36
John Huguet Cardona	23/07/36

Nicholas Cehelskyj	25/05/51
Nicholas Konrad	26/06/41
Peter Verhun	07/02/37
Romanus Lysko	14/10/49

Religious:-

Clement Šeptyckyj	01/05/51
Joachim Senkivskyj	26/06/41
John Ziatyk	17/05/52
Laurentia Harasymiv	26/08/52
Leonidas Fedorov	07/03/35
Olympia Bidà	28/01/52
Severian Baranyk	26/06/41
Tarsicia Mackiv	18/07/44
Vitalis-Vladimir Bajrak	16/05/46
Zenobius Kovalyk	30/06/41

Layman:-

Vladimir Pryjma	26/06/41

VIETNAM

Saints (117):-

Agnes Lê Thị Thành	12/07/1841
Andrew Dũng Lạc	21/12/1839
Andrew Nguyễn Kim Thông Nam	15/07/1855
Andrew Trần Văn Trong	28/11/1835
Andrew Tường	16/06/1862
Anthony Nguyễn Đích	12/08/1838
Anthony Nguyễn Hữu Quỳnh	10/07/1840
Augustine Nguyễn Văn Mới	19/12/1839
Augustine Phan Viết Huy	13/06/1839
Augustine Schoeffler	01/05/1851
Bernard Vũ Văn Duệ	01/08/1838
Clement-Ignatius Delgado y Cebrián	12/07/1838
Dominic Bùy Văn Uy	19/12/1839
Dominic Cám	11/03/1859
Dominic-Nicholas Đinh Đạt	18/07/1839
Dominic Henares	25/06/1838
Dominic Huyên	05/06/1862
Dominic Mạo	16/06/1862
Dominic Mậu	05/11/1858
Dominic Nhi	16/06/1862
Dominic Ninh	16/07/1862
Dominic Ngôn	22/05/1862
Dominic Nguyễn	16/06/1862
Dominic Nguyễn Văn Hạnh	01/08/1838
Dominic Nguyễn Văn Xuyên	26/11/1839
Dominic Phạm Trọng Khảm	13/01/1859
Dominic Toại	05/06/1862
Dominic Trạch	18/09/1840
Dominic Tước	02/04/1839

Emmanuel Lê Văn Phụng	13/07/1859
Emmanuel Nguyễn Văn Triệu	17/09/1798
Emmanuel Phụng	13/07/1859
Francis-Xavier Cần	20/11/1837
Francis Đỗ Minh Chiểu	25/06/1838
Francis Gil de Frederich	22/01/1745
Francis-Xavier Hà Trọng Mậu	19/12/1839
Francis Jaccard	21/09/1838
Francis Trần Văn Trung	06/10/1858
Hyacinth Castañeda	07/11/1773
Isidore Gagelin	17/10/1833
James Đỗ May Năm	12/08/1838
Jerome Hermosilla	01/11/1861
John-Louis Bonnard	01/05/1852
John-Baptist Cơn	08/11/1840
John-Charles Cornay	20/09/1837
John Đạt	28/10/1798
John Baptist Đinh văn Thành	28/04/1840
John Đoàn Trinh Hoan	26/05/1861
John-Theophanes Vénard	02/02/1861
Joseph Đặng Đình Viên	21/08/1838
Joseph-Mary Díaz Sanjurjo	20/07/1857
Joseph Đỗ Quang Hiền	09/05/1840
Joseph Fernández	24/07/1838
Joseph Hoàng Lương Cành	05/09/1838
Joseph Lê Đăng Thị	24/10/1860
Joseph Marchand	30/11/1835
Joseph Nguyễn Đình Nghi	08/11/1840
Joseph Nguyễn Duy Khang	06/12/1861
Joseph Nguyễn Đình Uyển	03/07/1838
Joseph Nguyễn Văn Lựu	02/05/1854
Joseph Phạm Trọng Tả	13/01/1859
Joseph Tuân	07/01/1862
Joseph Tuấn	30/04/1861
Joseph Túc	01/06/1862
Laurence Nguyễn Văn Hưởng	27/04/1856
Luke Thìn	13/01/1859
Luke Vũ Bà Loan	05/06/1840
Martin Tạ Đức Thịnh	08/11/1840
Martin Thọ	08/11/1840
Matthew Alonso de Leziniana	22/01/1745
Matthew Lê Văn Gẫm	11/05/1847
Matthew Nguyễn Văn Phượng	26/05/1861
Melchior García Sampedro	28/07/1858
Michael Hồ Đinh Hy	22/05/1857
Michael Nguyễn Huy Mỹ	12/08/1838
Nicholas Bùi Viết Thể	13/06/1839
Paul Hạnh	28/05/1859
Paul Lê Bảo Tịnh	06/04/1857
Paul Lê Văn Lộc	13/02/1859
Paul Nguyễn Ngân	08/11/1840
Paul Nguyễn Văn Mỹ	18/12/1838